The Complete Poems of Shakespear

CW00642426

Although best known for his plays, William Shakespeare (1564–1616) was also a poet who achieved extraordinary depth and variety in only a few key works. This edition of his poetry provides detailed notes, commentary and appendices resulting in an academically thorough and widely readable edition to Shakespeare's poetry.

The editors present his non-dramatic poems in the chronological order of their print publication: the narrative poems *Venus and Adonis* and *The Rape of Lucrece*; the metaphysical 'Let the Bird of Loudest Lay' (often known as *The Phoenix and the Turtle*); all 154 Sonnets and *A Lover's Complaint*. In headnotes and extensive annotations to the texts, Cathy Shrank and Raphael Lyne elucidate historical contexts, publication histories and above all the literary and linguistic features of poems whose subtleties always reward careful attention.

Substantial appendices trace the sources for Shakespeare's narrative poems and the controversial text *The Passionate Pilgrim*, as well as providing information about poems posthumously attributed to him and the English sonnet sequence. Shrank and Lyne guide readers of all levels with a glossary of rhetorical terms, an index of the poems (titles and first lines) and an account of Shakespeare's rhymes informed by scholarship on Elizabethan pronunciation. With all these scholarly resources supporting a newly edited, modern-spelling text, this edition combines accessibility with layers of rich information to inform the most sophisticated reading.

Cathy Shrank is Professor of Tudor and Renaissance Literature at the University of Sheffield, UK.

Raphael Lyne is a Fellow of Murray Edwards College and a Reader in Renaissance Literature in the Faculty of English at the University of Cambridge, UK.

LONGMAN ANNOTATED ENGLISH POETS

General Editors: Paul Hammond and David Hopkins
Founding Editors: F. W. Bateson and John Barnard

Other titles available:

ROBERT BROWNING: POEMS VOLS 1–4 and SELECTED POEMS
Edited by John Woolford, Daniel Karlin and Joseph Phelan

THE COMPLETE POEMS OF JOHN DONNE
Edited by Robin Robbins

DRYDEN: POEMS VOLS 1–5 and SELECTED POEMS
Edited by Paul Hammond and David Hopkins

THE POEMS OF ANDREW MARVELL
(Revised Edition)
Edited by Nigel Smith

MILTON: PARADISE LOST
(Second Edition)
Edited by Alastair Fowler

MILTON: COMPLETE SHORTER POEMS
(Second Edition)
Edited by John Carey

THE POEMS OF ALEXANDER POPE, VOL. 3: THE DUNCIAD
Edited by Valerie Rumbold

THE POEMS OF SHELLEY, VOLS 1–4
Edited by Michael Rossington, Jack Donovan and Kelvin Everest

SPENSER: THE FAIRIE QUEENE
(Revised Second Edition)
Edited by A. C. Hamilton

TENNYSON: A SELECTED EDITION
(Revised Edition)
Edited by Christopher Ricks

https://www.routledge.com/Longman-Annotated-English-Poets/book-series/LAEP

The Complete Poems of Shakespeare

Edited by Cathy Shrank and Raphael Lyne

Routledge
Taylor & Francis Group

LONDON AND NEW YORK

First published 2018
by Routledge
2 Park Square, Milton Park, Abingdon, Oxon OX14 4RN

and by Routledge
711 Third Avenue, New York, NY 10017

Routledge is an imprint of the Taylor & Francis Group, an informa business

© 2018 selection and editorial matter, Cathy Shrank and Raphael Lyne

The right of Cathy Shrank and Raphael Lyne to be identified as the authors of the editorial material has been asserted in accordance with sections 77 and 78 of the Copyright, Designs and Patents Act 1988.

British Library Cataloguing-in-Publication Data
A catalogue record for this book is available from the British Library

Library of Congress Cataloging-in-Publication Data
Names: Shakespeare, William, 1564–1616, author. | Shrank, Cathy,
    editor. | Lyne, Raphael, editor.
Title: The complete poems of Shakespeare / [edited by] Cathy
    Shrank and Raphael Lyne.
Description: Abingdon ; New York : Routledge, 2017. | Series:
    Longman annotated English poets | Includes bibliographical
    references and index.
Identifiers: LCCN 2017003335 | ISBN 9780415737074 (hardback :
    alk. paper) | ISBN 9780582784109 (pbk. : alk. paper) | ISBN
    9781317481355 (mobipocket/kindle) | ISBN 9781315707945
    (Master) | ISBN 9781317481379 (pdf)
Subjects: LCSH: Shakespeare, William, 1564–1616–Poetic works. |
    Shakespeare, William, 1564–1616–Criticism and interpretation.
Classification: LCC PR2841 .S57 2017 | DDC 822.3/3—dc23
LC record available at https://lccn.loc.gov/2017003335

ISBN: 978-0-415-73707-4 (hbk)
ISBN: 978-0-582-78410-9 (pbk)
ISBN: 978-1-315-70794-5 (ebk)

Typeset in Bembo Std
by Swales & Willis Ltd, Exeter, Devon, UK

Printed and bound by CPI Group (UK) Ltd, Croydon, CR0 4YY

Contents

List of figures   vii

A note from the General Editors   ix

Acknowledgements   xi

Introduction: editorial procedures   xiii

Venus and Adonis (ed. Raphael Lyne)   1

Lucrece (ed. Raphael Lyne)   105

'Let the Bird of Loudest Lay' (ed. Raphael Lyne and Cathy Shrank)   251

Shakespeare's Sonnets (ed. Cathy Shrank)   269

A Lover's Complaint (ed. Cathy Shrank)   625

Appendix 1 (Raphael Lyne): *Venus and Adonis*: principal source   663

Appendix 2 (Raphael Lyne): *Lucrece*: principal sources   673

Appendix 3 (Cathy Shrank): *The Passionate Pilgrim*   685

Appendix 4 (Cathy Shrank): Shakespeare's sonnets in manuscript   715

Appendix 5 (Cathy Shrank): *Shakespeare's Sonnets* and English sonnet sequences in print (to 1640)   729

Appendix 6 (Cathy Shrank): poems posthumously attributed to Shakespeare   735

    'Upon a Pair of Gloves' 736
    Verses on the Stanley tomb 737
    'Shall I die?' 738
    'An Epitaph on Elias James' 741
    'An Epitaph on John Combe' 742
    Another epitaph on John Combe 743
    'On Ben Jonson' 743
    'Upon the King' 744

Shakespeare's epitaph on himself 744
'To the Queen' 745

Appendix 7 (Raphael Lyne and Cathy Shrank): Shakespeare's rhymes   747
Glossary of rhetorical terms   769
Bibliography   771
Index of first lines and titles   779

Figures

1.1 William Shakespeare, *Venus and Adonis* (London: Richard Field, 1593), sig. G3r; Bodleian Library copy, classmark Arch.Ge.31(2). Used with permission of the Bodleian Library   95

1.2 William Shakespeare, *Venus and Adonis* (London: R. Bradocke, 1602?), sig. D1r; Bodleian Library copy, classmark Arch.Gg.4(2). Used with permission of the Bodleian Library   95

2.1 William Shakespeare, *Lucrece* (London: Richard Field, 1594), sigs D4v–E1r; Folger Shakespeare Library copy, classmark STC 22345, Copy 2. Used with permission of the Folger Shakespeare Library   155

4.1 William Shakespeare, *Shakespeare's Sonnets* (London: George Eld, 1609), T.T.'s dedication; Folger Shakespeare Library copy, classmark STC 22353. Used with permission of the Folger Shakespeare Library   278

4.2 William Shakespeare, *Shakespeare's Sonnets* (London: George Eld, 1609), sigs H2v–H3r; Folger Shakespeare Library copy, classmark STC 22353. Used with permission of the Folger Shakespeare Library   553

4.3 William Shakespeare, *Shakespeare's Sonnets* (London: George Eld, 1609), sigs H4v–I1r; Folger Shakespeare Library copy, classmark STC 22353. Used with permission of the Folger Shakespeare Library   577

A note from the General Editors

Longman Annotated English Poets was launched in 1965 with the publication of Kenneth Allott's edition of *The Poems of Matthew Arnold*. F.W. Bateson wrote that the 'new series is the first designed to provide university students and teachers, and the general reader with complete and fully annotated editions of the major English poets'. That remains the aim of the series, and Bateson's original vision of its policy remains essentially the same. Its 'concern is primarily with the *meaning* of the extant texts in their various contexts'. The two other main principles of the series were that the text should be modernised and the poems printed 'as far as possible in the order in which they were composed'.

These broad principles still govern the series. Its primary purpose is to provide an annotated text giving the reader any necessary contextual information. However, flexibility in the detailed application has proved necessary in the light of experience and the needs of a particular case (and each poet is by definition, a particular case).

First, proper glossing of a poet's vocabulary has proved essential and not something which can be taken for granted. Second, modernisation has presented difficulties, which have been resolved pragmatically, trying to reach a balance between sensitivity to the text in question and attention to the needs of a modern reader. Thus, to modernise Browning's text has a double redundancy: Victorian conventions are very close to modern conventions, and Browning had firm ideas on punctuation. Equally, to impose modern pointing on the ambiguities of Marvell would create a misleading clarity. Third, in the very early days of the series Bateson hoped that editors would be able in many cases to annotate a *textus receptus*. That has not always been possible, and where no accepted text exists or where the text is controversial, editors have been obliged to go back to the originals and create their own text. The series has taken, and will continue to take, the opportunity not only of providing thorough annotations not available elsewhere, but also of making important scholarly textual contributions where necessary. A case in point is the edition of *The Poems of Tennyson* by Christopher Ricks, the second edition of which (1987) takes into account a full collation of the Trinity College Manuscripts, not previously available for an edition of this kind. Yet the series' primary purpose remains annotation.

The rationale for the present edition of *The Complete Poems of Shakespeare* is that as the knowledge, requirements and expectations of readers change from generation to generation, and as scholars make further discoveries, new editions are needed. The text of Shakespeare's poems is presented here in a form which sensitively modernises spelling and punctuation, while the annotation pays particular attention to elucidating the complexities of Shakespeare's language in particularly rich detail, and to charting connections of thought and phrasing between Shakespeare's poetry and the work of his contemporaries. It therefore not only presents Shakespeare's work to the modern reader, but also draws that reader into the rich, complex, and sometimes strange habits of thought which characterised the Elizabethan world.

Paul Hammond
David Hopkins

Acknowledgements

The debts accrued during the preparation of this edition are numerous. Like all editors of Shakespeare's texts, we owe much to our predecessors, from the eighteenth-century Edward Capell onwards. It is humbling to realise what they achieved without the electronic resources that have enabled much of the work on this edition. Even our most recent fellow-editors (Colin Burrow, Katherine Duncan-Jones, Henry Woudhuysen), working in the early 2000s, did not then have access to the full range of resources that we have had at our fingertips: the on-line Catalogue of English Literary Manuscripts; Phases I and II of EEBO-TCP; an increasing wealth of high-quality digitised images released by leading research libraries, such as the Folger Shakespeare Library, Washington D.C., to name but a few. The general editors of Annotated English Poets, Paul Hammond and David Hopkins, have provided meticulous comments on multiple drafts: we take full responsibility for the errors that remain, but the edition would have been a much, much poorer thing without their input. We have also benefitted from the support of our home institutions (the Universities of Cambridge and Sheffield) in terms of study leave and conference funding, and from the generous advice of friends and colleagues, on matters ranging from sixteenth-century lutes to phonetics, from the composition of early modern ink to the placement of individual marks of punctuation: in particular, Sylvia Adamson, Gavin Alexander, Alan Bryson, Colin Burrow, Ben Burton, Susan Fitzmaurice, Iona Hine, Danny Karlin, John Kerrigan, Micha Lazarus, Hester Lees-Jeffries, Andrew Linn, Steve May, Chris Montgomery, Subha Mukherji, Marcus Nevitt, Emma Rhatigan, Jenny Richards, Elizabeth Scott-Baumann, Ranjan Sen, Tim Shephard, Rosie Shute, Quentin Skinner, Felix Sprang, Graham Williams and Andrew Zurcher. As always, the largest debt of gratitude goes to our families (Clare, Thomas and Sophie; Phil, Ellen and Meg) who have had to live with this project for far too long.

Introduction

Editorial procedures

Canon

This edition contains Shakespeare's non-dramatic poetry: the two narrative poems from the mid-1590s (*Venus and Adonis*, *Lucrece*), 'Let the Bird of Loudest Lay' (aka 'The Phoenix and the Turtle'), appended to Robert Chester's *Love's Martyr* (1601), and the *Sonnets* and *A Lover's Complaint* (printed together in 1609). *The Passionate Pilgrim* (the entirety of which is falsely ascribed to Shakespeare during his lifetime) and poems in manuscript attributed to Shakespeare appear in appendices; the attributions are discussed in those locations.

Copy-texts

The texts are all based on their first editions, which – in the case of 'Let the Bird of Loudest Lay', *Shakespeare's Sonnets*, and *A Lover's Complaint* – are also the only editions printed in Shakespeare's lifetime.

Modernising spelling and punctuation

In general, spelling has been modernised in accordance with headwords in the *OED*. When this edition was being prepared, 34 per cent of the works on Early English Books Online were available as searchable keyed text via EEBO-TCP (Phases I and II). This resource was therefore used to check language use (for example, regarding the printing of reflexive pronouns, discussed below). Whilst a negative result on EEBO-TCP does not prove that a word or spelling was not in use, a positive result shows that it was, and the resource has consequently been an invaluable supplement to reference works such as the OED. During the preparation of this volume, OED was also in the process of being revised: OED^3 indicates updated entries from the 3rd edition; OED without superscript numbering indicates entries from the 2nd edition (which remains available to on-line users, even after entries have been updated).

Occasionally, older forms (e.g. 'forbod', 'daffed') have been preserved, because full modernisation affects the sonic quality of the verse in those instances. Some aspects of the texts, which are fluid in the original, have been standardised. The exclamation 'O'/'Oh' appears in both forms in the original texts, even within the same work. To twenty-first-century readers, the different spellings can have different connotations, with 'Oh' being read as a sigh, 'O' as a more histrionic utterance (OED categorises 'O' as 'Now chiefly *poet.* and *rhetorical*'); in the sixteenth and seventeenth centuries, however, 'Oh' and 'O' were interchangeable, and to avoid tempting over-reading of the different spellings, all instances have been regularised as 'O'.

Twenty-first-century readers might similarly find a cognitive difference between 'myself' and 'my self', where the former is read neutrally as a reflexive pronoun, the latter as expression of 'my being'. In early modern print, the reflexive pronoun is almost always spaced as two words. A search on EEBO-TCP of texts printed by Richard Field before 1594 (the year he printed *Lucrece* and the year after *Venus and Adonis*) reveals that there are 389 usages of 'thy self/thy selfe' and 381 instances of 'my self/my selfe', compared to one usage of 'thyself/thyselfe'; 'myself/myselfe' does not appear. Figures for George Eld, up to 1609 when he printed *Shakespeare's Sonnets*, are similar: there are 272 occurrences of 'thy self/thy selfe' and 574 of 'my self/my selfe', compared to seven instances of 'myself/myselfe', and none of 'thyself/thyselfe'. With few exceptions (discussed in notes), reflexive pronouns are consequently modernised as one word.

Poetry in sixteenth- and seventeenth-century manuscripts is typically only lightly punctuated (punctuation is often omitted at the end of lines of verse, for example, as can be seen in the transcriptions from manuscript in Appendix 4); much of the punctuation in the copy-texts would therefore have been added by the compositors in the printing house, according to a rhetorical – rather than grammatical – system of punctuation. The policy adopted in this volume is to keep or supply such punctuation as aids the comprehension of a twenty-first-century reader. Quotation marks (not used in the sixteenth and early seventeenth centuries) have been added to indicate direct speech or thought.

For explanations of points of grammar, the main points of reference are Hope (2003), as the most up-to-date source at the time of writing, and Abbott (1884) as the most comprehensive.

Spelling and punctuation in the appendices

Primary texts in the appendices are in old spelling and punctuation, and editorial intervention has been kept to a minimum (namely, expanding tildes, to provide 'n' or 'm'; supplying missing end brackets; and standardising typography, by replacing the long 's' with modern 's').

Textual cruxes

Textual cruxes – those parts of the text where errors seem to have crept in – are discussed in the notes; there is only one instance (Sonnet 146.2) where a corrupted copy-text is signalled in the text itself, with the use of square brackets. When resolving textual cruxes, the editors have considered the processes of transmission in order to evaluate where, how, and if errors have occurred. Early printed texts were set manually – letter by letter – by compositors; for a first edition, this would involve reading from a handwritten document (later editions would be almost always set from an earlier printed edition). This handwritten document might be several removes from its author, and each time a document is copied increases the possibility for error, through misreading or mishearing a word (not all documents were copied by sight in this period). Attention has therefore been paid to the likelihood of various errors, be it the probability of a letter, or a syllable, being misread, or misheard, as another, or the possibility of the compositor inserting a piece of type upside-down (an error which in the case of 'u' and 'n' is likely to go unnoticed without careful proof-reading). When assessing the possible errors that have been introduced during the production and reading of handwritten documents, we have assumed that these would have been written in a sixteenth-century 'secretary' hand: a cursive script, which – for speed – was most commonly used in the period. Many of the letter forms used in secretary hand differ from modern-day handwriting; a useful introduction and accompanying visual material can be found at 'English Handwriting: An Online Course': https://www.english.cam.ac.uk/ceres/ehoc/.

Guides to rhyme and metre

English pronunciation has changed quite significantly since the sixteenth century, when Shakespeare's accent would have been shaped. Many of the words which – to Elizabethan and Jacobean ears – could have sounded as full rhymes now appear to us only as eye rhymes. A list and explanation of these appears in Appendix 7.

In the texts that follow, accents show where a word should be stressed only when (i) a syllable which is usually silent in modern pronunciation needs to be sounded for metrical purposes (e.g. '-tunèd', Sonnet 8.5), and (ii) marking such a stress does not risk confusing the reader (as we felt it did with a word like 'annexions', which needs to be sounded as four syllables in *A Lover's Complaint*, l. 208). In cases where stresses differ from usual modern pronunciation and accents are not marked in the text (e.g. with 'annexions', or the stress on the first syllable of 'antique'), guidance on scansion is provided by the notes.

The number of syllables which need to be stressed is not always consistent: 'heaven' and 'flower', for example, can be pronounced with either one or two syllables: contrast Sonnets 14.8 and 17.3 ('heaven'); *Venus and Adonis*, ll. 8, 1055 ('flower'). In the interest of presenting a clear and uncluttered text, we have kept the marking of elisions to a minimum, only including them when the alternative poses a potential stumbling block to the reader. For example, 'blustering' (*Lucrece*, l. 115) needs to be pronounced as two syllables (and is spelled 'blustring' in the 1594 quarto) but – since twenty-first-century English naturally accommodates a disyllabic pronunciation – this has not been marked in the text. In contrast, 'stolen' (Sonnet 31.6) needs to be pronounced as one syllable, counter to the disyllabic pronunciation that is customary in twenty-first-century English (it is spelled 'stolne' in the 1609 quarto). In this, and other such cases (e.g. 'present'st', Sonnet 70.8), the elision has therefore been marked. Where an elision is needed for purposes of scansion but is not shown in the text, guidance has been given in the notes, with the exception of 'every', which is always disyllabic (never tri-syllabic): it is therefore noted here, rather than in a note at each occurrence.

Venus and Adonis

Text, publication and reception

Venus and Adonis (1593) was the first work printed under Shakespeare's name. London theatres were closed for large parts of 1592–4, which may have led Shakespeare, already a working playwright, to turn to narrative poetry. He may also have wanted to present a poem to Henry Wriothesley, the Earl of Southampton, in the hope of further patronage as the earl came of age. *Venus and Adonis* was the second work dedicated to Wriothesley, who would also be the dedicatee of *Lucrece*. The first was John Clapham's *Narcissus* (1591), another Ovidian story of doomed love. Clapham's poem may have been intended to send a message to the young earl from his guardian William Cecil, Lord Burghley. Southampton had refused to marry Elizabeth Vere: comparison with Narcissus could then be a rebuke. Without clearly either endorsing or opposing this possible point in Clapham's poem, *Venus and Adonis* (like Sonnets 1–17) revisits its interest in coming-of-age, willingness and wilfulness.

The signed dedication to Southampton is a strong indication that the 1593 first quarto (Q), of which only one copy survives in the Bodleian Library, Oxford, was (i) authorised by Shakespeare and (ii) based on a manuscript deriving from the author or someone close to him. Its lack of obvious errors also points this way. Accordingly, Q is the basis of this and all other editions, and its readings are preferred unless there is compelling evidence to the contrary. There are only two places in the text where another word is chosen: one of these derives initially from Q7 (on which see below; l. 1054), the other from H.N. Hudson's Victorian edition (l. 466).

Q was printed by Richard Field, who had claimed rights over the work in the register of the Stationers' Company on 18 April 1593 (Arber 1875–94, ii.630). It is reasonable to assume it was written shortly before. Like Shakespeare, Field was from Stratford-upon-Avon, and he was only three years older (baptised 1561; died 1624). This connection may lie behind their collaboration on Shakespeare's first venture into print. However, by 1593 Field was a well-established figure in London printing. He became a freeman of the Stationers' Company in 1587, and in the same year Thomas Vautrollier (to whom he had been apprenticed) died. Soon after, Field began collaborating with his widow Jacqueline, who took over Vautrollier's business, and in 1589 they were married. This made Field one of the leading printers in England, especially of foreign-language books (ODNB), and before *Venus and Adonis* he had printed Puttenham's *Art of English Poesy* (1589) and Sir John Harington's translation of *Orlando Furioso* (1591). Thus his credentials as a prestigious printer and/or publisher of literature were established, and afterwards these credentials grew further, for example with Spenser's *Faerie Queene* (1596), Sidney's *Arcadia* (1598) and Robert Chester's *Love's Martyr* (1601), which included 'Let the Bird of Loudest Lay'.

In June 1594 Field passed on the right to publish *Venus and Adonis* to John Harrison the elder, but continued as its printer for the next three editions (1594–6). Harrison also employed Field to print *Lucrece* (1594). With sixteen editions before 1640, *Venus and Adonis* proved popular:

'the best-selling poetry book of its time' (Erne and Badcoe 2014: 53). We follow usual editorial practice in designating these as a numbered sequence Q, Q2, Q3, etc., even though from Q3 onwards the books are actually in the smaller octavo format. William Leake received the right to publish from Harrison in 1596, and held it until 1617. There is a problematic group of editions dating from, or claiming to date from, 1602. Q7, a unique copy in the Bodleian Library, was probably printed for Leake in that year by Richard Bradock, though it lacks a title-page. Another printer, Robert Raworth, took the extraordinary risk of producing a version of the text (Q8) without licence, *c.* 1607, presenting it as a book of 1602. He was found out and the book was 'suppressed'; he did not print another book for 25 years (Erne and Badcoe 2014: 53). When Henry Lownes printed Q9, *c.* 1608, we assume he did this with Leake's permission, but this edition too is dated 1602, as is Q10, which survives only as a title-page in the British Library. (Not all editors include this in their sequence of editions; we follow Burrow in doing so.) The most satisfactory explanation why even legitimate editions came out with false dates is that this was a tactic to deflect attention away from newly published erotic content: Richard Bancroft, Archbishop of Canterbury 1604–10, supervised the printing industry more closely than some predecessors (Erne 2013: 149–53).

Although Q is by far the most authoritative of the early texts, other editions are featured in the notes as sources of significant variants, some of which offer insights into the difficulties of Q's readings. In general these variants arise from misreadings of, or apparently deliberate changes to, the most recent text to be published. However, Roe (1992: 293) suggests that Q6 may have paid attention to more than just Q5, which is distinctively error-strewn. Q7 is the most interesting of the later editions: it seems to have benefited from insightful copy-editing, resolving many of the errors that were the legacy of Q5, sometimes so as to restore Q's reading, sometimes to supply its own. Q7 also emends some readings that had survived since Q, often with a view to clarifying and simplifying the text. See 54, 126, 142, 272, 542, 547, 632, 760, 780, 872–3, 1050, 1054 (where it is the source of one of only two accepted emendations of Q), 1101nn.

Other early editions are mentioned in the notes as follows: Q2 at ll. 156, 484, 1113; Q3 at l. 1031; Q4 at l. 160; Q5 at ll. 142, 547; Q6 at l. 996; Q9 at ll. 899, 909; Q13 at l. 605.

Duncan-Jones ('Much Ado', 1993) has shown that there was an immediate literary response in Thomas Edwards' *Cephalus and Procris* (1593), Michael Drayton's *Piers Gaveston* (1593) and Thomas Heywood's *Oenone and Paris* (1594); on which see 229–40n. According to Gabriel Harvey, 'the younger sort takes much delight in Shakespeare's Venus, and Adonis' (Duncan-Jones and Woudhuysen 2007: 490); this 'sort' is exemplified by the young men of the *Parnassus Plays*, who quote the poem approvingly, one promising that 'to honour [Shakespeare, I] will lay his *Venus and Adonis* under my pillow' (Leishman, ed., 1949: 193). Roberts' survey of the reception of Shakespeare's poems contrasts the intimate familiarity with which male readers approached and quoted *Venus and Adonis* (2003: 62–101), with the wary approaches of female readers (pp. 20–61) who had to negotiate its possible threats to virtue. The focus on erotic qualities, however, is a unifying theme in contemporary accounts of the poem's enthusiastic reception.

This carried on into the next generation. Richard Braithwaite's conduct manual *The English Gentleman* (1630) portrays young men 'carrying about them (even in their naked bosoms, where chastest desires should only lodge) the amorous toys of *Venus and Adonis*: which poem, with others of like nature, they hear with such attention, peruse with such devotion, and retain with such delectation, as no subject can equally relish their unseasoned palate' (sig. E2v). *Venus and Adonis* turns up in a more unlikely location, but with similar implications, in Thomas Robinson's *The Anatomy of the English Nunnery at Lisbon* (1622): 'after supper it is usual for him [i.e. the nuns' confessor, during his visits] to read a little of *Venus and Adonis*, the jests of George Peele, or some such scurrilous book: for there are few idle pamphlets printed in England which he hath not in the house . . . If I should repeat all their unchaste practices, I should make the Christian reader blush at them' (sig. D1r).

This image of the poem is reflected, with less moralistic disapproval, and with the genders of the lover and the object of desire often reversed, when it is mentioned in the theatre. See the references to Thomas Heywood's *Fair Maid of the Exchange* (1607) and Gervase Markham's *The Dumb Knight* (1608) at 229–40n; also, somewhat later, James Shirley's *The Ball: A Comedy* (1639), where Coronell flightily asks to swear by '*Venus and Adonis* then, / Or Ovid's wanton Elegies, Aristotle's / Problems, Guy of Warwick, or Sir Bevis, / Or if there be a play-book you love better, / I'll take my oath upon your epilogue'. Lucina responds: 'You're very merry' (sig. H1r).

Manuscript quotations also focus on the erotic: see the notes at 91–102, 229–40, 517–22. See also, however, 529–34n: one of the poem's rhetorical set-pieces caught the attention of multiple readers. Indeed, the other quality prized in its early reception was wit (both as humour and as ingenuity). *Venus and Adonis* is the first work mentioned in relation to Meres' famous 'sweet witty soul' comment (see 472n). John Davies' satirical *A Scourge for Paper-Persecutors* (1625) puts the two at odds: 'Fine wit is shown therein: but finer 'twere / If not attired in such bawdy gear. / But be it as it will: the coyest dames, / In private read it for their closet-games: / For, sooth to say, the lines so draw them on, / To the Venerian speculation, / That will they, nill they (if of flesh they be) / They will think of it, sith loose thought is free' (sig. A4r).

Sources and contexts

The principal source is the story of Venus and Adonis in Book 10 of Ovid's *Metamorphoses*. See Appendix 1 for a text of Arthur Golding's Elizabethan translation. Shakespeare and many of his readers would have known this work in Latin, in translation, and as part of a widespread Ovidian influence in Elizabethan poetry that peaked in the 1590s (Carter 2011; Moss 2014). Ovid's stories frequently combine moments of tragic pain and loss on the one hand, with wit, rhetorical display, and a light and often humorous tone, on the other. *Venus and Adonis* has more of a reputation for the latter, but both these qualities are crucial to its Ovidian inheritance. The story of Adonis is one of several key episodes in the *Metamorphoses* that feature young men, sex, violence and gods, such as Actaeon and Narcissus (in Book 3), Hermaphroditus (Book 4), Cyparissus and Hyacinthus (Book 10). All these stories underlie, explicitly at times, *Venus and Adonis*. The last pair are both part of Orpheus' song in Book 10, as is Adonis, and in this book Ovid gives him a problematic genealogy, with Pygmalion both his great-grandfather and his great-great-grandfather owing to the incestuous relationship of Cinyras and Myrrha.

The pertinence of Adonis' incestuous birth in Shakespeare's poem, with its self-standing story, is debatable, and no more than slight. Nevertheless the stories were readily linked in Elizabethan poetry, as in Thomas Peend, *The Pleasant Fable of Hermaphroditus and Salmacis* (1565): 'What did Adonis' mother, in her father old perceive: / Why she should seek by incest vile, her mother's bed for to defile' (sig. B5r). In Abraham Fraunce's *The Third Part of the Countess of Pembroke's Yvychurch, Entitled Aminta's Dale* (1592), in which a translation of the Ovidian section features, his origin is marvelled at: 'Myrrha, made Myrrh-tree, brought forth incestuous offspring, / And yet most delicate, most sweet, most beautiful offspring, / Dame Nature's darling, heav'ns joy, world's wonder, Adonis' (M1v).

There are many other versions of the Adonis story before and after the *Metamorphoses*, and sometimes these are cited as possible sources for Shakespeare's deviations from Ovid. For example, see 1111–16n on the possible influence of a Greek poem, thought in Shakespeare's time to be by Theocritus, which imagines the boar trying to kiss Adonis. Burrow suggests Giovanni Tarchagnota's *L'Adone* (Venice, 1550) as a parallel for Venus complaining against Death, though he doubts Shakespeare had read the poem (Burrow 2002: 224). Mythological manuals and compendia, such as Natale Conte's *Mythologiae*, or Abraham Fraunce's *Aminta's Dale* (as above) were widely read as well (see Hulse 1978). None of these alternative sources seems strictly necessary in order to understand how Shakespeare developed the story from Ovid.

As Weaver, *Untutored Lines*, shows (2012: 70–93), the Venus and Adonis story featured in Aphthonius' *Progymnasmata* (a set of rhetorical exercises) as an instance of *chreia* (anecdote): Aphthonius tells a different story, about Ares' violent jealousy, Venus hurting her foot when rushing to help Adonis, and her blood turning white roses red. There is a longer version in Camerarius' *Elementa Rhetoricae* (1545), which incorporates more Ovidian elements (e.g. the boar, storytelling). See Weaver on how these manuals, and the role of the story therein, relate to the transition between boyhood and manhood (2012: 70).

Venus and Adonis is a poem of its own moment as well as existing in a long-standing tradition. The Garden of Adonis in Spenser's *Faerie Queene* III.vi (1590) portrayed the dying-reviving hero amid a paradise of plenty and rebirth. The early 1590s saw the height of the Elizabethan vogue of the epyllion, short narrative poems on mythical themes (as in Clark, ed., *Amorous Rites* (1994), and Donno, ed., *Elizabethan Minor Epics* (1963)). Thomas Lodge's *Scilla's Metamorphosis* (1589) started the immediate vogue, though the Ovidian fashion was older (*The Fable of Ovid Treating of Narcissus* by T.H. [probably Thomas Hackett], 1560, and Peend's *Hermaphroditus and Salmacis*, 1565). John Clapham's *Narcissus* (1591; claimed by Martindale and Burrow (1992) as a 'pre-text' for *Venus and Adonis*) pursued the trend in Latin. Christopher Marlowe's *Hero and Leander* was first published in 1598 but must have been written before 1593 when Marlowe died, and the many debts attested in the notes show that Shakespeare knew and admired this poem, and in *Venus and Adonis* he meets its challenge in various ways. One facet of *Hero and Leander*, distinctively in the epyllion tradition, is its openness to sexuality of diverse kinds: Shakespeare's poem's candid attention to Adonis' youthful body follows Marlowe's homoerotic presentation of Leander.

The legacy of Ovid reached Shakespeare also through his *Amores*, which alongside other Latin lyrics were direct and indirect models for Shakespeare's presentation of love. Catullus' kiss poems (5 and 7 especially) are invoked by *Venus and Adonis*, probably as a result of the voluminous intervening tradition of neo-Latin *Basia*. Poets such as Joannes Secundus (see Wong 2013) elaborated hugely on the intensity, the gender dynamics and the humour found in Catullus. These motifs were taken on by the early English sonnet sequences, for example in Sir Philip Sidney's *Astrophil and Stella*, which is another vital reference point for the style and mood of *Venus and Adonis*. This sequence is also a major conduit into English for the devotion, desperation and inventiveness of sonnets in Italian and French (Petrarch and Ronsard especially). It is a saturated tradition, and *Venus and Adonis* gives a sense of that saturation, while also reversing some of its key dynamics: to make the desperate lover a woman, and indeed into a goddess, and the beautiful object into a man, overturns the usual Petrarchan scene.

The language of *Venus and Adonis* is not only derived from mythical and erotic traditions. As many citations in the notes attest, its lexis is that of early Shakespeare – of the history plays as well as the comedies. It contains detailed vocabulary relating to everyday Elizabethan life at various social levels: animals, hunting, war, the law and economics. It also turns frequently to a proverbial style, whether to achieve a wise tone of its own, or to portray its characters' attempts at wisdom.

The final obligatory context in which to understand *Venus and Adonis* is provided by *Lucrece*. The notes attest frequently to the two poems' shared vocabulary and interests. The dedication to *Venus and Adonis* offers a duality (if we take *Lucrece* to be the 'graver labour') that is hard to resist, in which *Venus and Adonis* is a comic forbear. On the other hand, it may suggest a more troubling affinity, in which (as in McGee 2012) the problems of sex and power in the earlier poem resonate. It also explores psychological depths that the later poem would revisit at greater length. Commenting on ll. 1037–53, Burrow says that this is 'the part of the poem from which Shakespeare learnt most in his later works . . . a radically disturbing picture of the mind . . . a central preoccupation of Shakespeare's next poem, *Lucrece*' (2002: 40).

Style and rhetoric

Shakespeare follows Lodge's *Scilla's Metamorphosis* in using a six-line stanza rhyming *ababcc*. Although this form is known as a sixain, or *sesta rima*, it is just as often called the '*Venus and Adonis* stanza' in English, testimony to its virtuosic use in the poem. George Puttenham's *Art of English Poesy* (1589) offers one contemporary view of an everyday, flexible form: 'the third ['proportion' of a 'staff', i.e. stanza, is] by *sixain* or six verses, and is not only most usual but also very pleasant to the ear' (sig. M1v). In *Venus and Adonis* the stanza allows for copious juxtaposition and antithesis, especially between quatrain and couplet (see Lyne 2014). This is one aspect of the witty style of the poem. Another is its rhetorical display, especially in figures of repetition and excess (antimetabole, epizeuxis, hyperbole, pleonasm and polyptoton all feature). Although the wit of *Venus and Adonis* has been valued throughout its reception history, and Duncan-Jones is right to note that in its time it 'exemplified the rhetoric of courtship' (1993: 497), its rhetoric has also been seen as something that stifles the individuality of Adonis (Dubrow 1987; Kiernan 1995).

Display and excess are features of the poem's many similes and comparisons. The characteristic vivid instruction to 'Look how' introduces several analogies (see 67n). Similes are often hyperbolic at first glance, but a reader's sense of proportion (what is exaggerated, and what is not) may need to be calibrated to suit the strength of a goddess' passion (see for example ll. 16, 78, 193–8, 389, 755, 815–16, 1057 and notes). Three extended depictions of animals (the horse, ll. 259–324; the boar, ll. 615–38; the hare, ll. 673–708) replace Ovid's inset story, told by Venus, about the transformation of Atalanta and Hippomenes into lions. These vivid depictions are tours-de-force of visual and other sensory description (*enargeia*), but their attention to animal experience (and the points Venus tries to make, especially about the horse's sexual appetite) fills out the poem's serious interest in nature and the difficulty of determining what constitutes natural behaviour.

Venus and Adonis

Title-page

Vilia. . . aqua 'Let the common sort wonder at worthless things. May golden Apollo provide me with cups full of the Muses' water'. The epigraph (from Ovid, *Amores*, 1.15.35–6) presents the poem as an ambitious, classically oriented work, with aspirations to an elite readership. The source in the *Amores* also suggests that wit and eroticism will feature.

VENUS AND ADONIS

Vilia miretur vulgus: mihi flavus Apollo
Pocula Castalia plena ministret aqua.

LONDON
Imprinted by Richard Field, and are to be sold at
the sign of the white greyhound in
Paul's Churchyard.
1593

Dedication

Henry Wriothesley See headnote.

I know not how I shall offend This phrase may be conventional modesty, but it might be genuinely tentative. Park Honan (*ODNB*) takes it to indicate that Shakespeare 'barely knows' the earl at the time of the dedication.

unpolished OED³ 2, 'not carefully finished; not skilfully performed; crude, inelegant, unfinessed', combines both elements of this term. Compare the 'untutored lines' of the *Lucrece* dedication.

only. . . pleased if your Honour seems at all pleased with it.

idle hours modestly demeaning the worth of the poem again. 'Idle' primarily suggests an unproductive waste of time (see l. 422 and note), but may also suggest the unoccupied leisure associated with wealth (in tune with the dedication's aspirations).

graver labour more serious work; usually taken to mean *Lucrece*, and to cast *Venus and Adonis* as an immediate predecessor to something more substantial. OED has this as first citation for 'grave, *adj.*1 and *n.*5', 'of works [. . .] weighty, important'. Burrow (2002: 173) notes the Latin word 'gravior' underlying related uses around poetry and the aspiration towards epic: e.g. the 'bigger notes' (translating 'graviore sono') in Edmund Spenser, *Virgil's Gnat* (1595) l. 11, and the 'graver verse' (translating 'plectro graviore') which Orpheus remembers using to describe an epic battle, in Golding's *Metamorphoses*, 10.155.

An EEBO-TCP search of uses of 'graver' before 1594 confirms that the usage here is innovative, though 'graver studies' is a common phrase. There is a notable precedent in Gabriel Harvey, *Four Letters, and Certain Sonnets* (1592): 'graver tragedies' as opposed to 'pelting comedies' (sig. G2v); also in George Puttenham's *Art of English Poesy* (1589) on how altering line length 'doth alter the nature of the poesy, and make it either lighter or graver' (sig. M1v).

first heir of my invention This was the first printed book featuring Shakespeare's name; the phrase invites the reader to approach *Venus and Adonis* as an early work. 'Invention' suggests his creative effort and skill (OED 4), but also *inventio* in rhetoric, i.e. the technique of gathering material and arguments for the orator's case (OED 1d).

ear plough (OED³ 'ear, *v.*1', 1a).

survey examination, perusal, perhaps specifically 'literary examination' (OED 4a). In the light of the agricultural metaphor being developed, a survey of land (OED 5a) is also evoked.

hopeful expectation Although any connection between Wriothesley and the young man of the *Sonnets* is conjectural, the concept of 'hopeful expectation' is central to Sonnets 1–17 and their many links to *Venus and Adonis*. The closing lines of this dedication seem warily to acknowledge the world expects things of the earl that might not come to pass.

TO THE RIGHT HONOURABLE
Henry Wriothesley, Earl of Southampton,
and Baron of Titchfield.

Right Honourable, I know not how I shall offend in dedicating my unpolished lines to your Lordship, nor how the world will censure me for choosing so strong a prop to support so weak a burden; only if your Honour seem but pleased, I account myself highly praised, and vow to take advantage of all idle hours, till I have honoured you with some graver labour. But if the first heir of my invention prove deformed, I shall be sorry it had so noble a godfather, and never after ear so barren a land, for fear it yield me still so bad a harvest. I leave it to your Honourable survey, and your Honour to your heart's content, which I wish may always answer your own wish, and the world's hopeful expectation.

Your Honour's in all duty,
William Shakespeare.

Venus and Adonis

1 ***Even as*** 'Even' is monosyllabic here. More often than not these words introduce a comparison in Shakespeare (as at ll. 55, 338, 458; or in *Two Gentlemen of Verona*, 2.4.192, where Proteus starts a soliloquy 'Even as one heat another heat expels [...]'). This poem full of comparisons and similes feints in that direction, but the tense of the verb 'had ta'en' clarifies this is a temporal clause, establishing the time at which the story starts.

purple-coloured Most straightforwardly, this refers to the red colour of the morning sun, but also evokes blushes (as Burrow 2002: 175 notes, the word 'purpureus' is prominent in Ovid's *Amores*, e.g. 1.3.13, of a blush). Purple itself suggests regality (OED^3 1a). In the poem, it is used also of blood ('purple tears', l. 1054) and the flower into which Adonis is turned (l. 1168). Elsewhere Shakespeare uses it of blood, grapes, violets and the dawn. The red morning sky is proverbially ominous (Dent M1175: 'a red morning foretells a stormy day'). In Chapman's continuation of *Hero and Leander* this is linked to a lover's complexion: 'And all the air she purpled round about, | And after it a foul black day befell, | Which ever since a red morn doth foretell' (III, 176–8). The other crucial context is Matthew 16:2–3, where Jesus says 'When it is evening, ye say, fair weather: for the sky is red. And in the morning ye say, today shall be a tempest; for the sky is red and louring'. Compare l. 453. However, the ominous message of a red morning sky is subsidiary to the main point, which is that the sun-god is red-faced after a night of passion.

2 ***ta'en*** taken.

weeping dewy; Roe wonders whether the personified morning is weeping over the sun-god's departure (1992: 79). Having the sun and the morning as lovers (as at ll. 855–6) evokes no particular myth: Phoebus (Apollo) has many lovers, but the Dawn (Eos) is not one of them. Her most famous lover (Tithonus, granted eternal life but not eternal youth) is almost an antithesis of Adonis.

3 ***Rose-cheeked Adonis*** At this point a difference between 'rose' and 'purple' separates the youthful glow of Adonis from the guiltier flush of the sun-god; proliferating play on red and white throughout the poem challenges such fine-tuning (see l. 10 and note). The phrase is used by Marlowe, *Hero and Leander*, ll. 91–3, describing a festival in Sestos that celebrates Adonis: 'The men of wealthy Sestos every year, | (For his sake whom their goddess held so dear, | Rose-cheeked Adonis) kept a solemn feast'. The red rose is associated with the story of Venus and Adonis because in some versions its colour derived from blood spilled by one or the other, as in Aphthonius (see headnote) or Barnabe Barnes, *Parthenophil and Parthenophe* (1593), Ode 16.21–2: 'Her forehead was like to the rose | Before Adonis pricked his feet' (sig. S1v).

hied him hurried.

4 ***love*** primarily refers to love in the abstract. At various points in the poem (including here, tenuously) the word could refer to the goddess of love, Venus herself.

laughed to scorn derided; mocked disdainfully.

5 ***Sick-thoughted*** love-sick.

makes amain unto hurries towards him forcefully: 'makes unto' is equivalent to 'makes for', and 'amain' means violently or swiftly. Baldwin (1950: 10–11) notes the resemblance between Venus and the rapacious Salmacis in Ovid's myth of Hermaphroditus (*Metamorphoses*, 4.285–388, Golding, 4.352–481).

8 ***fields'*** Burrow (2002) has 'field's'; the difference is minimal. Modernised spelling requires a decision one way or another.

flower disyllabic; apart from this instance, and possibly the rhyme-words at ll. 65, 946, 1188, the word is monosyllabic in the poem. Here it foreshadows Adonis' ultimate metamorphosis.

compare The word and its cognates appear also at the very end of the poem (ll. 1172, 1176; and at 701). On comparison in the poem, see headnote.

9 ***Stain*** cause of humiliation; OED cites this line for 'stain, *n.*', 3c, 'One who eclipses or casts into the shade'. He tarnishes their reputations, because he is more beautiful than they are. A possible echo of the word 'disdain' foreshadows that word's importance later in the poem; see l. 33 and note.

more lovely than a man 'Man' here could denote a mortal, an adult, or the male sex in general.

10 ***white and red*** After the red hues of the first stanza, the poem's key paired colours appear in the second (see ll. 35, 36, 76, 345–8, 467–8, 902, 1168, 1169). It is telling that they are initially linked to clichés of love poetry and female blazon: doves (which will eventually carry Venus out of the poem, l. 1190) and roses. These are both proverbial: Dent D573.2, 'as white as a dove', and R177, 'as red (ruddy) as a rose'. Compare *Lucrece*, ll. 11, 71 and notes. They are also ubiquitous

Even as the sun with purple-coloured face
Had ta'en his last leave of the weeping morn,
Rose-cheeked Adonis hied him to the chase;
Hunting he loved, but love he laughed to scorn.
    Sick-thoughted Venus makes amain unto him,   5
    And like a bold-faced suitor 'gins to woo him.

'Thrice fairer than myself' (thus she began),
'The fields' chief flower, sweet above compare,
Stain to all nymphs, more lovely than a man,
More white and red than doves or roses are: 10
    Nature, that made thee with herself at strife,
    Saith that the world hath ending with thy life.

'Vouchsafe, thou wonder, to alight thy steed,
And rein his proud head to the saddle-bow.

in love poetry. See Marlowe's translation of the *Amores*, 3.3.5–6: 'Fair white with rose red was before commixed: | Now shine her looks pure white and red betwixt', and *Astrophil and Stella*, 9.5–8: 'The door by which sometimes comes forth her grace, | Red porphyre is, which lock of pearl makes sure: | Whose porches rich (which name of cheeks endure) | Marble mixed red and white do interlace'. The profusion of this pair of colours in Shakespeare's poem, however, is distinctive. There may be some play on the colours in the Tudor rose, and the civil war which preceded the Tudor dynasty (compare l. 764 and note).

11–12 *Nature. . . life* The argument here (that self-absorption is culpably unproductive) resembles that of the procreation sonnets (1–17; especially 1), but without the procreation.

11 *at strife* in competition. Nature has made Adonis so lovely that he surpasses the rest of nature. 'Strife' predominantly denotes discord, but can suggest natural, creative energy amid contention, something the OED does not acknowledge. Compare Marlowe's use of the word as Hero half-resists Leander's sexual advances: 'She trembling strove, this strife of hers (like that | Which made the world) another world begat, | Of unknown joy' (ll. 775–7; on this passage see l. 337 and note). Compare *Timon of Athens*, 1.1.37–8, the Poet speaking: 'It tutors nature. Artificial strife | Lives in these touches, livelier than life'; also l. 291, and *Lucrece*, l. 1377.

12 *hath ending with thy life* will die when you do. The hyperbolic and apocalyptic tone here will return at the end of the poem, but is familiar from love poetry with or without tragedy. Burrow (2002: 176) compares

Sonnet 11 and *Romeo and Juliet*, 1.1.215–24 (on Rosaline's beauty); compare also *Antony and Cleopatra*, 4.15.67–8: 'there is nothing left remarkable | Beneath the visiting moon'. In the key seduction passage of *Hero and Leander* Marlowe also turns to the idea: 'All heaven would come to claim this legacy, | And with intestine broils the world destroy, | And quite confound nature's sweet harmony' (ll. 250–2).

13 *Vouchsafe* give consent; OED *v.* 2a suggests the word was becoming more clearly associated with condescension (compare 'deign', l. 15) in Shakespeare's time.
    alight climb down from; usually intransitive, here transitive.

14 *proud* 'full of vigour, mettle or beauty' is Schmidt's paraphrase for one complex of uses in the poem: compare ll. 14, 260, 288, 300, 884, 923. Other senses of the word arise at l. 309 ('full of esteem, elated, haughty'), and l. 113 ('selfish cold, unkind'); Schmidt's paraphrases in all cases help organise the many nuances of the word seen under OED[3] 'proud, *adj.*, *n.*, and *adv.*'. See also 'pride', at ll. 278, 420, 762. For the word's appearances in *Lucrece*, see 37n. The nuances of the word are important in the poem, where (from Venus' point of view) sexual vigour must not be handled selfishly. The word is associated with Adonis in *Hero and Leander*, 9–14: 'The outside of her garments were [. . .] bordered with a grove, | Where Venus in her naked glory strove | To please the careless and disdainful eyes | Of proud Adonis that before her lies'.
    saddle-bow 'the arched front part of a saddle' (OED[3]). Fixing the reins here restrains a horse.

15 *meed* reward.

16 *thousand* The number recurs at ll. 240, 477, 517, 682, 775, 907, 1130. Kisses are counted also at ll. 22, 517–22 ('thousand [...] ten hundred [...] twenty hundred'). Kisses are counted most famously in Catullus, poems 5 and 7, which must be evoked here, and in the long tradition of neo-Latin *Basia* (most influentially by Joannes Secundus, on which see headnote and ll. 64–6, 84, 1187–8 and notes). This tradition often tends towards excess in the counting and the passion described, but to treat this as straightforwardly hyperbolic may be problematic when the goddess of love – whose capacity and appetite are supernatural – is concerned. Compare *Lucrece*, l. 456 and note.

honey secrets sweet, intimate knowledge; the next stanza expands upon the hint of cloying here and in 'smother', l. 18. For more honey in the poem, see ll. 452, 538, and compare Sonnet 65.5 and note.

18 *set* seated (down), following 'sit' in l. 17. OED notes under both 'sit' and 'set' that there is overlap between the two words in Shakespeare's time. Shakespeare plays on the interaction of transitive and intransitive meanings, and on the linguistic nicety.

smother Compare l. 1035 and note.

19–20 *And yet not cloy. . . plenty* It is common to portray desire as insatiable. There is a specific connection here with the story of Narcissus in Ovid. The resonant line is *Metamorphoses*, 3.466 ('inopem me copia fecit'; Golding, 3.587, 'my plenty makes me poor'), where Narcissus cannot get enough of his reflection. *Antony and Cleopatra*, 2.2.234–5 plays on a similar theme: 'Age cannot wither her, nor custom stale | Her infinite variety'. See also *Lucrece*, ll. 97, 557, on Tarquin's appetite, and Sonnet 1.5–7, though Venus is planning a captivating effect, rather than observing it.

19 *loathed satiety* fullness or over-fullness that causes disgust. 'Satiety' ('sacietie', Q) needs to be pronounced with three syllables, unless 'loathed' is disyllabic, in which case 'satiety' must be elided into two. Metrical over-fullness is thematically apt; four words rhyming on unstressed syllables – satiety, plenty, variety, twenty; eleven syllables in each line – suit the suggestion of luxurious excess.

22 *twenty* the poem's favourite number, and a numerical measure of hyperbole; see ll. 522 (with 'hundred'), 575, 775 (with 'thousand'), 833–4 (three times) and Sonnet 152.6. On the tradition of counting kisses in the neo-Latin *Basia* genre, especially in the poems of Joannes Secundus, see 16n.

23 *an hour but short* only an hour long; compare 'short time', *Lucrece*, l. 1573 and note.

24 *wasted* This word may not seem pejorative (especially given that an immortal must have a different attitude to time). Compare *Merchant of Venice*, 3.4.11–12: 'companions | That so converse and waste the time together'. In the case of Celia in *As You Like It*, 2.4.94–5 ('I like this place, | And willingly could waste my time in it'), the word reflects her insensitivity to rural poverty as well as charming optimism.

beguiling (i) fooling; (ii) cheating; but see also OED 'beguile, *v.*' 5, 'To divert attention in some pleasant way from (anything painful, or irksome)'. Shakespeare seems to stretch this word away (as he may do with 'wasted') from its pejorative core meanings. Line 23's 'seem' leaves it unclear whether time itself is being fooled, or whether the lovers deceive only themselves.

sport play (with erotic implications). There is a cluster of uses early in the poem (ll. 105, 124, 154) with approximately this sense, but Adonis would prefer another kind of sport (hunting). The last appearance of the word (l. 844) is a sardonic reflection on lovers in general, and on Venus' uses of the word earlier in the poem. Compare *Lucrece*, l. 992.

25 *With this* (i) having said this; (ii) at that moment. The poem uses 'with this' (see ll. 811, 1121) and 'by this' (which can mean 'meanwhile', see l. 175 and note) as ways of propelling the narrative along. See l. 39 and note.

26 *precedent* president Q; sign, indication (OED³ 3). In this line Adonis' sweat is taken to be a predictive indication of his sexual vigour. *Othello* also falsely connects moisture and wantonness: 'Thy hand is moist, my lady [...] | This argues fruitfulness and liberal heart' (3.4.36, 38). In misreading the sweaty palm, the narrative voice seems to merge with Venus' perspective. Compare ll. 139–44, and *Lucrece*, l. 1261.

pith strength (suggesting he is firm and substantial).

livelihood liveliness.

27 *calls it balm* deems it (i.e. Adonis' sweat) a perfumed, health-giving ointment. Many Shakespearean uses of the word relate to monarchy, e.g. *Richard II*, 4.1.207: 'With mine own tears I wash away my balm',

If thou wilt deign this favour, for thy meed   15
A thousand honey secrets shalt thou know.
   Here come and sit, where never serpent hisses,
   And being set, I'll smother thee with kisses.

'And yet not cloy thy lips with loathed satiety,
But rather famish them amid their plenty,   20
Making them red, and pale, with fresh variety:
Ten kisses short as one, one long as twenty.
   A summer's day will seem an hour but short,
   Being wasted in such time-beguiling sport.'

With this she seizeth on his sweating palm,   25
The precedent of pith and livelihood,
And, trembling in her passion, calls it balm,
Earth's sovereign salve to do a goddess good.
   Being so enraged, desire doth lend her force,
   Courageously to pluck him from his horse.   30

Over one arm the lusty courser's rein,
Under her other was the tender boy,

where its two meanings (curative ointment; anointing oil) overlap.

28 **sovereign salve** picking up on 'balm', his sweat is now seen as the most pre-eminent ('sovereign') ointment ('salve') in the world, such that it can even cure a goddess. EEBO-TCP has 36 uses of the phrase in 32 different works before 1593, which suggests that it was well-known.

29 **enraged** in a state of feverish passion; it need not imply anger. In Thomas Thomas' *Dictionarium* (1587) it is part of the gloss for Latin 'lymphatus': 'mad, furious, enraged, bestraught, outrageous, fantastical: fallen out of his wit by seeing some thing'. Compare *Lucrece*, l. 424.
lend her endow her with; as at l. 775. In the poem the word has other meanings relating to granting and bestowing (ll. 315, 539, 756, 790) and as an opposite to borrowing (l. 961). Given the poem's interest in giving and taking (especially of sexual favour), this knot of meanings is suggestive.
her i.e. Venus, though it could conceivably (but awkwardly) be a possessive pronoun where a feminine 'desire' is lending the 'force' in question.

30 **Courageously** passionately (rather than bravely). 'Courage' is a repeated and varying word in the poem, suggesting sexual desire, bravery and high spirits. See Richard Huloet's *Abecedarium Anglico Latinum* (1552), where it is glossed as 'Animus, Audatia, Spiritus' (where 'animus' and 'spiritus' both suggest 'spirit', and 'audatia' is 'boldness'). It is used of humans and animals: see ll. 276, 294, 556, 1158.
pluck remove; a key word in *Venus and Adonis*. Flowers are plucked before their time. This word, part of the poem's exploration of the question of ripeness in relation to physical love, recurs at ll. 416, 528, 574, 946, 1150. Compare 'crops', used at l. 946, and when Venus picks the flower at l. 1175.

31 **Over one arm** The goddess is able to carry Adonis under one arm, and to control the horse with the other.
lusty vigorous, with sexual overtones.
courser 'a large powerful horse, ridden in battle, in a tournament, etc.; a charger' (OED *n.*2 1), but see also OED 1b, 'since 17th c. usually taken as: A swift horse, a racer'.

32 **tender** delicate, youthful (OED *adj.* (and *adv.*) and *n.*3, 4), but other meanings of the word are in play here, e.g. he is not feeling tender towards others (OED 8a); he is physically immature (OED 4 again).

33   **dull** lacking in lust and lustre; picked up by 'leaden' in the next line.

33   **disdain** a key word in the poem. It means contempt generally, but is frequently associated with contempt of a lover or love in general; see also ll. 112, 241, 358, 394, 501, 761, and *Lucrece*, l. 691. See *Astrophil and Stella*, 5th song, 28 (addressing his muse): 'Since she [i.e. Stella] disdaining me, doth you in me disdain'. In *Hero and Leander* the word is used when Leander is compared to a horse: 'For as a hot proud horse highly disdains, | To have his head controlled, but breaks the reins, | Spits forth the ringled bit, and with his hooves | Checks the submissive ground' (ll. 625–8); here it collocates with 'proud', as it does in the quotation at 14n. See also ll. 263–70 and note.

34   **leaden** unresponsive, the first citation in OED for 2c, 'with allusion to the want of elasticity in the metal: Inert, spiritless, depressing'. See *Richard III*, 3.1.176, 'if he be leaden, icy, cold, unwilling' (not in an erotic context).
   unapt Schmidt's paraphrase, 'not propense or ready', is incisive but shades of meaning are important here because of the implications of Adonis' unaptness: ill-suited (because he is too young), ill-adapted (because he is unwilling), perhaps also incapable. Other uses in Shakespeare tend to mean ill-suited by age or temperament; see *Lucrece*, l. 695, and *1 Henry IV*, 1.3.1–2, 'My blood hath been too cold and temperate, | Unapt to stir at these indignities'. Compare Marlowe, *Elegies*, 2.1.3–6: 'So *Cupid* wills, far hence be the severe, | You are unapt my looser lines to hear. | Let maids whom hot desire to husbands lead, | And rude boys touched with unknown love me read'.
   toy dally, play (sexually); compare l. 106, and *Lucrece*, l. 214.

35–6   **She red. . . he red** On red and white, see l. 10 and note. This couplet offers a slightly false opposition between an outward redness and an inward '**frosty**' whiteness (and coldness). The interplay between pronouns, a repeating feature of the poem's language, suggests a balance between the protagonists that is actually far from equal.

37   **studded** This line is the first citation for OED 'studded' 1a, 'Set with or as with studs or large-headed nails'; see also *The Taming of the Shrew*, Induction, 2.41–2: 'Thy horses shall be trapped, | Their harness studded all with gold and pearl'. The word encompasses rugged practicality and ornate decoration.
   ragged rough, with sharp projections (OED³ 2a).

38, 40   **love. . . prove** On the rhyme, see Appendix 7; this is a common one in Elizabethan love poetry, as at *Astrophil and Stella*, 10.13–14: 'Reason thou kneeled'st, and offered'st straight to prove | By reason good, good reason her to love'.

38   **quick** swift (but compare ll. 140, 547).

39   **stallèd up** halted; with 'up' 'stall' usually means that the animal is put in an actual stall (OED 'stall', *v*.1', 8a), but alone it can mean 'stop' more generally.
   even emphatically pronounced with two syllables; the only time 'even' is disyllabic in the poem, except perhaps at l. 495; see 493, 495n.
   now Duncan-Jones and Woudhuysen note the forty-seven uses of this word in the poem, which 'propel' its action, and make it seem 'enacted, not narrated in retrospect' (2007: 136).

40   **To. . . prove** She starts to try ('prove', on which see l. 597 and note) to restrain Adonis into sexual compliance; 'tie' turns him into a beast of burden like his horse.

41   **Backward she pushed** Burrow compares Ovid's *Metamorphoses*, 10.557 for Venus squashing Adonis into place: 'pressitque et gramen et ipsum', 'she lay down on the ground and him' (2002: 177). Golding seems nonplussed by this: 'they sat them down anon' is his version (10.645). Shakespeare picks up, and enhances, the physical inequality.
   would be wanted to be.
   thrust Duncan-Jones and Woudhuysen cite *Romeo and Juliet* 1.1.17–18 (Sampson's coarse promise to 'thrust [Montague's] maids to the wall'), 'for the word's evident sexual connotations' (2007: 136), though this is the only other Shakespearean use of the word that tends in this direction.

42   **governed** overpowered, exceeded.

43–4   **So. . . down** As soon as he was down, she lay alongside him. Their brief wrestle ends with him 'down' as soon as they engage, and they end up lying opposite one another, on their sides. Golding gives a different and even less

Who blushed and pouted in a dull disdain,
With leaden appetite, unapt to toy;
    She red, and hot, as coals of glowing fire,   35
    He red for shame, but frosty in desire.

The studded bridle on a ragged bough,
Nimbly she fastens (O how quick is love!).
The steed is stallèd up, and even now
To tie the rider she begins to prove: 40
    Backward she pushed him, as she would be thrust,
    And governed him in strength, though not in lust.

So soon was she along, as he was down,
Each leaning on their elbows and their hips;
Now doth she stroke his cheek, now doth he frown,   45
And 'gins to chide, but soon she stops his lips,
    And kissing speaks, with lustful language broken,
    'If thou wilt chide, thy lips shall never open.'

He burns with bashful shame, she with her tears
Doth quench the maiden burning of his cheeks;
Then with her windy sighs and golden hairs   50
To fan and blow them dry again she seeks.
    He saith she is immodest, blames her miss;
    What follows more, she murders with a kiss.

clear picture, 'lying upward with her head upon his lap along' (10.646). Compare the posture of l. 594.

45 ***Now doth she stroke*** The shift into the historic present tense here is also seen in *A Lover's Complaint*, l. 299.

46 ***stops*** physically closes or fills with a kiss (see OED 8b). The same idea features in *Much Ado About Nothing*: Beatrice tells Hero she should 'stop his [Claudio's] mouth with a kiss' 2.1.310–11; Benedick turns the tables on her – 'Peace, I will stop your mouth' – in 5.4.97.

47–8 ***And. . . open*** words and kisses interfere with one another, as at *Metamorphoses*, 10.559 ('interserit oscula verbis', 'she mingled kisses with her words'). The broken/open rhyme appears in Sonnet 61.1, 3, but nowhere else in Shakespeare; compare also ll. 451–3. The vowels are the same, but the consonants are not; something 'broken' suits an interrupted rhyme scheme.

50 ***maiden burning*** virginal blushing. Venus' feminine tears meet Adonis' feminine blush.

51 ***windy sighs*** The sighs of Petrarchan love poetry are traditional (as are the golden hairs which follow). Compare 'Glaucus Complaint', 4, in Thomas Lodge's *Scilla's Metamorphosis* (1589): 'Why fail my plaints when pensive I rehearse them | To wound thine ears? When as my words exceed them, | And that my sighs instead of winds do lead them' (D1r). EEBO-TCP offers only one precedent for the precise phrase, in Thomas Kyd's *Spanish Tragedy* (1592) 3.13.166: 'By force of windy sighs thy spirit breathes'. See also *Hamlet*, 1.1.79: 'windy suspiration of false breath'.

53 ***miss*** mistake, inappropriate action. OED[3] cites this line under *n*.1, 4a, 'Wrong, wrongdoing; sin, sinfulness; offence, injury; a wrong, a misdeed'.

54 ***murders*** murthers Q; smothers Q7. See l. 906 and note.

55–60 **Even as. . . Even so. . .** The first extended simile of the poem compares Venus to a rapacious predator. Compare *Astrophil and Stella*, 14.1–3: 'Alas have I not pain enough my friend, | Upon whose breast a fiercer gripe [vulture] doth tire | Than did on him who first stale down the fire [i.e. Prometheus]'. The energetic attention to mood, action, and the particularity of the bird foreshadows later excursions into the animal world (the horse, the hare and the boar).

55 **empty** i.e. hungry.
   sharp by fast rendered keen by starvation (OED 'sharp, *adj.* and *n.*1', A4f; compare *Lucrece*, l. 422); but perhaps vicious; perhaps even angular, bony, sharp-formed.

56 **Tires** pulls at, from French 'tirer', to pull. The word is used in falconry, OED *v.*2, II.2.

58 **gorge** gullet.

59 **Even** monosyllabic here (as it is in l. 55 above).

61 **content** acquiesce (OED 2c, which cites this line), or perhaps 'to make [Venus] happy'; pronounced with emphasis on the second syllable.

63 **steam** breath (hot, after physical strain).
   prey Q pray. Along with 'heavenly' and 'grace' in the next line, the possible wordplay on 'pray' corroborates an idolatrous religious frame of reference for the boy's panting breath.

64–6 **heavenly. . . showers** 'it' is his breath, praised here as a source of tiny drops of lovely '*moisture*'. The '*air of grace*' suggests something freely given, or perhaps even by divine forces (as in God's 'grace'). The physical intimacy of this near-kiss echoes the tradition of the post-Catullan, neo-Latin *Basia*, on which see 16n. 'Heavenly' is disyllabic, i.e. 'heav'nly'.

65–6 **flowers. . . showers** probably monosyllabic. All instances of these plurals are monosyllabic in the poem; the only clearly disyllabic instance of the singular is 'flower', l. 8. Compare ll. 944, 946, and 1187, 1188, and notes.

66 **So** provided that.
   distilling condensing into droplets.

67 **Look how. . .** Compare 'look' at ll. 79, 289, 299, 529, 815, 925.

69 **Pure shame** (i) shame alone; (ii) undiluted shame, with the sense also that this is innocent shame.
   awed cowed, overcome. OED links 'awe, *v.*' and 'awed, *adj.*' (for which there are no

citations before 1642) with fear or reverence, neither of which is clearly apt here.
   fret become irritated, angry (OED, 'fret, *v.*1', 9a); the word can suggest violent agitation in Elizabethan English. Compare ll. 75, 621, and *Lucrece*, l. 648, but also l. 767, where it means 'corrode'.

70 **angry** Anger, like disdain (see l. 33 and note) is frequently a quality of Elizabethan love-objects. See *Astrophil and Stella*, 73.12–14: 'O heav'nly fool, thy most kiss-worthy face, | Anger invests with such a lovely grace, | That Anger's self I needs must kiss again'.

71–2 **Rain. . . bank** The couplet resembles both proverb and simile, but ends up a rather inscrutable analogy. The point might be that his eyes are overflowing with liquid, the fretting having caused an excess; or it might be that his beauty is now overflowing like a river, exacerbated by emotion.

71 **rank** swollen (and thus liable to overflow, OED *adj.* and *adv.* 8a), rather than 'disgusting' (morally, or physically, OED 11).

72 **Perforce** inevitably (OED[3] 2), but with some evocation of its original sense 'violently' (OED 1). The concatenation with 'force' adds a sententious note.

73 **Still** always, continually; in l. 75 it has this meaning as well, though with more of its modern senses ('nonetheless' or 'yet').

73–4 **prettily. . . pretty** suggests mutual femininity.

75 **lours** scowls. Both 'lours' and 'lowers' are acceptable modern spellings for Q's 'lowres': the former is chosen to fit with an internal rhyme between later 'louring' and 'sour[ing]' in ll. 183–5, and because the latter's optical closeness to 'lowers' (i.e. reduces height) adds nothing here. It also fits better with the monosyllabic pronunciation required. Compare Sonnet 149.7.
   frets See l. 69 and note.

76–7 **crimson. . . pale. . . red. . . white** Another balancing of the two colours (see l. 10 and note) starts like a new variation on the theme, but then the verbal repetition is immediately restored.

78 **best is bettered** Hyperbole (here combined with *polyptoton*) is a typical mode for poetic lovers, but again pointedly so for a goddess whose power is, in the mortal world, excessive. 'More' is used here as a comparative adjective equivalent to 'greater'. An EEBO-TCP search uncovers no other use of 'best is bettered' before 1700. Compare Sonnet 75.8.

Even as an empty eagle, sharp by fast,   55
Tires with her beak on feathers, flesh, and bone,
Shaking her wings, devouring all in haste,
Till either gorge be stuffed, or prey be gone:
 Even so she kissed his brow, his cheek, his chin,
 And where she ends, she doth anew begin.   60

Forced to content, but never to obey,
Panting he lies, and breatheth in her face.
She feedeth on the steam, as on a prey,
And calls it heavenly moisture, air of grace,
 Wishing her cheeks were gardens full of flowers,   65
 So they were dewed with such distilling showers.

Look how a bird lies tangled in a net:
So fastened in her arms Adonis lies.
Pure shame and awed resistance made him fret,
Which bred more beauty in his angry eyes: 70
 Rain added to a river that is rank
 Perforce will force it overflow the bank.

Still she entreats, and prettily entreats,
For to a pretty ear she tunes her tale.
Still is he sullen, still he lours and frets,   75
'Twixt crimson shame and anger ashy pale.
 Being red she loves him best, and being white,
 Her best is bettered with a more delight.

Look how he can, she cannot choose but love,
And by her fair immortal hand she swears   80
From his soft bosom never to remove,
Till he take truce with her contending tears,
 Which long have rained, making her cheeks all wet,
 And one sweet kiss shall pay this countless debt.

79 **Look how he can** whatever expression he has on his face.

80 **by her. . . hand** Swearing 'by the hand' was a common and potentially formal (legal) way of making a promise (Burrow 2002: 179). *Much Ado About Nothing* (see l. 46) provides two perspectives on the formula: 'By this hand, I love thee', 4.1.324–5, but also more ominously 'By this hand, Claudio shall render me a dear account', 4.1.332–3.

81 *remove* move (herself), withdraw.

82 **take truce with her contending tears** agree not to fight with her tears, which are battling against him (another military metaphor, which Roe (1992: 83) sees also in the 'remove' of l. 81 and the swearing of l. 80). The love-truce metaphor features in *Hero and Leander*, ll. 761–2: 'Yet there with Sisyphus he toiled in vain, | Till gentle parley did the truce obtain'.

84 **And one sweet kiss. . . debt** In the neo-Latin *Basia* tradition the idea of debt and payment around kisses is an important trope; see 16n.

countless comptlesse Q; too great to count. First citation in OED.

86 **dive-dapper** diuedapper Q; a small water-
bird, also known as a dabchick. The simile
seems like a simple evocation of nature, as
does the pun on 'duck' in l. 87. However
there is a metamorphic hint here. In Ovid
Aesacus turns into a diving bird (*mergus*),
perhaps a cormorant: 'His head is from his
shoulders far: of sea he is most fain. | And
for he underneath the waves delighteth for
to drive | A name according thereunto the
Latins do him give' (Golding, 11.916–18).

87 **Who** i.e. 'which'; these are regularly inter-
changed in Elizabethan English. In *Venus
and Adonis* various things (perhaps somewhat personified thereby) have the pronoun
'who' (see Hope 2003: 108–10); compare
ll. 306, 630, 891, 956, 968, 1041, 1043. See
Lucrece, 296n.

88 **offers** acts as if he intends to yield (see OED³
5b), rather than verbally proposes to do so.

89 **pay** payment.

90 **winks** blinks, closes his eyes (as opposed to
a more knowing, one-eyed modern wink).
Later (ll. 96, 121) this wink might suggest
artful coquettishness, youthful playfulness,
modesty or fear, depending on the figure winking and the observer; when Venus
alludes to it (ll. 121–2) she takes it, characteristically, as the first of these. 'Wink' could be a
variant form of 'winch' (meaning 'to shrink,
wince'; OED 'wink', v.2). However, OED's
roughly contemporary example from
Sylvester's Du Bartas (1611: Q6r) is affected
by the need for a rhyme: 'That boisterous
Adam's body did not shrink | For northern
winds, nor for the southern wink'.

91–102 **Never did. . . have** These lines are copied into
Folger MS X.d.562, probably sometime in
the 1630s, with the blunt rhyming couplet
'wherefore did Venus love Adonis | but for the
member where no bone is' (CELM ShW 31.5).

91 **passenger** traveller, '*esp.* a traveller on foot',
says OED³ 3a.

92 **good turn** i.e. the kiss, the benefit for her in
the bargain Adonis proposed. Burrow (2002:
180) notes an innuendo ('good turn' meaning sexual intercourse) with reference to
Antony and Cleopatra, 2.5.58–9: Cleopatra
asks what 'good turn' binds Antony to
Octavia, and the messenger replies 'For the
best turn i' th' bed'. In *Measure for Measure*
the bawd Pompey uses it in this way (4.2.59).
Alternatively, Venus might thirst for (i.e. as a
result of) his deft turn away from her, but this
seems less convincing.

93 **help** the thing which would help her.

94 **water. . . fire** In the post-Petrarchan tradition
water and fire appear in many paradoxical
relations, as in Samuel Daniel's *Complaint
of Rosamond*, ll. 393–6: 'Whose pure clear
streams, which lo so fair appears, | Wrought
hotter flames, O miracle of love, | That kin-
dles fire in water, heat in tears, | And makes
neglected beauty mightier prove'. Compare
Sonnet 154.14.

95 **'gan she cry** she began to exclaim.
flint-hearted unrelenting (see l. 199, and for
Adonis' hard heart more generally, ll. 375,
426, 500).

96 **coy** modest, bashful.

98 **Even. . . war** In Ovid's *Metamorphoses*
(4.171–89; Golding, 4.206–28) the affair
between Venus and Mars ends badly when
Hephaestus, the jealous husband, catches the
lovers in a net. Whether, as Burrow says, she
'omits' the story of the capture, is debatable,
since it may not have happened yet, and the
myth of Mars and Venus is often evoked
without it (2002: 180). It stirs the erotic imagination of Mardian the eunuch in *Antony and
Cleopatra*, who thinks about 'What Venus did
with Mars' (1.5.17). 'Even' is monosyllabic.
direful dreadful, fearsome.

99 **sinewy** sinowie Q; disyllabic.
bow a gesture of military submission.

100 **jar** fight, quarrel (OED *n*.1, 6a).

101 **slave** A common motif in love poetry,
though usually from the perspective of the
lover welcoming or decrying servitude. See
Astrophil and Stella, 2.9–11: 'Now even that
footstep of lost liberty | Is gone, and now
like slave-born *Muscovite*, | I call it praise to
suffer tyranny'. See also 'servile' at ll. 112,
1161, and compare Sonnets 57.1, 133.4.

102 **unasked** not asked for (OED, 'unasked, *adj*.',
2a, where this line is cited); but perhaps it
could suggest 'without asking' or 'without
having asked'; Shakespeare's only use of the
word.
shalt In the voice of a goddess, the modality
of 'shalt' is double-edged, as prediction over-
laps with command.

103 **altars** Mars makes an offering like a worshipper at the altar of Venus. The 'altars' may
be metaphorical for the lovers' bed, and are
a familiar motif in love poetry. See Richard
Barnfield, *The Affectionate Shepherd* (1594),
'Sonnet', 5–6: 'Here on love's altar I do offer
up | This burning heart for my soul's sac-
rifice' (sig. G1r). The goddess' altar features

Upon this promise did he raise his chin,   85
Like a dive-dapper peering through a wave,
Who being looked on, ducks as quickly in:
So offers he to give what she did crave,
    But when her lips were ready for his pay,
    He winks, and turns his lips another way.   90

Never did passenger in summer's heat
More thirst for drink, than she for this good turn.
Her help she sees, but help she cannot get;
She bathes in water, yet her fire must burn.
    'O pity!', 'gan she cry, 'flint-hearted boy,   95
    'Tis but a kiss I beg, why art thou coy?

'I have been wooed as I entreat thee now,
Even by the stern and direful god of war,
Whose sinewy neck in battle ne'er did bow,
Who conquers where he comes in every jar.   100
    Yet hath he been my captive and my slave,
    And begged for that which thou unasked shalt have.

'Over my altars hath he hung his lance,
His battered shield, his uncontrollèd crest,
And for my sake hath learned to sport, and dance,   105
To toy, to wanton, dally, smile, and jest,
    Scorning his churlish drum and ensign red,
    Making my arms his field, his tent my bed.

in *Hero and Leander*, ll. 209–11: 'This sacrifice (whose sweet perfume descending, | From *Venus* altar to your footsteps bending) | Doth testify that you exceed her far'.
lance has phallic implications.

104 **uncontrollèd crest** decoration on helmet (e.g. of feathers), here with a phallic innuendo. 'Uncontrollèd' suggests both untidiness and indomitability (and see l. 270, and *Lucrece*, l. 645).

105 **sport** play; see l. 24 and note.

106 **toy** dally, play (compare l. 34).
wanton act wantonly; Shakespeare uses the word as noun and verb (the earliest OED[3] citation for which is 1589), as well as adjective. It is non-sexual in *The Winter's Tale* (2.1.17, about Mamillius playing) but is frankly lascivious in *Titus Andronicus* (2.1.21, where Aaron waits 'to wanton with this queen'). In *The Taming of the Shrew*, Induction, 2.50–2, it is associated with a picture of Venus and Adonis: 'Adonis painted in a running brook, | And Cytherea [i.e. Venus]

all in sedges hid, | Which seem to move and wanton with her breath'.

107 **churlish** 'rough, rude, brutal' (Schmidt); in Thomas Cooper's *Thesaurus Linguae Romanae et Britannicae* (1578) it appears in definitions of the Latin 'asper', 'barbarus' and 'rusticus' (i.e. physically rough, culturally barbarous, rustic). Compare ll. 134, 616: it is used of Mars here, then in contrast with Venus herself, then of the boar.
ensign red The colour of Mars' flag matches that of blood; another instance of the pervasive red and white pattern in the poem.

108 **field** battlefield. Both 'arms' and 'field' evoke heraldry. This does not add a great deal to the effect of this particular line, but the cumulative effect of heraldic references across the poem as a whole (alongside the ubiquitous play on red and white) adds to its powerful visual impression. Duncan-Jones and Woudhuysen note that the line has a chiasmic structure (2007: 142). Compare *Lucrece*, l. 58 and note.

109–11 *overswayed. . . obeyed* probably pronounced 'overswayèd', 'obeyèd'. When the -ed ending comes at the end of a line, scansion does not always help determine pronunciation. However, there is good reason to trust the orthography of Q in the case of *Venus and Adonis*. In all the instances where an -ed ending should not be sounded for the sake of rhyme ('cooled', l. 387, rhyming with 'would'; 'marred', l. 478, with 'hard'; 'distressed', l. 814, with 'breast'; 'cursed', l. 887, with 'first'; 'dismayed', l. 896, with 'afraid'; 'drowned', l. 984, with 'ground'; 'accurst', l. 1120, with 'first'; 'excelled', l. 1131, with 'beheld'; 'o'er-strawed', l. 1143, with 'fraud'; 'conveyed', l. 1192, with 'aid'), the spelling fits the pronunciation ('coold', 'mard', 'distrest', 'curst', 'dismayd', 'drownd', 'accurst', 'exceld', 'ore-strawd', 'conuaide'). The spelling of these words ('ouer-swayed', 'obayed') therefore suggests that the -ed should be sounded. This will be marked in the notes in the other cases (ll. 625–7, 925–7) but not in the text; the distinction is not quite certain enough to justify putting 'overswayèd', etc., and thus complicating our modernised text. Compare *Lucrece*, 50–2n.

109 *overruled* was so dominant. OED³ 1, 'to have overall authority', allows for a rare intransitive use of the verb; OED³ 3, 'to prevail over [. . .] dominate', closer in meaning, does not note intransitive uses.
overswayed ruled over; Shakespeare's only use. 'He' could be used as an emphatic alternative to 'him' (on which see Hope 2003: 84).

110 *prisoner* disyllabic.
red rose chain Garlands of flowers make appropriate bonds for use by the goddess of love. Her colour is the same as that of Mars' flag; this match may suggest the contradictoriness of nature, or the intersections between violence and love.

111 *Strong. . . obeyed* Even the best strengthened (tempered) steel gives way to the better power of Mars. The *polyptoton* ('Strong [. . .] stronger strength'; see l. 78) in this line seems to aim for grandeur (as does the alliteration in the last line of the stanza, 'her that foiled the god of fight').

112 *servile to* enslaved by; compare l. 1161, and 'slave', l. 112.

coy disdain These words have both already been used of Adonis (ll. 33, 96), and for Venus to use them of herself asserts her superiority. Duncan-Jones and Woudhuysen note that 'coy' can imply disdain (OED 3; 2007: 143); the *pleonasm* adds to Venus' assertiveness.

113 *proud* selfishly unkind; see l. 14 and note.
nor. . . not The double negative, common in Shakespeare, does not imply a positive. See Hope (2003: 171); also ll. 126, 409.

114 *mastering* defeating, conquering; pronounced with two syllables here.
fight war.

115–20 *Touch. . . eyes* This stanza is difficult to punctuate in a modernised edition. All the lines in Q end in commas except for the final question mark, and there is a case for emending them (as in the text). However, it should be noted that the hasty unfolding of the thought process, the profusion of monosyllables, and the non-sequitur in this argument, fit with the looser organisation resulting from commas.

116 *fair* beautiful (Venus is faux-modest here) but also pale in colour, a pun which allows the white and red interplay to emerge again.

119 *eyeballs* eyes; earliest citation in OED³ (though 'ball of the eye', s.v. 'ball, *n*.1', 14, meaning the pupil or visible part of the eye, is older). It sounds more comically anatomical to modern readers than it would have to Shakespeare's first readers.
there thy beauty lies This refers to his reflection in her eyes. It may also suggest that vision originates in the eyes; see l. 487 and note.

121 *ashamed. . . wink* Venus offers a second interpretation of the wink, now a sign of shame.

123 *Love. . . twain* The best time for celebrating Love (by kissing, etc.) is when there are just two people present. Love is personified as male (Cupid) here.

124 *our sport is not in sight* nobody can see what we are getting up to; or less probably 'our sport is not just in looking at one another' (Duncan-Jones and Woudhuysen 2007: 143). 'Play' and 'sport' both have erotic implications; see l. 24 and note.

125 *blue-veined* describing the petals of the violet flower, which have blue markings.

'Thus he that overruled, I overswayed,
Leading him prisoner in a red rose chain.   110
Strong-tempered steel his stronger strength obeyed,
Yet was he servile to my coy disdain.
   O be not proud, nor brag not of thy might,
   For mastering her that foiled the god of fight.

'Touch but my lips with those fair lips of thine: 115
Though mine be not so fair, yet are they red;
The kiss shall be thine own as well as mine.
What seest thou in the ground? Hold up thy head,
   Look in mine eyeballs, there thy beauty lies:
   Then why not lips on lips, since eyes in eyes?   120

'Art thou ashamed to kiss? Then wink again,
And I will wink, so shall the day seem night.
Love keeps his revels where there are but twain;
Be bold to play, our sport is not in sight.
   These blue-veined violets whereon we lean   125
   Never can blab, nor know not what we mean.

'The tender spring upon thy tempting lip
Shows thee unripe; yet mayst thou well be tasted.
Make use of time, let not advantage slip,

Shakespeare associates blue veins with the female body: with breasts in *Lucrece*, l. 419, and with eyelids in *Cymbeline*, 2.2.22–3 ('these windows, white and azure laced | With blue of heaven's own tinct').

126 **Never. . . mean** On the double-negativity of 'nor know not', perhaps emphatic here, see l. 113 and note. Q7 changes to 'nor know they', which suggests it may have seemed awkward to an early reader.

127 *tender spring* the first soft growth of facial hair; the phrase recurs in a different context at l. 656. EEBO-TCP has no earlier or contemporary uses relating to facial hair.

128 *unripe* Adonis is not physically mature, and yet Venus does not see this as a reason to leave him alone. See l. 524 for the other key appearance of the word. The world-view put forward by Venus (perhaps as a persuasive tactic; perhaps because this is an immortal's way of thinking) resembles that in Spenser's Garden of Adonis, where all seasons coincide:

'There is continuall Spring, and harvest there | Continuall, both meeting at one tyme' (*Faerie Queene* III.vi.42.1–2). In the Garden pleasure is like a harvest: 'There wont fayre Venus often to enjoy | Her deare Adonis joyous company, | And reape sweet pleasure of the wanton boy' (III.vi.46.1–3). Compare *The Passionate Pilgrim*, 5.

129–32 **Make. . . time** The 'carpe diem' ('seize the day') motif is frequently found in love poetry, though usually aimed at a woman. The phrase itself comes from Horace's *Odes* 1.11.8, where it encompasses the sexual and the philosophical (an Epicurean acceptance of the good things at hand, at least as much as a rapacious attitude towards opportunities for pleasure). This is a key theme of Venus': compare ll. 163–74, 405; see also *Hero and Leander*, ll. 325–30, especially 327–8: 'The richest corn dies, if it be not reaped, | Beauty alone is lost, too warily kept'.

129 *advantage* opportunity.

130 **Beauty. . . wasted** As in the first group of the Sonnets (1–17; especially 1.5–8, 9.11–12), which aim to persuade the young man to marry and have children, Ovid's Narcissus is the model of a young men who wastes beauty 'within itself'.

131 **flowers** monosyllabic here.
prime time of perfection, perhaps maturity (OED³ 9a or 9b); but also with the sense of 'springtime' (OED³ 8). Compare *Lucrece*, l. 332.

133 **hard-favoured** ugly (compare l. 931, and *Lucrece*, l. 1632). Burrow's suggestion of a hint of 'tyrannical rigour' seems apt (2002: 182).

134 **Ill-nurtured** badly looked-after (physically), badly brought-up (temperamentally).
churlish see l. 107 and note.

135 **O'er-worn** worn out (compare the effect of 'Time's injurious hand' at Sonnet 63.2).
rheumatic dripping with rheum, catarrh; associated with old age; here stressed on first syllable.

136 **Thick-sighted** having poor vision; perhaps myopic, though Roe suggests 'blurry-eyed' (1992: 87), perhaps hampered by old age causing the surface of the eye to thicken (compare Sonnet 3.11–12). In *2 Henry IV*, 3.2.313, Falstaff seems to be referring to indistinct sight in general. In *Julius Caesar*, 5.3.21, however, Cassius seems specifically short-sighted. He needs help to survey the battlefield, because 'My sight was ever thick'.
lean thin, but can also denote barrenness and sterility, as in *1 Henry IV*, 2.1.116: 'lards the lean earth'. Used in contrast with Venus here, it is used later of Death (l. 931).
juice vigour, liveliness (OED 4a) and, perhaps, more literally, moistness, which is associated with sexual vigour at ll. 25–6. On the voice/juice rhyme, see Appendix 7.

138 **defects** stressed on the second syllable.

139–44 **Thou. . . melt** Venus' blazon (descriptive catalogue) of herself emphasises conventional signs of youth and beauty, alongside things particular to her in this poem. The 'marrow burning' suggests sexual vigour, as at *All's Well That Ends Well*, 2.3.281: 'spending his manly marrow' (see OED³ 'marrow', *n*., 1b, and 1d, 'the innermost part of a person's being', where this line is cited).

140 **grey** perhaps similar to blue eyes in the present day, in that (i) the same colour may have been named differently by the Elizabethans, and (ii) they are both by-words for

attractiveness in love poetry. See Gascoigne, *A Hundred Sundry Flowers* (1573) in an 'Allegoria' warning against tempting women: 'Hir eyes as grey as glass, hir teeth as white as milk, | A ruddy lip, a dimpled chin, a skin as smooth as silk' (sig. N4v). Shakespeare picks up 'grey as glass' in *Two Gentlemen of Verona*, 4.4.192 (Julia on Sylvia): 'Her eyes are grey as glass, and so are mine'.

140 **quick** lively (as well as fast); compare l. 38 and note, l. 547.

141 **as the spring** Beauty is often cast as spring-like, but this is not the same as seeing it growing 'yearly'. Venus cannot be implying an annual cycle, wherein she is less beautiful in the winter, since she is immortal.
yearly yearelie Q; there is a pun here on 'yarely' (quickly, nimbly). OED lists 'yeerlie' as an alternative spelling in Shakespeare's time, though his uses (*Tempest*, 1.1.3, and *Antony and Cleopatra*, 2.2.218) both appear as 'yarely' in the First Folio.

142 **plump** not pejorative, though in Shakespeare's time it could still mean 'rude, unrefined' (OED³ 1a). Variations in early editions suggest that readers might have stumbled on the word. In Q5 it is 'plumbe'; Q7 emends to 'plum', often an alternative form of 'plump' (OED³ 'plum, adj.1', 1). In *Hero and Leander* it is compatible with Leander's beauty: 'The god put *Helle's* bracelet on his arm, | And swore the sea should never do him harm. | He clapped his plump cheeks, with his tresses played' (ll. 663–5).

143 **with** by.

144 **dissolve. . . melt** 'Dissolve' and 'melt' are often interchangeable in Elizabethan English. Here they both stand for the passionate merging of flesh that Venus proposes. In the poem these two words shift meanings. See 'melt' and its cognates at l. 315 (for sweating), l. 750 (melting), l. 982 (evaporating), l. 1073 (melting) and l. 1166 (disappearing). See also 'dissolve' at l. 565.

145 **discourse** speak at length, tell stories; stressed on second syllable.
enchant charm. This line is cited as the first instance of OED 3; the word's magical connotations still signify ('originally with conscious metaphor'). Compare *Lucrece*, 1521n.

146 **trip upon the green** dance or flit on the grass. See *A Midsummer Night's Dream* 2.1.99–100, where the 'quaint mazes in the wanton

Beauty within itself should not be wasted: 130
    Fair flowers that are not gathered in their prime
    Rot and consume themselves in little time.

'Were I hard-favoured, foul, or wrinkled old,
Ill-nurtured, crooked, churlish, harsh in voice,
O'er-worn, despisèd, rheumatic, and cold,   135
Thick-sighted, barren, lean, and lacking juice;
    Then mightst thou pause, for then I were not for thee,
    But having no defects, why dost abhor me?

'Thou canst not see one wrinkle in my brow;
Mine eyes are grey and bright, and quick in turning;   140
My beauty as the spring doth yearly grow;
My flesh is soft and plump, my marrow burning;
    My smooth moist hand, were it with thy hand felt,
    Would in thy palm dissolve, or seem to melt.

'Bid me discourse, I will enchant thine ear,   145
Or like a fairy trip upon the green,
Or like a nymph, with long dishevelled hair,
Dance on the sands, and yet no footing seen.
    Love is a spirit all compact of fire,
    Not gross to sink, but light, and will aspire.   150

'Witness this primrose bank whereon I lie,
These forceless flowers like sturdy trees support me.
Two strengthless doves will draw me through the sky,

green. | For lack of [fairies'] tread, are undistinguishable'.

147 **dishevelled** Compare *Lucrece*, l. 1129; Shakespeare's only two uses. In Elizabethan English it means that no head-dress was worn, but not that the hair was untidy (OED 2).

148 **footing** footprint (OED³ 7a). The 'elves' move with 'printless foot' in *The Tempest*, 5.1.34. See ll. 722 and 1028.

149–50 **Love. . . aspire** Love is composed of the lightest of the four elements – made of fire, resembling air, not at all 'gross' like earth (or water). 'Aspire' captures both the upward desire and (etymologically) the breathy manner of movement. Fire and air are set apart at *Antony and Cleopatra*, 5.2.289–90: 'I am fire and air; my other elements | I give to baser life'. The four elements, and their hierarchy in the natural order, are described in Ovid, *Metamorphoses*, 1.26–31; Golding, 1.25–32.

149 **compact** composed (OED *adj.*1, 2); stressed on second syllable.

151–6 **Witness. . . thee?** In *A Midsummer Night's Dream* the fairies are able to consort with humans, but they also seem tiny, harvesting bees and acorns. A related ontological clash is evident in *Venus and Adonis*, where the goddess is huge and strong, but also strangely light so that primroses hold her up like 'sturdy trees' (see l. 1028). Primroses are a bed for lovers also in *A Midsummer Night's Dream*, 1.1.214–15: 'often you and I | Upon faint primrose beds were wont to lie'.

152 **forceless** weak, lacking strength. On *-less* words, see *Lucrece*, 2n.
flowers monosyllabic.

153 **strengthless** as 'forceless', l. 152 (see note), denoting the lack of strength required to carry her. Compare *Lucrece*, l. 709, where the word has a slightly different sense.

154 *even where I list to sport me* wherever I wish to amuse myself. See l. 24 and note. 'Even' is monosyllabic.

155–6 *Is. . . thee* If love weighs so little (or, is so insignificant), sweet boy, can it be that you think you would find it a burden ('*heavy*' as in 'serious')? Roe sees the sense 'unconstrained' in 'light' (perhaps sexually so, OED, *adj*.1, 14b), and thus 'heavy' suggests oppression (1992: 88).

156 *should* Q2's 'shouldst' suggests that a contemporary reader could expect a regular second person ending here. 'Should' could be a variant second person form, or an error, but more likely it is a subjunctive form (i.e. a grammatical form of the verb tending, as the OED says, 'to express a wish, command, exhortation, or a contingent, hypothetical, or prospective event'). In Elizabethan English the subjunctive form was more common than it is today, but still rare (see Hope 2003: 156–8). See also ll. 369, 445, 676, 775.

157 *affected* in love with (compare OED³ *adj*.1, 2a, 2b), frequently seen in Shakespeare, as in *Two Gentleman of Verona*, 2.1.84: 'In conclusion, I stand affected to her'. In *Hero and Leander* the word features in a passage Shakespeare found memorable: 'It lies not in our power to love, or hate, | For will in us is over-ruled by fate. | When two are stripped, long ere the course begin | We wish that one should lose, the other win. | And one especially do we affect | Of two gold ingots like in each respect, | The reason no man knows, let it suffice, | What we behold is censured by our eyes. | Where both deliberate, the love is slight, | Who ever loved, that loved not at first sight?' (ll. 167–76). The last line is quoted by Phebe in *As You Like It*, 3.5.82.

158 *seize love upon* fall in love with. Two mirroring parts of the body choose one another in a Narcissistic way.

159 *thyself. . . thyself* Doubled reflexive pronouns are a feature of the poem (see ll. 161, 763, 1129; and compare *Lucrece*, ll. 29, 157, 160, 998, 1196, 1566). This is a witty rhetorical touch in keeping with its Ovidian style. However, as Langley (2009: 66–103) argues, they may also indicate a self-destructive, inward-turning tendency.

160 *Steal. . . theft* Capture yourself in love, and then complain about your own loss of freedom. Q4 amends to 'complain of', which is a possible sign that 'complain on' seemed archaic, as Burrow (2002: 183) suggests (though Abbott, § 181, says 'on' is 'frequently used' where modern English uses 'of').

161–2 *Narcissus. . . brook* The story of Narcissus, already hinted at (see ll. 29–30 and note, 130), is now mentioned explicitly. The drowned Narcissus of *Hero and Leander*, ll. 74–5 ('That leapt into the water for a kiss | Of his own shadow') and *Lucrece*, ll. 265–6 is a presence here.

161 *himself himself* On reflexive pronouns, see l. 159 and note.

162 *died to kiss* died in his attempt to kiss. *shadow* reflection (OED 5a; see also l. 1099). Compare *Julius Caesar*, 1.2.56–8, where Cassius says Brutus has 'no such mirrors as will turn | Your hidden worthiness into your eye, | That you might see your shadow'. The word 'shadow' has other meanings in the poem (as set out by Schmidt): 'shade', ll. 176, 191, 315; 'figure of the body projected on the ground by the interception of light', l. 706; 'spirit', l. 1001; and the verb 'to hide', l. 533. Compare l. 488 and note, on 'shine'.

163–74 *Torches are made. . . left alive* The arguments advanced here recall ll. 129–32, *Hero and Leander*, ll. 223–54, and Sonnets 1–17 (urging the young man to marry and procreate).

164 *Dainties* delicacies (food). *beauty for the use* proverbial (Dent B170, 'beauty is made for use'). Venus sets up false parallels, and the open-endedness of the key term 'use' reveals to the reader the typically opportunistic and self-serving side to the erotic strand in the 'carpe diem' tradition (compare ll. 129–32, 768, and notes). See OED³ *n*., 1c, for the erotic tendency of 'use', and compare Sonnet 2.9 and note, 4.7 and note.

165 *bear* produce leaves or fruit (OED 42a), but also perhaps carry a load: strong, sappy plants have qualities that suit them to certain work.

166 *Things. . . abuse* Things which only grow to benefit themselves (compare l. 1180, and Sonnet 94.10) are an affront to the whole idea of growth. *themselves* On reflexive pronouns, see l. 159 and note.

168 *get* beget.

From morn till night, even where I list to sport me.
   Is love so light, sweet boy, and may it be,   155
   That thou should think it heavy unto thee?

'Is thine own heart to thine own face affected?
Can thy right hand seize love upon thy left?
Then woo thyself, be of thyself rejected;
Steal thine own freedom, and complain on theft.   160
   Narcissus so himself himself forsook,
   And died to kiss his shadow in the brook.

'Torches are made to light, jewels to wear,
Dainties to taste, fresh beauty for the use,
Herbs for their smell, and sappy plants to bear: 165
Things growing to themselves are growth's abuse.
   Seeds spring from seeds, and beauty breedeth beauty:
   Thou wast begot, to get, it is thy duty.

'Upon the earth's increase why shouldst thou feed,
Unless the earth with thy increase be fed?   170
By law of nature thou art bound to breed,
That thine may live, when thou thyself art dead;
   And so in spite of death thou dost survive,
   In that thy likeness still is left alive.'

By this the lovesick queen began to sweat,   175
For where they lay the shadow had forsook them,
And Titan, tired in the midday heat,
With burning eye did hotly overlook them,

169–70 *increase. . . increase* productivity, generation (of fruits etc. in the first case, offspring in the second; indeed the word can mean 'offspring', OED *n*.6); stressed on the second syllable. Adonis' descendants might feed the earth through their presence, or their labour, but also through their deaths (compare *3 Henry VI*, 2.3.15, 'Thy brother's blood the thirsty earth hath drunk'). Human bodies seem particularly earth-bound and mortal at this moment, even though a kind of immortality ('in spite of death', l. 173) is the promise being made. Roe notes an echo of Genesis 9:1, where God tells Noah and his sons to 'bring forth fruit, and multiply, and replenish the earth' (1992: 88).

172 *thine* your descendants.

175 **By this** at that time; compare ll. 697, 877, 973, 1165, and 25 and note.

176 *the shadow had forsook them* they were no longer in the shade (OED 'shadow', 11a; compare l. 162 and note). The shade is made into the subject, if not personified.

177 **Titan** the sun, Apollo; one of Venus' fellow deities (her half-brother).
tired fatigued (by its journey across the sky); but it might play on 'tired', short for 'attired', since the sun is covered in the 'midday heat'. There are no other uses of 'tired' in this latter sense in Shakespeare; Leontes' accusation 'thou art woman-tired', *Winter's Tale*, 2.3.75, is most likely equivalent to hen-pecked, with 'tire', from falconry, meaning 'tear'.

178 **hotly** eagerly, passionately, jealously; there is some tautology in the idea of the sun doing things 'hotly'.
overlook look down from above (OED³ 1a, where this line is cited).

179 *team* the horses that pull the chariot of the sun.

180 *Venus'* Scansion requires 'Venus'' to be disyllabic and 'Adonis'' to be trisyllabic. Q simply has 'Venus' without an apostrophe. See also ll. 248, 816 (Venus'); ll. 261, 378, 978, 1172 (Adonis').

181 *lazy sprite* casual, sluggish spirit (sprite being a synonym thereof).

182 *disliking* disapproving; first citation for OED 'disliking, *adj.*', 'showing dislike or aversion'.
eye look, expression (OED³ 'eye, *n.*1', 4a, 4b); compare Scroop's 'dull and heavy eye', *Richard II*, 3.2.196. An EEBO-TCP search reveals no other use of the phrase *disliking eye* before 1700.

183 *louring* glowering; see l. 75 and note.
o'erwhelming hanging down, overlooking gloomily (as Schmidt suggests).
fair sight beautiful appearance (see OED³ 'sight, *n.*1', 3, and compare 'wanton sight', *Lucrece*, l. 104).

184 *blot* cover up, obscure (OED 5b, first citation).

185 *Souring* i.e. his cheeks take on a sour expression (perhaps pursing up as if he had eaten something sour). The OED has *Venus and Adonis* as the first citation for this rare transitive use (*v.*, 4c); it compares *Richard II*, 2.1.166–9, 'England's private wrongs [...] have made me sour my patient cheek'. In Q there is a gap between 'so' and 'wring' as if they are two words, perhaps revealing that 'souring' struck the compositor as an unlikely word. Q's version is nearly viable, but would require further emendation, and 'souring' chimes with 'louring'.
Fie see OED: an 'exclamation expressing, in early use, disgust or indignant reproach'; all of Shakespeare's uses strike this tone. See ll. 212, 611, 1021.

186 *remove* leave, get out of the sun; see OED³ 1a.

187 *young, and so unkind* Venus associates youth with kindness, by which she implies sexual compliance; the word resonates in *Venus and Adonis* (see ll. 204, 310, 312, 318, 478; and see *Lucrece*, l. 253n). Cognates of 'kind' draw in a range of meanings: what is natural, fundamental to most concepts of kindness, is

complex here as in *King Lear* (see 1.1.106, 'so young, and so untender?').

188 *bare* worthless, lacking substance (OED *adj.*, *adv.*, and *n.*, A10b, where this line is cited), shameless.
to be gone to get away.

189–91 *sigh. . . hairs* Venus deploys the clichéd sighs and golden hair of Petrarchan love (compare ll. 51–2).

189 *gentle* tender, meek, as at l. 278; but there are other overlapping senses elsewhere in the poem. It suggests loveliness, amiability at ll. 403, 653, 801, 853, and harmlessness at l. 883. Several meanings coincide in flattery at l. 1001, when Venus addresses Death.

190 *descending* setting.

191 *shadow* shade; compare l. 162 and note.

193–8 *The. . . sun* Adonis is seen as a sun more powerful than Phoebus in the sky, who merely warms the goddess' back. The combination of eyes and fire is traditional, a 'standard Petrarchism' (Burrow 2002: 185), and resonant with Neo-Platonist images of love (Roe 1992: 90). Even clichés, however, are sharpened when spoken by the goddess of love herself.

193 *shines. . . shines* a word that becomes prominent later in the poem; see l. 488 and note.

194 *lo* A 'favourite word' of the poem (Burrow 2002: 185), and of the demonstrative, authoritative goddess herself (ll. 259, 280, 320, 853, 1128, 1135, 1185).

196 *darts* sends rapidly (the first reference for the '*transf.* and *fig.*' OED 3); see l. 817.

197 *done* over, finished; see l. 749, and *Lucrece*, l. 23.

199 *obdurate* stressed on second syllable, as at *Lucrece*, l. 429.
flinty See l. 95 and note.

200 *at rain relenteth* is eroded (OED³ 1a) over time by rain; Venus suggests that nothing at all can wear Adonis down. The idea is proverbial (Dent D618, 'constant dropping wears the stone'); compare *Lucrece*, ll. 560, 959, and *A Lover's Complaint*, ll. 290–1.

201 *a woman's son* mortal, but also connected to womanhood and thus the world of emotion. Roe (1992: 90) and Burrow (2002: 186) note the pointedness of these lines if

Wishing Adonis had his team to guide,
So he were like him, and by Venus' side.   180

And now Adonis with a lazy sprite,
And with a heavy, dark, disliking eye,
His louring brows o'erwhelming his fair sight,
Like misty vapours when they blot the sky,
    Souring his cheeks, cries, 'Fie, no more of love,   185
    The sun doth burn my face, I must remove.'

'Ay me,' quoth Venus, 'young, and so unkind,
What bare excuses mak'st thou to be gone?
I'll sigh celestial breath, whose gentle wind
Shall cool the heat of this descending sun;   190
    I'll make a shadow for thee of my hairs;
    If they burn too, I'll quench them with my tears.

'The sun that shines from heaven, shines but warm,
And lo, I lie between that sun, and thee.
The heat I have from thence doth little harm;   195
Thine eye darts forth the fire that burneth me;
    And were I not immortal, life were done,
    Between this heavenly and earthly sun.

'Art thou obdurate, flinty, hard as steel?
Nay, more than flint, for stone at rain relenteth.   200
Art thou a woman's son and canst not feel
What 'tis to love, how want of love tormenteth?
    O had thy mother borne so hard a mind,
    She had not brought forth thee, but died unkind.

'What am I that thou shouldst contemn me this?   205
Or what great danger dwells upon my suit?
What were thy lips the worse for one poor kiss?

(as in Ovid) Adonis' mother is Myrrha (see headnote). Compare the use of the phrase, in a similar context, in Sonnet 41.7.

202 *want of love tormenteth* lack of love is torture.

204 *unkind* a resonant word; see l. 187 and note. Venus wants to equate natural behaviour with sexual compliance.

205 *contemn me this* (i) scornfully refuse me in this way, where 'this' may simply be 'thus' (see OED, *adv*.1, where this is the latest citation);

perhaps (ii) deny me this [request], where the verb could be taking a double object.

206 *dwells upon* accompanies, with the additional sense 'awaits you (if you submit)'. Shakespeare's uses of 'dwell upon' tend to fit OED 5, 'to spend time upon or linger over', but this seems to relate to OED 7, 'to remain [. . .] reside', used figuratively.

207 *What were thy lips the worse?* How will it cost your lips anything?
poor meagre.

208 ***Speak. . . mute*** Speak justly, but tell me kind things that will please me; otherwise be quiet.

fair. . . fair This word could work as a noun (if Adonis is called, or referred to as, 'fair [one]'), adjective (as it must be in the second appearance, meaning 'kind' and/or 'true'; these two meanings may be opposed here) or adverb (equivalent to 'fairly'). Its possibilities are worked on by Helena in *A Midsummer Night's Dream*, 1.1.181–2: 'Call you me fair? That fair again unsay. | Demetrius loves your fair: O happy fair!'. See also ll. 1083, 1086, *Lucrece*, l. 346, and Sonnets 18.7, 21.4. Elsewhere in Shakespeare there is wordplay on 'fair' meaning 'pretty', and 'fair' meaning 'just' (as at *Troilus and Cressida*, 3.1.43–9: 'Fair be to you my lord, and to all this fair company', etc.). If the first 'fair' is an adverb, then this wordplay arises as she wishes him to do justice, but only pleasing justice; if it is a vocative noun used to address Adonis, it signifies prettiness both times, and he is asked to make mind and body conform. The choice made here – adverb, then adjective – conveys a brief attempt to turn to justice as a principle.

209 ***again*** in return.

210 ***interest*** i.e. the profit on a loan; pronounced disyllabically here. While usury (money-lending) had a low reputation in the period, it is evoked in love poetry as a way of figuring the exchanges involved. Compare Sonnets 4.7 and note, 6.5, 134.10.

twain two.

211–16 ***Fie. . . direction*** The juxtaposition of humans with lifeless artworks evokes the premise, if not the transformation, in the story of Pygmalion in *Metamorphoses* 10. Compare ll. 289–94, especially l. 292 and note; also *Lucrece*, l. 1374; and the statue scene (5.3) of *The Winter's Tale*.

211 ***Fie*** see l. 185 and note.

lifeless liuelesse Q.

senseless unfeeling, lacking senses (OED 1d); compare *Lucrece*, l. 1564.

212 ***dull*** unresponsive.

213 ***Statue*** perhaps stressed on the second syllable for the metre (Q's spelling 'statüe' may

suggest this), but more likely this should be read as a scornful trochee.

contenting making happy.

215 ***complexion*** appearance, constitution (of bodily qualities, humours, etc.). The OED shows the word ranging from inward to outward qualities. Compare *Hamlet*, 1.4.27–8 ('their o'ergrowth of some complexion | Oft breaking down the pales and forts of reason'), and Sonnets 18.6, 99.4, 132.14.

216 ***For men. . . direction*** True men seek out kisses by natural inclination. 'Even' here mildly intensifies (like 'indeed'), or means 'solely', and is pronounced with one syllable. 'Direction' usually suggests purpose or instruction, as do Shakespeare's other uses (though it may suggest an impulse at *Troilus and Cressida*, 2.3.30–1, 'Let thy blood be thy direction till thy death!'). However, OED 7 ('disposition, turn of mind') and OED 9 (scientifically, 'the particular course or line pursued by any moving body') shade towards natural inclination (though the first citations are *c.* 1639 and 1665 respectively).

217 ***chokes*** constrains, silences (OED 6a, where this is cited).

219 ***blaze forth her wrong*** proclaim (OED 'blaze', *v.*, 2b; the word derives from blowing a trumpet, and relates to the heraldic 'blazon') her sense of indignation at having been wronged.

220 ***Being judge in love*** Despite having control over love; Shakespeare does not use the 'judge in. . .' formula anywhere else, and an EEBO-TCP search, uncovering no other instances before *Venus and Adonis*, suggests the phrase 'judge in love' is Shakespeare's innovation. The idea that judges cannot handle their own cases is proverbial: see Dent M341, 'no man ought to be judge in his own cause', but Dent does not cite this line. Compare *Merchant of Venice*, 2.9.61–2: 'To offend and judge are distinct offices | And of opposed natures'.

right justify, vindicate (see OED³ 13b, but also OED³ 11a: 'set in order').

cause case.

221 ***fain would*** very much wanted to.

Speak fair, but speak fair words, or else be mute.
　　Give me one kiss, I'll give it thee again,
　　And one for interest, if thou wilt have twain.　　　　　　　210

'Fie, lifeless picture, cold and senseless stone,
Well-painted idol, image dull and dead,
Statue contenting but the eye alone,
Thing like a man, but of no woman bred.
　　Thou art no man, though of a man's complexion,　　　　　215
　　For men will kiss even by their own direction.'

This said, impatience chokes her pleading tongue,
And swelling passion doth provoke a pause.
Red cheeks and fiery eyes blaze forth her wrong;
Being judge in love, she cannot right her cause.　　　　　　220
　　And now she weeps, and now she fain would speak,
　　And now her sobs do her intendments break.

Sometime she shakes her head, and then his hand;
Now gazeth she on him, now on the ground;
Sometime her arms enfold him like a band;　　　　　　　　225
She would, he will not in her arms be bound;
　　And when from thence he struggles to be gone,
　　She locks her lily fingers one in one.

222 **intendments** the things she was planning to say (OED 5). There is legal resonance here (OED 4, what the law intends, 'the sense in which the law understands a thing').

223–8 **Sometime. . . one in one** The drama of this episode is captured rhetorically and comically with the use of *zeugma*. The balanced clauses and the pattern of pronouns create the potential for a witty, Ovidian tone (see headnote), distancing the struggle being depicted.

225 **band** OED cites this line under 'band, *n*.1', 2a: 'The tie of straw with which sheaves are bound, a rope of hay used by the hay-binder, and *gen*. a rope or string of straw, rushes, or similar material'. This seems unnecessarily specific for this broad simile; 'band' *n*.1 covers a range of things which bind.

228 **lily fingers** The whiteness of the lily is proverbial (Dent L296); see *A Midsummer Night's Dream*, 3.1.93: 'Most radiant Pyramus, most lily-white of hue'; compare ll. 362, 1053, and *Lucrece*, ll. 72, 386, 478. Compare also Thomas Lodge, *Scilla's Metamorphosis*: 'The stately robe she [i.e. Venus] wore upon her back | Was lily white, wherein with coloured silk | Her nymphs had blazed the young Adonis' wrack, | And Leda's rape by swan as white as milk, | And on her lap her lovely son was placed, | Whose beauty all his mother's pomp defaced' (C1r).

229–240 *Fondling. . . bark* This section was widely quoted in the early reception of the poem. Duncan-Jones shows that Thomas Heywood responded to this passages in *Oenone and Paris* (1594), with Oenone offering instead to be Paris' 'barge' (1993: 495–6). In Heywood's *Fair Maid of the Exchange* (1607) this is the part that comes to the minds of two characters discussing seduction, one of whom 'never read any thing but *Venus and Adonis*', the other deeming it 'the very quintessence of love' (sig. G3r). It also appears in Gervase Markham's *The Dumb Knight* (1608) where the poem is summed up as 'maids' philosophy' (sig. F1r). These lines are copied in Cambridge University Library MS MM.3.29, fol. 63v, possibly *c.* 1596, and (among other extracts) in the early seventeenth-century commonplace book Somerset Heritage Centre MS DD/SF/10/5/1, fol. 33r (CELM ShW 32.5, 35.5).

229 *Fondling* a term of endearment, 'darling', from the adjective 'fond', as in OED *n.*1, 2, 'one who is fondly loved'. However, there is no citation there for this meaning before 1640 and so the closely related OED 1 'a fond or foolish person' needs to be considered. Editors prefer this meaning, but Duncan-Jones and Woudhuysen say 'here meant affectionately' (2007: 153); Burrow notes it is Shakespeare's only use (2002: 187). An EEBO-TCP search reveals that the sense of foolishness is indeed dominant at the time, but that it may shade towards affection, as perhaps in Bartholomew Griffin's *Fidessa* (1596), where it is used of the speaker himself: 'Winged with sad woes, why doth fair *Zephyr* blow | Upon my face [. . .] | No fondling, no it is to cool the fire, | Which hot desire within thy breast hath made' (B6r).
hemmed confined.

230 *circuit* space encircled by a boundary (OED 2).
ivory white. For the proverbial whiteness of ivory, see Dent I109, 'as white as ivory', and compare l. 363, and *Lucrece*, ll. 407, 464, 1234.
pale fence. Her white arms, locked together, make an enclosure. Burrow (2002: 187) notes the possessive and legal claim made by surrounding something with a 'pale' (OED³ *n.*1, 4a, 'a district of territory within determined bounds'); compare *1 Henry VI*, 4.2.45, 'bounded in a pale'. 'Pale'

is a noun here, and 'ivory' an adjective, but there is some ambiguity with 'pale' a possible adjective, and 'ivory' a possible noun. Compare *The Winter's Tale*, 4.3.4, 'For the red blood reigns in the winter's pale'.

231 *park* hunting reserve, often royal (OED³ 1a, a legal term), where deer are kept.
deer The spelling in Q, 'deare', keeps the deer-dear wordplay in view (see l. 239).

234 *pleasant fountains* Probably her genitalia, as in Nashe's *Choice of Valentines*, ll. 111–14, where a woman's body is likened to 'the bending of an hill, | At whose decline a fountain dwelleth still, | That hath his mouth beset with ugly briars | Resembling much a dusky net of wires'. Fountains are a typical feature of idealised landscapes. However, from this point on the elaborate conceit degenerates (in a funny and ingenious way) into opaque innuendo. Compare the 'valley-fountain' of Sonnet 153.4, and *A Lover's Complaint*, ll. 285–6.

235 *limit* boundary.
relief pasture (extending the deer metaphor); see OED³ 'relief, *n.*2', 5a: 'Of a hare or hart: the action or an act of seeking food, feeding or pasturing'. Burrow emphasises the danger implied (2002: 187); hounds have better scent of hares seeking 'relief' in George Gascoigne's *Art of Venery, or Hunting* (1575: sig. L6r): 'It is most certain that hounds will have better scent of an hare when she goeth towards the relief, than when she goeth towards her form, yea although she go sooner to the one than to that other: and the reason is, that when a hare is in the field and relieveth, she coucheth low upon the ground with her body, and passeth oftentimes over one plot of ground'. Shakespeare also draws on more familiar meanings of 'relief', suggesting satisfaction. Furthermore, OED³ 'relief, *n.*3' (1a, 'Moulding, carving, stamping, etc., in which the design stands out from a plane surface') connects with the contours of l. 236, as if Venus is depicting herself as a sculpture to be appreciated. This meaning has no OED citation before 1606, but the first (from Ben Jonson's *Hymenaei*, 1606) comes from the world of stage sets. The word and the idea were also available in foreign languages, as in John Florio's Italian dictionary, *A World of Words, or Most Copious, and Exact Dictionary*

'Fondling,' she saith, 'since I have hemmed thee here
Within the circuit of this ivory pale,   230
I'll be a park, and thou shalt be my deer:
Feed where thou wilt, on mountain, or in dale;
   Graze on my lips, and if those hills be dry,
   Stray lower, where the pleasant fountains lie.

'Within this limit is relief enough,   235
Sweet bottom grass and high delightful plain,
Round rising hillocks, brakes obscure and rough,
To shelter thee from tempest and from rain:
   Then be my deer, since I am such a park;
   No dog shall rouse thee, though a thousand bark.'   240

At this Adonis smiles as in disdain,
That in each cheek appears a pretty dimple;
Love made those hollows, if himself were slain,
He might be buried in a tomb so simple,
   Foreknowing well, if there he came to lie,   245
   Why there love lived, and there he could not die.

These lovely caves, these round enchanting pits,
Opened their mouths to swallow Venus' liking:

(1598), which has '*Rilévo*, raising, relief, [...] raised or embossed work. [...] Also an easing of a man'.

236 ***bottom grass*** grassy areas at the lower altitudes. For landscape-related senses, see OED[3] '*bottom, n. and adj.*' 2, river or lake bed; 3, deep place; 6a, 'low-lying land, a valley, a dell'. The reader's imagination is comically tested (and perhaps erotically tempted) by the parts of the body being hinted at (though the current obvious anatomical sense of 'bottom', OED[3] 8, was not yet established).

237–8 ***Round... rain*** The '*hillocks*' are non-specific and may make the description more comic, and less erotic; and the '*brakes*' '*obscure*' ('hidden thickets') even more so, though editors usually see these as pubic hair, following Partridge (1990: 237). It is not clear how the 'tempest, and... rain' operate within or outside the metaphor.

239 ***deer*** Q has 'deare' again (see l. 231).

240 ***rouse*** disturb, but specifically a hunting term (OED[3] 2a), 'cause (game) to rise or emerge from cover'.

though a thousand bark even if a thousand dogs were to start barking. 'Bark' may be a subjunctive form (see 156n).

241 ***as in disdain*** 'As' might mean 'as if', or it might suggest a simile, but it becomes clear that his smile is actually disdainful.

242 ***That*** so that (see ll. 509, 599, 830, 1140).

243–6 ***Love... die*** This aetiological fable might seem to arise from Venus' passion, but it is spoken by the narrative voice.

243 ***if himself*** so that if he himself (i.e. Love).

244 ***simple*** plain, uncontrived; compare the word's other appearance in the poem, at l. 795 (where it describes the disguise of plainness adopted by lust when it took true love's place in the world). See also Sonnet 66.11, 138.8, and *A Lover's Complaint*, l. 320.

246 ***Why*** exclamatory rather than interrogative.

247 ***caves... pits*** the dimples, becoming larger and more ominous.

248 ***swallow Venus' liking*** receive and consume the desire (in the form of her gaze) of the goddess. The possessive 'Venus'' here has two syllables (see l. 180 and note).

249 **how doth she now for wits?** could there be any reason left in her now? On 'wit' in the poem, see l. 472 and note.

250 **at first** at her first rejection by Adonis.
what needs what need is there of.

251 **in thine own law** in your own sphere of influence. Compare the 'law of nature', l. 171.
forlorn wretched; often applied to lovers, but less clearly so here (or at *Lucrece*, l. 1500), than at ll. 725 or 1026.

254 **the more increasing** continuing to increase.

255 **The time is spent, her object will away** She has run out of time, and the person to whom her affection is directed wants to escape. For 'object' see OED³ 3, and compare *A Midsummer Night's Dream*, 4.1.170–1: 'The object and the pleasure of mine eye | Is only Helena'.

256 **twining** winding, embracing. The word evokes the natural world; compare l. 873. In *Hero and Leander* the word arises when Mercury is wooing a country maid: 'And sweetly on his pipe began to play, | And with smooth speech, her fancy to assay, | Till in his twining arms he locked her fast, | And then he wooed with kisses' (ll. 401–4). This passage proved suggestive to Shakespeare, which may suggest a parallel between a god pursuing an innocent girl, and the scenario of *Venus and Adonis*. See ll. 278, 318, 435 and notes.
doth urge releasing demands that she let him go.

257 **remorse** compassion.

259 **neighbours by** stands nearby (OED³ *v.*, 4a, where this is the earliest citation).

260 **breeding jennet** A jennet is a horse, usually a light and speedy one, Spanish in origin. 'Breeding' suggests that this is a mare kept in order to have foals, and perhaps that she is in season at the point where she intervenes.
proud vigorous; can suggest the mare is in season (OED³ *adj.*, *n.*, and *adv.*, 7a), and sexually aroused (OED³ 7b); compare Sonnet 151.10, and see l. 14 and note.

261 **Adonis'** said with three syllables; see l. 180 and note.
trampling need not suggest destructive intent (see OED 'trample', 1a), but

conveys the weight and violence of the tied-up horse's pacing.
courser see l. 31 and note.

263–70 **The strong-necked steed. . . controllèd with** The description evokes the *Hero and Leander* simile quoted in 33n. Ovid's *Amores* 3.4, which compares passion to a horse fighting its constraints, probably 'lies behind' both passages (Duncan-Jones and Woudhuysen 2007: 156).

264 **straight** immediately.

265 **Imperiously** in a lordly, haughty way; pronounced with four syllables (compare l. 996).

266 **girths** straps around his belly that hold a saddle in place (OED *n.*1, 1a). They are 'woven' either for strength or decoration (or both); Burrow suggests that the adjective means that they are not made of leather (2002: 189).

267–8 **The. . . resounds** He strikes the earth on which he stands so hard that the subterranean caves echo thunderously.

267 **bearing** supporting, but also perhaps 'enduring', and being marked by, his hooves, or 'producing', in association with the 'womb' of l. 268.

268 **womb** see OED³ 'womb', 4, for comparable figurative uses; compare *Lucrece*, l. 549, and *A Lover's Complaint*, l. 1; also *Titus Andronicus* 2.3.239–40, where a 'deep pit' is a 'swallowing womb', and Hotspur's vivid conception in *1 Henry IV*, 3.1.27–30: 'oft the teeming earth | Is with a kind of colic pinched and vexed | By the imprisoning of unruly wind | Within her womb'.

269 **iron. . . teeth** Burrow (2002: 189) compares Dido's horse at Virgil, *Aeneid*, 4.135; 4.146 in the Phaer-Twyne translation (1573): 'on the foamy bit of gold with teeth he champs' (sig. I3v).
'tween between.

269, 270 **teeth, with** On the rhyme, see Appendix 7; Shakespeare does not rhyme with either of these words anywhere else.

270 **Controlling. . . controllèd with** overpowering the thing that was restraining him (for both senses of 'control', see Schmidt). The *polyptoton* here provides a wittily resounding end to the stanza.

271 **braided hanging mane** The horse's mane has been plaited to enhance its appearance.

Being mad before, how doth she now for wits?
Struck dead at first, what needs a second striking?   250
   Poor queen of love, in thine own law forlorn,
   To love a cheek that smiles at thee in scorn.

Now which way shall she turn? What shall she say?
Her words are done, her woes the more increasing,
The time is spent, her object will away,   255
And from her twining arms doth urge releasing.
   'Pity,' she cries, 'some favour, some remorse!'
   Away he springs, and hasteth to his horse.

But lo, from forth a copse that neighbours by,
A breeding jennet, lusty, young, and proud,   260
Adonis' trampling courser doth espy,
And forth she rushes, snorts, and neighs aloud.
   The strong-necked steed, being tied unto a tree,
   Breaketh his rein, and to her straight goes he.

Imperiously he leaps, he neighs, he bounds,   265
And now his woven girths he breaks asunder.
The bearing earth with his hard hoof he wounds,
Whose hollow womb resounds like heaven's thunder.
   The iron bit he crusheth 'tween his teeth,
   Controlling what he was controllèd with.   270

His ears up-pricked, his braided hanging mane
Upon his compassed crest now stand on end.
His nostrils drink the air, and forth again,
As from a furnace, vapours doth he send.

272 **compassed** curving. The adjective can denote a designed quality (OED 1, here through combing and shaping) or roundedness (OED 3a).
   crest neck; see OED *n*.1, 8a: 'the ridge or surface line of the neck of a horse, dog, or other animal; sometimes applied to the mane which this part bears'.
   stand Shakespeare uses what looks like a singular verb with a plural subject (Hope 2003: 161–3 argues that it is an alternative plural form), but not vice versa, as seems the case here. Compare ll. 272, 705, 840. Q7's variant ('stands') attests to the difficulty here, and is followed by subsequent early editions. However, 'stand'

should be taken as following two subjects ('ears' and 'mane').
273 **drink the air** breathe deeply (see OED 'drink', *v*.1, 1c for figurative use of the verb). Compare *Timon of Athens*, 1.1.83 ('drink the free air'), and *The Tempest*, 5.1.102–3 ('I drink the air before me, and return | Or ere your pulse twice beat'); the speakers there (the Poet; Ariel) are both rhetorically extravagant. An EEBO-TCP search for the phrase 'drink the air' reveals no non-Shakespearean use before 1656.
274 **As. . . send** The simile diverts attention from the whole to its parts, adding vividness in comparing the horse's respiration to a hot machine.

275 **His. . . fire** For this to be metrically regular, all three syllables of 'scornfully' must be pronounced. The friction with its natural stresses and those of 'glister' might convey haughtiness (though Roe 1992: 94 suggests that a compositor may have reversed the two words in error).
glisters sparkles. See the country maid in *Hero and Leander*, ll. 389–90: 'Whose careless hair, instead of pearl t'adorn it, | Glistered with dew, as one that seemed to scorn it'; this quotation comes very near the lines quoted in 256n.

276 **hot courage, and his high desire** The natural epithets are swapped. The horse displays an excess of choler, a humoral imbalance different from the one Venus sees in Adonis (who is cooled by phlegm).
courage See l. 30 and note.
high This suggests that in the horse desire may be elevated towards nobility (though it may just measure intensity). Since the horse will be held up as an exemplar for Adonis these nuances are significant.
desire This need not only refer to sexual desire, though this is its dominant and emerging sense in the period.

277 **told** counted (OED³ 'tell, *v*.', 17a; and see l. 520). The simile draws attention again to the question of what constitutes acting naturally.

278 **gentle majesty and modest pride** The second pair may be oxymoronic, although it may square with modesty (see 'modest', OED³ 1, 'Avoiding extremes of behaviour; well-conducted, temperate') to be as proud as you deserve to be. 'Gentle [i.e. noble] majesty' has a less pressing contrast, though majesty might denote a fearsome edge that contrasts with some senses of gentleness. On 'gentle' in the poem, see l. 189 and note.
pride See l. 14 and note.

279 **curvets** prances; the earliest citation of the verb in OED. It is a technical term from the Italian *corvetta*, so again training and spontaneity are juxtaposed. Compare the portrayal of a horse at *A Lover's Complaint*, ll. 107–9; and see l. 284. Edward Topsell, *The History of Four-Footed Beasts* (1607), puts the curvet in context: 'At last he put spurs unto him, and made him run, leap, career, and curvet, to the terror at the first of all the beholders, and afterward to their singular admiration and praise of himself' (sig. 2D4r).

280 **As who should say** (i) as if he were saying; (ii) as if he wanted to say; compare *Lucrece*, l. 320.
tried proven, demonstrated by example (OED 'try, *v*.', 7a).

282 **breeder** the jennet, a mare ready to breed. OED 1a, 'that which breeds or produces offspring', has *Titus Andronicus*, 4.2.68, 'the fair-faced breeders of our clime', as its first citation. An EEBO-TCP search reveals a majority of uses denoting humans breeding animals, rather than to any animals breeding themselves. However, there are precedents, e.g. Thomas Elyot's *Dictionary* (1538), which has '*Sali*, a kind of birds, which be great breeders'.

283 **What recketh he** what does he care for.
stir agitation.

284 **flattering** disyllabic here.
'Holla' A rider's cry, urging the horse to stop (compare *As You Like It*, 3.2.244–5: 'Cry "holla!" to thy tongue, I prithee. It curvets unseasonably').
Stand i.e. stop.

285 **curb** part of the horse's harness, a chain joined to the bit.

286 **caparisons. . . trappings** Both these words denote ornamental coverings placed over horses' saddles. The former, the OED suggests, is a recent borrowing from French or Spanish (compare 'curvet', l. 279); the latter is an older word of Germanic origin.

288 **For nothing. . . agrees** Nothing else is agreeable to his disdainful outlook; or perhaps nothing else suits his impressive appearance (depending on how 'sight' is taken).
proud See l. 14 and note.

289 **Look when a painter** another comparison with a visual cue (see l. 67 and note). The description of the horse that follows resembles that of the ideal stallion in Thomas Blundeville's *Art of Riding* (1566: sig. C4r–D1v). Topsell (1607: sig. 2C4v) provides a briefer resumé of the ideal horse (though even this list cannot compete for economy with Shakespeare's stanza): 'now followeth the form or outward proportion of the body, which ought to be great and solid, his stature answerable to his strength, his sides large, his buttocks round, his breast broad, his whole body full and rough, with knots of muscles, his foot dry and solid, having a high hoof at the heel. The parts of his beauty are these, a little and dry head, the skin almost cleaving to the bones, short and pricked ears, great eyes, broad nostrils, a long and large mane and tail, with a solid and fixed rotundity of his hooves, and such a one, as thrusteth his head deep into the water when he drinketh, his ribs and loins like an ox's, a smooth and straight back, his hips long, broad,

His eye, which scornfully glisters like fire,   275
Shows his hot courage and his high desire.

Sometime he trots, as if he told the steps,
With gentle majesty and modest pride.
Anon he rears upright, curvets, and leaps,
As who should say, 'Lo, thus my strength is tried,   280
    And this I do, to captivate the eye
    Of the fair breeder that is standing by.'

What recketh he his rider's angry stir,
His flattering 'Holla', or his 'Stand, I say'?
What cares he now, for curb, or pricking spur,   285
For rich caparisons, or trappings gay?
    He sees his love, and nothing else he sees,
    For nothing else with his proud sight agrees.

Look when a painter would surpass the life,
In limning out a well-proportioned steed,   290
His art with nature's workmanship at strife,
As if the dead the living should exceed:
    So did this horse excel a common one,
    In shape, in courage, colour, pace and bone.

and fleshy, his legs large, fleshy and dry, the sinews and jointures thereof great and not fleshy near the hooves: that the hinder part of his body be higher than his forepart, like as in a hart, and this beauty better appeareth in a lean body than in a fat, for fatness covereth many faults'.

would surpass the life would like to (or, seeks to) improve on nature. EEBO-TCP has no similar combinations of 'surpass' with 'life'. This suggests that the tone may be comically pretentious here. One of Shakespeare's two other uses of the verb, in *The Winter's Tale*, 3.1.1–3, also involves an elevated tone (where Cleomenes and Dion discuss the Delphic oracle): 'The climate's delicate, the air most sweet, | Fertile the isle, the temple much surpassing | The common praise it bears'.

290 **limning out** painting. OED's first citation for the general sense 'paint' ('limn, *v*.', 3a); earlier meanings are limited to illuminating letters (OED 1) and adorning with gold (OED 2).

291 **nature's** could be capitalised as a personification. **at strife** See l. 11 and note. The contention between art and nature appears here and later in the mention of fake grapes that seem real to birds (ll. 601–4). As Burrow (2002: 191) notes,

Spenser's Bower of Bliss is the Elizabethan epitome of the contention between art and nature: 'That nature had for wantonesse ensude | Art, and that Art at nature did repine; | So striving each th'other to undermine, | Each did the others worke more beautify' (*Faerie Queene*, II.xii.59.3–6).

292 **the dead** The phenomenal liveliness of the horse is at issue in this comparison, and artworks are frequently described as 'dead'. Compare ll. 211–16. In Spenser's *Faerie Queene* (II.ix.2.1–4; see 291n for a reference to the same book) Guyon compares the image on his shield with the real thing: 'Fayre Sir (sayd he) if in that picture dead | Such life ye read, and vertue in vaine shew, | What mote ye weene, if the trew lively-head | Of that most glorious visage ye did vew?'.

293 **excel** used transitively and comparatively (OED 2a).

294 **courage** See l. 30 and note.
pace stride, its way of running and walking (OED³ *n*.1, 4a).
bone bone structure, bodily frame (OED 3a). Compare *Troilus and Cressida*, 3.3.171–2: 'beauty, wit, | High birth, vigour of bone'.

295 *fetlocks* The fetlock is a joint in the lower leg of a horse; the word also refers to the hair that grows there (OED 1a).

shag equivalent to 'shaggy', here suggesting abundance and health more than roughness.

296 *full* plump, rounded (OED *adj.*, *n.*3, and *adv.*, A10a), but other senses of 'full' (complete, abundant) are pertinent.

297 *crest* See l. 272 and note.

passing strong superlatively strong (referring to his legs).

299 *Look. . . lack* See l. 67 and note. The reader is invited to visualise the courser as something emphatically present in the poem. There may be an innuendo here, in that the only thing that a stallion *'should have'*, but which has been omitted, is a penis. However, the couplet is liable to perform a summary role, so it mainly refers to the whole range of attributes.

300 *proud* See l. 14 and note.

301 *scuds* runs quickly (Shakespeare's only use of the word). It is used of a horse in John Studley's translation of Seneca's *Agamemnon* (1581): 'He is escaped and gone, and with unmeasurable might | The Chariot horse with rein at will do scud out of my sight' (sig. X7r).

301–2 *stares. . . starts. . . stirring* The alliteration has a slightly comical effect, but also conveys skittish animal instinct in action.

301 *stares* This has a particular equine resonance, in that it can denote the way a horse's coat stands on end (OED³ 4).

303 *bid the wind a base* to challenge the wind to a race; see OED³ 'base, *n.*3', a chasing game. See Marlowe's *Edward II*, 4.2.65–6: 'We will find comfort, money, men and friends | Ere long, to bid the English king a base'.

304 *where* alternative form of 'whether'; Malone emends to 'whe'er', which Schmidt takes as meaning 'which of the two'. It could also stand for 'whither' (OED 3). Compare Sonnet 59.11.

they presumably Venus and Adonis, looking on.

whether also a sixteenth-century spelling of 'whither' (on the sound of which see Appendix 7). It is unclear if they are wondering (i) which of the two, run or fly, or (ii) whither he is running or flying.

306 *who* i.e. which (see l. 87 and note).

307 *unto* stressed on second syllable, to fulfil the rhyme with 'woo her'.

308 *as if she knew his mind* It is not clear what there is to know, or how she might know it. 'Mind' may just means his purpose or intention, or his physical desire, in which case there seems little doubt that she would know about it more simply than is implied by the speculative 'as if'. Perhaps 'mind' reaches to encompass the horse's cognition, the way he is thinking.

309 *proud* See l. 14 and note.

310 *outward strangeness* a show of indifference, negativity (OED, 'strangeness', 2a). See l. 524; compare *Troilus and Cressida*, 3.3.50–1: 'We'll [. . .] put on | A form of strangeness as we pass along'. See also Thomas Watson's *Hekatompathia* (1582), preface to poem 16, explaining how its bird conceit portrays 'her strangeness, and drawing back from a due acceptance of his service' (sig. C1r).

unkind cruel, but with the usual possibility of meaning 'unnatural', 'unfitting to her nature' (see l. 187 and note, especially in relation to the equation of naturalness with sexual compliance).

311 *Spurns at* kicks out at; poised between literal and figurative usage (see OED 'spurn, *v.*1', 3). See *Lucrece*, l. 880.

312 *Beating. . . heels* kicking back at him as he tries fondly to embrace her. The fact that he is approaching from this angle, and her response, are two equine details amid the anthropomorphism. Topsell (1607: sig. 3E4v) offers a vivid image of a mule kicking back like this: 'He ought not to be under three years old, nor yet brought unto a mare which never knew male, for such a one will beat him away with her heels and mouth, and bring him into perpetual hatred with that kind'. The image may also recall the resistance of Saul in Acts 26:14; Nicholas Udall's translation of Erasmus' *Paraphrase* on the New Testament (1548) elaborates on the verse as follows: 'For it shall be hard and painful for thee, to beat thy heels against the prick. For thy striving is not against man, but against God' (sig. 3E4r).

kind fond; but also natural (which in Venus' view, entails being sexually desirous).

313 *like a melancholy malcontent* like a discontented person suffering from an excess of choler (black bile). Usually a simile would compare a human phenomenon to an animal action in order to characterise

Round-hoofed, short-jointed, fetlocks shag, and long,   295
Broad breast, full eye, small head, and nostril wide,
High crest, short ears, straight legs, and passing strong,
Thin mane, thick tail, broad buttock, tender hide:
    Look what a horse should have, he did not lack,
    Save a proud rider on so proud a back.   300

Sometime he scuds far off, and there he stares;
Anon he starts, at stirring of a feather.
To bid the wind a base he now prepares,
And where he run, or fly, they know not whether;
    For through his mane and tail the high wind sings,   305
    Fanning the hairs, who wave like feathered wings.

He looks upon his love, and neighs unto her;
She answers him, as if she knew his mind.
Being proud as females are, to see him woo her,
She puts on outward strangeness, seems unkind,   310
    Spurns at his love, and scorns the heat he feels,
    Beating his kind embracements with her heels.

Then, like a melancholy malcontent,
He vails his tail that, like a falling plume,
Cool shadow to his melting buttock lent;   315
He stamps, and bites the poor flies in his fume.
    His love, perceiving how he was enraged,
    Grew kinder, and his fury was assuaged.

the former. With the roles reversed, this simile looks like over-extended anthropomorphism. The two key words naturally associate, and alliterate, but they have no etymological connection. As several of Shakespeare's dramatic characters show (with Hamlet the arch-example; see also Richard III) the two personality types, unified by their pessimistic, discontented outlook, frequently collocate. However, EEBO-TCP offers no uses of the phrase before Shakespeare. The malcontent figure is often associated with a rebellious political tendency, but that sense is not strong here.

314 *vails* lowers (OED 'vail, *v.*2', 1c).
plume feather.
315 *shadow* shade (see l. 162 and note).
melting sweating (OED³, 'melt, *v.*1', 2e; though this precedes the first citation, from 1614); see l. 144 and note.
lent see l. 29 and note.

316 *fume* rage; or perhaps the 'fume' is his breath, and these are the flies drawn to the moisture, now vulnerable to snapping teeth. From its basic meaning (smoke) 'fume' comes to mean various literal and figurative vapours; compare *2 Henry VI*, 1.3.150–1, which connects bad temper with horses: 'She's tickled now; her fume needs no spurs, | She'll gallop far enough to her destruction'. In Thomas Cooper's *Thesaurus* (1578) the gloss on 'excandescere' reads 'to be very angry: to be in a fume'.
317–18 *His love. . . assuaged* The jennet's return to acquiescence is abrupt (and matched by a move to the past tense).
318 *fury* fierce passion (as opposed to anger; but both are found under OED 1a); as in *Hero and Leander*, ll. 415–16: 'Herewith he stayed his fury, and began | To give her leave to rise'. This quotation comes from a passage that proved suggestive to Shakespeare, as in 256n.

319 *testy* irritable.
 goeth about to take him sets out to capture him.
320 *unbacked* riderless, never been ridden (first citation in OED); but perhaps also not yet mated (with the courser at least).
321 *Jealous* wary, apprehensive; see OED 'jealous', 5a.
 catching i.e. being caught.
323 *As* 'As' equals 'As if' (see Abbott, § 107; compare ll. 336, 357, 473, 630, 968) but there is the possibility that it is causal, i.e. 'Since'.
 wood puns on 'wood' (often spelled 'wode') meaning 'mad' (OED, 'wood, adj., n.², and adv.'). Compare Demetrius in *A Midsummer Night's Dream*, 2.1.196–7: 'here am I, and wode within this wood, | Because I cannot meet my Hermia'. See l. 323.
 hie them hurry.
324 *Outstripping. . . them* The sudden appearance of the crows (carrion birds, though the particular significance of the choice of bird, if any, is unclear) places the horses' passionate flight back in the natural world. It is uncertain why the crows strive to overtake or at least keep up with them while flying above (the former the more likely sense of '*overfly*', OED³ 1a).
325 *swollen with chafing* bursting with anger; perhaps also bruised by his struggle with the horse (OED, 'chafe, v.', 4a, 'to rub so as to abrade or injure the surface'). 'Swollen' has one syllable here; Q spells it 'swolne'.
326 *Banning* cursing (OED 'ban, v.', 2a). Compare *1 Henry VI*, 5.3.42: 'Fell banning hag, enchantress, hold thy tongue!', and 'ban', *Lucrece*, l. 1460.
 boisterous disyllabic here.
327–8 *And. . . blest* And then it seemed like a good opportunity again, to try to win favour for heartfelt passion with words.
328 *love* could be treated as a personification and capitalised; this is frequently a difficult judgement in the poem, where Venus is both goddess and victim of love. Compare cases at ll. 412, 448–50, 471, 585, 610, 632, 794, 814, 985, 1012.
329–30 *For. . . tongue* The opinion of lovers is that the heart is particularly disadvantaged when it is forbidden the help of speech. OED³ says '*aidance*' is a Shakespearean coinage, and EEBO-TCP has no earlier result. Compare *2 Henry VI*, 3.2.165, 'aidance 'gainst the enemy', which is the first citation.

330 *barred* bard Q.
331 *stopped* blocked, sealed (OED, 2a). These images are proverbial (Dent O89.1: 'an oven dammed up bakes soonest'; S929: 'the stream stopped swells the higher'; and compare G449 'grief pent up will break the heart'). Compare *Titus Andronicus*, 2.4.36–7, 'Sorrow concealed, like an oven stopped, | Doth burn the heart to cinders where it is', and *Hamlet*, 1.2.159, 'break my heart, for I must hold my tongue'; also *Lucrece*, ll. 645, 1118.
 stayed dammed, from a general sense of 'hold back' in OED 'stay, v.1', 20a. The alliteration and parallel meaning of 'stopped' and 'stayed' partly explains the unusual usage.
334 *Free. . . assuage* The stanza as a whole restates the argument of ll. 329–30, and its focus is Venus' silently brewing passion. The narrative voice expounds her principle that the answer to desire is to give it a '*vent*', an outlet (see OED, 'vent, n.2', 1a, where this is cited: 'the action of emitting or discharging').
 fire disyllabic; Q's spelling is 'fier'.
335 *attorney* representative (especially legal), perhaps advocate (OED 4, no reference after Shakespeare); i.e. the tongue, which speaks for the heart. Compare *Astrophil and Stella*, 6th song, 13–14: 'Thus doth the voice and face, | These gentle Lawyers wage'.
336 *breaks* i.e. the heart is broken by emotional desperation; but it may have legal resonance, as in OED 'break, v.', 15b, which is transitive, and relates to the violation of contracts, or 11b (as noted by Burrow 2002: 193, Duncan-Jones and Woudhuysen 2007: 163) which relates to going bankrupt. Perhaps the client is driven to abandoning his silent lawyer.
 as desperate in his suit There is no need for this to be expressed as a simile, but it is in keeping with the profusion of similes in *Venus and Adonis*. 'Desperate' is disyllabic here.
 as as if (see l. 323 and note); perhaps 'because'.
337 *glow* OED 'glow, v.1', 5 covers the basic sense of bodily heat and colour; sense 6 has 'to burn with the fervour of passion and emotion'. In l. 339 it is revealed that this is an angry glow, but its initial appearance is tellingly ambiguous: this could look like shame, or lust (see l. 29), depending partly on the observer's expectation. Shakespeare uses 'glow' of shame (*King John*, 4.1.113), scorn (*As You Like It*, 3.4.54) and anger

His testy master goeth about to take him,
When lo the unbacked breeder, full of fear,   320
Jealous of catching, swiftly doth forsake him;
With her the horse, and left Adonis there.
 As they were mad, unto the wood they hie them,
 Outstripping crows, that strive to overfly them.

All swollen with chafing, down Adonis sits,   325
Banning his boisterous and unruly beast;
And now the happy season once more fits,
That lovesick love by pleading may be blest.
 For lovers say, the heart hath treble wrong,
 When it is barred the aidance of the tongue.   330

An oven that is stopped, or river stayed,
Burneth more hotly, swelleth with more rage:
So of concealèd sorrow may be said,
Free vent of words love's fire doth assuage;
 But when the heart's attorney once is mute,   335
 The client breaks, as desperate in his suit.

He sees her coming, and begins to glow,
Even as a dying coal revives with wind,
And with his bonnet hides his angry brow,
Looks on the dull earth with disturbèd mind,   340
 Taking no notice that she is so nigh,
 For all askance he holds her in his eye.

O what a sight it was wistly to view
How she came stealing to the wayward boy,
To note the fighting conflict of her hue,   345

(*Julius Caesar*, 1.2.183). There is a telling precedent in the seduction passage of *Hero and Leander* (on which see 11n): 'the more she strived | The more a gentle pleasing heat revived, | Which taught him all that elder lovers know. | And now the same 'gan so to scorch and glow | As in plain terms (yet cunningly) he craved it' (ll. 551–5).

338 **Even. . . wind** Even as a fading ember can be rekindled by increased ventilation. This simile for Adonis' reddening evokes a move from death to revival, which does not match Adonis' feelings. 'Even' is monosyllabic.

339 **bonnet** a hat, without the feminine or childish connotations it holds today. Often brimless, but at l. 1088 Adonis' clearly has a brim.

340 **dull** inanimate.

341 **nigh** near.

342 **askance** indirectly (compare *Lucrece*, l. 637, where 'askance' is a verb), 'with a side-long glance' (Schmidt); often implies scorn (OED[3] *adv.* and *adj.*, A1b).

343 **wistly** 'with close attention; intently' (OED); could be applied to Venus or the poetic eye viewing her. Compare *Lucrece*, l. 1355.

345 **fighting conflict** tautologous; attention is drawn to a vivid but hard-to-imagine visual scene.

hue complexion: on her face the competing colours, white and red as ever, seem to be at war. See l. 10 and note; and as a comparison to ll. 345–8, *Lucrece*, ll. 52–73.

347 ***But now... by and by*** At one moment... and then at the next.

351 ***heaveth*** lifts; probably not with the modern sense of strain, since this is not usual in Shakespeare's time. Compare l. 482, *Lucrece*, ll. 111, 638 (both 'heaved-up'), 413, 586, and *A Lover's Complaint*, l. 15.

353 ***tenderer*** disyllabic here.

353–4 ***print... dint*** 'Print' hints at a long-lasting mark. 'Dint' is also 'a mark or impression made by a blow or by pressure' (OED 3), but this meaning may have only recently emerged, in Shakespeare's time, from the word's predominant meaning 'a stroke or blow' (OED 1a). The first citation is from Spenser's 1590 *Faerie Queene*, I.i.1.2–3: 'Ycladd in mightie armes and silver shielde, | Wherein old dints of deepe woundes did remaine'. Spenser's use is evidently closer to the idea of a blow. The OED notes the overlap between this sense of 'dint' and 'dent, *n.*1', 4a. It seems likely that the first readers of *Venus and Adonis* would not have found the word obscure, but they may have registered an incongruity between its violent suggestion and the softness of snow (and Adonis' cheek).

354 ***apt*** liable (OED, 'apt', 4b, of things, 4c, of people), i.e. to physical impression. Within the simile aptness is purely physical, but the word has moral ramifications in *Venus and Adonis*: Adonis is not 'apt', as in 'inclined'. For 'unapt', compare l. 34 and note.
new-fallen 'fallen' is pronounced with one syllable here.

355–60 ***Oh... rain*** After brief flurries of martial ('war') and then legal ('petitioner... suing') language, the action involved (Adonis pretends not to see her, l. 357, and then scorns her entreaties, l. 358) is seen as a dramatic performance.

356 ***petitioners... suing*** Venus' eyes are the 'petitioners' doing the 'suing', i.e. they are begging, bringing a case, before a recalcitrant judge.

357 ***as*** as if (see l. 323 and note).

359 ***dumb*** silent; it has all been done in looks, like a dumb-show (a mime of a play's plot before the action proper, as in *Hamlet*, 3.2.135, s.d.).
acts continues the dramatic theme; '*his*' (i.e. its, a regular form of the neuter genitive, as

in Hope 2003: 87; and see ll. 570, 756, 944, 960, 1140) refers back to the 'dumb-play'. There is also a pun on the 'acts' that Adonis will not consent to.

360 ***chorus-like*** they have the function of a dramatic chorus, to describe and comment on the action.

361 ***Full*** very.

362–3 ***A... band*** These two metaphorical analogies for one white hand held in another make up a tour-de-force combining four embodiments of whiteness. The first sees a proverbially white flower (see 228n) held captive ('***prisoned***'; which again brings to mind Venus' power) in a prison made of proverbially white snow (Dent S591, 'as white as the snow'; see also *Lucrece*, 196n). (A possible pun on a windy 'gale' is helped by the Q spelling 'gaile'.) The second, less troubling to the senses, has one coveted white substance held in another, with the 'band' suggesting a setting or decoration for an ivory ornament. 'Alabaster' is a mineral used in carving and jewellery, and so white as to be a synonym for whiteness in Shakespeare's time (see Dent A95.2, 'as white as alabaster', compare *Lucrece*, l. 419). Roe observes 'the delicacy by which degrees of whiteness are measured' (1992: 98), and Mortimer (2000: 84) proposes a difference between the delicate ivory of Adonis and the imposing alabaster of Venus. Burrow gets closer in saying that this passage 'invites the reader to make infinitesimal discriminations between varieties of perfect whiteness' (2002: 195). These proverbial comparisons are conventional in Elizabethan love poetry when praising female beauty. See *Astrophil and Stella*, 9.1–4: 'Queen Virtue's court, which some call Stella's face, | Prepared by Nature's chiefest furniture, | Hath his front built of alabaster pure; | Gold is the covering of that stately place', and 32.9–11: 'Vouchsafe of all acquaintance this to tell, | Whence hast thou ivory, rubies, pearl and gold, | To show her skin, lips, teeth and head so well?'.

363 ***alabaster*** alablaster Q.

364 ***friend*** As well as standing in contrast to 'foe', this also evokes the common sixteenth-century sense of 'sexual partner' (OED[3] *n.* and *adj.* A6).

How white and red each other did destroy;
    But now her cheek was pale, and by and by
    It flashed forth fire, as lightning from the sky.

Now was she just before him as he sat,
And like a lowly lover down she kneels;   350
With one fair hand she heaveth up his hat,
Her other tender hand his fair cheek feels:
    His tenderer cheek receives her soft hand's print,
    As apt as new-fallen snow takes any dint.

O what a war of looks was then between them,   355
Her eyes petitioners to his eyes suing;
His eyes saw her eyes, as they had not seen them,
Her eyes wooed still, his eyes disdained the wooing;
    And all this dumb-play had his acts made plain
    With tears, which chorus-like her eyes did rain.   360

Full gently now she takes him by the hand,
A lily prisoned in a gaol of snow,
Or ivory in an alabaster band,
So white a friend engirts so white a foe.
    This beauteous combat, wilful and unwilling,   365
    Showed like two silver doves that sit a-billing.

engirts ingirts Q; an alternative spelling of 'engirds', which means 'surrounds' (as with a girdle, or a garland, or in military uses). Compare *Lucrece*, ll. 221, 1173 (both in negative, invasive senses).

365 ***wilful. . . unwilling*** This is more balanced than the preceding opposition, since 'wilful' can simply mean willing (OED *adj.*1, *adv.*, and *n.*, A3), but it is destabilised by the sexual senses of 'will' (on which there is play in the Sonnets, see 57.13 and note). Venus wilfully presses her case, and it 'takes an effort to exclude' (Burrow 2002: 195) the pejorative hint of obstinacy. Adonis, more neutrally, is unwilling to assent, or to be approached.

unwilling see Marlowe, *Elegies*, 1.2.13–18, for the combination of unwillingness in love with a horse analogy: 'Young oxen newly yoked are beaten more | Than oxen which have drawn the plough before. | And rough jades' mouths with stubborn bits are torn, | But managed horses' heads are lightly born. | Unwilling lovers, love doth more torment | Than such as in their bondage feel content.' The word reappears late in the poem (l. 1051), used to describe the light thrown on Adonis' wound.

366 ***Showed like*** had the appearance of. Compare *Lucrece*, l. 252, and *Richard II*, 2.2.14–15: 'Each substance of a grief hath twenty shadows, | Which shows like grief itself, but is not so'.

a-billing kissing, inasmuch as birds kiss. This is the first citation for OED 'bill, *v.*2', 2: 'to stroke bill with bill, as doves'. EEBO-TCP, however, has one precedent, in Lyly's *Sapho and Phao* (1584): 'for pigeons after biting fall to billing' (D1v). OED 3, 'to caress, make show of affection', cites *Troilus and Cressida*, 3.257, first: 'What, billing again?'. The hands look like the lovers should: turtle-doves were often invoked as types of the faithful lover.

367 *engine* 'agent, instrument, tool, or means' (OED³ 13b). This could refer to her tongue, or perhaps her voice; the thing that acts upon or delivers her thoughts. At *Titus Andronicus*, 3.1.82 it is gruesomely clear that the tongue is meant by 'that delightful engine of her thoughts'.

368 *mover* someone who moves (and who, therefore, lives); first citation in OED for this general use ('mover', 3). Earlier senses entail instigating or creating the movement involved, and tend towards divine creation (especially sense 1a).
mortal round the earth (a common sixteenth-century sense; OED³ 'round, *n.*1' 10); the world of mortals. 'Mortal' and 'mover' alliterate and offer to associate; but they are etymologically unconnected. The nuances of mortality are vital to the poem, though the word is not used very often (see ll. 618, 953, 996, 1018).

370 *thy heart my wound* if you had a wounded heart like mine.

371 *For. . . thee* In return for one look in your lovely eyes, I would ensure you received any remedy you need.
help remedy, the thing that would help you (OED, 5a). Compare Drayton, *Idea*, 61.1: 'Since there's no help, come let us kiss and part'.

372 *bane* harm.

374 *Give. . . it* i.e. she will let go of his hand if he will let go of her heart (or if he will give her what she desires).

375 *steel* harden, make like steel (OED 2a). The wordplay with 'steal', which must be a near-equal exchange before the next line's elaboration, is easier within early modern spelling conventions (Q's 'steele' could be 'steal' easily enough).

376 *grave* engrave, incise marks upon (OED, 'grave, *v.*1', 5b, metaphorically).

377 *groans* a characteristic sound of a lover (predominantly in grief, but also suggestive of pleasure). See *Astrophil and Stella*, 40.1: 'As good to write as for to lie and groan'. The generic pain of the word's early appearances in the poem (also at l. 785) is replaced by specific fear and grief (ll. 829, 940, 1044).
regard care about, have regard for.

378 *Adonis'* three syllables; see l. 180 and note.

379 *For shame* Q has no speech marks, and 'he cries' is not bracketed as previous attributions of direct speech have been.

Thus it is not simple to determine where the speaking starts in this line. Adonis could be exclaiming out of embarrassment rather than criticising the goddess for her lack of modesty (as in 'shame on you!').

380 *day's delight* pleasure the day had to offer (i.e. hunting). Compare 'world's delight', *Lucrece*, l. 385.

381 *bereft him* deprived of him.

382 *hence* i.e. 'go away from here!'.

384 *palfrey* a horse for everyday riding rather than war, and often associated with women. This may imply that Adonis is 'over-delicate' (Roe 1992: 100) but the distinction is not so clear. Burrow notes Phaer's *Aeneid*, 9.282, using 'palfrey' of a war-horse (2002: 196).

387 *Affection* passion, rather than loving attachment, though the word can mean both (compare l. 569, and *Lucrece*, l. 271).
coal specifically a 'glowing ember; a piece of carbonised fuel burning or smouldering without flame' (OED³ 1a), though the cold, non-burning sense (OED³ 1b) is also current. See *Lucrece*, l. 47, and compare the metaphorical use in *Astrophil and Stella*, 35.5–6: 'What Nestor's counsel can my flames allay, | Since reason's self doth blow the coal in me?'.

388 *suffered* (i) allowed, (ii) endured; the word has both senses, and they both contribute here.

389 *The sea. . . none* In the voice of a goddess the proverbial reference to the boundlessness of the sea (Dent S169.1, 'as boundless as the sea') has additional force. Compare *Twelfth Night*, 2.4.100: '[my love] is all as hungry as the sea'.

390 *no marvel though* it is no wonder that; see Sonnet 148.11.

391 *jade* contemptuous name for a horse (OED 'jade, *n.*1', 1a). See *Lucrece*, l. 707.

392 *Servilely* slavishly.

393 *fair* proper, beautiful; an appropriate lover is the reward ('fee') his youth deserves.

394 *disdain* See l. 33 and note; thus far 'disdain' has characterised Adonis' demeanour against love; now it is turned in love's favour.

395 *thong* leather cord, i.e. his rein.
bending crest curving neck (suggests submission); see l. 272.

396 *Enfranchising* liberating; 'enfranchise' can be used generally to mean 'free' (OED, 2a) but it comes with political resonance

Once more the engine of her thoughts began:
'O fairest mover on this mortal round,
Would thou wert as I am, and I a man,
My heart all whole as thine, thy heart my wound;   370
    For one sweet look thy help I would assure thee,
    Though nothing but my body's bane would cure thee.'

'Give me my hand,' saith he, 'why dost thou feel it?'
'Give me my heart,' saith she, 'and thou shalt have it.
O give it me lest thy hard heart do steel it,   375
And being steeled, soft sighs can never grave it.
    Then love's deep groans I never shall regard,
    Because Adonis' heart hath made mine hard.'

'For shame,' he cries, 'let go, and let me go!
My day's delight is passed, my horse is gone,   380
And 'tis your fault I am bereft him so.
I pray you hence, and leave me here alone,
    For all my mind, my thought, my busy care,
    Is how to get my palfrey from the mare.'

Thus she replies, 'Thy palfrey, as he should,   385
Welcomes the warm approach of sweet desire.
Affection is a coal that must be cooled,
Else suffered it will set the heart on fire.
    The sea hath bounds, but deep desire hath none,
    Therefore no marvel though thy horse be gone.   390

'How like a jade he stood tied to the tree,
Servilely mastered with a leathern rein,
But when he saw his love, his youth's fair fee,
He held such petty bondage in disdain,
    Throwing the base thong from his bending crest,   395
    Enfranchising his mouth, his back, his breast.

'Who sees his true love in her naked bed,
Teaching the sheets a whiter hue than white,

(originally, freeing slaves, OED 1a; see 'servilely', l. 392, and 'bondage', l. 394). Venus
blurs animal instinct and human social life.
397–400 **Who. . . delight?** The 'who. . . but' form
of question is not idiomatic in mod-
ern English, but natural in Elizabethan
English. The subject changes between the
two clauses, from the person seeing his
true love naked, to the parts of his body
that would surely wish to emulate the
eye's close contact.

397 **naked bed** bed in which one sleeps naked (as
was customary in Shakespeare's time; OED[3]
'naked, *adj.* and *n*.1', 1b). There is no inherent erotic implication; see Richard Edwards
in *The Paradise of Dainty Devices* (1576): 'In
going to my naked bed, as one that would
have slept, | I heard a wife sing to her child,
that long before had wept' (F1v).
398 **Teaching** showing.
   whiter. . . than white See *Lucrece*, l. 472 and
   note.

399 *full* fully.

400 *agents* i.e. the parts of the body; see OED[3], 'agent, *n*.1 and *adj*.', 5, 'the means by which something is done', which cites *Two Gentleman of Verona*, 1.3.46, 'here is her hand, the agent of her heart'. Compare also *Coriolanus*, 1.1.123–4, where the citizen responds to the fable of the belly, 'The former agents, if they did complain, | What could the belly answer?'.
like delight similar pleasure.

401 *so faint that dares not* so cowardly, weak-willed (OED 'faint, *adj*.', 3), that he does not dare.

402 *touch the fire* Presumably the 'touch' suggests closeness rather than actual contact.

403 *excuse* make excuse for, absolve, justify (OED 2a).
courser Burrow (2002: 197) surely overstates the 'metamorphosis' from a palfrey (see l. 384 and note), but now Venus wishes to praise the horse, its grandest name returns (see l. 31 and note).
gentle On the word's appearances in the poem, see l. 189 and note.

404 *learn of* learn from.

405 *on presented joy* of an opportunity for pleasure; for the 'carpe diem' tradition, see ll. 129–32 and note. This is the second OED[3] citation for 'presented, *adj*.', but without committing to the apposite sense, 'present' as in 'in the moment'. Various senses from the verb 'present' are pertinent, e.g. to offer, to bring into the presence of.

406 *proceedings* conduct, actions (OED 2a). See l. 898, and compare Achilles in *Troilus and Cressida*, 5.7.7: 'Follow me, sirs, and my proceedings eye'. Most of Shakespeare's uses have associations with law, politics or plotting.

408 *once made perfect* if you learn the lesson properly once (specifically by heart, like an actor, OED[3] 'perfect, *adj*., *n*. and *adv*.', A4b).

409–14 *I know. . . breath* The monosyllables here suggest a blunt attitude towards love, but there is considerable rhetorical skill in the repetition and *polyptoton* deployed (as Duncan-Jones and Woudhuysen (2007: 168) show).

409 *nor. . . not* The double negative is not unusual in Elizabethan grammar (see l. 113 and note), but it is emphatic here.

411 *'Tis much. . . owe it* Love makes you very indebted to another person, and I will not become indebted to you.

412 *My love. . . disgrace it* The desire I feel towards love [or perhaps, the homage I will pay] is only a desire to demean love's reputation. The two 'loves' remain abstract, but there is a possibility of personification (see 328n). The line is not easy to punctuate; we have removed Q's comma after the third 'love', but kept the one after the second.

414 *with a breath* within (OED 16c) the time-scale of a breath; in modern idiom, 'in a heartbeat'. Compare *Henry VIII*, 1.4.30: 'He would kiss you twenty with a breath'.

415–20 *Who wears. . . strong* This stanza is a counterpart to Venus' 'carpe diem' theme. Adonis makes a case for letting things reach maturity.

416 *plucks* see l. 30 and note. The word can be suggestive of lost virginity, as at *Pericles*, 4.6.42, 'never plucked yet'; see Williams, *Dictionary of Sexual Language*, 1059–60.

417 *springing* The OED cites this line for 'springing', 1a, 'Of plants, etc:. Sprouting, growing'; but accompanied by non-specific 'things' it must extend into the territory of OED 1b, figurative uses relating to 'beginning to develop, rising'.
any jot diminished harmed or lessened in any way.

418 *prove nothing worth* turn out to be worthless; on 'prove', see l. 597 and note.

419 *colt* a young horse, but also used of a young man (OED 2c); suggestive of unruly sexuality.
backed and burdened broken in (i.e. by wearing a saddle, OED 'back, *v*.', 10) and made to carry a load.

420 *pride* spirit, vigour (OED[3] *n*.1, 8). Like 'courage' (see l. 30 and note), this word is adapted to the poem's themes and to the depiction of the horse; see l. 14 and note.
waxeth grows.

421 *wringing* squeezing.

422 *idle* futile, unproductive (OED 2a); see ll. 770, 848, and compare the use of 'idle' in the dedication.
theme subject. Puck's epilogue to *A Midsummer Night's Dream* uses the same phrase when asking for forgiveness: 'While these visions did appear, | And this weak and idle theme, | No more yielding but a dream, | Gentles, do not reprehend' (5.1.426–9). Weaver (2012) sees 'theme' as a key word

But when his glutton eye so full hath fed,
His other agents aim at like delight?   400
    Who is so faint that dares not be so bold
    To touch the fire, the weather being cold?

'Let me excuse thy courser, gentle boy,
And learn of him, I heartily beseech thee,
To take advantage on presented joy.   405
Though I were dumb, yet his proceedings teach thee:
    O learn to love, the lesson is but plain,
    And once made perfect, never lost again.'

'I know not love,' quoth he, 'nor will not know it,
Unless it be a boar, and then I chase it.   410
'Tis much to borrow, and I will not owe it;
My love to love, is love but to disgrace it,
    For I have heard, it is a life in death,
    That laughs and weeps, and all but with a breath.

'Who wears a garment shapeless and unfinished?   415
Who plucks the bud before one leaf put forth?
If springing things be any jot diminished,
They wither in their prime, prove nothing worth.
    The colt that's backed and burdened being young,
    Loseth his pride, and never waxeth strong.   420

'You hurt my hand with wringing, let us part,
And leave this idle theme, this bootless chat.
Remove your siege from my unyielding heart,
To love's alarms it will not ope the gate.
    Dismiss your vows, your feignèd tears, your flattery,   425
    For where a heart is hard they make no battery.'

evoking the rhetorical tradition following the classical *Progymnasmata*, on which see headnote. See also *Lucrece*, l. 822.
    bootless unprofitable.

423 **Remove. . . siege** Venus' attempt to woo Adonis is likened to a castle siege, aiming to end resistance by a combination of violence and persistence. Seduction is likened to a siege at *Lucrece*, l. 221, and is a common motif in love poetry, as in *Romeo and Juliet*, 1.1.212–13: 'She will not stay the siege of loving terms, | Nor bide th' encounter of assailing eyes'.
    Remove raise. See OED³, 'remove', *v.*, 6a, for the word used specifically for the raising of a siege. Compare *Lucrece*, l. 243 and note.

424 *alarms* originally, a battle cry, 'to arms!', but then used more generally of assaults and the noise of battle.
    ope open.

425–6 *flattery. . . battery* both pronounced disyllabically here.

426 *battery* bombardment; implicitly, an effective (metaphorical) bombardment, as in OED 3a: 'A succession of heavy blows inflicted upon the walls of a city or fortress by means of artillery; bombardment'. See *A Lover's Complaint*, ll. 23, 277, and *3 Henry VI*, 3.1.37: 'Her sighs will make a battery in his breast'.

429   **mermaid's voice** mermaids were thought to draw sailors to their deaths with physical and vocal beauty. Compare *Lucrece*, l. 1411, and *3 Henry VI*, 3.2.186, 'I'll drown more sailors than the mermaid shall'.

430   **I had. . . bearing** Even before you spoke, I was already struggling to carry the weight of my desire; now it has become unbearable. 'Pressing' was a method of execution in Elizabethan England, wherein weights were loaded on a victim's chest until agonising suffocation occurred. Compare *Othello*, 3.4.177: 'I have this while with leaden thoughts been pressed'.

430–2   **bearing:. . . wounding** It is clearest to have ll. 431–2 as an elaboration on the 'voice' of l. 429, so Q's comma at the end of l. 430 is changed to a colon. Both lines in the couplet seem compressed into their eleven syllables: l. 431 requires 'melodious' to be read as three syllables, 'heavenly' as two. Too many of the monosyllables in l. 430 seem to require stress in reading. The rhyme words end the lines with unstressed syllables.

431   **Melodious. . . sounding** In *A Midsummer Night's Dream*, 4.1.116–18, Hippolyta wistfully remembers the harmonious discord (a typical oxymoron to describe music) of the sound of hunting dogs: 'every region near | Seemed all one mutual cry. I never heard | So musical a discord, such sweet thunder'. The couplet is all the object of 'bearing' in l. 430, but it gathers its own musical momentum, especially in the sonorous monosyllables of l. 432.

432   **Ears'. . . heart's** There are no apostrophes in Q, so it is unclear whether to take these as singular or plural. Here they are treated in accordance with the individual body, which has two ears and one heart, and with the plural of l. 433. The point of the line is that Adonis' voice is pleasing to her ears, but what he says wounds her heart profoundly.
sore could be noun (i.e. wound) or more likely adjective (painful), so 'deep sore' parallels 'deep sweet'.

433–50   **Had I no eyes. . . the feast** The exploration of the senses, and the different things to which they are attracted, is traditional in love poetry, to separate out different aspects of a lover's appeal, or to compare them with one another. The culmination of this tradition in Elizabethan England is George Chapman's *Ovid's Banquet of Sense* (1595), in which the Roman poet himself is drawn into intimate sensory contact with the object of his illicit affection. Chapman's poem is a more orderly Neo-Platonic ascent through the senses; in Venus' fervid, hyperbolic version touch comes early. Compare also the masque of the senses in *Timon of Athens*, 1.2.122–30. Although Roe (1992: 103) notes that 'banquet' (l. 445) was the regular Elizabethan translation of Plato's *Symposium*, the Neo-Platonic content of this part of *Venus and Adonis* seems fragmentary (nevertheless, see Roe 1992: 19–21). *Hero and Leander*, ll. 85–6, offers a parallel for treating sensory experience as a feast: 'A pleasant smiling cheek, a speaking eye, | A brow for love to banquet royally'.

433   **no eyes but ears** no eyes, and only ears; but with the paradoxical sense also that if the only eyes she had were ears, then she would love the sound of him.

434   **inward beauty and invisible** Both adjectives used equally of 'beauty'; Roe is probably right to see further Neo-Platonic possibilities here (1992: 103), but again these are fragmentary echoes.

435   **parts** physical features, attributes. The usage is common but the appearance in a key passage of *Hero and Leander* (see l. 256 and note) is significant: 'As shepherds do, her on the ground he laid, | And tumbling in the grass, he often strayed | Beyond the bounds of shame, in being bold | To eye those parts, which no eye should behold' (ll. 405–8).

436   **that were but sensible** (i) that had any kind of feeling; (ii) that only had the capacity to feel by touch. See OED 7a, which cites Philemon Holland's translation of Pliny's *Natural History* (1601): 'That sponges have life, yea and a sensible life, I have proved heretofore' (sig. 2O2r). Compare *Love's Labour's Lost*, 4.2.26–7: 'he is only an animal, only sensible in the duller parts'.

437   **Though neither** although I had neither.

439   **feeling** touch.
bereft taken from.

443   **stillatory** a still, i.e. an apparatus for distilling liquids such as perfume (compare Sonnet 5).

'What, canst thou talk?', quoth she, 'hast thou a tongue?
O would thou hadst not, or I had no hearing.
Thy mermaid's voice hath done me double wrong;
I had my load before, now pressed with bearing: 430
    Melodious discord, heavenly tune harsh-sounding,
    Ears' deep sweet music, and heart's deep sore wounding.

'Had I no eyes but ears, my ears would love
That inward beauty and invisible;
Or were I deaf, thy outward parts would move   435
Each part in me, that were but sensible;
    Though neither eyes, nor ears, to hear nor see,
    Yet should I be in love by touching thee.

'Say that the sense of feeling were bereft me,
And that I could not see, nor hear, nor touch,   440
And nothing but the very smell were left me,
Yet would my love to thee be still as much:
    For from the stillatory of thy face excelling,
    Comes breath perfumed that breedeth love by smelling.

'But O what banquet wert thou to the taste,   445
Being nurse and feeder of the other four!
Would they not wish the feast might ever last,
And bid Suspicion double-lock the door,
    Lest Jealousy, that sour unwelcome guest,
    Should by his stealing in disturb the feast?'   450

Best pronounced with two syllables ('still't'ry') for the metre. A precedent for the metaphor, in Thomas Drant's 'Wailings of Jeremiah', in *A Medicinable Moral* (1566), focuses on the liquid, rather than the perfume, that results from distillation: 'Mine eye, like stillatory runs, | and weeps, and knows no rest' (sig. K7r).

excelling outstanding; outstandingly beautiful in this case. Burrow picks up 'vestigial play on exhaling' (2002: 199).

444 *perfumed* stressed on second syllable.
smelling being smelled; Abbott, § 372, suggests Shakespeare uses -*ing* for a passive participle form.

446 *Being. . .four* The combination of 'banquet' with 'nurse and feeder' works best if the subject here is Adonis, who nourishes all the senses but is a particular feast for taste. The participle 'Being' could apply to taste itself, which might provide nourishment, through eating, for all the senses to thrive.

447 *they* i.e. the other four senses.

448–50 *And bid. . .feast* Venus' tour of the senses climaxes with the thought that the senses would seek to guard Adonis from anyone else's jealous eyes. Personification is again an issue: one could refrain from capitalising 'jealousy', or 'suspicion', but this time Venus deploys these personifications as parts of her hyperbolic seduction (see 328n).

448 *double-lock* The OED cites this as the first instance of 'double-lock' in its modern sense (i.e. to lock with two turns of the key), though this may be unnecessarily specific.

451 *ruby-coloured portal* i.e. his lips and/or mouth, with red again a dominant colour. Ruby-red is conventional, as in *Astrophil and Stella*, 32.9–11, quoted in 362–3n.

451, 453 *opened. . . betokened* on the rhyme, compare ll. 47–8 and note.

452 *honey* sweet and delightful (OED 'honey, n. and adj.', B1), and perhaps persuasive ('honey-tongued', see *Love's Labour's Lost*, 5.2.334). See 16n.

453 *Like a red morn* A surprising simile (a mouth like a morning) is paired with something proverbial and familiar. See l. 1 and note.
ever yet betokened has always signified.

454 *Wrack* shipwreck (OED *n.*2, 1a), or destruction generally (see l. 558).

456 *flaws* squalls, gusts of wind (OED *n.*2).
herdmen could be modernised to 'herdsmen' (Shakespeare's own usage in later works, e.g. at *Winter's Tale*, 4.4.336), but this affects the sound more than it helps readability.

457 *ill presage* bad omen; 'presage' accented on second syllable.
advisedly attentively, warily (OED 'advisedly, *adj.*', 1a, 1b). Compare *Lucrece*, l. 180 and note.
marketh notes.

458–61 *Even as. . . Or as. . . Or as. . . Or like* The first simile at least is proverbial (Dent R16, 'little rain allays winds', and C24, 'after a calm comes a storm'). Compare *Lucrece*, ll. 1788–90 and *3 Henry VI*, 1.4.145–6: 'For raging winds blows up incessant showers, | And when the rage allays, the rain begins'.

458 *Even* monosyllabic here.

459 *grin* primarily OED *v.*2, 1, 'Of persons or animals: To draw back the lips and display the teeth', but with the double-edged comfort offered by association with 1b, 'forced or unnatural smile'. Death is 'grim-grinning' at l. 933. It is often used of dogs; compare *2 Henry VI*, 3.1.18, 'Small curs are not regarded when they grin', but also 4.1.76–7, 'And thou that smil'dst at good Duke Humphrey's death, | Against the senseless winds shalt grin in vain'.

461 *like. . . a gun* A bullet can hit its target before the sound of the fired gun arrives.
of from (Abbott, § 166).

462 *struck* The line is cited under OED 34a, 'To hit with a missile', as a figurative use.
ere before.

463 *flatly* (i) on her back (this line is cited for the relevant OED sense 1); perhaps (ii) abruptly (as in OED 3, 'In a plain, blunt, or decisive manner; without ambiguity, qualification, or hesitation'). The fall recalls *Hero and Leander*, ll. 485–6: 'By this, sad Hero, with love unacquainted, | Viewing Leander's face, fell down and fainted'.

464 *For looks. . . reviveth* The narrative voice picks up the proverbial tone and the rhetorical turn here: the figure in question ('looks. . . love, . . . love. . . looks') is *antimetabole*.

465 *recures the wounding of a frown* heals the wound caused by (or embodied in) a frown; another motif familiar from love poetry. 'Recure' can suggest 'restore to a normal or sound condition' (OED³ 1b), but is often just a synonym for 'cure' (OED³ 1a). Compare Sonnet 45.9 and *Richard III*, 3.7.125–6, 130–1: 'This noble isle doth want her proper limbs; | Her face defaced with scars of infamy [. . .] | Which to recure, we heartily solicit | Your gracious self'.

466 *blessèd* The word conveys paradoxical, incredulous appreciation of the way that her fainting wins her more attention from Adonis.
bankrupt Q bankrout. See *Lucrece*, ll. 140, 711.
loss One of only two substantive changes to the Q text made in this edition, and the only one absent from all the early texts. Henry N. Hudson ed., *Complete Works* (1881) prudently completes the bankruptcy metaphor. Q's 'love' is not utterly impossible, but much less congruent than 'loss'. Roe suggests the copyist's eye was drawn to the word 'love' which appears twice in l. 464 (1992: 104); Burrow's suggestion, that the double long 's' of manuscript 'losse' might have resembled a 'v', seems less likely (2002: 200).

467–8 *The silly boy. . . red* The poem's colours, white and red (see l. 10 and note), reappear in a travestied form.

467 *silly* ignorant (OED³ *adj., n.* and *v.*, 5a), but also pitiable; compare ll. 1016, 1098, 1151, a cluster of uses late in the poem.

468 *Claps* smacks (OED 'clap, *v.*1', 6).

469 *brake* broke: one of several preterite forms available in 1593, though it has been seen as 'already archaic' by Duncan-Jones and

Once more the ruby-coloured portal opened,
Which to his speech did honey passage yield,
Like a red morn that ever yet betokened
Wrack to the seaman, tempest to the field,
    Sorrow to shepherds, woe unto the birds,   455
    Gusts, and foul flaws, to herdmen, and to herds.

This ill presage advisedly she marketh,
Even as the wind is hushed before it raineth;
Or as the wolf doth grin before he barketh;
Or as the berry breaks before it staineth;   460
    Or like the deadly bullet of a gun,
    His meaning struck her ere his words begun.

And at his look she flatly falleth down,
For looks kill love, and love by looks reviveth.
A smile recures the wounding of a frown,   465
But blessèd bankrupt, that by loss so thriveth!
    The silly boy, believing she is dead,
    Claps her pale cheek, till clapping makes it red,

And all amazed, brake off his late intent,
For sharply he did think to reprehend her,   470
Which cunning love did wittily prevent:
Fair fall the wit that can so well defend her!
    For on the grass she lies as she were slain,
    Till his breath breatheth life in her again.

Woudhuysen, who compare *Comedy of Errors*, 5.1.48, *Richard III*, 3.7.41, and *1 Henry IV*, 1.1.48 (2007: 173).

    intent i.e. as the next line says, he previously ('late') intended to 'reprehend' her.

470 **did think** had intended.

471 **cunning love** need not be Venus herself, love personified, but rather the love that has overtaken her (on personification, see 328n).

    wittily ingeniously. The OED records positive and pejorative senses; this instance seems neutral. On 'wit' and its cognates in the poem, see l. 472 and note.

472 **Fair fall the wit that can so well defend her** Good luck to the quick thinking that can get her so smartly out of a bad situation. *Fair fall*, hyphenated in Q, is a neat way of saying 'may good come to it' (OED 'fall, *v.*', 46d). Compare *King John*, 1.1.78

('Fair fall the bones that took the pains for me!'), and *Love's Labour's Lost*, 2.1.124 ('Fair fall the face it covers!').

    wit ingenuity; but 'wit' can mean many things, helpfully paraphrased by Schmidt as including 'mental faculty' and 'imaginative and inventive faculty'. The word and its cognates cover a range of meanings in the poem; see ll. 249, 471, 472, 690, 838, 850, 1008. Francis Meres' famous comment in *Palladis Tamia* makes *Venus and Adonis* the first example of Shakespeare's Ovidian wit. 'As the soul of Euphorbus was thought to live in Pythagoras: so the sweet witty soul of Ovid lives in mellifluous and honey-tongued Shakespeare, witness his *Venus and Adonis*, his *Lucrece*, his sugared Sonnets among his private friends, &c.' (sig. 2O1v).

473 **as** as if (see l. 323 and note).

475–80 **He wrings. . . still** For the same revival technique, see *2 Henry VI*, 3.2.34: 'Rear up his body, wring him by the nose!'.

476 **pulses** i.e. the places where pulses can be felt (OED³ 1c).

477 **chafes** rubs; but evidently not kissing her yet, since that comes in l. 479. However, see *2 Henry VI*, 3.2.141–2: 'Fain would I go to chafe his paly lips | With twenty thousand kisses'.

478 **unkindness** See l. 187 and note.
marred made worse; or simply 'caused'. The mend-mar antithesis also appears in *Lucrece*, l. 578, and Sonnet 103.9–10.

479 **by her good will** if she has her own way. Compare *The Tempest*, 3.1.30–1: 'for my good will is to it, | And yours it is against'.

480 **so** as long as (or perhaps, 'so that').
still always.

482 **two blue windows** eye-lids, or perhaps the eyes themselves. Compare *Cymbeline*, 2.2.22–3 (see 125n), and *Antony and Cleopatra*, 5.2.316: 'Downy windows, close'.
faintly. . . upheaveth Although 'upheaveth' need not denote strain (see l. 351 and note), the weakness suggested by 'faintly' suggests unusual effort. Duncan-Jones and Woudhuysen's detection of possible play-acting here is feasible (2007: 174).

483 **fresh array** new appearance (OED 'array, n.', 8a, 'a condition of special preparation, or which has been attained by special preparation'); or perhaps attire (OED 11a).

484 **earth** Early editions from Q2 onwards amend to 'world', which might actually be preferred, other things being equal: the liquid 'l' sounds flow better than the repeated 'th'. However, this does not constitute a compelling reason to depart from Q.

485 **glorifies** adorns, brings glory to (OED 1a).

486 **illumined with** lit up by.
eye singular standing for plural, for the purpose of rhyme.

487 **beams** emanations of the eyes through which it was thought, by early modern science, vision worked (OED, 21). The debate between intromissive vision (where the eye received images) and extramissive vision (where, as here, the eye emitted beams) had been established in classical times: Aristotle favoured the former, Euclid the latter. Compare *Lucrece*, ll. 228 and note, 1090,

Sonnet 43.4, 114.8, and *Love's Labour's Lost*, 4.3.27–8: 'thy eye-beams, when their fresh rays have smote | The night of dew that on my cheeks down flows'.

hairless an incidental detail which maintains an interest in the specifics of Adonis' physical development. There may be a faint pun on 'heirless' (Duncan-Jones and Woudhuysen 2007: 174). The OED has this as the second citation, the first being a dictionary, R. Huloet's *Abcedarium Anglico Latinum* (1552), entry for 'depilis': 'Hairless or without hair, or having no hair'. An EEBO-TCP search, which uncovers no other uses before Shakespeare, suggests that this is a rare word.

488 **shine** 'the light emitted by a celestial body' (Schmidt); a noun here and at l. 728, a verb at ll. 193, 492, 861. As in l. 487, the poem makes a lot of light emitted, received and conferred. Compare l. 162 and note, on 'shadow'.

489 **lamps** eyes, which shine like lamps. OED 'lamp. n.1', 2b, cites *The Comedy of Errors*, 5.1.316: 'My wasting lamps some fading glimmer left'. See also l. 1116.

490 **Had not his clouded with** had his not been clouded by. The poem has numerous clouds (literally in the environment, and metaphorically in the emotions): see ll. 533, 725, 820, 972, and compare *Astrophil and Stella*, 97.9–11: 'Even so (alas) a Lady, Dian's peer, | With choice delights and rarest company, | Would fain drive clouds from out my heavy cheer'.
brow's Q's 'browes' could be singular or plural.
repine vexation; Shakespeare's only use of the noun, and the first citation in OED³. Compare the verb in *1 Henry VI*, 5.2.20 with a slightly different sense: 'Let Henry fret and all the world repine'.

491 **crystal** clear, transparent. See also ll. 633, 957, 963, and compare *Lucrece*, l. 1251. Contemporary astronomy described a crystalline sphere in the heavens, and crystal eyes were a commonplace of love poetry (as at Sonnet 46.6).

491 **Shone** See l. 488 and note.

493, 495 **heaven. . . even** could be pronounced as one or two syllables. 'Heaven' appears as both in the poem; 'even' is always monosyllabic except at l. 39. Spelling offers

He wrings her nose, he strikes her on the cheeks,   475
He bends her fingers, holds her pulses hard,
He chafes her lips, a thousand ways he seeks
To mend the hurt that his unkindness marred.
　　He kisses her, and she by her good will
　　Will never rise, so he will kiss her still.   480

The night of sorrow now is turned to day:
Her two blue windows faintly she upheaveth
Like the fair sun, when in his fresh array
He cheers the morn, and all the earth relieveth;
　　And as the bright sun glorifies the sky,   485
　　So is her face illumined with her eye,

Whose beams upon his hairless face are fixed,
As if from thence they borrowed all their shine.
Were never four such lamps together mixed,
Had not his clouded with his brow's repine;   490
　　But hers, which through the crystal tears gave light,
　　Shone like the moon in water seen by night.

'O where am I?', quoth she, 'In earth or heaven,
Or in the ocean drenched, or in the fire?
What hour is this, or morn, or weary even?   495
Do I delight to die, or life desire?
　　But now I lived, and life was death's annoy;
　　But now I died, and death was lively joy.

'O thou didst kill me, kill me once again!
Thy eyes' shrewd tutor, that hard heart of thine,   500
Hath taught them scornful tricks, and such disdain
That they have murdered this poor heart of mine,
　　And these mine eyes, true leaders to their queen,
　　But for thy piteous lips no more had seen.

no distinction: Q has 'heauen' and 'euen'
whatever the pronunciation.

494 *the fire* Within classical mythology fire is
not as typical of Hell as it is in Christianity.
It is, more generally, the last of the four
elements she evokes: earth, air ('heaven'),
water ('ocean') and fire.

495 *weary* fatigue-inducing (OED 5).
　　even evening.

497–8 *But now. . . But now* just recently. . . and
then.

497 *death's annoy* a cause of annoyance to
death (see OED 'annoy, *n*.', 2; compare l.
587, and Sonnet 8.4).

498 *death was lively joy* oxymoronic; again
Venus gives a rhetorical climax to an emotional descant.

500 *shrewd* malicious (OED 1a).

503 *true leaders* faithful and/or accurate
guides.

504 *piteous* pitying.
　　had would have.

505 **Long. . . cure** Venus credits Adonis' lips with her restoration to life, and opportunistically suggests they should continue kissing themselves in order to ensure they also receive the 'cure'. As Burrow notes, a lover's lips kiss themselves at Sidney, *Astrophil and Stella*, 43.11: 'With either lip he doth the other kiss' (2002: 202).

506 **crimson liveries** the red surfaces of their lips; 'liveries' (disyllabic here) means 'uniforms', or less figuratively, 'characteristic coverings' (OED³ 1). Compare l. 1107 (Adonis' 'beauteous livery'), *Lucrece*, ll. 1054 ('slander's livery') and 1222 ('sorrow's livery'), and Sonnet 2.3; also *A Midsummer Night's Dream*, 2.1.111–13: 'the spring, the summer, | The childing autumn, angry winter, change | Their wonted liveries'. It is a familiar motif in love poetry; see Richard Barnfield's *Affectionate Shepherd*: 'And last of all, in black there doth appear | Such qualities, as not in ivory; | Black cannot blush for shame, look pale for fear, | Scorning to wear another livery' (sig. D2r).
wear wear away, becoming less red and visually arresting.

507 **verdour** vitality; the word derives from French *vert*, so compare 'green', Sonnet 63.14.

508 **drive infection. . . year** His lips, and their kiss, are attributed power to keep away a disease. This line may allude to the period of plague experienced by London in 1592–4, which caused theatres to close and may have caused Shakespeare to turn to narrative poetry (ODNB).
dangerous year somewhat obscure, but probably reflects that the plague came and went, and that any given year could seem dangerously prone to the disease. An EEBO-TCP search suggests that this was not a common phrase. One of only two earlier citations associates it with the 'climacteric', the culminating year of one's life; see Thomas Cooper's *Thesaurus* (1578), entry for 'climactericus annus'.

509 **That the star-gazers, having writ on death** so that astrologers, who have foretold destruction.

511 **seals** The whole stanza depends on the initial tactile metaphor. The meeting of lips is likened to the meeting of a seal (Adonis') with wax (Venus', which receive the imprint). The kiss-as-seal metaphor is a commonplace of Elizabethan love poetry. Compare Sonnet 142.7 (and note), and the 'Sundry sweet Sonnets' that accompany Lodge's *Scilla's Metamorphosis*: 'What sport may equal this, to see two pretty doves | When neb to neb they join, in fluttering of their wings, | And in their roundelays with kisses seal their loves?' (sig. D4v).
imprinted Compare *Hero and Leander*, ll. 65–9: 'I could tell ye, | How smooth his breast was, and how white his belly; | And whose immortal fingers did imprint, | That heavenly path, with many a curious dint, | That runs along his back'.

512 **bargains** agreements, transactions (OED 2a), to be finalised with seals. Venus hopes to make many deals of this sort, in order to win many kisses.
still always.

513 **contented** See Sonnet 151.11n, for Booth's suggestion that there may at times be an echo of 'cunt' in this word.

514 **So** provided that.
good dealing fair behaviour (with a hint of the mercantile); the preceding line oddly has Venus planning to sell herself. When she begins to contemplate penalising Adonis in the next stanza the monetary conceit takes another sharp turn.

515 **for fear of slips** just in case anything should go wrong. See OED 'slip, *n*.3', 10b ('A mistake or fault in procedure'); perhaps 10a ('An error in conduct'), for which compare *Hamlet*, 2.1.22: 'such wanton, wild, and usual slips'. Alternatively, the line may suggest a fear of false, counterfeit kisses, as in OED 'slip, *n*.4', 'a counterfeit coin', which has its first citation from Robert Greene, *A Disputation, Between A Hee Conny-Catcher, and a Shee Conny-Catcher* (1592): 'and therefore even as to a whore, so I give thee hire, which is for every time a slip, a counterfeit coin, which is good enough for such a slippery wanton' (E4r). For more forgery in the poem, see ll. 729–30 and note.

516 **seal manual** seal made with his own hand; a technical term, but amenable to figurative use, as in *Richard II*, 4.1.25–6, 'There is my

'Long may they kiss each other for this cure!   505
O never let their crimson liveries wear!
And as they last, their verdour still endure,
To drive infection from the dangerous year,
    That the star-gazers, having writ on death,
    May say the plague is banished by thy breath.   510

'Pure lips, sweet seals in my soft lips imprinted,
What bargains may I make still to be sealing?
To sell myself I can be well contented,
So thou wilt buy, and pay, and use good dealing,
    Which purchase if thou make, for fear of slips,   515
    Set thy seal manual on my wax-red lips.

'A thousand kisses buys my heart from me,
And pay them at thy leisure, one by one.
What is ten hundred touches unto thee?
Are they not quickly told, and quickly gone?   520
    Say for non-payment, that the debt should double,
    Is twenty hundred kisses such a trouble?'

'Fair queen,' quoth he, 'if any love you owe me,
Measure my strangeness with my unripe years.

gage, the manual seal of death, | That marks thee out for hell'. This seems more specific than a 'signature' (as suggested by Burrow 2002: 203, and Roe 1992: 106, in the light of OED³, 'manual, *adj.* and *n.*', A1b).
wax-red Red, as well as being the typical colour of lips, and a key motif in *Venus and Adonis*, was the usual colour of sealing wax.

517–22 ***A thousand. . . trouble*** The numbered kisses recall Catullus and the post-Catullan *Basia* tradition, as at l. 16 and note. These lines appear in two MS song-books (with music, in the first case): Bibliothèque Nationale, Paris, Département de Musique, MS Conservatoire Rés. 1186, fol. 56v (incipit only), and BL Add. MS 24665, fol. 72v–73r (CELM ShW 32.8, 33).

517 ***buys*** singular verb perhaps follows a singular thousand, though in modern usage it would be a plural verb. Hope (2003: 161–3) argues that such forms are alternative plurals, not actually singular forms;

compare ll. 1024, 1128. The verbs are singular also in ll. 519, 522.

518 ***And*** so.

519 ***touches*** i.e. kisses, but in the financial context there may be some connection to meanings of 'touch' related to touchstones used to test the quality of gold (OED 'touch, *n.*', 5a; and perhaps particularly 5b, genuine currency as opposed to 'slips', for which see l. 515).

520 ***told*** counted; see 277n.

521 ***for non-payment*** as a result of non-payment.

522 ***twenty*** See l. 22 and note: again the counting of kisses, a feature of the erotic wit of the post-Catullan kiss-poem tradition (on which see 16n), is a feature of *Venus and Adonis*.

523–8 ***Fair queen. . . taste*** Again Adonis presents himself as unready for love, using the key concepts of ripeness and prematurity.

524 ***Measure my strangeness with my unripe years*** Realise that my unwillingness to get involved is consistent with my immaturity. On 'strangeness', see l. 310 and note. On 'unripe'; see l. 128 and note.

525 ***know myself*** The nearest Shakespeare gets elsewhere to this idea of coming to know oneself is *Henry VIII*, 3.2.378–9: 'I know myself now; and I feel within me | A peace above all earthly dignities'. Here Wolsey, however, is emerging from a lack of self-understanding, rather than coming to his first mature self-awareness. On reflexive pronouns in the poem, see l. 159 and note.

know suggests intimate knowledge and sexual experience. It resonates with Genesis 4:1, where Adam 'knew' (from the Vulgate 'cognovit') his wife; compare *All's Well That Ends Well*, 5.3.289: 'if ever I knew man, 'twas you'. Compare also Sonnet 129.13.

526 ***No fisher. . . forbears*** Every fisherman refrains from taking immature, undersized fish. Adonis may justly call himself 'unripe' but he is no 'fry' (OED 'fry', *n*.1', 3: 'young fishes just produced from the spawn'). He is, after all, old enough to hunt boar without parental supervision.

ungrown not yet fully grown; earliest instance in OED and EEBO-TCP.

527 ***mellow*** ripe (OED³ 1a). Compare the complaint of Daphnis in Richard Barnfield's *Affectionate Shepherd*: 'I have fine orchards full of mellowed fruit; | Which I will give thee to obtain my suit' (sig. B2r).

green green in colour, unripe. See OED³ A5a; the word is specifically pertinent to plums, but can imply unripeness generally. Compare l. 806, and *Antony and Cleopatra*, 1.5.73–4: 'my salad days, | When I was green in judgement'.

528 ***plucked*** see l. 30 and note.

529–34 ***Look. . . goodnight*** These lines, a 'chronography' (description of the time of day), are the most quoted in the early MS reception of the poem: in Huntington HM 116, p. 32; in Rosenbach Library MS 239/27, p. 166; and in Rosenbach Library MS 1083/16, p. 175, where a version of Sonnet 106 is also found (all verse miscellanies; CELM ShW 34, 35, 35.5).

529 ***Look*** look how; see l. 67 and note.

the world's comforter i.e. the sun.

531 ***owl. . . shrieks*** proverbially a bad omen (Dent R33, 'the croaking raven (screeching owl) bodes misfortune (death)'); compare *Lucrece*, l. 165, and 'Let the Bird of Loudest Lay', ll. 5–6.

533 ***coal-black clouds, that shadow heaven's light*** The meteorology is not clear here. It seems to imply that at night the sun is blocked by black clouds, but perhaps the clouds are incidentally present, and represent a further deterioration of the environment. On clouds, see l. 490 and note.

shadow hide; compare *Lucrece*, l. 1416, and *Titus Andronicus*, 2.1.130: 'there serve your lust, shadowed from heaven's eye'. See also l. 164 and note.

534 ***goodnight*** two words in Q, but one word at ll. 535, 537; the OED³ lemma is 'goodnight' though it cites hyphenated and two-word examples.

538 ***honey fee of parting tendered is*** The sweet price paid at the moment of leaving (i.e. an embrace) is offered. 'Fee', and 'tendered' (OED 'tender', *v*.1'; but the sense of softness contributes something too), return us to the deal-making world of ll. 511–16. On honey, see 16n.

539 ***lend*** bestow upon; but Venus expects to receive this embrace back with interest.

540 ***Incorporate*** fused into one body; pronounced with three syllables here, 'incorp'rate'. Compare *Comedy of Errors*, 2.2.122–3: 'undividable incorporate, | [. . .] better than thy dear self's better part', and *Romeo and Juliet*, 2.6.36–7: 'you shall not stay alone | Till Holy Church incorporate two in one'. The word has legal resonance (OED *adj*.1, 2) and mythical connections, for example with the story of Salmacis and Hermaphroditus, for which see Ovid, *Metamorphoses*, 4.274–388 and Golding, 4.347–481. It lies behind a merging of bodies in Spenser's *Faerie Queene*, 1590 text, III.xii.46.1–4: 'Had ye them seene, ye would have surely thought, | That they had beene that faire Hermaphrodite, | Which that rich Romane of white marble wrought, | And in his costly Bath caused to bee site: | So seemd those two, as growne together quite'.

grows to grows into.

face, Q has a full stop at the end of this stanza, where modern usage, and the 'breathless' continuation of sense, would prefer a comma.

541 ***disjoined*** broke away; the first citation for OED 5b.

542 ***heavenly moisture*** compare l. 64; the narrative voice echoes Venus' reported praises (e.g. ll. 439–44). 'Heavenly' is disyllabic here.

moisture, that Q has no comma here, in which case 'that' here could stand for 'of that'. Q7 adds a characteristically shrewd

Before I know myself, seek not to know me: 525
No fisher but the ungrown fry forbears;
   The mellow plum doth fall, the green sticks fast,
   Or, being early plucked, is sour to taste.

'Look, the world's comforter, with weary gait,
His day's hot task hath ended in the west.   530
The owl (night's herald) shrieks, 'tis very late:
The sheep are gone to fold, birds to their nest,
   And coal-black clouds, that shadow heaven's light,
   Do summon us to part, and bid goodnight.

'Now let me say goodnight, and so say you: 535
If you will say so, you shall have a kiss.'
'Goodnight', quoth she, and ere he says 'Adieu',
The honey fee of parting tendered is:
   Her arms do lend his neck a sweet embrace;
   Incorporate then they seem, face grows to face,   540

Till breathless he disjoined, and backward drew
The heavenly moisture, that sweet coral mouth,
Whose precious taste her thirsty lips well knew,
Whereon they surfeit, yet complain on drouth.
   He with her plenty pressed, she faint with dearth,   545
   Their lips together glued, fall to the earth.

Now quick desire hath caught the yielding prey,
And glutton-like she feeds, yet never filleth.

comma that places 'mouth' and 'moisture' in apposition (as in Roe's text, and here), both objects of 'drew'.

coral red; the comparison is conventional in love-poetry, and proverbial (Dent C648.1). Compare *Lucrece*, l. 420; and Sonnet 130.2 and note.

544 ***Whereon they surfeit. . . drouth*** They overfill themselves [with the 'heavenly moisture' of Adonis' breath], but they still complain that they are in a state of drought and dearth. The Q spelling 'drouth' (which is listed alongside 'drought' as an alternative lemma in OED), is retained for the sake of the rhyme. The paradox recalls Ovid's Narcissus (see ll. 19–20 and note).

surfeit The word reappears at ll. 602, 743, 803. It connotes greed, excess and dissatisfaction, and is thematically in tune with a poem featuring rapacious passion. Its four

appearances are all grouped in the middle of the poem.

complain on (i) complain of; (ii) complain about, as at l. 160.

545 ***plenty*** (i) physical magnitude; (ii) strength of her passion.

pressed oppressed, burdened (and see l. 430).

547 ***quick*** lively, vigorous (compare l. 38 and note, and l. 140). On the association of speed with desire and thought, see Sonnet 45.4.

the Q5 erroneously gives 'his'; Q7 miscorrects to 'her' and is followed by subsequent early editions. Although Q does not make this a possessive pronoun, the genders of the possessives in other editions may be revealing. Venus' desire has masculine characteristics.

yielding See *Lucrece*, ll. 1036, and 1658, where Lucrece denies her compliance, 'accessory yieldings', in the rape.

548 ***filleth*** becomes full, satisfied.

550 *insulter* 'triumphing enemy' (Schmidt); the first citation in OED (for 'one who insults') and Shakespeare's only use. This seems like a coinage to capture a problematic situation wherein the goddess of love is arguably guilty of a sexual assault, and the poem's witty tone does not entirely contain it. EEBO-TCP has only one precedent, in Thomas Rogers' *Anatomy of the Mind* (1576), where it arises in a definition of 'insultation', i.e. taking pleasure in others' misfortune (sig. B8r). Uses of the verb 'insult' to mean physical rather than verbal assault are dated by OED post-1638 (sense 3) but see *Titus Andronicus*, 3.2.71: 'Give me thy knife, I will insult on him'. Compare *Lucrece*, l. 509.

551 *vulture thought* rapacious desire (Roe 1992: 108). Her strategy is vulture-like: she wants to scavenge whatever she can. Compare *Lucrece*, l. 556, which uses 'vulture' as a modifier for the rapist's 'folly', and the eagle simile at l. 55.
   pitch fix, settle (OED³, *v*.2, 19a); Burrow detects a pun (via the vulture) on 'pitch' (OED³ *n*.2, 21a), the height to which a falcon soars (2002: 205).

552 *draw . . . dry* suck out all the moisture (see l. 542) from his lips. This stanza evokes the neo-Latin *Basia* tradition (on which, see 16n) in its combination of wit and predatory violence.
   treasure Duncan-Jones and Woudhuysen (2007: 180) note that elsewhere Shakespeare may associate 'treasure' with a woman's sexual parts (see Sonnet 136.5; *Lucrece*, l. 16 and note), but here it seems more that the narrative voice is luxuriating in what Adonis has to offer.

553 *spoil* plunder (OED 1a). See *Lucrece*, ll. 553, 1172.

554 *blindfold* 'with the mind blinded; without perception; without forethought, heedless, reckless' (OED 2); two words in Q.
   forage plunder; nearly as violent, and just as unromantic, as 'spoil' (OED 2a, 'a raid for ravaging the ground from which the enemy draws supplies').

555 *reek* steam (OED³ 'reek, *v*.1', 2), not 'stink'; but also associated with blood (OED³ 2b), and, perhaps the primary meaning here, sweat (OED³), as in *King Lear* 2.4.30–1: 'a reeking post, | Stewed in his haste, half breathless'. Compare the same pairing in *Julius Caesar*, 3.1.158, in the context of sacrifice: 'whilst your purpled hands do reek and smoke', and see also Sonnet 130.8, *Lucrece*, l. 1377.
   smoke 'give off or send up vapour . . . steam' (OED 2a); effectively a synonym for 'reek' here. See *Lucrece*, l. 438.

556 *careless* reckless.
   desperate disyllabic here.
   courage See l. 30 and note, and especially l. 276.

557 *Planting oblivion* causing her to forget herself and her surroundings. See OED³ 'plant, *v*.', 3a 'to instil (an idea or feeling)'; compare *Lucrece*, l. 887.

558 *blush* See l. 69 and note.
   honour's wrack the ruin (OED 'wrack, *n*.1', 3a) of good faith, and her good name.

561 *chasing* being chased; for the grammar, compare l. 444 and note.

562 *like . . . dandling* like a fractious baby who is calmed by rocking.

564 *not all she listeth* not as much as she desires.

565 *What wax so frozen* The physical properties of wax are often the focus of attention in love poetry (as at ll. 511–16), especially its tactile quality and its ability to be made more malleable. This is proverbial: Dent W136, 'soft wax will take any impression'. Compare *Lucrece*, ll. 1240–3, and (for 'frozen') 247.
   dissolves melts, or at least softens; see l. 144 and note.
   tempering manipulation; as in OED 'temper, *v*.', 9, '. . . to fit, adapt, conform, accommodate, make suitable'. See also OED 13, specifically relating to wax; several meanings of the word relate to the imposition of a more useful or pliant state. Pronounced with two syllables here.

567 *Things out of hope . . . venturing* Things that seem unachievable can often be achieved if you make a bold attempt (proverbial; Dent N319, 'nothing venture nothing have'). On 'venturing', which is disyllabic here, see *Lucrece*, 148–9n.
   compassed attained, achieved (OED 'compass, *v.1*', 11a).

568 *Chiefly . . . commission* Especially in the case of love, where things tend to be taken further than they should be.
   leave permission (see OED³ 'leave, *n*.1', 1a).
   commission authority (OED³ 'commission, *n*.1', 1a). Most of Shakespeare's uses of 'commission'

Her lips are conquerors, his lips obey,
Paying what ransom the insulter willeth: 550
   Whose vulture thought doth pitch the price so high
   That she will draw his lips' rich treasure dry.

And having felt the sweetness of the spoil,
With blindfold fury she begins to forage.
Her face doth reek and smoke, her blood doth boil,   555
And careless lust stirs up a desperate courage,
   Planting oblivion, beating reason back,
   Forgetting shame's pure blush and honour's wrack.

Hot, faint, and weary with her hard embracing,
Like a wild bird being tamed with too much handling,   560
Or as the fleet-foot roe that's tired with chasing,
Or like the froward infant stilled with dandling,
   He now obeys, and now no more resisteth,
   While she takes all she can, not all she listeth.

What wax so frozen but dissolves with tempering,   565
And yields at last to every light impression?
Things out of hope are compassed oft with venturing,
Chiefly in love, whose leave exceeds commission.
   Affection faints not like a pale-faced coward,
   But then woos best, when most his choice is froward.   570

When he did frown, O had she then gave over,
Such nectar from his lips she had not sucked.
Foul words and frowns must not repel a lover:
What though the rose have prickles, yet 'tis plucked.
   Were beauty under twenty locks kept fast,   575
   Yet love breaks through, and picks them all at last.

are official, though compare *As You Like It*, 4.1.138–9: 'I might ask you for your commission; but I do take thee, Orlando, for my husband'. The tone is shifting here towards the military boldness of ll. 569–70.

569 *Affection* passion, desire; see l. 387.

570 *choice* the object of its choice (i.e. Adonis, in this case).
froward unwilling, but the OED and Shakespeare's other uses all have a pejorative note, as at l. 562. Affection itself might be froward – in the less pejorative sense of

'bold' – here, but it seems as if the narrative voice has again taken Venus' side.

571 *gave over* desisted.

572 *had not* would not have.

573 *Foul* harsh.

574 *plucked* See l. 30 and note, and ll. 131–2 and note; the word is natural here, used of a flower. The line is proverbial again: Dent R182; 'no rose without a thorn'; see also *Lucrece*, l. 492.

575 *twenty* See l. 22 and note.

576 *at last* in the end.

577 **For pity now. . . him** Now (finally) she feels enough pity that she can no longer keep him there against his will.
    For pity i.e. out of pity, but Duncan-Jones and Woodhuysen suggest also the sense 'What a pity that [. . .]' (2007: 182).

578 *fool* a term of endearment (OED *n.*1 and *adj.*, A1c) as well as pity. See *King Lear* 5.3.306, 'And my poor fool is hanged!'. 'Fool' can also convey censure and insult. At this point the narrative voice, the reader's inference, and Venus' influence might all inflect 'fool' differently.

580 **look well to her heart** take good care of her heart (which he is carrying away with him). The giving and receiving of a lover's heart is a commonplace of love poetry, as at Sonnet 22.11–14.

581 **The which** which.
    by Cupid's bow Venus protests about the abduction of her heart ('encaged' in Adonis' own 'breast') by invoking her own son. This is a typical lover's vow, as at *Midsummer Night's Dream* 1.1.169: 'I swear to thee, by Cupid's strongest bow'. Compare ll. 947–8. Cupid's bow defeats Hero in Marlowe's poem, ll. 369–72: 'Cupid beats down her prayers with his wings, | Her vows above the empty air he flings: | All deep enraged, his sinewy bow he bent, | And shot a shaft that burning from him went'.

583 *waste* spend (a period of time), but with some pejorative force, including the sense 'waste away' where 'this night' would not be a direct object (Roe 1992: 109).

584 *watch* remain sleepless, keep a vigil (OED 2a; 1a more generally).

585 *love's master* Again this could be capitalised as a personification of 'love' (see 328n).

586 *make* (i) arrange; (ii) attend.
    match appointment, arrangement (OED 'match, *n.*1', 9); the word carries pertinent implications of marriage, suitable partnership and rivalry.

589 *pale* pallor (OED[3], *n.*2), though Hope (2003: 101–2) treats this as an adjective acting as a head of a noun phrase.

590 *lawn* fine linen cloth, typically white (proverbially so; Dent L119.1). See *Lucrece*, ll. 258–9, and *The Winter's Tale*, 4.4.218: 'lawn as white as driven snow'. The image of a red rose being covered in white material plays on texture as well as colour. As l. 591 shows, her cheek should not be so white: the 'sudden pale' 'usurps' her face.

592 *yoking* guiding and constraining (like the yoke does to the oxen, a metaphor for embracing).

593, 594 *neck. . . back* A full rhyme may be possible in Elizabethan pronunciation, but see Appendix 7 for some doubts.

594 **He on her belly falls, she on her back** Compare ll. 43–4. In *Hero and Leander* Marlowe set a precedent with his two lovers (of equal inexperience in that case) stumbling into sex.

595 *lists* the venue for a jousting competition.

596 **Her champion mounted** The jousting analogy becomes stretched. Adonis is the 'champion' who has been transitively been 'mounted' (OED[3] 'mount, *v.*', 13b), i.e. given something to ride (Venus taking the role of horse). However, the agent engaged in seeking a sexual ('*hot*', OED[3] *adj.* and *n.*, A8c) encounter is Venus herself, and Adonis is a very passive champion. The OED cites ll. 595–8 for 'mount, *v.*', 14a, 'to climb on to (a partner or mate) for the purpose of sexual intercourse', referring specifically to l. 598, but recognising the extended word-play. Compare also l. 1191.

597 **All is imaginary she doth prove** The line's difficulty hinges on the sense of 'prove', an important word in the poem (ll. 40, 418, 597, 608; and 'proof' at l. 626). Does Venus (1) *test* and/or spuriously (2) *prove true* all her false erotic hopes; or does she (3) *experience* only imaginary things or (4) *discover* that they are only imaginary. (3) and to a lesser extent (4) are favoured by commentators, and (3) especially seems clearest.
    All is (i) that all is; (ii) all that is. It depends on how 'prove' is taken; see previous note.
    imaginary Lovers are prone to excesses of imagination, as in *Astrophil and Stella*, 38.5–8: 'The first that straight my fancy's error brings | Unto my mind, is Stella's image, wrought | By Love's own self, but with so curious draught, | That she, methinks, not only shines but sings'. In *Venus and Adonis* the word and its cognates cover a range of

For pity now she can no more detain him;
The poor fool prays her that he may depart.
She is resolved no longer to restrain him,
Bids him farewell, and look well to her heart,   580
    The which, by Cupid's bow, she doth protest,
    He carries thence encagèd in his breast.

'Sweet boy,' she says, 'this night I'll waste in sorrow,
For my sick heart commands mine eyes to watch.
Tell me, love's master, shall we meet tomorrow,   585
Say, shall we, shall we, wilt thou make the match?'
    He tells her 'No': tomorrow he intends
    To hunt the boar with certain of his friends.

'The boar!', quoth she, whereat a sudden pale,
Like lawn being spread upon the blushing rose,   590
Usurps her cheek; she trembles at his tale,
And on his neck her yoking arms she throws.
    She sinketh down, still hanging by his neck;
    He on her belly falls, she on her back.

Now is she in the very lists of love,   595
Her champion mounted for the hot encounter:
All is imaginary she doth prove.
He will not manage her, although he mount her,
    That worse than Tantalus' is her annoy,
    To clip Elysium, and to lack her joy.   600

hopes and fears: see ll. 668, 721, 975. It also plays an important role in *Lucrece*: see ll. 702, 1422, 1428, 1622.

598 **manage** control, with a sexual innuendo not marked by OED[3] or evident in Shakespeare's other uses (compare *A Lover's Complaint*, l. 112). The word originates in horsemanship (see OED[3] 1a and etymology), and comes to mean 'control' generally.

599 **That** so that.

Tantalus' no apostrophe in Q. In classical visions of hell there are some archetypal punishments. Tantalus, who (in some stories) fed his son to the gods at a banquet, is tortured forever by water and/or fruit that is just out of reach. See *Lucrece*, l. 858, and *Hero and Leander*, ll. 557–60: 'She, with

a kind of granting, put him by it, | And ever as he thought himself most nigh it, | Like to the tree of Tantalus she fled, | And seeming lavish, saved her maidenhead'.

annoy frustration (OED 1a).

600 **clip** embrace.

Elysium paradise, her heart's desire. In classical mythology Elysium is where the blessed go after death. Antedates first citation in OED, which (for the figurative use) is *Henry V*, 4.1.271, but see William Warner's *Pan His Syrinx* (1584): 'These considerations (my dear Arbaces) at the first urged of necessity, and then used as necessary, besides the place itself, which seemed a second Elysium, or of pleasure, and plenty, Nature her storehouse' (sig. Y2r).

601–4 ***Even so. . . berries saw*** An ambitious simile
that draws numerous aspects of the poem
together: visual imagination, sensory frustration and animal experience. The famous
story of the Greek artist Zeuxis (or Apelles),
who was able to paint fruit so realistic
it could draw a crowd of birds, celebrates
human skill. The key classical source for
this archetypical clash of art and nature in a
trompe l'oeil is Pliny, *The History of the World*,
trans. Philemon Holland, 1601: 'Zeuxis for
proof of his cunning, brought upon the scaffold a table, wherein were clusters of grapes
so lively painted, that the very birds of the
air flew flocking thither for to be pecking at
the grapes' (sig. 2Z4r). In the notes to Book
33 of Harington's translation of Ariosto's
Orlando Furioso (1591) he says the 'story of
the strife betweene Zeuxis and Parrhasius'
is 'well known, I think to all' (sig. Aa4r). See
Sonnet 47.6 and note.

601 ***Even*** monosyllabic here.

602 ***Do surfeit. . . eye*** become visually sated; on
'surfeit', see l. 544 and note, and compare
'pine and surfeit', Sonnet 75.13.
pine starve (OED³ 3a).
maw stomach; but it can mean throat or
gullet (OED³ 'maw, *n.*1', 3a), which takes it
closer to the organs of taste.

603 ***Even*** monosyllabic here.
mishaps misfortunes.

604 ***helpless*** OED cites this as the first instance
of sense 3, 'Affording no help; unavail-
ing, unprofitable'. An EEBO-TCP search
confirms that this usage is unusual but
not unprecedented. See Henry Howard,
*A Defence of the Ecclesiastical Regiment in
England* (1574): 'these unskilful surgeons
leave such a scar behind them by reason of their helpless salve' (sig. B1r). It
is marginally preferable to treat it as an
adjective rather than an adverb. Compare
Richard III, 1.2.12–13: 'in these windows
that let forth thy life, | I pour the helpless
balm of my poor eyes', and *Lucrece*, ll. 756,
1027, 1056.

605 ***effects*** results of her actions, i.e. some sort
of manifestation on his part (Duncan-
Jones and Woudhuysen (2007: 185) suggest
an erection); perhaps more generally 'signs'

(OED³ 4a). Compare *Lucrece*, ll. 251, 1555.
Burrow notes Q13's 'affects', which may
suggest that the word struck an early
reader as unexpected and challenging
(2002: 207).

608 ***She hath assayed. . . proved*** She has tried
everything she could possibly try. On 'prove',
see 597n.

609 ***fee*** reward.

610 ***She's Love. . . not loved*** The line savours
the variation and triple repetition (*polyptoton*),
but continues the insidious proposition
of the preceding line. It makes an explicit
equation between Venus and love itself
(she being its personification, on which see
328n).

611 **Fie, Fie** On the exclamation, see l. 185 and
note. Doubled here, as at l. 1021, it is inten-
sified.

612 ***withhold*** detain, restrain (OED 1a).

615 ***what it is*** i.e. how dangerous it is.

616 ***churlish*** see l. 107 and note.
gore pierce, spear; in Shakespeare's time
this was used generally, but subsequently
it became associated with bulls and boars
(OED 'gore, *v.*1', 2a). Compare *Troilus
and Cressida*, 1.1.112, 'Paris is gored with
Menelaus' horn'.

617 ***tushes*** tusks.
whetteth still is always sharpening. Burrow
(2002: 208) cites Gascoigne for the belief
that the upper pair of a boar's four tusks
were for sharpening the lower pair: 'we call
them tusks or tushes, whereof the two highest do not hurt when he striketh, but serve
only to whet the other two lowest' (1575:
sig. K3v).

618 ***mortal*** death-dealing (OED³ 3a). Compare
3 Henry VI, 3.3.256–7: 'I came from Edward
as ambassador, | But I return his sworn and
mortal foe'. See l. 368 and note.
bent determined (of the metaphorical
'butcher'), but with a physical aspect.

619 ***bow-back*** curved back.

619–20 ***he hath a battle set. . . foes*** The boar has
bristles (on his back) set up like a battle-
formation of spears, always threatening his
enemies. Compare Ovid's Calydonian Boar,
Metamorphoses, 8.285; Golding, 8.379–80:
'And like a front of armed pikes set close in

Even so poor birds, deceived with painted grapes,
Do surfeit by the eye, and pine the maw;
Even so she languisheth in her mishaps,
As those poor birds that helpless berries saw.
    The warm effects which she in him finds missing,   605
    She seeks to kindle with continual kissing.

But all in vain, good queen, it will not be.
She hath assayed as much as may be proved;
Her pleading hath deserved a greater fee.
She's Love, she loves, and yet she is not loved: 610
    'Fie, fie,' he says, 'you crush me, let me go,
    You have no reason to withhold me so.'

'Thou hadst been gone,' quoth she, 'sweet boy, ere this,
But that thou told'st me thou wouldst hunt the boar.
O be advised, thou know'st not what it is,   615
With javelin's point a churlish swine to gore,
    Whose tushes never sheathed he whetteth still,
    Like to a mortal butcher bent to kill.

'On his bow-back he hath a battle set
Of bristly pikes that ever threat his foes.   620
His eyes like glow-worms shine, when he doth fret;
His snout digs sepulchres where'er he goes.
    Being moved he strikes whate'er is in his way,
    And whom he strikes, his crooked tushes slay.

battle 'ray | The sturdy bristles on his back stood staring up alway'.

619 **battle** This line is cited as the only instance of OED 'battle, *n*.', 8b, figurative use of 8a, 'a body or line of troops in battle array'.

621 **glow-worms** The common name for the firefly *lampyris noctiluca*, this is an available if not straightforward comparison for fiery eyes. The glow-worm's light stands out against the dark but is not very bright; in *Merry Wives of Windsor*, 5.5.78 we hear that 'twenty glow-worms shall our [fairy] lanterns be'. However, it does shine mysteriously and uncannily; thus the simile captures the frightening quality of the boar's eyes.

fret become agitated (OED 'fret, *v*.1', 9a); see l. 69 and note. The clause 'when … fret', between two commas in Q, could conceivably go with the main clause before or after it. It seems more balanced to take it with the first, and to punctuate accordingly.

622 **sepulchres** graves. A sepulchre can be a funeral monument as well as a simple hole in the ground; compare *A Lover's Complaint*, ll. 45–6, where the speaker figuratively imagines 'sepulchres' for trinkets that end up 'in mud'.

623 **moved** roused (e.g. to anger).

624 **whom** whomever.
    crooked (i) curved; (ii) malignant (Schmidt).

625–7 **armed, harmed** probably pronounced 'armèd', 'harmèd'; the Q spellings are 'armed', harmed'. See 109–111n on the reliability of Q's orthography in these cases. Duncan-Jones and Woudhuysen note the preponderance of feminine endings in the stanza (2007: 186).

626 **proof** protection, invulnerability (OED³ 9a); perhaps specifically armour (OED³ 9b, see *2 Henry VI*, 4.2.61). Perhaps, less simply, 'a state of having been tried and having stood the test... particularly applied to defensive arms tried and found impenetrable' (Schmidt). Most of Shakespeare's uses relate to logic, but see *Coriolanus*, 1.4.25, 'hearts more proof than shields', and also *Hamlet*, 3.4.37–8: 'If damned custom have not brassed it [Gertrude's heart] so | That it be proof and bulwark against sense'. On 'prove', see 597n.

627 **easily** pronounced with two syllables.

628 **ireful** angry.
on against.
venture See l. 567 and note.

629 **embracing** The bushes are liable to obstruct him, which Venus sees as an embrace. The couplet is hard to punctuate in such a way as to make it run smoothly.

630 **As fearful** as if they were fearful.
whom which; perhaps because the brambles and bushes are being personified (Duncan-Jones and Woudhuysen 2007: 187), though the pronoun is used of things in this period (see OED, 9a). See l. 87 and note.

632 **love's eyes** another case where the personification of love-as-Venus is unclear (see 328n); it could also be love-as-Cupid, or simply love-as-itself.
pays The plural noun is followed by what looks like a singular verb, not a significant anomaly in Shakespearean usage (see l. 517 and note), but altered in Q7 ('eye pays').
tributary gazes looks which pay tribute, or which are offered as a tribute (OED *adj.* and *n.*, 3). Compare Daniel, *Delia*, 50.5–6: 'These tributary plaints fraught with desire, | I send those eyes, the cabinets of love'.

633 **crystal** clear, shining; see Sonnet 46.6 and note.
eyne alternative plural form of 'eye', probably seeming archaic to Shakespeare's first readers (treated as 'marked', by Hope 2003: 66), though still current in poetry. Used as a rhyme word in eleven of thirteen

Shakespearean instances (see *Lucrece*, l. 643), the others being *Pericles*, 3.Prol.5 (Gower, and thus archaic), and *Lucrece*, l. 1229.

634 **full perfection** utter perfection. The phrase can also suggest full maturity, as in 'A letter written by one to a rich widow', in H.C.'s *The Forest of Fancy* (1577): 'Your years, which being at the full perfection, neither too young a wanton, or too old a dotard, but one that are both able for your experience, to minister good counsel to such an unskilful young man as I am, and also sufficiently satisfy me in all other things requisite for my young years' (sig. L4r).
amazes a stronger word in the sixteenth century; the OED cites this line under 'amaze, *v.*' 4, 'To overwhelm with wonder, to astound or greatly astonish'. In Thomas Thomas' *Dictionarium* (1587), it is part of the gloss for Latin 'terreo': 'to fear, to make afraid, to put one in a flight, to amaze'. Compare Sonnet 20.8 and note.

635 **having thee at vantage** (i) having you at his mercy; (ii) having the advantage over you in the fight.

636 **root. . . roots** This line is the second citation for OED³ 'root, *v.*2', 1b, referring to the way a pig searches in the ground for food.
mead meadow.

637 **loathsome** vile; see OED 1a, 'offensive to the senses', as well as 1b 'In a moral sense: hateful, distasteful, odious'.
cabin lair; the word can be used of an animal's home, as well as other temporary and rough dwellings (OED 4).

638 **naught to do with** (i) nothing in common with; (ii) no need of contact with.

639 **danger** power to cause harm (OED *n.* and *adj.* 1b).
by thy will voluntarily.

640 **They that. . .friends** As Burrow says, this sounds proverbial, although a precise analogue cannot be found (2002: 209).

641 **not to dissemble** to tell the truth (Burrow 2002: 209).

642 **feared thy fortune** feared what would happen to you.

643 **mark** notice.

645 **down right** straight down (OED 1). Q has two words; the OED lemma is 'downright', but it cites hyphenated and one-word examples.

647 **boding** presaging, portending. This is the first citation for the adjective in OED.

'His brawny sides, with hairy bristles armed,   625
Are better proof than thy spear's point can enter.
His short thick neck cannot be easily harmed;
Being ireful, on the lion he will venture.
    The thorny brambles, and embracing bushes,
    As fearful of him part, through whom he rushes.   630

'Alas, he naught esteems that face of thine,
To which love's eyes pays tributary gazes;
Nor thy soft hands, sweet lips, and crystal eyne,
Whose full perfection all the world amazes;
    But having thee at vantage (wondrous dread!)   635
    Would root these beauties, as he roots the mead.

'O let him keep his loathsome cabin still;
Beauty hath naught to do with such foul fiends.
Come not within his danger by thy will;
They that thrive well take counsel of their friends.   640
    When thou didst name the boar, not to dissemble,
    I feared thy fortune, and my joints did tremble.

'Didst thou not mark my face, was it not white?
Saw'st thou not signs of fear lurk in mine eye?
Grew I not faint, and fell I not down right?   645
Within my bosom whereon thou dost lie
    My boding heart pants, beats, and takes no rest,
    But like an earthquake shakes thee on my breast.

'For where love reigns, disturbing Jealousy
Doth call himself affection's sentinel,   650
Gives false alarms, suggesteth mutiny,
And in a peaceful hour doth cry "kill, kill",

649 **disturbing Jealousy** Jealousy, who (or which) gets in the way. Here it denotes a general 'suspicion; apprehension' (OED 5) rather than relating to a love rival. The personification is compared by Roe and Burrow to Rumour in Virgil (*Aeneid*, 4.173–95; Phaer-Twyne translation (1573) 4.185–209). Jealousy is personified in *Astrophil and Stella*, 78.5–7: 'A monster, other's harm, self-misery, | Beauty's plague, virtue's scourge, succour of lies: | Who his own joy to his own hurt applies'.
650 **affection's sentinel** passion's sentry guard.
650, 652 **sentinel. . . "kill, kill"** On the rhyme, see Appendix 7. But the command to 'kill' is so emphatic that some disruption to the rhyme may be pertinent.

651 **suggesteth mutiny** plants the idea that one's lover is being disloyal, i.e. unfaithful.
652 **peaceful** unthreatened.
    "kill, kill" an English battle cry, suited to a general charge (as noted by Burrow 2002: 210). Commonly found in military and historical writings, Golding uses the phrase in his depiction of the battle of Lapiths and Centaurs, *Metamorphoses*, 12.268–70: 'The death of him did set the rest | His double-limbed brothers so on fire, that all the quest | With one voyce cried out "kill kill"'. Marlowe also features it in Aeneas' description of the destruction of Troy in *Dido Queen of Carthage*, 2.1.189–90: 'And through the breach did march into the streets, | Where meeting with the rest, "kill kill" they cried'.

653 **Distempering** unsettling; pronounced here with three syllables, 'distemp'ring'. The word often refers to bodily humours, but can be used more generally (OED 'distemper, *v.1*', 5). See John Florio's *World of Words* (1598) in which it is part of the gloss to the Italian word 'passionare': 'to appassionate, to distemper, to perturb, to grieve, to vex'. Compare *Twelfth Night*, 2.1.4–5: 'the malignancy of my fate might perhaps distemper yours'.
gentle On the word's appearances in the poem, see 189 and note.

654 **air** Wells and Taylor's (2005) emendation 'earth' has no textual authority but is sensible: air often fans flames. However, it also cools things. It is possible that the goddess of love has her elements out of order.
abate lessen, quench.

655–8 **This. . .This. . .This. . .This. . .** for similar catalogues, see *Lucrece*, ll. 221–3, 689–91.

655 **bate-breeding** causing contention (OED 'bate, *n.1*', 1a).

656 **canker** a worm that eats buds, literally, or generally 'a malignant or destructive influence that corrodes or corrupts' (OED³ 4a). See l. 767, and Sonnets 35.4, 54.5, 70.7, 95.2, 99.12.
tender spring fresh and fragile youth, new growth; compare ll. 127, 801, and *Lucrece*, ll. 604, 869. It is often horticultural, as in Thomas Elyot's *Dictionary*, gloss for 'festuca': 'the young tender spring of a tree, or herb'. However, for the metaphorical use see Harington's translation of Ariosto: 'For entering first into my tender spring | Of youthful years, unto the court I came' (1591: sig. C5v).

657 **carry-tale** tell-tale, as at *Love's Labour's Lost*, 5.2.463–4: 'some carry-tale. . .some mumble-news'.
dissentious (i) given to quarrels; (ii) causing quarrels.

659 **Knocks at my heart** (i) beats at, but also (ii) tries to gain entry to, the heart. Compare *Measure for Measure*, 2.2.137–9: 'Go to your bosom; | Knock there, and ask your heart what it doth know | That's like my brother's fault'.

661 **And more than so. . . eye** In addition to this, jealousy gives me a vision [of something else].

662 **picture** combines the poem's interests in both visual representation and imagination.
chafing (i) raging, but also (ii) rough, bruising (compare ll. 325, 477).

663 **fangs** tusks.
on his back i.e. on the imaginary Adonis' back.

665–6 **Whose blood. . . head** Venus' fears are precisely realised at ll. 1055–6.

665 **flowers** monosyllabic here.

666 **hang the head** hang their heads. The scene of blood sprinkled on flowers, and the flowers grieving, brings into view other metamorphic myths (especially Hyacinthus) as well as foreshadowing Adonis' fate.

667–70 **What. . . divination** The structure of the questions here varies from edition to edition. Q has a question mark only after l. 667; for the modern reader it is better placed after l. 668.

667 **seeing thee so indeed** if I were actually to see you.

668 **That tremble at th' imagination** i.e. Venus is shaking at the unreal inner image ('imagination', OED³ 1b) of Adonis dead. For 'imagination' see l. 597 and note, and compare *Twelfth Night*, 3.4.375: 'Prove true, imagination, O, prove true'. If one rigorously counts ten syllables in a line, then 'imagination' accounts for six. Whether spun out syllabically, or anxiously brief, this word is heavily emphasised.

670 **divination** prophetic power (pronounced with five syllables).

671 **my living sorrow** (i) my sadness as I remain alive; (ii) my undying sorrow.

672 **encounter with** meet in a fight (OED *v.* 1a, 1b). Compare Golding's Ovid, 10.632, in a hunting context: 'Encounter not the kind of beasts whom nature armed hath'. See also l. 676 and note.

673–8 **But if. . . hounds** These lines advise a style of hunting which Venus pursues in Ovid's version of the story, *Metamorphoses*, 10.547–9; Golding, 10.621–3: 'she cheered the hounds with hallowing like a hunt, | Pursuing game of hurtless sort, as hares made low before, | Or stags with lofty heads, or bucks'.

673 **needs wilt** really must.

674 **Uncouple** release your dogs; usually they were tied in pairs until the hunt started (see OED 1a). The word is vividly used in the hare section of Gascoigne's *Art of Venery*:

Distempering gentle love in his desire,
As air and water do abate the fire.

'This sour informer, this bate-breeding spy,   655
This canker that eats up love's tender spring,
This carry-tale, dissentious Jealousy,
That sometime true news, sometime false doth bring,
    Knocks at my heart, and whispers in mine ear,
    That if I love thee, I thy death should fear.   660

'And more than so, presenteth to mine eye,
The picture of an angry chafing boar,
Under whose sharp fangs, on his back doth lie
An image like thyself, all stained with gore,
    Whose blood upon the fresh flowers being shed,   665
    Doth make them droop with grief, and hang the head.

'What should I do, seeing thee so indeed,
That tremble at th' imagination?
The thought of it doth make my faint heart bleed,
And fear doth teach it divination: 670
    I prophesy thy death, my living sorrow,
    If thou encounter with the boar tomorrow.

'But if thou needs wilt hunt, be ruled by me,
Uncouple at the timorous flying hare,
Or at the fox which lives by subtlety,   675
Or at the roe which no encounter dare.

'And I have seene hares oftentimes run into a flock of sheep in the field when they were hunted, and would never leave the flock, until I was forced to couple up my hounds, and fold up the sheep, or sometimes drive them to the cote: and then the hare would forsake them, and I uncoupled my hounds at her again and killed her' (sig. L3v). This section is close to that cited under ll. 685–9.
timorous flying fearful and prone to flight; a typical characteristic of hares, as in Topsell ('fearful and unarmed creature', 1607: sig. 2A1r), and proverbial (Dent H147, 'as fearful as a hare'). The other characteristic of the hare in Topsell is its association (shared with many other animals, but linked in the hare's case with fear) with lust: 'It falleth out by divine providence, that hares and other fearful beasts which are good for meat, shall multiply to greater numbers in short space' (sig. 2A2r). 'Timorous' is disyllabic here.

675 **subtlety** cunning. Gascoigne (1575: sig. N3r) mentions the stereotypical cunning of the fox in a poem: 'Reynard the Fox am I, a crafty child well known, | Yea better known than credited, with more than is mine own: | A bastard kind of court, mine ears declare the same, | And yet my wit and policy have purchased me great fame'. Overall, however, he is scornful of hunting foxes, classing them with other vermin.

676 **encounter** confrontation, fight. See a similar meaning (for the cognate verb) at l. 672, but a contrasting erotic sense for the noun at l. 576. It is ironically fitting that hunting and sex should be brought together in this word.

dare perhaps a subjunctive form (see 156n).

677 **downs** Venus prefers open land to forests, which are associated with hunting but also with violence in Ovid (and in *Titus Andronicus*).

678 **well-breathed** with good stamina (see OED³ 'well-breathed, *adj.*').

679 **on foot** running.

purblind with poor vision (OED³ 'purblind, *n.* and *adj.*', 2c). Hares were associated with bad eyesight, at close range at least; the first citation in OED³ (1a) is an alternative name for a hare. See Topsell 1607: sig. Z6v: 'The eyelids coming from the brows are too short to cover their eyes, and therefore this sense is very weak in them, and besides their overmuch sleep, their fear of dogs and swiftness, causeth them to see the less; when they watch they shut their eyes, and when they sleep they open them'. Elsewhere Shakespeare uses the word to mean 'blind', as in *Romeo and Juliet*, 2.1.12, where Cupid is Venus' 'purblind son and heir'.

680 **Mark** observe.

overshoot pass beyond (OED³ 1b). Steevens first proposed modernising Q's 'ouer-shut' in this way, and has been followed by later editors, though Malone preferred 'overshut', as in 'conclude'. Roe (1992: 114) and Burrow (2002: 211) see this as a hunting term, i.e. he is losing the things pursuing him: 'let him follow fair and easily, not making over much haste at first, nor making too much noise either with horn or voice: for at the first the hounds will easily overshoot a chase through too much heat' (Gascoigne, 1575: sig. L7r).

681 **care** Q has a comma at the end of this line. It is omitted here, so the 'care' is applied to the cranking and crossing' of l. 682. With the comma it would apply to the outrunning of the wind in l. 681, or might be more self-standing.

682 **cranks** twists and turns. This is the first citation for OED *v.*1; EEBO-TCP has no earlier uses. The noun 'crank', 'winding or crooked path', OED *n.*2, 1a, is older.

doubles zig-zags. OED has this as first citation for 'a sharp turn in running, as of a hunted hare' ('double, *n.*', 6). EEBO-TCP provides no earlier instance, but it is present as a noun in Gascoigne's *Art of Venery*: 'Mine opinion is that the best entering of hounds is at the hare,

for that is their very best beginning, for as much as thereby they shall learn all doubles, and turns' (1575: sig. C3r). Although 'cranks' is not found in Gascoigne, 'crosses' and 'doubles' do coincide: 'When you see that your hounds find where an hare hath passed at relief, upon the highway's sides, and hath much doubled and crossed upon dry places, and never much broken out nor relieved in the corn, it is a token that she is but lately come into those quarters' (sig. L1r).

683 **musets** gaps (in hedges or fences). The OED³ has this as its first instance for a word it traces back to Anglo-Norman 'mucette', a hiding place. Richard Barnfield's *Affectionate Shepherd* is the only comparable instance from 1594 or before in an EEBO-TCP search, and may well follow Shakespeare: 'hare-pipes (set in a muset hole)' (sig. C1v). It seems like a word from the English countryside that has found its way into the mouth of a classical goddess.

the which which.

684 **labyrinth t'amaze** The alternative scansion 'lab'rinth to amaze' is viable, but the text is preferred because of frequent elision of infinitives in Elizabethan verse. The only other instance of 'labyrinth' in Shakespeare's verse is trisyllabic: see *1 Henry VI*, 5.3.188–90: 'But, Suffolk, stay, | Thou mayest not wander in that labyrinth, | There Minotaurs and ugly treasons lurk'. In the only other instance of 'to amaze' in Shakespeare the infinitive must be elided: 'Let not our ships and number of our men | Be like a beacon fired t'amaze your eyes' (*Pericles*, 1.4.86–7).

amaze bewilder (with a pun on maze, 'labyrinth' in the same line).

685–9 **Sometime he runs. . . deer** The hare's tactics (hiding among sheep, in rabbit holes, taking advantage of dogs' attraction to deer) are noted by Gascoigne (1575: sig. L2v–L3v).

687 **conies** rabbits.

keep live.

688 **yell** noisy, barking assault; the word is associated with dogs also at *Love's Labour's Lost*, 4.2.58, 'the dogs did yell'. This is another instance of the hare's-eye-view, dominated by a terrifying sound that encompasses all the dogs' activity.

689 **sorteth** mixes into, accompanies (OED gives this as first citation for 'sort, *v.*1', 19).

Pursue these fearful creatures o'er the downs,
And on thy well-breathed horse keep with thy hounds.

'And when thou hast on foot the purblind hare,
Mark the poor wretch, to overshoot his troubles, 680
How he outruns the wind, and with what care
He cranks and crosses with a thousand doubles;
    The many musets through the which he goes
    Are like a labyrinth t' amaze his foes.

Sometime he runs among a flock of sheep, 685
To make the cunning hounds mistake their smell,
And sometime where earth-delving conies keep,
To stop the loud pursuers in their yell,
    And sometime sorteth with a herd of deer;
    Danger deviseth shifts, wit waits on fear. 690

For there his smell with others being mingled,
The hot scent-snuffing hounds are driven to doubt,
Ceasing their clamorous cry, till they have singled,
With much ado, the cold fault cleanly out.
    Then do they spend their mouths, echo replies, 695
    As if another chase were in the skies.

690 ***Danger. . . fear*** Dangerous situations call for resourceful tricks; cleverness is a servant to and/or accompanies fear. This sounds proverbial, though it does not appear in collections. For '***shifts***', compare *Lucrece*, l. 920.
    wit On this word and its cognates, see l. 472 and note.

692 ***snuffing*** sniffing. In Shakespeare's time the word 'snuff' could mean to inhale with 'an effort of inhalation' (OED 'snuff, *v*.2', 6a), and is thus different from senses of 'sniff' and 'snuff' which suggest a mainly olfactory purpose. Compare *Love's Labour's Lost*, 3.1.16–17: 'as if you snuffed up love by smelling love'. Here we have the dogs 'scent-snuffing', which mixes the two: a terrifying noise to a hare, and here a distinctively canine word.
    driven monosyllabic here.

693–4 ***till they. . . cleanly out*** until, after a lot of effort and fuss, they have accurately discerned the lost trail.

693 ***singled*** with or without 'out', a hunting term (OED, 'single, *v*.1', 2), for when one

deer out of a herd is selected for the chase. Compare *3 Henry VI*, 2.4.12–13 ('Nay, Warwick: single out some other chase, | For I myself will hunt this wolf to death'), and, in a hunting forest with great erotic threat, *Titus Andronicus*, 2.1.117–18 ('Single you thither then this dainty doe, | And strike her home by force').

694 ***cold fault*** lost scent; for the phrase see under OED 'fault', 8 ('break in the line of scent'); this is the first citation, and EEBO-TCP has no earlier uses.

695 ***spend their mouths*** bark excitedly, a hunting term (OED, 'spend, *v*.1', 9b, 'bark. . . on finding or seeing the game'). Compare *Troilus and Cressida*, 5.1.90–2: 'he will spend his mouth and promise, like Brabbler the hound'.

696 ***As if another chase were in the skies*** Compare *Titus Andronicus*, 2.3.17–19, where Tamora admires the cacophony of hunting: 'the babbling echo mocks the hounds, | Replying shrilly to the well-tuned horns, | As if a double hunt were heard at once'.

697 **By this** meanwhile (see l. 175 and note).
Wat a word for a hare (OED *n*.2) but probably best treated as a nickname for this one, although Q has lower-case 'w'.

698 **hinder legs** back (i.e. hind) legs.
listening disyllabic here.

699 **hearken** try to hear (an action which will later be emulated by Venus, ll. 868, 889).

700 **Anon** soon.
alarums barks, aggressive noises; see l. 424.

702 **passing bell** a bell rung to announce a death or to commemorate it at a funeral (OED³, 'passing bell'). Primarily this suggests a person in danger of death meeting a memento mori in the sound announcing someone else's death. However, it may also have been used for a bell rung in anticipation of death, as is perhaps implied in the Topsell quotation below, so it is feasible for a very ill person ('*one sore sick*') to hear it rung on their behalf. The doomed hare's predicament might go further, resembling a person somehow hearing the bell that announces their death has occurred. In Topsell the phrase arises in the context of hunting: 'being pursued with all the cries of hunters, ringing and echoing betwixt heaven and earth, dismaying him with the continual noise in his ears, no less dreadful and fearful then the voice of a passing bell to a sick man, or the sight of the executioner to a condemned caitiff, yet still he striveth until wearied and breathless, he be forced to offer up his blood and flesh to the rage of all the observant pedissequants [i.e. followers] of the hunting goddess Diana' (1607: N2r).

703 **bedabbled** spattered; compare *A Midsummer Night's Dream*, 3.2.443: 'Bedabbled with the dew and torn with briers', which is the first citation in OED. EEBO-TCP offers no uses of the word before *Venus and Adonis*, though OED 'dabble, *v*.1.', 'to wet by splashing', has its first citation from 1557.

704 **indenting** zig-zagging; from OED 'indent, *v*.1', 1a, to make tooth-shaped incisions in the edge of something (e.g. a document). Compare *As You Like It*, 4.3.112, of a snake, which 'with indented glides did slip away', and Golding, 7.1016: 'doubling and indenting still avoids his enemy's lips'.
with the way with its path, passage.

705 **envious briar** The thorny briars seem spiteful, in that they catch hold of him constantly.

do apparently a plural verb after the singular subject 'Each…briar', but the subject entails many briars engaged in the action. See l. 272 and note.

706 **shadow** See l. 162 and note.
stay stand still.

707 **For misery… many** when creatures are in a wretched state, everyone and everything is against them. Proverbial (Dent M194 'if a man once fall all will tread on him').

708 **being low** when they have really been trodden down.

710 **(Nay… rise)** In Q there are no parentheses, just a comma at the end. The punctuation here makes it clear that this interjection interrupts the flow of Venus' sentence.

712 **Unlike… moralise** You have heard me drawing moral conclusions, which is not my usual style at all. 'Moralise' can suggest 'to recognise the evil in', as at *Lucrece*, l. 104, but it is probably used here to suggest a pedantic and negative attitude when teaching by means of examples, as at *As You Like It*, 2.1.44, of the melancholic Jaques: 'Did he not moralise this spectacle?'. The word also refers back to the tradition of moralising classical texts, especially Ovid (see the extracts in Appendix 1). See 'comment', l. 714, and 'theme', l. 770, also contributing to the representation of this didactic Venus.

713 **Applying this to that, and so to so** Venus depicts herself in moralising mode, arguing by analogy, 'applying' one lesson to another. See OED³ 'apply, *v*.', 8: 'To give to (a general, theoretical, or figurative statement) a specific reference to a particular instance'.

714 **For love… woe** The modal force of 'can' is subtle: for Venus, it means that love has the authority to pronounce (and that she herself has that authority); for the reader, it might mean instead 'is liable to'.
comment deliver a moral commentary (compare l. 712 and note, and Sonnet 89.2).

715 **Where did I leave?** (i) Where did I leave off? (ii) Where did I interrupt myself? As Burrow notes (2002: 213), Leander becomes impatient 'ere halfe this tale was done', with an inset narrative in *Hero and Leander*, l. 685. Compare also Tarquin's interruption at *Lucrece*, l. 667.

'By this poor Wat, far off upon a hill,
Stands on his hinder legs with listening ear,
To hearken if his foes pursue him still.
Anon their loud alarums he doth hear,   700
　　And now his grief may be comparèd well
　　To one sore sick that hears the passing bell.

'Then shalt thou see the dew-bedabbled wretch
Turn, and return, indenting with the way;
Each envious briar his weary legs do scratch,   705
Each shadow makes him stop, each murmur stay,
　　For misery is trodden on by many,
　　And being low, never relieved by any.

'Lie quietly, and hear a little more,
(Nay do not struggle, for thou shalt not rise)   710
To make thee hate the hunting of the boar.
Unlike myself thou hear'st me moralise,
　　Applying this to that, and so to so,
　　For love can comment upon every woe.

'Where did I leave?' 'No matter where,' quoth he,   715
'Leave me, and then the story aptly ends.
The night is spent.' 'Why, what of that?', quoth she.
'I am', quoth he, 'expected of my friends,
　　And now 'tis dark, and going I shall fall.'
　　'In night', quoth she, 'desire sees best of all.   720

'But if thou fall, O then imagine this:
The earth, in love with thee, thy footing trips,
And all is but to rob thee of a kiss.
Rich preys make true men thieves: so do thy lips

No matter where It does not matter which point (you have reached).

716 *aptly* at an appropriate point. On aptness and timing, see l. 34 and note.

717 *spent* This cannot literally mean 'passed' or 'finished', as it is still dark (see l. 719), but Adonis is hyperbolic in his frustration.

718 *expected of* waited for by.

719 *going* (i) if I go; (ii) when I go; or (iii) taking the gerund-participle as such, 'as I walk along'.

720 *In night. . . all* This proverbial note (Dent N167, 'dark knight is Cupid's day') is shared by *Hero and Leander*, l. 191 ('dark night is Cupid's day'), and *Romeo and Juliet*, 3.2.8–10: 'Lovers can see to do their amorous rites | By their own beauties, or, if love be blind, | It best agrees with night'.

721 *imagine* On this word and its cognates, see l. 597 and note.

724 *Rich preys. . . thieves* proverbial (Dent P570, 'the prey entices the thief', also cited at Sonnet 48.14n). 'True men' is hyphenated in Q.

725–6 **Make modest Dian. . . forsworn.** Diana is Venus' opposite in the pantheon of the gods: she is the deity of chastity, hunting and the moon.

725 **cloudy** gloomy in mood (OED 6a), melancholy; compare *Lucrece*, ll. 115, 1084, but here Diana is equated with the moon, so the cloudiness can be more literal. On clouds in the poem, see l. 490 and note.
   forlorn See l. 251 and note.

726 **forsworn** having betrayed her vow (of chastity, if she stole a kiss).

727 **of this dark night** Venus toys with an aetiological fable (a reason 'of', i.e. 'for'), in which the dangerous darkness that has fallen is the result of Diana's shame.

728 **Cynthia** Diana (alternative name).
   shine See l. 488 and note.

729–30 **Till forging Nature. . . were divine** Until Nature is held to an account for an act of forgery (see OED, 'forge, *v*.1', 5a), in which heavenly patterns, which should have been reserved for gods, were given to mortals. Making coins was a royal prerogative, and this lies behind the 'forging. . . moulds' metaphor here. On counterfeit coins, see l. 515 and note. Thomas Smith, *The Commonwealth of England* (1589), offers another image of forging nature, this time creating things to a purpose: 'so nature hath forged each part to his office: the man stern, strong, bold, adventurous, negligent of his beauty, and spending. The women weak, fearful, fair, curious of her beauty, and saving' (p. 13).

730 **heaven** monosyllabic here.

731 **she framed** Nature created.
   in high heaven's despite against the will of the gods. 'Heaven' is monosyllabic.

733 **the Destinies** the fates; personified controllers of the future (see OED, 'destiny', 5). See l. 945, and *Hero and Leander*, ll. 377–80: 'Then towards the palace of the Destinies, | Laden with languishment and grief he flies. | And to those stern nymphs humbly made request, | Both might enjoy each other, and be blest'.

734 **cross** contravene, thwart, oppose (OED 14a, 14c); can suggest the creation of a hybrid (OED 16a), which connects with 'mingle' in l. 735.
   curious 'elegant, nice' (Schmidt); one tempting modern sense of 'curious' (OED 16a,

'exciting curiosity. . . strange') is dated by the OED post 1715; more pertinent is 4a ('ingenious') though there are other possibilities in the word relating to attentiveness, ingenuity and carefulness. Thomas Cooper's *Thesaurus* (1578) traces the range of the word in his definitions for 'accuratus' ('curious: exact: well handled: diligently and studiously done') and 'curiosus' ('curious: more careful than is seemly. Also in the good part, very careful and circumspect'). Compare *Lucrece*, l. 1300, and see also the *Hero and Leander* quotation at 511n.

735 **infirmities** fragile elements; primarily suggests physical weakness but this may be working to contrast the mortal with the divine.

736 **defeature** disfigurement; the first citation in OED 2. The earliest citation for the word (OED 1, 'undoing, ruin') is from Samuel Daniel in 1592. EEBO-TCP has no earlier uses. Daniel's word derives from OED 'defeat, *n*.1', which covers both 'undoing' and the modern military sense; it is used frequently in historical writing. Shakespeare's is linked (by the OED, convincingly) to 'defeat, *v*.', 3 ('to destroy the beauty, form, or figure of'). This is a Shakespearean coinage, but also a word that fits its speaker particularly well: for her, to be defective is to be defeated.

738 **mad mischances** capricious, irrational misfortunes. Roe (1992: 116) and Duncan-Jones and Woudhuysen (2007: 195) interpret this as 'accidents which drive the victim mad', but none of Shakespeare's other uses of the word 'mad' tends clearly in this direction.

739–44 **As burning. . . so fair** Venus marvels at the diseases which prey on mortality, which act as elaboration for the 'mischances' in the preceding stanza, and then as curses on nature, in revenge for overdoing Adonis' beauty.

739 **As** such as.
   agues feverish diseases; often used generally and synonymous with 'fevers', but also used specifically of a malarial disease (OED³ 1a).

740 **poisoning** disyllabic here.
   wood insane (OED, 'wood, *adj.*, *n*.2 and *adv.*', 1a). Compare *1 Henry VI*, 4.7.35–6: 'How the young whelp of Talbot's, raging-wood, | Did flesh his puny sword in Frenchmen's

Make modest Dian cloudy and forlorn,   725
Lest she should steal a kiss and die forsworn.

'Now of this dark night I perceive the reason:
Cynthia, for shame, obscures her silver shine,
Till forging Nature be condemned of treason,
For stealing moulds from heaven that were divine,   730
    Wherein she framed thee, in high heaven's despite,
    To shame the sun by day, and her by night.

'And therefore hath she bribed the Destinies
To cross the curious workmanship of nature,
To mingle beauty with infirmities,   735
And pure perfection with impure defeature,
    Making it subject to the tyranny
    Of mad mischances and much misery.

'As burning fevers, agues pale and faint,
Life-poisoning pestilence and frenzies wood,   740
The marrow-eating sickness whose attaint
Disorder breeds by heating of the blood,
    Surfeits, impostumes, grief, and damned despair
    Swear Nature's death for framing thee so fair.

blood!'. Roe deems this a *pleonasm* (1992: 117). See l. 323.

741–2 ***The marrow-eating. . . the blood*** 'Marrow' can mean bone marrow (OED[3] 1a) so this may be taken quite specifically to refer to a disease attacking bones. However, it is also used generally to mean the inner part or inner strength (compare l. 142). Commentators understandably consider venereal disease a likely candidate; Roe is perhaps going too far in registering significant irony in Venus complaining about venereal disease (1992: 117).

741 ***attaint*** infection, harm. The word can mean 'touch' (OED 1a), but compare *Lucrece*, ll. 825, 1072, where it has a moral aspect, and Sonnet 82.2.

743 ***Surfeits*** digestive disorders caused by over-indulgence (OED[3] 4a). On 'surfeit', see l. 544 and note.

impostumes abscesses, swellings; was used figuratively of moral contagion (OED 2a). The OED allows for this spelling and for

'imposthume', which is the more usual spelling post-1700, but for which there is no justification in the etymology (probably the word was confused gradually with 'post-humous'). Shakespeare's other uses are both in the singular: among a list of diseases in a curse by Thersites in *Troilus and Cressida* (5.1.19–20: 'wheezing lungs, bladders full of impostume, sciaticas') and, metaphorically, in Hamlet's reflection on Fortinbras' war against Poland, 4.4.27–9: 'This is the impostume of much wealth and peace, | That inward breaks, and shows no cause without | Why the man dies'.

grief, and damned despair two psychological symptoms, thought (as parts of melancholy) to have been caused by physiological disorder. 'Damned' is theologically precise rather than a generally derogatory term: losing trust in God's mercy (i.e. despair) must lead to damnation.

744 ***Swear Nature's death*** vow to destroy Nature.
framing creating.

745–6 *And not. . . under* Even the least harsh of these afflictions can ruin someone's beauty in a minute. 'Bring. . . under' may relate to OED³ 'bring under' ('bring, *v.*', 8d), i.e. put into subjection.

747 *Both* can be used in early modern England to refer to more than two things; compare Sonnet 83.14 and note.
favour grace and/or beauty.
savour fragrance.
hue complexion.

748 *gazer* observer.
late recently, the moment before.

749 *thawed* melted away (compare l. 565, where 'frozen' is used of wax). 'Wasted' and 'done' bluntly capture physical destruction, but 'thawed' lacks the sense of unfreezing, or of increasing acquiescence, that it has in other uses in Shakespeare and in OED. It makes the mortal body seem like a raw substance temporarily formed into a loveable shape.
done destroyed, finished; see l. 197 and note.

751 *despite of fruitless chastity* in defiance of unproductive virginity. Venus addresses Adonis in the spirit of Marlowe's Leander addressing Hero, ll. 317–20: 'Abandon fruitless cold virginity, | The gentle queen of love's sole enemy. | Then shall you most resemble Venus' Nun, | When Venus' sweet rites are performed and done'.

752 *Love-lacking vestals* unloved virgins, the word deriving from the Vestal Virgins of Rome (priestesses who tended a sacred flame and were obliged to remain chaste). Compare *Lucrece*, l. 883. They are a by-word for virginity, but the sacred perpetual flame, and its Vestal guardians, are associated with passion in Barnabe Barnes, *Parthenophil and Parthenope* (1593), Sonnet 22.1–4: 'From thine heart's ever-burning vestal fire, | The torch-light of two suns is nourished still. | Which in mild compass still surmounting higher | Their orbs with circled harmony fulfil' (sig. C2r).
self-loving nuns Venus, of course, is suspicious of chastity, and when contemplating nuns (the word has Christian connotations but is used of classical priestesses too, OED³ *n.*1, 1b) she considers it a kind of narcissism. Marlowe's Hero is a 'nun' of Venus (e.g. at *Hero and Leander*, l. 319;

see 751n). Duncan-Jones and Woudhuysen note that nuns are depicted masturbating ('self-loving') in reformation polemic (2007: 196).

753–4 *That on the earth. . . of sons* who would like to generate only an unfertile shortage of girls and boys in the world.

754 *sons* Q suns, perhaps enabling a pun alongside 'night' and 'light' in the following lines. Compare l. 863.

755 *prodigal* abundant, generous (OED³ *adj.*, *n.*, and *adv.*, 4a). However, other meanings of the word relate to wastefulness and extravagance, as in the Biblical parable of the Prodigal Son (Luke 15.11–32). This may be another word with a special inflection in Venus' lexicon: for her, prodigality lacks a pejorative side. Compare *Love's Labour's Lost*, 2.1.9–12, 'Be now as prodigal of all dear grace | As Nature was in making graces dear | When she did starve the general world beside | And prodigally gave them all to you', as near as Shakespeare comes elsewhere to using it positively, but Boyet is a flattering courtier.

755–6 *the lamp. . . his light* For Venus, this is a piece of proverbial wisdom (Dent C39, 'a candle (torch) lights others and consumes itself'), but for Adonis it may seem ominous. Roe (1992: 117) makes a link with the parable of the wise and foolish virgins (Matthew 25:1–13).

756 *Dries up* exhausts, expends.
his i.e. its; referring to the lamp.
lend See l. 29 and note.

757–62 *What is. . . slain* This stanza shares the message of Sonnets 1–17, and especially 1.14, 3.7–8, but the message is less focused on procreation as the main end, as Adonis notes in his counter-argument, ll. 791–2.

757 *swallowing grave* The body's mortality is apprehended in another innovative and shocking metaphor. An EEBO-TCP search does reveal an earlier instance, in Thomas Bentley's *Monument of Matrons* (1582): 'their throats [i.e. those of the ungodly] are like unto an open sepulchre, or swallowing grave' (O3r). Compare 'swallowing gulf', *Lucrece*, l. 557, and *Titus Andronicus*, 2.3.239–40 (see 268n). See also 'graves' at ll. 995, 1106; and Sonnet 77.6.

'And not the least of all these maladies,   745
But in one minute's fight brings beauty under:
Both favour, savour, hue, and qualities,
Whereat the th' impartial gazer late did wonder,
　　Are on the sudden wasted, thawed, and done,
　　As mountain snow melts with the midday sun.   750

'Therefore, despite of fruitless chastity,
Love-lacking vestals and self-loving nuns,
That on the earth would breed a scarcity
And barren dearth of daughters and of sons,
　　Be prodigal: the lamp that burns by night   755
　　Dries up his oil to lend the world his light.

'What is thy body, but a swallowing grave,
Seeming to bury that posterity,
Which by the rights of time thou needs must have,
If thou destroy them not in dark obscurity?   760
　　If so, the world will hold thee in disdain,
　　Sith in thy pride so fair a hope is slain.

So in thyself, thyself art made away,
A mischief worse than civil home-bred strife,
Or theirs whose desperate hands themselves do slay, 765

---

758 **posterity** descendants (OED³ 1). Compare *Lucrece*, l. 208, and Sonnets 3.8, 6.12.

759 **by the rights of time** (i) according to what is owed to time; (ii) according to the demands of time; perhaps (iii) according to the rules of time (OED, 'right, *n*.', 1). Compare *Hamlet*, 2.2.284: 'by the rights of our fellowship'. For 'time' Schmidt gives this line to illustrate his sense 'men, the world', comparing Sonnets 11.7, 70.6, 117.6. There may be a word-play on 'rites', as there could also be at Sonnet 17.11. 'Rites' can have sexual connotations, as in the *Romeo and Juliet* quotation at 720n, though the contribution of that aspect would be small here.

760 **dark obscurity** deep darkness ('obscurity', OED³ 4); compare *Titus Andronicus*, 5.2.36: 'no vast obscurity or misty vale'. Q7 registers the tautology in changing 'dark' to 'their'. This is the poem's only twelve-syllable Alexandrine line, which suits the sonorousness of Venus' message. See *Lucrece*, 354n.

761–2 **disdain. . . pride** Venus aims to jolt him out of his scorn by turning the key word 'disdain' (on which, see l. 33 and note) against him, with the thought that he will himself be scorned by the world.

762 **Sith** since.
pride selfishness; but can suggest sexual vigour. See l. 14 and note.

763 **thyself, thyself** On reflexive pronouns, see l. 159 and note.
made away killed (OED³, 'make away', 2). Compare *Titus Andronicus*, 2.3.189: 'Till all the Andronici be made away'.

764 **civil home-bred strife** civil war, pleonastically expressed. The chronological proximity to *Venus and Adonis* of the early histories, depicting the Wars of the Roses, may suggest additional resonance to the red and white pattern of the poem, on which see l. 10 and note.

765 **desperate** disyllabic here.

766 **butcher sire** murderous, violent father. Compare *Richard III*, 5.5.24–6: 'The brother blindly shed the brother's blood, | The father rashly slaughtered his own son, | The son, compelled, been butcher to the sire'.
reaves. . . of life kills ('reaves' means 'robs by force', OED³ 'reave, *v*.1', 3b). Compare *2 Henry VI*, 5.1.187: 'To reave the orphan of his patrimony'.

767 **cankering** corrosive, corrupting; see l. 656; disyllabic here.
frets corrodes gradually (OED 'fret, *v*.1', 3a); see l. 69 and note.

768 **gold** Venus tries to set up the idea that Adonis is hoarding his beauty and risking its loss, but she creates a fallacy, since gold is not vulnerable to rust.
put to use Though the fear of corrosion may be groundless, Venus' argument has a further turn, towards the concept of profit as a moral obligation: his wealth should not just stand still. The mobile word 'use' helps us see that Venus is motivated by a wish to 'use' her lover erotically (as in OED³ 'use, *n*.', 1c), as well as by revulsion and incomprehension at a mortal's attitude towards time. The line is proverbial (Dent M1053, 'money begets money') and its idea 'commonplace' (Duncan-Jones and Woudhuysen 2007: 197). Burrow (2002: 216) makes two comparisons: the Parable of the Talents, Matthew 25:14–30, and *Hero and Leander*, ll. 231–6: 'Vessels of brass, oft handled, brightly shine: | What difference betwixt the richest mine | And basest mould, but use? For both not used | Are of like worth. Then treasure is abused | When misers keep it; being put to loan, | In time it will return us two for one'. On 'use', compare l. 164 and note.

769 **Adon** stressed on first syllable.

770 **idle over-handled theme** time-wasting, repetitive subject-matter; see l. 422 and note.

771–2 **in vain. . . in vain** Adonis compares his fruitless attempt to appease Venus with a kiss to her fruitless pursuit despite resistance ('against the stream'). His advice shows he can be proverbial too: Dent S927 warns not to resist the inexorable, 'it is hard (folly, in vain) to strive against the stream'.

773 **desire's foul nurse** Like Venus, Adonis sees that night-time is when desire is nurtured (see figurative use of OED³ 'nurse, *n*.1', 1b); compare l. 720, and *Lucrece*, ll. 764–70.

The phrase 'foul nurse' appears in Gascoigne's *Art of Venery*: '[he must] tell a tale, which may such minds appal | As pass their days in slothful idleness, | The first foul nurse to worldly wickedness' (1575: sig. F7r).

774 **treatise** pious, didactic speech; 'treatise' usually refers to something written, OED 1a.

775 **have lent** had lent, in modern usage. This is a subjunctive form (see 156n) within a conditional clause. See l. 29 and note on 'lend'.
twenty thousand Adonis' hyperbole matches Venus' (see ll. 22, 522, and notes).

776 **every** disyllabic here.
moving affecting; see OED³ 4, which cites *Two Gentleman of Verona*, 5.4.55–6: 'If the gentle spirit of moving words | Can no way change you to a milder form'.

777 **mermaids' songs** Venus herself alluded to the mythical power of the mermaid's song (l. 429). The lack of an apostrophe in Q means the mermaid(s) could be singular or plural.

778 **Yet from mine ear. . . blown** Even so your attempt at seductive speech would be rejected by my ears. 'Blown' probably means 'blown away', as in OED 12a, 'to drive or carry (things) by means of a current of air'.

779 **heart stands armèd** The link between love and war is commonplace; Ovid's *Amores*, 1.9.1–2 states (in Marlowe's translation) that 'All lovers war, and Cupid hath his tent, | Attic [i.e. Atticus, the addressee], all lovers are to war far sent'.

780 **false** (i) treacherous; (ii) out of tune (Duncan-Jones and Woudhuysen 2007: 198).
there; Recent editors run on to the next stanza with a comma, where Q has a full stop. The halfway-house chosen by Q7 is preferred for poise and efficiency. A similar choice arises at l. 816, where Q7 has a colon.

781 **Lest the deceiving harmony** The first four lines follow from the previous stanza; the 'deceiving harmony' refers back to the 'tempting tune'.

782 **quiet closure** peaceful enclosed space (as in OED 'closure', 3; compare Sonnet 48.11).

784 **barred of** excluded from.

785 **groan** On groans, see l. 377 and note.

787 **reprove** rebuke; perhaps it also suggests 'disprove'.

788 **The path is smooth. . . danger** proverbial (Dent P101.1 'the path is smooth that leads to danger').

789 **device** 'manner of thinking, cast of mind' is Schmidt's paraphrase, generated by the context here. The OED's most pertinent and

Or butcher sire, that reaves his son of life.
 Foul cankering rust the hidden treasure frets,
 But gold that's put to use more gold begets.'

'Nay then', quoth Adon, 'you will fall again
Into your idle over-handled theme.   770
The kiss I gave you is bestowed in vain,
And all in vain you strive against the stream,
 For by this black-faced night, desire's foul nurse,
 Your treatise makes me like you worse and worse.

'If love have lent you twenty thousand tongues,   775
And every tongue more moving than your own,
Bewitching like the wanton mermaids' songs,
Yet from mine ear the tempting tune is blown;
 For know my heart stands armèd in mine ear,
 And will not let a false sound enter there;   780

'Lest the deceiving harmony should run
Into the quiet closure of my breast,
And then my little heart were quite undone,
In his bedchamber to be barred of rest.
 No, lady, no, my heart longs not to groan,   785
 But soundly sleeps, while now it sleeps alone.

'What have you urged, that I cannot reprove?
The path is smooth that leadeth on to danger.
I hate not love, but your device in love,
That lends embracements unto every stranger.   790
 You do it for increase, O strange excuse,
 When reason is the bawd to lust's abuse.

perhaps preferable sense is 'ingenuity' (as in OED 1a; see Schmidt's 'contrivance. . . stratagem'), which in Adonis' mind leads skittishly to promiscuity. This sense is more clearly pertinent at *Lucrece*, l. 535, and compare *Othello*, 2.3.388: 'Dull not device by coldness and delay'. 'Device' may also denote a witty poetic conceit (OED 10); compare George Puttenham, *The Art of English Poesy* (1589): 'It will be found our nation is in nothing inferior to the French or Italian for copy of language, subtlety of device, good method and proportion in any form of poem' (sig. H4v). It can also refer to a 'devised or fancifully invented' play or masque, as in *Love's Labour's Lost*, 5.2.669 ('I will forward with my device') and *A Midsummer Night's Dream*, 5.1.50–3: '"The riot of the tipsy Bacchanals, | Tearing the Thracian singer in their rage": | That is an old device; and it was played | When I from Thebes came last a conqueror'. These two resonant senses offer the possibility that Adonis should be read, with considerable irony, as complaining about the literary tradition of erotic love, and its corrupting effect.

790 **lends** On 'lend', see l. 29 and note.
 embracements Compare the erotic edge to this word in *Hero and Leander*, ll. 513–14: 'Sweet are the kisses, the embracements sweet, | When like desires and affections meet'.
792 **bawd** a pimp (usually female at the time).

793 **love to heaven is fled** The thought that some good quality, or good deity, has fled a fallen world, is found elsewhere in classical mythology. The goddess Astraea, justice, is said to have left the world in *Titus Andronicus*, 4.3.4: 'Terras Astraea reliquit', a quotation from Ovid, *Metamorphoses*, 1.150. **heaven** monosyllabic here.

794 **sweating** suggests perspiration from both desire and disease.
his name The complex web of personification around love has it masculine here (on the issue in general, see 328n). It could mean Cupid, or more likely, a more abstract personification which is masculine because Adonis is making a contrast with feminine lust. 'His' could also just be an alternative form of 'its' in sixteenth-century English. Venus is daringly connected with 'sweating lust', masquerading as love itself.

795 **simple semblance** harmless appearance, but for the resonance of 'simple' see l. 244 and note; Adonis emphasises simplicity to complement his emphasis on quietness and smallness, a riposte to the passion of Venus. EEBO-TCP has no earlier use of the phrase.

796 **blotting** often used of a moral stain, as in *Lucrece*, ll. 192, 1299, 1322, 1519.
blame censure, OED 1a.

797 **Which the hot tyrant. . . bereaves** Which that lustful, dominant force (i.e. lust) spoils, and then steals (or strips) away (OED 'bereave, *v.*' 1a). Compare *Lucrece*, l. 373. An EEBO-TCP search uncovers no other uses of the phrase 'hot tyrant'.

798 **As caterpillars. . . leaves** Caterpillars were often associated with voracious appetite; compare *Richard II*, 2.3.166, 'the caterpillars of the commonwealth', describing Richard's favourites, and *2 Henry VI*, 3.1.90, 'caterpillars eat my leaves away'.

799–804 **Love comforteth. . . forged lies** In this stanza Adonis undertakes a rhetorical *distinctio* (Burrow 2002: 217).

799 **sunshine after rain** a proverbial motif (Dent R8, 'after rain (showers) comes fair weather (the sun)').

801 **gentle** On the word's appearances in the poem, see l. 189 and note.

802 **Lust's winter. . . done** The cold, dead stage of lust arises before the hot and pleasurable

part is half finished. See OED 'winter, *n.*1', 1c, for figurative uses relating to 'a state of affliction or distress'; compare *Troilus and Cressida*, 4.5.24, 'I'll take that winter from your lips', and *Lucrece*, ll. 48–9.

803 **surfeits** overindulges; on the word, see l. 544 and note.

805–10 **More I. . . offended** Q's medial commas are retained here, except in l. 807, although a modernised text could be smoother without them. The pauses they create suit the conclusion of Adonis' preaching.

806 **text. . . orator** Adonis self-consciously portrays himself as a professional speaker delivering a planned speech, so he can then deny the sophistication that one might expect to go with it. 'Text' may suggest the Bible verse on which a sermon-writer would comment, or more generally a topic serving as the basis for an oration.
green unsophisticated, inexperienced (see l. 527 and note).

807 **sadness** seriousness.

808 **teen** grief (OED 3; but perhaps also 'irritation', 2a). Shakespeare's other uses suggest the former; compare *Love's Labour's Lost*, 4.3.161–2: 'O, what a scene of fool'ry have I seen, | Of sighs, of groans, of sorrow and of teen!', and see *A Lover's Complaint*, l. 192.

810 **burn themselves** cause pain to themselves; closest to OED, 'burn, *v.*1', 14a, a reflexive use.

811 **With this** having said this; see l. 25 and note. The immediacy of the present tense in **breaketh** moves the poem quickly on.

812 **bound** could be part of the verb 'bind', or 'bound, *v.*1', OED 2b, i.e. 'enclose'.

813 **laund** glade. Shakespeare's other use is in a hunting context, *3 Henry VI*, 3.1.2: 'through this laund anon the deer will come'.

814 **Love** personified here in the undignified figure of Venus; on personification, see 328n.

815–16 **Look how. . . Venus' eye:** for the colon, compare l. 780 and see note. This is another visual simile introduced with the invitation to 'Look' (see l. 67 and note), and another that challenges the reader. Shooting stars are fast, and disappear in a very short time; can Adonis really seem to recede so brightly and quickly? Two complementary conclusions offer themselves: first, we see

'Call it not love, for love to heaven is fled,
Since sweating lust on earth usurped his name,
Under whose simple semblance he hath fed 795
Upon fresh beauty, blotting it with blame,
    Which the hot tyrant stains, and soon bereaves,
    As caterpillars do the tender leaves.

'Love comforteth like sunshine after rain,
But lust's effect is tempest after sun; 800
Love's gentle spring doth always fresh remain,
Lust's winter comes, ere summer half be done;
    Love surfeits not, lust like a glutton dies;
    Love is all truth, lust full of forgèd lies.

'More I could tell, but more I dare not say: 805
The text is old, the orator too green.
Therefore in sadness now I will away;
My face is full of shame, my heart of teen;
    Mine ears, that to your wanton talk attended,
    Do burn themselves, for having so offended.' 810

With this he breaketh from the sweet embrace
Of those fair arms which bound him to her breast,
And homeward through the dark laund runs apace,
Leaves Love upon her back, deeply distressed.
    Look how a bright star shooteth from the sky: 815
    So glides he in the night from Venus' eye,

Which after him she darts, as one on shore
Gazing upon a late embarkèd friend
Till the wild waves will have him seen no more,
Whose ridges with the meeting clouds contend: 820

things from Venus' perspective, wherein speed and light are heightened; second, Adonis is running as quickly as he can.
816 **glides** moves smoothly; OED offers no sense of speed.
Venus' pronounced as two syllables; see l. 180 and note.
817–22 **Which. . . sight** The simile shifts from the manner in which Venus watches to the manner in which Adonis is swallowed up by darkness.
817 **darts** shoots, referring back to her 'eye' in l. 816; see l. 196. On the extramissive theory of vision implied here, see l. 487 and note. Compare *Astrophil and Stella*, 8th

song, 33–6: '*Stella*, in whose shining eyes, | Are the lights of *Cupid's* skies, | Whose beams, where they once are darted, | Love therewith is straight imparted'.
818 **late embarkèd friend** friend who has recently boarded a ship.
820 **Whose ridges. . . contend** The crests of the sea's waves are so high that they reach the clouds with which they come together and appear to fight. See *Lucrece*, l. 1439.
ridges waves; see OED³, 'ridge, *n*.1', 2a.
meeting first citation for OED³ 'meeting, *adj*.', 2a, 'that meets or comes together'.
clouds On clouds in the poem, see l. 490 and note.

821 *pitchy* black, like pitch (tar).

822 *Fold in* envelop; compare *Lucrece*, l. 675.

824 *flood* sea.

825 *'stonished* bewildered, dismayed (OED, 'astonished, *adj.*', 2, 3).

night-wanderers night-time travellers. Shakespeare's other use of the compound noun is *A Midsummer Night's Dream*, 2.1.39: 'You mislead night-wanderers, laughing at their harm'. For the adjectival form, compare *Lucrece*, l. 307, and *Hero and Leander*, l. 107: 'Not that night-wand'ring, pale and watery star' (i.e. the moon). 'Wanderers' is disyllabic here.

826 *mistrustful* See Hope (2003:46–8) on adjectives' 'location of effect'; in Shakespeare's English it is common for adjectives ending in *-ful* to locate their effect both inside and outside the object described. So, 'mistrustful' can mean 'suspicious' but here it means that it is liable to cause suspicion; this line is the first citation for OED 'mistrustful, *adj.*', 2, 'untrustworthy'.

827 *Even* monosyllabic here.

confounded (i) confused; (ii) astonished, amazed, in keeping with the parallel adjectives of ll. 823, 825. Compare ll. 882, 1048 where the verb suggests amazement, and in all cases the hint of destruction (OED 1, 'bring to ruin, destroy') adds an ominous note; compare *Lucrece*, 160n, and *Hero and Leander*, ll. 250–2, quoted at 12n.

828 *Having lost. . . way* Having lost the (metaphorical) light shed by Adonis' beauty, which enabled her to find the right path.

Having elided into one syllable.

discovery 'the act of showing or bringing to view. . . i.e. him who showed, by whose light she perceived her way' (Schmidt; akin to OED³ 1, '. . . the action of bringing to light something'). Trisyllabic here, 'discov'ry'.

829 *she beats her heart* she strikes her own breast in grief. Elsewhere Shakespeare portrays this as an excessive gesture. At *Much Ado*, 2.3.147, it is one of the symptoms Claudio cites when pretending that Beatrice is lovelorn; at *Hamlet*, 4.5.5 a gentleman says Ophelia 'beats her heart' in mad grief.

groans This refers to a sound of grief as a pain response from the heart itself, merging the physical and metaphorical. On groans in the poem, see l. 377 and note.

830–1 *all the neighbour caves. . . moans* Compare *A Lover's Complaint*, ll. 1–2. Venus is like Orpheus in Ovid (*Metamorphoses*, 10.86–105; Golding, 10.93–113) here, drawing a sympathetic audience from inanimate nature. The echoing scene recalls another Ovidian episode, that of Narcissus and Echo, especially *Metamorphoses*, 3.495–6; Golding, 3.622–3: 'Yet rueing his unhappy case, as often as he cried | "Alas", she cried "alas" likewise with shrill redoubled sound'. Burrow notes the connection with Clapham's *Narcissus*, where there is an echo poem (2002: 219; see headnote). Links continue throughout the lamenting, mourning and echoing of ll. 829–52. Compare the echoes of *Lucrece*, l. 1806.

830 *That* so that.

neighbour nearby.

as as if.

831 *verbal* (i) verbose, i.e. copious, as in OED *adj.* and *n.*, 1b, for which the first citation is *Cymbeline*, 2.3.105–6: 'You put me to forget a lady's manners | By being so verbal'; or (ii) verbatim (OED 5a; first citation from 1616), as suggested by Burrow (2002: 219): the point is the exact repetition rather than the echoes taking the form of words.

repetition Compare *Lucrece*, l. 1285, where the word suggests a 'recital' rather than an echo.

832 *Passion* expressions of passion, lamentation. OED³ 6d, 'literary composition or passage marked by deep or strong emotion; a passionate speech or outburst', cites *A Midsummer Night's Dream*, 5.1.315. Thisbe's 'passion', her speech about the dead Pyramus, 'ends the play'. See also l. 1059.

deeply is redoubled 'Deeply' fits the caves physically while also suggesting a sound (solemn, low) and strength of emotion.

833–4 *twenty. . . twenty. . . twenty* the poem's number again; see l. 22 and note.

835 *marking* noticing.

note tune.

836 *sings extemporally* improvises. 'Extemporally' is pronounced with four syllables here, 'extemp'rally'.

ditty song; although it did not have the air of triviality that the word has today, 'ditty'

So did the merciless and pitchy night
Fold in the object that did feed her sight.

Whereat amazed as one that, unaware,
Hath dropped a precious jewel in the flood,
Or 'stonished, as night-wanderers often are,   825
Their light blown out in some mistrustful wood,
    Even so confounded in the dark she lay,
    Having lost the fair discovery of her way.

And now she beats her heart, whereat it groans,
That all the neighbour caves, as seeming troubled,   830
Make verbal repetition of her moans;
Passion on passion deeply is redoubled:
    'Ay me', she cries, and twenty times, 'woe, woe',
    And twenty echoes, twenty times cry so.

She, marking them, begins a wailing note,   835
And sings extemporally a woeful ditty,
How love makes young men thrall, and old men dote,
How love is wise in folly, foolish witty.
    Her heavy anthem still concludes in woe,
    And still the choir of echoes answer so.   840

Her song was tedious, and outwore the night,
For lovers' hours are long, though seeming short.
If pleased themselves, others they think delight,

implies something short and informal in Shakespeare's time (OED 2a). Most of his uses of the word suggest this, although see *The Tempest*, 1.2.406–8: 'The ditty does remember my drowned father. | This is no mortal business, nor no sound | That the earth owes'.

837 **young men** hyphenated in Q.
thrall captive.
dote love foolishly.

838 **foolish witty** foolish when witty, complementary to 'wise in folly'; a double oxymoron. Compare 'Glaucus' Complaint' in Lodge's *Scilla's Metamorphosis*: 'Take pity Scilla, pity thou thy lover; | For thou art fair, and beauty should have pity. | Alas she flies, persuasions cannot move her, | She is too wanton, or too foolish witty' (D1r). Wise and witty are closely associated words but they are not synonyms: the attribution of wisdom to love is less secure than the

attribution of folly. On 'wit' and its cognates, see l. 472 and note.

839, 840 **still** always.

839 **anthem** song; typically church music, as in OED³ 1b, 'song consisting of verses or passages sung or chanted responsively by a choir divided into two parts'. See 'Let the Bird of Loudest Lay', l. 21, where it is clearly a mourning song, though it can serve other purposes. The 'choir of echoes' in l. 840 picks up the inflated Christian resonance.
concludes in woe finishes with a sad note, ends sadly.

840 **choir. . . answer** A plural verb follows a collective noun here; see l. 272 and note.

841 **tedious** long and boring, though the word can mean simply exhaustive, or elaborate; compare *Lucrece*, l. 1309.
outwore lasted through, wore out. Compare *Lucrece*, l. 123.

844 *such like. . . such like* the same. . . the same. There is a case for modernising these into single words, but the monosyllables contribute to the pacing of the line, which is stretched out and copious.
circumstance situation.
sport fun; see l. 24 and note.

845 *copious* fulsome, lengthy; perhaps richly ornamented. Erasmus' *De Copia* (1512) was an influential writing manual that promoted the value of an abundant style; lovers pursue it less practically than Erasmus advocated.

846 *End. . . audience* i.e. nobody is listening by the end.

847 *withal* with, perhaps more emphatic (Abbott, § 196).

848 *idle* (i) useless; (ii) meaningless; see l. 422 and note.
parasites flatterers (who just repeat and endorse what the powerful person has said); pronounced to rhyme with 'wits', and spelled 'parasits' in Q.

849 *Like shrill-tongued. . . call* Like loud, perhaps high-voiced (i.e. youthful) barmen, answering calls for drink. Tapsters in Shakespeare are notorious for cheating customers, but also for needing to gratify them. See Apemantus in *Timon of Athens*, 4.3.215–16, who says 'Thou gav'st thine ears (like tapsters that bade welcome) | To knaves and all approachers'. See also the efforts of Francis the drawer to meet the demands of Prince Hal and his friends in 1 *Henry IV*, 2.4.
answering disyllabic.

850 *humour* moods.
fantastic fanciful, capricious (OED 4b). Shakespeare's other use of the word with this sense comes in *Two Gentlemen of Verona*, 2.7.47–8: 'To be fantastic may become a youth | Of greater time than I shall show to be'.
wits On this word and its cognates, see l. 472 and note.

852 *say after her* repeat what she said.

853 *gentle* On the word's appearances in the poem, see 189n.
weary of rest tired of doing nothing. In the poem it is time for a change, and 'Lo' strikes the right note (see l. 194 and note). However, the paradox in 'weary of rest' means the lark starts the day in an odd mood; compare Sonnet 29.11–12.

854 *moist* damp.

cabinet nest; the word is used freely of small dwelling spaces, including animal dens (OED 1a). EEBO-TCP provides no earlier use of the phrase *moist cabinet*.

855 *whose* i.e. the morning's.
silver compare the silver morning of *Lucrece*, l. 24.

857 *behold* look at; but the sun's divine gaze changes everything it touches with light, and so older meanings of the word (OED 1–5), which are closer to the modern 'hold', are implied. Compare the description of the rising sun in Sonnet 33.1–4.

858 *cedar tops* the tops of cedar trees (which are associated with majesty, so the gold fits).
burnished polished.

859 *him* i.e. the sun.
good morrow a morning greeting.

860 *clear* (i) bright; (ii) shining; it evokes the etymologically linked Latin word 'clarus', which conveys both brightness and fame.

861 *lamp* heavenly body (OED 2a); compare *Macbeth*, 2.4.6–7, 'By the clock 'tis day, | And yet dark night strangles the travelling lamp'.
shining See l. 488 and note.

862 *beauteous* disyllabic.
influence trisyllabic. In Venus' theory of light, an original source (the sun) bestows its 'influence' on planets and stars. Compare the theory of vision at l. 487 and note. In astrology, too, power flows from the sun and planets into other things. 'Influence' is often used of stars, as in Sonnet 15.4, but it has an amatory and hyperbolic context in *Two Gentlemen of Verona*, 3.1.182–4: 'I leave to be, | If I be not by her fair influence | Fostered, illumined, cherished, kept alive'. See also *Hero and Leander*, ll. 543–7: 'Much more in subjects having intellect, | Some hidden influence breeds like effect. | Albeit Leander rude in love, and raw, | Long dallying with Hero, nothing saw | That might delight him more'.

863 *son* wordplay on 'sun', as at l. 754, and in Sonnet 7.
earthly mortal, terrestrial; as opposed to divine or heavenly. OED^3 *adj.* and *n.* A1a ('Of or relating to the earth, terrestrial; worldly, material. Hence: of or belonging to the material or lower elements of human nature; base, coarse') allows for a negative note, which might suit Venus' divine perspective. Compare Sonnet 17.8, *Lucrece*, l. 85.

In such like circumstance, with such like sport.
    Their copious stories, oftentimes begun,   845
    End without audience, and are never done.

For who hath she to spend the night withal,
But idle sounds resembling parasites?
Like shrill-tongued tapsters answering every call,
Soothing the humour of fantastic wits,   850
    She says ''Tis so', they answer all ''Tis so',
    And would say after her, if she said 'No.'

Lo here the gentle lark, weary of rest,
From his moist cabinet mounts up on high
And wakes the morning, from whose silver breast   855
The sun ariseth in his majesty,
    Who doth the world so gloriously behold,
    That cedar tops and hills seem burnished gold.

Venus salutes him with this fair good morrow:
'O thou clear god, and patron of all light,   860
From whom each lamp and shining star doth borrow
The beauteous influence that makes him bright,
    There lives a son that sucked an earthly mother
    May lend thee light, as thou dost lend to other.'

This said, she hasteth to a myrtle grove,   865
Musing the morning is so much o'erworn,
And yet she hears no tidings of her love.
She hearkens for his hounds, and for his horn:
    Anon she hears them chant it lustily,
    And all in haste she coasteth to the cry.   870

---

mother On the myth of Myrrha (Adonis' mother), and its pertinence, see headnote.

864 **other** i.e. others; see Abbott, § 12, for the use of 'other' as a plural pronoun.

865 **myrtle** tree associated with Venus.

866 **Musing. . . o'erworn** wondering how (perhaps wondering *that*) so much of the morning has been used up.

868 **hearkens** listens.

869 **Anon** and then.
chant it strike up (barking); often used of birds (OED 1b) but also of hounds (1c). On the 'indefinite object' 'it', see Hope (2003: 88).

870 **all in haste she coasteth** in a great hurry she travels. 'Coast' can just mean 'approach' (OED 8) but it has a specific meaning in hunting, OED 10: 'not to fly or run straight at; to keep at a distance'. This meaning is contrary to Venus' purposes, so the technicality may be less important than the atmosphere of hunting. See Gascoigne (1575: sig. L2v): 'And you must understand, that if you leese [i.e. lose] an hare at any time, let the huntsmen yet remember and mark which paths she bet [i.e. preterite of 'beat'], and what way she coasted: for another time if you find the same hare, she will doubtless keep the same places, and make the like doublings, crossings, &c.'. See also sig. L7v for another pertinent sense: 'again do mark which way an hare bendeth at the first, and coast before her to meet her'.

872–3 *catch. . . kiss. . . twined* Again the bushes want to hold on to passing figures. The shift in tenses from present to past helps convey the haste and immediacy (compare ll. 317–8). Nonetheless Q7's amendment to 'twine' is tempting, and at least it shows that early readers could be disarmed by rapid shifts of tense; Q's 'twin'd' may be an alternative spelling for the sake of rhyme; compare *Lucrece*, l. 1544.

874 *strict* tight, constricting.

875 *milch doe* female deer with milk to feed young. Venus resembles the deer at least in her urgency and concern, but the maternal context (see also ll. 974, perhaps 1119–20, 1178, 1185) problematises Venus' feelings towards Adonis.

dugs udders.

876 *brake* thicket.

877 *By this* just then (see l. 175 and note).

at a bay facing their quarry at close quarters, as in OED 'bay, *n*.4', 4 (where this line is cited). 'At bay' can be used of hunter or hunted in this situation. However, as the OED's headnote says, this often merges with 'bay' indicating barking (OED 1, from Italian *a bada*, and Latin *badare*, to open the mouth). Venus hears the barking of a critical moment in the hunt. Compare Gascoigne (1575: sig. K6v): 'For such a boar will seldom keep hounds at a bay, unless he be forced: and if he do stand at bay, the huntsmen must ride in unto him as secretly as they can without much noise'.

878–80 *like one. . . shudder* The simile recalls Virgil's *Aeneid*, 2.379–81; Phaer, 2.375–6 (1573: sig. D4v; as noted by Burrow 2002: 221): 'As one that unbethought hath happed some snake among the briars | To tread, and quickly starting back with trembling fear retires'. On the 'adder' / 'shudder' rhyme, see Appendix 7.

879 *Wreathed up* coiled (OED 'wreathe' *v*. 1a, 'to twist or coil').

fatal deadly, promising death.

just in his way right in front of him.

881 *Even so* just like this (reiterating the simile). 'Even' is monosyllabic.

timorous (i) fearful (i.e. the hounds are nervous of the boar), but also (ii) fear-inducing (OED 2). Venus' fear permeates the world around her. This effect is seen, though less clearly, in 'fearfully', l. 886.

882 *Appals* terrifies.

spirit elided into one syllable.

confounds puts into a state of confusion, horrifies.

883 *gentle chase* harmless thing to be hunted (OED, 'chase, *n*.1', 4a). EEBO-TCP has no earlier instances of the phrase. This conclusion and the beasts mentioned next echo Venus' practice and advice in Ovid, *Metamorphoses*, 10.537–47; Golding, 10.621–9: 'Pursuing game of hurtless sort [. . .] | Be bold on cowards (Venus said)' (ll. 622, 628). Compare ll. 673–8 above. On 'gentle' in the poem, see l. 189 and note.

884 *blunt* rough, harsh.

proud See l. 14 and note.

886 *aloud* loudly.

887 *cursed* vicious (OED 4b), perhaps also morally despicable.

888 *strain courtesy who shall* struggle to negotiate the etiquette of who should. An EEBO-TCP search reveals the phrase 'strain courtesy' is quite widely used before 1593 (33 hits in 28 records); Burrow (2002: 222) notes a pertinent appearance in Gascoigne (1575: sig. M6v). They do this out of fear, or at least, out of the fear that Venus projects from herself, on to them.

courtesy disyllabic here.

cope attack, tackle; see OED, 'cope, *v*.2', 7: 'to meet, meet with, come into contact with'. See *Lucrece*, l. 99.

889 *dismal* (i) depressing, dire (OED *n*. and *adj*., B4), but also (ii) ominous, sinister (OED B2), in keeping with the word's origin in the *dies mali* (unpropitious days) of the Medieval calendar. Compare *3 Henry VI*, 2.6.58–9: 'Now death shall stop his dismal threatening sound, | And his ill-boding tongue no more shall speak'.

890 *surprise* (i) mount a sudden attack on (OED 2a); (ii) capture, seize (OED 2b). Compare *Titus Andronicus*, 1.1.284, 'Treason, my lord! Lavinia is surprised!', which is the first citation for the latter sense in OED.

891 *Who* the heart, vividly personified as part of a dramatisation of inner processes. Compare l. 1043 (the heart again), and l. 956, where the pronoun 'who' is used in a less vivid personification; see also l. 87 and note.

892 *cold-pale* (i) pale with cold; or just (ii) cold and pale. It seems best to leave this

And as she runs, the bushes in the way,
Some catch her by the neck, some kiss her face,
Some twined about her thigh to make her stay.
She wildly breaketh from their strict embrace,
    Like a milch doe, whose swelling dugs do ache,   875
      Hasting to feed her fawn, hid in some brake.

By this she hears the hounds are at a bay,
Whereat she starts like one that spies an adder
Wreathed up in fatal folds just in his way,
The fear whereof doth make him shake and shudder: 880
    Even so the timorous yelping of the hounds
      Appals her senses, and her spirit confounds.

For now she knows it is no gentle chase,
But the blunt boar, rough bear, or lion proud,
Because the cry remaineth in one place,   885
Where fearfully the dogs exclaim aloud,
    Finding their enemy to be so cursed,
      They all strain courtesy who shall cope him first.

This dismal cry rings sadly in her ear,
Through which it enters to surprise her heart,   890
Who, overcome by doubt and bloodless fear,
With cold-pale weakness numbs each feeling part;
    Like soldiers when their captain once doth yield,
      They basely fly, and dare not stay the field.

Thus stands she in a trembling ecstasy,   895
Till cheering up her senses all dismayed,

hyphenated as in Q, a compound adjective, as it is treated in OED (as a 'special use' under 'cold, *adj.*'). The hyphenation may be compositorial, and the difference between two similar adjectival pairs in Shakespeare may be minimal: see *Titus Andronicus*, 5.3.152, 'take this warm kiss on thy pale cold lips', and *Richard II*, 1.2.33–4, 'That which in mean men we entitle patience | Is pale cold cowardice in noble breasts'. See also George Gascoigne's *A Hundred Sundry Flowers* (1573): 'But I will kiss these cold pale lips of thine, | And wash thy wounds with my waymenting [i.e. lamenting] tears' (sig. X1v).

894 *stay the field* remain in the battle.

895 *ecstasy* paralysis; OED 1 says this is to be 'beside oneself' in 'a frenzy or a stupor'.

Most of Shakespeare's uses incline towards frenzy, whereas here stupor seems more pertinent. Compare *Hamlet*, 2.1.99–100, 'This is the very ecstasy of love, | Whose violent property fordoes itself'; also *A Lover's Complaint*, l. 69. Spenser captures the dream-like quality at III.viii.22.7–9: 'He marveild more, and thought he yet did dreame | Not well awakte, or that some extasye | Assotted [i.e. beguiled] had his sence, or dazed was his eye'. Likewise the definition in Holland's translation of Plutarch's *Morals* (1603) emphasises the trance-like state: 'Ecstasy, A trance or transportation of the mind, occasioned by rage, admiration, fear, &c.' (5Z3v).

896 *cheering up* encouraging, rousing.

899 ***Bids them. . . no more*** Q9 and some later texts avoid the repetition by putting 'wills' for the second 'bids'; see l. 909 and note. Q's text draws attention to the image of a goddess requesting her faculties to come to order.

900 ***And with that word*** As with 'By this' in l. 877, Shakespeare again moves the action on rapidly (and into the past tense, 'spied'), a stark contrast with the long orations with which Venus occupied Adonis.

901 ***bepainted*** smeared.

902 ***Like milk and blood*** The white and red pattern, which had receded from view since l. 486, emphatically returns.

903 ***spread*** The subject of the verb is the boar's 'mouth' (l. 901), the sight of which spread (past tense) fear through her body.

905 ***now she will no further*** and then she decided not to run further.

906 ***retires*** returns (OED³ 7a); as at *Lucrece*, l. 962.
rate scold, berate (OED³ 'rate, *v*.1', 1). Compare *Lucrece*, l. 304.
murder murther Q. The word is spelled in both ways in Shakespeare's time, which suggests that the pronunciations of 'murder' and 'murther' were very similar in early modern English (see Kökeritz 1953: 320). See ll. 54 (Q 'murther'), 502 and 1031 (Q 'murdred'). It is part of the hyperbole of love in *Hero and Leander*, ll. 610–12: 'So beauty sweetly quickens when 'tis nigh, | But being separated and removed, | Burns where it cherished, murders where it loved'.

907 ***spleens*** impulsive feelings (this line is the first citation for OED 4a; EEBO-TCP has no earlier similar uses of the plural); the spleen was thought to be a source of capricious and/or melancholic thoughts. Compare *1 Henry IV*, 5.2.19: 'A hare-brained Hotspur, governed by a spleen', and also (more figuratively) Lysander in *A Midsummer Night's Dream*, 1.1.145–6, about 'sympathy in choice': 'Brief as the lightning in the collied [i.e. dark, coal-black] night | That, in a spleen, unfolds both heaven and earth' (this is cited under OED 7a, 'a fit of temper, a passion').

908 ***She treads. . . untreads*** She goes one way, and then retraces her steps; another variant on rhetorical repetition. See *Merchant of Venice* 2.6.10–12, for another use of the rare word 'untread' (*Venus and Adonis* is the first citation in OED). Gratiano seems to be remembering several things in *Venus and Adonis* when he says: 'Where is the horse that doth untread again | His tedious measures with the unbated fire | That he did pace them first?'.

909 ***more than haste*** extreme hurry (as at *Lucrece*, l. 1332).
mated combined. This is the first citation for OED³ 'mate, *v*.3', 4, so it is understandable that Q9, the compiler of which seems to have been attentive around these lines (see 899n), replaces it with 'marred'. This is closer to the meaning seen by most commentators (halted, thwarted; as in OED³ 'mate, *v*.1').

910 ***proceedings*** behaviour.

911 ***respects*** matters for consideration, concerns. See OED³, 'respect, *n*.', 4, as in *Hamlet*, 3.2.174: 'The instances that second marriage move | Are base respects of thrift, but none of love'.
respecting considering, paying attention to; compare *Lucrece*, l. 431.

913 ***kennelled in a brake*** having taken refuge in a thicket. OED cites this first under 'kennel', 2a: 'to put into, or keep in, a kennel' (transitive). However, it seems clear that it is being used figuratively – there is no actual kennel here – more like the intransitive 1a, which includes 'of a fox or other wild beast: to retreat into a lair'. The hunting dog has become the quarry.

914 ***caitiff*** wretch.

916 ***'Gainst venomed sores. . . plaster*** If there is a danger of poison (or infection) in a wound, this [licking] is the only truly effective cure. Compare l. 28; here too an EEBO-TCP search (on 'sovereign plaster') uncovers several earlier uses.
sovereign See OED, 'sovereign, *n*. and *adj*.', 2a, 'greatest, or most notable', and Schmidt's gloss 'supremely medicinal or efficacious' (as in OED B3). Compare Sonnet 153.8.
plaster cure; see OED 1b, 'a healing or soothing measure'.

917 ***sadly*** sorrowfully; see also l. 929 and note.
scowling sullen. Elsewhere Shakespeare uses it of humans, the sky and weather, but compare Golding's Ovid, 7.524–6: 'The currish Hell-hound Cerberus, who, dragging arseward still | And writhing back his scowling

She tells them 'tis a causeless fantasy
And childish error that they are afraid,
   Bids them leave quaking, bids them fear no more;
   And with that word she spied the hunted boar: 900

Whose frothy mouth bepainted all with red,
Like milk and blood being mingled both together,
A second fear through all her sinews spread,
Which madly hurries her she knows not whither:
   This way she runs, and now she will no further,   905
   But back retires to rate the boar for murder.

A thousand spleens bear her a thousand ways;
She treads the path that she untreads again.
Her more than haste is mated with delays,
Like the proceedings of a drunken brain,   910
   Full of respects, yet naught at all respecting,
   In hand with all things, naught at all effecting.

Here kennelled in a brake she finds a hound,
And asks the weary caitiff for his master,
And there another licking of his wound,   915
'Gainst venomed sores the only sovereign plaster;
   And here she meets another, sadly scowling,
   To whom she speaks, and he replies with howling.

When he hath ceased his ill-resounding noise,
Another flap-mouthed mourner, black and grim,   920
Against the welkin volleys out his voice;
Another, and another, answer him,
   Clapping their proud tails to the ground below,
   Shaking their scratched ears, bleeding as they go.

Look how the world's poor people are amazed   925
At apparitions, signs, and prodigies,
Whereon with fearful eyes they long have gazed,

eyes because he had no skill | To see the sun and open day'.

919 *ill-resounding* harshly echoing.

920 *flap-mouthed* with loose skin around its mouth (first reference in OED for this compound).
   black in mood, as much as in colour.

921 *Against the welkin* into the sky.
   volleys out his voice shouts out (barks) impetuously (OED 'volley, *v*.', 1a). The word evokes a cannon firing a volley of shot.

923 *Clapping. . . to* slapping. . . on; compare *2 Henry VI*, 5.1.154, '[a cur] hath clapped his tail between his legs'.
   proud See l. 14 and note.

925-7 *amazed, gazed* probably pronounced 'amazèd', 'gazèd'; the Q spellings are 'amazed', 'gazed'. See 109–111n on the reliability of Q's orthography in these cases.

925 *Look how* See l. 67 and note.

926 *prodigies* extraordinary things (often taken as portents).

928 ***Infusing them with*** (i) imputing to them (i.e. the signs); (ii) imbuing them with, the 'dreadful prophecies'. This line is cited under OED 5, 'to imbue or inspire (a person or thing) with some infused quality'.

929 ***sad*** (i) sorrowful, but also (ii) grave, serious.

930 ***it*** her breath, unusually the object of 'sighing'.
exclaims on Death denounces Death (personified). 'Exclaim' can be used with various prepositions: compare *1 Henry VI*, 3.3.60, 'all French and France exclaims on thee', and *Lucrece*, l. 757: 'she exclaims against repose and rest'.

931 ***Hard-favoured*** ugly. See l. 133, and *Lucrece*, l. 1632.
meagre thin, barren.

932 ***divorce of love*** force which causes lovers to separate.

933 ***Grim-grinning ghost*** alliteratively merges together the death's-head skull with a less corporeal spirit of death. EEBO-TCP has no earlier instance of the hyphenated compound 'grim-grinning'. Compare the wolf's grin at l. 459.
earth's worm hyphenated in Q. Death is likened to the proverbially lowly worm (though this does not show up as a proverb in Dent). He is already associated with the worms which consume corpses, as in *As You Like It*, 4.1.106–7: 'men have died from time to time, and worms have eaten them'.
what dost thou mean[?] (i) what are you trying to achieve? (ii) who do you think you are?

935–6 ***set. . . Gloss on*** gave shine to. The OED associates 'gloss, *v*.2' with false or superficial lustre; Shakespeare's uses tend in that direction, though with some of the double-edged note present here (compare *Much Ado*, 3.2.5–6, 'as great a soil in the new gloss of your marriage').

936 ***violet*** The key association of the violet here is its sweet smell, but it also evokes the impermanence of youth, as at Sonnet 99.1 and note.

937–8 ***it cannot be. . . at it*** cannot be possible that, if you had seen his beauty, you would attack him. A rhetorical *correctio*, curtailing the unthinkable.

939 ***thou hast no eyes to see*** Venus ingeniously accuses Death, imagined as a skull, of having no eyes. Cupid is the one traditionally blind in some myths; in comparison with love, death is usually thought to have better aim.

940 ***hatefully*** maliciously; Shakespeare's only use of the adverb.
at random (i) haphazardly – the modern meaning is current in Shakespeare's time; (ii) impetuously, violently (as in the older sense of the word, OED[3] *n.*, *adv.*, and *adj.* 1a).

941 ***mark*** target.
dart arrow; the word could denote a spear or javelin, but the 'mark' suggests archery.

942 ***infant's heart*** 'Infant' predominantly means a very young child, as in *As You Like It*, 2.7.143–4, 'mewling and puking in the nurse's arms'; compare l. 562. OED records figurative uses, a particular legal meaning (*n*.1 and *adj*., A2, equivalent to 'minor', 'in common law, one who has not completed his or her twenty-first year'), and Spenser's use to mean a young nobleman (OED 3; *Faerie Queene*, II.viii.56.1). Shakespeare's uses either refer to young children or are figurative. Venus exaggerates Adonis' youth for effect.

944–6 ***power. . .flower*** The rhyme words are probably disyllabic, though it is a marginal call, especially because the first 'power' in l. 944 is evidently monosyllabic. Spelling offers some corroboration, in that Q has 'power. . .flower' here, and the only disyllabic instance ('flower', 8) is 'flower' in Q, whereas other clearly monosyllabic instances of the singular (ll. 1056, 1168, 1171, 1177) are 'floure' in Q. The monosyllabic instance of 'pow'r' in l. 944, however, is also 'power' in Q. Compare 65–6n, and 1187–8n.

944 ***had lost his*** would have lost its.

945 ***Destinies*** fates, goddesses of fate; as at l. 733 and note.

946 ***crop*** This can be a violent and sexual term. It denotes murder at *Richard III*, 1.2.246–7: 'me, | That cropped the golden prime of this sweet prince'. See l. 1175.
pluck'st On 'pluck', see l. 30 and note.

947–8 ***Love's. . . dead*** Love poetry often laments the destructive influence of Cupid's arrow, but Venus portrays it in a positive light. It is golden here as at *Metamorphoses*, 1.470, and *A Midsummer Night's Dream*, 1.1.170: 'By the best arrow with the golden head'. See l. 581 and note.

Infusing them with dreadful prophecies:
    So she at these sad signs draws up her breath,
    And sighing it again, exclaims on Death.   930

'Hard-favoured tyrant, ugly, meagre, lean,
Hateful divorce of love' (thus chides she Death),
'Grim-grinning ghost, earth's worm, what dost thou mean,
To stifle beauty, and to steal his breath?
    Who when he lived, his breath and beauty set   935
    Gloss on the rose, smell to the violet.

'If he be dead – O no, it cannot be,
Seeing his beauty, thou shouldst strike at it!
O yes, it may, thou hast no eyes to see,
But hatefully at random dost thou hit.   940
    Thy mark is feeble age, but thy false dart
    Mistakes that aim, and cleaves an infant's heart.

'Hadst thou but bid beware, then he had spoke,
And hearing him, thy power had lost his power.
The Destinies will curse thee for this stroke: 945
They bid thee crop a weed, thou pluck'st a flower.
    Love's golden arrow at him should have fled,
    And not death's ebon dart to strike him dead.

'Dost thou drink tears, that thou provok'st such weeping?
What may a heavy groan advantage thee?   950
Why hast thou cast into eternal sleeping
Those eyes that taught all other eyes to see?
    Now Nature cares not for thy mortal vigour,
    Since her best work is ruined with thy rigour.'

Here, overcome as one full of despair,   955
She vailed her eyelids, who like sluices stopped

947 *fled* from 'fly', not 'flee'; a form of the past participle said by the OED to be 'rare and chiefly for rhyme'.

948 *ebon* black, as if made of ebony; or actually made of ebony.
dart See 941n.

950 *What* i.e. how (in more usual modern idiom).
groan On groans, see l. 377 and note.

952 *Those eyes. . . to see* Adonis' eyes have shown everyone else (i) what true beauty is; (ii) where their eyes should be looking. The repetition of 'eyes' is an instance of emphatic rhetorical *diacope*.

953 *Nature* personified here (see 'her', l. 954).
mortal vigour deadly power; the phrase is an oxymoron, but, with heavy paradoxical force, is also able to mean 'human liveliness'.

954 *rigour* severity, harshness.

955–60 *Here. . . again* Compare the description of the weeping youth in *A Lover's Complaint*, ll. 283–7.

956 *vailed* lowered (OED *v.*2), with some play on 'veiled'.
who which (see l. 87 and note).
sluices flood-gates (i.e. gates controlling the flow of water); see *Lucrece*, l. 1076.

957   *crystal tide* her tears; see l. 979 and *Lucrece*, 645n, on the word 'tide'.

958   *channel* i.e. the cleft between her breasts.

959   *silver rain* i.e. her tears again.

960   *his* referring to 'the silver rain'.
      course flow (suggesting also a watercourse).

961   *lend* See l. 29 and note.

962   *eye. . . eye* The rhetorical figure here is *antimetabole*.

963   *crystals* cited at OED *n.* and *adj.*, A3b, 'poet. An eye', but this does not explain the metaphor. One of the properties of crystals (a term used of numerous transparent minerals) was that they could be polished to a reflective surface. See l. 633 and note.

963–4   *sorrow. . . Sorrow* epizeuxis; 'often used as a rhetorical indicator of great passion in Shakespeare' (Burrow 2002: 225).

967   *Variable* Changeability is a feature of lovers, as in Barnabe Barnes, *Parthenophil and Parthenophe*, Canzone, 3.97–100: 'Because they were inconstant, and unstable, | In drought, in moisture, frosty cold, and heat, | Here with a sunny smile, their stormy threat: | Much like my lady's fancies variable' (sig. S1r).

968   *As striving* as if to compete.
      who a pronoun typical in Shakespearean personification (see l. 87 and note).
      become (i) suit; or perhaps (ii) adorn.

969   *entertained* (i) admitted; (ii) attended to. Compare *Lucrece*, l. 1629.

970–1   *That every. . . none is best* Each emotion ('sorrow' now stands for all of them) that comes before her seems like the strongest, but none is pre-eminent.

972   *clouds* On clouds in the poem, see l. 490 and note.
      consulting for plotting, conferring about. OED 1a allows for uses with prepositions, though 'for' is unusual.

973   *By this* at that moment (see l. 175 and note).
      hallow cry out (to encourage hunting dogs, OED 'hallow, *v*.2', 2).

974   *A nurse's song. . . well* The hallowing of the hunter is likened to a lullaby that soothes a baby, as at *Titus Andronicus*, 2.3.27–9: 'Hounds and horns and sweet melodious birds | Be unto us as is a nurse's song | Of lullaby to bring her babe asleep'. For Venus as the mother-figure, compare l. 875 and note.

975   *dire imagination she did follow* disastrous delusion (OED³ 'imagination', 4) that she had

been believing (but which this more positive sign is now striving to overcome). On 'imagination' and its cognates, see l. 597 and note.

977   *reviving* This works in two senses: joy itself is coming back, but it is also restoring Venus.

978   *flatters her* gives her false hope.

979–80   *Whereat her tears. . . glass* Tears are turned to pearls by Cupid in *Hero and Leander*, ll. 375–6: 'And as she wept, her tears to pearl he turned, | And wound them on his arm, and for her mourned'.

979   *tide* See l. 957 and *Lucrece*, 645n.

981   *orient drop* Pearls were often described as 'orient', i.e. eastern, as at *Richard III*, 4.4.321–2, which is also a comparison with tears: 'The liquid drops of tears that you have shed | Shall come again, transformed to orient pearl'. There is wordplay on 'orient' (rising, OED³ *n.* and *adj.*, B3a) with 'drop'.

982   *melts, as scorning it should pass* causes to evaporate, as if it were scornful at the thought that it might drop all the way down. This use of 'melt' (from liquid to vapour, or to nothing) is not covered by OED³ *v.*1, though it is close to 1f, 'disperse, cause to disappear'. Shakespeare does not use it elsewhere to suggest evaporation; see l. 144 and note.

983–4   *To wash. . . drowned* Venus' perspective impinges here. The ground is compared to a dirty woman who appears to be overcome with tears but is actually just drunk (a recurrence of the theme from ll. 849–50).

983   *sluttish* dirty; though morally disparaging meanings were current in the late sixteenth century. Compare Sonnet 55.4.

984   *drowned* soaked (OED 1b), but also overwhelmed, immersed (OED 'drown, *v*.', 6a).

985   *hard-believing* (i) sceptical; (ii) assuming the worst; the two possible meanings of this phrase are paraphrased in l. 986.
      love This is another case where the extent of personification is unclear (on which see 328n).
      strange perhaps with a hint of 'reluctant, unwilling' (OED 11b; Duncan-Jones and Woudhuysen 2007: 214).

987   *weal and woe* well-being and sadness. It was proverbial that women experienced extreme feelings (Dent W651, 'a woman either loves or hates to extremes'); compare *Much Ado About Nothing*, 5.1.177–8: 'if she did not hate him deadly, she would love him dearly'.

The crystal tide, that from her two cheeks fair
In the sweet channel of her bosom dropped;
    But through the flood-gates breaks the silver rain,
    And with his strong course opens them again.   960

O how her eyes and tears did lend and borrow,
Her eye seen in the tears, tears in her eye,
Both crystals, where they viewed each other's sorrow:
Sorrow, that friendly sighs sought still to dry,
    But like a stormy day, now wind, now rain,   965
    Sighs dry her cheeks, tears make them wet again.

Variable passions throng her constant woe,
As striving who should best become her grief.
All entertained, each passion labours so
That every present sorrow seemeth chief,   970
    But none is best; then join they all together,
    Like many clouds consulting for foul weather.

By this, far off she hears some huntsman hallow;
A nurse's song ne'er pleased her babe so well.
The dire imagination she did follow,   975
This sound of hope doth labour to expel.
    For now reviving joy bids her rejoice,
    And flatters her it is Adonis' voice.

Whereat her tears began to turn their tide,
Being prisoned in her eye, like pearls in glass.   980
Yet sometimes falls an orient drop beside,
Which her cheek melts, as scorning it should pass
    To wash the foul face of the sluttish ground,
    Who is but drunken when she seemeth drowned.

O hard-believing love, how strange it seems,   985
Not to believe, and yet too credulous!
Thy weal and woe are both of them extremes;
Despair and hope makes thee ridiculous.
    The one doth flatter thee in thoughts unlikely,
    In likely thoughts the other kills thee quickly.   990

988 *makes* a singular verb form after two subjects, not uncommon in Shakespeare (Hope 2003: 164).

989–90 *The one. . . quickly* Hope persuades her to trust in things that are not probable; despair tortures her beyond endurance about things that are probable. The opposition (chiastically arranged) pessimistically assumes that despair is more truthful than hope. Roe hears play on 'quickly' ('quick', meaning 'alive'), which would add a skittish quality to what is otherwise a sententious pronouncement (1992: 128).

991 **web** of fears, and also her unwise hostility towards death.

993 **all to naught** good for nothing.

995 **clepes** calls; this would probably have seemed an archaic word to most of Shakespeare's readers, or at least a formal one, which suits Venus' attempt at ingratiating grandeur. Hamlet uses it (1.4.19: 'they clip us drunkards') in a showy way; in *Love's Labour's Lost*, 1.1.239–40 it appears (in extra-archaic form, 'it is ycliped thy park') in a letter from the braggart Don Armado. Q's spelling, and the *OED* lemma, both justify 'clepes' as the form chosen here (as opposed to 'clips'). The *antimetabole* in the same line ('king of graves, grave of kings') also gives her apology an attempt at grandeur.

996 **Imperious** majestic, dominant (OED 2); pronounced with three syllables. Q6's adjustment to 'imperial' may suggest some unfamiliarity with the word or its sense here, though an EEBO-TCP search reveals many instances before Shakespeare.
supreme ruler, as in OED[3] 'supreme, *adj.* and *n.*', B1, 'supreme authority or ruler'; stressed on the first syllable. Compare *Lucrece*, l. 780.

999 **When as** when.

1000 **still** always.

1001 **gentle** kind, but also suggests 'noble'; on the word's range of meanings in the poem see 189n.
shadow spirit; perhaps ghost or phantom (Burrow 2002: 227), but not 'mere reflection of reality' (Roe 1992: 129), because Venus is flattering death here. Death is associated with the shadows (shades) that populate the classical underworld. See l. 162 and note.

1004 **Be wreaked** have revenge (OED, 'wreak, *v.*', 5a, 5b).

1005 **foul creature** i.e. the boar.

1006 **but** only.
act. . . author Venus portrays herself as the innocent performer of speeches written for her by the boar.

1007–8 **Grief hath. . . wit** proverbial (Dent, G446.1, 'grief has two tongues').

1008 **wit** intelligence; on this word and its cognates, see l. 472 and note.

1010 **suspect** suspicion (OED, *n.*1, 1a); emphasis on the second syllable. Shakespeare's uses of the noun are predominantly in early work, e.g. in *2 Henry VI*, 3.2.139: 'If my suspect be false, forgive me, God'.
extenuate excuse, 'treat as of trifling magnitude' (OED 7a). Mostly used by Shakespeare of laws and sins, but more generally in *Othello*, 5.2.342: 'Speak of me as I am; nothing extenuate'.

1012 **Death** capitalised, because this is manifestly a personification; on less clear cases of personification, see 328n.
insinuate ingratiate herself (OED 2b).

1013 **stories** tells of; a transitive verb (as at *Lucrece*, l. 106), followed by its three objects in the next line.

1016 **silly** feeble, ignorant; see 467–8n.

1017 **wail** bewail.

1018 **mutual overthrow of mortal kind** the universal end of the human race. EEBO-TCP has no earlier uses of the phrase 'mutual overthrow'. In the OED[3] 'mutual, *adj.* and *n.*', A1a, refers to 'two or more' parties: in Shakespeare it can be emphatically about two ('Let the Bird of Loudest Lay', l. 24) but, especially relating to battles, e.g. at *1 Henry IV*, 1.1.14 ('mutual well-beseeming ranks') it can encompass higher numbers. Schmidt paraphrases it as 'common'.

1020 **beauty dead. . . chaos comes again** Venus gives an idiosyncratic cosmology in which the survival of the universe depends on beauty (and thus on her lover); without it there is just a return to the void before creation, as imagined by Ovid's *Metamorphoses*, 1.5–9; Golding, 1.5–9: 'a huge rude heap, and nothing else but even | A heavy lump and cluttered clod of seeds together driven, | Of things at strife among themselves, for want of order due' (6–8). The echo in *Othello*, 3.3.91–2, 'when I love thee not, | Chaos is come again', links the idea to the attitude of the dangerously over-committed lover.

1021 **Fie, fie** On the exclamation, see l. 185 and note; doubled also at l. 611.
fond foolish.
Love She addresses love in general, but also herself; for this reason the word is capitalised, though in Q it is not.

1022 **hemmed with** surrounded by.

1023 **unwitnessèd** uncorroborated; Shakespeare's only use of the word.

Now she unweaves the web that she hath wrought:
Adonis lives, and Death is not to blame;
It was not she that called him all to naught;
Now she adds honours to his hateful name.
    She clepes him king of graves, and grave for kings,   995
    Imperious supreme of all mortal things.

'No, no,' quoth she, 'sweet Death, I did but jest;
Yet pardon me, I felt a kind of fear
When as I met the boar, that bloody beast,
Which knows no pity, but is still severe.   1000
    Then gentle shadow (truth I must confess),
    I railed on thee, fearing my love's decease.

''Tis not my fault, the boar provoked my tongue;
Be wreaked on him, invisible commander.
'Tis he, foul creature, that hath done thee wrong;   1005
I did but act, he's author of thy slander.
    Grief hath two tongues, and never woman yet
    Could rule them both, without ten women's wit.'

Thus hoping that Adonis is alive,
Her rash suspect she doth extenuate,   1010
And that his beauty may the better thrive,
With Death she humbly doth insinuate,
    Tells him of trophies, statues, tombs, and stories
    His victories, his triumphs, and his glories.

'O Jove,' quoth she, 'how much a fool was I,   1015
To be of such a weak and silly mind,
To wail his death, who lives, and must not die,
Till mutual overthrow of mortal kind?
    For he being dead, with him is beauty slain,
    And beauty dead, black chaos comes again.   1020

'Fie, fie, fond Love, thou art as full of fear,
As one with treasure laden, hemmed with thieves.
Trifles unwitnessèd with eye, or ear,
Thy coward heart with false bethinking grieves.'
    Even at this word she hears a merry horn,   1025
    Whereat she leaps, that was but late forlorn.

1024 **bethinking** surmises; OED, 'the action of considering, reflecting, or remembering'. **grieves** afflicts; the subject is 'Trifles' (with what looks like a singular verb, but see l. 517 and note) and the object 'heart'.

1025 **Even** monosyllabic here.
1026 **leaps** i.e. for joy, with excitement. **late** recently. **forlorn** see l. 251 and note.

1027 *As falcons to the lure* The predatory bird diving at the trainer's bait ('lure', OED *n.2*) is a difficult parallel for her movement here, but Venus is optimistic and purposeful in her flight.

1028 *The grass stoops not* i.e. it does not bend under her weight; a measure of speed, but also of Venus' fluctuating physical qualities (the flowers are said to hold her up at l. 152 as well). This recalls the speed of Atalanta and Hippomenes (whom Venus rewards, and then punishes) in *Metamorphoses*, 10.655, Golding, 10.767–9: 'A man would think they able were upon the sea to go, | And never wet their feet, and on the ails [i.e. the beard-like ends of the the grain-sheath] of corn also | That still is growing in the field'. Since Steevens and Malone it has been thought to recall Camilla in the *Aeneid*, 7.808–9, Phaer, 7.852–3, to which Ovid is surely alluding: 'She for a pastime would on crops upright of standing corn | Have flown, and with her tender feet have never an ear down borne' (1573: sig. X2r).

1029 *unfortunately* 'by ill fortune' (Schmidt); the sense is stronger than in modern usage. This is Shakespeare's only use of the adverb.

1030 *foul. . .fair* Various things are designated 'foul' by Venus in the poem (see ll. 133, 456, 573, 638, 767, 773, 972, 983, 1005, 1105) but here the contrast with 'fair' Adonis is most direct. The pairing is well-known from *Macbeth*, 1.1.12 ('fair is foul, and foul is fair') but is also a feature of Elizabethan love poetry, as at *Astrophil and Stella*, 8th song, 9–12: 'Him great harms had taught much care, | Her fair neck a foul yoke bare, | But her sight his cares did banish, | In his sight her yoke did vanish'.
on of.

1031 *eyes are murdered* Q3's 'as' makes this a slightly ungainly double simile. Here Q's drastic metaphor is retained, and punctuation is changed instead (a semi-colon at the end of the line rather than Q's comma).

1032 *Like stars ashamed of day* There are similes in *Venus and Adonis* that generate strange mismatches; but there are others, like this one, that deepen the scene with new consequence. Stars are absent in the day-time and their presence, rather than their

absence due to shame, may be the arresting thought; still the thoughts of cosmic rejection are sharp.

1033–8 *Or as the snail. . .her head* The use of *shelly* (first reference for OED 2a; only use in Shakespeare) draws attention to the novelty of the simile. Compare *Edward III*, 1.1.138 ('I will make you shrink your snaily horns') and *Love's Labour's Lost*, 4.3.334–5 ('Love's feeling is more soft and sensible | Than are the tender horns of cockled snails').

1035 *smothered up* covered up closely (OED 'smother, *v.*', 6b). For 'smother', compare l. 18.

1037 *his bloody view* the sight of him, covered in blood.

1038 *cabins* Shakespeare reconceives the eye-sockets as cave-like dwellings, see l. 637. Compare George Peele, *Sir Clyamon and Sir Clamydes* (1599): 'And dares not, with the seely snail, from cabin show my head, | Till Vesper I behold aloft in skies begin to spread' (sig. G2r). See also *Lucrece*, l. 379, where closed eyelids are likened to a prison.
head. Recent editions tend to have a comma at the end of the stanza here, because the sense runs on, but keeping Q's full stop is feasible: 'where' is connective but need not create a subordinate clause. The same applies in l. 1044, where Duncan-Jones and Woudhuysen (2007) have a comma, and Roe (1992) a semi-colon: it is even easier to keep the full stop there.

1039–44 *Where they resign. . .deadly groan* Another depiction of dynamic, divided inwardness, this time personifying the brain and heart (hence the 'Who' pronouns of ll. 1041 and 1043). The brain is like a court official, the heart like a king, confused and groaning. The potency of the body-as-state metaphor is evident when the citizens contest Menenius' application of it in *Coriolanus*, 1.1.

1039 *office* proper task.

1040 *disposing* management.

1041 *Who* i.e. which (see ll. 87 and note, and 891 and note on the personification of the heart, as seen also in l. 1043 shortly after this).

As falcons to the lure, away she flies;
The grass stoops not, she treads on it so light,
And in her haste unfortunately spies
The foul boar's conquest on her fair delight.   1030
    Which seen, her eyes are murdered with the view;
    Like stars ashamed of day, themselves withdrew;

Or as the snail, whose tender horns being hit,
Shrinks backward in his shelly cave with pain,
And there, all smothered up, in shade doth sit,   1035
Long after fearing to creep forth again:
    So at his bloody view her eyes are fled,
    Into the deep dark cabins of her head.

Where they resign their office and their light
To the disposing of her troubled brain,   1040
Who bids them still consort with ugly night,
And never wound the heart with looks again,
    Who like a king perplexèd in his throne,
    By their suggestion gives a deadly groan.

Whereat each tributary subject quakes,   1045
As when the wind imprisoned in the ground,
Struggling for passage, earth's foundation shakes,
Which with cold terror doth men's minds confound.
    This mutiny each part doth so surprise
    That from their dark beds once more leap her eyes,   1050

---

still always.
consort with keep the company of (OED 1).
ugly night Compare *Lucrece*, l. 925.
1043 *Who* i.e. which (see ll. 87, 891 and notes).
1044 *By their suggestion* at what the eyes are (i) prompting; (ii) showing.
    deadly death-like (OED 7c).
    groan. On groans, see l. 377 and note. On the punctuation, see l. 1038 and note.
1045 *tributary* who pays a tribute (a kind of tax); the parts of the body serve their monarch and contribute to his resources.
1046–8 *As when the wind. . . confound* The simile connects the cavernous noise (again groans and underground noises come together, as at ll. 267–8, 830–1) with the astonishment felt by the body. It was believed from Aristotle's *Meteorology* onwards that earthquakes were caused by underground winds.

See Arthur Golding, *A Discourse Upon the Earthquake* (1580): 'Earthquakes are said to be engendered by wind gotten into the bowels of the earth, or by vapours bred and enclosed within the hollow caves of the earth, where, by their striving and struggling of themselves to get out, or being haled [OED 'hale, *v.1*', 'draw or pull'] outward by the heat and operation of the sun, they shake the earth for want of sufficient vent to issue out at' (sig. B1v).
1050 *dark beds* eye-sockets (see l. 1038), with some suggestion of graves (Duncan-Jones and Woudhuysen 2007: 218).
    eyes, eies. Q. Q7 has a comma here. In this case the running-on of meaning necessitates a change in punctuation (see l. 1038 and note for a different conclusion in another case).

1051 ***threw unwilling light*** looked without wanting to; another instance of the extramissive theory of vision (see l. 487 and note), in which case it might also suggest unwillingness in the light itself (Roe 1992: 132).

1052 ***trenched*** gouged. This is the OED's first reference for 'trench', 1c (making a wound, as opposed to 1a, severing or dividing). An EEBO-TCP search confirms the unusual nature of the usage, but uncovers Thomas Heywood's translation of Seneca's *Thyestes* (1560): 'doth Tityus yet assay | With trenched heart and wounded womb to move the former ires?' (sig. D3r). It is another term with strong military associations; compare its appearance in MS variants of Sonnet 2, in Appendix 4.

1053 ***flank*** the body between the bottom rib and the hip. Often used of animals, it can nevertheless have an erotic sense, as in Thomas Watson's *Hekatompathia*, 75.4: 'Nor she, whose flanks he filled with fained heat' (K2r). A bawdy song in Sidney's *Countess of Pembroke's Arcadia* also features eroticised flanks: 'Yet never shall my song omit | Those thighs, for Ovid's song more fit; | Which flanked with two sugared flanks, | Lift up their stately swelling banks' (ed. Ringler, 1962: 85). Compare l. 1115.
wonted usual.

1053–4 ***lily white. . . With purple tears*** Purple can be more or less synonymous with red (OED³ *adj.* and *n.* A2a; see l. 1 and note), so the poem's habitual pair appears again. Calling the drops of blood 'tears' makes the white of his side resemble his cheek, the source of much whiteness earlier in the poem.

1054 ***was*** Q7; had Q. It takes too much ingenuity (perhaps 'had' stands for 'had been', or 'had drenched' comes to mean 'became wet') to make Q's reading work. Q7 provides the necessary clarification. Q's word

may have been generated by the rhyme with 'had trenched', l. 1052. Duncan-Jones and Woudhuysen note that amending 'With' to 'Which' would resolve some of the problem (2007: 219), but the link with l. 1053 then is less clear. See Figures 1.1 and 1.2.

1055–6 ***No flower. . . to bleed*** All these plants are covered in Adonis' blood, and seem to be shedding blood as well, foreshadowing his metamorphosis. This fulfils Venus' fears at ll. 665–6. 'Flower' here is monosyllabic.

1056 ***But*** which did not.

1057 ***sympathy. . . noteth*** The etymology of 'sympathy' in Greek – feeling or suffering with – is engaged here. This may be a case of pathetic fallacy, with Venus herself projecting her own emotions onto the environment (hence some irony in 'noteth'). Then again Venus, as a goddess, may be able to perceive the plants' feelings.

1058 ***Over one shoulder. . . head*** Roe suggests that this might have been a familiar and conventional stage gesture (1992: 132).

1059 ***passions*** pours out her emotions. The first citation in OED³ for this sense of the word (*v.*, 3, 'To show, express, or be affected by passion or deep feeling') is from *Love's Labour's Lost*, 1.1.260: 'with this I passion to say therewith'. See also *Two Gentleman of Verona* 4.4.167–8: ''twas Ariadne passioning | For Theseus' injury and unjust flight'. For the equivalent noun, see l. 832, and see Sonnet 20.2 and note.
doteth acts irrationally (and like an excessive lover).

1061 ***bow*** bend.

1062 ***Her eyes are mad, that they have wept till now*** Her eyes are furious that they have shed tears at any time before this.

1064 ***dazzling*** blurring, becoming dazzled (see OED *adj.*, 1); compare *3 Henry VI*, 2.1.25: 'Dazzle mine eyes, or do I see three suns?'.

And, being opened, threw unwilling light
Upon the wide wound that the boar had trenched
In his soft flank, whose wonted lily white
With purple tears, that his wound wept, was drenched.
    No flower was nigh, no grass, herb, leaf, or weed,   1055
    But stole his blood, and seemed with him to bleed.

This solemn sympathy poor Venus noteth;
Over one shoulder doth she hang her head.
Dumbly she passions, frantically she doteth,
She thinks he could not die, he is not dead.   1060
    Her voice is stopped, her joints forget to bow,
    Her eyes are mad, that they have wept till now.

Upon his hurt she looks so steadfastly,
That her sight, dazzling, makes the wound seem three,

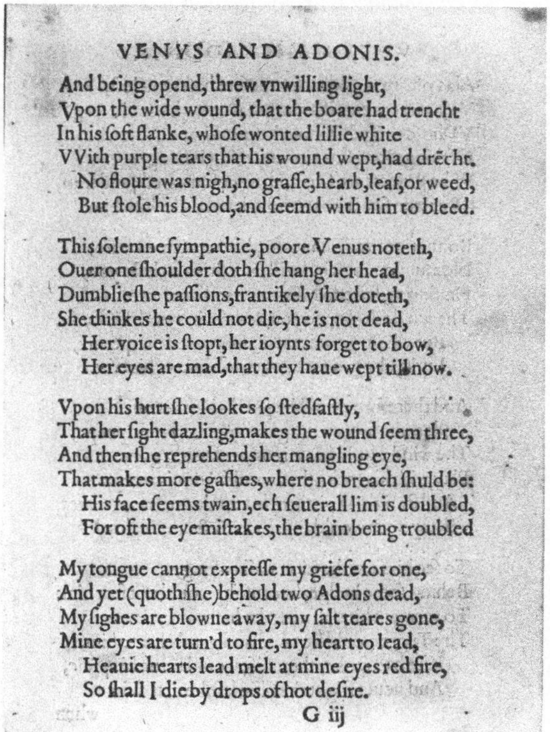

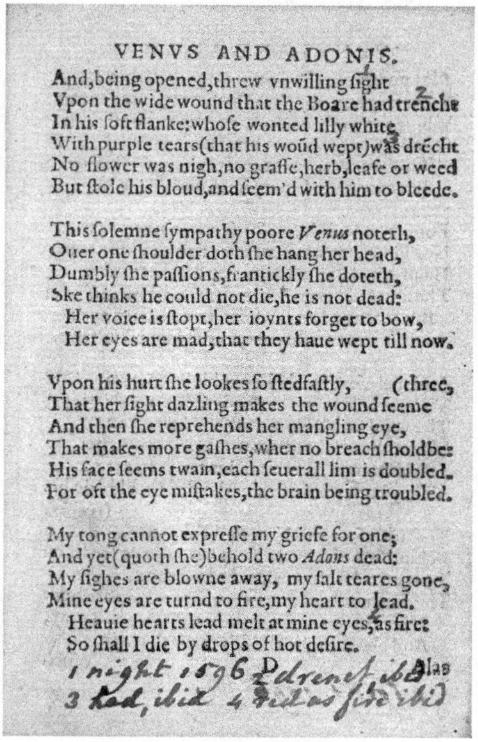

Figure 1.1 William Shakespeare, Venus and Adonis (London: Richard Field, 1593), sig. G3r; Bodleian Library copy, classmark Arch.Ge.31(2). Used with permission of the Bodleian Library

Figure 1.2 William Shakespeare, Venus and Adonis (London: R. Bradocke, 1602?), sig. D1r; Bodleian Library copy, classmark Arch.Gg.4(2). Used with permission of the Bodleian Library

1066 **breach** rupture, i.e. wound; the word is not often used of the body (see OED 7a), but compare *Troilus and Cressida* 4.5.245: 'the very breach whereout Hector's great spirit flew'. See l. 1175.

1067 **twain** double.
several individual, separate; disyllabic here.

1070 **Adons** stressed on first syllable; see l. 769.

1073 **melt** may it melt; see l. 144 and note.

1078 **Of things. . . ensuing** of things which happened long ago, or of anything that will happen in the future.
anything any thing Q.

1079 **flowers** monosyllabic here.
trim fine.

1081 **Bonnet nor veil** For Adonis' bonnet, see l. 339 and note.
wear will (need to) wear.

1082 **Nor. . . nor** neither. . . nor.
kiss i.e. burn or tan the skin, a characteristic metaphor. Compare *Hero and Leander*, ll. 27–30, where it is female whiteness that shuns the sun: 'She ware [i.e. wore] no gloves, for neither sun nor wind | Would burn or parch her hands, but to her mind, | Or warm or cool them, for they took delight | To play upon those hands, they were so white'.

1082–4 **you. . . you. . . you. . . you** addresses the 'creature(s)' of l. 1081.

1083 **fair** beauty; a noun, as at l. 1086; see l. 208 and note.

1084 **hiss** make a disapproving, derisive sound (OED 3).

1085 **sharp** (i) rough; (ii) cunning (in combination with the thieves of l. 1086). Not necessarily cold; here the sun and wind seem to be two properties of a skin-threatening summer day.

1087–92 **And therefore. . . tears** The tenderness of the elements towards Adonis echoes Neptune's playing with Leander's body in *Hero and Leander*, ll. 663–75.

1088 **gaudy** shining brightly. In Shakespeare's time it did not need to be disparaging, as in *Love's Labours Lost*, 5.2.802: 'Nip not the gaudy blossoms of your love'. Compare *Lucrece*, l. 272.

1089 **being gone** i.e. the bonnet being gone.

1091 **straight** immediately.

1092 **strive who** contend which of them (see l. 87 and note).

1094 **would not** did not want to.
fear frighten (OED 1a).

1095 **To recreate himself. . . sung** Whenever he (Adonis) entertained himself with singing. He is attributed an Orphic power to move wild beasts, though (as Roe notes, 1992: 134) this did not work on the boar.

1097 **had spoke** spoke.

1098 **silly** helpless; see 467n.

1099 **shadow** reflection; a hint towards the story of Narcissus. See l. 162 and note.

1100 **The fishes spread on it their golden gills** A striking image, not easily paraphrased. 'Spread' could mean 'displayed', i.e. they are offered as ornaments like flags or cloths (Burrow 2002: 232). Alternatively, the fish may press themselves as closely as they can onto Adonis' shadow. The Orphic effect of his beauty becomes hard to visualise here.

1101 **by,** Q7's comma, included here, clarifies that 'by' means 'nearby', rather than him being next to the birds.

1104 **sight** appearance (OED *n.*1, 3), the sight of him.

1105 **grim** fierce, cruel (OED *adj.* and *adv.*, A1a); used of a lion in a simile describing Tarquin in *Lucrece*, l. 421.
urchin-snouted with a nose like a hedgehog's (OED, 'urchin', 1a), a scornful comparison. It is not clear whether this is because it is bristly, prickly and/or pointed (Burrow 2002: 232).

1106 **downward** downward-pointing.
still always.

And then she reprehends her mangling eye,   1065
That makes more gashes, where no breach should be.
    His face seems twain, each several limb is doubled,
    For oft the eye mistakes, the brain being troubled.

'My tongue cannot express my grief for one,
And yet', quoth she, 'behold two Adons dead.   1070
My sighs are blown away, my salt tears gone,
Mine eyes are turned to fire, my heart to lead.
    Heavy heart's lead melt at mine eyes' red fire:
    So shall I die by drops of hot desire.

'Alas, poor world, what treasure hast thou lost,   1075
What face remains alive that's worth the viewing?
Whose tongue is music now? What canst thou boast,
Of things long since, or anything ensuing?
    The flowers are sweet, their colours fresh and trim,
    But true sweet beauty lived and died with him.   1080

'Bonnet nor veil henceforth no creature wear:
Nor sun, nor wind, will ever strive to kiss you.
Having no fair to lose, you need not fear:
The sun doth scorn you, and the wind doth hiss you.
    But when Adonis lived, sun and sharp air   1085
    Lurked like two thieves, to rob him of his fair.

'And therefore would he put his bonnet on,
Under whose brim the gaudy sun would peep;
The wind would blow it off, and being gone,
Play with his locks; then would Adonis weep,   1090
    And straight in pity of his tender years,
    They both would strive who first should dry his tears.

'To see his face the lion walked along
Behind some hedge, because he would not fear him;
To recreate himself when he hath sung,   1095
The tiger would be tame, and gently hear him.
    If he had spoke, the wolf would leave his prey,
    And never fright the silly lamb that day.

'When he beheld his shadow in the brook,
The fishes spread on it their golden gills;   1100
When he was by, the birds such pleasure took
That some would sing, some other in their bills
    Would bring him mulberries and ripe-red cherries:
    He fed them with his sight, they him with berries.

'But this foul, grim, and urchin-snouted boar,   1105
Whose downward eye still looketh for a grave,

1107 **beauteous livery** gorgeous outward show. His beauty is compared to a formal costume, but Shakespeare often uses the word metaphorically. Compare l. 506, Sonnet 4.5 and *Merchant of Venice*, 2.1.2, where Morocco claims 'the shadowed livery of the burnished sun'.
livery disyllabic.

1108 **Witness the entertainment that he gave** This is proved by the way he treated Adonis.
entertainment treatment; can be neutral in meaning at this time (OED 5), though here it is also a sardonic reflection on more welcoming senses of the word. Burrow connects 'entertainment' (i.e. 'reception') with the knightly implications of 'livery' via OED 2b, 'provision for the support of persons in service' (2002: 232).

1111–16 **'Tis true. . . soft groin** Venus expands upon her theory that the boar was just trying to kiss Adonis. This idea is shared with, and may derive from, a poem about the death of Adonis that was (dubiously) attributed to Theocritus in Shakespeare's time, and which had recently been published in the anonymous translation *Six Idyllia* (1588): 'I minded not to kill | But as an image still | I him beheld for love, | Which made me forward shove, | His thigh, that naked was, | Thinking to kiss alas' (sig. A8r). The poem features as an anonymous work in more modern editions, e.g. *Theocritus, Moschus, Bion*, ed. Hopkinson (2015: 543–7).

1113 **did** Q2's 'would' is preferred by Burrow, and it clarifies the boar's intentions (i.e. he did not want to, or was not trying to). However, it is not strictly necessary, and the auxiliary 'did' can at least imply intention here.
whet sharpen (ready to attack); see OED 1b, for its specific use of boars' tusks, and l. 617 and note.

1114 **there** to stay in that place; or perhaps adverbially, 'in that way' (Roe 1992: 135).

1115 **nuzzling** nousling Q. Cited under OED³ 'nuzzle, *v*.', 3a ('poke or push with the nose or snout'), but this word sits between (i) boar-like rooting around with the nose (OED³ 2a), and (ii) suggestions of physical intimacy that appear to originate in Elizabethan English (OED³ 5; first citation from 1597). It has an anthropomorphic quality, but just as much it evokes another animal's particular way of doing things.

flank See l. 1053; more delicate than the 'groin' which is revealed in the next line. The element of euphemism is clearer here than at the word's first appearance.

1116 **Sheathed** buried, thrust; see *Lucrece*, l. 1723 and note.
groin in Ovid, 'sub inguine' (10.715), and in Golding, 'in his cods' (10.839; i.e. testicles, OED, 'cod, *n*.1', 4a, 'not in polite use'). Shakespeare is less blunt than Golding but leaves the word to resonate at the end of the stanza. In *Aminta's Dale* (1592) Abraham Fraunce links the location of the wound to the fertility myth that underlies the story (especially in Spenser's version in *The Faerie Queene*): 'by Adonis is meant the sun; by Venus, the upper hemisphere of the earth (as by Proserpina the lower); by the boar, winter; by the death of Adonis, the absence of the sun for the six wintry months; all which time, the earth lamenteth: Adonis is wounded in those parts, which are the instruments of propagation: for, in winter the sun seemeth impotent, and the earth barren: neither that being able to get, nor this to bear either fruit or flowers' (sig. M3v).

1119–20 **never did he bless | My youth with his** Venus complains that she never experienced Adonis' youth completely, presumably because they never had sex. She balances 'my youth' with 'his', but the equation is false, since youth is not so fleeting to an immortal. Roe (1992: 135) sees the argument of Sonnets 1–17 recurring here again, i.e. 'bestow his likeness on me in the form of a child', which discovers a maternal motive in Venus (on which, see l. 875 and note). More likely the blessing is simply in the form of love, as in the 8th song of *Astrophil and Stella*, 5–8: 'Astrophil with Stella sweet, | Did for mutual comfort meet, | Both within themselves oppressed, | But each in the other blessed'.

1120 **the more am I accursed** I am all the more cursed as a result.

1121–2 **With . . . blood** Collatine does something similar in *Lucrece*, ll. 1774–5.

1121 **With this** at that moment; having said these words. See l. 25 and note.

1125 **heavy tale** sad, serious story.

1127 **coffer-lids** eye-lids, imagined as the lids of chests. Typically in Shakespeare these contain money, except in *Pericles* (3.1, 3.4)

Ne'er saw the beauteous livery that he wore;
Witness the entertainment that he gave.
  If he did see his face, why then I know,
  He thought to kiss him, and hath killed him so.   1110

''Tis true, 'tis true, thus was Adonis slain!
He ran upon the boar with his sharp spear,
Who did not whet his teeth at him again,
But by a kiss thought to persuade him there;
  And nuzzling in his flank, the loving swine   1115
  Sheathed unaware the tusk in his soft groin.

'Had I been toothed like him, I must confess,
With kissing him I should have killed him first;
But he is dead, and never did he bless
My youth with his; the more am I accursed.'   1120
  With this she falleth in the place she stood,
  And stains her face with his congealèd blood.

She looks upon his lips, and they are pale;
She takes him by the hand, and that is cold;
She whispers in his ears a heavy tale,   1125
As if they heard the woeful words she told.
  She lifts the coffer-lids that close his eyes,
  Where lo, two lamps burnt out in darkness lies.

Two glasses where herself herself beheld
A thousand times, and now no more reflect,   1130
Their virtue lost, wherein they late excelled,
And every beauty robbed of his effect;
  'Wonder of time,' quoth she, 'this is my spite,
  That thou being dead, the day should yet be light.

where the 'coffer' is Thaisa's (presumably improvised) coffin (for which sense, see OED 3; '*obs.*' and no citation after 1555).

1128 *lies* singular verb for plural (see l. 517 and note), completing the rhyme.

1129 *glasses* i.e. Adonis' eyes acting as mirrors.
herself herself On reflexive pronouns, see l. 159 and note.

1130 *and* and which.

1131 *virtue* power.
late until recently.

1132 *every beauty. . . effect* all their beautiful characteristics have lost their outward manifestation (OED[3] 'effect, *n.*', 4a; as suggested by Burrow 2002: 233). However, 'effect' could be glossed as 'efficacy' or 'effectiveness', or the line could mean that these beauties are simply no longer present (OED[3], 1a, 'The state or fact of being operative or in force').

1133 *Wonder of time* (i) marvel for all eternity, but more likely (ii) wonder of the world; see l. 759 and note. Francis Bacon's *Advancement of Learning* (1605) combines the two senses: 'Alexander the Great, and Caesar the dictator mentioned before, but now in fit place to be resumed, of whose virtues and acts in war, there needs no note or recital, having been the wonders of time in that kind' (sig. K1v).
this is my spite the thing which particularly seems to taunt (or hurt) me is.

1135–6 **prophesy. . . hereafter** Venus proclaims the story to be exemplary and to set a premise for all time. Aetiology is a feature of many stories in the *Metamorphoses* and in the epyllion tradition (as in *Hero and Leander*, ll. 386–484). Some of the things she promises have been evident earlier in *Venus and Adonis*, and the young man himself seems suspicious of love because it is already as she describes. Ovid has equivalents for the goddess' somewhat empty gesture, as when Apollo wears a laurel wreath in memory of Daphne (*Metamorphoses*, 1.557–65), and turns Hyacinthus into a flower (10.205–16).

1137–8 **It. . . end** The ideas are proverbial (Dent L510, 'love is never without jealousy'; L513, 'love is sweet in the beginning but sour in the ending').

1137 **waited on with** attended by.
jealousy As well as the suspicion, envy and possessiveness suggested by the word today, it also carried the sense of 'anger' (OED 1).

1138 **unsavoury** unpleasant.

1139 **Ne'er settled equally, but high or low** never settling into equilibrium; this might suggest love never arising (i) between social equals, or (ii) between those who love with equal intensity (both suggested by Roe 1992: 136).

1140 **That** so that.

1142 **Bud, and be blasted, in a breathing while** Bring forth flower-buds, and then wither (OED 'blast, *v*.', 7) in the time it takes to take a breath. The OED equates 'breathing-while' with 'breathing-space', i.e. a period of relief in which breathing is possible. However, rapidity is clearly the issue here, as it may be at *Richard III*, 1.3.60, where the King 'cannot be quiet scarce a breathing-while'.

1143 **o'er-strawed** strewn over, covered. This is an alternative spelling of 'overstrew', kept here for the rhyme with 'fraud'. The sense is most likely culinary, a sprinkle of sugar masking poison's taste; Roe, though, thinks it evokes an animal trap, with grasses covering a pit (1992: 136).

1144 **sweets** (i) sweet things to eat (OED *n*. 1b); or (ii) more generally, delightful things (OED 3a). See *Astrophil and Stella*, 79.1–2: 'Sweet kiss, thy sweets I fain would sweetly indite [i.e. express in poetic form], | Which even of sweetness sweetest sweetener art'.
the truest sight the most accurate and discerning vision.

1146 **Strike the wise dumb, and teach the fool to speak** The line combines two proverbs: (i) Dent L165, 'whom we love best to them we say least', for which see also Sonnet 23.13; and (ii) Dent L522, 'love makes men orators', for which see *Hero and Leander*, l. 556: 'Love always makes those eloquent that have it'.

1147 **sparing** abstemious.
too full of riot excessively committed to debauchery (OED³ 'riot, *n*.', 2a).

1148 **Teaching decrepit age to tread the measures** making infirm old people perform dance steps (OED³, 'measure, *n*.', 15a).

1149 **staring** 'looking fixedly with wide open eyes' (OED 1a), but suggesting OED 1b, 'frantic, wild', and perhaps boldness too (Roe 1992: 136, Burrow 2002: 234). Compare *King John*, 4.3.49: 'wall-eyed wrath or staring rage'.
ruffian disyllabic here.
in quiet peaceful.

1150 **Pluck down** overthrow. For the Biblical, ominous edge to 'pluck down', see Numbers 33:52: 'Ye shall then drive out all the inhabitants of the land before you, and destroy all their pictures, and break asunder all their images of metal, and pluck down all their high places'. On 'pluck', see l. 30 and note.

1151 **silly** feebly; see 467–8n.

1153 **where is** where there is.

1157 **Perverse** obstinate (OED³ 3); see *Romeo and Juliet*, 2.2.95–6: 'Or if thou thinkest I am too quickly won, | I'll frown and be perverse, and say thee nay'. Other meanings of 'perverse', e.g. OED³ 1a ('contrary, fickle, irrational') also create the necessary contrast.
toward willing, compliant (cited at OED 'toward, *adj.* and *adv*.', 4a).

1158 **Put** (It shall) change. The idea that love makes cowards dangerous is proverbial (Dent D216, 'despair (love) makes cowards courageous'). Compare *Lucrece*, ll. 271–3.

1160 **sire** father; compare ll. 764–6.

1161 **servile** See l. 112 and note, and 'slave', l. 102. This word denotes a more slavish state than 'subject'.
discontents bad moods (i.e. lovers are slaves to these), rather than malcontented people (OED³ 2b).

1162 **combustious** inflammable, liable to catch fire (only OED citation for sense 2; EEBO-TCP corroborates this).

1163 **Sith** since, because.
in his prime i.e. in Adonis' prime.

'Since thou art dead, lo here I prophesy: 1135
Sorrow on love hereafter shall attend;
It shall be waited on with jealousy,
Find sweet beginning, but unsavoury end;
   Ne'er settled equally, but high or low,
   That all love's pleasure shall not match his woe.   1140

'It shall be fickle, false, and full of fraud,
Bud, and be blasted, in a breathing while,
The bottom poison, and the top o'er-strawed
With sweets that shall the truest sight beguile.
   The strongest body shall it make most weak,   1145
   Strike the wise dumb, and teach the fool to speak.

'It shall be sparing and too full of riot,
Teaching decrepit age to tread the measures;
The staring ruffian shall it keep in quiet,
Pluck down the rich, enrich the poor with treasures.   1150
   It shall be raging mad and silly mild,
   Make the young old, the old become a child.

'It shall suspect where is no cause of fear;
It shall not fear where it should most mistrust;
It shall be merciful and too severe,   1155
And most deceiving, when it seems most just.
   Perverse it shall be, where it shows most toward,
   Put fear to valour, courage to the coward.

'It shall be cause of war and dire events,
And set dissension 'twixt the son and sire;   1160
Subject and servile to all discontents,
As dry combustious matter is to fire.
   Sith in his prime death doth my love destroy,
   They that love best, their loves shall not enjoy.'

By this the boy that by her side lay killed   1165
Was melted like a vapour from her sight,

1165 **By this** 'at that moment', but the hint of causation ('as a result of this') is significant (see l. 175 and note).

1166 **melted like a vapour** disappeared into the air like steam. For melt, see l. 144 and note. The phrase's resonance is suggested by its appearance in a prayer at the end of Jean Calvin's *Lectures or Daily Sermons* (1578): 'but rather always that we may be attentive unto thy providence: that we may know not only that our life doth hang by a thread, but that it is like a vapour vanishing away' (F3v). The insubstantiality of the metamorphosis and the flower that results is a key note in Ovid, *Metamorphoses*, 10.736–8; Golding, 10.860–3: 'Howbeit the use of them is short. | For why the leaves do hang so loose through lightness in such sort, | As that the winds that all things pierce, with every little blast | Do shake them off and shed them so as that they cannot last'.

1168 **A purple flower. . . chequered with white**
The red and white duality appears for the
last time (see l. 10 and note; and l. 1 and
note on purple), with the flower's mottled
('chequered') combination of colours matching Adonis' blood-spattered white cheek.
flower monosyllabic here.

1171 **new-sprung** Roe takes this to mean that the
flower is an entirely new creation (1992:
137), but a more straightforward sense,
'recently sprung', is available.
flower monosyllabic here.

1172 **Adonis'** said with three syllables; see l. 180
and note.
breath hints at the traditional name of the
flower, 'anemone', which means 'wind-
flower', and Ovid notes the appropriateness
of a flower which loses its petals all too
quickly in the wind (see l. 1166 and note).
Shakespeare does not name it.

1174 **reft** taken away.

1175 **crops** gathers the flower by cutting the stalk;
see l. 946 and note.
breach the broken-off edge of the stalk
(but see l. 1066, where the word is used of
Adonis' wound).

1176 **which she compares to tears** In the
Metamorphoses (10.499–500; Golding,
10.572), when Adonis' mother Myrrha is
changed into a tree, her sap is a relic of her
tears: 'Although that she | Together with her
former shape her senses all did lose, | Yet
weepeth she, and from her tree warm drops
do softly ooze'.

1177 **flower** monosyllabic here.
guise manner, style (OED 1a). Adonis used
to weep a lot, she claims.

1178 **issue** (i) offspring (see l. 875 and note, and
Sonnet 13.8); perhaps (ii) outcome; the
word describes the flower.
sweet-smelling not hyphenated in Q.

1180 **To grow. . . desire** This may mean 'he
wanted to keep himself for himself', with an
accusation of narcissism. However, the tone
here is less negative than at l. 166 (see note);
perhaps Venus now accepts, to some degree,
Adonis' wish to mature on his own terms.

1182 **blood** progeny, bloodline.

1184 **next of blood** next of kin.

1185 **Lo** See l. 194 and note.
cradle The final flourish of a maternity sub-
text that has recurred several times (see l.
875 and note).

1187–8 **There shall not. . . flower** the poem's last
kiss, and its last intersection with the *Basia*,
on which see 16n.

1187–8 **hour. . . flower** almost certainly monosyllabic. Spelling offers some corroboration,
in that Q has 'houre. . . floure' here, and
the only disyllabic instance ('flower', l. 8) is
'flower' in Q, whereas other clearly monosyllabic instances of the singular (ll. 1056,
1168, 1171, 1177) are 'floure' in Q. In *Venus
and Adonis* elsewhere 'hour' is always monosyllabic. On the rhyme, compare ll. 65–66n,
and 944–946n.

1189 **hies** hurries; see l. 3 and note. The poem
ends as it began.

1190 **silver doves** Venus' chariot was traditionally
pulled by birds (especially swans or doves).
See Thomas Lodge, *Scilla's Metamorphosis*:
'No sooner from her reverent lips were past
| Those latter lines, but mounting in the east,
| Fair Venus in her ivory coach did haste, |
And toward those pensive dames, her course
addressed; | Her doves so plied their waving
wings with flight, | That straight the sacred
goddess came in sight' (sig. C1r); also Thomas
Watson's *Hekatompathia* for silver doves in a
poem about Venus, 4.11–12: 'Then will I
say, the Rose of flowers is best, | And silver
Doves for birds excel the rest' (sig. A2v).

1190–2 **And. . . conveyed** Q has commas at the ends
of ll. 1190 and 1191 and one after 'chariot'
in l. 1192. It is difficult to repunctuate in a
way that captures (i) that 'mounted through
the empty skies | In her light chariot' is best
read as a subordinate clause depicting the
manner in which Venus is 'conveyed', and
(ii) the speed of motion, while (iii) allowing for the ambiguity in syntax ('mounted'
could be read as a main verb) still to function.
The solution here, to omit all three commas,
retains fluidity of movement and syntax.

1191 **mounted** flown upwards; compare l. 596 and
note.

1193 **Paphos** in Cyprus, the mythical birthplace
and home of Venus.

1194 **Means to immure herself** plans to hide away;
literally, to wall herself in. The earliest citation for 'immure' in OED is from 1583, for
the pertinent 3, '*transf.* and *fig.* To enclose'
etc. There is closure in her retreat from the
world, but it not clear that she will do what
she 'means' to do.

And in his blood that on the ground lay spilled
A purple flower sprung up, chequered with white,
   Resembling well his pale cheeks and the blood
   Which in round drops upon their whiteness stood.   1170

She bows her head, the new-sprung flower to smell,
Comparing it to her Adonis' breath,
And says within her bosom it shall dwell,
Since he himself is reft from her by death.
   She crops the stalk, and in the breach appears   1175
   Green-dropping sap, which she compares to tears.

'Poor flower,' quoth she, 'this was thy father's guise,
Sweet issue of a more sweet-smelling sire,
For every little grief to wet his eyes.
To grow unto himself was his desire,   1180
   And so 'tis thine, but know it is as good
   To wither in my breast, as in his blood.

'Here was thy father's bed, here in my breast;
Thou art the next of blood, and 'tis thy right.
Lo, in this hollow cradle take thy rest,   1185
My throbbing heart shall rock thee day and night;
   There shall not be one minute in an hour
   Wherein I will not kiss my sweet love's flower.'

Thus weary of the world, away she hies,
And yokes her silver doves, by whose swift aid   1190
Their mistress mounted through the empty skies
In her light chariot quickly is conveyed,
   Holding their course to Paphos, where their queen
   Means to immure herself, and not be seen.

Lucrece

Text, publication and reception

The first quarto edition of *Lucrece*, printed by Richard Field in 1594, has the one-word title adopted here. While the running-titles give the poem its more familiar title, *The Rape of Lucrece*, the title-page is at least as likely to have met with the author's approval. On 9 May 1594 a work entitled 'The Ravishment of Lucrece' was entered in the Stationers' Register (Arber 1875–94, ii.648), with copyright given to John Harrison. In June of the same year, Richard Field signed over the copyright of *Venus and Adonis* to Harrison (on Field, see the *Venus* headnote). So it seems very likely that in summer 1594 *Lucrece* and Q2 of *Venus and Adonis* were published in close proximity, with similar title-pages. The name-only title enhances that similarity. Both works were printed by Field; such collaborations and manoeuvres around the assignment of copyright were common practice among Elizabethan printers, who distributed risk and opportunity in complex patterns.

The work is dedicated, as was *Venus and Adonis*, to Henry Wriothesley, the Earl of Southampton. The circumstances a year later were somewhat different from those described in the *Venus* headnote. Shakespeare's address is less tentative, so it seems reasonable to infer a positive reception for his earlier poem; and in the case of *Lucrece* there is no theory of a thematic link between the poem and its dedicatee's life. One set of circumstances does unite *Lucrece* and *Venus and Adonis*, which is the continued closure of the theatres due to plague. This is alluded to in the poem (see 1479n).

Shakespeare's relationship with Field and the prestigious contact with Southampton make it very likely that Q was authorised. The text requires very little verbal emendation, with a few challenging readings (e.g. ll. 639, 1544, 1680), which in this edition are retained, and only one case where we come close to proposing a substantive change (from 'to this night' to 'too this night', l. 485) to usual editorial practice. Field makes a greater effort to produce a visually impressive text for *Lucrece* than he did for *Venus and Adonis*, with not entirely consistent results: for example, names and places are generally capitalised. Duncan-Jones and Woudhuysen (2007) make the case that this effort in presentation could well have had authorial input, and at least tacit consent; nevertheless, we have not preserved these effects in our modernised text. We have made a similar decision in relation to the double inverted commas marking *sententiae* at thirteen points in the text; see 87–8n.

In the course of printing Q the text was corrected. These press variants appear to result from a partial proofreading of the sheets as they emerged from the presses. There are corrections only on inner formes of gatherings B and H, and the outer formes of C, D, I, K and M. This may reflect a lack of trust in one compositor; or it may reflect the limited opportunity or stamina of the proofreader. As was normal practice, the existence of corrected sheets did not mean that uncorrected sheets were destroyed, and surviving copies of Q *Lucrece* are sometimes corrected to varying degrees. Nevertheless it is convenient in the notes to distinguish between 'Qc' (corrected) and 'Qu' (uncorrected) at those points, even though this does not denote a stable pair of categories.

The press corrections are sometimes perceptive adjustments (two of which are accepted in our text), and sometimes unnecessary interventions where poetic effects have led to unusual constructions. For this reason it seems very unlikely that the corrections were made by Shakespeare himself. See the notes on ll. 24, 31, 50, 125, 126, 396, 1118, 1182, 1335, 1350, 1774, 1776, 1832 for details of corrected and uncorrected versions (see Connor 2012).

Reception

Lucrece was not as popular in print as *Venus and Adonis*, but there were eight editions up to 1632. After the first, they were all in octavo format, but (as with *Venus and Adonis* from Q3 onwards) we follow the convention of continuing the naming sequence Q2, Q3, etc. Field only printed the first: Q2 (1598) was printed by Peter Short, Q3–4 (both 1600) by John Harrison Jr (the publisher's son) and Q5 (1607) by Nicholas Okes. Harrison kept copyright until 1 March 1614 (working on *Lucrece* with various printers), when it was assigned to Roger Jackson, who is responsible for Q6 onwards.

The later editions do not provide many significant alternative readings, but are mentioned in the notes on ll. 19, 21, 48, 134–6, 354, 639, 684, 782, 1661, 1680, 1832. The most significant is Jackson's first edition (Q6, 1616), which is the earliest to have *The Rape of Lucrece* and Shakespeare's name on the title-page. With evident (though not persuasive) efforts to revise the text, notes and a table of contents, it appears to be a concerted effort to reinvigorate interest in buying Shakespeare's poem (see Duncan-Jones 2001b).

It is not always clear whether the frequent allusions to the story of Lucrece in literature post-1594 have anything to do with Shakespeare's poem. Nonetheless it is certain that, like *Venus and Adonis*, it caused an immediate literary response, and there are clear signs of its impact. In Michael Drayton's *Matilda* (1594), Lucrece is described as 'Lately revived to live another age, | And here arrived to tell of Tarquin's wrong, | Her chaste denial, and the Tyrant's rage' (sig. B2r). In the same year, a commendatory poem by Hadrian Dorrell (possibly the author of the whole work; possibly a pseudonym) in *Willobie His Avisa* mentions the author's name: 'Though Collatine have dearly bought, | To high renown, a lasting life, | And found, that most in vain have sought, | To have a Fair, and Constant wife, | Yet Tarquin plucked his glistering grape, | And Shakespeare paints poor Lucrece' rape' (A4r).

Lucrece was evidently thought of in conjunction or contrast with *Venus and Adonis*. Gabriel Harvey's comment on 'the younger sort' preferring the latter (see *Venus* headnote) had 'the wiser sort' preferring the former (and *Hamlet*). Both poems are excerpted in anthologies such as John Bodenham's *Belvedere* (1600) and Robert Allott's *England's Parnassus* (1600), but *Lucrece* more so. The two are sharply combined in John Lane's *Tom Tell-Troth's Message* (1600), where the author relates 'lewd lechery': 'When chaste Adonis came to man's estate, | Venus straight courted him with many a wile; | Lucrece once seen, straight Tarquin laid a bait, | With foul incest her body to defile: | Thus men by women, women wronged by men, | Give matter still unto my plaintive pen' (F2r).

The tone of this early response is not always so serious. Robert Greene's *Honourable History of Friar Bacon and Friar Bungay* (1594) uses Lucrece as an exemplar of allure: 'How beauty played the housewife, how this girl | Like Lucrece laid her fingers to the work, | Thou wouldst with Tarquin hazard Rome and all, | To win the lovely maid of Fresingfield' (A4r). Nor is it always at all in tune with Shakespeare's emphasis: in the anonymous *Fancy's Ague-Fits, or Beauty's Nettle-Bed* (1599), an eclectic essay on the topic of love opines that 'Virtue, beauty, and honesty are the true allurers of love, and therefore Tarquin was not so much moved with the beauty of Lucrece as her chastity and honest demeanour, finding her well exercised and busied in her house, not idle and slothful as he had done many other' (D4r–v). This is, however, one of many cases where it is unclear whether an author had Shakespeare's poem in mind (and see 8n).

There were two significant retellings of the whole story within Shakespeare's lifetime. One was Thomas Middleton's *The Ghost of Lucrece* (1600), in which the spectral speaker rails against Tarquin in a way that is more closely affiliated to the female complaint tradition (see *A Lover's Complaint*, headnote) than *Lucrece*. Thomas Heywood's play *The Rape of Lucrece* (1608) presented the story for the popular audience at the Red Bull theatre. He expanded the Roman framework, giving more room for blaming Collatine, filling out the characterisation of Brutus, and adding other Roman lords including Publius Valerius (who is mentioned in the Argument but nowhere else), who sings a number of comic songs. The tone of the play is far more varied than that of Shakespeare's poem.

The legacy of *Lucrece* in Shakespeare's work is most palpable in two memories of Tarquin's silent, threatening entry to commit a terrible act. One is Macbeth's (cited in 162–8n), the other is Iachimo's, in *Cymbeline* (cited in 318n). The story's political import matters to Shakespeare's Romans, as when Brutus acknowledges his ancestor in *Julius Caesar*, 2.1.52–4: 'Shall Rome stand under one man's awe? What, Rome? | My ancestors did from the streets of Rome | The Tarquin drive, when he was called a king'.

As with *Venus and Adonis*, though less fittingly, manuscript quotations show an inclination towards the erotic. The lines where Lucrece's body is described most intimately are the only ones appearing twice in the Catalogue of English Literary Manuscripts (see 386–413n), though it is worth noting that these manuscripts are from the mid-seventeenth century, and may reflect quite different circumstances from the initial impact described above. See also the notes on ll. 365–71, 419–20, 869–82, 897–924, 1086–7 and 1330. The last is one of the earliest manuscript citations, in William Scott's *Model of Poesy* (1599). This manuscript discussion of poetics contains some of the earliest approving discussion of Shakespeare and *Lucrece* earns particular praise (ed. Alexander 2013: 12, 17, 41, 53).

Sources and contexts

The poem's two principal sources are the Roman authors Ovid and Livy. In the second book of his *Fasti* Ovid tells the story of Lucretia. Like the other stories in that epic-scale work, it illustrates the origins of a Roman festival, in this case the Regifugium (flight of the king), celebrated on 24 February. This context is emphasised at the beginning and end of the story, but the narrative itself draws out the emotion and the violence, and courts the erotic possibilities, which all feature in Shakespeare's version. Livy tells the story of Lucretia as part of his history of Rome. Writing in the reign of Augustus, Livy lauded the virtues of Rome's Republican past, and the depravity of the Tarquins was thus an important theme; Lucretia was one of a number of exemplars of Rome's preference for honour above all things. Livy's version, thus, more than Ovid's, focused on the political implications of the story.

The two were very likely to have been united in the experience of readers of the *Fasti* in Shakespeare's time, of whom Shakespeare himself was probably one. Classical texts were printed with commentaries, and one frequently present commentary was that of Paulo Marso (Paulus Marsus), first printed in 1482. Ann Moss points out its pedagogical purpose (1982: 17–18); Livy is quoted at length for the purpose of comparison throughout the Lucretia section. There was no translation of the *Fasti* in Shakespeare's time. The first, by John Gower, dates from 1640, and the pertinent section is printed in Appendix 2. The first full English translation of Livy was also still awaited, but came sooner; Philemon Holland's version appeared in 1600. However, William Painter had translated the Lucretia story in 1566 as part of a collection of prose fictions, and this version, also in Appendix 2, was known to Shakespeare.

Determining Shakespeare's precise debts is difficult because of the many interlocking strands of the literary tradition, but it seems best to take it that the 'graver labour' of *Lucrece* took in both Ovid and Livy. The notes record Shakespeare's fluctuating affinities with both, and record the importance of other versions of the story. One of these was Chaucer's *Legend of Good Women*, but there is barely anything to distinguish this from, for example, the version of the story in Gower's *Confessio Amantis*, in the background of *Lucrece*. The Christian tradition is dominated by St Augustine, who went against the grain of what he saw as a tradition tending to exonerate Lucrece. He argued that she was sinful either by committing suicide or adultery: if she was truly guiltless in the rape, then her suicide was unnecessary (see *The City of God*: 28–31; Donaldson 1982: 21–39). One important strand is a tradition in the visual arts that included high art (Titian, for the moment of violence; Cranach, for an extreme case of the tendency to feature Lucrece's nudity; see Donaldson 1982: 15–20) but also many manifestations in everyday decoration around Elizabethan London. The publisher Thomas Purfoot used images of Lucretia to identify his books: in the same year as *Lucrece* it appears on the title-page of Nicholas Malby's *Remedies for the Diseases in Horses* (1594). Shakespeare alludes to something similar when Malvolio recognises Olivia's seal in *Twelfth Night*, 2.5.90–1: 'the impressure her Lucrece, with which she uses to seal: 'tis my lady'.

One pressure point for considering the sources of the poem is the Argument. Its authorship is uncertain. The case against it being Shakespearean is that it presents the story with different emphasis and with a broader political framework. In that respect it most resembles Livy (including names, such as that of Publius Valerius, who is unmentioned in the poem), and could well result from someone consulting Painter's version or remembering the outline of the story. On the other hand, Shakespeare could well have opted himself to give his poem, which has a swift beginning and a very compact ending, a fuller frame. Some verbal links, such as the key word 'consent' used at pivotal moments (Arg.21, Arg.24; l. 1854), give greater weight to this possibility.

Shakespeare departs from all sources in elaborating at great length on the thoughts and the speech of both Lucrece and Tarquin. These dominate the poem, whereas the political context is handled much more briefly. Lucrece's appeal to Tarquin and his response (ll. 568–672) are the kind of expansion one might expect as a brief illustrative narrative becomes a dramatic minor epic. The long sections devoted principally to his weighing up of reasons for and against gratifying his lust (ll. 127–441), and her reaction to her violation (ll. 743–1582), however, are more striking additions. They do a great deal to unfold tragic psychology, but they create different kinds of risk in the reception of the poem: that Tarquin's point of view may infiltrate the reader's; and that Lucrece's gruelling exposition of hers may make readers less rather than more sympathetic.

The description of the painting of the Trojan War in Lucrece's house is another addition to the primary sources, but it has an extensive literary tradition behind it, out of which two cases stand out. In Virgil's *Aeneid*, 1.453–93, Aeneas views a temple frieze depicting the Trojan War; he is then able to tell more of the story, including key episodes (Sinon; the death of Priam), which takes up the whole of Book 2. Nearer in time to *Lucrece*, Samuel Daniel's *Complaint of Rosamond* (1592) features a casket depicting mythical scenes 'so rare, that art did seem to strive with nature, | T'express the cunning workman's curious thought'. The complaint tradition, as well as exemplary historical stories such as were featured in the various editions of *The Mirror for Magistrates* (from 1559 onwards; by William Baldwin et al.), are key generic contexts within Elizabethan writing.

Style and rhetoric

The pattern here, of classical sources and more recent work both contributing to *Lucrece*, is borne out in other ways. Duncan-Jones and Woudhuysen (2007: 16) compare the number of words with three or more syllables in *Lucrece* (640) and *Venus and Adonis* (300); even allowing for the greater length of the later poem, it has a more ornate, Latinate vocabulary. Nonetheless the affinity between the two poems (as noted in the *Venus* headnote) is manifest in a great deal of shared lexis. When this pertains to quasi-Petrarchist blazon and courtship, or to the erotic chase, then this results in some connections that do not fit straightforwardly into the elevated tragedy of *Lucrece*.

Although its language is not as persistently fashionable as that of *Venus and Adonis*, *Lucrece* also includes many words shared with Shakespeare's earlier plays, especially the early histories. It has more in common with the tragedies and Roman plays, however, in keeping with its subject matter. It also shows many signs of the linguistic energy of the early 1590s, with suggestive links with innovative uses of words by popular authors such as Robert Greene and Thomas Lodge, who are chroniclers of the world of crime.

Shakespeare did not repeat his use of the six-line stanza of *Venus and Adonis*. Instead he opted for a seven-line 'Rhyme Royal' stanza form rhyming *ababbcc*. This form had a more prominent and prestigious heritage, as described by Puttenham's *Art of English Poesy* (1589): 'the fourth ['proportion' of a 'staff', i.e. stanza] is in seven verses, and is the chief of our ancient proportions used by any rhymer writing anything of historical or grave poem, as ye may see in Chaucer and Lydgate, th'one writing the loves of Troilus and Cressida, th'other of the fall of Princes' (sig. M1v). The form lends itself to more complex organisations of syntax and thought, so there are fewer straightforward parallels (see Lyne 2014).

Many of the rhetorical features of *Venus and Adonis* are evident in *Lucrece* as well. There are many figures of repetition (*antanaclasis, epistrophe, pleonasm, polyptoton*) and excess (hyperbole; use of numbers). There are some extended and elaborated metaphors: the figure of the siege appears throughout the poem (see ll. 1, 221, 428–45, 464–83, 720–8, 1170–3, 1366–568). There are also many proverbial phrases. These are reached for in a variety of ways: they are embedded in the narrative voice's observations, in Tarquin's self-justification, and especially in Lucrece's pleas and castigations. The style of the poem becomes most intense and most problematic in the apparent excess of the heroine's rhetoric. It should be acknowledged that Lucrece 'pleads' (l. 544) in a formal sense; that she constructs her long deliberations, accusations and defences, according to the principles of legal argument (see Skinner 2014). Alongside this formality, her repetitions and proverbs can be seen as plangent but dignified, a controlled and deliberate vehicle for her overwhelming feelings.

As the notes attest at various points, the delicacy required in dealing with Lucrece's style is paralleled by a need for subtle judgement elsewhere. A poem on this subject – with its story of sexual violence – might be expected to be scrupulous about many things, such as the question of blame, the eroticisation of the scene, and the political resonance reaching from Rome into Elizabethan England. The last of these, as has been said above, is understated in comparison with all the main sources, except at the very end of the poem. More importantly, it courts difficulty on the other two counts, complicating the question of responsibility, tending towards voyeuristic physical description, sometimes at jarring moments, and ensuring that the reader's experience of the poem is intense and troubling.

LUCRECE.

LONDON.

Printed by Richard Field, for John Harrison, and are
to be sold at the sign of the white greyhound
in Paul's Churchyard. 1594.

Lucrece

Dedication

2–3 **Henry Wriothesley** See headnote. On similarities in tone and diction (probably generic)
between the dedication and one of the 'young
man' sonnets, see Sonnet 26.1n.

5 **dedicate** devote, offer.

without end The phrase is not uncommon, but
the echo of the *Book of Common Prayer* is suggestive: 'Glory be to the father, and to the son: and
to the holy ghost, as it was in the beginning, is
now, and ever shall be: world without end' (ed.
Cummings 2001: 44).

pamphlet The word was used of any short work,
but in the 1590s it particularly suggests (i) a
short printed book without a hard cover (OED³
1b), thus suited to more ephemeral and less
prestigious material, and (ii) a polemical work
(OED³ 2). Shakespeare's only other use of the
noun is set before the era of printing but (also
anachronistically) suggests the latter: *1 Henry
VI*, 3.1.1–7, 'Com'st thou with deep premedi-
tated lines, | With written pamphlets studiously
devised? | Humphrey of Gloucester, if thou canst
accuse, | Or aught intend'st to lay unto my
charge, | Do it without invention, suddenly, | As
I with sudden and extemporal speech | Purpose
to answer what thou canst object'. The distinction between 'pamphlets studiously devised' and
'extempore' suggests another quality: a pamphlet
may be the result of scholarly effort (polemicists
were often thought of as studious). The word
thus sits ambiguously in relation to the idea that
Lucrece fulfils the promise of a 'graver labour' in
the *Venus and Adonis* dedication, though that
possibility remains considerable, and 'pamphlet'
is at least partly a gesture of modesty.

without beginning Primarily, this is a modest
counterweight to a 'love... without end': it suggests a lack of foundation and substance, and no
claim to mastery over time. More specifically, it
may be an acknowledgement (i) that the poem
starts *in medias res*, in the haste of Tarquin's lust,

rather than (as the Argument does) explaining
the political and narrative context; and/or (ii)
that the poem has no preface other than its
Argument, no grand invocation or moral pro-
nouncements.

6 **moiety** part; see Sonnet 46.12.

warrant guarantee; this probably refers to a
favourable reception from Southampton for
Venus and Adonis.

7 **untutored** This parallels 'unpolished' in the
Venus and Adonis dedication: there the word
was ironic because the poem interacts so much
with contemporary poetic fashion; here the
word is ironic because *Lucrece* involves multiple classical sources. As with 'unpolished', this
is a modesty topos that would have been well
understood as such by readers. 'Untutored'
may well be Shakespeare's coinage; see Sonnet
138.3n.

8 **being... yours** i.e. Southampton is part of his
life in every respect, and Shakespeare is devoted
to him. The syntax is difficult, in that the subject of 'being' seems to be 'you' extracted from
'yours', and the subject of 'devoted' needs to
be 'I', but neither of these follows naturally in
English.

8–9 **show greater** produce a poem which is (i) better
and/or (ii) longer; or perhaps a greater achievement more generally.

9 **meantime** for the present.

bound (i) owed (OED *adj*.2 7a); (ii) bound as
an apprentice is to a master (7b); (iii) on its way
(OED *adj*.1, 2). In addition, Duncan-Jones and
Woudhuysen pick up a printing-related sense,
looking back to 'pamphlet' (2007: 233): perhaps
the implication is that the earl will of course
receive a bound copy.

11 **Your Lordship's... duty** The sign-off in the
Venus and Adonis dedication is very similar:
'Your Honour's in all duty'.

TO THE RIGHT
HONOURABLE HENRY
Wriothesley, Earl of Southampton,
and Baron of Titchfield.

The love I dedicate to your Lordship is without end, whereof this pamphlet without beginning is but a superfluous moiety. The warrant I have of your honourable disposition, not the worth of my untutored lines, makes it assured of acceptance. What I have done is yours, what I have to do is yours, being part in all I have, devoted yours. Were my worth greater, my duty would show greater; meantime, as it is, it is bound to your Lordship, to whom I wish long life still lengthened with all happiness.

Your Lordship's in all duty, William Shakespeare.

Argument

ARGUMENT summary.

1 **Lucius Tarquinius** King of Rome from *c.* 534 to 509 BCE. The story of his reign is told in Livy, 1.48–9.

Superbus the *cognomen* (rendered here as 'surnamed') of Lucius Tarquinius, earned when he took the throne in the way described here. See 'proud issue', l. 37 and note.

2 **Servius Tullius** King of Rome *c.* 578 to 535 BCE, whose daughter Tullia, according to Livy, conspired with her husband Lucius Tarquinius to kill her father, and drove over his corpse in her chariot (1.47).

3 **requiring** asking.

staying waiting.

suffrages votes; the ancient Roman monarchy was elective, though the consent of the people was often sought in a public and ritualised way. Shakespeare features the word elsewhere as something characteristic of Roman politics. Titus refers to the process in *Titus Andronicus*, 4.3.18–20, 'Ah, Rome! Well, well; I made thee miserable | What time I threw the people's suffrages | On him that thus doth tyrannise o'er me'; Coriolanus shies away from something similar (though in a Republican setting) in *Coriolanus*, 2.2.136–9, ' Let me o'erleap that custom; for I cannot | Put on the gown, stand naked, and entreat them | For my wounds' sake to give their suffrage. Please you | That I may pass this doing'.

possessed himself took possession (OED³ 9c, for this reflexive usage).

4 **Ardea** the capital of the Rutuli, one of the Italic peoples; it was situated on the coast twenty-five miles south of Rome.

5–6 **Sextus Tarquinius** the son of Lucius Tarquinius who gained notoriety by betraying the Gabii (see 1501–68n). In the poem he is always known as Tarquin.

7 **Collatinus** the son of Tarquinius Priscus, King of Rome before Servius Tullius. Q's spellings of the name 'Collatinus' and the place 'Collatium' always have one 'l', but the spelling chosen here is generally accepted as correct. The Latin form of his name appears in the poem five times (ll. 218, 232, 256, 829, 1817), the anglicised form 'Collatine' twenty-four times.

Lucretia This Latin form of her name appears twice in the poem (ll. 317, 510), the anglicised form 'Lucrece' thirty-four times.

8 **pleasant humour** jovial mood.

posted rode quickly; see l. 1 and note.

Rome The men ride to Rome, and the implication is that they see all their wives there; later, however, Lucrece is at Collatium (see Arg. 15 and note). Shakespeare may treat Collatium as part of Rome, or possibly we are meant to assume that the men's journey took in Collatium as well (which fits best with Arg.23). Both are more likely than Lucrece having taken her maids to Rome to spend the evening spinning.

9 **avouched** asserted.

finds a historic present tense, effectively equivalent to the past tense, but perhaps conveying extra vividness here. The historic present is frequently deployed by Roman historians.

11 **several** various.

disports recreations. Shakespeare's only other use of the noun is in *Othello*, 1.3.268–74, where the implication is sexual, but where Othello's language is so ornate that it is not a straightforward guide to usage: 'No, when light-winged toys | Of feathered Cupid seel [i.e. blind] with wanton dullness | My speculative and officed instruments, | That my disports corrupt and taint my business, | Let housewives make a skillet of my helm, | And all indign and base adversities | Make head against my estimation!'.

12 **fame** honour; but in the period fame is often seen as fickle, even to the point that the word can mean 'evil repute, infamy' (OED *n.*1 4). Shakespeare's uses of 'fame' are usually positive, but see *Comedy of Errors*, 3.2.19–20, 'Shame hath a bastard fame, well managed; | Ill deeds are doubled with an evil word'. The word weighs heavily throughout the poem (ll. 20, 53, 106, 1054, 1188, 1202, 1203, 1491, 1638).

Lucrece' the usual possessive form of the name (as at l. 36); in Q there is no apostrophe.

13 **smothering** (i) repress (OED 'smother, *v.*', 2c); (ii) conceal (2b); and in parallel with 'inflamed', (iii) extinguish (as one would put out a fire). OED has this as the earliest citation for (i), but the metaphorical quality, and the closeness to sense (ii), make this an unnecessarily over-specific definition.

for the present for the time being.

14 **privily** privately.

royally splendidly.

15 **lodged** 'receive into one's house for the night' (OED 'lodge, *v.*', 2a).

Collatium A town about nine miles east of Rome, but possibly merged into Rome by Shakespeare (see Arg.8n). The proper name is Collatia, but this is the form preferred in the poem too (ll. 4, 50). On spelling, see Arg.7n.

THE ARGUMENT

Lucius Tarquinius (for his excessive pride surnamed Superbus), after he had caused his own
father-in-law Servius Tullius to be cruelly murdered, and, contrary to the Roman laws and
customs, not requiring or staying for the people's suffrages, had possessed himself of the
kingdom, went, accompanied with his sons and other noblemen of Rome, to besiege Ardea.
During which siege, the principal men of the army meeting one evening at the tent of Sextus   5
Tarquinius the king's son, in their discourses after supper every one commended the virtues of
his own wife, among whom Collatinus extolled the incomparable chastity of his wife Lucretia.
In that pleasant humour they all posted to Rome, and intending by their secret and sudden arrival
to make trial of that which every one had before avouched, only Collatinus finds his wife
(though it were late in the night) spinning amongst her maids. The other ladies were all found   10
dancing and revelling, or in several disports, whereupon the noblemen yielded Collatinus the
victory, and his wife the fame. At that time Sextus Tarquinius, being enflamed with Lucrece'
beauty, yet smothering his passions for the present, departed with the rest back to the camp, from
whence he shortly after privily withdrew himself, and was (according to his estate) royally
entertained and lodged by Lucrece at Collatium. The same night he treacherously stealeth into   15
her chamber, violently ravished her, and early in the morning speedeth away. Lucrece in this
lamentable plight hastily dispatcheth messengers, one to Rome for her father, another to the
camp for Collatine. They came, the one accompanied with Junius Brutus, the other with Publius
Valerius, and finding Lucrece attired in mourning habit, demanded the cause of her sorrow. She,
first taking an oath of them for her revenge, revealed the actor and whole manner of his dealing,   20
and withal suddenly stabbed herself. Which done, with one consent they all vowed to root out
the whole hated family of the Tarquins; and, bearing the dead body to Rome, Brutus acquainted
the people with the doer and manner of the vile deed, with a bitter invective against the tyranny
of the king. Wherewith the people were so moved, that with one consent and a general
acclamation the Tarquins were all exiled, and the state government changed from kings to consuls.   25

15–16 **stealeth. . . ravished. . . speedeth** another
instance of changing tenses, with past and
historic present combined.

17 **one. . . another** In the poem she only sends
one letter, to Collatine (ll. 1331–5); we take
it that her father was with the Roman army,
as he is part of the 'other company', l. 1584.
In Livy Lucrece sends 'nuntium. . . eundem'
(the same messenger, or the same message);
Painter clarifies that there are two messengers,
'a post. . . and another' (1.58.5; Appendix 2).

18 **Junius Brutus** See 1734n.

18–19 **Publius Valerius** He is not mentioned in the
poem, but he is in Livy (1.58.5; see Appendix 2).

19 **habit** clothes; see the 'mourning black' of l.
1585.

20 **taking. . . revenge** extracting a promise from
them that they would avenge her. This concurs with Shakespeare's poem, but not with the
main sources, in having Lucrece obtain the
pledge before revealing the rapist's name (see
1681–98n).

actor perpetrator (OED[3] 3a).

whole manner of his dealing every detail of
what he had done.

21 **withal** moreover (OED *adv.* and *prep.* 1).

one consent The phrase, repeated at Arg.24, is
echoed by the 'consent' of l. 1854 (see note).

22 **bearing. . . Rome** This is the strongest indication
that Collatium and Rome are to be seen as physically separate; see ll. 1850–1, Arg.8 and note.

23 **bitter invective** This is completely missing
from the poem; on the politics of the poem
and the Argument, see headnote.

24 **one consent** See Arg.21n.

25 **state government** the government of the state.
This is the earliest citation for the phrase in
OED[3] 'state, *n.*', C3a. EEBO-TCP corroborates
this, though there are numerous uses in the early
seventeenth century. The earliest of these is from
Livy's *Roman History*, trans. Philemon Holland
(1600): 'he enacted certain laws very popular,
and namely, concerning the appeal from the
Consuls to the people, and the receiving of the
state-government from the said people, as Livius
and Dionysius do witness' (sig. 5P5r). This comes
in the section of the 'Chronology to the History
of Titus Livius' that concerns the consulship of
Brutus and Collatine, so perhaps Holland had
Shakespeare's poem in mind.

1 **besiegèd** the poem starts with a literal siege; see headnote, on the importance of the siege metaphor in the poem.

    Ardea disyllabic; emphasis on the first syllable; compare l. 1332.

    all in post in a great hurry. Painter's version of the story (see Appendix 2) may be the source of this phrase. The poem starts urgently (Roe: '*in medias res*. . . with remarkable economy', 1992: 143). For 'post', see also l. 926 and note.

2 **trustless** untrustworthy, treacherous (OED^3 3); perhaps also distrustful (since Tarquin is motivated by a wish to test Lucrece's reputation; OED^3 1). It is one of forty-seven uses of adjectives ending -*less* (Duncan-Jones and Woudhuysen 2007: 237). This is Shakespeare's only use of 'trustless' (compare 'bateless', l. 9; 'priceless', l. 17; 'wordless', l. 112; 'graceless', l. 246, 'ceaseless', l. 967; 'lightless', ll. 4, 1555, is only used in *Lucrece*). EEBO-TCP suggests that such compounds are uncommon outside Shakespeare as well: no prior instances of 'bateless' and 'wordless' appear, and only one of 'priceless' (also 1594).

    wings. . . desire linked to the hubris of Icarus by Roe (1992: 143), but more evocative of Cupid. Compare *1 Henry VI*, 2.5.15, 'swift-winged with desire', and *3 Henry VI*, 1.1.267, 'winged with desire'. The falseness of desire seems axiomatic (compare l. 642) but other uses of the 'wings of desire' trope in the period suggest the epithet is necessary. In Richard Edwards, *The Paradise of Dainty Devices* (1585), the wings suggest ambition: 'who seeks the way to win renown, | Or flyeth with wings of high desire' (sig. K4r). In a religious context, as in the 1570 *Godly Meditations*, attributed at the time to St Augustine, they can suggest a spiritual elevation: 'being lifted up out of this vale of misery and tears, with the wings of his godly desire, he may fly unto the heavenly kingdom' (sig. M1r).

3 **Lust-breathèd** 'animated or inspired by lust, or breathing lust' (OED 'breathed, *adj.*', 1b); Shakespeare's only use of the compound. OED sees this as a Shakespearean figurative adaptation of OED 1a, 'put into breath', as when animals are 'well-breathed'. Compare *Timon of Athens* 1.1.10–11, 'breathed, as it were, | To an untirable and continuate goodness'.

    host army.

4 **lightless** (i) giving no light; perhaps (ii) smouldering. The **fire** is lust. The phrase is a paradox verging on oxymoron. See 2n on the -*less* suffix, and compare l. 1555.

5 **lurks** The menacing note in the word recurs at ll. 362, 851, 1535, 1537.

    to aspire in order to rise up; looks back (through the Latin *aspiro*, 'breathe') to 'lust-breathèd'. The connection between 'aspire' and 'fire' is seen elsewhere in contemporary poetry. See Richard Stapleton's *The Phoenix Nest* (1593), 'For fancy's flames of fire, | Aspire, | Unto such furious power' (sig. I2v), and one of the shape poems ('the Spire or Taper called Pyramis') in Puttenham's *Art of English Poesy* (1589): 'For to aspire | Like stem of fire | In form of spire' (sig. N2r).

6 **girdle** encircle; Burrow suggests an ironic link between 'girdle' and chastity, in that the term used to denote Tarquin's overwhelming of Lucrece denotes a garment that protects her lower body (2002: 243); the '**flames**' of course suggest lust.

    waist 'Waist' is euphemistic here, and it also puns on the sound of 'waste' (as in destruction). In both respects, compare Sonnet 129.1.

7 **Lucrece** Elsewhere the name is stressed on the first syllable, and perhaps should be here, for emphasis after a caesura. Compare l. 512.

    chaste She is still 'chaste Lucrece' at the very end of the poem (l. 1839) but the definition of the word is tested in between.

8 **Haply. . . unhappily** By chance. . . disastrously (i.e. with 'unhappy' consequences). Livy (1.57.10, 'cum forma. . . castitas incitat', her chastity aroused him along with her beauty) and Ovid (*Fasti*, 2.765, 'verba placent. . . et quod corrumpere non est', 'her words pleased him, and so did the fact that she was incorruptible') both cite Lucrece's incorruptible chastity as part of her attractiveness to Tarquin. See Appendix 2.

    unhappily trisyllabic here, 'unhapp'ly'.

9 **bateless** 'that cannot be "bated" or blunted; unalterably keen' (OED 1; first citation). The metaphor in this line ('**edge. . . keen**') is of a sword, but there may also be a pun on his appetite's lack of appropriate 'bait' (Duncan-Jones and Woudhuysen 2007: 238; Roe 1992: 143). This is Shakespeare's only use of the word; on the -*less* suffix, see 2n.

    keen appetite compare Sonnet 118.1, 'to make our appetites more keen', and the exact phrase in *Merchant of Venice*, 2.6.8–9: 'Who riseth from a feast | With that keen appetite that he sits down?', where lust is clearly denoted by the culinary metaphors.

10 **let** forbear, cease.

LUCRECE

From the besiegèd Ardea all in post,
Borne by the trustless wings of false desire,
Lust-breathèd Tarquin leaves the Roman host,
And to Collatium bears the lightless fire,
Which, in pale embers hid, lurks to aspire   5
    And girdle with embracing flames the waist
    Of Collatine's fair love, Lucrece the chaste.

Haply that name of 'chaste' unhappily set
This bateless edge on his keen appetite,
When Collatine unwisely did not let   10
To praise the clear unmatchèd red and white,
Which triumphed in that sky of his delight,
    Where mortal stars as bright as heaven's beauties
    With pure aspects did him peculiar duties.

For he, the night before, in Tarquin's tent,   15
Unlocked the treasure of his happy state:
What priceless wealth the heavens had him lent

11 *clear* bright (OED *adj.*, *adv.*, and *n.* A1a), morally unsullied (OED 15a); also perhaps famous (OED 5; closest to the meaning of Latin *clarus*). See l. 382.
unmatchèd unrivalled (OED³ 1a), with some play on the appealing contrast between the 'red and white' (though the OED does not allow for this possible meaning, comparable to 'mismatched').
red and white i.e. her complexion. Compare ll. 54–77, 386, 477–83, 1234, 1510–12. Compare also *Venus and Adonis*, l. 10n; *Lucrece* here seems to respond to the earlier poem, and perhaps even to presume that its readers will recognise the connection through its characteristic colours.
12 *triumphed* shone gloriously (see OED 3 'to be in a state of pomp or magnificence'). The word suggests Collatine's boasting; or perhaps Lucrece's beauty is focalised through her husband's pride. Petrarch's *Trionfi*, however, included Lucrece in a 'triumph' of chastity. See Lord Morley's translation, *The Triumphs of Francis Petrarch* (1555): 'Lucretia on the right hand there she stood, | And sweet Penelope so mild of mood. | These twain had broken in pieces small | Love's bow, his darts, arrows and all, | And pulled his wings quite from his back' (sig. F4r).
sky of his delight i.e. the face he loved.

delight a multifaceted word in the poem, 'delight' and its cognates span innocent and guilty pleasures. See ll. 357, 385, 430, 487, 697, 742, 927.
13 *mortal stars* i.e. Lucrece's eyes, contrasted in their mortality (earthly; subject to death) with heaven's stars ('beauties').
14 *aspects* looks (OED 1a); probably stressed on second syllable. In astrology the word denotes 'the relative positions of the heavenly bodies as they appear to an observer on the earth's surface' (OED 4), and so it connects to the 'stars' of l. 13.
peculiar (i) private (OED³ 2a); (ii) perhaps also 'special... distinctive' (OED³ 1a).
duties signs of reverence.
16 *Unlocked the treasure* laid open the treasure-house, or treasure-chest (both OED 3), i.e. revealed private things. Compare ll. 33–5, 132, 280, 1056. The Sonnets explore the sexual connotations of the word, as at 2.6, 20.14 (see note), 52.2, and especially 136.5. See also *Venus and Adonis*, l. 552 and note, and *Cymbeline*, 2.2.41–2, 'I have picked the lock and ta'en | The treasure of her honour'; Iachimo, the speaker, refers to 'our Tarquin' earlier in the scene (2.2.12).
17 *priceless* possibly Shakespeare's coinage (first citation in OED³), and his only use; on the *-less* suffix, see 2n.
lent can but need not denote temporary donation (OED *v.*2, 1 does, OED 2 does not).

18 **possession** This word had legal resonance; Zurcher proposes a significant interplay between the ideas of possession in law, and possession in fact (2010: 169–74).

19 **Reckoning** disyllabic here.

high proud exalted and glorious (with the negative connotation of 'pride' a factor in both cases, see OED³, 'high', *adj.* and *n.2*, A11; and see 37n). Duncan-Jones and Woudhuysen hyphenate (2007: 239). From Q6 onward 'such high proud' became 'so high a', an indication that the double adjective seems to have caused some difficulty to early readers.

rate value, worth.

20 **espousèd to more fame** (i) married to a more famous woman; (ii) more famous.

21 **peer. . . peerless** there is play on 'peer' (a person of high rank, OED³ 3, rather than an equal) and 'peerless' (unrivalled; see 2n on the *-less* suffix; and 'unmatchèd', 11n). Like *Venus and Adonis* (see headnote), *Lucrece* uses rhetorical figures of doubling and expansion (in this case, *polyptoton*). From Q2 onwards 'peer' is changed to 'prince', as if a later hand sought to remove a perceived clumsiness.

23 **possessed** Compare Sonnet 129.9.

decayed mainly suggests a gradual decline (OED *v.* 1a), but can be more abrupt (OED 1b); compare l. 516 and note.

done finished, destroyed (compare *Venus and Adonis*, ll. 197, 749).

24 **As is. . . dew** Shakespeare uses a dew simile elsewhere, but not with the same sense of fleetingness. See *The Taming of the Shrew*, 2.1.172–3: 'I'll say she looks as clear | As morning roses newly washed with dew'; also *2 Henry VI*, 5.2.52–5: 'Tears virginal | Shall be to me even as the dew to fire, | And beauty, that the tyrant oft reclaims, | Shall to my flaming wrath be oil and flax'. For an equivalent simile, see Samuel Daniel's *Delia*, 42.1–4: 'Beauty (sweet Love) is like the morning dew, | Whose short refresh upon the tender green | Cheers for a time, but till the sun doth show, | And straight 'tis gone as it had never been'.

morning Qu; Qc's 'mornings' (i.e., 'morning's') appears to be a press correction. Although 'morning dew' is a stock phrase (as at *Titus Andronicus*, 2.3.201; *A Midsummer Night's Dream*, 4.1.121; *Romeo and Juliet*, 'morning's dew' in this case, 1.1.132), the line of three words premodifying 'dew' is awkward. The change is thus an understandable intervention, but not necessary. As Roe notes, both alternatives sound very similar (1992: 144).

silver i.e., causing a silvery gleam; compare *Venus and Adonis*, l. 855.

melting evaporating (compare *Venus and Adonis*, ll. 982, 1166, and notes.).

25 **Against** [when] exposed to (OED³ 12b, which cites Sonnet 73.3, 'boughs which shake against the cold').

26 **expired** stressed on the first syllable.

date period (of existence; OED³ *n.2*, 1).

ere well begun before it has properly started. Compare 'lent', l. 17 and note.

27 **owner's** primarily Collatine's, but this also suggests a question as to whether Lucrece possesses herself.

28 **fortressed** protected.

world of harms The phrase is unique in Shakespeare, and EEBO-TCP reveals no instance before *Lucrece*.

29 **of itself** by nature, by its own means. For the doubled reflexive pronouns, see 157n.

30 **orator** spokesperson; but 'orator' stands for persuasive words more generally, a pervasive concern in the poem. Compare ll. 268, 563–4, 815.

31 **apology** defence, justification; a technical term in classical and renaissance rhetoric, as in Plato's *Apology of Socrates* and Sidney's *Apology for Poetry*. This makes the press variant 'apologies' in Qc seem all the more like an error.

32 **set forth** The most pressing of a range of possible meanings are 'express in words', (OED³ 'to set forth', under 'set', *v.*), 'exhibit, display' (10), 'praise' (9, compare *Merchant of Venice*, 3.5.87, 90, 'let me praise you. . . I'll set you forth'). However, 'represent in art' (OED³ 6b), 'adorn' (7), 'publish' (a law, 4; a literary work, 5) are all pertinent, especially in the light of 'publisher' in the following line.

singular private (OED 8a) but also special (10), rare (11).

33 **publisher** someone who makes something public; OED 2a 'A person who prepares and issues a book or document to the public' has its first citation from 1579, so it contributes to the resonance here. Compare l. 1852 and note, and 32n.

34 **jewel** as at l. 1191; pronounced disyllabically.

35 **thievish ears** the ears of thieves (carrying through the 'jewel' metaphor, for which compare Sonnet 48.5–8).

In the possession of his beauteous mate;
Reckoning his fortune at such high proud rate
    That kings might be espousèd to more fame,   20
    But king nor peer to such a peerless dame.

O happiness enjoyed but of a few,
And, if possessed, as soon decayed and done
As is the morning silver melting dew
Against the golden splendour of the sun;   25
An expired date, cancelled ere well begun.
    Honour and beauty in the owner's arms
    Are weakly fortressed from a world of harms.

Beauty itself doth of itself persuade
The eyes of men without an orator.   30
What needeth then apology be made
To set forth that which is so singular?
Or why is Collatine the publisher
    Of that rich jewel he should keep unknown
    From thievish ears, because it is his own?   35

Perchance his boast of Lucrece' sovereignty
Suggested this proud issue of a king;
For by our ears our hearts oft tainted be.
Perchance that envy of so rich a thing,
Braving compare, disdainfully did sting   40
    His high-pitched thoughts, that meaner men should vaunt
    That golden hap which their superiors want.

36 **boast** Compare l. 1193, and note.
Lucrece' The possessive is without apostrophe or 's' in Q; but see l. 317.
sovereignty supreme excellence (Schmidt), pre-eminence (Burrow 2002: 245); but see 69n.
37 **Suggested** provoked, tempted (OED 2a).
proud This points back to the last name (*cognomen*) of Tarquin's father, Lucius Tarquinius Superbus (i.e., 'proud'). This resonance adds another aspect to the important set of implications carried by 'proud' and 'pride': sexual vigour, haughtiness, selfish unkindness. See also ll. 19, 298, 432, 437, 438, 662, 705, 712, 864, 944, 1259, 1371, 1449, 1669, 1809, and compare a related set of meanings in *Venus and Adonis*, 14n.
issue offspring.

39 **rich** precious (OED[3] 4a, of material things, 4b, of immaterial); compare *Romeo and Juliet*, 1.5.46, 'Beauty too rich for use, for earth too dear!'.
40 **Braving compare** defying comparison.
sting hurt, provoke; perhaps poison (Duncan-Jones and Woudhuysen 2007: 241, Roe 1992: 145).
41 **high-pitched** lofty, aspiring (first citation for OED[3], 'high-pitched', 1). The 'pitch' is the highest point in a falcon's flight before it swoops (OED[3] 'pitch', n.2, 21a; compare *Venus and Adonis*, l. 551), which suggests the threat Tarquin offers.
that i.e., with the thought that.
42 **hap** fortune, happiness (see l. 8 and note).
want lack, primarily; but for Tarquin to lack Lucrece is to 'want' (i.e. desire) her.

43 **untimely** ill-timed, inappropriate; also at an unnatural, ill-fated time (as in *Richard III*, 1.2.22, 'Prodigious, and untimely brought to light'). Compare ll. 570, 1178, 1675, 1720.

44 **timeless** hasty (as suggested by Duncan-Jones and Woudhuysen 2007: 241, Roe 1992: 145), though this is not listed in OED³. Of the senses found there, 'unseasonable' (2; as suggested also by Schmidt; see 43n) seems pertinent. Shakespeare's uses of the word usually have this sense, as at *3 Henry VI*, 5.6.42, 'orphans for their parents' timeless death'. Burrow's suggestion of 'remembered throughout time' is also useful (2002: 245; compare *Titus Andronicus*, 2.3.265, 'the complot of this timeless tragedy'). See 2n on the *-less* suffix.
    if none of those i.e., if neither the 'boast' (l. 36) nor 'envy' (l. 39) spurred him on.

45 **affairs** business; see especially OED³ 2c, relating to governance (compare *2 Henry VI*, 1.3.154, 'I come to talk of commonwealth affairs'), which sharpens the rebuke.
    state rank, position (Duncan-Jones and Woudhuysen 2007: 241), again with the possibility of evoking his public responsibility.

46 **Neglected all** all forgotten, ignored.
    with swift intent intending to act swiftly (Roe 1992: 145).

47 **coal** used metonymically for the heat of his passion. Since coal is the result of burning, and then cooling, and can then be reignited, it is a suggestive metaphor. Compare *Venus and Adonis*, l. 387.
    liver considered at the time to be the source of desire and other rash emotions. See 48n.

48 **wrapped in repentant cold** This may suggest that rash desire leads to cold repentance (a simpler way of putting it, as in Q3–4 which have 'repentance'), or that desire sometimes hides behind a pose of morality. See *The Tempest*, 4.1.55–6: 'The white cold virgin snow upon my heart | Abates the ardour of my liver'.

49 **spring** The seasonal metaphor opposes the lively 'spring' of desire with the 'cold' of chastity, but the positive connotations of 'spring' are mostly undone by 'hasty'. Compare *Venus and Adonis*, l. 802.
    still always.
    blasts withers (OED 9).

50–2 **arrived. . . strived** When the *-ed* ending comes at the end of a line, scansion does not always help determine whether or not the final syllable is sounded. As with *Venus and Adonis* (see 109–11n) there is good reason to trust the spelling in Q as a guide to pronunciation in such cases. When an *-ed* verb ending is rhymed with a noun or other word that determines its sound, the spelling appears to change accordingly. For cases where it is clear from rhyme and spelling that the *-ed* is not to be sounded, see ll. 90–1 guest / exprest, 361–2 espide / aside, 447–8 behold / controld, 678–9 controld / fold, 785–7 child / defil'd, 884–6 thawd / bawd / laud, 954–7 childe / wild / beguild, 1007–8 mist [missed] / list, 1255–8 kild / hild / fulfild, 1275–7 staide / maide, 1371–2 prowd / bow'd, 1395–8 behold, told, rold, 1444–7 steld / dweld / beheld, 1542–5 milde / beguild / defild, 1654–7 finde / mind / inclind, 1696–9 aide / bewraide / said. For cases where the *-ed* is to be sounded, see ll. 120–2 bed / questioned, 1185–8 dishonored / dead / bred, 1427–8 head / imagined, 1622–3 head / imagined. An exception to the clarity of this distinction comes with the *-ide* phoneme at ll. 424–5 qualified / side, 1749–50 abide / putrefied. Thus Q's spelling could be taken as a guide to the pronunciation of *-ed* here (where the Q spellings are 'arriued' and 'striued'), and at ll. 132–3, 272–3, 377–8, 415–18, 561–3, 657–8, 716–19, 898–901, 1112–13, 1353–6, 1450–2, 1527–9, 1532–3, 1581–2, 1724–7, 1742–3, 1752–5, 1801–4, 1833–4, 1836–9. This will be marked in the notes in each case, but not in the text; the distinction is not certain enough to justify putting 'arrivèd', etc., and thus complicating our modernised text. Compare *Venus and Adonis*, 109–11n.

50 **Collatium** Qu has 'Colatium' which is the usual name in the poem (as at l. 4). The Qc press variant 'Colatia' is the correct name for the town. See Arg.15n.

52 **Beauty. . .Virtue** an allegorical pairing, capitalised as they are in Q.

53 **underprop** support (e.g. with pillars).

55 **in despite** in (hostile) response.

56 **stain** colour, although OED 1a 'to deprive of colour', now obsolete, is pertinent since red is a more typical colour for a stain. See Lodge, *Scilla's Metamorphosis* (1589): 'whereas vermilion hue is stained in sight' (sig. E2v). The idea is powerful throughout the poem – see ll. 168, 196, 366, 655, 684, 1012, 1059, 1181, 1316, 1435, 1655, 1701, 1708, 1710,

But some untimely thought did instigate
His all too timeless speed, if none of those.
His honour, his affairs, his friends, his state,   45
Neglected all, with swift intent he goes
To quench the coal which in his liver glows.
    O rash false heat, wrapped in repentant cold,
    Thy hasty spring still blasts and ne'er grows old.

When at Collatium this false Lord arrived,   50
Well was he welcomed by the Roman dame,
Within whose face Beauty and Virtue strived
Which of them both should underprop her fame.
When Virtue bragged, Beauty would blush for shame;
    When Beauty boasted blushes, in despite   55
    Virtue would stain that o'er with silver white.

But Beauty, in that white intitulèd
From Venus' doves, doth challenge that fair field.
Then Virtue claims from Beauty Beauty's red,
Which Virtue gave the golden age to gild   60
Their silver cheeks, and called it then their shield,

1743, 1836 – where typically physical and moral redness or blackness are imposed on whiteness.

o'er over; '*that*' is the blush or Lucrece's face. Q1 has 'ore', its usual spelling of 'o'er', enabling a pun on metal 'ore' and heraldic 'or' (gold) more easily than the modern spelling. Malone amended to 'or', which makes 'that' a more straightforward deictic pronoun. Red and gold are interchangeable here (as are silver and white); see l. 60.

57–8 **in. . . doves** having a rightful claim (OED 'intitule, *v.*' 4a; 'entitled' became the regular form only after the eighteenth century) to whiteness because it is the colour of Venus' doves. '*Intitulèd*' is a technical term in keeping with the heraldic theme; its other use in Shakespeare ('a companion of the King's, who is intituled, nominated, or called, Don Adriano de Armado', Nathaniel in *Love's Labour's Lost*, 5.1.7–8) seems designedly pretentious.

58 **challenge** lay claim to (OED 5).

field i.e. Lucrece's face, with two heraldic overtones, (i) the field of a battle or joust, (ii) the 'surface of an escutcheon, shield, banner, etc., on which a charge is displayed, esp. with reference

to its colour' (OED[3] *n*.1 17a). Compare ll. 61, 64, and *Venus and Adonis*, l. 108 and note.

60 **golden age** the first era of the world in classical mythology, a time of natural perfection. See Golding's Ovid: 'Then sprang up first the golden age, which of itself maintained, | The truth and right of every thing unforced and unconstrained. | There was no fear of punishment, there was no threatening law, | In brazen tables nailed up, to keep the folk in law. | There was no man would crouch or creep to judge with cap in hand, | They lived safe without a judge, in every realm and land' (1.103–8; 1.89–93 in the Latin). It could also be a cliché, as perhaps in the nearest equivalent elsewhere in Shakespeare, where in his imaginary republic Gonzalo 'would with such perfection govern, sir, | T' excel the golden age' (*Tempest*, 2.1.168–9).

61 **silver** interchangeable with white.

shield protection, but continuing the heraldic theme. Pooler (1927) notes a possible source in *Astrophil and Stella*, 13.9–11: 'Cupid then smiles, for on his crest their lies | Stella's fair hair; her face he makes his shield, | Where roses gules are borne in silver field'.

63   **When** i.e. so that when.
      fence close in, defend. Burrow (2002: 247) sees
      another sense of 'fence' (sword-fighting, OED
      1b) adding contention here. OED's first refer-
      ence in this case is from *Merry Wives of Windsor*,
      2.3.15 ('Alas sir, I cannot fence') which would
      make this an early point for such implications
      to emerge. The tangle of protecting and con-
      testing, though, fits a rather elaborate extended
      analogy being foisted on Lucrece.

64   **heraldry** This makes the heraldic overtones of
      the preceding lines explicit, but this is not a
      heraldry put out by Lucrece's face, so much as
      one imposed upon it.

65   **Argued by** expressed in; but the next two
      lines are the 'argument' of Beauty and Virtue
      in another sense (each claiming the other's
      colour), so a contest is implied.

66   **colour** See 92n.

67   **world's minority** the earliest days of the world.

69   **sovereignty** power, dominion. Zurcher (2010:
      159–60) puts this word at the 'epicentre' of the
      poem's legal language and questions: power over
      the body, justice and the state are all at stake.

70   **seat** place of authority, throne.

71   **lilies. . . roses** See l. 386 and *Venus and Adonis*,
      ll. 345–8 for a parallel exploitation of these pro-
      verbial flower/colour matches (Dent L296, 'as
      white as a lily'; R177, 'as red (ruddy) as a rose').
      For roses, see *Lucrece*, ll. 258–9. Duncan-Jones
      and Woudhuysen (2007: 244) compare *Aeneid*,
      12.64–5, Lavinia's blush in front of Turnus: 'aut
      mixta rubent ubi lilia multa | alba rosa' (as
      when white lilies blush when mixed with many
      a rose'). Compare also Sonnet 98.9 and note.

72   **field** See 58n, here more clearly suggesting battle.

73   **pure ranks** The arrayed lilies and roses of the
      red and white in Lucrece's face are lined up for
      battle. Duncan-Jones and Woudhuysen (2007:
      244) are surely right to pick up on the buried
      oxymoron (where 'rank' suggests rotten; com-
      pare Sonnet 94.14, 'Lilies that fester').
      traitor in the sense that Tarquin's eye is not
      loyal to either red or white; also in that his eye
      is generally treacherous. In Renaissance poetry
      the eye was traditionally vulnerable to desire.

74   **it** Tarquin's 'eye'; the 'coward captive' of l. 75.

76   **would** would rather.

77   **triumph in** triumph over.

78   **shallow** inadequate, superficial (OED, 6a, 'Of
      thought, reasoning, observation. . .' has its first
      citation from the Countess of Pembroke's Psalms,
      c. 1595). Compare ll. 1016, 1329. Shakespeare's
      comparable usages elsewhere tend to relate to

inadequate reasoning, as at *1 Henry VI*, 2.4.16–18:
'I have perhaps some shallow spirit of judgement;
| But in these nice sharp quillets of the law, |
Good faith, I am no wiser than a daw.'

79   **niggard prodigal** ungenerous spendthrift (an
      oxymoron).

80   **high** noble, substantial (as opposed to 'shallow').

81   **barren** meagre, 'bare of intellectual wealth'
      (OED 6). See *Venus and Adonis*, dedication,
      where the poet's 'invention', if unpleasing to
      its patron, is 'so barren a land'. 'Barren' is used
      in the Sonnets to suggest the inadequacy of a
      lover's praise: 16.4, 76.1, 83.4.

82   **doth owe** ought to pay.

83   **answers with** pays in the form of (in Collatine's
      stead); see OED³ 'answer, *v.*', 26a, 26b, for
      debt-related senses.
      surmise brooding thoughts. OED 'surmise,
      n.' 4a, 'an idea formed in the mind [. . .] but
      without certainty. . .; a conjecture', is most
      pertinent. Compare l. 1579, where the word
      suggests contemplation, imaginative engage-
      ment and suspicion. Roe (1992: 148) prefers
      the sense of 'wonder, surprised admiration',
      which is consistent with *Macbeth*, 1.3.139–41:
      'My thought, whose murther yet is but fantas-
      tical, | Shakes so my single state of man that
      function | Is smothered in surmise'.

84   **In silent wonder of still-gazing eyes** with his
      ever-staring eyes silently marvelling (at the
      sight of Lucrece).

85   **earthly saint** Christian overtones gather in this
      stanza. 'Saint' can just mean a person living a
      holy life (OED B4a), though 'earthly' seems
      to be suggesting something more techni-
      cal and specific (i.e. that she is a saint in the
      mortal, terrestrial world, anticipating a place
      in heaven). For 'earthly', compare *Venus and
      Adonis*, l. 863.

86   **suspecteth** 'regards with mistrust' (Schmidt).

87–8 In Q there are double inverted commas
      marking these as *sententiae* (memorable moral
      sentences). This happens also at ll. 460, 528,
      530, 560, 831–2, 853, 867–8, 1109–18, 1125,
      1127, 1216 and 1687. There are none of these
      in *Venus and Adonis*, and Burrow concludes
      that since the same printer handled both
      works, the *Lucrece* markings were probably
      authorial rather than the work of a compositor
      (2002: 248). There is no modern equivalent of
      these gnomic markings, so in this edition they
      are omitted from the text. We follow Burrow's
      punctuation of ll. 87–8, where the colon at the
      end of l. 86 sets up two parallel *sententiae*.

Teaching them thus to use it in the fight:
When shame assailed, the red should fence the white.

This heraldry in Lucrece' face was seen,
Argued by Beauty's red and Virtue's white;   65
Of either's colour was the other queen,
Proving from world's minority their right;
Yet their ambition makes them still to fight,
    The sovereignty of either being so great
    That oft they interchange each other's seat.   70

This silent war of lilies and of roses,
Which Tarquin viewed in her fair face's field,
In their pure ranks his traitor eye encloses;
Where, lest between them both it should be killed,
The coward captive vanquishèd doth yield   75
    To those two armies that would let him go,
    Rather than triumph in so false a foe.

Now thinks he that her husband's shallow tongue,
The niggard prodigal that praised her so,
In that high task hath done her beauty wrong,   80
Which far exceeds his barren skill to show.
Therefore that praise which Collatine doth owe
    Enchanted Tarquin answers with surmise,
    In silent wonder of still-gazing eyes.

This earthly saint, adorèd by this devil,   85
Little suspecteth the false worshipper:
For unstained thoughts do seldom dream on evil;
Birds never limed no secret bushes fear.
So guiltless she securely gives good cheer
    And reverend welcome to her princely guest,   90
    Whose inward ill no outward harm expressed.

---

87 **unstained** morally uncorrupted.
   dream on have any conception of, have any inclination towards (OED³ 5); with the senses 'suspect'
(Roe 1992: 148) or 'imagine' (Duncan-Jones and
Woudhuysen 2007: 245) both pertinent.
88 **limed** trapped with sticky birdlime. The proverb
(Dent B394) is quoted in *3 Henry VI*, 5.6.13–14:
'The bird that hath been limed in a bush, | With
trembling wings misdoubteth every bush'.
   secret i.e. concealing a trap.
89 **So guiltless** (i) thus innocently; (ii) innocent in
this way.
   securely in a way 'free from care, apprehension,
or anxiety' (OED³, 'secure', *adj.*, *adv.*, and *n.*1,

A1a); but the modern sense ('Protected from
or not exposed to danger', OED³ 6a, first citation from 1572) may impinge ironically.
   gives good cheer welcomes.
90 **reverend** reverent; OED³ 'reverend', *adj.* and
n., 4 is a 'now rare' equivalent to reverent, but
OED³ does not list 'reverend' as an alternative
spelling under 'reverent, *adj.*'. Accordingly, the
spelling is unchanged from Q.
91 **inward ill** internal (with the implication
of 'hidden') tendency towards harm. The
poem uses the word 'inward' also at ll. 185,
1546, 1779 (and compare *Venus and Adonis*,
l. 434).

92 **coloured** disguised (OED³ *adj.* 4c) his 'inward ill' (l. 91). After the discussion of red and white in relation to Lucrece (the red of a blush conventionally reveals something inward) the colours here are more subtle and evasive. Throughout the poem there is interplay between natural colours (of skin, especially when caused by feeling) and rhetorical ones: for the former, see ll. 66, 257, 477, 708, 1593, 1600; and the latter, see ll. 267, 476, 481, 1497.

93 **pleats** folds (of metaphorical opulent cloth, standing for his royal power). Shakespeare's only use of the noun; but see *King Lear*, Q1 1.1.280: 'Time shall unfold what pleated cunning hides'. The 'pleat' metaphor was used by other writers to denote concealed thoughts and truths; see William Fisher's *Goodly Sermon Preached at Paul's Cross* (1592): 'Now then if it be such a fearful and horrible thing to look into the book of a guilty conscience in this life, what shame and confusion shall overwhelm us, in the life to come? When nothing shall be concealed, when all pleats and wrinkles shall be unfolded, when all counsels and secrets shall be discovered' (C1v–C2r).

94 **That** so that; as at ll. 177, 208, 467, 804, 1353, 1472, 1524, 1738, 1764.
inordinate 'unrestrained in passions' (OED 3). The sense is morally stronger than *2 Henry IV*, 3.2, where the King accuses his son of 'inordinate and low desires'.

97 **poorly rich** an oxymoron echoed at l. 140 and elaborated in the rest of l. 97.
wanteth in his store lacks despite his abundance. See l. 1837, and *Venus and Adonis*, ll. 19–20. Ovid's Narcissus is the key source ('inopem me copia fecit', *Metamorphoses*, 3.466), which may suggest the selfishness and self-destructiveness of Tarquin's desire.

98 **pineth** starves, longs; this line adds a proverbial nuance: Dent M1287, 'much would have more'.

99 **coped with** encountered. OED's first reference for 'meet with... have to do with' ('cope', *v*.2, 5). As Burrow asserts, the military associations of the word ('... come to blows, encounter, join battle...', OED 1) would have struck readers (2002: 249). Compare *Venus and Adonis*, l. 888.
stranger i.e. of a stranger, noun acting as adjective (Hope 2003: 58–9).

100 **parling** conversing; the word suggests 'parley', military negotiation. This is the first citation for the adjective in OED³, though EEBO-TCP reveals two earlier uses, of which the earliest is in George Turberville's *Heroycall Epistles* (1567): 'no marvel though | I sought to have thy parling voice his pledge' (sig. R8v).

101 **shining** gleaming (in his eyes). The adjective combines paradoxically with the more obviously related 'subtle... secrecies'.

102 **glassy margents of such books** Compare l. 1253, and *Romeo and Juliet*, 1.3.85–6: 'And what obscured in this fair volume lies | Find written in the margent of his eyes'. The meaning of books is glossed in the margins; so the eye (glassy is appearance) is the place in which an experienced viewer can see what a person really intends.

103 **touched** sensed, apprehended; OED 'touch, *v*.', 17a is predominantly used of immaterial touching, but is perhaps apt because the '**baits**' are metaphorical. There is an innuendo here on sexual touching (OED 2a).
hooks i.e. fish-hooks, picking up the metaphor from 'baits'.

104 **moralise** give a moral interpretation of, i.e. recognise the evil in; see *Venus and Adonis*, l. 712. Moralised interpretation might be carried out in the margins (see l. 102).
sight (i) appearance, as in OED³ 'sight, *n*.1', 3, as at *Venus and Adonis*, l. 183; (ii) way of looking at her (see OED³ 'sight, *n*.1', 7a, 11a).

105 **More... light** any more than his eyes were open to (the light of) moral scrutiny.

106 **stories** (i) praises; (ii) tells stories (like a historian). OED³ ('story, *v*.') only acknowledges the latter, but the former seems more apt here, as at *Cymbeline*, 1.4.32–4: 'how worthy he is I will leave to appear hereafter, rather than story him in his own hearing'. It is tempting to see deception in the stories, given the speaker, but Shakespeare's uses of the verb (the noun has a wider range of meanings) rarely carry this sense. Compare *Venus and Adonis*, l. 1013.

108 **decks** adorns richly (OED 2a).

110 **bruisèd arms** battered armour; the line recalls *Richard III*, 1.1.5–6: 'Now are our brows bound with victorious wreaths, | Our bruised arms hung up for monuments'.

111 **heaved-up** raised (without the modern sense of effort; see l. 638, and *Venus and Adonis*, l. 351).

112 **wordless** silent, speechless; first citation in OED³ (2a), and Shakespeare's only use. On the *-less* suffix, see 2n.
greets salutes (i.e. thanks).
heaven monosyllabic here.

For that he coloured with his high estate,
Hiding base sin in pleats of majesty;
That nothing in him seemed inordinate,
Save sometime too much wonder of his eye,   95
Which having all, all could not satisfy;
    But, poorly rich, so wanteth in his store
    That cloyed with much, he pineth still for more.

But she that never coped with stranger eyes
Could pick no meaning from their parling looks,   100
Nor read the subtle shining secrecies
Writ in the glassy margents of such books.
She touched no unknown baits, nor feared no hooks,
    Nor could she moralise his wanton sight
    More than his eyes were opened to the light.   105

He stories to her ears her husband's fame,
Won in the fields of fruitful Italy,
And decks with praises Collatine's high name,
Made glorious by his manly chivalry,
With bruisèd arms and wreaths of victory.   110
    Her joy with heaved-up hand she doth express,
    And wordless so greets heaven for his success.

Far from the purpose of his coming thither,
He makes excuses for his being there.
No cloudy show of stormy blustering weather   115
Doth yet in his fair welkin once appear,
Till sable Night, mother of dread and fear,
    Upon the world dim darkness doth display,
    And in her vaulty prison stows the day.

For then is Tarquin brought unto his bed,   120
Intending weariness with heavy sprite;

115 *cloudy* dark and threatening, gloomy in mood (OED 6a). Compare l. 1084, and *Venus and Adonis*, l. 725.
    blustering disyllabic here.
116 *welkin* sky, a metaphor for his face, which is not marred by tell-tale signs of 'stormy' emotions.
117 *sable* black.
    Night a capitalised personification here, as in Q, because of the vividness of 'mother' and 'stows' (l. 119).
118 *display* unfold (OED 1a, typically used of a banner or sail). Its modern meaning is also evident here; the nautical sense is picked up by 'stows', l. 119.
119 *in her vaulty prison stows the day* in her high-arching prison (the darkened heavens) she stashes away the light of day.
121 *Intending. . . sprite* pretending to be tired, and weary in his spirits. For 'intending', see OED 'intend, *v*.', 22; compare *Richard III*, 3.5.5, 8: 'I can counterfeit the deep tragedian [. . .] | Intending deep suspicion'.
    sprite spirit(s); compare l. 1728.

122 **questionèd** conversed with.

123 **wore out** passed (see *Venus and Adonis*, l. 841).

124 **life's strength** i.e. the vigour that keeps one awake.

125 **betakes** The verb originally means 'hand over, deliver; give up' (OED 1a), and 'commit or commend' (OED 2a), and comes to mean 'commit oneself, have recourse or resort to' in the sixteenth century (OED 4a), as here. 'Betakes' is the reading in Qu; Qc alters this and '*wakes*' (l. 126) to 'themselves betake... | minds that wake'.

126 **wakes** cannot sleep (OED 1a, 'remain awake; to keep oneself, or be kept, awake'). This may be a singular verb with a plural subject, according to modern usage, though Hope (2003: 161–3) argues that such forms (which are not uncommon in Shakespeare) are alternative plurals, not actually singular forms.

127 **one of which** i.e. Tarquin corresponds to one (in fact, all) of the 'thieves, and cares, and troubled minds' that night enlivens.

revolving turning over in his mind (OED³ 'revolve, *v.*', 9).

128 **his will's obtaining** getting what he desires.

130 **weak-built** lacking foundation.

131 **Despair... gaining** those who have no hope of profiting often trade (perhaps, illicitly) to pursue profit. The *polyptoton* ('gain... gaining') illustrates the 'revolving' of l. 127; see also the repetition 'death... death' in l. 133.

traffic This can just mean 'to trade, to buy and sell' (OED 1a), suggesting the persistence of those without hope; the pejorative sense (OED 2b, 'to have dealings of an illicit or secret character') suggests desperation turning to evil. The two senses interact at *Macbeth*, 3.5.3–5 ('how did you dare | To trade and traffic with Macbeth | In riddles and affairs of death?') and *Timon of Athens*, 1.1.158 ('since dishonour traffics with man's nature'). See also the mercantile metaphor of l. 1660. Compare Sonnet 4.9–10.

132–3 **proposed... supposed** On the sounding, or not, of final -*ed*, see 50–2n. Q's spellings are 'proposed' and 'supposed'.

132 **treasure** See 16n.

meed reward.

133 **Though... supposed** Although death follows inevitably, people do not believe (or imagine) any mortal threat. For '*adjunct*', see OED³ *adj.* and *n.*, A1, 'associated, connected; joined', but Shakespeare's use here and elsewhere suggests an immediate and automatic connection. Compare Sonnet 91.5, and *King John*, 3.3.57–8: 'Though that my death were adjunct to the act, | By heaven, I would do it'. For 'supposed', see also l. 377.

134–6 **Those... bond** This edition follows Malone in using brackets rather than Burrow in adding emphatic parenthetical dashes in line 135. Either solution clarifies the quibble in the line, that those who covet gain 'scatter and unloose' 'that which they possess' (i.e. their worldly belongings), but these are things that in truth 'they have not'. Underlying this is the idea that covetous people are alienated from their own possessions. The challenge of these lines is seen in early editions from Q6 onwards, which amend l. 135 to 'That oft they have not that which they possess'. An alternative is to preserve the 'agitated syntax [that] expresses the anxiety which surrounds loss and gain' (Duncan-Jones and Woudhuysen 2007: 250). Burrow (2002: 251) and Roe (1992: 150) cite Publilius Syrus as the source of the proverb; his *sententiae* were gathered in sixteenth-century collections, as in the expanded 1539 English translation of Erasmus' *Adagia*: 'Tam deest avaro quod habet quam quod non habet. The covetous man as well wanteth that he hath, as that he hath not. He useth no more his own than he doth other men's goods. So he lacketh them both alike' (sig. E3v).

134 **fond** foolishly in love.

136 **bond** ownership, but with a contrast between something bound in a 'bond', versus 'scatter and unloose'.

137 **hoping** hoping for, desiring.

138 **excess** having more than enough (which leads only to unhealthy overindulgence and its 'griefs'); may also suggest usury, but the OED's only citation ('excess, *n.*', 6c; *Merchant of Venice*, 1.3.61–2, 'I neither lend nor borrow | By taking nor by giving of excess') seems like a euphemistic usage rather than a distinct sense of the word.

139 **sustain** (i) 'suffer, undergo' (Schmidt); (ii) supply, satisfy (OED³ 2d).

140 **bankrupt** See l. 711, and *Venus and Adonis*, l. 466.

poor rich oxymoron; see l. 97.

141 **aim of all** every person's goal.

the life life.

142 **waning age** old age.

143 **thwarting strife** a frustrating, counterproductive struggle.

For after supper long he questionèd
With modest Lucrece, and wore out the night.
Now leaden slumber with life's strength doth fight,
    And every one to rest himself betakes,   125
    Save thieves, and cares, and troubled minds that wakes.

As one of which doth Tarquin lie revolving
The sundry dangers of his will's obtaining,
Yet ever to obtain his will resolving,
Though weak-built hopes persuade him to abstaining.   130
Despair to gain doth traffic oft for gaining,
    And when great treasure is the meed proposed,
    Though death be adjunct, there's no death supposed.

Those that much covet are with gain so fond
That what they have not (that which they possess)   135
They scatter and unloose it from their bond,
And so by hoping more they have but less;
Or gaining more, the profit of excess
    Is but to surfeit, and such griefs sustain
    That they prove bankrupt in this poor rich gain.   140

The aim of all is but to nurse the life
With honour, wealth and ease in waning age;
And in this aim there is such thwarting strife,
That one for all, or all for one we gage,
As life for honour in fell battle's rage,   145
    Honour for wealth, and oft that wealth doth cost
    The death of all, and all together lost.

So that in venturing ill we leave to be
The things we are, for that which we expect;

144 **gage** wager, risk (OED 2a). The earliest reference is from 1598, but OED 1a, 'to pledge or pawn', is close, and a *Hamlet* citation under 2a ('Against the which a moiety competent | Was gaged by our king' 1.1.90–1) is both pledge and risk.

145 **As. . . honour** as, for instance, we risk our lives in pursuit of honour.
fell savage.
battle's rage the turmoil of war, the heat of battle.

147 **all together** altogether Q1; the amendment is helpful because the sense of 'all together' ('all' suggesting every part of a thing, or every person involved) is absent from modern 'altogether'. The amendment also allows the repetition of 'all' to remain prominent.

148–9 **in venturing. . . expect** When we take an unwise (or sinful) risk, we abandon our true selves in favour of what we hope to gain. Compare *Venus and Adonis*, ll. 567, 628. OED 'venture, *v.*' focuses on risking loss but it is clear that venturing in pursuit of gain is implied by *Henry V*, 1.2.192: 'Others, like merchants, venter trade abroad'. See also *2 Henry IV*, 1.1.181–4: 'we ventured on such dangerous seas | That if we wrought out life 'twas ten to one, | And yet we ventured, for the gain proposed, | Choked the respect of likely peril feared'.

148 **venturing** disyllabic here.

150 **ambitious foul infirmity** this vile weakness, ambition. Ambition was reviled in Shakespeare's time more than it is today. Compare *Macbeth*, 1.7.25–8, 'I have no spur | To prick the sides of my intent, but only | Vaulting ambition, which o'erleaps itself | And falls on the other', and 2.4.28–9, 'Thriftless ambition, that wilt ravin up | Thine own live's means!'. This is the first instance of 'foul' in the poem, a word used more times in this poem than in any other Shakespeare work (twenty-three, including one 'fouler'; see ll. 173, 198, 199, 284, 346, 412, 546, 554, 574, 612, 629, 661, 700, 722, 799, 886, 1029, 1208, 1623, 1704, 1824, 1852). It represents a thread of revulsion running throughout.

151 **In having much** when (perhaps with the force 'even when') we possess a great deal.
   defect insufficiency (stressed on second syllable).

153 **all for want of wit** because of a lack of reason. Compare *Comedy of Errors*, 2.2.179–80: 'Who, all for want of pruning, with intrusion | Infect thy sap, and live on thy confusion'.

154 **Make. . . it** make what we have seem worthless in our own eyes because of our attempts to gain more.

155 **hazard** dangerous risk. Originally 'hazard' was a dice game, as referred to in *Richard III*, 5.4.9–10: 'Slave, I have set my life upon a cast, | And I will stand the hazard of the die'.
   must The modal verb can express obligation or compulsion, and it can also express possibility. Here, and at several points in the poem (see ll. 157, 182, 348, 383, 385, 512, 513, 612) there is a clash between the idea that an aspect of the rape is (i) overwhelmingly likely to happen, and (ii) something required of Tarquin, either by forces beyond his control, or by his own will. On the problems of attributing blame in the poem, see headnote.
   doting The word is often used of foolish lovers who are less culpable than Tarquin; compare ll. 643, 1064, and *Venus and Adonis*, ll. 837, 1059. Compare 'dote' at l. 207.

156 **Pawning** pledging. This could suggest a wager or an offer of security in a business transaction. Both senses are active when Imogen offers to 'pawn mine honour' for the safety of Iachimo's trunk in *Cymbeline*, 1.6.194. See also l. 1351.

157 **himself himself** The doubled reflexive pronouns balance Tarquin's lust against his honour. This is a characteristic stylistic feature of this poem and *Venus and Adonis*. See ll. 29, 160, 998, 1196, 1566, and *Venus and Adonis*, 161n.
   must See 155n.

158 **truth** trustworthiness.
   self-trust integrity, truth to oneself. However, this is the second citation in OED for 'self-trust' taken to mean 'self-confidence'. The first is Arthur Golding's translation of *The Sermons of Mr John Calvin upon [. . .] Deuteronomy* (1583): 'Let us understand that there is no strength in us, and that we must rid ourselves of all self-trust' (sig. A6v). There the sense clearly tends towards the negative, whereas in *Lucrece* it appears a more positive and necessary quality than the OED suggests.

159 **When. . . just** How can he expect someone he does not know to treat him honourably?

160 **confounds** destroys, obstructs. See also ll. 250, 290, 456, 1202, 1489, and see *Venus and Adonis*, 827n.

161 **hateful days** a life of infamy. The OED allows for 'hateful' to mean both 'full of hate' (1) and 'exciting hate' (2a), so the phrase can also suggest the self-disgust that follows sin. Compare *Titus Andronicus*, 3.1.131–2: 'Or shall we bite our tongues, and in dumb shows | Pass the remainder of our hateful days?'. The word 'hateful' runs through the poem: see ll. 240, 771, 849, 1698.

162–8 A vivid rhetorical *chronographia* (a description of a particular time), which pulls the narrative back into the moment. Burrow (2002: 252) notes the parallel with Virgil's *Aeneid*, 4.522–8; in the Phaer-Twyne translation (1573): 'Then was it night, and creatures all that weary were on ground | Did take their slumber sweet; both woods and seas had left their sound, | And waves of waters wild, when stars at midnight soft do slide, | When whist [silent] is every field, and beasts and birds of painted pride | In bushes broad that breed, and country fowls of land and lake, | By night in silence still are set on sleep, their ease to take, | Forgetting labours long, and care away from heart they shake. | But not so Dido could, nor never rest relieves her mind, | On sleep she never falls, her eyes or heart no night can find' (sig. L1v). Dido, a troubled and passionate lover with a role in the formative stories of Rome, is an interesting parallel for Tarquin. This moment is recalled by *Macbeth*, 2.1.49–56: 'Now o'er the one half world | Nature seems dead, and wicked dreams abuse | The curtained sleep; witchcraft celebrates | Pale Hecat's off'rings,

And this ambitious foul infirmity,   150
In having much, torments us with defect
Of that we have; so then we do neglect
 The thing we have, and all for want of wit
 Make something nothing, by augmenting it.

Such hazard now must doting Tarquin make,   155
Pawning his honour to obtain his lust,
And for himself himself he must forsake.
Then where is truth if there be no self-trust?
When shall he think to find a stranger just,
 When he himself himself confounds, betrays   160
 To slanderous tongues and wretched hateful days?

Now stole upon the time the dead of night,
When heavy sleep had closed up mortal eyes.
No comfortable star did lend his light,
No noise but owls' and wolves' death-boding cries: 165
Now serves the season that they may surprise
 The silly lambs; pure thoughts are dead and still,
 While Lust and Murder wakes to stain and kill.

And now this lustful lord leapt from his bed,
Throwing his mantle rudely o'er his arm,   170

and withered Murther, | Alarumed by his sen-
tinel, the wolf, | Whose howl's his watch, thus
with his stealthy pace, | With Tarquin's ravish-
ing strides, towards his design | Moves like a
ghost'. In the same year as the first printing
of *Lucrece* Thomas Nashe may have alluded
sardonically to this moment in *The Terrors
of the Night* (1594): 'By night time came the
Deluge over the face of the whole earth; by
night time Judas betrayed Christ; Tarquin ravished Lucretia. When any Poet would describe
a horrible Tragical accident; to add the more
probability & credence unto it, he dismally
beginneth to tell, how it was dark night when
it was done, and cheerful daylight had quite
abandoned the firmament' (1.386).

164 *comfortable* benevolent, offering comfort; the
predominant meaning in Elizabethan English,
pronounced here with four syllables.

165 *owls'. . . cries* Proverbially a bad omen
(Dent R33, 'the croaking raven (screeching
owl) bodes misfortune (death)'). Compare
Venus and Adonis, l. 531, and 'Let the Bird of
Loudest Lay', ll. 5–7. The proverbial resonance

justifies adding apostrophes to both Q's
'Owles, & wolues', although the comma after
'Owles' suggests otherwise, and see 166n.

166 *serves* is favourable (Schmidt).
 season time, moment.
 they The pronoun refers back most readily to
the wolves of l. 165, but the decision to attribute the 'death-boding cries' to both owls
and wolves means the pronoun here somewhat awkwardly takes in the owls as well.
 surprise (i) seize (OED 2b); (ii) catch unawares
(OED 3a).

167 *silly* feeble, defenceless, guileless.

168 *wakes* a singular verb after two subjects, not
uncommon in Shakespeare (Hope 2003: 164).
 stain defile; see 56n.

169 *leapt* a participle here (i.e. 'having leapt'); 'Is',
l. 171, is the main verb of the sentence. Both
modern spellings are possible ('leapt' and
'leaped'); the former is Q's.

170 *mantle* cloak.
 rudely roughly, hastily; the point is that
Tarquin is not dressing himself properly. See
'rude', l. 175.

172 **Th'one. . . th'other. . .** both elided, unlike the other instances of the formulation in the poem (ll. 1097, 1164, 1187, 1793).

173 **honest fear** i.e. fear which, in matters of sin, tends towards honesty and modesty.
charm spell, enchantment.

174 **betake him to retire** withdraw ('him' is reflexive). 'Betake' contributes more specific meaning at l. 125 (see note); here perhaps it helps to convey that 'honest fear' puts up some resistance.

175 **brainsick** mad; perhaps specifically obsessive, as in *1 Henry VI*, 4.1.111–13: 'Good Lord, what madness rules in brainsick men, | When for so slight and frivolous a cause | Such factious emulations shall arise!'.
rude rough, violent.

176 **falchion** specifically, a curved sword with its blade on the convex side; the word comes from Latin 'falx', a sickle. It is used, as here, to mean 'sword' in general. Compare ll. 506, 1046, 1626, and the wordplay with 'falcon' at l. 509; this suggests the two might have been pronounced similarly, as Cercignani (1981: 354) notes.
softly quietly.

177 **That** so that.

179 **lodestar** guiding star.
eye; Other editors change Q's full stop here to a comma, with the sense running on to the next line. The extra pause, however, is dramatic, and worth preserving.

180 **advisedly** deliberately, as if after consideration. This word focuses on the human ability to exercise reason. Here, as in some other instances in the poem, this is a compromised ability. Compare ll. 1488, 1527, 1816, 1849, and *Venus and Adonis*, l. 457. Compare also 'heedfully', l. 454.

181–2 The proverb 'In the coldest flint there is hot fire' (Dent F371) might be noted here.

182 **must** The sense of compulsion comes from his desire, but it is also part of the false parallel: the twisted logic derives this 'must' from the sparking flint; see 155n.

183 **premeditate** think over in anticipation. This suggests that Tarquin has not yet made up his mind. However, the word suggests something planned in advance (as in *Henry V*, 4.1.162–3: 'the guilt of premeditated and contrived murther').

184 **enterprise** as Burrow notes, 'could be used of daring military adventures' (2002: 254).

185 **inward mind** On 'inward', see also 91n. Shakespeare uses the phrase 'inward soul' elsewhere, for example at l. 1779.

188 **naked armour** oxymoronic: the metaphorical 'armour' with which he takes on this 'enterprise' (l. 184), i.e. lust, actually leaves him without any protection, and therefore 'naked'. The exposure of the body is suggestive in the sexual context of the poem. EEBO-TCP reveals no other use of the phrase.
still-slaughtered always destroyed. The point is that lust, destructive in itself, destroys itself when it is satisfied. There is no hyphen in Q.

189 **justly. . . unjust** The *polyptoton* suggests a pause in his thinking.

191 **darken** cast a shadow over (OED 9a), eclipse (OED 9b), both used by Shakespeare with metaphorical moral significance, as here. Compare *Antony and Cleopatra*, 1.4.10–11: 'I must not think there are | Evils enow to darken all his goodness', and 3.1.22–4: 'ambition | (The soldier's virtue) rather makes choice of loss | Than gain which darkens him'.

192 **unhallowed** wicked. The OED dates this figurative use (2; as opposed to the technical sense 1, 'not consecrated') to *The Troublesome Raigne of King John* (1591): 'His quarrel is unhallowed, false and wrong' (sig. F3v). Compare *Titus Andronicus*, 2.3.210: 'this unhallowed and blood-stained hole'. See ll. 392, 552.
blot stain, mar (morally). See also ll. 537, 948, 1299, 1322, 1519, *Venus and Adonis*, l. 796, and Sonnet 92.13 and note.

193–4 **divine. . . shrine;** Q has colons at the end of both lines. Previous editors have changed these to full stops, which makes the stanza rather static. A case could be made for keeping the first colon, or (as here) having a semi-colon at the end of l. 194.

195 **humanity** (i) kindness, 'the quality of being humane' (OED[3] 1a); (ii) humanity (in its modern sense, 'the condition, quality, or fact of being human', OED[3] 3a).

196 **spots** tarnishes (OED[3] 1a). The word and its derivatives (as noun and adjective too) appear seven times in *Lucrece* (also at ll. 685, 721, 821, 1053, 1172, 1656). See Sonnet 95.3 and note.
stains Like 'spot', 'stain' and its derivatives run throughout the poem; see 56n.
snow-white The compound is proverbial (Dent, S591); compare ll. 420, 1011. *Venus and Adonis* also plays on snow-whiteness; compare 362–3n.
weed garment (i.e. love should be clothed in chastity).

Is madly tossed between desire and dread:
Th' one sweetly flatters, th' other feareth harm;
But honest fear, bewitched with lust's foul charm,
    Doth too too oft betake him to retire,
    Beaten away by brainsick rude desire.   175

His falchion on a flint he softly smiteth,
That from the cold stone sparks of fire do fly,
Whereat a waxen torch forthwith he lighteth,
Which must be lodestar to his lustful eye;
And to the flame thus speaks advisedly: 180
    'As from this cold flint I enforced this fire,
    So Lucrece must I force to my desire.'

Here, pale with fear, he doth premeditate
The dangers of his loathsome enterprise,
And in his inward mind he doth debate   185
What following sorrow may on this arise.
Then, looking scornfully, he doth despise
    His naked armour of still-slaughtered lust,
    And justly thus controls his thoughts unjust:

'Fair torch, burn out thy light, and lend it not   190
To darken her whose light excelleth thine;
And die, unhallowed thoughts, before you blot
With your uncleanness that which is divine.
Offer pure incense to so pure a shrine;
    Let fair humanity abhor the deed   195
    That spots and stains love's modest snow-white weed.

'O shame to knighthood and to shining arms;
O foul dishonour to my household's grave;
O impious act including all foul harms;
A martial man to be soft fancy's slave!   200
True valour still a true respect should have;

197 **knighthood** chivalry; see ll. 569, 1694, 1697, and notes, and also the heraldic turn of ll. 204–10.
198 **household's grave** family tomb; perhaps, as Roe suggests, his family's ancestry (1992: 153). Shakespeare sees a tomb as a site of Roman honour also in *Titus Andronicus*, 1.1.350–3: 'This monument five hundred years hath stood, | Which I have sumptuously re-edified. | Here none but soldiers and Rome's servitors | Repose in fame'.
199 **including** encompassing.
    harms evil actions.

200 **soft fancy's slave** enslaved by weak, whimsical infatuation.
201 **true respect** due consideration, regard (for what is right); see OED[3] 'respect, *n.*', 3a, and *King John*, 4.2.213–14: 'dangerous majesty, when perchance it frowns | More upon humour than advised respect'. The phrase may also suggest, appropriately given the stanza's focus on reputation, proper admiration from others. The phrase recurs at l. 642 and l. 1347, but nowhere else in Shakespeare's work or in EEBO-TCP up to 1594.

202 *digression* 'moral deviation' (OED 1b). Compare *Love's Labour's Lost*, 1.2.116–17: 'I may example my digression by some mighty president [i.e. precedent]'.

203 *engraven* Shakespeare's only use; elsewhere he has 'engraved', perhaps for emphasis as well as for scansion. Picking up the 'arms' of l. 197, this suggests that Tarquin's face will bear the heraldic signs of his crime. The next stanza continues the heraldic theme. Compare Lucrece's sense of being marked at ll. 807–8.

204 *though* even if, even when.
scandal 'damage to reputation', OED 2a, where the earliest work cited is *The Comedy of Errors*, 5.1.13–15: 'I wonder much | That you would put me to this shame and trouble, | And, not without some scandal to yourself'. Earlier senses of the word all relate to religious lapses. This resonance, likely still current for Elizabethan readers, sharpens Tarquin's meaning here.

205 *eyesore* ugly flaw.
coat coat of arms.

206 *dash* a mark on a coat of arms, made by a herald as a formal record of the holder's transgression. Editors have followed Wyndham (1898) in linking this dash to the practice of 'abatement' as described in Guillim, *Display of Heraldry* (1610): 'An abatement is an accidental mark annexed to coat-armour, denoting some ungentleman-like, dishonourable, or disloyal demeanour, quality, or stain, in the bearer, whereby the dignity of the coat-armour is greatly abased' (sig. E1r). See also, on the same page: 'Diminution is a blemishing or defacing of some particular point or points of the escutcheon, by reason of the imposition of some stain and colour thereupon'. However, as the relevant entry in OED³ ('abatement, *n.*', 4) notes, it is uncertain whether this actually happened (except in the case of illegitimacy). See also l. 828 and note.
contrive devise.

207 *cipher me* show (i) to; (ii) for; or (iii) about me by means of a sign; for 'cipher', compare l. 1396. 'Me' is an indirect object of 'cipher', and is best thought of as a dative form, possibly an 'ethic dative' expressing the object's interest in what is being represented.

fondly. . . dote foolishly. . . love. See 'doting', l. 155, and note.

208 *That* so that.
posterity descendants (OED³ 1). Compare *Venus and Adonis*, l. 758, and Sonnets 3.8, 6.12.
note 'stigma, reproach' (OED³ 'note, *n.*2', 4a); or 'mark' more generally. Compare Sonnet 141.2.

209 *hold it for no sin* consider it not sinful (to disobey the fifth commandment, 'Honour thy father and thy mother').

211–14 As Burrow (2002: 255) notes, these lines build on the equivalent question in Ovid's version of the story: 'quid, victor, gaudes? haec te victoria perdet. | heu quanto regnis nox stetit una tuis!' (*Fasti*, 2.811–12; 'Why are you rejoicing, victor? This victory will destroy you. Alas, one night has cost your kingdom so much!'; see Appendix 2). The additional elements incorporated are (i) the Biblical question of Mark 8:36 ('For what shall it profit a man, though he should win the whole world, if he lose his soul?'), and (ii) the sense of waste after sexual fulfilment, as seen in Sonnet 129.

212 *froth* 'something. . . unsubstantial or of little worth' (OED 2a, where this is the first citation).

214 *toy* trivial thing; the word often has erotic implications. Compare *Venus and Adonis*, ll. 34, 106.

216 *fond* foolish.

217 *straight* immediately.
stricken strooken Q. The unusual participle form from 'strike' may simply be a case of *proparalepsis* (an additional syllable) for the sake of metre. However, alongside 'engraven', l. 203, it may suggest a particular emphatic or formal tone adopted by this speaker. There is no particular social or tonal pattern to Shakespeare's use of 'strucken' elsewhere, so the more modern form 'stricken' is preferred here.

218 *dream* subjunctive form of the verb (i.e. a grammatical form of the verb tending, as the OED says, 'to express a wish, command, exhortation, or a contingent, hypothetical, or prospective event'; in Elizabethan English the subjunctive form was more common than it is today, but still rare; see Hope 2003: 156–8).

Then my digression is so vile, so base,
That it will live engraven in my face.

'Yea, though I die the scandal will survive,
And be an eyesore in my golden coat.   205
Some loathsome dash the herald will contrive
To cipher me how fondly I did dote,
That my posterity, shamed with the note,
    Shall curse my bones, and hold it for no sin
    To wish that I their father had not been.   210

'What win I if I gain the thing I seek?
A dream, a breath, a froth of fleeting joy.
Who buys a minute's mirth to wail a week,
Or sells eternity to get a toy?
For one sweet grape who will the vine destroy,   215
    Or what fond beggar, but to touch the crown,
    Would with the sceptre straight be stricken down?

'If Collatinus dream of my intent,
Will he not wake, and in a desperate rage
Post hither, this vile purpose to prevent?   220
This siege that hath engirt his marriage,
This blur to youth, this sorrow to the sage,
    This dying virtue, this surviving shame,
    Whose crime will bear an ever-during blame.

'O what excuse can my invention make   225
When thou shalt charge me with so black a deed?
Will not my tongue be mute, my frail joints shake,

220 *Post* hasten; compare l. 1.
221–3 *This. . . This. . . This. . .* For similar constructions see ll. 689–91 and *Venus and Adonis*, ll. 655–8.
221 *siege* On the metaphor, see *Venus and Adonis*, 423n and headnote.
    engirt ingirt Q; surrounded. This can suggest military and non-military encirclement. Compare l. 1173, and *Venus and Adonis*, l. 364 and note.
    marriage trisyllabic.
222 *blur* stain, blemish (moral). Compare l. 522, and 192n on the comparable 'blot'.
    sage wise, but must also suggest 'old' (in contrast with 'youth'). The OED somewhat allows for this shading of meaning, in that

'sage, *adj.* and *n.2*' 1a allows for wisdom to come 'by experience'.
224 *ever-during* everlasting.
225 *invention* ability to construct a case (in his defence). Although this word is used of the poetic imagination, it resonates particularly here with the rhetorical 'inventio', the technique of constructing the matter of an argument. See *Venus and Adonis*, dedication, 11n., and compare Lucrece's 'inventions' at l. 1302.
226 *thou* Although this pronoun need not refer to anyone in particular (it could be an impersonal accuser, or his own conscience), it seems here that Tarquin suddenly imagines Collatine himself making the charge.

228 *forgo. . . light* become blind. This may suggest the beams of light emitted by the eyes that featured in the prevailing theories of vision in Shakespeare's time. See ll. 375 and note, 1090, and *Venus and Adonis*, 487n.

229 *still* always.

230 *extreme* stressed on first syllable.

231 *But* but only.

233 *betray my life* i.e. to kill me (or arrange for my death) through treachery.

235 *work upon* (i) seduce; (ii) rape. Shakespeare's only comparable use of the phrase, suggesting strong effects caused by the influence of another, is in *Othello*, 4.1.275–6, where Lodovico asks, 'did the letters work upon his blood, | And new-create this fault?'.

236 *quittal* repayment, requital. Shakespeare may have had Thomas Kyd's *Spanish Tragedy* 3.1.78–9 in mind when using this word for the only time: 'Let him unbind thee that is bound to death, | To make a quittal for thy discontent'. The OED[3] deems it 'rare', and an EEBO-TCP search reveals only three uses between Kyd and Shakespeare.

237 *kinsman* Collatine was distantly related to the Tarquins (see Argument).

238 *excuse* repeating the word from l. 235.
   end both 'purpose' (in that if Collatine were his enemy, there would be a point in raping Lucrece in revenge) and 'conclusion' (in that the resultant shame will last for ever).

239–41 *Shameful. . . own.* Q has colons in the middle of all three lines, and commas at the end of ll. 239 and 240. Editors alter punctuation in different ways to capture the internal debate, characteristic of Senecan-influenced drama. The practice here is to keep Q's medial colons, as all the following clauses are expansions or qualifications to some extent, and the parallelism between the lines is effective. The commas at the ends of ll. 239 and 240, however, are now semi-colons, to create the right degree of pause. Roe (1992: 155) and Duncan-Jones and Woudhuysen (2007: 258) aptly cite two passages that illustrate the dramatic quality of such rhetorically ornate self-examinations: *Richard III*, 5.3.182–6, 'What do I fear? Myself? There's none else by. | Richard loves Richard, that is, I am I. | Is there a murderer here? No. Yes, I am. | Then fly. What, from myself? Great reason why – | Lest I revenge. What, myself upon myself?', and Kyd's *Spanish Tragedy*, 2.119–24: 'Yet

might she love me for my valiancy – | Ay, but that's slandered by captivity. | Yet might she love me to content her sire – | Ay, but her reason masters his desire. | Yet might she love me as her brother's friend – | Ay, but her hopes aim at some other end'.

239 *fact* deed; compare l. 349. The word comes directly from Latin *factum*. This is Shakespeare's only use of the phrase 'if the fact be known', and EEBO-TCP reveals no other instance before 1693.
   known i.e. known about; shame depends on it being public knowledge.

240 *Hateful* See 161n.

241 *not her own* i.e. she is married.

242 *The. . . reproving* The worst thing that could happen is that Lucrece will refuse my advances and rebuke me for them.

243 *past. . . removing* beyond the ineffectual dissuasive power of reasoned argument. Tarquin may be imagining a continuation of his own internal debate (between his 'will' and 'reason'), or the future protestations of Lucrece. 'Removing' is a physical way of indicating persuasion, relating to 'move' used of emotions, and also to 'remove' as a term used for the raising of a siege (see OED[3] 6a). Compare *Venus and Adonis*, 423n, and *Romeo and Juliet*, 5.3.237: 'to remove that siege of grief from her'.

244 *sentence* maxim; a Latin *sententia*. See 87–8n. The word evokes legal verdicts too; in this line Tarquin undermines the resources of reason, making its 'sentence' not a judgement but something more like a 'saw' (see below).
   saw saying, proverb. In Jaques' 'seven ages' speech, 'saws' are associated with the fifth stage of life: 'the justice, | In fair round belly with good capon lined, | With eyes severe and beard of formal cut, | Full of wise saws and modern instances' (*As You Like It*, 2.7.152–5).

245 *painted cloth* Elizabethan houses were sometimes decorated with moral sentences painted onto cloth. Tarquin's scorn is mostly at the thought that he might be cowed by homespun wisdom, but also that these were cheap alternatives to tapestries. Other appearances of such cloths in Shakespeare are treated with similar humour. Pandarus in *Troilus and Cressida*, 5.10.45–6, says 'Good traders in the flesh, set this in your painted cloths'. In *As You Like It*, 3.2.273–5, Orlando retorts to Jaques, 'I answer you right painted cloth,

Mine eyes forgo their light, my false heart bleed?
The guilt being great, the fear doth still exceed;
   And extreme fear can neither fight nor fly,
   But coward-like with trembling terror die.   230

'Had Collatinus killed my son or sire,
Or lain in ambush to betray my life,
Or were he not my dear friend, this desire
Might have excuse to work upon his wife,   235
As in revenge or quittal of such strife.
   But as he is my kinsman, my dear friend,
   The shame and fault finds no excuse nor end.

'Shameful it is: ay, if the fact be known;
Hateful it is: there is no hate in loving;   240
I'll beg her love: but she is not her own.
The worst is but denial and reproving.
My will is strong past reason's weak removing:
   Who fears a sentence or an old man's saw
   Shall by a painted cloth be kept in awe.'   245

Thus graceless holds he disputation
'Tween frozen conscience and hot burning will,
And with good thoughts makes dispensation,
Urging the worser sense for vantage still;

from whence you have studied your questions'. Compare these simple works with the elaborate picture described at ll. 1366–568.

246 *graceless* wicked, lacking in divine grace. Other senses of the word are pertinent too: lacking in social decency; lacking in rhetorical skill. See l. 564 and note.
holds. . . disputation debates formally; see ll. 822, 1101.

247 *frozen* immobile, most likely in the sense that it is steadfast, but with the implication also that it is inert. Furthermore, set against the heat of the 'will', the 'frozen' conscience seems metaphorically ready to melt. A word which seems capable of praising conscience turns out, in two ways, to signal its weakness. Compare *Venus and Adonis*, l. 565 and note.

248 **makes dispensation** dispenses (i.e. he disregards 'good thoughts'). This may just be a formal way of saying 'dispense', but the word 'dispensation' resonates. This line is the first citation for OED 'dispensation, *n.*', 11, 'The

action of dispensing with anything; a setting aside, disregarding; a doing away with, doing without'. The word can also be used of distribution, ordering, of social and religious issues; it can also (OED 8, religious; OED 9, secular or legal) suggest a formal exemption, as in a Papal dispensation. See *Love's Labour's Lost*, 2.1.85–7: 'He rather means to lodge you in the field, | Like one that comes here to besiege his court, | Than seek a dispensation for his oath'. Compare also 'dispense', l. 1070.

249 *Urging. . . still;* either 'preferring a more evil way of thinking, always to his own advantage', or (especially if 'dispensation' is taken in its more technical sense) 'pressing a wicked interpretation (of the 'good thoughts', l. 248). . .'. Shakespeare frequently uses '*worser*' as an alternative form of 'worse'. Burrow's comma at the end of the line helps carry through the momentum of 'urging' (2002: 257). Nevertheless Q's full stop suggests a pause, hence the semi-colon here.

250 **confound** destroy; see 160n.

251 **effects** results; see l. 1555, *Venus and Adonis*, 605n.

252 **shows** appears; compare 'showed like', *Venus and Adonis*, l. 366. This whole stanza expresses a common anxiety about the art of rhetoric, in which the art of disputation can make 'vile' appear 'virtuous'. The specific trope is *paradiastole*, redescription of bad as good.

253 **kindly** The word suggests benevolence (OED³ *adv.* 4a) and natural, familial affection (OED³ 3), but the word's erotic potential (OED³ 'kind, *adj.* and *adv.*', 7c) also impinges. See Sonnet 134.6 and note. The meanings are played on in Henry Constable's *Diana* (1595): 'Women are kind by kind, | But coy by fashion' (sig. F4r); here Tarquin's unclear levels of self-knowledge and self-loathing make the word-play sharp and opaque. Compare *Venus and Adonis*, 187n.

254 **gazed for tidings** looked intently for signs of news.

   eager Roe suggests this 'has the appearance of a transferred epithet: i.e. "she *eagerly* gazed"' (1992: 156). Both sides of the exchange of gazes are eager, at cross-purposes. Tarquin's eagerness to see Lucrece is consistent with his desire for her.

255 **hard** bad.

256 **lies** dwells, sleeps; with a hint of lying dead.

257 **colour** On the word in *Lucrece*, see 92n.

258–9 **First. . . away** On the colours, see 11n; on roses and their proverbial redness, see 71n.

258 **lawn** fine linen cloth, typically white (proverbially so; Dent L119.1); see *Venus and Adonis*, l. 590.

259 **took** having been taken.

261 **it** Tarquin's hand; Lucrece's hand is trembling so much that it causes his to tremble too.

   loyal also used of Lucrece at ll. 1034, 1048.

262 **Which** i.e., most straightforwardly, her fear; but this could refer to the shaking of Tarquin's hand.

   struck her made her feel.

   sad (i) sorrowful; (ii) serious. The two predominant senses of 'sad' in the period (OED³ A.II and A.I respectively) are often in dialogue in the twenty-four appearances of the word and its cognates in the poem. See ll. 277, 556, 561 ('sadly'), 736 ('sadly'), 1081, 1110, 1129, 1131, 1147, 1179, 1212 ('sadly'), 1221, 1324, 1386, 1457, 1496, 1542 ('sober-sad'), 1590

('sad-beholding'), 1591, 1610, 1612, 1662, 1699. Overall there is a pattern that leads from the sad-sorrowful fate of Lucrece, to the sad-serious response of the Roman men, to the eventual expulsion of the Tarquins from Rome. As subsequent uses show, however, this process is not orderly or straightforward, and both Lucrece and Collatine find themselves caught in the multiple possibilities of 'sad'.

   it Lucrece's hand.

   rocked shook.

264 **cheer** expression (OED³ *n.*1, 1a), mood (OED³ 2a), rather than cheerfulness (OED³ 5); compare *A Midsummer Night's Dream*, 3.2.96: 'All fancy-sick she is and pale of cheer'.

265 **Narcissus** Narcissus, the young man who fell in love with his own reflection in classical mythology (and Ovid's *Metamorphoses* Book 3) is used as a negative example in *Venus and Adonis*, ll. 161–2.

266 **flood** pool, stream (in which Narcissus sees his reflection).

267 **colour** pretext (OED³ *n.*1, 9), or rhetorical ornament (OED³ 15). On the different meanings of 'colour' in the poem, see 92n.

268 **All. . . pleadeth** Tarquin repeats the narrative voice's description of beauty's persuasiveness at ll. 29–30.

269 **Poor. . . abuses** Worthless people feel sorry for their insignificant transgressions. A scornful dismissal of remorse, this is the second of three one-line statements with which Tarquin regains his defiance.

270 **shadows** unreal things.

271 **Affection** passion; as at l. 500, but compare l. 1060 (where Lucrece is describing Collatine's marital love). See *Venus and Adonis*, ll. 387, 569.

272–3 The force of the proverbial idea here (Dent D216: 'love makes cowards courageous') is not to liken Tarquin to a coward, but to say that if love makes cowards brave, then it must make non-cowards yet bolder. Compare *Venus and Adonis*, l. 1158.

   displayed. . . dismayed On the sounding, or not, of final -*ed*, see 50–2n. Q's spellings are 'displaide' and 'dismaide'.

272 **gaudy** bright, impressive (from Tarquin's perspective); perhaps also showy. See *Venus and Adonis*, l. 1088, where it seems less disparaging.

Which in a moment doth confound and kill   250
  All pure effects, and doth so far proceed
  That what is vile shows like a virtuous deed.

Quoth he, 'She took me kindly by the hand,
And gazed for tidings in my eager eyes,
Fearing some hard news from the warlike band   255
Where her beloved Collatinus lies.
O, how her fear did make her colour rise!
  First red as roses that on lawn we lay,
  Then white as lawn, the roses took away.

'And how her hand, in my hand being locked,   260
Forced it to tremble with her loyal fear!
Which struck her sad, and then it faster rocked
Until her husband's welfare she did hear;
Whereat she smilèd with so sweet a cheer,
  That had Narcissus seen her as she stood,   265
  Self-love had never drowned him in the flood.

'Why hunt I then for colour or excuses?
All orators are dumb when beauty pleadeth;
Poor wretches have remorse in poor abuses;
Love thrives not in the heart that shadows dreadeth.   270
Affection is my captain, and he leadeth;
  And when his gaudy banner is displayed,
  The coward fights and will not be dismayed.

'Then childish fear avaunt, debating die!
Respect and reason wait on wrinkled age!   275
My heart shall never countermand mine eye:
Sad pause and deep regard beseems the sage;

---

273 **dismayed** stronger in meaning in Shakespeare's time than it sometimes is today: see OED 'dismay, *v.*1', 1: 'to deprive of moral courage at the prospect of peril or trouble; to appal or paralyze with fear or the feeling of being undone; utterly to discourage, daunt, or dishearten'.

274 **avaunt** go away.
  debating die let there be no more argument or discussion.

275 **Respect** consideration (OED³ 3a); see 201n. Troilus uses the same pair of words, also disparagingly, at 2.2.49–50: 'reason and respect | Make livers pale and lustihood deject'.
  wait on let them accompany.

276 **countermand mine eye** revoke (or contradict) an order given by my eye.

277 **Sad . . . sage** Serious-minded hesitancy and profound consideration suit old wise men. See 222n on Tarquin's problematic negative association of wisdom with old age; while the word predominantly denotes wisdom, here again the opposition with 'youth' (l. 278) is clear. For 'regard', see l. 305.
  beseems a singular verb after two subjects, not uncommon in Shakespeare (Hope 2003: 164).

278 ***My. . . Youth*** I play the role of Youth, and will
drive these (i.e. 'sad pause' and 'deep regard',
l. 277) off the stage. This evokes a morality
play, in which allegorical characters (such as
'Youth') and violent symbolic action (beating
characters from the stage) are both found. An
apt comparison is the anonymous *Interlude of
Youth*, printed by John Waley in 1557.

279 ***pilot*** navigator (of a ship).

280 ***treasure*** The word can have a sexual sense in
Shakespeare; see l. 16 and note.

281 ***As corn. . . weeds*** proverbial (Dent W242,
'the weeds overgrow the corn').
heedful cautious.

282 ***almost*** perhaps 'all but' rather than 'very
nearly but not quite' (both OED³ 2a).
unresisted irresistible; but also suggesting that
Tarquin has failed to exert sufficient resistance
against his lust. This is Shakespeare's only use
of the word.

283 ***he*** Tarquin. The nearest possible antecedent is
(personified) 'lust', and at this point Tarquin is
becoming a personification of lust.
listening ear listening either (i) to the imagined voices in the inward debate preceding
this, or (more likely) (ii) for threatening noises
around the house.

284 ***foul hope. . . fond mistrust*** Tarquin is divided
between his hope for shameful pleasure, and
his foolish fear of being discovered. The two
paradoxical phrases result from epithets swap-
ping from more natural places: 'fond hope'
and 'foul mistrust'. Bassanio talks of the 'ugly
treason of mistrust', in *Merchant of Venice*,
3.2.28. See, however, Thomas Campion's *Two
Books of Airs* (1613): 'How oft have we even
smiled in tears, | Our fond mistrust repenting'
(sig. K1r). The idea of fond hope is at home
in tragic narratives, as in William Baldwin's
Mirror for Magistrates: 'Lo thus fond hope did
their both lives abridge' (sig. G1r).

285 ***servitors. . . unjust*** servants helping him in his
wickedness. This line is cited by OED under
'unjust, *adj.*' 1a, where it denotes an unjust person rather than an action (1b). In the poem
it seems rather to encompass both agent and
action. 'Servitor' is also used metaphorically at
Richard III, 4.3.51–2: 'I have learned that fearful
commenting | Is leaden servitor to dull delay'.

286 ***cross*** thwart (OED 14a).
opposite persuasion contradictory arguments.

287 ***league*** peace treaty (as with 'invasion' later in
the line, military language arises frequently).

290–1 ***That eye. . . That eye*** i.e. one of Tarquin's eyes
looks at an imaginary Lucrece 'within his
thought' (l. 288), and the other at an imaginary Collatine.

290 ***confounds his wits*** destroys his ability to reason (because of his lust). See 160n.

291 ***as more divine*** (i) being more religious (or
moral); perhaps (ii) as if it saw things in a more
religious and godly way. The nearest sense
in OED is 3, '. . . devoted to God; religious,
sacred', but here the word seems hyperbolic,
describing an unreachable moral state.

292 ***Unto. . . incline*** (i) will not turn back (or submit) to such a morally distorting sight; (ii) will
not yield to such a morally disgusting way of
thinking. '*View*' can mean 'sight' (OED³ 6a) or
'visual appearance' (OED³ 9a) but the sense
'particular manner or way of considering
or regarding a matter or question' is emerging
in this period (OED³ 14a, first citation 1573).
Shakespeare, however, does not use it this way
elsewhere (but compare l. 1261). Roe considers
that the question of whether Lucrece's appearance is culpable for causing lust (relative to
Collatine's, which inspires more moral thoughts)
is 'tactfully not pursued' (1992: 158); however, it
could also be said that it is edgily evoked.

293 ***pure*** unconditional. 'Pure' is opposed to 'false'
in l. 292, and 'corrupted' in l. 294. It has a legal
sense in the period ('absolute, unconditional',
OED³ 2b) as well as its more familiar sense
'free of moral corruption' (4a). It seems best
to allow this resonant word to contain both in
the complex, compact phrase 'pure appeal' (for
which EEBO-TCP offers no other instances).
appeal plea.
seeks to the heart looks to the heart for help
(see OED, 'seek, *v.*', 13c).

294 ***once corrupted*** (i) having been corrupted; (ii)
having been corrupted once.
worser part; the worse (less moral) side of the
case. On 'worser', see 249n. Q has a full-stop at
the end of the stanza, but the sense continues
dynamically, and so lighter punctuation is preferable. A comma is possible (as in Q3) but the
semi-colon recognises Q's pause to some extent.

295 ***heartens up*** encourages, emboldens. The word
plays on its subject, the heart. Shakespeare
only uses the word 'hearten' in one other
place (*3 Henry VI*, 2.2.78–9, 'cheer these
noble lords | And hearten those that fight
in your defence'), so the presence of 'up', the
first of three appearances of the word in the

My part is Youth and beats these from the stage.
　　Desire my pilot is, Beauty my prize;
　　Then who fears sinking where such treasure lies?　　　　　　280

As corn o'er-grown by weeds, so heedful fear
Is almost choked by unresisted lust.
Away he steals with open listening ear,
Full of foul hope, and full of fond mistrust;
Both which, as servitors to the unjust,　　　　　　　　　　　　285
　　So cross him with their opposite persuasion
　　That now he vows a league, and now invasion.

Within his thought her heavenly image sits,
And in the self-same seat sits Collatine;
That eye which looks on her confounds his wits;　　　　　　　290
That eye which him beholds, as more divine,
Unto a view so false will not incline,
　　But with a pure appeal seeks to the heart,
　　Which once corrupted takes the worser part;

And therein heartens up his servile powers,　　　　　　　　　295
Who, flattered by their leader's jocund show,
Stuff up his lust, as minutes fill up hours;

stanza, cannot be said to be anomalous. An
EEBO-TCP search reveals only two earlier
references for 'hearten up'; one coming in
a military context in John Stow's *Chronicles*
(1580): 'The Romans on the other side,
ascribing the praise of this victory, not to the
prowess of the Roman soldier, but to fortune, and the wiliness of their captain, used all
means possible, to hearten up and arm their
youth' (sig. C8r).
　　servile powers inferior faculties; here, his
passion or lustful appetite.
296　***Who*** frequently used as a pronoun for things
　　in Shakespeare, especially at the beginning of
　　a line, as at ll. 328, 388, 447, 461, 655, 1119,
　　1139, 1231, 1740, 1781, 1805; see Hope 2003:
　　108–10 and *Venus and Adonis*, 87n.
　　flattered encouraged.
　　jocund show cheerful, confident display.
297　***Stuff up*** bolster; the oldest meaning of 'stuff'
　　in OED is 'to furnish. . . with men, munitions,
　　and stores' ('stuff', *v.1*, 1a), so there is also a
　　small continuation of the military language.
　　as minutes. . . hours Roe (1992: 158) sees this
　　as a clock reference (the minute hand rising

to the top as the hour approaches), but this
may be anachronistic. The minute hand
was a recent invention (perhaps in a clock
designed by Jost Bürgi *c.* 1577), so it would
only recently have impinged upon an English
readership, if at all. Compare Sonnet 77.2, and
see *3 Henry VI*, 2.5.24–6: 'To carve out dials
quaintly, point by point, | Thereby to see the
minutes how they run: | How many make
the hour full complete'. In Thomas Fale's
Horologiographia: The Art of Dialing (1593: sig.
H2r): a minute is a subdivision of a degree on
a sundial, which works in hours. A mechan-
ical clock designed by the leading London
craftsman Bartholomew Newsam (British
Museum, item 1888.1201.126) has only one
hand, tracing the hours, the dominant design
of the time. However, John Blagrave's *Book of
the Making and Use of a Staff* (1590) wishes
for something like a minute hand: 'instead of
minute glasses, which as they say, they use at
the sea, I should like better of a clock or watch
that should turn the hand quite round about
the dial every hour to show the exact minute.
I have seen such ready made' (sig. H2r).

298 *as their captain* i.e. in the same way as the heart swells with excitement.

pride As in *Venus and Adonis* (see 14n) this word incorporates ideas of physical and sexual mettle (OED³ 'pride, *n*.1', 8), and sexual excitement (OED 11) and thus it suggests arousal as well as denoting the vaunting spirits of the 'servile powers'. See 37n.

299 *more. . . than they owe* His lust goes beyond the bounds of the 'tribute' it owes the heart, reaching a state of excessive excitement.

300 *reprobate* depraved; but perhaps the specific religious meaning 'rejected by God; *spec.* predestined by God to eternal damnation' weighs in pointedly here against the rising excitement. In one of Shakespeare's two other uses of the word, in *Measure for Measure*, 4.3.73–4 ('What if we do omit | This reprobate till he were well inclined') it is also possible to see a similar interplay between a statement about character and a stronger statement about the state of an immortal soul.

301 *marcheth* The verb recalls where he should properly be: with his army.

303 *enforced* forced open; but the word readily evokes and here prefigures rape (OED 9); compare 'enforcement', l. 1623.

retires draws back; OED³'s first citation for this transitive use, 5b, 'to draw or pull back'. This may be a singular verb with a plural subject, according to modern usage, though Hope (2003: 161–3) argues that such forms are alternative plurals, not actually singular forms. It may have been drawn into the singular by 'Each one'.

ward guard. The word has a technical physical sense, OED 'ward, *n*.2', 24a, 'each of the ridges projecting from the inside plate of a lock, serving to prevent the passage [of the wrong key]', alongside its general sense ('. . . look-out, watch, guard', OED 1).

304 *rate* scold, berate (OED³ 'rate, *v*.1', 1), as at *Venus and Adonis*, l. 906.

ill evil intent.

305 *creeping* See 1517n.

regard consideration, caution; see ll. 277, 1400.

306 *grates* rubs audibly against (OED, 'grate, *v*.1', 7b).

to have him heard (as if) in order to make people hear him.

307 *Night-wandering* See *Venus and Adonis*, l. 825 and note.

weasels In Shakespeare weasels are associated with bad temper ('saucy, and | As quarrelous as the weasel', *Cymbeline*, 3.4.158–9) and sly, murderous invasion, as at *Henry V*, 1.2.169–71:

'For once the eagle (England) being in prey, | To her unguarded nest the weasel (Scot) | Comes sneaking, and so sucks her princely eggs'. Roe (1992: 159) cites Roger Ascham's *Toxophilus* (1545) for its general suspicion of nocturnal creatures: 'For on the night-time and in corners, spirits and thieves, rats and mice, toads and owls, night-crows and polecats, foxes and foumarts [OED: another name for the polecat], with all other vermin, and noisome beasts, use most stirring, when in the daylight, and in open places which be ordained of God for honest things' (sig. E2r). In Alciato's *Emblemata* (Leyden, 1593), no. 126, weasels are considered bad omens in houses, and yet (as Burrow 2002: 260 notes, citing Aesop's *Fables*) they were also kept in houses to catch mice and rats. Both reputations are cited in Topsell: 'neither are they unthankful unto the countrymen in whose houses they lodge, for they kill, eat, and devour all manner of mice, rats, and moles, for because of their long slender bodies, they are apt to creep into the holes of the earth and narrow passages'. . . 'an unhappy, unfortunate, and unlucky beast' (sig. 3T4v–3T5r). Separately any one of these qualities might make weasels appropriate observers of Tarquin's entrance, and he shares most of them.

308 *pursues his fear* persists (nonetheless) in the course of action that frightens him.

310 *vents* openings (more often, outlets); see l. 1040.

311 *make him stay* prevent his progress; see l. 323.

313 *conduct* guide (OED, 'conduct, *n*.1', 3).

case matter; the formal tone of 'conduct' adds to the legal resonance.

314 *fond* foolish.

316 *being lighted* when it had reignited.

317 *Lucretia's* The Latin form of her name is used in the Argument and at l. 510. Shakespeare does not use the three-syllable 'Lucretia's', preferring in other cases the disyllabic 'Lucrece'.

glove Although Lucrece's glove serves a practical purpose, a glove was also a typical lover's token, as in *Troilus and Cressida*, 5.2.78–81: ' Thy master now lies thinking on his bed | Of thee and me, and sighs, and takes my glove, | And gives memorial dainty kisses to it, | As I kiss thee'.

wherein. . . sticks i.e. her embroidery needle has been left there for safe-keeping.

318 *rushes* rushes were used as floor-coverings. See *Taming of the Shrew*, 4.1.45–7: 'Is supper ready, the house trimmed, rushes strewed, cobwebs swept?', and most pertinently *Cymbeline*, 2.2.12–14:

And as their captain, so their pride doth grow,
Paying more slavish tribute than they owe.
 By reprobate desire thus madly led,   300
  The Roman lord marcheth to Lucrece' bed.

The locks between her chamber and his will,
Each one by him enforced, retires his ward;
But as they open they all rate his ill,
Which drives the creeping thief to some regard.   305
The threshold grates the door to have him heard;
 Night-wandering weasels shriek to see him there;
  They fright him, yet he still pursues his fear.

As each unwilling portal yields him way,
Through little vents and crannies of the place   310
The wind wars with his torch to make him stay,
And blows the smoke of it into his face,
Extinguishing his conduct in this case;
 But his hot heart, which fond desire doth scorch,
  Puffs forth another wind that fires the torch;   315

And being lighted, by the light he spies
Lucretia's glove, wherein her needle sticks.
He takes it from the rushes where it lies,
And, griping it, the needle his finger pricks,
As who should say, 'This glove to wanton tricks   320
 Is not inured; return again in haste,
  Thou seest our mistress' ornaments are chaste.'

But all these poor forbiddings could not stay him;
He in the worst sense consters their denial:

'Our Tarquin thus | Did softly press the rushes
ere he wakened | The chastity he wounded'.

319 **griping** grasping, seizing. Not 'gripping'; the
OED maintains a distinction between 'gripe'
and 'grip', as two verbs with separate etymological paths and marginally different meanings,
and cites Shakespeare consistently under 'gripe'.
needle elided with 'his'; Malone emended to
'neeld' to make it more clearly monosyllabic.
Although this is listed as an alternative form in
OED, the elision fits both the spelling in Q and
the pronunciation in l. 317.

320 **As who should say** (i) as if it were saying; (ii) as if
it wanted to say; compare *Venus and Adonis*, l. 280.

321 **inured** accustomed. Shakespeare's only use of
this form, though see *Twelfth Night*, 2.5.148–9:

'to inure thyself to what thou art like to be, cast
thy humble slough and appear fresh'.

322 **ornaments** accessories, equipment; OED[3]
'ornament, *n.*' 1a allows for uses that do not
imply display or decoration, but such implications are hard to dismiss here. Compare *1
Henry VI*, 5.1.52–4: 'The sum of money which
I promised | ... For clothing me in these
grave ornaments'.

323 **poor** ineffectual.
forbiddings Shakespeare's only use of the noun,
singular or plural.
stay stop, delay.

324 **worst sense** Compare 'worser' at ll. 249, 294.
consters construes (as it is given in Q3–5),
interprets.

326 **accidental things of trial** chance events that test him (i.e., that test his resolve).

327 **bars. . . hourly dial** the lines on the clock face which cause the clock's hand to stop. It seems probable that this refers to the hour hand of a clock reaching the bars that indicate the hourly divisions. These would not actually present an obstacle to the arm, but in an early modern clock the arm would move in a stop-start way, giving an appearance that the bars themselves prevented progress. See also 297n.

328 **lingering stay** protracted delay.
   let hinder.

329 **Till. . . debt** i.e. the hour hand cannot move until every minute has done its service. Compare the eagerness and excess in debt-paying in l. 299.

330 **So, so** OED lists this as the earliest instance of 'so, *adv.* and *conj.*', 5c, where it is seen as an 'introductory particle'. It notes that, along with 5d and 5e (expressions of approval or acceptance), such uses 'are common in Shakespeare's plays'. Compare *Henry VIII*, 1.1.219–20: 'So, so; | These are the limbs o' th' plot. No more, I hope?'.
   lets hindrances.
   attend the time serve the moment, i.e. the obstacles actually heighten the pleasure and anticipation.

331 **threat** threaten.

332 **more** greater.
   prime springtime; compare *Venus and Adonis*, l. 131 and note.

333 **sneapèd** nipped, pinched (by frost); compare *Love's Labour's Lost*, 1.1.100–1: 'like an envious sneaping frost | That bites the first-born infants of the spring'.

334 **pays the income** (i) pays for the entrance; (ii) pays the entrance-fee. The OED has this instance (Shakespeare's only use of the word) under 'income, *n.*1', 'coming in, entrance, arrival, advent', but sense 3, 'a fee paid on coming in or entering', is current in Shakespeare's time (first citation 1549).

335 **shelves** sandbanks.

336 **ere** before.

338 **of his thought** that he has been imagining (or planning).

339 **yielding** Compare l. 1658, where the noun 'yielding' is used more sharply in the context of the rape.

341 **So. . . wrought** wickedness has made him so unlike himself.

342 **prey to pray** Both words are spelled 'pray' in Q.

343 **heavens** monosyllabic here.
   countenance favour, sanction.

344 **unfruitful** unprofitable.

345 **solicited** petitioned.

346 **compass** possess; but the word has other complementary senses. The earliest citation for OED 'compass, *v.*1', 11b 'attain, obtain', is from *Two Gentlemen of Verona*, 2.4.213–14: 'If not, to compass her I'll use my skill'. See also, sense 2a, 'contrive, machinate'; 9, 'catch, seize'; and also 8b, 'embrace, encircle with the arms', for which compare Marlowe's *Dr Faustus*, 4.1.107, 'in mine arms I would have compassed him', and the Folio text of *Troilus and Cressida*, 1.3.275–6: 'a lady, wiser, fairer, truer | Than ever Greek did compass ['couple' in the Quarto version of the play] in his arms'.
   fair fair unblemished beauty. See OED³ 'fair, *adj.* and *n.*', 12, for the suggestion of moral purity. Compare *Venus and Adonis*, ll. 208, 1083, 1086.

347 **they** the heavens (target of his prayer in l. 342); 'th'eternal power' is a more recent antecedent, and a synonym for 'the heavens'. Compare the switch from singular to plural in *Richard III*, 1.3.216–18: 'If heaven have any grievous plague in store | Exceeding those that I can wish on thee, | O, let them keep it till thy sins be ripe' (as noted by Roe 1992: 161).
   stand. . . hour look favourably on the occasion. This use of 'auspicious' predates any in the OED; *All's Well That Ends Well*, 3.3.7–8, 'Fortune play upon thy prosperous helm | As thy auspicious mistress!', is cited under the pertinent sense, 2b. However, EEBO-TCP has a comparable instance in George Peele's *The Honour of the Garter* (1593): 'As if the same, | The same great Empress that we here enjoy, | Had climbed the clouds, and been in person there; | To whom the earth, the sea, and elements | Auspicious are' (sig. C3r–v).

348 **Even** monosyllabic here, as it is in every case in *Lucrece* except l. 498.
   must See 155n.

349 **fact** deed.

351 **Love and Fortune** The resonance here is both proverbial (Dent F601, 'Fortune favours the bold') and classical: in a gloss on Ovid's *Fasti*, 2.782 ('audentes forsque deusque iuvat', 'Fortune and God help the daring'), Marsus makes a link with the same proverb, and another 'Love makes a man daring' (*P. Ovidii Nasonis Fastorum*, 1527: 146). Elizabethan uses of the phrase suggest the nuances of Tarquin's

The doors, the wind, the glove that did delay him   325
He takes for accidental things of trial;
Or as those bars which stop the hourly dial,
   Who with a lingering stay his course doth let,
   Till every minute pays the hour his debt.

'So, so,' quoth he, 'these lets attend the time,   330
Like little frosts that sometime threat the spring
To add a more rejoicing to the prime,
And give the sneapèd birds more cause to sing.
Pain pays the income of each precious thing:
   Huge rocks, high winds, strong pirates, shelves and sands   335
   The merchant fears, ere rich at home he lands.'

Now is he come unto the chamber door
That shuts him from the heaven of his thought,
Which with a yielding latch, and with no more,
Hath barred him from the blessèd thing he sought.   340
So from himself impiety hath wrought,
   That for his prey to pray he doth begin,
   As if the heavens should countenance his sin.

But in the midst of his unfruitful prayer,
Having solicited th' eternal power   345
That his foul thoughts might compass his fair fair,
And they would stand auspicious to the hour,
Even there he starts. Quoth he, 'I must deflower.
   The powers to whom I pray abhor this fact;
   How can they then assist me in the act?   350

'Then Love and Fortune be my gods, my guide.
My will is backed with resolution:
Thoughts are but dreams till their effects be tried;

---

self-dramatisation here. EEBO-TCP reveals that it is a favourite of Robert Greene and Thomas Lodge, writers of romance and classically inspired erotic fiction. Compare Greene's *Pandosto*: 'which cross luck drove him into a great choler, that he began both to accuse love and fortune' (sig. C1r), and Lodge's *Scilla's Metamorphosis*: 'songs of remorse I warble now and then, | Wherein I curse fond Love and Fortune dureless' (sig. B3v).

352 **backed with** supported by.
   resolution pronounced with five syllables, which is rare in Shakespeare (compare *2 Henry VI*, 3.1.332, *Julius Caesar*, 2.1.113, *Othello*, 5.1.5).

As Burrow notes (2002: 263), Capell ('dauntless resolution') and Taylor ('constant resolution', by analogy with *Henry V*, 2.4.35) have proposed emendations to this line which would give it a feminine rhyme or make it an Alexandrine (see 354n), while Q6 emends l. 354 (see note).

353 **Thoughts. . . tried** Intentions are merely imaginary until we experience their consequences in action; a pragmatic thought often compared to Francis Bacon's essay 'Of Great Place': 'For good thoughts (though God accept them) yet towards men are little better than good dreams, except they be put in act' (1985: 34).
   effects See ll. 251, 1555.

354 **The blackest** Blacke Q6; see 352n.

with absolution by forgiveness; with a strong hint of a technical, Christian sense, where it means remission of sins, and with further specific Catholic resonance, where this is done by a priest after penitence. The idea does not follow from l. 353, and in spite of being orthodox doctrine, is not something that any Christian should plan on before committing a terrible sin. 'Absolution' and 'dissolution' in l. 355 are pronounced with five syllables. The lines are Alexandrines, with six rather than five feet. Perhaps this was done to help create a particularly sententious tone. Compare *Venus and Adonis*, 760n.

355 **hath dissolution** melts; see l. 247 and note, and on the pronunciation, see 354n.

356 **eye of heaven** sun. This common phrase (for a number of different celestial bodies) is used on four other occasions by Shakespeare: Sonnet 18.5, twice in *Richard II* (1.3.275, 3.2.37), and in *King John* (4.2.15). It is picked up in Middleton's sequel poem, *The Ghost of Lucrece*: 'But O my heaven, shall I forget thy spheres, | O spheres of heaven, shall I let pass your skies? | O skies which wears out time, and never wears, | Shall I make dim the tapers of your eyes? | O eyes of heaven, sun, moon, and stars that rise | To wake the day, and free imprisoned night, | Shall my oblivious vapour cloud your light?' (sig. C3r). 'Heaven' is monosyllabic here.

out extinguished (like a candle, as in *Macbeth*, 2.1.5, 'Their candles are all out', and 5.5.23, 'Out, out, brief candle!'); i.e. the sun has set.

357 **delight** See 12n. Compare Sonnet 129.

358 **plucked up** lifted; the word can denote 'sudden or forcible effort' (OED³ 'pluck, *v*.', 4a) and the preposition intensifies this. This may denote impatience and/or the physical force that lies ahead (compare l. 359). On 'pluck', see *Venus and Adonis*, 30n.

359 **with his knee. . . opens wide** The analogy between entering the chamber and the rape of Lucrece is clearer here.

360 **fast** (i) soundly (OED 'fast, *adv*.', 1b); (ii) securely (OED 2c). The second sense, though, has no OED citations after l. 1535, and would of course be ironic. Compare *Macbeth*, 5.1.8, 20, where the Gentlewoman sees Lady Macbeth as 'in a most fast sleep', and 'fast asleep'. The word has other resonances that add to the urgency and anxiety of the moment (fixedly and resolutely, OED 1a, 1c; stoutly and strongly, 1d; 'so as not to permit of escape', 2a; very nearby, 4a). Indeed, the buried possibility of speed (and the sense 'readily', 6c) make this word a source of tension.

364 **mortal** deadly.

sting Figuratively this suggests Tarquin's lust, as commentators note, but neither the OED definition nor any of Shakespeare's other uses of the word, though often figurative, is so clearly a synonym for lust or sin. Iago comes closest: 'we have reason to cool our raging motions, our carnal stings, our unbitted lusts', *Othello*, 1.3.329–31. Compare also 'the lurking serpent's mortal sting', *3 Henry VI*, 2.2.15. The 'sting' may suggest a physical assault from death, or from Tarquin's penis. The phrase is used in Spenser's depiction of Error, *Faerie Queene*, I.i.15.2–4: 'Her huge long taile her den all overspred, | Yet was in knots and many boughtes upwound, | Pointed with mortall sting'.

365–71 On these lines in manuscript, see 386–413n.

365 **stalks** walks stealthily, like a hunter or predator. The resonance with Chaucer's *Legend of Good Women*, l. 1781, 'And in the nyght ful thefly can he stalke', suggests criminal stealing as well.

367 **close** closed.

about around the bed.

368 **Rolling. . . eyeballs** This line is quoted to illustrate OED³ 'roll, *v*.2', 21b, where the gesture is associated predominantly with 'surprise or disapproval'. OED³ 21a, however, though intransitive, seems closer: 'often as a sign of injury or frenzy'. In *King John*, 4.2.191–2, 'Whilst he that hears makes fearful action | With wrinkled brows, with nods, with rolling eyes', fear and anxiety are suggested. In *A Midsummer Night's Dream*, 5.1.12–13, 'The poet's eye, in a fine frenzy rolling, | Doth glance from heaven to earth, from earth to heaven', there is a more positive sort of frenzy or madness. The figure of Dissemblance in *Faerie Queene*, III.vi.15.4–6 – appropriately enough, assailing the Knight of Chastity – has a comparable expression: 'He loured on

The blackest sin is cleared with absolution;
Against love's fire, fear's frost hath dissolution. 355
   The eye of heaven is out, and misty night
   Covers the shame that follows sweet delight.'

This said, his guilty hand plucked up the latch,
And with his knee the door he opens wide.
The dove sleeps fast that this night-owl will catch; 360
Thus treason works ere traitors be espied.
Who sees the lurking serpent steps aside;
   But she, sound sleeping, fearing no such thing,
   Lies at the mercy of his mortal sting.

Into the chamber wickedly he stalks, 365
And gazeth on her yet unstainèd bed.
The curtains being close, about he walks,
Rolling his greedy eyeballs in his head.
By their high treason is his heart misled,
   Which gives the watchword to his hand full soon 370
   To draw the cloud that hides the silver moon.

Look as the fair and fiery-pointed sun,
Rushing from forth a cloud, bereaves our sight;
Even so, the curtain drawn, his eyes begun
To wink, being blinded with a greater light. 375

her with dangerous eye-glance, | Showing his nature in his countenance; | His rolling eyes did never rest in place'. In *The Last Part of the Mirror for Magistrates* (1578), the paranoid tyrant Phereus is seen 'whirling in his head | His rolling eyen, he searcheth here, and there | The deep danger that he so sore did fear' (sig. T4r). Lust must also be a factor here. Compare also Sonnet 20.5.

369 **high treason** i.e the eyes now entirely betray their ruler, the heart, where previously they helped it (see 276n). Compare Sonnet 46.1 and note.

370 **watchword** verbal signal to begin an attack (OED 2a, and figuratively 2b, where this line is cited).
full soon immediately, or at last very shortly (as at *Romeo and Juliet*, 2.3.30: 'Full soon the canker death eats up that plant').

371 **draw . . . moon** pull the curtain that conceals Lucrece. She is figured here as the moon-goddess Diana, perhaps evoking Ovid's story of Actaeon, who saw the goddess bathing naked and was turned into a stag (*Metamorphoses*, Book 3).

372 **Look as** just as. See *Venus and Adonis*, l. 67 and note; this phrase is a characteristic invitation to witness and compare. The imperative compels the reader to invade Lucrece's privacy.

373 **bereaves** takes away. Compare *Venus and Adonis*, l. 797.

374 **Even** monosyllabic here.
begun i.e. began, an alternative preterite form.

375 **wink** close, blink. See *Venus and Adonis*, l. 90 and note.
greater light Perhaps Lucrece is brighter than the sun of ll. 372–3, or perhaps she emits more light than the eyes do in their beams. See l. 376, and compare 228n, and *Venus and Adonis*, 487n.

376 **that** the fact that.

reflects so bright The OED³ allows for 'reflect' to mean 'shine' (4b, citing *Titus Andronicus*, 1.1.225–6, 'whose virtues will, I hope, | Reflect on Rome'), but this may be a further twist on the 'eye-beams' theme, with Lucrece a wondrous mirror, sending back the rays of light.

377 **supposed** imagined; compare l. 133. On the rhyme with '**enclosed**' (l. 378), and the sounding, or not, of final -*ed*, see 50–2n. Q's spellings are 'supposed' and 'inclosed'.

379 **darksome prison** i.e. under the eyelids; compare the 'deep dark cabins' of *Venus and Adonis*, l. 1038. This is Shakespeare's only use of 'darksome'.

380 **period** end.

382 **clear** unstained, pure; see l. 11 and note.

383 **they** Tarquin's eyes.

must See 155n.

blessèd league holy covenant (of marriage); 'league' suggests a military pact. Compare l. 689.

384 **holy-thoughted** The only citation in OED for this compound describing the purity of Lucrece's thoughts; EEBO-TCP also has no other citations before Shakespeare (whose only use this is).

their sight i.e. to Tarquin's gaze.

385 **Must** See 155n.

sell This may suggest mercenary or mercantile exchange; or just 'give [...] in response to a demand [...] yield' (OED 1); or indeed 'give up treacherously [...] betray' (2a). Compare Sonnet 76.7.

world's delight her delight in the world. See 'earth's delight', l. 487, and compare 'day's delight' in *Venus and Adonis*, l. 380. In *Love's Labour's Lost*, 1.1.29–30 Dumain uses the phrase to suggest sensual pleasures: 'The grosser manner of these world's delights | He throws upon the gross world's baser slaves'. There may be a contrast here between the lawful pleasure she could have expected to enjoy, and the unlawful pleasure to which she is soon to be subjected. Compare also *Faerie Queene*, I.vii.39.103: 'What world's delight, or joy of living speech | Can heart, so plunged in sea of sorrows deep, | And heaped with so huge misfortunes, reach?'. On 'delight' itself, see 12n.

386–413 These lines (especially the first two stanzas) evidently appealed to early readers, an indication of the impact of the poem's erotic potential in spite of its overall emphasis. They are reprinted in *England's Parnassus* (1600: sig. 2C6v–7r). The first two stanzas appear in two verse miscellanies, probably from the mid-seventeenth century: British Library, Add. MS 27406, 74r (in this case, alongside ll. 365–71 and 419–20), and Rosenbach Museum & Library, MS 239/16, 146 (CELM ShW 2, 2.5). A version adapted into the six-line *Venus and Adonis* metre appeared in Sir John Suckling's *Fragmenta Aurea*, entitled 'A Supplement of an imperfect Copy of Verses of Mr Wil. Shakespeare's, By the Author'. Burrow (2002: 44), suggests that Suckling found these lines badly transcribed in manuscript and restored them thus, rather than them being the traces of an earlier version of *Lucrece*.

386 **lily. . . rosy** See 11n on the combination of red and white in the poem, and 71n on lilies and roses.

387 **Cozening** cheating; disyllabic here.

388 **Who** i.e. the pillow; see 296n.

therefore i.e. as a result of being deprived of a kiss.

in sunder into two parts.

389 **Swelling** The pillow rises up on either side of her head and hand pressing it down.

want his lack its.

391 **virtuous monument** This evokes the figures of wives on Tudor tombs, lying as if asleep with their heads on pillows alongside their husbands (as in the tomb of Sir Robert Oxenbridge and his wife at Hurstbourne Priors, Hampshire, made 1574) or alone like Lady Margaret Beaufort in Westminster Abbey. The Tarquinesque Iachimo in *Cymbeline*, 2.2.31–2 also makes this connection: 'And be her sense but as a monument, | Thus in a chapel lying!'. The 'virtuous monument' may also suggest an allegorical Virtue presented in the way Viola imagines a figure of Patience in *Twelfth Night*, 2.4.114–15: 'She sat like Patience on a monument, | Smiling at grief'.

392 **admired of** admired by.

unhallowed wicked; see 192n.

393 **Without** outside.

Whether it is that she reflects so bright
    That dazzleth them, or else some shame supposed,
    But blind they are, and keep themselves enclosed.

O had they in that darksome prison died,
Then had they seen the period of their ill;   380
Then Collatine again, by Lucrece' side,
In his clear bed might have reposèd still.
But they must ope, this blessèd league to kill,
    And holy-thoughted Lucrece to their sight
    Must sell her joy, her life, her world's delight.   385

Her lily hand, her rosy cheek lies under,
Cozening the pillow of a lawful kiss;
Who, therefore angry, seems to part in sunder,
Swelling on either side to want his bliss;
Between whose hills her head entombèd is,   390
    Where like a virtuous monument she lies,
    To be admired of lewd unhallowed eyes.

Without the bed her other fair hand was
On the green coverlet, whose perfect white
Showed like an April daisy on the grass,   395
With pearly sweat resembling dew of night.
Her eyes, like marigolds, had sheathed their light,

394 **whose** i.e. Lucrece's hand's.

395 **April daisy** As well as the colour contrast there is a suggestion of youthful vigour. In *Merry Wives of Windsor*, 3.2.66–9 'Fenton [. . .] has eyes of youth; he writes verses, he speaks holiday, he smells April and May'. April also suggests vigour in Sonnets 3.10, 98.2. Daisies were given various symbolic meanings, of which modesty and purity seem most apt here (Thomas and Faircloth 2014: ebook).

396 **pearly** Shakespeare's only use of the adjective. Qc has 'pearlie' rather than Qu's 'perlie'; the original spelling could evoke other words, though 'pearly' would still be the compelling possibility. Pearls are often associated with tears (as at l. 1553, and *Venus and Adonis*, l. 980), which are more easily idealised, but less often with sweat. An EEBO-TCP search only finds one example before Shakespeare, in *The Third Volume*

of [Holinshed's] Chronicles (1587): 'the more did he [the Duke of Brabant; this is his deathbed contrition] detest himself as a most miserable sinner: then might you have seen among much sweat which as pearls ran down his hair and beard' (sig. 6O2v).

397 **marigolds** The petals of marigolds close at night. See *The Winter's Tale*, 4.4.165–6: 'The marigold, that goes to bed wi' th' sun | And with him rises weeping'. Compare also Sonnet 25.6.

sheathed 'covered from view' (OED 'sheathe, *v*.1' 3b, where this line is the only citation). The word is most often used with weapons, as at l. 1723; compare its use of the boar's tusks in *Venus and Adonis*, ll. 617, 1116. The host in *The Merry Wives of Windsor*, 2.3.84–5, says 'sheathe thy impatience, throw cold water on thy choler', but this connects metaphorically to more violent contexts.

398 **canopied** covered, as if by a curtain, by her eyelids. Shakespeare uses the same metaphor in *Cymbeline*, 2.2.19–22 when Iachimo observes Imogen: 'The flame o' th' taper | Bows toward her, and would under-peep her lids, | To see th' enclosed lights, now canopied | Under these windows'.

400 **golden threads** On the poem's problematic Petrarchanisms (such as the golden hair of the beautiful woman) see headnote.
played. . . breath i.e. her hair moved, as if playing or dancing, when she breathed. Compare *A Lover's Complaint*, ll. 85–8.

401 **modest. . . modesty** a *chiasmus* of oxymorons (though 'wanton' could be used of innocent playfulness) continues the playful and yet ominous depiction of Lucrece's unwitting allure.

402 **life's triumph** (i) the highest achievement of life; (ii) life's proud performance, as in a Roman triumphal procession.
map image, representation, OED³ *n*.1, 5a; sleep presents a picture of death. For the face as a map, see l. 1712, and Sonnet 68.1. Compare *2 Henry VI*, 3.1.202–3: 'in thy face I see | The map of honour, truth, and loyalty'. EEBO-TCP reveals no instance of the phrase 'map of death' before Shakespeare. Compare Aemilia Lanyer, 'A Preamble of the Author Before the Passion', in *Salve Deus Rex Judaeorum* (1611), which may allude to Shakespeare: 'a matter far beyond my barren skill, | To show with any life this map of death' (sig. B2r).

402–3 **life's. . . death. . . death's. . . life's** another *chiasmus* (see l. 401).

403 **dim** dull, lifeless.
life's mortality human life (Schmidt); as Duncan-Jones and Woudhuysen note, there is an element of tautology here as a result of the need to complete the *chiasmus* (2007: 273). 'Mortality' may suggest 'human nature' or the term of human life; in either case the element of death (Latin 'mors') in the word is downplayed.

404 **Each** Both life and death.

406 **life. . . life** a final *chiasmus* in the stanza (as at ll. 401, 402–3).

407–8 **Her. . . unconquerèd** These lines recall the depiction of breasts and blue veins at *Hero and Leander*, ll. 757–61: 'For though the iv'ry mount be scaled, | Which is with azure circling lines empaled, | Much like a globe

(a globe may I term this, | By which love sails to regions full of bliss), | Yet there with Sisyphus he toiled in vain'. Duncan-Jones and Woudhuysen take it that the debt is probably Shakespeare's, but in doing so recognise that we cannot be sure of the compositional chronology (2007: 273). Nevertheless this is another way in which *Lucrece* recalls the epyllion tradition even beyond *Venus and Adonis*, wherein compare 'blue-veined', l. 125 and note. Compare too *Venus and Adonis*, l. 82 and note, where the lines from *Hero and Leander* may also be recalled.

407 **ivory** i.e. white (proverbially so, as in Dent I109, 'as white as ivory') and smooth. Compare ll. 464, 1234, and *Venus and Adonis*, l. 230 and notes.
globes The word can denote simply a 'spherical or rounded body' (OED³ 1), but the rest of the stanza shows that modern globes (spherical representations of the earth) are suggested here. This is Shakespeare's only use of the word in the plural; singular uses tend to suggest the planet earth rather than a map of it, except, in a bawdy context, in *The Comedy of Errors*, 3.2.113–15: 'No longer from head to foot than from hip to hip: she is spherical, like a globe; I could find out countries in her'.
circled surrounded; compare ll. 1229, 1587, and note.

408 **maiden** Although the word often means technical virginity, it is also used figuratively, and here denotes her chastity within marriage. The OED³ cites this line under *n*. and *adj*. B4, 'That has not been conquered, tried, worked, etc.... Of a town, castle, fortress, etc.: that has never been captured'; this is consistent with the conquering metaphor but unnecessarily specific. The moment probably elaborates Ovid's *Fasti*, 2.803–4, 'positis urgentur pectora palmis, | tunc primum externa pectora tacta manu' ('her breasts were eagerly touched by his outstretched hands, | which were then touched for the first time by a stranger's hand'). See Appendix 2.

409 **bearing yoke** The familiar image of marriage, likened to the yoking of oxen in pairs, suggests the dutiful work of honourable partnership although Shakespeare's other uses of the metaphor are negative. Hermia uses it of an unwelcome marriage in *A*

And canopied in darkness sweetly lay
Till they might open to adorn the day.

Her hair, like golden threads, played with her breath;   400
O modest wantons, wanton modesty,
Showing life's triumph in the map of death,
And death's dim look in life's mortality!
Each in her sleep themselves so beautify,
    As if between them twain there were no strife,   405
    But that life lived in death, and death in life.

Her breasts, like ivory globes circled with blue,
A pair of maiden worlds unconquerèd,
Save of their lord no bearing yoke they knew,
And him by oath they truly honourèd.   410
These worlds in Tarquin new ambition bred,
    Who like a foul usurper went about
    From this fair throne to heave the owner out.

What could he see, but mightily he noted?
What did he note, but strongly he desired?   415
What he beheld, on that he firmly doted,
And in his will his wilful eye he tired.

Midsummer Night's Dream, 1.1.79–82: 'So will I grow, so live, so die, my lord, | Ere I will my virgin patent up | Unto his lordship, whose unwished yoke | My soul consents not to give sovereignty'. Don Pedro uses it sardonically in *Much Ado About Nothing*, 1.1.260–1: 'Well, as time shall try | "In time the savage bull doth bear the yoke"'.

410 **by oath** i.e. within the vows of marriage.

411–12 **ambition. . . foul usurper** These terms resonate with the poem's political interests: Tarquin is a king but will be deemed illegitimate. Macbeth, who is an ambitious usurper, imagines himself stalking Duncan 'with Tarquin's ravishing strides' (see 162–8n).

412 **went about** conspired, prepared (OED³ 'go, *v.*', PV1, 5); but restless motion around Lucrece's bed seems pertinent here too (as at l. 367).

413 **this fair throne** i.e. Lucrece's breasts, but the stanza's extended usurpation metaphor is expansive enough that this could be taken to refer to her whole body or the marital bed.

heave move, lift; though the modern sense of strain and violence, not usually evident in Shakespeare's uses (see 111n), seems active here. Compare l. 586.

owner i.e. Collatine.

414 **noted** observed, perceived (OED³ 'note, *v.*2', 5a, 5b). This usage is recalled at *Cymbeline*, 2.2.24: 'To note the chamber, I will write all down'.

415–8 **desired. . . tired. . . admired** On the sounding, or not, of final *-ed*, see 50–2n. Q's spellings are 'desired', 'tyred', and 'admired'.

416 **firmly** (i) steadily; (ii) strongly.

doted Compare l. 155 and note.

417 **will. . . wilful** lust. . . lustful. *Polyptoton*, which in *Venus and Adonis* (ll. 78, 111, 270, 409–14, 610) often allows witty savouring of etymology, has a darker effect here.

tired wore out, exhausted, but with the sense of hawk-like feeding also contributing here (OED 'tire, *v.*2', 2a 'Of a hawk. . . to tear flesh in feeding'; see 2b and 2c for figurative uses of humans). Compare *Venus and Adonis*, ll. 56, 177.

418 **admiration. . . admired** On rhetorical polytoton, see 417n.

419–20 On these lines in manuscript, see 386–413n.

419 **azure** proverbially blue (Dent A411.2); Burrow draws attention to the expense of true azure, made from lapis lazuli, and to the commodification of Lucrece's beauty in the rest of ll. 419–20 (2002: 266). Compare 'blue-veined', *Venus and Adonis*, l. 125.

   alabaster proverbially white (Dent A95.2); compare *Venus and Adonis*, ll. 362–3 and note, and *Othello*, 5.2.4–5: 'that whiter skin of hers than snow, | And smooth as monumental alablaster'.

420 **coral** proverbially red (Dent C648.1); compare l. 1234, and *Venus and Adonis*, l. 542 and note. The connection to Sonnet 130.2 made there indicates that at this point in *Lucrece*, as so often in *Venus and Adonis*, the stereotypes of love poetry are in evidence.

   snow-white proverbial; see 196n.

421 **grim** fierce, cruel (OED *adj.* and *adv.* A1a); compare the boar in *Venus and Adonis*, l. 1105. The word's other possible senses (stern, merciless, repellent, formidable) are evident in the word's other appearances in the poem. See ll. 452, 769, 1451.

   fawneth o'er takes pleasure in. When used of an animal it need not have the negative connotations of OED 'fawn, *v.*1', 3a 'to court favour or notice by an abject demeanour'.

422 **Sharp** keen; compare *Venus and Adonis*, l. 55.

423 **stay** pause.

424 **rage** frenzy; can denote a range of different passions, not only anger. Compare l. 468 and see 'enraged' at *Venus and Adonis*, l. 29 and note.

   qualified moderated (OED³ 'qualify, *v.*', 9a), as at *King John*, 5.1.12–13: 'This inundation of mistempered humour | Rests by you only to be qualified'.

425 **Slaked** weakened, diminished (OED 'slake, *v.*1', 1a). Q's 'Slakt' could be a form of 'slacked' (i.e. slackened; see Q2–5, where the word is 'Slackt').

427 **uproar** violent insurrection (OED 1a, 1b; this line is cited among the figurative uses). Although the word can mean 'loud outcry' (OED 2a) or 'commotion, excitement'

(3a), all Shakespeare's uses tend towards the stronger sense. Compare *Macbeth*, 4.3.97–100: 'had I pow'r, I should | Pour the sweet milk of concord into hell, | Uproar the universal peace, confound | All unity on earth.'

   veins. The use of 'veins' to stand for 'blood' as a metaphor for passions is not common in Shakespeare, but see *Henry V*, 2.3.4–5: 'Nym, rouse thy vaunting veins; | Boy, bristle thy courage up'. Q's full-stop is retained to preserve the pause before the 'uproar' is elaborated, but a comma is also viable.

428 **straggling slaves** disorderly vagabond soldiers. Calling them 'slaves' may suggest enslaved soldiers, the lowest ranked; or it may simply be a term of general social disparagement, as in *Richard II*, 1.4.27: 'What reverence he did throw away on slaves'. 'Straggling' most readily suggests a chaotic lack of military formation here, but Shakespeare's only other use of the term (*Timon of Athens*, 5.1.6–7: 'He likewise enriched poor straggling soldiers with | Great quantity') suggests an abject state.

   pillage plunder.

429 **Obdurate** hard-hearted, lacking humane feeling (rather than having firmness of purpose); stressed on second syllable, as it is at *Venus and Adonis*, l. 199.

   fell savage.

   effecting carrying out.

430 **ravishment** (i) rape; (ii) plunder (OED³ 4); the first sense is dominant elsewhere and is clearly denoted by Shakespeare's only other use (l. 1128). The context allows the second, which would avoid a moment of tautology between the vehicle and tenor in the metaphor here; but that tautology itself suggests the horror of what lies ahead.

431 **respecting** regarding; compare *Venus and Adonis*, l. 911.

432 **pride** For this word's connotations, including sexual vigour as well as vaunting self-esteem, see 37n, and especially ll. 298, 437, 438.

   still always, at any moment.

433 **Anon** at once, forthwith.

   alarum the signal to attack (provided by the heart's drumbeat).

With more than admiration he admired
    Her azure veins, her alabaster skin,
    Her coral lips, her snow-white dimpled chin.   420

As the grim lion fawneth o'er his prey,
Sharp hunger by the conquest satisfied,
So o'er this sleeping soul doth Tarquin stay,
His rage of lust by gazing qualified:
Slaked, not suppressed, for standing by her side,   425
    His eye, which late this mutiny restrains,
    Unto a greater uproar tempts his veins.

And they, like straggling slaves for pillage fighting,
Obdurate vassals fell exploits effecting,
In bloody death and ravishment delighting,   430
Nor children's tears nor mother's groans respecting,
Swell in their pride, the onset still expecting.
    Anon his beating heart, alarum striking,
    Gives the hot charge, and bids them do their liking.

His drumming heart cheers up his burning eye;   435
His eye commends the leading to his hand;
His hand, as proud of such a dignity,
Smoking with pride, marched on to make his stand
On her bare breast, the heart of all her land,
    Whose ranks of blue veins, as his hand did scale,   440
    Left their round turrets destitute and pale.

---

434 **hot charge** command for a fierce attack; the phrase, which can refer to the attack itself, appears in military contexts and must have had some technical resonance. See Plutarch's Life of Brutus in North's translation of the *Lives* (1579): 'So they gave a hot charge upon them. But notwithstanding all the force they made, they could not break into the midst of their battle' (sig. 4X4r).

them i.e. his veins, standing for his lust (see l. 427 and note).

435 **cheers up** raises the spirits of; see OED[3] 'cheer, *v.*1', PV1, where the first citation is *2 Henry IV*, 4.1.143: 'My sovereign lord, cheer up yourself, look up'.

436 **commends the leading** entrusts command.

437 **as** (i) as if; (ii) being.

proud On this word's connotations, see 37n.

438 **Smoking** burning, steaming; compare *Venus and Adonis*, l. 555.

pride sexual arousal; see 37n, and l. 298.

make his stand hold his ground, prepare to fight.

440 **ranks. . . scale** On blue veins, see ll. 407–8 and note. The passage from *Hero and Leander* quoted there may be the source of 'scale', but that word also fits the military language of the stanza, as does 'ranks'.

441 **round turrets** nipples, or perhaps the whole breasts. The extended physical analogy resembles the 'park' section of *Venus and Adonis* (ll. 229–40).

destitute abandoned, deserted (OED A1a).

442 **They** the veins of Lucrece's breasts.

mustering assembling (OED³ 'muster, *v.*1', 3a), as in *Measure for Measure*, 2.4.20, 'Why does my blood thus muster to my heart?'. However, the word often refers to the gathering in readiness of an army (OED³ 2a), thus continuing the military thread: the veins have left their posts. Compare ll. 720, 773.

quiet cabinet i.e. her mind, or heart. A cabinet, as well as being a treasure-chest for jewellery, was a small room to which a nobleman or noblewoman would retire to do private business; hence it works as an analogy for sleep. Compare the sun's 'moist cabinet' at *Venus and Adonis*, l. 854, and the 'poisoned closet', l. 1659.

443 **governess** ruler, mistress; i.e. her reason, her consciousness. Shakespeare's only other use of the word is in *A Midsummer Night's Dream*, 2.1.103 ('the moon (the governess of floods)').

444 **beset** surrounded, assailed (OED 2a); perhaps besieged (OED 2b).

446 **amazed** bewildered.

breaks ope. . . locked-up i.e. she breaks out of the 'prison' of l. 379.

447 **Who** which (see 296n).

this tumult to behold in order to see the riot [that the reporting veins have described].

448 **dimmed and controlled** clouded and overwhelmed; the light of her eyes is overcome by that of the torch. Compare l. 375, where her eyes' light dominates.

450 **From forth** out of.

by. . . waking being woken by imaginary fear, i.e. a nightmare.

451 **ghastly sprite** terrifying spirit.

452 **grim** See 421n.

aspect stressed on second syllable.

453 **worser** See 249n.

taking (i) condition, plight (OED³ 'taking, *n.*', 4a); (ii) 'disturbed or agitated state of mind' (OED³ 4c), as at *Merry Wives of Windsor*, 3.3.180–1: 'What a taking was he in when your husband asked who was in the basket!'.

454 **heedfully** consciously, attentively, as at *Two Gentlemen of Verona*, 2.6.11: 'Unheedful vows may heedfully be broken'. Compare 'heedful', l. 495; and also 'advisedly', l. 180 and note.

455 **supposèd** imagined.

456 **Wrapped** consumed, absorbed. There is an aural link with 'rapt' (Q's spelling: 'wrapt') suggesting ravished, as in (i) being transported by intense emotion, OED³ 'rapt, *adj.*', 6; (ii) being raped (OED³ 3).

confounded confused.

thousand The number reappears at ll. 912, 963, 1373, and is used to denote a non-specific large number. Compare *Venus and Adonis*, l. 16 and note.

457 **Like. . . lies** Ovid's simile at this point is of lamb and wolf (II.799–800; see Appendix 2): 'sed tremit, ut quondam stabulis deprensa relictis | parva sub infesto cum iacet agna lupo' ('But she trembled as a little lamb does, when it lies below a wicked wolf, having been caught outside the fold'). Shakespeare simplifies the picture but adds that the bird's shivers come after death, not before it.

458 **winking** when her eyes close.

appears singular verb with a plural subject, according to modern usage. Hope (2003: 161–3) argues that such forms are alternative plurals, not actually singular forms.

459 **Quick-shifting antics** grotesque, rapidly changing shapes. 'Antics' may suggest performers playing ludicrous, disturbing roles (in line with OED 'antic, *adj.* and *n.*', B4); or the shows such performers create (OED B3); or it may suggest fantastic or monstrous shapes as found in architecture (OED B1). Shakespeare uses the word more often with the former sense, as at *Troilus and Cressida*, 5.3.85–6: 'Behold, distraction, frenzy, and amazement, | Like witless antics, one another meet'. For 'shifting', see l. 930, Sonnet 20.4.

ugly horrible, frightful; compare *Richard III*, 1.4.2–3: 'O, I have passed a miserable night, | So full of fearful dreams, of ugly sights'.

460 marked as a *sententia*. See 87–8n.

shadows delusions, insubstantial shows; as in *A Midsummer Night's Dream*, 5.1.423–4, the word can suggest actors ('If we shadows have offended, | Think but this, and all is mended'), which picks up an aspect of l. 459. Compare ll. 971, 1457.

461 **Who** which, referring most likely to her brain, the source of both 'forgeries' (l. 460) and 'sights' (l. 462); see 296n.

lights powers of sight, as in OED 'light, *n.*1', 4, 'power of vision, eyesight', but the phrase is obscure, and suggests both the light emitted or received by the eyes, depending on which theory of vision is implied.

462 **daunts** intimidates.

464 **Rude** brutal (Schmidt).

ram. . . ivory wall The touch of hand on breast is likened to a battering ram in a siege; similar images for the rape, all with the verb 'batter',

They, mustering to the quiet cabinet
Where their dear governess and lady lies,
Do tell her she is dreadfully beset,
And fright her with confusion of their cries.   445
She, much amazed, breaks ope her locked-up eyes,
   Who, peeping forth this tumult to behold,
   Are by his flaming torch dimmed and controlled.

Imagine her as one in dead of night,
From forth dull sleep by dreadful fancy waking,   450
That thinks she hath beheld some ghastly sprite,
Whose grim aspect sets every joint a-shaking.
What terror 'tis! But she in worser taking,
   From sleep disturbèd, heedfully doth view
   The sight which makes supposèd terror true.   455

Wrapped and confounded in a thousand fears,
Like to a new-killed bird she trembling lies.
She dares not look, yet winking there appears
Quick-shifting antics, ugly in her eyes.
Such shadows are the weak brain's forgeries,   460
   Who, angry that the eyes fly from their lights,
   In darkness daunts them with more dreadful sights.

His hand that yet remains upon her breast –
Rude ram to batter such an ivory wall –
May feel her heart, poor citizen, distressed,   465
Wounding itself to death, rise up and fall,
Beating her bulk, that his hand shakes withal.
   This moves in him more rage and lesser pity,
   To make the breach and enter this sweet city.

appear at ll. 723, 1171. The poem starts with another siege, at Ardea; see headnote, on the metaphor. On 'ivory', see 407n.

465 *citizen* i.e. the heart is an inhabitant of the besieged city within the 'wall' of l. 464. In Shakespeare 'citizen' tends to denote particular status and rights in relation to power, and so it evokes the poem's political context. See *Richard III*, 3.5.76–8: 'Tell them how Edward put to death a citizen, | Only for saying he would make his son | Heir to the Crown.'
distressed stronger in Elizabethan English than today; see OED 'distress, *v.*', 1a: 'To subject to severe strain or pressure (physical, financial, or other); to put to sore straits'. See ll. 1127, 1444, 1446.

466 *Wounding. . . death* i.e. the heart is beating so hard (see l. 467) that it is damaging itself.

467 *bulk* body, as in OED 'bulk, *n.*1', 2a, where this line is cited. Shakespeare's other uses of the word denote large size (OED 2c), but here it emphasises the palpability of the physical evidence of her distress.
withal as a result.

468 *rage* See 424n.
lesser less.

469 *breach* gap in the wall; see OED 7c, 'a gap in the fortification made by a battery', where the first citation is from 1598. Compare *Henry V*, 3.1.1–2: 'Once more unto the breach, dear friends, once more; | Or close the wall up with our English dead'. For 'breach', see also l. 809.
city The same metaphor is used at *A Lover's Complaint*, l. 176.

470 **trumpet** trumpeter (OED 4a, 4b).

471 **sound a parley** signal a wish to discuss peace terms.

heartless dejected, disheartened (OED³ 1b); compare l. 1392, and Shakespeare's only other use, at *Romeo and Juliet*, 1.1.66, 'What, art thou drawn among these heartless hinds?', where it inclines towards 'cowardly' (OED³ 1a). The 'white sheet' of l. 472 gives this sense more of a presence.

472 **white sheet** There is a problematic hint of surrender here (troops behind a white flag, continuing from the 'parley' of l. 471). For white set against whiter, compare *Venus and Adonis*, l. 398.

peers extends, makes peer out. This is the only transitive use cited under OED³ 'peer, *v*.3'; it is always intransitive elsewhere in Shakespeare.

473 **reason. . . alarm** cause of this sudden disturbance.

474 **dumb demeanour** (i) silent expression (i.e. a passionate, lustful look); (ii) silent behaviour (i.e. some sort of gesture).

475 **vehement prayers** most likely pronounced as two disyllables.

urgeth still continues to ask insistently.

476 **Under what colour** with what (deceptive) pretext. See OED³ 'colour', *n*.1', P2c, which cites *Two Gentlemen of Verona*, 4.2.3–4: 'Now I must be as unjust to Thurio, | Under the colour of commending him'. On the range of meanings of 'colour' in the poem, see 92n. Here a military sense of 'colour' seems especially relevant, i.e. OED³ 20a, 'a flag or ensign carried by a military regiment'. Compare *3 Henry VI*, 2.2.173, 'Sound trumpets! Let our bloody colours wave!'.

478 **for anger** out of anger.

478–9 **lily. . . rose** On lilies and roses, and the colour codes of *Lucrece* and *Venus and Adonis*, see 71n.

479 **her own disgrace** The rose blushes because Lucrece's red colour has embarrassed its own.

480 **loving tale** tale of love. Compare *Richard III*, 4.4.359, where coercive seduction is also in mind: 'Then plainly to her tell my loving tale'. In Robert Wilson's *Pleasant Comedy of Fair Em* (1591), the phrase is used to distinguish amatory talk from the soldier's typical mode: 'I cannot, Madam, tell a loving tale, | Or court my mistress with fabulous discourses, | That am a soldier sworn to follow arms' (sig. C4v).

481 **Under that colour** See 476n.

482 **fort. . . fault** There may be a pun here (Duncan-Jones and Woudhuysen 2007: 279 deem it 'just possible', citing Kökeritz 1953: 311).

484 **forestall** anticipate (OED 6), rather than obstruct; but compare l. 728.

mean subjunctive form of the verb (see 219n).

485 **to** There is a case for emending this to 'too'. Then Tarquin's point would be that her beauty has of course ensnared him, but now she must face the fact that it has trapped her as well. The natural stress of the line falls on this syllable, which would make no sense with 'to', but works well with 'too'. Although Q is mostly consistent in differentiating between the spellings of adverbial 'too' and prepositional 'to' in the modern way, there is one telling instance at l. 1801 where Q's 'to' must be amended. In Elizabethan English it is common to spell prepositional 'to' as 'too', so the spelling could easily have been altered – perhaps wrongly standardised – between manuscript and print. Another piece of evidence is that the formulation 'to this night' is only used in one other place by Shakespeare, *Romeo and Juliet*, 2.2.26–30: 'O, speak again, bright angel, for thou art | As glorious to this night, being o'er my head | As is a winged messenger of heaven | Unto the white-upturned wond'ring eyes | Of mortals'. The sense there, though also obscure, is not a close comparison. The phrase 'this night', however, is used without a preposition by Shakespeare many times to denote what in modern English would be 'on this night'. However, as in previous cases we have left Q unemended, either (i) taking this to be to be an unusual use of 'to' meaning 'in respect of', or 'on', or (ii) taking the preposition to follow 'ensnare', i.e. she has been tied 'to' the fate that follows. The latter is more straightforward, and the combination 'ensnare to' is rare but visible in Shakespeare's time. See William Touris, trans. Richard Robinson, *A Dial of Daily Contemplation* (1578): 'Mischief shall fall upon, and ensnare the wicked to his destruction' (sig. G2r). Other arguments against changing from 'to' to 'too' are (i) that the connective 'Where' in the next line works best if 'this night' is a noun phrase following 'to', rather than a temporal adverbial after 'too'; (ii) Tarquin has not said that her beauty has ensnared him, in which case the sense 'also' would follow more obviously; (iii) a parallel formulation, 'enchainèd me | To' appears at ll. 934–5. (This line appears in Figure 2.1.)

Lucrece   155

First, like a trumpet doth his tongue begin   470
To sound a parley to his heartless foe,
Who o'er the white sheet peers her whiter chin,
The reason of this rash alarm to know,
Which he by dumb demeanour seeks to show;
   But she with vehement prayers urgeth still   475
   Under what colour he commits this ill.

Thus he replies: 'The colour in thy face,
That even for anger makes the lily pale
And the red rose blush at her own disgrace,
Shall plead for me and tell my loving tale.   480
Under that colour am I come to scale
   Thy never-conquered fort; the fault is thine,
   For those thine eyes betray thee unto mine.

'Thus I forestall thee, if thou mean to chide:
Thy beauty hath ensnared thee to this night,   485

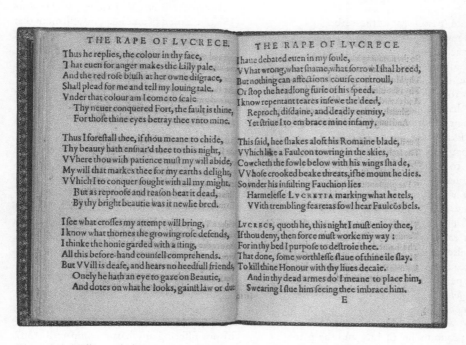

Figure 2.1 William Shakespeare, *Lucrece* (London: Richard Field, 1594), sigs D4v–E1r; Folger Shakespeare Library copy, classmark STC 22345, Copy 2. Used with permission of the Folger Shakespeare Library

486   *Where* i.e. wherein, during 'this night'.
   abide endure.

487   *marks . . . delight* chooses you as (i) a source of pleasure for my body (the 'earthly' part of him; for 'earth' in this sense, see OED³ 'earth, *n*.1', 14a and Sonnet 146.1); (ii) the source of my greatest worldly pleasure (see 'world's delight', l. 385). Compare Nicholas Breton, *The Countess of Pembroke's Love* (1592): 'What earth's delight, but is to me distress, | When nature's health doth prove the soul's annoy?' (sig. M2v).

488   *Which* i.e. 'my will'.
   all my might Tarquin seems to want to exonerate his intentions here. Shakespeare's uses of the phrase seem sardonic, as at *Merry Wives of Windsor*, 2.1.14–19 (Falstaff signing off a letter 'Thine own true knight, | By day or night, | Or any kind of light, | With all his might | For thee to fight, John Falstaff'), and Sonnet 80.3.

489   *reproof and reason* reproach and argument; the point is that moral and rational objections were both raised. Duncan-Jones and Woudhuysen note a possible link with *Edward III*, 2.1.291–2: 'I cannot beat | With reason and reproof fond love away' (2007: 280). See also 512n.
   beat preterite (past) form of the verb.

490   *newly bred* revived.

491   *crosses* obstacles.
   bring i.e. result in.

492–3   Both these ideas are proverbial. See Dent R182 ('no rose without a thorn') and B211 ('bees that have honey in their mouths have stings in their tails [tongues])'. For the former, see also *Venus and Adonis*, l. 574.

492   *defends* singular verb with a plural subject, according to modern usage. Hope (2003: 161–3) argues that such forms are alternative plurals, not actually singular forms.

493   *think* know that, believe that (as in OED³ 'think, *v*.2', 11, 12).

494   *beforehand counsel* anticipatory deliberation. 'Counsel' also suggests the advice a monarch should take. 'Beforehand' is usually an adverb, but Shakespeare's only other use is adjectival, as in *King John*, 5.7.110–11: 'O, let us pay the time but needful woe, | Since it hath been beforehand with our griefs'.

495   *Will* The pronoun 'he' (l. 496) and the pairing with 'Beauty' suggest that this should be capitalised as a personification, as it is in Q, with 'Will' and 'Beauty' shadowing Tarquin and Lucrece.
   heedful mindful, cautious; compare l. 454 and note.

496   *Only he hath* he only has.
   Beauty See 495n.

497   *on what he looks* on what he looks upon; Abbott § 394 notes Shakespeare's tendency to omit the second preposition in relative clauses.

498   *even* pronounced with two syllables here, uniquely in *Lucrece*.

500   *affection's course* passion's race; on 'affection', see 271n. The speed of this 'course' is described in l. 501. 'Affection' could be capitalised here (see 495n), though it is not in Q. Lust resembles a horse; compare ll. 705–7 and notes, and Sonnets 50, 51.

502   *ensue* follow, result from (OED 5a).

503   *disdain* (i) contempt; but here perhaps rather (ii) ignominy (Schmidt), as in OED 3b, 'the quality which excites aversion'. Compare l. 521.

506   *falcon* plays on falchion (l. 509); see 176n.
   towering high up, ready to swoop; disyllabic here. Compare *Macbeth*, 2.4.12: 'A falcon, towering in her pride of place'. This seems to have been a technical usage; in George Turberville's *Book of Falconry or Hawking* (1575) it is used of an eagle ('he affirmeth that the eagles do tower up and mount so high, of purpose for prospect, and to see from far', sig. A7v) and a lark ('it is a pleasure to take a lark towering or climbing', sig. F8r). Its metaphorical potential is captured in Thomas Lodge, *Phillis* (1593): 'My memory of sorrow doth expire, | And falcon-like I tower joy's heavens amain' (sig. F4v).

507   *Coucheth* causes to cower; the first reference for OED 'couch, *v*.1', 2. This is Shakespeare's only transitive use of the verb.

508   *Whose* i.e. the falcon's.
   threats gives this threat, that.
   mount flies up; subjunctive form of the verb (see 219n). The word also has a sexual sense, OED³ 14a, that intrudes here. Compare *Venus and Adonis*, 596n.

509   *insulting* vaunting, bragging (OED 'insult, *v*.', 1a). Compare *Venus and Adonis*, l. 550 and note.
   falchion See ll. 176 and note, 506.

510   *Harmless* (i) not having suffered any harm; (ii) not offering any harm; compare ll. 1507, 1723.

Where thou with patience must my will abide,
My will that marks thee for my earth's delight,
Which I to conquer sought with all my might;
    But as reproof and reason beat it dead,
      By thy bright beauty was it newly bred.   490

'I see what crosses my attempt will bring;
I know what thorns the growing rose defends;
I think the honey guarded with a sting;
All this beforehand counsel comprehends.
But Will is deaf, and hears no heedful friends,   495
    Only he hath an eye to gaze on Beauty,
    And dotes on what he looks, 'gainst law or duty.

'I have debated even in my soul
What wrong, what shame, what sorrow I shall breed,
But nothing can affection's course control,   500
Or stop the headlong fury of his speed.
I know repentant tears ensue the deed,
    Reproach, disdain, and deadly enmity;
    Yet strive I to embrace mine infamy.'

This said, he shakes aloft his Roman blade, `   505
Which, like a falcon towering in the skies,
Coucheth the fowl below with his wings' shade,
Whose crooked beak threats, if he mount he dies.
So under his insulting falchion lies
    Harmless Lucretia, marking what he tells   510
    With trembling fear, as fowl hear falcons' bells.

'Lucrece,' quoth he, 'this night I must enjoy thee;
If thou deny, then force must work my way;

---

511 **bells** Duncan-Jones and Woudhuysen take these to be bells attached to a falcon's legs so it can be found once it has taken its prey (2007: 281). The former interpretation is backed up by Turberville's *Book of Falconry or Hawking* (1575): 'She should also have two good bells, whereby she may be the better heard. For commonly when a sparrow-hawk taketh any prey, she will carry it into some thick bush to feed thereon, in such sort, that she cannot lightly be either heard or seen, and whiles she plumeth it, the plumage doth oftentimes cover both her eyes, or one of them, then to take away the said plumage, she straineth with one of her feet, and thereby her bells discover her' (sig. F5r).

512 **must** See 155n.

enjoy The sexual sense of the word is seen elsewhere in Shakespeare; the most apposite comparisons share the implication of rape and compulsion seen in this instance. See *Richard III*, 5.3.336–7, 'Shall these enjoy our lands? lie with our wives? | Ravish our daughters?', and, as Duncan-Jones and Woudhuysen propose, *Edward III*, 2.1.291: 'I must enjoy her' (2007: 281). See 489n.

513 **must** See 155n.

work my way allow me to achieve my aim.

514 *destroy* kill; however, as the OED's first meaning for 'destroy, *v.*' (1a, 'to pull down or undo (that which has been built); to demolish, raze to the ground') shows, this is part of the poem's siege theme.

515 *some. . . slay* The slave plot is common to all the key sources, but there is disagreement on whose slave it is. Ovid and Livy do not specify, but Painter makes it one of Tarquin's own (see Appendix 2). Shakespeare is closest to Chaucer's *Legend of Good Women*, ll. 1807–9: 'I shal in the stable slen thy knave, | And ley him in thy bed, and loude crye, | That I the fynde in swich avouterye [i.e. in such adultery]'. As Burrow (2002: 272) notes, this idea is prominent in the Lucrece entry in the 'Dictionarium Historicum et Poeticum' appended to Thomas Cooper's *Thesaurus Linguae Romanae et Britannicae* (1578): 'and with his sword drawn, menaced present death, unless she would condescend unto his pleasure, adding moreover, that he would kill one of her servants, and lay him in bed with her, and so spread abroad that he took them in adultery and slew them' (sig. ²L2v). It may lie behind a somewhat similar plot in *Macbeth*, where the hero blames Duncan's murder on his grooms. This does not appear in Holinshed (Macbeth's principal source), and is one of numerous suggestive links between play and poem (see 162–8n, 411–12n).

516 *decay* destruction; see OED 1b, where this line is cited, but (as OED 1a shows) the word was coming to denote a progressive decline in Shakespeare's time. Shakespeare's uses cover both senses; see ll. 713, 808, 947, 1168, and Sonnets 11.6, 13.9, 15.11, 16.3, 23.7, 64.10, 71.12, 80.14, 100.11.

520 *scornful mark* target of scorn. See OED[3] 'mark, *n.*1', 23b. EEBO-TCP does not reveal any other uses of the phrase.
   open watching, attentive.

521 *disdain* See 503n.

522 *blurred* stained (morally); compare l. 222. The OED credits Shakespeare with the first figurative use of the verb (sense 2) in this way, citing *Hamlet*, 3.4.40–1: 'Such an act | That blurs the grace and blush of modesty'.

nameless i.e. as the result of the loss of her reputation, her children will be deemed illegitimate, losing their father's name.

523 *obloquy* disgrace.

524 *cited up* referred to; see OED[3] 'cite, *v.*', 3, for the combination with 'up', which Shakespeare uses on one other occasion, *Richard III*, 1.4.14: 'and cited up a thousand heavy times'.

525 *succeeding times* the future; Shakespeare's only use of the phrase. Compare *Hero and Leander*, ll. 51–4: 'Amorous Leander, beautiful and young, | (Whose tragedy divine Musaeus sung), | Dwelt at Abydos, since him, dwelt there none, | For whom succeeding times make greater moan'. See also Sonnet 19.12 ('succeeding men').

526 *rest* remain.
   secret friend (i) friend who keeps secrets; (ii) secret lover; for the sexual sense of 'friend', see OED[3] 6, and *Venus and Adonis*, 364n.

527 *The fault. . . unacted* As Duncan-Jones and Woudhuysen note (2007: 282), Dent lists proverbs equivalent to this phrase (F104.1, 'A fault unknown is no fault', and S477, 'Sins are not known till they be acted'), but sees them as later than Shakespeare.

528, 530 marked as *sententiae*; see 87–8n.

528–9 *A little. . . enacted* A small fault, committed in order to achieve a significant positive outcome, is adopted as law. This is a variant on the proverbial 'the end justifies the means' (Dent E112).

530 *simple* medicinal substance derived from one plant (OED *adj.* and *n.* B6).
   compacted mixed.

531 *pure* beneficial, no longer poisonous.
   applied (i) mixed (as in OED[3] 1b, 'put close to'), (ii) placed on the skin (OED[3] 2a), or more generally (iii) used (OED[3] 10).

532 *His* its.

534 *Tender* receive favourably; see OED 'tender, *v.*2', 3b, where this is the last citation. This lemma in OED covers senses relating to gentleness and softness, whereas 'tender, *v.*1' includes senses relating to offering suits. Tarquin's use merges the two suggestively. Compare Surrey's translation of Virgil's *Aeneid* (1557): 'Achilles was to Priam not so stern. | For lo he,

For in thy bed I purpose to destroy thee;
That done, some worthless slave of thine I'll slay,   515
To kill thine honour with thy life's decay;
    And in thy dead arms do I mean to place him,
    Swearing I slew him, seeing thee embrace him.

'So thy surviving husband shall remain
The scornful mark of every open eye;   520
Thy kinsmen hang their heads at this disdain;
Thy issue blurred with nameless bastardy;
And thou, the author of their obloquy,
    Shalt have thy trespass cited up in rhymes,
    And sung by children in succeeding times.   525

'But if thou yield, I rest thy secret friend:
The fault unknown is as a thought unacted.
A little harm done to a great good end,
For lawful policy remains enacted.
The poisonous simple sometime is compacted   530
    In a pure compound; being so applied,
    His venom in effect is purified.

'Then, for thy husband and thy children's sake,
Tender my suit; bequeath not to their lot
The shame that from them no device can take,   535
The blemish that will never be forgot,
Worse than a slavish wipe or birth-hour's blot:
    For marks descried in men's nativity
    Are nature's faults, not their own infamy.'

Here, with a cockatrice' dead-killing eye,   540
He rouseth up himself, and makes a pause,

tendering my most humble suit, | The right, and faith, my Hector's bloodless corpse | Rendered, for to be laid in sepulture' (sig. C2v).
lot fortune, condition (OED[3] 6a).

535 *device* scheme, trick; compare *Venus and Adonis*, 789n. There is probably a link between the word and the heraldic devices (on which illegitimacy would be marked) evoked in ll. 204–10.

537 *slavish wipe* (i) a brand that marks the bearer as a slave; (ii) the mark of a whip or blow applied by master to slave. OED 2b cites this line uniquely ('a mark as of a blow or lash; a scar or brand'), alongside 2a,

'a slashing blow'. On branding, see l. 1091, Sonnet 111.5 and notes.
birth-hour's blot birthmark; on 'blot', see 192n.

538 *descried. . . nativity* evident when people are born. '*Nativity*' was used to mean a newborn's horoscope (OED[3] 4), so there may be a hint of astrological taint alongside the ominous birthmark.

539 *infamy* source of shame; compare l. 504.

540 *cockatrice'. . . eye* A cockatrice was a mythical monster, mostly serpent-like, which in heraldic representations had a cock's head, wings and feet. It had a proverbial power (Dent C496.2) to kill with its gaze.

542 **picture** image, ideal representation.
piety fidelity (OED³ 3), virtue (Schmidt).

543 **white hind** female deer, the whiteness of which denotes purity, as in Petrarch's poem 'Una candida cerva', *Rime Sparse*, 190.
gripe vulture (OED *n*.3, 2), or bird of prey generally; it can also mean a griffin (OED 1), which would complement the cockatrice. See l. 556, and compare *Venus and Adonis*, ll. 55–60, 551.

544 **Pleads** (i) begs for mercy; (ii) makes a plea as if in court (which the rest of the line shows to be in vain).
wilderness This imagines the absolute opposite of civilised Rome, a wasteland without laws. Compare *Titus Andronicus*, 3.1.53–4: 'dost thou not perceive | That Rome is but a wilderness of tigers?'.

545 **gentle right** (i) kind justice; (ii) claim to good treatment that belongs to those who are well-born.

548 **aspiring** soaring.

549 **womb** Winds were thought to come from inside the earth; compare *Venus and Adonis*, ll. 1046–8. For comparable uses of 'womb', see *Venus and Adonis*, l. 268 and note, and *A Lover's Complaint*, l. 1.
get breed.

550 **blows** blow Q. The emendation originated with Malone, and it clarifies that 'gust' is the subject. Reasons for keeping 'blow' would include (i) treating it as a subjunctive (see 219n), though this is not a typical use; (ii) taking 'some gentle gust' to be indeterminately singular or plural, and thus open to either verb form; (iii) taking it to be an authorial choice even if its grammar is obscure. This line is compressed on the printed page ('from' is printed 'frō'), which might explain a compositor's wish to lose a letter. Compare *Venus and Adonis*, l. 705 and note, where the singular noun was more easily taken to be a collective, amenable therefore to a plural verb form.
pitchy black (and thick) as pitch.
biding dwelling, resting place. Compare *King Lear*, 4.6.224, 'I'll lead you to some biding', Shakespeare's only other use of the noun.

551 **present** immediate.
fall rainfall; this line is the first citation for OED 'fall, *n*.1', 1d.
dividing separating (i) the clouds from the mountains; (ii) the clouds from one another.

552 **unhallowed** wicked; see 192n.
delays singular verb with a plural subject ('words'), according to modern usage. Hope (2003: 161–3) argues that such forms are alternative plurals, not actually singular forms.

553 **And . . . plays** alludes to the story of Orpheus and Eurydice in Ovid's *Metamorphoses* 10: after the death of Eurydice, the legendary poet-singer performs for Pluto (God of the Underworld), and moves him so much that he gives her back. The reprieve is only temporary, as is Tarquin's pause. Compare *Titus Andronicus*, 2.4.48–51: 'Or had he heard the heavenly harmony | Which that sweet tongue hath made, | He would have dropped his knife, and fell asleep, | As Cerberus at the Thracian poet's feet'.
moody This suggests Pluto's typically grim, irascible temperament.
winks sleeps (OED 'wink, *v*.1', 3).

554–5 The idea is proverbial; see Dent C127 ('as a cat plays with a mouse').

554 **dally** play.

555 **holdfast** firmly grasping; hyphenated in Q but not in the OED lemma.

556 **sad** serious, determined (in opposition to 'folly').
vulture folly predatory, mad lust; see 543n, and 'tyrant folly', l. 851. Compare also *Venus and Adonis*, l. 551, and *Macbeth*, 4.3.73–6: 'We have willing dames enough; there cannot be | That vulture in you, to devour so many | As will to greatness dedicate themselves, | Finding it so inclined'. None of Shakespeare's other uses has this link with lust, but compare 'the ravenous vulture of his love' in Middleton's *Revenger's Tragedy* (1607: sig. C2r).

557 **swallowing gulf** all-consuming (i) whirlpool (see OED 3a); (ii) abyss (OED 2a, 4a), i.e. of his appetite. OED 3b sees the metaphor effectively become part of anatomy, as in Spenser's *Shepherd's Calendar*, 'September', ll. 185–6, 'A wicked Wolf | That with many a Lamb had glutted his Gulf', and *Macbeth*, 4.1.23–4, 'maw and gulf | Of the ravined salt sea shark'. See also Shakespeare's other use of the phrase at *Richard III*, 3.7.128–9 ('shouldered in the swallowing gulf | Of dark forgetfulness and deep oblivion'), and 'swallowing grave', *Venus and Adonis*, l. 757 and note. Compare also Turberville's translation of Ovid's *Heroides* (1567): 'I have nor ship yleft, | Nor mates

While she, the picture of pure piety,
Like a white hind under the gripe's sharp claws,
Pleads in a wilderness where are no laws
    To the rough beast that knows no gentle right,   545
    Nor aught obeys but his foul appetite.

But when a black-faced cloud the world doth threat,
In his dim mist th' aspiring mountains hiding,
From earth's dark womb some gentle gust doth get,
Which blows these pitchy vapours from their biding,   550
Hindering their present fall by this dividing;
    So his unhallowed haste her words delays,
    And moody Pluto winks while Orpheus plays.

Yet, foul night-waking cat, he doth but dally,
While in his holdfast foot the weak mouse panteth;   555
Her sad behaviour feeds his vulture folly,
A swallowing gulf that even in plenty wanteth.
His ear her prayers admits, but his heart granteth
    No penetrable entrance to her plaining:
    Tears harden lust, though marble wear with raining.   560

Her pity-pleading eyes are sadly fixed
In the remorseless wrinkles of his face.
Her modest eloquence with sighs is mixed,

alive: the swallowing gulf | Hath every whit bereft' (sig. T5r). 'Swallowing' is disyllabic.
in plenty wanteth feels a lack even when it has more than enough. For the link with Narcissus, see 97n.

559 **No penetrable entrance to her plaining** no way in for the persuasive effect of her lament. On its own 'penetrable entrance' seems tautologous, but Shakespeare's other uses of 'penetrable' associate it with an ability to change or move the mind (as at *Richard III*, 3.7.224–5: 'I am not made of stone, | But penetrable to your kind entreaties') so in the phrase as a whole it adds something to the simple notion of an entrance. This line is cited at OED³ *adj.* and *n.* A2b, 'able to be penetrated, understood, etc., by thought or reasoning. . . able to be affected, susceptible'.

560 **harden lust** make lust more determined.
marble. . . raining The line is marked as a *sententia*; see 87–8n. See Dent D618 for

the proverbial 'constant dropping will wear the stone'. Compare ll. 592, 959, *Venus and Adonis*, l. 200 and note, and *A Lover's Complaint*, ll. 290–1.

561–3 **fixed. . . mixed** On the sounding, or not, of final *-ed*, see 50–2n. Q's spellings are 'fixed' and 'mixed'.

561 **pity-pleading** i.e. pleading for pity.

562 **In** on. Shakespeare uses 'fix' with 'in', 'on', 'upon' and 'to', without evident changes in the force of the word. Nevertheless here it may be that Lucrece's gaze is made to seem more obsessive by going more deeply 'in' than 'on'.
remorseless wrinkles pitiless frown. Shakespeare usually associates wrinkles with old age, as at Sonnets 3.12, 63.4, 77.5, 108.11, but also with mood, as at Sonnet 93.8. Hecuba's wrinkles in *Lucrece* are caused by grief and age, see l. 1452. There is no exact precedent for Tarquin's wrinkles, which most likely arise from the contortion of his face by lust.

564 *oratory* pronounced with four syllables.
grace pleasing (persuasive) quality (OED³ 13a). Compare ll. 246, 1319, and notes.

565 *period* pause at the end of a sentence (OED³ *n.*, *adj.*, and *adv.* A17b; as represented in writing by a full stop, OED³ A17a).
his its.

566 *sentence* In its most basic sense (OED 6a, 'a series of words in connected speech or writing') this can simply refer to her attempt to compose coherent speech. However it also refers to more structured rhetorical units, since 'sentence' is the English form of *sententia*; see 244n.
accent speech; compare 'accents', l. 1719. *Aposiopesis* is the rhetorical figure for this kind of curtailment.

568 *conjures* implores, beseeches (OED 4a).

569 *knighthood* See 197n.
gentry (i) gentlemanly rank; (ii) 'courtesy, generosity', characteristic of good breeding (OED 1c). Compare *Hamlet*, 2.2.21–3: 'If it will please you | To show us so much gentry and good will | As to expend your time with us a while'.

570 *untimely* unseasonable; the point is that Lucrece should never have to shed tears for such a cause, rather than that her current tears are inopportune or premature.

571 *holy human law* God's requirement that human beings should treat one another well. This evokes Matthew 7:12: 'Therefore whatsoever ye would that men should do to you, even so do ye to them: for this is the Law and the Prophets'.
troth good faith.

572 *heaven* pronounced with one syllable.

573 *borrowed* This invokes another thing that should sway Tarquin: the obligations of a guest who has been shown hospitality.
make retire return. The phrase can suggest an army's retreat, and thus it may add further military resonance. Compare William Garrard's *Art of War* (1591): 'The most fit and apt time when the soldiers must enter the skirmish, make retire, and give a fresh onset, ought to be showed and made manifest by the sound of trumpets to horsemen' (sig. Q3v). However, it could also appear in peaceful contexts; see the poem 'The Praise of Virginity', in Richard Stapleton's compilation *The Phoenix Nest* (1593): 'On Eastern

coast, she cast so great a light, | That Phoebus thought it time to make retire, | From Thetis' Bower, wherein he spent the night, | To light the world again with heavenly fire' (sig. N4v).

574 *stoop* yield (with a submissive bow, OED 'stoop', *v.*1, 2a).

576 *black payment* wicked recompense.
pretended offered (OED³ 2a).

577 *Mud not... thee* This idea became proverbial after Shakespeare, and perhaps because of him. See Dent D345: 'cast no dirt into the well that has given you water', and *Titus Andronicus*, 5.2.170: 'Here stands the spring whom you have stained with mud'. Compare also ll. 850, 1707, and Sonnet 35.2. This line is the first citation in OED³ for this sense of 'mud, *v.*1', 2a.

578 *Mar... amended* The mend-mar antithesis also appears in *Venus and Adonis*, l. 478, and Sonnet 103.9–10.

579 *End... ended* Stop aiming for the wrong target before you have taken your shot. 'Ill aim' also suggests evil intention. This kind of repetition (*polyptoton*) appears frequently in the poem, e.g. at ll. 700, 964, 978, 979, 980, 1019, 1045, 1337. Apart from the first and last, these are all in Lucrece's voice.

580 *woodman* hunter; the association between hunting and desire is a common motif in love poetry (as in Bates 2013).

581 *unseasonable* out of season (i.e. for hunting, because the doe is pregnant or with young). Shakespeare's closest comparable use of the word appears at *King John*, 4.2.18–20: 'This act is as an ancient tale new told, | And, in the last repeating, troublesome, | Being urged at a time unseasonable'.

582–5 The repetitive endings of these lines are a rhetorical *epistrophe*, repeating the same final word or words in successive clauses. See 579n.

585 *Thou... deceit* Lucrece's observation is paradoxical, in that deceit must by nature dissemble its nature. Her idea comes back in the Sinon section, ll. 1520–68.

586 *sighs like whirlwinds* The sighs and the hyperbole recall *Venus and Adonis* (e.g. l. 51). The idea may be echoed in Dekker's *Wonderful Year* (1603), where a storm, 'like a great-bellied wife, her sighs being whirlwinds, and her groans thunder, at length she fell in labour, and was delivered of a pale, meagre, weak child, named Sickness' (sig. B1v).

Which to her oratory adds more grace.
She puts the period often from his place,   565
   And midst the sentence so her accent breaks
   That twice she doth begin ere once she speaks.

She conjures him by high almighty Jove,
By knighthood, gentry and sweet friendship's oath,
By her untimely tears, her husband's love,   570
By holy human law and common troth,
By heaven and earth, and all the power of both,
   That to his borrowed bed he make retire,
   And stoop to honour, not to foul desire.

Quoth she: 'Reward not hospitality   575
With such black payment as thou hast pretended;
Mud not the fountain that gave drink to thee;
Mar not the thing that cannot be amended;
End thy ill aim before thy shoot be ended:
   He is no woodman that doth bend his bow   580
   To strike a poor unseasonable doe.

'My husband is thy friend: for his sake spare me;
Thyself art mighty: for thine own sake leave me;
Myself a weakling: do not then ensnare me;
Thou look'st not like deceit: do not deceive me.   585
My sighs like whirlwinds labour hence to heave thee;
   If ever man were moved with woman's moans,
   Be movèd with my tears, my sighs, my groans.

'All which together, like a troubled ocean,
Beat at thy rocky and wrack-threatening heart   590

---

heave move; though the modern sense of strain and violence, not usually evident in Shakespeare's uses (see 111n), seems active here. Compare l. 413.

587–8 **moved. . . movèd** swayed emotionally, persuaded; but propelled physically as well, in the light of the effort conveyed in l. 586.

588 **tears. . . sighs. . . groans** As Duncan-Jones and Woudhuysen note, these are the characteristic actions of lovers (2007: 288). Viola portrays Orsino's love for Olivia 'With adorations, fertile tears, | With groans that thunder love, with sighs of fire' (*Twelfth*

Night, 1.5.255–6). However, they seem to evoke grief readily as well, as at *2 Henry VI*, 3.2.60–3: 'Might liquid tears or heart-offending groans, | Or blood-consuming sighs recall his life, | I would be blind with weeping, sick with groans, | Look pale as primrose with blood-drinking sighs'. See also l. 1319.

590 **rocky. . . heart** Shakespeare uses the metaphor again at *A Lover's Complaint*, l. 291.
wrack-threatening which threatens shipwreck ('wrack' being Shakespeare's preferred variant spelling of 'wreck'); 'threatening' is pronounced with two syllables (Q 'threatning').

591–4 This merges the proverbial erosion of stone by water with the proverbial capacity of even the hardest hearts to soften. For the former, see l. 560 and note, and compare again *A Lover's Complaint*, l. 291. For the latter, see Dent H310.1 and H311, and see also l. 978.

591 *continual* pronounced with three syllables.

592 *convert* change.

594 *Melt* See *Venus and Adonis*, l. 144 and note.

596 *entertain* receive (as a guest); see l. 1629, and compare *Venus and Adonis*, l. 969.

597 *put on his shape* taken on his appearance; Lucrece questions rhetorically whether her attacker is a demon pretending to be Tarquin; compare l. 1529.

598 *host of heaven* The phrase is used to denote both (i) the multitude of angels that attend upon God, and (ii) the sun, moon and stars (see OED 'host', *n*.1, 3a). Shakespeare's other use of the phrase does not point clearly either way, but seems closer to the former: 'O all you host of heaven! O earth! What else? | And shall I couple hell?' (*Hamlet*, 1.5.92–3).
complain me lament; Shakespeare's only use of the reflexive phrase. EEBO-TCP has fifty instances of it in the century before, and sixty-five in the century after, a rough indication that the phrase was not especially distinctive or archaic.

600 *if the same* if you are what you seem to be.

602 *govern* control. Burrow (2002: 276) aptly quotes Pierre de la Primaudaye's *French Academy*, trans. Thomas Bowles (1586): 'As God is not touched with any affections or passions, but ruleth and governeth all things perfectly by his providence: so after his example a prince laying aside the perturbations of his soul must follow reason only in all his doings' (sig. 2T4v–2T5r). Lucrece makes in a private context what will be a powerful public argument against monarchy after her death. The idea was proverbial: Dent 275.1, 'Kings are gods on earth'.
everything Her point is not that monarchs should have absolute power, but that they should not omit to control themselves.

603 *be seeded* bear fruit, reach maturity; although none of the OED's senses for 'seed, *v*.' and 'seeded, *adj*.' quite fits the former. Compare *Troilus and Cressida*, 1.3.316–18: 'the seeded pride | That hath to this maturity blown up | In rank Achilles must or [i.e. either] now be cropped | Or shedding, breed a nursery of like evil'.
age old age, maturity.

604 *spring* youth; see l. 869, and *Venus and Adonis*, l. 656.

605 *hope* expectancy (of inheriting the crown).
outrage stressed on second syllable.

607 *be remembered* remember; Shakespeare's only use of this verb phrase.

608 *vassal* servile, inferior. OED cites this as the first usage of 'vassal' as an adjective (*n*. and *adj*., 4a); a keyword search of EEBO-TCP finds just one earlier instance: 'dominions over all under & vassal Princes', in John Bridges' *Defence of the Government Established in the Church of England* (1587), sig. 4P3v. Compare Sonnet 141.12.
actors perpetrators.
wiped away erased (from memory and/or reputation).

609 *Then* then it follows that.
in clay in the grave, even when they are dead and buried (OED 'clay, *n*.' 3). See *Henry V*, 4.8.122–4: 'Do we all holy rites: | Let there be sung *Non nobis* and *Te Deum*, | The dead with charity enclosed in clay', and Sonnet 71.10.

610 *only loved* loved only.

611 *happy* successful, secure.
still always.
feared for love treated with the awe and reverence that come from devotion. The question of whether monarchs should aspire to be loved or feared was influentially handled by Cicero's *De Officiis*, trans. Nicholas Grimald (1556): 'And certes of all things neither is there any fitter to maintain a power than to be loved, neither any unfitter than to be feared. Notably saith Ennius: Whom they fear, him they hate always the most: whom any man hateth, he wisheth him lost' (sig. i8r). Shakespeare elsewhere has characters approve of both. See *Henry V*, 2.2.25–8: 'Never was monarch better feared and loved | Than is your Majesty. There's not, I think, a subject | That sits in heart-grief and uneasiness | Under the sweet shade of your government'. Burrow (2002: 277) aptly quotes Guevara's *Dial of Princes*, trans. Thomas North (1557), which also asserts the need for both and then

To soften it with their continual motion,
For stones dissolved to water do convert.
O, if no harder than a stone thou art,
    Melt at my tears and be compassionate:
    Soft pity enters at an iron gate. 595

'In Tarquin's likeness I did entertain thee;
Hast thou put on his shape to do him shame?
To all the host of heaven I complain me;
Thou wrong'st his honour, wound'st his princely name.
Thou art not what thou seem'st, and if the same, 600
    Thou seem'st not what thou art, a god, a king;
    For kings like gods should govern everything.

'How will thy shame be seeded in thine age,
When thus thy vices bud before thy spring?
If in thy hope thou dar'st do such outrage, 605
What dar'st thou not when once thou art a king?
O be remembered, no outrageous thing
    From vassal actors can be wiped away;
    Then kings' misdeeds cannot be hid in clay.

'This deed will make thee only loved for fear, 610
But happy monarchs still are feared for love.
With foul offenders thou perforce must bear,
When they in thee the like offences prove.
If but for fear of this, thy will remove;
    For princes are the glass, the school, the book 615
    Where subjects' eyes do learn, do read, do look.

'And wilt thou be the school where Lust shall learn?
Must he in thee read lectures of such shame?
Wilt thou be glass wherein it shall discern

asserts that 'if the miserable Tarquin had been beloved in Rome, he had never been deprived of the realm, for committing adultery with Lucretia' (sig. m1r).

612 **With. . . bear** tolerate.
  perforce inevitably.
613 **When. . . prove** When they can demonstrate that you have committed the same crimes as them.
614 **If but** if only.
  will desire.
  remove (i) set aside; (ii) put an end to. See OED³ 'remove, *v*.', 4a, 6b, and *Othello*, 4.2.12–14: 'I durst, my lord, to wager she

is honest; | Lay down my soul at stake. If you think other, | Remove your thought; it doth abuse your bosom'. Compare l. 243 and note.

615–16 **For. . . look** Lucrece turns a proverbial idea (Dent K70: 'like prince like people') into a wrought couplet. Compare *2 Henry IV*, 2.3.21–2: 'He was indeed the glass | Wherein the noble youth did dress themselves'.
615 ***glass*** mirror; the word was often used in didactic contexts, as in the title of George Gascoigne's *Glass of Government* (1577).
618 ***lectures*** lessons (OED 5b).
619 ***discern*** perceive, find.

620   ***Authority*** (i) permission; (ii) guiding precedent.
warrant for blame authorisation for sin; 'warrant' suggests the written document itself (OED, 'warrant, *n*.1', 9a).

621   ***privilege*** permit, sanction. See OED³ 3, where the first citation is Samuel Daniel's *Complaint of Rosamond* (1594), sig. G6r: 'Kings cannot privilege a sin forbade'. Compare Sonnet 58.10.

622   ***back'st*** support.
laud praise; see l. 887.

623   ***bawd*** pimp, i.e. merely something that lures people into sin.

624   ***command*** control, power (over yourself); the first citation for OED 3a, 'The faculty of commanding; exercise of authority; rule, control, sway; *spec.* that of a military or naval commander'. For a comparable abstract use, see *Hamlet*, 2.2.26–9: 'Both your Majesties | Might, by the sovereign power you have of us, | Put your dread pleasures more into command | Than to entreaty'.
him God; this suggests the Christian God more than it does any Roman deity (e.g. Jupiter).

625   ***rebel will*** Compare 'rebel powers', Sonnet 146.2.

627   ***all that brood*** i.e. iniquity (l. 626), portrayed as multiple offspring; compare Sonnet 19.2.

628   ***office*** duty, function.

629   ***patterned*** given an example to follow; see l. 1350, and compare *Titus Andronicus*, 4.1.57–8: 'Patterned by that the poet here describes, | By nature made for murthers and for rapes'.

632   ***trespass*** sin; see also ll. 812, 1070, 1476, 1613.

634   ***partially*** in a way biased towards themselves.
smother hide, suppress; compare *1 Henry VI*, 4.1.109–10: 'Your private grudge, my Lord of York, will out, | Though ne'er so cunningly you smother it'.

636   ***wrapped. . . infamies*** (i) entirely covered by, (ii) thoroughly embroiled in, their disgraceful reputations. The use of 'wrap' with the two prepositions captures deep involvement in sin in *A Little Book of John Calvin's Concerning Offences*, trans. Arthur Golding (1567): 'But this happeneth through the lewdness of men, that as soon as Christ appeareth afar off, by and by they are wrapped in with Offences, or rather of themselves run headlong into them' (sig. A2v).

637   ***That*** who.
askance turn away; this is the first citation for the verb in OED³; EEBO-TCP offers no earlier uses. The adverb appears at *Venus and Adonis*, l. 342.
eyes! Q ends the stanza with a question mark. Although a question is a viable option, an exclamation is the better choice in a modernised text, and in Shakespeare's time question marks could be used to denote exclamations.

638   ***heaved-up*** raised-up; compare l. 111 and note.

639   ***rash relier*** either (i) 'headstrong dependant' (Burrow 2002: 278); or perhaps (ii) the thing you unwisely (and impetuously) depend on. The former is a more straightforward reading of the unusual word; this is the first citation for 'relier, *n*.' in OED³, and the only use in Shakespeare. An EEBO-TCP search reveals no earlier instances. From Q6 onwards it was emended to 'reply', which replaces one problem with another.

640   ***repeal*** recall (from banishment); see *Coriolanus*, 4.7.31–3: 'The tribunes are no soldiers, and their people | Will be as rash in the repeal, as hasty | To expel him thence'.

641   ***flattering*** (i) deceptively deluding; (ii) 'pleasing to the imagination' (OED 2a); disyllabic here.

642   ***true respect*** the regard which is properly owed him; see 201n.
prison imprison; Shakespeare's other uses of the verb are at *Venus and Adonis*, ll. 362, 980, and Sonnet 133.9.

643   ***doting*** Compare ll. 155, 1064.
eyne alternative plural form of 'eye', used for the sake of rhyme, and probably seeming archaic to Shakespeare's first readers (treated as 'marked', by Hope 2003: 66), though still current in poetry. See l. 1229, and *Venus and Adonis*, l. 633, Sonnet 113.14, and notes.

644   ***state*** (i) rank; (ii) condition.

645–6 The idea of these lines is proverbial; see Dent S929: 'The stream stopped swells the higher'. Compare ll. 1118–19, and *Venus and Adonis*, l. 331 and note.

645   ***uncontrollèd*** unrestrained, uncontrollable. For Shakespeare's only other use, see *Venus and Adonis*, l. 104 and note.

Authority for sin, warrant for blame,   620
To privilege dishonour in thy name?
    Thou back'st reproach against long-living laud,
    And mak'st fair reputation but a bawd.

'Hast thou command? By him that gave it thee,
From a pure heart command thy rebel will.   625
Draw not thy sword to guard iniquity,
For it was lent thee all that brood to kill.
Thy princely office how canst thou fulfil,
    When patterned by thy fault foul Sin may say
    He learned to sin, and thou didst teach the way?   630

'Think but how vile a spectacle it were
To view thy present trespass in another.
Men's faults do seldom to themselves appear;
Their own transgressions partially they smother;
This guilt would seem death-worthy in thy brother.   635
    O how are they wrapped in with infamies,
    That from their own misdeeds askance their eyes!

'To thee, to thee, my heaved-up hands appeal,
Not to seducing lust, thy rash relier:
I sue for exiled majesty's repeal;   640
Let him return, and flattering thoughts retire.
His true respect will prison false desire
    And wipe the dim mist from thy doting eyne,
    That thou shalt see thy state, and pity mine.'

'Have done,' quoth he. 'My uncontrollèd tide   645
Turns not, but swells the higher by this let.
Small lights are soon blown out, huge fires abide,
And with the wind in greater fury fret;

tide The tide is used by Shakespeare elsewhere to represent extreme passion, as at
Othello 3.3.453–60: 'Like to the Pontic Sea, |
Whose icy current and compulsive course
| Ne'er feels retiring ebb, but keeps due
on | To the Propontic and the Hellespont,
| Even so my bloody thoughts, with violent
pace, | Shall nev'r look back, nev'r ebb to
humble love, | Till that a capable and wide
revenge | Swallow them up'. Compare ll.
1667–71, 1789, and *Venus and Adonis*, l. 979.

646 *let* hindrance.
647–8 Again (see 645–6n) proverbial; see Dent
W448a, 'The wind puts out small lights but
enrages great fires'. There is a related idea,
on attempts at 'blunting' making desire more
'keen', at *A Lover's Complaint*, l. 161.
647 *lights* flames, such as the torch carried by
Tarquin.
648 *fret* rage, move agitatedly (OED, 'fret, *v*.1',
9a). Compare *Venus and Adonis*, l. 69 and
note.

649–51 This may well be the third proverbial idea in the stanza: see 'all rivers run into the sea' (Dent R140).

649 *petty* small.

650 *salt sovereign. . . haste* i.e. the sea, which is augmented in volume, but unaltered in its saltiness, by the influx of stream water (as his lust is fed but not mollified by her tears).

652–3 *sea. . . boundless flood* For another use of the sea as an image of power, compare Sonnet 80.5 and note, and see also 135.9n.

653 *flood* (i) water; the word could refer to the sea; (ii) tide (OED 1).

654 *misgoverning* Shakespeare's only use of the word; a politically resonating way of suggesting a lack of self-control. It may recall the title of Sir Thomas Elyot's *Book of the Governor* (1531), which set out the qualities of a good monarch. There is considerable emphasis on the need for royal self-control: 'They shall also consider that by their pre-eminence they sit as it were on a pillar on the top of a mountain, where all the people do behold them, not only in their open affairs, but also in their secret pastimes' (sig. N6r).

655 *Who* which; see 296n, though here there is a sense that the abstract nouns of the previous lines may be allegorically personified.
stain See 56n.
blood passions; compare l. 1655.

656 *petty* insignificant; the word reflects back sharply on Tarquin's own use, l. 649, and attempts to flatter Tarquin with the thought that he should be able to overcome these 'ills'.
good goodness.

657 *The sea. . . hearsed* The greatness of the sea (Tarquin) is confined, as if dead, within an ignominious, rank pool (of his sins). On the rhyme of *hearsed* with '*dispersed*' (l. 658), and the sounding, or not, of final -*ed*, see 50–2n. Q's spellings are 'hersed' and 'dispersed'. Compare 'inhearse', Sonnet 86.3 and note.
puddle Shakespeare's two other puddles are both disgusting: see *2 Henry VI*, 4.1.70–1: 'Poole! Sir Poole! lord! | Ay, kennel, puddle, sink, whose filth and dirt | Troubles the silver spring where England drinks'; and *Antony and Cleopatra*, 1.4.62–3: 'the gilded puddle | Which beasts would cough at'. This fits OED[3] 2a, 'impure, degrading, or morally

corrupting state or situation; corrupt or degraded behaviour or way of life'.
hearsed Shakespeare is credited by OED with the first use of 'hearse' as a verb. Compare Sonnet 86.3–4, where 'inhearse' appears in combination with 'womb' as well as 'tomb'.

659 *slaves* i.e. the 'petty ills' of ll. 653–5.

663 The idea is proverbial; Dent G437: 'the greater hides the less'.

664–5 Another proverbial idea underlies these lines, though Lucrece inverts the point: see Dent C208: 'high cedars fall when low shrubs remain'. The cedar is traditionally the tree of kings, as in *Cymbeline*, 5.5.453–4: 'The lofty cedar, royal Cymbeline, | Personates thee'.

666 *state* – 'exalted position' (OED[3] 15a); and then Tarquin interrupts Lucrece. Compare this to other interruptions at ll. 1534, 1716–18, and at *Venus and Adonis*, l. 715.

667 *heaven* pronounced here with one syllable.

668 *enforcèd hate* hatred pursued with force; see OED 'enforce, *v.*', 3a 'add force to', 4a 'press home'.

669 *coy* tentative.

670 *despitefully* maliciously; Shakespeare's only use of the adverb. His uses of the adjective gravitate towards the sense 'spiteful', but see *Titus Andronicus*, 4.4.50–1 ('Despiteful and intolerable wrongs! | Shall I endure this monstrous villainy?'), which seems stronger.

671 *rascal groom* low-born man-servant.

672 *doom* fate; the word also suggests the judgement that will fall on her (OED 2).

673 *light* torch.

675 *folded up* enveloped; compare l. 1073, *Venus and Adonis*, l. 822.

676 *tyrannise* 'exercise power. . . cruelly' (OED 3a), but the political resonance is pertinent, given the poem's wider context.

677 *wolf. . . lamb* For this archetypal pairing, see l. 878, the dog and the lamb at ll. 736–7, and (for its proverbial and Biblical resonances) Sonnet 96.9–10n.

678 *white fleece* i.e. her sheets, or nightwear, as in l. 680 and note.
controlled restrained (OED[3] 1); 'voice' is the subject of 'entombs' (l. 679).

679 *outcry* crying out. The word could denote any kind of exclamation, but Shakespeare's other use of the singular noun tends towards a more modern sense of riotous, public

The petty streams, that pay a daily debt
    To their salt sovereign, with their fresh fall's haste   650
    Add to his flow, but alter not his taste.'

'Thou art', quoth she, 'a sea, a sovereign king,
And lo, there falls into thy boundless flood
Black lust, dishonour, shame, misgoverning,
Who seek to stain the ocean of thy blood.   655
If all these petty ills shall change thy good,
    Thy sea within a puddle's womb is hearsed,
    And not the puddle in thy sea dispersed.

'So shall these slaves be king, and thou their slave;
Thou nobly base, they basely dignified;   660
Thou their fair life, and they thy fouler grave;
Thou loathèd in their shame, they in thy pride.
The lesser thing should not the greater hide:
    The cedar stoops not to the base shrub's foot,
    But low shrubs wither at the cedar's root.   665

'So let thy thoughts, low vassals to thy state –'
'No more,' quoth he, 'by heaven I will not hear thee!
Yield to my love; if not, enforcèd hate
Instead of love's coy touch shall rudely tear thee.
That done, despitefully I mean to bear thee   670
    Unto the base bed of some rascal groom
    To be thy partner in this shameful doom.'

This said, he sets his foot upon the light,
For light and lust are deadly enemies.
Shame folded up in blind concealing night,   675
When most unseen, then most doth tyrannise.
The wolf hath seized his pray; the poor lamb cries,
    Till with her own white fleece her voice controlled
    Entombs her outcry in her lips' sweet fold.

For with the nightly linen that she wears   680
He pens her piteous clamours in her head,

noise, rather than emotional pain. See *Romeo and Juliet*, 5.3.191–3: 'O, the people in the street cry "Romeo", | Some "Juliet," and some "Paris," and all run | With open outcry toward our monument'.
fold enclosure, playing on (i) a sheepfold, and (ii) a fold in fabric such as a bedsheet.

680 **nightly linen** Since she 'wears' this, it seems most likely it is her night-dress. This would evoke Lucrece's nakedness rather suddenly, which may give a reason why this might be her bed-sheets, with 'wears' used more loosely.
681 **pens** still within the metaphorical field following 'wolf', 'lamb' and 'fold'.

682 **Cooling. . . tears** The idea that tears might cool a lover is part of the erotic lyric tradition; compare its sardonic use in Herrick's 'To Dews', *Hesperides* (1648): 'I die here, | Unless you cool me with a Tear: | Alas! I call; but ah! I see | Ye cool, and comfort all, but me' (sig. E3v).

684 **prone** eager (OED³ 2). Shakespeare's uses of the word sometimes move beyond the sense 'disposed, inclined' (OED³ 1) towards something like this eagerness. See *Cymbeline*, 5.4.198–9: 'Unless a man would marry a gallows and beget young gibbets, I never saw one so prone'. Compare also Sonnet 141.6. The combination with 'lust' may well be original; EEBO-TCP has no other use of the phrase 'prone lust' before 1653. Q4's amendment to 'proud', and Q6's to 'foul', offer more predictable alternatives to what appears to have been an unusual choice.

685 **spots** As with 'stain', l. 684, these are physical and moral. See also l. 196, where the two are contiguous again, and note.
    could weeping purify if weeping could purify.

686 **should** would; but perhaps the sense 'ought to' is also pertinent.

687–700 These two stanzas, contrasting the enormity of Lucrece's loss with the ephemerality of Tarquin's gain, share interests with Sonnet 129.

688 **what. . . again** something he will want to relinquish (compare l. 730). The point is made bluntly by Ovid, *Fasti*, 2.811, 'Quid, victor, gaudes? haec te victoria perdet' ('why are you rejoicing in your victory? This victory will destroy you'; see Appendix 2).

689–91 **This. . . this. . . this** See 221–3n.

689 **league** (i) union; or perhaps (ii) truce.

691 **converts to** turns into; compare *Romeo and Juliet*, 1.5.91–2: 'this intrusion shall, | Now seeming sweet, convert to bitterest gall', and (more generally) Sonnet 129.
    disdain Compare *Venus and Adonis*, l. 33 and note.

692–3 **Chastity. . . before** Lust is 'poorer than before' by a similar logic to l. 688: it steals something that will not last, and will leave it even more bereft.

692 **rifled** robbed. The word, repeated at l. 1050, suggests an invasive search. Compare *Two Gentlemen of Verona*, 4.1.3–4 (an outlaw speaking), 'throw us that ye have about ye. | If not, we'll make you sit, and rifle you'.
    store possessions, riches.

693 **Lust, the thief** Although EEBO-TCP reveals no comparable instances of the idea before 1594, the poem 'Of Lust', in the anthology *Belvedere* (1600), says 'Lust lives by spoil, like thieves that rob true men' (sig. I4v). In the same volume there is also a poem 'Of Chastity' that includes a version of Shakespeare's couplet: 'When chastity is rifled of her store, | Lust, the proud thief, is poorer than before' (sig. D3v).

694 **Look as** see how; compare *Venus and Adonis*, l. 1 and note.

695 **Unapt for** unsuited to; see *Venus and Adonis*, 34n.
    tender acute, sensitive.

696 **Make** The plural verb takes both 'hound' and 'hawk' as its subjects (disregarding the 'or' of l. 694).
    balk (i) let slip (OED *v*.1, 2e); but more likely (ii) refuse (2c).

698 **surfeit-taking** over-indulging.

699–700 **His taste. . . devouring** What starts as a delicious taste becomes sour as the food is digested, and it ends up consuming the desire that was itself motivated by a wish to consume. Compare Sonnet 129.

701 **bottomless conceit** limitless imagination.

702 **still imagination** silent thought; the point is that even the most concerted effort of contemplation cannot conceive of the depths to which lust can go.

703 **his receipt** what he has drunk. This use of 'receipt' is cited in OED³ (1b) as an example of how the word can stretch from money to other things received.

704 **abomination** (i) detestable behaviour (OED³ 2); (ii) the detestable thing he has become (OED³ 3). Q's spelling 'abhomination' was common in the period, and suggested a folk etymology from the Latin *ab homine*, falling short of human, inhuman. Compare ll. 921, 1832 (same spelling).

Cooling his hot face in the chastest tears
That ever modest eyes with sorrow shed.
O that prone lust should stain so pure a bed!
    The spots whereof, could weeping purify,   685
    Her tears should drop on them perpetually.

But she hath lost a dearer thing than life,
And he hath won what he would lose again;
This forcèd league doth force a further strife,
This momentary joy breeds months of pain,   690
This hot desire converts to cold disdain.
    Pure Chastity is rifled of her store,
    And Lust, the thief, far poorer than before.

Look as the full-fed hound or gorgèd hawk,
Unapt for tender smell or speedy flight,   695
Make slow pursuit, or altogether balk
The prey wherein by nature they delight:
So surfeit-taking Tarquin fares this night;
    His taste delicious, in digestion souring,
    Devours his will that lived by foul devouring.   700

O deeper sin than bottomless conceit
Can comprehend in still imagination!
Drunken Desire must vomit his receipt
Ere he can see his own abomination.
While Lust is in his pride, no exclamation   705
    Can curb his heat, or rein his rash desire,
    Till like a jade Self-will himself doth tire.

705–7 These lines portray lust as a horse (though this is not explicit until l. 707); see l. 500 and note. This evokes the horse of *Venus and Adonis*, ll. 259–324.

705 *in his pride* at its height, in its pomp, vaunting itself; perhaps also sexually excited (OED³ *n*.1, 11), for which compare Sonnet 151.10. See *Venus and Adonis*, 14n, for the complex of meanings, including sexual senses, the word can have. Compare l. 1669.
exclamation cry of protest and/or reproach.

706 *curb* restrain. The metaphor is sometimes used in Shakespeare without a significant link with its origin (part of a horse's bit), as at *Troilus and Cressida*, 2.2.180–2: 'There is a law in each well-ordered nation | To curb those raging appetites that are | Most disobedient and refractory'. Here, however, that original sense is active. See *Venus and Adonis*, l. 285, and *A Lover's Complaint*, l. 163.

707 *jade* contemptuous name for a horse, often a 'worn-out' one (OED 'jade, *n*.', 1a). See *Venus and Adonis*, l. 391.
Self-will a personification of selfish lust. Compare 'self-willed', Sonnet 6.13.

708 *lank and lean* hollow and thin; the alliterative phrase appears elsewhere, as at *2 Henry VI*, 1.3.130: 'The commons hast thou racked; the clergy's bags | Are lank and lean with thy extortions'.

discoloured i.e. pale, without its vigorous appearance as a result of sexual exertion.

709 *heavy eye* The phrase can denote both grief and tiredness; the latter is obviously pertinent here, but the despondency of the spent lover has a melancholy aspect. Compare *Venus and Adonis*, l. 182 and note, where Shakespeare's other use of the phrase, in *Richard II*, is quoted.

knit brow Shakespeare's only use of an established phrase (see OED 'knit, *v*.', 4a) to denote the furrowed brow associated with a range of emotions: here it conveys depressed enervation.

strengthless pace weak, listless gait. For 'strengthless' (in a somewhat different sense) and 'pace', see *Venus and Adonis* 153n, 294n, respectively.

710 *recreant* (i) defeated; (ii) cowardly; (iii) treacherous; disyllabic here. OED³ 'recreant, *adj.* and *n*.' allows all three. Shakespeare's uses elsewhere tend towards (iii), but the 'feeble' state of desire here enhances the pertinence of (i) and (ii).

711 *bankrupt* Compare *Venus and Adonis*, l. 466, for this metaphor in the context of desire.

wails his case laments his situation.

712 *flesh being proud* As at l. 705 (see note), 'proud' can suggest sexual arousal. There is also a religious resonance in the idea of 'flesh', which stood for the corrupt worldly body in Elizabethan theology, and was regularly characterised as proud in its defiant sensuality. See *A Little Book of John Calvin's Concerning Offences*, trans. Arthur Golding (1567): 'Now this thing seemeth so intolerable to our proud flesh, that for very spite they gnash their teeth, as many as have not learned to deny themselves' (sig. B7v).

Grace continues the religious aspect of 'flesh'; see also l. 246 and note.

713 *there. . . that* in the flesh. . . the flesh.

decays See 516n.

714 *rebel* i.e. Desire.

remission forgiveness; but the word has specific Christian resonance, where it is the word for the expiation of sins, as in the absolution at Morning Prayer in the 1559 *Book of Common Prayer* (ed. Cummings 2011: 107).

715 *faultful* a rare and problematic word. This is the OED's second citation, the first being *The Troublesome Reign of King John* (1591): 'Such Meteors were the Ensigns of his wrath | That hastened to destroy the faultful Town' (sig. G2v). EEBO-TCP offers only one earlier use, in William Rankins, *The English Ape, the Italian Imitation, the Footsteps of France* (1588): 'the proud tongue that uttered her ambitious beauty (had it not been corrupted with ambition) might have pleaded in her behalf (if it had not seemed so faultful to the Goddess)' (sig. C1r). The OED's definition, 'faulty, culpable', seems understated for the context, so it is possible that the word should be equivalent to 'sinful'. Q's spelling 'fault-full' may also bring out that 'full' could suggest 'stuffed'; compare 'gorgèd', l. 694.

716–19 *chased. . . disgraced. . . defaced* On the sounding, or not, of final -*ed*, see 50–2n. Q's spellings are 'chased', 'disgraced' and 'defaced'.

716 *this accomplishment* the attainment of his goal; i.e. the rape.

717 *sounds this doom* proclaims this judgement. The use of 'sounds' evokes the apocalyptic trumpets of the book of Revelation, and helps the resonance of this 'doom' with the Last Judgement (OED 'doom, *n*.', 6). See also l. 924.

718 *through. . . times* forever.

719 *soul's fair temple* i.e. his body; see l. 1172 (where the body is Lucrece's). The idea of the body as temple recalls 1 Corinthians 3:16–17: 'Know ye not that ye are the Temple of God, and that the Spirit of God dwelleth in you? | If any man destroy the Temple of God, him shall God destroy, for the Temple of God is holy, which ye are'. Shakespeare picks up the idea at *Hamlet*, 1.3.11–14: 'For nature crescent does not grow alone | In thews and bulk, but as this temple waxes, | The inward service of the mind and soul | Grows wide withal'.

720–8 Tarquin's soul is conceived as a princess under siege.

720 *muster* See l. 442 and note.

721 *spotted princess* i.e. the defiled soul. On 'spot', see 196n.

And then with lank and lean discoloured cheek,
With heavy eye, knit brow and strengthless pace,
Feeble Desire, all recreant, poor and meek,   710
Like to a bankrupt beggar wails his case.
The flesh being proud, Desire doth fight with Grace,
    For there it revels, and when that decays,
    The guilty rebel for remission prays.

So fares it with this faultful lord of Rome,   715
Who this accomplishment so hotly chased;
For now against himself he sounds this doom,
That through the length of times he stands disgraced.
Besides, his soul's fair temple is defaced,
    To whose weak ruins muster troops of cares,   720
    To ask the spotted princess how she fares.

She says her subjects with foul insurrection
Have battered down her consecrated wall,
And by their mortal fault brought in subjection
Her immortality, and made her thrall   725
To living death and pain perpetual,
    Which in her prescience she controllèd still,
    But her foresight could not forestall their will.

Even in this thought through the dark night he stealeth,
A captive victor that hath lost in gain,   730
Bearing away the wound that nothing healeth,
The scar that will despite of cure remain,

722 *subjects* i.e. his lust.

724 *mortal fault* (i) deadly sin; (ii) sin that is characteristic of humans; see ll. 364, 715 and note. The word contrasts the body's mortality with the immortality of the soul (l. 725).

726 *pain perpetual* (i) the agony of shame when alive; (ii) everlasting punishment in hell. This is Shakespeare's only use of a phrase that is used (with 'pain' singular or plural) frequently in religious contexts, to the extent that it becomes part of a parody of alliteration in Thomas Wilson's *Art of Rhetoric* (1553): 'Some use overmuch repetition of some one letter, as pitiful poverty prayeth for a penny, but puffed presumption, passeth not a point, pampering

his paunch, with pestilent pleasure, procuring his passport to post it to Hell pit, there to be punished with pains perpetual' (sig. z1r).

729 *Even* pronounced with one syllable.
in this thought while thinking this.
he Tarquin; and henceforth 'she' now refers to Lucrece, not to the personified 'princess'.

730 *captive victor* This oxymoron recalls Ovid's *Fasti*, 2.811, quoted in 688n, where the same idea appears in a more expanded form.

731–2 The idea is proverbial: see Dent W929, 'Though the wound be healed yet the scar remains'. See Sonnet 34.8 and note.

731 *nothing* not at all.

732 *despite of cure* in spite of treatment or healing.

733 **spoil** plunder (OED 1a); but in this case the word also suggests the thing which has been plundered, i.e. Lucrece's body despoiled of its chastity ('victim', as Duncan-Jones and Woudhuysen 2007: 299 propose). Compare l. 1172; *A Lover's Complaint*, l. 154; and *Venus and Adonis*, l. 553. There is also a sense of 'ruin' in 'spoil': Lucrece is irrevocably damaged.
perplexed (i) bewildered; (ii) enmeshed.

734 **load of lust** (i) burden of the guilt caused by Tarquin's lust, but if the line contrasts with Tarquin's 'guilty mind', rather than complementing it, this may be less compelling; (ii) a physical burden left behind by lust, which might be the memory of the weight of his body, or indeed his child. The last of these is given more weight by the association of 'bear' with pregnancy. An EEBO-TCP search reveals no other use of 'load of lust', but Shakespeare uses 'load of wrath' at l. 1474. His other references to emotional loads, as at *Much Ado About Nothing*, 5.1.27–8 ('tis all men's office to speak patience | To those that wring under the load of sorrow'), describe the bearer's own feelings, not ones so wholly imposed by another.

736–7 **dog. . . lamb** Compare the wolf and the lamb at l. 677.

739 **desperate** despairing (OED *adj.*, *n.* and *adv.* A1a), pronounced here as two syllables. This was a stronger word than in modern usage, because it implied a loss of faith in God. See l. 1038, and Sonnet 147.7.

740 **faintly** (i) in a cowardly way (OED 2); but also (ii) feebly (picking up the physical depletion of ll. 708–9).

741 **exclaiming on** railing against; see l. 758.
direful dreadful, terrible.

743 **heavy convertite** sad penitent. 'Convertite' tends to denote someone who has changed religion, rather than undergone moral reform, as in OED's first citation, from Marlowe's *Jew of Malta* (1592) 1.2.82–3: '[GOVERNOR] Why, Barabas, wilt thou be christened? [BARABAS] No, governor, I will be no convertite'. EEBO-TCP has other uses before 1594, of which the earliest comes in John Jewel's *Defence of the Apology of the Church* (1567): 'But on th'other side, if they turn and repent, there are houses called Monasteries of the Convertites, and special provision and discipline for them, where they are taught how to bewail their unchaste life so sinfully passed over' (sig. 2h5r).

744 **castaway** one who is (i) rejected, (ii) damned. The word can suggest general rejection but OED's sense 'reprobate' (*adj.* and *n.*, Ba) denotes a specific religious sense, i.e. one who is abandoned utterly by God. 2 Corinthians 13:5 reads 'Prove yourselves whether ye are in the faith; examine yourselves; know ye not your own selves, how that Jesus Christ is in you, except ye be reprobates?' in the Geneva text, but in earlier English translations, such as Tyndale's, the last word is 'castaways'. This helps reveal the Christian resonance of '**hopeless**': despair (itself deriving from 'without hope') is the state of the reprobate. Compare 'cast away', Sonnet 80.13 and note.

745–6 In the traditional *aubade* lovers regret the coming dawn (as in Ovid's *Amores*, 1.13, or *Romeo and Juliet*, 3.5.1–13).

745 **looks for** watches for; probably in the sense that he wants the dawn to come.

747 **day. . . lay** The point of l. 746 is made explicit in proverbial form; compare Dent N179, 'what is done by night appears by day'.
scapes transgressions; can denote 'an outrageous sin' (OED 'scape, *n.*1', 2) as well as smaller slips, which are implied by Ovid's *Elegies*, 1.11.3: 'Thy service for night's scapes is known commodious'.

748 **true** honest.

749 **cunning brow** deceptive expression. This is the first citation for the figurative OED 'brow, *n.*1', 5b, 'as the seat of the facial expressions of joy, sorrow, shame, anxiety, resolution, etc.'. EEBO-TCP has no earlier instance of 'cunning brow'.

750 **They** Lucrece's eyes.
think not but cannot think otherwise than.

752 **would they still** they wished they could always.

754 **unfold** reveal.

755 **grave** etch.
water strong acid (that can corrode steel); see OED³ 'water, *n.*', 24, often in a compound, 'strong water, *n.*', a direct translation of Latin *aquafortis*, i.e. nitric acid. Compare Stephen Gosson, *The Ephemerides of Phialo* (1579): 'Some kind of water eats into steel, but it

Leaving his spoil perplexed in greater pain.
    She bears the load of lust he left behind,
    And he the burden of a guilty mind.   735

He like a thievish dog creeps sadly thence;
She like a wearied lamb lies panting there.
He scowls and hates himself for his offence;
She, desperate, with her nails her flesh doth tear.
He faintly flies, sweating with guilty fear;   740
    She stays exclaiming on the direful night;
    He runs, and chides his vanished loathed delight.

He thence departs a heavy convertite;
She there remains a hopeless castaway.
He in his speed looks for the morning light;   745
She prays she never may behold the day.
'For day,' quoth she, 'night's scapes doth open lay,
    And my true eyes have never practised how
    To cloak offences with a cunning brow.

'They think not but that every eye can see   750
The same disgrace which they themselves behold,
And therefore would they still in darkness be,
To have their unseen sin remain untold.
For they their guilt with weeping will unfold,
    And grave, like water that doth eat in steel,   755
    Upon my cheeks what helpless shame I feel.'

Here she exclaims against repose and rest,
And bids her eyes hereafter still be blind;
She wakes her heart by beating on her breast,
And bids it leap from thence, where it may find   760
Some purer chest to close so pure a mind.
    Frantic with grief thus breathes she forth her spite
    Against the unseen secrecy of night.

was never my fortune with any confection to pierce the heart of a stony Courtier' (sig. E6v).

756 *helpless* See ll. 1027 and note, 1056, and on -*less* compounds, 2n.

757 *exclaims against* accuses, rails against (compare l. 741).

    repose and rest She blames them because she was asleep when Tarquin entered her room.

758 *still* always.

761 *chest* (i) breast, enclosing her heart; or (ii) coffer, metaphorically representing a body, enclosing her mind; she wishes for one 'purer' than her own defiled one. Compare Sonnet 48.9.

    close enclose.

762 *spite* (i) hatred; (ii) injury (OED 1).

764–70 The complaint against night is compared by Burrow (2002: 285) to Spenser's *Faerie Queene*, III.iv.55–8: 'Under thy mantle black there hidden lye, | Light-shonning thefte, and traiterous intent, | Abhorred bloodshed, and vile felony, | Shamefull deceipt, and daunger imminent; | Fowle horror, and eke hellish dreriment' (58.1–5). Shakespeare himself parodies such complaints in *A Midsummer Night's Dream*, 5.1.170–1: 'O grim-looked night! O night with hue so black! | O night, which ever art when day is not!'.

765 *notary* clerk, secretary; either writing in, or accompanying, the 'register', depending on how it is taken.

766 *Black . . . tragedies* Duncan-Jones and Woudhuysen cite the possibility of a theatrical practice, first mentioned in this context by Malone, of hanging the stage of tragedies with black cloth (2007: 301). See Richard Verstegan, *Odes in Imitation of the Seven Penitential Psalms* (1601): 'Strange visions then there did appear to me: | A spacious Theatre first me thought I saw, | All hanged with black to act some tragedy' (sig. H1r).
fell savage.

767 *nurse* Compare night as 'desire's foul nurse', *Venus and Adonis*, l. 773.

768 *Blind muffled bawd* a pimp who is concealed ('blind, *adj.* and *adv.*', 9a) and covered up.
harbour shelter.
defame (i) disgrace; (ii) slander; the OED allows both. Shakespeare only uses the noun in *Lucrece*, three times (see also ll. 817, 1033).

769 *Grim* See l. 421 and note.
cave of death The phrase appears in the story of Salimbene and Angelica in William Painter's *Second Tome of the Palace of Pleasure* (1567): 'albeit she be alive, yet is she buried in the most obscure cave of death, having lost the honour which maketh Maidens march with head upright' (sig. 4Z2v). The chastity-related context makes this a suggestive precedent.

770 *close-tongued* secretive. Shakespeare modifies 'tongued' in other ways (long, honey, lewd, poisonous, trumpet, shrill, maiden); this is the only case of 'close'. OED and EEBO-TCP offer no earlier instances but the phrase 'close of tongue' is attested before 1594.

771 *vaporous* misty; as at *Measure for Measure*, 4.1.56–7: 'make haste, | The vaporous night approaches'. OED's first citation for this sense (3a), but EEBO-TCP reveals other meteorological uses, e.g. Andrew Borde's *Compendious Regiment or a Dietary of Health* (1547): 'misty and cloudy days, impetuous and vehement wind, troublous and vaporous weather is not good to labour in it to open the pores to let in infectious air' (sig. A3r).

772 *cureless* On -*less* compounds, see 2n.

773 *Muster . . . mists* See 442n, and, for the word 'musty' which merges the sounds of 'muster' and 'mists', l. 782.

774 War against time is a feature of Sonnets 15–16; compare also 745–6n, on the aubade tradition of Ovid, *Amores*, 1.13.
proportioned course regular passing.

777 *Knit* wind, weave.

778 *rotten* tainted, foul (OED³ *adj.*, *n.* and *v.* A2); compare Sonnet 34.4.
damps mists (see l. 771).
ravish 'spoil, corrupt' (OED³ 1c, where this is the first citation).

779 *exhaled* breathed out (of the earth).

780 *life of purity* the thing which gives life to purity, i.e. the sun. See OED³ 'life, *n.*', 5a.
supreme fair (i) beautiful ruler; (ii) greatest beauty; probably the former is more pertinent, but both words could be nouns as well as adjectives. For 'supreme', which is stressed on the first syllable, see *Venus and Adonis*, l. 996.

781 *arrive* arrive at.
noontide prick the point of noon (on a sundial). See also *3 Henry VI*, 1.4.33–4: 'Now Phaethon hath tumbled from his car, | And made an evening at the noontide prick'.

782 *musty* mouldy, mouldy-smelling. See ll. 773, 778 for the link with 'mists'; indeed, early editions from Q3 onwards have 'misty' here.
thick densely.

785 *but Night's child* merely the offspring of Night (i.e., just a secondary instance of its evil power).

786 *silver-shining queen* the moon; the Roman moon-goddess Diana was also the goddess of chastity.
distain (i) discolour, darken; (ii) defile.

787 *twinkling handmaids* i.e. the stars.

788 *peep* Compare *Macbeth*, 1.5.53–4, 'Nor heaven peep through the blanket of the dark | To cry "Hold, hold!"'. Modern uses of 'peep' often have a comic or belittling effect, but that is not the case here.

789 *co-partners* Shakespeare's only use of 'partner' with the prefix. In this case it does not seem to intensify the sense, as in the case in some of his other *co*-compounds (e.g. 'my co-mates

'O comfort-killing Night, image of hell,
Dim register and notary of shame,   765
Black stage for tragedies and murders fell,
Vast sin-concealing chaos, nurse of blame,
Blind muffled bawd, dark harbour for defame,
    Grim cave of death, whispering conspirator
    With close-tongued treason and the ravisher;   770

'O hateful, vaporous and foggy Night,
Since thou art guilty of my cureless crime,
Muster thy mists to meet the eastern light,
Make war against proportioned course of time;
Or if thou wilt permit the sun to climb   775
    His wonted height, yet ere he go to bed,
    Knit poisonous clouds about his golden head.

'With rotten damps ravish the morning air;
Let their exhaled unwholesome breaths make sick
The life of purity, the supreme fair,   780
Ere he arrive his weary noontide prick;
And let thy musty vapours march so thick
    That in their smoky ranks his smothered light
    May set at noon, and make perpetual night.

'Were Tarquin Night, as he is but Night's child,   785
The silver-shining queen he would distain;
Her twinkling handmaids too (by him defiled)
Through Night's black bosom should not peep again.
So should I have co-partners in my pain,
    And fellowship in woe doth woe assuage,   790
    As palmers' chat makes short their pilgrimage.

'Where now I have no-one to blush with me,
To cross their arms and hang their heads with mine,

and brothers in exile', *As You Like It*, 2.1.1); but compare 'Let the Bird of Loudest Lay', l. 51: 'Co-supremes and stars of love'.

790–1 Lucrece again turns to proverbial expression. See Dent C571, 'it is good to have company in trouble', and C566, 'good company makes short miles'.

791 *palmers'* pilgrims' (so-called because those who travelled to the Holy Land returned with a palm-leaf).

792 *Where* whereas.

793 *cross. . . arms* a gesture of anxiety, associated with the melancholy lover in another Shakespearean use of the motif, at *Love's Labour's Lost*, 3.1.17–19: 'with your hat penthouse-like o'er the shop of your eyes; with your arms crossed on your thin-bellied doublet like a rabbit on a spit'. The portrait of John Donne in the National Portrait Gallery, London (NPG 6790), painted *c.* 1595, depicts him with untied collar and folded arms, taken to be signs of love-melancholy. Compare also l. 1662.

hang. . . heads A gesture of grief in *Venus and Adonis*, ll. 666 and 1058, and a sign of weighty cares in *Titus Andronicus*, 4.4.69–71: 'Is warlike Lucius general of the Goths? | These tidings nip me, and I hang the head | As flowers with frost, or grass beat down with storms'. However, it is commonly used to denote shame, which is the main sense here (see OED 'hang, *v.*', 4b).

794 **mask their brows** conceal their expressions. 'Brow' in singular or plural can stand for facial expression (see l. 709 and note), but the 'brows' here could be more literal, no longer visible after the hanging of heads in l. 793, or indeed after pulling down a hat, as in the *Love's Labour's Lost* quotation in 793n.

796 Compare *A Lover's Complaint*, ll. 17–18, and *Twelfth Night*, 1.1.27–30: 'she will veiled walk, | And water once a day her chamber round | With eye-offending brine; all this to season | A brother's dead love'.
Seasoning salting.

798 **wasting monuments** decaying memorials; the motif of monuments succumbing to time, despite being built for posterity, was fertile material for renaissance writers, as in Spenser's *Ruins of Rome*, and Sonnet 55. The phrase could also mean 'draining reminders', which exhaust the griever. Compare l. 391, and *2 Henry VI*, 3.2.339–42: 'Give me thy hand, | That I may dew it with my mournful tears; | Nor let the rain of heaven wet this place | To wash away my woeful monuments'.

799 **reeking smoke** since 'reeking' meant 'smoking' (not 'foul-smelling'), this verges on tautology. EEBO-TCP has only one other use of the phrase, in Michael Drayton's *Barons' Wars* (1603): 'The elements together thrust in crowds, | Both Land and Sea hid in a reeking smoke' (sig. K4r).

800 **jealous** 'suspicious; apprehensive of evil, fearful' (OED 5a, where this line is cited).
that face i.e. Lucrece's.

802 **Immodestly** unchastely; there is a sharp irony here, in that the 'all-hiding cloak' of night currently preserves her modesty, in the visual sense at least.
martyred (i) slaughtered (OED³ 'martyr, *v.*', 1b); (ii) tormented (OED³ 2a); the sense of morally superior death for a cause is also pertinent here. Shakespeare uses the word most often in *Titus Andronicus*, a play set in pre-Christian Rome. Compare 3.1.106–7, 'Thou hast no hands to wipe away thy tears, | Nor tongue, to tell me who hath martyred thee', and 3.2.36–7: 'I can interpret all her martyred signs: | She says she drinks no other drink but tears', both quotations referring to the raped Lavinia.

803 **still** always.
place usual location, home.

804 **That** so that; see 94n.

805 **sepulchred** entombed; the earliest citations for the verb in OED are from Shakespeare, and EEBO-TCP reveals no earlier uses of the form 'sepulchred'. Compare *The Two Gentlemen of Verona*, 4.2.116–17: 'Go to thy lady's grave and call hers [i.e. her love] thence, | Or at the least, in hers sepulchre thine'. Here it is stressed on the second syllable.

806 **object** Could be adjective ('exposed', OED³ 1a) or noun ('something placed before or presented to the eyes or other senses', OED³ 1a). Shakespeare does not use the adjectival form anywhere else. Compare l. 1103.

807 **charactered** inscribed; probably pronounced with emphasis on the second syllable.

808 **decay** destruction, downfall; see 516n.

809 **breach . . . vow** Only Lucrece can break her marriage vow, but Tarquin is responsible for the 'breach' (an attack that comes from outside; on 'breach', part of the poem's siege vocabulary, see l. 469).
holy wedlock vow i.e. the holy vows of marriage.

811 **cipher** decipher. This is the only citation of this sense of 'cipher' in OED (4), which is in effect opposite to other senses that stress expression and encoding. Shakespeare does not use the word in this sense anywhere else; compare ll. 207, 1396. An EEBO-TCP search on forms of 'cipher' before 1594 also reveals no use with this sense, and yet the meaning does not seem obscure. It might best be thought of as an *aphaeresis* (omission of opening syllable) of 'decipher'.

812 **quote** 'read, interpret' (as suggested by Schmidt, following 'illiterate' and 'writ'). The closest sense in OED³ is 'notice' (5a), for which is cited *Romeo and Juliet*, 1.4.30–1: 'A visor for a visor! what care I | What curious eye doth cote [i.e. quote; the spelling in Q *Lucrece* is also 'cote'] deformities?'.

815 **deck** adorn.

817 **Feast-finding minstrels** roving entertainers, seeking out banquets at which to play.
tuning singing (OED 'tune, *v.*2', 4a); compare ll. 1107, 1465.
defame disgrace; see 768n.

818 **tie** compel. There may be an allusion here to the tradition of the 'Gallic Hercules' emblem, which portrayed the power of rhetoric as a physical link between the speaker's tongue and the listener's ears. See Puttenham's *Art of English Poesy* (1589):

To mask their brows and hide their infamy;
But I alone, alone must sit and pine, 795
Seasoning the earth with showers of silver brine,
    Mingling my talk with tears, my grief with groans,
    Poor wasting monuments of lasting moans.

'O Night, thou furnace of foul reeking smoke!
Let not the jealous day behold that face, 800
Which underneath thy black all-hiding cloak
Immodestly lies martyred with disgrace.
Keep still possession of thy gloomy place,
    That all the faults which in thy reign are made,
    May likewise be sepulchred in thy shade. 805

'Make me not object to the tell-tale day!
The light will show, charactered in my brow,
The story of sweet chastity's decay,
The impious breach of holy wedlock vow.
Yea, the illiterate that know not how 810
    To cipher what is writ in learned books
    Will quote my loathsome trespass in my looks.

'The nurse to still her child will tell my story,
And fright her crying babe with Tarquin's name;
The orator, to deck his oratory, 815
Will couple my reproach to Tarquin's shame;
Feast-finding minstrels, tuning my defame,
    Will tie the hearers to attend each line,
    How Tarquin wrongèd me, I Collatine.

'Let my good name, that senseless reputation, 820
For Collatine's dear love be kept unspotted.
If that be made a theme for disputation,

'At least ways, I find this opinion, confirmed by a pretty device or emblem that Lucianus allegeth he saw in the portrait of Hercules within the City of Marseilles in Provence: where they had figured a lusty old man with a long chain tied by one end at his tongue, by the other end at the people's ears, who stood afar off and seemed to be drawn to him by the force of that chain fastened to his tongue, as who would say, by force of his persuasions' (sig. R1v).
    attend give their attention to; see l. 1674.
820 *senseless reputation* (i) reputation for having no sensuality, as in OED 'sense, *n.*', 4b,

for which compare Sonnet 35.9; (ii) reputation without any meaning or substance, as in OED 'senseless, *adj.*', 4. On the -*less* suffix, see 2n.
821 *unspotted* untarnished, unblemished; on 'spot', see 196n.
822 *theme for disputation* subject for formal debate; see ll. 246, 1101, and compare 'idle theme', *Venus and Adonis*, l. 422. Saint Augustine's *City of God*, I.19, is a possible specific reference point for Lucrece's anxiety here (see headnote). The focus of the debate there is the morality of her suicide.

823 **root** i.e. of Collatine's family tree. Compare *Richard III*, 2.2.40–1: 'Edward, my lord, thy son, our king, is dead! | Why grow the branches when the root is gone?'.

825 **attaint** stain, disgrace. See l. 1027, and *Venus and Adonis*, l. 741.

828 **unfelt sore** A paradoxical pairing, verging on oxymoron; unlike Lucrece, Collatine will have no physical sensation to accompany his disgrace. The 'unseen' and 'invisible' shame of l. 827 tend towards the oxymoronic too.
    crest-wounding private scar The idea that a 'private' harm could wound the family's 'crest' (the heraldic, and therefore public, representation of its virtue) is also oxymoronic. See 206n. There may also be a suggestion of the cuckold's traditional horns here, adorning the 'crest' of his head.

829 **Reproach** shame; but this also implies Lucrece imagining a look of reproach from Collatine, aimed at her.

830 **mot** motto; Shakespeare's only use of this form. He only uses 'motto' in *Pericles*, 2.2 (three times, as Thaisa describes the pageant heraldry).

831–2 These lines are marked as *sententiae* (with l. 833 evidently part of the second). See 87–8n. Lucrece casts Collatine as a kind of unwitting cuckold: compare *Othello*, 4.1.67–9, 'There's millions now alive | That nightly lie in those unproper beds | Which they dare swear peculiar [i.e. privately theirs, as at l. 14 above]'. A similar idea appears in *The Winter's Tale*, 1.2.190–6: 'There have been | (Or I am much deceived) cuckolds ere now, | And many a man there is (even at this present, | Now, while I speak this) holds his wife by th' arm, | That little thinks she has been sluiced in 's absence, | And his pond fished by his next neighbour – by | Sir Smile, his neighbour'.

835 **bereft** taken away.

836 **drone-like** A drone is a male bee that consumes but does not make honey. The 'honey' is Lucrece's precious chastity, and she is unable to restore it. The drone is a byword for inactivity in the extended hive analogy in *Henry V*, 1.2.202–4: 'The sad-eyed justice, with his surly hum, | Delivering o'er to executors pale | The lazy yawning drone'. Compare also *Pericles*, 2.Prol.17–19: ' Good Helicane, that stayed at home, | Not to eat honey like a drone | From others' labours'. The idea is

identified as proverbial by Dent D612.1: 'to eat honey like a drone'. A link between honey and rape is made at *Titus Andronicus*, 2.3.131–2, 'But when ye have the honey we desire, | Let not this wasp outlive, us both to sting'.

837 **perfection** ideal complement, proper fruition; i.e. the honey, her chastity.

838–40 Compare *Two Gentlemen of Verona*, 1.2.103–4: 'Injurious wasps, to feed on such sweet honey, | And kill the bees that yield it with your stings!'.

838 **injurious** pronounced with three syllables.

839 **wandering** The wasp invades the hive rather than having one of its own; the word also suggests sinfulness (wandering from a virtuous path).

841 **wrack** destruction.

843 **put him back** turn him away.

844 **had been** would have been.
    disdain reject.

846 **unlooked-for** unexpected.

847 **profaned** desecrated.

848 **worm. . . bud** Shakespeare's other two uses of the 'worm'–'bud' pairing refer to destructive secrecy in love. See *Twelfth Night*, 2.4.110–12: 'she never told her love, | But let concealment like a worm i' th' bud | Feed on her damask cheek'; and *Romeo and Juliet* 1.1.149–52: 'But to himself so secret and so close, | So far from sounding and discovery, | As is the bud bit with an envious worm, | Ere he can spread his sweet leaves to the air'. Here, however, the idea is that something precious is being invaded and devoured, as it is in the uses of canker or canker-worm in Sonnets 35.4, 70.7, 95.2, 99.13.
    intrude 'enter forcibly' (OED 5a). This is the only citation in OED, a rare transitive use that captures the violence of the invasion being evoked here.

849 **cuckoos** Known for invading others' nests, as in *King Lear*, 1.4.215–6: 'The hedge-sparrow fed the cuckoo so long, | That it had it head bit off by it young'. Also linked to cuckoldry, a pun exploited in *Love's Labour's Lost*, 5.2.910–11: 'Cuckoo, cuckoo – O word of fear, | Unpleasing to a married ear!'.

850 **toads** Thought of as disgusting, and associated with sexuality in *Othello*, 4.2.61–2: 'a cistern for foul toads | To knot and gender in'.
    founts This is the first citation in the OED for this poetical variation on 'fountain', but

The branches of another root are rotted,
And undeserved reproach to him allotted,
　　That is as clear from this attaint of mine　　825
　　As I ere this was pure to Collatine.

'O unseen shame, invisible disgrace!
O unfelt sore, crest-wounding private scar!
Reproach is stamped in Collatinus' face,
And Tarquin's eye may read the mot afar,　　830
How he in peace is wounded, not in war.
　　Alas, how many bear such shameful blows,
　　Which not themselves but he that gives them knows.

'If, Collatine, thine honour lay in me,
From me by strong assault it is bereft:　　835
My honey lost, and I, a drone-like bee,
Have no perfection of my summer left,
But robbed and ransacked by injurious theft.
　　In thy weak hive a wandering wasp hath crept,
　　And sucked the honey which thy chaste bee kept.　　840

'Yet am I guilty of thy honour's wrack;
Yet for thy honour did I entertain him.
Coming from thee I could not put him back,
For it had been dishonour to disdain him.
Besides, of weariness he did complain him,　　845
　　And talked of virtue – O unlooked-for evil,
　　When virtue is profaned in such a devil!

'Why should the worm intrude the maiden bud,
Or hateful cuckoos hatch in sparrows' nests,
Or toads infect fair founts with venom mud,　　850
Or tyrant folly lurk in gentle breasts,
Or kings be breakers of their own behests?
　　But no perfection is so absolute
　　That some impurity doth not pollute.

an EEBO-TCP search reveals numerous earlier uses, including several in the works of Robert Greene and Thomas Lodge, and e.g. Thomas Watson's *Hekatompathia* (1582): 'I'll praise no star but Hesperus alone, | [...] Nor any spring but Acidalian fount' (sig. A2v). See also *A Lover's Complaint*, l. 283. Compare *3 Henry VI*, 4.8.54: 'You are the fount that makes small brooks to flow'. For the idea of muddied springs, see l. 577 and note.

venom poisonous (see OED 'venom, *n.* and *adj.*', B).
851 *folly* (i) wickedness, OED 'folly, *n.*1', 2a; (ii) lewdness, 3a. Compare 'vulture folly', l. 556, and l. 992.
　gentle noble.
852 *behests* commands, laws.
853–4 marked as a *sententia* (on l. 853 alone); see 87–8n.
853 *absolute* (i) complete; (ii) perfect.

855 *coffers up* hoards (OED, 'coffer, *v.*1', 1a, often with 'up'). Baldwin (1950: 135) cites a note on Luke 12:15 in the Geneva Bible that may have suggested 'coffers' and 'barns' (see l. 859) in relation to misers: 'Christ condemneth the arrogancy of the rich worldlings, who as though they had God locked up in their coffers and barns, set their whole felicity in their goods'.

856 *gouts* On the association between gout and miserliness, compare *A Lover's Complaint*, ll. 139–40.

858 *still-pining Tantalus* always starving Tantalus. In the classical underworld he is tortured forever by water and/or fruit that is just out of reach. Compare *Venus and Adonis*, l. 599 and note. Horace's *Satires* 1.1.68–78 tells the story as an illustration of a miser's fate, and this passage is quoted in Erasmus' *Adagia*, 2.6.14 ('Tantali Poenae'). See Thomas Drant's translation, *Horace his Art of Poetry, Epistles, and Satires Englished* (1567): 'I pray thee now, what cause hast thou to sport and pleasance take? | To fawn upon thy foolish gold which endless grief doth make. | For thou endurest Tantal's fate, and taking but his name, | This tale may well be told of thee, thou art the very same' (sig. I4v).

859 *barns* stores in a barn; the earliest citation for the verb in OED. See the Biblical quotation in 855n.

863 *mastered* possessed. The OED³ lists this as the first instance of sense 6a (for which it also cites Sonnet 106.8); however, the more usual sense (command, control) is close here.

864 *pride* (i) prime; (ii) arrogance. See 37n.
presently immediately.

866 *hold* keep.

867–8 marked as a *sententia* (see 87–8n), and proverbial; see Dent S1034.1, 'after sweet the sour comes'. Compare Sonnet 129.

867 *sweets. . . sours* Compare Sonnet 94.13.
sours sour things. This is Shakespeare's only use of the noun (though it is in regular use elsewhere).

869–82 These lines, and ll. 897–924, are excerpted in an early seventeenth century miscellany owned and possibly compiled by Richard Waferer of Buckinghamshire, now British Library, Add. MS 52585 (CELM ShW 3), 54r–v.

869 *wait on* accompany (see l. 275), or perhaps 'lie in wait for' (Burrow 2002: 290).

tender spring See *Venus and Adonis*, l. 656 and note.

870 This idea does not appear in Dent, but it is proverbial in tone at least. For other instances of weeds corrupting flowers, see Sonnet 69.12 and note.

874 *ill-annexèd* unfortunately linked. This is the only citation in OED for this unusual use of 'ill-, *comb. form*'. Compare 'annexed' at Sonnet 99.11.
Opportunity i.e the chance to sin. Most of Shakespeare's uses of the word are positive, but see *A Midsummer Night's Dream*, 2.1.217–19: 'To trust the opportunity of night, | And the ill counsel of a desert place, | With the rich worth of your virginity'; and *Troilus and Cressida*, 4.5.61–3: 'set them down | For sluttish spoils of opportunity, | And daughters of the game'. Burrow (2002: 291) suggests 'Occasion' is the more usual word in the emblematic tradition. For a similar attack on an abstract noun, compare the Bastard's speech about 'Commodity' in *King John*, 2.1.561–98. See also 886n.

875 *Or. . . or* either. . . or.
his. . . his referring back to 'good', l. 873.
quality nature (OED³ *n.* and *adj.* A1a); perhaps, more strongly, excellence of nature (1b), nobility.

877 *execut'st* makes happen.

878 *sets* The usual form of the verb would be 'set'st', but Shakespeare uses this form at times, here perhaps to be more euphonious. Compare l. 1134, and see Hope (2003: 161).
wolf. . . lamb On this pairing, see 677n.

879 *point'st* appoint. Q's spelling 'poinst' may be intended to make the line sound more smoothly.
season favourable time (OED 14).

880 *spurn'st at* show contempt to; originally, to kick, as at l. 1026 and *Venus and Adonis*, l. 331.

881 *cell* small room or dwelling; the word suggests poverty and isolation. Shakespeare's cells are inhabited by Veronese friars (*Two Gentlemen of Verona, Romeo and Juliet*), the dead (*Romeo and Juliet*), death itself (*Hamlet*), vengeance (*Othello*) and Prospero (*The Tempest*).

883 *vestal. . . oath* The vestal virgins, Roman priestesses of Vesta, were required to keep a vow of chastity, on pain of death. See *Venus and Adonis*, l. 752 and note.

'The aged man that coffers up his gold   855
Is plagued with cramps and gouts and painful fits,
And scarce hath eyes his treasure to behold;
But like still-pining Tantalus he sits,
And useless barns the harvest of his wits,
    Having no other pleasure of his gain   860
    But torment that it cannot cure his pain.

'So then he hath it when he cannot use it,
And leaves it to be mastered by his young,
Who in their pride do presently abuse it;
Their father was too weak, and they too strong   865
To hold their cursèd-blessèd fortune long.
    The sweets we wish for turn to loathèd sours
    Even in the moment that we call them ours.

'Unruly blasts wait on the tender spring;
Unwholesome weeds take root with precious flowers;   870
The adder hisses where the sweet birds sing;
What virtue breeds iniquity devours.
We have no good that we can say is ours,
    But ill-annexèd Opportunity
    Or kills his life, or else his quality.   875

'O Opportunity, thy guilt is great:
'Tis thou that execut'st the traitor's treason;
Thou sets the wolf where he the lamb may get;
Whoever plots the sin, thou point'st the season.
'Tis thou that spurn'st at right, at law, at reason,   880
    And in thy shady cell, where none may spy him,
    Sits Sin to seize the souls that wander by him.

'Thou mak'st the vestal violate her oath;
Thou blow'st the fire when temperance is thawed;
Thou smother'st honesty, thou murder'st troth;   885
Thou foul abettor, thou notorious bawd,

884 **blow'st the fire** fan the flames of passion.
thawed Temperance is represented as cold by nature. When temperance lapses and acquires the heat of passion, it is Opportunity who stokes the fire.
885 **murder'st** Q's spelling 'murthrest' (not 'murtherst', which would be more similar to Q's 'smotherst' earlier in the line) suggests an alternative modernised elision here: 'murd'rest'. Here we have chosen to represent the parallel between the two verbs in similar spelling, and thereby to be consistent with our treatment of verbs ending -*st* elsewhere. Compare l. 929.
troth (i) good faith; (ii) marital fidelity (OED³ 3).
886 **notorious bawd** The link between Opportunity and the work of a bawd was proverbial, as in Dent O70: 'Opportunity is whoredom's bawd'.

887 **plantest** establish (in the place properly held by 'laud'). Compare 'planting', *Venus and Adonis*, l. 557.
laud praise; perhaps praiseworthiness (OED 'laud, *n*.1', 1c).

889 **honey...gall** The frequently contrasted pair (sweet versus bitter) was linked proverbially, as in Dent H551.1, 'no honey without gall'. Shakespeare counterpoints them also in *Troilus and Cressida*, 2.2.14–15: 'You have the honey still, but these the gall; | So to be valiant, is no praise at all'.

892 **smoothing** flattering (OED 'smoothing, *adj*.', 2).
ragged rough, i.e. unworthy.

893 **wormwood** plant known for its bitter taste, as in the Nurse's tale of weaning Juliet, *Romeo and Juliet*, 1.3.30–2: 'When it did taste the wormwood on the nipple | Of my dug and felt it bitter, pretty fool, | To see it teachy [i.e. tetchy] and fall out wi' th' dug!'. The sugar/wormwood contrast is less common than honey/gall, but also sets sweet and bitter against one another. They combine neatly in George Abbot's *An Exposition Upon the Prophet Jonah* (1600): 'When Elias was chased by Jezebel, and was comfortless in the wilderness, he crieth: "Now it is enough, Lord take away my soul, for I am no better than my fathers". But if this gall and wormwood were turned into sugared honey, we should not hasten from this place; but yet we be not ready' (sig. P5r).

894 **violent...never last** That violent things could never last was proverbial, as in Dent N321, 'nothing violent can be permanent'.
vanities empty pleasures. Compare *Henry V*, 2.4.36–8: 'And you shall find his vanities forespent | Were but the outside of the Roman Brutus, | Covering discretion with a coat of folly'. (The Brutus in question is the one featured later in *Lucrece*.)

897–924 See 869–82n.

898–901 **obtained...chained...pained** On the sounding, or not, of final *-ed*, see 50–2n. Q's spellings are 'obtained', 'chained' and 'pained'.

899 **sort** choose, as in OED 'sort, *v*.1', 14a, where the first citation is Thomas Kyd's *Spanish Tragedy* (1592), 4.4.103–4: 'They had sorted leisure | To take advantage in my Garden plot | Upon my son'. See *Richard III*, 2.2.148–50:

'For by the way, I'll sort occasion, | As index to the story we late talked of, | To part the Queen's proud kindred from the Prince'.

901 **physic** medicine.

902 **halt** limp. The line combines three nouns with three verbs: lame/halt, blind/creep, poor/cry out seem the most natural pairings, though the orders of nouns and verbs do not match, and it would be quite possible for any of lame/blind/poor to halt/creep/cry out.

905 **pines** starves.

907 **Advice** i.e. medical advice, personified here (as is 'Justice' in the previous line).
sporting frolicking; the word suggests sexual licence as well as frivolity.

909 **rape** One of only two appearances of the word in the poem itself, except for the running-titles at the head of every page in Q; for the other see l. 1369.

910 **heinous** loathsome.

911 **have to do** get involved.

912 **crosses** obstacles.

914 **gratis** for free; the legal language of this stanza and the next becomes distinct at this point.
apaid satisfied; Shakespeare's only use of the word. The word derives from Latin *pax*, French *paix*, and suggests pacification. There is a strong play on 'pay'/'paid' (as with 'fee' in the previous line).

915 **As well...grant** Opportunity grants the case made as soon as he hears it in court (like a corrupt judge).
he i.e. Sin.

916 **else** otherwise.

917 **stayed** stopped; the specific legal sense (OED 'stay, *v*.1', 25a, halting a court process) is pertinent here. Shakespeare uses it with legal resonance and without: compare *2 Henry IV*, 4.3.72: 'Retrait is made and execution stayed', and 4.1.121–2: 'Then, then, when there was nothing could have stayed | My father from the breast of Bullingbrook'.

919 **subornation** bribery (e.g. to commit perjury).

920 **shift** subterfuge; the legal context means that the word implies a technical fraud, but it tends to be used more generally. Shakespeare's closest equivalent use is *Antony and Cleopatra*, 3.11.61–3: 'Now I must | To the young man send humble

Thou plantest scandal, and displacest laud.
    Thou ravisher, thou traitor, thou false thief,
    Thy honey turns to gall, thy joy to grief.

'Thy secret pleasure turns to open shame,   890
Thy private feasting to a public fast,
Thy smoothing titles to a ragged name,
Thy sugared tongue to bitter wormwood taste;
Thy violent vanities can never last.
    How comes it then, vile Opportunity,   895
    Being so bad, such numbers seek for thee?

'When wilt thou be the humble suppliant's friend,
And bring him where his suit may be obtained?
When wilt thou sort an hour great strifes to end,
Or free that soul which wretchedness hath chained?   900
Give physic to the sick, ease to the pained?
    The poor, lame, blind, halt, creep, cry out for thee,
    But they ne'er meet with Opportunity.

'The patient dies while the physician sleeps;
The orphan pines while the oppressor feeds;   905
Justice is feasting while the widow weeps;
Advice is sporting while infection breeds;
Thou grant'st no time for charitable deeds.
    Wrath, envy, treason, rape, and murder's rages,
    Thy heinous hours wait on them as their pages.   910

'When Truth and Virtue have to do with thee,
A thousand crosses keep them from thy aid;
They buy thy help, but Sin ne'er gives a fee.
He gratis comes, and thou art well apaid
As well to hear as grant what he hath said.   915
    My Collatine would else have come to me
    When Tarquin did, but he was stayed by thee.

'Guilty thou art of murder and of theft,
Guilty of perjury and subornation,
Guilty of treason, forgery and shift,   920
Guilty of incest, that abomination,
An accessory by thine inclination

treaties, dodge | And palter in the shifts
of lowness'. Compare *Venus and Adonis*,
l. 690.
921 **abomination** See 704n.
922 **accessory** someone who assists in a crime
    (OED³ 1); probably requires stress on the

first and third syllables (of four in this
case). Q's spelling is 'accessarie', and OED³
allows both spellings as lemmata; however,
it regards 'accessory' as the primary form,
hence the spelling here.
inclination natural disposition.

924 *general doom* Last Judgement; Shakespeare uses the phrase again in *Romeo and Juliet*, 3.2.67: 'Then, dreadful trumpet, sound the general doom'.

925 *copesmate* (i) 'partner, companion' (OED 2a); (ii) 'accomplice in cheating' (OED 3a). An EEBO-TCP search of uses before 1594 reveals a striking number of instances from the work of Robert Greene (12 of 39), e.g. in *Greene's Groat's-Worth of Wit* (1592): 'When she alights, I will conduct her to a chamber far from his lodging; but when the lights are out, and she expects her adulterous copesmate, yourself (as reason is) shall prove her bed-fellow' (sig. D1v). This suggests the word may have had a socially deprecatory aspect, belonging to the world of prose fiction tricks.
   ugly Night The phrase is also used in *Venus and Adonis*, l. 1041. 'Night' is capitalised in this edition (though not in Q) as a personification, in keeping with other personifications in Lucrece's speech.

926 *subtle* (i) cunning; (ii) 'Working imperceptibly or secretly; insidious' (OED³ 7a). The word can also be associated with movement, and while the relevant sense in OED³ (13) has no citation before 1654, two of Shakespeare's uses seem to tend in this direction, while having, especially in the first case, aspects of (i) and (ii). See *Twelfth Night*, 1.5.296–8: 'Methinks I feel this youth's perfections | With an invisible and subtle stealth | To creep in at mine eyes'; and *Macbeth*, 3.1.94–6: 'the valued file | Distinguishes the swift, the slow, the subtle, | The house-keeper, the hunter, every one'.
   post messenger. Specifically, the word was used in the sixteenth century to refer to courier riders, especially those working in relays (for the sake of speed) along 'post-roads'. See OED³ 'post, *n*.3', 2a, 2b, and 1n.
   carrier This can denote a carrier of mail, in keeping with 'post'. However, it may mean a generic menial carrier of 'care', looking ahead to 'packhorse', l. 928.
   grisly horrible, terrible.

927 *Eater of youth* Time as a devourer is a proverbial motif (Dent T326, 'time devours all things') with a significant place in Ovid's *Metamorphoses* ('tempus edax rerum', 'time the devourer of [all] things', 15.234; Golding's translation, 15.258); compare Sonnet 19.1 and note.

928 *watch of woes* (i) sentinel looking out for bad news; or perhaps (ii) guardian (OED 11, one of 'those who watch, for purposes of guarding and protecting life') of harm.
   packhorse drudge (OED³ 2). Compare Shakespeare's other use of the word, *Richard III*, 1.3.120–1: 'Ere you were queen, ay, or your husband king, | I was a pack-horse in his great affairs'.

928 *virtue's snare* The combination recurs in *Antony and Cleopatra*, 4.8.17–18: 'O infinite virtue, com'st thou smiling from | The world's great snare uncaught?'.

929 *murder'st* Q's spelling is 'murthrest', so there is a case for modernising to 'murd'rest'; compare l. 885 and note. Here consistency in modernising *-st* forms means 'murder'st' is preferred.

930 *injurious. . . Time* Shakespeare repeats this combination in *Troilus and Cressida*, 4.4.42–3: 'Injurious time now with a robber's haste | Crams his rich thievery up, he knows not how'; and in Sonnet 63.2. 'Injurious' is pronounced with three syllables, as at l. 838.
   shifting (i) deceptive, cheating; (ii) always in motion.

931 *since* i.e. since you are guilty.

933 *to repose* for rest.

934 *Cancelled* OED cites this use first under 'cancel, *v*.', sense 3b, 'frustrate, reduce to nought, put an end to, abolish', but in keeping with the legal language of surrounding lines, the more contractual sense 2a ('annul, repeal, render void') and the specific legal sense 1 ('deface or obliterate, properly by drawing lines across it lattice-wise. . . to annul, render void or invalid by so marking') come into view. Compare l. 1729.
   enchainèd Shakespeare's only use of enchained or enchain.

935 *date* period, duration (OED³ 'date, *n*.2', 1)

936–59 The description of Time here elaborates on the 'eater of youth' idea; see l. 927 and note.

936 *office* function.
   fine (i) bring an end to (OED³ 'fine, *v*.1', 3a); (ii) punish with a financial penalty (OED³ 'fine, *v*.2'). This is later than any citation under any sense of 'fine, *v*.1', but under the adjectival form there is Drayton's *Tragical Legend of Robert Duke of Normandy* (1596): 'In fined things such marvels infinite' (sig. D4r), which suggests that the archaic word still had a life in an elevated, tragic register.

To all sins past and all that are to come,
From the creation to the general doom.

'Misshapen Time, copesmate of ugly Night,   925
Swift subtle post, carrier of grisly care,
Eater of youth, false slave to false delight,
Base watch of woes, sin's packhorse, virtue's snare,
Thou nursest all, and murder'st all that are.
    O hear me then, injurious shifting Time,   930
    Be guilty of my death, since of my crime.

'Why hath thy servant Opportunity
Betrayed the hours thou gav'st me to repose,
Cancelled my fortunes, and enchainèd me
To endless date of never-ending woes?   935
Time's office is to fine the hate of foes,
    To eat up errors by opinion bred,
    Not spend the dowry of a lawful bed.

'Time's glory is to calm contending kings,
To unmask falsehood and bring truth to light,   940
To stamp the seal of time in aged things,
To wake the morn and sentinel the night,
To wrong the wronger till he render right,
    To ruinate proud buildings with thy hours,
    And smear with dust their glittering golden towers;   945

'To fill with worm-holes stately monuments,
To feed oblivion with decay of things,

937 **opinion** popular judgement, which was often represented as flawed by nature. Compare *Henry V*, 5.2.128–9: 'Rotten opinion, who hath writ me down | After my seeming'.
938 **spend** waste.
940 **bring. . . light** A proverbial idea (Dent T324: 'time brings the truth to light'). See also Spenser, *Faerie Queene*, I.ix.5.9: 'As time in her just term the truth to light should bring'.
941 **stamp. . . things** to endorse ancient things with its authority (like a king putting the royal seal on an authentic letter).
942 **sentinel** guard, watch over. This is the first citation in OED for a transitive use of the verb; Thomas Nashe's slightly earlier *Christ's Tears Over Jerusalem* (1593) is cited for the intransitive use: 'My vigilance should have

sentinelled for all your sleeps' (2.43). EEBO-TCP offers no earlier instances.
943 **wrong. . . right** harm the one who has done harm, until he puts things right.
944 **ruinate** reduce to ruins; see Sonnet 10.7 and note.
    with thy hours Lucrece emphasises that Time ruins things with slow decay rather than with violent action.
945 **smear with dust** Compare l. 1381, and Sonnet 55.4.
946 **worm-holes** This is the first citation of 'worm-hole, *n*.' in OED, and EEBO-TCP offers no earlier uses.
    monuments Either these are made of wood, or they are books (OED[3] 'monument', 3a), or the worm-holes are metaphorical.

948   **blot** See 192n.
      alter change, perhaps by 'razing', as at Sonnets 25.11, 122.7 (see notes).
      contents stressed on the second syllable.

949   **ancient ravens** On the similar longevity of crows, see 'Let the Bird of Loudest Lay', 17n. Here the point is that Time outlasts even the raven.

950   **old oaks** Oaks were thought of as long-lived trees. Compare *As You Like It*, 4.3.104–5: 'Under an old oak, whose boughs were mossed with age | And high top bald with dry antiquity'.
      cherish Emendations have been suggested, e.g. 'perish' (Johnson), 'blemish' (Oxford, Taylor), because this seems an abrupt shift to the nurturing effects of Time. However, the antithesis in the line (see note on 'springs' below), and the emphasis on proper growth in the stanza, diminish the need for any alteration.
      springs young plants, shoots (OED 'spring', *n*.1, 6a; in contrast with 'old oaks'). This is more straightforward than taking these as springs of water, in contrast with 'dry'. Shakespeare's other use of 'springs' with this sense is in *The Comedy of Errors*, 3.2.2–3: 'Shall, Antipholus, | Even in the spring of love, thy love-springs rot?'.

951   **spoil** probably 'destroy' (OED 'spoil, *v*.1', 11a) rather than 'damage' (10a).

952   **turn. . . wheel** The wheel of Fortune was a common and traditional image of the world's changeability.
      giddy rapidly circling, whirling (OED 2d).
      round i.e. 'the circumference, bounds, or extent of a circular object', OED³ *n*.1, 3.

953   **beldam** grandmother; although the word is used in the period to mean 'old woman' in general (as at l. 1458), this is its original sense.

954   **man a child** primarily, this refers to the re-infantilising effects of old age, which were proverbial (Dent 570, 'old men are twice children'). It may also imply the birth of children.

956   **tame the unicorn** The unicorn was said to be untameable, as in Topsell, *History of Four-Footed Beasts* (1607): 'It is said by Aelianus and Albertus, that except they be taken before they be two years old they will never be tamed; and that the Thracians do yearly take some of their Colts, and bring them to their King, which he keepeth for combat, and to fight with one another: for

when they are old, they differ nothing at all from the most barbarous, bloody, and ravenous beasts' (sig. 3S6r). Compare John Lyly's *Euphues* (1578), where the idea is also used to attribute great efficacy, in this case to 'labour', whereby 'the fierce Unicorn is tamed, the wildest Falcon is reclaimed, the greatest bulwark is sacked' (sig. K1v).

957   **To mock. . . beguiled** (i) to confound the treacherous who catch themselves in their own traps; or (ii) to make fools of the sophisticated who confuse themselves with their overthinking.

958   **increaseful** fruitful; apparently Shakespeare's coinage (first citation in OED; no earlier use in EEBO-TCP).

959   **waste** wear away; see l. 560 and note.

960   **pilgrimage** course, progress. The idea may still have evoked religious controversy (pilgrimage being a Catholic practice attacked in the Reformation), but the word was used figuratively, as of a metaphorical river current in *Two Gentlemen of Verona*, 2.7.28–32: 'He makes sweet music with the enamelled stones, | Giving a gentle kiss to every sedge | He overtaketh in his pilgrimage; | And so by many winding nooks he strays | With willing sport to the wild ocean'. Compare also Ben Jonson's *Volpone*, 2.2.195–6: 'So short is this pilgrimage of man (which some call life)', and Sonnets 7.8, 27.6.

962   **retiring** returning; as at *Venus and Adonis*, l. 906.

963   **thousand thousand** See 456n.

964   **Lending. . . lends** Giving the wisdom (of hindsight, with the benefit of a 'retiring minute') to anyone who lends to people who cannot pay back. The *polyptoton* of this line is repeated more emphatically soon after (see 969n).

965   **one hour** for one hour.

966   **prevent** (i) anticipate (OED³ 1a); (ii) 'preclude the occurrence of' (9a); in this case it is a combination of both, rather than either/or.
      shun thy wrack avoid the destruction you have caused.

967   **Thou. . . eternity** Compare Sonnet 77.8.
      ceaseless never-stopping. This is Shakespeare's only use of 'ceaseless'; on the -*less* suffix, see 2n.
      lackey Shakespeare's uses of 'lackey' bring out its derogatory note; compare *Richard III*, 5.3.315–17: 'Remember whom you are to cope withal: | A sort of vagabonds,

To blot old books and alter their contents,
To pluck the quills from ancient ravens' wings,
To dry the old oaks' sap and cherish springs,   950
   To spoil antiquities of hammered steel,
   And turn the giddy round of Fortune's wheel;

'To show the beldam daughters of her daughter,
To make the child a man, the man a child,
To slay the tiger that doth live by slaughter,   955
To tame the unicorn and lion wild,
To mock the subtle in themselves beguiled,
   To cheer the ploughman with increaseful crops,
   And waste huge stones with little water drops.

'Why work'st thou mischief in thy pilgrimage,   960
Unless thou couldst return to make amends?
One poor retiring minute in an age
Would purchase thee a thousand thousand friends,
Lending him wit that to bad debtors lends.
   O this dread night, wouldst thou one hour come back,   965
   I could prevent this storm and shun thy wrack.

'Thou ceaseless lackey to eternity,
With some mischance cross Tarquin in his flight;
Devise extremes beyond extremity
To make him curse this cursèd crimeful night;   970
Let ghastly shadows his lewd eyes affright,

rascals, and runaways, | A scum of Bretons, and base lackey peasants'.

968 *cross* obstruct.

969 *extremes. . . extremity* The former (though not so much the latter) is used at times in Shakespeare to refer specifically to physical hardships, as at *Troilus and Cressida*, 4.2.101–2: 'Time, force, and death, | Do to this body what extremes you can'. For 'extremity', see also l. 1337. The use of *polyptoton* here and in several other lines nearby conveys the psychological intensity of the moment; see also ll. 964, 970, 978–80, 981–7.

970 *crimeful* full of crimes, characterised by crimes; OED³ and EEBO-TCP have this as the first use of the word. The line involves another *polyptoton* (see 969n).

971–94 The curses are reminiscent of those aimed at the King in the roughly contemporary *Richard III*. Compare 1.3.216–32: 'If heaven have any grievous plague in store | Exceeding those that I can wish upon thee, | O, let them keep it till thy sins be ripe, | And then hurl down their indignation | On thee, the troubler of the poor world's peace! | The worm of conscience still begnaw thy soul! | Thy friends suspect for traitors while thou liv'st, | And take deep traitors for thy dearest friends! | No sleep close up that deadly eye of thine, | Unless it be whilst some tormenting dream | Affrights thee with a hell of ugly devils! | Thou elvish-marked, abortive, rooting hog! | Thou that wast sealed in thy nativity | The slave of nature and the son of hell! | Thou slander of thy mother's heavy womb! | Thou loathed issue of thy father's loins! | Thou rag of honour! thou detested –'.

971 *shadows* delusions; see l. 460 and note.
lewd wicked, lustful.

973   **Shape. . . devil** Give every bush the appearance of a foul, misshapen demon. The idea behind the line is proverbial (Dent B738, 'He thinks every bush a bear') as well as memorable from *A Midsummer Night's Dream*, 5.1.22: 'How easy is a bush supposed a bear'.
  hideous Compare Sonnet 5.6 and note.
  shapeless unshapely (OED 2). Compare 'misshapen Time', l. 925, and *Comedy of Errors*, 4.2.19–20: 'He is deformed, crooked, old, and sere, | Ill-faced, worse bodied, shapeless everywhere'.

974   **restless** 'affording or yielding no rest' (OED³ 1b). On the *-less* ending, see 2n.
  trances This seems to be a late instance of OED 'trance, *n.*1', 1: 'A state of extreme apprehension or dread' (latest reference in OED is 1577). Shakespeare's other two uses, however, one of which is l. 1595, have their modern sense, a loss of consciousness.

975   **bedrid** bedridden; although the word technically modifies the 'groans', it refers to Tarquin himself, groaning in bed if Lucrece's curse is successful.

976   **bechance** befall; see *3 Henry VI*, 1.4.6: 'My sons, God knows what hath bechanced them'.
  pitiful dreadful, i.e. the kind of thing that would arouse pity in other circumstances.

977   **moan** 'lament, grieve' (OED³ 2a).

978–80   **Stone. . . wildness** *Polyptoton* again (see 969n).

979   **to him** towards him; perhaps 'when they meet him'.

980   **tigers** Generally associated with viciousness, but particularly with vengeful female rage, as in *3 Henry VI*, 1.4.137, 154–6, 'O tiger's heart wrapped in a woman's hide! [. . .] But you are more inhuman, more inexorable, | O, ten times more, than tigers of Hyrcania. | See, ruthless queen, a hapless father's tears!', and 'that ravenous tiger Tamora', *Titus Andronicus*, 5.3.195.

981–7   **Let him. . .** As at ll. 969 and 978–80 (see 969n) repetition, here in the form of *anaphora* and *polyptoton* ('Disdain. . . disdainèd'), as well as playing on 'time', conveys the passion of Lucrece's curse.

981   **curlèd hair** This is probably a scornful reflection on the fashionable styling of a young aristocrat's hair, rather than a description of natural curls, though 'curled' could mean either. Compare *Othello*, 1.2.67–8: 'So opposite to marriage that she shunned | The wealthy curled darlings of our nation'.

985   **orts** scraps (of food).

989   **resort** gather.

990–2   Lucrece takes three lines to reiterate two commonplaces about the passing of time: Dent H747, 'Hours of pleasure are short', and Dent H747.1, 'Hours of sorrow are long'. The monosyllables of l. 990 may help to distend the moment; compare l. 1575 and note. The point may be that it is too late for such oft-learned lessons to be learned by Tarquin.

990   **mark** observe, realise.

992   **folly** mad lust (as at ll. 556, 851).
  sport The word is turned sardonically in *Venus and Adonis* as well; see 24n.

993   **unrecalling** irrevocable; Shakespeare's only use, and the first citation of two in OED³; EEBO-TCP reveals no earlier uses. Abbott, § 372, suggests Shakespeare uses *-ing* for a passive participle form. Duncan-Jones and Woudhuysen offer an alternative, which is that 'unrecalling' describes Tarquin, failing to remember his better nature, as he commits his 'crime' (2007: 318).

994   **time. . . time** For a similar repetition, see l. 1570.

996   **that** to whom.

997   **At his own shadow** Lucrece again turns to a proverbial register: see Dent S261, 'To be afraid of his own shadow'. Duncan-Jones and Woudhuysen also cite Dent T112, 'The thief does fear every bush and officer', which links back to l. 973 and note (2007: 318). On Lucrece's speech, and her use of proverbial language, see headnote.

998   **Himself himself** See 157n.

999   **wretched. . . wretched** despicable, hateful (OED 4).

1000   **who so base would** who is so reprehensible that they would.

1001   **slanderous** disgraceful (OED 1a); compare *Richard II*, 1.1.60–1: 'I do defy him, and I spit at him; | Call him a slanderous coward, and a villain'.
  deathsman executioner. In *Measure for Measure* Pompey the bawd becomes an executioner's assistant as an alternative to

And the dire thought of his committed evil
Shape every bush a hideous shapeless devil.

'Disturb his hours of rest with restless trances;
Afflict him in his bed with bedrid groans;   975
Let there bechance him pitiful mischances
To make him moan, but pity not his moans;
Stone him with hardened hearts harder than stones,
    And let mild women to him lose their mildness,
    Wilder to him than tigers in their wildness.   980

'Let him have time to tear his curlèd hair;
Let him have time against himself to rave;
Let him have time of Time's help to despair;
Let him have time to live a loathèd slave;
Let him have time a beggar's orts to crave,   985
    And time to see one that by alms doth live
    Disdain to him disdainèd scraps to give.

'Let him have time to see his friends his foes,
And merry fools to mock at him resort;
Let him have time to mark how slow time goes   990
In time of sorrow, and how swift and short
His time of folly and his time of sport;
    And ever let his unrecalling crime
    Have time to wail th' abusing of his time.

'O Time, thou tutor both to good and bad,   995
Teach me to curse him that thou taught'st this ill.
At his own shadow let the thief run mad,
Himself himself seek every hour to kill.
Such wretched hands such wretched blood should spill,
    For who so base would such an office have   1000
    As slanderous deathsman to so base a slave.

'The baser is he, coming from a king,
To shame his hope with deeds degenerate;

imprisonment, an indication of the low
status of the job.
so base a slave such an immoral wretch, i.e.
Tarquin.
1002 **coming from** being a descendant of.
1003 **shame** ruin.
his hope (i) the expectations people had of
him; (ii) the expectations he had of himself.

degenerate falling shamefully short of his
nature. This points to the betrayal of qualities he should have inherited from his noble
family (his *genus*), as *1 Henry IV*, 3.2.122–
4, 128: 'Why, Harry, do I tell thee of my
foes, | Which art my nearest and dearest
enemy? | Thou that art like enough [...] |
To show how much thou art degenerate'.

1005 *begets him hate* makes him hated. The familial aspect of 'begets' connects with 'degenerate', l. 1003.

1006 *waits on* accompanies. The phrase may (sardonically in this case) suggest the work of a servant (see OED 'wait on', 10, in 'wait, *v.*1').
state rank.

1007 *presently* immediately.
missed This plays on 'mist' (the spelling in Q).

1008 *them* themselves.
list wish.

1009–11 *coal-black. . . snow-white* Both proverbial (CC14; S591, as at 196n); the proverbial voice may be a way of portraying Lucrece's righteous candour.

1009 *mire* mud; but the word conveys a swamp-like mass (OED³ 1a) and its moral sense ('undesirable state or condition [. . .] formerly esp. of sin or moral degradation', 1b) was well established in Shakespeare's time. Compare *Timon of Athens*, 1.2.58, 'Honest water, which ne'er left man i' th' mire'.

1010 *unperceived* The adjective refers to the 'mire' on the feathers, but it is applied to the crow, i.e. the crow will escape notice for the fact of its dirty feathers.

1012 *silver* white; see l. 56.

1013 *grooms* servants.
sightless invisible (OED 2); on -*less* compounds see 2n.
glorious day Monarchs were often likened to suns, a motif that recurs in *Richard II*, as in 3.2.47–52: 'when this thief, this traitor Bullingbrook, [. . .] Shall see us rising in our throne, the east, | His treasons will sit blushing in his face, | Not able to endure the sight of day'.

1016 *shallow* Cited as first instance of OED 'shallow, *adj.* and *n*.3', A6c, 'wanting in depth of mind, feeling, or character', though the difference between this and A6a, '[lacking depth in] thought, reasoning, knowledge, observation, or feeling' is slight. Compare *Two Gentlemen of Verona*, 1.1.21–2, which is cited under 6a: 'That's on some shallow story of deep love: | How young Leander crossed the Hellespont'. See also, in the same play 1.2.7–8, 'I'll show my mind | According to my shallow simple skill', and 4.2.96–7, 'Think'st thou I am so shallow, so conceitless, | To be seduced by thy flattery?'.

1017 *Unprofitable* useless (OED³ 2).
arbitrators judges.

1018 *skill-contending schools* academic settings where students compete to show off their rhetorical aptitude. In Shakespeare's time this would have evoked universities or the Inns of Court, centres of legal training; the idea seems to be raised disparagingly here.

1019 *where leisure serves* when there is free time in which to do so.
debaters Shakespeare's only use of the word in singular or plural. The OED cites this as the earliest use of the word in its modern sense (2, 'one who takes part in debate'), and thus perhaps a pivotal usage between this and its older sense (1, 'one who contends or strives; a quarrelsome or contentious person'). However, the modern sense is a small stretch from readily available senses of the verb 'debate', and EEBO-TCP has three earlier instances in John Bridges, *A Defence of the Government Established in the Church of England for Ecclesiastical Matters* (1587), e.g. in a marginal note: 'If the debaters should be moderate men, then should our brethren use more moderation in their terms and not be so peremptory in their dealing' (sig. A8r). Compare 'debate', l. 1421.

1020 *clients* 'a person [. . .] using the services of a lawyer' (OED³ 2a).
mediators intercessors; those who (in this context) go between the 'clients' and the judge. Shakespeare's other use of the word suggests a technical register, as Iago scornfully complains in *Othello*, 1.1.14–16: 'And, in conclusion, | [Othello] Nonsuits my mediators; for, "Certes," says he, | "I have already chose my officer."'

1021 *force not. . . straw* have no regard whatsoever for argument. For 'force' see OED *v.*1, 14a, 'to attach force or importance to'. The worthlessness of a straw was proverbial (Dent S918, 'not worth a straw').

1024 *uncheerful* cheerless; Shakespeare's only use of the word.

1025 *cavil with* object to, quibble with. Shakespeare's uses of 'cavil' usually suggest pedantic attention to detail, as in *1 Henry IV*, 3.1.127–8: 'But in the way of bargain, mark ye me, | I'll cavil on the ninth part of a hair'.

1026 *spurn at* show contempt to; originally, to kick; see l. 880 and note.
confirmed irrevocable. OED 'confirm, *v.*', 2a, means to ratify or establish in a technical

The mightier man, the mightier is the thing
That makes him honoured or begets him hate,   1005
For greatest scandal waits on greatest state.
   The moon being clouded presently is missed,
   But little stars may hide them when they list.

'The crow may bathe his coal-black wings in mire,
And unperceived fly with the filth away;   1010
But if the like the snow-white swan desire,
The stain upon his silver down will stay.
Poor grooms are sightless night, kings glorious day;
   Gnats are unnoted wheresoe'er they fly,
   But eagles gazed upon with every eye.   1015

'Out, idle words, servants to shallow fools,
Unprofitable sounds, weak arbitrators!
Busy yourselves in skill-contending schools;
Debate, where leisure serves, with dull debaters;
To trembling clients be you mediators.   1020
   For me, I force not argument a straw,
   Since that my case is past the help of law.

'In vain I rail at Opportunity,
At Time, at Tarquin, and uncheerful Night;
In vain I cavil with mine infamy,   1025
In vain I spurn at my confirmed despite;
This helpless smoke of words doth me no right.
   The remedy indeed to do me good
   Is to let forth my foul defilèd blood.

'Poor hand, why quiver'st thou at this decree?   1030
Honour thyself to rid me of this shame,

legal sense, which is in keeping with the preceding lines.
   despite condemnation.

1027 *helpless* offering no help, as at l. 1056; compare also l. 756, and see *Venus and Adonis*, 604n, on the extent of Shakespeare's innovation in using it with this sense. On *-less* compounds, see 2n.
   smoke of words The metaphor primarily suggests the insubstantiality of words. Elsewhere Shakespeare links words and smoke in order to convey obscurity and a sense of threat, as in *King John*, 2.1.229–30: 'They shoot but calm words folded up in smoke, | To make a faithless error in your ears'. See also *Love's Labour's Lost*, 3.1.63–5,

where Don Adriano de Armado develops the metaphor: 'Sweet smoke of rhetoric! | He reputes me a cannon, and the bullet, that's he; | I shoot thee at the swain'. Compare 'wind of words', l. 1330.
   doth me no right brings me no justice.

1028 *remedy* The word's medical (OED^3 2) and legal (OED^3 3) resonances are both active here.

1029 *let forth* Bloodletting was an established medical 'remedy', but Lucrece is patently thinking of suicide here.
   foul defilèd (i) shamefully polluted, with 'foul' taken adverbially; (ii) polluted and corrupted.

1030 *decree* judgement.

1031 *to rid me* by ridding me.

1033 *defame* disgrace; see l. 768 and note.

1034 *loyal* faithful. The OED's first citation for this sense (1) is *Othello* 4.2.34–5, 'Your wife, my lord, your true | And loyal wife'. An EEBO-TCP search reveals six instances of the phrase 'loyal wife' (which recurs at l. 1048) in five works before 1594 (though none of 'loyal dame'). For example, see William Painter, *The Second Tome of the Palace of Pleasure* (1567): 'I have lost the hope which I had of thee, thou the favour of the king and of thy brethren [...] I an unfaithful husband, thou a most pure and loyal wife' (sig. 5G2v).

dame mistress.

1036 *yielding* See 'yieldings', l. 1658 and note.

1037 *betumbled* 'tossed in confusion, disordered' (OED, where it is the only citation, and EEBO-TCP has no others). The sexual sense of 'tumble' is attributed to Shakespeare by the OED ('tumble, *v.*', 9a, citing *Hamlet*, 4.5.62–3, 'Quoth she, "Before you tumbled me, | You promised me to wed."'). However, earlier uses of the word, sometimes intransitive, tend in this metaphorical direction. A vivid example comes in the 1583 edition of Foxe's *Acts and Monuments*, where the martyr John Bradford tells of spiritual struggles in a letter: 'I hide me with Adam in the garden, I play not only Samuel running to Eli, but I play Jonah running to the sea, and there I sleep upon the hatches tumbling in Jezebel's bed' (vol. 2, sig. 4I5r).

1038 *desperate* despairing; pronounced here with two syllables. The emotion is transferred from her to the 'instrument' (see OED *adj.*, *n.*, and *adv.* A1b). It may also suggest 'extremely reckless or violent' (OED A4a). See 739n.

1039 *imparteth* provides.

1040 *more vent* a larger outlet; see l. 310. Compare 'hole', l. 1175.

1042 *Etna* The Sicilian volcano was certainly famous, but more for its ferocity than for the evanescence of its smoke. Compare *Titus Andronicus*, 3.1.241–2, 'Now let hot Aetna cool in Sicily, | And be my heart an ever-burning hell!'. Etna is featured in Ovid's *Metamorphoses*, 15.340–55, where, in keeping with the poem's emphasis on change, the point is that its power will not last forever. See Golding's translation, 15.375–84: 'Mount Etna with his burning ovens of brimstone shall not bide | Ay [i.e. always] fiery: neither was it so forever erst [i.e. in the past]. For whether | The earth a living creature be, and that to breathe out hither | And thither flame, great

store of vents it have in sundry places, | And that it have the power to shift those vents in divers cases, | Now damming these, now opening those, in moving to and fro: | Or that the whisking winds restrained within the earth below, | Do beat the stones against the stones, and other kind of stuff | Of fiery nature, which do fall on fire with every puff: | As soon as those same winds do cease, the caves shall straight be cold'.

consumes vanishes, disperses. Compare OED[3], 'consume, *v.*1', 1, 'to cause to evaporate or disappear; to disperse', which is, however, transitive; also *1 Henry VI*, 5.4.92, 'Break thou in pieces and consume to ashes', which is intransitive, but relates to destruction by fire.

1043 *fumes* issues, rises (OED 3a, for which this is the first citation).

1045 *mean* means.

hapless unfortunate; on *-less* compounds, see 2n; the proximity of 'happy' may draw extra attention to the compound form (as with 'peer...peerless', l. 21).

1046 *falchion* sword; see 176n.

1048 *loyal wife* See 1034n.

1050 *true* (i) authentic, merited; (ii) loyal, chaste.

type (i) symbolic role, as in OED 1a; perhaps (ii) sign, as in OED 3, 'distinguishing mark or sign'. The latter sense might suit the tangibility of 'rifled'. Compare *3 Henry VI*, 1.4.121–3, which is cited under OED 3: 'Thy father bears the type of King of Naples, | Of both the Sicils and Jerusalem, | Yet not so wealthy as an English yeoman'. See also *Richard III*, 4.4.242, 244–5: 'Th' advancement of your children [...] Unto the dignity and height of fortune, | The high imperial type of this earth's glory'. The phrase 'true type', however, was linked more to OED 1a, as in Lodowick Lloyd, *The Consent of Time* (1590): 'Jacob was the true type of the church of God, Christ being the head thereof' (sig. B4r).

rifled robbed; see 692n.

1053 *To clear* by clearing.

spot stain (moral); see 196n.

1054 *badge of fame* a symbol of good reputation. A 'badge' was 'an identifying mark worn by a knight and his retainers' (OED[3] 1a). Usually it would not be at odds with heraldic livery as it is here.

slander's livery Lucrece accepts the shameful uniform given to her by slander now she has become its servant, but she hopes by her suicide to embellish it. For other

For if I die, my honour lives in thee,
But if I live, thou liv'st in my defame.
Since thou couldst not defend thy loyal dame,
    And wast afeard to scratch her wicked foe,   1035
    Kill both thyself and her for yielding so.'

This said, from her betumbled couch she starteth,
To find some desperate instrument of death;
But this, no slaughterhouse, no tool imparteth
To make more vent for passage of her breath,   1040
Which thronging through her lips so vanisheth
    As smoke from Etna that in air consumes,
    Or that which from dischargèd cannon fumes.

'In vain', quoth she, 'I live, and seek in vain
Some happy mean to end a hapless life.   1045
I feared by Tarquin's falchion to be slain,
Yet for the self-same purpose seek a knife.
But when I feared I was a loyal wife –
    So am I now – O no, that cannot be:
    Of that true type hath Tarquin rifled me.   1050

'O that is gone for which I sought to live,
And therefore now I need not fear to die.
To clear this spot by death, at least I give
A badge of fame to slander's livery,
A dying life to living infamy.   1055
    Poor helpless help, the treasure stolen away,
    To burn the guiltless casket where it lay.

metaphorical liveries, see l. 1222, and *Venus and Adonis*, 506n.

1055 **dying life** 'an immortal reputation acquired through dying' (Burrow 2002: 300). This takes the phrase 'dying life' differently from its common sense in the period, where it denotes a living death, a life that is equivalent to death. In order to parallel l. 1054, 'life' here is taken as something positive, counter-active to 'living infamy', going beyond even 6a, 'a sense of vitality or energy', to suggest a praiseworthy existence.
living infamy everlasting disrepute.

1056 **helpless help** ineffectual aid; i.e. it does no good to kill the body once its value ('treasure', i.e. virtue) has been taken away. An EEBO-TCP search for the phrase reveals seven citations before 1650, all after Shakespeare. It compresses characteristic stylistic features of the poem (repetition of 'help'; oxymoron; *-less* compound, on which see 2n). Compare 'lifeless life', l. 1374, and 1045n, on 'happy...hapless'. The idea behind ll. 1056–7 is also proverbial; compare Dent S838 'when the steed is stolen [it is too late to] shut the stable door'.
treasure See 16n.
stolen monosyllabic here.

1057 **guiltless casket** i.e. her body, a metaphorical chest containing the 'treasure' of her chastity. 'Guiltless' denotes her innocent state, but also puns on 'gilt-less', lacking in the gold decoration one might expect on a noblewoman's casket. The word 'giltless' is not in OED, but in a poem with many *-less* compounds (see 2n), it is not an abstruse coinage. Shakespeare puns on guilt and gilt at *Henry V*, 2.Prol.23–7, where conspirators 'Have, for the gilt of France (O guilt indeed!) | Confirmed conspiracy with fearful France', and *Richard II*, 2.1.294–5, 'Wipe off the dust that hides our sceptre's gilt, | And make high majesty look like itself'.

1059   **troth** marital fidelity (OED[3] A3).

1061   *flatter* deceive (with the thought that any child resulting is legitimate).

1062   *bastard graff* illegitimate child. The metaphor is from horticulture, where a '*graff*' is a young shoot inserted into a mature plant with the aim of producing hybrid stock (the modern word is 'graft'). Lucrece's concern about pregnancy is not present in Shakespeare's sources. Shakespeare returns to the link between grafting and illegitimacy elsewhere, as in *2 Henry VI*, 3.2.212–15, 'Thy mother took into her blameful bed | Some stern untutored churl; and noble stock | Was graft with crab-tree slip, whose fruit thou art, | And never of the Nevils' noble race'; *Richard III*, 3.7.126–7, 'Her face defaced with scars of infamy, | Her royal stock graft with ignoble plants'; and as part of the debate between Polixenes and Perdita, *The Winter's Tale*, 4.4.82–5, 'carnations and streaked gillyvors | (Which some call nature's bastards). Of that kind | Our rustic garden's barren, and I care not | To get slips of them'.

1063   *stock* (i) trunk, stem (into which a 'graff' is placed; see 1062n); (ii) ancestry, bloodline.

1064   *doting* (i) loving; (ii) foolish. The two senses often combine, as love is frequently seen as foolish. Compare ll. 155, 643.

1066   *state* i.e. the condition of being a cuckold.

1067   *interest* Collatine's stake in, or right to, Lucrece's chastity, and/or (since they are fundamentally linked) her offspring. Compare ll. 1619, 1797.

1068   *Basely. . . gold* There is play on the idea of base metal, which tends to refer to metals less prestigious than gold and silver (see OED[3] 'base metal, *n.*'). For a possible play on 'base' and 'noble', see also l. 660.
       stolen monosyllabic here.

1069   *For me* as for me.

1070   *trespass* sin; see 632n.
       dispense [with] pardon; see the phrasal verb 'dispense with', 7, under OED 'dispense, *v.*'. Compare 'makes dispensation', l. 248 and *Measure for Measure*, 3.1.134–5: 'Nature dispenses with the deed so far, | That it becomes a virtue'.

1071   *Till life. . . offence* Until I pay, with my life, the debt owed to death as a result of the crime that I was forced to do. For '*acquit*' in

this sense, see OED[3] 2a, and the more general 2c, 'pay or atone for', where this line is cited.

1072   *attaint* stain, disgrace; see l. 825.

1073   *fold* cover up; compare l. 675.
       cleanly coined artfully forged. 'Coined' could just suggest 'manufactured', while 'cleanly' could denote neatness and/or that the excuses have been created to give an impression of purity. However, the alliterative phrase is clearly pejorative in Barnabe Rich's *The Adventures of Brusanus Prince of Hungaria* (1592): 'This accusation thus cleanly coined between them, the Duke intended the very next day to make riddance of his wife' (sig. P3r); likewise the 'cleanly coined lies' of Nashe's *Christ's Tears over Jerusalem* (1594: 2.172).

1074   *sable ground* black background (heraldic terms).

1075   *abuses* transgressions, crimes; the word has a specifically sexual sense as well (OED[3] 6a, 'sexual violation, *esp.* rape'). Compare Sonnets 4.5, 121.10.

1076   *sluices* flood-gates; see *Venus and Adonis*, l. 956.

1079   *By this* meanwhile, by this time; see ll. 1268, 1772.
       Philomel the nightingale, whose story is one of the most influential rape-narratives in Ovid's *Metamorphoses* (6.424–676). In it, Philomela is raped by her brother-in-law, Tereus, and her tongue is cut out to prevent her speaking. She finds a way of informing her sister Procne by weaving a tapestry, and they take revenge on Tereus by feeding him the body of his son Itys. The two sisters are transformed into birds, Procne into a swallow and Philomela into a nightingale. The story's interest in rape and secrecy brings it close to *Lucrece*; it is also very influential on *Titus Andronicus*, which Shakespeare wrote around the time of *Lucrece* (c. 1592–4), and where the Ovidian story is referred to several times (3.1.26–43, 4.1.41–58, 5.2.194–5).

1080   *well-tuned* melodious; compare *Titus Andronicus*, 2.3.17–19, 'And whilst the babbling echo mocks the hounds, | Replying shrilly to the well-tuned horns, | As if a double hunt were heard at once', and Sonnet 8.5.
       warble tune, song.

'Well, well, dear Collatine, thou shalt not know
The stainèd taste of violated troth.
I will not wrong thy true affection so,
To flatter thee with an infringèd oath.   1060
This bastard graff shall never come to growth:
   He shall not boast who did thy stock pollute,
   That thou art doting father of his fruit.

'Nor shall he smile at thee in secret thought,   1065
Nor laugh with his companions at thy state;
But thou shalt know thy interest was not bought
Basely with gold, but stolen from forth thy gate.
For me, I am the mistress of my fate,
   And with my trespass never will dispense,   1070
   Till life to death acquit my forced offence.

'I will not poison thee with my attaint,
Nor fold my fault in cleanly coined excuses;
My sable ground of sin I will not paint
To hide the truth of this false night's abuses.   1075
My tongue shall utter all; mine eyes, like sluices,
   As from a mountain spring that feeds a dale,
   Shall gush pure streams to purge my impure tale.'

By this, lamenting Philomel had ended
The well-tuned warble of her nightly sorrow,   1080
And solemn night with slow sad gait descended
To ugly hell, when lo, the blushing morrow
Lends light to all fair eyes that light will borrow;
   But cloudy Lucrece shames herself to see,
   And therefore still in night would cloistered be.   1085

nightly night-time (OED³ 1a; the first citation of 'nightly' meaning 'every night', 1b, comes from 1599).

1082 *blushing morrow* the reddish light of dawn. Compare *Venus and Adonis*, ll. 1–2 and notes.

1083 *light will borrow* want to make use of light.

1084 *cloudy* gloomy; see l. 115 and note.

   shames. . . see is ashamed to see herself. The intransitive use of 'shame' (OED 1a) is common in the period.

1085 *still* may mean 'always', but probably has its modern sense: she wants the darkness of night to continue.

would would like to.

cloistered shut in; the word's association with the enclosure (and chastity) of monks and nuns is pertinent here too. The OED (under 'cloister, v.' and 'cloistered, adj.') suggests uses beyond the monastic context are rare and recent, but EEBO-TCP provides a number of instances, including William Painter, *The Second Tome of the Palace of Pleasure* (1567): 'The Roman maidens were cloistered within their fathers' Palaces, still at their mothers' elbows, and notwithstanding were so well brought up, that those of best civility and finest trained-up in our age, shall not be the second to one of the least perfect in that City' (sig. 3C4r).

1086–7 A version of these lines has been written on the initial leaf in a volume of courtly works, dating from *c.* 1597, now Alnwick Castle, MS 525 (CELM ShW 5).

1088 *eye of eyes* i.e. the sun, source of the daylight. This does not seem to be a common phrase (no appearances before Shakespeare in EEBO-TCP).

1089 *peeping* The OED³ has this as its second citation for the noun ('peeping, *n.*2'), and the first is dated 1593, which gives the impression that it is a recent innovation. However EEBO-TCP has somewhat earlier instances, such as John Bridges, *A Defence of the Government Established in the Church of England for Ecclesiastical Matters* (1587): 'O Brethren, Brethren, it is more than high time to look to such a Seignory, the very peeping out of whose heads, and the first appearing in the Discoursing of them, shall begin his course, on this course fashion' (sig. 3H7v). The suggestion of voyeurism recognised by the OED, though absent from the Bridges example, is clearly there in *Lucrece*.

1090 *tickling beams* i.e. the sunbeams which irritate someone trying to keep their eyes closed.

1091 *Brand* Branding with a hot iron was a punishment for several offences in Elizabethan England; see Sonnet 111.5 and note. Shakespeare associates it with prostitution at *Hamlet*, 4.5.118–21, although this was not the usual contemporary practice: 'That drop of blood that's calm proclaims me bastard, | Cries cuckold to my father, brands the harlot | Even here between the chaste unsmirched brow | Of my true mother'. More important than any particular offence specified by the punishment is the feeling that daybreak will reveal her sin. Compare also 'slavish wipe', l. 537.

1092 *naught to do* nothing to do with; usually in Elizabethan English the phrase includes 'with' or equivalent, as at *Venus and Adonis*, l. 638. Compare also *Richard III*, 1.1.99–101, where the phrase is full of innuendo: 'Naught to do with Mistress Shore? I tell thee, fellow, | He that doth naught with her (excepting one) | Were best he do it secretly alone'. Abbott, § 200, notes

Shakespeare's practice of omitting prepositions in similar cases.

1093 *cavils* See 1025n.

1094 *fond, and testy* foolish and irritable; for the pairing compare *Two Gentlemen of Verona*, 1.2.57–9: 'Fie, fie, how wayward is this foolish love, | That (like a testy babe) will scratch the nurse, | And presently, all humbled, kiss the rod!'.

1095 *wayward once* having misbehaved once.

1096 *bear them mild* behave mildly; 'them' is reflexive, equivalent to 'themselves'.

1097 *Continuance* persistence; pronounced with three syllables.
the one. . . the other i.e. the 'old woes'. . . the 'infant sorrow'.

1098 *plunging still* constantly thrashing about; this reading fits best with the point of the next line. 'Plunging' could suggest diving (rather too purposeful), ducking or sinking (not consistent with the 'too much labour' of the next line).

1100 *drenchèd* submerged (OED 'drench, *v.*', 2).
sea of care The idea was proverbial ('sea of troubles', Dent S177.1; as in *Hamlet*, 3.1.58: 'take arms against a sea of troubles').

1101 *Holds disputation* debates formally, as at l. 246; compare also l. 822.

1103 *No object but* every single thing she looks at.

1104 *shifts* passes from view.
straight immediately.

1106 *mad* (i) lacking self-control; (ii) 'extravagant, wild' (Schmidt).
affords provides (OED³ 3a).

1107 *tune* sing; compare l. 1465. The OED has this as the earliest instance of 'tune, *v.* 2', 4a, but EEBO-TCP provides possible earlier uses, such as Thomas Lodge, *Phillis* (1593): 'The birds methinks, tune nought but moan, | The winds breathe nought but bitter plaint' (sig. C3v).

1109–18 marked as *sententiae*; see 87–8n.

1109 *mirth* gaiety (OED³ 4a).
search probe (OED 8). This sense of 'search' tends to go with wounds and sores, but it offers an apt sense that the reaching into and revealing are unpleasant and painful. Compare *Troilus and Cressida*, 2.2.15–17, which is less negative: 'modest doubt is called | The beacon of the wise, the tent

Revealing day through every cranny spies,
And seems to point her out where she sits weeping;
To whom she sobbing speaks: 'O eye of eyes,
Why pry'st thou through my window? Leave thy peeping,
Mock with thy tickling beams eyes that are sleeping;   1090
  Brand not my forehead with thy piercing light,
  For day hath naught to do what's done by night.'

Thus cavils she with every thing she sees;
True grief is fond, and testy as a child
Who, wayward once, his mood with naught agrees.   1095
Old woes, not infant sorrows, bear them mild:
Continuance tames the one, the other wild,
  Like an unpractised swimmer plunging still,
  With too much labour drowns for want of skill.

So she, deep drenchèd in a sea of care,   1100
Holds disputation with each thing she views,
And to herself all sorrow doth compare.
No object but her passion's strength renews,
And as one shifts, another straight ensues.
  Sometime her grief is dumb and hath no words;   1105
  Sometime 'tis mad and too much talk affords.

The little birds that tune their morning's joy
Make her moans mad with their sweet melody.
For mirth doth search the bottom of annoy;
Sad souls are slain in merry company;   1110
Grief best is pleased with grief's society.
  True sorrow, then, is feelingly sufficed
  When with like semblance it is sympathised.

[i.e. probe] that searches | To th' bottom of the worst'; but see also *Titus Andronicus*, 2.3.262: 'Now to the bottom dost thou search my wound'.
bottom depths.
annoy pain, suffering (OED 1a). The word is stronger than its modern sense; see l. 1370, and Sonnet 8.4.
1110 *slain* tormented; this line is listed under varied figurative uses of OED 'slay, *v*.1', 5b; the archaic sense 11 (last citation 1568), 'to overcome with affliction or distress', helps clarify that the word can denote suffering as well as death.

1111 For the proverbial note here, see 790–1n.
1112 *feelingly* emotionally; compare l. 1492.
sufficed satisfied. On the sounding, or not, of final -*ed*, in 'sufficed' and 'sympathised' (l. 1113) see 50–2n. Q's spellings are 'suffiz'd' and 'simpathiz'd'.
1113 *When . . . sympathised* when it receives sympathy from something that has a similar expression. For 'sympathised', compare Sonnet 82.11.
semblance 'a person's appearance or demeanour, expressive of his thoughts, feelings etc.' (OED 3a), rather than 'likeness' (OED 5); compare ll. 1246, 1453, 1759.

1114 *in ken* within sight. The OED cites the *Lucrece* line as the first instance of 'ken, *n.*1', 3, but the closely related sense 2a, 'Range of sight or vision', is better attested: an EEBO-TCP search reveals a concentration of uses of the phrase meaning 'within sight' by Robert Greene, in five works dating from 1587–92.

1115 *pines* starves; compare l. 858 and note.

1116 *salve* healing ointment.

1117 *that would* that which would.

1118–19 The proverbial idea is shared with ll. 645–6 (see note).

1118 *roll* Qc has 'roll'; Qu has 'rowle'.
gentle smoothly flowing; cited as the first instance of OED *adj.* and *n.* A.6b, referring specifically to rivers. An EEBO-TCP search for the phrase 'gentle flood' and variant forms reveals twenty instances after *Lucrece*, but none before.
flood (i) deluge, as in the modern sense of 'flood', which makes the phrase 'gentle flood' somewhat oxymoronic; (ii) tide (OED 1a), or flowing water more generally.

1119 *Who* which; see 296n.
stopped dammed, blocked.
bounding confining (i.e. they hold in the water); compare l. 1669.

1120 *dallied* (i) played; (ii) delayed.
nor. . . nor neither. . . nor.

1121–2 *entomb. . . breasts* This echoes the description of the sleeping Lucrece (ll. 389–90), with the words 'entomb' and 'swelling' both specific verbal connections.

1122 *hollow swelling* i.e. the birds' breasts inflate (perhaps with a suggestion of pride) as they sing.

1124 *stops* interruptions. There are three current musical senses of 'stop, *n.*2': 'the closing of a finger-hole. . . in a wind instrument so as to alter the pitch'; the equivalent on an organ; 'the act of pressing with the finger on a string of the violin, lute etc.' (15a, 16, 15d respectively). None of these, however, relates specifically to the breaks in sound evoked here.
rests silent intervals ('rest, *n.*1', 6a); also a musical term.

1125 marked as a *sententia*; see 87–8n.
brooks tolerates.

1126 *Relish* sing; the line is cited under OED[3] 'relish, *v.*2', to 'sing. . . warble', the verb related to 'relish, *n.*3', an ornamental

musical trill. The word could suggest a more general sense of making things delightful, as in 'relish, *v.*1', 2b. However, Shakespeare does use the verb on one other occasion, relating to birds, plainly to denote singing, at *Two Gentlemen of Verona*, 2.1.18–21: 'first, you have learned, like Sir Proteus, to wreathe your arms, like a malcontent; to relish a love-song, like a robin-redbreast'.
pleasing ears ears which are pleased thereby; on this 'confusion' in passive and active participles, see Abbott, § 372.

1127 marked as a *sententia*; see 87–8n.
dumps mournful song (OED 'dump, *n.*1', 3). Compare *Much Ado About Nothing*, 2.3.70–1: 'Sing no more ditties, sing no moe, | Of dumps so dull and heavy'.
time is kept with tears tears provide the rhythm.

1128 *Philomel* See 1079n.

1129 *dishevelled* Shakespeare's only other use is in *Venus and Adonis*, l. 147 (see note); the word need not denote untidiness, just the lack of any head-dress.

1130 *languishment* distress, sorrow; see l. 1141. Shakespeare's only other use of the word may be in *Titus Andronicus*, 2.1.110–11: 'A speedier course than lingering languishment | Must we pursue, and I have found the path', and it appears also in *Edward III*, 2.1.94 (as noted by Duncan-Jones and Woudhuysen 2007: 329); in both cases questions of authorship are complex.

1131 *strain. . . strain* musical phrase. . . squeeze out. The rhetorical figure here is *antanaclasis* (for which, compare l. 1233).

1132 *deep groans* Compare the 'deep groans' of *Venus and Adonis*, l. 377, and see note: there they are characteristic of lovers.
diapason accompanying tune, specifically an octave below the main melody. OED has this as the first citation for 1c, which refers to a musical part of this sort, rather than to the interval between notes. Compare, for example, another description of avian song in Robert Saltwood's *A Comparison Between Four Birds, the Lark, the Nightingale, the Thrush and the Cuckoo* (1533): 'The cuckoo began then readily to sing, | A fair key taking of mean time, | The diapason now and then touching | The lark in her voice anon did climb. | The nightingale reported him | A standing

'Tis double death to drown in ken of shore;
He ten times pines that pines beholding food;   1115
To see the salve doth make the wound ache more;
Great grief grieves most at that would do it good;
Deep woes roll forward like a gentle flood,
    Who, being stopped, the bounding banks o'erflows;
    Grief dallied with nor law nor limit knows.   1120

'You mocking birds,' quoth she, 'your tunes entomb
Within your hollow swelling feathered breasts,
And in my hearing be you mute and dumb.
My restless discord loves no stops nor rests;
A woeful hostess brooks not merry guests.   1125
    Relish your nimble notes to pleasing ears;
    Distress likes dumps when time is kept with tears.

'Come Philomel, that sing'st of ravishment,
Make thy sad grove in my dishevelled hair.
As the dank earth weeps at thy languishment,   1130
So I at each sad strain will strain a tear,
And with deep groans the diapason bear;
    For burden-wise I'll hum on Tarquin still,
    While thou on Tereus descants better skill.

'And whiles against a thorn thou bear'st thy part,   1135
To keep thy sharp woes waking, wretched I,
To imitate thee well, against my heart
Will fix a sharp knife to affright mine eye,
Who, if it wink, shall thereon fall and die.

tenor song. The thrush | Joined in fellowship in that bush' (sig. B3r).

1133 **burden-wise** as a bass-line. 'Burden' denotes an 'undersong' (OED 9) rather than a refrain (OED 10) here. The OED notes, though, that the musical sense of 'burden' results from a somewhat confused anglicisation of the French word 'bourdon' (OED 'bourdon', *v.*2), rather than from a link with any sense of loading; nonetheless the pun is active here. Shakespeare's musical uses of 'burden' tend to denote refrains, but see *As You Like It*, 3.2.247–8: 'I would sing my song without a burthen; thou bring'st me out of tune'.

1134 **Tereus** Philomel's rapist; see 1079n.
    descants sing a higher variation. On the form of the verb (rather than the usual 'descant'st') see 878n.

better skill more skilfully. On the omission of the preposition 'with' in the adverbial phrase, see Abbott, § 340.

1135 **whiles** not an unusual form for Shakespeare (though less common than 'while', which accounts for nearly 80 per cent of cases), but the only instance in *Lucrece* (there are none in *Venus and Adonis*).
    against a thorn i.e. pressing against a sharp thorn into order to stay awake and keep singing. Dent lists the idea as proverbial, N183, 'to sit (sing) like a nightingale, with a thorn against one's breast'. Compare *The Passionate Pilgrim*, 20.9–11.
    bear'st thy part keep singing your part in the song.

1139 **Who** which, i.e. the heart; see 296n.
    if it wink if the eye closes. Compare l. 375 and note, for 'wink'.

1140   *means* methods; there may be hint of 'mean, *n.* 2', 'lament or complaint; a mournful sound', though all OED³'s citations from the period are Scottish in origin. There may alternatively be some musical play on 'mean, *n.*3', 9a, 'the middle part in three-part polyphonic music'. It is presumably with this sense that Biron says 'nay, he can sing | A mean most meanly', *Love's Labour's Lost*, 5.2.327–8.

   frets raised bars or rings (made of gut in early examples) on the finger-boards of stringed instruments; they guide the musician's fingering. Shakespeare exploits the pun on 'fret' meaning 'worry' more obviously in *Hamlet*, 3.2.370–2 ('Call me what instrument you will, though you can fret me, yet you cannot play upon me'), but it is a factor here too.

1141   *heartstrings* hyphenated in Q, but given here according to the OED³ lemma. Shakespeare exploits the interplay between the anatomical sense (i.e. the veins and arteries thought to support the heart, OED³ 1), and its musical resonance elsewhere, as in *Richard III*, 4.4.365: 'Harp on it still shall I till heart-strings break'. This and the *Lucrece* instance both pre-date the OED³'s earliest (1602) for sense 2b, with a 'punning allusion to stringed musical instruments'. EEBO-TCP has still earlier cases, such as Thomas Lodge, *Euphues' Shadow* (1592): 'Every one in the company was delighted with this ditty, only Harpaste counted all strings out of tune, since her heart strings were out of temper' (sig. C4r).

   languishment See l. 1130 and note.

1142   *for* because.

1143   *As shaming* as if ashamed (that); compare 'as', l. 437, and 'shames', l. 1084 and note.

1144   *desert* uninhabited wilderness.

   seated from the way situated away from the road (i.e. away from where anyone might pass). An EEBO-TCP search for the phrase reveals no other cases, which suggests that it is an unusual formulation (perhaps compressed by metre; or by Lucrece's sonorous tone, in line with the alliteration of 'deep dark desert').

1147   *stern* cruel (OED *adj.*, *n.*2, and *adv.*, A3); describing the 'creatures'.

   kinds natures.

1148   *gentle* kind, tender (OED *adj.* and *n.*, A8).

1149–53   The image of the deer recalls *Venus and Adonis* by evoking the fear of the chase (especially Venus' description of the timid hare, ll. 673–708, running as if in a maze), and by the use of an extended comparison.

1149   *at gaze* staring; Shakespeare's only use of the phrase. It is particularly associated with deer (OED 'gaze, *n.*', 3b); compare Robert Greene, *Greene's Mourning Garment* (1590): 'I noted oft that beauty was a blaze, | I saw that love was but a heap of cares, | That such as stood as Deer do at the gaze, | And sought their wealth amongst affectious tares [i.e. weeds]' (sig. H3v).

1151   *encompassed with* surrounded by.

1153   *in mutiny* in 'a state of discord' (OED³ 1). Compare *Henry VIII*, 3.2.120, 'There is a mutiny in 's mind'. See also l. 426, and *Venus and Adonis*, ll. 651, 1049.

1155   *reproach's debtor* (i) is in thrall to shame; (ii) is trapped within shame. It is unclear whether 'is shamed' and 'reproach's debtor' are equivalent or significantly distinct; probably the former, since l. 1154 bemoans the difficulty of deciding between the two.

1157   *with. . . pollution* the contamination of my soul to go along with my already contaminated body. The grammar is compact; it is simplest to take 'body' as equivalent to 'body's'. Her orthodox, Christian point is that committing suicide would undoubtedly damn her soul. Q's spelling 'pollution' helps the rhyme with 'confusion'.

1158   *half* i.e. the purity of the body but not of the soul.

1159   *confusion* destruction.

1160   *conclusion* experiment (OED 8a, and 8b, specifically with 'try'). Compare *Antony and Cleopatra*, 5.2.354–6, 'for her physician tells me | She hath pursued conclusions infinite | Of easy ways to die', and *Hamlet*, 3.4.194–6, 'Let the birds fly, and, like the famous ape, | To

These means, as frets upon an instrument,   1140
Shall tune our heartstrings to true languishment.

'And for, poor bird, thou sing'st not in the day,
As shaming any eye should thee behold:
Some dark deep desert seated from the way,
That knows not parching heat nor freezing cold,   1145
Will we find out; and there we will unfold,
    To creatures stern, sad tunes to change their kinds;
    Since men prove beasts, let beasts bear gentle minds.'

As the poor frighted deer that stands at gaze,
Wildly determining which way to fly,   1150
Or one encompassed with a winding maze,
That cannot tread the way out readily:
So with herself is she in mutiny,
    To live or die, which of the twain were better,
    When life is shamed and death reproach's debtor.   1155

'To kill myself,' quoth she, 'alack what were it,
But with my body my poor soul's pollution?
They that lose half with greater patience bear it
Than they whose whole is swallowed in confusion.
That mother tries a merciless conclusion,   1160
    Who, having two sweet babes, when death takes one
    Will slay the other, and be nurse to none.

'My body or my soul, which was the dearer,
When the one pure the other made divine?
Whose love of either to myself was nearer,   1165
When both were kept for heaven and Collatine?
Ay me, the bark pilled from the lofty pine,

try conclusions in the basket creep, | And break your own neck down'.

1164 When. . . divine i.e. 'the body's purity made the soul worthy of heaven' (Duncan-Jones and Woudhuysen 2007: 331).

1165 Whose. . . nearer Which of them (body and soul) did I love more? For 'whose', meaning 'which', see Abbott, § 264. Burrow (2002: 305) suggests that the pronoun follows the 'semi-personification' of l. 1164.

1166 heaven monosyllabic.

1167, 1169 pilled stripped (OED³, 'pill', *v*.1, 2b); the word is associated with bark, rind and skin. Shakespeare uses it figuratively elsewhere: *Richard III*, 1.3.154–5, 'Hear me, you wrangling pirates, that fall out | In sharing that which you have pilled from me!'. The OED³ distinguishes 'pill' from 'peel', and amendment of either instance to 'peeled' might avoid the repetition. Burrow (2002: 305) suggests the alternative to emendation is 'to accept that this is unusually slack writing'; alternatively, it could be seen as Lucrece emphasising, even labouring, the metaphorical link she has made (with 'bark' repeated too).

1169 **bark** i.e. her body (bark-like because it surrounds her soul).

1170–3 On the importance of the siege metaphor in the poem, see headnote.

1171 **mansion** This word is usually used by Shakespeare to suggest a large house (as at Sonnets 95.9, 146.6), but in the period it can denote any kind of dwelling (OED³ 1b).
battered On the verb 'batter', and its connection with rape, see l. 464 and note.

1172 **temple** See 719n.
spotted blemished, i.e. morally corrupted. On 'spot', see 196n.
spoiled plundered; compare l. 733.

1173 **Grossly** both (i) indecently (OED 7a) and (ii) obviously (OED 2). Compare *All's Well That Ends Well*, 1.3.177–9, 'and thine eyes | See it so grossly shown in thy behaviours | That in their kind they speak it', and Sonnet 99.5.
engirt surrounded; see 221n.

1175 **hole** Compare *Julius Caesar* 5.1.30–2, where Antony uses 'hole' to draw attention to the bathetic physicality of murder: 'In your bad strokes, Brutus, you give good words; | Witness the hole you made in Caesar's heart, | Crying "Long live! hail, Caesar!"'.

1176 **convey** The word has unruly implications (OED v.1, 6a, 6b, 'with a connotation of secrecy', a euphemism for 'steal'); compare *Merry Wives of Windsor*, 1.3.29–30: '"Convey," the wise it call. "Steal"? foh! a *fico* [i.e. a fig] for the phrase!'.

1178 **Have** has; subjunctive form of the verb, see 219n.
untimely see 43n.

1181 **bequeath** In Thomas Nashe's *Summer's Last Will and Testament* (printed 1600, but written *c.* 1592–3, according to ODNB) and Donne's 'The Will', the sardonic potential of the fictional will genre comes to the fore. Lucrece's starts with some bitter wit but by the end (see ll. 1198–204 especially) it proposes the foundation for revenge.

1182 **by** In the uncorrected Q, this is 'for', probably as a result of eye-skip within the line.

1183 **writ in my testament** See 1181n, on 'bequeath'; the suggestion here is that the (imaginary) document is to be written in her blood.

1186 **'Tis honour. . . life** The idea is proverbial; see Dent H576, 'it is better to die with honour than to live with shame'.
deprive take away (OED 5; as at l. 1752).

1187 **The one. . . the other** honour. . . life (as in l. 1186).

1188 **of shame's ashes. . . bred** This evokes the legend of the phoenix, though the element of transformation here (from 'shame' to 'fame') is not part of that myth.

1190 **so dead** having died in this way.

1191 **jewel** i.e. her chastity.

1193 **resolution** See 1200n.
thy boast something for you to boast about. This line is cited as the first instance of OED 3c, referring to the cause or occasion of boasting. However, it does not seem clear that this cannot mean, more simply, the content of an 'expression of ostentation' (OED 3a). Compare *Cymbeline*, 5.5.162–3, 'beauty that made barren the swelled boast | Of him that best could speak', but especially l. 36, where Collatine unwisely boasts of Lucrece's beauty, and helps precipitate the events that cause the new boast proposed here.

1195 **used** dealt with.

1197 **so** refers not simply to the act of killing, but also to the confusion of 'friend' and 'foe' (Tarquin is both to Collatine) in l. 1196. On the length of Lucrece's deliberation before her suicide, see headnote; and compare ll. 1364–5.

1198 **abridgement** summary, shortened version.

1199 **My soul. . . ground** A verb (e.g. 'I commend') needs to be understood to complete the clause. It is characteristic of the language of wills, especially in a 'brief abridgement', that things are expressed compactly.

1200 **resolution** The repetition (from l. 1193) is significant: Lucrece sets herself up as an example of firm purpose for her avengers. On this turn in her 'will', see 1181n.

1202 **fame** reputation.
confound destroy.

1203 **disbursèd** given away. The OED cites this line as the first instance of the figurative use (*v.*, 2) of a word usually referring to money, but straightforwardly applicable to the distribution of a dead person's goods. However, this obvious figurative use was established earlier, as in Erasmus, *The First Tome or Volume of the Paraphrase of Erasmus upon the New Testament*, trans. Nicholas Udall (1548): 'he signifieth it to concern such, as have the dispensation and disbursing of God's word committed unto them' (sig. 2P5r).

His leaves will wither and his sap decay;
So must my soul, her bark being pilled away.

'Her house is sacked, her quiet interrupted,   1170
Her mansion battered by the enemy;
Her sacred temple spotted, spoiled, corrupted,
Grossly engirt with daring infamy;
Then let it not be called impiety,
    If in this blemished fort I make some hole   1175
    Through which I may convey this troubled soul.

'Yet die I will not, till my Collatine
Have heard the cause of my untimely death,
That he may vow, in that sad hour of mine,
Revenge on him that made me stop my breath.   1180
My stainèd blood to Tarquin I'll bequeath,
    Which by him tainted shall for him be spent,
    And as his due writ in my testament.

'My honour I'll bequeath unto the knife
That wounds my body so dishonourèd.   1185
'Tis honour to deprive dishonoured life:
The one will live, the other being dead.
So of shame's ashes shall my fame be bred,
    For in my death I murder shameful scorn;
    My shame so dead, mine honour is new born.   1190

'Dear lord of that dear jewel I have lost,
What legacy shall I bequeath to thee?
My resolution, love, shall be thy boast,
By whose example thou revenged mayst be.
How Tarquin must be used, read it in me: 1195
    Myself thy friend will kill myself thy foe,
    And for my sake serve thou false Tarquin so.

'This brief abridgement of my will I make:
My soul and body to the skies and ground;
My resolution, husband, do thou take;   1200
Mine honour be the knife's that makes my wound;
My shame be his that did my fame confound;
    And all my fame that lives disbursèd be
    To those that live and think no shame of me.

1205   *oversee* supervise the execution of; see OED³ 'overseer, *n*.', 1b. Compare *The Troublesome Reign of King John* (1591): 'A Will indeed, a crabbed Woman's will, | Wherein the Devil is an overseer, | And proud dame Elinor sole Executress' (sig. C2v).

1206   *How. . . see it!* This could be either an exclamation or an incredulous question (Q's question mark can mark either), interrupting the 'will' metaphor with a savage pun.
        overseen deceived (OED³ 1a); Shakespeare's only use of the word.

1207   *slander* disgrace.

1208   *free it* absolve it; for the grammar here, see Abbott, § 417. The 'it' stands for 'my life's foul deed', removed from its natural place in the clause.

1209   *Faint not* do not give in to weakness.

1212   *plot of death* plan for death, suicide plan. Compare, however, *King Lear*, 3.6.89, where it means a conspiracy to murder: 'I have o'erheard a plot of death upon him'.

1213   *brinish pearl* salty tears ('pearl' acting as a collective noun). The phrase 'brinish tears' is commonplace in the period, as at *3 Henry VI*, 3.1.40–1, 'And Nero will be tainted with remorse | To hear and see her plaints, her brinish tears', and see OED 1b. For 'brinish', compare *A Lover's Complaint*, l. 284.

1214   *untuned* discordant; the musical sense looks back to the birdsong of ll. 1121–48.

1215   *hies* hurries.

1216   marked as a *sententia*; see 87–8n. The speed of thought was proverbial, as in Dent T240, 'as swift as thought'. Compare especially *Love's Labour's Lost*, 5.2.260–1, 'their conceits have wings | Fleeter than arrows, bullets, wind, thought, swifter things'.
        fleet swift. OED cites this line as the first instance of the compound 'fleet-winged'; EEBO-TCP corroborates.

1218   *meads* meadows.

1219   *Her mistress* to her mistress.

1220   *slow* (i) hesitant; (ii) sympathetically measured. In *Twelfth Night*, 3.4.72–4, this quality is characteristic of formal, respectable behaviour, with 'a sad face, a reverend carriage, a slow tongue, in the habit of some sir of note, and so forth'. The Q version of the phrase is 'soft slow-tongue'.

1221   *sorts* fits.

1222   *For why* for which reason; it is better to take 'her face' to refer to the maid, sympathetically taking on the expression of sadness she sees in her mistress, rather than to take it to refer to Lucrece herself (in which case 'for why' would mean 'because'). Compare *Titus Andronicus*, 3.1.226–7, 230–1: 'She is the weeping welkin, I the earth: | Then must my sea be moved with her sighs [. . .] For why my bowels cannot hide her woes, | But like a drunkard must I vomit them'.
        sorrow's livery the outward show appropriate to sorrow; for the heraldic metaphor, see also 1054n.

1223   *audaciously* boldly, frankly. The OED currently lists *Love's Labour's Lost*, 5.2.104, 'Yet fear not thou, but speak audaciously', as the earliest instance, but EEBO-TCP has twelve instances before 1594, of which the earliest is Philip Melanchthon et al., *A Famous and Godly History Containing the Lives and Acts of Three Renowned Reformers*, trans. Henry Bennet (1561): 'who after they shall cease to fear Luther's censure and severe correction, will not stick audaciously to corrupt this doctrine of us faithfully taught' (sig. H4v).

1224   *suns* eyes.
        cloud-eclipsèd The idea that the face's sun-like light might be clouded over by sadness was familiar in the period, especially in love poetry. Compare George Gascoigne's *Hundred Sundry Flowers* (1573): 'There is no cloud that can eclipse so bright a sun as she' (sig. T2v).

1225   *over-washed* flooded.

1226–7   This simile of the evening dew parallels the beginning of *Venus and Adonis*, where the dew falls at the 'weeping morn' (l. 2).

1228   *Even* monosyllabic here.
        'gan began to.

1229   *circled* Shakespeare uses the word to mean both 'surrounded' (as at l. 407, and see 'circles', l. 1587), and 'circular' (OED 3; see *Romeo and Juliet*, 2.2.109–10, 'th' inconstant moon, | That monthly changes in her circled orb'). The former might suggest her eyes are moistened all around, or puffed up with crying; the latter might suggest their rounded shape, or that they are wide open with emotion.
        eyne eyes; elsewhere used by Shakespeare for the sake of rhyme, except at *Pericles*,

'Thou, Collatine, shalt oversee this will –   1205
How was I overseen that thou shalt see it!
My blood shall wash the slander of mine ill;
My life's foul deed, my life's fair end shall free it.
Faint not, faint heart, but stoutly say "So be it."
    Yield to my hand, my hand shall conquer thee: 1210
    Thou dead, both die, and both shall victors be.'

This plot of death when sadly she had laid,
And wiped the brinish pearl from her bright eyes,
With untuned tongue she hoarsely calls her maid,
Whose swift obedience to her mistress hies,   1215
For fleet-winged duty with thought's feathers flies.
    Poor Lucrece' cheeks unto her maid seem so
    As winter meads when sun doth melt their snow.

Her mistress she doth give demure good-morrow
With soft, slow tongue, true mark of modesty,   1220
And sorts a sad look to her lady's sorrow,
For why her face wore sorrow's livery,
But durst not ask of her audaciously
    Why her two suns were cloud-eclipsèd so,
    Nor why her fair cheeks over-washed with woe.   1225

But as the earth doth weep, the sun being set,
Each flower moistened like a melting eye:
Even so the maid with swelling drops 'gan wet
Her circled eyne, enforced by sympathy
Of those fair suns set in her mistress' sky,   1230
    Who in a salt-waved ocean quench their light,
    Which makes the maid weep like the dewy night.

A pretty while these pretty creatures stand
Like ivory conduits coral cisterns filling.
One justly weeps, the other takes in hand   1235

3.Prol.5 (where the speaker Gower's diction is archaic). See 643n.

enforced forced to act; on 'enforced', compare l. 303 and note.

sympathy 'conformity; agreement of disposition' (Schmidt; as in OED 2).

1230 **Of** with.

1231 **quench** extinguish, douse.

1233 **pretty. . . pretty** sizeable (OED³ 4a). . . attractive, admirable. The trope at work here is *antanaclasis.*

1234 **Like. . . filling** The idea is that their eyes have turned red through weeping. The metaphor is of a fountain, which has a main tank (a 'cistern') into which channels of water ('conduits') feed. On red and white in the poem, see 11n; for 'coral', see l. 420 and note; for 'ivory', see l. 407 and note.

1235 **justly** with good reason.

takes in hand presumes, claims. See OED³ 'hand, *n.* P2 p.(a)(i)' for 'take in hand' meaning 'to take the charge or responsibility of'.

1236 ***company. . . spilling*** keeping her company while she weeps.

1237 ***gentle sex*** Shakespeare's only use of the phrase, and EEBO-TCP offers no instances before 1594. However, OED 'gentle, *adj.* and *n.*', 8, offers Philip Stubbes, *The Anatomy of Abuses* (1583): 'but yet (such is the magnificency and liberality of that gentle sex) that I trust I shall not be unrewarded at their hands' (sig. E7v), which suggests that the phrase was in use, if not commonplace.

1238 ***to guess at*** (i) in order to intuit; (ii) in intuiting.
       smarts sufferings.

1240 ***marble*** associated with masculine resolve elsewhere in Shakespeare; compare *Antony and Cleopatra*, 5.2.238–41, 'I have nothing | Of woman in me; now from head to foot | I am marble-constant; now the fleeting moon | No planet is of mine', and *Measure for Measure*, 3.1.229–30, 'and he, a marble to her tears, is washed with them, but relents not'.
       waxen minds i.e. easily imprinted and moulded. Compare *Twelfth Night*, 2.2.29–30: 'How easy is it for the proper-false | In women's waxen hearts to set their forms!'. The idea was proverbial and well established: Dent 135.1, 'as soft as wax', gives Caxton's *Game and Play of the Chess* (1474) as the earliest citation. While this case refers clearly to women, citations under Dent's next proverb, W136, 'soft wax will take any impression', refer to children and young men, so the idea is not only aimed at one sex. *Venus and Adonis*, l. 565, works with the same proverbial idea.

1241 ***as marble will*** in the shapes desired by marble (which, in the metaphor, forms an impression, as a seal would).

1242 ***The weak oppressed*** when the weak are oppressed; the repetition of 'press' in both 'oppressed' and 'impression' continues the wax theme of ll. 1240–1.
       strange kinds (i) unnatural dispositions; (ii) dispositions different from their own.

1243 ***skill*** craftiness; the OED does not record a pejorative sense of skill, but the pairing with 'fraud' requires something threatening. Compare *A Lover's Complaint*, l. 125, and

Two Gentlemen of Verona, 2.4.213–14, 'If I can check my erring love, I will; | If not, to compass her I'll use my skill'.

1246 ***semblance*** image, likeness (OED 5).

1247 ***smoothness*** This is the first OED citation for the figurative use of the noun (1b), but this is a difficult distinction to maintain. Compare, for example, Marlowe, *Tamburlaine Part I* (1590), 2.1.21–2: 'His lofty brows in folds do figure death, | And in their smoothness amity and life'.
       champaign open land; the implication is that the territory is fertile, available for use, as in *King Lear*, 1.1.64, 'With shadowy forests and with champains riched'.
       plain could be noun or adjective, going with 'champaign' to similar effect.

1248 ***Lays open*** reveals.
       worms used generally of 'any small creeping animal' (Schmidt; as in OED 2a).

1250 ***Cave-keeping*** cave-dwelling; the only citation in OED (or EEBO-TCP) for this compound. Compare *Cymbeline*, 4.2.298–9, 'I thought I was a cave-keeper, | And cook to honest creatures', and (for another Shakespearean -*keeping* compound) *Two Gentlemen of Verona* 1.1.2, 'Home-keeping youth have ever homely wits'.
       obscurely invisibly, in darkness.

1251 ***crystal walls*** i.e. the clear, transparent (i) eyes, which is consistent with the use of 'crystal' in *Venus and Adonis* (see l. 491 and note), or (ii) faces, which perhaps works better with 'walls'.
       mote speck of dust. The word is common, but may evoke Matthew 7:3, 'And why seest thou the mote, that is in thy brother's eye, and perceivest not the beam that is in thine own eye?'.
       peep appear.

1253 ***women's faces. . . books*** Compare l. 102 and note; here, however, the emphasis is on legibility. See also *Macbeth*, 1.5.62–3: 'Your face, my thane, is as a book, where men | May read strange matters'.

1254 ***No man inveigh*** let no one rail.

1257 ***worthy*** worthy of.
       held Q's 'hild' is an unusual sixteenth-century spelling, not used anywhere else in Shakespeare's work. Nevertheless it is seen elsewhere, and reflects the pronunciation of

No cause but company of her drops' spilling.
Their gentle sex to weep are often willing,
    Grieving themselves to guess at others' smarts,
    And then they drown their eyes, or break their hearts.

For men have marble, women waxen minds,   1240
And therefore are they formed as marble will:
The weak oppressed, th' impression of strange kinds
Is formed in them by force, by fraud, or skill.
Then call them not the authors of their ill,
    No more than wax shall be accounted evil   1245
    Wherein is stamped the semblance of a devil.

Their smoothness, like a goodly champaign plain,
Lays open all the little worms that creep;
In men, as in a rough-grown grove, remain
Cave-keeping evils that obscurely sleep.   1250
Through crystal walls each little mote will peep;
    Though men can cover crimes with bold stern looks,
    Poor women's faces are their own faults' books.

No man inveigh against the withered flower,
But chide rough winter that the flower hath killed;   1255
Not that devoured, but that which doth devour
Is worthy blame. O let it not be held
Poor women's faults that they are so fulfilled
    With men's abuses: those proud lords, to blame,
    Make weak-made women tenants to their shame.   1260

The precedent whereof in Lucrece view,
Assailed by night with circumstances strong
Of present death, and shame that might ensue

the relevant vowels (see Appendix 7); it is printed as 'held' in Q5, which may be a further indication that it is untypical.

1258 *fulfilled* filled up (OED 'fulfil, *v*.', 1); the physicality of this sense of the word evokes, uncomfortably, both physical violation and pregnancy.

1259 *abuses* transgressions, particularly perversions (OED[3] 2a), sexual violations (6a).
lords See 1260n.
to blame at fault, i.e. the ones who are truly 'to blame'.

1260 *tenants* The point of distinction between lord and tenant here is that women are forced to take temporary possession of the shame of lust, which is truly owned by men.

1261 *precedent* illustrative example; compare *Venus and Adonis*, l. 26 and note.
view observe; an imperative addressed to the reader.

1262–3 *circumstances. . . death* a situation offering a compelling threat of immediate death; this refers to Tarquin's threat to kill her if she resisted. Compare 'dreadful circumstance', l. 1703, and *Othello*, 3.3.406–8, 'If imputation and strong circumstances | Which lead directly to the door of truth | Will give you satisfaction, you might have't'.

1264 **that her death** her death itself.

1266 **dying fear** (i) 'paralysing fear' (Burrow 2002: 310); (ii) fear of death; neither of which is very close to any OED sense of 'dying'. Compare *Measure for Measure*, 2.3.40–2, 'O injurious love, | That respites me a life whose very comfort | Is still a dying horror!'; and Spenser's *Faerie Queene*, I.ix.30.4–6, 'But I more feare-full, or more lucky wight, | Dismayd with that deformed dismall sight, | Fledd fast away, halfe dead with dying feare'. The two possibilities map onto differences between sources that have a bearing on Lucrece's agency: (i) in Chaucer's *Legend of Good Women*, 1816–17, she faints 'in a swogh [i.e. swoon]...and wex so dead' when assaulted by Tarquin; (ii) in Livy and Ovid the fear of infamy after death may overcome her resistance.

1268 **By this** at this, by this time; compare l. 1079 and note.

  bid bade; an alternative preterite form.

1269 **poor counterfeit** (i) pitiable imitator; (ii) inadequate copy; both referring to the maid. The former seems more likely, because the narrative voice has been sympathetic to her thus far.

  complaining lamentation.

1270 **on what occasion** for what reason.

1272 **of my sustaining** at what I am enduring.

1273 **small avails** brings little help to.

1278 **The more. . . negligence** which does my negligent laziness all the more discredit; i.e. the maid should have been awake to tend to their guest's needs before he departed.

1279 **with the fault. . . dispense** I can make this much excuse for my failing. 'Fault' here is a much lighter thing than it is in most of the poem's uses of the word (see ll. 527, 715, 724, and notes).

1283 **know** understand.

  heaviness sadness.

1285 **repetition** recital (OED³ 2); compare *Venus and Adonis*, l. 831, where the word suggests a more basic echo, and *Richard III*, 1.3.164–5, 'But repetition of what thou hast marred, | That will I make before I let thee go'.

1287 **deep** grievous, deeply felt.

1292 **by and by** shortly.

1295 **cause** reason (for writing).

  craves requires.

1298 **Conceit** thought, ideas.

1299 **What wit. . . will** Burrow (2002: 312) is right to cite the figure of *aporia* here. See Peacham (1577), 'when we show that we doubt either where to begin for the multitude of things, or what to say or do, in some strange and doubtful manner' (sig. M1v). However, there is an important distinction between the poet's *aporia*, a rhetorical device, and Lucrece's unfeigned, traumatised inability to commit to expression. The 'wit'–'will' opposition is famous from Sidney's *Defence*, 2004: 79: 'our erected wit maketh us know what perfection is, and yet our infected will keepeth us from reaching unto it'.

  wit intellect.

  straight immediately.

  will emotion.

1300 **too curious-good** expressed (i) over-ingeniously; (ii) over-fastidiously. See OED 'curious, *adj.*', 2, 4, and *Venus and Adonis*, l. 734 and note.

  ill badly put.

1301 **press** crowd; the simile evokes the crowd of actual people whose scrutiny Lucrece fears. Compare l. 1408, and the simile in *King John*, 5.7.16–20: 'his siege is now | Against the mind, the which he pricks and wounds | With many legions of strange fantasies, | Which in their throng and press to that last hold, | Confound themselves'.

1302 **inventions** attempts to express herself; see l. 225 and note.

  which. . . before competing to go first.

1303 **At last** A formula Shakespeare turns to at the beginnings of lines in the last third of the poem, as noted by Duncan-Jones and Woudhuysen 2007: 340; compare ll. 1366, 1501, 1567, 1597, 1790.

1305 **Health to thy person** Shakespeare uses the 'health to' greeting elsewhere, though not this precise formula. Compare *1 Henry VI*, 1.1.57, 'My honourable lords, health to you all!'. In Antonio Guevara, *The Dial of Princes*, trans. Thomas North (1568), it is used (as in *Lucrece*) as a way of starting letters between Romans: 'Marcus Aurelius Emperor of Rome, tribune of the people, high bishop, second consul and monarch of all the Roman empire, wisheth to thee Pulio his old friend, health to thy person, and prosperity against thy evil fortune' (sig. K5v).

  vouchsafe t'afford be so gracious as to offer. The formality is conventional for letters of this time, but it also conveys the hesitant composition of the letter.

By that her death to do her husband wrong.
Such danger to resistance did belong   1265
    That dying fear through all her body spread,
    And who cannot abuse a body dead?

By this, mild patience bid fair Lucrece speak
To the poor counterfeit of her complaining:
'My girl,' quoth she, 'on what occasion break   1270
Those tears from thee that down thy cheeks are raining?
If thou dost weep for grief of my sustaining,
    Know, gentle wench, it small avails my mood;
    If tears could help, mine own would do me good.

'But tell me, girl, when went' – and there she stayed   1275
Till after a deep groan – 'Tarquin from hence?'
'Madam, ere I was up,' replied the maid,
'The more to blame my sluggard negligence.
Yet with the fault I thus far can dispense:
    Myself was stirring ere the break of day,   1280
    And ere I rose was Tarquin gone away.

'But Lady, if your maid may be so bold,
She would request to know your heaviness.'
'O peace!' quoth Lucrece. 'If it should be told,
The repetition cannot make it less;   1285
For more it is than I can well express,
    And that deep torture may be called a hell
    When more is felt than one hath power to tell.

'Go, get me hither paper, ink, and pen –
Yet save that labour, for I have them here.   1290
What should I say? One of my husband's men
Bid thou be ready, by and by, to bear
A letter to my lord, my love, my dear.
    Bid him with speed prepare to carry it,
    The cause craves haste, and it will soon be writ.'   1295

Her maid is gone, and she prepares to write,
First hovering o'er the paper with her quill.
Conceit and grief an eager combat fight;
What wit sets down is blotted straight with will.
This is too curious-good, this blunt and ill;   1300
    Much like a press of people at a door
    Throng her inventions, which shall go before.

At last she thus begins: 'Thou worthy lord
Of that unworthy wife that greeteth thee,
Health to thy person; next, vouchsafe t' afford   1305

1306 *wilt* would, would wish to.

1307 *present* immediate.

1308 *So I commend. . . grief* 'I commend me' means 'I ask that you remember me kindly' (OED 'commend, *v.*', 5). The location of the house, conventionally added at the end of a letter, is replaced by 'in grief'.

1309 *tedious* long, gruelling; see l. 1379, and *Venus and Adonis*, l. 841 and note.

1310 *tenor* (i) summary, import (OED *n.*1 and *adj.*, A1a); (ii) transcript (OED, 1b), either sense having legal resonance; perhaps also (iii) quality, character, nature (OED 3). The former's lack of exactness fits better with 'uncertainly', l. 1311. Q's 'tenure' is one of the Elizabethan spellings of 'tenor', and no sense of modern 'tenure' is helpful here. On 'tenor' and 'tenure', compare Sonnet 61.8n.

1311 *uncertainly* (i) 'without definite result, course, or aim' (OED 2); (ii) 'not so as to convey certain knowledge' (Schmidt); (iii) 'in an uncertain manner' (OED 1), referring back to Lucrece's difficulty in composition.

1312 *schedule* note (OED 1). Often these were short additions or summaries, but in Shakespeare they can be long; see *2 Henry IV*, 4.2.166–9: 'Then take, my Lord of Westmerland, this schedule, | For this contains our general grievances: | Each several article herein redressed, | All members of our cause'. Compare also *A Lover's Complaint*, l. 43. The alliteration with 'short' may well not have existed in Elizabethan English, as the Q spelling 'Cedule' may indicate pronunciation (most likely with a soft 'c').

1313 *quality* nature.

1314 *make discovery* disclose.

1315 *gross* See l. 1173 and note.
abuse offence, fault.

1316 *Ere. . . excuse* Before she had stained with her blood the letter which exonerates her from the stain of rape. Schmidt's suggestion that the second 'stained' means 'caused by a stain' helps clarify this concentrated line, which might also be taken to mean, problematically, that her excuse is itself contaminated. Editors have suggested emendations to avoid this, and the verbal repetition: 'stained. . . strained' (Sewell), 'stained. . . stain's' (Wells and Taylor). The latter especially seems viable, and the *polyptoton* is characteristic of the speaker's style, but the change is not necessary. See 56n.

1317 *Besides* There is no comma in Q, so 'besides' could be a preposition. However, it works best to take it as an adverb, meaning 'in addition to this': we have heard what Lucrece manages to convey in her letter, and now we hear that she has held back far more.
life and feeling best taken as a *hendiadys*, the 'lively feeling', the 'feeling life', i.e. the emotional core.

1318 *by* present, nearby.

1319 *grace* adorn; compare ll. 246, 564. The pairing with 'disgrace' (l. 1322) is comparable with 'peer. . . peerless', 'hap. . . hapless' (see 1045n), where a word and its antonym are brought together.
fashion style, form; or perhaps 'action or process of making' (OED 1).

1322 *blot. . . blot* stain on her reputation ('suspicion', l. 1321). . . disfigure. See 192n.

1323 *action* (i) deeds; the primacy of deeds over words was proverbial (Dent W820, 'not words but deeds'), compare l. 1348; perhaps (ii) gesture (OED³ 19a), for which compare *Hamlet*, 3.2.17–19: 'Suit the action to the word, the word to the action, with this special observance, that you o'er-step not the modesty of nature'. In the play the context is literally theatrical-rhetorical, in the poem it would be metaphorically so.
become suit.

1324–6 This is a miniature version of the *paragone*, a feature of classical and renaissance poetics, in which the relative merits of verbal and visual art were competitively compared. Shakespeare's most elaborate *paragone*, other than the implicit one involved in the painting on Lucrece's wall, ll. 1366–568, is the argument between poet and painter in *Timon of Athens*, 1.1.1–94.

1324 *hear* to hear (the 'to' carries over from the first word of the line).

1326 *heavy* (i) important; (ii) sad, serious.
motion action; in Elizabethan English it could denote 'a show or entertainment; *spec.* a puppet-show' (OED³ 8a), which would be in keeping with the play on 'part' in the next lines.

1327 *every part. . . part of woe* each part of the body. . . a sorrowful role; this takes 'motion' in its simplest sense. If 'motion' is taken as a 'show' (see 1326n), then the *antanaclasis* here would be different: 'each role [in the

(If ever, love, thy Lucrece thou wilt see)
Some present speed to come and visit me.
   So I commend me, from our house in grief:
   My woes are tedious, though my words are brief.'

Here folds she up the tenor of her woe,   1310
Her certain sorrow writ uncertainly.
By this short schedule Collatine may know
Her grief, but not her grief's true quality.
She dares not thereof make discovery,
   Lest he should hold it her own gross abuse,   1315
   Ere she with blood had stained her stained excuse.

Besides, the life and feeling of her passion
She hoards, to spend when he is by to hear her,
When sighs and groans and tears may grace the fashion
Of her disgrace, the better so to clear her   1320
From that suspicion which the world might bear her.
   To shun this blot, she would not blot the letter
   With words, till action might become them better.

To see sad sights moves more than hear them told,
For then the eye interprets to the ear   1325
The heavy motion that it doth behold,
When every part a part of woe doth bear.
'Tis but a part of sorrow that we hear:
   Deep sounds make lesser noise than shallow fords,
   And sorrow ebbs, being blown with wind of words. 1330

Her letter now is sealed, and on it writ
'At Ardea to my lord with more than haste'.
The post attends, and she delivers it,
Charging the sour-faced groom to hie as fast

show]... a portion of the sorrow'. The third sense of 'part' required in l. 1328 makes the first suggestion more likely.

1328 *part* small portion.
1329 *sounds* waters, straits; the word typically refers to narrow sea-channels (which may indeed be deep), but its presence here is partly for the word-play with 'noise'. The point is proverbial, as in Dent W123, 'shallow waters make the greatest sound'.
1330 This line is quoted in William Scott's *Model of Poesy* (ed. Alexander 2013: 28), on which see headnote. It is said to illustrate that 'it is an ease to the person affected [by 'calamities and losses'] to unload the burden of his affections and pour out his passion in complaint'.
ebbs diminishes.
being monosyllabic.
blown blown away.
wind of words The idea tends to suggest a lack of substance.
1332 *Ardea* As Burrow (2002: 313), says, this line recalls l. 1.
more than haste extreme hurry (as at *Venus and Adonis*, l. 909); compare 'in post', l. 1.
1333 *post* messenger.
attends (i) ready; (ii) waiting; see 1334n.
1334 *groom* servant.
hie hurry.

1335 *lagging* habitually slow; the point is that a high wind causes birds to fly faster, and Lucrece wishes her servant could also be propelled with unusual speed.

blast wind; Qc's singular noun seems more apt than Qu's 'blasts', not least because it completes the rhyme.

1336 *but* only.

1337 *Extremity* intense distress; but it may be better to leave the nature of the extremity general, in order to make the most of a near-pleonasm with 'extremes'. This word is a specific link with Sonnet 51 (l. 7), the general theme of which is closely related to this passage.

still always.

1338 *homely* (i) unsophisticated, humble (OED³ 2b), as at *Macbeth* 4.2.68–9, 'If you will take a homely man's advice, | Be not found here'; (ii) unattractive, plain-looking (OED³ 2c), as at *Winter's Tale*, 4.4.425–6, 'I'll have thy beauty scratched with briers and made | More homely than thy state'. The former is simpler, and denotes his social standing; the latter would connect to ll. 1334 and 1345 as part of a harsh representation of the servant.

villein Q's 'villaine' could be modernised to 'villain' as well. The OED distinguishes the two, with 'villein' denoting bonded service, and 'villain' denoting roguishness and criminality.

curtsies Both men and women curtsied in the period.

1339 *blushing on her* blushing as he looked at her. The OED has this as the only instance of this sense ('blush, *v.*, 3b: 'look on her with a blush'), and an EEBO-TCP search does not reveal any earlier uses.

1340 *or. . . or* either. . . or.

1342 *lie* The subject is singular, but the plural 'they' and 'bosoms' may explain the unexpected verb form.

1345 *silly* simple; see ll. 1334, 1338, and notes.

God wot God knows. Shakespeare uses 'God knows' itself much more often (eighteen times); his two other uses of 'God wot' suggest that this is an archaic or demotic phrase, so it creates a frank tone with which to exclaim at the painful delicacy of the moment. Compare the Third Citizen in *Richard III*, 2.3.18, 'Stood the state so? No, no, good friends, God wot'; and a ballad quoted in *Hamlet*, 2.2.415–20, 'Why – | "As by lot, God wot," | and then, you know, | "It came to pass, as most like it was" – the first row of the

pious chanson will show you more'. The narrative voice may therefore borrow its register from the servant.

defect a lack (in the groom); stressed on second syllable.

1347 *true respect* proper concern; see l. 201 and note.

1348 *talk in deeds* let their actions speak louder than words; see 1323n, where the same proverbial thought is put less plainly.

saucily insolently.

1350 *this. . . the* Qc changes to 'the. . . this', which is not a thoughtless intervention but misses the deictic point of the first 'this'.

pattern model.

worn-out long past. This is the only OED citation for this figurative sense of 'worn-out, *adj.*', 4, and the earliest citation of all, but the verb 'wear out' is often used figuratively before 1594. Compare Orlando's praise of Adam's service in *As You Like It*, 2.3.56–8, 'how well in thee appears | The constant service of the antique world, | When service sweat for duty, not for meed!'.

1351 *Pawned* pledged (as security); compare l. 156.

to gage as pledge.

1352 *kindled. . . kindled* awakened. . . roused; *antanaclasis* again.

1353 *That* so that.

1353–6 *blazed. . . gazed. . . amazed* On the sounding, or not, of final *-ed*, see 50–2n. Q's spellings are 'blazed', 'gazed' and 'amazed'.

1354 *as knowing* because he knew about.

1355 *wistly* 'with close attention; intently' (OED); see *Venus and Adonis*, l. 343.

1356 *amazed* (i) confused; (ii) afraid.

1359 *long she thinks* perhaps simply 'she thinks it will be [such] a long time', but see the phrase 'think long' in OED³ 'think, v.2', 13b, 'to grow weary with waiting. . . to be impatient; to long, yearn'. Compare *Romeo and Juliet*, 4.5.41–2, 'Have I thought long to see this morning's face, | And doth it give me such a sight as this?'. There is a simpler 'thinks. . . long' combination at l. 1572.

1360 *duteous* dutiful.

scarce is gone has only just left.

1361 *entertain* 'occupy. . . while away' (OED 9b); compare Sonnet 39.11.

1362 *stale* tedious, wearing; compare *Hamlet* 1.2.133–4, 'How weary, stale, flat and unprofitable | Seem to me all the uses of this world!'

1363 *tired* pronounced with two syllables; perhaps 'tirèd'.

As lagging fowls before the northern blast.   1335
   Speed more than speed but dull and slow she deems:
   Extremity still urgeth such extremes.

The homely villein curtsies to her low,
And, blushing on her with a steadfast eye,
Receives the scroll without or yea or no,   1340
And forth with bashful innocence doth hie.
But they whose guilt within their bosoms lie
   Imagine every eye beholds their blame;
   For Lucrece thought he blushed to see her shame,

When, silly groom, God wot, it was defect   1345
Of spirit, life, and bold audacity.
Such harmless creatures have a true respect
To talk in deeds, while others saucily
Promise more speed, but do it leisurely.
   Even so this pattern of the worn-out age   1350
   Pawned honest looks, but laid no words to gage.

His kindled duty kindled her mistrust,
That two red fires in both their faces blazed;
She thought he blushed, as knowing Tarquin's lust,
And blushing with him wistly on him gazed.   1355
Her earnest eye did make him more amazed;
   The more she saw the blood his cheeks replenish,
   The more she thought he spied in her some blemish.

But long she thinks till he return again,
And yet the duteous vassal scarce is gone;   1360
The weary time she cannot entertain,
For now 'tis stale to sigh, to weep, and groan.
So woe hath wearied woe, moan tired moan,
   That she her plaints a little while doth stay,
   Pausing for means to mourn some newer way.   1365

At last she calls to mind where hangs a piece
Of skilful painting made for Priam's Troy,

1364 *stay* stop. Lucrece pauses her speech to find further 'means to mourn'.

1366–442 The *ekphrasis* (rhetorical description of a work of art) of the painting on Lucrece's wall allows Shakespeare to represent her suffering mind at work, and to link his poem with the literary tradition past and present. On possible sources of this section in Virgil's *Aeneid* and Daniel's *Complaint of Rosamond*, see headnote. The story of Troy is also one culmination of the siege metaphor in the poem, on which, again, see headnote.

1366 *piece* The OED[3] notes a specific pertinent sense, 'An item of artistic composition', 1c.

1367 *made for* depicting.

1368 **the which** which (i.e. Troy).
drawn (i) assembled, drawn up; (ii) represented.

1369 **rape** abduction (since it is usually thought that Helen was a willing participant in sexual relations). One of only two uses of the word in the poem; see l. 909 and note.

1370 **cloud-kissing Ilion** The phrase recalls *Doctor Faustus*, 12.81–2, 'Was this the face that launched a thousand ships, | And burnt the topless towers of Ilium?': again Shakespeare uses the ekphrasis to put his poem into conversation with the literary tradition (see 1366–568n). Compare *Hamlet*, 3.4.58–9, 'A station like the herald Mercury | New lighted on a heaven-kissing hill'.
annoy harm. See l. 1109 and note.

1371 **conceited** imaginative, artful; see l. 1423.

1372 **As** that; see Abbott, §109.

1374 **In scorn of** in defiance of.
lifeless life a kind of life which is not actually alive; on the inanimate nature of art, see *Venus and Adonis*, 211–16n. An EEBO-TCP search for the phrase reveals no instances before Shakespeare; it combines characteristic stylistic features of the poem (repetition; paradox; *-less* compound, on which see 2n). Compare 'helpless help', l. 1056 and note. Q's spelling is 'liueless', as it is in *Venus and Adonis*, l. 211; the OED sees 'liveless' as an alternative spelling of 'lifeless'. Compare *Henry V*, 4.2.53–5, 'Description cannot suit itself in words | To demonstrate the life of such a battle, | In life so liveless [*sic*] as it shows itself'.

1375 **dry drop** i.e. of paint; but the phrase has an oxymoronic quality.
weeping tear OED lists this line under 'weeping, *adj.*', 3a, 'abundant weeping. Rarely in *sing.*'. It may be easier, in the light of Abbott, § 372, just to take 'weeping' as a passive participle, 'being wept'.

1377 **reeked** steamed; compare *Venus and Adonis*, l. 555 and note. This is evidently a difficult thing to depict, hence the 'strife'.
strife effort; see *Venus and Adonis*, ll. 11, 291 and notes. This predates the first citation for the pertinent OED 4, which is *All's Well That Ends Well*, 5.Epil.3–4, 'Which we will pay, | With strife to please you, day exceeding day'.

1378 **gleamed forth** This line is cited as the first instance of OED 'gleam, *v.*1' 1b, the 'quasi-transitive' use of the verb. EEBO-TCP has no other use of the phrase. It suggests the impression of light projecting, remarkably, from the picture.
ashy pale; see l. 1512 and note.

1379 **tedious** long, wearisome; see l. 1309 and note.

1380 **pioneer** 'A member of an infantry group going with or ahead of an army or regiment to dig trenches, repair roads, and clear terrain in readiness for the main body of troops. Also: a soldier specialising in digging mines during a siege' (OED[3] *n.* and *adj.*, A1a). Like 'loop-holes' (l. 1383), though to a lesser extent, the word is from a technical military register, but Hamlet plays on it when he address the underground ghost in 1.5.162–3, 'Well said, old mole! canst work i' th' earth so fast? | A worthy pioner! [*sic*]'.

1383 **loop-holes** narrow holes in the walls, for looking through or for firing missiles (like arrow-slits); Shakespeare's only use of the word. It has technical resonance, as in William Garrard, *The Art of War* (1591): 'the shot, as well Musket as Arquebusiers, must be upon the brink of the Ditch, always shooting and defending, that not one of the town do so much as appear at their defences or loop-holes' (sig. 2Q3v).

1384 **lust** pleasure, enthusiasm (OED 1a).

1385 **sweet** delightful.
observance attention to detail (OED[3] 3); compare *Hamlet*, 3.2.17–19, quoted in 1323n.

1388 **triumphing** (i) appearing gloriously, as in l. 12 and note; (ii) rejoicing. The word is stressed on the second syllable.

1389 **quick bearing** lively demeanour.

1390 **interlaces** inserts (OED 3).

1392 **heartless peasants** cowardly louts; 'peasant' may suggest rusticity but it may just be a scornful way of denoting the lowest social ranks. Compare the disdain for those of common birth also evident in the presentation of Lucrece's manservant (ll. 1334, 1338, 1345).

1393 **he** Although allowing that the impersonal pronoun was often 'he' in Elizabethan English, Burrow (2002: 317) wonders whether this masculine turn 'opens a gap

Before the which is drawn the power of Greece,
For Helen's rape the city to destroy,
Threatening cloud-kissing Ilion with annoy,   1370
  Which the conceited painter drew so proud,
  As heaven, it seemed, to kiss the turrets bowed.

A thousand lamentable objects there,
In scorn of nature, art gave lifeless life;
Many a dry drop seemed a weeping tear,   1375
Shed for the slaughtered husband by the wife.
The red blood reeked to show the painter's strife,
  And dying eyes gleamed forth their ashy lights,
  Like dying coals burnt out in tedious nights.

There might you see the labouring pioneer,   1380
Begrimed with sweat and smearèd all with dust,
And from the towers of Troy there would appear
The very eyes of men, through loop-holes thrust,
Gazing upon the Greeks with little lust.
  Such sweet observance in this work was had   1385
  That one might see those far-off eyes look sad.

In great commanders grace and majesty
You might behold, triumphing in their faces;
In youth, quick bearing and dexterity;
And here and there the painter interlaces   1390
Pale cowards marching on with trembling paces,
  Which heartless peasants did so well resemble,
  That one would swear he saw them quake and tremble.

In Ajax and Ulysses, O what art
Of physiognomy might one behold!   1395

between the abstract, ideal observer and the female Lucrece'.

1394–407 Ajax, Ulysses and Nestor are three of the most famous characters in the literature of the Trojan War, and all feature in *Troilus and Cressida*. The first two are involved in a legendary confrontation and debate over which should inherit the armour and weapons of the dead Achilles. This episode is part of Ovid's *Metamorphoses*, Book 13, and is thus likely to have been well-known to Shakespeare. The portraits of the two heroes have a notable precedent in Golding's moralising Epistle to his translation of the *Metamorphoses*, ll. 248–55: 'Ulysses doth express | The image of discretion, wit, and great advisedness, | And Ajax on the other side doth represent a man | Stout, heady, ireful, halt of mind, and such a one as can | Abide to suffer no repulse. And both of them declare | How covetous of glory and reward men's natures are. | And finally it sheweth plain that wisdom doth prevail | In all attempts and purposes when strength of hand doth fail'. Nestor is the voice of old age, experience and wisdom in the Greek army.

1395 *physiognomy* the art of judging character from a person's face; the skill is possessed by the painter, who has managed to convey personality in appearance.

1396 *either. . . either's* each one. . . his.
  ciphered communicated, expressed; compare l. 207.

1397 *face* i.e. faces; the singular helps the scansion, and may be carried over from the 'either. . . either's' structure of the previous line.
  manners 'habitual behaviour or conduct; morals' (OED³ 4a). Compare *2 Henry VI*, 5.1.157–8, 'Hence, heap of wrath, foul indigested lump, | As crooked in thy manners as thy shape!'.
  expressly told clearly revealed.

1398 *blunt* (i) rough, without refinement (OED *adj.* and *n.*1, A4a); (ii) harsh, unfeeling (OED 4b).
  rigour cruelty, hard-heartedness (OED³ 1a, 2).

1399 *sly Ulysses* The hero's cleverness has positive and negative qualities. Golding's Epistle (see 1394–407n) stresses the former, but in his translation of Book 13 (ll. 68, 155, 913) Golding calls him 'sly' three times. Compare *3 Henry VI*, 3.2.188–90, 'I'll play the orator as well as Nestor, | Deceive more slily than Ulysses could, | And, like a Sinon, take another Troy'.

1400 *regard* consideration; compare ll. 277, 305.
  smiling government (i) good-humoured self-control; or (ii) 'affable leadership' (Burrow 2002: 317), depending on whether this develops the mildness of his 'glance', or portrays the public face of the consummate politician. In the latter case, the phrase may hint at the duplicity of those who, like Claudius, 'may smile, and smile, and be a villain' (*Hamlet*, 1.5.108).

1401 *pleading* arguing a case.

1403 *sober action* dignified movements.

1404 *charmed the sight* captivated the viewer's attention.

1405 *silver-white* The two colours are often interchangeable, and the link is proverbial (Dent S453, 'as white as silver'). However, attention here is focused on the prowess of the painter in the ingenious production of precise colour in art.

1406 *Wagged* Burrow (2002: 317) doubts there is a comic tone here; 'wag' can simply mean 'move' (OED 1). However, Nestor can be a figure of mockery, as in *Troilus and Cressida*, 1.3.165–6, 'Now play me Nestor, hem, and stroke thy beard, | As he being dressed to some oration'. Wagging beards are disparaged at *Coriolanus*, 2.1.86–7, 'When you speak best unto the purpose, it is not worth the wagging of your beards', and a traditional song in *2 Henry IV*, 5.3.32–4, associates them with festivity: ''Tis merry in hall when beards wag all, | And welcome merry Shrove-tide. | Be merry, be merry'.

1407 *purled* curled, swirled; see OED³ 'purl, *v.*2', 2a, 'to be emitted in a swirling stream', where this is the first citation; the word is usually used of water. There is some contribution from senses of 'purl, *v.*1' relating to embroidering and edging; the word suggests the craftedness of this shape.

1408 *press* crowd; see l. 1301 and note.

1410 *jointly* together; see l. 1846.
  several graces different benevolent attitudes; for this sense of 'grace', see OED³ 2b (bestowed by a person rather than a deity), and compare *Macbeth*, 1.6.29–30, 'we love him highly, | And shall continue our graces towards him'. Shakespeare almost always uses the word to mean 'attractive qualities' (OED 13a), and this sense contributes here too: the listeners are visually appealing.

1411 *mermaid* mermaids were famous for the beguiling power of their songs; see *Venus and Adonis*, l. 429 and note.

1412 *high. . . low* in (i) social distinction, which looks back to 'graces' and ll. 1387–93; (ii) physical position, which looks forward to ll. 1413–14.
  nice precise.

1414 *mock the mind* to deceive the viewer's perception. An exchange in *The Winter's Tale* shows 'mock' used comparably. Paulina says 'prepare | To see the life as lively mocked as ever | Still sleep mocked death', and Leontes later adds 'The fixture of her eye has motion in't, | As we are mocked with art' (5.3.18–20, 67–8).

1416 *shadowed* hidden. Compare *Venus and Adonis*, l. 533.

1417 *being* monosyllabic here.
  thronged crowded out. Compare ll. 1301 and note, 1408.
  bears back retreats.

The face of either ciphered either's heart;
Their face their manners most expressly told:
In Ajax' eyes blunt rage and rigour rolled,
    But the mild glance that sly Ulysses lent
    Showed deep regard and smiling government.   1400

There, pleading, might you see grave Nestor stand,
As 'twere encouraging the Greeks to fight,
Making such sober action with his hand
That it beguiled attention, charmed the sight.
In speech it seemed his beard, all silver-white,   1405
    Wagged up and down, and from his lips did fly
    Thin winding breath, which purled up to the sky.

About him were a press of gaping faces,
Which seemed to swallow up his sound advice,
All jointly listening, but with several graces,   1410
As if some mermaid did their ears entice;
Some high, some low, the painter was so nice.
    The scalps of many, almost hid behind,
    To jump up higher seemed to mock the mind.

Here one man's hand leaned on another's head,   1415
His nose being shadowed by his neighbour's ear;
Here one being thronged bears back, all bollen and red;
Another, smothered, seems to pelt and swear;
And in their rage such signs of rage they bear
    As, but for loss of Nestor's golden words,   1420
    It seemed they would debate with angry swords.

bollen swollen; monosyllabic. This is Shakespeare's only use of the word.

1418 *pelt* strike out, perhaps physically (OED³ 'pelt, *v*.1', 1a), though the OED³ takes its cue from 'swear' and gives this line as the first citation for 3a, 'throw out abuse; to show signs of anger, to fume'.

1419 *rage. . . rage* The repetition draws further attention to the painter's skill at conveying emotions in 'signs'.

1420 *As, but for loss of* as if, were it not that they would lose.

golden words The phrase was associated with wisdom (as well as with, for example, flattery). Compare Heinrich Bullinger, *Fifty Godly and Learned Sermons*, trans. H.I. (1577): 'Let us hear, I beseech you, the golden words of Solomon the wisest among all men' (sig. 2B3r).

1421 *debate* fight (OED 1); compare 'debaters', l. 1019.

1422–8 Gombrich (1960: 211) established a link between this stanza and an ancient Greek (*c.* third century CE) collection of essays describing artworks. Philostratus, *Imagines*, 1.4, features a painting by Menoeceus: 'This is the siege of Thebes, for the wall has seven gates; and the army is the army of Polyneices, the son of Oedipus, for the companies are seven in number. Amphiaraüs approaches them with face despondent and fully aware of the fate in store for them; and while the other captains are afraid – that is why they are lifting their hands to Zeus in prayer – Capaneus gazes on the walls, resolving in his mind how the battlements may be taken with scaling ladders. As yet, however, there is no shooting from the battlements, since the Thebans apparently hesitate to begin the combat. The clever artifice of the painter is delightful. Encompassing the walls with armed men he depicts them so that some are seen in full figure, others with the legs hidden, others from the waist up, then only the busts of some, heads only, helmets only, and finally just spear-points. This, my boy, is perspective; since the problem is to deceive the eyes as they travel back along the proper receding planes of the picture' (trans. Fairbanks, 16–17). Though not printed in England, the *Imagines* were widely enough available to be on the curriculum at St John's College, Cambridge, where Thomas Jenkins, master at Shakespeare's grammar school in Stratford, had studied (Burrow 2002: 318). The dense intertextuality here (possibly signalled by the echo of *Imagines* in 'imaginary', l. 1422) may explain the stanza's pause on this detail. Another reason is offered by Cheney (2008: 53), who views the spear brandished here as Shakespeare's signature.

1422 *imaginary work* (i) work of the imagination, as in OED[3] 3, 'of the nature of an image or representation', where this is the first citation; also perhaps (ii) work for the imagination, as in OED[3] 2, where 'imaginary' can mean 'imaginative'. See Sonnet 27.9n, and *Venus and Adonis*, l. 597.

1423 *Conceit deceitful* see 'conceited', l. 1371, and 'mock the mind', l. 1414 and note. Here the qualities of art observed in Sidney's *Defence of Poesy* are concentrated in a word-play based on the *-ceit* morpheme: it is a creation of something, and it also feigns something unreal.

so compact so well composed (of diverse elements). Compare *King Lear*, 1.2.6–9, 'Why bastard? Wherefore base? | When my dimensions are as well compact, | My mind as generous, and my shape as true, | As honest madam's issue?'. Shakespeare's only use of 'compact' in an artistic context comes in *As You Like It*, 2.7.5–6, 'If he, compact of jars, grow musical, | We shall have shortly discord in the spheres'. Compare also *A Midsummer Night's Dream*, 5.1.7–8: 'The lunatic, the lover, and the poet | Are of imagination all compact'. While the sense of 'compact' here is different, its collocation with 'imagination' (see 'imaginary', l. 422), and the presence of a character named Philostrate, suggest that the connections with Philostratus described in 1422–8n may have remained in Shakespeare's mind.

kind natural (OED[3] *adj.* and *adv.* 1a), appropriate (1b), and thus perhaps naturalistic.

1424 *Achilles. . . spear* The line is an example of, and explains, the rhetorical figure metonymy, where a part, aspect or quality of something can stand for the whole. Achilles was strongly associated with his spear, as in *2 Henry VI*, 5.1.100–1, 'Whose smile and frown, like to Achilles' spear, | Is able with the change to kill and cure'. It is not explicit how Lucrece knows that the spear is Achilles': its size or a painted name-label might validate her identification, but an interesting possibility is that she has noticed that Achilles is missing and infers his presence.

1425 *Gripped* See l. 319 and note, where 'griped' is preferred. Q's 'Grip't' could be modernised to either form, which are distinguished by the OED. Where 'gripe' suggests the motion of seizing, 'grip' has its modern sense, as here.

1426 *eye of mind* mind's eye. The idea and related phrases were well-known before Shakespeare; see William Painter, *The Second Tome of the Palace of Pleasure* (1567): 'In like manner the virtuous and shamefaced dames, have not their eyes of mind so blindfold, but that they see whereunto those frank services, those disloyal faiths and vices coloured and stuffed with exterior virtue do tend' (sig. 4A4r–v). See also *Hamlet*, 1.1.112, where Horatio says 'A mote it is to trouble the mind's eye'; in the next scene Hamlet uses the phase, 'In my mind's eye, Horatio' (1.2.185).

For much imaginary work was there,
Conceit deceitful, so compact, so kind,
That for Achilles' image stood his spear,
Gripped in an armèd hand; himself behind   1425
Was left unseen, save to the eye of mind:
    A hand, a foot, a face, a leg, a head,
    Stood for the whole to be imaginèd.

And from the walls of strong-besiegèd Troy,
When their brave hope, bold Hector, marched to field,   1430
Stood many Trojan mothers, sharing joy
To see their youthful sons bright weapons wield;
    And to their hope they such odd action yield
    That through their light joy seemèd to appear,
    Like bright things stained, a kind of heavy fear.   1435

And from the strand of Dardan where they fought
To Simois' reedy banks the red blood ran,

1427–8 These are pictorial versions of rhetorical *synecdoche*, where a part is taken for the whole. The trope is closely related to metonymy (see l. 1424).

  1429 **strong-besiegèd** intensely besieged; the phrase 'strongly besieged' is well attested before 1594 (twenty-four hits in an EEBO-TCP search; none for 'strong-besieged', with or without hyphen).

  1430 **Hector** The greatest warrior of the Trojans, and one of the fifty sons of King Priam; his rivalry with Achilles, ending in Hector's death, is central to Homer's *Iliad*.

  1433 **hope** optimism; Hector may alternatively be 'their hope' in OED sense 4b, 'a person or thing that gives hope'.
    odd action unfitting gestures.
    yield supply.

  1434 **light** i.e. light-hearted; the opposite of 'heavy', l. 1435.

  1436 **strand of Dardan** Trojan coast. Dardanus, son of Zeus, was the legendary ancestor of the Trojans, and from his name derived the Latin *Dardanus*, an adjective attached to Trojans and Troy. Although the OED offers no pre-Shakespearean uses of the adjective or noun, it is in use before 1594, especially in translations of Latin, such as Ovid's *Heroical Epistles*, trans. Turbervile (1567): 'We shall to Troy flit in haste | by mean of wind and oar.

| Thou like a stately Queen | through Dardan streets shalt ride' (sig. M7r).

1437 **Simois** a river flowing on the Trojan plain; usually pronounced with three syllables, but disyllabic here. As with 'Dardan' (l. 1436) the word appears mostly in translations (of Virgil and Ovid especially) before 1594, but see the interesting quotation from St Augustine in Ludwig Lavater's *Of Ghosts and Spirits*, trans. Robert Harrison (1572): 'For who is he (saith Augustine) that will be afraid to call a man painted, a man, considering that without staggering, we are accustomed to give each thing his proper name, as soon as we behold the picture of the same: as when we take the view of a painted table, or wall, we say straight way, this is Tully, this is Sallust, he Achilles, that other Hector, this is the flood called Simois, that place termed Rome, whereof these things be ended no other than painted Images, of those things whose names they bear' (sig. R2r–v). Shakespeare's other reference to Simois comes in *The Taming of the Shrew*, 3.1.31–3, '"*Hic ibat*," as I told you before, "*Simois*," I am Lucentio, "*hic est*," son unto Vincentio of Pisa, | "*Sigeia tellus*," disguised thus to get your love'. (He is quoting, and pretending to translate, Ovid's *Heroides*, 1.33–4, on which see also 1485n.)

1439 **ridges** crests; see *Venus and Adonis*, l. 820.

1440 **gallèd** chafed (by the waves); compare *Henry V*, 3.1.11–14, 'let the brow o'erwhelm it | As fearfully as doth a galled rock | O'erhang and jutty his confounded base, | Swilled with the wild and wasteful ocean'.

then Q than; a variant spelling in the period.

1444, 1446 **all distress** utmost sorrow; the second instance is an emphatic reference back to the first.

1444 **stelled** portrayed, delineated (OED 3). This use antedates the first citation in OED for this sense, which is Giovanni Paolo Lomazzo, *A Tract Containing the Arts of Curious Painting, Carving, Building*, trans. Richard Haydocke (1598): 'Wherefore before you begin to Stell, delineate and trick out the proportion of a man, you ought to know his true quantity and stature' (sig. B2v). EEBO-TCP does not offer any earlier uses, and it is not clear in the OED how this technical use relates to the sense 1, which is deemed a predominantly Scottish word, meaning 'fix, post, place' (and which itself could serve here in *Lucrece*). See Sonnet 24.1 and note.

1445 **some** i.e. some 'distress', but not the 'all distress' that she is looking for.

1447 **despairing** The adjective could be made to apply to Lucrece or Hecuba.

Hecuba the Queen of Troy, and an exemplar of extreme grief at the deaths of her husband Priam and their sons (including Hector, Paris and Troilus). In *Titus Andronicus*, 4.1.18–21, Shakespeare had made her an exemplar for Young Lucius: 'For I have heard my grandsire say full oft, | Extremity of griefs would make men mad; | And I have read that Hecuba of Troy | Ran mad through sorrow'. Later Shakespeare went further, making her a figure of mad grief in the Player's speech in *Hamlet* ('Run barefoot up and down, threat'ning the flames | With bisson rheum, a clout upon that head | Where late the diadem stood',

2.2.505–7), and also a test case for the human capacity for sympathy with art: 'What's Hecuba to him, or he to Hecuba, | That he should weep for her?' (2.2.559–60). Her story had been told shortly before *Lucrece* in a poem by Thomas Fenne entitled 'Hecuba's Mishaps' (*Fenne's Fruits*, 1590: 2B3v–2G3v), and in George Peele's *Tale of Troy* (1589).

1449 **Which** (i) Priam, with the pronoun equivalent to 'Who', on which see Abbott, § 265; or (ii) Priam's wounds, standing for him, in keeping with the earlier interest in metonymy and *synecdoche* (ll. 1424, 1427–8).

Pyrrhus The son of Achilles, and the brutal killer of Priam in Virgil's *Aeneid* Book 2, Marlowe's *Dido Queen of Carthage* (where the posture here has a precedent, 'treading upon his breast', 2.242), and in the Player's speech in *Hamlet*, where he is said to 'make malicious sport | In mincing with his sword her husband's [Priam's] limbs' (2.2.513–14).

1450 **anatomised** 'la[id] open minutely... analyse[d]' (OED 3a). On the sounding, or not, of final *-ed*, in 'anatomised' and '**disguised**' (l. 1452) see 50–2n. Q's spellings are 'anathomiz'd' and 'disguiz'd'.

1451 **ruin** 'destructive influence' (OED³ 7a).

wrack destruction.

grim See 421n.

1452 **chaps** cracks (OED 'chap, *n*.1', 1b); Q's 'chops' is an alternative spelling. Compare Sonnet 62.10 and note.

1453 **semblance** 'outward aspect', appearance (OED 2a).

1454 **blue blood** This refers to the colour of her blood as it appears through the skin; trauma and old age have changed it to black. There was no association between this phrase and aristocracy in Shakespeare's time.

1455 **Wanting** lacking.

spring The metaphor has Priam as a source for the moisture in her veins. The word may also suggest spring-like youthfulness, on which see l. 869, and *Venus and Adonis*, l. 656 and note.

shrunk pipes i.e. her shrunken veins.

Whose waves to imitate the battle sought
With swelling ridges, and their ranks began
To break upon the gallèd shore, and then   1440
   Retire again, till meeting greater ranks
   They join, and shoot their foam at Simois' banks.

To this well-painted piece is Lucrece come,
To find a face where all distress is stelled.
Many she sees where cares have carvèd some,   1445
But none where all distress and dolour dwelled,
Till she despairing Hecuba beheld,
   Staring on Priam's wounds with her old eyes,
   Which bleeding under Pyrrhus' proud foot lies.

In her the painter had anatomised   1450
Time's ruin, beauty's wrack, and grim care's reign.
Her cheeks with chaps and wrinkles were disguised;
Of what she was no semblance did remain.
Her blue blood, changed to black in every vein,
   Wanting the spring that those shrunk pipes had fed,   1455
   Showed life imprisoned in a body dead.

On this sad shadow Lucrece spends her eyes,
And shapes her sorrow to the beldam's woes,
Who nothing wants to answer her but cries,
And bitter words to ban her cruel foes.   1460
The painter was no god to lend her those,
   And therefore Lucrece swears he did her wrong,
   To give her so much grief and not a tongue.

'Poor instrument,' quoth she, 'without a sound,
I'll tune thy woes with my lamenting tongue,   1465
And drop sweet balm in Priam's painted wound,

1457 *shadow* image, representation; see 460n.
The suggestion of ghostliness is also pertinent to this dehumanised figure.
    spends wears out (OED *v.*1, 5a); perhaps with weeping, perhaps with intense scrutiny.
1458 *shapes* adapts.
    beldam's old woman's; compare l. 953.
1459 *wants* lacks.
1460 *ban* curse (OED 2a); compare 'banning', *Venus and Adonis*, l. 326.
1463 *tongue* voice.

1464 *instrument* musical instrument (introducing a metaphor that continues into l. 1465).
1465 *tune* sing, perform, as at l. 1107 (see note).
1466 *balm* ointment; proverbially sweet (Dent B63.1, 'as sweet as balm'). Her tears are probably indicated here; compare *Richard III*, 1.2.12–13: 'Lo, in these windows that let forth thy life | I pour the helpless balm of my poor eyes'.
    painted i.e. (i) with blood, and (ii) in paint.

1467   **rail on** rant at.

1471–7   The turn towards Helen amid the ruins of Troy follows Virgil's *Aeneid* 2; see Phaer-Twyne (1573): 'And now alone was left but I [Aeneas, narrating here], when Vesta's temple stair | To keep, and secretly to lurk all couching close in chair | Dame Helen I might see to sit, bright burnings gave me light | Where ever I went, the ways I passed, all thing was set in sight. | She fearing her the Trojans' wrath, for Troy destroyed to wreak, | Greeks' torments, and her husbands' force whose wedlock she did break | The plague of Troy, and of her country monster most untame: | There sat she with her hated head, by the altars hid for shame' (E3r–v). In this stanza Lucrece recognises her own interest in the Trojan story, when she blames Paris' destructive lust (though she also blames Helen, the '**strumpet**').

1471   **stir** trouble, disturbance (i.e. the war).

1472   **That** so that.

1473   **fond** foolish, lustful.

1474   **load of wrath** Compare the 'load of lust' carried by Lucrece, l. 734 and note.

1475   **Thy eye** Burrow (2002: 321) suggests two plausible and linked reasons for this unusual alternative to 'thine eye': (i) scornful emphasis, (ii) symmetry with 'Thy heat', l. 1473. The form is used by Shakespeare elsewhere (though much less often than 'thine eye'), without apparent strong cause. See Sonnet 46.13, 14n, and *Love's Labour's Lost*, 4.2.115, 'Thy eye Jove's lightning bears, thy voice his dreadful thunder'.

1479   **plague** calamity (OED^3 2), but given the outbreaks of plague that hit London in 1592–4, and which may have led to Shakespeare's turn to poetry (see headnote), the word has contemporary resonance. It was a commonplace that such diseases were punishments for sin; see for example Anthony Anderson, *An Approved Medicine against the Deserved Plague* (1593): 'And now my beloved, and important charge, I beseech you by the mercies of God, remember with me, there is no plague but for sin, and the Lion roareth not, without his prey' (sig. A4v).
   moe more; archaic form kept for the sake of the rhyme. Compare l. 1615.

1480   **light** fall (OED 10c); compare *The Merchant of Venice*, 3.1.94–5, 'no satisfaction, no revenge, nor no ill luck stirring but what lights a' my shoulders'.

1482   **guilty woe** the misery that comes with guilt. The *polyptoton* of antonyms created by the combination with 'guiltless' in the same line is characteristic of the poem's style (see 1319n; and on *-less* compounds, 2n).

1484   **To plague. . . in general** To punish all for one person's transgression. Compare *King John*, 2.1.183–7: 'I have but this to say, | That he is not only plagued for her sin, | But God hath made her sin and her the plague | On this removed issue, plagued for her, | And with her plague, her sin'.

1485–7   **Here. . . Here** Duncan-Jones and Woudhuysen note two Troy-related precedents for the repeated deixis (pointing out) here (2007: 355). One is in Ovid, *Heroides*, 1.33–4, which is quoted during the seductive Latin lesson of *The Taming of the Shrew*, 3.1.27–9, already cited at 1437n: 'Here, madam: | "*Hic ibat Simois; hic est Sigeia tellus; | Hic steterat Priami regia celsa senis*"'. Turberville (1567) translates thus: 'Here Simois (saith he) did flow, | here is Sigeian land: | And here the aged Priam's hall | and princely house did stand' (sig. A2r). The other is a '*hic*. . . *hic*. . .' construction in *Aeneid*, 2.29–30, translated by Phaer-Twyne (1573): thus: 'Here lay the men of Dolop land, here fierce Achilles fought, | Here stood their ships, and here to try were wont the armies stout' (sig. C4r).

1486   **manly Hector faints** Like many renaissance narrative paintings, this one depicts different moments in time across the Trojan War; Hector dies before Priam, and so, according to narrative chronology, should not be fainting (perhaps physically; perhaps losing heart) here. **sounds** faints, swoons. The OED lists 'sound, *v.*4' as a distinct lemma, so Q's form is preferred here to other viable modernisations, such as 'swounds' or indeed 'swoons'. This is a typical lover's gesture; Troilus swoons several times in Chaucer's *Troilus and Criseyde*, and see *A Lover's Complaint*, l. 305.

1487   **bloody channel** a stream of blood; unless the 'channel' suggests some pre-existing watercourse that has become 'bloody',

And rail on Pyrrhus that hath done him wrong,
And with my tears quench Troy that burns so long;
    And with my knife scratch out the angry eyes
    Of all the Greeks that are thine enemies.   1470

'Show me the strumpet that began this stir,
That with my nails her beauty I may tear.
Thy heat of lust, fond Paris, did incur
This load of wrath that burning Troy doth bear;
Thy eye kindled the fire that burneth here,   1475
    And here in Troy, for trespass of thine eye,
    The sire, the son, the dame, and daughter die.

'Why should the private pleasure of some one
Become the public plague of many moe?
Let sin alone committed light alone   1480
Upon his head that hath transgressèd so.
Let guiltless souls be freed from guilty woe:
    For one's offence why should so many fall,
    To plague a private sin in general?

'Lo, here weeps Hecuba, here Priam dies,   1485
Here manly Hector faints, here Troilus sounds,
Here friend by friend in bloody channel lies,
And friend to friend gives unadvisèd wounds,
And one man's lust these many lives confounds.
    Had doting Priam checked his son's desire,   1490
    Troy had been bright with fame, and not with fire.'

Here feelingly she weeps Troy's painted woes:
For sorrow, like a heavy-hanging bell,
Once set on ringing, with his own weight goes;
Then little strength rings out the doleful knell.   1495
So Lucrece, set a-work, sad tales doth tell

such as a stream or a gutter (OED 'channel, *n*.1', 3a).

1488 *unadvisèd* unintentional; see 180n.

1489 *confounds* destroys.

1490 *doting* foolish.
    checked (i) restrained; (ii) reproved. Paris resembles Tarquin, in that his sexual desire brought disaster down on his city and family.

1492 *feelingly* (i) 'from or with personal feeling, knowledge, or experience' (OED³ 4);

(ii) 'with feeling or emotion; in a manner displaying emotion' (OED³ 5, where this line is listed). Compare l. 1112.

1494 *on ringing* a-ringing.

1495 *knell* can be used for any bell's ring, but especially associated with funerals; compare *Macbeth*, 4.3.170–1, 'the dead man's knell | Is there scarce asked for who'.

1496 *a-work* to work (Q has 'a worke').

1497 **pencilled** painted. This is the first OED[3] citation for the adjective in this sense (2), and EEBO-TCP concurs. The verb, however, has considerably older citations. Compare *Timon of Athens*, 1.1.156–60 (soon after the *paragone* section discussed at 1324–6n): 'The painting is almost the natural man; | For since dishonour traffics with man's nature, | He is but outside; these pencilled figures are | Even such as they give out'.
pensiveness melancholy.
coloured painted.

1498 **looks** expressions.

1499 **throws. . . round** casts her gaze all over the painting.

1500 **who** whoever.

1501–68 The story of Sinon, the Greek soldier who pretends to betray his army, and persuades the Trojans to take in the fateful horse, is told by Aeneas in *Aeneid*, 2.57–198. Several details in *Lucrece* have precedents here; see Phaer-Twyne translation (1573): 'Behold the shepherds in this while a young man have ycaught, | And pinioned with his hands behind unto the king him brought. | That for the nonce had done himself by yielding to be take | To compass this, and to the *Greeks*, Troy open wide to make. | A fellow sly, and stout of mind, and bent in both to try, | To win by guile, or if he fail, with certain death to die. | On every side about him drew the Trojan youth to see, | And some of them to scorn him 'gan, but now take heed to me: | You shall perceive the treasons false of Greeks, and of this one | Conjecture all. | For as unarmed in the midst all vexed there he stood, | And with his eyes on Trojan men did look with piteous mood: | Alas (quod he) what ground may me, what sea may me receive?' (sig. B4v). This episode is recalled in *Titus Andronicus*, 5.3.80–7, in a context which also links Sinon's violation of Troy with an act of rape: 'Speak, Rome's dear friend, as erst our ancestor [i.e. Aeneas], | When with his solemn tongue he did discourse | To love-sick Dido's sad attending ear | The story of that baleful burning night, | When subtle Greeks surprised King Priam's Troy. | Tell us what Sinon hath bewitched our ears, | Or who hath brought the fatal engine in | That gives our Troy, our Rome, the civil wound'. See also the quotation from *3 Henry VI* quoted in 1399n. Lucrece fixates on this image because, like Sinon, Tarquin does not reveal his cruel intentions. There is a further link between Sinon and Tarquin, made explicit in Paolo Marso's commentary on the *Fasti* (1527: sig. G12r): Sextus Tarquinius (the Tarquin of *Lucrece*) pretended to join the Gabii in their fight against the Romans, who were ruled by his father Tarquinius Superbus, and, like Sinon, betrayed them; Marso notes the resonance with the *Aeneid*.

1501 **bound** tied up as a prisoner; see 1501–68n for the binding of Sinon in Virgil's *Aeneid*.

1502 **piteous looks** 'piteous' can mean 'affected by pity' (OED[3] 1) and 'arousing pity' (OED[3] 2), so these expressions could be on the Trojans' faces, or on Sinon's, respectively.
Phrygian Trojan.

1503 **showed content** appeared contented; the artist has somehow managed to convey that Sinon's 'cares' are false, and he wants to be taken in by the sympathetic Trojans.

1504 **blunt swains** simple shepherds (who capture Sinon and hand him over to Priam).

1505 **mild** even-tempered; see ll. 1520, 1542.

1507 **hide deceit** As Duncan-Jones and Woudhuysen note, this hints at the artist's proverbial need to conceal art itself (Tilley, A335, 'it is art to hide art'), as well as at the falsely honest appearance of the image of Sinon (2007: 357).
harmless show (i) 'appearance of harmlessness' (Duncan-Jones and Woudhuysen 2007: 357); perhaps (ii) harmless picture, since the threat offered by Sinon, unlike that offered by Tarquin, is non-existent. See 'shows', l. 1580.

1508 **An humble** Shakespeare uses this form on seven other occasions, e.g. in *Titus Andronicus*, 4.3.117, 'thou hast made it like an humble suppliant'.
wailing weeping. This is the OED's earliest citation for 'wail *v.*', 1c, 'to weep', however, compare the (technically adjectival, but closely related) use in George Gascoigne's *Hundred Sundry Flowers* (1573): 'But eke we must with wailing eyes behold | Their bodies dead' (sig. V2v).

1509 **unbent** not furrowed as a result of suffering; perhaps, less literally, the 'brow unbent' suggests an unbowed expression, not ground down by hardship. This is the only citation

To pencilled pensiveness and coloured sorrow;
She lends them words, and she their looks doth borrow.

She throws her eyes about the painting round,
And who she finds forlorn, she doth lament.   1500
At last she sees a wretched image bound,
That piteous looks to Phrygian shepherds lent;
His face, though full of cares, yet showed content.
    Onward to Troy with the blunt swains he goes,
    So mild that patience seemed to scorn his woes.   1505

In him the painter laboured with his skill
To hide deceit, and give the harmless show
An humble gait, calm looks, eyes wailing still,
A brow unbent that seemed to welcome woe,
Cheeks neither red, nor pale, but mingled so   1510
    That blushing red no guilty instance gave,
    Nor ashy pale the fear that false hearts have.

But like a constant and confirmèd devil
He entertained a show so seeming just,
And therein so ensconced his secret evil   1515
That jealousy itself could not mistrust
False creeping craft and perjury should thrust
    Into so bright a day such black-faced storms,
    Or blot with hell-born sin such saint-like forms.

for OED 2, 'not wrinkled or knit'. Although an EEBO-TCP search reveals no earlier uses, the idea of a bent brow is common. For the link between 'unbend' and mood, compare Robert Southwell's *Mary Magdalen's Funeral Tears* (1591): 'Dost thou look that she should answer, for thee I seek, or for thee I weep? Unless thou wilt unbend her thoughts, that her eyes may fully see thee' (sig. G4v).

1510–12 On red and white in the poem, see 11n.

1511 *guilty instance* sign, evidence (OED 7) of guilt; EEBO-TCP has no other uses of the phrase, so it may not have specific legal resonance.

1512 *ashy pale* proverbial (see Dent, A339, 'as pale as ashes'); compare l. 1378.

1513 *constant and confirmèd* unrelenting and incorrigible; both words suggest, more simply, an unchanging aspect that contrasts with the Devil's reputation for deceptive changeability.

1514 *entertained* put on.

seeming apparently.

just trustworthy.

1515 *ensconced* sheltered, hid; the word (which, according to OED and EEBO-TCP, was a recent addition to English) originally meant 'to fortify', and this is listed as the earliest figurative use. Compare Sonnet 49.9.

1516 *jealousy* suspicion.

mistrust suspect that.

1517 *False creeping* deceitful, stealthy; for 'creeping', see ll. 305 and 1627, and 'creeps', l. 1575.

craft cunning. Capitalised, as is 'perjury', in Q, so both could be treated as personifications.

thrust insinuate (OED 7b); this seems the most apt sense, but the violence and penetration latent in the word threaten to emerge.

1518 *black-faced* threatening, but also literally black (or at least dark grey), as storm-clouds are.

1519 *blot* See 192n.

1520 *mild* see l. 1505 and note.

1521 *Sinon* first named here; on his history and importance in the poem, see 1501n.
enchanting beguiling. The word retains its menacing, magical sense; Shakespeare exploits this interplay between charm and dangerous magic also in *Antony and Cleopatra*, 1.2.128: 'I must from this enchanting queen break off'. Compare *Venus and Adonis*, 145n.

1522 *after* later.

1523 *wildfire* Q 'wild fire'; OED allows the hyphenated form as well. The OED lists this, in parentheses (second instance from 1699), as the first instance of the phrase 'like wildfire', meaning 'with immense rapidity and effect' (5c). EEBO-TCP provides an earlier instance, in William Charke's *An Answer for the Time, unto the Foul and Wicked Defence of the Censure* (1583): 'your seditious books like wild fire, would not have come tumbling forth so fast' (sig. B2r). However, it is probably better to see the sense of destructive speed as a by-product of the word's primary meaning here, which is 'a composition of highly inflammable substances, readily ignited and very difficult to extinguish' (OED 3). Compare Marlowe's *Dido Queen of Carthage*, 2.2.216–18, 'And after him [Pyrrhus; see 1449n] his band of Myrmidons, | With balls of wildfire in their murdering paws, | Which made the funeral flame that burnt fair Troy'.

1524 *that* so that; see 94n.
skies heavens, gods.

1525 *fixèd places* Stars were thought to have immutable places in the heavens; changes would accompany or foretell cataclysmic events. Compare *A Midsummer Night's Dream*, 2.1.153–4, 'certain stars shot madly from their spheres, | To hear the sea-maid's music'.

1526 *glass* mirror; Troy was as constant and glorious as the stars.

1527–9 *perused. . . abused* On the sounding, or not, of final -ed, see 50–2n. Q's spellings are 'perus'd' and 'abus'd'.

1527 *advisedly* carefully; but the word suggests wary, meticulous and informed qualities to her attention at this point. See 180n.

1529 *some shape. . . abused* another (innocent) person's shape had been falsely represented as Sinon's; compare l. 597.

1530 The proverbial wisdom underlying this line is contradictory. See Dent F3, 'a fair face must have good conditions (cannot have a crabbed heart)'; but F5, 'fair face foul heart', points in another direction.
lodged housed, contained.

1532–3 *spied. . . belied* On the sounding, or not, of final -ed, see 50–2n. Q's spellings are 'spied' and 'belied' here, so there may be a case for 'spièd' and 'belièd'.

1533 *was belied* was lying. The sense 'was proved false' is tempting, but deemed later by OED³ (1624 for the verb 'belie', 7; 1718 for the equivalent adjective 'belied'); an EEBO-TCP search reveals no instances before 1594. Shakespeare tends to use the passive construction to mean 'is lied about'; see Sonnet 130.14.

1534 *guile –* The rhetorical figure for such curtailment is *aposiopesis*; compare ll. 666, 1716–18.

1536 *the while* meanwhile.

1538 *forsook* gave up.

1539 *turned it* changed its meaning.

1540 *But* but that.

1541 *even* monosyllabic here.

1542 *sober-sad* See 262n, on 'sad'.
mild See l. 1505.

1543 *travail* labour.
fainted lost heart.

1544 *armèd to beguild* equipped to deceive; this takes Q's 'beguild' as an alternative spelling for 'beguile', perhaps for the sake of rhyme. Compare *Venus and Adonis*, l. 873 (see note), and *Tottel's Miscellany*, which includes a similar rhyme: 'So was the house defiled | Of Collatine: so was the wife beguiled [sp. begilde]' (sig. X3v; as noted by Duncan-Jones and Woudhuysen 2007: 361). The alternative would be to see it as a use of 'begild', to cover (metaphorically or not) in gold. OED records no use of 'begild' until 1600, but it cites an instance of 'begilded' from 1594. An earlier instance in John Hawkins, *A True Declaration of the Troublesome Voyage* (1569), 'Fair words begilded [begylded]' (marginal note on sig. B1r), suggests a part of 'begild', but is close to 'beguile' as well. A similar overlap between 'guile' and 'gild' appears at Sonnet 28.12 (see note).

1546 *him* Sinon.

The well-skilled workman this mild image drew   1520
For perjured Sinon, whose enchanting story
The credulous old Priam after slew;
Whose words like wildfire burnt the shining glory
Of rich-built Ilion, that the skies were sorry,
    And little stars shot from their fixèd places,   1525
    When their glass fell wherein they viewed their faces.

This picture she advisedly perused,
And chid the painter for his wondrous skill,
Saying some shape in Sinon's was abused:
So fair a form lodged not a mind so ill.   1530
And still on him she gazed, and gazing still,
    Such signs of truth in his plain face she spied
    That she concludes the picture was belied.

'It cannot be', quoth she, 'that so much guile –'
She would have said 'can lurk in such a look',   1535
But Tarquin's shape came in her mind the while,
And from her tongue 'can lurk' from 'cannot' took.
'It cannot be' she in that sense forsook,
    And turned it thus: 'It cannot be, I find,
    But such a face should bear a wicked mind.   1540

'For even as subtle Sinon here is painted,
So sober-sad, so weary, and so mild,
As if with grief or travail he had fainted,
To me came Tarquin armèd to beguild
With outward honesty, but yet defiled   1545
    With inward vice. As Priam him did cherish,
    So did I Tarquin; so my Troy did perish.

'Look, look, how listening Priam wets his eyes
To see those borrowed tears that Sinon sheds!
Priam, why art thou old and yet not wise?   1550

---

cherish 'entertain kindly' (OED 3); compare l. 1629, and *1 Henry IV*, 3.3.170–2, 'Hostess, I forgive thee. Go, make ready breakfast; love thy husband, look to thy servants, cherish thy guesse [i.e. guests]'.

1547 **my Troy did perish** On the siege metaphor, here explicitly used to link Troy's fall with the rape, see headnote.

1549 **borrowed** assumed, fake.
sheds Q 'sheeds' clarifies the rhyme (the same one as Sonnet 34.13–14; see Appendix 8).

1550 **old. . . not wise** Shakespeare also overturns the proverbial link between age and wisdom (Dent O37, 'older and wiser') in *King Lear*, as in 1.5.45: 'Thou shouldst not have been old till thou hadst been wise'.

1551 *falls* lets fall (OED 49a). Compare *Troilus and Cressida*, 4.1.70–3, 'For every false drop in her bawdy veins, | A Grecian's life hath sunk; for every scruple | Of her contaminated carrion weight, | A Trojan hath been slain'; although Lucrece turns to blame Helen to some extent (see 1471–7n), Sinon is her particular focus.

1553 *pearls* tears, as at l. 1213.

1554 *balls. . . fire* See the 'wildfire' of l. 1523 and note.

1554–5 *quenchless. . . lightless* unextinguishable. . . dark (Hell's fires produce no light). On -*less* compounds, see 2n; for 'lightless' see also l. 4 and note.

1555 *effects* (i) qualities (OED³ 2a); (ii) phenomena (4a); i.e. Sinon and his kind emulate the lightlessness of hell as they conceal their destructive impulses. For 'effects', compare ll. 251, 353, and *Venus and Adonis*, l. 605. See also *Measure for Measure*, 3.1.23–5, 'Thou art not certain; | For thy complexion shifts to strange effects, | After the moon'.

1558 *such unity do hold* are brought together in one body.

1560–1 *flatter. . . water* On the rhyme, see Appendix 7.

1560 *doth flatter* fosters deceptively. The singular verb may follow Sinon, rather than his 'tears'; on the grammar, see Hope (2003: 161–2).

1561 *he. . . his* Sinon. . . Priam's.

1564 *senseless* lacking in feeling because he is merely an artistic representation; but also because he is heartless. Compare *Venus and Adonis*, l. 211, and *Two Gentlemen of Verona*, 4.4.198–9 (Julia here addressing Silvia's picture), 'Come, shadow, come, and take this shadow up, | For 'tis thy rival. O thou senseless form, | Thou shalt be worshipped, kissed, loved and adored'.

1565 *unhappy* 'causing misfortune or trouble' (OED 1a).

1566 *herself herself* See 157n.

1567 *with this gives o'er* finishes with these words.

1568 *sore* grievous, severe (OED 1a).

1570 *time. . . time* Compare the similar repetition at l. 994. Here the reflexive quality of repetition is more functional, conveying the length of her complaint as passing time even tires itself out.

1571 *looks for* looks forward to.

1572 *thinks too long* Compare 'long she thinks', l. 1359.

remaining probably refers to 'night' and 'morning', rather than to Lucrece herself, in which case it would mean 'still alive'.

1573 *in sorrow's. . . sustaining* when one is enduring painful sorrow. The particular contrast with *Venus and Adonis*, ll. 23–4, where time seems short during pleasure, stands for a general difference between the explorations of time in the two poems.

1574 *heavy* intense, oppressive; but the line depends on a play on OED *adj.* and *n.* A28, 'weighed down by sleep, weariness'.

1575 *watch* stay awake, cannot sleep; the monosyllables of the line give it an appropriately ponderous effect (as at ll. 990–2; see note).

1576 *Which* i.e. her 'woe'.
overslipped her thought passed by without her noticing; Shakespeare's only use of 'overslip'.

1577 *That* refers back to 'all this time', l. 1576.

1578 *brought* removed, relieved.

1579 *surmise of* meditation on, contemplation of (see OED 4a, 5a); but other key senses of the word (allegation, suspicion; 2, 3a) contribute, because this word stands for a complex activity in which Lucrece has used the picture both to savour and avoid her predicament. Compare l. 83, Sonnet 117.10, and *Macbeth*, 1.3.139–42, 'My thought, whose murther yet is but fantastical, | Shakes so my single state of man that function | Is smothered in surmise, and nothing is | But what is not'.
detriment loss, harm; Shakespeare's only use of the word.

1580 *shows* representations, i.e. the picture; see 'harmless show', l. 1507.

1581–2 The proverbial 'I am not the first (and shall not be the last)' (Dent F295) underlies this line. Compare *Richard II*, 5.5.23–30, 'Thoughts tending to content flatter themselves | That they are not the first of Fortune's slaves, | Nor shall be the last [. . .] And in this thought they find a kind of ease, | Bearing their own misfortunes on the back | Of such as have before endured the like', and the more straightforward consolation claimed at *King Lear*, 5.3.3–4, 'We are not the first | Who with best meaning have incurred the worst'.
cured. . . endured On the sounding, or not, of final -*ed*, see 50–2n. Q's spellings are 'cured' and 'endured'.

For every tear he falls, a Trojan bleeds;
His eye drops fire, no water thence proceeds.
　　Those round clear pearls of his that move thy pity
　　Are balls of quenchless fire to burn thy city.

'Such devils steal effects from lightless hell:　　　　　　　1555
For Sinon in his fire doth quake with cold,
And in that cold hot burning fire doth dwell.
These contraries such unity do hold
Only to flatter fools and make them bold;
　　So Priam's trust false Sinon's tears doth flatter,　　　1560
　　That he finds means to burn his Troy with water.'

Here, all enraged, such passion her assails
That patience is quite beaten from her breast.
She tears the senseless Sinon with her nails,
Comparing him to that unhappy guest　　　　　　　　　　1565
Whose deed hath made herself herself detest.
　　At last she smilingly with this gives o'er:
　　'Fool, fool,' quoth she, 'his wounds will not be sore.'

Thus ebbs and flows the current of her sorrow,
And time doth weary time with her complaining;　　　　　1570
She looks for night, and then she longs for morrow,
And both she thinks too long with her remaining.
Short time seems long in sorrow's sharp sustaining:
　　Though woe be heavy, yet it seldom sleeps,
　　And they that watch see time how slow it creeps.　　　1575

Which all this time hath overslipped her thought
That she with painted images hath spent,
Being from the feeling of her own grief brought
By deep surmise of others' detriment,
Losing her woes in shows of discontent.　　　　　　　　1580
　　It easeth some, though none it ever cured,
　　To think their dolour others have endured.

But now the mindful messenger come back
Brings home his lord and other company,
Who finds his Lucrece clad in mourning black,　　　　　1585

1583 *mindful* responsible, attentive to his task; Shakespeare's only use of the word.
come having come.
1585 *mourning black* This has not been mentioned before this point; see l. 680 and note, for her white 'nightly linen'. The detail may come from Ovid's *Fasti*, 2.817–18 (see Appendix 2) or from Chaucer's *Legend of Good Women*, 1829–32, where she receives Collatine 'al dischevele, with hire heres cleere, | In habit swich as women used tho | Unto the buryinge of hire frendes go, | She sit in halle with a sorweful sighte'.

1586   **tear-distainèd** tear-stained.

eye singular stands for the plural here, and helps the rhyme.

1587   **Blue circles** shadows around her eyes caused by weeping, which now seem to weep; compare ll. 1229, 407–8 (for the blue circles around Lucrece's breasts) and notes.

1588   **water-galls** 'secondary or imperfectly formed rainbows' (OED³ 1); the meteorologically precise point is that Lucrece's face, 'dim' as it is, cannot produce a full rainbow. This rare word has a precedent in the Phaer-Twyne translation of *Aeneid* 12 (1573): 'And through the thick'st of all the host holds on his frantic pace, | And on each side the ray [array] of enemies' ranks he doth displace. | Like as a rock that from a lofty mount doth headlong fall, | Enforced with rage of wind, or else with showers, and water gall' (sig. 2N1v).

dim element gloomy sky (i.e. her face). The word 'element' is in place amid the elevated register of *Lucrece*, but the Clown in *Twelfth Night*, 3.1.57–9, considers it hackneyed: 'who you are, and what you would, are out of my welkin – I might say "element," but the word is overworn'.

1589   **new storms** more tears.

to in addition to.

1590   **sad-beholding** (i) looking gravely; (ii) appearing sorrowful; on 'sad', see 262n.

1592   **sod** boiled; in contrast with 'raw'. Shakespeare's other use of the word is in *Love's Labour's Lost*, 4.2.22–3, 'Twice sod simplicity, *bis coctus* [Latin: 'twice cooked']! | O thou monster Ignorance, how deformed dost thou look!'. Since Holofernes here may be using 'sod' as a word appropriate to the Latinless Dull, it is possible that its use in *Lucrece* brings in a rough register (which may be extended by the physicality and alliteration of 'red and raw').

1595   **acquaintance** friends, acquaintances; the singular use as a collective noun (OED³ 2b) was common in the period.

1596   **wondering. . . chance** (i) amazed at having met together by chance; (ii) wondering at or about each other's fortunes.

1598–9   In Ovid's *Fasti* Lucrece's husband and father question her together (Appendix 2); in Chaucer's *Legend of Good Women*, ll. 1833–4, 'her friends' ask 'what hire eylen [i.e. ail] myghte'; but in Livy, as here, Collatine alone asks (see Appendix 2). His question, 'whether all things were well', is notably brief in comparison.

1598   **uncouth** (i) unknown (OED 1); (i) unpleasant (OED 4a).

1599   **befallen** disyllabic here.

1600   **spite** injury.

spent exhausted.

1602   **Unmask** Reveal the nature of, explain.

dear dear Shakespeare uses double 'dear' elsewhere, as in *Richard II*, 2.1.57–8: 'This land of such dear souls, this dear dear land, | Dear for her reputation through the world'. However, he does not repeat this formulation of adjective and noun.

moody heaviness melancholy (OED 'moody, *adj.*', 4a; compare l. 553) sorrow; melancholy was thought to be a heavy humour. Compare *Comedy of Errors*, 5.1.78–80, 'what doth ensue | But moody and dull melancholy, | Kinsman to grim and comfortless despair'.

1603   **tell thy grief** tell us what you are grieving about. On grief as physical pain as well as mental pain, see Sonnet 34.9n.

1604   **Three times** Ovid's Lucretia 'ter conata loqui, ter destitit' (2.823, 'three times she tried to speak, three times she stopped'; see Appendix 2). The triple effort has an epic quality, most immediately because of Virgil's *Aeneid*, 2.792–4, Phaer-Twyne (1573): 'Three times about her neck I [Aeneas; reaching out for his wife Creusa] sought mine arms to set, and thrice | In vain her likeness fast I held, for through my hands she flies | Like wavering wind, or like to dreams that men full swift espies' (sig. F2r). In the *Aeneid* the key phrase, *ter conatus*, is repeated when Aeneas reaches out for his father's shade in the underworld (6.700).

gives. . .fire tries to light the fuse of her sorrow. In the metaphor, continued in the 'discharge' of l. 1605, the expression of her sorrow is a fire-arm that proves difficult to fire.

1606   **addressed** prepared; but OED³ 16 'to send, aim' may also contribute here, as an extension of the 'fire. . . discharge' metaphor.

1608   **ta'en prisoner** The metre demands that this phrase should occupy only three syllables, hence the elision of 'ta'en' (Q 'tane'), and the disyllabic 'prisoner'.

And round about her tear-distainèd eye
Blue circles streamed, like rainbows in the sky.
    These water-galls in her dim element
    Foretell new storms to those already spent.

Which when her sad-beholding husband saw,   1590
Amazedly in her sad face he stares:
Her eyes, though sod in tears, looked red and raw,
Her lively colour killed with deadly cares;
He hath no power to ask her how she fares.
    Both stood like old acquaintance in a trance,   1595
    Met far from home, wondering each other's chance.

At last he takes her by the bloodless hand
And thus begins: 'What uncouth ill event
Hath thee befallen, that thou dost trembling stand?
Sweet love, what spite hath thy fair colour spent?   1600
Why art thou thus attired in discontent?
    Unmask, dear dear, this moody heaviness,
    And tell thy grief, that we may give redress.'

Three times with sighs she gives her sorrow fire,
Ere once she can discharge one word of woe.   1605
At length addressed to answer his desire,
She modestly prepares to let them know
Her honour is ta'en prisoner by the foe,
    While Collatine and his consorted lords
    With sad attention long to hear her words.   1610

And now this pale swan in her watery nest
Begins the sad dirge of her certain ending:
'Few words', quoth she, 'shall fit the trespass best,
Where no excuse can give the fault amending.

1609 **consorted** united in comradeship. Shakespeare tends to use the word negatively, as at *Richard II*, 5.3.137–9, 'But for our trusty brother-in-law and the abbot, | With all the rest of that consorted crew, | Destruction straight shall dog them at the heels'. Here the formal, Latinate word suits the Roman context and the formality of the moment.
1610 **sad** See 262n.
1611 **swan** Swans were traditionally reputed to sing before death (as in the proverb 'like a swan, he sings before death', Dent S1028). Compare 'Let the Bird of Loudest Lay', l. 15, and *Othello*, 5.2.247–8: 'Hark, canst thou hear me? I will play the swan, | And die in music'.

1612 **certain ending** inevitable death.
1613 **trespass** sin, crime.
1614 **give. . . amending** make amends for the crime, make good the wrong. This is Shakespeare's only use of 'amending', and EEBO-TCP suggests that the formula 'give... amending' in this sense is a rare one (no instances before 1700). This may help explain the altered appearance of ll. 1613–14 in 'Of the Tongue, etc.', a composite poem in John Bodenham's anthology *Belvedere, or, The Garden of the Muses* (1600): 'Few words do ever fit a trespass best, | Where no excuse can give the fault amends' (sig. M5v). The next line in that poem is *Lucrece*, l. 1220.

1615   *moe* The archaic form of 'more'; compare l. 1479.

depending waiting for relief; see OED 'depend, *v.*1', 7, 'to be in suspense or undetermined, be waiting for settlement (as an action at law, a bill in parliament, an appointment, etc.)'.

1618   *it* the tongue (l. 1617).

1619–20   *in the interest. . . came* intruded upon your right to your marriage bed; for 'interest', see also ll. 1067, 1797.

1622   *what* whatever.

1623   *enforcement* use of force, violence; the OED does not list 'rape' as one of the word's meanings, but all variations on 'force' have that potential in *Lucrece*. Compare also *Richard III*, 3.7.7–8, 'Th' unsatiate greediness of his desire, | And his enforcement of the city wives'.

1626   *falchion* sword; see 176n.

1627   *creeping* See 1517n.

1629   *entertain* receive; compare l. 596 and *Venus and Adonis*, l. 969, but see especially 'cherish', l. 1546 and note, where the language of hospitality is similarly corrupted.

1631   *contradict* oppose, speak out against; compare *Henry VIII*, 2.4.27–9, 'When was the hour | I ever contradicted your desire? | Or made it not mine too?'.

1632   *hard-favoured* rough-looking, ugly; for the term, compare *Venus and Adonis*, ll. 133, 931. In Tarquin's earlier threats the groom's looks have not been mentioned: he is 'worthless', l. 515, and 'rascal', l. 671.

1633   *yoke. . . will* submit your will to my desire.

liking Multiple implications of the word are gathered under OED 'liking, *n.* 1', 4b and 5: taste, preference, will and choice. Compare *Much Ado About Nothing*, 1.1.314–15, 'But lest my liking might too sudden seem, | I would have salved it with a longer treatise'; also *All's Well That Ends Well*, 3.5.53–4, 'the King had married him | Against his liking'.

will here with its modern sense, i.e. 'the action of choosing', 'intention' (OED 5a, 5b).

1635   *fulfil* perform.

1639   *With this* at these words.

1643   *rest upon record* remain in the written record; perhaps, more simply, 'be remembered', but Shakespeare tends to use 'record' for something written. Compare the complex of the word's meanings in Sonnets 55.8, 59.5, 122.8; the stress falls on the second syllable.

1645   *adulterate* adulterous.

1648   *bloody* bloodthirsty, cruel (OED³ *adj., n.,* and *adv.* A4a).

judge Tarquin plays the incompatible parts of both judge and witness (with 'evidence to swear', l. 1650).

forbod an older form of 'forbade' which was current in 1594; see *A Lover's Complaint*, l. 164.

1650   *scarlet lust* The colour is fitting, in that red is associated with passion (see 11n); but an EEBO-TCP search does not reveal any other examples of the phrase. One key reference point is the Whore of Babylon in Revelations 17:4: 'And the woman was arrayed in purple and scarlet, and gilded with gold, and precious stones, and pearls, and had a cup of gold in her hand, full of abominations, and filthiness of her fornication'. This association with lust is evident in *Romeo and Juliet* 2.5.70–1 ('Now comes the wanton blood up in your cheeks, | They'll be in scarlet straight at any news'), where the Nurse sees Juliet's desire for Romeo. Compare also 'scarlet ornaments', lips, in Sonnet 142.6. The legal metaphor in these lines (see 'judge', l. 1648 and note) connects with 'scarlet' through the ceremonial robes worn by judges and others (OED 3).

evidence witness (OED 7a, where this is the first citation).

1651   *poor* (i) inferior; or (ii) 'poor' can be read as a pitying epithet, qualifying a personified beauty; compare Sonnet 67.7.

purloined stolen; OED³ cites this line as the earliest instance of 'purloin, *v.*', 3, where the stealing is metaphorical, but EEBO-TCP has other examples. See, for example, Seneca, *Ten Tragedies*, trans. Jasper Heywood et al.: 'No lady's lust hath ravished yet Atrides in his life, | Nor privily purloined his heart betrothed to his wife' (sig. U4v); or Jean Calvin, *Sermons. . . upon the Book of Job*, trans. Arthur Golding (1574): 'Wherefore as often as we be tempted to put our trust in creatures and earthly things: let us call to mind that it is a robbing of God of his honour, and a purloining of it from him' (sig. 2O8r).

1652   *robbed* Now the judge has become victim as well as witness in the trial (both

In me moe woes then words are now depending,   1615
    And my laments would be drawn out too long
    To tell them all with one poor tirèd tongue.

'Then be this all the task it hath to say:
Dear husband, in the interest of thy bed
A stranger came, and on that pillow lay   1620
Where thou wast wont to rest thy weary head;
And what wrong else may be imaginèd
    By foul enforcement might be done to me,
    From that, alas, thy Lucrece is not free.

'For in the dreadful dead of dark midnight,   1625
With shining falchion in my chamber came
A creeping creature with a flaming light,
And softly cried, "Awake, thou Roman dame,
And entertain my love, else lasting shame
    On thee and thine this night I will inflict,   1630
    If thou my love's desire do contradict.

'"For some hard-favoured groom of thine," quoth he,
Unless thou yoke thy liking to my will,
I'll murder straight, and then I'll slaughter thee,
And swear I found you where you did fulfil   1635
The loathsome act of lust, and so did kill
    The lechers in their deed. This act will be
    My fame, and thy perpetual infamy."

'With this I did begin to start and cry,
And then against my heart he set his sword,   1640
Swearing, unless I took all patiently,
I should not live to speak another word.
So should my shame still rest upon record,
    And never be forgot in mighty Rome
    Th' adulterate death of Lucrece, and her groom.   1645

'Mine enemy was strong, my poor self weak,
And far the weaker with so strong a fear.
My bloody judge forbod my tongue to speak;
No rightful plea might plead for justice there.
His scarlet lust came evidence to swear   1650
    That my poor beauty had purloined his eyes,
    And when the judge is robbed, the prisoner dies.

breaches of legal practice). Q's spelling 'rob'd' may allow a pun on the ceremonial dress suggested by 'scarlet', l. 1650. The punishment for robbery in Elizabethan England could be death. **prisoner** disyllabic.

1654 **refuge** defence, excuse, 'in which a person takes refuge' (OED³ 3c); compare *1 Henry VI*, 5.4.65, 68–9, ' Now heaven forfend, the holy maid with child? [...] She and the Dolphin have been juggling. | I did imagine what would be her refuge'.

1655–6 The plea is shared with Livy (see Appendix 2).

1655 **my gross blood** (i) all the blood in my body; (ii) all my descendants; the two are closely enough connected, and the idea of blood so resonant, that both are conveyed; see l. 655. For this sense of 'gross' ('entire, total, whole', OED *adj.* and *n.*4, 6a), compare *As You Like It*, 4.1.193–5, 'the most unworthy of her you call Rosalind, that may be chosen out of the gross band of the unfaithful'. Other senses of 'gross' could be engaged here: Lucrece's blood has been rendered monstrous (OED 4) by the rape.

1656 **spotless** unblemished, uncorrupted. On 'spot', see 196n, and on *-less* compounds, see 2n.

1657 **forced** raped; compare l. 1623 and note, for the less explicit 'enforcement'.

1658 **accessory yieldings** consenting surrenders, surrenders that assisted the criminal. On 'accessory' (Q 'accessarie') see 922n, and Sonnet 35.13. Compare *Richard III*, 1.2.189–91, 'This hand which for thy love did kill thy love, | Shall for thy love kill a far truer love; | To both their deaths thou shalt be accessory'. This is Shakespeare's only use of 'yielding' in the plural; compare ll. 339, 1036, *Venus and Adonis*, l. 547, and *Measure for Measure*, 2.4.103–4, 'Redeem thy brother | By yielding up thy body to my will'. The metre requires that 'accessory' should be stressed on the first and third syllables.

1659 **poisoned closet** i.e. her corrupted body. A 'closet' was 'a private room' (OED 1a) or 'a private repository of valuables' (OED 3a), and was often associated with the heart, as at Sonnet 46.6 (see note). Compare *Edward III*, 2.1.433–4 ('An honourable grave is more esteemed | Than the polluted closet of a king'), and the 'quiet cabinet', l. 442.

1660 **hopeless. . . loss** The metaphor sees Collatine as a merchant who has lost enough to make him 'hopeless'; this evokes the 'interest' of l. 1619. Compare the mercantile and nautical metaphors surrounding both Collatine and Tarquin: 'treasure. . . priceless wealth', ll. 16–17, 'traffic. . . treasure', ll. 131–2, 'pilot. . . treasure', ll. 279–80. The other use of 'hopeless' in the poem ('hopeless castaway', l. 744) suggests shipwreck, which was a cause of mercantile loss.

1661 **declined** bent down; Q2's 'inclined' is more likely to result from the memory of 'inclined' (l. 1657) than any difficulty in the word. Compare *Winter's Tale*, 2.3.13–16, 'To see his nobleness, | Conceiving the dishonour of his mother! | He straight declined, drooped, took it deeply, | Fastened and fixed the shame on't in himself'.

1662 **wreathèd** crossed. Q's 'wretched' could be a misreading, replacing a relatively unusual word with a thematically if not specifically appropriate one; in manuscript 'wreched' and 'wrethed', for example, could easily be confused. It may also have resulted from eye-slip between this line and 'wretched' in l. 1665. The emendation was first made in Dyce's 1866 edition, in response to a suggestion from Walker (1860). For this gesture in Shakespeare, deemed typical of the lover, see l. 793 and note, and *Love's Labour's Lost*, 4.3.132–4, 'Did never sonnet for her sake compile, | Nor never lay his wreathed arms athwart | His loving bosom to keep down his heart'. (This is cited under OED, 'wreathed, *adj.*', 2, with the date given as 1598, whereas scholars usually prefer a date of 1594–5 for the play.)

1663 **new** recently.
waxen grown, become. Compare *2 Henry VI*, 3.2.76, 'What? art thou like the adder waxen deaf?'. In modern usage wax and paleness are associated, but this does not work in Elizabethan English: wax in regular use was usually red or yellow in colour. Of the many instances of 'wax' near 'pale' (138 before 1594, in a 'near.3' EEBO-TCP search), most of which have a similar formula to this line, none gives any suggestion of a play on the paleness of wax.

1667–71 The Thames in London is a tidal river, and so the phenomenon described here, though not always 'violent roaring', would have been familiar to many of Shakespeare's readers. On 'tide', see 645n.

1668 **his** its (as at l. 532).

'O teach me how to make mine owne excuse,
Or at the least this refuge let me find:
Though my gross blood be stained with this abuse, 1655
Immaculate and spotless is my mind,
That was not forced, that never was inclined
    To accessory yieldings, but still pure
    Doth in her poisoned closet yet endure.'

Lo, here the hopeless merchant of this loss, 1660
With head declined and voice dammed up with woe,
With sad set eyes and wreathèd armes across,
From lips new waxen pale begins to blow
The grief away, that stops his answer so.
    But wretched as he is he strives in vain: 1665
    What he breathes out, his breath drinks up again.

As through an arch, the violent roaring tide
Outruns the eye that doth behold his haste,
Yet in the eddy boundeth in his pride
Back to the strait that forced him on so fast, 1670
In rage sent out, recalled in rage being past:
    Even so his sighs, his sorrows make a saw,
    To push grief on, and back the same grief draw.

Which speechless woe of his poor she attendeth,
And his untimely frenzy thus awaketh: 1675
'Dear lord, thy sorrow to my sorrow lendeth

1669 *eddy* 'water that by some interruption in its course, runs contrary to the direction of the tide or current' (OED 1), rather than a whirlpool.
  boundeth in his pride (i) leaps with all his vigour (on 'pride' and 'proud', see 37n); (ii) constrains his force (Schmidt, on 'pride'). These two senses are actually complementary, in that controlling the course of a river can increase the force of its flow. For the latter sense of 'bound', see l. 1119, and *Troilus and Cressida*, 4.5.127–9, 'my mother's blood | Runs on the dexter cheek, and this sinister | Bounds in my father's', which OED credits as the first instance of 'bound, *v*.1', 2b, 'enclose, confine, contain. . . with *in*'. However, compare Nashe's *Unfortunate Traveller* (1594): 'his bases were the banks or shores that bounded in the streams' (2.274).

1670 *strait* narrow channel.
1672 *his sighs. . . saw* His sighs give a saw-like motion to his sorrows, moving them back and forth, in and out; the metaphor also suggests his extreme sighing causes rasping pain.
1674 *poor she* i.e. Lucrece.
  attendeth observes.
1675 *untimely* ill-timed, inappropriate; see 43n. Shakespeare mostly uses the word to mean 'premature', often with a pejorative implication.
  frenzy trance; the context does not suggest the wild activity usually associated with the word (see the 'frenzies wood' of *Venus and Adonis*, l. 740). Of Shakespeare's other uses, the closest is *Twelfth Night*, 5.1.281–2, 'A most extracting frenzy of mine own | From my remembrance clearly banished his'.

1677 **slaketh** is diminished by; see 425n.

1678 **sensible** intensely felt. This line is the earliest citation for OED *adj.* and *n.* A6, but for an instance before *Lucrece*, see Giovanni Boccaccio, *Amorous Fiametta*, trans. Bartholomew Yong (1587): 'The force of love is felt more sensibly and stronger in them that seek to expel it' (sig. D2v).
passion emotion.

1679 **feeling painful** This compound, of which an EEBO-TCP search has no other instances, suggests (i) acutely painful (Duncan-Jones and Woudhuysen 2007: 369), and also (ii) sensitive to its own pain (Burrow 2002: 330). Compare *Measure for Measure*, 1.2.36–7, ' I think thou dost; and indeed with most painful feeling of thy speech'.

1680 **drown on woe** drown in woe; Q3's 'one woe' creates a neat parallel construction, and 'on' is a known Elizabethan spelling of 'one'. However, the change is unnecessary, as is Malone's replacement of 'on' with 'in' because 'drown on' is an occasional alternative to 'drown in' in the period. See John Stow, *Chronicles* (1580): 'On the 25th day of November was the Lord Fitzwater drowned on the sea, and much other harms were done by tempest' (sig. 2R6v). The use of 'on' with 'drown' need not only refer to immersion in liquid; it can also denote shipwreck on solid ground, resulting in drowning. See William Martyn, *History and Lives of the Kings of England* (1615): 'Henry Holland, his son, was attainted when King Edward the Fourth reigned, and was drowned on Calais Sands' (sig. 2V3r).

1681–98 Livy 1.58 (see Appendix 2) provides a precedent for this appeal; however, in Livy Lucrece names Tarquin before securing the pledge offered at ll. 1695–7.

1681 **when** if
charm influence, bewitch.

1682 **For** for the sake of.
she for 'she' in place of 'her', see Hope (2003: 86–7).
attend me give me your attention.

1683 **suddenly** immediately.

1684 **his own** i.e. Tarquin is an enemy to himself.
defend (i) vindicate; (ii) protect, an impossibility that suggests an extra edge to 'Suppose': Collatine may feel he can help, but he cannot.

1687 **For. . . iniquity** marked as a *sententia*; see 87–8n. The idea is proverbial (Dent P50, 'pardon makes offenders'), as in *Romeo and Juliet*, 3.1.197, 'Mercy but murders, pardoning those that kill'.

1690 **plight** pledge (OED³ 3).

1691 **venge** avenge.

1694 **Knights. . . harms** The Roman *equites* were often seen as equivalent with English knights, as in Thomas Smith's *Commonwealth of England* (1589): 'No more are all made knights in England that may dispend a knight's land or fee, but they only whom the king will so honour. The number of *Equites* was uncertain, and so it is of knights, at the pleasure of the Prince. *Equites Romani* had *equum publicum* [i.e. horses paid for by the state]. The knights of England have not so, but find their own horse themselves in peace time, and most usually in wars' (sig. D4r). The line is reminiscent of medieval chivalry, which suggests an appropriate sense of honour and obligation, but which is also anachronistically out of place in ancient Rome.

1697 **knighthood** See ll. 197, 1694 and note.
imposition 'action of imposing or laying as a burden, duty, charge, or task; the action of inflicting, levying, enjoining, or enforcing' (OED 4a).

1698 **bewrayed** revealed.

1699 **sad** See 262n.

1700 **protestation** declaration (OED³ 1); see l. 1844.

1702 **quality** nature.

1703 **dreadful circumstance** Compare ll. 1262–3 and note.

1706 **terms** words (Shakespeare's usual sense), arguments, circumstances (OED 10).
this chance my misfortune; the thing that has happened to me.

1707 See l. 577, where Lucrece pleads not to have her fountain muddied, and l. 1734, for the 'purple fountain' of blood from which Brutus draws the knife, and notes.

1709–10 Livy 1.58 (see Appendix 2 for Painter's version), quoted in Marso's commentary, provides a precedent for this offer of comfort.

1709 **With this** at these words.

1710 **Her body's stain. . . clears** her uncorrupted mind (i) exonerates her of, or (ii) purifies, the violation of her body.

Another power; no flood by raining slaketh.
My woe too sensible thy passion maketh
   More feeling painful. Let it then suffice
   To drown on woe one pair of weeping eyes.   1680

'And for my sake, when I might charm thee so
(For she that was thy Lucrece now attend me),
Be suddenly revengèd on my foe,
Thine, mine, his own. Suppose thou dost defend me
From what is past, the help that thou shalt lend me   1685
   Comes all too late; yet let the traitor die,
   For sparing justice feeds iniquity.

'But ere I name him, you fair lords', quoth she,
Speaking to those that came with Collatine,
'Shall plight your honourable faiths to me,   1690
With swift pursuit to venge this wrong of mine;
For 'tis a meritorious fair design
   To chase injustice with revengeful arms;
   Knights by their oaths should right poor ladies' harms.'

At this request, with noble disposition,   1695
Each present lord began to promise aid,
As bound in knighthood to her imposition,
Longing to hear the hateful foe bewrayed.
But she, that yet her sad task hath not said,
   The protestation stops. 'O speak,' quoth she,   1700
   'How may this forcèd stain be wiped from me?

'What is the quality of my offence,
Being constrained with dreadful circumstance?
May my pure mind with the foul act dispense,
My low-declinèd honour to advance?   1705
May any terms acquit me from this chance?
   The poisoned fountain clears itself again,
   And why not I from this compellèd stain?

With this they all at once began to say
Her body's stain her mind untainted clears,   1710
While with a joyless smile she turns away
The face, that map which deep impression bears

1712 **map** See 402n on the face as a map. As Duncan-Jones and Woudhuysen note, the 'deep impression' suggests an engraved map, with the tears acting like acid, etching lines (2007: 372). Compare *Twelfth Night*, 3.2.78–80, 'He does smile his face into more lines than is in the new map, with the augmentation of the Indies', which shares the link between facial lines and the lines on a map, if not the suggestion of engraving.

1713 *in it* it in Q; Malone's emendation, proposed by Capell, has been accepted by all recent editors.

1714–15 A repeating concern of Lucrece's, but Livy 1.58, quoted in Marso's commentary, gives a specific precedent for the phrasing here. See Appendix 2 for Painter's version, 'for no unchaste or ill woman shall hereafter take example of Lucrece'.

1715 *By my. . . giving* will claim that my pardon can be given to them too.

1716–22 On the rhetorical figure for such curtailment, *aposiopesis*, compare ll. 666, 1534 and notes. There is a precedent for her hesitation at this point in Ovid, *Fasti*, 2.825–7; see Appendix 2.

1719 *accents* sounds (OED³ 4b); the word encompasses more and less articulate vocalisations, and here suggests words half-formed, broken attempts to speak. Compare *Coriolanus*, 3.3.54–6, 'do not take | His rougher accents for malicious sounds, | But as I say, such as become a soldier'. Compare 'accent', l. 566.

1720 *Untimely breathings* (i) premature intakes of breath (as if she is about to start), or perhaps (ii) irregular breathing (though this sense of 'untimely' is not noted by OED). Shakespeare does not use the plural form of the noun anywhere else.
sick 'deeply affected by some strong feeling' (OED *adj.* and *n.* A4a).
assays attempts.

1723–4 *sheathèd. . . harmless. . . harmful. . . unsheathed* This version of an *antimetabole* at a moment of crisis in the poem uses antonyms rather than repetitions of the same words. It is thus characteristic of the dense, tense style of this part of the poem. On the rhyme of 'unsheathed' with '*breathed*' (l. 1726) and '*bequeathed*' (l. 1727), and on the sounding, or not, of final -*ed*, see 50–2n. Q's spellings are 'unsheathed', 'breathed', 'bequeathed'.

1723 *sheathèd* buried; see 397n, and compare other Shakespearean uses of the metaphor at *Venus and Adonis*, l. 1116, Titus Andronicus, 2.1.54–6, 'Not I, till I have sheathed | My rapier in his bosom, and withal | Thrust these reproachful speeches down his throat', and *Romeo and Juliet*, 5.3.203–5, 'This dagger hath mista'en, for,

lo, his house | Is empty on the back of Montague, | And it mis-sheathed in my daughter's bosom!'.
harmless innocent; the contrast with 'harmful' puts more emphasis on the suffix here (on -*less* compounds, see 2n); compare ll. 510, 1507.

1724 *unsheathed* freed; the soul is released from its containment, figured as a scabbard.

1725 *did bail* released (OED 'bail, *v*.1', 2a; the word usually suggests a security payment, but that does not seem pertinent here); compare Sonnet 133.10 and note.

1727 *bequeathed* See 1181n on Lucrece's earlier oral testament.

1728 *wingèd sprite* i.e. her soul; compare l. 122. The phrase may be Shakespeare's; EEBO-TCP offers no other instance before 1594. Shakespeare's other uses of 'sprite' refer to more Puck-like spirits, 'that shrewd and knavish sprite | Called Robin Goodfellow' (*A Midsummer Night's Dream*, 2.1.33–4); however 'sprite' and 'spirit' are etymologically linked and were used with many overlapping meanings in the period.

1729 *Life's lasting date* everlasting life; her uncorrupted soul remains immortal. For 'date' meaning 'duration', see also ll. 26, 935.
cancelled destiny a fate (i.e. her sorrow; or her life) that has been annulled (by her suicide). For 'cancelled', see l. 934 and note, where Lucrece fears that her pain will be everlasting.

1730 *Stone-still, astonished* The line exploits a word-play found in Spenser's *Faerie Queene*, II.vi.31.9, 'Wherewith astonisht, still he stood, as senselesse stone'. There is no etymological link between 'stone' and 'astonished' (the latter probably more related to 'stun'). For 'astonished', see Sonnet 86.8.

1731 *crew* company; in Elizabethan English the word could imply military or nautical organisation, or informal disreputability, depending on context, but it could also have a neutral sense, as here.

1733 In Ovid, *Fasti*, 2.835–6 both Collatine and Lucretius (Lucretia's father) fall on Lucrece's body ('ecce super corpus. . . virque paterque iacet'; see Appendix 2).
self-slaughtered First citation in OED for the adjective, and *Hamlet* is the first citation

Of hard misfortune, carved in it with tears.
 'No, no,' quoth she, 'no dame hereafter living
 By my excuse shall claim excuse's giving.'   1715

Here, with a sigh as if her heart would break,
She throws forth Tarquin's name: 'He, he', she says,
But more than 'he' her poor tongue could not speak,
Till, after many accents and delays,
Untimely breathings, sick and short assays,   1720
 She utters this: 'He, he, fair lords, 'tis he
 That guides this hand to give this wound to me.'

Even here she sheathèd in her harmless breast
A harmful knife that thence her soul unsheathed;
That blow did bail it from the deep unrest   1725
Of that polluted prison where it breathed.
Her contrite sighs unto the clouds bequeathed
 Her wingèd sprite, and through her wounds doth fly
 Life's lasting date from cancelled destiny.

Stone-still, astonished with this deadly deed,   1730
Stood Collatine and all his lordly crew,
Till Lucrece' father, that beholds her bleed,
Himself on her self-slaughtered body threw,
And from the purple fountain Brutus drew
 The murderous knife, and as it left the place,   1735
 Her blood in poor revenge held it in chase;

---

for the noun ('Or that the Everlasting had not fixed | His canon 'gainst self-slaughter!' 1.2.131–2); but the phrase was probably in use before Shakespeare. The one pre-1594 instance arising in an EEBO-TCP search covering all forms is in Anthony Anderson, *The Shield of Our Safety* (1581): 'Thus you see how Samson's life and death is sanctified, being the shadow of Christ, and delivered from the ignominy of self-slaughter' (sig. M1r). This quotation offers a useful reminder that in Christian doctrine suicide is sinful; see 822n.

1734 ***purple fountain*** i.e. her bleeding wound. Compare *Romeo and Juliet*, 1.1.83–5, 'you beasts! | That quench the fire of your pernicious rage | With purple fountains issuing from your veins'; see also l. 1707,

and the quotation from *Titus Andronicus* in 1738n.

Brutus Lucius Junius Brutus was the nephew of Tarquinius Superbus, and thus a cousin of Sextus Tarquinius. He earned the cognomen Brutus (stupid, irrational) by pretending to be thus in order to avoid arousing the hatred of the King, the murderer of Brutus' brother. Having thrown off this disguise (see ll. 1814–16) he led the revolt against the Tarquins, expelling them from Rome, and becoming Consul (along with Lucretius Tarquinius Collatinus, Lucrece's husband) in 509 BCE.

1736 ***held it in chase;*** pursued it. Q ends the stanza with a full-stop but a semi-colon, or indeed a comma, better enables the sense to continue across to the next stanza.

1738 **rivers. . . crimson blood** Compare *Titus Andronicus*, 2.4.22–5, 'Alas, a crimson river of warm blood, | Like to a bubbling fountain stirred with wind, | Doth rise and fall between thy rosed lips, | Coming and going with thy honey breath'. Of Shakespeare's fourteen uses of 'crimson', nine refer to blood, four to complexion (blushes, red lips; see *Venus and Adonis*, ll. 76, 506) and one to a rose.

that so that.

1740 **Who** which; but it is 'her' body, so Lucrece and her body may be combined in the pronoun.

late-sacked island As Burrow (2002: 333) suggests (following Woodbridge 1991), the idea of Lucrece as an invaded and despoiled island may have resonated with the English, or British, idea of a body politic, only a few years after the Spanish Armada of 1588.

vastly desolately. This is Shakespeare's only use of the adverb, OED's only citation for this sense (1a), and the only one for any sense before 1664; an EEBO-TCP search reveals no use before *Lucrece*. Behind it lies the Latin adjective *vastus* (which denoted both empty and devastated).

1741 **Bare** This may hint at Lucrece's nakedness; Shakespeare omits a scruple present in Ovid, *Fasti*, 2.833–4 (see Appendix 2) and in Chaucer's *Legend of Good Women*, ll. 1856–60: 'And as she fel adoun, she kaste her lok [i.e. look], | And of her clothes yet she hede tok. | For in her fallynge yet she had a care, | Lest that hir fet or suche thyng lay bare; | So well she loved clennesse and eke trouthe'.

1742–3 **remained. . . stained** On the sounding, or not, of final *-ed*, see 50–2n. Q's spellings are 'remain'd' and 'stain'd'.

1743 **some looked black** Lucrece's blood may be black because (i) it has been discoloured by sin; (ii) it has been altered by traumatic experience, like Hecuba's, l. 1454 and note; or (iii) because she is suffering from melancholy (Duncan-Jones and Woudhuysen 2007: 374). The first of these seems most likely.

that false Tarquin stained (i) that was the blood which false Tarquin polluted; (ii) that blood served as an accusation or reproach to false Tarquin. The construction is opaque but (i) seems the dominant

sense, balancing the stained blood with the 'pure and red' of l. 1742.

1744 **About** around.

face surface.

1745 **watery rigol** a circle of watery serum (surrounding the clot of 'black blood'). OED[3] cites an earlier instance from 1459–60 and conjectures origins and contexts for the word, but nonetheless Shakespeare's two uses of the word ('this golden rigol' is the crown in *2 Henry IV*, 4.5.36) seem unusual. This earlier instance especially uses the word to register a strange phenomenon.

1747–50 In addition to the spilling of blood, which is inevitable, both *Venus and Adonis* and *Lucrece* share an aetiological and metamorphic turn. Compare *Venus and Adonis*, ll. 1135–64. While the medical literature of the period is often concerned with the wateriness or otherwise of blood, Shakespeare's phenomenon is better thought of as allegorical, rather than scientific, in character.

1747 **as** as if.

1748 **token** evidence.

1751 **Lucretius** Lucrece's father, Spurius Lucretius Tricipitinus, is first named here.

1752 **deprived** taken away; see 1186n. On the rhyme with '**unlived**' (l. 1754) and '**derived**' (l. 1755), and on the sounding, or not, of final *-ed*, see 50–2n. Q's spellings are 'depriued', 'unliued', and 'deriued'.

1754 **unlived** 'deprived of life' (OED 1); this appears to be a neologism. The first citation in OED is from 1642, and no candidate arises from an EEBO-TCP search. The word 'unliving' was well established, but has a distinct sense ('not living or alive; lifeless', OED). This part of the poem has a concentration of linguistic innovation (see ll. 1678, 1679, 1745, 1756), appropriately enough as it seeks to find its register for extreme sorrow.

1755 **to this end** (i) for such a death; (ii) for such a purpose.

1756 **predecease** die before; another possible neologism. This is the first citation in OED[3] (EEBO-TCP corroborates this); the first citation for 'predeceased' is *Henry V*, 5.1.70–3, 'Will you mock at an ancient tradition, begun upon an honourable respect, and worn as a memorable trophy of predeceased valour, and dare not avouch in your deeds any of your words?'.

And, bubbling from her breast, it doth divide
In two slow rivers, that the crimson blood
Circles her body in on every side,
Who like a late-sacked island vastly stood   1740
Bare and unpeopled in this fearful flood.
   Some of her blood still pure and red remained,
    And some looked black, and that false Tarquin stained.

About the mourning and congealèd face
Of that black blood a watery rigol goes,   1745
Which seems to weep upon the tainted place,
And ever since, as pitying Lucrece' woes,
Corrupted blood some watery token shows,
   And blood untainted still doth red abide,
    Blushing at that which is so putrefied.   1750

'Daughter, dear daughter,' old Lucretius cries,
'That life was mine which thou hast here deprived.
If in the child the father's image lies,
Where shall I live now Lucrece is unlived?
Thou wast not to this end from me derived: 1755
   If children predecease progenitors,
    We are their offspring and they none of ours.

'Poor broken glass, I often did behold
In thy sweet semblance my old age new-born,
But now that fair fresh mirror, dim and old,   1760
Shows me a bare-boned death by time outworn.
O, from thy cheeks my image thou hast torn,
   And shivered all the beauty of my glass,
    That I no more can see what once I was.

Q1's spelling 'praedecease' draws attention to the Latinate nature of the compound. Duncan-Jones and Woodhuysen believe the spelling to be compositorial rather than authorial (2007: 489).

1758–9 These lines share one of the key motifs of the procreation sonnets, 1–17, especially 3.9–10, namely the parental joy in a child's resemblance. However, the idea is over-turned by premature death.

1758 *glass* mirror. For the idea that children were mirrors to their parents, compare Sonnet 3, esp. ll. 9, 10 and notes.

1759 *sweet semblance* beautiful appearance; compare Sonnet 13.4.

1761 *Shows me* (i) reveals that I am; (ii) portrays me as.
   bare-boned death i.e. the death's head skull; rather than rejuvenating her father with its youth, Lucrece's face is now a memento mori. Compare the even more threatening figure of death in *King John*, 5.2.176–8, 'in his forehead sits | A bare-ribbed death, whose office is this day | To feast upon whole thousands of the French'.
   outworn wasted, worn out; compare Sonnet 68.1.

1763 *shivered* shattered.

1764 *That* so that.

1766 *surcease* cease; the repeated '*sur-*' prefix in the line emphasises the contrast between 'surcease' and 'survive'. Shakespeare makes a different play on the word in *Macbeth*, 1.7.2–4, 'If the assassination | Could trammel up the consequence, and catch | With his surcease, success'.

1772 *By this* at these words. Other uses of 'By this' (see l. 1079 and note) suggest 'meanwhile', but this is a moment of intervention.

1773 *give. . . place* acknowledge his precedence in grief.

1774–5 Venus acts similarly in *Venus and Adonis*, ll. 1121–2.

1774 *then* Qc; Qu has 'than'.
key-cold The phrase was a common and proverbial (Tilley K23) way of denoting emotional and spiritual indifference as well as physical, metallic cold. Both Shakespeare's uses (see also *Richard III*, 1.2.5, 'Poor key-cold figure of a holy king') are focused on the physical.

1776 *counterfeits to die* imitates death (by lying still on the ground).
a space for a while (OED³ 'space, *n.* 1', P2a). Shakespeare does not use this phrase elsewhere, but compare *Richard III*, 4.1.78–9, 'Within so small a time [Even in so short a space, Q] my woman's heart | Grossly grew captive to his honey words'. The length of the 'short period of time' in the OED definition might suggest something momentary, or somewhat more extended, in which case the uncomfortable possibilities latent in 'counterfeits' (that this is a performance of emotion, rather than something spontaneous) would come to the surface.
a space, Qc; Qu has a full-stop.

1777 *possess* control.

1780 *served. . . arrest* (i) forced his tongue to be silent by means of legal restraint; (ii) imposed a cessation of speech upon his tongue. The former depends on a loose sense of legal arrest, the latter on OED 'arrest, *n.*1', 1, 'stoppage, stop, halt, delay', for which compare Sonnet 74.1 and note.

1781 *Who* which.
mad raging, furious.
use (i) purpose (OED³ 13a); (ii) ability to be used (14b); (iii) function (17).

1784 *so thick come* arriving in such a rush; it seems best to take this as an instance of OED 'thick, *adj.* and *n.*', A5a, 'Existing or occurring in large numbers in a relatively small space, or at short intervals; densely

arranged, crowded'. However, the sense of 'thick' that pertains most often to the voice in the period is 8, 'not clear; hoarse; having a confused or husky sound; indistinct, inarticulate', which is viable, though it does not pick up 'throng'. Compare *Cymbeline*, 3.2.56–8, where copiousness is implied: 'say, and speak thick | (Love's counsellor should fill the bores of hearing, | To th' smothering of the sense)'; also *2 Henry IV*, 2.3.23–5, where husky indistinctness is implied: 'He [Hotspur, a role model for young men] had no legs that practised not his gait; | And speaking thick (which nature made his blemish) | Became the accents of the valiant'.

1787 *tore* savaged, mauled. OED 'tear, *v.*1', 3b, 'tear the name of', means to blaspheme against, and this adds further edge to Collatine's imprecation. The phrase was used of slanderous attack more generally, as in William Baldwin, *The Last Part of the Mirror for Magistrates* (1578): 'Now farewell Baldwin, shield my torn name, | From slanderous trump of blasting black defame' (sig. R2v).

1788–90 These lines draw on proverbs; see *Venus and Adonis*, 458–61n, Sonnet 90.7, and also Tilley T275, 'after wind comes rain'.

1789 *tide* See ll. 645, 1667 and notes.

1790 *busy* frenetic, non-stop.

1791 *son* i.e. son-in-law.
strife competitive effort (see OED 'strife, *n.*', 3).

1792 *Who should* i.e. to see which of them would.

1794 *the claim. . . lay* the thing to which they lay claim. Compare 'interest', ll. 1067, 1619, 1797.

1795 Q's punctuation ('The father saies, shee's mine, ô mine shee is') does not make it clear who says 'O mine she is'. The lack of punctuation at the end of the line corroborates the idea that this is probably Collatine's reply, which then continues in l. 1796.

1797 *sorrow's interest* my (i) claim, or (ii) right, to sorrow; for 'interest', see ll. 1067, 1619–20. The word's different applications in the poem have in common an emphasis on rightful possession.

1798 *only mine* mine alone.

1799 *wailed* mourned.

1801 *too late* perhaps (i) after the point at which the rape could have been prevented; but more likely (ii) so recently. The latter would lose some of the parallelism in 'too early. . . too late', but other possible Shakespearean

'O Time, cease thou thy course and last no longer,   1765
If they surcease to be that should survive.
Shall rotten death make conquest of the stronger,
And leave the faltering feeble souls alive?
The old bees die, the young possess their hive,
    Then live, sweet Lucrece, live again and see   1770
    Thy father die, and not thy father thee.'

By this starts Collatine, as from a dream,
And bids Lucretius give his sorrow place;
And then in key-cold Lucrece' bleeding stream
He falls, and bathes the pale fear in his face,   1775
And counterfeits to die with her a space,
    Till manly shame bids him possess his breath,
    And live to be revengèd on her death.

The deep vexation of his inward soul
Hath served a dumb arrest upon his tongue,   1780
Who, mad that sorrow should his use control,
Or keep him from heart-easing words so long,
Begins to talk; but through his lips do throng
    Weak words, so thick come in his poor heart's aid
    That no man could distinguish what he said.   1785

Yet sometime 'Tarquin' was pronouncèd plain,
But through his teeth, as if the name he tore.
This windy tempest, till it blow up rain,
Held back his sorrow's tide to make it more;
At last it rains, and busy winds give o'er.   1790
    Then son and father weep with equal strife
    Who should weep most, for daughter or for wife.

The one doth call her his, the other his,
Yet neither may possess the claim they lay:
The father says 'She's mine.' 'O mine she is,'   1795
Replies her husband. 'Do not take away
My sorrow's interest; let no mourner say
    He weeps for her, for she was only mine,
    And only must be wailed by Collatine.'

'O,' quoth Lucretius, 'I did give that life   1800
Which she too early and too late hath spilled.'

instances of 'too late' as 'so recently' involve similar patterns. See *3 Henry VI*, 2.5.92–3, 'O boy! thy father gave thee life too soon, | And hath bereft thee of thy life too late', and *Romeo and Juliet*, 1.5.139, 'Too early seen unknown, and known too late!'.

spilled destroyed; the metaphor takes 'life' to be synonymous with blood. On the rhyme with '**killed**' (l. 1803) and '**filled**' (l. 1804), and on the sounding, or not, of final *-ed*, see 50–2n. Q's spellings are 'spil'd', 'kil'd' and 'fild'.

1803   **owed** owned.
  that the thing which.
1805   **dispersed** scattered; the adjective is transferred from the 'clamours', i.e. they are scattered through the air. Possibly the adjective could apply to the air, in that it has been 'driven asunder' (OED 1a) by their cries. The metre requires that 'dispersed' is pronounced on the first syllable.
  who which.
  life her soul, the 'wingèd sprite' of l. 1728.
1806   The air echoes the cries of Collatine and Lucretius exactly. Compare the echo song in *Venus and Adonis*, ll. 830–1 (see note, on the tradition underlying it).
1808   **emulation** competition; see 'strife', l. 1791. Compare *Troilus and Cressida*, 4.5.122–3: 'The obligation of our blood forbids | A gory emulation 'twixt us twain'.
1809   **clothe** adorn, cover; this is the point at which Brutus throws off his disguise of foolishness, and recovers his intelligence and status; see 1734n.
  state prestige.
  pride dignity.
1810   **Burying** pronounced with two syllables.
  folly's show display of foolishness and/or stupidity; see 1734n.
1812   **silly** frivolous, ridiculous (OED³ *adj.*, *n.*, and *adv.*, A6a).
  idiots fools (OED³ A3); the word can denote the professional fools who are evoked here, but it also suggests unintentionally absurd and unintelligent figures. Shakespeare's other uses of 'idiot' all tend in the latter direction.
1813   **sportive** jesting.
1814   **shallow** superficial (OED *adj.*1 and *n.*3, 6).
  habit (i) demeanour; (ii) pose; it can also suggest clothing (OED 1), and the physical verb ('throws...by') brings that sense to the surface.
  by away.
1815   **policy** (i) prudence, shrewdness (OED³ 5a); (ii) contrivance, cunning (OED³ 3).
  him himself.
1816   **advisedly** prudently; see 180n.
1819   **unsounded** unfathomed; nobody has measured the depths of Brutus' mind. Compare *2 Henry VI*, 3.1.56–7, 'Gloucester is a man | Unsounded yet and full of deep deceit'.

See also *Two Gentlemen of Verona*, 3.2.77–80, 'For Orpheus' lute was strung with poets' sinews, | Whose golden touch could soften steel and stones, | Make tigers tame, and huge leviathans | Forsake unsounded deeps to dance on sands'. Here there is wordplay on another sense of 'unsounded', OED *adj.*2, 'not sounded, uttered, or pronounced'; this sense resonates in *Lucrece* too, as Brutus too has never truly spoken until this point.
1820   **set. . . to school** teach. . . a lesson.
1821–41 Livy 1.59.4 (see Appendix 2) states that the Romans were affected by the fact that Brutus, an unlikely source, was urging them to take revenge. His opening idea is proverbial; see Dent D125, 'to lament the dead avails not and revenge vents hatred'.
1821   **Why** come on!
1822   **help. . . help** There is a case for emending the first of these to 'heal' (as suggested by Walker 1860), which fits well with wounds, and avoids awkward repetition; compositorial eye-slip might have caused the doubling. However, the parallel is not so awkward as to require amendment.
  grievous heinous; there is no etymological link between 'grief' and 'grievous', but there is word-play nonetheless.
1825   **childish humour** immature behaviour; compare *3 Henry VI*, 5.4.37–8, 'Why, courage then! what cannot be avoided, | 'Twere childish weakness to lament or fear'.
1826   **so** in this way.
1829   **relenting** softening; see OED³ 'relent, *v.*1', 2 for transitive use. Shakespeare does not use it transitively anywhere else; compare *Venus and Adonis*, l. 200.
1832   **That. . . suffer** i.e. asking them to allow.
  abominations, See 704n. Qu has no punctuation after this word; Qc provides a full stop. Q3 is the first edition to give a comma.
1834   **chased** to be chased (following 'suffer'). There may be some word-play on 'chaste' here, emphasising the proper purity of Rome. On the rhyme with '*disgraced*' (l. 1833), and on the sounding, or not, of final *-ed*, see 50–2n. Q's spellings are 'disgraced' and 'chaced'.

'Woe, woe,' quoth Collatine, 'she was my wife;
I owed her, and 'tis mine that she hath killed.'
'My daughter' and 'My wife' with clamours filled
    The dispersed air, who, holding Lucrece' life,   1805
      Answered their cries, 'My daughter' and 'My wife'.

Brutus, who plucked the knife from Lucrece' side,
Seeing such emulation in their woe,
Began to clothe his wit in state and pride,
Burying in Lucrece' wound his folly's show.   1810
He with the Romans was esteemèd so
    As silly jeering idiots are with kings,
      For sportive words and uttering foolish things.

But now he throws that shallow habit by,
Wherein deep policy did him disguise,   1815
And armed his long-hid wits advisedly,
To check the tears in Collatinus' eyes.
'Thou wrongèd lord of Rome,' quoth he, 'arise.
    Let my unsounded self, supposed a fool,
      Now set thy long-experienced wit to school.   1820

'Why, Collatine, is woe the cure for woe?
Do wounds help wounds, or grief help grievous deeds?
Is it revenge to give thyself a blow
For his foul act, by whom thy fair wife bleeds?
Such childish humour from weak minds proceeds.   1825
    Thy wretched wife mistook the matter so,
      To slay herself that should have slain her foe.

'Courageous Roman, do not steep thy heart
In such relenting dew of lamentations,
But kneel with me and help to bear thy part,   1830
To rouse our Roman gods with invocations,
That they will suffer these abominations,
    Since Rome herself in them doth stand disgraced,
      By our strong arms from forth her fair streets chased.

1835   ***Capitol*** The Capitoline is one of the seven hills of Rome. It was an important religious centre, the site of temples to Jupiter, Juno and Minerva; the Tarquins, including Tarquinius Superbus (the father of the Tarquin of *Lucrece*), commissioned some of these. In *Titus Andronicus*, 1.1.39, 41–3, this religious association is invoked, 'Let us entreat [...] in the Capitol and Senate's right, | Whom you pretend to honour and adore, | That you withdraw you, and abate your strength'. However, even here the association between the Capitoline and the Senate, and thus the political heart of Rome, is evident. The Roman Senate building, the *Curia Julia*, was at the foot of the Capitoline Hill. In *Julius Caesar* the Capitol is frequently invoked, as the place to which Caesar may or may not go on the fateful day. It is clear in that play that it is the location of Republican politics, as in *Julius Caesar*, 1.2.185–8, 'Cicero | Looks with such ferret and such fiery eyes | As we have seen him in the Capitol, | Being crossed in conference by some senators'. The extent to which this moment in *Lucrece* has political resonance is crucial: the more Brutus is invoking a political spirit, the more the poem associates the fall of the Tarquins with Republicanism; this is, after all, very late in the poem, and while much has been said about the responsibilities of monarchs, there has been little anti-monarchical sentiment.

1836–9   ***stained. . . maintained. . . complained***   On the sounding, or not, of final -ed, see 50–2n. Q's spellings are 'stained', 'maintained' and 'complained'.

1836   ***chaste blood*** The phrase in the oath is used by Painter (Appendix 2, translating 'castissimum. . . sanguem', 'most pure blood', Livy 1.59.1) and in Chaucer's *Legend of Good Women*, 1862, 'by hir chaste blood'; Ovid has the same idea, 'castam cruorem', *Fasti*, 2.841 (see Appendix 2).

1837   ***fat*** fertile (OED, *adj.* and *n*.2, A9a).
store abundance; see l. 97 and note.

1838   ***country*** national; see OED³ 'country, *n*. and *adj*.', C1a.
rights The primary sense is 'legal entitlement' (OED³ 8), but the homophony with 'rites' adds to the sense that these are sacred things by which one would swear.

1839   ***that*** Technically it was Lucrece who complained, but the pronoun merges her with her soul.
complained lamented (OED 1a).

1841   ***true*** faithful.

1842–8   The stanza closely follows Livy (see Appendix 2) in dwelling on the Roman lords' amazement that Brutus should be the one giving this exhortation. Ovid (*Fasti*, 2.845–6; see Appendix 2) depicts Lucrece's eyes and hairs posthumously stirring in assent.

1843   ***end*** complete.

1844   ***protestation*** declaration; as at l. 1700.

1845   ***allow*** (i) 'approve of, sanction; to receive with favour or approval' (OED³ 1a); (ii) commend (OED³ 2); see Sonnet 112.4.

1846   ***jointly*** together; see l. 1410.

1847   ***deep*** solemn, profound.

1849   ***advisèd doom*** considered judgement. Compare l. 180 and note, and *Richard II*, 1.3.188–9, 'Nor never by advised purpose meet | To plot, contrive, or complot any ill', and Sonnet 49.4; also *As You Like It*, 1.2.83–4, 'Firm and irrevocable is my doom | Which I have passed upon her; she is banished', and Sonnet 145.7.

1850   ***conclude*** resolve (OED 12a).

1850–1   The display of Lucrece's body contravenes her wish for obscurity in her dishonoured state, but it helps to motivate the Romans to expel the Tarquins. In Ovid's *Fasti*, 2.849, her wound is revealed on the way to her funeral, to general outrage ('volnus inane patet'; the gaping wound appears); in Livy 1.59.3 she is displayed in the forum at Collatia (for both, see Appendix 2). In Chaucer's *Legend of Good Women*, ll. 1865–8, she is put on show in Rome, where her death occurs: 'And openly the tale he tolde hem alle, | And openly let cary her on a bere | Thurgh al the toun, that men may see and here | The horryble dede of hir oppressyoun'. Shakespeare, then, may offer a particularly purposeful journey and display, but this depends on whether Collatium is seen as part of Rome or not. In Arg.8, Arg.15 (and notes) it seems possible that it is; Arg.22, which describes the equivalent moment to ll. 1850–1, does most to separate them.

1851   ***thorough*** through, perhaps with the suggestion of 'throughout'.

1852   ***publish*** make public; there is an echo of l. 33 (see note).

1853   ***with speedy diligence*** This could refer to the publishing of Tarquin's offence, or to the consent; Q has a comma before and after the phrase. The punctuation of this edition

'Now, by the Capitol that we adore,   1835
And by this chaste blood so unjustly stained,
By heaven's fair sun that breeds the fat earth's store,
By all our country rights in Rome maintained,
And by chaste Lucrece' soul that late complained
    Her wrongs to us, and by this bloody knife,   1840
    We will revenge the death of this true wife.'

This said, he struck his hand upon his breast,
And kissed the fatal knife to end his vow,
And to his protestation urged the rest,
Who, wondering at him, did his words allow.   1845
Then jointly to the ground their knees they bow,
    And that deep vow which Brutus made before
    He doth again repeat, and that they swore.

When they had sworn to this advisèd doom
They did conclude to bear dead Lucrece thence,   1850
To show her bleeding body thorough Rome,
And so to publish Tarquin's foul offence;
Which being done, with speedy diligence
    The Romans plausibly did give consent
    To Tarquin's everlasting banishment.   1855

reflects a preference for giving of consent, where the speed seems more fitting. The emphasis on rapidity might (i) recall the beginning of the poem, 'in post' (l. 1) and/or (ii) reflect the ready enthusiasm of the Romans for the political change being proposed.

1854 *plausibly* 'with applause; approvingly' (OED³ 1); compare the 'general acclamation' in the Argument, ll. 25–6. Shakespeare does not use the adverb anywhere else, and his only use of 'plausible' has a different meaning; compare *Measure for Measure*, 3.1.243–4, 'Go you to Angelo; answer his requiring with a plausible [i.e. believable] obedience'. Thus it is hard to know whether to take this as literal applause or not. The Roman context may suggest a greater presence for the Latin root, *plaudo*, which in Thomas Cooper's *Thesaurus Linguae Romanae et Britannicae* (1578) is translated as 'To rejoice with countenance: to clap the hands together for joy' (sig. 5D3v); this suggests that it is best to think of physical applause underlying Shakespeare's adverb.
consent This echoes a phrase, 'with one consent', used twice in the Argument

(ll. 21, 24). Burrow (2002: 338) sees this as 'a strong piece of evidence for the consistency of political outlook of poem and argument'. 'Consent', which points towards Republican values, is a resonant enough political word that it can bear this weight, but it is isolated and not much anticipated by earlier parts of *Lucrece*.

1855 *Tarquin's* Q has no possessive apostrophe, so this could refer to Sextus Tarquinius in the singular, or the Tarquins collectively. The former is in keeping with the vast majority of the poem, which focuses on an individual outrage; the latter is in keeping with the brief but vital political turn at the end of the poem. The Argument, l. 25, says that 'the Tarquins were all exiled'; other parallels at the end of the poem (see 1854n) add to the possibility that the plural and its implications should be chosen. However, l. 1855 says 'Tarquins', not 'the Tarquins', and the singular thus sounds more natural, especially in a modern version; in original spelling there was no need to decide either way, which in this case is a productive ambiguity.

'Let the Bird of Loudest Lay'

Title, publication in *Love's Martyr* and authorship

Since 1807, when the title first appeared in two Boston editions of Shakespeare's *Poems and Works*, 'Let the Bird of Loudest Lay' has often been known as 'The Phoenix and the Turtle' (i.e. turtle-dove), with or without the second definite article (Rollins 1938: 560–1). Prior to that, there was an editorial tradition of printing 'Let the Bird of Loudest Lay' as the twentieth poem in *The Passionate Pilgrim* (e.g. Malone 1780; see Rollins 1938: 560).

The poem first appeared in a supplement to Robert Chester's *Love's martyr: or, Rosalin's Complaint. Allegorically shadowing the truth of love, in the constant fate of the phoenix and turtle*, printed in 1601 for the bookseller Edward Blount by Richard Field (who also printed *Venus and Adonis* – see headnote to that poem – and *Lucrece*). There are three extant copies of *Love's Martyr*: in the Huntington Library, Folger Shakespeare Library and National Library of Wales (imperfect). There are no known manuscript copies.

Chester's sequence of poems uses a loose and digressive narrative about Dame Nature's search for a suitable mate for the phoenix (lest she die without issue) to bring together a diverse range of material, from Arthurian legend to catalogues of plants, minerals, animals and birds. The work is dedicated to the Welsh gentleman Sir John Salusbury (*c*. 1566–1612), himself an amateur poet (his verses are printed in Brown 1913). Salusbury, whose family seat was at Lleweni, Denbighshire, was descended (via an illegitimate son) from Henry VII (Duncan-Jones and Woudhuysen 2007: 98). He was educated at Jesus College, Oxford and the Middle Temple, where he was admitted on 19 March 1595, the same month that he became an Esquire of the Body to Elizabeth I; he was knighted in June 1601 – the year in which *Love's Martyr* was printed – for his loyalty to Elizabeth during the Essex revolt, a rebellion in which his own cousin, Owen Salusbury, one of Essex's supporters, was killed (Duncan-Jones and Woudhuysen 2007; Hume 1989; *ODNB*). The knighthood completed the restoration of the family's fortunes, which had suffered after the execution of his elder brother, Thomas, for his involvement in the Babington Plot to assassinate Elizabeth I in 1586.

There is some debate about the identity of the poet Robert Chester. Grosart (1878) proposed Robert Chester of Royston, Hertfordshire (1566–1640), an identification dismissed by Brown (1913), who instead argued that the author of *Love's Martyr* was closely linked not to south-east England but Lleweni, where Salusbury lived. Little is known of this other 'Denbighshire' Chester (whose signature differs from the Royston Chester; Brown 1913: li). The lack of documentary evidence for the Denbighshire Chester has led Duncan-Jones and Woudhuysen (2007: 106) to suggest that critics have been too quick to dismiss Grosart's candidate (who was – like Salusbury – a member of the Middle Temple). Nonetheless, both *ODNB* and Borukhov (2009) have found evidence that places a Robert Chester (other than the Royston one) within Salusbury's household, perhaps serving as a chaplain or secretary, since four surviving documents associated with the

Salusbury household are written, or signed by, this other Denbighshire Chester, most significantly (i) a memorandum of fees paid by Salusbury in 1601, when he was knighted, and (ii) a series of poems on members of Salusbury's family preserved in Christ Church, Oxford MS 184, including a Christmas-time poem, 'A poor shepherd's introduction made in a merriment [. . .] at the house of the right worshipful John Salusbury of Lleweni' (Borukhov 2009: 78).

Two additional factors make it unlikely that the Royston Chester was the author of *Love's Martyr*: (i) the Royston Chester was an esquire; that social status is nowhere asserted in *Love's Martyr*, as one would expect, if its author held that rank, nor in the documents the Denbighshire Chester wrote and signed (Borukhov 2009: 79); (ii) it is likely that the author of *Love's Martyr* was Welsh, since the title-page presents Chester as a 'British', not 'English', poet, an adjective which was strongly associated with Wales in the sixteenth century (see, for example, William Averell's *An Excellent History [. . .] of Charles and Julia, two British, or rather Welsh lovers* (1581)). Borukhov further argues that some of the spellings in *Love's Martyr* ('voutsafe' for 'vouchsafe'; 'vading' for 'fading') 'suggest the influence of the Welsh language' (2009: 79). (As William Salesbury's 1550 *Brief and plain introduction, teaching how to pronounce the letters of the British tongue (now commonly called Welsh)* explains, the English digraph 'ch' – as in 'church' – does not appear in sixteenth-century Welsh, and 'f' is pronounced 'v' (sigs B2v, B4v), although Salesbury notes the latter also occurs in some English dialects.)

How 'Let the Bird of Loudest Lay' came to be published with *Love's Martyr* is unclear. It is part of a series of poems, also dedicated to Salusbury, appended to that volume and divided from Chester's verses by an internal title-page, which announces that:

> Hereafter follow diverse Poetical Essays on the former Subject; viz: the Turtle and Phoenix. Done by the best and chiefest of our modern writers, with their names subscribed to their particular works: never before extant. And (now first) consecrated by them all generally, to the love and merit of the true noble knight, Sir John Salusbury. *Dignum laude virum Musa vetat mori*. ['The Muse will not let the man who deserves praise perish', Horace, *Odes* 4.8.28] MDCI. [1601].

Pagination and signatures follow straight on from *Love's Martyr*, so it is clear the 'Poetical Essays' were intended to be joined with Chester's work at the inception of that publication. The presence of these additional poems is also advertised on the title-page to the whole volume, which declares that 'To these [Chester's poems] are added some new compositions, of several modern writers whose names are subscribed to their several works, upon the first subject: viz. the Phoenix and Turtle.'

The contents of these 'Diverse Poetical Essays' comprise the following:

No.	Title	Incipit	pp.	Attribution
(i)	'Invocatio, Ad Apollinem & Pierides' [Invocation, to Apollo & the Muses]	'Good Fate, fair Thespian Deities'	167	'Vatum Chorus' [the chorus of poets] (p. 167)
(ii)	'To the worthily honoured knight Sir John Salusbury'	'Noblest of minds, here do the Muses bring'	168	'Vatum Chorus' (p. 168)
1	'The first'	'The silver vault of heaven, hath but one eye'	169	'Ignoto' [Unknown] (p. 169)
2	'The burning'	'Suppose here burns this wonder of a breath'	169	

3		'Let the bird of loudest lay'	170–1	'William Shakes-peare' (p. 172)
4	'Threnos'	'Beauty, Truth, and Rarity'	172	
5	'A narration and description of a most exact wondrous creature, arising out of the Phoenix and Turtle Dove's ashes'	'O 'twas a moving *Epicedium* [funeral ode]!'	173	'John Marston' (p. 176)
6	'The description of this perfection'	'Dares then thy too audacious sense'	174	
7	'To perfection. A sonnet'	'Oft have I gazed with astonished eye'	174–5	
8	'Perfectioni hymnus' [A hymn to perfection]	'What should I call this creature'	175–6	
9	'Peristeros: or the male Turtle'	'Not like that loose and parti-livered sect'	176	'George Chapman' (p. 176)
10	'Praeludium' [Prelude]	'We must sing too? What subject shall we choose?'	177–8	
11	'Epos' [Song]	'Not to know vice at all, and keep true state'	178–82	'Ben: Johnson' (p. 182)
12	'The Phoenix analysed'	'Now, after all, let no man'	182	
13	'Ode ἐνθουσιασικὴ [sic]' [Inspired ode]	'Splendour! O more than mortal'	182–3	'Ben: Johnson' (p. 183)

This table presents as straightforward two issues which are debateable: first, whether or not 'Let the Bird of Loudest Lay' and 'Threnos' are one or two poems; and secondly, if they are two poems, whether the attribution 'William Shakes-peare' (which appears after the 'Threnos') applies to both. Although in the text that follows in this edition, 'Let the Bird of Loudest Lay' and 'Threnos' have been given through-lineation, the poems can be seen as two separate items (as in the table), owing (i) to the difference in their poetic form (although sharing the same metre, their rhyme schemes are, respectively *abba* and *aaa*); and (ii) the *mise-en-page*, which inserts a decorative border at the head of the page, above the 'Threnos'. However, 'Let the Bird of Loudest Lay' and 'Threnos' are closely linked: the 'Threnos' supplies the 'threne' promised in in l. 49, and – unlike the other poems in the volume – both verses treat the Phoenix as dying without issue.

Although the attribution of 'Let the Bird of Loudest Lay' to Shakespeare is less certain than those of other poems where his name appears on a title-page, the presence in the 'Poetical Essays' of other named writers (all prominent metropolitan poet-playwrights by this time) makes it extremely likely that it is his (see also comments under 'Form and style' below). The verses in 'Poetical Essays' appear to be grouped by author: the collection begins with two preliminary verses by the 'chorus' of poets; it ends with a cluster by Jonson. It is also a collection which seems concerned with attribution: the anonymous poems are subscribed 'Ignoto', not simply left unascribed, and it is quite conventional in both print and manuscript miscellanies for a subscription to cover all the poems between it and a prior subscription, although admittedly that convention is complicated here by the appearance of two separate attributions to poems by Jonson.

The presence of Shakespeare, Jonson, Chapman and Marston in a volume by an otherwise amateur and probably provincial poet is intriguing. *Love's Martyr* was Chester's only print publication. The whole of the 1601 volume, including the 'Poetical Essays', may have been Chester's project, but other potential candidates have greater influence and better connections. Hume (1989) argues that it was the poetry-loving Salusbury who contacted the 'modern' poets who contributed the 'Poetical Essays', since he was acquainted with the London theatrical scene through his late brother-in-law Ferdinando Stanley, fifth earl of Derby (1559?–1594), one-time patron of Chapman and the playing company Strange's Men. Salusbury may also have known Marston, since both men were members of Middle Temple, a fact that leads Duncan-Jones (2001a: 143) to propose that it was Marston who was responsible for assembling the authors of the 'Poetical Essays'.

Jonson provides another, alternative link between Salusbury and the other poets, and consequently may have acted as broker: an autograph copy of Jonson's 'Ode to James, Earl of Desmond' appears in a miscellany owned by the Salusbury family (Christ Church, Oxford, MS 184, which also preserves Chester's lyrics on the Salusbury family), and drafts of Jonson's 'Praeludium' and 'Epos' are found in National Library of Wales MS 5390D, compiled by members of the Salusbury family in the early to mid-seventeenth century (CELM). Jonson would go on to collaborate with Chapman and Marston on *Eastward Ho!* in 1605 and was a notorious friend and rival of Shakespeare (Bland 2000; Hume 1989; Williams 1981–2). As Burrow suggests (2002: 88–9), it was possible that, in 1601, Jonson and Chapman were both actively looking for a new patron in the aftermath of the Essex revolt: Chapman had dedicated his translation of the first seven books of Homer's *Iliad* to Essex in 1598, and Bland (2000) argues that Jonson had been angling for Essex's patronage immediately prior to the earl's fall. In these circumstances, the recently honoured Salusbury, with his taste for poetry and record as a literary patron in the second half of the 1590s, may have looked a promising prospect: other books dedicated to Salusbury include Robert Parry's *Sinetes' Passions* (1597) and William Rankins' *Seven Satires* (1598). Certainly, the publication of *Love's Martyr*, which refers to 'Sir John Salusbury', must postdate his knighthood in June 1601.

Whatever the cause and motivation for assembling this 'chorus' of poets, the presentation of their contributions undoubtedly lives up to their soubriquet of 'modern', a term which in the late sixteenth century indicated not so much being 'current' as looking back to the ancient past in order to move forward (see Withington 2010: 73–101), as in Robert Barret's 1598 *Theorike and Practike of Modern Wars*, which promotes Roman military practices and rigour as a model that contemporary armies should follow. In the 'Poetical Essays', this modish classicism is reflected in the ostentatiously Latin and Greek vocabulary used to describe the poetic offerings: 'epicedium', 'epos', 'praeludium' and 'threnos' would all have been unusual terms for most readers, as would 'peristeros' (the Greek for dove/pigeon) and the (mistranscribed) Greek in the title of the final ode. These 'modern' poems also make an odd fit with Chester's part of the volume, which is much more backwards-looking in its orientation, with its use of more traditional vernacular forms (e.g. allegorical poetry, verse dialogue) and motifs (e.g. 'Dame Nature', Arthurian legend).

Despite the presence of the 'Poetical Essays' by 'the best and chiefest of our modern writers', the volume was not a commercial success, although the poet William Drummond includes 'loves martir' among his 1606 list of 'books read by me' (National Library of Scotland, MS 2059, fol. 362r). The initial print-run clearly did not sell out, since the collection was reissued by the printer Edward Allde for the bookseller Matthew Lownes in 1611 using leftover sheets from the 1601 edition, omitting Chester's name from the title-page and with a new title – *The annals of great Britain. Or, a most excellent monument wherein may be seen all the antiquities of this kingdom* – presumably designed to exploit the early seventeenth-century antiquarian interest in British history. Only one known copy of *The Annals*, held by the British Library, survives.

'Let the Bird of Loudest Lay' was also reprinted in Benson's 1640 *Poems* (where the first line reads 'Let the bird of lowest lay', sig. K6v). Benson accepts Shakespeare's authorship of both 'Let the Bird' and the 'Threnos', which he prints consecutively (although divided by a ruled line).

Date

'Let the Bird of Loudest Lay' was probably written specially for the 1601 volume: certainly it would seem to respond to Chester's contribution in the way that the phoenix and turtle-dove are uncharacteristically gendered female and male respectively and not, as usual, the other way round. Nevertheless, some critics, including Brown (1913) and Honigmann (1985: 90–113) date it and much of *Love's Martyr* to the 1580s, connecting the volume with Salusbury's marriage in 1586 to Ursula Stanley (the illegitimate but acknowledged daughter of Henry Stanley, fourth earl of Derby); for Honigmann the poem thus becomes evidence to corroborate his theory that Shakespeare's 'lost years' in the 1580s were spent in the household of the Derbyshire Stanleys (a Catholic family).

However, as Burrow (2002: 84) argues, it was unlikely that *Love's Martyr* was written before 1590: its combination of allegory with chorographic, historical, encyclopaedic and erotic strains would seem to place it as a work postdating Spenser's *Faerie Queene*, the first three books of which were published in 1590. Burrow also finds parallels in the works of Samuel Daniel, published from 1592 onwards, and allusions to both *Venus and Adonis* ('under this | Fair Venus from Adonis stole a kiss', sig. C1v), and *Lucrece* (sig. A4v), both of which were printed in the mid-1590s. Jove's description of the Isle of Paphos – where 'The crocodile and hissing adder's sting | May not come near this holy plot of ground; | No nightworm in this continent may sing, | Nor poison-spitting serpent may be found' (sig. C2r) – is also reminiscent of the fairies' song in *A Midsummer Night's Dream* (printed in 1600): 'You spotted snakes with double tongue [. . .] | Newts and blind-worms, do no wrong, | Come not near our fairy queen' (2.2.9–12). See also 'Form and style', below. Furthermore, the title-page to *Love's Martyr* announces the 'Diverse Poetical Essays' as 'new compositions'. The fact that this is patently designed to advertise the volume does not necessarily discredit this information; Field could, for example, have chosen to promote the work with the much-used formulation 'never before imprinted' (as Thorpe does for the 1609 edition of *Shakespeare's Sonnets*).

Contexts and readings

'Let the Bird of Loudest Lay' has a history of perplexing readers and critics: it seems to invite allegorical interpretation, and it follows *Love's Martyr*, which belongs even more clearly to the allegorical tradition (although there is no critical consensus as to the allegorical meaning of Chester's poem). *Love's Martyr* combines two myths: that of the faithful turtle-dove, true to its dead mate, and that of the unique phoenix who, after a lifespan of five or six hundred years, burns to ashes, from which a new phoenix (or the old phoenix rejuvenated) hatches. The conventional turtle-dove of love poetry is female, but that of *Love's Martyr* and the accompanying 'Poetical Essays' is male.

'Let the Bird of Loudest Lay' complicates these mythological elements still further, since there is no indication that a new phoenix will rise from the ashes (Ellrodt 1962; Copland 1965; Schwartz 1969; McCoy 1997). This lack of an heir is emphasised by the fact that the funeral ceremonies in Shakespeare's poem have to be performed by other birds summoned for the occasion and not, as in myth, by the new phoenix, who usually carries the ashes of the old phoenix to the temple of the sun (Ovid, *Metamorphoses*, 15.391–407; Golding, 15.431–48). Shakespeare seems to be rebuked for failing to mention the new phoenix in Marston's poem that follows: 'can blackest Fate consume | So rare creation? No' ('O 'twas a moving *Epicedium*!', ll. 2–3).

Critics have argued for diverse allegorical interpretations of Shakespeare's Phoenix and Turtle. Knight (1955), for example, sees the Turtle as Shakespeare himself, or as his personified love for the young man to whom he addressed many of his sonnets. However, there are two main strands of interpretation: one looks to the dedicatee, the other to Elizabeth I; Duncan-Jones and Woudhuysen (2007) connect both strands, by placing *Love's Martyr* and the 'Poetical Essays' in the political context of summer and autumn 1601, when Salusbury was first waiting for Elizabeth to summon parliament, and then attempting to be elected as MP for Denbighshire, an election which was abandoned after 'violent scuffles between hundreds of rival supporters in the churchyard [at Wrexham]', meaning that when Parliament opened on 27 October, it still lacked a member for Denbighshire (107–8).

In the Salusbury-related readings, Sir John is the Turtle, the Phoenix either his wife Ursula (Brown 1913; Buxton 1980; Honigmann 1985), or Dorothy Halsall, Salusbury's sister-in-law, named through acrostics in Salusbury's 'Poesy 1', printed in *Sinetes' Passions* in 1597 (sigs D7r–v; see Williams 1981–2). However, it is hard to see how Shakespeare's poem with its emphasis on married chastity could be appropriate either to a marriage that had produced, by 1601, eleven children, or to an adulterous (and technically incestuous) liaison.

The Stanley connection – combined with the ritualistic elements of 'Let the Bird of Loudest Lay', with its invocation of the Latin mass – also provides fertile ground for those such as Honigmann (1985) who are interested in Shakespeare's Catholic affiliations and potential sympathies. The poem's potential for such 'recusant' readings is illustrated by Finnis and Martin (2003), who argue that the Phoenix is the Catholic widow Anne Line/Lyne, executed in 1601, and the Turtle, her husband Roger, who died in 1595. However, the theory is so specific that Finnis and Martin have to identify particular readers to whom it would have been meaningful, namely the circle of Edward Somerset, the fourth Earl of Worcester, who – whilst conformist – had Catholic leanings, and who is unsteadily identified with the eagle of l. 11.

The most common reading of Shakespeare's Phoenix is as a representation of Elizabeth I. Elizabeth used the iconography of the phoenix (Yates 1947; Strong 1963), coupling her phoenix emblem with the motto *Semper eadem* (always the same), or occasionally with the motto *Sola phoenix omnis mundi* (the only phoenix in the whole world). An oil painting, associated with Nicholas Hilliard, known as the Phoenix portrait (National Portrait Gallery 190, *c.* 1575) uses the symbol on a medallion worn on the queen's bodice. Another image of Elizabeth, the Phoenix Jewel (British Museum, SLMisc.1778, *c.* 1570–80), has a phoenix rising from flames on the back and a portrait of the queen on the front. Elizabeth also appears as a phoenix in Shakespeare and Fletcher's *Henry VIII* (1612), where Cranmer prophesies the succession of James I to the English throne (5.4.39–47).

For those critics who read Elizabeth into Shakespeare's Phoenix, the Turtle can stand for the love and fidelity of her subjects (Axton 1977; Hume 1989), or her faithful knight, Sir John Salusbury (Harrison 1951), or Robert Devereux, Earl of Essex (Grosart 1878; Matchett 1965; Oakeshott 1975; McCoy 1997). The latter is unlikely: Essex was executed early in 1601, making a work about him at this time extremely provocative and dangerous. Moreover, as Hume (1989) points out, Salusbury had helped to suppress the Essex Rebellion (and had been rewarded for this service), and is therefore an unlikely dedicatee for a volume celebrating Essex and his relationship with Elizabeth. A further problem with all three theories is that, if Elizabeth is indeed Shakespeare's Phoenix, then her death is being commemorated two years before it occurred, and after the extension of the Treason laws in 1571, it was treasonable to 'compass, imagine, invent, devise or intend the death or destruction, or any bodily harm tending to death, destruction, maim or wounding of the royal person' (Elton 1982: 73).

Thomas Churchyard's 'A few plain verses of truth against the flattery of time' and 'Verses of value', in *Churchyard's Challenge* (1593: sigs 2D4v–2E1r, 2E2r–2E3v), depict the living queen as a phoenix to celebrate her uniqueness and durability; nevertheless – unlike Shakespeare's poem – Churchyard's never mention the phoenix's death. Axton (1977) meets the objection that Elizabeth is still alive in 1601 by drawing attention to the lines by Ignoto preceding 'Let the Bird of Loudest Lay', which ask the reader to imagine the burning has already occurred ('Suppose here burns the wonder of a breath', l. 1). However, this does not detract from the fact that Shakespeare's poem portrays the Phoenix as a 'dead bird' (l. 67), a treasonable act if it signifies Elizabeth.

Elizabeth was not the only contemporary figure celebrated through this image. The poet Philip Sidney was figured as a phoenix in John Phillip's 1587 elegy, *The life and death of Sir Philip Sidney*, where 'sweet Sidney' is described as 'This Phoenix [. . .] the flower of courtesy, who in his lifetime gave a perfect light in his conversation [behaviour] to lead men to virtue [. . .] that by his example they might both learn to fear God, to glory in sincerity, to abound in loyalty, & to become careful lovers of their native country' (fol. 2r). Another elegy for Sidney in R[ichard] S[tapleton]'s *The Phoenix Nest* (1593) – 'An Elegy, or friend's passion, for his Astrophil' – includes a varied cast of birds, many of whom appear in 'Let the Bird of Loudest Lay', including a swan, eagle and (female) turtle-dove ('Example of immortal love', sig. B1v), who gather to mourn the (male) phoenix (Rollins 1931: 9–15). Duncan-Jones (2001a: 142) also points out that Salusbury's mother was commemorated after her death in 1591 as 'Britannica Phoenix' (the British, or Welsh, phoenix). The phoenix had more general, long-standing associations with love poetry too, found, for example, in Petrarch's *Rime Sparse* (*Rime*, 185, 210, 321) and Chaucer's *Book of the Duchess*, which respectively compare Laura and Blanche to the phoenix to compliment their beauty and uniqueness. *Rime Sparse* 135 also compares the speaker's love to the phoenix, burning and being reborn.

The poem has an important degree of neo-Platonic resonance (a further link with Petrarch's *Rime Sparse*) as it probes the notion of a transcendent love. It also sets up theological echoes, especially relating to the mystery of the Trinity, which again connect back to the multifarious phoenix, since the bird was used by the Church Fathers as an emblem of Christ's resurrection, and in medieval bestiaries to represent Christ himself (McMillan 1972). There is controversial potential in the poem's evocation of religious ceremony in an anti-Catholic age, and the phoenix was also associated with the Virgin Mary (see Shahani 1946). Yet none of the many meanings inherent in the phoenix offers the allegorical key to unlock Shakespeare's poem. Bednarz (2012) argues persuasively that the pursuit of specific allegory has not been fruitful; rather, the poem honours Salusbury, not by encoding political themes, but by fulfilling what Bednarz takes to be Salusbury's commission, i.e. to write about 'the truth of love'.

Form and style

'Let the Bird of Loudest Lay' is written in catalectic trochaic tetrameter (which omits the final, unstressed syllable), a form used by Sidney in the 'Eighth Song' in *Astrophil and Stella*, to which Everett (2001) argues Shakespeare is indebted, and by Shakespeare for the fairies' songs in *A Midsummer Night's Dream* (first performed c. 1595), 2.2.10–26; 5.1.371–422. The poem draws together different types of style, syntax and vocabulary, from the artfully Latinate to the monosyllabic Anglo-Saxon. The first fifty-two lines are in quatrains rhyming *abba*; the last fifteen – the 'threnos' – are in rhyming triplets (and can even be seen as a separate, but related, poem; see above). Garber (1984) usefully divides the poem into three sections: lines 1–20 are ceremonial and express simple ideas in complex ways through *periphrasis*; lines 21–52 (the anthem) express complex, contradictory ideas in deceptively simple terms; the final section (the threnos) continues from the anthem in exploring Reason's inability to deal with the martyrdom of the two birds.

It is probable that 'Let the Bird of Loudest Lay' was written within a year of *Hamlet* (c. 1600–1), and the two works have many words and themes in common, including problematic funeral scenes, an interest in confounded reason, and self-consciously technical philosophical vocabulary. Kermode (2000: 71) sees the poem sharing the deepening linguistic richness of *Hamlet* and *Twelfth Night* (1601); Schwartz (1969) and Campbell (1970) find further similarities with *Troilus and Cressida* (*c.* 1602) and *Othello* (*c.* 1603–4); see also Jackson (2001) for links between the vocabulary of the poem and Shakespeare's seventeenth-century plays. The poem shares numerous interests with the *Sonnets*, including the notion of transcendent love, the closeness of lovers, and the interaction of reason and passion. However, it is the link with *Hamlet* that is most evident and suggestive (see notes on ll. 1, 6, 7, 12, 16, 17, 26), which offers further corroboration for a date of composition *c.* 1600–1 (rather than earlier), and also an important connection between the two as experiments in words and thoughts that tend to evade conclusive action.

The poem's style is widely recognised as being unlike anything else Shakespeare wrote, even the songs in the plays, though the lament 'Fear no more the heat of the sun' in *Cymbeline* (4.2.258–81) has something of its reverent tone. Lewis (1980: 508–9) calls it a 'metaphysical poem', which 'we could not have guessed, I think, from internal evidence [. . .] was by Shakespeare'. Halliday (1964: 368) goes further, seeing the poem's un-Shakespearean qualities as evidence of its misattribution. However, it seems more likely that Shakespeare – writing outside his usual playhouse milieu – adopts and explores the uncharacteristic but fashionable tone and modes of thought of metaphysical poetry, a style associated with the Inns of Court, a key location in the production of *Love's Martyr* and its 'Poetical Essays', dedicated to, and including work by, Middle Templars.

There are a number of correspondences between Donne's poems, which epitomise the metaphysical style, and 'Let the Bird of Loudest Lay'. Bednarz (2012) argues that its depiction of mutuality influenced poems like Donne's 'The Canonization', where passion transforms the lovers, who die in flames (albeit the temporary death of orgasm), and whose love is similarly described as 'mysterious', or beyond reason. The most resonant section of 'The Canonization' (ll. 19–27) also refers to an eagle, dove (i.e. turtle) and phoenix. The general approach and strategy of 'Let the Bird of Loudest Lay' is similarly akin to Donne in the metaphysical mode it assumes, as Shakespeare addresses abstract principles, drawing on a range of semantic fields, from the alchemical (e.g. 'essence', 'simple', 'compounded', ll. 26, 44) to the mathematical and logical (see notes to ll. 26, 27, 28, 37, 42). The poem reaches a very different destination from Donne's metaphysical experiments, however. Hyland (2003: 202–3) sees it as an act of deliberate competition, an attempt to 'out-Donne Donne' (some of Donne's poetry was circulating in manuscript by 1601), and Underwood (1974: 260–2) makes pertinent distinctions between Donne's worldly, sexual work – which synthesises metaphysics and baser desires with dazzling wit – and Shakespeare's poem, which remains unworldly and symbolic.

1 **lay** song; the word was in common use in the period as a synonym for song (including bird song, as at Sonnet 98.5), but it could have an archaic quality, as at *Pericles*, 5.0.4, where it is spoken by the medieval poet Gower. In *Hamlet* it is used of elegy: the 'melodious lay' for Ophelia at 4.7.182. Bates (1955: 24–7) identifies the '**bird of loudest lay**' as a cock, citing *Hamlet*: 'The cock, that is the trumpet to the morn' (1.1.150). The bird has also been identified as a crane, described by Chaucer as 'the geaunt [giant], with his trompes sound' (*Parliament of Fowls*, l. 344); a nightingale; and even the phoenix itself, thanks to the poem *De Ave Phoenice* (attributed, possibly dubiously, to the third-century Latin philosopher Lactantius), which refers to the 'wonderful' [mira] voice of the phoenix (l. 46); compare Thomas Watson, *Hekatompathia*, Passion 11.3, which describes the 'wondrous force' of his mistress' voice, who is then being compared to a phoenix (1582: sig. B2r). However, of all the potential birds, the phoenix is the least likely, since it is dead and – in Shakespeare's poem – has no heir; the exact identity of the bird is probably less significant than the alliterative patterning of the line.

2 **sole Arabian tree** a palm tree, the traditional perch of the phoenix, deemed unique because the phoenix is unique. See *Tempest*, 3.3.21–4 ('Now I will believe | That there are unicorns; that in Arabia | There is one tree, the phoenix' throne, one phoenix | At this hour reigning there') and John Florio's *World of Words*: '*Rasin* [...] a tree in Arabia, whereof there is but one found, and upon it the Phoenix sits' (1598: sig. 2C8v). The words for phoenix and palm tree are etymologically connected in Greek and Hebrew; see Pliny's *History of the World*, trans. Philemon Holland: 'The bird Phoenix, which is supposed to have taken that name of this date tree (called in Greeke φοῖνιξ) for it was assured to me, that the said bird died with that tree, and revived of itself as the tree sprung again' (1601: sig. 2L2r). Garber (1984: 7) argues that the tree is 'sole' because it is now alone, deprived of its former inhabitant.

3 **Herald** For the role of Elizabethan heralds in arranging participating state events, see 9n.
sad serious.
trumpet trumpeter; compare *King John*, 1.1.27–8: 'Be thou the trumpet of our wrath, | And sullen presage of your own decay'.

4 **To** The verb *obey* is regularly used with preposition *to* in Elizabethan English, although (as Duncan-Jones and Woudhuysen 2007 note) the only other Shakespearean usage is at *Troilus and Cressida*, 3.1.150–2: 'His stubborn buckles [...] | Shall more obey than to the edge of steel'.
wings *synecdoche* for birds; the summoned birds – like the Phoenix and Turtle they mourn (l. 61) – are said to be '*chaste*'. The gathering of birds for another bird's funeral has a comic analogue in Ovid, *Amores*, 2.6, a poem that features a turtle-dove (whose loyal love is mentioned, ll. 12–16) helping to mourn a parrot, who will encounter the phoenix in Elysium (l. 54). Statius' *Silvae* 2.4 is a burlesque response to Ovid's mock-heroic poem and also features a comparable cast of birds.

5 **shrieking harbinger** the ominous owl, who is the forerunner (harbinger) of dire events, as in Chester's *Love's Martyr* ('The filthy messenger of ill to come | The sluggish Owl is, and to danger some', sig. R1r) or Chaucer's *Parliament of Fowls* ('The oule ek, that of deth the bode bryngeth', l. 343). Compare *Lucrece*, l. 165; *Venus and Adonis*, l. 531; *Midsummer Night's Dream*, 5.1.376–8: 'the screech-owl, screeching loud, | Puts the wretch that lies in woe | In remembrance of a shroud'.

6 **Foul** a possible pun on 'fowl'.
precurrer precursor, forerunner (compare 'harbinger', l. 5); this is the only instance of the word cited in OED[3] (a full-text search of EEBO-TCP provides no earlier citations either), but the word relates to 'precursor' (of which it may be a misspelling), 'precurrent' and 'precurse'; compare *Hamlet*, 1.1.121–3: 'And even the like precurse of feared events, | As harbingers preceding still the fates | And prologue to the omen coming on'. The collocation of 'precurse' and 'harbinger' is one of a number of echoes between the two works.
the fiend presumably, the Devil.

7 **Augur** prophet or soothsayer; in Roman times, the augur would divine the future by observing the flights and actions of birds (and other portents). Most of Shakespeare's uses of augur/augury are in classical contexts, although see Sonnet 107.6 (which seems to refer to recent events) or Hamlet's 'We defy augury. There is special providence in the fall of a sparrow' (5.2.219–20).
fever's end the end of illness, either by a cure, or in death.

8 **troop** company.

9 **session** sitting of a court or parliament, one of the ways in which Shakespeare's scene recalls Chaucer's *Parliament of Fowls*; for the potential

'Let the Bird of Loudest Lay'

> Let the bird of loudest lay,
> On the sole Arabian tree,
> Herald sad and trumpet be:
> To whose sound chaste wings obey.
>
> But thou, shrieking harbinger,   5
> Foul precurrer of the fiend,
> Augur of the fever's end,
> To this troop come thou not near.
>
> From this session interdict
> Every fowl of tyrant wing   10
> Save the eagle, feathered king:
> Keep the obsequy so strict.
>
> Let the priest in surplice white,
> That defunctive music can,

significance of parliament to the poem's 1601 context, and the dedication to Salusbury, see above 'Contexts and readings'. There follows a string of political vocabulary (interdict, tyrant, king), a strand in the poem highlighted by McCoy (1997). The heirless Phoenix leaves a problem of succession, which also threatened England in 1601, with its heirless and ageing queen. At times of unsettled succession in England, it was a herald's role to summon parliament to settle the matter.

    interdict prohibit; the only other occurrence of the word in Shakespeare (albeit in a different form) is at *Macbeth*, 4.3.106–7 ('the truest issue of thy throne | By his own interdiction stands accused').

10 ***fowl of tyrant wing*** bird of prey.

11 ***eagle*** The eagle is the only bird of prey to be exempted from the ban on 'tyrant' birds, owing – presumably – to its traditional regal status (as in Chester, *Love's Martyr*: 'The princely Eagle, of all birds the king', sig. Q3v).

12 ***obsequy*** funeral rites; Shakespeare uses this noun in seven other instances; in every other instance, in the plural.

    strict limited in number; see *Hamlet*, 5.1.226–7, where the Doctor discusses the limits on the 'obsequies' for Ophelia ('Her obsequies have been as far enlarged | As we have warranty').

13 ***surplice white*** loose white garment worn by clerics in church services; the swan is to act the part of priest because its plumage is white. Ecclesiastical vestments had been a point of contention in the earlier Elizabethan church, with puritan elements condemning remnants of Catholic formality. In 1601 the issue was less current, but this and other ceremonial features in the poem – such as the use of the Latin *requiem* (l. 16) – could have seemed controversial.

14 ***defunctive*** related to dying (a showy Latinism); this is the first citation in OED, and a full-text search of EEBO-TCP reveals no earlier examples. Shakespeare uses 'defunct' as an adjective at *Henry V*, 4.1.21 ('defunct and dead') and *Othello*, 1.3.263–4 ('the young affects | In me defunct'), and the noun 'defunction' as technical political jargon in *Henry V*, 1.2.57–8 ('Four hundred one and twenty years | After defunction of King Pharamond').

    can is skilled in; the word is of Old English derivation and – in the sense used here – was already archaic by the late sixteenth century; see Edmund Spenser, *Shepheardes Calender*, 'January', note by E.K. on l. 10: 'couthe: cometh of the verb "conne", that is, to know or to have skill'. Its proximity to the Latinate 'defunctive' shows Shakespeare experimenting with different strains of vocabulary.

15 **death-divining** refers to bird lore, where the swan senses its imminent death and sings its 'swan-song'; see *Lucrece*, ll. 1611–12.

16 **requiem** first word of the Latin Mass for the Dead ('Requiem aeternam dona eis, Domine', 'Give them eternal rest, O Lord'). In Protestant England, funeral rites would be spoken in English. Shakespeare's only other usage of this word is at *Hamlet*, 5.1.236–8, where the Doctor forbids Ophelia the full funeral rites: 'We should profane the service of the dead | To sing a requiem and such rest to her | As to peace-parted souls'.
lack his right not be properly observed (punning on 'rite'). The swan-priest's presence is necessary to ensure the full performance of the ceremony, hence it is 'his' (the swan's) right/rite; alternatively, 'his' is the neuter 'its' (as is possible in Elizabethan English), in which case the requiem itself lacks its 'right'. McCoy (1997) argues that the funeral rites are as 'maimed' as those of Ophelia in *Hamlet*, 5.1 (see above).

17 **treble-dated** refers to the reputedly long life of the crow; Pliny cites Hesiod on the belief that the crow lives nine times as long as a human (Pliny, *History*, trans. Holland, 1601: sig. Q6v). Like the swan and the cock, the crow is listed as a prophetic bird in Vincenzo Cartari's mythological handbook, *Le imagini degli dei degli antichi* (1571): see Eriksen (1981: 194).

18 **sable** black; the word appears nine other times in Shakespeare's works, four of which are in *Hamlet* (1.2.241, 2.2.452, 3.2.130, 4.7.80, the latter two referring to suits of black clothing, appropriate – as here – for mourning). The word is often used in rhetorically heightened or poetic situations (e.g. the 'Pyrrhus' speech, *Hamlet*, 2.2.452; Don Armado's letter, *Love's Labours Lost*, 1.1.231; Gower's prologue, *Pericles*, 5.0.19).
gender offspring (that which has been engendered, OED^3 2b).

19 **With . . . tak'st** refers to the belief, alluded to in Pliny's *History* (trans. Holland 1601: sig. 2A6v), that ravens reproduced by the male breathing into the female's beak; this chaste method of reproduction prefigures the union of the Phoenix and Turtle. Pliny treats this as popular misconception, arguing that ravens kiss (bill) like pigeons. This line also echoes lines from the burial service in the Elizabethan *Book of Common Prayer*: 'The Lord giveth, and the Lord taketh away' (2011: 171; see Davies 1995).

21 **anthem** a song of praise, particularly a passage of scripture set to music; anthems were part of the burial service in the *Book of Common Prayer*. The anthem in 'Let the Bird' may comprise l. 22, ll. 22–4, or ll. 22–52 (see Garber 1984).

22 **Love . . . dead** The singular verb (is) for what looks like a plural subject (Love and Constancy) is not unusual in Elizabethan English (see Hope 2003: 161–3), but it may suggest that Love and Constancy have become one indivisible unit.

23 **Phoenix** mythical bird; see 'Contexts and readings' (above). The Phoenix and the Turtle are both capitalised and italicised throughout Shakespeare's poem, as they are in *Love's Martyr* and the 'Poetical Essays' in general.
Turtle turtle-dove, a bird celebrated for its constancy to its mate; see *The Winter's Tale*, 5.3.132–5: 'I, an old turtle, | Will wing me to some wither'd bough, and there | My mate (that's never to be found again) | Lament till I am lost'.

24 **mutual** See Donne, 'The Dissolution' (which almost certainly postdates 'Let the Bird of Loudest Lay'): 'She's dead; and all which die | To their first elements resolve; | And we were mutual elements to us, | And made of one another' (ll. 1–4). Despite the mutuality of their love, however, one of Donne's lovers outlives the other.

25 **as** (i) with the result that; (ii) as if.

26 **essence** being, existence (OED 1a); Shakespeare plays on the complexity of this word at *Hamlet*, 3.4.187–8: 'I essentially am not in madness, | But mad in craft'. The theological sense of the word – 'denoting that in respect of which the three persons in the Trinity are one' (OED 4b) – is relevant here, since the Phoenix and Turtle form an equally mysterious two-in-one. 'Essence' also refers to those 'indispensable attributes' of a being or object which 'are sufficient for a valid definition' (OED 7a), a meaning with obvious resonance in a section of the poem that starts to wrestle with the process of categorising something that defies categories (see Cunningham 1952: 265).

27 **distincts** individual entities; Thomas Aquinas uses the term *distinctio* (distinction) to describe the persons of the Trinity: 'we can [. . .] use the word "distinction" [*distinctio*] on account of relative oppositions [. . .] we must avoid "separation" [*separatio*] and "division" [*divisio*] as implying a whole divided into parts' (*Summa Theologiae*, 6.89: cited by Burrow 2002: 374–5). See Ben Jonson, 'To the Holy Trinity', *Underwood* 1.1, ll. 39–40 ('Distinct

Be the death-divining swan,   15
Lest the requiem lack his right.

And thou, treble-dated crow,
That thy sable gender mak'st,
With the breath thou giv'st and tak'st,
'Mongst our mourners shalt thou go.   20

Here the anthem doth commence:
Love and Constancy is dead,
Phoenix and the Turtle fled
In a mutual flame from hence.

So they loved, as love in twain   25
Had the essence but in one,
Two distincts, division none:
Number there in love was slain.

Hearts remote, yet not asunder;
Distance and no space was seen   30

in persons, yet in unity | One God to see') and Richard Hooker's version of Aquinas in *Laws of Ecclesiastical Polity* (5.244), where the Trinity is seen as a 'mystical association', a suggestive phrase for the Phoenix and Turtle as well. This is the only citation in OED for 'distinct' as noun; no other Elizabethan instances are revealed by a full-text search of EEBO-TCP.

division none The Phoenix and Turtle can no more be separated into their different parts than can the Trinity. The indivisibility of the Phoenix and Turtle makes them transcend categorisation, since, in logic, division is companion and aid to definition. According to Thomas Wilson's *Rule of Reason*, 'as a definition [. . .] doth declare what a thing is, so the division sheweth how many things are contained in the same' (1551: sig. E1v).

28 ***Number . . . slain*** As two-in-one, the Phoenix and Turtle disrupt the principle that everything has an individuated entity and can be counted. The two birds have also become one, which – according to mathematical principles – is no number (see Sonnets 8.14, 136.8 and notes). This connects with an image of love in Plato's *Symposium* (sections 189c–193d), where Aristophanes the comic dramatist describes love

as a deep need to rejoin the other halves of the creatures humans once were, before the gods punished them by splitting them into two. The fifteenth-century neo-Platonist Marsilio Ficino (1433–99) embraced this theory in his own *Commentary on Plato's Symposium on Love*, developing the idea of love as a transcendent force, connecting earthly life to heavenly ideals. Shakespeare is not necessarily proposing or even engaging with this philosophy as philosophy, but Bradbrook (1951: 34) is justified in calling this 'Shakespeare's one work in the Platonic mode'. See also Petronella (1975), which compares the poem with Donne's 'The Ecstasy' (probably composed 1605–13).

29 ***asunder*** separate; Burrow (2002: 375) notes that this echoes the Anglican marriage service from the *Book of Common Prayer*: 'Those whom God hath joined together, let no man put asunder' (2011: 159). In 'Let the Bird of Loudest Lay' celebration of the union of the Phoenix and Turtle coincides with celebration of their deaths; the two birds thus embody the marriage vow to remain together 'till death us depart'.

30 ***Distance and no space*** This is a quibble on meanings of 'distance': there is difference between them (OED 2) but no measurable space (OED 3).

31 **queen** Usually, the faithful turtle-dove is depicted as female (see above, 'Contexts and readings'); here, however, and throughout the *Love's Martyr* collection, the Turtle is male (to a female Phoenix).

32 **But** except; the union would be a miracle in any except these two birds.

34 **right** that which the Turtle owns (OED³ 9a) or is due to him (OED³ 11a), prefiguring ideas of possession found in 'mine' and 'property', ll. 36–7; alternatively, the Turtle's 'right' could refer to 'that which is proper for or incumbent on [him] to do' (OED³ 2).

35 **Flaming** glowing (OED 3a); in flames (OED 1a).

36 **mine** Each bird belongs to the other (where 'mine' is a possessive); or, each bird was a source of riches to the other (*n.*, OED³ 1c, citing Ben Jonson, *Epicoene* (first performed 1609), 4.6.48: 'so rich a mine of virtue'); compare *Antony and Cleopatra*, 4.6.30–1: 'O Antony, | Thou mine of bounty'. Constable (1989) also suggests the alternative reading 'mien' ('mien, *n.*1', OED³ 1: 'look, bearing'), where the union of the two birds is prefigured in the way that they come to reflect one another's appearance. 'Mien' is not a word that Shakespeare uses elsewhere, however.

37 **Property** 'right to possession' (OED³ 4); 'any attribute, characteristic, or quality of an object' and, in Aristotelian logic, 'a characteristic which is peculiar to a particular kind of thing but is not part of its essence or definition' (OED³ 1c); as such, it features as one of the (four or five) 'predicables' which 'shew the largeness and narrowness of words, how far they do extend, and how much they comprehend in them' (Wilson, *Rule of Reason*, 1551: sig. B4v) and thus serve as a way of arriving at knowledge about the nature of a thing. The Phoenix and Turtle disrupt 'property', defying definition and Aristotelian logic.
appalled weakened, enfeebled (OED 6).

38 **That . . . same** See the penultimate line of *De Ave Phoenice*: 'ipse quidem, sed non eadem est' ('it itself, but not the same'), cited by Garber (1984: 10). The treatment of the phoenix myth in *De Ave Phoenice* is also resonant with Shakespeare's poem in its depiction of the phoenix as a paradox ('she is offspring to herself'), as defying categorisation ('whether male or female or neither'), and as achieving love in death ('Death for her is Venus').

39 **Single . . . name** It is also possible to punctuate this line 'Single natures, double name'. Modernised punctuation requires imposing a choice between possibilities in a poem where the distinction between single and plural is being eroded. The verb that follows is singular ('was'), and this provides the simplest concrete grounds for the choice made here, but see above, l. 22n.

40 **Neither . . . called** As Garber (1984: 11) points out, 'numbers should be the most explicit, as they are the least adorned, of words'. This statement, however, 'effectively demonstrates that there are some conditions for which the very concept of number is useless'.

41 **confounded** both 'confused' (OED 1) and a synonym for 'founded as metals be, thawed, undone' (Florio, *World of Words*, 1598: sig. M2r); logical tools, habitually used by the personified Reason for defining experience, are ineffectual when it comes to describing the Phoenix and Turtle in their two-in-oneness.

42 **division grow together** The primary sense, where division is 'the action of dividing or the state of being divided' (OED 1a), is congruent with the series of paradoxes to which this line belongs. Just as Reason is confused, single nature has a double name, and simplicity is compounded, so here the action of dividing becomes the means of coming together. However, the paradoxical sense of division is also latent in the use of the term in arithmetic. According to Robert Recorde's *The Ground of Arts teaching [. . .] Arithmetic*, division is not 'when one thing is parted into diverse and many parts', but 'contrary ways it bringeth many parcels into few, but yet so that these few be taken together are equal in value to the other many' (1543: sig. I3r).

43 **To . . . neither** Neither of the two was wholly distinct from the other, but nor were they one single indistinguishable being. Duncan-Jones and Woudhuysen (2007: 426) draw attention to parallels with Michael Drayton's *Mortimeriados*, ll. 2379–80: 'fire seemed to be water, water flame, | Either or neither, yet both the same' (1596: sig. Q1v).

44 **Simple . . . compounded** This line can be read both as a paradox – 'simple' being something that is 'not compounded' (Florio, *World of Words*, 1598: sig. 2H2r) – or as a description of the alchemical process, in which 'simples' are pure ingredients or elements that can be combined to make 'compounds' ('simple, *adj.* and *n.*', OED B7a).

45 **it** Reason; the next three-and-a-half lines are spoken by Reason.
twain couple.

46 **concordant** harmonious, a quality impossible in a single object ('one'), which explains why Reason is 'confounded'.

'Twixt this Turtle and his queen:
But in them it were a wonder.

So between them love did shine
That the Turtle saw his right
Flaming in the Phoenix' sight: 35
Either was the other's mine.

Property was thus appalled
That the self was not the same:
Single nature's double name
Neither two nor one was called.   40

Reason in itself confounded
Saw division grow together –
To themselves yet either neither,
Simple were so well compounded –

That it cried, 'How true a twain   45
Seemeth this concordant one.
Love hath reason, Reason none,
If what parts can so remain.'

Whereupon it made this threne
To the Phoenix and the Dove,
Co-supremes and stars of love,   50
As chorus to their tragic scene:

47 **Love . . . Reason** Reason is habitually pitched against love, or passion, in Renaissance thought, reason being a sign of 'erected wit', and passion, of 'infected will' (for a notable instance in Sidney's *Defence of Poesy*, see Alexander 2004: 10); compare the proverb 'Love is without reason' (Dent L517). Yet, as Janakiram (1980: 225–8) argues, within neo-Platonic thought, love and reason are not necessarily in conflict. Perfect love transcends 'common reason', which is governed by prudence, and is associated instead with 'uncommon reason', which aspires to higher things.

48 **what. . . remain** what separates also remains together.

49 **threne** a song of lamentation; not a common word in sixteenth-century English (and not used elsewhere by Shakespeare); one precedent is Robert Southwell's *Saint Peter's Complaint*: 'My threnes an endless alphabet do find' (1595: sig. A4v).

51 **Co-supremes** a paradox, since 'supreme' is a superlative, defined in Robert Cawdrey's *Table Alphabetical* as meaning 'highest, or greatest' (1604: sig. H8v). Here, that superlative is made equal with another. This is the earliest use of the term 'co-supreme' cited by the OED; a full-text search of EEBO-TCP reveals no other earlier examples. For Shakespeare's use of the 'co-' prefix, see *Lucrece*, 789n.
stars superlative examples, 'in various figurative and similative contexts' ('star, *n*.1', OED 4).

52 **chorus . . . scene** In classical tragedy, the Chorus commented on the action of the play. The description of the deaths of the Phoenix and Turtle as 'tragic' raises the question of whether this scene is tragic for them, although they have transcended the world, or for those left bereft.

53–67 The *threnos* – a song of lamentation – is spoken by Reason.

53–4 **Beauty, Truth, . . . Rarity, | Grace** These can be read as personifications of these qualities, which are embodied in the Phoenix and Turtle (beauty and rarity in the Phoenix, truth and grace in the Turtle); Beauty is certainly referred to as 'she' at l. 63. The pairing of Beauty and Truth is very important in the Sonnets (14.11, 14; 54.1–2, 13–14; 60.10–11; 101; 137.12) as in much love poetry of the period.

55 *enclosed* in the urn.

59–61 **Leaving . . . chastity** The fact that the Phoenix and Turtle have left no children is not a sign of their infertility or incapacity, but a result of their chastity. In leaving the Phoenix without issue, Shakespeare here diverges from the phoenix myth, from the ending of Chester's poem, and from the other 'Poetical Essays', which celebrate the birth of the new Phoenix.

62 **Truth . . . be** Truth may appear to be true, but since truth died with the two birds, it cannot be truth itself. Reason imagines the world as a lesser place without the Phoenix and the Turtle.

63 **Beauty . . . she** Again, just as truth is only an imitation after the immolation of the Phoenix and Turtle, so beauty may boast of being beautiful, but real beauty has died; compare Sonnet 104.14.

67 **For . . . prayer** For Davies (1995: 529), the final line hints at the pre-Reformation practice of intercession for the souls of the dead, a ritual at odds with Protestantism. Garber (1984: 15) argues that the *threnos* – which proclaims the birds to be 'dead' – cannot be taken as authoritative, because it is spoken by Reason, whose methods have been shown to be ineffectual.

Threnos

'Beauty, Truth, and Rarity,
Grace in all simplicity,
Here enclosed, in cinders lie.   55

'Death is now the Phoenix' nest,
And the Turtle's loyal breast
To eternity doth rest.

'Leaving no posterity,
'Twas not their infirmity: 60
It was married chastity.

'Truth may seem, but cannot be;
Beauty brag, but 'tis not she:
Truth and Beauty buried be.

'To this urn let those repair   65
That are either true or fair:
For these dead birds, sigh a prayer.'

William Shakespeare

Shakespeare's Sonnets

The 1609 Quarto (Q)

The publication of *Shakespeare's Sonnets* by Thomas Thorpe in 1609 raises a number of challenging questions regarding (1) whether or not the publication was authorised, and (2) the identity of 'Mr W.H.', named in the printer's dedication.

Despite Sidney Lee's categorisation of Thorpe as 'predatory' (*DNB*), there is little evidence to suggest that he was a particularly unscrupulous or piratical publisher. There are three incidents which are often cited as evidence of Thorpe's malpractice (e.g. Vickers 2007: 8–9): (1) Thorpe's entry in the Stationers' Register on 23 June 1603 of a panegyric to James I, a poem which had already been registered to Gregory Seton; Thorpe's entry was subsequently cancelled; (2) Thorpe's attempt to profit from Thomas Coryat's notoriety in 1611, when he reprinted (without licence) the preliminaries from *Coryat's Crudities* as *The Odcombian Banquet*; and (3) Thorpe's acquisition from Edward Blount of Christopher Marlowe's translation of Lucan, which Thorpe printed in 1600, with a dedication to Blount 'in regard of [his] old right in it' (sig. A2r). Nevertheless, the Stationers' Register is peppered with examples of fines being exacted for infringing copyright or printing without licence, and Thorpe was not out-of-line with the sometimes sharp practice of his fellow-stationers, whilst the suggestion that he obtained Marlowe's *Lucan* by underhand means does not sit easily with his regular co-operation with Blount in the years that followed (e.g. in publishing Ben Jonson's *Sejanus*, 1605 ('Thorpe, Thomas', *ODNB*), and John Healey's translation of *Epictetus*, 1610). Indeed, if the publication of the sonnets was authorised, then Thorpe would have been a likely person for Shakespeare to approach, since he had been Jonson's regular publisher since *Sejanus* (bringing out *Hymenaei*, 1606; *Volpone*, 1607; *Characters of Two Royal Masques*, 1608). Jonson – unlike Shakespeare – also paid close attention to the printing of his own works and would have been unlikely to entrust them to a disreputable publisher. Certainly, there was nothing irregular in the way that Thorpe established his right to publish *Shakespeare's Sonnets*: 'a book called SHAKESPEARE's *sonnets*' was entered in the Stationers' Register in Thorpe's name on 20 May 1609, for a standard sum of 6 old pence (Arber 1875–94, iii.410). Nor is there any evidence that Q was suppressed after its publication, as Dover Wilson suggests (1963: xlii): ESTC lists twelve surviving copies, a large number (compare the three copies of the first 1591 edition of Philip Sidney's *Astrophil and Stella*, which was recalled), and to date no additional archival evidence of post-publication censorship has come to light.

The fact that Shakespeare did not supply a dedication to Q is one of the main arguments used by those critics who think that the publication of *Shakespeare's Sonnets* was unauthorised. Printers' or publishers' dedications were not unusual in the period, but they generally supplement an authorial one. However, as Duncan-Jones suggests (1997a: 59), Thorpe may have supplied the dedication (on Shakespeare's authority) because Shakespeare was away from London at the time of printing; both Henry Constable's *Diana* (1592) and Edmund Spenser's *Amoretti* (1595) have prefaces by their printers rather than their authors, and both poets were absent from London while their works were printed (see Appendix 5). The closure of the London theatres in May 1609 due to a prolonged outbreak of plague meant that Shakespeare would have had little reason to stay in London and was probably in Stratford that summer, while Q was being printed: when the Stratford court records document Shakespeare's recovery of a debt from John Addenbrooke on 7 June 1609 (just over a fortnight after Thorpe registered his ownership of the sonnets) they describe Shakespeare as 'nuper in curia domini Jacobi' ('lately at the court of King James'; Halliwell 1848: 228), which could imply that he had recently returned from there to Stratford.

The other key objection to Q being authorised is that some features of the printed text suggest that the manuscript was not a fair copy but retains evidence of partial revision; i.e. it was not in the polished state that would be expected of a text that an author has released for printing. However, once eye-skips and other compositorial errors are ruled out, there is little evidence of incomplete revision: for example, only 25.9, 11 provide an example of a non-rhyming pair which must originate with the copy-text (those at 69.1, 3 and 113.6, 8 can be explained by compositorial error; see notes on those sonnets). Other 'slips' (e.g. that Sonnet 96 repeats the couplet from Sonnet 36; the presence of a fifteen-line sonnet, 99; the missing couplet in 126) may in fact be intentional. For a further defence of the authorised nature of Q, see Duncan-Jones 1983.

Printing Q

Q was printed for Thorpe in George Eld's workshop; Eld worked with Thorpe throughout the latter's career as a publisher (ESTC attests to twenty collaborations between Eld and Thorp/ Thorpe, between 1605 and 1624, the year before Thorpe's death). Jackson's widely accepted analysis of the spelling, punctuation and typographical spacing of the quarto indicates that it was set by two compositors: A and B, with the latter setting most of the volume. According to Jackson (1975), built on and revised by Blakemore Evans (1996: 276–80), pages set by A include Sonnets 1; 2.1–12; 7.10–14; 8; 9; 31.9–14; 32; 33; 34; 35; 36; 37; 38; 39; 40; 41.1–2; 53.3–14; 54; 55; 56; 57; 58; 59; 60.1–5; 86.12–14; 87; 88; 89; 90; 91.1–8; 94; 95; 96; 97; 98; 99; 100; 101; 102; 103.1–8; 113.4–14; 114; 115.1–9; 144.6–14; 145; 146.1–11; 149.3–14; 150; 151; 152; 153 (i.e. part or all of fifty-one sonnets); and *A Lover's Complaint* ll. 216–78, ll. 279–*c*. 203. The rest are assigned to B.

Although no holograph or early scribal copy of Shakespeare's sonnets survives, poetry in manuscript was usually very lightly pointed in this period, and often lacked punctuation at the end of the line: this would be introduced by compositors, and as Ingram and Redpath point out (1985: 350), 'Q often prints commas at the ends of lines which modern readers would rightly regard as enjambed. Such cases occur in about forty sonnets out of 154'. Both of Q's compositors also have a tendency to end quatrains with strong marks of punctuation (full stops, colons, question marks). Shakespeare made much less experimental use of the sonnet form than, for example, Sidney; where Sidney's syntax frequently runs over the end of a rhyming unit, Shakespeare tends to use the quatrain as a unit of utterance. Nonetheless, this feature of Shakespeare's sonnets is exaggerated by the heavy end-stopping introduced by Q's compositors.

Q is not carefully printed, particularly in comparison to the quartos of *Venus and Adonis* and *Lucrece*, produced by Richard Field in 1593 and 1594. Instances of errors which must be due to the compositors include transposed type (e.g. 'wiht' for 'with', 23.14; 'stainteh' for 'staineth', 33.14) and missing letters (e.g. 'mighst' for 'mightst', 41.9, 96.11); other errors in Q probably result from a compositor's eye-skip (e.g. the repetition of the rhyme word 'loss' at 34.10 and 12, and the phrase 'my sinfull earth' at 146.1 and 2), and both compositors recurrently misread a scribal abbreviation of 'thy' as 'their' (see 26.12n). Nor do the surviving copies bear witness to many stop-press corrections, which suggests that Q was not proof-read attentively. Rollins (1944: 2.5) lists just six definite stop-press corrections: the correction of a catchword at sig. F3r; two changes to punctuation (at 27.6 and 150.6); the emendment of 'seife' to 'selfe' at 47.10; the correction of 'proface' to 'profane' (89.11); and an alteration to the number of Sonnet 116 (erroneously 119 in all but one copy).

Q exists in two issues, with different booksellers, William Aspley and John Wright, named on the title-page of the two versions. The use of two booksellers, based in different city streets, would have helped maximise sales of Q (Aspley was at the sign of the Parrot in St Paul's Churchyard; Wright next to Christchurch, near Newgate). It might also be testimony to business connections and loyalties. Wright frequently sold books printed by Eld: ESTC lists fourteen separate titles (aside from the *Sonnets*) in the years up to and including 1609, the earliest of which was printed in 1606. Aspley had strong connections with Thorpe but worked with Eld much less frequently: the ESTC lists just four works besides the *Sonnets* printed by Eld and sold by Aspley, and one of these was *Eastward Ho!* by George Chapman, Ben Jonson and John Marston, co-published with Thorpe in 1605. Aspley had co-published Marston's *The Malcontent* with Thorpe in 1604, and Thorpe may have worked in Aspley's shop ('Thorpe, Thomas', *ODNB*): two out of three of Thorpe's earliest publications had originally been entered in the Stationers' Register to Aspley, and all three were sold in Aspley's shop; i.e. of the two booksellers, one (Wright) had a much stronger relationship with Eld, the other (Aspley) with Thorpe. Whilst many of the works in both Aspley's and Wright's shops were religious (reflecting the high proportion of religious works in this period), the two booksellers also stocked a strong list of more literary and dramatic works. Wright's stock included Christopher Marlowe's *Dr Faustus* (1609), printed by Eld, and *King Leir* (1605). As well as the ventures with Thorpe mentioned above, Aspley had co-published Shakespeare's *Much Ado* and *2 Henry IV* in 1600 with the bookseller Andrew Wise; and he would go on to be one of the four booksellers involved in the printing of Shakespeare's First Folio in 1623.

Date

The printing of *Shakespeare's Sonnets* in 1609 appears belated, occurring as it does over a decade after the sonnet boom of the mid-1590s (see Appendix 5). It has been argued (e.g. Duncan-Jones 1983: 12) that its publication was due to an outbreak of plague in 1608–9, which led to the closure of the London theatres by injunction in May 1609. (The turn to non-dramatic poetry with *Venus and Adonis* in 1593 had similarly coincided with the closure of the playhouses during a time of plague.) Although Shakespeare was a substantial property-owner by 1609, the closure of the theatres may still have caused financial difficulties, particularly as his playing company, having taken possession of Blackfriars in 1608, now had two playhouses lying unused; and Shakespeare's pursuit of Addenbroke for debt in June 1609 (see above) may indicate that he was in need of ready money. Turning to previously unpublished material may have provided a short-term solution.

Some of Q's sonnets at least must have existed in draft at least a decade before they were printed. By 1598, when they were mentioned in Francis Meres' *Palladis Tamia*, Shakespeare was known to have authored some 'sugared sonnets', circulated 'among his private friends' (sigs 2O1v–2O2r), and versions of two sonnets (138 and 144 in Q) were printed by William Jaggard in 1599 in *The Passionate Pilgrim* (see Appendix 3). The choice of a predominantly 'English' form of sonnet is also characteristic of sonnet sequences from the mid-1590s (see Appendix 5).

Stylometric analysis has been used to date the sequence, through identifying 'early rare words' (words occurring between three and nine times in works known to have been written before 1600) and 'late rare words' (occurring between three and nine times in works known to have been written after 1600); see Hieatt et al. 1987; Jackson 1999b, 2001, 2005. On the basis of this work, there is scholarly consensus that the sonnets fall into four groups:

1   Sonnets 1–60: written in 1590s (Hiett et al. 1987 posit 1591–5; Jackson, 1595–6); revised after 1600.
2   Sonnets 61–103: written in early- to mid-1590s (Hiett et al. 1987 posit 1591–5; Jackson, 1594–5, and 1598–1600 for the 'rival poet(s)' series, 78–86).
3   Sonnets 104–126: written *c.* 1600.
4   Sonnets 127–154: written in early 1590s (1591–5).

The order in which the sonnets appear in Q is therefore unlikely to be the order in which they were composed; however, it is probable that the order is authorial, not least because of the numerological significance that attaches to some of the sonnets (e.g. 12, 60, 63). Moreover, the fact that there are no known manuscript copies of Shakespeare's sonnets before the 1610s (see Appendix 4) implies that their circulation in the 1590s and early 1600s was very restricted. The copy that Thorpe acquired must therefore have been close to Shakespeare's original. For a fuller defence of the authority of Q's sequence, see Jackson 1999a.

Shakespeare's sonnets and the literary tradition

In the *Sonnets*, Shakespeare draws on a well-established lyric tradition, reworking motifs such as love-as-hunt (Sonnet 129), the court of love, where judgement is passed on various body parts (Sonnet 46), or the exchange of hearts (Sonnet 22). Many of these conventions feature in Petrarchan poetry, as do the insomniac lover (Sonnet 27), the tyrannical mistress (Sonnet 131), and the self-consciousness of the poetic voice as a writer of verse (passim). Shakespeare's plays periodically mock sonneteering, as the clichéd activity of the besotted; see, for example, Don Armado in *Love's Labours Lost*, probably written *c.* 1595, contemporaneously with many of the sonnets (see above, 'Date'): 'Assist me, some extemporal god of rhyme, for I am sure I shall turn sonnet. Devise, wit, write, pen, for I am for whole volumes in folio' (1.2.183–5). Shakespeare's sonnets are not parodic: they contain no moments akin to Sidney's *Astrophil and Stella* 9, which pushes the blazon to parodic excess; however – like many collections and sequences of sonnets – they are self-consciously engaged with, and testing, the possibilities and uses of the form.

Petrarchism was popularised in English through the publication of *Songs and Sonnets* (aka *Tottel's Miscellany*) in 1557, a volume – containing the poems of Thomas Wyatt and Henry Howard, Earl of Surrey – which would go through at least eleven editions before 1590, and which became a byword for love poetry: witness the inexperienced wooer Slender declaring 'I had rather than forty shillings I had my Book of Songs and Sonnets here' in *Merry Wives* (1.1.198–9). The Elizabethan miscellanies by Barnabe Googe (*Eclogues, Epitaphs and Sonnets*, 1563) and George Turberville (*Epitaphs, Epigrams, Songs and Sonnets*, 1567, 1570), early responses to *Tottel*, have a loose understanding of the term 'sonnet' (which is applied to poems of varying length), but their homosocial use of the 'sonnet' as verses exchanged between men and, in particular, as a vehicle for doling out advice to youthful addressees is especially pertinent to Sonnets 1–17 (see Shrank 2008); the juxtaposition of sonnets and epitaphs in those collections is also suggestive, in light of the emphasis on commemoration in *Shakespeare's Sonnets*.

The print publication of Sidney's *Astrophil and Stella* in 1591 helped to establish both the primacy of the fourteen-line form and a vogue for English sonnet sequences (as opposed to collections of sonnets; see Appendix 5 for further information about English sonnet sequences in print). In such a self-reflexive genre, it is difficult to ascertain direct borrowings and allusions, but Shakespeare's sonnets have particularly strong resonances with images found in Constable's *Diana* (see Shakespeare, Sonnets 24, 99, 106, 128), Richard Barnfield's 'Certain Sonnets' (see Shakespeare, Sonnet 46) and Samuel Daniel's *Delia*, especially – in their imagining of the now-youthful subject in old age – *Delia* 30–4 (see Shakespeare, Sonnets 2–3, 5). Elizabethan sonnets periodically reflect on the immortalising power of verse (see, for example, Spenser, *Amoretti* 75; Daniel, *Delia* 34); however, this is a much more sustained feature of *Shakespeare's Sonnets* than in other contemporaneous collections and sequences, and here Shakespeare draws on classical texts, such as Horace, *Odes* 3. Other sources to which the *Sonnets* are recurrently indebted include Ovid's *Metamorphoses*, the Bible, and (for Sonnets 1–17) Thomas Wilson's translation of Erasmus' 'Epistle to persuade a young man to marriage' and Christopher Marlowe's *Hero and Leander*, although as Blakemore Evans notes (1996: 119) the borrowing may have been the other way round (depending on the dating of those sonnets).

The genre of *A Lover's Complaint* and the literary tradition to which it belongs are discussed in the headnote to that poem.

W.H.

The identity of 'W.H.', to whom Q is dedicated, has been the cause of much speculation. It is possible that the dedicatee and addressee are different persons, and that poems composed for and about one addressee may have been revised for, and readdressed to, another in the years that followed (as happens, for example, with sonnets in Spenser's *Amoretti*, printed in 1595). The main contenders for 'W.H.' and/or the youthful addressee of the sonnets are:

1   Henry Wriothesley, third Earl of Southampton (1573–1624), to whom Shakespeare had dedicated both *Venus and Adonis* (1593) and *Lucrece* (1594). The main objections to this theory are that the initials are transposed; that 'Mr' was not an appropriate title for an aristocrat like Southampton; and that after 1594 there is little evidence of Southampton's continued patronage of, or contact with, Shakespeare, although – since many of the sonnets appear to have been written in the 1590s (see above), this does not preclude Southampton as their inspiration and – if 'W.H.' is also the youthful friend – their addressee. The composition of Sonnets 1–17 (probably in the early 1590s) would tally with a period immediately after Southampton had refused to marry Elizabeth Vere, granddaughter of his guardian William Cecil, Lord Burghley; as a royal ward, Southampton consequently faced paying a fine of £5,000. Southampton eventually married Elizabeth Vernon in 1598, when she was pregnant with his first child. Some critics find an allusion to Wriothesley in the opening sonnet; see 1.2n.

2   William Herbert, third Earl of Pembroke (1580–1630). The other main contender for both the dedicatee and youthful addressee, Pembroke refused a series of advantageous marriages: to Elizabeth Carey in 1595; Bridget Vere in 1597; Sir William Hatton's widow, Elizabeth (née Cecil), in 1598; a niece of Charles, Lord Howard in 1599; and Mary Fitton in 1601 (despite the fact that she was pregnant with his child). He married Mary Talbot (the Earl of Shrewsbury's daughter) in 1604. Herbert was a generous patron of the arts: in 1609 he gave £100 to the Bodleian Library, Oxford, for the purchase of books (see Duncan-Jones 1997a: 58); he would go on to be the co-dedicatee (with his brother Philip) of Shakespeare's First Folio, in which John Heminges and Henry Condell thank the Herbert brothers for the 'favour' shown both to Shakespeare's plays 'and their author living' (sig. A2r). Duncan-Jones also suggests that the use of 'adventurer' in the dedication (l. 10) may reflect Herbert's incorporation as a member of the Virginia Company on 27 May 1609 (a week after *Shakespeare's Sonnets* had been entered in the Stationers' Register). However, as with Southampton, 'Mr' would not be used for an aristocrat, although Duncan-Jones (a keen advocate for Herbert as 'W.H.') argues that 'one obvious function of the "Mr." would be to indicate that the sonnets

dedicated to him had their origin, or "begetting", in the period before his inheritance of the Earldom of Pembroke [in January 1601]' (1997a: 59). The fusing of Herbert's 'When mine eyes, first admiring your rare beauty' and Shakespeare's Sonnet 106 into a composite poem in MS Rosenbach 1083/16 is discussed in Appendix 4.

Other candidates for 'W.H.' include:

3   A boy-actor, Willy Hughes (see 20.7n), a theory first propounded by the eighteenth-century critic Thomas Tyrwhitt and popularised through Oscar Wilde's *The Portrait of Mr W.H.* (1889), where the obsessional search for Willy Hughes proves fatal for at least one protagonist.

4   'William Himself' or a misprint for 'W. Sh.'/'W. S.', resulting from a compositor picking up the wrong piece of type or misreading a capital 'S' as 'H' in his copy (Foster 1987a, developing a nineteenth-century theory); however, it is hard to think of another example of a work being dedicated to its own author, and since Thorpe wrote the dedication, he would presumably have noticed the error on receipt of the copies.

5   Shakespeare's brother-in-law William Hathaway.

6   The stationer William Hall; Fleissner (1980) points to a potential pun in the juxtaposition 'W.H. ALL.' in the dedication, but it is unclear why Hall, who acquired his own printing press in 1608, would give copy to a rival to print and reap the profits of.

7   The London stationer William Holme. Caveney (2015) points to Holme's potential connections with Thorpe, through their shared roots in Chester, where 'they both had close relatives who were sheriffs and mayors of the city' (p. 120) and, through the printer Adam Islip, with Eld. Caveney argues that Thorpe and Eld found the manuscript of the *Sonnets* amongst Holme's belongings after he died in August 1607, along with seven play scripts that they went on to enter in the Stationers' Register later that summer/autumn. However, it is unclear why they would wait a further two years before registering and publishing the *Sonnets* or why they would need to withhold Holme's identity in the dedication.

For these last three identifications (5–7), 'begetter' is understood as indicating the person who procured the manuscript for the printer.

The sonnets and biographical readings

The fact that Thorpe's dedication is addressed – like many of the ensuing sonnets – to a man, described as the 'only begetter' of the sonnets (which can be read as the 'inspiration' for the sonnets), encourages readers to make a biographical connection between the dedicatee and the young man of the sonnets (although – as noted above – 'begetter' may indicate 'procurer'). The sonnets certainly toy with elements of Shakespeare's biography: the poet-speaker refers to himself as 'Will' (Sonnets 135, 136) and there are possible references to the acting profession at 110.2 and 111.4. However, as Kerrigan notes, 'The text is neither fictive nor confessional. Shakespeare stands behind the first person of his sequence as Sidney had stood behind Astrophil – sometimes near the poetic "I," sometimes farther off, but never without some degree of rhetorical projection' (1986: 11).

After the 1609 Quarto

Shakespeare Sonnets and *A Lover's Complaint* (the narrative poem appended to it) were not republished in Shakespeare's lifetime. Neither reappeared in print until *Poems: Written by Wil. Shakespeare. Gent.*, printed in 1640 by Thomas Cotes for John Benson, who entered the work in the Stationers' Register on 4 November 1639. Benson made numerous alterations. He corrected some verbal errors and introduced new ones; he rearranged the order of the sonnets, omitting eight and combining all but thirty-one of the remaining sonnets into longer poems comprising two to five sonnets each, to which he gave descriptive headings; he interspersed the sonnets with non-Shakespearean poems from the 1612 *Passionate Pilgrim* (see Appendix 3); and on three occasions he altered male pronouns to female ones, although he did not – as is sometimes claimed – systematically seek to eradicate traces of the male addressee. Benson, like Thorpe, has been depicted as an unscrupulous printer, desecrating Shakespeare's sonnets to conceal their origin. More recent criticism (e.g. de Grazia 2000; Baker 1998; Shrank 2009) has attempted to rehabilitate Benson, arguing that Benson's treatment of the 1609 *Sonnets* is not an act of either piracy or literary barbarism, but printed legally and fashioned in response to mid-seventeenth-century literary tastes and practices. Since the sonnets did not circulate extensively in manuscript (see Appendix 4), Benson's edition sheds a rare light on how the sonnets were read in the seventeenth century; information about how he grouped the sonnets, and the titles he gave them, is consequently included in the notes below.

The 1640 *Poems* also had more influence than Q over the reception of Shakespeare's sonnets in the centuries after his death. Even after Bernard Lintott printed a facsimile edition of Q in *c.* 1710, eighteenth-century editions continued to follow Benson's *Poems*, until Edmond Malone's 1780 edition restored Q's text and order as well as addressing many of Q's textual cruxes, frequently drawing on emendations that Edward Capell made to a copy of Lintott's edition (now Capell MS 4 in the Wren Library, Trinity College, Cambridge). Although he reproduced Q's text almost exactly (including the retention of its italics, see 1.2n), Lintott, even more than Benson, heterosexualises the sonnets, subtitling his edition '*I. One Hundred and Fifty Four Sonnets, all of them in Praise of his Mistress. II. A Lover's Complaint of his Angry Mistress*'.

Shakespeare's Sonnets

Title-page

SHAKESPEARE'S SONNETS The title is unusual for a sonnet sequence in having the name of its author as part of its title, rather than a pair of lovers or the name of the female Muse/beloved (see Appendix 5). The prominence of Shakespeare's name (which also appears two leaves later, as an internal title, above the first sonnet) is probably a marketing strategy: Shakespeare's name had featured on the title-pages to his plays since 1598 (by the beginning of 1609, at least ten of his plays were in print under his name, many in more than one copy), and the power of Shakespeare's name to sell books is indicated by the appropriation of his name to *The London Prodigal* (1605) or by the way that the title-page of the 1599 *Passionate Pilgrim* attributes that work wholly to him, although only five of its twenty poems (1–3, 5, 16) can be linked securely to Shakespeare and a number are demonstrably not by him, but by contemporaries including Richard Barnfield and Christopher Marlowe (see Appendix 3).

Never before imprinted another marketing strategy; printers regularly advertised the novelty of their wares in this way.

G. Eld George Eld.

T.T. Thomas Thorpe; Thorpe used Eld to print the majority of the books for which he held a licence. For further information on Thorpe, see headnote, above.

William Aspley A variant imprint of this edition gives John Wright as book-seller. For further information on Aspley's and Wright's business connections with (respectively) Thorpe and Eld, see headnote ('Printing Q'), above.

SHAKESPEARE'S
SONNETS
Never before imprinted.

AT LONDON
By *G. Eld* for *T. T.* and are
to be sold by *William Aspley.*
1609.

Dedication

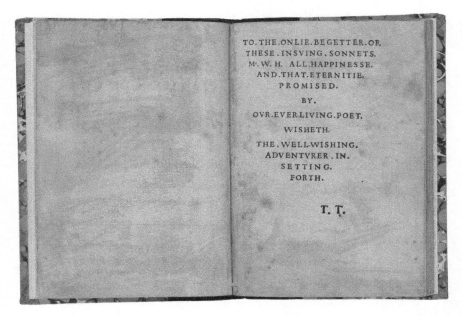

Figure 4.1 William Shakespeare, *Shakespeare's Sonnets* (London: George Eld, 1609), T.T.'s dedication; Folger Shakespeare Library copy, classmark STC 22353. Used with permission of the Folger Shakespeare Library

This fourteen-line dedication has, in Rollins' words, 'caused the spilling of more ink, the utterance of more futile words, than almost any other personage or problem of Q' (1944: 2.166). The mystery is increased, perhaps purposefully, by the use of initials (compare George Gascoigne's teasing use of initials in *Adventures of Master F.J.* in *Hundred Sundry Flowers*, 1573) and by the convoluted syntax, which places the subject of the sentence ('the adventurer') after the main verb ('wisheth'), contravening the usual English word order. Written in capital letters and with a point between each word, the dedication resembles an inscription in stone and further disrupts reading, since the stops do not indicate the end of a sentence. The layout is unusual, but not unique: Ben Jonson's dedication to 'the two famous universities' of the quarto of *Volpone* (1607), printed – like Q – by George Eld for Thomas Thorpe, is formatted in a similar fashion (albeit without the stops). Jonson's *Sejanus* (1605), also printed by Eld for Thorpe, contains a proclamation (sig. M1r), printed in capitals and with stops (as in Q).

The lack of an authorial dedication is one key piece of evidence used to argue that Q was unauthorised; for details of other sonnet sequences containing non-authorial dedications (some of which were definitely authorised), see Appendix 5. Whether or not it was sanctioned by Shakespeare, the dedication responds creatively and sensitively to the sequence it introduces, picking up on its themes of immortality and pseudo-memorialisation: the dedication promises 'Mr W.H.' posthumous fame (an 'eternity') that it actually denies, by suppressing his full identity, just as Shakespeare's sonnets do to the youthful addressee.

1 **ONLY.** 'sole' (OED[3] 2a) or 'peerless' (OED[3] 3a); Duncan-Jones (1997a: 108) highlights the possibility of interpreting 'only' as double-edged: W.H. might have been instrumental in begetting the sonnets, but he has *only* produced sonnets, not children. For the use of 'only' to indicate 'peerless', compare 1.10.

Shakespeare's Sonnets

TO. THE. ONLY. BEGETTER. OF.
THESE. ENSUING. SONNETS.
MR. W.H. ALL. HAPPINESS.
AND. THAT. ETERNITY.
PROMISED.   5
BY.
OUR. EVER-LIVING. POET.
WISHETH.
THE. WELL-WISHING.
ADVENTURER. IN.   10
SETTING.
FORTH.

T.T.

BEGETTER. 'the agent that originates, produces or occasions' (OED 2); this could indicate (i) the inspiration for these sonnets; (ii) the individual who procured the manuscript and passed it to Thorpe, a reading which questions the authority of this volume (see headnote, above); or even (iii) the author (if 'W.H' is read as 'William Himself'). The use of 'begetter' to suggest 'procurer' is extremely rare, however: a search of EEBO-TCP produces no examples between 1500–1610 of 'begetter' being used of someone who procures something (rather than being responsible in some figurative or literal way for producing it). Rather, the dominant meaning in the period conveys procreation (literal or figurative).

3 **MR. W.H.** the 'only begetter'; for a summary of the main candidates for W.H., see headnote above.

4 **THAT. ETERNITY.** the eternity promised by the poet in many of the sonnets that follow (e.g. 18, 19, 60, 63, 101); as Blakemore Evans points out (1996: 116), 'that' implies 'that kind of', i.e. a particular type of eternity, rather than '*the* eternity' that would be expected if the 'ever-living poet' (l. 7) refers to God.

7 **OUR. EVER-LIVING. POET.** Most commentators agree that this refers to Shakespeare; Foster (1987a: 46) argues that 'ever-living' is normally used only for God or the dead (but see l. 4n, above).

8 **WISHETH.** The subject of this verb is 'adventurer' (l. 10).

10 **ADVENTURER.** 'a person who undertakes or invests in a commercial adventure or enterprise' (OED³ 1); i.e. Thorpe, the publisher, who – like a Merchant Adventurer – was risking his capital in this commercial 'venture', with no guarantee of a return. The description of publishing as adventuring (i.e. something which involves risk, 'adventure, *v.*' OED³) is fairly common in early modern dedications; see Thomas Achelley, *Key of Knowledge* (1572), sig. C2r ('I have compiled this little book of prayers [...] which I have adventured to publish under the patronage of your Ladyship's name'); William Byrd et al., *Musica Transalpina* (1588), sig. A2v: 'I kept them [my songs] (or the most of them) for a long time by me, not presuming to put my sickle in another man's corn, till such time as I heard, that the same being dispersed into many men's hands, were by some persons altogether unknown to the owner, like to be published in print, which made me to adventure to set this work in hand'.

11–12 **SETTING. | FORTH.** common sixteenth- and seventeenth-century term for printing a book, and one which continues the metaphor of adventuring from l. 10.

14 **T.T.** Thomas Thorpe; Thorpe customarily used initials to sign his name in prefatory material (usually 'T. Th.' or 'Th. Th.').

Shakespeare's Sonnets The title of the work, which prominently names Shakespeare, appears in Q both here, immediately above the text, and on the title-page; the stress on Shakespeare as the author of these sonnets indicates his marketability (see note on title-page, above); compare Benson's 1640 edition, where the title, 'Poems: Written by Wil. Shakespeare. Gent', appears three times before we get one line of Shakespeare's verse.

Sonnets 1–126: These are generally regarded as being addressed to a man (although a number of sonnets lack pronouns specifying the gender of the addressee; see Dubrow 1996). The identity of this youth has been the cause of much speculation (see headnote, above). Whilst it does not necessarily follow that the same person inspired, or is addressed in, all the sonnets, once gathered into and read in one volume, the natural and dominant impression created is that a single man is being addressed.

   Shakespeare's Sonnets is unusual, but not unique, in containing sonnets (other than commendatory verses) which are about, or addressed to, a man, and many of which adopt the language of adoration, yearning and despair found in the many amorous sonnets written to or about women in this period. Richard Barnfield's 'Certain Sonnets', printed in his *Cynthia* volume in 1595 (dedicated to William Stanley, sixth Earl of Derby), weaves an intensely homoerotic narrative about the poet-speaker's desire for 'Ganymede', which includes a sonnet about a wet dream (Sonnet 6) and a blazon of Ganymede's body (Sonnet 17), which exceeds convention – and anything found in *Shakespeare's Sonnets* – by invoking not just visual and aural senses (capable of being experienced at a distance), but also ones of taste and touch.

Sonnets 1–17, often dubbed the 'procreation sonnets', urge a young man to marry, in order to produce children. Many of the analogies used to convince the youth are drawn from Desiderius Erasmus' 'Epistle to persuade a young man to marriage', which appears, translated into English, in Thomas Wilson's *Art of Rhetoric* (1553), sigs F1v–I2v; one of the first extended manuals of rhetoric in English, this volume was reprinted throughout the sixteenth century and may be the source which Shakespeare used. Some of the motifs – of usury, music, and aristocratic dwellings – found in these sonnets are also reminiscent of those in Leander's seduction speech in Christopher Marlowe's *Hero and Leander* (printed in 1598, but circulating in manuscript from the early 1590s), particularly ll. 229–58 (see 4.1n, 8.9–10n, 8.14n, 9.12n, 10.7n). There are also recurrent echoes of Venus' attempts to seduce Adonis in Shakespeare's earlier narrative poem.

1

Benson combines Sonnets 1–3 under the title 'Loves cruelty'.

[1] The sonnet is unnumbered in Q.

1 *creatures* probably living things in general (OED³ 3a), rather than humans specifically (OED³ 2a).

increase 'the production of offspring' (OED 2b); Burrow (2002: 382) points to the possibility of a play on 'increase' as the 'advancement' (OED 4) or profit that might result from writing poems to a patron (as here).

2 *That* so that.

thereby by means of increase, but also 'by means of fairest creatures'.

beauty's rose the epitome of beauty; compare *Antony and Cleopatra*, 3.13.20–1: 'Tell him he wears the rose | Of youth upon him'. Barnabe Barnes uses the phrase to express superlative beauty in *Parthenophil and Parthenophe*, Sonnet 45.1–2: 'Sweet beauty's rose in whose fair purple leaves | Love's queen in richest ornament doth lie' (1593: sig. E1v). There is a long tradition of using roses to symbolise exceptional (and often youthful) beauty; see, for example, Geoffrey Chaucer's description of Cleopatra in *Legend of Good Women* (1385), l. 613: 'Sche was fayr as is the Rose in may'. This is the first of nine sonnets featuring roses (others being 35, 54, 67, 95, 98, 99, 109, 130, of which only 130 falls in the sonnets to/about the mistress). In all of them, 'rose' is capitalised (in 35, it falls at the start of a line), but so too are other words indicating species of plants/animals, such as 'lilies' (98.9, 99.6) and 'lambs' (96.9, 10); 1.2 is the only instance of 'rose' being italicised as well as capitalised, which in Q frequently indicates a proper name (e.g. 'Adonis', Q53.5) or a 'learned' term, etymologically derived from Greek or Latin (e.g. 'interim', Q56.9); however, Q's use of capitals and italics occasionally seems random (e.g. 'statues', Q55.5, 'autumn', Q104.5) or unnecessary (e.g. 'audit', a well-established term, Q4.12). The italics were probably present in the manuscript from which Q was copied: setting text in italics required compositors to use a different case of type and therefore entails extra work which they are unlikely to initiate without a prompt from the copy in front of them. There is a critical tradition of reading the capitalisation of 'rose' as an indication

that it here refers to a Platonic idea of beauty (see Wyndham 1898; Young 1937). Proponents of the earl of Southampton as 'Mr W.H.' claim that his family name 'Wriothesley' could be pronounced 'Rose-ly'; however, evidence suggests that the sixteenth- and seventeenth-century pronunciation was actually 'Risley' (see Rowse 1965: 106); until the early sixteenth century, the family name was plain 'Writh', until gentrified by Southampton's great-great-uncle, Thomas.

3 *as* while.

riper older; the adjective suggests fruit rather than the flowers of l. 2; as ll. 2–3 move from blossoming to ripeness to *decease* (l. 3), they evoke the proverb 'Soon ripe soon rotten' (Dent R133).

should shall, ought to.

4 *His, his* neuter, as well as masculine, pronoun in early modern English.

tender youthful (OED A4), kind, loving (OED A8a); Mahood (1957: 92) and editors following her draw attention to the potential, intralingual pun on *tender heir* and 'tender air'; compare *Cymbeline*, 5.5.446–9: 'The piece of tender air, thy virtuous daughter, | Which we call *mollis aer*, and *mollis aer* | We term it *mulier*; which *mulier* I divine | Is this most constant wife'. The 'tender heir' who will 'bear' the thing that will preserve the father's memory is a 'tender air', i.e. *mulier*, the Latin for wife. The accessibility of the pun is dependent on the reader knowing Latin (more usually a male accomplishment in early modern England).

bear his memory (i) perpetuate his father's memory; (ii) resemble his father; 'bear' retains some sense of giving birth ('bear, *v*.1', OED 43a): in this case, the offspring will generate anew his father's memory.

5 *contracted* 'betrothed' (OED 2a), but also 'narrowed, shortened, shrunken' (OED 5a). This latter sense is the first hint that the addressee is being accused of narcissism: ll. 5–8 evoke the tale of Narcissus from Ovid's *Metamorphoses* 3 (a sixteenth-century schoolroom text), in which Narcissus pines away, having fallen in love with his own reflection; one of the key features stimulating Narcissus's self-love are 'his ardent eyes which like two stars full bright and shining be' (Golding, 3.526; sig. F5r; 'geminum, sua lumina, sidus', Ovid, 3.420).

6 *Feed'st . . . fuel* The image is that of a candle; see Clifford's death in *3 Henry VI*, 2.6.1: 'Here

Shakespeare's Sonnets

[1]

From fairest creatures we desire increase,
That thereby beauty's rose might never die,
But as the riper should by time decease,
His tender heir might bear his memory: 4
But thou, contracted to thine own bright eyes,
Feed'st thy light's flame with self-substantial fuel,
Making a famine where abundance lies,
Thyself thy foe, to thy sweet self too cruel.   8
Thou that art now the world's fresh ornament,
And only herald to the gaudy spring,
Within thine own bud buriest thy content,
And, tender churl, mak'st waste in niggarding: 12
   Pity the world, or else this glutton be,
   To eat the world's due, by the grave and thee.

burns my candle out'. Like Narcissus (see 1.5n, above), the addressee of the sonnet is accused of consuming himself; compare Golding's similarly alliterative translation of this line from Ovid's *Metamorphoses*: 'He is the flame that sets on fire and thing that burneth too' (3.536; sig. F5r). At the root of the term '*self-substantial*' lies the word 'substance' ('riches, possessions', OED³ 12b), hinting at the fact that, in remaining unmarried and without an heir, the addressee lives parasitically off his family property.

7 *Making. . . lies* Golding's Narcissus laments that 'my plenty makes me poor' (3.587; sig. F6r); Shakespeare's introduction of the term '*famine*' suggests that the youth's self-love has wider ramifications than self-annihilation alone, anticipating the instruction in ll. 13–14 to 'Pity the world'.

9 *fresh* 'untainted' (OED A6a), 'not sullied' (OED A9a), 'blooming, looking healthy or youthful' (OED A9b); the word resonates with the vernal and floral imagery around which this sonnet is structured.

10 *only* 'peerless' (OED³ 3a); compare the use of the adjective in the phrase 'the only begetter' (dedication, l. 1), or *Hamlet*, 2.2.401–2: 'For the law of writ and the liberty: these are the only men'.
herald messenger: the young man is sent by spring to announce that season's imminent arrival.

gaudy brilliantly or richly attired; the word does not here have the negative connotations that it does in modern English; compare *Love's Labours Lost*, 5.2.802: 'Nip not the gaudy blossoms of your love'. Etymologically related (via Anglo-French) to the Latin *gaudium* ('joy'), the word evokes a sense of festivity or joy (see *Antony and Cleopatra*, 3.13.182: 'Let's have one other gaudy night'), a sense still used by Oxford colleges for celebratory dinners ('gaudy, *n.*', OED 5a). 'Gaudy' is also associated with 'gaudy-green', cloth dyed with weld (*Reseda Luteola*), a plant which produces a yellow-green dye, a colour evoking the new growth of spring.

11 *bud* unopened flower; Williams (1997) suggests that this might also allude to a penis.
buriest here pronounced as two syllables.
content (i) happiness; (ii) the offspring that this prospective father currently contains within him.

12 *tender churl* echoes l. 4, but here applied to the young man, who has so far failed to provide the 'tender heir'; the juxtaposition of 'tender' and 'churl' – 'a term of disparagement' ('churl, *n.*', OED 5), with connotations of low-birth, lack of breeding, and (OED 6) miserliness – can be read as an oxymoron or as pointedly stripping away the positive meanings of 'tender' present in l. 4, so that the addressee is merely 'youthful' or 'immature' (OED 4). The tight-fistedness

potentially conveyed by 'churl' anticipates 'niggarding', and is a combination found in Miles Coverdale's 1535 translation of Isaiah 32:5: 'Then shall the niggard be no more called gentle, nor the churl liberal'. The use of financial imagery and distinction between hoarding and investment also occur in Sonnets 2, 4.

mak'st waste in niggarding a paradox: by hoarding ('niggarding') himself, instead of procreating, the youth both squanders ('waste[s]') the qualities he has (and should invest in the next generation) and causes destruction ('waste') by depriving the world of fruit. Compare the description of Rosaline in *Romeo and Juliet*, 1.1.218–20, who 'in that sparing [i.e. not marrying] makes huge waste; | For beauty starved with her severity | Cuts beauty off from all posterity'.

14 ***To. . . thee*** The unborn offspring ('the world's due', i.e. a debt he owes to the world) are consumed first by the youth who refuses to breed and then, with his demise, by the grave. Compare *Venus and Adonis*, ll. 757–62. Dying is proverbially expressed as 'pay[ing] one's debt to nature' (Dent D168).

[1]

From fairest creatures we desire increase,
That thereby beauty's rose might never die,
But as the riper should by time decease,
His tender heir might bear his memory: 4
But thou, contracted to thine own bright eyes,
Feed'st thy light's flame with self-substantial fuel,
Making a famine where abundance lies,
Thyself thy foe, to thy sweet self too cruel.   8
Thou that art now the world's fresh ornament,
And only herald to the gaudy spring,
Within thine own bud buriest thy content,
And, tender churl, mak'st waste in niggarding: 12
    Pity the world, or else this glutton be,
    To eat the world's due, by the grave and thee.

2

CELM lists thirteen manuscript texts for Sonnet 2, all transcribed after Q; see Appendix 4.

Daniel, *Delia*, Sonnets 30–4 similarly use winter imagery and a vision of the (female) addressee's faded beauty to attempt to coerce her into modifying her behaviour. The solution offered in *Delia* 34.9 – that the poetry 'may remain thy lasting monument' – is not one that Q's sequence offers until 15.14, although it becomes the standard way in which the poet-speaker promises to defeat time from Sonnet 18 onwards.

Benson combines Sonnets 1–3 under the title 'Loves cruelty'.

1 *forty winters* i.e. 'When you are old'; 'forty' is a Biblically large and formulaic number (e.g. 'forty days and forty nights', Genesis 7:4; the 'forty years' the Israelites stayed in the wilderness, Exodus 16:35). However, if read literally, as imagining a time forty years hence, the number appropriately places the young man (who, having had time to display his reluctance to marry, must be in his late teens at least) in old age ('senectute'), which according to Thomas Elyot's *Castle of Health* lasts from 40 to 60 years, and is followed by 'age decrepit' (1539: sigs B2v–B3r). The choice of 'winters' to represent the passing of the years enforces the destructiveness of time and contrasts with the spring evoked in Sonnet 1.
besiege The military metaphor continues in l. 2 with 'field' and 'trenches'.

2 *dig. . .field* The image of the wrinkled face as a ploughed field is not uncommon in late sixteenth-century poetry; see Daniel, *Delia*, 4.7–8 ('all the world may view | Best in my face, how cares have tilled deep furrows'); and Michael Drayton, *Idea, the Shepherd's Garland*, Eclogue 2: 'The time-ploughed furrows in thy fairest field' (1593: sig. B4r). Compare the agricultural metaphor at 22.3, and the militaristic ones (see below) at 60.10.
field (i) agricultural field, ploughed by time; (ii) battlefield, dug with defensive trenches, which connects with 'besiege' above; (iii) heraldic term, to mean the surface of the shield on which charges or bearings are depicted, anticipating 'livery' in l. 3.

3 *youth's proud livery* the splendid appearance of youth; the fact that this beauty is imagined as clothing points to its impermanence. 'Proud' suggests haughtiness (OED³ A1a) as well as splendour (OED³ A5b); i.e. youthful beauty makes the addressee arrogant; 'proud' can also mean 'full of sap; luxuriant in growth' (OED³ A6d), continuing the imagery of plants from l. 2 as well as Sonnet 1. 'Livery' is pronounced as three syllables.

4 *tattered weed* a ragged piece of clothing, contrasting with 'youth's proud livery' (l. 3), but also continuing the potentially botanical strain of 'beauty's field'; 'tottered' in Q, an acceptable variant of 'tattered' in sixteenth- and seventeenth-century English, but now obsolete.
worth value, merit; a significant term within the *Sonnets*, worth and its derivatives appear thirty-two times in twenty-four sonnets (2.4; 16.11; 25.9; 26.12; 37.4; 38.6, 9; 39.1; 48.6; 52.7, 13; 60.14; 62.7, 8; 70.6; 72.4, 14; 74.13; 79.6; 80.5, 11; 82.6; 83.8, twice; 87.3, 9; 100.3; 103.3; 106.12; 116.8; 150.13, 14); twenty-three of these sonnets and thirty occurrences are in the first 126 sonnets, those seen as addressed to, or about, the youth; there are particularly dense clusters around Sonnets 37–39, 70–74, 79–83.

5–8 *Then. . . praise* alludes to the parable of the talents (Matthew 25:14–30), where God is figured as a master who gives his servants money: the two that 'occup[y]' the money and, by putting it to use, double the sum are rewarded; the 'unprofitable' servant who hoards his share is punished.

6 *lusty* 'beautiful' (OED 2a), 'healthy, strong, vigorous' (OED 5); an adjective particularly associated with youth (as in the title of the mid-sixteenth-century morality play, *Lusty Juventus* [juventus = youth]); also 'lustful' (OED 4).

7 *thine own deep-sunken eyes* contrast with the 'bright eyes' of 1.5.

8 *all-eating* all-consuming, devouring everything.
thriftless 'worthless' (OED 2), 'wasteful, improvident' (OED 3), because the youth has hoarded up his beauty, rather than putting it to 'use' (l. 9) through procreation.

9 *use* 'the act of [. . .] employing [. . .] a thing for any (esp. a beneficial or productive) purpose' (OED³ 1a); in this case, the addressee is instructed to use his attractive body to

2

When forty winters shall besiege thy brow,
And dig deep trenches in thy beauty's field,
Thy youth's proud livery so gazed on now
Will be a tattered weed of small worth held: 4
Then, being asked where all thy beauty lies,
Where all the treasure of thy lusty days,
To say within thine own deep-sunken eyes
Were an all-eating shame and thriftless praise.   8
How much more praise deserved thy beauty's use
If thou couldst answer, 'This fair child of mine
Shall sum my count and make my old excuse',
Proving his beauty by succession thine.   12
    This were to be new made when thou art old,
    And see thy blood warm when thou feel'st it cold.

procreate. 'Beauty is made for use' is proverbial; see *Venus and Adonis*, 164n. The financial connotations of 'use' (lending money for interest, i.e. accruing profit from its use) surface explicitly in Sonnet 6. 'Use' can also imply sexual activity; see *King Lear*, 4.6.161–3: 'Why dost thou lash that whore? Strip thine own back, | Thou hotly lusts to use her in that kind | For which thou whip'st her'.

10–11 **'This. . . excuse'** Q does not mark direct speech.

11 **sum my count** 'tot up my account'.
make my old excuse 'justify how I have spent my beauty when I am old'; 'old' here stands for 'in my old age'; the alternative and ostensibly more straightforward meaning of 'make my usual excuse' does not make sense in this context.

12 **Proving** There is an on-going concern in the *Sonnets* with the idea of demonstrating, or proving, something through trial and experience; the verb 'prove' and its related terms ('approve', 'proof') appear twenty-four times in twenty-one sonnets (2.12; 8.14; 10.12; 26.14; 32.13; 39.9; 42.8; 48.14; 70.5; 72.4; 88.4; 110.8, 11; 116.13; 117.10, 13; 125.4; 129.11, twice; 136.7; 147.7; 151.4; 153.7; 154.13). Erasmus' 'Epistle on marriage' (a key source for Sonnets 1–17, see headnote to Sonnets 1–17) is also motivated by a desire to 'prove' its case, the word appearing twice in its opening peroration: 'I will

neither wish that the love of your friends [. . .] nor yet mine authority that I have over you should do me any good at all [. . .] if I shall not prove unto you by most plain reasons that it will be both much more honest, more profitable, and also more pleasant for you to marry than to live otherwise. Yea, what will you say, if I prove it also to be necessary for you at this time to marry?' (Wilson, *Art of Rhetoric*, sig. F2r).

by succession 'according to the customary or legal principle by which one succeeds another in an inheritance, an office, etc. by inherited right' (OED 5b, citing this line).

13 **were** would be.
new made made again (in the child); rejuvenated.

14 **And. . . cold** Early modern medical theory held that you were hot and moist in youth, and that you cooled and dried with age (see Elyot, *Castle of Health*, sigs B2v–B3r); in this line, even though the aged father's blood runs colder, when he looks at his son he will see his own blood still warm, because he shares the same blood as his son. For the belief that a son shares his father's blood, see *Henry V*, 3.1.17–18 ('On, on, you noblest English, | Whose blood is fet from fathers of war-proof!') or Laertes' assertion, when seeking his father's revenge: 'That drop of blood that's calm proclaims me bastard' (*Hamlet*, 4.5.118).

3

Benson combines Sonnets 1–3 under the title 'Loves cruelty'.

1, 9 *glass* mirror; both (i) a symbol of vanity (see the description of Pride in Edmund Spenser's *Faerie Queene*, I.iv.10.6–7: 'And in her hand she held a mirrhour bright | Wherein her face she often vewed fayne') and (ii) a genre of early modern writing with a didactic function (where the image is an exemplary one), as in the best-selling *Mirror for Magistrates* (various editions 1559–1621) or William Averell's *Dial for Dainty Darlings* (1584), subtitled *A glass for all disobedient sons to look in, A mirror for virtuous maids*. Daniel's *Delia* 29 similarly begins with the image of the addressee gazing in her mirror ('O why doth Delia credit so her glass?', l. 1); this sonnet immediately precedes, and leads into, a mini-sequence imagining the addressee's (Delia's) lost youth and beauty (see headnote to Sonnet 2). Shakespeare makes recurrent use of the trope of the glass or mirror in the first 126 sonnets; see 22.1; 62.9; 103.6, 14.

2 *another* another face; early modern spacing of compound words is not systematic (see discussion of the *-self* suffix in the notes on modernising principles, introduction, p. xiv); however Q's 'an other' also holds open the sense of 'another person'.

3 *Whose* refers to 'the face' (l. 1), not to 'another'.
fresh 'not deteriorated or changed by lapse of time' (OED A7a), 'not faded or worn' (OED A8), 'looking healthy or youthful' (OED A9b).
repair condition (*n*.2, OED³ 4); whilst the phrase 'fresh repair' could indicate the 'recent' 'action of repairing a damaged, worn, or faulty object or structure' ('fresh, *adj*.', OED 2a; 'repair, *n*.2', OED³ 2a), the context makes this meaning unlikely. Booth (1977: 139) suggests an intralingual pun on 'père' (French for father), citing *All's Well*, 1.2.30–1: 'It much repairs me | To talk of your good father'.
renewest 'make[s] (something) new, or like new, again; [...] restore[s] to the same condition as when new, young, or fresh' ('renew, *v*.1', OED³ 1a), 'replace[s] with something new or fresh of the same kind' (OED³ 5a).

4 *beguile the world* cheat the world of what it is owed (compare Sonnet 1.14); 'beguile' suggests that this trickery is done charmingly (OED 4, 5).

unbless some mother deprive a woman (a mother *in potentia*) of the blessing of children; this is the first recorded usage in OED of 'unbless', although the word appears in John Brooke's translation of Pierre Viret's *Christian Disputations* (1579: sig. U3r), where it is also used in the context of sexual intercourse ('They [adulterers] may well go to bless the beds of the spouses, for to learn the way, and to unbless them afterwards'). For the idea of conception as a blessing, see *Hamlet*, 2.2.184–6: 'Conception is a blessing, but as your daughter may conceive, friend, look to't'.

5 *uneared* The word has two different, but mutually enforcing, meanings: (i) unfruitful (corn or wheat is 'eared' when it has set seed, 'ear, *v*.2', OED³); (ii) 'unploughed, untilled' ('uneared, *adj*.', OED), from the Old English 'erian', to plough; for the sexual connotations of ploughing, see *Antony and Cleopatra*, 2.2.228: 'He ploughed her, and she cropped'. Compare Wilson's translation of Erasmus' epistle on marriage: 'What punishment is he worthy to suffer, that refuseth to plough that land, which being tilled, yieldeth children' (*Art of Rhetoric*, sig. H1v). Shakespeare uses 'ears' as a synonym for 'ploughs' in *All's Well*, 1.3.44–5 (in a passage about the benefits of being a willing cuckold): 'He that ears my land spares my team, and gives me leave to inn [harvest] the crop'.

6 *husbandry* 'tillage or cultivation of the soil' (OED 2a); continues the agricultural imagery – and bawdy innuendo – of l. 5; compare *Measure for Measure*, 1.4.43–4: 'her plenteous womb | Expresseth his full tilth and husbandry'. In Sonnet 3 (unlike *Measure for Measure*, where it describes Juliet's pregnancy, conceived out of wedlock), the word plays on the meaning of 'husband' as a married man. A further meaning of 'husband' ('to use, spend, or apply economically; [...] to save, lay by a store of') is also relevant ('husband, *v*.', OED 2).

7 *fond* 'foolish' (OED A2), 'loving' (OED A5a).
tomb more specific than 'grave'; OED defines 'tomb' as 'a monument erected to enclose or cover the body and preserve the memory of the dead; a sepulchral structure raised above the earth' (OED 2); that sense of a tomb as an architectural structure is its usual sense in Shakespeare; see, for example, *1 Henry VI*, 2.2.12–13: 'I'll erect | A tomb, wherein his corpse shall be interred'.

3

Look in thy glass and tell the face thou viewest,
Now is the time that face should form another,
Whose fresh repair, if now thou not renewest,
Thou dost beguile the world, unbless some mother: 4
For where is she so fair whose uneared womb
Disdains the tillage of thy husbandry?
Or who is he so fond will be the tomb
Of his self-love to stop posterity?   8
Thou art thy mother's glass, and she in thee
Calls back the lovely April of her prime;
So thou through windows of thine age shalt see,
Despite of wrinkles, this thy golden time.   12
   But if thou live rememb'red not to be,
   Die single, and thine image dies with thee.

7–8 the tomb. . . posterity Compare *Venus and Adonis*, ll. 757–8 (lines also evoked by 1.14).

8 *Of* The word can serve two different grammatical functions; (i) as a conjunction ('because of' the youth's self-love he will stop prosperity); (ii) as a genitive ('the tomb | Of his self-love'). Q has a comma after tomb, but it frequently has commas where modern readers would enjamb the lines (see 152.3–4n), and – as a discreet utterance – line 7 seems incomplete without an explanation of what is entombed.

stop posterity cut off the family line (stop = 'put an end to', OED 23a); compare Volumnia threatening the tribune Sicinius in *Coriolanus*, 4.2.26: 'He'ld make an end of thy posterity'.

9 *mother's glass* For the concept of offspring as mirrors to their parents, see l. 10n (below) and Lucretius' lament in *Lucrece*, ll. 1758–9.

10 *Calls back* 'Remember' as a meaning of 'call back' is not cited by OED before 1851 ('to call back', in 'call, *v.*', OED 4); however the verb 'recall' could mean 'remember' (OED[3] 4a) from the late sixteenth century, and 'call to mind/remembrance' was in use from the fifteenth century ('call, *v.*', OED 20b). Since the mother's image is actually in front of her (in the form of her son), the physical sense of 'to summon (a person) to return' ('to call back', OED 2) is also appropriate. In making the son the mirror to a mother, not a father, the sonnet modifies the usual pattern found, for example, in Erasmus' 'Epistle to persuade a young man to marriage': 'what man can be grieved that he is old when he seeth his own countenance, which he had being a child, to appear lively in his son?' (trans. Wilson, *Art of Rhetoric*, sig. H3r). It may be that the androgyny hinted at here pre-empts that of Sonnet 20, although *Lucrece* also blurs divisions of gender, as Lucretius describes his daughter as a 'broken glass' in which he 'often did behold | [. . .] his] old age new born' (ll. 1758–9).

lovely 'lovable; deserving of love or admiration' (OED[3] A2), 'beautiful' (OED[3] A3a); compare 5.2.

April month epitomising spring; 'In the April of one's age' was proverbial (Dent A310); compare Daniel, *Delia* 31.9: 'No April can revive thy withered flowers'.

prime 'early adulthood' (*n.*1, OED[3] 8), a sense that builds on the meaning of 'prime' as 'spring' (OED[3] 7); 'prime' also means the 'best or most flourishing stage' (OED[3] 9a), i.e. 'the prime of life'. Compare 12.3.

11 *windows of thine age* aged eyes; early modern glass was translucent rather than transparent (as in 1 Corinthians 13:12: 'now we see through a glass darkly'); the image thus conveys the bleared eyesight that comes with old age. In Sonnets 1–17 the youth is periodically described (as here) in terms of a house, a

290 Shakespeare's Sonnets

further reminder of the youth's responsibilities for maintaining the family property as well as the dynastic line. The correlation between property, status and inheritance is evident from fathers' advice to their sons during this period; see, for example, William Cecil's opinion that 'that gentleman which [. . .] sells an acre of land loses an ounce of credit, for gentility is nothing but ancient riches' or Walter Ralegh's explanation of why a widow should not inherit the family seat: 'Thy house and thy estate, which liveth in thy son and heir, not in thy wife, is to be preferred' (Wright 1962: 10, 22).

12 *wrinkles* Following Aristotle, early modern medical theory held that eyesight was diminished in old age because 'the skin in the eyes, like that elsewhere, gets wrinkled and thicker in old age' (*De Generatione Animalium* 780a, 31–3; p. 501).

golden time youth; compare *Richard III*: 'the golden prime of this sweet prince' (1.2.247).

13 *rememb'red* Q's spelling 'remembred' has the same number of syllables as 'remembered', but possibly (i) suggests a slightly different pronunciation, and (ii) puns on 'bred' (although see also 29.13, where no such pun seems intended).

14 *image* (i) appearance; (ii) copy (i.e. son, who – unborn – will die with the friend); for that second sense, see *Winter's Tale*, 5.1.127: 'Your father's image is so hit in you'.

3

Look in thy glass and tell the face thou viewest,
Now is the time that face should form another,
Whose fresh repair, if now thou not renewest,
Thou dost beguile the world, unbless some mother: 4
For where is she so fair whose uneared womb
Disdains the tillage of thy husbandry?
Or who is he so fond will be the tomb
Of his self-love to stop posterity?   8
Thou art thy mother's glass, and she in thee
Calls back the lovely April of her prime;
So thou through windows of thine age shalt see,
Despite of wrinkles, this thy golden time.   12
    But if thou live rememb'red not to be,
    Die single, and thine image dies with thee.

4

Benson combines Sonnets 4–6 under the title 'Magazine [store] of beauty'.

1 ***Unthrifty*** 'Unprofitable, wasteful; harmful' (OED 1a), because the youth's beauty is not put to use (compare 2.5–12); the term may also suggest 'unchaste, wanton' (OED 3), although this meaning was archaic by the end of the sixteenth century: of the fifty-one usages that show up in EEBO-TCP for 1590–9, the primary meaning is predominantly one of waste and extravagance (usually coupled with idleness or other financial mismanagement, such as gambling). This opening word thus establishes the financial imagery that runs through this sonnet and which appears in almost every line: 'spend' (l. 1); 'legacy' (l. 2); 'bequest', 'lend' (l. 3); 'frank', 'lends' (l. 4); 'niggard' (l. 5); 'bounteous largess' (l. 6); 'profitless usurer', 'use' (l. 7); 'sum' (l. 8); 'traffic' (l. 9); 'audit' (l. 12); 'used', 'executor' (l. 14). This imagery develops the financial thread of Sonnet 2 (where the cognate term 'thriftless' features at 2.8), and the idea in Sonnet 3 of beauty being left as an inheritance to posterity; both these themes are pursued in Sonnet 6. These motifs, of lending for profit and of ensuring a legacy, are reminiscent of Leander's seduction speech in Marlowe's *Hero and Leander* (especially ll. 234–5 'treasure is abused, | When misers keep it'), composed before Marlowe's death in May 1593.

1–2 ***spend | Upon thyself*** 'Spend' can mean 'ejaculate' (see 129.1n; 149.7–8n; *All's Well*, 2.3.281: 'Spending his manly marrow in her arms'). 'Spend | Upon thyself' would thus imply masturbation (the antithesis of procreative intercourse). The primary meaning, however, indicates self-absorption: the youth's attention is expended ('spend, *v.*1', OED 3) on himself alone and is therefore squandered (OED 10a). As the sonnet develops, the financial sense (of dispensing money) is also activated.

2 ***thy beauty's legacy*** both the beauty that the youth has received from either nature ('Nature's bequest', l. 3) or his own parents, and the beauty that he should pass on to his heir.

3 ***lend*** For the idea that life is something on loan, see Desiderius Erasmus, *Mimi Publiani*,

translated by Richard Taverner: '*Homo vitae commodatus, non donatus est.* Man is lent unto life and not given. As who should say, life is granted but for a time and in such wise as he that lent it may lawfully require it again when him lusteth' (1539: sig. C8r). See also Daniel, *Delia* 34.7: 'Here see the gifts that God and nature lent thee'.

4 ***frank*** 'liberal, bounteous, generous' (*adj.*2, OED 2a); the word – paired and alliterating with 'free' at the end of the line – also plays on the older sense, already archaic by the end of the sixteenth century, of 'free in condition; not in serfdom or slavery' (OED 1a), a meaning often found in the phrase 'frank and free'.

those are those who are.

free There are multiple meanings at play here. The word echoes the dual meanings of 'frank' at the start of the line, indicating 'not [...] in servitude or subjection to another' (OED³ A1a) and 'honourable, generous, magnanimous' (OED³ A3b), qualities that would have been expected of someone (like the youth) who is 'of noble birth' (OED³ A3a). As with 'unthrifty' (l. 1), there is also a suggestion of sexual licentiousness ('sexually promiscuous or available', OED³ A19); see *1 Henry VI*, 5.4.82: 'It's a sign she hath been liberal and free'.

5–6 ***Then. . . give*** Like 2.5–8, these lines allude to the parable of the talents (Matthew 25:14–30).

5 ***beauteous*** pronounced as two syllables; aside from the *Sonnets*, Shakespeare uses the word twenty-nine times; eighteen of these uses describe women (or aspects of women); nine, objects or abstractions; only two describe men: the seducer in *A Lover's Complaint* (l. 99) and Adonis (*Venus and Adonis*, l. 1107), both of whom (in their androgynous beauty) have much in common with the youth of the *Sonnets*. 'Beauteous' is used in the *Sonnets* more than in any other work (nine times); five of these instances describe the youth or some quality of his (here at 4.5; 10.7; 41.6; 54.13; 84.13); the other four occurrences describe things (night, day, beauty, spring) made beauteous by association (27.12; 34.1; 54.1; 104.5); none of the instances occurs in the sonnets to or about the mistress.

niggard miser (OED³ A1a); compare 'waste in niggarding' (Sonnet 1.12).

4

Unthrifty loveliness, why dost thou spend
Upon thyself thy beauty's legacy?
Nature's bequest gives nothing but doth lend,
And being frank she lends to those are free: 4
Then, beauteous niggard, why dost thou abuse
The bounteous largess given thee to give?
Profitless usurer, why dost thou use
So great a sum of sums, yet canst not live? 8
For having traffic with thyself alone,
Thou of thyself thy sweet self dost deceive;
Then how, when Nature calls thee to be gone,
What acceptable audit canst thou leave? 12
    Thy unused beauty must be tombed with thee,
    Which usèd lives th' executor to be.

abuse misuse (OED³ 1a), but also continues the vein of sexual innuendo running through the poem (OED³ 4: 'to inflict a sexual act regarded as illicit or unnatural', a sense which could also be used reflexively, 'to behave in a licentious manner; [...] to masturbate').

6 ***bounteous largess*** the beauty given to the youth, but which he is refusing to pass on to the next generation; the phrase is pleonastic, since largess is necessarily bountiful. 'Bounteous' is pronounced as two syllables.

7 ***Profitless usurer*** oxymoronic, because a usurer lends money for profit. Usury was a controversial issue in the late sixteenth century: trade required money-lending, but it contravened Biblical strictures; see Jones 1989. Usurers were stereotyped as misers (see Shylock in *Merchant of Venice*, or Marlowe's Barabas in *Jew of Malta*), and the phrase consequently harks back to 'beauteous niggard' (l. 5).

use The primary meaning suggests waste ('consume, expend [...], exhaust, wear out', OED³ 12); however, as elsewhere in this sonnet, other meanings are also at play. There is sense of irony conveyed by the contradictory possibilities of the verb 'use', since the youth wastes what he should 'put to practical or effective use' (OED³ 15a). As with 'unthrifty', 'spend', 'free', 'abuse' and, later, 'traffic', a sexual reading is possible

('to have sexual intercourse with', OED³ 14b): interpreted this way, the youth is wanton ('unthrifty', l. 1; 'free', l. 4), but is not spending his seed in a legitimate womb, which will produce profit in the form of an heir.

8 ***sum of sums*** phrase deriving from the Latin *summa summarum*, i.e. the grand total, made up of smaller quantities; here, it describes the youth's beauty (his 'bounteous largess').

live Within the financial metaphor, this means 'sustain oneself' (*v.*1, OED³ 2a), but within the context of the sonnet (and the procreation sonnets in general) it means to live on in posterity, through producing a child.

9 ***traffic*** commerce (OED 1), trade (OED 2a), continuing the financial imagery of this sonnet; the word can also imply sexual traffic (see Partridge 1990: 204); as such, this echoes the potential reading of ll. 1–2 as masturbation ('spend | Upon thyself').

10 ***of thyself*** by your own actions; perhaps also the replica of the self that would be created in a son; for the idea of a son as a second self, compare 6.7, 10.13, 13.7.

deceive cheat, defraud (OED 4); in this case, the youth defrauds himself of a son.

11 ***how*** Duncan-Jones suggests that 'how' is redundant (the question, 'what...?' follows in l. 12), but that its insertion may emphasise the

'searching nature of the question' (1997a: 118). Alternatively, 'how' could indicate (i) an exclamation; or (ii) 'by what means' or 'at what rate or price' (*adv.*, OED 1a, 6).

12 *audit* official examination of financial accounts; here the addressee is being constructed as either an executor, summing up the assets of a dead person, or as a steward, producing an account of the wealth of an aristocratic household, thus picking up on a motif that runs through Sonnets 1–17 (especially 10, 13) where the fair youth is imagined in terms of a country house (the family seat), which he holds in lease for the next generation. Failure to produce an 'acceptable audit' could be punished with imprisonment (Sokol 2000: 17). The necessity of giving an audit, accounting for the use to which gifts have been put, recalls the parable of the talents (Matthew 25:14–30), where the servants are called upon to give an oral reckoning, which is how an audit would have originally been delivered: 'audit' derives from the Latin *auditus*

(hearing), and is capitalised and italicised in Q, as is the frequently the case with proper nouns or (as here) a foreign coinage; see also 126.11.
leave Audits are usually given, rather than left (Duncan-Jones 1997a: 118); 'leave' suggests (i) the fact that the young man will depart from this world; (ii) the legacy (currently an empty one) that he will leave behind.

13 *unused* because not put out for profit (i.e. the production of an heir); 'unused' can also mean 'unusual' (OED 3), pointing to the youth's exceptional beauty and emphasising the loss to the world should he not reproduce it in the next generation.

14 *uséd* invested, put to use (through procreation).
th' executor the 'person appointed by a testator to execute or carry into effect his will after his decease' (OED 3a), here, a son; the word carries on the imagery of legacies and wills begun in Sonnet 1, and present in this sonnet from l. 2. Some editors (following Malone, following Capell) emend to 'thy executor'.

4

Unthrifty loveliness, why dost thou spend
Upon thyself thy beauty's legacy?
Nature's bequest gives nothing but doth lend,
And being frank she lends to those are free: 4
Then, beauteous niggard, why dost thou abuse
The bounteous largess given thee to give?
Profitless usurer, why dost thou use
So great a sum of sums, yet canst not live?   8
For having traffic with thyself alone,
Thou of thyself thy sweet self dost deceive;
Then how, when Nature calls thee to be gone,
What acceptable audit canst thou leave?   12
    Thy unused beauty must be tombed with thee,
    Which usèd lives th' executor to be.

5

Blakemore Edwards (1996: 119) highlights the relationship between Sonnets 5–6 ('man and the seasons'), Sonnet 7 ('man, day and night') and Ovid's *Metamorphoses*, 15.177–229 (Golding, 15.196–251; sig. 2C5r–v), lines which treat of change and the destructiveness of time. The analogy between human life and the seasons was commonplace. See George Gascoigne, 'Gascoigne's Gardenings' (the quotation below also appears – under the heading 'Life' – in the printed commonplace book *England's Parnassus*, 1600: sig. M5r):

> [. . .] The restless life which men here lead
> May be resembled to the tender plant:
> In spring it sprouts, as babes in cradle breed;
> Flourish in May, like youths that wisdom want;
> In autumn ripe, and rots lest store wax scant;
> In winter shrinks and shrouds from every blast,
> Like crooked age, when lusty youth is past.
> (*Hundreth Sundry Flowers*, 1573: 399)

Benson combines Sonnets 4–6 under the title 'Magazine of beauty' ('Magazine' = store).

1 *hours* pronounced as two syllables; since the sonnet proceeds to talk about the seasons, as well as indicating 'time', 'hours' may also refer to the mythological *Horae*, 'female divinities supposed to preside over the changes of the seasons' ('hour, *n.*', OED 6); although this usage is not attested in OED before Milton's *Comus* (1637), the emphasis on classical literature in the grammar school curriculum may have made this secondary meaning available to educated readers.
gentle 'noble' (OED A1d), 'tender' (OED A5); the word is recurrently associated with the youth (see 20.3; 40.9; 41.5; 79.2; 96.2). Unlike many of the epithets associated with the youth, this one is also used in sonnets traditionally associated with the mistress (see 128.3, 11; 151.3). For sexual connotations of the word, see 20.3n.
frame 'shape' (OED³ 5a), 'make' (OED³ 7), but also in the specific sense 'prepare (timber) for use in building' (OED³ 4a), an architectural meaning with particular resonance in the context of a series of sonnets addressed to an aristocratic youth, with responsibilities towards the upkeep of his house (both his family seat and his dynastic line).

2 *lovely* 'lovable; deserving of love or admiration' (OED³ A2), 'beautiful' (OED³ A3a); compare 3.10.

gaze 'that which is gazed or stared at' (OED 1), i.e. the youth; it may also refer to the youth's gaze (his eyes).
dwell linger (OED 5), but – coming so close to 'frame' (l. 1) – it may also evoke the idea of reside (OED 7).

3 *tyrants* Time is portrayed as a tyrant in Sonnets 16 and 115; compare Daniel, *Delia* 30.5–7: 'Then beauty [. . .] | Whose glorious blaze the world doth so admire, | Must yield up all to tyrant Time's desire'.

4 *unfair* 'deprive of fairness or beauty' (OED); a Shakespearean coinage and the only citation for the verb in OED; a keyword search of EEBO-TCP reveals no earlier instances.
fairly doth excel 'is outstandingly beautiful', but other senses of 'fairly' – 'by proper or legal means; legitimately' (OED³ 4a), 'in accordance with what is right or just' (OED³ 4b) – are also invoked, suggesting that the way in which the hours 'unfair' the youth is unjust (as are the actions of tyrants, to which they are compared).

5 *Time. . . summer* Q is not consistent in the capitalisation of words such as 'time' and 'summer' in cases where they could be read as personifications (here Q capitalises summer, but not time); capitalisation may also be a reflection of compositorial, rather than authorial, practice.
leads summer on Time guides summer in the dance of the seasons (compare 'To the Queen', l. 7, Appendix 6), but also 'lures, entices', as in *Merry Wives*, 2.1.95–6: 'lead him on with a fine-baited delay'.

6 *hideous* 'causing dread or horror' (OED A1); here pronounced as two syllables. Shakespeare does not use this word lightly: compare 'a hideous shapeless devil' (*Lucrece*, l. 973); 'hideous death' (*King John*, 5.4.22); 'the hideous god of war' (*2 Henry IV*, 2.3.35).
confounds defeats utterly, destroys (OED 1); continues the portrayal of time as a tyrant (see notes on ll. 3–4, above); the verb and its cognate terms are also used to describe the destructive effects of time/age at 60.8, 63.10, 64.10.
him summer, often depicted as male; see Thomas Nashe, *Summer's Last Will and Testament* (1592) or Spenser, *Faerie Queene*, VII.vii.29 ('Cantoes of Mutabilitie').

7 *Sap. . . frost* On a literal level, this refers to how plants are affected by winter (the sap retreats and the leaves fall); however, lying behind the sonnet is the notion of the seasons of human life: for the

5

Those hours, that with gentle work did frame
The lovely gaze where every eye doth dwell,
Will play the tyrants to the very same
And that unfair which fairly doth excel: 4
For never-resting Time leads summer on
To hideous winter and confounds him there,
Sap checked with frost, and lusty leaves quite gone,
Beauty o'er-snowed, and bareness everywhere.   8
Then, were not summer's distillation left
A liquid prisoner pent in walls of glass,
Beauty's effect with beauty were bereft,
Nor it, nor no remembrance what it was.   12
    But flowers distilled, though they with winter meet,
    Lose but their show; their substance still lives sweet.

idea that the human body grows colder with age, see 2.14n.

checked stopped; the first citation in OED for 'checked' as an adjective meaning 'stopped' is 1793 (*adj*.1, OED 1a), but that sense of the verb was in use from the fourteenth century ('check, *v.*1' OED 3).

lusty pleasant (OED 2), beautiful (OED 2a), 'full of healthy vigour' (OED 5); compare 2.6 and note.

8 **o'er-snowed** Given as first citation in OED³; the only Shakespearean usage; a keyword search of EEBO-TCP reveals no earlier instances. The word evokes both the once-summery landscape covered in snow, and a once-young head now covered with white hair; compare Daniel, *Delia* 33.14, 34.1 ('When winter snows upon thy golden hairs') and Golding's translation of Ovid, *Metamorphoses* 15.212–13, to which this sonnet alludes (see headnote): 'Then ugly winter last | Like age steals on with trembling steps, all bald, all overcast | With shirl [rough] thin hair as white as snow' (Golding, 15.233–5; sig. 2C5v).

bareness Gildon 1710 emends to 'barrenness'; Q's 'barenes' is a feasible early modern spelling of 'barrenness'; however, by the late sixteenth century, puns on the two words rely on their orthographic differentiation, even as they play on their inter-relation; see, for example, Thomas

Middleton, *The Wisdom of Solomon Paraphrased*: 'barenes and barrennes is vertues grace' (1597: sig. E2v; original spelling retained); W.I., *The Whipping of the Satyr* makes similar use of orthography in a similar pun (1601: sig. F1v). Gildon's emendation also disrupts the metre.

9 **distillation** 'the product of distilling' (OED 4), i.e. the essence; the product being distilled here is 'beauty's rose' (1.2); rose-water was frequently used in early modern medicine and cookery.

10 **liquid.... glass** A number of editors note the probable allusion to Cecropia's speech on marriage in Philip Sidney's *Arcadia*: 'Have you ever seen a pure rosewater kept in a crystal glass, how fine it looks, how sweet it smells while that beautiful glass imprisons it? Break the prison, and let the water take his own course, doth it not embrace dust and lose all his former sweetness and fairness? Truly so are we, if we have not the stay, rather than the restraint, of crystalline marriage' (1590: sig. 2L6r). Shakespeare uses the same image, but makes it emblematic, not of marriage per se, but of the procreation it legitimates (the child who will preserve his father's beauty).

prisoner pronounced as two syllables.

pent confined; not a common Shakespearean word (it appears eight times across all his works), it also appears at 133.13.

11 **Beauty's effect. . . bereft** If left undistilled, the essence of beauty would be 'quite gone' ('bereft', OED 2) at the same time as ('with') beauty itself; compare the description of Rosaline in *Romeo and Juliet*, 1.1.215–16 (see also 1.12n): 'O, she is rich in beauty, only poor | That, when she dies, with beauty dies her store'.

12 **Nor it. . . was** The main verb – e.g. 'remains' – is missing (appropriate in a sonnet in which everything, including language, is being stripped back to 'bareness everywhere', l. 8).

   nor no double negative, used for emphasis, and quite usual in sixteenth- and early seventeenth-century English; see Blake 2002: 211.

   remembrance (i) memory; (ii) reminder, token by which to remember someone/something, as in *Hamlet* 3.1.92–3: 'My lord, I have remembrances of yours | That I have longed long to redeliver'.

13 **flowers** here pronounced as one syllable.

   meet The word contains a sense of military encounter (OED³ 6a).

14 **lose** Q has 'leese', an acceptable early modern variant for 'lose'; modernising the spelling here effaces both the assonance with 'meet' and 'sweet', and a potential play on (i) 'lees' (the dregs left behind in distillation) and (ii) 'lease'; compare 13.5.

   substance 'nature or essence' (OED³ I), but – considering the way in which Sonnets 1–17 recurrently use the young man's duty to his family estate as a tool of persuasion – the word also suggests 'material possessions, [. . .] goods, estate' (OED³ 12a). The contrast between 'substance' and 'show' is proverbial (Dent S408, S951: 'More show than substance'; 'Lose not the substance for the shadow').

   still 'without change, interruption, or cessation' (OED 3a); the word also puns on the still in which distillation takes place and echoes 'distilled' in l. 13, performing a verbal distillation, extracting 'still' from the adjective 'distilled'. For a similar play on still/distilled, see 119.2, 4.

5

Those hours, that with gentle work did frame
The lovely gaze where every eye doth dwell,
Will play the tyrants to the very same
And that unfair which fairly doth excel: 4
For never-resting Time leads summer on
To hideous winter and confounds him there,
Sap checked with frost, and lusty leaves quite gone,
Beauty o'er-snowed, and bareness everywhere.   8
Then, were not summer's distillation left
A liquid prisoner pent in walls of glass,
Beauty's effect with beauty were bereft,
Nor it, nor no remembrance what it was.   12
    But flowers distilled, though they with winter meet,
    Lose but their show; their substance still lives sweet.

6

Benson combines Sonnets 4–6 under the heading 'Magazine of beauty' ('Magazine' = store).

1 ***Then*** The conjunction is here causative ('that being the case'), and links Sonnet 6 back to Sonnet 5, a connection that is further indicated by the shared vocabulary and ideas, including winter/summer and distillation; the imagery of usury, posterity and inheritance also connects this sonnet to Sonnet 4, so that the three sonnets work as a triad, with Sonnet 6 drawing together threads from both, as Benson reflects in his 1640 edition, where he combines all three sonnets into one poem.

ragged 'rough or shaggy like an animal' (OED[3] 1a), 'having a rough, irregular, or uneven surface, edge, or outline' (OED[3] 2, a sense often used of plants), 'torn, frayed, worn' (of a garment, OED[3] 6a); possibly also a transferred epithet, referring to the effect of winter's hand in making summer ragged. Q's spelling 'wragged' is unusual (a search of EEBO-TCP produces just one other example, from 1675, aside from Q and Benson's 1640 edition, based on Q).

hand As Burrow points out (2002: 392) 'hand' could also mean handwriting, so that winter is imagined scoring lines in the youth's face; compare 19.10.

deface (i) 'mar the face, features, or appearance of' (OED 1a); (ii) 'blot out, obliterate, efface (writing, marks)' (OED 3a).

3 ***vial*** a vessel for liquids (e.g. perfume); here, a woman's womb; compare John Lydgate's praise of the Virgin Mary: 'O glorious viole [vial], O vitre [glass] inviolable' (*A Balade in Commendation of Our Lady*, l. 113).

treasure 'furnish or endow with treasures' (OED 3, citing this instance as the first usage of this sense of the verb); the dominant modern sense ('cherish', OED 4) is not cited before 1907.

4 ***beauty's treasure*** the youth's beauty which he is being commanded to bestow upon a woman, by impregnating her; it is also possible to read 'beauty' as referring to a woman: the treasure that he is to bestow upon her is her due (hence the use of the possessive). Emilia in *Othello* indicates the possibility of reading 'treasure' as 'semen', as she complains about philandering husbands who 'pour our treasures into foreign laps' (4.3.88). Q's 'beautits' – a compositorial error – was emended to 'beauties' by Benson in 1640, and to 'beauty's' by Gildon in 1714.

self-killed Orgasm was known as a 'little death' and it was believed that every orgasm shortened one's life-span (see John Donne, 'The Canonization' (1604?), l. 21: 'We're tapers too, and at our own cost die'). 'Self-killed' thus hints at masturbation; see 4.1–2n, 4.9n. Suicide was also strongly connected in the period with self-love (see Langley 2009), epitomised by Narcissus' self-consumption in *Metamorphoses* 3.

5–6 ***That use. . . loan*** Using one's property (here, the friend himself) for profit ('use, *n*.', OED[3] 15b) cannot be considered wrong (***'forbidden usury'***) if it advantages those who have to pay the debt. Elizabethan attitudes to usury were ambivalent (see 4.7n): the Usury Act of 1571 stated that 'all usury, being forbidden by the law of God, is a sin and detestable', yet at the same time legalised charging interest of up to 10 per cent. The sexual sense of 'use' (OED[3] 1c) is relevant here.

6 ***happies*** makes happy (the first citation in OED[3] for its use as a verb is Nicholas Breton's *Mad Cap's Messsage*, 1600: sig. E1r).

willing Booth (1977: 142) points up sexual resonances of this word (see Sonnet 135 and notes).

7 ***That's. . . thee*** The line explains how the youth might meet the conditions of permissible usury laid out in ll. 5–6, i.e. by lending out a part of himself (his semen), a debt which will be repaid in the form of a son. 'That's' thus works as a relative pronoun, linking back to 'That use'.

breed another thee The phrase continues the usury motif by evoking the way in which usury allows money to reproduce itself; the verb 'breed' is also reminiscent of Shakespeare's most famous usurer, Shylock: 'ANTONIO: [. . .] is your gold and silver ewes and rams? SHYLOCK: I cannot tell, I make it breed as fast' (*Merchant of Venice*, 1.3.95–6). For the idea of a son as a second self, see 4.10n.

8 ***ten for one*** ten children, produced by one father; alludes to the fact that 10 per cent was the maximum interest that could be charged under the 1571 Usury Act (see note on ll. 5–6, above).

9 ***than*** in Q 'then', a standard variant spelling of 'than'; grammar requires 'than' (to complete the comparative clause); the original spelling allows that whilst also retaining a temporal sense ('at that time in the future, as opposed to now').

6

Then let not winter's ragged hand deface
In thee thy summer ere thou be distilled:
Make sweet some vial; treasure thou some place
With beauty's treasure ere it be self-killed.   4
That use is not forbidden usury
Which happies those that pay the willing loan;
That's for thyself to breed another thee,
Or ten times happier be it ten for one.   8
Ten times thyself were happier than thou art,
If ten of thine ten times refigured thee;
Then what could death do if thou shouldst depart,
Leaving thee living in posterity?   12
   Be not self-willed, for thou art much too fair
   To be death's conquest and make worms thine heir.

10 *refigured* OED cites this line to support the definition 'to figure again; to represent in a different shape or form' ('refigure, *v*.', OED³ 1); considering the mathematical multiplications in ll. 7–10, the word may also play on the meaning of 'figure' as 'calculate' ('figure, *v*.', OED 12b). OED does not cite any instances of the verb 'figure' in this sense before the late nineteenth century; however, the noun 'figure' to mean 'numerical symbol' (OED 19a) – 'originally applied to the ten syllables of the so-called Arabic notation' – was in use from the early thirteenth century.

11 *depart* Although, in context, the word means 'leave', it also echoes the marriage service in the *Book of Common Prayer*: 'till death us depart [i.e. separate]' (2011: 159).

12 *Leaving* (i) continues the idea of departure (from l. 11); and (ii) recalls the inheritance imagery of Sonnet 4, as the youth will bequeath ('leave, *v*.1', OED 2a) himself as a legacy.

   posterity (i) descendants (OED³ 1); compare *Lucrece*, l. 208, and *Venus and Adonis*, l. 758; (ii) 'all future generations of people collectively' (OED³ 2a).

13 *self-willed* 'wilful or obstinate in the pursuit of one's own desires or opinions' (OED); echoes – both verbally and conceptually – 'self-killed' (l. 4). For the sexual resonances of 'will', see Sonnet 135 and notes; 'willing', l. 6 (above); and

Lucrece, l. 707. Q's spelling 'selfe-wild' may also reflect a sense of the friend's savagery towards himself (in his refusal to self-perpetuate); however, when contracting an *-ed* ending to 'd', Q's compositors tend not to retain a double *ll* (see 17.2n). 'Self-willed' therefore seems the primary meaning, to be prioritised when modernising.

   fair beautiful, but also contains a secondary sense of being just or fair-minded: the sonnet thus uses wordplay to portray the youth as too honourable to squander his beauty and deny it to subsequent generations; early modern praise poetry was frequently used to prescribe the desired behaviour, rather than describe the reality.

14 *conquest* something that is conquered; the word has amorous and/or sexual connotations; see, for example, *Richard III*: 'Bound with triumphant garlands will I come | And lead thy daughter to a conqueror's bed; | To whom I will retail my conquest won, | And she shall be sole victoress' (4.4.333–6).

   worms symbolic of the levelling effect of death, which effaces all differences of wealth, status or beauty; see *Hamlet*, 4.3.21–4: 'Your worm is your only emperor for diet: we fat all creatures else to fat us, and we fat ourselves for maggots; your fat king and your lean beggar is but variable service, two dishes, but to one table'.

7

Printed as a single sonnet by Benson entitled 'Quick prevention'.

1 *orient* east; here pronounced as two syllables not three.

gracious light the sun, which is the central metaphor of this sonnet, although the word 'sun' does not appear until the homophonic pun on 'son' in l. 14. 'Gracious' – denoting something that imparts 'grace' – had more weight than now. As a quality associated with royalty (OED³ 2c), it pre-empts the 'majesty' of l. 4; as a quality associated with the divine (OED³ 4), it contributes to the religious, and specifically Christian, resonances of much of the vocabulary of this sonnet ('sacred', l. 4; 'pilgrimage', l. 8; 'converted', l. 11; and 'heavenly hill', l. 5, possibly evoking the site of Christ's crucifixion). The central metaphor – of the sun, which rises in the east – is also one with Christian application (Christ as the resurrected Son).

2 *each under-eye* all mortal eyes, distinguished by the adjective 'under' from the eye above, i.e. the sun; for the sun as the eye of heaven, see 18.5. Mortal eyes are 'under' both because of their physical location, under the sun, and their status as the sun's subjects (a position that becomes clear by the time we get to 'homage', l. 3, and 'majesty', l. 4).

3 *homage* in feudal law, 'formal and public acknowledgement of allegiance, by which a male tenant declares himself the vassal of the king or the lord from whom he holds land; the existence of such a relationship, typically entailing payment oaths of fidelity, or obligations of service' (OED³ 1); the eyes do 'homage' because, unable to stare directly at the brightening sun, they have to look down (like people bowing before a monarch).

4 *sacred majesty* Compare *King Lear*, 1.1.109: 'by the sacred radiance of the sun'.

5 *having climbed* refers to the sun, not the 'under-eyes'.

steep-up precipitous; compare *Passionate Pilgrim*, 9.5 (Appendix 3) and *Othello*, 5.2.280: 'Wash me in steep-down gulfs of liquid fire!'. The image also echoes Golding's translation of Ovid's *Metamorphoses* 15.226–7: 'wearing out his middle age apace, | Through drooping age's steepy path he runneth out his race' (15.248–9; sig. 2C5v).

heavenly here pronounced as two syllables.

6 *middle age* the prime of youth; Shakespeare here uses the tri-partite division of the ages of man (which goes back to Aristotle's discussion in *Rhetoric*, Book 2), where the stages of life were 'youth, the prime of life, and old age' (2.12.2).

7 *Yet* pleonastic with 'still' (i.e. continually, to the present time), rather than being used to mean 'nevertheless'.

8 *Attending on* paying attention to, watching, but also continues the metaphor of the sun as sovereign, who is waited on by mortal eyes, as a monarch would be by servants.

pilgrimage course, progress; see *Lucrece*, l. 960 and note.

9–12 *But. . . way* These lines refer to the proverb 'The rising, not the setting, sun is worshipped by most men' (Dent S979). Owing to the fact that the image of the sun is frequently used as a figure for the ruler, the proverb has obvious potential for political resonance, as can be seen in Plutarch's 'Life of Pompey', when Pompey warns the dictator Sulla 'how men did honour the rising, not the setting of the sun: meaning thereby, how his own honour increased, and Sulla's diminished' (Thomas North's 1579 translation, p. 684). Compare *Julius Caesar*, 5.3.60–3: 'Cassius is no more. O setting sun, | As in thy red rays thou dost sink tonight, | So in his red blood Cassius' day is set! | The sun of Rome is set. Our day is gone'.

9 *highmost pitch* at the highest point.

car a literary or poetic term for chariot, 'esp. of war, triumph, splendour, or pageantry', often used of the chariot of Phaethon or the sun (OED³ 1b). Either the adjective '*weary*' is transferred to the chariot from the driver and team of horses, or 'car' is understood as a collective term, encompassing the driver and team of horses as well as the vehicle itself.

10 *reeleth* totters ('reel, *v*.1', OED³ 3b).

11 *(fore duteous)* The brackets are in Q. Some editors insert an apostrophe ('fore) to indicate the elision of 'afore'; others hyphenate the phrase, so that it becomes a compound adjective (see 86.2n). Neither emendation is necessary: in the sixteenth and early seventeenth centuries, the adverbial form could quite properly be spelled 'fore'.

converted turned away, looking in another direction; in the context of the sonnet, with its recurrent religious imagery, the word-choice

7

Lo, in the orient when the gracious light
Lifts up his burning head, each under-eye
Doth homage to his new-appearing sight,
Serving with looks his sacred majesty;   4
And having climbed the steep-up heavenly hill,
Resembling strong youth in his middle age,
Yet mortal looks adore his beauty still,
Attending on his golden pilgrimage: 8
But when from highmost pitch with weary car
Like feeble age he reeleth from the day,
The eyes (fore duteous) now converted are
From his low tract and look another way: 12
    So thou, thyself outgoing in thy noon,
    Unlooked on diest unless thou get a son.

also brings into play a secondary meaning: 'To cause to turn to and embrace a (specified) religious faith, usually implying that the turning is to truth from error or ignorance' ('convert, *v.*', OED 9a).

12 *tract* path (*n.*3, OED 8).

13 *outgoing* The word captures the way in which, even in his prime, the youth is subject to the transience of time. He outgoes (surpasses) himself (OED³ 3), even as at the peak of his life he is on the journey towards death when he will outgo (go forth from) this life (OED 1). Duncan-Jones (1997a: 124) draws attention to a potential reference to masturbation, with the friend wasting himself even in his prime (alluding to the common early modern

belief that every ejaculation diminished a man's life-span); '*noon*' – Duncan-Jones points out – could indicate an erection (thanks to the upright hand of a clock at twelve); compare Sidney's *Astrophil and Stella*, 76.9 ('But lo, while I do speak, it groweth noon with me') and *Romeo and Juliet*, 2.4.112–13: 'the bawdy hand of the dial is now upon the prick of noon'.

14 *Unlooked on* unregarded.
    diest here pronounced as one syllable.
    get acquire, beget.
    son The controlling metaphor of the sonnet (the sun) is named, through a homophone, in the final word. Compare the pun at *Venus and Adonis*, l. 863.

8

A version of this sonnet (probably copied *c.* 1630–50) appears in BL Additional MS 15,226, fol. 4v, entitled '*In laudem Music[a]e et opprobrium Contemptori[s] eiusdem*' ('In praise of music and in disapproval of he who despises it'); see Appendix 4.

A sonnet about music is appropriately placed as the eighth in the sequence, bearing in mind the reliance of Western music on the idea of the octave; compare the positioning of Sonnet 12, which uses the motif of the clock, and Sonnet 60, with its references to minutes.

Benson combines Sonnets 8–12 under the title 'An invitation to marriage'.

1 ***Music to hear*** either (i) when there is music for you to hear; or (ii) you who are music to hear. Even with the elision of the main verb ('hear'st') to one syllable, this line (like l. 3) has eleven syllables, with sadly/gladly forming feminine rhymes.
   sadly 'mournfully' (OED³ 9a); it was commonplace to portray music as something that induces sadness: see *As You Like It*, 2.5.12–13 ('I can suck melancholy out of a song, as a weasel sucks eggs', 2.5.11–12); *Merchant*, 5.1.69 ('I am never merry when I hear sweet music'). Burrow (2002: 396) cites the motto of the musician John Dowland: *Semper Dowland semper dolens* ('always Dowland, always doleful').

2 ***Sweets*** pleasures, delights (OED 3a); 'sweet sounds' (OED 5a, citing only Spenser, *Faerie Queene*, I.xii.39.6).

3, 4 ***receiv'st*** listen to (OED³ 9c).

4 ***annoy*** The word is stronger than in its modern sense, indicating 'a mental state akin to pain arising from the involuntary reception of impressions [. . .], which one dislikes; [. . .] discomfort, vexation, trouble' (OED 1a). Lavinia's rape is descried as the 'root of [her] annoy' (*Titus Andronicus*, 4.1.49); see also *Lucrece*, ll. 1109, 1370.

5 ***true concord*** perfect agreement, harmony; 'concord' is both a legal (OED 3) and, appropriately, a musical term (OED 5).
   well-tunèd Compare *Lucrece* l. 1080 and note, although here the term indicates more than simply 'melodious', capturing also the action of tuning the strings that has produced the harmony.

6 ***unions*** musical chords or harmonies; since 'union' also means 'marriage' (OED 5), there is a play on 'married' (i.e. joined), which follows; compare *King John*, 2.1.444–7: 'Two such controlling bounds shall you be, kings, | To these two princes, if you marry them. | This union shall do more than battery can | To our fast-closed gates'. Duncan-Jones (1997a: 126) points to a possible allusion to Cecropia's speech on marriage in Sidney's *Arcadia* (which may also be alluded to at 5.10): 'And is a solitary life as good as this? Then can one string make music as a consort?' (1590: sig. 2L6v).

7 ***They*** the sounds which produce 'concord'; the way in which the sonnet switches between plural and singular subjects ('music', 'concord', 'sounds') points up the paradoxical way in which a single, unified thing is the result of plural things acting in harmony.

7–8 ***confounds | In singleness*** By remaining single (and not producing legal issue) the young man is being destructive; compare 5.6. The unnaturalness of what he is doing is also conveyed by the other meanings of 'confound' which may be present besides 'destroy' (OED 1): namely, 'throw [. . .] into [. . .] disorder' (OED 5), 'mingle' (OED 6).

8 ***parts*** (i) musical parts ('part, *n*.1', OED³ 13); (ii) roles (i.e. of husband, father, OED³ 12b); (iii) personal qualities or attributes; abilities, talents (OED³ 15); compare the use of 'parts' in 17.4 and 69.1.
   bear The verb keeps ideas of procreation to the fore.

9–10 ***Mark. . . ordering*** The strings of the lute are organised into between six and ten pairs ('courses'). The two strings in each course are tuned to the same note, but each course is tuned to a different note from the others. Left unstopped (i.e. with no fingers placed on the strings), each course will form consonant intervals with some of the other courses. Lines 9–10 may refer (i) to the pair of strings within a single course, tuned to the same note; (ii) to sympathetic resonance: when plucking one course on the lute, other courses tuned to notes consonant with the plucked course would also resonate, more faintly, because of the mathematical relationship underlying musical harmony, as described by Pythagoras; the metaphor of musical harmony is thus

8

Music to hear, why hear'st thou music sadly?
Sweets with sweets war not, joy delights in joy:
Why lov'st thou that which thou receiv'st not gladly,
Or else receiv'st with pleasure thine annoy? 4
If the true concord of well-tunèd sounds
By unions married do offend thine ear,
They do but sweetly chide thee, who confounds
In singleness the parts that thou shouldst bear. 8
Mark how one string, sweet husband to another,
Strikes each in each by mutual ordering,
Resembling sire, and child, and happy mother,
Who all in one, one pleasing note do sing, 12
    Whose speechless song being many, seeming one,
    Sings this to thee: 'Thou single wilt prove none.'

extended to harmonious relations between spouses. Of these options, (ii) is more likely, because it was unusual for composers to require performers to pluck just one string in a course; generally, each course was treated as a single item. Alternatively, (iii) 'ordering' could indicate the skilled fingering which produces a harmonious ('mutual') sound; see the lute lesson in *Taming of the Shrew*, where Bianca is 'To learn the order of [Hortensio's] fingering' (3.1.65). There are possible echoes in this line of Marlowe's *Hero and Leander* ('Like untuned golden strings all women are, | Which long time lie untouched, will harshly jar', ll. 229–30).

10 **Strikes** A musical instrument (such as a lute) is struck to produce a note, but 'strikes' also has sexual overtones; see *Titus Andronicus* 2.1.129–30: 'There speak, and strike, brave boys, and take your turns, | There serve your lust'. (Sexual innuendo is also evident in Bianca's lute lesson, cited above, ll. 9–10n)

11 **sire** father.

12 **Who . . . sing** Some critics (see Baldwin 1950: 175) argue that this line alludes to the family motto of Henry Wriothesley, earl of Southampton (one of the candidates for 'Mr W.H'; see headnote): 'Ung par tout, tout part ung' ('one for all, all for one').

note Booth (1977: 146) suggests that – owing to a similarity of pronunciation – early modern readers 'may have heard a complex play on *not*, *note*, and "knot"' (as in a marriage knot).

13 **speechless song** without words; only the instrumental part of the music is being played.
being many, seeming one because in harmony.

14 **'Thou . . . none.'** 'unmarried, you will turn out to be ['prove', OED[3] 3d] nothing'; since these words are spoken by the music, 'none' might also indicate that the youth will lack the harmony of the music he hears, because he is single. Lying behind this utterance is the commonplace that 'one is no number' (Dent O54), a motif also found amongst the sonnets to the mistress (136.8), where the poet-speaker uses the figure to argue that she can accommodate one more lover (himself). Marlowe uses the same proverb (which can be traced back to Aristotle's *Metaphysics* XIV.I.ii (1088a)) as part of Leander's speech of seduction: 'One is no number; maids are nothing then, | Without the sweet society of men' (*Hero and Leander*, ll. 255–6). Bearing in mind the echo in l. 9 (see note above) to a slightly later part of this same speech, it is possible that Shakespeare had this section of Marlowe's poem in mind when composing this sonnet. The speech marks are editorial.

9

Benson combines Sonnets 8–12 under the title 'An invitation to marriage'.

2 **consum'st** The senses evoked by the word include: (i) 'destroy, corrode, wear away; (of fire) to burn up' ('consume, *v.*1', OED³ 2a); (ii) 'eat' (OED³ 6a); (iii) 'use up (esp. a commodity or resource)' (OED³ 6b); (iv) 'spend (money), esp. wastefully; to squander (goods)' (OED³ 7a). Meaning (i) recalls 1.6; (ii) 1.7, 1.14; (iii) and (iv) the economic imagery in 1.12, 2.5–11, 4.1–14, 6.3–12.

3 **issueless** without children.
hap chance, happen (verb).

4 **makeless** without a mate ('make'), i.e. without a husband.

5 **still** without cessation, always.

6 **form** image, likeness (OED 2); 'in the Scholastic philosophy: The essential determinant principle of a thing' (OED 4a). Compare 13.8.

7 **private widow** ordinary widow, as opposed to the widowed world, whose grief is public, shared by all; Booth (1977: 147) suggests that 'private' forms an intralingual pun, drawing on the Latin verb 'privare' (to bereave).

8 **By** by means of.

9–10 **Look. . . it** 'Whatever a prodigal ['**unthrift**, *n.*', OED 3a] spends, it is not lost to the world, but is redistributed' ('his' is a neuter pronoun); this is contrasted with the impact of the young man's prodigality (ll. 11–12), which causes the utter destruction of his beauty, of which no trace will be left posthumously unless he procreates.

11 **waste** (i) 'useless expenditure or consumption, squandering' (OED 5a); (ii) 'gradual loss or diminution from use, wear and tear, decay or natural process' (OED 9a). The word continues the financial imagery of ll. 9–10 (and Sonnets 1–17 in general) and conveys a sense of the ageing process.

12 **unused. . . it** Beauty will be destroyed if it is not put to use, a word which includes the idea of putting out to usury (i.e. the young man's replication of his beauty by producing an heir). The line replays the argument of Sonnet 4; the usury motif also appears at 6.5. There is a parallel in Leander's seduction speech in Marlowe's *Hero and Leander*: 'Beauty alone is lost, too warily kept' (l. 328).
so thus, in this way.

13 **toward** here pronounced as one syllable.

14 **himself** could refer to both the bosom ('himself' as neuter pronoun) or the young man.
murderous shame a shameful, murderous act (compare 10.5). Since this sonnet describes the fact that the young man is failing to procreate, it is possible to read 'murderous shame' as hinting at masturbation; see 4.1–2n, 9n; 6.4n; 7.13n. In Q's sequence, 'shame' is picked up in the opening line of the next sonnet. 'Murderous' (spelled 'murdrous' in all three instance in Q) is here pronounced as two syllables (other instances are 10.5, 129.3).

9

Is it for fear to wet a widow's eye
That thou consum'st thyself in single life?
Ah, if thou issueless shalt hap to die,
The world will wail thee like a makeless wife;   4
The world will be thy widow and still weep
That thou no form of thee hast left behind,
When every private widow well may keep,
By children's eyes, her husband's shape in mind.   8
Look what an unthrift in the world doth spend
Shifts but his place, for still the world enjoys it,
But beauty's waste hath in the world an end,
And kept unused the user so destroys it: 12
    No love toward others in that bosom sits
    That on himself such murderous shame commits.

10

Benson combines Sonnets 8–12 under the title 'An invitation to marriage'.

1 *For shame* 'Shame on you[!]' ('shame, *n.*', OED 14b); 'from a sense of shame' (OED 13a); in Q's sequence, the word 'shame' links with the preceding sonnet (9.14).

2 *unprovident* improvident; recalls the financial imagery of the preceding sonnets in Q's sequence (esp. 1, 4, 9), which have established the prodigality of the young man.

3 *Grant* agree (OED 1).
beloved of many Compare 31.1.

5 *possessed with* 'inhabited and controlled by a demon or spirit' (OED³ 2).
murderous hate Compare 'murderous shame' (9.14); 'murderous' is pronounced as two syllables; see 9.14n.

6 *stick'st not* do not hesitate, do not scruple ('stick, *v.*1', OED 15a).

7 *beauteous* two syllables; for the association with youth, see 4.5n.
roof head (standing in as *synecdoche* for the whole of the youth's body); as in 3.11, 5.1 and 13.9–12 (see notes), the youth is being figured as the family house, reminding him of his duty both to continue the lineage of his dynastic house and to maintain the fabric of the family seat (which may be put at risk of neglect and decay if he fails to provide an heir). Compare Wilson's translation of Erasmus' epistle on marriage (*Art of Rhetoric*, sig. I2r): 'Seeing also you are a man of great lands and revenues by your ancestors, the house whereof you came, being both right honourable and right ancient, so that you could not suffer it to perish, without your great offence and great harm to the common weal'.
ruinate 'reduce to ruins' (OED³ 2a); a possible echo of Leander's seduction speech in *Hero and Leander*: 'Who builds a palace and rams up the gate | Shall see it ruinous and desolate. | Ah, simple Hero, learn thyself to cherish, | Lone women like to empty houses perish' (ll. 239–42). Edmund Spenser's *Ruins of Rome* (in *Complaints* 1591) may also be an influence: 'time in time shall ruinate | Your works and names' (7.10–11). Compare too *Lucrece*, l. 944 (also describing the effect of time).

8 *repair* renovate (by having a son and heir); Duncan-Jones (1997a: 130) cites Fynes

Moryson on Charles Blount for a contemporary use of house-building as an analogy for continuing the family line: Blount 'chose to be drawn with a trowel in his hand, and this mot[to]: *Ad reaedificandam antiquam domum*, to rebuild the ancient house: for this noble and ancient barony was decayed' (*An Itinerary*, 1617: sig. 2F3r). See also 3.3n for the possibility of an intralingual pun on 'père' (French for father).

9 **O** The ejaculation appears sixty-fives times in Q, and – in the *Sonnets* (fifty instances) – it is almost always positioned at the start of a quatrain or couplet (exceptions being 92.11, 95.4, 132.10, 138.11; and its appearance mid-line at 126.9 and 149.1). Jackson convincingly uses the 'O'/'Oh' spellings as a key piece of evidence for identifying the hands of the two compositors: pages assigned to B always use 'O'; of the nineteen occurrences on pages probably set by A, seventeen are spelled 'Oh' (the exceptions being at 92.11, *Lover's Complaint*, l. 264).
change. . . mind 'Change your attitude (towards marriage), so that I can change my opinion (that you are selfish)'; this is the first appearance in Q's sequence of the pronoun 'I'.

10 *fairer lodged* housed in more attractive surroundings (i.e. in the youth, under his 'beauteous roof').

11 *presence* appearance ('demeanour, carriage, esp. when stately or impressive; nobleness or handsomeness of bearing or appearance', OED³ 5a); the word also has regal or aristocratic connotations (OED³ 2a).
gracious (i) 'characterized by or exhibiting kindness, courtesy, or generosity of spirit' (OED³ A2a), a sense which renders the word pleonastic with 'kind'; (ii) 'kind, indulgent, or benevolent to others of lower (social) status' (OED³ A2b), hence not only evoking the noble status of the youth (OED³ A2c), but also prescribing his reaction to the plea (that the young man should procreate) made by the poet-speaker, the youth's social inferior. The word and its cognates are recurrently associated with the youthful friend; compare 17.6; 40.13; 53.13; 62.5; 78.8, 12; 79.2; 96.2–4; 103.12.
kind benevolent (OED 5a), affectionate (OED 6); in a sonnet about continuing the family line, the word also plays on its associations with 'kindred' (kindness being the

10

For shame deny that thou bear'st love to any,
Who for thyself art so unprovident;
Grant, if thou wilt, thou art beloved of many,
But that thou none lov'st is most evident: 4
For thou art so possessed with murderous hate
That 'gainst thyself thou stick'st not to conspire,
Seeking that beauteous roof to ruinate
Which to repair should be thy chief desire.   8
O change thy thought, that I may change my mind;
Shall hate be fairer lodged than gentle love?
Be as thy presence is, gracious and kind,
Or to thyself at least kind-hearted prove: 12
  Make thee another self for love of me,
  That beauty still may live in thine or thee.

quality you should show your kin) and on acting 'in accordance with nature or the usual course of things' (OED 1a), i.e. producing offspring, something that the youth is currently – and unnaturally – failing to do. Compare Hamlet's bitter pun on his uncle-step-father: 'A little more than kin, and less than kind' (1.2.65).

13 **another self** a son (see 4.10n); however, it was also an early modern commonplace to describe a friend as a second self (see Cicero, *On Friendship*, 21.80; Dent F696; Sonnet 22.3n); this second meaning gains retrospective purchase in the light of the ambiguities of l. 14, which sees the first hint that the sequence will begin to move away from counselling marriage and procreation to a celebration of friendship. Kerrigan (1986: 186) draws attention to a third possibility: that 'another self' might indicate 'change your ways', as in Henry V's description of his reformation in *2 Henry IV*, 5.5.57–8: 'For God doth know, so shall the world perceive | That I have turned away my former self'.

love of me The first point in Q's sequence where the poet-speaker indicates that there is a close, personal relationship between him and the young man.

13, 14 **me. . . thee** This is the commonest rhyme pair in the *Sonnets*, occurring twenty-three times (in either order); the usage is densest in Sonnets 1–60, appearing in fifteen rhyme pairs (3.6 per cent of rhymes) as opposed to five in Sonnets 61–126 (1.1 per cent), and three in Sonnets 127–154 (1.6 per cent).

14 **That** so that.
   still always.
   in thine or thee That the youth's beauty will continue through his heirs ('in thine') fits the logic both of the sonnet and the sequence to this point; however, the suggestion that beauty may also live on 'in thee' is problematic, since it seems to go against the argument hitherto that it can only be preserved through procreation. Kerrigan (1986: 186) posits that 'thee' can be understood as 'your-children-who-are-you', but the line can also be read as an early sign that the sequence will abandon its focus on the need for procreation, and will focus instead on (an intense) friendship, and what the poet-speaker can do to ensure the addressee's eternity. In Q's sequence from this sonnet onwards (with its first introduction of the pronoun 'I'), the poet-speaker starts to insert himself more forcefully into the poems, drawing attention to the immortalising power of his verse (see for example, 15.14), until by Sonnet 18, the theme of procreation has fallen away entirely.

11

Benson combines Sonnets 8–12 under the title 'An invitation to marriage'.

1–2 **As. . . departest** 'As quickly as you will dwindle [referring to the early modern belief that a man's life-span was shortened with every ejaculation as well as the more general effect of ageing], as quickly you will grow in a child, who is created out of the semen which you have parted with' ('depart, *v*.', OED 12b); 'thine' could refer both to the offspring and to the wife whose womb he has impregnated (since wives were legally the possession of their husbands); reading 'thine' as the wife's womb activates the meaning of 'fast' as 'firm' (OED I), whereby the man's semen – which early modern medical theory held solely responsible for the production of a child – is securely rooted in the wife's womb. 'Depart' is also a frequent synonym for die (OED 7) and thus reminds the young man that he needs to produce an heir in order to leave something of himself behind after death; 'depart' may also echo the marriage service ('till death us depart'); compare 6.11n.

3 **blood** (i) 'the fluid which sustains life [. . .]; (metonymically) life' (OED³ 4) that the young man bestows upon the wife in the form of his semen, which creates new life; (ii) 'the inherited characteristic' (OED³ 5a), which the young man will pass to his offspring; (iii) when coupled here with the adjective '*fresh*', it indicates the next generation.

youngly while young.

4 **Thou mayst call thine** Although the youth has parted from ('departest', l. 2) his semen, he will still be able to call it his, since it will have been transformed into his children.

convertest turn from (i.e. get older).

5 **Herein** in this course of action (i.e. procreation).

increase (i) procreation (OED 2b); (ii) offspring (OED 6); (iii) growth in wealth, honour (OED 4).

6 **Without this** contrasts with 'Herein' (l. 5) and presents what will happen if the young man does not follow the suggested course of action and fails to produce a child.

cold decay harks back to Sonnet 6 and the depiction of old age as winter; the phrase could also refer to death itself.

7 **If . . . cease** Compare Wilson's translation of Erasmus' epistle on marriage: 'Let it be forbidden

that man and woman shall not come together, and within few years all mankind must needs decay forever' (*Art of Rhetoric*, sig. H4v).

so in this way.

times future generations, the human era.

8 **threescore** sixty years, cutting short the biblical life-span of 'three-score years and ten'; Psalm 90, in which this phrase appears (v.10), is about brevity of life.

make the world away destroy humankind ('the world'); l. 8 echoes and reinforces the argument of Sonnet 1.

9 **Nature** Q is inconsistent about the capitalisation of words like 'nature'; it is not capitalised at this point in Q, but the feminine pronouns in ll. 11, 13 here give Nature the force of a personification rather than an abstraction.

store (i) stock laid up for future use (OED 7a); (ii) animals kept for breeding, as in 'store-cattle' (OED C1c); (iii) 'accumulated goods or money' (OED 5a); for that last meaning, see, for example, *Antony and Cleopatra*, 4.1.15: 'Feast the army; we have store to do't'.

10 **Harsh** 'of rough aspect' (OED 2c).

featureless 'ugly' (OED 1, one of two instances cited by OED); the word also appears in this sense in Gervase Markham's *Tragedy of Sir Richard Grinvile*, where the earth's 'cold, dry carcass' is described as 'featureless, unfair' (1595: sig. B4r).

rude 'ignorant', 'uncultured' (OED³ A3a, A4), with connotations of low birth (OED³ A4a).

barrenly perish die without issue (because Nature refuses to breed from those who are 'harsh, featureless, and rude').

11 **Look whom** whomsoever (compare 'Look what', 9.9); Capell and a number of modern editors (e.g. Ingram and Redpath) introduce a comma (there is none in Q), so that 'Look' becomes admonitory, or commands the addressee's attention.

endowed The choice of word continues the motif of property that runs through the first seventeen sonnets.

the more 'Thee' could be spelled 'the' in early modern orthography; Capell and Sewell (1726) accordingly emend Q's 'the' to 'thee', so that the line means that Nature gives the youth even more than those to whom she had bestowed most. However, most modern editors retain Q's 'the', so that the youth is included in a general statement, which argues that Nature

11

As fast as thou shalt wane, so fast thou grow'st
In one of thine, from that which thou departest,
And that fresh blood which youngly thou bestow'st
Thou mayst call thine, when thou from youth convertest.   4
Herein lives wisdom, beauty, and increase;
Without this, folly, age, and cold decay.
If all were minded so, the times should cease,
And threescore year would make the world away.   8
Let those whom Nature hath not made for store –
Harsh, featureless, and rude – barrenly perish;
Look whom she best endowed, she gave the more,
Which bounteous gift thou shouldst in bounty cherish.   12
    She carved thee for her seal and meant thereby
    Thou shouldst print more, not let that copy die.

gives more (including powers of generation and thus offspring) to those she has already favoured most.

12 ***in bounty cherish*** The youth should look after the 'bounteous gift' that Nature has bestowed on him by being liberal with it. As Booth points out, since 'cherish' can mean 'to keep or guard carefully' (OED 5), 'this phrase embodies the paradox of several previous sonnets, that of keeping by giving, increasing by diminishing' (1977: 151), a theme invoked by the recurrent recourse to the parable of the talents (see 2.5–8n, 4.5–6n).

13 ***seal*** The engraved stamp from which impressions are made, e.g. when sealing documents with wax; the implication is that Nature has created the youth in her own image.

14 ***print more*** The youth is ordered to reproduce more images of himself (and Nature) by having children. Compare *Winter's Tale*, 5.1.124–6: 'Your mother was most true to wedlock, Prince, | For she did print your royal father off, | Conceiving you'.

copy 'the original writing, work of art, etc. from which a copy is made' (OED A8a); the word also evokes its primary sense of 'plenty, abundance' (OED A1a), and is etymologically linked to the Latin *copia*. By reproducing himself, the youth thus preserves and perpetuates Nature's abundant gifts currently lodged in him.

12

Sonnet 12 draws together the themes of Sonnets 5–7. Like 5 and 73, this sonnet echoes the passage in Ovid, *Metamorphoses* 15.199–213 where the stages of human life are compared to the passing of the seasons (Golding, 15.221–35; sig. 2C5v). The destructiveness of time is a recurring theme of the *Sonnets*; compare 15–16, 19, 55, 60, 63–5, 77, 100, 115–16, 123.

Benson combines Sonnets 8–12 under the title 'An invitation to marriage'.

1 **count the clock** count the chimes telling the hour; a sonnet that begins with an allusion to a clock, with twelve hours marked out on its dial, is appropriately placed as the twelfth in the sequence.
2 **brave** splendid, showy (OED A2); as Burrow points out (2002: 404) the word holds connotations of 'courageous resistance to insurmountable forces' (see 12.14, 15.8).
   hideous slurred, to produce two syllables; compare 5.6 and note.
3 **violet** Here pronounced as three syllables. Violets are a springtime flower, associated with humility, modesty, and chastity; see Lydgate, *History of Troy*, 3: 'vyolettes / of parfyte [perfect] chastyte' (1513: sig. Q6v). Shakespeare generally depicts violets as a fragile flower; see esp. *Hamlet*, where Laertes considers Hamlet's affection for Ophelia 'a violet in the youth of primy nature' (1.3.7), and the violets 'withered all' when Polonius dies (4.5.185). Shakespeare also associates the flower with innocence; see *Hamlet*, 5.1.238–40: 'Lay her i' th' earth, | And from her fair and unpolluted flesh | May violets spring!'.
   past prime (i) past its best ('prime, *n.*1', OED³ 9a); (ii) after spring (OED³ 7) is over.
4 **sable** black.
   are silvered o'er Q has 'or siluer'd ore'. Most editors follow Malone's emendation, 'all silvered o'er', which parallels 'all girded up' (l. 7), a repetition which has been read as both counting against the emendation (Sisson 1953: 1.209–10) and in favour of it (Duncan-Jones 1997a: 134); Ingram and Redpath (1985) suggest 'o'er-silver'd all', making the same correction but inverting the order and thus avoiding the repetition with l. 7. The emendation made here follows Gildon 1714. It is problematic because it causes the line to deviate from the pattern of past-participial constructions in ll. 2–8; however, it has been chosen in the light of the likelihood of potential

misreadings made by a copyist or compositor. A lower-case secretary 'a' could easily be misread as 'o' (producing 'or' from 'ar', a feasible spelling of 'are'); mistaking a secretary 'l' for 'r' is much less probable. The reading here is similar to Blakemore Evans' conjecture (1996: 125) of 'o'er-silvered are' (which merely inverts the order but is based on the same principles of likely copying errors). Considering probable copying/compositorial mistakes also stacks the odds against 'ensilvered o'er' (Wells and Taylor 2005), since neither a secretary 'r' or 'l' resemble 'n'; Burrow (2002: 404) also argues that 'ensilvered' is not cited by OED after 1382; EEBO-TCP reveals no instances, either. In contrast, 'silvered over' is relatively common: compare *Merchant of Venice*, 2.9.69 ('silver'd o'er'). Tucker defends Q's reading on the grounds that '*Or* may be the heraldic colour "gold," and "gold silver'd o'er with white" is exactly right' (Rollins 1944: 2.33); however, the line quite clearly states that the hair in question is dark (sable), not golden, nullifying this argument.
5 **barren** recalls the threat of 11.10 ('barrenly perish').
6 **erst** before, earlier.
   canopy shelter; the first OED citation for 'canopy' as a verb; a keyword search of EEBO-TCP reveals no earlier usages.
7 **girded** tied firmly ('gird, *v.*1', OED 5a).
8 **bier** could simply mean a 'handbarrow' (OED 1); however, it was strongly associated with transporting dead bodies (OED 2); compare *Hamlet*, 4.5.165: 'They bore him bare-faced on the bier'. The harvest homecoming thus also figures as a funeral procession, an added reminder of the oblivion facing the youth and his line should he fail to reproduce.
   beard the awn [bristly growth] on grass crops like barley and oats (OED 6a), but continuing the metaphoric conflation of humans and the seasons (most adult men in the period were bearded).
9 **question make** speculate about.
10 **thou . . . go** Multiple meanings are at play: (i) 'you must join the ranks of things destroyed by time'; (ii) 'you insist on exposing yourself to time-wasting activities and opportunities'; Burrow (2002: 404), here highlights the echo of *Twelfth Night*, 3.1.130: '*Clock strikes*. The clock upbraids me with the waste of time'; (iii) the line also makes the youth's passage through time into a metaphorical journey through the areas ('wastes') ruined by time.

12

When I do count the clock that tells the time,
And see the brave day sunk in hideous night;
When I behold the violet past prime,
And sable curls are silvered o'er with white;   4
When lofty trees I see barren of leaves,
Which erst from heat did canopy the herd,
And summer's green all girded up in sheaves
Borne on the bier with white and bristly beard: 8
Then of thy beauty do I question make
That thou among the wastes of time must go,
Since sweets and beauties do themselves forsake,
And die as fast as they see others grow;   12
   And nothing 'gainst Time's scythe can make defence,
   Save breed to brave him, when he takes thee hence.

11 **sweets** (i) pleasures, delights (OED 3a); compare 8.2; (ii) fragrant flowers (OED 7); see Gertrude at Ophelia's grave, *Hamlet*, 5.1.243: '[*Scattering flowers.*] Sweets to the sweet, farewell!'.
themselves forsake leave their sweetness and beauty behind, i.e. cease to be sweet or beautiful.
12 **And. . . grow** Compare 11.1.
others other sweets and beauties.
13 **nothing** a potential pun on vagina, whereby sexual reproduction offers the only way to conquer time; compare *Hamlet*, 3.2.117–19: 'OPHELIA: I think nothing, my lord. HAMLET: That's a fair thought to lie between maids' legs'.
Time's scythe Time was often depicted iconographically with a scythe (see 60.12, 100.13–14,

123.14) or sickle (116.10, 126.2). Here the reaping implement also harks back to the imagery in ll. 7–8. Time is capitalised in Q; whilst Q is not consistent in capitalising words like 'time' and 'summer' in instances where they could be read as personifications (see 5.5n), here the coupling with 'scythe' pushes the word towards a personification.
14 **Save** except.
brave 'challenge, defy' (OED 1); the word echoes l. 2 and transforms the futile defiance of 'brave day' into something more hopeful and achievable. Ingram and Redpath (1985) compare the revision of the meaning of the word 'state' in 29.2, 14.

13

Benson combines Sonnets 13–15 under the title 'Youthful glory'.

1 **you** This is the first sonnet in Q's sequence in which the youth is addressed as 'you'. Whilst 'thou' is the more informal second-person singular pronoun, by the late sixteenth century, 'you' and 'thou' were becoming interchangeable. In Sonnets 13–126, Shakespeare oscillates between 'thou' and 'you' when addressing the youth (thirty-three of sonnets of these sonnets use 'you'). From Sonnets 127–152, only 'thou' is used, with one exception (145, an anomalous sonnet; see notes). Other sonneteers of 1580s and 1590s similarly alternate between the two forms; compare, for example, Sidney's *Astrophil and Stella* 59, where Stella is addressed with both 'you' and 'thou' forms. The frequent alternation between pronouns – and the widespread nature of the phenomenon – should caution us against reading into these pronoun-choices a change in attitude to the young man. Rather, the choice may come down to euphony; see Burrow (2002: 406) and Vickers (1989: 47–8). Certainly l. 2 would be ungainly – thanks to four repetitions of 'th-' in close proximity – if it read 'No longer thine than thou thyself here live'.

2 **No longer. . . live** As in Sonnet 10, the youth is figured as the inhabitant of a mansion (his own body); the depiction of that tenancy as finite pre-empts the image of leasehold in ll. 5–6.

3 **this coming end** death; the proximal deictic 'this' is used to impress upon the youth how close it is (contrast the effect of 'that').

4 **semblance** appearance. Duncan-Jones (1997a: 136) posits that the word, 'with its connotations of "seeming", suggests something fragile and provisional about this beauty', but this reading does not accord with usages elsewhere by Shakespeare (e.g. *Lucrece*, l. 1759).
some other a child.

5 **lease** Property is held 'in lease' for a finite term, and in Shakespearean usage tends to imply impermanence; see 146.5.

6 **determination** end; in legal language, the point at which a lease expires.
were would be.

7 **Yourself again** plays on the idea of a son as a second self; see 4.10n. Q's 'you selfe' (first emended by Benson) is clearly an error.
Yourself. . . your self See note on modernising the '-self' suffix (introduction, p. xiv).

8 **your sweet issue. . . bear** (i) your children should resemble you; (ii) the line anticipates the time when his children pass on his image to the subsequent generation.
form image, likeness (OED 2); 'in the Scholastic philosophy: The essential determinant principle of a thing' (OED 4a). Compare 9.6.

9–12 **Who. . . cold** continues the motif whereby the youth and the dynasty ('house') he should maintain are imagined architecturally, as an actual house; see Sonnet 10 and l. 2n above.

10 **husbandry** 'the administration and management of a household' (OED 1), but also a pun on husband, as in spouse.

12 **barren rage** The rage causes barrenness.

13 **unthrifts** spendthrifts; compare 9.9.

13–14 **O. . . so** There are various ways of punctuating this couplet: (i) a colon at the end of l. 13 (Ingram and Redpath, Duncan-Jones, Burrow) indicates that the youth is required to acknowledge the truth of the preceding statement about 'unthrifts'; this renders l. 14 a statement of fact, rather than something the youth is prompted to recall; (ii) a break can come after 'unthrifts' (Kerrigan, exclamation mark; Blakemore Evans, colon), in which case the youth is invited to remember that he had a father. Burrow (2002: 406) argues forcefully for (i), observing that the construction created by (ii) 'is too commonplace a thought to warrant the strenuous enjambment required to make it possible'. He also suggests that 'You had a father' is a 'set phrase for egging on young men to woo', citing Shallow urging Slender to woo Ann Page in *Merry Wives* ('She's coming; to her, coz. O boy, thou hadst a father!' 3.4.36–7); this set phrase 'is broken if Q's comma is not hardened'. Nonetheless, this edition follows Booth, retaining Q's punctuation (with the single addition of a comma after 'love'), since it leaves open the various interpretations.

13

O that you were yourself; but, love, you are
No longer yours than you yourself here live;
Against this coming end you should prepare,
And your sweet semblance to some other give.   4
So should that beauty which you hold in lease
Find no determination; then you were
Yourself again after your self's decease,
When your sweet issue your sweet form should bear.   8
Who lets so fair a house fall to decay,
Which husbandry in honour might uphold
Against the stormy gusts of winter's day
And barren rage of death's eternal cold?   12
   O none but unthrifts, dear my love, you know,
   You had a father, let your son say so.

14

Benson combines Sonnets 13–15 under the title 'Youthful glory'.

1 **pluck** gather (OED³ 1a); the verb potentially belittles astrological learning as 'pluck' can suggest that something is easily taken. Compare other Shakespearean usages, e.g. *2 Henry VI*, 5.1.1–2 ('From Ireland thus comes York to claim his right, | And pluck the crown from feeble Henry's head'); *1 Henry 4*, 1.3.201–2: 'By heaven, methinks it were an easy leap, | To pluck bright honour from the pale-faced moon'.

2 **methinks** it seems to me.
have astronomy have knowledge of astrology (i.e. how the stars affect, or predict, human affairs).

3–7 **But not. . . well** a summary of the type of things (e.g. famines, whether spring will be wet or dry, the weather, rulers' fortunes) that almanacs and fortune-tellers predict.

4 **quality** characteristic (OED³ A7a), i.e. what the seasons will be like.

5 **Nor can. . . tell** 'nor can I predict precisely ['*to brief minutes*'] what will happen'; 'brief minutes' points to the fleetingness of time.

6 **Pointing** The word is usually glossed as 'appointing'. Blakemore Evans notes that 'were it not for the rhyme-scheme, we might suppose that lines 5 and 6 had been transposed, since 6 follows more naturally on 4, and 5 could well serve as an introductory line to 7' (1996: 127). However, the muddled description of the powers and remit of astrology, which veers between prophecy and predicting the weather, is in-line with the slightly comic and dismissive tone established in l. 1. The sonnet is not preoccupied with giving an accurate and logical account of astrology; rather, it uses astrology as a vehicle for depicting the youth, hyperbolically, as the poet-speaker's universe.
his its ('his' was a neuter, as well as masculine, pronoun in early modern English).

7 **it** fortune.

8 **By oft. . . find** 'By frequent predictions which I read in the stars'. This line is the only citation in OED³ for '**predict**' as a noun. 'Predict' is rarely used as an English word in Elizabethan and Jacobean English (as opposed to a Latin abbreviation); only six out of 1781 instances in EEBO-TCP before 1609 are in English phrases; none of these instances is a noun. Duncan-Jones, following Gildon 1714, offers an alternative, emending Q's 'oft predict' to 'aught predict' (i.e. 'anything that I find predicted'), on the grounds that (i) 'oft' is rarely used as an adjective (there are no comparable Shakespearean usages); (ii) 'a compositor or copyist could easily hear or misread "ought" as "oft"'; and (iii) OED has two citations from mid-1570s where 'aught' is spelled 'oft' (1997a: 138; 'aught, *n*.2', OED Aβ). Gildon spells 'aught' as 'ought', an acceptable variant spelling until the nineteenth century.

9–10 **thine eyes. . . constant stars** Comparing the beloved's eyes to stars is a Petrarchan commonplace (see, for example, Petrarch, *Rime Sparse* 189.12: 'Celansi i duo mei dolci usati segni'; 'My two usual sweet stars are hidden', trans. Durling). The conceit of this sonnet – where the only stars that matter are the eyes of the young man – may owe something to Sidney's *Astrophil and Stella* 26.13–14, where Astrophil 'fore-judge[s]' his 'after-following race, | By only those two stars in Stella's face'. See also Sidney, *Arcadia*: 'O sweet Philoclea [. . .] thy heavenly face is my astronomy' (1590: sig. 2L3r).

10 **read such art** discover such knowledge.

11 **As** introduces the knowledge that the poet-speaker has discovered.

11–12 **truth. . . convert** Truth and beauty will prosper if the youth abandons his narcissism and turns instead to procreation (compare use of 'store' in 11.9).

13 **prognosticate** foretell (OED³ 1b).

14 **Thy end. . . date** The conjunction, and shared fate, of truth and beauty in ll. 11, 14 echo 'Let the bird of loudest lay', ll. 62–4.
end death.
doom 'final fate, destruction, ruin, death' (OED 4b, with this line as the first citation).
date 'the limit or end of a period of time or of the duration of something' (*n*.2, OED³ 5).

14

Not from the stars do I my judgement pluck,
And yet methinks I have astronomy,
But not to tell of good or evil luck,
Of plagues, of dearths, or seasons' quality;   4
Nor can I fortune to brief minutes tell,
Pointing to each his thunder, rain, and wind,
Or say with princes if it shall go well
By oft predict that I in heaven find.   8
But from thine eyes my knowledge I derive,
And, constant stars, in them I read such art
As truth and beauty shall together thrive
If from thyself to store thou wouldst convert: 12
    Or else of thee this I prognosticate,
    Thy end is truth's and beauty's doom and date.

15

Benson combines Sonnets 13–15 under the title 'Youthful glory'.

1 *consider* consider that; there may be a play on 'stars' (l. 4), owing to theories about the etymology of the word, which according to the Roman grammarian Festus (author of *De verborum significatu*) 'derived from *sidus, sider* – star, constellation' ('consider, *v.*', OED).

every thing The spacing follows Q; some editors elide to 'everything'.

2 *Holds in perfection* stays at the point of perfection.

3–4 *huge stage. . . comment* The image of the world as a stage was a commonplace; see *As You Like It*, 2.7.139–40 ('All the world's a stage, | And all the men and women merely players'); Dent W882: 'This world is a stage and every man plays his part'. Here the metaphor is extended so that the stars are depicted as spectators; compare Walter Ralegh's 'What is our life?' ll. 5–6: 'Heaven the spectator is | Who sits and views whoso'er doth act amiss'.

4 *influence* technical astrological term: 'the supposed flowing or streaming from the stars or heavens of an ethereal fluid acting upon the character and destiny of men, and affecting sublunary things generally' (OED 2a). It is '*secret*' because this process is 'hidden' (OED A1) to humankind (although astrologers claim to reveal it).

comment probably meant in its earliest sense: 'devise, contrive, invent (especially something false or bad)' (OED 1), otherwise – as Blakemore Evans points out (1996: 128) – there is a potential discrepancy between the verb 'comment' (if understood in its dominant modern sense, of 'remark upon') and the active intervention implied by 'secret influence'.

6 *Cheerèd. . . sky* The metre requires that 'cheered' be disyllabic, with the stress on the final syllable, and that '*even*' be pronounced as one syllable.

checked Compare 5.7.

selfsame sky the heavens, the astrological bodies which were believed to influence the quality of the seasons; see 14.4, 6.

7 *Vaunt. . . sap* (i) boast about ('vaunt, *v.*', OED 1) their youthful vigour; (ii) boast during their youthful vigour (where 'in' is temporal).

at height decrease start to fade at the very moment that they reach their peak.

8 *wear. . . memory* Youthfulness is figured as splendidly ostentatious clothing ('*brave state*') that is worn out to such a degree that it fades from recollection. Compare *King Lear*, 4.6.134–5: 'O ruined piece of nature! This great world | Shall so wear out to nought'. Ingram and Redpath (1985: 35) suggest that there is a latent allusion to the second-hand clothes, passed on by noblemen, worn by players on-stage.

9 *conceit* thought (OED 1a); apprehension, understanding (OED 2a).

inconstant stay flux (playing on the contradiction between 'inconstant' and 'stay'); compare Golding's translation of Ovid's *Metamorphoses* 15.177–8: 'In all the world there is not that that standeth at a stay. | Things ebb and flow, and every shape is made to pass away' (Golding, 15.197–8; sig. 2C5r). Compare 60.1–4 and note. For the influence of *Metamorphoses* 15 on Sonnets 1–17, see headnote to Sonnet 5.

stay 'continuance in a state' (*n.*3, OED 6c, citing this example).

10 *rich in youth* (i) full of youth; (ii) splendid during the period of youthfulness; (iii) the phrase also continues the motif of clothing apparent in l. 8, so that 'youth' becomes a piece of attire, worn temporarily. There is a potential pun (the word 'you' appears 'in youth').

11 *Where* in the poet-speaker's sight.

wasteful causing destruction (OED 1).

Time. . . Decay In Q, neither Time nor Decay is capitalised here, although Time is at l. 13 (for the inconsistency of Q's capitalisation, see 5.5n). The anthropomorphic activity (debating) given to Time and Decay in this line justifies capital letters here too, to bring out the personifications. Bearing in mind the theatrical metaphor running through this sonnet, 'Time' and 'Decay' can also be seen as allegorical figures in a morality drama.

debateth (i) contends ('debate, *v.*1', OED 1); (ii) disputes, argues (OED 4a); (iii) discusses (OED 5a); (i) places Time and Decay at odds with each other about which of them will 'change your day of youth'; in (ii) and (iii), Time and Decay deliberate (with varying degrees of acrimony) about how to 'change your day of youth to [. . .] night'.

15

When I consider every thing that grows
Holds in perfection but a little moment,
That this huge stage presenteth naught but shows
Whereon the stars in secret influence comment;   4
When I perceive that men as plants increase,
Cheerèd and checked even by the selfsame sky,
Vaunt in their youthful sap, at height decrease,
And wear their brave state out of memory;   8
Then the conceit of this inconstant stay
Sets you most rich in youth before my sight,
Where wasteful Time debateth with Decay
To change your day of youth to sullied night,   12
    And all in war with Time for love of you,
    As he takes from you, I engraft you new.

12 *day. . . night* for the metaphorical use of times of day to signify the various life-stages, see 7.9–10 and *Richard III*, 4.4.16: 'Hath dimmed your infant morn to aged night'.
sullied 'soiled, polluted [...] made gloomy or dull' (OED a, citing this line).

13 *in war* at war; contrasts with 'in love'.

14 *engraft* horticultural practice, where a shoot from one tree or plant is inserted into another, to rejuvenate it; once the graft has taken, the old branch is then cut out. Compare Wilson's translation of Erasmus' epistle on marriage: 'even as a young graff [graft] buddeth out when the old tree is cut down' (*Art of Rhetoric*, sig. H3r). Booth (1977: 158) also suggests a pun on the Greek *graphein* (to write). 10.14 offered a hint that procreation was not the only way to cheat death (see 10.14n); however, this is the first of the sonnets in Q's sequence to make no mention at all of sexual reproduction. Sonnet 16 draws back from this suggestion, but 15 nevertheless pre-empts the abandoning of the procreative theme after 17, when it is initially joined, and subsequently supplanted by, an insistence on the poet's power to achieve eternity (for themselves and others); see Sonnets 18–19, 55, 60, 63, 65, 81. The eternising power of poetry in the face of the destructiveness of time is a motif found in Horace (e.g. *Odes* 3) and Ovid (*Metamorphoses* 15), as well as more contemporaneous works such as Spenser's *Ruins of Time* (in *Complaints* 1591).

16

Benson combines Sonnets 16 and 17 under the title 'Good admonition'.

1 *But wherefore* 'but why'; continues – and revises – the argument of Sonnet 15.
   a mightier way a more powerful way of defeating time and decay than the poetry offered in Sonnet 15; 'mightier' is slurred, so that it becomes two syllables.

2 *bloody tyrant Time* The description of Time as a tyrant recurs; see 5.3, 115.9.

3 *fortify yourself* strengthen yourself; the image of fortification follows on from that of war in l. 2.

4 *means. . . rhyme* The contrast of 'means more blessèd' (i.e. marriage) with 'barren rhyme' – i.e. verses that are both infertile ('barren, *adj.*', OED AI) and inadequate, 'bare of intellectual wealth, destitute of attraction or interest (OED A6) – equates being 'fortunate' ('blessed, *adj.*', OED 3a) with having children; compare 'unbless some mother' at 3.4. Marriage is also 'more blessèd' than poetry because the marriage service included a blessing (*Book of Common Prayer* 2011: 160).

5 *stand. . . top* The cycle of life (where the 'top' or zenith is the prime of life) is here reminiscent of the wheel of fortune (see Thomas Wyatt's 'Stand whoso list upon the slipper top | Of court's estates', ll. 1–2); like the wheel of fortune, the wheel of life inevitably turns, and what is at the top must come down.
   happy Whilst the dominant modern meaning, 'glad' (OED³ A5a) is pertinent here, so too are other, earlier meanings – 'lucky' (OED³ A2a), 'blessed' (OED³ A1b) – in which the word's etymological connection to ideas of good fortune (good 'hap') is more strongly present.

6 *unset* OED cites this line as the only instance of OED 5c: 'unfurnished with plants'. However OED 5b ('not planted') adequately expresses the sense here, whereby unmarried women are depicted as 'maiden gardens' because – as virgins – their wombs have not yet received the male seed (semen) which will bring forth 'living flowers' (l. 7).

7 *With virtuous wish* virtuous because any children would be born within wedlock.
   flowers here pronounced as one syllable.

8 *Much liker* more similar.
   painted Writing could be described as painting (see 'paint, *v.*1', OED³ 1d: 'to set down (written text)').

counterfeit 'image, likeness, portrait' (OED B3a); however, the negative connotations of the word ('a false or spurious imitation', OED B1) are also pertinent, resonating with the inadequacies of art in the face of nature that are expressed in the comparisons established in ll. 1, 4 and here in l. 8. The shortcomings of art are explored further in Sonnet 24.

9 *lines of life* (i) bloodlines, lines of family descent ('line, *n.*2', OED 24a), which will ensure that the youth is rejuvenated in his descendants; (ii) the contours or outlines of the youth (OED 14a), which will be reproduced in his children (compare *Cymbeline*, 4.1.9–10: 'The lines of my body are as well drawn as his').
   that life your life.
   repair 'restore (a damaged, worn, or faulty object or structure) to good or proper condition by replacing or fixing parts' (*v.*2, OED³ 1a); 'renew' (OED³ 2b); compare 10.8 and note.

10 *Which. . . pen* Q's punctuation, which brackets off 'Time's pencil or my pupil pen', has been retained here, on the grounds that a copyist/compositor is unlikely to misread, or introduce, parentheses. The line is puzzling, but no more so than when editors remove the brackets.
   this As punctuated in Q, the referent of 'this' is supplied by the parenthesis. Neither Time nor the poet-speaker will be able to rejuvenate the youth.
   pencil 'a paintbrush made with fine hair tapered to a point, esp. a small brush suitable for delicate work' (OED³ 1a); as such it symbolises the discipline of fine art, which is being compared with the literary arts, represented by 'my pupil pen'. Burrow (2002: 412) contextualises this within the formalised debates ('paragone') about the respective merits of sister arts, citing *Timon*, 1.1.1–94.
   pupil This could indicate that the procreation sonnets (1–17) are an early work, produced by an inexperienced writer, who is still a 'pupil' in the art, but it is more likely to continue the humility topos of l. 4 ('barren rhyme'). For the association between sonnets and youthful inexperience, see 22.1n.

11 *fair* beauty (a noun; *n.*1, OED³ B1); compare 18.7, 10; 21.4; 68.3; 70.2; 83.2; *Lover's Complaint*, l. 206.

12 *in eyes of men* (i) before men's eyes (who will be able to assess the youth's 'outward fair', l. 11); (ii) in the opinion of the world (who will judge the youth's 'inward worth', l. 11).

13 *To. . . still* replays the idea found in a number of the previous sonnets in Q's sequence (see 11.12n)

16

But wherefore do not you a mightier way
Make war upon this bloody tyrant Time,
And fortify yourself in your decay
With means more blessèd than my barren rhyme? 4
Now stand you on the top of happy hours,
And many maiden gardens, yet unset,
With virtuous wish would bear your living flowers,
Much liker than your painted counterfeit: 8
So should the lines of life that life repair
Which this (Time's pencil or my pupil pen)
Neither in inward worth nor outward fair
Can make you live yourself in eyes of men. 12
   To give away yourself keeps yourself still,
   And you must live drawn by your own sweet skill.

that by giving himself away – in marriage, through sexual intercourse that leads to pro-creation – the young man will paradoxically be able to keep hold of what he has (beauty, youth) because it will be recreated in a son. 'To give yourself away' echoes the marriage service in the *Book of Common Prayer*: 'who giveth this woman to be married unto this man?' (2011: 158).

14 **drawn** i.e. reproduced in his children. Puns on pens and penises were fairly common in the period. See, for example, Gascoigne's *Adventures of Master F.J.*: 'the secretary, having been of long time absent, and thereby his quills and pens not worn so near as they were wont to be, did now prick such fair large notes that his mistress liked better to sing faburden under him than to des-cant any longer upon F.J.'s plain song' (1573: 272); or Gratiano's jealous threat at *Merchant of Venice*, 5.1.236–7: 'let me not take him then, | For if I do, I'll mar the young clerk's pen'.

17

Sonnet 17 is the last of the so-called 'procreation sonnets'. From Sonnet 18 onwards, any promise of eternity comes through the powers of poetry.

Benson combines Sonnets 16 and 17 under the title 'Good admonition'.

1–4 **Who. . . parts** Ingram and Redpath interfere with Q's punctuation (moving the question mark to the end of l. 1 and making ll. 3–4 parenthetical) in order to emend what they regard as 'the unintelligible clash of tenses' between 'will' (l. 1) and 'were' (l. 2). However, whilst modern syntax requires 'would', not 'will', Elizabethan modal constructions were less rigid, and 'will' is acceptable here. Most editors now follow Q's punctuation (as here), leaving the question mark at the end of l. 2.

2 **filled** Q's 'fild' could also be modernised to 'filed', i.e. polished, refined; the ambiguity arises because neither of the two compositors who set Q tend to retain a double *l* before the contracted *-ed* ending: of the sixteen instances across the volume, there is only one such example ('call'd', *Lover's Complaint*, l. 181); the more usual practices are reflected by the spelling of 'distil'd' (Q5.13; Q6.2) 'cauld' (Q49.4), 'miscalde' (Q66.11) and 'cal'd' (Q105.1). The spelling 'fild' also appears at Q86.13 (where it definitely indicates 'filled') and Q63.3 (where it is slightly more ambiguous, but probably indicates 'filled'; see 63.3n). The one occasion on which the word 'filed' appears unambiguously, it is spelled 'fil'd' (Q85.4), but Burrow (2002: 414) is possibly crediting the compositors with too much orthographic care when he suggests that the inclusion of the apostrophe is a deliberate attempt to distinguish the contracted forms of 'filed' and 'filled'.

deserts excellent qualities ('desert, *n*.1', OED 1b).

3 **yet** at present; harks back to the 'pupil pen' (16.10), which possibly implies that the poet is still learning his craft and thus hopes to do better in the future.

heaven pronounced as one syllable.

tomb Where in 3.7, it was the youth who was portrayed as his own tomb, here it is the poet-speaker who constructs a tomb out of his own verses, because his poetry can only

commemorate the youth, not renew him. For the difference between 'tomb' and 'grave', see 3.7n.

4 **parts** personal qualities or attributes; abilities, talents ('part, *n*.1', OED³ 15); compare the use of 'parts' in 8.8 and 69.1. There may also be a play on body parts, such as those figured in an effigy on top of a tomb.

5 **write the beauty** As Kerrigan notes (1986: 195), 'a direct object declares the poet's radical ambition: not to write about but inscribe beauty on the page'.

6 **fresh** new, novel (OED A1a), vigorous (OED A10a).

numbers metrical feet, i.e. poetry; obvious play on the verb '**number**' (enumerate) that follows.

7–8 **'This. . . faces.'** The quotation marks are editorial.

7 **This poet** Burrow (2002: 414) highlights the potential use of the word 'poet' as a term of abuse, citing Ben Jonson's *Discoveries* ('He is upbraidingly called a poet', *Works*, 7.509), and George Puttenham's *Art of English Poesy*: 'commonly who so is studious in th' art or shows himself excellent in it, they call him in disdain a fantastical; and a light-headed or fantastical man (by conversion) they call a poet' (1589: 14).

8 **heavenly** pronounced as two syllables.

touches strokes of a pen, pencil, or some other tool (OED 10a, citing *Timon* 1.1.37–8 as the first example: 'Artificial strife | Lives in these touches, livelier than life').

9 **papers** verses in manuscript, like the 'sugared sonnets' circulated 'among [Shakespeare's] private friends' (Meres, *Palladis Tamia*, 1598: sigs 2O1v–2O2r); compare Daniel, *Delia* 36.1–2: 'O be not grieved that these my papers should | Bewray unto the world how fair thou art'.

10 **of less. . . tongue** more talkative than honest; compare the proverb 'Old men and far travellers may lie by authority' (Dent M567).

11 **true rights** the praise that the youth deserves; possible pun on 'rites' (i.e. worshipful ceremonies); compare 23.6.

poet's rage the *furor poeticus* ('poetic, prophetic [. . .] enthusiasm or inspiration', 'rage, *n*.', OED³ 8); this type of inspiration is tinged with suggestions of madness; see *Midsummer Night's Dream*: 'I never may believe | These antic fables, nor these fairy toys. | Lovers and madmen have such

17

Who will believe my verse in time to come
If it were filled with your most high deserts?
Though yet, heaven knows, it is but as a tomb
Which hides your life and shows not half your parts. 4
If I could write the beauty of your eyes
And in fresh numbers number all your graces,
The age to come would say, 'This poet lies:
Such heavenly touches ne'er touched earthly faces.' 8
So should my papers (yellowed with their age)
Be scorned, like old men of less truth than tongue,
And your true rights be termed a poet's rage
And stretchèd metre of an antique song. 12
But were some child of yours alive that time,
You should live twice: in it, and in my rhyme.

seething brains' (5.1.2–4); 'The poet's eye, in a fine frenzy rolling' (5.1.12).

12 **stretchèd** 'strained beyond normal or natural limits' (OED 4a, with this cited as the first usage). Ingram and Redpath (1985: 42) also suggest that it may refer to the long lines of fourteeners and poulters' measure (alternating lines of twelve and fourteen syllables) that had been popular in mid-sixteenth-century verse but which, by the end of the century, were passing out of fashion.

antique 'old-fashioned' (OED A3a); a play on 'antic' (of which it is a homophone), meaning 'grotesque' or 'bizarre' (OED A1); stressed on the first syllable.

14 **it** a child; this is the last time that Q alludes to the possibility of procreation as a way to cheat death; from this point on in Q's sequence, it is poetry ('*rhyme*') that is presented as a means to eternity.

rhyme verse; a potentially disparaging description; compare 'rhymers', 38.10; *Antony and Cleopatra*, 5.2.215 ('scald rhymers'), and Sidney's *Astrophil and Stella*, 15.5–6: 'You that do dictionary's method bring | Into your rhymes, running in rattling rows'.

18

Sonnet 18 is omitted from Benson's 1640 edition of the *Poems*, as is Sonnet 19. Benson's edition tends to group together, under a thematic title, sonnets which are adjacent in Q's sequence. Sonnets 18 and 19 share the topic of time; as Alden argues (1916: 29), it is likely that, under Benson's editorial *modus operandi*, these sonnets would have been paired together; that both are missing from *Poems* suggests that their omission may be accidental. It is clear from the reduplication of much of the spelling, punctuation and italicisation – as well as a good number of Q's errors – that the 1640 *Poems* were set directly from Q (although 138 and 144 were taken from the 1612 edition of *Passionate Pilgrim*). Alden posits that the text for *Poems* was prepared by clipping a couple of copies of Q, and pinning or pasting together the pairs or groups of sonnets. In the case of 18 and 19, the resulting paper containing both sonnets may then have been lost in the printing house, and – since the first seventeen sonnets are not printed in Q's order – their absence could easily have been overlooked. This theory might also account for the omission of 75 and 76 (another potential pair), and four single sonnets: 43, 56, 96 and 126, although Alden also suggests that the last two may have been left out intentionally, as 'imperfect' copies (96 repeats the couplet in 36; 126 is only twelve lines long). Certainly, in *Poems*, Q's sequence of Sonnets 41–45 is interrupted by the inclusion of poems from *Passionate Pilgrim*; Sonnets 50–59 appear in three separate clusters (the last of which comprises 55 and 52), and Sonnets 70–79 in two separate clusters, neither of which follows Q's numerical order. The way in which Benson's order disrupts Q's in these three cases makes it feasible that a pair or single sonnet might be overlooked in the process of setting the pages.

Although Sonnets 18–19 discard – and even contradict – the focus on procreation found in 1–17, they continue the theme of immortality and, in particular, the eternising power of verse also found in 15–17; see 15.14n.

1 **summer's day** proverbially perfect; see Dent S966.1 ('As fair as the summer's day(s)'), S967 ('As good (etc.) as one shall see in a summer's day'). 'Day' can also mean a period of time, as in *2 Henry VI*, 2.1.2: 'I saw not better sport these seven years' day'.

2 **lovely** 'loving, kind, affectionate' (OED³ A1a); 'lovable' (OED³ A2).

temperate 'of persons [...] Keeping due measure, self-restrained, moderate' (OED 1a); 'of the weather [...] neither too hot nor too cold; of mild and equable temperature' (OED 3a).

3 **Rough...May** Compare *Cymbeline*, 1.3.33–7: 'or ere I could | Give him that parting kiss [...] | [...] comes in my father , | And like the tyrannous breathing of the north | Shakes all our buds from growing'.

darling dearly-loved (OED B1).

May Owing to the shift from the Julian to the Gregorian calendar, adopted in Britain in 1752, Shakespeare's May would have begun ten days later, meaning that May would have been a warmer month overall than now.

4 **lease** a temporary and limited period of possession; compare 13.5.

date 'the limit, term, or end of a period of time, or of the duration of something' (*n*.2, OED³ 5); here the end of 'summer's lease'. Compare 14.14.

5 **Sometime** sometimes; play on 'sometime' in l. 7.

eye of heaven the sun; see *Lucrece*, 356n, and compare 'each under-eye' in 7.2n.

7 **dimmed** because obscured by clouds.

fair...fair beautiful thing... beauty. For 'fair' as a noun, see 16.11n.

sometime at some point in time.

8 **untrimmed** 'deprive[d] of trimness or elegance; [...] strip[ped] of ornament' (*v.*, OED 1, with this as first citation of 'untrim' as a verb, although it had been in use as an adjective since the early sixteenth century); used only once elsewhere by Shakespeare, in its more usual adjectival form, in *King John*, 3.1.208–9: 'the devil tempts thee here | In likeness of a new untrimmed bride'.

10 **Nor lose possession** contrasts with temporary possession ('summer's lease') in l. 4. Q has 'loose', an acceptable early modern spelling of 'lose' and the usual spelling in Q; this is the first of eleven instances in Q of 'loose'/ 'loosing' to mean 'lose'/ 'losing' (the others being Q39.6; Q42.9, 10, 11; Q64.14; Q88.8; Q95.14; Q102.12; Q119.4; Q134.12); the modern spelling 'lose' is used only once (at Q125.6).

fair beauty (noun); see 16.11n.

ow'st owns (OED³ 1a); in a subsidiary sense, the youth is also indebted (OED³ 3b) to nature for the gift of beauty granted him.

18

Shall I compare thee to a summer's day?
Thou art more lovely and more temperate:
Rough winds do shake the darling buds of May,
And summer's lease hath all too short a date;   4
Sometime too hot the eye of heaven shines,
And often is his gold complexion dimmed,
And every fair from fair sometime declines,
By chance or nature's changing course untrimmed: 8
But thy eternal summer shall not fade,
Nor lose possession of that fair thou ow'st;
Nor shall Death brag thou wand'rest in his shade,
When in eternal lines to time thou grow'st.   12
    So long as men can breathe or eyes can see,
    So long lives this, and this gives life to thee.

11 *wand'rest. . . shade* echoes Psalm 23:4: 'Yea, though I should walk through the valley of the shadow of death, I will fear no evil'.

12 *eternal lines* lines of verse; contrast 'lines of life' (16.9), where their primary meaning was lines of genealogical descent; in Sonnet 18, however, there is no reference to any other immortality besides that granted by poetry.

to time thou grow'st The youth is here imagined as a graft (see 15.14), bound by 'lines' (used in grafting to tie the shoot to the stock) and becoming 'by degrees ineradicably fixed *into*, vitally or indissolubly united *to* [. . .] something, as by the process of growth' ('grow, *v.*', OED 3a).

14 *this* proximal deictic, indicating 'this poem', or this collection of sonnets.

19

Omitted from 1640 *Poems*; see headnote to 18. For the immortalising power of poetry in the face of the destructiveness of time, see 15.14n.

1   *Devouring Time* proverbial (Dent T326: 'Time devours all things'); also echoes Ovid's 'edax rerum' (15.234; 'the eater up of things', Golding's translation, 15.258; sig. 2C6r); see *Love's Labours Lost*, 1.1.4 ('cormorant devouring Time') and the description of time in *Lucrece*, ll. 925–59, esp. 'eater of youth', l. 927. Of the three instances of 'time' in this sonnet, only one (l. 13) is capitalised in Q; for Q's sporadic use of capitalisation, see 5.5n.

    paws animal feet with claws and pads ('paw, *n.*1', OED[3] 1a); compare *Titus Andronicus*, 2.3.151–2: 'The lion, moved with pity, did endure | To have his princely paws pared [trimmed] all away'.

3   *keen* savage (OED A2c), sharp (OED A3a, citing this as an example).

4   *phoenix* mythical bird, fabled to live for over 500 years, after which it rejuvenates itself by burning itself on a funeral pyre, before rising – renewed – from the ashes; Ovid tells of the phoenix in *Metamorphoses* 15.391–407 (Golding 15.432–48; sig. 2C8r–v). For more details, see notes to 'Let the bird of loudest lay'. In that poem, as here, Shakespeare omits a reference to the bird's reincarnation: the phoenix's burning seems final, although the inclusion of the phoenix may pre-empt the eternity offered in l. 14.

    in her blood The phoenix literally burns in her own blood, but also 'in her prime' ('blood, *n.*', OED[3] P1b). The phoenix is usually imagined as male, but is female in the Latin poem *De Ave Phoenice* [*About the Bird, the Phoenix*] attributed to Lucius Caecilius Firmianus Lactantius (*c.* 240–*c.* 320 CE) and in Joshua Sylvester's translation of Guillaume du Bartas' *Divine Weeks and Works* (1605: sigs N3r–N4r). The use of the image of the phoenix as a symbol of Queen Elizabeth's longevity and uniqueness (see, for example, the British Museum's Phoenix Jewel, *c.* 1570–80, and Nicolas Hilliard's Phoenix Portrait *c.* 1575) may also have increased the likelihood by the late sixteenth century of describing the bird as female.

5   *fleet'st* pass rapidly; compare Thomas Wyatt: 'My pleasant days they fleet away and pass' ('Love, fortune and my mind', *Tottel* [95], l. 9). Some editors follow Dyce 1857, emending to 'fleets', to make a full rhyme with sweets.

6   *swift-footed Time* Time was proverbially swift-footed; see Dent T327 ('Time flees away without delay'), *As You Like It*, 3.2.306 ('the swift foot of Time'), and Daniel, *Delia* 31.11 ('swift speedy Time').

7   *sweets* Compare 8.2, 12.11; as in 12.11, it could indicate 'fragrant flowers' (OED 7) as well as 'pleasures or delights' (OED 3a). The word also looks back to the 'sweet brood' of l. 2.

8   *heinous* 'hateful, odious; highly criminal or wicked; infamous, atrocious' (OED 1): not a word to use lightly, as Shakespearean usage confirms; see, for example, *King John* 4.2.71 ('The image of a wicked heinous fault'); *King Lear*, 5.3.92 ('Thy heinous, manifest, and many treasons'); *Merchant of Venice*, 2.3.16–17 ('Alack, what heinous sin is it in me | To be ashamed to be my father's child!').

10   *Nor . . . no* The double negative is here used for emphasis.

    antique ancient, with a play on 'antic'; see 17.12n; stressed on the first syllable.

11   *thy course* passage of time; the primary meaning – 'the action of running; a run; a gallop on horseback' (OED 1) – continues the motif of 'swift-footed Time'.

    untainted untouched by time (i.e. left looking young, beautiful and unblemished); Booth (1977: 162) also points to a possible play on the jousting term 'taint' (a 'hit' in tilting), an image which fits with the image of time galloping on horseback (see note above).

12   *pattern* 'something shaped or designed to serve as a model from which a thing is to be made' (OED[3] A1a).

    succeeding men subsequent generations; compare *Lucrece*, l. 525. In Sonnets 1–17, 'succeeding' would have summoned up ideas of familial descent, but by this stage in Q's sequence the debate has moved on to promoting literary, rather than biological, reproduction.

13   *old* acknowledging Time's antiquity, but also potentially familiar, 'designating a friend, acquaintance, or enemy of long standing' (OED[3] 13b), and even derogatory.

14   *My love* both the beloved and the affection felt by the poet-speaker.

19

Devouring Time, blunt thou the lion's paws
And make the earth devour her own sweet brood;
Pluck the keen teeth from the fierce tiger's jaws
And burn the long-lived phoenix in her blood;   4
Make glad and sorry seasons as thou fleet'st
And do whate'er thou wilt, swift-footed Time,
To the wide world and all her fading sweets;
But I forbid thee one most heinous crime: 8
O carve not with thy hours my love's fair brow,
Nor draw no lines there with thine antique pen;
Him in thy course untainted do allow
For beauty's pattern to succeeding men.   12
    Yet do thy worst, old Time: despite thy wrong,
    My love shall in my verse ever live young.

20

The only one of the *Sonnets* to use feminine rhymes throughout.

Printed by Benson as a single sonnet entitled 'The exchange'.

1 *with* by.

Nature's not capitalised in Q (either here, or at l. 10); for Q's inconsistency regarding capitalisation of personifications or probable personifications, see 5.5n.

painted (i) drawn (i.e. Nature is depicted as an artist, creating life; compare the use of 'drawn' in 16.14); (ii) made up with cosmetics (see 21.2, 83.1–4). There is an inherent tension here: painting in sixteenth- and early seventeenth-century literature almost always suggests something false and unnatural; here the painting is done by Nature herself. Compare *Twelfth Night*, 1.5.239–40: ''Tis beauty truly blent, whose red and white | Nature's own sweet and cunning hand laid on'.

2 *master mistress of my passion* 'Master mistress' (often hyphenated by editors) is the focus of much debate about the sexuality articulated in these sonnets. Those who would deny the possibility of the speaker's homosexuality or bisexuality read this line as a literary joke, where Shakespeare is twisting the usual sonnet conventions by addressing an amorous poem to a man, not a woman, since 'passion' can mean 'a literary composition [. . .] marked by deep or strong emotion; a passionate speech' (OED³ 6d) as well as 'strong [. . .] emotion' (OED³ 6a), 'strong affection; love' (OED³ 8a) and 'sexual desire or impulses' (OED³ 8b). Thomas Watson's *Hekatompathia*, one of the earliest sonnet sequences in English, calls its poems 'passions', and the protagonist of Thomas Lodge's *True and Historical Life of Robert, Duke of Normandy* carves a 'devout passion' (a devotional poem) in the bark of pine tree (1591: sig. F2r). 'Passion' is used in *A Midsummer Night's Dream*, 5.1.288, 315, and *Venus and Adonis*, l. 832 to denote a passionate speech, and – at *Venus and Adonis*, l. 1059 – as a verb to indicate 'pour out emotion'; see note on that line. Of course, accepting that 'passion' might indicate a 'literary composition' does not preclude that it here also expresses love and desire.

3 *gentle* Hammond (2012: 456) draws attention to a sense which is not specified in OED but which – arising from OED A5 ('soft, tender; yielding to pressure, pliant') and OED A8 ('kind') – suggests sexual availability; compare 41.5.

3–4 *acquainted* | *With* accustomed to (OED³ A4); probable pun on 'quaint', used until at least the end of the sixteenth century as a term for female genitalia ('quaint, *n.*1', OED³).

4 *false women's fashion* a stereotypical depiction of women as (i) deceitful; (ii) artificial (i.e. wearing cosmetics); (iii) fickle (iterating '*shifting change*'). The inconstancy of women was proverbial: see Dent W673 ('A woman's mind and winter wind change oft'), W703.1 ('Women are oft unstable'), Tilley W674 ('A woman's mind (A woman) is always mutable'). The stereotype was also endorsed by early modern medical theory; see for example the debate in Robert Greene's *Mamillia*, Part 2, where the Marquise is required to rebuff the opinion that: 'Socrates, Plato, yea, and Aristotle himself [. . .] assigned this as a particular quality appertaining to womankind, namely to be fickle and inconstant, alleging this astronomical reason: that Luna [the Moon], a feminine and mutable planet hath such predominant power in the constitution of their complexion because they be phlegmatic, that of necessity they must be fickle, mutable and inconstant' (1593: sig. H1v).

5 *rolling* wandering, roving (i.e. to other lovers); see *Lucrece*, 368n.

6 *Gilding* in a positive sense, tingeing with a golden colour or light ('gild, *v.*1' OED, 4a), whereby the youth's eye beautifies – makes golden – whatever it falls upon (i.e. the youth's eye is like the sun); however, the superficiality inherent in gilding lends the word more negative resonances, including 'to give a specious brilliance or lustre to' (OED 5). 'Gilding' can also be deceptive, as in the phrase 'gilding over': 'to cover with gilding, to hide defects' (OED 7). These negative aspects are not prominent here, but see *Lover's Complaint*, l. 172, a poem which – as its headnote argues – re-evaluates the qualities lauded in this sonnet.

it the youth's eye.

7 *man in hue* 'Man' can be understood as 'human' (i.e. the youth is not here – as elsewhere – lent an air of divinity), but structurally the phrase

20

A woman's face with Nature's own hand painted
Hast thou, the master mistress of my passion;
A woman's gentle heart, but not acquainted
With shifting change as is false women's fashion;   4
An eye more bright than theirs, less false in rolling,
Gilding the object whereupon it gazeth;
A man in hue, all hues in his controlling,
Which steals men's eyes and women's souls amazeth.   8
And for a woman wert thou first created,
Till Nature as she wrought thee fell a-doting,
And by addition me of thee defeated,
By adding one thing to my purpose nothing.   12
    But since she pricked thee out for women's pleasure,
    Mine be thy love, and thy love's use their treasure.

responds to, and revises, the opening phrase ('A woman's hand'), so it makes more sense to read it in gendered terms; men and women also form a contrasting pair in l. 8. In early modern English, 'hue' could mean both 'form, shape, figure; appearance' ('hue, *n*.1', OED 1a) or 'complexion' (OED 2); i.e. the youth is manly in appearance and/or complexion (whereby a male aristocratic complexion might be expected to be darker than that of the female counterpart, who would try to avoid becoming weather-beaten and would whiten her skin with make-up). Baldwin (1950: 165) also suggests that 'hue' could be seen as an Englishing of the Italian term *sprezzatura*, citing Hoby's translation of Baldassare Castiglone's *Courtier* (1561), where a courtier is described as having 'a certain grace and (as they say) a hue'; in this reading, the youth would have about him a 'certain something' ('je ne sais quoi') that makes him compellingly attractive. Kerrigan (1986: 200) suggests that 'early readers would have been struck by the comparative strangeness of *hue*. Though revived later, and now common, the word had fallen into disuse by the 1590s, except in some verse'. However, the keyword searches now available through EEBO-TCP reveal that the word is more common than Kerrigan

suggests, in both verse and prose (186 hits in 72 records, from 1590–9, including sermons, histories, biblical commentaries and religious controversy; instances of 'Hugh', 'hue and cry', and typographical errors have been removed from these results).

all. . . controlling The hues could be the youth's own; i.e. he has power – control – over his appearance, be it pale or blushing, so that – like Shakespeare's Cleopatra – part of the youth's compelling beauty comes from his 'infinite variety' (*Antony and Cleopatra*, 2.2.235). Alternatively (and more probably), he has control over the appearance of others, causing them to blush or whiten. In Q 'hues' is italicised and (like all italicised words in Q) capitalised; often, this seems to indicate a name (as in 135 and 136), although words other than proper nouns are also italicised (e.g. 'alchemy', Q114.4; 'heretic', Q124.9). Nonetheless, this hint at a pun on a proper name has prompted various editors and critics to search the historical records for a 'William Hughes' and promote him as a candidate for Mr. W.H. (see headnote to the *Sonnets*).

8 **Which** can be used of animate as well as inanimate beings in early modern English (e.g. 'I am married to a wife | Which is as dear to me as life itself', *Merchant of Venice*, 4.1.282–3;

'The mistress which I serve', *Tempest*, 3.1.6); i.e. here it might refer to 'A man', 'hue', or 'controlling'.

steals men's eyes Compare *Pericles* 4.1.40–1: 'That excellent complexion, which did steal | The eyes of young and old'.

women's souls amazeth The soul was seen as the seat of the emotions (OED³ 3a); see, for example, *As You Like It* 1.1.165–6 ('My soul [...] hates nothing more than he') and the descriptions of wooing in *Merchant of Venice*, 5.1.19 ('Stealing her soul with many vows of faith') and *Midsummer Night's Dream*, 1.1.106–8 ('Demetrius [...] | Made love to Nedar's daughter, Helena, | And won her soul'). The youth's effect thus appears to be even more profound for women than that it was for men: men appreciate him visually; women are stirred to their emotional and spiritual core. This reading is enhanced by the choice of the verb 'amazeth', which was a stronger word than today, meaning 'to stun or stupefy' (OED 1), 'to overwhelm with wonder' (OED 4): Romeo is 'amazed' after the death of Tybalt (*Romeo and Juliet*, 3.1.134); Paulina promises 'more amazement' before she awakens Hermione's statue (*Winter's Tale*, 5.3.87); see also *Venus and Adonis*, l. 634 and note.

9 **for a woman** as a woman.

10 **wrought** made.

fell a-doting became infatuated with; the line recalls Ovid's myth of Pygmalion, who fell in love with the statue he made (see *Metamorphoses* 10). 'Doting' also implies foolishness; see Wilson's *Art of Rhetoric*: 'In the doting world, when stocks were saints' (sig. V1v). 'Dote' and its derivatives are used recurrently of the poet-speaker's infatuation with the mistress (131.3, 141.4, 148.5), but this is the only occurrence in the first 126 sonnets (those seen as being addressed to, or about, the friend).

11 **by addition** (i) by adding something (a penis); (ii) by honouring you; compare *Troilus and Cressida*, 4.5.140–1: 'I came to kill thee, cousin, and bear hence | A great addition earned in thy death'.

defeated disappointed, defrauded, cheated ('defeat, *v.*', OED 7a).

12 **one thing** penis; compare Wilson's translation of Erasmus' epistle on marriage (a source for images in Sonnets 1–17; see headnote to Sonnet 1): 'all men would think you were not worthy to have the thing, if either you could not, or you would not use it, and occupy it [...] it is not like that Nature slept or forgot herself when she made this one thing' (*Art of Rhetoric*, sig. G3r–v).

to my purpose nothing 'of no use to me'; also puns on 'nothing' as a term for female genitalia (see 12.13n).

13 **pricked** (i) selected (names on a list would be marked with a puncture; see *Julius Caesar*, 4.1.1: 'These many then shall die, their names are pricked'); (ii) marked out the outline, as if preparing a sketch. 'Prick' was also common slang for penis (see Partridge 1990: 167) and thus as a verb for sexual intercourse; see Thomas Wyatt 'She sat and sewed' (*Tottel* [67]), in which the God of Love makes the woman stab her finger with a needle 'To feel if pricking were so good indeed' (l. 8).

14 **love. . . love's use** The line draws a distinction between affection (unconsummated) and sexual intercourse; 'love's use' may imply reproduction, as earlier in Q's sequence (see 2.9n).

treasure The sonnet ends with a final bawdy pun (compare 136.5); 'treasure' is frequently used by Shakespeare when describing the sexual conquest of women; see *Titus Andronicus*, 2.1.130–1 ('There serve your lust, shadowed from heaven's eye, | And revel in Lavinia's treasury'); *Measure for Measure*, 2.4.96 ('You must lay down the treasures of your body'); *Cymbeline*, 2.2.42 ('The treasure of her honour'); *Lucrece*, l. 280. Here Shakespeare inverts that usual dynamic, so that the 'treasure' is not something taken from women, but which they gain.

20

A woman's face with Nature's own hand painted
Hast thou, the master mistress of my passion;
A woman's gentle heart, but not acquainted
With shifting change as is false women's fashion; 4
An eye more bright than theirs, less false in rolling,
Gilding the object whereupon it gazeth;
A man in hue, all hues in his controlling,
Which steals men's eyes and women's souls amazeth. 8
And for a woman wert thou first created,
Till Nature as she wrought thee fell a-doting,
And by addition me of thee defeated,
By adding one thing to my purpose nothing. 12
    But since she pricked thee out for women's pleasure,
    Mine be thy love, and thy love's use their treasure.

21

The first sonnet in Q's sequence in which the primary addressee is not the youth.

Printed by Benson as a single sonnet entitled 'True content'.

1 *So* At first glance, when read in Q's sequence, this appears to point back to Sonnet 20, particularly thanks to the recurrence of 'painted' in l. 2 (compare the use of 'So' in 134.1). However, as the sonnet unfolds it becomes apparent that 'So' sets up a comparison between the poet-speaker and the type of hackneyed poet he here derides. The critique does not seem to be of a specific rival poet, but of clichéd poets in general (although see l. 14n, below); compare Sidney, *Astrophil and Stella* 15, which mocks inferior poets who, imitating 'poor Petrarch's long deceased woes', 'wring' poetic tropes ('every flower [...] which grows') into their verses and 'dictionary's method bring | Into [their] rhymes, running in rattling rows' (ll. 3–7). *Muse* poet, by *metonymy* (*n*.1, OED³ 4). Shakespeare uses the word 'Muse' seventeen times in the *Sonnets*, more than any other work, which is unsurprising, considering the frequent use of sonnets to reflect self-consciously on the creative process. Within the *Sonnets*, 'Muse' usually indicates 'creative faculty' or 'creative powers' (thirteen instances: 32.10; 38.1, 13; 79.4; 82.1; 85.1; 100.1, 5, 9; 101.1, 5, 13; 103.1), rather than 'source of inspiration' (one instance: 78.1), or the classical deities who presided over the different branches of the arts (two instances: 38.9; 85.4).

2 *Stirred* moved ('stir, *v*.', OED 1a); the word may also suggest physical attraction; compare *Pericles* 4.2.142–4: 'thunder shall not so awake the beds of eels as my giving out her beauty stirs up the lewdly inclined'.
   painted beauty (i) beauty represented in painting or writing (see 24.1n); (ii) an artificial beauty, created by use of cosmetics (in contrast to the youth 'with Nature's own hand painted', 20.1); the use of make-up is frequently lambasted in Shakespeare's plays; see, for example, *Hamlet*, 3.1.142–4: 'I have heard of your paintings [...] God hath given you one face, and you make yourselves another'.

3 *Who* The subject is 'that Muse' (i.e. that other type of poet).

3–4 *heaven...rehearse* That other type of poet compares the beloved with sacred things for rhetorical effect ('*ornament*') and describes every beautiful thing ('*every fair*') in comparison with his beloved ('*his fair*'); 'rehearse' further denigrates the accomplishment of this versifying, implying (i) repetition and that what is said is not original, but 'previously said, heard, written' (OED³ 3); and (ii) tedium, since it could also mean 'describe at length' (OED³ 1a). 'Heaven' is pronounced as one syllable. For the use of 'fair' as a noun, rather than an adjective, see 16.11n.

5 *couplement of proud compare* refers to the Petrarchan conceits, common in Elizabethan poetry, which yoke together ('couple') dissimilar objects because they share one particular element (e.g. coral and lips, because both are red); see Sonnet 130. A list of such comparisons follows in ll. 6–7. 'Proud' means 'splendid' (OED³ A5b), describing the hyperbolic comparisons.

6–7 *sun...flowers* the type of clichéd and exaggerated comparisons frequently found in Elizabethan verse; see, for example, Watson, *Hekatompathia*, Passion 7.9–11: 'On either cheek a rose and lily lies | [...] Her lips more red then any coral stone' (1582: sig. A4r). Watson also repeatedly refers to the beloved as a 'second sun', as in Passion 35.1–4: 'When first mine eyes were blinded with desire, | They had new-seen a second sun whose face | Though clear as beaten snow, yet kindled fire | Within my breast, and moult my heart apace' (sig. E2r).

7 *rare* 'exceptional' (OED³ 4a), 'of uncommon excellence' (OED³ 5a).
   flowers pronounced as one syllable.

8 *rondure* sphere, roundness; the word is not used elsewhere by Shakespeare, and is the first citation in OED³; a keyword search of EEBO-TCP reveals no earlier instances, although 'roundure' (which has a separate entry in OED/OED³) appears in *King John*, 2.1.259 ('the roundure of your old-faced walls'), spelled 'rounder' in the 1623 Folio. The choice of word is perhaps intended to capture the inflated diction of the hackneyed poetry that the poet-speaker here mocks.
   hems confines ('hem, *v*.1', OED 3).

21

So is it not with me as with that Muse,
Stirred by a painted beauty to his verse,
Who heaven itself for ornament doth use,
And every fair with his fair doth rehearse,   4
Making a couplement of proud compare
With sun and moon, with earth and sea's rich gems,
With April's first-born flowers, and all things rare
That heaven's air in this huge rondure hems.   8
O let me, true in love, but truly write,
And then, believe me, my love is as fair
As any mother's child, though not so bright
As those gold candles fixed in heaven's air: 12
    Let them say more that like of hearsay well;
    I will not praise that purpose not to sell.

10 *then* both temporal (when that happens) and causative (on account of that).
fair beautiful, with suggestions of a fair complexion.

11 *any mother's child* The gender of the child is not specified, and throughout the poem there is no explicit indication of whether or not the beloved is male or female. Some critics (see Pooler 1931) argue for altering the position of this sonnet within the sequence, particularly since the insistence on the beloved being 'as fair' as others is reminiscent of Sonnets 127 and 131–132, about the dark-haired mistress. For use of the phrase 'any mother's child', compare 'every mother's son' in *Midsummer Night's Dream*, 1.2.78, 3.1.73. That both times this phrase is given to the 'rude mechanicals' indicates its colloquial nature, perhaps in deliberate contrast to the type of pretentious neologisms (e.g. 'rondure', l. 8) employed by lesser poets.

12 *gold. . . air* stars; 'fixed' to distinguish them from planets (which were 'wandering stars').

13 *like of* like.
hearsay information transmitted orally, with the strong implication that it is less trustworthy than a written report.

14 *I will. . . sell* proverbial; see Dent P546 ('He praises who wishes to sell') and *Love's Labours Lost*, 4.3.235–6: 'Fie, painted rhetoric! O, she needs it not. | To things of sale a sellers' praise belongs'. Duncan-Jones (2010: 153) suggests that this may be a 'sidelong allusion' to George Chapman, whose name means 'merchant' or, more contemptuously, 'pedlar' (OED 1a, 2); see headnote to Sonnet 79.

22

Printed by Benson as a single sonnet entitled 'Strong conceit'.

1 **glass** mirror. Shakespeare also uses the mirror-glass as the opening image of Sonnet 3; the difference between the two sonnets – as here the poet-speaker looks in the mirror – is a sign of the way in which the poet-speaker has started by this stage in Q's sequence to acquire a more central role, as a protagonist, rather than as a commentator.

old The first of the sonnets in Q to suggest that the poet-speaker is old. If, as most commentators agree, most of the sonnets were composed before 1596 (see headnote to *Sonnets*, 'Date'), Shakespeare would have been in his early thirties, which would not have counted as 'old', even within the reduced life expectancy of the early modern world (see 7.6n). Blakemore Evans (1996: 135) and Burrow (2002: 424) both suggest that it is conventional for sonneteers to lament their old age, yet there is a contrary convention of portraying sonneteering as a youthful activity; see, for example, Petrarch's portrayal of the *Rime Sparse* as the product of 'my first youthful error' ('mio primo giovenile errore', 1.3); Turberville's description of his 'few sonnets' as 'the unripe seeds of [his] barren brain' is also typical of the way in which sixteenth-century collections of sonnets are introduced and excused (*Epitaphs, Epigrams, Songs and Sonnets*, 1567: sig. *5r).

2 **youth and thou** Since the sonnets vary in whether they address the youth as 'you' or 'thou', there is a potential play on the 'you' in 'youth'; compare 15.10n.

of one date last as long as each other; 'date' = duration (*n*.2, OED³ 1).

3 **in thee** The youth has become the poet-speaker's mirror and is thus being figured as a second self; for the proverbial notion that a friend is a second self, see 10.13n. The replacement of the idea of a son as a second self (found, for example, at 6.7) with that of a friend indicates how Q's sequence has now firmly left behind the theme of procreation. For the motif of a friend as a second self, compare 39.2, 62.13, 133.6, 134.3.

time's furrows wrinkles; compare 2.2.

4 **look I** I anticipate.

expiate end (OED 7); from the Latin *piare* (to appease by sacrifice), 'expiate' usually means 'cleanse' or 'purify' (OED 2); the unusual usage here probably derives from (a misreading of?) Marlowe's *Dido* (printed in 1594), 5.1.316–17: 'Cursed Iarbas, die to expiate | The grief that tires upon thine inward soul' (also cited by OED under sense 7, as first usage). The only other Shakespearean usage is as an adjective (indicating the appointed time); see *Richard III*, 3.3.24: 'Make haste, the hour of death is expiate'.

5–14 **For. . . again** Booth (1977: 170) suggests that these lines are influenced by Ephesians 5:25–33, a passage which – with its emphasis on husband and wife becoming one flesh – formed part of the marriage service in the *Book of Common Prayer* (2011: 162–3). However, the controlling image of the sonnet from l. 7 onwards is not the joining of flesh into one body, but the exchange of hearts, which remain in separate bodies. For the exchange of hearts, compare Sonnet 133 (where the friend's and poet-speaker's hearts are exchanged in a complicated triangular relationship with the mistress).

5 **cover** Bearing in mind the reference to the 'seemly raiment' (l. 6), 'cover' here would seem to mean 'clothe' (*v*.1, OED 3a).

6 **but** merely.

seemly. . . heart The friend's beautiful body is a 'pleasant' or 'handsome' garment, clothing the poet-speaker's heart ('seemly', OED 2), but it is also a 'decorous' and 'appropriate' garment (OED 3, 4), which strengthens the idea that the youth and the poetic speaker complement each other.

7 **as thine in me** Exchanging hearts was a conventional motif of love poetry (see Thomas Wyatt, 'My heart I gave thee, not to do it pain'; *Tottel* [100]) and is an idea expressed through the proverb 'The lover is not where he lives but where he loves' (Dent L565).

9–10 **be of. . . will** 'take care of yourself, as I will take care of myself – not for my own sake, but for yours' (because his breast is 'bearing' the other's heart, l. 11); '**wary**' indicates 'cautious, careful' (OED 2a), but also 'careful in expenditure, thrifty' (OED 4).

22

My glass shall not persuade me I am old,
So long as youth and thou are of one date,
But when in thee time's furrows I behold,
Then look I death my days should expiate: 4
For all that beauty that doth cover thee
Is but the seemly raiment of my heart,
Which in thy breast doth live, as thine in me.
How can I then be elder than thou art? 8
O therefore, love, be of thyself so wary
As I, not for myself, but for thee will,
Bearing thy heart, which I will keep so chary
As tender nurse her babe from faring ill: 12
    Presume not on thy heart when mine is slain;
    Thou gav'st me thine not to give back again.

11 **Bearing** carrying, although the movement of the subsequent line into a simile about nursing children does activate a subsidiary sense of bearing offspring, in which the friend's heart becomes a substitute child; together with ll. 3 and 12 (see notes), this reworking of reproductive motifs into expressions of friendship shows how Q's sequence has, by now, turned its back on the procreative arguments of Sonnets 1–17.
chary 'carefully' (OED 8, quasi-*adv*); the multiple resonances of the word are evident in its adjectival senses: precious (OED 3), careful in preserving (OED 5), careful not to waste (OED 6).

12 **nurse her babe** Child-rearing is here a simile, not an objective as it was in Sonnets 1–17; see notes on ll. 3 and 11 (above).

13 **Presume** 'lay presumptuous claim to' (OED³ 1a), 'count upon' (OED³ 3), 'take for granted' (OED³ 7).

13–14 **Presume. . . again** As Blakemore Evans notes, the couplet 'hints at the fear that the youth's love is less committed than the poet's' (1996: 135).

23

For the motif of the tongue-tied lover, see Petrarch *Rime Sparse* 49, in which the poetic speaker berates his uncommunicative tongue (translated by Thomas Wyatt as 'Because I still kept thee from lies and blame', *Tottel* [48]) and Anon, 'The complaint of a lover with suit to his love for pity': 'And when that I, ere this, my tale could well by heart | And that my tongue had learned it, so that no word might start, | The sight of her hath set my wits in such a stay | That to be lord of all the world, one word I could not say' (*Tottel* [168], ll. 31–4).

Printed by Benson as a single sonnet entitled 'A bashful lover'.

1 **unperfect** 'not thoroughly accomplished or practised in a skill' (OED³ 4); not used elsewhere by Shakespeare, but compare the use of the antonym 'perfect' in *Love's Labours Lost*, 5.2.558–9, where Costard comments on his performance as Pompey: 'I hope I was perfect. I made a little fault in "Great".'

2 **with** as a result of.
   besides his part out of his part; i.e. he forgets his lines.

3–4 **Or. . . heart** These lines introduce a second simile (that of a wild beast, bursting – '*replete*' – with rage); ll. 7–8 respond to this simile; ll. 5–6 to that of the dumbstruck actor in ll. 1–2.

4 **Whose** The antecedent could either be 'thing' or 'rage'.
   weakens. . . heart The destructive effects of excess are indicated by *Hamlet*: 'For goodness, growing to a pleurisy, | Dies in his own too much' (4.7.117–18). 'Heart' can here be the bodily organ, placed under too much strain, or it might have a more figurative sense, of 'courage, spirit' (OED³ A11a) or 'purpose' (OED³ A7).

5 **fear of trust** 'Trust' can mean (i) 'confidence' in something/someone (OED 1a); (ii) 'fidelity, reliability, loyalty, trustiness' (OED 4); (iii) 'The condition of having confidence reposed in one' (OED 5a), i.e. the poet-speaker might be anxious about his own capabilities, or his own trustworthiness, or that of the youth; or he might be apprehensive about living up to the responsibility with which he has been entrusted. The phrase plays on a typical Petrarchan oxymoron: the poetry of Thomas Wyatt, for example, works the oxymoron both ways: 'fearful trust' ('Though this thy port', l. 7) and 'trusty fearfulness' ('My galley charged', *Tottel* [50], l. 8).

forget omit (OED 2a), forget how (OED 3c).

6 **perfect** (i) remembered fully (contrast 'unperfect', l. 1); (ii) performed correctly.
   rite Q's spelling (right) is an acceptable sixteenth-century variant of 'rite', but it also highlights a secondary sense whereby the proper performance of this ritual (rite) is love's due (right). In *All's Well*, 'rite of love' means sexual intercourse (2.4.41); however the emphasis in this sonnet on verbal communication renders this meaning unlikely here.

8 **O'ercharged** overburdened.
   burden 'burthen' in Q, an acceptable sixteenth-century variant.

9 **books** writings; this might refer to these sonnets in particular, or the poet-speaker's writings more generally. Sewell 1726 emends Q's 'books' to 'looks' (as does Capell); 'looks' would certainly be more conventional; compare John Davies, *Wit's Pilgrimage*, 62.9–10, in which another tongue-tied lover bemoans the fact that he cannot 'interplead' with his beloved 'But merely by the mean of speaking-looks' (1605: sig. F1v). However, Sewell's emendation undercuts Sonnet 23's preoccupation with a changing notion of eloquence. Classical rhetoric was divided into five parts: *inventio* (invention), *dispositio* (arrangement), *elocutio* (style), *memoria* (memory) and *pronuntiatio* (delivery). By the sixteenth century, though, eloquence increasingly took a written form, and this is reflected here in a sonnet which acknowledges its speaker's inadequacies in the parts of eloquence which relate to oral performance (memory fails in ll. 1–2, 5); pronunciation in l. 10 ('dumb presagers'). Nevertheless, he still confidently lays claim to an 'eloquence' that comes in written form.

10 **presagers** signs; editors who adopt Sewell's emendation ('looks', l. 9) seize on this problematic word, which usually means someone or something 'which presages or predicts something' (OED³ 1), arguing that books – presumably already written or printed – cannot be said to predict something. See, however, Shakespeare's use of the related word 'presage' (noun and verb) to mean 'indicate/indication' – devoid of a sense of futurity – at *Antony and Cleopatra*, 1.2.47 ('There a palm presages chastity') and *Twelfth Night*, 3.2.64–5 ('the youth bears in his visage no great presage of cruelty').
    breast heart, by *synecdoche*.

23

As an unperfect actor on the stage,
Who with his fear is put besides his part,
Or some fierce thing replete with too much rage,
Whose strength's abundance weakens his own heart;　　　　4
So I, for fear of trust, forget to say
The perfect ceremony of love's rite,
And in mine own love's strength seem to decay,
O'ercharged with burden of mine own love's might:　　　　8
O let my books be then the eloquence
And dumb presagers of my speaking breast,
Who plead for love and look for recompense
More than that tongue that more hath more expressed.　　　　12
　　O learn to read what silent love hath writ;
　　To hear with eyes belongs to love's fine wit.

11 **Who** The antecedent is 'books'.
　　plead The legal sense ('To address the court as an advocate, [. . .] to maintain or urge the claim', OED³ 2a) is relevant here.
　　recompense 'compensation or return for trouble, exertion, services, or merit' (OED³ 3).
12 **More. . . expressed** The poet-speaker looks for more recompense than someone ('that tongue') who has managed to articulate a greater love in a greater quantity of words. 'That tongue' may point to a specific rival (as in 78–80, 82–86, sonnets which replay some of the anxieties explored here regarding the power of the poet-speaker's words). However, in Q's sequence, 'that tongue' is more likely to generate a connection back to the general type of glib and superficial poet derided in 21 ('that Muse', 21.1).
13 ***silent love*** True love was often depicted as proverbially silent; see Sidney, *Astrophil and*

Stella 54.13–14 ('Dumb swans, not chattering pies [magpies], do lovers prove, | They love indeed, who quake to say they love'); Dent L165 ('Whom we love best to them we can say least') and the supporting quotations, esp. Marlowe, *Hero and Leander*, l. 186: 'True love is mute'.
　　hath writ has written (past tense); this poet-speaker has a body of compositions already behind him.
14 ***To hear with eyes*** because reading; rebuffs the proverb 'love is blind' (Dent L506); instead, love is seen to have sharpened the lover's acumen ('***wit***', OED 5a).
　　with. . . wit In Q 'wit' and 'wiht' respectively; the compositor probably misread the manuscript (where 'wᵗ' would be the standard abbreviation for 'with') and then inserted the 'h' in the wrong place when trying to correct the error.

24

Printed by Benson as a single sonnet entitled 'A masterpiece'.

1 *eye* plural eyes; compare 'Mine eyes', l. 10.

painter The verb 'to paint' could refer to writing (*v.*1, OED³ 1d); more specifically, it could also mean 'to flatter' (OED³ 6b).

stelled Q's 'steeld' was first emended thus by Capell and is generally accepted by editors; Ingram and Redpath (1985: 60, 62) lay out an extensive list of arguments for and against the emendation, and retain 'steel'd' on the grounds that, when two alternatives make sense, it is proper to retain the original reading. Duncan-Jones more decisively opts for 'steeled', highlighting the association with mirrors ('to steel' is to back a mirror with steel, OED 1b), which would fit with the idea of the beloved being reflected in the poet-speaker's eyes (1997a: 158). However, the dominant image in l. 1 is not that of mirrors but of painting, and 'stelled' is an artistic term ('to portray, delineate', OED 3) that fits more appropriately here. Moreover, whilst there is no equivalent Shakespearean usage of 'steeled', there is an exact parallel to 'stelled' in *Lucrece*, l. 1444 (see note on that line). An earlier meaning of 'stell' as 'fix' (OED 2a) is also pertinent here, as the poet-speaker endeavours to embed permanently the youth's form within his heart. 'Stelled' makes a better rhyme with 'held' for modern readers; however, as Kökeritz indicates, early modern pronunciation is more flexible, and 'held' elsewhere rhymes with 'field', 'filed' and 'killed' (1953: 188). For the effect of early modern pronunciation on Shakespeare's rhymes, see Appendix 7.

2 *table* This could mean a notebook (compare Sonnet 122.1–2, and *Hamlet*, 1.5.107:'My tables – meet it is I set it down'); this reading is bolstered by a Biblical parallel in Proverbs 3:3: 'write them upon the table of thine heart'. However, in light of the reference to the frame that follows (l. 3) and the image of the eye as painter (l. 1), 'table' is more likely to indicate 'a board or other flat surface on which a picture is painted' (OED³ 3).

3 *frame* It could be an easel (OED³ A3b) or a picture frame, 'a surrounding structure [. . .] in which something, esp. a picture, pane of glass, etc. is set' (OED³ A8). There is also a play on 'frame' as 'the human body' (OED³ A4; compare 59.10).

4 *perspective* 'The art of drawing solid objects on a plane surface so as to give the same impression of relative position, size, or distance' (OED³ 3a); also 'A picture or figure designed to appear distorted or confused except when viewed from a certain position, or presenting totally different aspects from different positions' (OED³ 2b); compare *Richard II*, 2.2.18–20: 'Like perspectives, which rightly [directly] gazed upon | Show nothing but confusion; eyed awry | Distinguish form'. Stressed on the first syllable.

5 *through the painter* (i) by means of the painter's skill; (ii) bearing in mind the location of the picture – in the poet speaker's bosom (l. 7) – through the outer layers of the poet-speaker's flesh and bone, to the heart.

5, 6 *you. . . your* The change from 'thou' and 'thy' used elsewhere in the poem is possibly for reasons of euphony ('must thou' is much more awkward to say, because of the oral movement necessary to switch from 't' to 'th'); see 13.1n.

7 *bosom's shop* The conceit of the beloved's image hanging in the lover's bosom can be found in, amongst other places, Constable's *Diana* (1592), 9.1–4:

> Thine eye the glass where I behold my heart,
> Mine eye the window, through the which thine eye
> May see my heart, and there thyself espy
> In bloody colours how thou painted art.
> (sig. C1r)

shop workshop (OED 3a); the commercial connotations of shop (as a place of sale, OED 2a) do not seem pertinent here.

still probably temporal ('constantly', OED 3a) rather than indicating a lack of motion (OED 2).

8 *his* its (referring to the poet-speaker's breast).

windows eyes (compare 3.11).

glazèd. . .eyes The poet-speaker's eyes are 'glazèd' with the friend's eyes because the friend's eyes are reflected in his. There is a possibly play on the verb 'glaze', meaning 'to stare' (*v.*2, OED).

24

Mine eye hath played the painter and hath stelled
Thy beauty's form in table of my heart;
My body is the frame wherein 'tis held,
And perspective it is best painter's art,   4
For through the painter must you see his skill
To find where your true image pictured lies,
Which in my bosom's shop is hanging still,
That hath his windows glazèd with thine eyes.   8
Now see what good turns eyes for eyes have done:
Mine eyes have drawn thy shape, and thine for me
Are windows to my breast, wherethrough the sun
Delights to peep, to gaze therein on thee.   12
    Yet eyes this cunning want to grace their art:
    They draw but what they see, know not the heart.

9 *good turns* alludes to the proverb 'one good turn deserves another' (Dent T616); Q hyphenates 'good-turns', creating a compound noun.

10 *drawn* (i) delineated (OED 4); (ii) extracted (OED 1a).

13 *cunning* skill.

want lack.

14 ***They. . . heart*** The last line undermines the confidence of the preceding thirteen lines: the friend's image might be engraved in the poet-speaker's heart, but the friend's heart remains a closed book.

25

Printed by Benson as a single sonnet entitled 'Happiness in content'.

1 *in . . . stars* whose stars are favourable; as Kerrigan points out (1986: 206) 'the astrological allusion scornfully severs advancement from merit, attributing success to chance' (and thus also devolves the poet-speaker from any responsibility for his own lack of worldly success).

3 *of* from.

4 *Unlooked for* The phrase works in two senses: (i) qualifying 'joy', it means 'unexpected[ly]' (OED 2a, quasi-*adv.*); this is the usual sense in which Shakespeare deploys this phrase (as either an adjective or an adverb); compare *1 Henry IV*, 5.3.60–1 ('honour comes unlooked for') and *Richard II*, 1.3.154–5 ('A heavy sentence [. . .] | And all unlooked for from your Highness' mouth'); (ii) qualifying 'I' (l. 3), it means 'unregarded' (OED 1b), which is how most editors gloss it.

joy in take pleasure in, rejoice (OED 1); there is also a potential astrological allusion: planets 'joy' 'when they are in those houses [sections of the sky] where they are most powerful and strong' (OED 2c); Edward Phillips' *New World of English Words* (1658) is the first citation for this usage in OED, but the entry for 'joy' as a noun includes a fifteenth-century usage in this astrological sense (OED 7); see also 'joie', *Medieval English Dictionary*, sense 8 (source accessed 14.7.2015).

honour The word has shifted from a noun indicating public acclaim or external signs of rank in l. 2 to a verb expressing private devotion.

most The poet-speaker delights (i) in the one whom he most honours; (ii) because he honours this person more than anyone else does.

5 *princes* could indicate male or female rulers in early modern usage.

favourites pronounced as three syllables.

leaves petals (see note on 'marigold', l. 6, below).

6 *But* merely.

marigold The petals of pot marigolds (calendulas) open and shut with the sun; see Thomas Hill, *Profitable Art of Gardening*, which tells how the marigold 'is named the husbandman's dial, for that the same so aptly declareth the hours of the morning and evening by the opening and shutting of it. Also named the sun's

flower, for that after the rising of the sun unto noon, this flower openeth larger and larger, but after the noontime unto the setting of the sun, the flower closeth and shutteth more & more' (1568: sigs Q3r–v). See also Watson, *Hekatompathia*, Passion 9.1–6:

> The marigold so likes the lovely sun
> That when he sets the other hides her face,
> And when he 'gins his morning course to run,
> She spreads abroad and shows her greatest grace;
> So shuts or sprouts my joy as doth this flower,
> When my She-sun doth either laugh or lour. (1582: B1r)

In terms of Shakespeare's simile here, princes' favourites are like marigolds: they are glorious when their prince (the sun) smiles on them, and they wither up when out of favour.

7 *And . . . burièd* Compare 1.11; since the pronouns are plural, the line must refer to the impact on the courtiers of the withdrawal of princely favour, rather than to the influence of the sun on the marigold (which is singular). '*Pride*' is pejorative, whether it refers to the courtiers' external show – their 'pomp, ostentation' (*n.*1, OED³ 6a) – or their 'inordinate self-esteem' (OED³ 1a); both senses are pertinent here.

9 *painful* painstaking, diligent (OED³ 4b); inflicting pain (OED³ 2b).

warrior pronounced as two syllables.

famousèd made famous, celebrated ('famous, *v.*', OED 1).

worth This fails to rhyme with 'quite' in l. 11. Most editors consequently emend this to 'might' (following Capell) or 'fight' (following Malone); a more select band follows Collier (1878) and emends 'quite' to 'forth'. There is obviously an error here; however, it is unlikely to be a compositorial one: it is hard to see how 'might' or 'fight' could be misread (or misheard) as 'worth', or 'quite' as 'forth'; 'mi' could feasibly be misread as 'wo', but Sisson's suggestion (1953) that the rest of the word is illegible because mutilated at the end of the line (and thus near the edge of

25

Let those who are in favour with their stars
Of public honour and proud titles boast,
Whilst I, whom fortune of such triumph bars,
Unlooked for joy in that I honour most;   4
Great princes' favourites their fair leaves spread
But as the marigold at the sun's eye,
And in themselves their pride lies burièd,
For at a frown they in their glory die.   8
The painful warrior famousèd for worth
After a thousand victories, once foiled,
Is from the book of honour razèd quite,
And all the rest forgot for which he toiled: 12
    Then happy I that love and am beloved
    Where I may not remove, nor be removed.

the manuscript leaf) is unconvincing, since l. 9 is by no means the longest in the poem. The mistake must therefore be in the copy itself, possibly the result of a process of revision remaining incomplete. Any substitutions for 'worth' or 'quite' are conjectural, and it is more honest (and interesting) to preserve Q's reading, which seems to show the sonnet in a process of transition (although ingenious readers might also argue that a failed rhyme is entirely appropriate here, in the light of the human failure that the sonnet discusses).

10 *foiled* (i) defeated ('foil, *v*.1', OED 4a); (ii) dishonoured (OED 7).

11 *razèd* Q's spelling, 'rased', is an acceptable alternative for 'razed', meaning 'scraped clean' (OED³ 1); to erase writing from a document, ink would be scraped off with a knife, and Shakespeare regularly uses 'raze' in this sense; see, for example, *Macbeth*, 5.3.42 ('Raze out the written troubles of the brain'); *Richard II*, 2.3.74–5: ''Tis not my meaning | To raze one title of your honour out'.
quite completely.

13 *happy* In a sonnet which reflects on the role of fortune, this must play on 'hap' (luck).

13, 14 *beloved. . . removed* Some editors (e.g. Booth) mark a stress on the final syllable of both words, on the grounds that Q usually elides an unstressed '-ed' ending. However, few orthographic rules in Q are entirely consistent, and here – neither metrically nor for the purpose of rhyme – is there any need to sound the final -*ed*. Compare 27.2, 4; 41.6, 8; 45.9, 11; 133.6, 8.

14 *remove* 'depart' (OED³ 1a) or 'change one's place of residence' (OED 1b); i.e. transfer affections to another; compare 116.4.

26
Printed by Benson as a single sonnet entitled 'A dutiful message'.

1 **Lord** unambiguously identifies the addressee as male, the first such marker in Q's sequence since Sonnet 20; for those critics who propose that the fair youth is Southampton or Pembroke, this title is also an appropriate indication of the addressee's aristocratic status.
vassalage A vassal is 'In the feudal system, one holding lands from a superior on conditions of homage and allegiance' (OED A1a). Critics frequently draw attention to the similarities between this sonnet and the dedicatory epistle to Southampton in *Lucrece*, often as evidence for Southampton's candidature as the fair youth of the *Sonnets*. However, a note of homage and humility – the 'subordination, homage, or allegiance' that characterises 'vassalage' (OED 2a) – is conventional in dedications of this period; Nashe characteristically takes this language of clientage to the edge of parody in *Terrors of the Night* (1594): 'Much more may I acknowledge all redundant prostrate vassalage to the royal descended family of the Careys' (1.375). It therefore seems wiser to read the parallels between the *Lucrece* dedication and this sonnet (particularly strong in ll. 5–8) as generic, rather than indicating a connection with a particular individual.
3 **ambassage** 'message conveyed by an ambassador' (OED 2); here, this sonnet.
4 **witness. . . wit** The sonnet professes to be unconcerned about displaying the poet's skill; the play on 'wit' in this line showcases the very cleverness that this false modesty alleges to disclaim; see also note on 'show it, bestow it' (ll. 6, 8).
6 **bare** meagre; but pre-empts the motifs of nakedness and clothing that follow in ll. 8, 11.
wanting lacking.
it duty.
6, 8 **show it. . . bestow it** Particularly when read aloud, there is a play on 'show wit', 'bestow wit', a further display of the poet-speaker's verbal skill and mental agility, notwithstanding the humility expressed.
7 **But** except.
conceit thought (OED 1a), understanding (OED 2a), opinion (OED 4a); in the context of a poem about verbal dexterity, the meaning

'ingenious or witty [. . .] expression' (OED 8a) is also strong (possibly implying that the addressee is also – if not a poet – a competent composer of verses, like many educated men and women of the period).
8 **In thy soul's thought** The phrase locates both where the 'good conceit' (l. 7) originates (the addressee's innermost feelings) and where the poet-speaker wishes his duty to be bestowed.
(all naked) The parentheses are in Q. The phrase modifies (i) duty (called 'bare' in l. 6), with 'naked' conveying vulnerability and defencelessness, and/or (ii) 'soul's thought', in which case 'naked' would suggest the unadorned nature of 'soul's thought'.
bestow it provide with a resting place (OED 3a).
it duty (as in l. 6).
10 **Points on** shines its rays on; compare *Richard II*, 1.3.146–7: 'his golden beams to you here lent | Shall shine on me and gild my banishment'.
fair aspect Astrologically, 'aspect' is 'the relative position of the heavenly bodies' (OED 4); a 'fair' aspect is one in which the conjunction of heavenly bodies, the positions of which were believed to influence human affairs, promises to be favourable. The adjective 'fair', however, reminds us that the star that guides is also the 'fair' youth, and 'aspect' could here mean gaze (OED 1a) or appearance (OED III); compare Petrarch *Rime Sparse* 189.12, where the lover is in a boat lost in stormy seas at night, and his 'two usual sweet stars', which should guide him, 'are hidden' ('Celansi i duo mei dolci usati segni'). 'Aspect' is stressed on the second syllable.
11 **puts apparel on** clothes; words were commonly described as clothing; see quotation from Thomas Wyatt's *Defence* (1541), cited at 76.6n.
tattered 'tottered' in Q, an acceptable Elizabethan variant for 'tattered'; see 2.4n.
12 **thy** The emendation from Q's 'their' was first made by Capell and has generally been followed by editors since. There are fourteen other instances when Q's compositors may have misread 'thy' as 'their' (although not every instance is accepted as an error by all editors); the others are at 27.10; 35.8 (twice); 37.7; 43.11; 45.12; 46.3, 8, 13, 14; 69.5; 70.6; 128.11, 14. The error (if it is

26

Lord of my love, to whom in vassalage
Thy merit hath my duty strongly knit,
To thee I send this written ambassage
To witness duty, not to show my wit;   4
Duty so great, which wit so poor as mine
May make seem bare, in wanting words to show it,
But that I hope some good conceit of thine
In thy soul's thought (all naked) will bestow it,   8
Till whatsoever star that guides my moving
Points on me graciously with fair aspect,
And puts apparel on my tattered loving
To show me worthy of thy sweet respect.   12
    Then may I dare to boast how I do love thee;
    Till then, not show my head where thou mayst prove me.

an error) probably arose from misreading a contracted form of 'thy' ('y^i' or 'y^{ie}') as a contracted form of 'their' ('y^r'). Both these contractions are much rarer than contractions for 'the' ('y^e') or 'that' ('y^t'), but they were nonetheless in use in handwritten documents, as Blakemore Evans shows through his analysis (1996: 281) of compositorial errors in *Edward III*, where 'their' is twice misread as 'thy', and 'your' as 'their' in 2.1 (a scene possibly authored by Shakespeare).
respect (i) 'gaze' (OED^3 1); (ii) 'regard; notice' (OED^3 3); (iii) as 'the influence of a celestial object on terrestrial phenomena' (OED^3 2) the word continues the motif of figuring the youth as a heavenly body, determining the fate of the poet-speaker. Notions of 'deferential regard' (OED^3 10a) are not appropriate here, because of the social disparity between poet-speaker and the youth.

13–14 **love me. . . prove me** From the first rhyming pair (vassalage/ambassage), this sonnet has employed a higher proportion of feminine rhymes than many of Shakespeare's other sonnets (where monosyllabic or unambiguously masculine rhymes dominate).

14 **not. . . head** possibly invoking the proverb 'he dares not show his head' (Dent H246), sometimes used of those who were afraid of being arrested for debt.
prove 'establish as true' (OED^3 1); 'try, test' (OED^3 II).

344 Shakespeare's Sonnets

27

The insomniac lover, who cannot fall asleep for thinking – or seeing an image – of their beloved is a recurrent trope of love poetry. See Sonnets 43, 61; Sidney, *Astrophil and Stella* 38, 39; and Petrarch, *Rime Sparse* 164 – translated by Surrey as 'Alas so all things now do hold their peace' (*Tottel* [10]) – where the peace of the beasts and birds, and stillness of heaven, earth and wind are contrasted with the lover who wakes, thinks, burns and weeps. Virgil's Dido provides a classical precedent: 'when all have gone their ways, and in turn the dim moon sinks her light, and the setting stars invite sleep, along she mourns in the empty hall, and falls on the couch [Aeneas] has left. Though absent, each from each, she hears him, she sees him' ('post ubi digressi, lumenque obscura vicissim | luna premit suadentque cadentia sidera somnos, | sola domo maeret vacua stratisque relictis | incubat. illum absens absentem auditque videtque', *Aeneid* 4.80–3).

Benson combines Sonnets 27–29 under the title 'A disconsolation'.

2 **dear** precious.
   repose place of rest (OED³ 6a, with 1621 as the first citation for this usage; however *Tempest*, 2.1.310 – 'Whiles we stood here securing your repose' – could be read in this sense).
   travail Q's 'trauaill' can indicate both labour and travel (compare 34.2, 50.2); as such, the word is a bridge between between 'toil' (l. 1) and 'journey' (l. 3).
2, 4 **tirèd. . . expirèd** Stressing the *-ed* ending produces a pair of eleven-syllable lines; the rhyme works without the additional stress, but the consistent distinction in Q between the spelling 'tired', when the word is disyllabic (here; Q50.5), and 'tyr'd' (Q66.1, 13), when it is not, suggests that a stressed ending is appropriate here (all instances appear on pages set by Compositor B).
3 **journey** a mild pun on 'a day's labour' (OED 5) or a distance travelled in a day (OED 2a); compare Thomas Wyatt, 'So feeble is the thread', l. 20, describing the movement of the sun: 'From east to west, from west to th' east so doth his journey lie' (*Tottel* [104]).
4 **work** exercise (OED³ 11b).
   body's work physical labour ('toil', l. 1).
   expirèd ended, playing on the idea of sleep as a little death.
5 **far** afar.

6 **Intend** (i) 'proceed on (a journey, etc.)' (OED 6a); compare *Antony and Cleopatra*, 5.2.200–1 ('Caesar through Syria | Intends his journey'); (ii) 'turn one's thoughts to' (OED 12); (iii) 'have in the mind a fixed purpose' (OED 18). There are close links between the meanings of the word resonant here, its Latinate etymology, and various common Latin phrases in which it is embedded: sense (i) picks up on *iter intendere*; senses (ii) and (iii) on *intendere animum*.
   zealous pilgrimage The choice of adjective both strengthens and complicates the devotional note present in 'pilgrimage', since 'zealous' was a word frequently used of keen reformers – as in 'A zealous favourer of the Gospel, and of the godly preachers thereof' (George Whitney, *Choice of Emblems*, 1586: sig. ★3r) – precisely the sort of people who would deplore the practice of going on pilgrimages. Pilgrimage continues the motif of journeying, and the idea of the lover making a pilgrimage to the shrine of their saintly beloved is a frequent trope of love poetry. Compare *Two Gentlemen of Verona*, 2.7.28–32 (cited at *Lucrece*, 960n) and *Romeo and Juliet*, 1.5.93–106 (the sonnet shared by the eponymous lovers at their first meeting).
8 **Looking** The subject is 'thoughts' (l. 5).
9 **Save** except.
   soul's imaginary sight imagination, the faculty 'whereby the soul beholdeth the likeness of bodily things when they are absent' (Stephen Batman, *Batman upon Bartholomew*, 1582: sig. D1v). 'Imaginary' here means 'of the imagination' (see OED³ A2); compare *Lucrece*, l. 1422.
10 **thy** 'their' in Q; Ingram & Redpath are rare examples of editors who reject Capell's emendation to 'thy', arguing that 'their' refers back to thoughts (l. 5); however, the distance between the pronoun and its referent (five lines) renders this unlikely, and 'thy' is elsewhere mistaken for 'their' in Q; see 26.12n.
   shadow 'a delusive semblance or image' (OED 6a), 'a spectral form, phantom' (OED 7). Compare 37.10; 43.5; 61.4; 98.14.
   sightless view Compare Petrarch, *Rime Sparse* 134.9 ('Veggio senza occhi'), translated by Thomas Wyatt as 'Without eye, I see' ('I find no peace', l. 9; *Tottel* [49]).
11 **like a jewel** Compare *Romeo and Juliet* 1.5.45–6: 'It seems she hangs upon the cheek of night | As a rich jewel in an Ethiop's ear'. Elizabethans believed that some jewels emitted light; see

27

Weary with toil, I haste me to my bed,
The dear repose for limbs with travail tirèd,
But then begins a journey in my head
To work my mind, when body's work's expirèd;   4
For then my thoughts (from far where I abide)
Intend a zealous pilgrimage to thee
And keep my drooping eyelids open wide,
Looking on darkness which the blind do see;   8
Save that my soul's imaginary sight
Presents thy shadow to my sightless view,
Which like a jewel (hung in ghastly night)
Makes black Night beauteous and her old face new.   12
    Lo, thus by day my limbs, by night my mind,
    For thee, and for myself, no quiet find.

Titus Andronicus, 2.3.227, where Bassanius' corpse wears 'a precious ring that lightens all this hole'.

ghastly 'causing terror' (OED 1a); 'influenced by GHOST, *n*. [...]) Like a spectre' (OED 2a).

12 **beauteous** pronounced as two syllables; the word is strongly associated with the youth; see 4.5n.

old face Night (Nox) is depicted as old because she is 'the most ancient of all the deities' (Christopher Irving, *A Catechism of Mythologies*, 1822: 46). Compare Spenser, *Faerie Queene*, where Night is 'most auncient Grandmother of all' (I.v.22.2).

14 **For. . .for** on account of . . . on behalf of: the word looks the same in the two instances, but has a different meaning.

28

Benson combines Sonnets 27–29 under the title 'A disconsolation'.

1 **How. . . return** links this sonnet to 27, and in particular the journey described there.

happy 'Happy' in this period is strongly linked to ideas of 'good fortune' (OED³ AI); however, the dominant sense here is 'satisfied, content' (OED³ A5a).

plight 'bodily or physical condition' (*n*.2, OED³ 2a); 'plight' is not necessarily negative in sixteenth- and early seventeenth-century English.

2 **debarred** prevented, forbidden.

3 **by** (i) at; (ii) through the agency of.

5 **either's** spelled 'ethers' in Q; altered to 'others' by Benson.

6 **Do. . . me** Although they are rivals, day and night make an agreement (sealed by a handshake) to torment the poet-speaker.

7 **The one. . . the other** day and night, respectively: the one, the day, tortures the poetic speaker with 'toil'; the other, the night, torments him by allowing him time to remember how far he is from the youth, his friend.

8 **still** always (temporal); even (indicating distance).

thee? In Q, the question mark comes at the end of l. 2; many editors place it at the end of l. 4. Placing it here emphasises the length of what is, syntactically, one complete sentence, the duration of which is mimetic of the length of the poet-speaker's sorrows, extended still further because of the lack of any relief through sleep.

9 **I. . . him** (i) 'I flatter the day by telling him that you are bright (like him)'; (ii) 'I tell the day that you are bright in order to please him'. Some editors place 'to please him' between commas, which ensures that it qualifies 'I tell the day'. The lack of punctuation here follows Q and keeps both possibilities open.

10, 12 **heaven. . . even** Because both words come at the end of the line, it is difficult to determine the scansion and whether they are sounded as two syllables – to make a feminine rhyme – or whether they are elided ('heav'n'; 'ev'n'). 'Heaven' is pronounced as both one and two syllables within the *Sonnets* (and is spelled the same – 'heauen' – in both cases). The same rhyme appears at 132.5, 7.

11 **So** in a similar way.

swart-complexioned dark-faced.

12 **twire** peer, peep (*v*.1, OED 1).

gild'st Q has 'guil'st' ('beguile[s], deceive[s]', 'guile, *v*.', OED), meaning to 'make the time pass pleasantly' as in *A Midsummer Night's Dream*, 5.1.40–1: 'How shall we beguile | The lazy time, if not with some delight?'. Most editors follow Malone, following Capell, and emend (as here) to 'gild'st', on the grounds that (i) it is possible that the compositor misread 'ld' as 'il' (both 'l' and 'd' are looped in a secretary hand, and an 'l' is often a shortier, stubbier letter, so that it could be mistaken for 'i'); and (ii) although beguiling the evening makes sense, the idea that the beloved proves a suitable substitute for the absent stars because he gilds the evening makes more sense still. There is, moreover, a semantic correlation between 'gild' and 'beguile', even if there is no etymological connection, and 'guild' and 'guilt' are recorded by OED as feasible early modern spellings of (respectively) the present and past tense of 'gild, *v*.1'; compare *Lucrece*, l. 1544 and note.

even The two instances of 'even' to mean 'evening' are both spelled 'eauen' in Q (the other instance is at Q132.7), which may be designed to accentuate the rhyme (see Appendix 7) or to distinguish it from 'even' (the adverb), always spelled 'euen' in Q. 'Eauen' is an unusual spelling for 'even[ing]': there are fewer than ten occurrences in a full-text search of EEBO-TCP before 1609 (once false results – curtailed 'heaven', the adjective 'even' – are removed); certainly, it is not a spelling practice associated with Eld's printing house and may originate in the manuscript from which Q is taken.

13 **draw** draw out, extend.

14 **grief's** Since there were no possessive apostrophes in early modern English, it is impossible to tell whether Q's 'greefes' indicates a singular (grief's) or plural (griefs').

length Some editors, following Capell, emend this to 'strength'. However, a compositor is unlikely to misread the consonantal string 'str' for the single character 'l'. If the objection is to the semantic similarity of 'length' and 'longer', then this is a poem which makes frequent use of repetition, presumably to capture the tedious oppression of both day and night.

28

How can I then return in happy plight
That am debarred the benefit of rest,
When day's oppression is not eased by night,
But day by night and night by day oppressed, 4
And each (though enemies to either's reign)
Do in consent shake hands to torture me,
The one by toil, the other to complain
How far I toil, still farther off from thee? 8
I tell the day to please him thou art bright
And dost him grace when clouds do blot the heaven;
So flatter I the swart-complexioned night:
When sparkling stars twire not, thou gild'st the even. 12
   But day doth daily draw my sorrows longer,
   And night doth nightly make grief's length seem stronger.

29
Benson combines Sonnets 27–29 under the title 'A disconsolation'.

1 **disgrace** disfavour (see OED 1, 2a); in the late sixteenth century/early seventeenth century, the condition was strongly associated with the withdrawal of favour by someone 'in a powerful or exalted position' and the concomitant 'degradation, dishonour, or contumely' (OED 1).
Fortune capitalised in Q; for the inconsistent use of capitals in Q, see 5.5n.
men's eyes public esteem.
2 **outcast** 'socially despised; exiled from or ostracized by society; abject, [...] or neglected' (OED³ 1).
state condition.
3 **heaven** pronounced as one syllable.
bootless 'without [...] remedy' (*adj*.1, OED 2); 'unavailing, useless' (OED 3); compare Job 30:20 (a possible influence on ll. 1–4 more generally): 'When I cry unto thee, thou dost not hear me, neither regardest me, when I stand up'. Job also epitomises the man who weeps because of his afflicted condition.
5 **one... hope** (i) someone with better prospects; (ii) Burrow (2002: 438) also suggests 'someone blessed by having a greater capacity for hope'.
6 **Featured** 'fashioned, formed' (OED 1a), with a suggestion that the appearance that is envied is a 'comely' one (OED 1b).
7 **this man's... that man's** Up until this point, theoretically, 'one' (l. 5), 'him' and 'him' (l. 6) could refer to the same (supremely fortunate) man; however the deictics 'this' and 'that' strongly indicate that the poet-speaker is comparing himself enviously to a whole variety of men, and finding himself lacking in some way against them all, which heightens the sense of inadequacy expressed.
art skill.
scope (i) 'opportunity or liberty to act' (*n*.2, OED 7a); (ii) 'reach or range of mental activity' (OED 6a, citing this line); (iii) 'purpose, aim' (OED 2a).

10 **Haply** by chance, but with a play on 'happily'.
state state of mind, but looks back to l. 2 and anticipates l. 14.
11 **(Like... arising)** Q places the parentheses as here; some editors move the closing bracket after 'earth' (l. 12), so that it is the lark which rises from 'sullen earth', rather than the poet-speaker's 'state'; that certainly makes sense, and the enjambment created has the added advantage of mimicking the lark soaring upwards from the earth. However, since Q's reading also makes sense, the original reading has been preserved. The lark was famed for its early morning song; see *Venus and Adonis*, ll. 853–4, and *Cymbeline*, 2.3.20–1: 'Hark, hark, the lark at heaven's gate sings, | And Phoebus [the sun-god] 'gins arise'. Further to that – as a bird which nests on the ground and yet quickly rises to the heights in flight – it can also denote someone of low social status (like the poet-speaker) who receives rapid promotion; compare *Henry VIII*, 2.3.93–4, where the Old Lady comments on Anne Boleyn's swift rising through the social ranks on the wings of Henry's favour: 'With your theme, I could | O'ermount the lark'.
12 **sullen** gloomy, denoting both its dull colour (OED A4a) and its allegedly melancholic or 'sluggish' condition (OED A3a); early modern medical theory, dominated by the concept of the four bodily humours, associated earth (the heaviest of the elements) with melancholy (see 44.11n), which was produced by an excess of black bile and which – along with phlegm – was seen as one of the two more lethargic humours (in contrast to the active humours of blood and choler); in this way, the 'sullen earth' shares characteristics with the poet-speaker's despondency before he remembers his beloved.
13 **wealth** well-being (OED 1a), although the word also evokes a secondary sense of 'prosperity' (OED 3a), which is the sense in which Shakespeare habitually uses it, both elsewhere in the *Sonnets* and more generally.

29

When in disgrace with Fortune and men's eyes,
I all alone beweep my outcast state
And trouble deaf heaven with my bootless cries
And look upon myself and curse my fate,   4
Wishing me like to one more rich in hope,
Featured like him, like him with friends possessed,
Desiring this man's art and that man's scope,
With what I most enjoy contented least;   8
Yet in these thoughts myself almost despising,
Haply I think on thee, and then my state
(Like to the lark at break of day arising)
From sullen earth sings hymns at heaven's gate;   12
    For thy sweet love rememb'red such wealth brings
    That then I scorn to change my state with kings.

30

Benson combines Sonnets 30–32 under the title 'The benefit of friendship'. The sonnet is an example of what Henry Peacham categorises as '*anamnesis*' or '*recordatio*', 'a form or speech by which the speaker calling to remembrance matters past, doth make recital of them. Sometime matters of sorrow' (*Garden of Eloquence*, 1593: sig. M2v).

1 **sessions** 'continuous series of sittings or meetings of a court' (OED 3a); love poetry frequently invokes a court setting or trial (see Thomas Wyatt, 'Mine old dear en'my'; *Tottel* [64]; a translation of Petrarch, *Rime Sparse* 360). Such legal imagery is parodied in *Gulling Sonnets* (Grosart 1876b), probably written *c.* 1594 by the lawyer-poet John Davies: 'Into the Middle Temple of my heart | The wanton Cupid did himself admit' (7.1–2).

2 **summon** 'call together by authority for action or deliberation' (OED 1a); 'cite by authority to attend at a place named, esp. to appear before a court or judge to answer a charge or to give evidence' (OED 2a); continues the legal idiom begun with 'sessions' (l. 1); see also l. 7n (below).

   remembrance of things past recalls Wisdom 11:10 (one of the apocryphal books of the Bible): 'their grief was double with mourning, and the remembrance of things past'. The phrase also appears in the conclusion to Thomas Wyatt's *Quiet of Mind* (1528), a translation of a section of Plutarch's *Moralia*, in which the 'pleasant remembrance of things past' (sig. D3r) is recommended as a means of achieving a Stoic resilience. Whilst the initial remembrance here causes the opposite effect, in the couplet, the thought of the friend does bring the desired quietude (albeit one which relies on attachment, rather than a Stoic detachment from worldly things).

3 **sigh** sigh for.

4 **And. . . waste** Modernising requires that decisions be taken about which word in this line functions as a possessive noun. In Q, there are two alternative readings: 'And with old woes' new wail my dear times waste' (i.e. reiterating old woes, I waste dear times) or the version given here, in which 'wail' is a verb, and 'dear time's waste' a noun phrase. '*Dear*'

can mean both 'beloved' (OED A2a) and 'precious, valuable' (OED A4a), initiating a strand of financial imagery which continues to the end of the sonnet. 'Waste' denotes both 'squandering' (OED 5a) and 'destruction' (OED 6a). Whilst 'waste' is not necessarily negative in the period (see OED), the predominant attitude to waste in Sonnets 1–17 ensures that, read in Q's sequence, these more neutral meanings of 'waste' are unlikely to be to the fore.

5 **drown an eye** weep.

   flow fill with tears (OED 12).

6 **dateless** 'having no limit or fixed term; endless' (OED[3] A1); compare *Richard II*, 1.3.151: 'The dateless limit of thy dear exile'.

7 **cancelled** 'annulled, made void' (OED); the word comes with legal and financial implications, linking two strands of vocabulary running through this sonnet; 'cancel, *v.*': 'of legal documents, deeds, etc.: To annul, render void or invalid [by crossing or striking out]' (OED 1a).

8 **expense** loss (OED 1d), with strong financial connotations, as in 'spending, laying out (of money)' (OED 1a).

   many a slurred into two syllables.

   sight also a valid spelling of 'sigh' in Elizabethan English, so that the poet-speaker bemoans both the sighs that he has spent and the fact that he has lost the sight of friends now dead.

9–12 **Then. . . before** Blakemore Evans draws attention to the use in these lines of *polyptoton* and *diacope* (1996: 142); such rhetorical tropes capture repetition and reiteration of remembering and re-remembering these old woes.

9 **grievances** injuries (OED 1); troubles, sufferings (OED 2).

   foregone past; this is first cited instance in OED, but a keyword search of EEBO-TCP shows it being used in a similar sense in Richard Cavendish's *Image of Nature*, where 'foregone' translates 'praecedentibus' (from the Latin 'praecedo', 'to go before'), in the phrase 'foregone merits' (1571: sigs P7r, Q1r, Q1v).

10 **heavily** 'laboriously, sluggishly' (OED 2), 'with sorrow, grief' (OED 3).

30

When to the sessions of sweet silent thought
I summon up remembrance of things past,
I sigh the lack of many a thing I sought
And with old woes new wail my dear time's waste;   4
Then can I drown an eye (unused to flow)
For precious friends hid in death's dateless night
And weep afresh love's long since cancelled woe
And moan th' expense of many a vanished sight;   8
Then can I grieve at grievances foregone
And heavily from woe to woe tell o'er
The sad account of fore-bemoanèd moan,
Which I new pay as if not paid before.   12
    But if the while I think on thee (dear friend)
    All losses are restored, and sorrows end.

---

tell o'er (i) relate over again; (ii) sum up; the financial resonances of this second meaning pre-empt 'account' and 'pay' (ll. 11, 12).

11 ***account*** (i) narrative; (ii) financial reckoning; the two meanings keep in play the possibilities of 'tell o'er' (l. 10).

fore-bemoanèd already lamented; only instance cited in OED; a keyword search of EEBO-TCP reveals no earlier usages.

13 ***the while*** meanwhile.

(dear friend) The first time that the address 'friend' is used in Q's sequence. 'Dear' can indicate both affection and a sense in which this relationship is costly (emotionally) for the poet-speaker.

14 ***restored*** compensated or made good ('restore, *v*.1', OED³ 1a); the financial resonances of this word are strong, thanks to 'account' and 'pay' in ll. 11–12.

31

Sonnet 31 continues on from Sonnet 30, explaining why and how 'all losses are restored' (30.14); in the process, it becomes clear that these losses ('precious friends hid in death's dateless night', 30.6) have not simply been 'compensated for' – the apparent meaning at 30.14 – but that the lost things have been returned ('restore, *v.* 1', OED³ 2). The sonnet has affinities with the description of the seducer in *Lover's Complaint*, ll. 253–80.

Benson combines Sonnets 30–32 under the title 'The benefit of friendship'.

1 **bosom** seat of emotions; used as a *synecdoche* for the youth.
   endearèd The first usage of the verb 'endear' to mean 'render (a person) dear to another' cited by OED is 1611 (sense 3), although OED citations often lag behind actual usage, and a keyword search of EEBO-TCP shows 'endear' being used to mean 'make beloved' by the early seventeenth century; see Ben Jonson, *Cynthia's Revels* (performed 1600): 'I would have you direct all your courtship thither; if you could but endear yourself to her affection, you were eternally engallanted', 4.3.2–3). Nonetheless, the dominant meaning here (particularly in the light of the financial imagery of Sonnet 30) relates to its more usual sixteenth-century senses of 'enhance the price of' and 'enhance the value of' ('endear, *v.*', OED 1, 2a).
3 **love. . . parts** As in Sonnet 30, the sonnet deploys *polyptoton* and *diacope* (see 30.9–12n). Q capitalises 'Loue' and 'Loues', suggesting personification (although see note about Q's capitals at 5.5n). The idea of Love as a sovereign (or tyrant) ruling over the lover is a poetic commonplace; see Henry Howard, 'Love that doth reign and live within my thought' (*Tottel* [6]), a translation of Petrarch, *Rime Sparse* 140.
   parts attributes, personal qualities (*n.*1, OED³ 15); compare 17.4.
5 **many a** slurred into two syllables; compare 30.8n.
   obsequious 'dutiful' (OED³ 1a), with a particular sense of being 'dutiful in performing obsequies or showing respect for the dead' (OED³ 1b); here pronounced as three syllables.
6 **dear** 'beloved' (OED A2a), 'precious, valuable' (OED A4a), 'costly' (OED A6a).

religious 'devout' (OED³ 2a), 'scrupulous, exact, strict, conscientious' (OED 4a); the phrase 'religious love' recurs, with an ironic twist, in *A Lover's Complaint*, l. 250.
stol'n Since tears are 'spent' (see Daniel, *Delia* 11.2: 'Tears, vows, and prayers have I spent in vain'), poetically, they become a form of tribute or payment, as in *Delia* 21.1–4: 'These sorrowing sighs, the smokes of mine annoy; | These tears, which heat of sacred flame distils, | Are these due tributes that my faith doth pay | Unto the tyrant'. Here, love has pilfered these valuable items. 'Stolen' is pronounced as one syllable in all five instances in which it appears in the *Sonnets*, which may be reflected in Q's spelling 'stolne', a form used by both compositors (including B, who is generally less sensitive to metrical issues). The Quartos of Shakespeare's plays consistently use the spelling 'stolne' (even in prose); however, a keyword search of EEBO-TCP also indicates that 'stolne' was the preferred spelling in this period (779 hits in 361 records, 1590–1609, to 194 hits in 123 records for 'stolen').
7 **interest** something that someone has a right to (OED 1); in this case, the dead have a right to their friends' tears, which continues the idea of tears as tributes. Here pronounced as two syllables.
   which refers to 'all those friends' (l. 4).
8 **But** merely.
   removed absent.
   there in your bosom (as in l. 3); Gildon's emendation to 'thee' (1710) is followed by most editors, on the grounds that 'there' is 'comparatively flat' (Blakemore Evans 1996: 143) and is a possible compositorial misreading of 'thee', comparable to the frequent thy/their confusion (see 26.12n). However, since Q's 'there' makes sense, the original reading is to be preferred; moreover, the dramatic shock of the shift to 'Thou' at the start of the subsequent line would be diminished if 'there' was changed to 'thee'.
9 **Thou art. . . live** Contrast the depiction of the youth as his own grave/tomb at 1.11–14; 3.7–8. As Burrow (2002: 442) points out, 'there is something at once resurrective and vampiric' created by the unexpected use of 'live' at the end of a line containing the words 'grave' and 'buried'.
10 **trophies** In ancient Greek and Roman history, spoils of war would be hung from a tree or monument as 'trophies' or tokens of victory

31

Thy bosom is endearèd with all hearts,
Which I by lacking have supposèd dead,
And there reigns love and all love's loving parts,
And all those friends which I thought burièd.   4
How many a holy and obsequious tear
Hath dear religious love stol'n from mine eye,
As interest of the dead, which now appear
But things removed that hidden in there lie?   8
Thou art the grave where buried love doth live,
Hung with the trophies of my lovers gone,
Who all their parts of me to thee did give;
That due of many now is thine alone.   12
    Their images I loved I view in thee,
    And thou (all they) hast all the all of me.

(OED³ 2a); compare *Titus Andronicus*, 1.1.387–8: 'There lie thy bones, [. . .] | Till we with trophies do adorn thy tomb'.
   lovers can mean 'friends' in this period, as well as more amorous or sexual relationships.
11 **parts of** portion of, share in ('part, *n*.1', OED³ 10a).
12 **That due of many** the debt owed to many; compare 'world's due', 1.14.
13 **Their. . . loved** 'Their images that I loved'; 'images' may hint that the poet-speaker's love has, in the past, been directed towards false idols.

14 **all the all of me** contrasts with 'parts of me' (l. 11); Kerrigan argues (1986: 215) that 'the all of all' is 'a stock tag (used, for example at *Love's Labours Lost*, 5.1.109) meaning "summary conclusion"', thus producing word-play at the sum and conclusion of this sonnet. However, 'the all of all' is not as common as Kerrigan suggests (and in *Love's Labours Lost* is used of a character – Armado – whose grandiose style of speaking is a source of humour). The main effect of this phrase here is hyperbole.

32

A copy of this sonnet, *c.* 1650, entitled 'A sonnet', exists in Folger MS V.a.162, fol. 26r; see Appendix 4.

Benson combines Sonnets 30–32 under the title 'The benefit of friendship'.

1   *well-contented day* 'day' indicates (i) the poet-speaker's lifetime (OED³ 16a); and (ii) 'a day formally designated or agreed for a payment, [. . .] etc., to take place' (OED³ 12a), i.e. the termination of the poet-speaker's life, when he pays his ultimate debt, which f its with the meaning of 'content' as 'to satisfy (a person) by full payment' (OED 4a).

2   *that churl Death* Although not capitalised in Q (the typography of which is admittedly no clear guide on this matter), there is a strong sense of personification here. 'Churl' figures Death disparagingly as a 'rude, low-bred fellow' (OED 5) or, in the light of the financial resonances of 'contented', as a 'miser' (OED 6).

3   *by fortune* by chance.
resurvey read over again (OED³ 1); this line is the first cited usage in OED; a keyword search of EEBO-TCP reveals no earlier instances.

4   *rude* 'lacking in elegance or polish; deficient in literary merit' (OED³ A11a).
lover See 31.10n.

5   *Compare them with* 'read them in the context of'.
bettering of the time conveys the sense that culture – including literary style – is always improving and becoming more sophisticated; the time-frame imagined in this sonnet (where the friend in the future re-reads poems composed much earlier) curiously mirrors the situation of a reader in 1609, perusing a collection of sonnets (a genre which had its heyday in the 1590s, which is when many of these sonnets too would seem to have been written). Duncan-Jones (1997a: 29) argues that the sonnet sequence was enjoying 'a second wave' *c.* 1609, but see discussion of dating in headnote and the survey of sonnet sequences in Appendix 5. 'Bettering' is here pronounced as two syllables.

7   *Reserve* preserve from decay (OED³ 8b); keep (OED³ 6b); compare 85.3.
for my love (i) out of love for me; (ii) because of my love for you, which these lines of poetry show.
rhyme poetic style.

8   *height* great achievements.
happier more fortunate.

9   *vouchsafe* grant 'in a gracious or condescending manner' (OED 2).
but only, just.

10–14   *'Had. . . love'* Quotation marks have been added to indicate direct thought.

10   *Muse* creative powers; for Shakespeare's use of the word in the *Sonnets*, see 21.1n.
growing burgeoning; continues the idea (found in l. 5 and later in l. 13) that each age improves culturally on the one before.

11   *A dearer birth than this* If the poet-speaker had lived, he would have brought out a poem of more value ('dearer') than this one. The creative process is frequently figured as giving birth; see Sidney, *Astrophil and Stella* 1.12, where Astrophil describes himself as 'great with child to speak, and helpless in my throes'. Compare 38.11; 59.3–4; 76.8; 77.11; 78.10; 86.4.

12   *march in ranks* in step with; implies a sense of equality, where the poet-speaker would have been on a par with the later poets, here imagined as being better equipped ('*of better equipage*') than their predecessors. Compare Thomas Nashe's preface to Robert Greene's *Menaphon*, where Thomas Watson's *Amyntas* and *Antigone* are said to 'march in equipage of honour, with any of our ancient poets' (1589: sig. A1r).

13   *better prove* For the belief that each age improves on the one that went before, see notes on l. 5 and 10, above.

14   *for his love* See note on l. 7, above.

32

If thou survive my well-contented day,
When that churl Death my bones with dust shall cover,
And shalt by fortune once more resurvey
These poor rude lines of thy deceasèd lover,   4
Compare them with the bettering of the time,
And though they be outstripped by every pen,
Reserve them for my love, not for their rhyme,
Exceeded by the height of happier men.   8
O then vouchsafe me but this loving thought:
'Had my friend's Muse grown with this growing age,
A dearer birth than this his love had brought
To march in ranks of better equipage: 12
    But since he died, and poets better prove,
    Theirs for their style I'll read, his for his love.'

33

A copy, *c.* 1650s, appears in Folger MS V.a.148, fol. 23r; see Appendix 4.

Benson combines Sonnets 33–35 under the title 'Love's relief'.

1-8 *Full. . . disgrace* These lines reflect the proverb 'The morning sun never lasts a day' (Tilley S978). See also Thomas Howell, *H. his Devises*, 'Reply to [E.L.]', a poem about friendship built out of proverbial sayings: 'Not ay doth prove the glorious morning show | The fairest day' (1581: sig. G3r).

1 *Full* very.

many a slurred into two syllables; compare 31.5.

glorious pronounced as two syllables.

2 *Flatter. . . eye* As well as 'court' ('flatter, *v*.1', OED 2) and 'beguile' (OED 5), the less usual meaning of 'flatter' as 'stroke lightly and caressingly' (OED 1b) is also possible here. For the sun as eye of heaven and for the regal connotations of the sun, see 7.2n and compare *Edward III*, 1.2.141–2 (a scene possibly by Shakespeare): 'Let not thy presence, like the April sun, | Flatter our earth and suddenly be done'.

4 *alchemy* Compare *King John*, 3.1.77–80: 'To solemnize this day the glorious sun | Stays in his course and plays the alchemist, | Turning with splendour of his precious eye | The meagre cloddy earth to glittering gold'. By the sixteenth century, alchemy – characterised by the search to turn base metals into gold – had become intellectually and morally suspect, as in John Harington's 'Brief and Summary Allegory', appended to his translation of *Orlando Furioso*: 'Though the show of it were glorious, the substance of it was dross, and nothing but alchemy and cozenage' (1591: sig. 2M4v).

5-8 *Anon. . . . disgrace* There are a number of Shakespearean parallels to these lines, including *1 Henry IV*, 1.2.197–9: 'Yet herein will I imitate the sun, | Who doth permit the base contagious clouds | To smother up his beauty from the world'. The fact that the speaker of these lines (Prince Hal) is the heir apparent to the throne endorses the link between sun and sovereignty.

5 *Anon* soon.

basest (i) lowest ('base, *adj.*', OED³ A1), indicating the lowest stratum of clouds; (ii) darkest (OED A5); (iii) lowliest (OED A6b), particularly in comparison to the 'sovereign' sun. The adjective also keeps in play the alchemical motif (which sought to turn 'base metals' to gold).

6 *rack* 'a mass of cloud moving quickly' (*n*.2, OED³ 2a); 'a bank of cloud' (OED³ 2b).

7 *forlorn* because deprived of the sight of the sun; stressed on the first syllable.

hide governed by 'have I seen' (l. 1).

8 *Stealing* The choice of word suggests furtive movement. Compare Bertram preparing to 'steal away' to the war (*All's Well*, 2.1.33) or Amiens and the first lord 'steal[ing] behind' Jacques, to eavesdrop, in *As You Like It* (2.1.30).

to west because the sun travels from east to west.

disgrace dishonour, ignominy (OED 3), disfigurement (OED 6).

9 *my sun* the friend.

11 *out alack* expression of despair; compare Richard Robinson, *Certain Selected Histories*: 'But "Out alack," this harper says' (1577: sig. A3r).

12 *region* the upper atmosphere; see *Hamlet*, 2.2.486–7: 'anon the dreadful thunder | Doth rend the region'. The word is here used adjectivally, as in *Hamlet*, 2.2.579: 'region kites'.

13 *no whit* not a bit.

14 *Suns. . . world* (i) great men (who are above lesser men); (ii) pun, through homophone, on 'sons of the world', i.e. mere mortals.

stain 'lose [. . .] lustre' (OED 2); 'blemish [. . .,] discolour' (OED 4a); the word also hints at moral failings on the part of the friend: 'defile or corrupt morally' (OED 5a); 'of the conscience: to suffer stain' (OED 5c).

heaven's pronounced as one syllable.

staineth 'of the sun, etc.: To deprive (feebler luminaries) of their lustre' (OED 1b).

33

Full many a glorious morning have I seen
Flatter the mountain tops with sovereign eye,
Kissing with golden face the meadows green,
Gilding pale streams with heavenly alchemy,   4
Anon permit the basest clouds to ride
With ugly rack on his celestial face,
And from the forlorn world his visage hide,
Stealing unseen to west with this disgrace: 8
Even so my sun one early morn did shine
With all triumphant splendour on my brow;
But out alack, he was but one hour mine,
The region cloud hath masked him from me now.   12
    Yet him for this my love no whit disdaineth:
    Suns of the world may stain when heaven's sun staineth.

34

Benson combines Sonnets 33–35 under the title 'Love's relief'.

1–2   *Why. . . cloak* evokes the proverb 'Although the sun shines leave not your cloak at home' (Dent S968) and follows on from Sonnet 33, where the friend was figured as the sun.

1   *beauteous* pronounced as two syllables; the word is strongly associated with the youth; see 4.5n.

2   *travel* 'trauaile' in Q, which in Elizabethan spelling could indicate both 'travel' and 'travail' (labour); see 27.2n.

3   *base clouds* See 33.5n; 'base clouds' may suggest that the friend has been led astray by unsuitable companions, like those whom Prince Hal describes as 'base contagious clouds', obscuring his true nature in *1 Henry IV*, 1.2.198. Here these 'base clouds' intervene between the sun (the friend) and the poet-speaker.

4   *bravery* 'display, show, ostentation; splendour' (OED 3a); the word may be pejorative; here pronounced as two syllables (as indicated by Q's 'brau'ry').

    rotten (i) 'Of air or water: [. . .] tainted; foul' (OED³ 2); compare *Lucrece*, ll. 778–80; (ii) wet, rainy (OED³ 8).

    smoke vapour (OED 3a); it was believed that plague and other diseases were caused by vapours; see, for example, John Stockwood's translation of Johann von Ewich's *The duty of a faithful and wise magistrate in preserving and delivering the commonwealth from infection in the time of the plague* (1583: fols 37r, 55v, 83r).

6   *rain* figuratively, the tears shed by the poet-speaker because of the actions of the friend; it was a poetic commonplace to describe a lover's tears as rain; see Petrarch *Rime Sparse* 189, translated by Wyatt as 'My galley charged with forgetfulness' (*Tottel* [50]), l. 9: 'A rain of tears' ('pioggia di lagrimar').

7   *salve* 'healing ointment for application to wounds or scars' (*n*.1, OED 1a); a subsidiary sense ('A remedy (esp. for spiritual disease, sorrow, and the like)', OED 2a) is also relevant.

8   *heals* Tucker renders Q's 'heales' as 'heles', which derives from the Old English *helian* and means 'To hide, conceal; to keep secret', 'To cover' ('hele, heal, *v*.2', OED 1a, 2),

instances of which occur into the nineteenth century (particularly sense 2). However, if there is any play on this meaning, it is surely subsidiary to the sense of 'heals' as a synonym for 'cures', not least because of the proverbial nature of the line, as in Dent W929: 'Though the wound be healed yet the scar remains'; compare *Lucrece*, ll. 731–2 and Thomas Wyatt's 'Sighs are my food' (*Tottel* [116]), another poem about betrayal, ll. 7–8: 'Sure I am, Brian, this wound shall heal again: | But yet, alas, the scar shall still remain'.

    disgrace dishonour (OED 3), disfigurement (OED 6); cause of shame or dishonour (OED 5); compare 33.8.

9   *shame* 'the painful emotion arising from the consciousness of something dishonouring [. . .] in one's own conduct or circumstances' (OED 1a).

    physic medicine; since such physic was often purgative, there is a suggestion that the poet-speaker is imagining a medicine that would flush out his grief (only, of course, the friend's sense of shame does not manage to work in this way).

    grief can denote physical pain (OED 5a) as well as mental pain (OED 7a); see, for example, Falstaff questioning whether honour can 'take away the grief of a wound' (*1 Henry IV*, 5.1.132).

10   *still* (i) nevertheless; (ii) 'without change, interruption, or cessation' (OED 3a).

11   *Th' offender's* This term places the blame for injury squarely on the friend.

12   *offence's* Since Q has no possessive apostrophes, when modernising, decisions need to be made about whether or not to render Q's 'offences' singular or plural; it seems likely that here 'offence' is meant to be singular, since it works as a synonym for 'disgrace' (l. 8) and 'shame' (l. 9).

    cross Q's 'losse' is emended to 'cross' by Capell, an emendation followed by Malone and most subsequent editors (as here); the rhyme pair cross/loss appears in the same position (ll. 10, 12) in Sonnet 42. The image of bearing a cross is reminiscent of Christ's walk to Calvary; see John 19:17: 'And he bore his cross, and came into a place named of dead men's skulls, which is called in Hebrew, Golgotha'. For the more general application of 'bearing one's cross' to indicate a 'trial or

34

Why didst thou promise such a beauteous day
And make me travel forth without my cloak
To let base clouds o'ertake me in my way,
Hiding thy bravery in their rotten smoke? 4
'Tis not enough that through the cloud thou break
To dry the rain on my storm-beaten face,
For no man well of such a salve can speak
That heals the wound and cures not the disgrace; 8
Nor can thy shame give physic to my grief:
Though thou repent, yet I have still the loss;
Th' offender's sorrow lends but weak relief
To him that bears the strong offence's cross. 12
    Ah, but those tears are pearl which thy love sheds,
    And they are rich and ransom all ill deeds.

affliction [. . .] to be borne with Christian patience' ('cross, *n*.', OED 10a), see Matthew 10:38: 'And he that taketh not his cross, and followeth after me, is not worthy of me'.

13 **pearl** Pearls were precious; see, for example, Matthew 13:46 ('a pearl of great price'); *Othello*, 5.2.347–8: 'the base Indian, threw a pearl away | Richer than all his tribe'. Powdered, pearl was also used medicinally, and therefore continues the healing imagery of ll. 8–9.
   thy love your love for me.

13, 14 **sheds. . . deeds** A full rhyme is possible in Elizabethan pronunciation; see Appendix 7. Q's spelling – 'sheeds' – an older variant of 'sheds' – shows the rhyme more clearly and is retained by some editors for that reason.

14 **they** the pearls.
   rich powerful (OED³ A1b); valuable, precious (OED³ A4a); abundant (OED³ A8a).

ransom 'atone or pay for' (OED³ 1c); should Q's 'loss' in l. 12 be an error for 'cross' (the result of a compositor's eye-skip), the choice of verb here continues the Christ-like imagery, since it was a word frequently employed of Christ's Passion; see, for example, Matthew 20:28: 'the Son of Man came not to be served, but to serve, and to give his life for the ransom of many'. The potential references to Christ are not theologically consistent: like Christ, the poet-speaker bears the cross for another's wrong-doing, but it is the offender himself (the friend) who performs the Christ-like action of redeeming the offence. However, the poet-speaker does tend to exonerate the young friend, perhaps over readily; see, for example, 35, which follows in Q's sequence.

35

Benson combines Sonnets 33–35 under the title 'Love's relief'.

1 **No more** no longer; the sonnet continues on from the previous two sonnets, moving from berating the friend for his transgression to excusing it; the concluding couplet of Sonnet 34 – where the friend's tears ransom his ill deeds – prepares us for this shift.

2 **Roses have thorns** proverbial; see Dent R182: 'No rose without a thorn'.

   silver. . . mud See *Lucrece*, 577n.

3 **stain** 'obscure the lustre of' (OED 1c); 'blemish [. . .], discolour' (OED 4a); compare 33.14.

4 **canker** 'a caterpillar or other insect larva which attacks plants, esp. the buds and leaves' (OED³ 3); proverbial: 'the canker soonest eats the fairest rose' (Dent C56); compare 70.7, 95.2, 99.13; *Lucrece*, l. 848; and *Two Gentlemen of Verona*, 1.1.42–3: 'in the sweetest bud | The eating canker dwells'. The suggestion is that it is the most beautiful flowers that are most susceptible.

5 **make faults** do wrong; the line alludes to another proverb: 'Every man has his faults' (Dent M116).

   even The word occurs twenty-two times in the *Sonnets*; usually it is monosyllabic (see, for example, 33.9). This is one of four instances where it is pronounced as two syllables (the others coming at 39.5, 41.11, 48.13); in all four cases (which appear in the 1–60 group, probably composed in the early-to-mid 1590s) the use of 'even' is emphatic.

   in this (i) in doing this, i.e. excusing you; (ii) in this poem.

6 **Authorising. . . compare** 'justifying your transgression by drawing comparisons' (to roses, which cannot help having thorns; to fountains, which cannot be held responsible for the presence of mud; to the sun and moon, which have no power to stop eclipses; and to buds, which cannot help having a canker). There is a possible play on the word 'author', as the poet-speaker uses his verses to excuse the friend's sins; 'authorise' also had legal senses ('to make legally valid', OED³ 4; 'to give legal or formal authority (to do something)', OED³ 3b), initiating a thread of legal vocabulary that runs to the end of the sonnet. For the use of 'compare' to mean 'comparison', see 21.5. 'Authorising' is stressed on the second syllable.

7 **My self corrupting** As Hammond notes (2012: 178), 'several meanings are possible:

(i) my self-corrupting; (ii) corrupting myself; (iii) corrupting my self'. See introduction p. xiv for note on modernising 'self' and '-self' constructions.

   salving anointing a wound with a salve or healing unguent ('salve, *v.*1', OED 1a); there seem no grounds to follow Capell's emendation of 'in salving', which makes the line hypermetrical.

   amiss error, fault (OED C).

8 **Excusing. . . are** Offering an apology for the faults of objects in ll. 2–4 more than those faults require (because they are not actually culpable at all); '**their. . . their**' follows Q; many editors follow Malone (following Capell) and emend to 'thy. . . thy' (for the frequent confusion of thy/their, see 26.12n). Some editors (e.g. Wyndham) retain the second 'their', so that it refers back to the faults of the objects mention in ll. 2–4. Duncan-Jones opts for 'these. . . these', suggesting that the compositor may have misread 'theis' (a viable spelling for 'these') as 'their' (1997a: 180). 'These' has the additional advantage of keeping it open as to which 'sins' this line refers: (i) the faults of the objects in ll. 2–4 (which are not sins at all), or (ii) the friend's sins. However, Q's reading has been followed here, on the grounds that (i) since Q's reading makes sense, there is no need to alter it; (ii) emending to 'thy' makes an awkward shift between the singular sin attributed to the friend in Sonnet 34 and in l. 9 ('thy sensual fault'). In Q's reading, l. 8 contrasts with, rather than explains, l. 7: the poet-speaker compromises himself by excusing the friend's (great) fault and by condemning as 'sins' things which are not transgressions but natural occurrences.

9 **sensual fault** a moral failing due to a desire to gratify some appetite (including sexual appetite).

   bring in sense provide rational arguments (to excuse the sensual fault); however, within the context (in a poem about how the poet-speaker is corrupted by the friend's moral failings even as he seeks to excuse them), the meaning of 'sense' as 'the faculties of the mind' (OED 7a) becomes tainted with its alternative meaning of 'the faculties of corporeal sensation considered as channels for gratifying the desire for pleasure and lusts of the flesh' (OED 4a). Several editors note a possible play on 'incense', often used to disguise foul smells. As the poet-speaker wrestles to exonerate the friend, the

35

No more be grieved at that which thou hast done:
Roses have thorns, and silver fountains mud,
Clouds and eclipses stain both moon and sun,
And loathsome canker lives in sweetest bud.   4
All men make faults, and even I in this,
Authorising thy trespass with compare,
My self corrupting salving thy amiss,
Excusing their sins more than their sins are: 8
For to thy sensual fault I bring in sense –
Thy adverse party is thy advocate –
And 'gainst myself a lawful plea commence.
Such civil war is in my love and hate   12
    That I an accessory needs must be
    To that sweet thief which sourly robs from me.

artificiality of his language heightens: the *diacope* of l. 8 ('sin. . . sins') is followed here by *polyptoton* of 'sensual' and 'sense'. See also l. 10n (below) and 43.4n.

10 *adverse party* opponent; contributes to a string of legal vocabulary ('advocate', l.10; 'lawful plea', 'commence' (the legal term for beginning an action), l. 11; 'accessory', l. 13); this cluster of legal vocabulary is also fore-shadowed (less obviously) by 'Authorising' and 'trespass' (l. 6).
advocate 'person employed to plead a cause on behalf of another in a court of law' (OED³ 2a); more generally 'one who pleads for or speaks on behalf of another' (OED³ 4a); the paradox of having one's adversary as one's advocate is compounded by the repetition of the shared prefix ad-.

12–14 *Such. . . me* It is not clear whether the last three lines are the plea itself, or whether they are an explanation of why the poet-speaker might be embarking on a plea against himself. If they are the plea, then it has turned into an attempt to exonerate the accused (the poet-speaker) who is also, confusingly, the accuser. There are plenty of instances in *Shakespeare's Sonnets* where the couplet completes a sentence begun in the third quatrain

with an additional clause; this is one of very few instances where the end of l. 12 comes mid-clause; see also Sonnet 154.

12 *civil war* internecine conflict between the poet-speaker's love for his friend and hate at what he (the friend) has done; possible play on 'civil' as opposed to 'criminal' law, and the civility, or courtesy, with which this war is conducted.

13 *accessory* in law, 'a person who incites or assists someone to commit an arrestable offence, or who knowingly aids someone who has committed such an offence [. . .]. Also more general: a person who accedes to an act or undertaking [. . .]; an adherent' (OED³ 1); the poet-speaker is complicit in the crime because he attempts to excuse his friend. See *Lucrece*, ll. 922, 1658, and notes.

14 *sweet thief* the friend; compare 40.9, 99.2.
sourly peevishly; Shakespeare only uses the adverb here, at 41.8, and *Coriolanus*, 5.3.13, where Martius describes his rejection of Menenius – which left the old man with 'a cracked heart' (5.3.9) – as 'show[ing] sourly to him'. The concept of sourness is not used lightly by Shakespeare; see, for example, *Lucrece*, ll. 699, 867; *Richard II*, 3.2.136 ('sourest and most deadly hate'); *Romeo and Juliet*, 5.3.82 ('sour misfortune's book').

36

Benson combines Sonnets 36–37 under the title 'Unanimity'.

1 **Let me confess** Following on from Sonnet 35, the legal resonances of this phrase are strong. 'Let me' can also be read as introducing a hypothetical situation, in which the poet-speaker rehearses parting from the youth.

   twain separated (OED A3a), with a pleonastic play on 'two'; compare *Troilus and Cressida*, 3.1.101–2: 'She'll none of him. They two are twain'.

2 **undivided** 'not separated or parted from each other' (OED 1b); 'shared or held jointly' (OED 3a).

   one The one-ness of lovers was a motif of love poetry; see Petrarch, *Rime Sparse* 48.5–6: 'Love [...] on whom my one soul in two bodies depends' ('Amor [...] al qual un'alma in due corpi s'appoggia'). Booth (1977: 192) also points to the possible influence of Ephesians 5:25–33, which depicts man and wife as one flesh and which formed part of the marriage service in the *Book of Common Prayer*. See 22.5–14n, 39.2n.

3 **blots** moral stains, faults ('blot, *n*.1', OED 2a); it is not clear what faults are referred to here: (i) the poet-speaker's 'disgrace with Fortune' (29.1); (ii) the friend's actions lamented in Sonnets 33–35 (which the poet-speaker shares because he and the friend are one); (iii) the fault committed in Sonnet 35 when the poet-speaker endeavours to excuse his friend's fault; (iv) 'blots' could also indicate 'imputation[s] of disgrace, defamation[s]' (OED 2b).

4 **borne** endured; recalls 'bears' in 34.12.

5 **one respect** (i) mutual consideration for one another ('respect, *n*.', OED³ 3a); (ii) the

same quality (OED³ 6a); (iii) the same aim (OED³ 4).

6 **separable spite** adverse or hostile situation ('spite'), which causes us to be apart; OED cites this as the sole instance of 'separable' as 'capable of separating' (OED 2); 'separable' is pronounced as four syllables. 'Spite' occurs five times in the *Sonnets*, with the greatest cluster between Sonnets 36 and 40 (36.6, 37.3, 40.14); the two remaining instances are both in Sonnet 90 (ll. 3, 10).

7 **sole** singular, unique (OED 5c); there is also a sense in which love's effect is 'solitary' (OED 2a), because it continues to exist even when the poet-speaker and his friend are apart, divided from each other.

   effect workings ('the state or fact of being operative or in force', OED³ 1); although old-fashioned by the late sixteenth century, the meaning 'essential part' (OED 3c) also seems pertinent here.

8 **love's delight** the pleasure of being together.

9 **evermore** (i) continually (OED 2); (ii) at any future time (OED 3b).

   acknowledge publicly recognise.

10 **bewailèd guilt** This may refer to the sin to which the poet-speaker became an accessory in 35.13; however, bearing in mind the focus on social status in the lines that follow, it seems more likely that this refers back to the inferior social status ('disgrace') lamented in Sonnet 29.

11 **public kindness** 'kindness to me in public'.

12 **Unless. . . name** 'unless you are prepared to damage your standing'.

13–14 **But. . . report** 'Do not acknowledge me publicly: I love you in such a way that – since you are mine – your reputation ['report', OED³ 5] is also my reputation'. '**Being**' is monosyllabic. This couplet is repeated in the same position in 96. See 96.13–14n.

36

Let me confess that we two must be twain,
Although our undivided loves are one:
So shall those blots that do with me remain,
Without thy help, by me be borne alone.   4
In our two loves there is but one respect,
Though in our lives a separable spite,
Which though it alter not love's sole effect,
Yet doth it steal sweet hours from love's delight.   8
I may not evermore acknowledge thee,
Lest my bewailèd guilt should do thee shame,
Nor thou with public kindness honour me,
Unless thou take that honour from thy name: 12
    But do not so; I love thee in such sort
    As, thou being mine, mine is thy good report.

37

Vendler sees 37 and 38 as intervening disruptively between Sonnets 36 and 39, and suggests that, in arranging Q's sequence (be it by Shakespeare or not), 'earlier and less practiced sonnets' have been inserted at this point (1997: 191); but, as Burrow suggests (2002: 454), Sonnets 37–38 'continue the wounded selflessness at the end of 36, in which the poet takes surrogate delight in the success of the friend, and they prepare for the suggestion in 39 that praise of the friend is in fact self-praise'.

Benson combines Sonnets 36–37 under the title 'Unanimity'.

1–2 *As. . . youth* reworks the idea captured in 2.13–14, but framed as a simile and with the poet-speaker (not the friend) taking the role of the old man deriving joy from watching energetic youth.

3 *made lame* handicapped; compare the Quarto version of *King Lear*: 'A most poor man, made lame by Fortune's blows' (sig. I4v; the Folio *King Lear* has 'made tame to', 4.6.221). Twentieth-century editors get much fun out of mocking overly literal interpretations of this phrase by the eighteenth- and nineteenth-century editors who read it as indicating that the poet is lame, just as 'it has also been revealed that he once resided in Bath and in Wells (26, 153, 154) and in Southern Europe (33)' (Ingram and Redpath 1985: 88).

dearest (i) most grievous ('dear, *adj.* 2', OED 2); (ii) most heartfelt ('dear, *adj.*1', OED A7a, citing only examples from Shakespeare); the choice of word also captures the paradoxical nature of this experience, which costs the poet-speaker dear, but is also – in some ways – treasured by him, since he would rather feel this pain than never to have known the friend at all.

spite malice (referring back to 36.6 and the 'separable spite' which has separated them).

4 *Take. . . of* 'get all my consolation from'.

worth 'Worth' and its derivatives appear thirty-two times in twenty-four sonnets (see 2.4n). Its appearance here initiates a concentrated cluster (see 38.6, 9; 39.1).

5 *wit* wisdom (OED 6a), intellectual ability (OED 5a).

6 *any of these all* any one of those qualities listed in l. 5.

or all or all of those qualities taken together.

or more or other qualities not listed in l. 5; 'more' may mean 'better' as well as 'more' in number.

7 *Entitled. . . sit* 'Justifiably take a place among your attributes'. Q has 'Intitled in their parts, do crowned sit'; most editors (as here) follow Capell's emendment of 'their' to 'thy', on the grounds that: (i) Q's compositors seem to confuse 'their' and 'thy' with some regularity (see 26.12n); (ii) the argument demands that the qualities listed at l. 5 are explicitly connected with the youth, which is achieved by 'thy' but not by 'their'; (iii) whilst '*parts*' could indicate the 'roles' ('part, *n.*1', OED³ 12b) assumed by the youth's qualities (listed at l. 5), the sense of prestige that is introduced through '*Entitled*' and '*crownèd*' makes a theatrical metaphor unlikely. It thus seems more probable that the 'parts' belong to the youth, be it the beauty of his body parts (OED³ 4) which ennoble the qualities listed, or his 'personal qualities or attributes' (OED³ 15), which are also praised at 17.4.

8 *engrafted to this store* refers to the practice of inserting a shoot from one tree or plant into another (compare 15.14); here, the poet-speaker's love is engrafted onto the 'sufficient or abundant supply' ('store', OED 4a) that is provided by the friend's plentiful attributes (i.e. beauty, birth, wealth, wit). The image also puns on 'stock', which is both a synonym for 'store' and the horticultural term for the plant onto which a stem is grafted.

9 *then* (i) at that time; (ii) as a result of.

10 *shadow. . . substance* The contrast between shadow and substance was proverbial; see Dent S951 ('Lose not the substance for the shadow'), or *1 Henry VI*, 2.3.50–1 (the culmination of a play on shadow/substance): 'I am but shadow of myself. | [. . .] my substance is not here'. Shakespeare also plays on shadow/substance in Sonnet 53. In Sonnet 37, the usual dynamic is inverted, so that rather than substance creating a shadow, substance (sustenance, strength) is provided by the shadow; 'this shadow' refers to the 'image' that the poet-speaker has conjured of the friend's qualities, and may also imply a sense of 'protection' (OED 11a) that this thought lends the poet-speaker. For the neo-Platonic resonances of 'substance' and 'shadow', see 53.1n. The risk that the shadow might be a 'delusive semblance' (OED 6a) hangs over this line,

37

As a decrepit father takes delight
To see his active child do deeds of youth,
So I, made lame by Fortune's dearest spite,
Take all my comfort of thy worth and truth;   4
For whether beauty, birth, or wealth, or wit,
Or any of these all, or all, or more,
Entitled in thy parts do crownèd sit,
I make my love engrafted to this store: 8
So then I am not lame, poor, nor despised,
Whilst that this shadow doth such substance give
That I in thy abundance am sufficed
And by a part of all thy glory live.   12
    Look what is best, that best I wish in thee;
    This wish I have, then ten times happy me.

despite the poet-speaker's seeming confidence here; compare 27.10; 43.5; 61.4; 98.14.

11 *abundance* plenty.
   sufficed satisfied (OED).
12 *part* portion; play on 'parts' (l. 7).
13 *Look what* seek what, i.e. whatever; compare 9.9.
   in thee to belong to you.

14 *This. . . me* This line can be read hypothetically ('if I have this wish, then I will be tenfold happier') or as if the wish has already been fulfilled and the poet-speaker is now experiencing this tenfold happiness. Through the adjective 'happy', the poet-speaker attempts to redefine his situation as a fortunate one ('happy, *adj.*', OED[3] A2), in the teeth of Fortune's spite (l. 3).

38

Benson combines Sonnets 38–40 under the title 'A congratulation'.

1, 13   *Muse* creative faculty; for Shakespeare's use of the word in the *Sonnets*, see 21.1n.
  want lack.
  subject to invent material for poetic invention, alluding to '*inventio*', one of the five parts of classical rhetoric (see note on l. 8, below).

2   *that* who.

3   *argument* theme, subject (OED 6).
  excellent Stronger in early modern usage than today, 'excellent' indicates superlative praise (someone who is 'preeminent, superior, supreme', OED A1).

4   *vulgar paper* poetry that is 'ordinary' or 'commonplace' ('vulgar, *adj.*', OED 10a).
  rehearse relate, describe.

5   *aught in me* 'anything in my poetry' ('in me' works by *metonymy*; compare the use of 'in Shakespeare' or 'in Chaucer' to mean in works by them).

6   *stand. . . sight* 'withstand your scrutiny' ('stand against', phrasal verb in 'stand, *v.*', OED 1); as usage elsewhere by Shakespeare indicates, 'stand against' is more combative than the habitual gloss 'meets your eye' suggests. See, for example, *1 Henry IV*, 4.3.37, 40: 'stand against us like an enemy'; 'You stand against anointed majesty'.

7   *dumb* reticent (OED A3a), lacking in eloquence; emended by Gildon 1710 to 'dull'.
  to thee addressing you; about you.

8   *invention* One of the five parts of classical rhetoric, *inventio* is 'the finding out of apt matter [. . .] a searching out of things true, or things likely, the which may reasonably set forth a matter' (Wilson, *Art of Rhetoric*, 1553: sig. ²A3v).

9   *the tenth Muse* The nine Muses ('those old nine', l. 10) were classical deities, regarded as inspirers of learning and the arts; their names first appear in Hesiod; later writers assigned each of them a particular function: Clio (Muse of history), Thalia (comedy), Melpomene (tragedy), Euterpe (music), Terpsichore (dancing); the remaining four – Erato (lyric poetry), Polyhymnia (hymns), Urania (astronomy), Calliope (epic poetry) – 'appear less frequently in English literature'

('muse, *n.*1', OED³). Michael Drayton, *Idea's Mirror*, Amour 8, describes his mistress as a tenth muse (1594: sig. B4v); John Davies ridicules Drayton's sonnet in *Epigrams and Elegies*, 'In Decium 25' (1599?: sig. C1r). The classical Muses were all female; in Q's sequence (where – although the gender of each sonnet's addressee is not always stipulated – there is nothing to indicate that the addressee has changed from male to female), casting the (male) addressee as a Muse may suggest the androgyny also explored in Sonnet 20. For Shakespeare's use of the word 'Muse' in the *Sonnets*, see 21.1n.
  ten times more conventional expression of a great quantity (compare 37.14), as well as a play on the tenth Muse.
  worth value, merit; for the clustering of the term 'worth' within the *Sonnets*, see 2.4n.

10   *rhymers* derogatory term for poets; see 17.14n.
  invocate invoke, call upon; Shakespeare uses the verb rarely (there are two other instances: *1 Henry VI* 1.1.52; *Richard III*, 1.2.8); in both of those, it describes summoning a ghost. As an obviously Latinate word, it may be used to mock those inferior poets ('rhymers') who try to bring a false lustre to their works by using such neologisms unnecessarily; the next line provides a literal translation of 'invocate' ('calls on') to show how plain English is sufficiently poetic, at least when being used in relation to such a superlative subject.

11   *he. . . thee* the poet who invokes you as a Muse.
  bring forth This suggests giving birth; compare *Macbeth*, 1.7.72: 'Bring forth men-children only'. Childbirth is a conventional metaphor for producing poetry; see 32.11n and l. 14n (below).

12   *Eternal numbers* poetry that will last forever ('numbers' is a term for metre; see 17.6 and note).
  outlive long date outlast even a time of expiry set far in the future.

13–14   *If. . . praise* Compare Daniel's dedicatory sonnet in the 1594 edition of *Delia*, ll. 13–14: 'Whereof, the travail I may challenge mine, | But yet the glory (Madam) must be thine' (sig. A2r).

38

How can my Muse want subject to invent
While thou dost breathe, that pour'st into my verse
Thine own sweet argument, too excellent
For every vulgar paper to rehearse?   4
O give thyself the thanks if aught in me
Worthy perusal stand against thy sight,
For who's so dumb that cannot write to thee,
When thou thyself dost give invention light?   8
Be thou the tenth Muse, ten times more in worth
Than those old nine which rhymers invocate,
And he that calls on thee, let him bring forth
Eternal numbers to outlive long date.   12
   If my slight Muse do please these curious days,
   The pain be mine, but thine shall be the praise.

13 *slight* insignificant, flimsy.
  curious 'difficult to satisfy; particular; nice, fastidious' (OED 2); the readership which was imagined as becoming increasingly more sophisticated through time in Sonnet 32 is here imagined as becoming overly sophisticated and hypercritical; 'curious' is slurred into two syllables.

14 *pain* effort; may also suggest the pains of childbirth.

39

In Q's sequence, this sonnet marks a return to the theme of separation found in Sonnet 36 (with which it also shares three rhyme pairs: me/thee; one/alone; twain/remain). Vendler consequently sees Sonnets 37–38 as insertions which disrupt Q's sequence (see headnote to 37); however, like Sonnet 38, Sonnet 39 explores the role of poetry in negotiating a relationship between poet and subject; it reflects on separation, but does so in the light of his role as a poet discussed in Sonnet 38.

Benson combines Sonnets 38–40 under the title 'A congratulation'.

1   *worth* value, merit.
    with manners decently, with propriety; as the sonnet develops, it becomes apparent that this means without it being self-praise.

2   *all . . . me* possibly a deliberate echo of Ovid's 'parte [. . .] meliore mei' (15.875), referring to the soul, which Golding translates as 'the better part of me' (15.989; sig. 2D7v); the phrase also plays on the proverbial understanding of a friend as a second self (see 22.3n), an idea that is central to the sonnet as a whole, with additional wordplay in the inherent contrast between 'all' and 'part'. 'Half', a synonym for part, is also used elsewhere by Shakespeare to indicate 'wife' (reflecting the way in which the *Sonnets* recurrently invert gender roles); see *Julius Caesar*, 2.1.271–5, where its use is strongly reminiscent of Ephesians 5:25–33, a passage that features in the marriage service in the *Book of Common Prayer* (see 22.5–14n, 36.2n):

> PORTIA I charm you [. . .]
> By all your vows of love, and that great vow
> Which did incorporate and make us one,
> That you unfold to me, your self, your half,
> Why you are heavy.

The phrase 'better part of me' is repeated at 74.8.

4   *mine own* my own praise.

5   *Even for this* for this very reason; 'even' is here disyllabic, and therefore more emphatic than the elided form usual in Q; see 35.5n; it is also the sole instance of 'even' appearing at the start of a line, forcing the foot to become a trochee, which again adds emphasis.
    divided apart, but with strongly negative resonances: 'split, cut, or broken into pieces; incomplete, imperfect' (OED 1a).

6   *dear* precious, but also costly because of the pain it causes.
    lose. . . one (i) lose the reputation for being united as one; (ii) lose the ability to classify it in this way; the *pleonasm* 'single one' emphasises the oneness of this union even as that oneness is threatened.

8   *That due. . . alone* what is your right (i.e. praise), and your right alone (i.e. without the poet-speaker sharing it because he and the friend are one).

9–14   *O absence. . . remain* The addressee changes from the friend to absence.

11   *entertain the time* while away the time; compare *Lucrece*, l. 1361.

12   *so* (i) in this way; (ii) used as an intensifier.
    dost as in Q, so that 'absence' is the subject. Malone emends to 'doth' (with the subject being 'love'); other editors follow Capell in emending to 'do' (with either 'time and thoughts' or 'thoughts of love' as the subject). Q's reading is retained because it is not easy to misread a secretary 'st' for 'th', as the 'h' has a distinctive descender; nor does a secretary 't' resemble the characteristic long 's' found in sixteenth-century handwriting. Further to that, Q's reading makes sense: absence beguiles lovers into wasting time by thinking of their absent beloved.

13   *make one twain* make one thing (our love) two.

14   *By praising. . . remain* By praising the friend, the poet-speaker makes him seem present, even though he is absent ('hence', from here). If 'here' refers not just to the poet-speaker's geographical location but also, specifically, to this poem, then the lyric serves in a similar way to a letter, conventionally understood as

39

O, how thy worth with manners may I sing,
When thou art all the better part of me?
What can mine own praise to mine own self bring,
And what is 't but mine own when I praise thee?   4
Even for this, let us divided live,
And our dear love lose name of single one,
That by this separation I may give
That due to thee which thou deserv'st alone.   8
O absence, what a torment wouldst thou prove,
Were it not thy sour leisure gave sweet leave
To entertain the time with thoughts of love,
Which time and thoughts so sweetly dost deceive,   12
    And that thou teachest how to make one twain
    By praising him here who doth hence remain.

a way of making absent friends present; see Jerome (1963: 46), Letter 8, which begins 'The comic poet Turpilius, speaking of the exchange of letters, says: "It is the only thing which makes the absent present"' ('Turpilius comicus tractans de vicissitudine litterarum: sola, inquit, res est, quae homines absentes praesentes faciat'; Jerome 1996: 31). This idea is picked up by Desiderius Erasmus in his influential letter-writing manual, *De conscribendis epistolis* (1534). See also John Donne, 'To Mr Henry Wotton' (1598), ll. 1–2: 'Sir, more than kisses, letters mingle souls, | For, thus friends absent speak'.

40

Sonnets 40–42 rehearse a situation analogous to that in 133–134, 144, which respond to the friend's affair with the poet-speaker's mistress; the gender of the appropriated lover is not specified in this sonnet, but becomes clear (in Q's sequence) in 41–42.

Benson combines Sonnets 38–40 under the title 'A congratulation'.

1 *Take* 'accept' (OED 39a), 'seize, capture' (OED 2a), 'appropriate' (OED 15a), 'captivate, delight, charm' (OED 10a); Partridge (1990: 197) highlights the sexual connotations ('take carnal possession of'). The duality of this first word sets the tone for the sonnet that follows, which – as Ingram and Redpath note – is dependent on ambiguity (1985: 94), particularly as regards 'love', which encompasses (i) emotion; (ii) a term of address (used for the friend); (iii) the mistress stolen from the poet-speaker.
all my loves 'all the kinds of love I have', i.e. affection and actual lovers; there is extended play on shifting meanings of 'my love' within the sonnet; see ll. 3, 5.
1, 3 *my love* the friend.
2 *then* (i) causative (in that case); (ii) temporal (at that time).
3 *No love* (i) no lover; (ii) no affection.
4 *All . . . thine* 'all that I had was yours'; echoes the marriage service in the *Book of Common Prayer:* 'with all my worldly goods, I thee endow' (2011: 159).
5–8 *Then . . . refusest* quatrain using four feminine rhymes; unusual in the *Sonnets.*
5 *for my love* (i) 'out of love for me'; (ii) 'in place of my love for you'; (iii) 'to win more love from me'; the phrase recurs in l. 6, but with a quite different meaning again (where 'for' means 'because').
my love The second occurrence in this line refers to the mistress.
receivest 'accept (a person) in [. . .] some relationship' ('receive, v.', OED³ 2a); the choice of word makes the youth seem a passive recipient of the woman's transferred attentions, but it also implicates him as the receiver of stolen goods ('receive, v.', OED³ 9d); tax collectors (never anyone's heroes) were also known as 'receivers' ('receiver, n.1', OED 1a).
6 *I cannot . . . usest* The attempt to excuse the friend ('I cannot reproach you for taking my lover because you are merely making use of

my love/my lover') is undercut by the sexual connotations of 'use' ('who could blame you for sexually enjoying my lover').
7 *if . . . deceivest* 'this self' (as in Q); editors (following Malone) frequently emend to 'thyself', although Q makes sense: 'this self' is here the poet-speaker, playing on the idea of friends (or lovers) as two halves of the same self; see 22.3n.
8 *wilful* 'obstinately self-willed or perverse' (adj.1, OED A1a); other Shakespearean usages recurrently link this quality (i) to youth ('wilful boy', *3 Henry VI*, 5.5.31; 'wilful youth', *Merchant of Venice* 1.1.146) and (ii) with strongly negative concepts ('wilful disobedience', *1 Henry VI*, 4.1.142; 'wilful abuse', *2 Henry IV*, 2.4.311–12; 'wilful adultery', *Henry V*, 2.1.37; 'wilful choler', *Romeo and Juliet*, 1.5.89). Since 'will' can mean sexual desire (see notes on Sonnets 134–136), 'wilful' also here suggests 'lustful'.
taste trial, test (n.1, OED 2a); relish, enjoyment (OED 7b).
what thyself refusest As Burrow notes (2002: 460), 'these are very obscure lines'. The primary meaning of 'refuse' is here 'reject' (Schmidt, 3; see 'refuse, v.1', OED³ II). 'To avoid, eschew, refrain from (sin, error, etc.)' (OED³ 3a) and 'To decline to give or grant' (OED³ 14a) are also relevant. One way of reading this line is that while the friend refuses to enter into a sexual relationship with the poet-speaker, he is engaged in one with the mistress. Alternatively, if we find a play in this sonnet between the self and the true self, then here the friend is doing something (having a sexual relationship with the mistress) from which his ideal self would abstain.
9 *gentle* 'well-born' (OED A1a(a)); 'kind' (OED A8); the phrase *gentle thief* echoes 'sweet thief' in 35.14; see also 99.2.
10 *steal thee* 'steal for yourself'; prepositions could be omitted in Shakespearean English when pronouns could be interpreted as a dative; see Blake (2002: 179), and compare *Hamlet*, 1.3.51: 'O, fear me not' (i.e. 'for me').
all my poverty 'the little I have'.
11 *And yet* even so.
love here an abstraction.
13 *Lascivious* lustful (both 'inclined to lust', OED 1a, and 'inciting to lust', OED 1b); here slurred into three syllables. The surprising conjunction with '*grace*' (elegance, OED³ 14a) anticipates the oxymoron '*ill well shows*' (evil looks good, with the emphasis on external appearance).
14 *spites* injuries, insults, reproaches (OED 1a).

40

Take all my loves, my love, yea take them all;
What hast thou then more than thou hadst before?
No love, my love, that thou mayst true love call;
All mine was thine before thou hadst this more: 4
Then if for my love thou my love receivest,
I cannot blame thee, for my love thou usest;
But yet be blamed, if thou this self deceivest
By wilful taste of what thyself refusest.   8
I do forgive thy robb'ry, gentle thief,
Although thou steal thee all my poverty;
And yet love knows it is a greater grief
To bear love's wrong than hate's known injury.   12
    Lascivious grace, in whom all ill well shows,
    Kill me with spites, yet we must not be foes.

372 Shakespeare's Sonnets

41

Benson combines Sonnets 41 and 42 under the title 'Loss and gain'.

1 **pretty** (i) slight, insignificant, owing to the proverb 'little things are pretty' (Dent T188); (ii) ingenious, artful (OED³ 1b); (iii) charming (OED³ 2b); (iv) considerable (OED³ 4a); the opening image of the sonnet to some extent disrupts expectations, 'petty wrongs' being the obvious and orthographically similar phrase that is here evaded.
liberty licence (OED³ 5a); strongly associated with sexual indulgence, as in the Lawrence Andrewes' sermon (1618) cited by OED³: 'we demean ourselves with such liberty (nay, licentiousness rather)'.

2 **sometime** sometimes (OED 1a); at some time or other (OED 5a).
absent from thy heart If the sonnets are read as a narrative, following Q's sequence, the exchange of hearts described in Sonnet 22 has proved less than permanent.

3 **thy years** your youth.
full well befits The subject is 'wrongs' (l. 1); third person plurals ending in -s are possible in Elizabethan English; see Hope 2003: 61–3.

4 **still** continually.

5 **Gentle . . . won** (i) 'you are kind [OED A8] and therefore winnable'; (ii) 'you are well-born [OED A1a(a)] and therefore worth winning'; (iii) 'you are pliant [OED A5] and therefore winnable'. The line echoes and subverts the proverb 'All women may be won' (Dent W681); compare *1 Henry VI* 5.3.79: 'She is a woman; therefore to be won'. For the sexual connotations of 'gentle', see 20.3n.

6 **Beauteous** pronounced as two syllables; a word frequently used to describe the friend (see 4.5n).
assailed an image of military assault, conventionally used of wooing/seduction (see *Cymbeline* 1.4.125: 'What lady would you choose to assail?'), but here applied to a man, not – as usual – to a woman. 'Assailed' (like 'prevailed', l. 8) is spelled with an -ed ending in Q; usually this indicates that the final syllable should be stressed (e.g. 'tired', 'expired', Q27.2, 4); unstressed -d endings are habitually indicated by the omission of that penultimate 'e', an omission

sometimes signalled by an apostrophe (e.g. 'dimm'd', 'untrim'd', Q.18.6, 8), sometimes not (e.g. 'foild', 'toild', Q.25.10, 12). However, few orthographic rules in Q are entirely consistent: for example, both compositors spell a trisyllabic 'unfathered' with an -ed ending at Q97.10, Q124.2; compare the spelling of the disyllabic 'yellowed' (Q17.9), 'tottered' (Q26.10) and 'flattered' (Q138.14). Here – neither metrically nor for the purpose of rhyme – is it necessary to sound the final -ed. Compare 25.13, 14; 45.9, 11; and 133.6, 8.

7 **when . . . woos** The blame is placed squarely on the woman; for further attempts to exonerate the friend (at least partially) see 11n (below).
what woman's son Contrast Venus' astonishment at the lack of ardour shown by Adonis (*Venus and Adonis*, ll. 201–2).

8 **sourly** peevishly, disagreeably; another term (like 'spites', see 36.6n) which clusters around these sonnets, also occurring at 35.14 and (as 'sour') at 39.10; 'sourly' is disyllabic.
he emended to 'she' by Malone and others; retaining Q's 'he' reveals the strain in the attempt to exonerate the friend: the woman might have begun the seduction, but the man sees it through. A further argument for retaining 'he' when the reader might expect 'she' is that it is another instance within the sonnet where expectations have been subverted: compare 'pretty', not 'petty' (l. 1), and the manipulation of the proverb in l. 5.
prevailed succeeded ('prevail, v.', OED³ 3). Another meaning, suggested by Ingram and Redpath (1985: 96) – where 'prevailed' means 'refrain from responding till he has worn her down, and she has ceased wooing him' – is possible only until the reader reaches l. 9, where 'but yet' needs to function as a contradiction ('even so').

9 **Ay me** Alas.
seat place; the sexual application of the term is apparent from *Othello*, 2.1.295–6: 'I do suspect the lusty Moor | Hath leaped into my seat'.
forbear 'do without', 'keep away from' (OED 4a, 4c).

10 **chide** scold, rebuke; frequently used of a superior chastising an inferior (see *Antony and Cleopatra*, 4.1.1: 'He calls me boy, and chides'), so that the friend is put in the position of a parent reproaching his wayward children.

41

Those pretty wrongs that liberty commits,
When I am sometime absent from thy heart,
Thy beauty and thy years full well befits,
For still temptation follows where thou art.   4
Gentle thou art and therefore to be won;
Beauteous thou art, therefore to be assailed;
And when a woman woos, what woman's son,
Will sourly leave her till he have prevailed?   8
Ay me, but yet thou might'st my seat forbear
And chide thy beauty and thy straying youth,
Who lead thee in their riot even there
Where thou art forced to break a two-fold truth: 12
   Hers, by thy beauty tempting her to thee;
   Thine, by thy beauty being false to me.

11 **Who** The referents are 'thy beauty' and 'thy [. . .] youth'; almost personified, these qualities are represented as beings independent from the youth (note the use of 'who' not 'which'); the poet-speaker thus attempts to exonerate the friend from full responsibility for his actions (compare the effect of 'art forced', l. 12).
   riot debauchery (OED³ 2a); the action of a hound following the scent of an animal other than the intended prey (OED³ 5); riot is often associated with youth; see Tilley Y47 ('Youth riotously led breeds a loathsome old age') and the use of 'Riot' as the Vice figure in *The Interlude of Youth* (1557?); riot is also recurrently associated with Prince Hal's youth (see *1 Henry IV*, 1.1.85; *2 Henry IV*, 4.4.62, 5.5.62; *Henry V*, 1.1.56).
   even pronounced as two syllables (not, as usual in the *Sonnets*, elided); for the use of the disyllabic 'even' for emphasis, see 35.5n.
12 **truth** troth, pledge (OED 2a).
13–14 **Hers. . . thee. . . Thine. . . . me** The pronouns at the beginnings and ends of these lines embody the love triangle, in which both the mistress and the friend break their pledges of loyalty to the poet-speaker.

42

The sonnet continues from Sonnet 41.

Benson combines Sonnets 41 and 42 under the title 'Loss and gain'.

1 **hast** have; possess carnally; see also 'hath' (l. 3); compare 129.6, 10 and notes.
all my grief (i) 'the whole cause for my pain'; (ii) 'the entirety of my suffering'.

2 **dearly** fondly, but with a play on 'costly' (because of the subsequent pain caused).

3 **of my wailing chief** 'the main ['chief'] cause of my lamenting'.

4 **touches** affects, hurts.
nearly intimately.

5 **Loving offenders** The friend and the mistress transgress or offend because they love; the phrase also anticipates the poet-speaker's far-fetched and sophistical attempt to extend that love towards himself. The strained conceit that loving someone's mistress (or wife) is not a betrayal but a sign of friendship is exposed in *All's Well*, 1.3.46–51: 'He that comforts my wife is the cherisher of my flesh and blood; he that cherishes my flesh and blood loves my flesh and blood; he that loves my flesh and blood is my friend: *ergo*, he that kisses my wife is my friend. If men could be contented to be what they are, there were no fear in marriage'.
excuse ye attempt to clear you from blame ('excuse, *v.*', OED 1a); the excuses that endeavour to do this follow in ll. 6–12.

7 **even so** in a similar way; i.e. just as you love her because I love her ('for my sake'), so she loves you because I love you; 'even' needs to be elided into one syllable for metrical purposes, making an eleven- (rather than twelve-) syllable line, to match l. 5.
abuse injure, hurt, wrong (OED³ 6); mislead, cheat, deceive (OED³ 3a).

8 **Suffering** allowing ('suffer, *v.*', 13a); here pronounced as two syllables.
for my sake because she loves me, and you and I are one.
approve try, test (*v.*1, OED 8); experience (OED 9).

9 **thee** the friend.
my love's my mistress'.

9, 10, 11 **lose. . . losing. . . lose** spelled 'loose' and 'loosing' in Q, a variant of 'lose' and 'losing' (see 18.10n); the dominant sense of the verbs here is 'loss' (in light of the play on 'loss', ll. 9, 10); however, modernising necessarily removes the play on 'loose', whereby the poet-speaker can console himself with the delusion that he voluntarily loosed the bonds that held friend and mistress to him. For the play on loose/lose, compare *Hamlet*, 2.2.162 (where there is a potential pun on 'lose' and 'loose my daughter'); Ben Jonson's elegy, composed after the death of his eldest boy in 1603: 'O, could I lose all father now' ('On my first son', l. 5, spelled 'loose' in the 1616 Folio); and Sonnets 88.8n; 134.12n.

10 **losing her** 'in my losing her to him'.
found recovered.

11 **both twain** each of the two; pleonastic for emphasis. 'Both' is repeated three times in two lines: the poet-speaker keeps coming back to a word that acknowledges a twosome that excludes him; the thrice-repeated insistence that they act like this 'for my sake' (ll. 7, 8, 12) is an inadequate attempt to buttress the poet-speaker against the recognition of this two-ness.
lay on me 'burden me with'.
cross 'trial or affliction viewed in its Christian aspect, to be borne for Christ's sake with Christian patience' (OED 10a); 'annoyance; misfortune, adversity' (OED 10b); see also 34.12n. Duncan-Jones (1997a: 194) points out the resonances here with Simon of Cyrene, who was made to carry Christ's cross.

13 **my friend. . . one** The one-ness of the friend and poet-speaker is stressed in a number of the sonnets immediately preceding this in Q's sequence (36, 37, 39, 40).

14 **flattery** cited in OED as one of two instances (both Shakespearean) of the meaning 'gratifying deception, delusion' (OED 2), the other being *Othello*, 4.1.127–9 ('She is persuaded I will marry her, out of her own love and flattery, not out of my promise'); compare 138.14. 'Flattery' is here pronounced as two syllables.

42

That thou hast her, it is not all my grief,
And yet it may be said I loved her dearly;
That she hath thee is of my wailing chief,
A loss in love that touches me more nearly. 4
Loving offenders, thus I will excuse ye:
Thou dost love her because thou know'st I love her,
And for my sake even so doth she abuse me,
Suffering my friend for my sake to approve her. 8
If I lose thee, my loss is my love's gain,
And, losing her, my friend hath found that loss;
Both find each other, and I lose both twain,
And both for my sake lay on me this cross. 12
    But here's the joy: my friend and I are one;
    Sweet flattery! Then she loves but me alone.

43

There is a similar consideration of sleep, sight, night, day, light and dark in Sonnet 27.

Omitted from Benson; see headnote to Sonnet 18.

1 **wink** close my eyes (*v*.1, OED 1a); reworks the proverb 'Although I wink I am not blind' (Dent W500).

2 **unrespected** (i) without noticing; (ii) unworthy of respect (because not the friend).

3 **sleep, in dreams** Contrast Sonnet 27, where the poet-speaker was unable to sleep, but saw visions of the friend in his mind's eye.

4 **darkly bright** bright although in darkness; eyes were thought to emit as well as receive light.

    bright. . . directed This is obscure and is complicated by the various ways of reading 'bright': (i) as adjectival (bright eyes have a focus in the dark of night that they lack during the day); (ii) as adverbial, so that they see 'brilliantly, clearly' ('brightly, *adj.*', OED); (iii) as part of a compound adverb ('bright-in-dark'). The basic meaning would seem to be that, at night, the poet-speaker's eyes are bright because they send out beams of light towards the friend (for the belief that eyes emit beams, see *Venus and Adonis*, 487n). However, in some ways the meaning is less important than the show of verbal dexterity; this sonnet is thick with rhetorical devices, which indicates both the artifice of the poet-speaker's attempts to console himself and his endeavours to recapture the friend's attention. This line, for example, features oxymoron (bright, dark); *diacope* ('bright, are bright'); *polyptoton* (darkly, dark); *antimetabole* ('darkly bright, are bright in dark').

5 **Then** (i) at that time; (ii) as a result.

    shadow 'an unreal appearance; a delusive semblance or image' (OED 6a); compare 27.10; 37.10; 61.4; 98.14.

    shadows. . . bright 'illuminates the shady parts'; the meaning of shadow has shifted from 'image' to 'gloom' or 'darkness' (an example of *antanaclasis*; see also 'form form', l. 6).

6 **thy shadow's form** your actual shape ('form') which has produced this shadow.

form happy show 'make a pleasing spectacle'; more rhetorical flourishes on the part of the poet-speaker, as '*form form*' functions as both *antanaclasis* and *epizeuxis*.

7 **clear** 'bright' (OED A1a); 'fully light, bright; opposed to dusk or twilight' (OED A2a); hyperbolically, the friend's mere image is said to be still brighter ('*clearer*'); the moral connotations of 'clear' ('unspotted, unsullied, free from fault, offence, or guilt', OED A15a) show the levels of the poet-speaker's self-delusion, or willing blindness, as – in Q's sequence – the choice of adjective would seem to go counter to the accusations of moral fault made in the preceding sonnets.

8 **unseeing eyes** because asleep; compare 'sightless eyes' (l. 12) and 'sightless view' (27.10), although in Sonnet 27 sight was impeded not by sleep, but by the darkness.

8, 11 **shade** shadow; since seen at night, there is also a suggestion of 'ghost'; compare 61.5–8.

8, 12 **?** Punctuated as in Q; question marks in early modern punctuation could also indicate an exclamation, which would be an alternative way of reading these lines; however a question mark also keeps to the fore the sense that the poet-speaker is addressing the youth, and desires to elicit a response.

10 **living day** contrasts with 'dead night' (l. 11): days are full of life; nights are associated with dead things.

11 **dead night** contrasts with 'living day' (l. 10), but might also indicate 'in the middle of the night' (see *Lucrece*, l. 162).

    thy Almost all editors accept Capell's emendation to Q's 'their'; for their/thy error in Q, see 26.12n.

    imperfect because only the shadow of reality.

    shade image; if Capell's emendation is accepted (as here), this is the image of the youth; if Q's 'their' is allowed to stand, this would be the image of the youth which appears to the poet-speaker's eyes (where 'their' refers to 'eyes').

12 **heavy** deep (OED A13a); in a sonnet which harps on 'light' and 'dark', there is additional wordplay here, since 'heavy' is also the opposite of 'light'; 'heavy' is often used in Shakespeare to indicate sadness (see the responses to the dying Antony in *Antony*

43

When most I wink, then do mine eyes best see,
For all the day they view things unrespected;
But when I sleep, in dreams they look on thee,
And, darkly bright, are bright in dark directed.   4
Then thou, whose shadow shadows doth make bright,
How would thy shadow's form form happy show
To the clear day with thy much clearer light,
When to unseeing eyes thy shade shines so?   8
How would (I say) mine eyes be blessèd made
By looking on thee in the living day,
When in dead night thy fair imperfect shade
Through heavy sleep on sightless eyes doth stay?   12
    All days are nights to see till I see thee,
    And nights bright days when dreams do show thee me.

and Cleopatra, 4.14.134, 4.15.40: 'Most heavy day!' 'A heavy sight'). Whilst sleep is welcomed by the poet-speaker, this sense of 'heavy' (albeit subsidiary here) may hint at the poet-speaker's underlying sorrow.
stay remain.

13–14 *All. . . me* The fact that the poet-speaker only sees the friend in his dreams indicates that they are currently separated, a theme that continues in Sonnet 44. The order of 'thee' and 'me' has been inverted (presumably to avoid a monorhyme with l. 13) and the dominant sense is 'show you to me', but it may also suggest that poet-speaker (deludedly) hopes that he might appear in the friend's dreams.

44

Benson combines Sonnets 44 and 45 under the title 'Melancholy thoughts'. The two sonnets are closely linked both to each other and to Sonnets 50–51 by themes of separation and the four elements (see l. 11n, below); all four sonnets also share thematic and verbal connections with *Henry V*, 3.7.11–40, a eulogy on a horse delivered by either the dauphin (in F) or Bourbon (in Q), a tribute which parodies the language and practice of sonneteering, Bourbon/the dauphin having 'once writ a sonnet in his [horse's] praise' (3.7.39).

1 *dull . . . flesh* The contrast between 'thought' and the materiality of the body ('flesh') is heightened by the choice of adjective ('dull'), which means both 'slow of understanding' (OED 1) and 'inert, sluggish, inactive; heavy' (OED 3a).

2 *Injurious* The word could simply mean 'detrimental' (OED 3), but the sense of grievance found in its primary sense of 'wrongful; hurtful or prejudicial to the rights of another' (OED 1) is relevant here; pronounced as three syllables.
stop my way bar my passage.

3 *For then* because in that case.
despite of in spite of.

4 *limits* regions, as in *1 Henry IV*, 3.1.71–2: 'The Archdeacon hath divided it | Into three limits very equally'.
where to where.
stay reside (*v.*1, OED 8a), but also contains an accusation of tarrying or lingering (OED 7a).

5 *No matter then* (i) it is of no concern at that time; (ii) it is of no concern in that case; there is a play on 'matter' as in 'substance' (l. 1).

6 *farthest . . . from* the part of the world most distant from.

7 *nimble thought* The speed of thought is proverbial; see Dent T240: 'As swift as thought'.

8 *he* thought (l. 7).
would wishes to.

9 *thought . . . thought* The poet-speaker is destroyed by the realisation that he is not thought, but flesh, and therefore unable to span great distances in an instant.

11 *so much. . . wrought* This line alludes to the theory that everything, including the human body, was composed of the four elements (fire, air, earth and water). The balance of these elements within the body was believed to determine health and temperament. The poet-speaker defines himself as being made up of earth and water, the two heaviest elements, and ironically those that separate him from the friend ('sea and land', l. 7). Contrast the description of the horse in *Henry V*, 3.7.21–2 ('He is pure air and fire; and the dull elements of earth and water never appear in him') and *Antony and Cleopatra*, 5.2.289–90: 'I am fire and air; my other elements | I give to baser life'. See also 45.1–8.

12 *attend. . . leisure* (i) literally, wait for time to pass; (ii) metaphorically, waiting on Time, who – as Ingram and Redpath note (1985: 102) – is represented as a great man, with the power to grant or refuse petitions, and where the poet-speaker's petition (to be reunited with his friend) comprises his '*moan*' or complaint.

13 *naught* nothing; Gildon's emendation of Q's 'naughts' (1710) is generally accepted by editors. Both Duncan-Jones (1997a) and Hammond (2012) stick out against this trend and retain 'naughts', which could mean (i) wrongs (OED³ B2a) or (ii) things of no worth or value (OED³ B2b), although such nominal usages are rare: a keyword search of EEBO-TCP reveals just three instances prior to 1609 where 'naughts' could be read as a noun, and it is not a form that Shakespeare uses elsewhere. Retaining 'naughts' is also problematised by the contradictory 'But' in l. 14.
by through the operation of.
elements so slow i.e. earth and water; see l. 11n, above.

14 *heavy* sad (*adj.*1, OED A25a; compare 43.12n), but also weighty (OED A1a) because composed of water, one of the heavier elements (see l. 11n, above).
badges tokens, emblems.
either's of earth's and water's (the tears are wet, like water, and heavy like earth).

44

If the dull substance of my flesh were thought,
Injurious distance should not stop my way,
For then despite of space I would be brought
From limits far remote, where thou dost stay;   4
No matter then although my foot did stand
Upon the farthest earth removed from thee,
For nimble thought can jump both sea and land
As soon as think the place where he would be.   8
But ah, thought kills me that I am not thought,
To leap large lengths of miles when thou art gone,
But that, so much of earth and water wrought,
I must attend time's leisure with my moan,   12
    Receiving naught by elements so slow
    But heavy tears, badges of either's woe.

45

Benson combines Sonnets 44–45 under the title 'Melancholy thoughts'.

For the connections of Sonnets 44–45 with Sonnets 50–51 and *Henry V*, 3.7.11–40, see headnote to Sonnet 44.

1   ***The other two*** i.e. the elements of air and fire (the other two, earth and water, having featured in the preceding sonnet, of which this is a continuation).
   slight 'lacking in solid or substantial qualities' (OED A3b); contrasts with the 'dull substance' (44.1) of the poet-speaker's flesh (comprised of the heavy elements of earth and water); as Hammond suggests (2012: 198) the long 's' in Q – which would also have been in the manuscript copy – may produce a visual pun on 'flight', 'fast-moving' (*adj.*, OED 1a).
   purging The choice of the term to describe the cleansing effects of fire anticipates the concern with physical and mental health from l. 7 onwards, since purges played a key role in early modern medicine as a means by which to rid the body of any excessive humours and restore its proper balance.

3   ***The first. . . the other*** Air is identified with thought, fire with desire.
   desire wish (OED 1a); the sexual implications (of 'lust', OED 2) are inevitably present.

4   ***present–absent*** Most editors follow Malone in hyphenating these words. (i) Thought and desire are simultaneously both here (with the poet-speaker) and elsewhere (with the friend); (ii) thought and desire, as they shuttle between the poet-speaker and the friend, are alternately present and absent. Compare Stella's 'absent presence' in Sidney's *Astrophil and Stella* 106.1, a more usual formulation of presence in absence, because it is the thought of the beloved that is continually present (despite their physical absence), rather than the bifurcation of the speaker that we find here.
   swift Both thought and desire are associated with speed: see Dent T240 ('As swift as thought'; compare 44.7n); *1 Henry VI*, 2.5.15 ('swift-winged with desire'); *Venus and Adonis*, l. 547.
   slide The choice of verb implies effortless movement.

5   ***For*** as in Q; Tucker emends to 'Forth'; Ingram and Redpath's 'so' is more plausible, since the long 's' could be mistaken for an 'f', and if spelled 'soe' – as is common in Elizabethan English – the secretary 'e' could be misread as 'r'.
   these quicker elements air and fire (represented by thought and desire); 'quicker' implies both 'swifter' and 'more alive'; 'quick' also has specialised meanings when applied to fire ('burning strongly', OED³ 11b) and air ('sharp, piercing', OED³ 17c; see *Pericles*, 4.1.27–8: 'The air is quick there, | And it pierces and sharpens the stomach').

6   ***to thee*** The phrase both attaches to 'embassy' (as its destination) and modifies 'love' (indicating 'affection for you'). The idiom of embassy is also used at 26.3.

7   ***life. . .four*** Every living being is composed of the four elements; see 44.11n. 'Being' is monosyllabic.

7–8   ***with two. . . melancholy*** With air and fire absent, only the elements of earth and water remain; according to the humoral theory on which the early modern understanding of mind and body depended, the resulting dominance of the heavy elements would make the body and mind likewise prone to heaviness (see 29.12n), and melancholy is a state of mind traditionally associated with the element of earth (Porter 1999: 58) and with reflections on death (see Robert Burton, *Anatomy of Melancholy*, 1621: Subsect II, 'Symptoms or Signs in the Mind'). 'Melancholy' could be pronounced as three syllables ('melanc'ly') to retain a decasyllabic line; alternatively, if all four syllables are pronounced (requiring a stress on both the first and third syllable), the effect of elongating, and slowing, the line, could be seen to be mimetic of melancholy.

9   ***life's composition*** the combination of the four elements necessary for life; spelled 'liues composition' in Q, possibly reflecting late sixteenth-century pronunciation.
   recured restored to health ('recure, *v*.', OED³ 1a) (by the return of the missing two elements); compare *Venus and Adonis*, l. 465 and note.

9, 11   ***recured. . . assured*** Some editors place a stress on the final syllable, on the grounds that an *-ed* ending in Q usually indicates a stress, but see 41.6n.

45

The other two, slight air and purging fire,
Are both with thee, wherever I abide;
The first my thought, the other my desire,
These present-absent with swift motion slide; 4
For when these quicker elements are gone
In tender embassy of love to thee,
My life, being made of four, with two alone
Sinks down to death, oppressed with melancholy, 8
Until life's composition be recured
By those swift messengers returned from thee,
Who even but now come back again assured
Of thy fair health, recounting it to me. 12
    This told, I joy, but then no longer glad,
    I send them back again and straight grow sad.

10 *messengers* i.e. air and fire (thought and desire).
11 *even but now* at this very moment; 'even' is pronounced as one syllable.
assured certain.
12 *thy* Q has 'their'; most editors (following Malone, following Capell) emend as here; for the thy/their error, see 26.12n.
fair Duncan-Jones (1997a: 200) suggests a play on 'fire' + 'air'.

13 *joy* rejoice.
14 *straight* immediately.
sad With air and fire (thought and desire) sent back to the friend, the poet-speaker regresses into his previously melancholic state. 'Sad' plays on its meanings of both 'sorrowful' (OED[3] 5a) and 'heavy' (OED[3] 8b), since the poet-speaker has (voluntarily) rid himself of the lighter elements.

46

Benson combines Sonnets 46–47 under the title 'Two faithful friends'.

1   *Mine eye. . . war* A conflict between the eyes (organs of external sense) and the heart (the seat of inner feeling and thought) is conventional in love poetry; more, usually, however, the conceit portrays the eyes as betraying the heart into loving; see Petrarch, *Rime Sparse* 84.1–2 ('Eyes, weep; accompany the heart, which suffers death through your fault' ['Occhi, piangete, accompagnate il core | che di vostro fallir morte sostene']); Watson, *Hekatompathia*, Passion 59, in which 'the Author [. . .] accuseth his own eyes, as the principal or only cause of his amorous infelicity, wherein his heart is so oppressed continually with evils' (1582: sig. H2r); Constable, *Diana* (1592), 12.4, where 'traitor eyes my heart's death did conspire' (sig. C2v); the quotation from Barnfield, l. 9n, below; and *Lucrece*, ll. 368–9. Shakespeare's use of the motif, in which heart and eyes struggle to possess the beloved, is closer to Michael Drayton's in *Idea's Mirror* (1594), Amour 33.1–3: 'Whilst thus mine eyes do surfeit with delight, | My woeful heart imprisoned in my breast | Wishing to be transformed to my sight' (sig. F1r). 'Eye' can denote plural eyes; see 24.1n.
    mortal deadly, fatal; this is hyperbolically portrayed as a fight to the death.

2   *conquest* spoils of war, booty (OED 4); compare *Julius Caesar*, 1.1.32–3: 'What conquest brings he home? | What tributaries follow him to Rome?'.
    thy sight 'sight of you'; l. 3 indicates that it is a picture of the friend at which the poet-speaker is looking (in Q's sequence, the poet-speaker is at this stage parted physically from the friend; see Sonnets 44–45, 47). The friend's picture also features in 47.5–6.

3, 8   *thy* In Q, 'their'; for the frequent thy/their error, see 26.12n. The compositor makes the same error at ll. 13, 14 below.

3   *bar* obstruct, prohibit; the word has legal connotations ('to arrest or stop (a person) by ground of legal objection from enforcing some claim', OED 5a) which are relevant in the light of the legalistic vocabulary that has taken hold by l. 5.

4   *freedom. . . right* the liberty to enjoy something to which one is legally entitled; the phrase contributes to the legalistic imagery.

5   *plead* 'maintain or urge the claim, or state the case, of a party to a suit' (OED3 2a); the legal connotations hinted at in ll. 2–4 are by this stage in the poem indisputable and unambiguous.
    lie reside.

6   *closet* 'a private room' (OED 1a); a box or cabinet used as 'a private repository of valuables' (OED 3a); the 'closet of the heart' was also used in the sixteenth century to refer to the pericardium (OED 6a), the sac enclosing the heart. The construction of the heart as a room is similar to the description of the heart as the 'bosom's shop' in 24.7. See also *Lucrece*, l. 1659 and note.
    pierced It was believed in this period that eyes emitted, as well as received, rays; see 43.4n.
    crystal clear; the word is often associated with eyes in Shakespearean usage; see, for example, *Cymbeline*, 5.4.81 ('Thy crystal window ope; look out'); *Two Gentlemen of Verona*, 2.4.89 ('her crystal looks'); *Venus and Adonis*, ll. 633, 963.

7   *defendant* the eye, which has to answer the case brought against it by the heart; the conceit continues the legal motif.
    plea legal suit or action.

9   *find* spelled 'ſide' (side) in Q; OED cites these lines from Q as the only instance of the meaning 'to assign to one of two sides or parties' ('side, *v.*1', OED 5). The evidence for this meaning is consequently rather thin: the nearest parallel in Shakespeare to such a usage would be *Coriolanus*, 1.1.191–4 ('They'll sit by th' fire, and presume to know | What's done i' th' Capitol [. . .] side factions, and give out | Conjectural marriages'), where 'side' indicates 'to support or countenance' (OED 3). Most modern editors consequently follow Malone (following Capell) and emend 'side' to ''cide' (i.e. decide), on the grounds that (i) 'deside' was an acceptable early modern spelling of 'decide', and (ii) Shakespeare frequently coins aphetic forms (Abbott 1884: § 460). However, this edition (like Duncan-Jones 2010) accepts the emendation proposed by Hammond 2008, which argues that Q's 'side' is a misreading of 'finde': 'f' and the long 's' are easily mistaken for each other in secretary hand, and it is similarly easy to miss the tilde over a vowel that is often used to supply 'n' or 'm'. The same error expanding a tilde

46

Mine eye and heart are at a mortal war
How to divide the conquest of thy sight:
Mine eye, my heart thy picture's sight would bar;
My heart, mine eye the freedom of that right.   4
My heart doth plead that thou in him dost lie
(A closet never pierced with crystal eyes),
But the defendant doth that plea deny
And says in him thy fair appearance lies.   8
To find this title is impanellèd
A quest of thoughts, all tenants to the heart,
And by their verdict is determinèd
The clear eye's moiety and the dear heart's part,   12
    As thus: mine eye's due is thy outward part,
    And my heart's right thy inward love of heart.

seems to have been made at 67.6 and 77.10; and Hand D, possibly Shakespeare's, certainly uses tildes in the manuscript of *Thomas More* (BL MS Harley 7368, fols 8r, 8v: 'vppõ' for 'vppon', i.e 'upon'). 'Find' in this context would thus mean 'agree upon and deliver' a verdict (OED 17d), and fits the legal vocabulary adopted in this sonnet. Hammond (2012: 200) also points to a parallel usage of 'find' at 92.11, and (2002: 81) to its appearance in the first of the 'Certain Sonnets' in Richard Barnfield's *Cynthia* volume, ll. 9–10: 'Conscience the judge, twelve reasons are the jury; | They find mine eyes his beauty t'have let in' (1595: sig. B6r). Barnfield's sonnet is also constructed around the conceit of the lover's eyes being put on trial and may have been an influence on Shakespeare's poem.
  title legal right of possession.
  impanellèd the formal term for enrolling a jury.
10 *quest* jury.
  tenants. . . heart The jury assembled is not impartial since the thoughts which comprise its members all owe allegiance (as 'tenants') to their landlord, the heart, which is traditionally depicted as the organ of thought as well as feeling (see 69.2). For the imagery of tenancy, compare Barnes, *Parthenophil and Parthenophe*, Sonnet 20.1–3: 'These eyes, thy beauty's tenants, pay due tears | For occupation of mine heart, thy freehold, | In tenure of love's service' (1593: sig. C1v).

11 *determinèd* settled, with a strong sense of this being a judicial decision.
12 *moiety* in 'legal or quasi-legal use', half (OED3 1a), but often used more loosely – as here – to mean 'share or portion' (OED3 2b) or 'small or lesser share' (OED3 2a); compare *Lucrece*, dedication, l. 6. Here pronounced as two syllables.
  part share.
13 *As thus* The couplet sums up the verdict of the jury.
  due 'that to which one has a right legal or moral' (OED 2a).
  outward part external appearance; the eye is thus granted the right to exercise its faculty (of sight) which the heart had sought to deny it.
13, 14 *thy* Malone 1790 emends Q's 'their' to 'thine' because in both cases the pronoun precedes a vowel. However, Shakespeare sometimes uses 'thy' for 'thine' before words beginning with a vowel (see 14.14, 56.2, 61.1, 79.1, 87.2; *Lucrece*, l. 1475 and note) and most editors follow Capell's 'thy' for reasons of euphony. For the frequent thy/their error, see 26.12n, and note on ll. 3, 8, above.
14 *inward. . . heart* The biased jury allots the greatest prize to the heart, who is allowed to enjoy the friend's love, whereas the eye merely enjoys his external appearance. Logically, however, it could not be otherwise. Each organ ends up acting in its proper function: the heart feels; the eye sees.

47

This sonnet continues from the preceding one.

Benson combines Sonnets 46–47 under the title 'Two faithful friends'.

1 *a league is took* an alliance is made; 'took' is an acceptable past participle in Elizabethan usage; compare *Measure for Measure*, 2.2.74–5 ('He that might the vantage best have took | Found out the remedy').

2 *And each. . . other* The line echoes the proverb 'one good turn asks (requires, deserves) another' (Dent T616), which is also alluded to at 24.9; '*now*' contrasts this friendly co-operation with the enmity of Sonnet 46. The line is reminiscent of the conclusion to Drayton, *Idea's Mirror*, Amour 33.14, which (like Sonnet 46, see headnote) describes the envious contention between hand and eye; by the end of that poem, however, 'Each one of these doth aid unto the other lend' (1594: sig. F1r).

4 *Or* or when.
with sighs Whilst the primary meaning of the line requires the reading 'smother with sighs', there is a productive ambiguity which hints at the self-indulgence of the love-struck, who are 'in love with sighs'.

5 *my love's picture* Coupled with 'painted banquet' (l. 6), this would seem to be a real picture, as opposed to an image in the mind's eye; see also 46.3.
feast The idea of 'feasting on your sight' returns in Sonnet 75.

6 *painted banquet* 'Banquet' in this period often indicated 'a course of sweetmeats, fruit, and wine' (OED 3a), allowing a potential reference to the tale of the famous Greek artist Zeuxis, highlighted by Kerrigan (1986: 231): 'Zeuxis, for proof of his cunning, brought upon the scaffold a table, wherein were clusters of grapes so lively painted that the very birds of the air flew flocking thither for to be pecking at the grapes' (Pliny, *The History of the World*, trans. Philemon Holland, 1601: sig. 2Z4r). Compare *Venus and Adonis*, ll. 601–2, lines which foreground the ultimate inadequacy of a feast that is merely painted.

8 *doth. . . part* The eye joins the heart in thinking of love. The echo of 46.12 reminds readers of the dispute now resolved.

10 *Thyself* 'Thy seife' in most copies of Q, except in the Rosenbach Library copy, which has been corrected in press and reads 'thy selfe'.
are as in Q; some editors follow Malone (following Capell) and emend this to 'art' for grammatical reasons; however Shakespeare does sometimes use this form for the second person singular before consonants, presumably for reasons of euphony.

10, 12 *still* constantly.

11 *no* Q has 'nor'; editors generally follow either Benson's emendation to 'not' or Capell's 'no'. Either is graphically possible: 'noe' is a common Elizabethan spelling of 'no', and both a secretary 'e' and 't' (in 'not') can easily be misread as 'r'. Blakemore Evans (1996: 156) also suggests 'ne'er' as a potential reading (citing the spelling 'ner' in *First Part of the Troublesome Reign of King John*, 1591, 3.4).

12, 13 *them. . . they. . . they* thoughts.

47

Betwixt mine eye and heart a league is took,
And each doth good turns now unto the other:
When that mine eye is famished for a look,
Or heart in love with sighs himself doth smother,   4
With my love's picture then my eye doth feast
And to the painted banquet bids my heart;
Another time mine eye is my heart's guest
And in his thoughts of love doth share a part.   8
So either by thy picture or my love,
Thyself away are present still with me,
For thou no farther than my thoughts canst move,
And I am still with them, and they with thee;   12
   Or if they sleep, thy picture in my sight
   Awakes my heart, to heart's and eye's delight.

48

Printed by Benson as a single sonnet entitled 'Careless neglect'.

1 *careful* The meaning 'full of care' is live for the duration of l. 1; however, l. 2 fixes its meaning as 'painstaking'.
took my way set out on a journey.

2 *trifle* a thing of little value or importance.
truest firmest, most secure.

3 *to my use* for my use, profit; for sexual resonances of 'use' see 2.9n.

3–4 *stay | From* remain out of.

4 *hands of falsehood* untrustworthy, thieving hands.
sure safe.
wards (i) places of shelter, protection ('ward, *n*.2', OED 8c); (ii) store cupboards, wardrobes (OED 22; compare 52.10); (iii) in the light of the image of the locked chest that follows (l. 9), the specialist meaning of 'wards' is also relevant: 'the ridges projecting from the inside plate of a lock, serving to prevent the passage of any key the bit of which is not provided with incisions of corresponding form and size' (OED 24a).
of trust? trustworthy, strong; a postmodifying prepositional phrase (just as 'chain of gold' = 'golden chain'); however, as well as mirroring the construction 'hands of falsehood', it also keeps in play the sense of 'trust' as a noun, reminding us that ultimately what will keep the youth safe, and for the poet-speaker's own use, is his trustiness. Q ends this sentence with a question mark, which in early modern punctuation can also signal an exclamation mark (which is how many editors choose to modernise it here). Q's question mark has been retained, however, because this rhetorical question – like many in the *Sonnets* – is hedged with doubt and the certainty that it at first seems to assert is soon undermined.

5 *to whom* 'compared to whom', but also contains a suggestion (particularly in Q's sequence) that the jewels are mere trifles in the estimation of the richer, more privileged friend.
jewels pronounced as two syllables.

6 *worthy* 'valuable', with a possible play on 'distinguished' (bearing in mind the elevated social status of the youth).
grief cause of suffering.

7 *best of dearest* the most treasured thing among all the poet-speaker's most precious things; 'dearest' may hold some negative connotations: if the jewels are costly ('dear') in terms of their expense, then the friend is also dear because of what he has 'cost' the poet-speaker emotionally.
care (i) sorrow; (ii) responsibility; (iii) 'anxious concern' (Schmidt, 2).

8 *vulgar* common, ordinary.

9 *chest* puns on chest as a box (for keeping jewels safe) and as the thorax, which contains the heart but which cannot be locked. Shakespeare uses this term for the thorax in *Lucrece* (l. 761) in a similar quibble, and in *Troilus and Cressida*, 1.3.163 ('From his deep chest laughs out a loud applause') and 4.5.10 ('Come, stretch thy chest'). For the image of the thorax as a lockable container, compare 46.6. The idea of the futility of trying to lock up love is also expressed in *Venus and Adonis*, ll. 575–6.

10 *Save* except.

11 *gentle closure* Compare *Venus and Adonis*, l. 782.

12 *at pleasure* as you desire ('pleasure' contains a sense of sexual pleasure).
come and part come and go.

13 *even* pronounced as two syllables; for the emphatic effect of a disyllabic 'even', see 35.5n.
thence from there ('the gentle closure of my breast', l. 11).

14 *truth. . . dear* Honesty itself becomes dishonest to gain such a valuable prize. Compare *Venus and Adonis*, l. 724 and *As You Like It*, 1.3.110: 'Beauty provoketh thieves sooner than gold'. See also Dent P570: 'The prey entices the thief'.

48

How careful was I, when I took my way,
Each trifle under truest bars to thrust,
That to my use it might unusèd stay
From hands of falsehood, in sure wards of trust?   4
But thou, to whom my jewels trifles are,
Most worthy comfort, now my greatest grief,
Thou best of dearest and mine only care,
Art left the prey of every vulgar thief.   8
Thee have I not locked up in any chest,
Save where thou art not, though I feel thou art,
Within the gentle closure of my breast,
From whence at pleasure thou mayst come and part;   12
    And even thence thou wilt be stol'n, I fear,
    For truth proves thievish for a prize so dear.

49

Blakemore Evans notes that the sonnet disrupts a sequence on travel (1996: 157); however Burrow highlights the numerological appropriateness of its position within the sequence, since 49 (as 7 × 7) was regarded as a 'minor climacteric or point of crisis in body's development' (2002: 478); 63 (7 × 9) was the 'grand climacteric' (see headnote to 63).

Printed by Benson as a single sonnet entitled 'Stout resolution'.

1 *Against* in preparation for (OED³ A10); in defence against (OED³ A5a).
2 *defects* faults; stressed on the second syllable.
3 *Whenas* at the time when.
   hath . . . sum has made the final reckoning (i.e. closed the account).
4 *Called* summoned.
   audit In the context of the financial imagery in the preceding line, the dominant meaning is 'the official examination of accounts' (OED 2); however, by the end of the sonnet, the audit starts to resemble 'a judicial hearing of complaints' (OED 1).
   advised respects judicious considerations; compare *King John*, 4.2.214 ('More upon humour than advised respect') and *Lucrece*, l. 1849.
5 *strangely* 'in an unfriendly or unfavourable manner; with cold or distant bearing' (OED 2); compare 89.8, 110.6, and *2 Henry IV*, 5.2.63–4, when the newly-crowned (and reformed) Henry V encounters his former critics: 'You all look strangely on me, [. . .] | You are, I think, assured I love you not'.
6 *that . . . eye* The image reworks the idea of the friend as the sun, found at 33, 34.1–6; for the idea of the sun as the eye of heaven, see 18.5.
7 *converted* changed.
8 *Shall . . . gravity* 'will find reasons for behaving with staid solemnity'; compare *Julius Caesar*, 4.2.20–1 on the souring friendship between Brutus and Cassius: 'When love begins to sicken and decay | It useth an enforced ceremony'. Both 'settled' and 'gravity' imply age. See *Julius Caesar*, 2.1.148–9, where 'gravity' is used as a counterpoint to youth ('Our youths and wildness shall no whit appear, | But all be buried in his

gravity'), and *Hamlet*, 4.7.78–81, where a similar contrast is established: 'youth no less becomes | The light and careless livery that it wears | Than settled age his sables and his weeds, | Importing health and graveness'.

9 *ensconce me* fortify myself; compare *Lucrece*, l. 1515 and note. A 'sconce' is 'a small fort or earthwork' (n.3, OED 1a). The protection provided by this modest fortification is further undercut by the line that follows, which reveals that the fortress is merely self-belief.
10 *desert* merit, worth; the shadow of the homophone, the adjective 'desert' ('deserted, forsaken, abandoned', OED 1), hangs over this line, further undermining the protection offered by 'ensonce me' (l. 9).
11–12 *And this . . . part* The poet-speaker clearly raises ('*uprear[s]*') his hand, but why he does so is less obvious. Most editors interpret these lines as indicating that the poet-speaker lifts his hand either (i) in violence against himself (pre-empting 'guard', l. 12); or (ii) to take the oath before testifying against himself in court (anticipating the legal language of ll. 13–14). However, as Hammond (2012: 206) points out, these readings contradict ll. 9–10. The poet-speaker could here be referring to the way in which his hand acts against him in writing this sonnet, which acknowledges that he has no legal claim on the friend. Alternatively, Ingram and Redpath (1985: 114) suggest that '*against*' here means 'in front of' (OED³ 12a) and '*guard*' 'protect or defend from' (OED 1c).
12 *lawful reasons* arguments which would stand up in court.
   on thy part (i) on your side (where 'on thy part' qualifies 'lawful reasons'); (ii) on your behalf (where 'on thy part' qualifies 'to guard', and the poet-speaker warding off the friend's reasons for rejecting him is seen to be in the longer term interest of the friend).
13 *thou . . . laws* 'you have legal right on your side'.
14 *why to love* 'why you should love me'.
   allege The primary meaning ('to declare on oath before a tribunal, to submit as legal evidence or testimony', v.1, OED³ 1a) continues the strain of legal vocabulary.

49

Against that time (if ever that time come)
When I shall see thee frown on my defects,
Whenas thy love hath cast his utmost sum,
Called to that audit by advised respects;   4
Against that time when thou shalt strangely pass
And scarcely greet me with that sun, thine eye,
When love, converted from the thing it was,
Shall reasons find of settled gravity;   8
Against that time do I ensconce me here
Within the knowledge of mine own desert,
And this my hand against myself uprear
To guard the lawful reasons on thy part: 12
   To leave poor me thou hast the strength of laws,
   Since why to love I can allege no cause.

no cause As with 'allege' the legal resonances are strong, the legal meaning of 'cause' being 'good, proper or adequate ground of action' (OED 3b); i.e. here the poet-speaker confesses that he has no grounds on which to argue that the friend should love him. However, Kerrigan (1986: 233) suggests that the line also critiques the friend, even as he is excused, citing Cordelia's 'No cause, no cause' (*King Lear*, 4.7.74) as an iteration of the mysteries of true love. If love, as Cordelia shows, cannot be calculated, how can it then be based on reasons?

50

Benson combines Sonnets 50–51 under the title 'Go and come quickly'; for the connection of both sonnets to Sonnets 44–45, see headnote to Sonnet 44.

1 *heavy* (i) sadly; (ii) sluggishly; (iii) because the melancholy that afflicts him is associated with earth, the heaviest of the four elements; see 45.7–8n.

2–4 *When...friend* The end of the journey will not bring rest and ease, because the poet-speaker will be reminded of how far he is from his friend. Q has no quotation marks round the direct speech in l. 4.

5 *tirèd* (i) weary; (ii) an aphetic form of 'attired'; the description can apply to both horse and rider.

6 *duly* Most editors accept Benson's emendation, which changes Q's 'duly' to 'dully'. 'Dully' encapsulates the sluggish pace and the gloominess of the rider, which the horse is made to mirror; the horse is also described as 'dull bearer' in 51.2. However, throughout Q, adverbs such as 'fearfully', 'wrongfully' and 'shamefully' – formed from adjectives which can be spelled with either a single or double 'l' in early modern spelling – are consistently spelled -*lly* (see Q66.5, 7; Q80.8; Q99.8; Q113.4). A full-text search of EEBO-TCP reveals no Shakespearean texts where 'dully' is spelled 'duly'; nor are any examples of this variant found in texts printed in Eld's workshop, 1605–15. Any substitution of 'duly' for 'dully' cannot be attributed to a variation in spelling, therefore, and would have to stem from a misreading (by the compositor or an earlier copyist), although it is not easy to mistake a

single for a double 'l' in secretary hand, thanks to the letter's distinctive and characteristic loops (as seen in the additions by Hand D, possibly Shakespeare's, in *Thomas More*, BL MS Harley 7368). Q's 'duly' ('dutifully', 'accordingly') also makes sense and has therefore been retained. It may be that Shakespeare intended a pun which is flattened through modernisation.

to bear in bearing.

that weight the woe in l. 5.

7 *instinct* As Kerrigan points out (1986: 233–4), in good horsemanship horse and rider should operate as one; compare *Lover's Complaint*, l. 107 or *Hamlet*, 4.7.85–8: 'He grew unto his seat, | And to such wondrous doing brought his horse, | As he had been incorpsed and demi-natured | With the brave beast'. The mute understanding between horse and rider imagined here extends to the poet-speaker feeling the pain of being spurred (l. 12) and hearing his own grief in the horse's groans (ll. 11, 13). For an analogous poem of the similarities between the horse and its rider (ridden by love), see Sidney, *Astrophil and Stella* 49. 'Instinct' is stressed on the second syllable.

wretch sometimes used with a degree of pity and affection; see *Hamlet*, 4.7.182 (where Gertrude describes Ophelia as 'the poor wretch') and *Romeo and Juliet*, 1.3.44 (where the Nurse remembers the infant Juliet as a 'pretty wretch').

8 *being* here pronounced as one syllable.

made from made away from.

11 *heavily* sorrowfully.

14 *onward...behind* The deictics are both temporal and spatial.

joy (i) happiness; (ii) the friend, who is the source of happiness.

50

How heavy do I journey on the way,
When what I seek (my weary travel's end)
Doth teach that ease and that repose to say,
'Thus far the miles are measured from thy friend.'   4
The beast that bears me, tirèd with my woe,
Plods duly on, to bear that weight in me,
As if by some instinct the wretch did know
His rider loved not speed being made from thee: 8
The bloody spur cannot provoke him on
That sometimes anger thrusts into his hide,
Which heavily he answers with a groan
More sharp to me than spurring to his side,   12
    For that same groan doth put this in my mind:
    My grief lies onward, and my joy behind.

51

The sonnet follows on from Sonnet 50. The use of equine imagery in the sonnet is reminiscent of *Henry V*, 3.7.11–40; see headnote to Sonnet 44.

Benson combines Sonnets 50–51 under the title 'Go and come quickly'.

1   *Thus* The manner in which the imagined excuse is made follows in ll. 3–4.
    my love my affection, rather than the beloved.
    slow offence the behaviour of the horse, described as a 'dull [sluggish] bearer' in l. 2; see 50.6n.

2   *speed* Although the horse moves slowly, it is still too fast for the poet-speaker because the journey is taking him away from his friend (see 50.8).

3–4 '*From...need.*' Q has no quotation marks round direct speech.

4   *posting* 'speedy travelling; hastening, haste, hurry' (*n.*2, OED 2).

6   *swift extremity* the utmost speed; on the return journey, even this will seem slow (just as on the outward journey, even going slowly feels too quick). Compare *Lucrece*, ll. 1336–7.

7   *though...wind* The wind was proverbially swift (see Dent W411: 'As swift as the wind'); even travelling at that speed, the poet-speaker will want to go faster.

8   *no...know* 'I will not feel as if I am moving' (even though travelling at the speed of something with wings).

10 *perfect'st* spelled 'perfects' in Q (possibly for purposes of euphony); precedent for 'perfects' as an elided form of 'perfectest' is supplied by Blakemore Evans (1996: 159), whose supporting citations include Drayton's *Idea, The Shepherd's Garland* (1593), Eclogue 5 ('But since unperfect are the perfects colours', 1593: sig. F1v) and John Davies' 'Song of Contention', l. 3: 'Women excel the perfects' men in this' (Grosart 1876b). 'Perfectest' exaggerates the superlative form already provided in 'perfect'; Shakespearean precedent for this form of the superlative can be found in *Macbeth*, 1.5.2 ('the perfect'st report') and *Much Ado*, 2.1.306 ('Silence is the perfectest heralt [herald] of joy').
    being pronounced as one syllable.

11 *neigh* Spelled 'naigh' in Q, this is one of the *Sonnets'* celebrated textual cruces. Most

editors modernise as 'neigh', so that desire is figured as a horse; compare Petrarch, *Rime Sparse* 98 (adapted by Thomas Wyatt as 'Though I myself be bridled of my mind'), another poem about separation and which draws an analogy between the addressee's war-horse and his heart. 'Neigh' suggests a state of excitement, or even sexual arousal, as with Adonis' horse who 'neighs' with desire in *Venus and Adonis*, l. 265. However, arguments have been made for emending this line, the two main alternatives being (i) 'weigh', where the compositor, or an earlier copyist, misread 'w' as 'n' (Burrow 2002; see also Jackson 1990); and (ii) 'rein' (modernised from a conjectured 'raign', Wells and Taylor 2005), where the compositor, or an earlier copyist, misread 'r' as 'n', and the final 'n' as 'h'. Q's version is entirely consistent with the imagery of the sonnet, however, and only needs the insertion of single comma (after 'neigh', to make the rest of the line parenthetical); therefore the original reading is here preferred.
    no dull flesh Unlike the horse, desire is not weighed down by physical matter; compare the treatment of the four elements in Sonnets 44–45.
    fiery 'ardent, eager' (OED 5a); 'of a horse: mettlesome, spirited' (OED 5c); desire is also aligned with the element of fire in 45.1–3.
    race rapid forward movement (*n.*1, OED³ I), 'path' (OED 5a); may also contain the sense of a 'contest' (OED 13a), as desire competes with the horse.

12 *love, for love* affection (compare l.1), which is prompted by (i) affection; (ii) charity (compassion for the horse); (iii) love (for the friend).
    jade 'a contemptuous name for a horse', be it 'of inferior breed', 'ill-conditioned, wearied, or worn-out' (*n.*1, OED 1).

13–14 '*Since...go.*' The couplet is the excuse provided for the horse; there are no quotation marks in Q.

13 *wilful* wilfully, deliberately (the adjective acts as an adverb).

14 *Towards* here pronounced as one syllable.
    give...go The poet-speaker hyperbolically imagines himself able to dispense with the horse's services, as he will be carried along by the wings of his desire.

51

Thus can my love excuse the slow offence
Of my dull bearer, when from thee I speed:
'From where thou art, why should I haste me thence?
Till I return of posting is no need.'   4
O what excuse will my poor beast then find,
When swift extremity can seem but slow?
Then should I spur, though mounted on the wind,
In wingèd speed no motion shall I know;   8
Then can no horse with my desire keep pace;
Therefore desire (of perfect'st love being made)
Shall neigh, no dull flesh in his fiery race,
But love, for love, thus shall excuse my jade: 12
   'Since from thee going he went wilful slow,
    Towards thee I'll run and give him leave to go.'

52

Printed by Benson as a single sonnet entitled 'Familiarity breeds contempt'.

1   *So. . . rich* 'I am just like the rich man'; throughout the sonnet, the poet-speaker imagines himself enjoying the accoutrements of the wealthy (treasure, jewelled necklaces, expensive clothes, a wardrobe).
    blessèd 'bringing, or accompanied by, blessing or happiness' (OED 4a).

2   *bring him to* bring him to the sight of.
    sweet. . . treasure There is a potentially erotic charge to the image (particularly when qualified by 'sweet', with its allusions to the sense of taste); for the bawdy connotations of 'treasure', see 20.14n.

4   *For* for fear of; compare *Two Gentlemen of Verona*, 1.2.133: 'Yet here they shall not lie, for catching cold'.
    seldom pleasure infrequent delight; this line provides the key argument of the sonnet, as the poet-speaker (absent from his friend) tries to find some comfort in convincing himself that if you see or experience something too often, the pleasure loses its edge. The sentiment is also proverbial (Dent P417: 'Pleasure the rarer used the more commendable').

5   *Therefore* for this reason.
    feasts feast days (holidays); compare *1 Henry IV*, 3.2.57–9 (lines which also associate rareness and solemnity): 'and so my state, | Seldom but sumptuous, showed like a feast, | And won by rareness such solemnity'.
    solemn sumptuous (OED 4a); as Booth (1977: 223) notes, there may be some etymological play on the Latin 'sollemnis' ('solus' + 'annus' = 'whole year'); this derivation is now questioned (see OED) but was believed valid in Shakespeare's lifetime; see the gloss on 'solennel' in Randle Cotgrave's *Dictionary of the French and English Tongues*: 'Solemn (not altogether as we do commonly understand it, but) annual, yearly' (1611: sig. 4D5r).
    rare infrequent (OED³ A3d), splendid (OED³ A5b); compare *1 Henry IV*, 1.2.204–7: 'If all the year were playing holidays, | To sport would be as tedious as to work; | But when they seldom come, they wished for come, | And nothing pleaseth but rare accidents'. This is the speech in which Hal reveals his future plans of 'reformation' (1.2.213), and – as in this sonnet – he moves from the comparison between workdays and holidays to the image of a jewel, which 'Shall show more goodly and attract more eyes | Than that which hath no foil to set it off' (1.2.214–15).

6   *in. . . set* Duncan-Jones (1997a: 214) notes how, in the light of this line, the sonnet appears at a numerologically appropriate point in Q's sequence (there being 52 weeks in a year).

7   *stones of worth* precious gems.
    thinly placèd sparsely distributed.

8   *captain* chief, principal (OED).
    carcanet 'ornamental collar or necklace, usually of gold or set with jewels' (OED 1a).

9   *So* like this (the same construction as in l. 1).
    keeps Time both 'withholds' or 'detains' the friend, but as time is figured as the poet-speaker's 'chest', it also contains him; however, unlike the rich man of ll. 1–4, the poet-speaker cannot access this chest with a key; the strain of the analogy thus starts to show, particularly as – in Q's sequence – Sonnet 48 has already revealed that the friend is not something which can be locked away securely in a chest.

10 *wardrobe* in this period, a room for storing clothes or armour, rather than a cupboard.

11 *To. . . blest* Some exceptional and important occasion will be made even more exceptional (by the production of this sumptuous article of clothing). The choice of the word '*instant*' ('an infinitely short space of time', OED 2) hints at the fragility and transience of such moments.

12 *unfolding* The wardrobe is anthropomorphised: not only does it contain the garment, it is then imagined unwrapping and displaying the folds of cloth.
    imprisoned pride the magnificence (i.e. the garment) which had been locked away inside.

13 *scope* opportunity.

14 *Being. . . hope* 'To possess you is to feel elation ['triumph, *v*.', OED 4]; not to have you is to be able to wish for you' (a state which is seen as having its own particular pleasure, in anticipation, and another instance of strained optimistic thinking on the part of the poet-speaker).

52

So am I as the rich whose blessèd key
Can bring him to his sweet up-lockèd treasure,
The which he will not every hour survey,
For blunting the fine point of seldom pleasure.   4
Therefore are feasts so solemn and so rare,
Since, seldom coming, in the long year set
Like stones of worth they thinly placèd are,
Or captain jewels in the carcanet.   8
So is the time that keeps you as my chest,
Or as the wardrobe which the robe doth hide
To make some special instant special blest,
By new unfolding his imprisoned pride.   12
    Blessèd are you whose worthiness gives scope,
    Being had, to triumph; being lacked, to hope.

53

Kerrigan (1986: 237) draws attention to the similarities of Sonnet 53 with Orlando's lyrics in praise of Rosalind in *As You Like It*, 3.2.141–52, which parody the hyperbolic tendencies of the besotted lover, who imagines that their beloved 'comprises all worldly beauty':

> Therefore heaven Nature charged
> That one body should be filled
> With all graces wide-enlarged.
> Nature presently distilled
> Helen's cheek, but not her heart,
> Cleopatra's majesty,
> Atalanta's better part,
> Sad Lucretia's modesty.
> Thus Rosalind of many parts
> By heavenly synod was devised,
> Of many faces, eyes, and hearts,
> To have the touches dearest prized.

For another instance of the proximity between the *Sonnets* and parodies of amorous verse, see headnote to Sonnet 44.

Benson combines Sonnets 53–54 under the title 'True admiration'.

1 *substance* (i) the material of which a body is formed (OED[3] 7a); (ii) essence (OED[3] 6b). Some commentators hear a play on 'substance' as in wealth (the friend is a 'man of substance'). However, the dominant framework invoked, thanks to the appearance of 'shadows' (l. 2), is neo-Platonic thought. As Plato's allegory of the Cave explains (*Republic*, VII), what we perceive as reality are mere shadows ('eidola') of the true essence of things (the 'idea'); here, the youthful friend is the true essence of things, and everything else in the natural world, a reflection of him. *whereof* of what.

2 *strange* 'other than one's own' (OED 2); i.e. these shadows do not belong to the youthful friend.
shadows The primary sense here is of parasitic companions (OED 8a), whose ultimate unreliability is underscored by the meaning of shadows as 'delusive semblance[s]', 'vain and unsubstantial object[s] of pursuit' (OED 6a). See also note on 'substance' (l. 1 above) for the evocation of neo-Platonic thought: next to the 'substance' of the youth, his companions seem like 'mere shadows'.
tend attend, follow like servants.

3 *Since. . . shade* Everyone (apart from the youth) has only one shadow; the meaning of 'shadow' has here shifted to 'the dark figure which a body "casts" or "throws" upon a surface by intercepting [the light]' (OED 4a). This use of *antanaclasis*, combined with the repetition of 'every' and 'one', marks this line as one of those moments in the *Sonnets* where the poet-speaker indulges in rhetorical display (here making a simple statement sound complex).

4 *And. . . lend?* The second part of this line is obscure (in line with the tendency of this poem to complicate apparently simple statements, as in l. 3); it is obvious from the first part that the friend has some unique power to do something, despite the fact that he is a single being ('but one'); however, the second part of the line is problematic because 'lend' is normally a transitive verb: you lend something, and most uses also indicate to whom you lend it. This sentence might mean: (i) the friend casts every shadow (because the youth is the essence, and everything else in the world, a reflection of that); (ii) the youth lends something (presumably his beauty) to every shadow (i.e. everything else in the natural world). Booth (1977: 225) and Burrow (2002: 486) both allow readings whereby it is the youth who adopts the likeness of all other (beautiful) things, but this requires either an unprecedented meaning of 'lend' (to indicate 'borrow') or an inversion of the usual English word-order (beyond what is usual, even in poetry), so that 'every shadow' becomes the subject. This difficult line seems to continue an ongoing interest in the *Sonnets* (e.g. at 18 and 130) and *Venus and Adonis* with the processes and problems of comparison.

5 *Adonis* The archetypically beautiful youth of classical mythology, with whom Venus falls in love (see Ovid, *Metamorphoses* 10); describing Adonis is, of course, what Shakespeare has done in *Venus and Adonis* (1593). Comparing the beloved to figures from classical literature was a commonplace of love poetry; see Orlando's lyrics in *As You Like It*, cited above, or Barnfield's homoerotic Sonnet 12 in the 'Certain Sonnets' section of his *Cynthia* volume, ll. 1–4: 'Some talk of Ganymede, th' Idalian Boy, | And some of fair Adonis make their boast, | Some talk of him whom lovely Leda lost, | And some of Echo's love that was so coy' (1595: sig. C3v).

53

What is your substance, whereof are you made,
That millions of strange shadows on you tend,
Since every one hath, every one, one shade,
And you, but one, can every shadow lend? 4
Describe Adonis, and the counterfeit
Is poorly imitated after you;
On Helen's cheek all art of beauty set,
And you in Grecian tires are painted new. 8
Speak of the spring and foison of the year:
The one doth shadow of your beauty show,
The other as your bounty doth appear,
And you in every blessèd shape we know. 12
 In all external grace you have some part,
 But you like none, none you, for constant heart.

counterfeit imitation (OED B1); the reference to 'painted' in l. 8 also activates the meaning of 'counterfeit' as 'picture' (OED B3a); Q's spelling ('counterfet') points to the full rhyme made with 'set' (l. 7); see Appendix 7.

6 **poorly. . . you** is a feeble copy, modelled on ('*after*') you; there is a sense in which Shakespeare could be pointing, self-referentially, to his own description of Adonis in *Venus and Adonis* as a pale imitation of the youth of the *Sonnets*. (This is not to imply that the youth is Southampton, one of the candidates for 'Mr. W.H.'; Southampton is the dedicatee of *Venus and Adonis*, not its subject.)

7 **Helen's cheek** Helen was renowned to be the most beautiful woman in the world and as such was the cause of the Trojan War (see Christopher Marlowe, *Dr Faustus*, 5.1.99–100: 'Was this the face that launched a thousand ships, | And burnt the topless towers of Ilium?'). The invocation in this sonnet of the epitome of both male and female beauty – Adonis (l. 5) and Helen – recalls the androgynous beauty of the 'master-mistress' of Sonnet 20.
cheek face (by *synecdoche*).
all. . . set 'place all art associated with depicting beauty'; that the beauty has to be added hints at the use of cosmetics; Shakespeare's own portrayal of Helen in *Troilus and Cressida* (probably written after these sonnets, *c.* 1602) is certainly

unflattering, her value residing less in her intrinsic beauty than the fact that men are prepared to die for her: as Troilus notes, 'Helen must needs be fair, | When with your blood you daily paint her thus' (1.1.90–1).

8 **And. . . new** 'the resulting picture of Helen will resemble you, painted in Grecian dress' ('*tire*' could also mean a head-dress); 'new' means 'afresh' or 'again' (OED³ 2).

9 **foison** plentiful harvest (OED 1b); see *Tempest*, 4.1.110–11: 'Earth's increase, and foison plenty | Barns and garners never empty'. There is a self-referentiality here: the first eighteen sonnets make recurrent recourse to images of the seasons – including autumn and **spring** – when discussing the youth's beauty.

10 **The one** spring.
shadow mere image.

11 **The other** foison (i.e. autumn).
bounty munificence, generosity; compare *Antony and Cleopatra*, 5.2.86–8: 'For his bounty, | There was no winter in 't; an autumn it was | That grew the more by reaping'.

12 **And . . . know** (i) 'we recognise ['know'] you in all beautiful things' ('**blessèd shape**' being something that gives pleasure; here, in the context of a sonnet about 'external grace' and beauty, the pleasure is presumably caused by visual stimulation); (ii) 'you appear in all the beautiful things we know'.

13 ***all external grace*** all things which are visually beautiful.
part share.

14 ***you . . . heart*** The *antimetabole* ('you like none, none you') emphasises the uniqueness: the youth resembles nobody, and nobody resembles him in his fidelity and loyalty; for the *Sonnets'* concern with the problems of comparison, see Sonnets 18, 130 and note on l. 4, above. Praise of the friend's 'constant heart' is at odds with his portrayal else-where: within Q's sequence, this might be the result of the poet-speaker's strained attempts to look on the bright side (compare Sonnet 52). It is possible to produce a more sardonic reading if 'like' serves as a verb (you like no one because of their constant heart, and equally no one likes you for that reason); the friend has beauty, but not constancy. Booth (1977: 226) also points to the possibility of '***constant heart***' sounding like 'con-stant art' (i.e. continual artifice). However, in Q's sequence, Sonnet 54 would seem to run counter to this more cynical reading, as it naively and optimistically asserts the inward beauty which truth supplies.

53

What is your substance, whereof are you made,
That millions of strange shadows on you tend,
Since every one hath, every one, one shade,
And you, but one, can every shadow lend?   4
Describe Adonis, and the counterfeit
Is poorly imitated after you;
On Helen's cheek all art of beauty set,
And you in Grecian tires are painted new.   8
Speak of the spring and foison of the year:
The one doth shadow of your beauty show,
The other as your bounty doth appear,
And you in every blessèd shape we know.   12
    In all external grace you have some part,
    But you like none, none you, for constant heart.

54

Benson combines Sonnets 53–54 under the title 'True admiration'.

1, 13   ***beauteous*** pronounced as two syllables; the word is strongly associated with the youth; see 4.5n.

2   ***By*** as a result of.
that. . . give? 'Truth' (fidelity, loyalty) embellishes external beauty, by adding internal beauty; the superlative quality of the resulting beauty is reflected in the *polyptoton* of l. 1 ('beauty beauteous'). Most editors emend Q's comma at the end of the line to an exclamation mark. However, Q does not always put a question mark where one is needed (see, for example, Q84.4, Q92.13, Q103.10). Recognising the interrogative note sounded here highlights the way in which the sonnet assumes an audience, inviting them to draw on a common stock of experience or wisdom ('As sweet as a rose' was proverbial; see Dent R178). This dynamic is then enforced by the plural first-person pronoun in l. 3: 'fairer *we* it deem'.

3   ***rose*** Here, as elsewhere in Q, capitalised; see 1.2n.
fair beautiful.

4   ***For*** because of.

5   ***canker blooms*** flowers of wild roses (dog roses), which have no scent (rather than alluding to the 'canker', a caterpillar, which destroys buds, as in 35.4); Duncan-Jones (1997a: 218) suggests that this may refer to the colloquial name for wild red poppies, citing the index of John Gerard's 1636 *Herbal*. Poppies have a much richer colour than dog roses, which would fit with the statement that they '***have full as deep a dye***' as garden roses. However, poppies do not 'hang on [. . .] thorns' (l. 7), and whilst wild roses are not strongly coloured, neither were Elizabethan roses as brightly coloured as today's hybrids, cultivated for that purpose. The botanical accuracy is less important than the overall rhetorical argument that visual beauty is inferior to that which is combined with internal beauty.

6   ***tincture*** 'in early chemistry [. . .] The (supposed) essential principle of any substance obtained in solution. Also, the extraction of this essential principle' (OED 7a); the word

thus anticipates the distilling imagery with which the sonnet concludes.

7   ***Hang. . . thorns*** Wild roses grow on thorny stems, just like domesticated roses; invokes another proverb: 'No rose without a thorn' (Dent R182). Duncan-Jones' suggestion (1997a: 218) that 'thorns' could suggest 'stalks' is unconvincing: it relies on a line from Dumaine's sonnet in *Love's Labours Lost* (4.3.110), in which (i) the 'blossom' described is unspecified (and therefore could be a rose); and (ii) Dumaine's versifying serves more as a vehicle for parodying clichéd amorous verse than a reliable guide to botanical terms, particularly as, in Dumaine's poem, 'thorn' is needed to make the rhyme.
wantonly playfully; the word does not suggest lasciviousness in this context.

8   ***summer's breath*** gentle summer's breeze; compare 65.5.
maskèd concealed (by their calyxes); possibly also a play on 'damask' (i.e. 'blush-coloured', OED B8), a description often used of roses and in poetic descriptions of a lover's complexion; see *Love's Labours Lost*, 5.2.295–7 ('Fair ladies masked are roses in their bud; | Dismasked, their damask sweet commixture shown, | Are angels vailing clouds, or roses blown') and Shakespeare's parody of this convention in 130.5–6.
discloses opens up, unfurls (OED³ 2a).

9   ***for*** because.
virtue. . . show 'Their only merit ['virtue', OED³ 6a] is their appearance'.

10   ***unwooed*** not sought after.
unrespected (i) unnoticed (OED³ 1); (ii) not held in respect or regard (OED³ 2).

11   ***Die to themselves*** perish alone and without issue; compare 94.10. As Blakemore Evans notes, this also recalls the self-annihilation of the 'sweet self' in Sonnet 4, 'which is followed by the distillation imagery of 5 and 6, here repeated in line 14' (1996: 162). The lack of issue – and the echoes of the procreation sonnets – hint at an autoerotic reading ('die' being a common euphemism for orgasm). In light of the focus on colour in l. 5, there may also be a play here on 'dye'.

12   ***Of. . . made*** Unlike wild (canker) roses, scented roses are made into perfumes after being plucked; the line recollects Sonnets

54

O how much more doth beauty beauteous seem
By that sweet ornament which truth doth give?
The rose looks fair, but fairer we it deem
For that sweet odour which doth in it live.   4
The canker blooms have full as deep a dye
As the perfumèd tincture of the roses,
Hang on such thorns and play as wantonly
When summer's breath their maskèd buds discloses;   8
But, for their virtue only is their show,
They live unwooed and unrespected fade,
Die to themselves. Sweet roses do not so;
Of their sweet deaths are sweetest odours made: 12
　　And so of you, beauteous and lovely youth,
　　When that shall vade, by verse distils your truth.

5–6, only without the imperative to breed. The deaths of scented roses are 'sweet' because they end up in rosewater or syrups, which are sugared.

13　*so of you* The youth is identified with the scented roses (worthy of distillation) rather than with the 'canker blooms'.
　lovely 'beautiful' (OED³ 3); 'lovable; deserving of love or admiration' (OED³ 2); 'affectionate' (OED³ 1a); 'amorous' (OED³ 1b); compare 126.1.
14　*that* beauty.
　vade a variant spelling of 'fade', but also a distinct word, as can be seen by its use to rhyme with 'fade' in Spenser's *Faerie Queene*,V.ii.40.2, 5 and *Ruins of Rome*, 20.13–14; derived from the Latin *vadere*, it means depart, i.e. in this context, to die.

by verse. . . truth 'Your truth will be extracted by my poetry and concentrated in it' (thus preserving it for future generations). 'Truth' could here indicate 'faithfulness' (OED 1a) or 'true likeness'; in Q's sequence, the confident assertion of the youth's faithfulness is soon to be disappointed and the 'truth' that the poetry distils is his lack of truth. The theme of achieving immortality through verse recapitulates Sonnets 15–19, and in Q's sequence, becomes a recurrent motif from this point on, until Sonnet 126. Some editors follow Capell's emendation, changing 'by' to 'my', since 'distil' is usually a transitive verb, although Booth (1977: 227) cites its use as an intransitive in King James Bible (1611): 'My doctrine shall drop as the rain, my speech shall distil as the dew' (Deuteronomy 32:2).

55

Printed by Benson as a single sonnet entitled 'A living monument'.

The motif of immortality achieved through verse continues from the conclusion to the previous sonnet; it is also a recurrent theme of poetry from the classical period onward (see 15.14n). Propertius' *Elegies* 3.2 has been suggested as a possible source for Shakespeare's treatment of this theme (which celebrates the immortality of the beloved, rather than the poetry itself); however, as Kerrigan notes (1986: 241), Propertius was not widely read in the period, and Shakespeare is more likely to be indebted to (i) Horace's *Odes* and (ii) the closing lines of Ovid's *Metamorphoses*. These texts are frequently echoed in literature of the period, e.g. in Whitney's *Choice of Emblems*, 'Scripta manent', 'Penna gloria perennis' (1586: sigs R2r, 2B2v). The borrowing may therefore not be at first-hand.

(i) Exegi monumentum aere perennius
regalique situ pyramidum altius,
quod non imber edax, non Aquilo inpotens
possit diruere aut innumerabilis
annorum series et fuga temporum
Non omnis moriar multaque pars mei
vitabit Libitinam; usque ego postera
crescam laude recens [. . .].

I have finished a monument more lasting than bronze and loftier than the Pyramids' royal pile, one that no wasting rain, no furious north wind can destroy, or the countless chain of years and the ages' flight. I shall not altogether die, but a mighty part of me shall escape the death-goddess. On and on shall I grow, ever fresh with the glory of after time. (Horace, *Odes*, 3.30.1–8)

(ii) Iamque opus exegi, quod nec Iovis ira nec ignis
nec poterit ferrum nec edax abolere vetustas.
cum volet, illa dies, quae nil nisi corporis huius
ius habet, incerti spatium mihi finiat aevi:
parte tamen meliore mei super alta perennis
astra ferar, nomenque erit indelebile nostrum,
quaque potet domitis Romana potentia terris,
ore legar populi, perque omnia saecula fama,
siquid habent veri vatum praesagia, vivam.
(Ovid, *Metamorphoses*, 15.871–9)

Now I have brought a work to end which neither Jove's fierce wrath,
Nor sword, nor fire, nor fretting age with all the force it hath
Are able to abolish quite. Let come that fatal hour
Which (saving of this brittle flesh) hath over me no power
And at his pleasure make an end of mine uncertain time;
Yet shall the better part of me assured be to climb
Aloft above the starry sky, and all the world shall never
Be able for to quench my name. For look how far so ever
The Roman empire by the right of conquest shall extend,
So far shall all folk read this work. And time without all end
(If poets as by prophecy about the truth may aim)
My life shall everlastingly be lengthened still by fame. (Golding, 15.984–95; sigs 2D7v–8r)

1 ***gilded*** frequently used in Shakespeare to suggest a fragile, transient beauty – as in *Coriolanus*, 1.3.60–1 ('gilded butterfly), *King Lear*, 4.6.112 ('the small gilded fly'), *Titus Andronicus*, 3.2.61 ('his slender gilded wings') – or a veneer, disguising the true quality beneath, as in *Hamlet*, 3.3.58 ('Offence's gilded hand may shove by justice') and Goneril's description as 'this gilded serpent' in *King Lear*, 5.3.84. Here the gilt is both temporary (like all earthly things, except poetry) and at odds with the decay that it encloses. Compare 101.11.

monuments 'monument' in Q, and (following Malone) emended for the rhyme; a plural was often formed in sixteenth- and early seventeenth-century manuscripts by an '*es*'-hook, and it may be that the compositor mistook this for a flourish or for a terminal 'e', which was becoming much rarer in printed texts by the end of the sixteenth century (see 113.10n). Compare also 126.8n.

2 ***powerful*** Pronounced as two syllables; Q's 'powrefull' may result from the compositor's spelling preference rather than an endeavour to show the elison: Compositor A (who probably set this line) consistently favours 'powre' and 'flowre' in contrast to B's 'power' and 'flower'.

55

Not marble, nor the gilded monuments
Of princes shall outlive this powerful rhyme,
But you shall shine more bright in these contents
Than unswept stone, besmeared with sluttish time.   4
When wasteful war shall statues overturn,
And broils root out the work of masonry,
Nor Mars his sword, nor war's quick fire shall burn
The living record of your memory.   8
'Gainst death and all oblivious enmity
Shall you pace forth; your praise shall still find room,
Even in the eyes of all posterity
That wear this world out to the ending doom.   12
    So, till the judgement that yourself arise,
    You live in this and dwell in lovers' eyes.

In all of Compositor A's instances, power and flower need to be monosyllabic, so it is difficult to prove this thesis either way in his case; however, Compositor B regularly uses the spellings 'power' and 'flower' regardless of the number of stressed syllables, including 124.4, where – of the two instances of 'flower – metrically, the first needs to be monosyllabic, the second, disyllabic.
rhyme poetry, i.e. this sonnet and/or the collection more generally.

3 **in these contents** what is contained in this verse; 'contents' is stressed on the second syllable.

4 **unswept stone** a stone monument (e.g. a tombstone) has become dusty with neglect; compare *Coriolanus*, 2.3.119: 'The dust on antique time would lie unswept'.
besmeared Compare *Lucrece*, l. 945 (also describing the effects of time) and l. 1381.
sluttish grimy (OED 2); compare *Venus and Adonis*, l. 983. As Burrow (2002: 490) notes, '*time*' is not the agent, doing the smearing, but the substance with which the stone is besmeared.

5 **wasteful** causing destruction; the word is used of time at 15.11.

6 **broils** tumults; habitually used in Shakespeare to indicate civil, rather than foreign, wars; e.g. *1 Henry IV*, 1.1.47–8: 'It seems then that the tidings of this broil | Brake off our business for the Holy Land'.
root out destroy, eradicate.
work of masonry work made of stone, by a mason.

7 **Nor . . . nor** neither. . . nor.
Mars his sword the sword of Mars, the Roman god of war; noun + 'his' was a common way of making a genitive in early modern English.
quick when applied to fire, means fierce or 'burning strongly' (OED³ A11b); 'living record' (l. 8) also possibly activates a pun on 'quick' as 'living' (OED³ A1a), as in the phrase 'the quick and the dead'.
shall burn *zeugma*, with the verb serving both fire and sword; obviously, swords do not burn, but the destructiveness of a commonplace combination of fire and sword is clear enough.

8 **The living record** i.e. the poem ('this powerful rhyme', l. 2); 'record' usually suggests (as here) a written record; compare *2 Henry VI*, 4.7.14: 'Burn all the records of the realm'. 'Record' is stressed on the second syllable.

9 **all oblivious enmity** 'all the hostile forces (like war, time, neglect) which cause oblivion and eradicate memory'; Malone's compound 'all-oblivious' – followed by some editors – changes the nature of 'all', so that it qualifies 'oblivious' (i.e. indicating 'completely oblivious') rather than enmity. Precedent for 'oblivious' to mean 'causing oblivion' can be found in *Macbeth*, 5.3.43–4: 'some sweet oblivious antidote' with which the physician might 'cleanse the stuffed bosom'. Ingram and Redpath (1985: 129) suggest that 'all oblivion's enmity' is a possible reading; there is no possessive apostrophe

in early modern punctuation, and substituting 'u' for 'n' is a common compositorial error (resulting from either inverted type or mistaking 'n' for 'u', easily done when reading secretary hand). The precedent in *Macbeth*, however, makes emendation unnecessary. 'Oblivious' is three syllables.

10   *pace forth* stride out (to meet the enemy).
     praise praiseworthiness (OED³ 3a), virtue, merit (OED³ 3c).
     still continually; nevertheless.
     room (i) space (*n.*1, OED³ A1); position, authority (OED³ 10b).

11   *Even* used for emphasis; here pronounced as one syllable.
     in. . . posterity 'in the opinion of future generations'; 'eyes' reminds us that they will have read about the friend in this 'powerful rhyme'.

12   *That* The antecedent is unclear: it could be eyes or posterity (if the latter is treated as a collective plural).
     wear. . . out (i) 'survive', as in OED 16 'to come safe through, "weather" (a storm, an attack of sickness)'; the first citation for this sense (1617) post-dates Q, but the dates of first citations in

OED are not always accurate; (ii) an alternative (and contradictory) sense, 'destroy, exhaust' (OED 11a), is also possible; compare *King Lear*, 4.6.134–5: 'This great world | Shall so wear out to naught'.
     ending doom day of judgement, end of the world.

13   *judgement* day of judgement.
     that when, as in *As You Like It*, 3.2.176–8: 'I was never so berhymed since Pythagoras' time, that I was an Irish rat, which I can hardly remember'.
     yourself arise It was believed that on the day of judgement the souls of the dead would be reunited with their bodies; when the youth is resurrected, it will consequently be as himself, in his body (which is uniquely and distinctively beautiful).

14   *live in* survive in, inhabit (compare 'dwell' in the same line).
     this this verse.
     lovers' eyes (i) other lovers, who read poetry that reflects their own situation; (ii) those who have read about you and who have fallen in love with you as a result.

55

Not marble, nor the gilded monuments
Of princes shall outlive this powerful rhyme,
But you shall shine more bright in these contents
Than unswept stone, besmeared with sluttish time. 4
When wasteful war shall statues overturn,
And broils root out the work of masonry,
Nor Mars his sword, nor war's quick fire shall burn
The living record of your memory. 8
'Gainst death and all oblivious enmity
Shall you pace forth; your praise shall still find room,
Even in the eyes of all posterity
That wear this world out to the ending doom. 12
    So, till the judgement that yourself arise,
     You live in this and dwell in lovers' eyes.

56

Omitted from Benson; see headnote to Sonnet 18.

1 *love* the emotion, rather than the beloved; this could also be read as Love personified.

2 *edge* keenness; appetite is often likened to a knife (see also 'sharpened', l. 4). Compare 118.1–4; *Lucrece*, l. 9.

appetite bodily cravings (including sexual desire).

3 *Which* i.e. appetite.

but only for.

allayed satisfied.

4 *sharpened. . . might* 'is renewed in all its previous strength'.

his its.

5 *So* i.e. like appetite.

love the beloved.

6 *even* pronounced as one syllable.

wink close (as if drowsing off after a heavy meal); Booth, with his habitual eye for innuendo, draws attention to the belief that sexual activity weakened your eyesight (1977: 231, 442), citing Francis Bacon's *Sylva Sylvarum, or A Natural History*: 'It hath been observed by the ancients that much use of Venus doth dim the sight' (1627: sig. Z2r).

7 *see* open your eyes (in contrast to winking of the previous day).

7–8 *kill | . . . love* destroy (i) love (which is imagined as a 'spirit'); (ii) the animating principle ('spirit') which causes love.

8 *The spirit. . . dullness* 'Spirit' can be pronounced as one syllable ('sprite') and 'perpetual' elided into three syllables, thus making an eleven-syllable, feminine-rhymed line, mirroring l. 6.

dullness 'sluggishness' (OED 2), 'gloominess of mind or spirits: now esp. as arising from want of interest' (OED 3); also recalls the knife analogy of ll. 2–4, as a blade can be said to be 'dull' (i.e. blunt).

9 *Let* allow (i.e. imagine that).

sad heavy, sorrowful; the word appears seven times in the *Sonnets* (30.11; 45.14; 56.9; 57.11; 65.2; 107.6; 153.12) and 'sadly', once, 8.1; all but one of these usages (153.12) falls in the sonnets to/about the youth, and the use of the word is clustered most intensely at this stage of Q's sequence.

interim an intervening period of time (here, the interval of time between meetings); the word is a sixteenth-century coinage and the use of italics in Q suggests that the compositor viewed it as an unfamiliar, foreign word (see 1.2n) or, more likely, that it is signalled as such in the manuscript from which Q was set. Here pronounced as two syllables.

like the ocean be The poet-speaker suggests comparing their temporal separation (the 'sad interim') to a spatial one (the ocean, i.e. a large expanse of water).

10 *parts the shore* 'divides the land at the coast'; the image is one of an estuary or a strait, which divides two lovers, a situation reminiscent of the story of Hero and Leander (retold by Marlowe) where the lovers live on either side of the Hellespont. The theme of separation, which is introduced in this quatrain and continues into the couplet, does not grow logically out of ll. 1–8.

two, contracted new, a pair of newly betrothed lovers.

12 *Return of love* (i) the physical return of the beloved; (ii) reciprocation of affection.

13 *As* Some editors follow Malone, following Capell, and emend Q's 'As' to 'Or'; graphically, 'Or' is not similar enough to 'As' to make this a likely compositorial error; even if – as is probable – the manuscript copy began each line with a letter in lower case (as does Hand D, possibly Shakespeare's, in the manuscript of *Thomas More*, BL MS Harley 7368), 'r' is not readily mistaken for 's' in secretary hand (which would probably be the sigma-style 's' in a terminal position). Q's 'As' can be read as introducing another analogy, whereby – instead of being compared to the ocean – their separation is to be viewed as winter.

it i.e. the interim.

being pronounced as one syllable.

care sorrow, grief (*n*.1, OED 1a).

14 *wished* wished for.

rare splendid; the couplet reworks the sentiment of 52.4, and the proverb 'Pleasure the rarer used the more commendable' (Dent P417). The poet-speaker here likens two things which are not entirely comparable: summer always follows winter, but lost love is not always recovered.

56

Sweet love, renew thy force; be it not said
Thy edge should blunter be than appetite,
Which but today by feeding is allayed,
Tomorrow sharpened in his former might.   4
So, love, be thou; although today thou fill
Thy hungry eyes even till they wink with fullness,
Tomorrow see again and do not kill
The spirit of love with a perpetual dullness.   8
Let this sad interim like the ocean be,
Which parts the shore where two, contracted new,
Come daily to the banks, that when they see
Return of love, more blest may be the view;   12
   As call it winter, which being full of care,
   Makes summer's welcome thrice more wished, more rare.

57

Benson combines Sonnets 57–58 under the title 'The force of love'. The two sonnets share vocabulary ('slave', 'hours', 'times', 'absence', 'stay', 'will', 'ill') and the motifs of waiting and of service/servitude.

1 **slave** Love poetry of the period frequently describes the lover as his mistress' slave, i.e. 'one who is [...] entirely subject to another person' (OED 1a), or 'who submits in a servile manner to the authority or dictation of another' (OED 2a); see Watson, *Hekatompathia*, Passion 18.9: 'A slave to beauty's will, a witless toy' (1582: sig. C1v). Compare also the physician William Bullein on the transformative effects of love: 'It altereth complexions, manners and conditions, and maketh of free men slaves, of wise men fools' (*Bullein's Bulwark* 1562: sig. ²N2v).

1–2 **tend | Upon** wait on; the sonnet plays on two senses of 'waiting': serving and hanging around.

2 **hours and times** occasions.
   desire (i) wishes; (ii) sexual desire, lust.

3 **I ... spend** The poet-speaker's time is of no value to him, unless he is devoting it to serving the youth; that this sonnet is addressed to the youth, rather than the mistress, is suggested by (i) its placing in Q's sequence; (ii) the use of the term 'affairs' in l. 10 (see note below).

4 **services** The word is used in a number of contexts which resonate with the language of this sonnet: (i) the duties performed for a master or superior ('service, *n*.1', OED 6b); (ii) sexual services (Partridge 1990: 181; OED 6c); (iii) religious devotions (OED 14), fitting with the liturgical language of l. 5; (iv) the devotions of a lover (OED 10).
   require (i) need; (ii) demand.

5 **world-without-end hour** time which appears endless; compare *Love's Labours Lost*, 5.2.788–9: 'A time methinks too short | To make a world-without-end bargain in'. The phrase is liturgical, borrowing from the doxology recurrently used in the services set down in the *Book of Common Prayer*: 'As it was in the beginning, is now, and ever shall be: world without end' (see, for example, 2011: 7, 14).

6 **my sovereign** the youth; considering the youth's power over the poet-speaker's health and well-being (see, for example, Sonnet 45), then there may be a play here on the meaning of 'sovereign' as an 'efficacious or potent' remedy (OED B3).

for you (i) for you in person (i.e. waiting for the friend to return); (ii) until it is time to do you services.

7 **Nor think** 'Nor dare I think' (parallel in construction to ll. 5, 9); the apparent reluctance to acknowledge the unpleasantness of something which is clearly unpleasant is indicative of the way in which the poet-speaker presents (but is also aware of) himself as subject to the youth.

9 **question with** 'To ask questions of; to hold a conversation with; (also) to discuss or debate with' ('question', OED³ 1).
   jealous The word has a number of meanings which are relevant here, and which extend beyond the dominant modern meaning (namely, 'troubled by the belief, suspicion, or fear that the good which one desires to gain or keep for oneself has been or may be diverted to another', OED 4). These other meanings are (i) 'devoted' (OED 1b); (ii) 'ardently amorous; covetous of the love of another' (OED 2); (iii) 'vigilant or careful in guarding; suspiciously careful or watchful' (OED 3); (iv) 'suspicious, [...] fearful' (OED 5a).

10 **affairs** concerns, business; the meaning 'love affair' (or adulterous liaison) was not live in this period; as Blakemore Evans suggests (1996: 165), the choice of this word helps confirm that the addressee is the male friend (since business was predominantly regarded as a male activity in the period).
   suppose imagine, guess at (OED³ 5a).

11 **sad** See 56.9n.

12 **Save** except.
   happy fortunate as well as joyous.

13 **So true** (i) so loyal; (ii) so complete.
   a fool is love 'Love' can indicate 'my love for you' or the spirit/idea of love. Love (and lovers) were proverbially foolish; see, for example, Dent L505.2 ('Love is a madness (lunacy)') and L517 ('Love is without reason'). The image of the fool – a household retainer – is also appropriate in a sonnet about service.
   will (i) 'desire, wish' (*n*.1, OED 1a); (ii) 'carnal desire or appetite' (OED 2); (iii) 'command' (OED 3b; compare 'require', l. 4); (iv) 'wilfulness' (OED 9a). The word is capitalised in Q, but not italicised (as it is in Sonnets 135, 136 and 143, where it is a play on Shakespeare's first name).

14 **he** love.

57

Being your slave, what should I do but tend
Upon the hours and times of your desire?
I have no precious time at all to spend,
Nor services to do till you require;   4
Nor dare I chide the world-without-end hour
Whilst I (my sovereign) watch the clock for you,
Nor think the bitterness of absence sour
When you have bid your servant once adieu;   8
Nor dare I question with my jealous thought
Where you may be, or your affairs suppose,
But like a sad slave stay and think of naught,
Save where you are how happy you make those.   12
   So true a fool is love, that in your will
   (Though you do anything) he thinks no ill.

58

Benson combines Sonnets 57–58 under the title 'The force of love'.

1   **That god** Love.
    forbid Booth (1977: 233) suggests this is 'the standard Renaissance form for the past tense of "to forbid"'; it is also possible to read this as a subjunctive ('May that god forbid'), which lends a greater urgency and immediacy to the sonnet, which then operates as an appeal to Love to prevent the poet-speaker displaying his jealousy.

2   **I. . . thought** (i) I should think to; (ii) in my mind; (iii) in my anxiety and distress (see 'thought, *n.*', OED³ 8a, which cites John Ponet's *Short Treatise of Politic Power*, 1556: 'pined away for thought').
    control (i) 'curb' (OED 4b); (ii) 'reprove' (OED 3a); (iii) the earliest meaning, 'to check or verify [. . .] (payments, receipts, or accounts generally)' (OED 1) is also pertinent here, and anticipates the financial imagery of 'th' account of hours' (l. 3).
    times of pleasure Compare 57.2; in both poems, 'desire' and 'pleasure' may be understood sexually.

3   **at your hand** in person from you.
    account report (of what the youth has been doing); the financial sense of the word is also in play here; see note on 'control', l. 2 above.

4   **vassal** 'a humble servant or subordinate; one devoted to the service of another' (OED 2b); 'a base or abject person; a slave' (OED 3); compare 'Being your slave' (57.1). The poet-speaker describes himself as bound 'in vassalage' at 26.1 and as a 'vassal wretch' to his mistress at 141.12.
    stay your leisure Although the sense of 'wait until you are free' is primary, 'stay' may hold some hints of wishful thinking, that the poet-speaker might 'stop' ('stay, *v.*1', OED 1a) the youth's leisure activities. The issue of when a servant should speak out and intervene in his master's affairs to avert disaster was a crucial dilemma in a political system dependent on counsel; see, for example, Thomas Elyot, *Pasquil the Plain* (1533), where the issue forms the main topic discussed in Part 2.

5   **suffer** 'endure, hold out, wait patiently' (OED 6).

beck 'the slightest indication of will or command, and transf. absolute order or control' (*n.*2, OED 2).

6   **Th' imprisoned. . . liberty** The absence of the youth, which results from his freedom, restricts what the poet-speaker feels able to do, so that the experience of separation is akin to being imprisoned. For the comparison of love to a prison, see Petrarch, *Rime Sparse* 89.1: 'Fleeing the prison where Love had kept me' ('Fuggendo la pregione ove Amor m'ebbe'). 'Liberty' can suggest licence (libertinism) as well as freedom; see *Hamlet*, 2.1.22–6:

> POLONIUS [. . .] such wanton, wild, and usual slips
> As are companions noted and most known
> To youth and liberty.
> REYNALDO As gaming, my lord.
> POLONIUS Ay, or drinking, fencing, swearing, quarrelling,
> Drabbing – you may go so far.

7   **And. . . check** This edition here follows Q's punctuation (with the sole omission of its terminal comma), which keeps open what Booth calls 'the range of the line' (1977: 235) and allows two possible readings: (i) where 'tame' is a verb governed by 'let me' (l. 5), and 'patience tame' and 'to sufferance bide' become the second and third actions in a series of three pleonastic phrases (emphasising the poet-speaker's abject submission); understood thus, the line means 'allow me to tame patience, to withstand every rebuff, with endurance'; (ii) where 'patience tame' is a compound adjective, describing the poet-speaker; understood thus, the line means 'let me, as tame as patience in the face of suffering, endure each rebuff'. Few editors (Duncan-Jones being an exception) retain Q's punctuation: the most standard renditions of this line are: (a) 'And, patience-tame to sufferance, bide each check' (which follows reading (ii) above); (b) 'And patience, tame to sufferance, bide each check' (where patience is inured to suffering); Burrow objects to this second reading (b) on the grounds that it 'introduces an additional grammatical subject which diminishes the intensive focus on "I" and "you" in the sonnet, and also allows the

58

That god forbid, that made me first your slave,
I should in thought control your times of pleasure,
Or at your hand th' account of hours to crave,
Being your vassal bound to stay your leisure.   4
O let me suffer (being at your beck)
Th' imprisoned absence of your liberty,
And patience tame, to sufferance bide each check
Without accusing you of injury.   8
Be where you list, your charter is so strong
That you yourself may privilege your time
To what you will; to you it doth belong
Yourself to pardon of self-doing crime.   12
    I am to wait, though waiting so be hell,
    Not blame your pleasure, be it ill or well.

poem to drift into abstraction at its centre' (2002: 496).

patience The word as used here is very close to its etymological roots (from the Latin *patior*, I suffer).

sufferance 'patient endurance, forbearance' (OED 1), 'the suffering or undergoing of pain, trouble, wrong' (OED 2a); there is a degree of *pleonasm* with 'patience'; 'sufferance' is here pronounced as two syllables.

bide 'withstand' (OED 7), 'endure' (OED 9a).

check 'reproof' (*n*.1, OED B4a), 'rebuff' (OED B5a).

8 *injury* The dominant sense in the late sixteenth/early seventeenth century was 'wrongful action or treatment' (OED 1), rather than a sense of physical hurt (as now).

9 *where you list* 'wherever you like' (implies the company that the youth associates with as well as locations he visits).

charter 'a written document delivered by the sovereign or legislature: granting privileges to, or recognizing rights of, the people, or of

certain classes or individuals' (*n*.1, OED 1a); compare 87.3 and *As You Like It*, 2.7.47–9: 'I must have liberty | Withal, as large a charter as the wind, | To blow on whom I please'. Considering that the youth has been cast in the role of 'sovereign' (57.6) or feudal overlord (with the word 'vassal', l. 4), there may be a suggestion that, in granting himself privileges, he abuses his power. OED cites this line as an example of sense 3 ('privilege; immunity; publicly conceded right'), but it is important to recognise the primary force of the term in order to understand its figurative use in the context of this sonnet.

10–11 *privilege. . . will* 'license your time to be spent as you please'; Malone's emendation of 'To' to 'Do' (followed by some early editors) is unnecessary. For 'privilege', see *Lucrece*, 621n.

12 *self-doing* done to yourself, done by yourself.
crime wrong-doing (not necessarily illegal).

13 *I. . . wait* 'I have to wait'.

59

Printed by Benson as a single sonnet entitled 'The beauty of nature'.

1   *nothing new* alludes to the debate about whether time was cyclical or linear; Pythagorean and Stoic philosophy advocated the idea that history was cyclical, but the most well-known source for this concept in the sixteenth century would probably have been Ecclesiastes 1:9–10, which the *Book of Common Prayer* ordained should be read at various points during the liturgical year: 'What is it that hath been? That that shall be. & what is it that hath been done? That which shall be done: and there is no new thing under the sun. Is there any thing, whereof one may say, Behold this, it is new? It hath been already in the old time that was before us'.

3   *labouring* It was a common poetic conceit to imagine the process of composition as giving birth; see 32.11n; 'labouring' is here pronounced as two syllables.

  invention one of the five parts of rhetoric; compare 38.8 and note.

  bear amiss In the context of the birthing imagery in ll. 3–4, the phrase suggests miscarriage, or at least that this twice-born child comes out 'faultily, defectively' the second time round ('amiss', OED A2).

4   *second. . . child* a work that has already been written by someone else.

5   *record* memory, recollection (*n*.1, OED³ A10a); stressed on second syllable. 'Record' usually suggests a written document, and Shakespeare often describes memory as something written; see *Hamlet*, 1.5.98–9: 'Yea, from the table of my memory | I'll wipe away all trivial fond records'.

6   *Even of* as far as; 'even' is pronounced as one syllable.

  five hundred. . . sun 500 years (the 'courses of the sun' being the annual passage of the sun, which – in the geocentric understanding of the universe – would take a calendar year to return to the same position at the same time of day); the sonnet here alludes to the idea of the 'Great Year', 'after which all the heavenly bodies were supposed to return to their original positions' ('year', OED³ 2b). The length of the Great Year was variously calculated as being between 540 and 600 years. Kerrigan (1986: 247) suggests that Shakespeare is using 'hundred' in its older sense:

the 'long hundred' of 'six score, or a hundred and twenty' ('hundred', OED 3). Five of such hundreds equate to 600 (and the end of a Great Year). Whether or not Shakespeare's calculations are precise, l. 6 alludes to a time centuries previously, when the stars were in the same configuration as the sonnet's 'now'.

7   *image* a written rather than pictorial depiction.
  antique ancient; stressed on the first syllable.

8   *Since. . . done* 'since thoughts [or memories ('mind, n.1', OED³ 6a, 3)] were first put in writing ['character', OED³ 4d, citing this line as first usage]'. The sixteenth century saw a shift in the meaning of the term character, from 'a disctinctive mark' (OED³ 1) to a 'sign or symbol used in writing' (OED³ 3b), letters of the alphabet (OED³ 4a), 'a particular person's' or 'general [. . .] style of handwriting' (OED³ 4b, 4c) as well as writing in general (OED³ 4d); over the same period, the word also came to indicate 'characteristic' and 'distinctive nature' (OED³ 7a, 8a, 8b), and – from that – 'The sum of the moral and mental qualities which distinguish an individual or people' (OED³ 9a). Shakespeare uses the word in all these senses, but predominantly to indicate writing of some kind, be it letters in general or an individual's handwriting.

9   *old world* Compare the curiosity about the different perceptions of 'the old age' in 127.1.
  say record in writing.

10   *this. . . frame* 'this well-put-together miracle of your form'; 'composèd' gestures towards the act of writing poetry, as if the friend were a literary composition.

11   *we* people of Shakespeare's time (as opposed to 'they' of 'the old world').
  we are Metrically, this needs eliding (we're).
  mended amended, improved.
  whe'er whether; spelled 'where' in Q, a common Elizabethan contraction of 'whether' (see *Venus and Adonis*, 304n); most editors emend as here, making ll. 11–12 into three parallel clauses.

12   *whether. . . same* 'or whether the cyclical nature of events ['revolution', OED³ 4a] means that we nowadays are just the same as them in the past'.

13   *wits* clever people (OED 9).

14   *subjects worse* inferior topics, but the phrase also hints that such subjects might be 'even worse' than the youth, which chimes with the criticism that both precedes and follows this sonnet in Q's sequence.

59

If there be nothing new, but that which is
Hath been before, how are our brains beguiled,
Which, labouring for invention, bear amiss
The second burden of a former child?   4
O that record could with a backward look,
Even of five hundred courses of the sun,
Show me your image in some antique book,
Since mind at first in character was done,   8
That I might see what the old world could say
To this composèd wonder of your frame;
Whether we are mended, or whe'er better they,
Or whether revolution be the same.   12
   O sure I am the wits of former days
   To subjects worse have given admiring praise.

60

Sonnet 60 addresses the immortality offered by verse in face of the destructiveness of time, an ongoing theme of the *Sonnets*; see 15.14n.

Benson combines Sonnets 60 and 63–66 under the title 'Injurious Time'.

1–4   *Like. . . contend* These lines are indebted to Ovid's *Metamorphoses* 15.177–85 (Golding 15.197–205, sig. 2C5r): 'In all the world there is not that that standeth at a stay. | Things ebb and flow, and every shape is made to pass away. | The time itself continually is fleeting like a brook, | For neither brook nor lightsome time can tarry still. But look, | As every wave drives other forth, and that that comes behind | Both thrusteth and is thrust itself, even so the times by kind | Do fly and follow both at once and evermore renew. | For that that was before is left, and straight there doth ensue | Another that was never erst'. Compare 15.9.

1   *Like as* just as.

     towards pronounced as one syllable.

2   *our minutes* breaking down a lifetime into minutes, not hours or days, emphasises the brevity of life; most sixteenth- and seventeenth-century timepieces did not have a minute hand (see *Lucrece*, 297n), so their passing would also be less perceptible. The choice of minutes is numerologically appropriate here (there being sixty minutes in each hour). There is a possible sonic play on 'hour' in 'our'.

     end death, but also suggests 'aim' or 'purpose (OED 14a), as if the minutes want to die.

3   *Each* can refer to both minutes and waves.

4   *In sequent toil* 'labouring after one another in turn'; this line is the first cited usage in OED for 'sequent, *adj.*', sense 3b ('Characterized by continuous succession; forming an unbroken series or course'); Burrow (2002: 500) suggests that Shakespeare imports the word directly from Ovid's Latin (*Metamorphoses* 15.183: 'tempora sic fugiunt pariter pariterque sequuntur' ['time both flees and follows']). 'Sequent toil' also works as a metaphor for imitation: the poem's work, following Ovid, is its 'sequent toil' (see Lyne 2001: 153).

     forwards an adverb, as all the waves press onwards (Schmidt).

     contend strive; 'contend' also suggests 'combat', pre-empting 'fight', l. 7.

5–12   *Nativity. . .mow* These lines draw on Ovid's *Metamorphoses* 15.218–36 (Golding, 15.240–60; sig. 2C5v): 'Dame Nature put to cunning hand and suffered not that we | Within our mother's strained womb should ay distressed be, | But brought us out to air and from our prison set us free. | The child, newborn, lies void of strength. Within a season, though, | He, waxing four-footed, learns like savage beasts to go. | [. . .] From that time growing strong and swift, he passeth forth the space | Of youth, and also wearing out his middle age apace, | Through drooping age's steepy path he runneth out his race. [. . .] And Helen, when she saw her aged wrinkles in | A glass, wept also, musing in herself what men had seen [. . .] | Thou, Time, the eater-up of things, and Age, of spiteful teen, | Destroy all things. And when that long continuance hath them bit, | You leisurely by lingering death consume them every whit'. Compare 63.4–5 and note.

5   *Nativity* the time of birth, by extension here 'a new-born child'; editors often note that the astrological meaning ('a horoscope', OED[3] 4) is activated by 'crookèd eclipses' (l. 7), but see note below.

     once at one time (OED[3] A1a), as soon as (OED[3] B).

     main of light 'Main' ('broad expanse', OED[3] 5c) is usually used of the sea (thus recalling the imagery of ll. 1–4) and is here transferred to the expanse of the sky that provides light, capturing the moment at which the new-born child emerges from the darkness of the womb.

6   *Crawls* The choice of verb – associated with babies – compresses the passage of time, as the imagined subject moves directly from infancy to maturity in the space of half a line; compare the effect of 'minutes', l. 2 and note.

     wherewith with maturity.

     being pronounced as one syllable.

7   *Crookèd eclipses* frequently glossed as meaning malign astronomical conjunctions ('crooked' = perverse, awry, OED 3a); however, the subject of ll. 5–8 is the passage of time and the ageing process, which affects all people, regardless of the stars. It seems more logical to read this as a reference to the 'loss of brilliance or splendour' ('eclipse', OED 2a)

60

Like as the waves make towards the pebbled shore,
So do our minutes hasten to their end,
Each changing place with that which goes before,
In sequent toil all forwards do contend.   4
Nativity, once in the main of light,
Crawls to maturity, wherewith being crowned
Crookèd eclipses 'gainst his glory fight,
And Time that gave doth now his gift confound.   8
Time doth transfix the flourish set on youth
And delves the parallels in beauty's brow,
Feeds on the rarities of nature's truth,
And nothing stands but for his scythe to mow.   12
    And yet to times in hope my verse shall stand,
    Praising thy worth, despite his cruel hand.

that comes with age, reading 'crooked' as 'bent or bowed with age. Hence transf. as an epithet of *age*' (OED 2a).

his the once new-born child's (Nativity's).

glory splendour.

8 *Time* capitalised, as here, by many editors (although not in Q), as the context implies personification. For the inconsistent use of capitalisation in Q, see 5.5n.

gift of the years of life; compare Job 1:21, used as part of the Burial Service in *Book of Common Prayer*: 'the Lord giveth, and the Lord taketh away' (2011: 171).

confound destroy; compare 5.6; 63.10; 64.10.

9 *transfix* pierce through (i.e. destroy); this is the only Shakespearean usage of the word.

flourish. . . youth 'flourish' suggests '"bloom" (of youth)' (OED 2a); however a more negative meaning ('ostentatious embellishment; gloss, varnish', OED 3) may be present in its conjunction with 'set on', which implies something added (like cosmetics), rather than something inherent in a youthful face.

10 *delves the parallels* digs wrinkles; 'parallels' are military trenches (OED³ A3), extending the

militaristic vein found in 'contend' (l. 4) and 'fight' (l. 7); compare 2.2.

11 *rarities* exceptional specimens.

of nature's truth nature's true image (rather than a counterfeit); the phrase also appears, in conjunction with youth, in *All's Well*, 1.3.132–3: 'It is the show and seal of nature's truth, | Where love's strong passion is impressed in youth'.

12 *stands* exists (OED 23b).

but except.

scythe Time was conventionally depicted with a scythe; see 12.13n.

12, 14 *his* Time's.

13 *to times in hope* (i) 'future, hoped-for, ages'; (ii) 'in hope' also attaches itself to the wish that 'my verse shall stand' (i.e. 'hopefully my verse will survive'), undermining the certainty of that statement, particularly in the light of the use of 'stands' in l. 12, where all things stand merely to be cut down by Time's scythe.

14 *despite. . . hand* i.e. despite the actions of the scythe (l. 12) that Time holds in his hand; 'cruel' is disyllabic.

61

Printed by Benson as a single sonnet entitled 'Patiens Armatus' ('man in armour, patiently suffering'), which probably refers to the image of the watchman in l. 12. Benson gives two other sonnets Latin titles ('Sat fuisse', Sonnet 62; 'Nil magnis invidia', Sonnet 70). All three Latin titles are borrowed from Henry Parrot's *Cures for the Itch: Characters, Epigrams, Epitaphs* (1626), a collection of prose characters, epigrams, and mostly satirical epitaphs.

Sonnet 61 plays on a theme common to love poetry, where the lover is kept awake at night by thoughts of their beloved. See headnote to Sonnet 27.

1   *will* wish.
     image likeness.

1, 3 *open. . . broken* For the rhyme, see *Venus and Adonis*, 47–8n.

2   *heavy eyelids* Compare 'drooping eyelids', 27.7.

4   *shadows* delusive semblances or images (OED 6a); compare 27.10; 37.10; 43.5; 98.14.
     mock delude (OED³ 1a).

5   *spirit* 'immaterial being' (OED 1d), but also hints at a ghostly or supernatural presence (OED 3a).

6   *far from home* As in Sonnets 44–45, 47–48, 50–52, the poet-speaker is physically separated from the friend.

7   *shames and idle hours* a *hendiadys*: the shameful deeds done in idle hours.

8   *scope and tenure* Q's 'tenure' is often modernised to 'tenor' (of which 'tenure' is a feasible early modern spelling), so that 'scope and tenor' means 'aim' ('scope, *n*.2', OED 2a) and 'purport' ('tenor, *n*.1', OED 1a); compare *Lucrece*, 1310n. Certainly 'tenor' is a more usual Shakespearean word than 'tenure' (of which there is only one other instance, in *Hamlet*, 5.1.98–100: 'Why may not that be the skull of a lawyer? Where be his quiddities now, his quillities, his cases, his tenures, and his tricks?'). Nonetheless, retaining 'tenure' – a word relating to the possession of property in English law (OED 1a) – reflects the way in which Shakespeare's sonnets recurrently express loving relationships in terms of property and/or legal rights (see, for example, Sonnets 87, 92, 133–134 and notes). 'Scope'

can also be used in a spatial sense: the Anglo-Irish usage of 'scope' ('A tract (of land); esp. a piece of land belonging to an individual', OED 10) might be a little obscure; however OED 7a ('room for exercise, opportunity or liberty to act') and OED 9a ('a (large) space, extent, tract, or area') were more established in sixteenth-century English. Shakespeare elsewhere uses 'scope' to mean both (i) aim and (ii) room or licence to act: for (i), see *Richard II*, 3.3.112–13 ('His coming hither hath no further scope | Than for his lineal royalties'); for (ii), see *Measure for Measure*, 1.3.35 (''twas my fault to give the people scope'); see also 29.7 and note. There is also a potential play on a more literary meaning of 'scope' as 'the subject, theme, argument chosen for treatment' (OED 3a), a usage which often occurs in relation to sermons, a genre in which the people addressed are not infrequently reprimanded for their faults, a dynamic that might be captured (perversely) in a jealous lover's admonitions.
     jealousy See 57.9n.

10, 11 *my love. . . Mine own true love* my affection; the alternative reading (my beloved) would contradict the argument propounded in the sestet: namely that – despite attempts in the octet to imagine that the friend's affections are so strong that he can project himself as a spirit which disrupts the poet-speaker's sleep and spies on him – it is the poet-speaker's emotions alone that disturb him. Nonetheless, the unwillingness to relinquish such wishful thinking and the simultaneous exposure of such self-delusion have been explored elsewhere; see Sonnets 41–43, 52 and notes.

11   *defeat* destroy (OED 1), frustrate (OED 5).

12   *To* in order to.
     watchman 'one who watches over or guards a person or thing, a guardian' (OED 3a); more specifically, 'a constable of the watch who [. . .] patrolled the streets by night to safeguard life and property' (OED 4). The word suggests the proverb 'One good friend watches for another' (Dent F716).

13   *For thee* (i) on your behalf; (ii) because of you; (iii) literally watching for you, in case you come.

61

Is it thy will thy image should keep open
My heavy eyelids to the weary night?
Dost thou desire my slumbers should be broken,
While shadows like to thee do mock my sight?   4
Is it thy spirit that thou send'st from thee
So far from home into my deeds to pry,
To find out shames and idle hours in me,
The scope and tenure of thy jealousy?   8
O no, thy love, though much, is not so great;
It is my love that keeps mine eye awake,
Mine own true love that doth my rest defeat,
To play the watchman ever for thy sake.   12
    For thee watch I, whilst thou dost wake elsewhere,
    From me far off, with others all too near.

watch (i) remain awake (OED 1a); (ii) be on the lookout (OED 4a); (iii) fulfil the duties (of vigilance and protection) of the watchman of l. 12 (OED 6a).

wake The activity is obviously related to 'watch', key meanings being 'remain awake' (OED 1a) and 'stay awake for the purpose of watching or tending' (OED 2a); however, the word also has an 'unfavourable implication: to sit up late for pleasure or revelry' (OED 1d); see *Hamlet*, 1.4.8: 'The King doth wake tonight and takes his rouse'.

14 *with. . . near* Sonnets 41–42 suggest that the friend is sexually active with the poet-speaker's mistress; here the plural 'others' hints at more promiscuous behaviour; compare 69.14 and note.

62

Printed by Benson as a single sonnet entitled 'Sat fuisse' ('it is enough to have existed'); for Benson's use of Latin titles, see headnote to Sonnet 61.

1   ***self-love*** In the octet, this looks like narcissism, the sin of which the friend was accused in 3.8; the sestet then redefines 'self-love' as love of the friend, who is a second self (see 22.3n). As Hammond (2012: 232) points out 'inordinate self-love was considered to be not a separate sin but the root of all sin by St Augustine (*De Civitate Dei* 14.28) and St Thomas Aquinas (*Summa Theologica* 2.1. q.77 art.4)'.
   possesseth occupies, has hold of; the word was used of supernatural forces from the sixteenth century (OED³ 4) and for diseases from the early seventeenth century (OED³ 2c), a usage which pre-empts 'remedy', l. 3.
   eye eyes; for the use of the singular form to denote a plural, see 46.1; in a poem about self-love, there is a possible play on the homophone 'I'.
2   ***all my every part*** The *pleonasm* of 'all' and 'every' is emphatic; compare *King John*, 4.2.38–9: 'all and every part of what we would | Doth make a stand at what your Highness will'.
3   ***remedy*** cure; sin was often figured as a disease; see, Anthony Marten (trans.), *The Tranquillity of the Mind*: 'In the leaden lethargy and disease of sin [lay hold] upon the quick remembrance of mercy by Christ' (1570: sig. A3v); John Donne, *Devotions*, Expostulation 1: 'I fall sick of sin, and am bedded and bedrid, buried and putrified in the practice of sin, and all this while have no presage, not pulse, no sense of my sickness' (1624: sigs B6r–v).
4   ***grounded inward*** 'deeply or strongly founded' ('grounded, *adj*.1', OED 1a) in the 'inner or inmost part' ('inward', OED 1a); compare one of the collects in the Communion Service in the *Book of Common Prayer*: 'Grant, we beseech thee, almighty God, that the words which we have heard this day with our outward ears, may through thy grace be so grafted inwardly in our hearts' (2011: 139).
5   ***Methinks*** it seems to me.
   gracious attractive; the use of the word as a 'courteous epithet' for the socially elite (OED³ A2c) foreshadows the move in the sestet, when it is revealed that the qualities the poet-speaker values are reflections of his (aristocratic) friend's

attributes. For the use of 'grace/s' and 'gracious' to describe the friend and his attributes, see 10.11n.

6   ***true*** correct, perfect; compare *King Lear*, 1.2.8–9: 'my shape as true, | As honest madam's issue'.
   truth fidelity (OED 1a): the ambiguity of whether this denotes loyalty to the friend, or the perfection of the poet-speaker's face (celebrated in l. 5) captures the play between the narcissistic sounding octet and the sestet, which defines self-love as praising someone else.
   account importance, value.
7   ***for myself*** (i) to satisfy myself; (ii) by myself.
8   ***other*** others.
   surmount surpass; compare *1 Henry VI*, 5.3.191: 'Bethink thee on her virtues that surmount'.
9   ***glass*** mirror; compare 22.1.
10 ***Beated*** an acceptable sixteenth-century variant of the past participle ('beaten'); for the use of an -*ed* ending where modern English uses -*en*, see *Troilus and Cressida*, 1.3.101 ('shaked'); it is therefore unnecessary to emend the line, as was the practice among eighteenth- and nineteenth-century editors. The face is 'beaten' because weather-beaten (see also notes on 'chapped' and 'tanned').
   chapped spelled 'chopt' in Q, a variant of 'chapped', meaning 'fissured, cracked', possibly by 'exposure to frost' (*adj*.1, OED 1a), thus complementing the weathering effect of the sun conveyed by 'tanned'; compare *As You Like It*, 2.4.50, where Touchstone praises a lover's chapped hands (also spelled 'chopt' in F), and the description of Hecuba in *Lucrece*, l. 1452.
   tanned antiquity browned by years of exposure to the sun; 'beaten' and 'tanned' are also terms to describe the processes by which animal hide is turned into leather (capturing the way in which skin does appear more 'leathery' with age). Editors frequently note that Shakespeare would have known about the tanning process since his father, John, was a glover.
   antiquity old age (OED 2); the first example for this usage cited by OED is from *2 Henry IV* (1598; printed 1600).
11 ***quite. . . read*** 'interpret in completely the opposite way'.
12 ***Self. . . iniquity*** 'To love oneself in such a way (or to such an extent) would be sinful.'
13 ***thee (my self)*** invokes the proverb 'A friend is one's second self' (Dent F696); see 22.3n, and note on l. 1, above. As the line plays on the

62

Sin of self-love possesseth all mine eye,
And all my soul, and all my every part;
And for this sin there is no remedy,
It is so grounded inward in my heart.   4
Methinks no face so gracious is as mine,
No shape so true, no truth of such account,
And for myself mine own worth do define,
As I all other in all worths surmount.   8
But when my glass shows me myself indeed,
Beated and chapped with tanned antiquity,
Mine own self-love quite contrary I read;
Self so self-loving were iniquity: 12
    'Tis thee (my self) that for myself I praise,
    Painting my age with beauty of thy days.

distinction between 'my self' (a self which
is viewed as a distinct entity) and 'myself', it
highlights the challenges of modernising '-*self*'
constructions; see note on modernising the -*self*
suffix (introduction, p. xiv).
for myself (i) instead of myself; (ii) to satisfy myself
(recalling meaning (i) in l. 7).

14 ***Painting. . . days*** The idea of old age being rejuvenated by youth is raised in 2.13–14 in relation
to the friend's imagined offspring, and in 37.1–2
(where the poet-speaker compares himself to a
father); that idea is in play here, although the
choice of the word 'painting' suggests that this
borrowed youth is a mere veneer.

63

Benson combines Sonnets 60 and 63–66 under the title 'Injurious Time'; the immortalising power of verse in the face of the destructiveness of time is a recurrent theme of the *Sonnets*; see 15.14n.

Graziani (1984) notes the appropriateness of the placing of this sonnet in Q's sequence, since the 'grand climacteric', the major crisis in the development of the human body, occurred aged 63. See Constable's headnote to Sonnet 63 in National Art Library MS Dyce 44: 'When I had ended this last sonnet and found that such vain poems as I had by idle hours writ did amount just to the climaterical number 63, methought it was high time for my folly to die and to employ the remnant of wit to other calmer thoughts, less sweet and less bitter' (fol. 42v).

1   *Against* in preparation for the time when; compare *Midsummer Night's Dream*, 3.2.99: 'I'll charm his eyes against she do appear'.
    my love my beloved.

2, 5, 10   *Time's. . . Age's* Q capitalises 'Ages' (twice), but not 'times'; many editors capitalise 'Time's', but not 'age's'; for the inconsistency of capitalisation to indicate personification, see 5.5n.

2   *injurious* 'wilfully inflicting injury or wrong' (OED 1); compare 44.2; *Troilus and Cressida*, 4.4.42–3 ('Injurious time now with a robber's haste | Crams his rich thiev'ry up'); *Lucrece*, l. 930; Spenser, 'Ruins of Rome' (in *Complaints*, 1591), 27.6 ('The which injurious time hath quite outworn'). The word is here pronounced as three syllables.
    o'er-worn 'threadbare' ('overworn', OED[3] 1a); rather than describing fallen masonry, 'crushed' (l. 2) would thus convey the effect of cloth being compressed and the nap being worn away at the folds.

3   *drained his blood* Early modern medical theory held that the amount of blood in the body diminished with age; hence the belief that in old age you were 'cold and dry', properties which are exactly opposite to those of blood, which is 'hot and wet' (see Elyot, *Castle of Health* 1539: sigs F1r–v).
    filled Spelled 'fild' in Q, this could also be modernised as 'filed' (see also 17.2n); 'filled' complements 'drained'; 'filed' would either suggest that the hours score lines in the friend's brow with a file (although files more usually smooth things), or work as an aphetic form of 'defiled' ('file, *v*.2', OED).

4–5   *when. . . night* Compare Sonnet 7.5 and note; like that sonnet, these lines show the influence of Ovid *Metamorphoses* 15.226–7 (Golding, 15.248–9; sig. 2C5v); see also Sonnet 60.5–12 and note; 73.1–8 and note.

5   *travailed* 'Travel' and 'travail' are interchangeable in early modern English, and many twentieth- and twenty-first-century editors modernise Q's 'trauaild' as 'travelled'. The primary meaning here is 'journeyed'; however Q's form has been retained because 'travelled' risks flattening the meaning for modern readers, whilst 'travailed' conveys both 'travel' and 'travail' (and thus the effort involved in labouring onwards 'to Age's steepy night').
    steepy steep, precipitous (OED 1), evoking the downward trajectory of the sun towards evening; compare 7.5 for the upward trajectory of the sun, travelling towards noon/ the prime of life. The word also conveys a sense of being 'steeped' (soaked, immersed) in Age's night.

8   *Stealing away* initially suggests 'creeping away', but the appearance of 'treasure' later in the line requires us to reinterpret the word as 'pilfering'; the double meaning of 'steal' is also active in 77.7–8; 92.1; 104.9–10.

9   *For* against, in preparation for.
    fortify build defences; compare 16.2–4, where offspring rather than 'barren rhyme' would allow the youth to 'fortify' himself against 'this bloody tyrant, Time'.

10   *confounding* destroying; the term 'confound' and its variants are used of Time, and the effects of time, at 5.6, 60.8, 64.10.
    cruel pronounced as two syllables.

11   *That* so that.

12   *My sweet love's* refers (i) to the beloved, as in l. 1; (ii) to the poet-speaker's affection.
    though. . . life 'he cuts' is understood.

13   *black lines* lines of verse; compare 65.14.

14   *still* (i) constantly, forever; (ii) even so.
    still green The phrase can refer to both the lines of poetry and the friend. Aside from indicating 'freshness', there may be a specific reference to writing, as iron gall ink tends to be blacker when first used and then fades to a greenish brown (Andrew Zurcher, private correspondence).
    green The colour is associated with spring and thus with youth; compare 104.8.

63

Against my love shall be as I am now,
With Time's injurious hand crushed and o'er-worn,
When hours have drained his blood and filled his brow
With lines and wrinkles, when his youthful morn   4
Hath travailed on to Age's steepy night,
And all those beauties whereof now he's king
Are vanishing, or vanished out of sight,
Stealing away the treasure of his spring: 8
For such a time do I now fortify
Against confounding Age's cruel knife,
That he shall never cut from memory
My sweet love's beauty, though my lover's life.   12
   His beauty shall in these black lines be seen,
   And they shall live, and he in them, still green.

64

Benson combines Sonnets 60 and 63–66 under the title 'Injurious Time'.

1, 12　***Time's. . . Time*** Q italicises the second, but not the first instance; for the inconsistency of capitalisation to indicate personification, see 5.5n.

1　***fell*** cruel, savage (OED A1); angry (OED A3).

defaced destroyed, disfigured; compare 6.1.

2　***rich*** splendid, costly.

proud magnificent, splendid (OED³ A5b); enforces 'rich', but also has negative connotations of 'arrogant' (OED A1a), indicative of the empty vanity of worldly things which will not last.

cost (i) expense (*n.*2, OED 1b); (ii) costly thing (OED 4, citing this example); the combination of 'rich proud cost' is echoed at 91.10.

outworn wasted, worn out (OED³ 1); compare *Lucrece*, l. 1761. The juxtaposition with 'rich proud cost' makes clothing the dominant image (compare 'o'erworn', 63.2 and note), but 'buried age' and 'brass' (l. 4) also activate the image of funeral monuments, the inscriptions on which become worn away with time (to the point of illegibility, thus negating their commemorative purpose).

buried age former ages (antiquity), now forgotten ('buried' in oblivion).

3　***sometime*** once (qualifying the 'lofty towers', rather than the verb 'see').

down razed demolished, levelled to the ground; 'down' intensifies the action already present in 'razed'.

4　***brass*** emblematic of durability; compare *Richard II*, 3.2.168: 'brass impregnable'. By the early seventeenth century, 'brass' was also being used to describe 'a sepulchural tablet [. . .], bearing a figure or inscription, laid down on the floor or set up against the wall of a church' (OED 2a).

eternal qualifies 'brass'; the phrase (including the Latinate inversion of noun and adjective) is indebted to Horace's 'aere perennius' ('more lasting than bronze/brass', *Odes* 3.30.1); see headnote to Sonnet 55; however, some of its force also attaches to 'slave', so that brass becomes forever enslaved to 'mortal rage'.

mortal (i) fatal; (ii) human; Shakespeare uses 'mortal' in both these senses within the *Sonnets*: for sense (i), see 46.1; sense (ii), 7.7. 'Mortal', meaning 'subject to death' (OED 2a), also forms an antithesis with 'brass eternal'.

rage violent action (OED³ 2a).

5　***hungry ocean*** Compare *Twelfth Night*, 2.4.100, where Orsino describes his love as 'all as hungry as the sea'.

5–6　***gain | Advantage on*** acquire superiority over ('advantage', OED³ 4b, citing these lines).

7　***win of*** encroach upon (*v.*1, OED 10, citing this example).

watery pronounced as two syllables.

main sea; compare 60.5 and note.

8　***Increasing. . . store*** As one side gains, the other loses, and vice versa. The erosion of the land by the sea, and the opposing extrusion of the land is emblematic of mutability; see Ovid *Metamorphoses* 15.261–5 (Golding, 15.287–91; sig. 2C6r–v): 'Even so have places oftentimes exchanged their estate. | For I have seen it sea which was substantial ground alate [of late] | Again where sea was, I have seen the same become dry land, | And shells and scales of seafish far have lain from any strand, | And in the tops of mountains high old anchors have been found'. Compare also *2 Henry IV*, 3.1.45–53: 'O God, that one might read the book of fate, | And see the revolution of the times | Make mountains level, and the continent, | Weary of solid firmness, melt itself | Into the sea, and other times to see | The beachy girdle of the ocean | Too wide for Neptune's hips; how chance's mocks | And changes fill the cup of alteration | With divers liquors!'.

9　***interchange of state*** exchange of condition ('state', OED³ 1a); possibly echoes Golding 15.287, cited above (l. 8n); for the multivalency of 'state', see note on l. 10, below.

10　***state itself*** 'Itself' brings out the sense that this indicates the very concept of 'state', be it the body politic (OED³ 26a), 'existence' (OED³ 6a), 'standing or position' (OED 14a), 'high rank, greatness, power' (OED 15b), 'splendour' (OED 16), 'territory' (OED 25).

confounded to decay Compare the use of 'confound' to describe the destructive effects of time in 5.6, 60.8, 63.10. 'Decay' could be a

64

When I have seen by Time's fell hand defaced
The rich proud cost of outworn buried age,
When sometime lofty towers I see down razed,
And brass eternal slave to mortal rage;   4
When I have seen the hungry ocean gain
Advantage on the kingdom of the shore,
And the firm soil win of the watery main,
Increasing store with loss, and loss with store;   8
When I have seen such interchange of state,
Or state itself confounded to decay,
Ruin hath taught me thus to ruminate:
That Time will come and take my love away.   12
   This thought is as a death, which cannot choose
   But weep to have that which it fears to lose.

noun (indicating the condition to which 'state' is brought) or an infinitive verb, indicating the process of decay which 'state' undergoes.

12 ***my love*** (i) my affection; (ii) my beloved.

13–14 ***cannot choose | But*** must.

14 ***weep to have*** (i) weep while in possession; (ii) weep in a desire to possess.
it 'this thought' (l. 13).

65

Benson combines Sonnets 60 and 63–66 under the title 'Injurious Time'.

1 *Since* 'Since there is neither'; 111.11 shows a similar ellipsis of 'there is'; 86.9 and 141.9, a similar ellipsis of 'neither'.

brass. . . stone. . . earth. . . sea The same things are subject to time's destructive powers in Sonnet 64: 'brass' (64.4); 'stone' ('lofty towers', 64.3); 'earth' ('firm soil', 64.7); 'boundless sea' ('watery main', 64.7).

2 *sad* sorrowful (OED³ 5a); serious, and 'often coupled with *wise* or *discreet*' (OED³ 3b), thus conveying a sense of authority; also 'firmly established in purpose or condition' (OED³ 2a); ironically, the only thing which is unchanging is change itself.

mortality the condition of being mortal, and subject to death; in the case of inorganic materials like brass, 'death' must be equivalent to destruction and decay, but the transferral of a condition (mortality) which cannot logically pertain to such inanimate objects is an indication of the ruinous effects of time.

o'ersways 'exercise[s] power or dominion over' (OED³ 1a); 'overrule[s]' (OED³ 1b); i.e. 'sad mortality' is a stronger authority than brass and the other elements in l. 1, since all those things are subject to mutability.

power pronounced as one syllable.

3 *with* against.

this rage Compare 64.4.

hold a plea a legal phrase (from the post-classical Latin *placitum tenere*) meaning 'try an action' ('plea', OED³ 2b); the legal language continues with 'action' (l. 4).

4 *action* (i) legal process, lawsuit (OED³ 1), continuing on from 'hold a plea', l. 3; (ii) agency (OED³ 13); (iii) 'the exertion of energy or influence; working, operation' (OED³ 15a); (iv) 'a military engagement, a battle' (OED³ 7), pre-empting the imagery of l. 6.

flower pronounced as one syllable.

5 *honey breath* There is a hint of cliché; compare *Venus and Adonis*, ll. 16, 452, 538; *Romeo and Juliet* 5.3.92 ('Death, that hath sucked the honey of thy breath'); *Titus Andronicus* 2.4.25 ('thy honey breath'); Marlowe and Barnfield take this conventional image to almost comical extremes: see Marlowe, *Hero and Leander*, ll. 21–3 ('Many would praise the sweet smell as she passed, | When 'twas the odour which her breath forth cast; | And there for honey, bees have sought in vain'); Barnfield, 'Certain Sonnets', 8.14 ('honeycombs from his lips dropping be') and 17.10 ('His mouth a hive, his tongue a honeycomb', 1595: sigs C1v, C6r).

6 *wrackful* (i) vengeful (*adj*.1, OED 1); or more likely, (ii) a variant of 'wreckful', meaning 'destructive' (*adj*.3, OED 2); OED cites this line for (ii). There are no other Shakespearean usages of either 'wrackful' or 'wreckful', and searches in EEBO-TCP confirm that usage of the word is rare (appearing in eleven other works 1473–1609); most of these usages suggest (ii), as in Arthur Brooke's *Romeus and Juliet*: 'wrackful bar [sandbar]' and 'wrackful shore' (1562: sigs C7r, E6v). However, Thomas Andrewe's *Unmasking of a feminine Machiavel* also uses it in conjunction with the destructive effects of time (in images similar to those used here and elsewhere, e.g. 63.14, 123.2), as it boasts about the ability of poetry to make the woman's infamy known to future generations: 'Though wrackful time brass monuments devour, | Verse shall survive unto the latest hour; | And when the proud pyramids to dust | Age shall outwear, & steel consume with rust, | Then like Apollo's laurel, ever green, | Shall verse be verdant, and unchanged be seen' (1604: sig. C4r).

siege of siege by.

battering pronounced as two syllables, as is perhaps suggested by Q's spelling 'battring', although Compositor B (who probably set this page) does not consistently use spelling to show similar elisions (see, for example, 'bettering', which needs to be pronounced as two syllables, at Q82.8).

7 *rocks impregnable* continues the metaphor of the siege from l. 6; compare *Richard II*, 3.2.167–70, which combines the image of brass and castle walls: 'As if this flesh which walls about our life | Were brass impregnable; and humoured thus, | [Death] Comes at last, and with a little pin | Bores through his castle wall, and farewell king!'.

stout strong; able to resist.

8 *gates of steel* Compare *Troilus and Cressida*, 3.3.121. The image is Virgilian, describing the gates in front of the temple of Mars in *Aeneid* 7 (translated Thomas Phaer, 1558: sig. U3r). 'Steel' is often used by Shakespeare as the epitome of hardness; see 112.8n.

decays destroys.

65

Since brass, nor stone, nor earth, nor boundless sea,
But sad mortality o'ersways their power,
How with this rage shall beauty hold a plea,
Whose action is no stronger than a flower?   4
O how shall summer's honey breath hold out
Against the wrackful siege of battering days,
When rocks impregnable are not so stout,
Nor gates of steel so strong but time decays?   8
O fearful meditation; where, alack,
Shall Time's best jewel from Time's chest lie hid?
Or what strong hand can hold his swift foot back,
Or who his spoil o'er beauty can forbid?   12
    O none, unless this miracle have might,
    That in black ink my love may still shine bright.

9 *fearful* 'causing fear; inspiring terror, reverence, or awe' (OED 1); stronger than in modern usage; Shakespeare often uses the term to describe wars and battles; see, for example, *Cymbeline*, 4.3.7; *2 Henry IV*, Induction.12; *Henry V*, 1.1.44.

9–10 *where. . . hid?* The friend is depicted as a beautiful gem, lent to the world by Time for a while; Time now seeks to reclaim him and to lock him away in his treasure chest; compare 52.9. 'Chest' in this period could mean coffin; see 'chest, *n*.1', OED 3, citing Holland's translation of Pliny's *History*: 'One Cn. Terentius [. . .] as he digged [. . .] lit upon a chest, wherein lay the body of Numa' (1601: sig. 2L5v).

11 *swift foot* Time was proverbially swift; see 19.6 and note.

12 *spoil* spoliation (OED 2a), with a play on plunder (OED 1), reminding us of the war imagery of l. 6.

o'er Q's 'or' is problematic; Capell's suggestion (followed here) is based on the hypothesis that the copy-text had 'ore' (a feasible early modern spelling of 'o'er'). Most modern editors follow Malone's emendation to 'of', but it is unlikely that a compositor or copyist would misread 'f' (which has a prominent ascender and descender in secretary hand) as 'r' (which remains on the line, except in the 'long r' form, which was rare by the mid-sixteenth

century, let alone the later sixteenth or early seventeenth century, when the manuscript underlying Q was produced). Ingram and Redpath note that 'on' is 'graphically more plausible than *of*, which has, however, more linguistic probability' (1985: 152); this observation is backed up by the OED citations under 'spoil', but the emendation to 'of' is nonetheless unconvincing, for the palaeographical reasons cited. Booth's defence of retaining Q's 'or' maintains that the construction is a *zeugma*, whereby 'no one can prohibit time's ravages or exclude the beloved's beauty from time's ravages' (1977: 247).

13 *this miracle* (i) that 'black ink' can make his beautiful beloved 'shine bright' (black customarily understood as being antithetical to beauty; see Sonnet 127 and notes); (ii) the immortalisation of the beloved through verse.

might power, efficacy; bearing in mind the tentative nature of this statement (which begins with 'unless'), there may be a pun on the homophone 'might', anticipating 'may' in l. 14.

14 *That. . . bright* Compare 63.13 and note; the immortalising power of poetry is a frequent theme of the *Sonnets*; see 15.14n.

love (i) beloved (the dominant sense, as in 63.13), but also (ii) the poet-speaker's affections.

66

Benson combines Sonnets 60 and 63–66 under the title 'Injurious Time'.

Burrow (2002: 512) argues that 'the timbre of the poem points to a date after 1603', (i) because 'limping sway' may allude to James I's 'ungainly walk', the result of a childhood injury; and (ii) 'complaints about the disregard of merit are common in the Jacobean period, as are lists of generalised abuses linked by anaphora'. However, there is a well-established pre-Jacobean tradition of using *anaphora* as a satirical tool to depict a world-turned-upside-down; see, for example, Thomas Churchyard, *Davy Dyker's Dream* (*c.* 1551), in which thirteen couplets make use of anaphora (through the repetition of 'when') to imagine an ideal polity 'When justice joins to truth, and law looks not to meed [reward, bribery], | And bribes help not to build fair bowers, nor gifts great gluttons feed', 'When riches wrongs no right, nor power poor puts back, | Nor covetous creeps not into court, nor learned, livings lack' (ll. 9–10, 17–18). The evils listed by Churchyard are typical of this type of complaint, as they focus on just reward, true-dealing (in personal relationships, commerce and the law), charity, and the correct exercise of authority. The preoccupation with these same social wrongs can be seen in *Hamlet*, 3.1.69–76 (the resemblance of which to Sonnet 66 is often noted by editors): 'For who would bear the whips and scorns of time, | Th' oppressor's wrong, the proud man's contumely, | The pangs of despised love, the law's delay, | The insolence of office, and the spurns | The patient merit of th' unworthy takes, | When he himself might his quietus make | With a bare bodkin; who would fardels bear, | To grunt and sweat under a weary life'. See also *Lucrece*, ll. 848–910.

1 **Tired with** tired of; compare Gower's prologue to *Pericles*, 2.0.37: 'Fortune, tired with doing bad'.
  these indicates the evils to follow, rather than pointing back to the previous sonnet.
2 **As** such as, for instance.
  desert merit, by extension a deserving person; some editors choose to capitalise 'Desert', along with all the other qualities listed here, so that they become personifications. Q capitalises 'Nothing' (l. 3), 'Folly' (l. 10), 'Truth' and 'Simplicity' (l. 11); for Q's inconsistent capitals and the problems of assigning personifications, see 5.5n.

3 **needy nothing** a term of contempt, and the opposite of 'desert'; compare *Cymbeline*, 3.4.132, where the villain Cloten is described as 'that harsh, noble, simple nothing', and *Hamlet*, 4.2.28–30: 'The King is a thing [...] | Of nothing'. Editors sometimes gloss this as 'people who have need of nothing', but this dilutes the contemptuous force of 'trimmed in jollity' (see below).
  trimmed dressed, but with connotations of ornamentation or even frippery, particularly as it is a 'needy nothing' who is squandering the little they have on overly fine clothes; see 'trim, *v.*' (OED 8): 'to decorate (a hat, garment, etc.) with ribbons, laces, feathers, flowers, braids, embroideries, or the like'. Compare the complaint voiced in *Davy Dyker's Dream*, ll. 15–16, which imagines a time 'When pride which picks the purse gapes not for garments gay | No javels [rascals] wear no velvet weeds, nor wandering wits bear sway'.
  jollity 'splendour, magnificence; finery of dress or array' (OED 7, citing this line).
4 **faith** (i) fidelity; (ii) (religious) belief; (iii) an oath; a concern with faith is expressed in the opening line of Churchyard's *Davy Dyker's Dream*, which anticipates a time 'When faith in friends bear fruit'.
  unhappily 'unluckily; by misfortune or mischance; regrettably' (OED 1a); 'mischievously, maliciously' (OED 3a).
  forsworn perjured (OED 1); abandoned, repudiated ('forswear, *v.*' OED 1, 2).
5 **gilded** The word inevitably retains its negative connotations of a superficial, or even deceptive attractiveness; see *Troilus and Cressida*, 4.4.105 ('some with cunning gild their copper crowns') and *A Lovers' Complaint*, l. 172, where 'gilded' plays on 'beguiling' (l. 170).
  misplaced wrongly bestowed; compare Ecclesiastes 10:5–6: 'There is an evil that I have seen under the sun, as an error that proceedeth from the face of him that ruleth. Folly is set in great excellency, and the rich set in the low place'.
6 **maiden virtue** This image works both literally (describing virginity) and metaphorically, whereby virtue is like a virgin.
  rudely (i) violently (OED³ 2); (ii) discourteously (OED³ 3).

66

Tired with all these, for restful death I cry:
As to behold desert a beggar born,
And needy nothing trimmed in jollity,
And purest faith unhappily forsworn,   4
And gilded honour shamefully misplaced,
And maiden virtue rudely strumpeted,
And right perfection wrongfully disgraced,
And strength by limping sway disablèd,   8
And art made tongue-tied by authority,
And folly (doctor-like) controlling skill,
And simple truth miscalled simplicity,
And captive good attending captain ill.   12
    Tired with all these, from these would I be gone,
    Save that to die, I leave my love alone.

strumpeted brought into the condition of a strumpet (a whore), either (i) in actuality ('strumpet, *v.*', OED 1), or (ii) by ruining the woman's reputation (OED 2, citing this line), as happens to Hero in *Much Ado*, Desdemona in *Othello*, Hermione in *Winter's Tale*, Imogen in *Cymbeline*. The former maps on to sense (i) of 'rudely' (above); the latter, sense (ii). Although the first cited usage for the verb 'strumpet' in OED is Thomas Heywood's *Rape of Lucrece* (1608), this usage is probably predated by Shakespeare's *Comedy of Errors* (also cited), since – whilst the earliest play-text is in the 1623 Folio – its first recorded performance was in December 1594. No earlier usages of 'strumpet' as a verb are revealed by a search of EEBO-TCP.

7 ***right*** true (OED³ A1c); 'wrongfully' also activates additional, subsidiary meanings ('just; morally good', OED³ A5a; 'correct', OED³ 6a).

8 ***strength*** power.
limping sway ineffectual (halting) authority; Duncan-Jones (1997a: 242) reads this as an allusion to 'the power exercised over young male courtiers by the ageing Elizabeth during the last years of her reign, the most conspicuous example being the house arrest imposed on the Earl of Essex in 1600/1'.
disablèd The primary meaning of the verb 'disable' is 'to incapacitate legally; to pronounce

legally incapable; to hinder or restrain (a person or class of persons) from performing acts or enjoying rights which would otherwise be open to them; to disqualify' (OED³ 1); there is thus less of a seeming paradox than might at first appear in 'limping sway' having the capacity to nullify 'strength'; 'disablèd' is pronounced as four syllables.

9 ***art*** 'skill [. . .], esp. as result of knowledge or practice' (*n.*1, OED³ 1).
tongue-tied by authority (i) censored by the powers-that-be (as sometimes happened to Elizabethan dramatists); (ii) impeded by the weight of tradition and precedent; compare Sidney, *Astrophil and Stella*, 1.11 ('And others' feet still seemed but strangers in my way'), where Astrophil's ability to write is hampered by his studying other writers.

10 ***folly (doctor-like)*** Folly is like an academic doctor or a learned man ('doctor', OED 2a), rather than a medical practitioner; academic doctors are a recurrent butt of Erasmus' satire in *The Praise of Folly*, where Folly imagines herself 'clad in doctor-like apparel' (trans. Thomas Chaloner, 1549: sig. Q2v). See also the citation from Ecclesiastes, l. 5n, above. The complaint about folly acquiring the position that should be accorded to wisdom is akin to Churchyard's wish, in *Davy Dyker's Dream*, for a time 'When wisdom walks aloft, and folly sits full low' (l. 7).

controlling (i) regulating ('control, *v.*', OED 1); (ii) rebuking (OED 3a); (iii) exercising power over, commanding (OED 4a); (iv) curbing, hindering (OED 4b); (v) overpowering (OED 5).

11 *simple. . . simplicity* As the plain ('simple') truth is renamed ignorance ('simplicity'), the sonnet employs *paradiastole*, another much-used rhetorical figure in this type of socio-political complaint; see, for example, Thomas Wyatt's 'Mine own John Poins' (*Tottel* [125]), ll. 64–75, where the poetic speaker deplores those who redefine vices as virtues, for example, relabelling flattery ('favell') 'eloquence', and cruelty 'zeal of justice'. The *paradiastole* is further underlined by the *polyptoton* of 'simple' and 'simplicity'. 'Simple-truth' is hyphenated in Q, and thus transformed into a compound noun (as is 'captive-good' in l. 12).

12 *captive. . . ill* Goodness, like a prisoner of war ('captive', OED A1a), is enslaved to – and waits upon – wickedness, who is figured as military leader; 'captain' also indicates 'chief, principal' ('captain, *adj.*', OED 1); compare 52.8. The word play on 'cap-' enforces the paradox; compare 35.10 and note.

13 *Tired. . . these* As Burrow points out (2002: 512), 'The repetition of the first line (*epimone*) closes the sonnet off without allowing it to progress forwards'.

14 *Save* except.
to die if I die.
my love my beloved.
alone Kerrigan (1986: 257) points to the word play with 'all these', which the beloved ('all one') outweighs.

66

Tired with all these, for restful death I cry:
As to behold desert a beggar born,
And needy nothing trimmed in jollity,
And purest faith unhappily forsworn,   4
And gilded honour shamefully misplaced,
And maiden virtue rudely strumpeted,
And right perfection wrongfully disgraced,
And strength by limping sway disablèd,   8
And art made tongue-tied by authority,
And folly (doctor-like) controlling skill,
And simple truth miscalled simplicity,
And captive good attending captain ill.   12
    Tired with all these, from these would I be gone,
    Save that to die, I leave my love alone.

67

Benson combines Sonnets 67–69 under the title 'Glory of beauty'.

1 **Ah. . . live** (i) 'Why is he [the friend] obliged to live in a corrupted world?', a question which links back to the evils lamented in Sonnet 66; (ii) 'Why should he keep such bad company?', which criticises the friend (compare 69.14). '**Infection**' can imply more than a medical condition, indicating 'moral contamination; corruption of character or habits by evil influences' (OED³ 6) or 'corruption of faith or loyalty by heretical or seditious principles' (OED³ 8); as such, the word is closely connected to 'impiety' (l. 2). The meaning of the verb 'live' and its derivatives shifts through the sonnet (here it means 'dwell', *v.*1, OED³ 8a); see ll. 6, 9, 10, 12 and notes on ll. 9, 12.

2 **grace** (i) 'show favour to' (OED³ 2b); (ii) 'adorn, embellish' (OED³ 3a); (iii) 'gratify, delight' (OED³ 6).

3 **That** with the result that.

4 **lace** (i) interlace, entwine; (ii) decorate (i.e. sin is beautified by the friend's society, like a piece of clothing ornamented with lace or embroidery). **society** The word can suggest more than 'company' (OED³ 5a): it could also indicate a confederation or alliance (OED³ 2a, 2b).

5 **false painting** (i) cosmetics, which were used by men as well as women in this period; (ii) a pictorial representation, which falls short of the friend's true beauty; although many modern editors rule out an allusion to portraiture here, there are references to visual depictions of the friend in 46.3; 47.5–10, 13. The inability of the figurative arts to capture the friend's beauty is described in 53.5–8.

6 **dead seeming** lifeless appearance; Q has 'seeing'; however 'seeing' is not used elsewhere by Shakespeare to mean 'appearance'; Q's reading is probably the result of compositorial error, the compositor having failed to notice a tilde (which in early modern manuscript and print supplies either an 'm' or 'n') over the second 'e'; see 46.9n and 77.10n for evidence of a similar error. **of** from. **hue** appearance, complexion, colour; see 20.7n.

7 **poor beauty** an inferior (presumably artificial) kind of beauty; alternatively, 'poor' can be read as a pitying epithet, qualifying beauty, and thus personifying it; compare *Lucrece*, l. 1651.

8 **Roses. . . true** reactivates the neo-Platonic imagery invoked in Sonnet 53 (see notes on that poem); the youth's bloom ('rose') is 'true' because it is the 'idea' or essence of the rose (compare 'beauty's rose' in 1.2), in contrast to the mere imitations ('of shadow').

9 **live** survive (*v.*1, OED³ 6a); see note on l. 1, above. **bankrupt** initiates a strand of financial vocabulary: 'beggared' (l. 10); 'exchequer' (l. 11); 'lives', 'gains' (l. 12); 'stores', 'wealth' (l. 13).

10 **Beggared** destitute; the antecedent is Nature. OED cites this line as the first figurative usage of the adjective, and *Henry V* as the first literal usage (the word appears in the 1623 Folio, but not in the 1600 Quarto); however, the verb 'beggar' was in use from the early 1520s. **blush** show red.

11 **exchequer** treasury. **but** except.

12 **proud of many** a problematic phrase; Capell suggests emending 'proud' to 'prov'd' (see also 129.11n); however, Shakespeare uses neither 'prove of' nor 'proved of' anywhere else. Kerrigan has "'prived", an aphetic form of 'deprived', which continues the financial vein instigated by 'bankrupt', on the grounds that – as 'i' and 'o' are easily mistaken in secretary hand – 'priud' and 'proud' could 'look alike' (1986: 259). Q's reading has been retained here, since it is possible to make sense of it, as either (i) Nature being swollen (pregnant) with many offspring; or (ii) taking pride in her many offspring. **lives** supports oneself by means of a source of income (*v.*1, OED³ 2a); see notes on ll. 1, 9.

13 **stores** supplies (i.e. with beauty) (OED 1a); keeps for future use (OED 4a); compare 11.9; 68.13.

14 **days long since** Compare 'days outworn', 68.1. **these last so bad** these recent, corrupt times; there is a potential millenarian edge here; Blakemore Evans (1996: 174) points to a possible allusion to 2 Timothy 3:1–4: 'This know also, that in the last days [of the world] shall come perilous times. For men shall be lovers of their own selves, covetous, boasters, proud, cursed speakers, disobedient to parents, unthankful, unholy, without natural affection, truce-breakers, false accusers, intemperate, fierce, despisers of them which are good, traitors, heady, high-minded, lovers of pleasures more than lovers of God'.

67

Ah, wherefore with infection should he live,
And with his presence grace impiety,
That sin by him advantage should achieve
And lace itself with his society?   4
Why should false painting imitate his cheek
And steal dead seeming of his living hue?
Why should poor beauty indirectly seek
Roses of shadow, since his rose is true?   8
Why should he live, now Nature bankrupt is,
Beggared of blood to blush through lively veins,
For she hath no exchequer now but his,
And, proud of many, lives upon his gains?   12
    O him she stores, to show what wealth she had
    In days long since, before these last so bad.

68

Benson combines Sonnets 67–69 under the title 'Glory of beauty'. A copy of this poem (transcribed *c.* 1650s) exists in Folger MS V.a.148, fol. 22v; see Appendix 4.

1   *Thus* for this reason, linking this sonnet to the preceding one.
    outworn 'wasted, destroyed, or obliterated as by wear, or by the action of time, [. . .] obsolete' (OED³ 1); compare 64.2.

1, 13 *map* image, epitome (*n.*1, OED³ 5a), embodiment (OED³ 5b); see *Lucrece*, l. 402 and note.

2   *as flowers do now* As the sonnet progresses, it becomes clear that it is the natural, unadorned beauty of flowers (rather than simply their transience) that is alluded to here (in contrast to the artificial beauty of 'now' that the poet-speaker laments); compare 127.5–8. The line echoes Job 14:2 ('He shooteth forth as a flower, and is cut down: he vanisheth also as a shadow, & continueth not'), a verse which is paraphrased in the Burial Service in the *Book of Common Prayer*: 'he cometh up, and is cut down like a flower; he flyeth as it were a shadow, and never continueth in one stay' (2011: 171).
    flowers pronounced as one syllable.

3   *bastard* counterfeit (OED B4); i.e. created by cosmetics; in *Winter's Tale*, Perdita calls 'Nature's bastards' flowers, such as carnations, whose beauty has been created by human interference (4.4.83).
    signs devices or tokens (as in heraldry).
    fair beauty (a noun, rather than an adjective); see 16.11n.
    borne Q's spelling 'borne' indicates both 'born' and 'borne'; the former resonates with 'bastard'; the latter with 'signs'.

4   *inhabit* dwell, but with a possible pun on 'habit' (i.e. apparel, OED I).

5–7 *Before. . . head* Wigs were made from human hair, including that taken from corpses; compare *Merchant of Venice*, 3.2.92–6: 'So are those crisped snaky golden locks, | Which make such wanton gambols with the wind | Upon supposed fairness, often known | To be the dowry of a second head, | The skull that bred them in the sepulchre'. This speech of Bassanio's, like this sonnet, critiques 'outward shows' and the way in which 'The world is still deceived with ornament' (3.2.73–4).

6   *right* rightful possession.

8   *beauty's dead fleece* the hair of l. 5; the phrase (particularly following 'golden tresses') parallels another of Bassanio's speeches from *Merchant of Venice*, in which he describes how Portia's 'sunny locks | Hang on her temples like a golden fleece' (1.1.169–70). Bassanio's speech explicitly invokes the voyage of Jason and the Argonauts to bring back the golden fleece from 'Colchis' strond' (1.1.171).
    gay The word holds a strong suggestion of 'showy' (OED³ 1a) as well as 'beautiful' (OED³ 2); it is often used by Shakespeare in a slightly pejorative sense: see 146.4; *Antony and Cleopatra*, 3.13.25–6 ('I dare him therefore | To lay his gay comparisons apart'); *Comedy of Errors*, 2.1.94 ('Do their gay vestments his affections bait?').

9   *holy* sinless (OED A4).
    antique hours time long-past (compare 'days outworn', l. 1).

10   *all* any; compare 74.2.
    itself The antecedent is beauty (l. 2).
    true unadorned.

11   *green* youthfulness, vitality (*n.*1, OED B2c); compare its appearance, as an adjective, at 63.14.

12   *no old* no old beauty.

13   *store* keeps for future use (OED 4a); compare 11.9; 67.13.

13, 14 *Nature. . . Art* The interaction between art and nature, and whether nature was a manifestation of divine art or required human art to 'improve it', were topics of philosophical and literary interest in the early modern period. See, for example, Perdita's and Polixenes' discussion about art and nature in *Winter's Tale*, 4.4.85–99. Whilst capitalisation is not a reliable indication of personification in Q (see 5.5n), it is worth noting that both words are capitalised here.

14   *of yore* in the past, with a possible pun on 'your'.

68

Thus is his cheek the map of days outworn,
When beauty lived and died as flowers do now,
Before these bastard signs of fair were borne,
Or durst inhabit on a living brow;   4
Before the golden tresses of the dead,
The right of sepulchres, were shorn away
To live a second life on second head,
Ere beauty's dead fleece made another gay: 8
In him those holy antique hours are seen
Without all ornament, itself and true,
Making no summer of another's green,
Robbing no old to dress his beauty new;   12
    And him as for a map doth Nature store,
    To show false Art what beauty was of yore.

69

Benson combines Sonnets 67–69 under the title 'Glory of beauty'.

1 ***parts*** (i) body parts; (ii) personal qualities or attributes.

2 ***Want*** lack.
thought of hearts The heart was seen as the seat of thoughts and emotions; see 46.1 and note.
mend improve.

3 ***due*** Q's 'end' is clearly faulty, as it mars the rhyme; Gildon (1714) was the first to suggest 'due', which is adopted (as here) by most editors. 'End' is probably the result of eye jump from either ll. 2 or 4; alternatively, it may result from the combination of a turned letter ('u' for 'n') and a momentary failure on the compositor's part to set the type in the inverted order required. The other suggestion, that 'in Elizabethan secreatry hand a *d* and an *e*, if hastily written and hastily read, might well be confused, as might a *u* and an *n*' (Ingram and Redpath 1985: 160) is less convincing: whilst 'u' and 'n' are indeed often indistinguishable, 'd's and 'e's would have to be very carelessly written to be readily confused, and the overall coherence of Q does not suggest such a poorly penned manuscript.

4 ***Uttering*** pronounced as two syllables, as is perhaps suggested by Q's spelling 'Vttring', although Compositor B (who probably set this page) does not consistently use spelling to show similar elisions (see, for example, 'bettering', which needs to be pronounced as two syllables, at 82.8).
even pronounced as one syllable.

5 ***Thy outward*** your outward appearance; for the use of 'outward' as a noun, see 125.2. Q has 'their'; for the recurrent compositorial error, confusing 'their' and 'thy', see 26.12n (although here, 'their' could refer back to 'parts', l. 1). Malone (1790) emends 'thy' to 'thine' (as is usual before a vowel), but see 46.13n.
outward praise (i) praise of the youth's external appearance; (ii) public praise; (iii) superficial praise (as opposed to sincere feeling, which would be 'inward'); for (iii) compare *Coriolanus*, 1.6.77: 'If these shows be not outward'. Ingram and Redpath (1985: 160) suggest an aural pun on 'uttered' (the acceptable sixteenth-century spelling of 'outward' as 'utwarde' points to the phonetic similarity between the two words).

6 ***those same tongues*** people who comment on the friend (by *synecdoche*).

7 ***accents*** tones (OED³ 4a); words (OED³ 4b).
confound overthrow (OED 1a); confute (OED 3b).

10 ***in guess*** by estimating.

11 ***Then, churls, their thoughts*** There are no commas in Q; Blake (1998) argues that this consequently forms a possessive phrase (churls' thoughts) similar to the use of 'his' in 'Purchas his Pilgrimage'. However, punctuation is not necessarily reliable in Q, and this sonnet is, as Booth notes, 'sloppily printed throughout' (1977: 253). Inserting commas (as here) makes the term of abuse ('churls') parenthetical, qualifying either the people ('tongues', l. 6) or 'their thoughts'.

12 ***To. . . weeds*** Compare 94.13–14 (where the accusation is in the mouth of the poet-speaker, not of these anonymous critics). '***Flower***' (pronounced as one syllable) initially indicates 'the best part' (compare *Coriolanus*, 1.6.32, where Martius is called 'flower of warriors'); however, during the course of the line, the organic sense of 'flower' is activated, anticipating the final couplet. Weeds are recurrently used by Shakespeare as an emblem of corruption; see *Lucrece*, l. 870; *Richard II*, 3.4.37–9 ('I will go root away | The noisome weeds which without profit suck | The soil's fertility from wholesome flowers'), lines about literal flowers/weeds which provoke a metaphorical response from the gardener's helper: 'the whole land | Is full of weeds, her fairest flowers choked up' (3.4.43–4).
rank festering (OED³ 12); compare *Hamlet*, 1.2.135–7: ''Tis an unweeded garden | That grows to seed, things rank and gross in nature | Possess it merely'.

13 ***odour. . . show*** For another use of this analogy of the inter-relationship between the scent and appearance of a flower, see Sonnet 54.

14 ***soil*** solution; Benson (1640) is the first editor to emend Q's 'solye' (a non-word) to 'soil' (of which 'soyle' is an acceptable early modern variant); Gildon (1710) substitutes 'toil'; Malone, 'solve'. However, these further emendations are unnecessary. This line is cited by OED as the only instance of 'soil' to mean 'solution' (*n*. 5); but Puttenham's *Art of English Poesy* (printed in 1589) is cited as an example of the noun 'assoil' (of which 'soil' would be an aphetic form), in his

69

Those parts of thee that the world's eye doth view
Want nothing that the thought of hearts can mend:
All tongues (the voice of souls) give thee that due,
Uttering bare truth, even so as foes commend. 4
Thy outward thus with outward praise is crowned,
But those same tongues that give thee so thine own
In other accents do this praise confound
By seeing farther than the eye hath shown. 8
They look into the beauty of thy mind
And that in guess they measure by thy deeds;
Then, churls, their thoughts (although their eyes were kind)
To thy fair flower add the rank smell of weeds; 12
But why thy odour matcheth not thy show,
The soil is this, that thou dost common grow.

explanation of the 'riddle' or 'enigma', 'of which the sense can hardly be picked out, but by the party's own assoil' (1589: 157). Admittedly, this again is the sole example cited, but the verb 'soil', meaning 'to resolve, clear up, expound, or explain; to answer (a question)' was in use from the late fourteenth century until the early seventeenth century ('soil, *v.* 2', OED 3); see Cotgrave, *Dictionary*: 'Souldre, to [...] resolve, clear, or soil, a doubt' (1611: sig. 4E2r). 'Soil' also resonates with the vegetative imagery of flowers and weeds, and hints at some kind of moral stain, as in *Troilus and Cressida* 2.2.148: 'the soil of her fair rape'.

common grow Compare Fulke Greville, *Caelica* (composed *c.* 1590), 37.13–14: 'While that fine soil, which all these joys did yield, | By broken fence is proved a common field' (*Works* 1633: sig. 2D1v). 'Common' indicates (i) that the friend is accessible to, or belongs, to many (like common land or a prostitute; compare 137.10 and note); and (ii) that, in being so, he is 'of merely ordinary or inferior quality' (OED A14a); (iii) 'common' was often used of sexual promiscuity (OED A6b). 'Grow' means 'become', but it also continues the vein of vegetative imagery.

70

Printed by Benson as a single sonnet entitled 'Nil magnis Invidia' ('no envy for the great'); for Benson's use of Latin titles, see headnote to Sonnet 61. This sonnet answers the envious tongues of Sonnet 69.

1 ***thou are*** Often altered by editors to 'thou art', Q's 'thou are' is unusual, but not unprecedented; a search of EEBO-TCP reveals over 100 usages in almost 100 texts (once false results are weeded out), including early editions of Shakespeare's plays: *Shrew* (Q); *2 Henry VI* (Q2); *Merry Wives, All's Well, Romeo and Juliet, Julius Caesar* (all F). However, it is possible that the compositor misread the terminal 't' as an 'e' (an easy mistake when reading secretary hand, in which the letter 't' is relatively short, and 'e' can be formed with two strokes, which sometimes resemble a 't' in which the cross stroke has become detached from its body).

   defect fault; stressed on the second syllable.

2 ***slander's mark*** proverbial; see Dent E175: 'Envy (Calumny) shoots at the fairest mark' (i.e. target).

   the fair people with beauty (both inward and outward); for the use of 'fair' as a noun, see 16.11n.

3 ***The ornament. . . suspect*** (i) beauty is forever open to suspicion ('suspect'), a conceit that is encapsulated in the proverb 'Beauty and chastity (honesty) seldom meet' (Dent B163); (ii) beauty is suspect because it might be created ('ornament[ed]') by cosmetics.

3, 13 ***suspect*** stressed on the second syllable.

4 ***crow. . . air*** 'Suspect' is here figured as a crow, an ill-omened bird; see Pliny, *History*: 'These birds all of them keep much prattling and are full of chat, which most men take for an unlucky sign and presage of ill fortune' (trans. Holland, 1601: sig. 2A6v). Compare *Macbeth*, 3.2.50–3 (immediately before Banquo's murder): 'Light thickens, and the crow | Makes wing to th' rooky wood; | Good things of day begin to droop and drowse, | Whiles night's black agents to their preys do rouse'.

   heaven's sweetest air The air that the crow contaminates is not just 'sweet': it is the 'sweetest' air; compare 'sweetest buds' in l. 7.

5 ***So*** provided that; the rest of the sonnet (and the friend's reputation) rests on this conditional.

   but only.

approve prove, demonstrate (*v.*1, OED 1); compare the herald's announcement of Mowbray's intention 'to approve | Henry of Herford [. . .] | To God, his sovereign, and to him disloyal' (*Richard II*, 1.3.112–14).

6 ***Thy*** Q has 'Their'; for the frequent compositorial confusion of 'their' for 'thy', see 26.12n.

   worth a recurrent word in *Sonnets* (see 2.4n); in Q's sequence, its appearance here marks the beginning a particularly dense cluster (see 72.4, 14; 74.13).

   wooed of time (i) tempted by the immorality of the age (see Sonnets 66 and 67); (ii) courted by Time, which has showered gifts upon you (including the gift of youth itself; see, for example, the portrayal of Time in 60.8). The phrase is puzzling, and there is a tradition of emending it: a manuscript conjecture in the Bodley-Caldecott copy of Q suggests reading 'of time' as 'oftime' (i.e. frequently); in his first edition, Malone conjectured 'void of crime' (1780: 637n), but withdrew it in the second; Capell suggests 'wood [mad] oftime'.

7 ***For*** because.

   canker vice Vice is depicted as a caterpillar ('cankerworm'); see 35.4n and 95.1–3.

8 ***present'st*** offer.

   prime youth; see 3.10 and note.

9 ***the ambush. . . days*** traps or temptations encountered in youth.

10 ***Either. . . . charged*** If every syllable is sounded as in standard English, this line is hypermetrical; however, 'Either' or 'being' could be elided into one syllable.

   assailed attacked; compare 41.6.

   charged The primary meaning is 'assaulted' (continuing the military language of 'ambush', 'assailed', 'victor'); there may be a secondary sense (of 'accused') at play.

11–12 ***Yet. . . enlarged*** 'Even being good ['***this thy praise***'] is not sufficient ['***so thy praise***'] to prevent ['***tie up***'] envious attacks, because envy will always be (i) increasing; or (ii) at liberty'. Compare the proverb 'Envy never dies' (Tilley E172) and Spenser's depiction of the Blatant Beast, who is chained by Calidore, but then breaks free (*Faerie Queene*, VI.xii.23–40).

13 ***of ill*** of ill-doing.

14 ***kingdoms of hearts*** sovereignty over all hearts.

   owe possess (OED[3] 1).

70

That thou are blamed shall not be thy defect,
For slander's mark was ever yet the fair;
The ornament of beauty is suspect,
A crow that flies in heaven's sweetest air.   4
So thou be good, slander doth but approve
Thy worth the greater, being wooed of time,
For canker vice the sweetest buds doth love,
And thou present'st a pure unstainèd prime.   8
Thou hast passed by the ambush of young days,
Either not assailed, or victor, being charged,
Yet this thy praise cannot be so thy praise
To tie up envy, evermore enlarged.   12
    If some suspect of ill masked not thy show,
    Then thou alone kingdoms of hearts shouldst owe.

71

Benson combines Sonnets 71, 72 and 74 under the title 'A Valediction'. A manuscript copy of this poem (transcribed *c.* 1650) exists in MS Folger V.a.162, fol. 12v; see Appendix 4.

As Duncan-Jones points out (1997a: 252), the way in which this poem turns to thoughts of death is numerologically appropriate, since the sequence has now exceeded the natural lifespan, of 'three score years and ten' (i.e. 70) set down in the Bible (Psalm 90:10).

2 ***Than*** Q's 'Then' is a variant spelling of 'than'; however, modernising it here does lose the double valency it holds in old spelling, whereby – as well as completing the relative clause established by 'no longer' (l. 1) – it also indicates temporality: when I am dead, then you will hear the bell toll.
   surly stern, gloomy (OED 4, citing this example).
   sullen 'of a deep, dull or mournful tone' (OED A3b).
   surly sullen bell Compare *2 Henry IV*, 1.1.101–3: 'his tongue | Sounds ever after as a sullen bell | Rememb'red tolling a departing friend'. Church bells were rung to mark a parishioner's death. Mourners could then pay for an annual bell to be rung in remembrance, or commission an extended tolling of the bell, as Shakespeare did at St Saviour's, Southwark for his brother Edmund, an actor, on 31 December 1607, paying twenty shillings for a ceremony which included 'a forenoon knell of the great bell' (Schoenbaum 1978: 29).

3 ***warning*** notice (of the poet-speaker's death), but also functioning as a memento mori, warning

others to be mindful of their own mortality; Donne, *Devotions*, Meditation 17: 'Never send to know for whom the bell tolls; it tolls for thee' (1624: 416).

4 ***vile world*** Compare *2 Henry VI*, 5.2.40: 'O, let the vile world end'.
   vildest Q's spelling is common early modern variant for 'vilest'; most editors (from Gildon on) modernise; Ingram and Redpath (who do not) argue that the 'heaviness' of the older form 'better suits the line' (1985: 164). Peacham uses the expansion of 'vile' to 'vilde' as an example of 'paragoge', where an extra sound is added for the purpose of metre or 'to make the verse more fine' (*Garden of Eloquence*, 1577: sigs E2v, E1v). Shakespeare frequently uses the d-form of this word (see Kökeritz 1953: 299). Q's spelling has here been retained because it affects the sound of the line. For the contemptibility of worms – as the lowest of the low – see Psalm 22:6, in which David describes himself as 'a worm, & not a man: a shame of men, and the contempt of the people'.

6 ***so*** (i) so much; (ii) in such a way.

8 ***woe*** woeful, sorrowful; compare *Tempest*, 5.1.139: 'I am woe for 't'.

10 ***compounded*** combined; compare *2 Henry IV*, 4.5.115: 'Only compound me with forgotten dust'.
   clay For the association of clay and the grave, see *Lucrece*, 609n.

11 ***rehearse*** utter (OED³ 2), repeat (OED³ 3).

12 ***even with*** at the same time as; 'even' is pronounced as one syllable.

13 ***look into*** 'examine or investigate (a matter, subject, issue)' ('to look into', OED³ 3, in 'look').

71

No longer mourn for me when I am dead
Than you shall hear the surly sullen bell
Give warning to the world that I am fled
From this vile world with vildest worms to dwell: 4
Nay, if you read this line, remember not
The hand that writ it, for I love you so
That I in your sweet thoughts would be forgot,
If thinking on me then should make you woe. 8
O if (I say) you look upon this verse
When I (perhaps) compounded am with clay,
Do not so much as my poor name rehearse,
But let your love even with my life decay, 12
    Lest the wise world should look into your moan
    And mock you with me after I am gone.

72

Benson combines Sonnets 71, 72 and 74 under the title 'A Valediction'.

1 *task* command.

recite As well as meaning 'speak of' (OED[3] 2a), 'list' (OED[3] 2b) or 'describe' (OED[3] 3), the word has a strong legal resonance relevant here: 'To state (a relevant fact) in a deed or other legal document' (OED 1).

2–3 *love | After my death* Q has no punctuation after 'love', allowing 'after my death' to attach to both 'love' and 'forget'. A number of editors place a comma after 'love', restricting the sense.

4 *worthy* Kerrigan (1986: 264) points to a potential quibble on 'worth thee'.

prove 'demonstrate the truth of by evidence' (OED[3] 1); Q has a full-stop after 'prove', disrupting the syntax, which continues into the second quatrain.

5 *virtuous* (i) powerful (OED[3] 8a); (ii) morally good (OED[3] 2a), making 'virtuous lie' an oxymoron; 'virtuous' is here pronounced as two syllables.

7 *hang more praise* alludes to the practice of hanging commemorative verses on biers; see *Much Ado* 5.3.3–10, where Claudio reads an epitaph which he then hangs on Hero's tomb.

I Presumably chosen for the purposes of rhyme, 'I' is irregular, but not ungrammatical (see Abbott 1884: §§ 205, 209). The pronoun, particularly in a rhyming position, also draws attention to the poet-speaker, in a sonnet which (as Fineman describes it) is 'a praise of the poet's own self' (1986: 164).

8 *niggard* miserly.

9 *in this* in this way.

10 *of me untrue* (i) untruly about me (adverb, describing the friend speaking); (ii) about me, who is unfaithful (adjective, describing the poet-speaker).

11 *My name be buried* let my name be buried.

12 *nor. . . nor. . .* neither. . . nor. . .

13 *that which I bring forth* i.e. his writings.

14 *so should you* (i) so would you be ashamed; (ii) so you ought to be ashamed.

nothing worth 'Nothing' could be pronounced 'noting' in the period, so it is possible to hear an implied criticism of the friend, who loves things (people, poems) 'noting' his 'worth'.

72

O lest the world should task you to recite
What merit lived in me that you should love
After my death (dear love) forget me quite,
For you in me can nothing worthy prove,   4
Unless you would devise some virtuous lie
To do more for me than mine own desert,
And hang more praise upon deceasèd I
Than niggard truth would willingly impart: 8
O lest your true love may seem false in this,
That you for love speak well of me untrue,
My name be buried where my body is
And live no more to shame nor me, nor you.   12
    For I am shamed by that which I bring forth,
    And so should you, to love things nothing worth.

73

Benson combines Sonnets 73 and 77 under the title 'Sunset'. For Shakespeare's portrayal of sonneteering as an activity conducted by an ageing poet, see 22.1n.

1–8 *That time. . . rest* Like Sonnets 5, 7, 12, 60 and 63, in comparing the ageing process to the passing of the day and/or the seasons, the octave echoes Ovid, *Metamorphoses*, 15.199–227 (Golding, 15.221–49; sig. 2C5r–v).

3 *against* in anticipation of; compare 63.1.

4 *Bare ruined choirs* Q has 'bare rn'wd quiers', emended by Benson (1640) to 'bare ruin'd quires' (an emendation generally followed by subsequent editors, although Capell suggests 'Barren'd of quires'). Q's spelling 'rn'wd' may be a combination of (i) transposition of characters (a mistake that the same Compositor, B, made at Q23.14 ('wiht' for 'with') and Q33.14 ('stainteh' for 'staineth')); (ii) misreading 'u' as 'n' (an easy mistake in secretary hand); and (iii) misreading the minims 'in' as 'w' (again, easily done with secretary hand); 'ruin'd' is thus converted to 'rn'wd'. 'Quires' is an acceptable alternative spelling of 'choirs': 'that part of a church appropriated to the singers; *spec.* the part eastward of the nave, in which the services are performed, separated from the rest of the building by a screen or screens, usually of open work; the chancel' (OED 2a). The leafless branches of the wintry tress, silhouetted against the sky, can be seen to resemble the open work on these screens. Compare *Cymbeline*, 3.3.42–4: 'our cage | We make a choir, as doth the prisoned bird, | And sing our bondage freely'. Describing the choirs as 'bare ruined' also evokes those monastic churches and abbeys deconsecrated during the dissolution of the monasteries under Henry VIII, many of which were then allowed to fall into disrepair or were plundered for their lead, stone and other materials; Giacomo Saranzo (Venetian ambassador to England, 1553–7) describes London as 'deformed' ('deformata') as a result (Alberi 1853: 51); Stow's *Survey of London* also gives occasional glimpses of the destruction, as in the description of the chapel in Pardon Churchyard: 'In the year 1549, on the tenth of April, the said chapel by commandment of the Duke of Somerset, was begun to be pulled down, with the whole cloister, the *Dance of Death* [a wall painting], the tombs, and monuments, so that nothing thereof was left, but the bare plot of ground' (1598: 265). Q's 'quiers' may also suggest a secondary sense of 'quires' (gatherings) of paper, a sense also activated by 'leaves' (l. 2) and the explicit reference to the poet-speaker's writings at the end of Sonnet 72.

late lately.

5 *such day* such a day.

8 *Death's second self* The subject is 'night' (l. 7); however, there may be an indirect allusion to sleep, conventionally depicted as 'the elder brother of death' (Tilley S526).

seals up (i) encloses or confines (as in a coffin); (ii) the verb may refer to the practice of 'seeling' a hawk's eyes, by sewing the lids together ('seel, *v.*2', OED 1); see *Macbeth*, 3.2.46–7: 'Come, seeling night, | Scarf up the tender eye of pitiful day'.

10 *his* its (referring to the fire, l. 9).

12 *Consumed. . . by* Compare Sonnet 1.6.

73

That time of year thou mayst in me behold
When yellow leaves, or none, or few do hang
Upon those boughs which shake against the cold,
Bare ruined choirs, where late the sweet birds sang.   4
In me thou seest the twilight of such day
As after sunset fadeth in the west,
Which by and by black night doth take away,
Death's second self that seals up all in rest.   8
In me thou seest the glowing of such fire
That on the ashes of his youth doth lie,
As the death-bed whereon it must expire,
Consumed with that which it was nourished by.   12
   This thou perceiv'st, which makes thy love more strong,
   To love that well, which thou must leave ere long.

74

Benson combines Sonnets 71, 72 and 74 under the title 'A Valediction'. Kerrigan (1986: 266) notes how the Ovidian resonances of Sonnet 73 are here replaced (from l. 5 onwards) by the Biblical imagery of Job 17.11–16: 'My days are past, mine enterprises are broken, and the thoughts of mine heart have changed the night for the day, and the light that approached, for darkness. Though I hope, yet the grave shall be mine house, and I shall make my bed in the dark. I shall say to corruption, "Thou art my father", and to the worm, "Thou art my mother and my sister." Where is then now mine hope? Or who shall consider the thing that I hoped for? They shall go down into the bottom of the pit; surely it shall lie together in the dust'.

1 *But* links Sonnet 74 to the preceding sonnet.
   contented 'satisfied', but with a sense of resignation ('limiting one's desires, willing to put up with something', OED 1a). Malone (followed by many subsequent editors) inserts a colon after 'contented': this is unnecessary; Ingram and Redpath (1985: 170) argue that such an abrupt break in the first line is found nowhere else in the *Sonnets* (but see 117.1).
   fell fierce, savage; compare the description of 'Time's fell hand' (64.1).
   arrest (i) the act of stopping (*n*.1, OED 1); (ii) death is figured as an officer, taking the poet-speaker into custody; compare *Hamlet*, 5.2.336–7: 'this fell sergeant, Death, | Is strict in his arrest'. Sense (ii) is developed in the subsequent line. See too *Lucrece*, l. 1780 and note.

2 *all* any; compare 68.10.
   bail 'security given for the release of a prisoner from imprisonment, pending his trial' (*n*.1, OED 5a).
   carry me away Blakemore Evans speculates as to whether this might be an allusion to the Vice in a morality play, 'who conventionally sometimes carried a sinner away to Hell on his shoulders at the conclusion of the play' (1996: 180).

3 *line* line of verse, i.e. poem.
   interest right of ownership (see OED 1a); 'interest' is here pronounced as three syllables.

4 *memorial* (i) reminder; (ii) physical object by which someone's memory is preserved.

5 *reviewest. . . review* 'review' implies close scrutiny; since copyists in this period frequently emended the works they transcribed, OED[3] sense 4a may

be pertinent: 'To look over or through (a document, book, etc.) in order to correct or improve it; to revise'. Blakemore Evans (1996: 180) finds the repetition 'rhetorically flat' and – although he retains Q in his text – he conjectures in the notes that 'review' (spelled 'reuew' in Q) may be a compositorial misreading of 'renew' ('n' being easily mistaken in secretary hand for 'u', which would serve as 'v' in early modern orthography); in this reading, ll. 5–6 would thus mean 'When you look over these lines, you give new life to the precise part which was dedicated to you'.

6 *was* which was.
   consecrate dedicated (with strong connotations of a religious devotion).

7 *The earth. . . earth* The line echoes the Burial Service in the *Book of Common Prayer*: 'earth to earth, ashes to ashes, dust to dust' (2011: 172).
   his its.

8 *spirit* monosyllabic; sometimes used in the *Sonnets* to suggest a poet's creative powers; compare 80.2, 85.7, 86.5.
   better part The phrase was used at 39.2, to refer to the friend as second self.

9 *then* both temporal (when I die) and causative (therefore).
   but only.
   the dregs of life the first of three noun phrases in apposition (the second and third being 'prey of worms' and 'coward conquest of a wretch's knife'); compare *Macbeth*, 2.3.95–6: 'The wine of life is drawn, and the mere lees [dregs] | Is left this vault to brag of'.

10 *prey of worms* conventional image of the ultimate fate of all human bodies; see 6.14 and note.

11 *The coward. . . knife* Shakespeare often uses 'coward' as an adjective: see *As You Like It*, 3.5.13 ('coward gates'); *Cymbeline*, 4.4.37 ('coward hares'). The 'wretch' is Death or his alter-ego, Time. Time has a knife at 100.14 and at 63.10 (where he appears as 'confounding Age'). 6.14 provides another useful parallel (as it does for the preceding line). 'Conquest' describes either (i) the poet-speaker's body, taken as 'booty' (OED 4), or (ii) Death's/Time's 'action of overcoming' the poet-speaker (OED 2). The line has been read as allusion to the infamous stabbing of Shakespeare's contemporary, and fellow-playwright, Christopher Marlowe by Ingram Frizer in a Deptford tavern in 1593 (see Jackson

74

But be contented when that fell arrest
Without all bail shall carry me away;
My life hath in this line some interest,
Which for memorial still with thee shall stay.   4
When thou reviewest this, thou dost review
The very part was consecrate to thee:
The earth can have but earth, which is his due;
My spirit is thine, the better part of me.   8
So then thou hast but lost the dregs of life,
The prey of worms, my body being dead,
The coward conquest of a wretch's knife,
Too base of thee to be rememberèd.   12
    The worth of that, is that which it contains,
    And that is this, and this with thee remains.

2005, which argues that Shakespeare makes frequent allusions to this event in 1598–1600).

12 *of thee* by thee.

rememberèd Q has 'remembred', but the word needs to be pronounced as four syllables if the line is not to be lacking metrically; the stressed ending is also necessary to make the rhyme with 'dead'.

13 *The worth. . . contains* The value of a body ('that') is the spirit ('that which') it contains.

14 *that* the poet-speaker's spirit.

this this poem (or the *Sonnets* more broadly); despite the evocation of the Burial Service in l. 7, the immortality that the poem imagines is a secular, rather than a Christian, one.

75

Omitted from Benson's 1640 edition; see headnote to Sonnet 18.

2 ***sweet seasoned*** (i) temperate; (ii) sweetly flavoured or spiced, picking up on 'food' (l. 1) and anticipating the feasting imagery in ll. 9–10.

   showers pronounced as one syllable.

3 ***for*** (i) to achieve; (ii) for the sake of; 'instead of' – sometimes proposed by editors – does not fit with the simile that follows.

   peace of you (i) balm of your company; (ii) the contentment and tranquillity you embody. The phrase is unusual: Malone suggests changing it to 'price' or 'sake' (1780: 641n); Staunton, to 'prize'; Tucker, to 'piece'. Most editors leave well alone, as 'peace' works structurally, as a contrast to 'strife', as well as providing an aural pun on the homonym 'piece'.

   hold such strife experience such conflicting feelings.

5 ***proud*** a sexual resonance is possible; see OED³ A7b; 151.10 and note.

   enjoyer the only Shakespearean usage of this word; for the sexual connotations of 'enjoy', see 129.5n.

   anon straightaway.

6 ***Doubting*** dreading ('doubt, *v.*', OED 5); compare *Macbeth*, 4.2.67: 'I doubt some danger does approach you nearly'.

   filching age thieving age; part of the poet-speaker's recurrent lament for the times in which he lives; see 67.14.

   treasure For the depiction of his love as a treasure, see Sonnets 48, 52.

7 ***counting best*** thinking it best.

8 ***bettered*** thinking it better; *Venus and Adonis*, l. 78, makes a similar play on 'best' and 'bettered'.

9 ***Sometime*** sometimes; compare 18.5.

9–10 ***all full . . . starvèd*** Compare the analogy of looking and feasting/fasting at 47.3–6, 56.1–6. 'Clean' is adverbial ('completely').

10 ***for a look*** (i) for a glance from you; (ii) for a sight of you.

11 ***Possessing or pursuing*** Compare the exploration of desire in 129.9.

12 ***Save*** except.

   what is had 'what I have had from you'. For the sexual connotations of 'have', see 129.6, 10n.

   or . . . took 'or what must be taken from you' (possibly because the friend does not give it willingly). OED does not record the use of 'take' in a sexual sense until 1915 (OED 14c); however, that sexual potential seems to have been available to Shakespeare and his contemporaries; for example, Touchstone – a character who is fond of innuendo – declares that he 'will not take her on gift of any man' at *As You Like It*, 3.3.68; see also Partridge 1990: 197.

13 ***pine and surfeit*** starve and feed to excess; compare *Venus and Adonis*, l. 602. 'Pine' can also mean 'languish with desire' (OED³ 7).

   day by day (i) every day; (ii) changing from one day to the next.

14 ***Or . . . or*** either . . . or.

   gluttoning feeding voraciously ('glutton, *v.*', OED).

   all The youth is described as the poet-speaker's 'all' at 109.14 and 112.5.

   all away left with nothing (mirroring 'pine' as 'gluttoning' mirrors 'surfeit').

75

So are you to my thoughts as food to life,
Or as sweet seasoned showers are to the ground;
And for the peace of you I hold such strife
As 'twixt a miser and his wealth is found: 4
Now proud as an enjoyer, and anon
Doubting the filching age will steal his treasure;
Now counting best to be with you alone,
Then bettered that the world may see my pleasure;   8
Sometime all full with feasting on your sight,
And by and by clean starvèd for a look;
Possessing or pursuing no delight,
Save what is had, or must from you be took.   12
    Thus do I pine and surfeit day by day,
    Or gluttoning on all, or all away.

76

Omitted from Benson's 1640 edition; see headnote to Sonnet 18. As in Sonnet 32, the poet-speaker ostensibly denigrates his poetic skill (particularly in relation to the fashionable writings of his contemporaries), but ends up asserting the worth of his own poetry, not only for the sincere love it expresses but also (more subtly) because he has the ability to distil that love into words. In Q's sequence, this sonnet pre-empts the 'rival poet(s)' group which follows soon after (78–80, 82–86). Duncan-Jones points out that Sonnet 76 'resumes the theme of 38', a poem exactly 38 poems previously in Q (1997a: 262). Both sonnets are concerned with the skill of the poet-speaker and the subject-matter of his verse, and share four key words (*invention*, *sweet*, *write*, *argument*).

1 *barren* The poet-speaker called his verses 'barren' at 16.4; here, they are 'deficient', but only of a quality ('pride') that can be viewed negatively.

new novel; whilst the poet-speaker seems to denigrate his verses, novelty is not necessarily to be admired and can be suggestive of superficiality; see Thomas Wyatt's 'Each man me telleth, I change must my device' (*Tottel* [46]) and 'They flee from me' (*Tottel* [52]), where the former lover grants herself 'leave' to use newfangledness' (ll. 18–19).

pride splendour (*n*.1, OED³ 6a); ostentatious adornment (OED³ 6c, citing this example); compare 103.2.

2 *So far from* so lacking in.

variation variety (e.g. of style, syntax, verse forms, vocabulary); unlike *Shakespeare's Sonnets*, many contemporaneous collections or sequences of sonnets display a great variety of rhyme schemes (see, for example, Sidney, *Astrophil and Stella*; Mary Wroth, *Pamphilia to Amphilanthus*, printed in *Urania* in 1621). Variety – for example of syntax or vocabulary – was also seen as a marker of an accomplished written style; to enable the desired variety, in 1512 Desiderius Erasmus supplied the schoolboys of St Paul's with the textbook *De copia rerum ac verborum* [*Copiousness of Words and Things*] which, amongst other things, taught pupils how to say 'thank you for your letter' in Latin in over 140 different ways and became a staple classroom text-book in schools across England.

quick change lively alteration; see Puttenham, *Art of English Poesy*, which recommends 'giving [sentences] ornament or efficacy by many manner of alterations in shape, in sound, and also in sense, sometime by way of surplusage, sometime by defect, sometime by disorder [. . .] in this or that sort tuning or tempering them, by amplification, abridgement, opening, closing, enforcing, meekening, or otherwise disposing them to the best purpose' (1589: 133). As Kerrigan (1986: 269) notes, 'or quick change' also glosses 'variation' and resembles the way in which Puttenham Englishes rhetorical terms (such as '*hyperbole* or the over-reacher', '*ironia* or the dry mock').

3 *with the time* following the fashion of the times.

glance aside change direction sharply; 'glance' implies rapid movement, and hence critiques the fickleness of those who follow ever-changing fashion.

4 *methods* 'way[s] of doing [some]thing, esp. according to a defined and regular plan' (OED³ 2a); Shakespeare lived in an age which was systematising poetic composition; vernacular treatises on the recommended method of writing verse had been printed from 1575 onwards (the first being George Gascoigne's 'Certain notes of instruction concerning the making of verse or rhyme in English', printed in his *Posies*). The largest, and probably most influential of these, Puttenham's *Art of English Poesy*, describes poetry as 'now an Art', whereas previously it 'were none, until by studious persons [it was] fashioned and reduced into a method of rules and precepts' (1589: 3). Sidney critiques those who try to write poetry by the book in *Astrophil and Stella* 15, where he denigrates 'You that do dictionary's method bring | Into your rhymes, running in rattling rows' (ll. 5–6). 'Method' was also originally a medical term (OED³ 1a), indicating 'a recommended or prescribed medical treatment for a specific disease', which resonates with the chemical meaning of 'compounds'. This sense is secondary, but demonstrates the verbal variety and dexterity of the poet-speaker, despite his demurring.

compounds strange newly coined compound words; Shakespeare was himself keen on coining new compounds; two appear in Sonnet 82, for example (82.8, 82.12), a poem which – like this one – compares the poet-speaker's literary style with the 'strained', artificial 'touches' of other poets (82.10).

76

Why is my verse so barren of new pride,
So far from variation or quick change?
Why with the time do I not glance aside
To new-found methods and to compounds strange?   4
Why write I still all one, ever the same,
And keep invention in a noted weed,
That every word doth almost sell my name,
Showing their birth and where they did proceed?   8
O know, sweet love, I always write of you,
And you and love are still my argument;
So all my best is dressing old words new,
Spending again what is already spent: 12
    For as the sun is daily new and old,
    So is my love still telling what is told.

5 **all one** always the same; appropriately pleonastic with 'ever the same'.
6 **invention** See 38.8n.
  noted notorious, recognisable.
  weed apparel; clothing was often used as a metaphor for verbal or literary style; see, for example, l. 11 below ('dressing') and Wyatt's *Defence* (1541): 'Because I am wont sometime to rap out an oath in an earnest talk, look how craftily they have put in an oath to [...] make the matter seem mine; and because they have guarded [ornamented] a naughty garment of theirs with one of my naughty guards [trimmings] they will swear and face me down that that was my garment' (Muir 1963: 199).
7 **That** so that.
  sell Q's 'fel' invites correction; Capell's conjecture, 'tell', is followed by Malone and most subsequent editors. However, it seems more likely that a compositor would have misread a long 's' as 'f' than as a secretary 't' (which – unlike a secretary 'f' – does not descend below the line): mistaking 's' for 'f' is one of the commonest copying mistakes when reading secretary hand. 'Sell' can mean 'betray' (OED 2a; Schmidt, 1), which would make sense here; see, for example, *Lucrece*, l. 385; *Coriolanus*, 5.6.46–7 ('He sold the blood and labour | Of our great action'). As Duncan-Jones notes (1997a: 262), in his prefatory poem to the first Folio of Shakespeare's plays, Ben Jonson stresses the distinctive character

of Shakespeare's verse: 'Look how the father's face | Lives in his issue, even so, the race | Of Shakespeare's mind and manners brightly shines | In his well-turned and true-filed lines' (sig. A4v), i.e. Here, thanks to his recognisable style, every word betrays ('sell[s]') their author.
8 **birth** parentage; for the use of birthing imagery to describe the creative process, see 32.11n.
  where from where.
9 **of** (i) about; (ii) derived from; in both cases, the friend is the poet-speaker's Muse, but (ii) makes the poet more dependent on his subject.
10 **argument** subject matter.
11 **all my best** (i) the best that I can do; (ii) all my best work.
  dressing arranging; the choice of word also continues the metaphor of literary style as clothing (see note on l. 6, above).
12 **spent** (i) paid (a *polyptoton* with 'spending'); (ii) worn out, exhausted (a form of *antanaclasis*, also with 'spending'); the rhetorical flourish proves that the poet-speaker is far from lacking 'variation or quick change' (l. 2); compare the use of rhetorical figures in Sonnet 43.
13–14 **For. . . told** The poet-speaker sets up a simile that, on close examination, does not hold true: the sun will always appear fresh in the morning; whether his poetry does is in the eye of the beholder.
14 **telling** (i) relating; (ii) counting (picking up on 'spending' in l. 12).

77

Benson combines Sonnets 73 and 77 under the title 'Sunset'.

1 **glass** mirror; Shakespeare makes recurrent use of the figure of the glass or mirror in the first 126 sonnets; see 3.1n.

  wear Q has 'were', a feasible variant of 'wear', which is how most editors (as here) modernise it. (The argument used by some that 'wear' is necessary for the rhyme does not hold, as 'were' and 'bear' can rhyme in Elizabethan pronunciation as they do at 13.6, 8; see Appendix 7). The original spelling and punctuation thus allow a dual resonance, lost when modernised: the glass shows the friend how his youthful charms are 'wearing out', but also reminds him of what they once 'were'.

2 **Thy dial** 'Shady stealth' in l. 7 hints at a sundial, but here 'thy' suggests a more personal timepiece. Shakespeare uses 'dial' for both: in *As You Like It*, 2.7.20, Touchstone 'drew a dial from his poke'; in *3 Henry VI*, 2.5.24 'To carve out dials quaintly' indicates a more monumental stone sundial. 'Dial' is also used – like 'mirror' – as a title for didactic works (see 3.1n). The inconsistency and imprecision about what kind of time-keeping instrument is intended does not impede the key message of this sonnet: namely, that a visible record of time passing should act as a memento mori for the friend. Kerrigan (1986: 271) notes how ll. 1–2 are linked metaphorically by the way in which the friend is invited to learn a lesson from both the face he sees in the mirror and the face ('dial') of the timepiece. 'Dial' is here two syllables (as it is at l. 7).

  minutes Q's spelling, 'mynuits', is unusual; there may be a possible play on the French 'minuits' (midnights), implying that the friend has employed his time unprofitably, staying up late, an activity that habitually comes in for moral censure; see 61.13 and note. However, 'mynuit' – although unusual – is the regular spelling employed by Q (at Q14.5, Q126.8 and, at Q60.2, 'minuites'); besides *Shakespeare's Sonnets*, just one other example of *mynuit/mynuits* shows up in EEBO-TCP for the years up to and including 1609: Thomas Kyd's *First Part of Jeronimo* (printed [by William Jaggard] for Thomas Pavyer, 1605); there are a further three instances of *minuit/minuits* (all other occurrences are in either French or Latin). Of these, one – George Chapman's continuation of Marlowe's *Hero and Leander* – has a possible play on 'midnight': 'had that kind minuit lasted' (1598: sig. N2v).

waste pass away (OED 14), but with the possibility of negative connotations of frittering away the time profitlessly; see 30.4 and note, and compare *Richard II*, 5.5.49: 'I wasted time, and now doth time waste me'.

3 **vacant leaves** blank pages; the sonnet is usually read as accompanying the gift of a blank notebook; compare Sonnet 122, where the poet-speaker apologises for having lost, or given away, a manuscript book given him by the friend.

4 **of** from.

  this book Up to this point in Q's sequence, 'this' has recurrently been used to indicate the poet-speaker's own verse (18.14; 26.3; 35.5; 55.2, 14; 71.5, 9; 74.3, 5). As the sonnet progresses, however, the meaning of 'this book' becomes more clearly the blank notebook in which the friend is encouraged to write. The two senses do not necessarily conflict if the sonnet is imagined as being written on the first leaf of the otherwise blank notebook.

  this learning this lesson; the lesson imparted is either that stated in ll. 5–8 (that time will take its toll on the young friend), or – if 'this book' also refers to this sonnet (see note above) – it comprises the rest of the sonnet in its entirety.

  mayst thou taste: The modal auxiliary 'may' in early modern English could be used to indicate (i) the ability (power) to do something; (ii) permission to do something; or (iii) possibility; see Adamson et al. 2001: 218–23. Here, meaning (i) might be dominant: the friend can experience or put to the test ('taste') the lesson the poem is about to impart; however, the confidence of that message is undermined by meaning (iii), which introduces a note of hesitancy: perhaps he may learn; perhaps he may not. The verb 'taste' increases the potential for doubt: the friend is not imagined drinking deeply from learning's well, but merely sampling (tasting) it. Q has a full-stop after 'taste'; this edition follows most modern editors in putting a colon, to highlight the way in which 'this learning' anticipates the lessons imparted in the ensuing lines.

6 **mouthèd** gaping (OED[3] 2, citing this as the first instance); the comparison of mouths to graves was an established one, used elsewhere by Shakespeare. See, for example, *Henry V*, 1.2.230–2: 'Either our history shall with full mouth | Speak freely of our acts, or else our grave, | Like Turkish mute, shall have a tongueless mouth'. See also 'swallowing grave', *Venus and Adonis*, l. 757 and note.

  give thee memory remind you.

77

Thy glass will show thee how thy beauties wear,
Thy dial how thy precious minutes waste,
The vacant leaves thy mind's imprint will bear,
And of this book, this learning mayst thou taste: 4
The wrinkles which thy glass will truly show,
Of mouthèd graves will give thee memory;
Thou by thy dial's shady stealth mayst know
Time's thievish progress to eternity.   8
Look what thy memory cannot contain,
Commit to these waste blanks, and thou shalt find
Those children nursed, delivered from thy brain,
To take a new acquaintance of thy mind.   12
        These offices, so oft as thou wilt look,
        Shall profit thee and much enrich thy book.

7 **shady stealth** slow-moving shadow. The phrase also anticipates 'Time's thievish progress' (l. 8), a play on the double meaning of 'steal' that is active at 63.8; 92.1; and 104.9–10. For the slowness of the dial hand on an individual timepiece, see 60.2n, 104.9–10n, and *Lucrece*, 297n.
mayst See note on 'mayst thou taste', l. 4, above.

8 **Time's. . . eternity** Compare *All's Well*, 2.1.165–6 ('four and twenty times the pilot's glass | Hath told the thievish minutes how they pass') and *Lucrece*, l. 967.

9 **Look what** whatever (compare 9.9); it is also possible read 'Look' as an imperative ('ensure that') and 'what' as a relative linking to the next clause.

10 **Commit to** write down in; it was standard practice in the early modern period for educated people to keep commonplace books in which they would note, or copy down, useful sentences ('sententiae'); see *Hamlet*, 1.5.107–8: 'My tables [i.e. notebook] — meet it is I set it down | That one may smile, and smile, and be a villain'.
waste blanks empty sheets; 'Q' has 'blacks', which could be easily mistaken for 'blanks', particularly if the 'n' was supplied in the manuscript by a tilde over the 'a' (i.e. blãcks). The compositor of *Hamlet* Q2 makes a similar mistake at 2.2.325, putting 'black verse' (sig. F2r) where F1 and Q1 have 'blanke verse'; see also 46.9n and 67.6n. 'Blancks' was an acceptable early modern variant of 'blanks'; compare the spellings 'banck' and 'thanck' in the additions made to the

manuscript of *Thomas More* by Hand D, possibly Shakespeare's (BL MS Harley 7368, fols 8r, 8v).

11 **Those children. . . brain** The idea of composition as giving birth was commonplace; see 32.11n.

12 **To take. . . mind** Reading his own words, the friend will become acquainted with himself in a new way; the writings are thus reflections of himself, as children are in Sonnets 1–17.

13 **These offices** these duties (OED³ 3a), referring to the threefold contemplation that the poet-speaker has recommended, namely looking at a mirror, a timepiece, and the friend's own writings. The liturgical sense of 'office' (an authorised form of divine service, OED 1) is also pertinent, as the friend is being instructed to go through a series of defined and regular processes, attending to the mirror, timepiece and notebook.
so oft as often.

14 **Shall profit. . . book** 'Profit' (as in moral or intellectual improvement) was a much-stated aim of reading in this period, and sixteenth- and early seventeenth-century title-pages conventionally promise their contents to be 'both pleasant and profitable' or (for dryer, more moralistic works) simply as 'very profitable to read'. The friend is thus to benefit from reading his own words, whilst the notebook will also become more useful ('profitable') as he fills its pages. If the 'book' includes the poet-speaker's sonnets, then there is also a sense in which the friend's writing will enhance the value of the poet-speaker's poems too (either by annotation, or by juxtaposing them with his own thoughts).

78

Benson combines Sonnets 78–79 under the title 'Retaliation'.

This is the first in a sequence (78–80, 82–86) often referred to as the 'rival poet(s) sonnets'. Much critical ink has been spent debating the identity of the rival poet or poets (see headnote to Sonnet 79); over the course of these sonnets, however, the poet-speaker slides between depicting one rival and (as in this sonnet) multiple competitors, perhaps indicating that the figure of the rival functions more as a device than an allusion to a particular individual or individuals. Elizabethan sonneteers often set themselves in competition with other poets; this is usually done by critiquing those literary competitors, not – as here – denigrating one's own poetic powers. See, for example, Sidney's scorn for lesser poets in *Astrophil and Stella* 15 ('You that do search for every purling spring') or Daniel's *Delia* 46.1–2, which distinguishes itself from the poetry of 'others' who 'sing of knights and palladines | In aged accents, and untimely words'.

1 *Muse* source of poetic inspiration; for Shakespeare's use of the word in the *Sonnets*, see 21.1n.

2 *fair* favourable, benign (OED³ AII); liberal (OED³ 5); 'fair' also reminds us of the friend's (blonde) beauty which inspires the poet-speaker.
   assistance In a poem about patronage, the help alluded to could encompass material benefit; 'fair assistance' could thus mean 'liberal reward' (see above), as well as poetic inspiration.
   in my verse in composing my verse.

3 *As* that.
   alien belonging to another (OED³ A1a); Q italicises 'alien', indicating that it is viewed (by poet, copyist or compositor) as a rare word. Although the word was in use from the mid-fourteenth century, a keyword search of EEBO-TCP indicates that between 1563 and 1609 the adjectival use of 'alien' was uncommon, the dominant usages being the noun 'alien' – to indicate 'foreigner', as distinct from 'denizen' (a naturalised foreigner) and native 'subject' – and the verb 'alien' (i.e. alienate). This is the only example of Shakespeare using the word as an adjective.
   hath got my use has adopted my practice (i.e. of addressing works to you).

3, 7, 11 *pen. . . feathers. . . style* Booth (1977: 269–70) draws attention to the relationship between these three words: 'pen' derives from the Latin *penna* (feather); 'style' from the Latin *stilus* (a writing implement); feather quills were the standard writing implement in this period.

4 *under thee* (i) under your name; (ii) under your protection and patronage; (iii) in your service; more than one meaning can be present.
   disperse 'distribute, put into circulation' (OED 4b); this could indicate both print and manuscript publication.

5 *on high* (i) in the heavens (compare 29.12); (ii) loudly.

5–6 *the dumb. . . ignorance* anticipates the poet-speaker's description of his 'rude ignorance' (l. 14); he thus aligns himself (with excessive modesty) with the ignorant and ineloquent; in contrast, his new rivals ('every alien pen') are, by implication, 'the learnèd' (l. 7) and those who have 'grace' (l. 8).

7 *added feathers* refers to the practice of 'imping' in falconry, where feathers are attached to a bird's wing to replace broken ones. Borrowed, or pilfered, plumage was often used as a metaphor for plagiarism; Ralph Brooke accused William Camden of having 'feathered [his] nest' with 'plumes' pilfered from the Henrician antiquary John Leland (*Discovery of Certain Errors*, 1599: sig. L4r), and Shakespeare was described in *Greene's Groatsworth of Wit* as 'an upstart crow, beautified with our feathers' (1592: sig. F1v).
   learnèd's Q's 'learneds' could potentially be modernised as 'learned'st'; see 51.10n. However, there are no comparable examples of this superlative in EEBO-TCP.

8 *given. . . majesty* This is the last of four examples which demonstrate the transformative (and improving) power of the poet-speaker's Muse and addressee: inspired by the friend, (i) the dumb learn to sing (l. 5); (ii) the ignorant rise (l. 6); (iii) the learned soar even higher than before (l. 7); and (iv) in this line, charm ('grace') becomes even more magnificent, acquiring a 'double majesty'. For the inspirational power of the friend (able to make the dumb eloquent), see 38.7–8.

78

So oft have I invoked thee for my Muse
And found such fair assistance in my verse
As every alien pen hath got my use
And under thee their poesy disperse.   4
Thine eyes, that taught the dumb on high to sing
And heavy ignorance aloft to fly,
Have added feathers to the learnèd's wing
And given grace a double majesty.   8
Yet be most proud of that which I compile,
Whose influence is thine and born of thee;
In others' works thou dost but mend the style,
And arts with thy sweet graces gracèd be;   12
    But thou art all my art and dost advance
    As high as learning my rude ignorance.

9 *compile* compose original work (OED 3), but the choice of word may be chosen by the poet-speaker to downplay his own originality and poetic skill; the primary and oldest senses of the word emphasise synthesis, rather than invention, indicating 'to collect and put together' (OED 1) and 'to make, compose or construct (a written or printed work) by arrangement of material collected from various sources' (OED 2a). The Latin *compilare* (from which the word probably derives, via French) means 'to plunder'. Shakespeare only uses the word in two other places: 85.2 (another of the rival poet(s) group) and (three times) in *Love's Labours Lost*, a play which often features, and mocks, derivative and hackneyed compositions, where it appears at 4.3.131–2 ('Longaville | Did never sonnet for her sake compile'); 5.2.52 (where Katherine calls Dumaine's verses 'vildly compiled'); and 5.2.886–7 (which announces that Holofernes, the pedant, and the schoolmaster Sir Nathaniel, have 'compiled' a dialogue 'in praise of the owl and the cuckoo' to end the show).

10 *influence* 'the inflowing, immission [insertion], or infusion (into a person or thing) of any kind of divine, spiritual, moral, immaterial, or secret power or principle; that which thus flows in or is infused' (OED 3);

the usage is also suggestive of the influence of the stars over human affairs (OED 2c), so that the friend is figured like a heavenly body; see 15.4n.

born of thee a twist on the conventional depiction of the creative process as giving birth (see 32.11n); here the poet-speaker's compositions are depicted as the offspring of his Muse, not of himself. Q's spelling 'borne' may also suggest 'carried'.

11 *but* only.
mend improve; compare 69.2, 103.9.

12 *arts* literary or rhetorical skills.
gracèd adorned, embellished ('grace, *v.*', OED³ 3a); *polyptoton* with 'graces'.

13 *thou . . . art* 'you provide my entire skill'; the use of *antanaclasis* indicates that the poet-speaker is far from artless.
advance 'raise or promote (a person) in rank or office' (OED³ 10a).

14 *learning* 'knowledge [. . .] acquired by systematic study; also, the possession of such knowledge, learnedness' (OED 3a).
rude ignorance pleonastic, for emphasis; literally meaning 'unlearned lack of knowledge' ('rude', OED³ A3; 'ignorance', OED 1a); 'rude' also contains a sense of social inferiority; see the 'rude mechanicals' ('a crew of patches [. . .] | That work for bread upon Athenian stalls') in *Midsummer Night's Dream* (3.2.9–10).

79

Benson combines Sonnets 78–79 under the title 'Retaliation'. This is the second of the 'rival poet(s)' grouping (78–80, 82–86; see headnote to Sonnet 78). However, whilst Sonnet 78 suggested plural poets, this sonnet evokes a single rival, who intrudes into the poem from the end of the first quatrain, variously described as 'another' (l. 4), 'a worthier pen' (l. 6), 'thy poet' (l. 7), and through the pronouns 'he' and 'him' (ll. 8–11, 13–14). Christopher Marlowe, Ben Jonson, Edmund Spenser and George Chapman have all been put forward as candidates for this rival poet; Rollins summarises the arguments for these, and other, writers (1944: 2.277–94).

1   *Whilst I alone* This contrasts with the present time, now 'every alien pen hath got my use' (78.3).
      call upon Compare 'invoked' (78.1); there is a similar play on 'invocate' and 'call upon' in 38.10–11, another sonnet in which the poet-speaker reflects on his relationship with his Muse.
      aid Poets regularly call upon the aid of their Muse in such poetic invocations (a convention of epic poetry in particular), but in the context of a series of sonnets about patronage, the word holds a strong sense of material or financial aid.
2   *My verse. . . gentle grace* (i) when my poetry enjoyed your exclusive patronage ('grace' here used in the sense of 'favourable regard'; OED³ 2b); (ii) when only my poetry treated of your charms ('grace', OED³ 14a). 'Gentle' has a number of resonances here, including 'well-born' (OED A1a(a)) and 'generous' (OED A3a), as well as 'courteous' (OED A3c) and 'kind' (OED A8).
3   *gracious numbers* 'Gracious' can mean (i) enjoying favour (OED³ A1c); (ii) elegant, graceful (OED³ A1a); and (iii) having the 'pleasing qualities' that are 'likely to find grace or favour' (OED³ A1b); in senses (ii) and (iii), the poet-speaker's verses ('numbers') have acquired key characteristics of their subject (for the association of the friend with grace, see 10.11n); this transference helps prepare the ground for ll. 7–11, where the rival poet 'robs' qualities from the patron he describes.
      decayed deteriorated ('decay, *v.*', OED 1a); preceding sonnets in Q's sequence have recurrently associated 'decay' with the ruinous effects of time (see 11.6, 13.9, 15.11, 64.10, 71.12). In a poem which expresses anxiety about waning

patronage, the sense of 'decay' as 'decline from prosperity or favour' (OED 1b) is also relevant.
4   *Muse* creative faculty; for Shakespeare's use of the word in the *Sonnets*, see 21.1n.
      doth. . . place 'allows someone else supremacy'; position in a procession was dependent on status and was often fiercely contested; in 1591, for example, Lady Frances Cooke complained to William Cecil that Lady Cheke 'taketh great advantage. For she doth not only offer me all the wrong and disgrace she can in court, in taking place afore me [. . .], but she openly publisheth to everybody, that I have no place at all' (Strype 1705: 135). Place is here given to 'another', indicating that the multiple rivals of Sonnet 78 have here been narrowed down to one particular competitor (see headnote).
5   *thy lovely argument* the lovely subject matter ('argument') of you, who are lovely; see 38.3.
6   *travail* labour or toil (*n*.1, OED 1), 'the outcome, product, or result of toil or labour [. . .] esp. a literary work' (OED 3).
      a worthier pen reminiscent of the poet-speaker's expression of his inadequacy in Sonnet 32; 'worthier' is two syllables. 'Worth' and its derivatives are recurrent words in *Sonnets* (see 2.4n); 'worthier' here marks the start in Q's sequence of a particularly dense cluster (80.5, 11; 82.6; 83.8, twice; 87.3, 9).
7   *thy poet* the rival poet.
      invent The word here plays on its primary meaning, 'discover' (OED 1), and its literary sense of 'compose' (OED 2b); the rival poet finds out the friend's qualities: he does not need to 'fabricate' them (OED 2c). For 'invention' as one of the parts of rhetoric, see 38.8n.
7, 8 *of thee. . . thee of* The reversal of the phrase in the same foot in adjoining lines mirrors the reciprocity of this action, as what the rival poet writes about ('of') the friend is actually stolen from ('of') him.
8   *pays. . . again* The rival poet merely pays back (in praise) what he has taken (in inspiration); the idea is repeated in l. 14.
9   *lends* grants (OED 2a), but – in close proximity to words like 'robs' (l. 8), 'pay(s)' (ll. 8, 14), 'stole' (l. 9), 'afford' (l. 11) and 'owes' (l. 14) – there is a strong play on the financial sense of the word.
10   *behaviour* 'good manners, elegant deportment' (OED 1e), as well as 'manner of conducting oneself in the external relations of life; demeanour, deportment, bearing, manners' (OED 1a).

79

Whilst I alone did call upon thy aid
My verse alone had all thy gentle grace,
But now my gracious numbers are decayed,
And my sick Muse doth give another place.   4
I grant (sweet love) thy lovely argument
Deserves the travail of a worthier pen,
Yet what of thee thy poet doth invent,
He robs thee of and pays it thee again;   8
He lends thee virtue and he stole that word
From thy behaviour; beauty doth he give
And found it in thy cheek; he can afford
No praise to thee but what in thee doth live.   12
    Then thank him not for that which he doth say,
    Since what he owes thee, thou thyself dost pay.

---

11 *cheek* face (by *synecdoche*).
afford supply (OED³ 3b); however, 'afford' also casts the ability, or gratitude, of the rival poet in a negative light: it is what he can 'manage to give' or 'spare' (OED³ 5). See l. 9n, for the financial imagery at play in this latter part of the sonnet.

14 *owes* is obliged to pay.
thyself As is standard in Q, 'thy self' is printed as two separate words, potentially activating a reading which highlights the way in which the friend pays his self ('thy self') to himself ('thyself'). See note on modernising the *-self* suffix, p. xiv.

80

Benson combines Sonnets 80–81 under the title 'Lovesick'.

This is the third sonnet in the 'rival poet(s)' grouping (78–80, 82–86). As Booth notes, the sonnet includes a number of words 'used elsewhere in sexual senses' (e.g. 'use', 2.9n; 'spends', 4.1–2n; 'will', 135 passim; 'pride', 151.10n; 'ride', 137.6n); 'none of them is fully activated here, but their concentration gives the poem vague sexual overtones' (1977: 273).

1 *faint* 'lose heart or courage' (OED 1), 'grow weak' (OED 2a); a homophonic pun on 'feint' (deceive) is possible.
2 *a better spirit* a superior, or at least more assertive, writer; particularly in relation to the feebleness of 'faint' (l. 1), 'spirit' implies someone with 'mettle; vigour of mind; ardour; courage; disposition or readiness to assert oneself or to hold one's own' (OED 13a); compare 85.7, 86.5. Following on from 79.4, the rival is here clearly identified as a single poet. 'Spirit' is monosyllabic; see 56.8n.
use your name The allusion to patronage – addressing works to a patron, or issuing them under their name and protection – is dominant here, but the meaning of 'use' as 'consume, expend' (OED³ 12) is also resonant, particularly following on from the pecuniary imagery of 79.8–14.
3 *spends* expends, employs (*v*.1, OED 3), utters (OED 9a), but it could also imply 'exhaust' (OED 5a) or 'waste' (OED 10a).
might poetic powers.
4 *To make me* This could indicate intention on the part of the 'better spirit' (that he intends to silence his competitor) or simply the debilitating effect of this rivalry on the poet-speaker.
tongue-tied Compare 85.1.
fame honour, reputation.
5 *worth* merit (*n*.1, OED 3a), but the financial sense (of price, OED 1a) is also pertinent (see note on 'use', l. 2, above).
(wide as the ocean is) Duncan-Jones (1997a: 270) highlights the use of images of the sea to indicate the munificence proper to royalty and aristocrats, citing *Lucrece* (see ll. 652–3), and Daniel's *Delia* 1.1: 'Unto the boundless ocean of thy beauty'. A bawdy twist on this laudatory language is provided by 135.9–10.

6–13 *The humble. . . cast away* For other instances of Shakespeare's use of extended nautical metaphors to express social hierarchies, see *Merchant of Venice*, 1.1.8–14 (where 'rich burghers on the flood' 'Do overpeer the petty traffickers') and *Troilus and Cressida*, 1.3.34–45, which contrasts 'shallow bauble boats' with 'those of nobler bulk' (see also note on l. 7, below).
6 *humble* 'Humble' acquires the force of a superlative (humblest) through the way in which it is balanced with 'proudest'; for other examples of this type of construction, see Abbott 1884: § 398.
proudest the most magnificent or splendid ('proud', OED³ 5b), but also with a strongly negative sense of most haughty or arrogant (OED³ 1a); compare 'goodly pride' (l. 12) and 86.1.
sail ship, by *synecdoche*.
7 *saucy* 'applied to a ship or boat [. . .] presumptuous, rashly-venturing' (OED 2d, citing this line as the first example); compare *Troilus and Cressida*, 1.3.42–5: 'Where's then the saucy boat | Whose weak untimbered sides but even now | Corrivalled greatness? Either to harbour fled, | Or made a toast for Neptune'.
bark small boat.
inferior pronounced as three syllables.
8 *main* open sea (*n*.1, OED³ 5a); compare 64.7.
wilfully gladly (OED 1a); voluntarily (OED 2a); with desire, longingly (OED 3); perversely, obstinately (OED 5); there is also a possible play on 'Will' (as in Sonnet 135).
9 *shallowest help* slightest aid; unlike Nestor's description of the storm in *Troilus and Cressida*, 1.3 (see note on l. 7, above), the 'saucy bark' here has an advantage over the larger vessel: as the smaller boat needs less water to float, it can be sustained by even the 'shallowest help' that the patron affords; 'shallowest' is here slurred into two syllables.
10 *soundless deep* unfathomable waters out in the open sea (contrasting with the shallows of l. 9).
11 *wrecked* 'wrackt' in Q, a variant form of wrecked (see 'wrack, *v*.2', OED).
worthless Wrecked (and out of favour), the 'saucy bark' is no longer supported by the friend's excellence (the 'worth' in ll. 5–6 that bore afloat both proud and humble ships); he consequently lacks worth and is 'worthless'.
12 *tall* handsome (OED A2b); also used specifically of ships to mean 'high, lofty' (OED A7a).

80

O how I faint when I of you do write,
Knowing a better spirit doth use your name,
And in the praise thereof spends all his might
To make me tongue-tied speaking of your fame.   4
But since your worth (wide as the ocean is)
The humble as the proudest sail doth bear,
My saucy bark (inferior far to his)
On your broad main doth wilfully appear.   8
Your shallowest help will hold me up afloat,
Whilst he upon your soundless deep doth ride,
Or (being wrecked) I am a worthless boat,
He of tall building and of goodly pride.   12
    Then if he thrive and I be cast away,
    The worst was this: my love was my decay.

building frame (Schmidt, 1); 'style of construction [...] (e.g. of a ship)' (OED 1b).
pride splendour (*n*.1, OED³ 6) and 'exalted position' (OED³ 7b), but more negatively, it also indicates 'inordinate self-esteem' (OED³ 1a) and 'arrogant [...] behaviour' (OED³ 2).
13 ***cast away*** rejected ('cast away', in 'cast, *v*.2', OED 2), but also continues the nautical metaphor ('to wreck (a ship)', OED 5); the sense of 'waste' (OED 4) is also relevant, and this is its dominant sense elsewhere in Shakespeare's works; see *King John*, 2.1.334 ('France, hast thou yet more blood to cast away?') and *Twelfth Night*, 1.5.172–3 ('I would be loath to cast away my speech'). *As You Like It*, a play with a strong economic undercurrent about the proper use of resources, uses the phrase four times (more than any of the other plays), three of which are in this sense: 'thy words are too precious to cast away upon curs' (1.3.4–5); 'I will not cast away my physic but on those that are sick' (3.2.358–9); 'to cast away honesty upon a foul slut were to put good meat into an unclean dish' (3.3.35–7). For the theological resonances of 'cast away', see *Lucrece*, 744n.
14 ***my love*** (i) my affection; (ii) my beloved.
decay ruin; see also 79.3 and note.

81

Benson combines Sonnets 80–81 under the title 'Lovesick'. This poem comes between the clusters of the 'rival poet(s)' sonnets (78–80, 82–86). It does not directly mention a literary rival, instead confidently announcing the power of poetry, although its assertion of the value of poetry means that it is not out of place in a mini-sequence which is so concerned with the dynamics of patronage. The faith that the sonnet expresses in the commemorative potential of poetry has much in common with Sonnet 18, the couplet of which has a strong resonances with ll. 9–14 of this sonnet; see also 15.14n.

1–2 *Or. . . Or* Whether. . . Or; see 'Or, *conj.*1', OED[3] 3b and *Merchant of Venice*, 3.2.63–4: 'Tell me where is fancy bred | Or in the heart or in the head?'

1 *make* write, compose (OED 4a); 'maker' was a term used for poet in this period; see the opening sentences of Puttenham's *Art of English Poesy*: 'A poet is as much to say as a maker. And our English name well conforms with the Greek word: for of *poeien* to make, they call a maker *Poeta*' (1589: 1). Many of the poems posthumously attributed to Shakespeare are epitaphs; see Appendix 6.

2 *rotten,* Until the later twentieth century, many editors replaced Q's comma with a semi-colon, rendering ll. 1–2 – as Ingram and Redpath note – 'a platitude of high banality' (1985: 186).

3 *From hence* from here, 'here' being this world, this sonnet, or both.

4 *in me each part* all my qualities and attributes; 'part' may also indicate 'role' (as in *As You Like It*, 2.7.142: 'one man in his time plays many parts').

5–6 *Your name. . . die* The irony is that Shakespeare's name survives, whilst that of the anonymous addressee has been the subject of centuries of conjecture.

5 *from hence* (i) from this time forth (shifting the meaning of 'from hence' in l. 3 from a spatial to a temporal sense); (ii) from this poem or sequence of sonnets.

7 *earth* ground, but also the world of man.
yield primarily, 'grant' (OED 10b), but the proximity to 'earth' brings out the agricultural sense ('produce, bear, generate', OED 8a), whereby the grave becomes a grim harvest.
but only.
common grave an undistinguished grave, possibly containing more than one body (like a pauper's grave, or the mass burials in times of plague) and probably unmarked, the lack of headstone contrasting with the way in which the addressee is imagined as lying '*entombèd in men's eyes*' (l. 8), evoking the image of an effigy recumbent on a tomb. Shakespeare himself was not buried in a 'common grave', but (by virtue of his position as holder of church tithes) inside the church of Holy Trinity, Stratford-upon-Avon, where an elaborate stone effigy was erected (this was in place before 1623).

8 *lie* The sonnet keeps offering seeming alternatives ('or. . . or') which transpire on closer examination to be far from symmetrical (see Burrow 2002: 542); here, readers might anticipate that 'die' (l. 6) will be balanced with some indication of life, but the rhyme 'lie' encapsulates how this sonnet confounds expectations: both poet-speaker and his subject are imagined as dead; it is just the nature of their subsequent commemoration that differs.

9 *monument* The type of monument shifts from the architectural edifice of l. 8 (where the addressee 'entombèd [. . .] shall lie') to a written memorial; 'monument' could indicate both kinds of memorial; see, for example, the recurrent use of the word in John Bale's edition of *The Laborious Journey of Johan Leland* (1549), where it is used 22 times in 128 pages as a synonym for 'book'.
gentle noble (OED A3a); kind (OED A8). The poet-speaker's verse has acquired a key characteristic of its subject matter; compare 79.3 and note.

10 *o'er-read* read over.

11 *tongues-to-be* the tongues of future generations, as yet unborn (parallel to 'eyes not yet created', l. 10).
being (i) existence; (ii) essence.
rehearse recite (OED[3] 4a); describe at length (OED[3] 1a); there is a possible pun on 'rehearse' as 're-inter, 're-bury'; see 'hearse, *v.*' OED 1c, and compare *Merchant of Venice*, 3.1.89–90: 'Would she were hearsed at my foot, and the ducats in her coffin!'.

12 *breathers* living people; a Shakespearean coinage (a claim made by OED and backed up by keyword searches on EEBO-TCP); Shakespeare also uses the word in this sense in *As You Like It*, 3.2.280–1 ('I will chide no breather in the world but myself') and *Antony and Cleopatra*, 3.3.20–1 ('She shows a body rather than a life, | A statue, than a breather'). A fourth instance, in

81

Or I shall live your epitaph to make,
Or you survive when I in earth am rotten,
From hence your memory death cannot take,
Although in me each part will be forgotten.   4
Your name from hence immortal life shall have,
Though I (once gone) to all the world must die;
The earth can yield me but a common grave,
When you entombèd in men's eyes shall lie: 8
Your monument shall be my gentle verse,
Which eyes not yet created shall o'er-read,
And tongues-to-be your being shall rehearse,
When all the breathers of this world are dead;   12
    You still shall live (such virtue hath my pen)
    Where breath most breathes, even in the mouths of men.

Measure for Measure, 4.4.26–8, indicates 'speaker' ('my authority bears of a credent bulk, | That no particular scandal once can touch | But it confounds the breather'), a meaning which anticipates the couplet of this sonnet.

this world this present age.

dead; Q's comma allows l. 12 to be read with either l. 11 or l. 13; most editors disambiguate (as here) by inserting a semi-colon or full-stop. Booth is a rare example of editor who retains Q's unprescriptive punctuation, arguing that 'the syntax of lines 11–13 is [...] demonstrative of the almost supernatural "virtue" of the speaker's pen: the lines expand as they are read, so that each in effect speaks twice' (1977: 279). However, as Blakemore Evans points

out, 'the implied finely balanced intentionality on Shakespeare's part hangs on a very slender thread – the Q pointing, which is frequently uncertain, particularly in the indiscriminate use of commas' (1996: 188).

13 **virtue** power.

14 **Where. . . men** The friend will be spoken about by subsequent generations, and thus his memory will live on. Compare 18.13–14. The orality of the act of commemoration imagined here provides a secular alternative to the annual obits outlawed, with varying degrees of success, by the Elizabethan Church (see Heal 2003: 456).

breath (i) breath of life; (ii) speech.

even pronounced as one syllable.

82

Benson combines Sonnets 82–85 under the title 'In praise of his love'. This is the fourth sonnet in the 'rival poet(s)' grouping (78–80, 82–86).

1 *grant* concede.
   married irrevocably tied, as if married, which – according to the marriage ceremony in the *Book of Common Prayer* – would require the friend to 'forsak[e] all other' (2011: 158).
   Muse creative faculty; for Shakespeare's use of the word in the *Sonnets*, see 21.1n.

2 *attaint* dishonour, or imputation of dishonour (OED 6); compare Daniel's *Complaint of Rosamond*, l. 26 ('Her legend justifies her foul attaint'); Shakespeare uses the word to indicate infection at *Venus and Adonis*, l. 741.
   o'erlook peruse, read through.

3 *dedicated words* (i) devoted words; (ii) writings dedicated to the friend; see 78.4n, 80.2n.

4 *Of* about.
   blessing Syntactically, the subject could either be (i) 'writers' (l. 3), who benefit ('bless') their books by addressing them to patrons through the dedication, or (ii) the 'fair subject' (l. 4), whose very presence as dedicatee exalts the book. To 'bless' is strongly connected with the idea of religious rites that will protect something, or someone, from evil agencies (see *v.*1, OED 1a, 2a); protection was repeatedly what dedicatees were called upon to provide for the books presented to them, and for the writers who presented them. 'Bless' also conveys a sense of reward: 'confer well-being upon; "to make happy; to prosper, make successful" (Johnson)' (OED 7a).

5 *as fair. . . hue* Your mind ('knowledge') is as beautiful and just ('fair') as you are blonde and beautiful ('fair') in appearance and complexion ('hue'); 'just' anticipates the legal sense of 'finding' (l. 6); for 'hue', see 20.7n.

6 *Finding* (i) discovering; (ii) the legal sense, of delivering a verdict (like a jury), is also pertinent ('find, *v.*', OED 17d); see 46.9n. The antecedent of 'Finding' is unclear, but from ll. 7–8 it would appear to be 'thou' rather than 'I'.
   limit region (OED³ 3a); compare 44.4: the friend's worth is envisaged as a territory, which lies beyond the reach of the poet-speaker's praise. Although not strictly logical, the phrase

also benefits from the primary sense of 'limit' as 'boundary' (OED³ 2a), whereby the friend's worth passes the bounds of the poet-speaker's ability to praise him.

7 *art enforced* 'thou art enforced'; the syntax of this sonnet is recurrently compacted, so that it becomes elliptical (compare the way in which the antecedents of 'blessing', l. 4, and 'finding', l. 6, are omitted).

8 *Some fresher stamp* some newer creation; 'stamp' is 'an instrument for making impressions' (*n.*3, OED 5a), 'esp. a die or the apparatus used in stamping a device upon a coin, token, medal or the like' (OED 5b). Shakespeare's use of 'stamp' and its derivatives often exploits metaphors of coining; see, for example, *Cymbeline*, 2.5.2–6: 'We are all bastards, | And that most venerable man which I | Did call my father, was I know not where | When I was stamped. Some coiner with his tools | Made me a counterfeit'. For the use of words as currency, see *Twelfth Night*, 3.2.22: 'some excellent jests, fire-new from the mint'.
   the time-bettering days Compare 32.5; 'time-bettering' (a Shakespearean coinage) could be seen as one of the 'compounds strange' that the poet-speaker presented as a marker of his more accomplished rivals in 76.4; see also 'true-telling', l. 12. 'Bettering' is here pronounced as two syllables.

9 *they have devised* The number of rivals has expanded again, from a single 'better spirit' in 80.2, to a plural 'they' (compare the plural 'others' imagined in Sonnet 78).

10 *strainèd touches* The phrase plays on words associated with music: 'strainèd' could indicate 'having a strain or melody' (OED 8); 'touches', the notes produced by touching a musical instrument (OED 8a). However, the compositions of these rival poets are also 'far-fetched, forced' ('strained', OED 5; citing this line as the first usage).
   lend bestow (*v.*2, OED 2a); however, the primary meaning of the verb – 'to grant the temporary possession of' (OED 1a) – is also resonant, further underlining the insubstantial nature of rhetoric's 'strainèd touches'.

11 *truly fair* Genuinely ('truly', OED 5a) lovely, the friend does not need artifice to beautify him.

82

I grant thou wert not married to my Muse,
And therefore mayst without attaint o'erlook
The dedicated words which writers use
Of their fair subject, blessing every book.   4
Thou art as fair in knowledge as in hue,
Finding thy worth a limit past my praise,
And therefore art enforced to seek anew
Some fresher stamp of the time-bettering days.   8
And do so, love; yet when they have devised
What strainèd touches rhetoric can lend,
Thou, truly fair, wert truly sympathised
In true plain words by thy true-telling friend,   12
   And their gross painting might be better used
   Where cheeks need blood; in thee it is abused.

truly sympathised accurately represented ('truly', OED 4a; 'sympathize, *v.*', OED 3b); compare *Lucrece*, l. 1113, and *Richard II*, 5.1.46–7: 'the senseless brands will sympathize | The heavy accent of thy moving tongue'.

11, 12 ***truly. . . truly. . . true*** Despite the poet-speaker's assertion (l. 12) that his words are 'plain' (i.e. eschewing rhetorical artifice and therefore implying honesty), there is considerable word-play at work in these lines: (i) *polyptoton* ('truly' and 'true'); (ii) *diacope* ('truly', 'truly'); (iii) the repetition of 'truly' also serves as a kind of *antanaclasis*, as 'truly' shifts from 'genuinely' (OED 5a) to 'accurately' (OED 4a).

12 ***true-telling*** Another Shakespearean coinage; see note on 'time-bettering', l. 8, above.

13 ***gross painting*** (i) a crude pictorial representation, lacking skill; (ii) cosmetics, laid on thickly; the image critiques the excessive rhetorical ornamentation used by the rival poets, which – it is implied – is not handled deftly. For the association of cosmetics and (a strained) rhetorical artifice, see Sonnet 21.

14 ***need*** lack.

83

Benson combines Sonnets 82–85 under the title 'In praise of his love'. This is the fifth sonnet in the 'rival poet(s)' grouping (78–80, 82–86).

1 *painting* (i) cosmetics; (ii) verbal ornamentation; continues argument from 82.13–14

2 *fair* a noun: beauty (both internal and external); see 16.11n.

3 *found* See 82.6n.
   exceed surpass; compare 82.6.

4 *barren* sterile, meagre, unprofitable; compare the poet-speaker's description of his 'rhymes' at 16.4.
   tender a legal term, indicating 'an offer of money, or the like, in discharge of a debt or liability' (*n*.2, OED 1b); Polonius exposes the fact that 'tenders' are not as substantial as actual payment in *Hamlet*, 1.3.105–7: 'think yourself a baby | That you have ta'en these tenders for true pay, | Which are not sterling'.
   debt obligation, duty (continuing the financial imagery).

5 *have. . . report* 'I have been inactive and/or remiss ['sleep, *v*.', OED 4a, 5] in praising you.'

6 *being* pronounced as one syllable.
   extant (i) existing (i.e. being alive); (ii) 'continuing to exist', having 'escaped the ravages of time' (OED 4b); (iii) prominent (OED 2).

7 *modern* (i) current day (OED³ 3a); (ii) everyday, ordinary, commonplace (OED³ 4); both meanings co-exist: what is from the present day is also commonplace or trite; compare

Shakespeare's recurrent use of the word in this sense in, for example, *King John*, 3.4.39–42, where Constance contrasts 'a modern invocation' with 'a passion' which would 'shake the world', or *All's Well*, 2.3.1–4: 'we have our philosophical persons, to make modern and familiar, things supernatural and causeless. Hence it is that we make trifles of terrors'.

9 *This silence* i.e. when the poet-speaker 'slept in your report' (l. 5).
   impute ascribe.

10 *glory* 'something that brings honour and renown; a subject for boasting' (OED 3); the poet-speaker is akin to Cordelia in *King Lear*, 1.1, whose muteness is truer than the eloquent flattery of her sisters.

10, 11 *being dumb. . . being mute* These clauses qualify 'I' (not glory or beauty).

12 *others. . . tomb* 'Other writers attempt to immortalise you, but they merely succeed in creating an ostentatious but lifeless monument'; compare 17.1–4, and contrast the living memorial promised in 81.9–14.

14 *both your poets* It is possible that this indicates the poet-speaker and the rival poet of Sonnet 80; however, l. 12 refers to plural rivals ('others') and 'both' can govern more than two objects in early modern English: see OED B1b; *Venus and Adonis*, l. 747; *1 Henry VI*, 5.5.107–8: 'Margaret shall now be Queen, and rule the King; | But I will rule both her, the King, and realm'.

83

I never saw that you did painting need,
And therefore to your fair no painting set;
I found (or thought I found) you did exceed
The barren tender of a poet's debt: 4
And therefore have I slept in your report,
That you yourself, being extant, well might show
How far a modern quill doth come too short,
Speaking of worth, what worth in you doth grow.   8
This silence for my sin you did impute,
Which shall be most my glory, being dumb,
For I impair not beauty, being mute,
When others would give life and bring a tomb.   12
    There lives more life in one of your fair eyes
    Than both your poets can in praise devise.

84

Benson combines Sonnets 82–85 under the title 'In praise of his love'. This is the sixth sonnet in the 'rival poet(s)' grouping (78–80, 82–86).

1-2 **Who. . . praise** 'Who is there who lavishes praise upon you who can say better than this. . .' Malone inserts a question mark after 'most', so that 'Who is it that says most?' becomes a separate question. This emendation is not necessary, however (ll. 1–2 make sense without it), and such a strong break in the first line is unusual in Shakespeare's sonnets; see 74.1n.

2 **rich** splendid; compare 85.2.

you alone only you, but there may be a hint that you are yourself only when alone (i.e. when not in the company of other friends or poets).

you, Some editors (following Gildon 1710) insert a question mark after 'you', which makes ll. 3–4 a separate question; punctuated thus it could be the rival poets who hoard a precious 'store' (presumably of poetic invention). However, the punctuation adopted here better suits the context of the *Sonnets*, where the friend has (in Sonnets 1-17) shown a tendency to retain a monopolistic hold on his 'store' of perfection.

3 **confine** enclosed space (*n.*2, OED 5); stressed on the second syllable.

immurèd walled (from the Latin *im* + *murus*); in close proximity to the verb 'grew', the image is that of a walled garden, or the *hortus conclusus* of medieval poetry (a site symbolic of purity), as in the thirteenth-century *Roman de la Rose*.

store abundance (OED 4a); accumulated goods (OED 5a); compare 37.8.

4 **should example** should exemplify, furnish a model or pattern (OED 1).

equal like, peer.

grew The past tense is necessary to make the rhyme, but it also suggests that it is only in the past that anyone might have matched the friend.

5 **Lean. . . dwell** The line is thick with word-play: (i) 'Lean penury' hovers between *pleonasm* ('poor poverty', 'meagre dearth') and personification; (ii) 'penury' quibbles on 'pen', as well as contrasting with 'rich' (l. 2); (iii) whilst pen indicates 'writer' (by *metonymy*), it also (iv) puns with 'confine', as its conjunction with 'dwell' activates a secondary sense of 'pen' as enclosure.

6 **his** its (the pen's).

subject refers to ordinary, commonplace subject matter, from whom the friend is distinguished in l. 7 ('But. . .').

8 **so** (i) in this way; (ii) to such an extent.

dignifies ennobles (OED 1a).

9 **but. . . writ** Compare Sidney's *Astrophil and Stella*, 3.12–14: 'in Stella's face I read | What love and beauty be; then all my deed | But copying is, what in her Nature writes'.

10 **clear** (i) bright, lustrous (OED A4a); (ii) 'Of the complexion [. . .] bright, fresh, and of pure colour' (OED A4d); (iii) illustrious (OED A5); (iv) 'free from fault, guilt, or offence' (OED A15a).

11 **counterpart** copy (OED 2); the earliest citation for this sense in OED is 1676, but the word derives from a legal term (OED 1) for the matching part of an indenture: 'a deed between two or more parties [. . .] executed in two or more copies, all having their tops or edges correspondingly indented or serrated for identification and security' ('indenture', OED 1a). 'Counterpart' in this sense was also in figurative use before the first citation (1617) listed in OED; see I.S., 'Sonnet', in Francis Davison's *A Poetical Rhapsody*: 'if your heart be not the counterpart | Of my true heart's indented chaste desire' (1602: sig. L5r). In Shakespeare's usage here (and in later senses of the word) there is thus a slide from something matching another thing (and making a pair with it) to something replicating that other thing.

fame make famous (*v.* 1, OED 3).

wit talent, genius (OED 5a), but perhaps with particular attention to verbal dexterity ('quickness of intellect or liveliness of fancy, with capacity of apt expression', OED 7).

12 **style** potential quibble with 'pen' ('style' deriving from the Latin *stilus*, or writing implement); see l. 5n., above.

13 **beauteous** pronounced as two syllables; the word is strong associated with the friend; see 4.5n.

blessings (i) the attributes bestowed on the friend by nature (see OED 4a); (ii) the favours the friend bestows on others, in his role as patron (see OED 4b).

curse The stark contrast with 'blessings' indicates how far, and how suddenly, the final ten words of the sonnet depart from preceding lines,

84

Who is it that says most, which can say more
Than this rich praise: that you alone are you,
In whose confine immurèd is the store
Which should example where your equal grew?   4
Lean penury within that pen doth dwell
That to his subject lends not some small glory;
But he that writes of you, if he can tell
That you are you, so dignifies his story.   8
Let him but copy what in you is writ,
Not making worse what nature made so clear,
And such a counterpart shall fame his wit,
Making his style admirèd everywhere.   12
    You to your beauteous blessings add a curse,
    Being fond on praise, which makes your praises worse.

which have done nothing to prepare us for this change in direction.

14 ***Being fond on*** having strong liking for (OED A6a), with 'fond' implying foolish infatuation (OED A2); 'Being' is monosyllabic.

praise. . . worse It is unclear whether the friend is (i) too quick to praise others, or (ii) too eager to be praised. Either way, the amount of praise he either lavishes on others (sense i), or demands (sense ii), means that – viewed through the economic lens of supply and demand – the commendations given/received are cheapened. As Ingram and Redpath point out (1985: 193), it may also be that (iii) the friend is too quick to praise others, because he wishes to be praised; or (iv) that others rush to praise him, because he is known to lavish praise.

85

Benson combines Sonnets 82–85 under the title 'In praise of his love'. This the seventh sonnet in the 'rival poet(s)' grouping (78–80, 82–86). The conceit of the lover whose sincerity is indicated by his inarticulacy can be found in Sidney's *Astrophil and Stella*, 54.13–14, which declares 'Dumb swans, not chattering pies, do lovers prove, | They love indeed, who quake to say they love'. The sentiment is also proverbial; see Dent L165: 'Whom we love best to them we can say least'.

1   *tongue-tied* Compare *Midsummer Night's Dream*, 5.1.104–5: 'Love, therefore, and tongue-tied simplicity | In least speak most, to my capacity'. The poet-speaker describes himself as 'tongue-tied' at 80.4, 140.2; art itself is tongue-tied at 66.9. Sonnet 23 finds the poet-speaker struggling to articulate words.
Muse creative faculty; for Shakespeare's use of the word in the *Sonnets*, see 21.1n.
in manners decently, with propriety; compare 39.1.
holds her still keeps quiet (OED 2a); compare 83.9; Muses are conventionally feminine ('her'); see 38.9n.

2   *comments* expository treatises (OED 1).
richly splendidly, sumptuously (with a potential suggestion of over-ornamentation); compare 84.2.
compiled composed, but with a possible slur about a lack of originality; see 78.9n.

3   *Reserve* 'set aside for future use, [...] store up' (*v.*1, OED³ 3a); eighteenth-, nineteenth-century and early twentieth-century editors recurrently emend this word, suggestions including 'Preserve' (Gildon 1714); 'Deserve' (Dowden); 'Treasure' (Tucker); see Rollins 1944: 1.215.
their In light of the frequent compositorial confusion of 'thy'/'their', 'their' could read 'thy' (see 26.12n), although this would have the disadvantage of addressing the friend with both 'your' and 'thy' in the same sentence; the use of pronouns was fluid (see 13.1n), and Sidney's Astrophil addresses Stella as both 'thee' and 'you' within the same sonnet (*Astrophil and Stella* 59), but not within the same sentence. Blakemore Evans (1996: 192) plausibly suggests that Q's 'their' could be a misreading in the manuscript of the common abbreviation 'yʳ' or 'yoʳ', i.e. 'your'

('y' often served as 'th', a hangover from the Old English thorn), nonetheless Q's reading has been retained because it is not nonsensical, since 'comments' (l. 2) can function as the antecedent of 'their'.
character 'feature, characteristic, trait' (OED³ 7a); the proximity to 'quill' also activates a pun on 'character' as 'handwriting' (OED³ 4b), Shakespeare's habitual usage of the word (see 59.8n), as in *Twelfth Night*, 5.1.345–6: 'this is not my writing, | Though I confess much like the character').
with golden quill in an ornate, 'aureate' (golden) style.

4   *precious* indicates value, following on from 'golden'; but can also suggest 'aiming at or affecting refinement in manners, language, etc.; fastidious, particular' (OED³ 3).
all the Muses all nine classical Muses, patronesses of various arts and branches of learning; see 38.9n; for Shakespeare's use of the word 'Muse' in the *Sonnets* more generally, see 21.1n.
filed polished; compare 'polished', 'well-refined' (l. 8). Jackson (2005: 236) notes how this line echoes Meres' praise of Shakespeare in *Palladis Tamia*: 'the Muses would speak with Shakespeare's fine filed phrase, if they would speak English' (1598: sig. 2O2r).

5   *good. . . good* The balance of this line, which poises thoughts against words, pivots on the shifting nuances of that repeated word 'good': 'good thoughts' being true currency (just as genuine coins are 'good', OED³ A24), versus a worth that is purely external and superficial.

5, 13   *other. . . others* The literary rivals are once again imagined as plural (as in Sonnets 78, 82, 83); 'other' is plural (a relic of the inflected *othere* in Middle English); compare 62.8.

6   *like. . . 'Amen'* The poet-speaker (modestly) compares himself to the unlearned ('*unlettered*') parish clerk whose duty it was to lead the congregation in its responses (but does not need to understand what has been said); see *Richard II*, 4.1.172–3: 'God save the King! Will no man say amen? | Am I both priest and clerk?'. The speech marks are added.
still always.

7   *hymn* song of praise; proponents of George Chapman as the rival poet note that he had published *The Shadow of the Night: Containing*

85

My tongue-tied Muse in manners holds her still
While comments of your praise, richly compiled,
Reserve their character with golden quill
And precious phrase by all the Muses filed.   4
I think good thoughts whilst other write good words,
And like unlettered clerk still cry 'Amen'
To every hymn that able spirit affords
In polished form of well-refinèd pen.   8
Hearing you praised, I say ''Tis so, 'tis true',
And to the most of praise add something more;
But that is in my thought, whose love to you
(Though words come hindmost) holds his rank before.   12
   Then others for the breath of words respect;
   Me for my dumb thoughts, speaking in effect.

Two Poetical Hymns in 1594; but Edmund Spenser (one of many other candidates) had published *Four Hymns* in 1596; see also 86.5–12n, and headnote to Sonnet 79.

that able spirit affords (i) 'which some capable person accomplishes'; (ii) alternatively, 'that' could be demonstrative (indicating a specific 'able spirit'); whilst grammatically possible, (ii) is less likely, considering that this allusion comes between two references to plural 'others' (ll. 5, 13). For a discussion of 'spirit', see 80.2n. 'Spirit' is monosyllabic; see 56.8n.

8 **polished. . . well-refinèd** pleonastic, for emphasis (stressing the elegant, rhetorical accomplishment of these rival pens); see also 'filed', l. 4.
pen writer (by *metonymy*), as at 84.5.

9 **''Tis. . . true'** speech marks added; ''Tis true' works as a loose Englishing of 'Amen' ('So be it; truly').

10 **the most of** the utmost, highest.

11 **to you** for you; directed to you.

12 **Though words. . . before** As in 79.4, the image is that of a procession, in which place is accorded by status; the poet-speaker's words lag behind others, but his love is such that it holds its place at the fore; 'his' can be the neuter pronoun 'its' in early modern English.

13 **respect** value (an imperative verb).

14 **in effect** 'in reality (opposed to *in show, in words*)' (in 'effect, *n.*', OED[3]); compare *Troilus and Cressida*, 5.3.108–9: 'Words, words, mere words, no matter from the heart; | Th' effect doth operate another way'.

86

Benson combines Sonnets 86–87 under the title 'A Resignation'. The eighth and last in the 'rival poet(s)' grouping (78–80, 82–86), this sonnet explains the silence (or writer's block) confessed at 83.9 and in 85.

1 **proud full sail** Compare 80.5–13, especially 'proudest sail' (80.6 and note).

2 **prize** trophy; combined with the nautical metaphors, the image is that of a merchant adventurer; a bawdy parallel is provided by Pistol in *Merry Wives*, 2.2.135–6: 'This punk is one of Cupid's carriers. | Clap on more sails, pursue; up with your fights; | Give fire! She is my prize, or ocean whelm them all!'.

(all-too-precious) 'Precious' conveys both emotional and financial value. Q's brackets possibly indicate a compound adjective (compare 7.11n): there are 45 instances of brackets in Q. In the majority of cases, they enclose additional information, rather than performing the grammatical function of indicating a compound adjective, and the compound adjective 'doctor-like' appears hyphenated and within brackets at Q66.10. Q's brackets have therefore been retained, as they have in every other instance where they appear in Q.

3 **ripe** mature; ready for dispersal (like seeds, OED³ A1a).

inhearse a Shakespearean coinage, indicating 'put in a hearse'; 'hearse' in this period could indicate a range of funereal equipment (including the pall cloth and the framework supporting the pall; see OED 2a–5); here, it would seem to be used in the general sense of 'bier, coffin; vaguely, a tomb, grave' (OED 5) in which the 'ripe thoughts' are enclosed. Shakespeare also uses this term in *1 Henry VI*, 4.7.44–6: 'Doubtless he would have made a noble knight. | See where he lies inhearsed in the arms | Of the most bloody nurser of his harms!'. See also *Lucrece*, l. 657.

4 **womb** The shift from 'sail' (l. 1) to 'womb' is reminiscent of *Midsummer Night's Dream*, 2.1.128–31 ('we have laughed to see the sails conceive | And grow big-bellied with the wanton wind; | [...] (her womb then rich with my young squire)'); the shift from 'tomb' (l. 3) to womb, of *Romeo and Juliet*, 2.3.9–10 ('The earth that's nature's mother is her tomb; | What is her burying grave, that is her womb').

The image of literary composition as giving birth was common (see 32.11n); if composition is giving birth, then the brain is (logically) the womb. This idea is treated with comic pedantry by Holofernes in *Love's Labours Lost*, where 'forms, figures, shapes, objects, ideas, apprehensions, motions, revolutions [...] are begot in the ventricle of memory, nourished in the womb of pia mater [membrane in the brain], and delivered upon the mellowing of occasion' (4.2.66–70).

5–12 **Was. . . thence** From Minto (1874) onwards, these lines are cited in support of George Chapman's identification as the rival poet; see Rollins 1944: 2.284–5. The key points of the argument in favour of Chapman's identification are: (i) the title-page of Chapman's *Shadow of the Night* (1594) had claimed 'Versus mei habebunt aliquantum Noctis' ('my verses will have something of the night'); compare l. 7; (ii) the dedication to that work portrays literary accomplishment as something that is attained with 'invocation, fasting, watching [i.e. staying up late; see l. 7]' and features a personified 'skill' which feeds, vampire-like, on writers, 'having drops of their souls like an heavenly familiar' (sig. A2r); see 'familiar' in l. 9 and note; (iii) Chapman also gives a supernatural motivation to his creative decisions (compare l. 5): in *Euthymiae Raptus* (1609: sigs A3v–A4r, B3r) Chapman claimed to have been inspired by the 'spirit' of Homer in his translation of the *Iliad*, a task he began in 1594, and seven books of which were printed in 1598, and he writes of being 'drawn by strange instigation' to finish Marlowe's *Hero and Leander* (1598: sig. E3v); (iv) Chapman's translation of Homer's epic could be seen as 'proud [i.e. splendid]' (l .1), and – in fourteeners – its lines were 'full' (l .1). See also l. 7n, below.

5 **spirit** monosyllabic; sometimes used in the *Sonnets* to suggest a poet's creative powers or informing genius; compare 80.2, 85.7 and *Antony and Cleopatra*, 2.3.20–1: 'Thy daemon, that thy spirit which keeps thee, is | Noble, courageous, high unmatchable'. Here, in the context of poetic rivalry, it also suggests 'mettle; vigour of mind [...] disposition or readiness to assert oneself or to hold one's own' (OED 13a).

spirits two syllables; supernatural beings, 'freq. conceived as troublesome, terrifying, or hostile

86

Was it the proud full sail of his great verse,
Bound for the prize of (all-too-precious) you,
That did my ripe thoughts in my brain inhearse,
Making their tomb the womb wherein they grew?   4
Was it his spirit, by spirits taught to write
Above a mortal pitch, that struck me dead?
No, neither he, nor his compeers by night
Giving him aid, my verse astonishèd.   8
He, nor that affable familiar ghost
Which nightly gulls him with intelligence,
As victors of my silence cannot boast;
I was not sick of any fear from thence.   12
    But when your countenance filled up his line,
    Then lacked I matter; that enfeebled mine.

to mankind' (OED 3a); compare 'ghost', l. 9.
See *1 Henry VI*, 5.3.10–11, where Joan calls on
'familiar spirits, that are culled | Out of the
powerful regions under earth'.

6 *pitch* highest point (OED³ 23); the rival poet
exceeds a 'mortal pitch' – what a human can
achieve – because (like Marlowe's Dr Faustus),
he has supernatural help.
dead 'bereft of sensation or vitality; benumbed,
insensible' (OED B2).

7 *compeers* companions (OED 2a), i.e. the 'spirits' of l. 5; Jackson (2005: 238) suggests that
Shakespeare gets this 'unusual' word from
Meres, but Meres (1598: fols 218v, 286r) uses
it in the sense of 'equal' (OED 1) rather than
'companion'; the word also appears – indicating 'companion' – in a number of other books
that we know Shakespeare read, including
Thomas North's 1579 translation of Plutarch's
Lives (sig. 4X5r) and Edward Hall's *Union of
the [. . .] Families of Lancaster & York* (1548: sig.
2F2r).
by night In the twentieth century, this was
sometimes read as an allusion to the 'School
of Night', a coterie of writers – including
Chapman – who centred on Walter Ralegh
(see Bradbrook 1936). However, the existence
of this coterie, and the sixteenth-century use
of this label, have been since discredited.

8 *astonishèd* stunned, paralysed ('astonish, *v.*',
OED 1a); compare *Lucrece*, l. 1730.

9 *He, nor* neither he nor.
affable The adjective, indicating a ghost who
is 'friendly, good-natured' (OED³ 1), is at odds
with the standard (Protestant) belief that ghosts
were diabolic in origin; see Ludwig Lavater, *Of
Ghosts and Spirits Walking by Night*, which catalogues a variety of monsters and apparitions,
noting that although 'some are only fabulous,
or false: yet notwithstanding, it may be, that
the devil doth deceive men under the forms
of them' (1572: sig. A4r); but see note on 'gulls',
l. 10, below.
familiar 'friendly or affable' (OED³ B2b), and
thus pleonastic with 'affable', but also used in
phrases such as 'familiar spirit', i.e. the (evil)
spirits that obey and assist witches (OED³
A3a); 'familiar' could also imply 'domestic',
'belonging to, or relating to one's household'
(OED³ B3a).

10 *gulls* deceives (*v.*3, OED 1); the word could
also indicate 'gorges' (*v.*1, OED 2); however,
Shakespeare always uses the word and its
derivatives in the former sense; see *Henry V*,
2.2.121 ('that same demon that hath gulled
thee thus'); *Twelfth Night*, 2.3.134–7 ('if I do
not gull him [. . .] do not think I have wit
enough to lie straight in my bed'). If gulls does
mean 'deceives', this complicates the meaning
of 'affable' (l. 9), since – if the ghost is knowingly tricking the rival poet – it cannot be
genuinely friendly or good-natured towards

him, but only has an appearance of being so, like the 'courteous destroyers, affable wolves' in *Timon* 3.6.95; i.e. the ghost conforms to (Protestant) beliefs about the diabolic origins of ghosts, and their deceptive purpose. (The ghost cannot be read as being 'affable' to the poet-speaker, because of the way that l. 11 positions it as being hostile to him.)

intelligence information, news; the term is strongly associated with 'information of military value' (OED³ 6a), a sense in which Shakespeare frequently uses it (see, for example, *Henry V*, 2.0.12; *King John*, 4.2.116); as such, it pre-empts 'victors' (l. 11), as if the rival poet and his 'familiar ghost' were strategising against the poet-speaker as in a military campaign.

11 **victors. . . boast** They cannot brag that they are the cause of the poet-speaker's silence.

12 **sick of** sick because of; compare *Twelfth Night*, 1.5.90: 'you are sick of self-love, Malvolio'; the poet-speaker's Muse is described as 'sick' at 79.4.

13 **countenance** (i) face (*n.*1, OED 5); (ii) patronage (OED 8a); Shakespeare uses the word in both senses, and puns on the two meanings in *1 Henry IV*, 1.2.28–9: 'our noble and chaste mistress the moon, under whose countenance we steal'.

filled up Malone modernises Q's 'fild up' as 'fil'd [filed] up'; 'filled' seems more likely, however, as (i) 'filed up' (polished up) is not early modern idiom (whereas 'filled up' is common); (ii) 'filled' recalls 'full' from l. 1; (iii) 'filled' is also spelled 'fild' at Q17.2; compare *Lucrece*, l. 1804.

line verse.

14 **that** that fact: either (i) that the rival's line is filled with the friend's 'countenance' (l. 13), or (ii) that the poet-speaker 'lacked matter'. Grammatically, 'that' could also refer to 'his line' (l. 13); however this seems unlikely logically, because of the poet-speaker's insistence (ll. 9–11) that neither the rival poet nor his familiar spirits can claim to be the reason for his silence.

86

Was it the proud full sail of his great verse,
Bound for the prize of (all-too-precious) you,
That did my ripe thoughts in my brain inhearse,
Making their tomb the womb wherein they grew? 4
Was it his spirit, by spirits taught to write
Above a mortal pitch, that struck me dead?
No, neither he, nor his compeers by night
Giving him aid, my verse astonishèd. 8
He, nor that affable familiar ghost
Which nightly gulls him with intelligence,
As victors of my silence cannot boast;
I was not sick of any fear from thence. 12
    But when your countenance filled up his line,
    Then lacked I matter; that enfeebled mine.

87

Benson combines Sonnets 86–87 under the title 'A Resignation'. This poem has an unusually high frequency of feminine rhymes for one of Shakespeare's sonnets (twelve, all double rhymes, ten of them ending *-ing*; see also Sonnet 20; here, the feminine rhymes soften the effect of the end-stopped lines. Compare Daniel, *Delia* 27, where there are twelve feminine rhymes, eight ending *-ing*; Daniel clearly became dissatisfied with the effect, revising away the feminine rhymes in subsequent editions, halving the amount in 1594, and removing all of them in 1601.

1   *dear* (i) beloved; (ii) costly; compare 'all-too-precious', 86.2; (iii) Shakespeare sometimes transfers the epithet 'to the subject of the feeling' (OED A3), so that it means 'affectionate, loving': see *Hamlet*, 1.2.110–11 ('with no less nobility of love | Than that which dearest father bears his son'); *Tempest*, 1.2.178–9 ('Bountiful Fortune | (Now my dear lady)').

   possessing The first of a series of words with legal resonances, particularly relating to land tenure ('charter', 'releasing', l. 3; 'bonds', 'determinate', l. 4; 'hold', 'granting', l. 5; 'patent', l. 8; 'misprision', l. 11; 'judgement', l. 12). The primary meaning of 'possess, *v.*' is 'to own, to have or gain ownership of [. . .]; to hold as property' (OED³ 1a). Compare 18.10.

2   *like enough* likely enough, probably.

   estimate (i) attributed value (OED 1b); (ii) reputation (OED 1c); both (i) and (ii) rely on the opinions of others, rather than indicating true, essential worth.

3   *charter. . . releasing* A charter is (i) a privilege (*n.*1, OED 3); (ii) a document or deed that relates to the conveyance of landed property (OED 2b). The image works in different ways, depending whether sense (i) or (ii) is understood: (i) the privilege, which the friend has because of his merits ('worth'), remits him from any obligations (see 'releasing', below); (ii) the charter, which had conveyed a right of possession upon the poet-speaker (to enjoy his friend's merit), allows the friend to release himself because the poet-speaker can no longer afford to meet the terms of that bond (the beloved has become 'too dear for [his] possessing', l. 1). See also 58.9 and note.

   releasing a legal term, indicating remission from an obligation (OED³ 1).

4   *bonds in thee* (i) claims to ownership over you; (ii) mutual ties that bind me to you; compare 117.4; 134.8. A bond is a term in English law indicating a 'deed, by which A (known as the *obligor*) binds himself, his heirs, executors, or assigns to pay a certain sum of money to B (known as the *obligee*), or his heirs, etc. A may bind himself to this payment absolutely and unconditionally, in which case the deed is known as a single or simple bond (*simplex obligatio*): bonds in this form are obsolete. Or a condition may be attached that the deed shall be made void by the payment, by a certain date, of money, rent, etc. due from A to B, or by some other performance or observance, the sum named being only a penalty to enforce the performance of the condition, in which case the deed is termed a penal bond' (OED 9a). Considering that these bonds are 'determinate', the 'bonds' would here seem to be 'penal'. Shakespeare was aware of the distinction; see *Merchant of Venice*, 1.3.144–5: 'Go with me to a notary, seal me there | Your single bond'.

   all (i) every one; (ii) completely.

   determinate terminated (used of the expiry of a legal bond); compare 13.6 and note.

5   *hold* (i) possess (continuing the vein of vocabulary relating to ownership of property; see OED 6a); (ii) embrace.

   thy granting your consent; the word plays on the legal sense of 'a conveyance of such property (viz. incorporeal hereditaments) as can pass only by deed' ('grant, *n.*1', OED 4b). Legally, an 'incorporeal hereditament' has 'no material existence in itself, but atta[ches] as a right or profit to some actual thing' ('incorporeal, *adj*', 3).

6   *that riches* 'Riches' could be treated as a singular noun up to the early nineteenth century; compare *Richard II*, 3.4.60: 'too much riches'.

7   *cause* (i) motive (OED 3a); (ii) 'good, proper, adequate ground of action' (OED 3b), of the sort that might lead you to take legal action and 'plead a cause' (see OED 7a).

   fair gift i.e. 'that riches' (l. 6); the gift is 'fair' because it is 'generous' (OED³ 5), but it is also 'beautiful' (OED³ 1), because it comprises the friend.

   wanting lacking.

8   *patent* 'document conferring some privilege, right, office, title, or property' (OED³ 1a).

87

Farewell, thou art too dear for my possessing,
And like enough thou know'st thy estimate;
The charter of thy worth gives thee releasing:
My bonds in thee are all determinate.   4
For how do I hold thee but by thy granting,
And for that riches where is my deserving?
The cause of this fair gift in me is wanting,
And so my patent back again is swerving.   8
Thy self thou gav'st, thy own worth then not knowing,
Or me to whom thou gav'st it, else mistaking;
So thy great gift, upon misprision growing,
Comes home again, on better judgement making.   12
    Thus have I had thee as a dream doth flatter:
    In sleep a king, but waking no such matter.

back . . . swerving reverting (i.e. the privileges granted by the patent have reverted to the friend); however, 'swerve' also carries connotations of disloyalty or inconstancy (OED 3b(b)): see *Henry V*, 2.2.133 ('Constant in spirit, not swerving with the blood'); *Winter's Tale*, 2.1.92–3 ('she's | A bed-swerver').

9 **Thy self** Whilst 'thyself' is always written as two words in Q (as is usual in the period), here 'thy self' helps convey the sense that the 'self' is a distinct entity: in giving 'himself', the friend had given 'his self'; see also 79.14n and the note on modernising the *-self* suffix (p. xiv).

9–10 **thy own worth . . . mistaking** 'Or' in l. 10 indicates that 'either' has been elided before 'thy own worth', so that the two lines are held up as alternatives: 'you gave yourself to me, either because you were unaware of your own value, or because you overestimated my value, to whom you gave it'.

11 **upon misprision growing** based on error; continues the strand of legal imagery, the primary sense of 'misprision' being '*Law*. A wrongful act or omission' (OED³ 1a); the legal phrase 'misprision of the clerk' (to indicate a clerical error) is also relevant (OED³ 2a).

12 **on . . . making** the friend having made a better judgement; the grammatical awkwardness

(strictly speaking, the subject of the clause is 'thy great gift') is imposed by the need to fit the rhyming pattern of feminine rhymes.

13 **Thus . . . flatter** Compare *Romeo and Juliet*, 5.1.1–2: 'If I may trust the flattering truth of sleep, | My dreams presage some joyful news at hand'.

   flatter beguile (*v.*1, OED 7a).

14 **a king** having the absolute sovereignty of a king (i.e. here holding rights of possession over the friend); 'As merry (happy) as a king' is proverbial (Tilley K54). The epigram 'To our English Terence, Mr Will: Shakespeare', by John Davies of Hereford, makes much of the fact that Shakespeare took the part of kings on stage: 'Some say (good Will) [. . .] | Had'st thou not played some kingly parts in sport | Thou hadst been a companion for a king, | And been a king among the meaner sort' (*Scourge of Folly*, 1611: sig. F6v).

   waking The internal rhyme highlights the wordplay on 'king'. Duncan-Jones (1997a: 284) suggests that the 'elevenfold repetition of the particle *-ing* hints at "ingle", = a boy favourite, a catamite ([*n*.2] OED)', and that 'such innuendo may also be underlined by the "feminine" rhymes [see Sonnet 20] and the word *had* in the previous line'.

88

Benson combines Sonnets 88–91 under the title 'A request to his scornful love'.

1 *disposed* Benson was the first editor to correct Q's 'dispode'.

   set me light consider me (i) of small importance ('light, *adj*.1', OED 13a); (ii) fickle (OED 16).

2 *place. . . scorn* 'hold my good qualities up for ridicule'.

4 *virtuous* slurred into two syllables.

   though (i) although; (ii) even if (looking to a hypothetical scenario in the future).

   forsworn perjured.

6 *Upon thy part* The dominant sense is 'in your defence', but it is possible to read this as a hint that the 'faults concealed' are ones committed 'on your side', 'by you'.

   set down Etymologically equivalent to 'depose' (which derives from the Latin *deponere*), the word is suggestive of the act of making a deposition ('a statement in answer to interrogatories, constituting evidence, taken down in writing to be read in court as a substitute for the production of the witness', OED 5a), particularly when in proximity to 'attainted' (l. 7), which has legal resonances.

7 *attainted* (i) condemned; (ii) accused; (iii) infected; this latter sense implies that the dishonour inflicted is not necessarily as a result of faults that the poet-speaker himself has committed, but that he has been stained by close association; compare 35.5–8.

8 *That* so that.

   losing 'loosing' in Q, a common variant for 'losing' (see 18.10n); however, modernising here flattens the play on words – between 'loosing' ('releasing') and 'losing' ('destroying'; 'lose, *v*.1', OED 2a) – that is permissible in early modern spelling; see 42.9, 10, 11n.

10 *For* because.

   bending [. . .] on turning to.

12 *double vantage me* advantage me twice: first, because the poet-speaker thinks of his friend, an activity which is always welcomed (compare 29.10); secondly, because the poet-speaker and the friend are one (see 39.2n), anything that benefits the friend benefits the poet-speaker too.

13 *so* (i) to such an extent; (ii) in such a way.

14 *for thy right* (i) to help your rightful cause; (ii) because of the privileges and immunity you enjoy.

   bear all wrong (i) take responsibility for all wrongdoing; (ii) endure all injustice.

88

When thou shalt be disposed to set me light
And place my merit in the eye of scorn,
Upon thy side against myself I'll fight
And prove thee virtuous, though thou art forsworn.   4
With mine own weakness being best acquainted,
Upon thy part I can set down a story
Of faults concealed wherein I am attainted,
That thou in losing me shall win much glory;   8
And I by this will be a gainer too,
For, bending all my loving thoughts on thee,
The injuries that to myself I do,
Doing thee vantage, double vantage me.   12
    Such is my love, to thee I so belong,
    That for thy right, myself will bear all wrong.

89

Benson combines Sonnets 88–91 under the title 'A request to his scornful love'. This sonnet continues from Sonnet 88.

1 *Say* (i) utter, speak; (ii) suppose that; however, sense (ii) only lasts until l. 2, where the presence of 'will' (rather than 'would') undermines the hypothetical.
for because of.
fault a multivalent word, with meanings including 'deficiency' (OED 1a), 'defect' (OED 3), 'transgression' (OED 5a), 'error' (OED 5b).

2 *comment* expound upon, with a potentially moralising edge; compare *Venus and Adonis*, l. 714 and note.

3 *straight* straightaway.
halt limp; a line interpreted by some as evidence that Shakespeare was lame (see Rollins 1944: 1.223–4); the line in fact reveals the opposite, as it suggests that poet-speaker is so craven that he will act exactly as friend demands (he only limps after the friend has said that he is lame). The poet-speaker imagines himself lamed by Fortune at 37.3. 'Lameness' could also play on the poetic humility adopted in Sonnets 76–80, 82–86, punning on the idea of inept metrical feet; compare *As You Like It*, 3.2.169, where Rosalind mocks the 'lame' feet of Orlando's verses.

4 *reasons* arguments.

6 *set a form* lend propriety to (form = 'due shape, proper figure', OED 8).
desirèd change presumably the friend's wish to cool, or end, his relationship with the poet-speaker.

6, 8 *change. . . strange* The same rhyme pair appears in this position in Sonnet 93; in Q's sequence Sonnets 89, 92 and 93 form a cluster of sonnets concerned with change (see 92.9, 10; 93.3, 6).

7 *will* (i) wish (*n.*1, OED 1a); (ii) intention (OED 7a); the word may also suggest sexual appetite (OED 2), and pun – as in Sonnets 135 and 136 – on the poet-speaker's name.

8 *acquaintance strangle* Compare *Antony and Cleopatra*, 2.6.120–2: 'you shall find the band that seems to tie their friendship together will be the very strangler of their amity'.
strange unfamiliar (as if I did not know you); compare 49.5.

9 *thy walks* your haunts.

11 *too much profane* too impious, ribald, coarse (OED³ A3); derived from the Latin *profanus* ('outside the temple'), the choice of word might also suggest that the poet-speaker is excluded from the privileged circles around the friend. The Folger-Mildmay copy of Q reads 'proface' (all the other extant copies read 'profane', as the result of a stop-press correction), although, on the principle of *lectio difficilor* (whereby the more unusual or difficult reading is probably correct, because copyists and compositors are more likely to emend – consciously or not – to something familiar), Blakemore Evans argues that 'proface' (a toast, meaning 'May it do you good!', OED³ A) may actually be the correct reading, incorrectly emended by a proof-corrector (1996: 197); the line would consequently have meant 'being overly familiar in saluting you by your "sweet belovèd name"'; Blakemore Evans cites *2 Henry IV*, 5.3.28 ('Proface! What you want in meat, we'll have in drink') in support of this thesis.
it your name.

12 *haply* by chance, perhaps; there is a potential, ironic pun on 'happily'.

13 *vow* promise, swear.
debate strife, conflict (both physical and verbal).

14 *him whom* whomever (in this case, the poet-speaker).

89

Say that thou didst forsake me for some fault,
And I will comment upon that offence;
Speak of my lameness, and I straight will halt,
Against thy reasons making no defence.   4
Thou canst not (love) disgrace me half so ill,
To set a form upon desirèd change,
As I'll myself disgrace, knowing thy will:
I will acquaintance strangle and look strange,   8
Be absent from thy walks, and in my tongue
Thy sweet belovèd name no more shall dwell,
Lest I (too much profane) should do it wrong
And haply of our old acquaintance tell.   12
    For thee, against myself I'll vow debate,
    For I must ne'er love him whom thou dost hate.

90

Benson combines Sonnets 88–91 under the title 'A request to his scornful love'.

1 **Then** therefore; continues from 89.14 (as the repetition of 'hate' confirms); as Kerrigan points out (1986: 286), '*when* and the double *now*, | *Now* [ll. 1, 2] quibble on the temporal sense of *Then*'.

1–4 **Then. . . after-loss** The lines follow Q's punctuation (with the exception of the replacement of the colon at the end of l. 4); it would be possible to punctuate these lines more definitively, with a semi-colon at either (i) the end of l. 1 or (ii) l. 2.

2 **bent** determined.
   cross thwart.

3 **spite of Fortune** The juxtaposition of 'fortune' with the human emotion of 'spite' tips this towards personification and the idea of fortune as a vindictive goddess; compare 37.3.
   make me bow force me to adopt a position of submission.

4 **drop in** The phrase is obscure: 'drop in' did not in 1609 have its later meaning of 'call unexpectedly [. . .], pay a casual visit'; despite OED giving this line as the first citation for this meaning, it is not until the later seventeenth century and eighteenth century that this meaning takes hold ('drop in', in 'drop, *v.*', OED 2). EEBO-TCP searches of texts before 1609 reveal no such usages. Its usage here is probably similar to that in *Antony and Cleopatra*, 3.13.158–61, where it indicates 'fall upon': 'if I be so, | From my cold heart let heaven engender hail, | And poison it in the source, and the first stone | Drop in my neck'.
   for as.

after-loss a loss felt at a future date; this coinage does not appear elsewhere in Shakespeare's works, or EEBO-TCP searches, although Shakespeare uses a similar principle to forge other 'compounds strange' (76.4), such as 'after-love' and 'after-debts': see *Richard II*, 5.3.35 ('To win thy after-love I pardon thee'); *Two Gentlemen of Verona*, 3.1.95 ('scorn at first makes after-love the more'); *All's Well*, 4.3.226 ('He ne'er pays after-debts, take it before').

5 **'scaped** aphetic form of the past participle of the verb to 'escape', here used in its primary sense of 'g[o]t free from detention or control, or from an oppressive or irksome condition' (OED 1a); the word anticipates the militaristic imagery of l. 6.

6 **rearward** rearguard; 'the part of an army or fleet stationed behind the main body' (*n.*1, OED³ 1a).
   conquered woe grief which has been overcome (because the sufferer had recovered from it).

7 **Give. . . morrow** proverbial; see Dent N166 ('A blustering night a fair day'), *Lucrece*, ll. 1788–90. Compare the use of meteorological metaphors to express the friend's favour, and withdrawal of favour, in Sonnets 33–34.

8 **linger out** protract.
   purposed intended.

11 **onset** (i) beginning; (ii) the first assault; compare *King John*, 2.1.325–7: 'Heralds, from off our towers we might behold, | From first to last, the onset and retire | Of both your armies'.
   shall 'stall' in Q; first corrected to 'shall' by Benson.

13 **strains** (i) types, kinds; (ii) pressures, exigencies; (iii) lyrically, a passage of music or verse.

90

Then hate me when thou wilt, if ever, now,
Now while the world is bent my deeds to cross,
Join with the spite of Fortune, make me bow,
And do not drop in for an after-loss. 4
Ah, do not, when my heart hath 'scaped this sorrow,
Come in the rearward of a conquered woe;
Give not a windy night a rainy morrow
To linger out a purposed overthrow. 8
If thou wilt leave me, do not leave me last,
When other petty griefs have done their spite,
But in the onset come; so shall I taste
At first the very worst of Fortune's might, 12
    And other strains of woe, which now seem woe,
    Compared with loss of thee, will not seem so.

91

Benson combines Sonnets 88–91 under the title 'A request to his scornful love'.

1 *birth* 'high birth' is understood; see l. 9.
skill encompasses more than manual dexterity, indicating knowledge and powers of discrimination.

2 *body's force* There are no apostrophes in Q marking the possessive. Most editors follow Capell's 'body's' for Q's 'bodies'.

3 *new-fangled ill* It was commonplace to mock those who enthusiastically adopted the latest ('new-fangled') fashions; see, for example, the critique of Gnatho's dress in Elyot's *Pasquil the Plain*: 'What have we here? A cap full of aglets & buttons; this long ostrich feather doth wonderfully well; the tyrf [turn-up] of the cap turned down afore like a prentice hath a marvellous good grace: but this long gown with straight sleeves is a non sequitur' (1533: sig. A3v). A similar mood is found in Kent's attack on the sycophantic courtier Oswald in *King Lear*. 'A tailor made thee. [. . .] A stone-cutter or a painter could not have made him so ill' (2.2.54–9).

4 *horse* plural horses, as in *Taming of the Shrew*, 3.2.204–5: 'Grumio, my horse.' 'Ay, sir, they be ready'. Hunting, hawking and horsemanship were three key 'gentlemanly' delights. See, for example, Wyatt's depiction of country pleasures in 'Mine own John Poins': 'This maketh me at home to hunt and hawk [. . .] | No man doth mark whereso I ride or go, | [. . .] I may leap both hedge and dyke full well' (*Tottel* [125], ll. 80, 83, 88).

5 *every. . . pleasure* It was believed that the ratio of the four bodily humours determined both health and psychological make-up

(see 29.12n); each 'humoral' type or complexion had a tendency, and therefore a particular pleasure, connected ('*adjunct*') to it. For Shakespeare's use of 'adjunct', see *Lucrece*, 133n.
his its.

7 *particulars* single things (contrast with 'general', l. 8); points back to the things listed in ll. 1–4.
not my measure (i) not fitted to me (like garments, made to measure); (ii) not the things I measure happiness against; (iii) inadequate for me.

8 *one general best* a single, all-embracing, superlative pleasure (in contrast to which the 'particular' pleasures enjoyed by others look trivial).

9 *better* 'bitter' in Q; Benson emends to 'better' in 1640 ('e' and 'i' are easily mistaken in many secretary hands).

10 *prouder* more splendid.
garments' cost Compare 64.2. There are no apostrophes in Q marking the possessive; 'cost' must be a noun rather than a verb (and Q's 'garments' a possessive) because of the parallel structure of ll. 9–11, which aligns 'cost' with 'high birth' (l. 9), 'wealth' (l. 10), 'hawks' and 'horses' (l. 11), as it recapitulates five of the eight 'particulars' listed in ll. 1–4.

12 *having* For the sexual potential of this word, see 129.6, 10n.
pride 'a person of whom, or thing of which, any person or group of people is proud; that which causes a feeling of pride in its possessor; (hence) the foremost, best, or most distinguished of a class, country, etc.' (*n*.1, OED[3] 4).

13–14 *Wretched. . . make* Compare 64.13–14.

91

Some glory in their birth, some in their skill,
Some in their wealth, some in their body's force,
Some in their garments, though new-fangled ill,
Some in their hawks and hounds, some in their horse,   4
And every humour hath his adjunct pleasure
Wherein it finds a joy above the rest;
But these particulars are not my measure;
All these I better in one general best.   8
Thy love is better than high birth to me,
Richer than wealth, prouder than garments' cost,
Of more delight than hawks or horses be;
And having thee, of all men's pride I boast,   12
    Wretched in this alone: that thou mayst take
    All this away, and me most wretched make.

92

Benson combines Sonnets 92–95 under the title 'A lover's affection though his love prove unconstant'.

1   *But* nevertheless; this sonnet continues from Sonnet 91.
      do thy worst Compare 19.13.
      steal thyself away (i) withdraw surreptitiously (compare 33.8); (ii) rob me of your love (the friend's love is described as 'richer than wealth' at 91.10). The double meaning of 'steal' is exploited at 63.8; 77.7; 104.9–10.

2   *term of life* duration of (my) lifetime; 'term' is a legal phrase (see OED 4b), used – amongst other things – to denote the duration of legal possession of land (OED 6).
      assurèd pledged (OED A3), or, more specifically, betrothed (OED A4).

4, 8 *depends. . . depend* (i) contingent on (*v.*1, OED 2a); (ii) 'rest entirely on [. . .] for maintenance, support, supply' (OED 4).

5   *the worst of wrongs* i.e. your loss (see l. 1).

6   *the least of them* i.e. the slightest coolness on your part, which would be the most trivial of the wrongs mentioned in l. 5.

7   *I see* I perceive.
      state condition.

8   *humour* (i) 'temporary state of mind or feeling; mood' (OED³ 5a); (ii) whim (OED³ 6a); see also 91.5n.

9   *vex* trouble (OED 1a); distress deeply (OED 3a); the word is stronger than in modern usage: when Cloten plans to murder Posthumous and rape Imogen, he does so to 'vex' Imogen (*Cymbeline*, 3.5.142), and Aaron predicts that his account of the rape and murder of Lucius' family will 'vex [his] soul' (*Titus Andronicus*, 5.1.62). See also 135.3, 148.10.

10   *Since. . . lie* 'because my life depends on your inconstancy' (which is why the friend's 'inconstant mind' cannot 'vex' the poet-speaker in l. 9); whilst the word 'revolt' is strongly associated with rebellion, here it is being used, as in *King John*, 3.1.322 ('O foul revolt of French inconstancy'), as a synonym for changeability, drawing on the etymology of the word (*révolter*, French for 'to turn'), semantic origins which Shakespeare exploits in *3 Henry VI*, 1.1.151: 'All will revolt from me and turn to him'. Sonnet 92 forms a cluster

with Sonnets 89 and 93 expressing anxiety about the idea of change (see 89.6; 93.3, 6).

11   *title* legal right to the possession of property, and evidence of such.

11, 12 *happy* The three repetitions of the adjective play on the various meanings of the word. The 'happy title' is 'fortuitous' (OED³ 3) and 'fortunate' (OED³ 1a); the poet-speaker is both 'fortunate' and 'glad' (OED³ 5a) to have the friend's love; and he is 'glad' to die for it.

12   *die!* The exclamation mark is in Q, one of ten in the volume (the others are at Q95.4, Q103.5, Q120.12, Q123.1, Q148.1; *A Lover's Complaint*, ll. 53, 54, 166, 285). The idea of dying for love is a commonplace of amorous verse; see Henry Howard's translation of Petrarch's *Rime Sparse* 140 ('Love, that liveth and reigneth in my thought', *Tottel* [6]): 'Sweet is his death, that takes his end by love' (l. 14). 'Die' has potential sexual connotations (see 6.4n), particularly in proximity to 'have' (see 129.6, 10n).

13   *blessèd fair* The OED cites this line as the first (and only) usage of 'blessed' in a quasi-adverbial sense; however, the phrase hovers between a compound adjective ('blessed-fair', which is how it is punctuated by Malone and many subsequent editors) and an adjectival phrase, in which 'blessed' acts almost as an intensifier.
      fears Blakemore Evans conjectures that Q's 'fears' might be a compositorial misreading of (or typographical error for) 'bears', comparing the line to *Lucrece*, ll. 853–4 (1996: 199–200); however, as 'fears' makes sense, neither this edition nor Blakemore Evans' emends the line.
      blot stain, blemish; in Shakespearean usage the word is strongly connected with sins such as murder (*1 Henry IV*, 1.3.162–3) and adultery (*Comedy of Errors*, 2.2.140); it is also a recurrent word in *Lucrece*, blot and its derivatives appearing five times in that poem in this moral sense (ll. 192, 537, 1299, 1322, 1519).

14   *mayst be* The friend's infidelity could be hypothetical, imagined as a future possibility; or it could be occurring in the present, as yet undetected by the poet-speaker. Sonnet 93 continues this uncertainty.
      yet (i) nevertheless; (ii) as yet.

92

But do thy worst to steal thyself away,
For term of life thou art assurèd mine,
And life no longer than thy love will stay,
For it depends upon that love of thine.   4
Then need I not to fear the worst of wrongs,
When in the least of them my life hath end;
I see a better state to me belongs
Than that which on thy humour doth depend.   8
Thou canst not vex me with inconstant mind,
Since that my life on thy revolt doth lie;
O what a happy title do I find,
Happy to have thy love, happy to die!   12
    But what's so blessèd fair that fears no blot?
    Thou mayst be false, and yet I know it not.

93

Benson combines Sonnets 92–95 under the title 'A lover's affection though his love prove unconstant'.

1   **So. . . true** continues from 92.13–14; '**supposing**' can indicate either (i) an involuntary belief, where the poet-speaker 'thinks' (OED³ 3) his friend is faithful; (ii) a voluntary and deliberate act which frames the friend's fidelity as a hypothesis (OED³ 1). 'So' can mean (i) therefore; (ii) in this way (a way demonstrated by the poem that follows).

2   **deceivèd husband** Since inheritance in early modern England was patrilineal and wives were the legal possession of their husbands, cuckoldry (and the subsequent risk of bringing up another man's child) was a legally and socially disruptive act and was consequently a frequent motif of early modern literature; Shakespeare recurrently uses the fear (rather than fact) of cuckoldry as a plot device, with results that are comic (e.g. Master Ford in *Merry Wives*) as well as tragic (*Othello*). Shakespearean characters also repeatedly joke about cuckoldry, even when there is no apparent reason to do so, so that the allusion – as here – is not structurally necessary, but reveals a cultural concern with legitimacy; see, for example, the exchange at *Much Ado*, 1.1.104–5:

> DON PEDRO I think this is your daughter.
> LEONATO Her mother hath many times told me so.

so (i) in this way; (ii) in order that; as Burrow points out (2002: 566), sense (ii) 'reinforces the suggestion of *supposing*, that the poet is deliberately deceiving himself'.
love's face (i) the appearance of love, an appearance that might be false; see *Macbeth*, 1.4.11–12 ('There's no art | To find the mind's construction in the face'); (ii) the beloved's face (a meaning which develops in ll. 3–4).

3   **still. . . me** 'to me' works twice: i.e. 'it appears to me to be love towards me'; '**seem**' is often used, by Shakespeare and other writers, to alert readers to falsity; see, for example,

Hamlet's outburst at his mother's choice of the word 'seems' at *Hamlet*, 1.2.76: 'Seems, madam? nay, it is, I know not "seems"'.
altered new (i) recently changed; (ii) changed into something different; Sonnet 93 concludes a cluster (with Sonnets 89 and 92) which meditates anxiously on change (see 89.6; 92.9, 10; l. 6, below).

4   **Thy looks. . . place** Compare 61.14.
looks (i) features; (ii) glances.

5   **For** because.

6   **in that** in 'thine eye' (l. 5).

6, 8   **change. . . strange** The same rhyme pair appears in this position in Sonnet 89 (in which the poet-speaker, as here, worries about the friend's potential withdrawal of affection).

7   **many's looks** in many people's features (the contrast with the friend is established in l. 9, beginning 'But').

8   **moods** anger (*n*.1, OED³ 2b); external expressions of feeling (Schmidt, 3).
wrinkles strange 'wrinkles' would here seem to be a synonym for 'frowns', which effect a coldness and distance between once familiar friends (i.e. make them 'strange' to one another); compare the situation imagined at 49.5–6.

9   **heaven** pronounced as one syllable.
in at.

10, 12   **should** the past tense of 'shall', denoting what heaven has decreed shall happen (and has therefore happened); 'should' can also imply 'ought to'.

11   **heart's workings** the operation of the heart, i.e. what is truly thought or felt (the heart being regarded as the seat of thoughts and emotions; see 46.1n). There are close parallels to this phrase at *Love's Labours Lost*, 4.1.33 ('the working of the heart') and *Othello*, 3.3.123 ('working from the heart').

12   **thence** from the heart.

13   **How like. . . grow** The attractive appearance of the tree from which Eve plucked the forbidden fruit is noted in Genesis 3:6: 'So the woman (seeing that the tree was good for meat, and that it was pleasant to the eyes, & a tree to be desired to get knowledge) took of the fruit thereof, and did eat, and gave also

93

So shall I live, supposing thou art true,
Like a deceivèd husband, so love's face
May still seem love to me, though altered new:
Thy looks with me, thy heart in other place.   4
For there can live no hatred in thine eye,
Therefore in that I cannot know thy change;
In many's looks the false heart's history
Is writ in moods and frowns and wrinkles strange;   8
But heaven in thy creation did decree
That in thy face sweet love should ever dwell;
Whate'er thy thoughts or thy heart's workings be,
Thy looks should nothing thence but sweetness tell.   12
    How like Eve's apple doth thy beauty grow,
    If thy sweet virtue answer not thy show.

to her husband with her, and he did eat'. The comparison to Eve's apple suggests that the friend's beauty is dangerously tempting, since – by offering Adam the fruit – Eve 'entice[d] her husband to sin' (chapter heading to Genesis 3). *grow* (i) become; (ii) flourish.

14 *If. . . show* Compare 69.13. The potential for the appearance of apples to be deceiving was proverbial; see Dent A291.1 ('An apple may be fair without and bad within') and *Merchant of Venice*, 1.3.101 ('A goodly apple rotten at the heart').

94

Benson combines Sonnets 92–95 under the title 'A lover's affection though his love prove unconstant'.

Sonnet 94 is widely regarded as one of the most enigmatic of Shakespeare's sonnets; ambivalence arises from whether the type of men described are being lauded or criticised (or somewhere in between). Whilst some critics question the authority of Q's sequence (and even whether it is a sequence at all), it is evident that some sections at least form mini-sequences; this sonnet is in such a cluster (Sonnet 92 is clearly linked to Sonnet 91 by its opening 'But'; Sonnet 93 is connected to Sonnet 92 by its initial 'So'; Sonnet 95 expands on 94.13–14; whilst Sonnet 96 meditates on the 'faults' that have been an on-going concern of all these sonnets). Sonnet 94 is unusual in the *Sonnets* overall (not just this mini-sequence) in its avoidance of personal referents, such as the pronouns 'I', 'you', 'thou'; whilst its governing conceits (inheritance and husbandry, ll. 5–8; flowers, ll. 9–12) are those recurrently applied to the friend, the subject of this sonnet is kept decidedly impersonal; see also Sonnet 129. Prynne 2001 provides an extended commentary on this one sonnet, and draws particular attention to its affinities with some of the poems of Thomas Wyatt, verses which – like this sonnet – pay close attention to structures of power and where political and amorous discourses are often blurred.

1   **They. . . none** See Dent H170 ('To be able to do harm and not to do it is noble'); Dent also cites Sidney's *Arcadia* – 'the more power he hath to hurt, the more admirable is his praise, that he will not hurt' (1590: sig. Z1r) – and Ben Jonson's *Case is Altered* (performed 1597; printed 1609), 1.5.67–8: 'The property of the wretch is, he would hurt and cannot; of the man, he can hurt, and will not'. As Duncan-Jones (2010: 298) notes, the Latin version of this motto ('*posse et nolle, nobile*') 'was adopted as a personal motto by Sir John Salusbury of Lleweni', for whom Shakespeare wrote 'Let the Bird of Loudest Lay' (see headnote to that poem). In this sonnet, the political resonances of this proverb are transmuted into a discussion of those who have emotional power over others. Compare Francis Beaumont, *Maid's Tragedy*, Act 5, perhaps a deliberate echo of this sonnet – 'Those have most to power to hurt us that we love: | We lay our sleeping lives within their arms' (1619: sig. L2r). Prynne (2001: 7) draws attention

to resonances with Wyatt's 'Mine Own John Poins' (*Tottel* [125]) – 'It is not because I scorn or mock | The power of them whom fortune here hath lent | Charge over us, of right to strike the stroke' (ll. 7–9) – and the opening of Wyatt's 'They flee from me' (*Tottel* [52]), where 'Wyatt invests the same opening pronoun with a comparably abrupt and obscured intensity' (2001: 3). '**Power**' is here pronounced as one syllable. '**Hurt**' encompasses both physical pain and mental distress (OED³ 3a, 4a). The capacity of the beloved to inflict pain on the lover is a commonplace of amorous verse. See, for example, Wyatt's translation of Petrarch, *Rime Sparse* 21 ('How oft have I, my dear and cruel foe' (*Tottel* [96]), cited by Prynne 2001: 13), ll. 13–14: 'So shall it be great hurt unto us twain | And yours the loss, and mine the deadly pain'.

2   **That. . . show** Like much in this sonnet, this line can be read both positively and negatively; leading on from l. 1, it appears commendable: such powerful men look dangerous, but they restrain themselves (a good thing). However, following from Sonnet 93, with its anxiety about duplicity and the mismatch between outward appearance and inward emotion, the line appears more critical: the unpredictability resulting from such a disjunction between the appearance and action of those in authority is also profoundly unsettling, particularly in a context (a discussion of power) which inevitably raises the image of courtly politics, where the receipt of favour was notoriously fickle; see, for example, Wyatt's description of the 'slipper[y] wheel | Of high estate' ('Stand whoso list', *Tottel* [118], l. 1).

3–4   **Who. . . slow** These lines echo and combine two proverbs: 'as steadfast as stone' (Dent S878.2) and 'as cold as a stone' (S876). Again, the implications of these lines are ambiguous. It was the role of a leader to 'move' others; see, for example, the much-cited 'foundation' myth for human civilisation, related in classical texts such as Cicero's *De Inventione* (I.ii.2–3) and recycled in humanist works such as Wilson's *Art of Rhetoric*, which describes how God 'stirred up his faithful and elect to persuade with reason all men to society, and gave his appointed ministers knowledge both to see the natures of men, and also granted them the gift of utterance, that they might

94

They that have power to hurt and will do none,
That do not do the thing they most do show,
Who, moving others, are themselves as stone,
Unmovèd, cold, and to temptation slow: 4
They rightly do inherit heaven's graces
And husband nature's riches from expense;
They are the lords and owners of their faces,
Others but stewards of their excellence.   8
The summer's flower is to the summer sweet,
Though to itself it only live and die,
But if that flower with base infection meet,
The basest weed outbraves his dignity: 12
　　For sweetest things turn sourest by their deeds;
　　Lilies that fester smell far worse than weeds.

with ease win folk at their will and frame them by reason to all good order' (1553: sig. A3v); compare Thomas Elyot, *Governor* (1531: sig. F5r). The image of the fixed ruler and mobile subjects could thus be seen as an emblem of good governance, a dynamic also reflected in another potential interpretation of '***stone***' as a 'lodestone', or magnet. Yet the image of someone impassively controlling the emotions of others is also disturbing; this is, after all, what Iago does to Othello. The 'cold' nature of such imagined leaders also evokes Angelo in *Measure for Measure*, whose chilly self-control is such that he 'scarce confesses | That his blood flows; or that his appetite | Is more to bread than stone' (1.3.51–3), and of whom it is rumoured 'that when he makes water his urine is congealed ice' (3.2.110–11). Angelo is also a fitting archetype for this sonnet because, like the festering lilies of l. 14, his succumbing to temptation takes him below the moral level of those he has previously condemned (see l. 14n). '***To temptation slow***' contains its own ambiguities: the dominant sense is 'not susceptible' ('slow', OED 5a) to temptation, but 'slow' could also suggest 'sluggish; lacking in promptness' (OED 2a). Nor is 'being slow' to succumb to temptation synonymous with being resistant to it. The religious resonance of 'temptation' – with its

echo of the Lord's Prayer ('Lead us not into temptation', l. 9) – is compounded by 'inherit heaven's graces', in l. 5 (see note, below). The youth is associated with temptation at 41.4. 'Temptation' is also a word that recurs in *Measure for Measure*, where it is strongly associated with sexual temptation (2.2.158, 181).

5 ***rightly*** (i) properly; (ii) truly; (iii) wisely; (iv) justly; (v) by rights; Ingram and Redpath (1985: 214) argue that Shakespeare never uses 'rightly' in 'the moral or legal sense of "rightfully", "justly", "legitimately", or "of right"', and hence they attempt to restrict its meaning to 'truly', 'really', or 'indeed'; however, as Booth points out (1977: 306), even 'if there were reason to believe that uniqueness argues the nonexistence of unique instances, one might note that two of Shakespeare's other twenty-five uses of "rightly" pun on "justly" [*1 Henry IV*, 2.4.319–25 (the 'meteors' (pustules) on Bardolph's face portend 'choler [. . .] if rightly taken', to which Hal responds 'No, if rightly taken, halter [i.e. the gallows]'); *2 Henry IV*, 5.2.65–6 ('I am assured, if I be measured rightly, | Your Majesty hath no just cause to hate me')], and that seven others appear in suggestive contexts of justice'.

inherit 'come into possession of, as one's right or divinely assigned portion' (OED 3); see Matthew 25:34: 'Then shall the King say to them on his right hand, "Come ye blessed of my Father: inherit ye the kingdom prepared for you from the foundations of the world'"; this allusion is strengthened by the reference to 'heaven's graces' that follows; the catechism included in the order of service for confirmation in *The Book of Common Prayer* describes the respondent as 'an inheritor of the kingdom of heaven' (2010: 151). However, 'inherit' (read as 'to take or receive property [. . .] by legal descent or succession', OED 2a) also prepares us for the imagery of holding and managing landed estates in ll. 6–8 (imagery which recapitulates key motifs of Sonnets 1–17; see notes on l. 6, below).

heaven's pronounced as one syllable.

6 **husband** 'manage as a good householder or steward; to manage with thrift and prudence' (OED 2); compare the use of 'husbandry' at 3.6, 13.10.

nature's riches The *Sonnets* recurrently features Nature as a benefactress, albeit one vulnerable (as here) to financial exigencies: she lends liberally at 4.3–4; at 67.9, she is 'bankrupt'.

expense 'wasteful expenditure, extravagance' (OED 1a); compare the recurrent use of 'spend' to indicate 'waste, squander' (e.g. 4.1, 9.9, 146.6).

7–8 **They. . . excellence** These lines set up a distinction between those who have possession (i.e. control) of how they appear to the world (and who are figured as '**lords and owners**'), and those who do not (presumably because they are reliant on the favour of others, and therefore need to fawn, or at least modulate their demeanour according to another's mood) and who are described as '**stewards**', officers employed to manage another's household affairs (OED 1). 'Faces' could be neutral ('the countenance [. . .] as expressive of feeling or character', OED³ 2a) or negative ('pretence', OED³ 14). The antecedent of '**their excellence**' is ambiguous: it could be (i) the worth and beauty of the 'lords and owners' (a reading strengthened by the potential play on the honorific title 'your excellency'); (ii) the stewards, whose possession of such excellence is rather more tenuous.

8 **but** only.

9, 11 **flower** although he is not directly addressed in this sonnet (see headnote), the friend is recurrently associated with, or compared to, flowers (e.g. 5.13; 16.7; 69.12), especially roses (1.2; 35.2; 54.3, 6, 11; 67.8; 95.2; 98.10; 99.8; 109.14). See also note on l. 14, below. 'Flower' is pronounced as one syllable in both instances. The final quatrain shifts markedly in both focus and imagery, from the powerful men (plural) discussed in the first two quatrains to a singular 'flower'.

9, 13 **sweet. . . sweetest** The first usage relates to smell; the second (opposed to 'sourest') to taste.

10 **to itself** (i) for itself; (ii) by itself; both indicate that it remains unpollinated; compare the sterility of the odourless dog roses, dying 'to themselves' at 54.9–11; compare too 4.9–10, and Venus' critique of 'Things growing to themselves' at *Venus and Adonis*, l. 166.

11,12 **base. . . basest** Like 'sweet' and 'sweetest' (ll. 9, 13) the meaning shifts; 'base' indicates 'vile' ('morally low', OED³ A9); 'basest', lowliest, lowest in social status (OED³ A6a).

11 **infection** disease; Geoffrey Hill (1984: 153) points to the potential play on the etymology of the word, drawn from the Latin 'inficere' (to dip in, stain); as such, it gestures towards the idea of a (moral) stain or 'blot' found at 92.13, 95.11.

12 **outbraves** surpasses; the word is often used of beauty or clothing (OED³ 2b), which activates a pun on 'weed' (as clothing as well as plant). The verb appears in suggestive conjunction with lilies (l. 14) in the preface to John Gerard's *Herbal*: 'The lilies of the field outbraved him' (1597: sig. B5v).

dignity excellence (OED 1).

13 **For. . . deeds** The line combines two proverbs: 'What is sweet in the mouth is oft sour (bitter) in the maw [stomach]' (Dent M1265); 'The corruption of the best is worst' (Dent C668). There may also be an echo of 'Love is sweet in the beginning but sour in the ending' (Dent L513).

deeds The primary sense of the word conveys a sense of deliberate and intentional action: 'that which is done, acted, or performed by an intelligent or responsible agent' (OED 1a).

14 **Lilies. . . weeds** The stench of lilies was proverbial; see Dent L297 ('The lily is fair in show but foul in smell'); see also *Batman upon Bartholomew*: 'The lily flower smelleth full sweet, while it is whole and not broken, and

94

They that have power to hurt and will do none,
That do not do the thing they most do show,
Who, moving others, are themselves as stone,
Unmovèd, cold, and to temptation slow: 4
They rightly do inherit heaven's graces
And husband nature's riches from expense;
They are the lords and owners of their faces,
Others but stewards of their excellence.   8
The summer's flower is to the summer sweet,
Though to itself it only live and die,
But if that flower with base infection meet,
The basest weed outbraves his dignity: 12
    For sweetest things turn sourest by their deeds;
    Lilies that fester smell far worse than weeds.

stinketh full foul if it be broken and froted [rubbed] with hands' (1582: sig. 3E6v). The line appears exactly as here in *Edward III* (1596), 2.1.451, a play thought to contain scenes by Shakespeare, in a speech in which the Earl of Warwick argues that 'The greater the man, the greater is the thing, | Be it good or bad, that he shall undertake' (2.1.434–5), a sentiment that accords with l. 13, above. This is the first mention of 'lilies' in Q's sequence; they also appear (both times in conjunction with roses) at 98.9, 99.6. Lilies are recurrently associated with purity – and particularly sexual purity – in Shakespearean usage (hence the greater impact of their corruption here); Imogen is described as a 'fresh lily' and 'sweetest, fairest lily' (*Cymbeline*, 2.2.15; 4.2.201); the young Elizabeth described as 'a virgin |

A most unspotted lily' (*Henry VIII*, 5.4.60–1); and the Princess' virginity is compared to 'the unsullied lily' (*Love's Labours Lost*, 5.2.352).

fester putrefy, rot (OED 2); the word is strongly associated with wounds (OED 1a, b) and, in Shakespearean usage, with bodily corruption: see, for example, *Henry V*, 4.3.88 (where the bodies of the dead 'Must lie and fester'), *1 Henry VI*, 3.1.191 (where 'festered' limbs 'rot but by degree'), and *Romeo and Juliet*, 4.3.42–3 ('Where bloody Tybalt [...] | Lies festering in his shroud'). Prynne (2001: 82) draws attention to the use of word in Wyatt's translation of the third Penitential Psalm (Psalm 38): 'And of my flesh each not well-cured wound | That festered is by folly and negligence, | By secret lust hath rankled under skin' (ll. 345–7; 1549: sig. C2r).

95

Benson combines Sonnets 92–95 under the title 'A lover's affection though his love prove unconstant'.

1 **lovely** 'lovable' (OED³ A2), 'beautiful' (OED³ A3a).

2 **like. . . rose** As Booth points out (1977: 309), '**canker[s]**' (caterpillars or larvae; cankerworms [OED³ 3]) 'attack roses in the bud – when they are still immature and show promise of greater beauty to come [...] the extent of devastation is not visible until the matured rose opens [...] only a small hole, a small *spot* [l. 3], betrays the presence of the worm'. Compare 35.4 (and note), 70.7, 99.13. For the recurrent use of flower imagery in relation to the friend, see 94.9n. Q capitalises 'Rose', as it recurrently does for words indicating species; see 1.2n.

3 **spot** stain, tarnish (OED 1a); more vituperative than in modern usage, as can be seen from its use (as a noun) in Antony's attack on Cleopatra in *Antony and Cleopatra*, 4.12.33–6 ('Let him take thee | And hoist thee up to the shouting plebeians! | Follow his chariot, like the greatest spot | Of all thy sex'), or Gertrude's self-hatred in *Hamlet*, 3.4.89–91: 'Thou turn'st my eyes into my very soul, | And there I see such black and grained spots | As will not leave their tinct'. The word and its derivatives recur throughout *Lucrece* (ll. 196, 685, 721, 821, 1053, 1172, 1656), associated each time with a moral blemish.

budding name youthful ('budding') reputation; compare 35.4, where the 'canker lives in sweetest bud'.

4 **sweets** (i) delights (OED 3a; as at 8.2; 12.11; 19.7; 102.12); (ii) 'substances having a sweet smell; fragrant flowers or herbs' (OED 7), a possibility also available at 12.11; compare Gertrude's 'sweets to the sweet', as she scatters flowers on Ophelia's grave (*Hamlet*, 5.1.243).

enclose! The exclamation mark is in Q (one of ten in the volume; see 92.12n).

6 **lascivious** pronounced as three syllables.

comments The word was much more closely tied to written commentary than in modern usage; the 'tongue' (l. 5) that 'tells the story' is consequently figurative rather than literal (indicating a poet whose main medium is now writing rather than oral delivery); certainly comments are not associated (as now)

with being 'off-the-cuff' or 'throwaway'; rather, 'comments' indicate 'expository treatise[s]' and 'commentaries' (OED 1), or 'the expository or critical matter added to illustrate the text of a book' (OED 3); see, for example, John Dickenson's discussion of the challenges of translating the 'comment', sometimes 'more obscure than the text itself', in his English version of Louis Le Roy's *Aristotle's Politics* (1598: sig. A4v).

sport recreation, with a potential sexual resonance (particularly in proximity to 'lascivious'); see *Othello*, 2.3.16–17: 'He hath not yet made wanton the night with her; and she is sport for Jove'. This is one of two occurrences in the *Sonnets*, the other being in the following sonnet (96.2).

7 **praise,** The comma is in Q; recent editors are divided between those who follow Q (as here) and those who adopt a semi-colon at the end of l. 7 (punctuation first suggested by Capell), which leaves l. 8 as a free-standing unit, but flattens what Ingram and Redpath (1985: 218) call the 'meandering flow' of ll. 7–8.

8 **Naming. . . report** Naming you gives a gloss of praise to bad accounts (of your behaviour).

9–10 **O. . . thee** For the comparison of the youth to a mansion or family seat, see 10.7n; like the preceding sonnet (94), Sonnet 95 recapitulates some of the key motifs of Sonnets 1–17. Compare also *Romeo and Juliet*, 3.2.84–5 ('O that deceit should dwell | In such a gorgeous palace!'). 'Those vices' are the 'sins' of l. 4.

11–12 **Where. . . see!** These lines share the concerns of Sonnet 93. Line 11 has strong echoes of Hebrews 10:20: 'through the veil, that is, his flesh'. As with 'spot' (l. 3), 'blot' has a moral force that is weaker in modern usage; see 92.13n. The exclamation mark at the end of l. 12 is in Q (one of ten in the volume; see 92.12n).

12 **turns** The subject of the verb is probably 'veil' (l. 11), however 'turns' could also be the old third-person plural still found in Elizabethan English, with 'all things' as the subject (see Abbott 1884: § 333).

13 **privilege** special licence or advantage.

14 **The hardest. . . edge** The line sounds proverbial, although no exact match has been found; compare Dent I92 ('Iron with often handling is worn to nothing'); *Hamlet*, 1.3.77 ('borrowing

95

How sweet and lovely dost thou make the shame,
Which, like a canker in the fragrant rose,
Doth spot the beauty of thy budding name?
O in what sweets dost thou thy sins enclose!   4
That tongue that tells the story of thy days
(Making lascivious comments on thy sport)
Cannot dispraise but in a kind of praise,
Naming thy name, blesses an ill report.   8
O what a mansion have those vices got,
Which for their habitation chose out thee,
Where beauty's veil doth cover every blot,
And all things turns to fair that eyes can see!   12
    Take heed (dear heart) of this large privilege:
    The hardest knife ill-used doth lose his edge.

dulleth th' edge of husbandry'); Thomas Nashe, *Christ's Tears over Jerusalem* (1593): 'No sword but will lose his edge in long striking against stones' (2.37). There is a possible sexual resonance here (namely that the friend's potency is put at risk by his promiscuity): '***knife***' is used in a bawdy context at *Romeo and Juliet*, 2.4.201–3 ('There is a nobleman in town [...] that would fain lay knife aboard; but she, good soul, had as lieve see a toad'); '***edge***' at *Hamlet*, 3.2.249–50 ('It would cost you a groaning to take off mine edge'); for the sexual connotations of '***used***', see 6.5n.
his its.

96

Omitted from Benson's 1640 *Poems*; see headnote to Sonnet 18. The sonnet continues the concerns of Sonnet 95, with which it shares vocabulary.

1　*thy fault is youth* The 'Homily of Whoredom and Uncleanness' (*Certain Sermons or Homilies*, 1547) critiques those who excuse wantonness (as 'Some' do here) as 'a pastime, a dalliance, and but a touch of youth, not rebuked but winked at' (sig. S4v).
　　wantonness lasciviousness (OED³ 2), but it could also indicate recklessness (OED³ 1a), extravagance and self-indulgence (OED³ 4a), or capriciousness (OED³ 4b).

2　*thy grace* your charm, attractiveness, but with a strong sense of the friend's higher social status (evoking as it does the honorific title 'your grace'); the idea that the friend's aristocratic rank helps gloss over his faults is enhanced by the simile that follows, ll. 5–8.
　　gentle sport recreation befitting someone gentle-born; 'sport', however, carries connotations of sexual activity; see 95.6n. For the sexual connotations of 'gentle', see 20.3n.

3　*of more and less* by people of both higher and lower social rank.

4　*to thee resort* flock to you; consort with you; compare the 'vices' that 'chose out thee' (95.9–10).

5　*thronèd queen* For the ability of majesty to lend an attractive gloss, see Sidney's *Arcadia*: 'she was a queen and therefore beautiful' (1590: sig. K5r).

6　*basest* least valuable.

7　*So* in this way (leading on to the second part of the simile that began with 'As', l. 5).

8, 10　*translated. . . translate* change(d); a word often used of metamorphosis, as in *Midsummer Night's Dream*, 3.1.118–19: 'Bless thee, Bottom, bless thee! Thou art translated!'

9　*stern* grim.
　　betray deceive.

9–10　*How. . . translate?* These lines draw on a series of proverbs: l. 9 on the enmity between wolves and lambs (see Dent L36, 'The lamb is more in dread of the wolf than of the lion'); l. 10 on the proverbial disguise of wolves in sheep's clothing ('like a lamb' here indicates 'to look like a lamb'): see Aesop's fables; Dent W614 ('A wolf in lamb's skin'); Matthew 7:15: 'Beware of false prophets, which come

to you in sheep's clothing, but inwardly they are ravening wolves'. The image of the predatory wolf and the lamb, his victim, occurs in *Lucrece*, ll. 677, 878.

11　*gazers* those who see only the outward appearance of the lamb (rather than the wolf within); there is a possible pun on 'grazers'; compare *Winter's Tale*, 4.4.109–10: 'I should leave grazing, were I of your flock, | And only live by gazing'.
　　might'st Q's 'mighst' is a compositorial error, corrected by Lintott (in the first edition to reprint this poem, since it is omitted from Benson's 1640 *Poems*).
　　lead away mislead, lead astray; the friend's power to move others (see 94.3 and note) is here being abused; compare Cicero, *De Inventione* I.ii.3, which describes how, after eloquence had been used to lead men to civility and to bring about the foundation of cities, 'a certain agreeableness of manner – a depraved imitation of virtue – acquired the power of eloquence'.

12　*state* (i) condition, which might relate to someone's physical or financial well-being (OED³ 1b); (ii) stature, bodily form (OED³ 5b); (iii) social standing, high rank (OED³ 14a, 15a); (iv) magnificence, of clothing, lifestyle, etc. (OED³ 16); '*the strength of all thy state*' could thus indicate both 'the power of your social position' and 'of your external beauty'.

13–14　*But. . . report* The same couplet appears at the end of Sonnet 36. Hypotheses about why this should occur include (i) that Thorpe's copy-text for Sonnet 96 was incomplete, missing a couplet, which was then supplied from Sonnet 36 (Dowden 1881: 32); (ii) printer's error, arising when the last two lines of 96 dropped out; when resetting them, the printer mistakenly copied the proofs of Sonnet 36 instead, the only other sonnet in Q in which the last nine lines appear 'at the head of a page on the outer leaf of a quire' (John Sampson, *TLS*, 2 Oct 1919: 532). See Rollins (1944: 1.238) for a summary of arguments. Beeching (1904) also posits that the insertion of the couplet here must be corrupt, because it repeats the sound of the 'b' rhyme from the first quatrain. However, twelve other couplets repeat rhyme sounds from preceding quatrains within the *Sonnets*; in seven cases, one rhyme word is repeated exactly (3.9/14;

96

Some say thy fault is youth, some wantonness,
Some say thy grace is youth and gentle sport;
Both grace and faults are loved of more and less:
Thou mak'st faults graces that to thee resort.   4
As on the finger of a thronèd queen
The basest jewel will be well esteemed,
So are those errors that in thee are seen
To truths translated and for true things deemed.   8
How many lambs might the stern wolf betray,
If like a lamb he could his looks translate?
How many gazers might'st thou lead away,
If thou wouldst use the strength of all thy state?   12
　　But do not so; I love thee in such sort,
　　As thou being mine, mine is thy good report.

43.3/13;   51.6/13;   90.6/13;   133.2/14; 135.1/14; 136.2/14); in three cases, both couplet rhymes repeat, exactly, previous rhyming pairs (24.2/4; 46.10/12; 134.5/7); in the remaining two cases (4 and 97), the couplet shares the rhyme sound without repeating the actual rhyme word. Other editors and critics (e.g. Brooke 1936) suggest that the repetition is deliberate; as Kerrigan (1986: 297) argues, the same couplet concludes two groups of sonnets which are critical of the friend (35–36, 92–96): 'The common couplet makes the two groups rhyme, as it were, pointing up their relationship with a duplication entirely consistent with the intricate, echoing, repetitive mode of these late sonnets, reconsidering early concerns'.

14 ***report*** reputation (OED³ 5).

97

97–98 form a pair of 'separation' sonnets (compare 27–28, 43–45); the separation may be physical or (following from Sonnets 92–96) an emotional estrangement. Like Sonnets 94–95, Sonnet 97 echoes some of the themes and language of Sonnets 1–17: here, the use of seasonal imagery, married with a troubled sense of procreation.

Benson combines Sonnets 97–99 under the title 'Complaint for his love's absence'.

1 **absence** separation; see headnote.
2, 3, 4 **?** The question marks are in Q; most editors turn them into exclamation marks, on the grounds (i) that punctuation marks are regularly muddled up in the compositor's case; (ii) that the exclamation mark was a typographic novelty, used only rarely in Q (see 92.12n); and (iii) that 'How' and 'What' indicate exclamations rather than questions. As at 43.8, 12, this edition retains Q's punctuation, since questions – even rhetorical ones – endeavour to make a connection with an addressee in a way that exclamations do not, and such a desire to reach out to the friend is entirely consistent with the poet-speaker's strategy.
2 **the pleasure. . . year** qualifies 'thee'; this could suggest either (i) 'you, who encapsulate all that is delightful about the swiftly-passing year'; or (ii) 'you who delight the swiftly-passing year'; time also 'fleet'st' at 19.5.
3 **What freezings. . . seen** Freezing was a stereo-typical state experienced by the unrequited lover; see Googe's witty parody of Petrarchan cliché: 'Two lines shall tell the griefs that I by love sustain. | I burn, I flame, I faint, I freeze, of Hell I feel the pain' (*Eclogues, Epitaphs, and Sonnets*, 1563: sig. G6v). Shakespeare here extends the conceit, so that – estranged from the beloved – the poet-speaker experiences an emotional winter, characterised by 'freezings' and '**dark days**' (because the days are shorter during winter in the northern hemisphere). For the absence of the beloved as the absence of light, compare Sidney, *Astrophil and Stella* 91.
4 **old December's** As the epitome of winter, December is conventionally personified as old. Compare Ovid, *Metamorphoses* 15.212–13 (Golding 15.233–5; sig. 2C5v): 'Then ugly winter last | Like age steals on with

trembling steps, all bald, or overcast | With shirl [rough] thin hair as white as snow'.
bareness everywhere The exact phrase appears at 5.8; as at 5.8, Gildon (1710) emends to 'barrenness' (of which 'bareness' is an acceptable sixteenth-century spelling); see 5.8n.
5, 9 **yet** nevertheless.
5 **this time removed** the time of physical or emotional separation ('absence', l. 1); Antonio uses 'removed' to express emotional distance in *Twelfth Night*, 5.1.89, when he describes Sebastian as 'a twenty years removed thing'.
summer's time Bearing in mind the pro-creation imagery that follows ll. 5–7, there may be a quibble here on 'time' as 'period of gestation' (OED³ A24); compare *Winter's Tale*, 2.2.23, where Hermione 'is, something before her time, delivered'.
6–10 **The teeming. . . fruit** For the contrast between the flourishing summer and the poet-speaker's downbeat mood, see Petrarch *Rime Sparse* 310: 'Zephyrus [the west wind] returns and leads back the fine weather and the flowers and the grass [. . .] But to me, alas, come back heavier sighs' (ll. 1–2, 9–10) ['Zefiro torna e 'l bel tempo rimena | e i fiori et l'erbe [. . .] | Ma per me, lasso, tornano i più gravi | sospiri'].
6 **teeming** fertile (*adj.*1, OED 2a, citing *Richard II*, 2.1.51 – 'this teeming womb of royal kings' – as the first example in this sense).
big heavily pregnant.
increase Compare 1.1, 11.5.
7 **wanton** (i) sexually promiscuous (OED³ A3a); (ii) playful, sportive (OED³ A4c), frolicsome (OED³ A4b); (iii) 'profuse in growth, luxuriant' (OED³ A7a); compare *Richard II*, 1.3.214: 'Four lagging winters and four wanton springs'.
burden 'burthen' in Q, an acceptable early modern variant for 'burden' (i.e. the child in the womb, OED 4a).
prime spring (*n.*1, OED³ 7); 'prime' becomes the husband, with autumn as the widowed wife, bearing his posthumous child (the harvest).
9 **this abundant issue** the harvest.
10 **But** only.
orphans The term could be used of children lacking only one parent; see OED³ A1.
unfathered 'deprived of a father' (*adj.*2, OED); compare 124.2.

97

How like a winter hath my absence been
From thee, the pleasure of the fleeting year?
What freezings have I felt, what dark days seen?
What old December's bareness everywhere?   4
And yet this time removed was summer's time,
The teeming autumn big with rich increase,
Bearing the wanton burden of the prime,
Like widowed wombs after their lords' decease: 8
Yet this abundant issue seemed to me
But hope of orphans and unfathered fruit,
For summer and his pleasures wait on thee,
And, thou away, the very birds are mute,   12
    Or if they sing, 'tis with so dull a cheer
    That leaves look pale, dreading the winter's near.

11 *For* because.
   his (i) its; (ii) alternatively, there is a mild personification of summer; for summer as male, see 5.6n.
   wait on attend; for the power of the friend to draw people and things into his service, see 53.2.
12 *thou away* you being away.
   the very. . . mute Compare 73.4.

13 *cheer* mood (*n*.1, OED 3a).
14 *That* with the result that.
   leaves. . . near Compare 73.2–3; leaves fade and lose their summer colour once the autumn chill sets in; however, the line also hints at personification, as if the leaves grow pale with fear as they anticipate winter's approach.

98

Benson combines Sonnets 97–99 under the title 'Complaint for his love's absence'. Sonnet 98 continues on from Sonnet 97 in its exploration of the seasons as a means of expressing the feelings of the poet-speaker when separated from the friend.

2 **proud pied** splendid and parti-coloured, presumably referring to the variety of colours (including subtly different greens) visible in a spring landscape; hyphenated (as a compound adjective) by many editors from Malone onwards.
   April the month which epitomises spring (as December does winter, in 97.4); see the opening of Chaucer's *Canterbury Tales*, ll. 1–2: 'Whan that Aprill with his shoures soote | The droghte of March hath perced to the roote'. For the image of April as well-dressed, see *Romeo and Juliet*, 1.2.27–8: 'well-apparelled April on the heel | Of limping winter treads'.
   trim dress, array (OED 4a).
3 **spirit** here pronounced as one syllable; see 56.8n.
4 **That** so that.
   heavy Saturn Saturn was the planet believed to increase the amount of black bile in the body, which in turn produced melancholy (i.e. a 'heavy' mood; see 29.12n); compare the adjective 'saturnine' ('sluggish, cold, and gloomy in temperament', OED A1b). Saturn was also associated with winter (see Stephen Batman, *The Golden Book of the Leaden Gods*, 1577: sig. C1v) and with old age (see Chaucer, *Knight's Tale*, ll. 2443–52).
   laughed and leapt 'To laugh and leap' (Dent L92a.1) was a proverbial expression of joy.
5 **Yet** nevertheless.
   nor. . . nor neither. . . nor.
   lays songs; already slightly archaic, or poetic, by the late sixteenth century; Shakespeare's Gower, for instance, uses the word at *Pericles*, 5.0.4. Shakespeare uses the word three times in the *Sonnets*, all three instances appearing in close proximity in Q's sequence, the other two occurrences being 100.7 and (in a rhyming position) 102.6.
6 **Of. . . hue** flowers which are different in scent and colour ('hue').
   different pronounced as two syllables.
   flowers pronounced as one syllable.
7 **any summer's story** a cheerful story, since 'a sad tale's best for winter' (*Winter's Tale*, 2.1.25); compare 'summer songs' (*Winter's Tale*, 4.3.11).

8 **proud** 'of a plant, crop, etc.: full of sap; luxuriant in growth' (OED[3] A6d).
   lap metonym for earth; compare *Richard II*, 5.2.46–7: 'Who are the violets now | That strew the green lap of the new-come spring?'.
9 **lily's white** Since Q has no apostrophes marking the possessive, Q's 'lilies white' could be (i) a noun phrase (in which the adjective and noun are inverted, for the purpose of the rhyme); (ii) a plural possessive (lilies' white); (iii) the singular possessive, in which 'lily' is representative of lilies in general; (iii) has been chosen here, because of the probably parallel with the singular 'rose' of l. 10. Lilies were proverbially the epitome of whiteness (see Dent L296) and were conventionally used as a sign of beauty (particularly in conjunction with roses) in amorous verse; see, for example, Richard Alison, *An Hour's Recreation in Music*, Song 19: 'There is a garden in her face, where roses and white lilies grow' (1606: sig. D2r). Shakespeare draws on this convention when describing Lucrece's beauty (seen through Tarquin's eyes) in *Lucrece*, ll. 71, 386.
10 **vermilion** bright red or scarlet; roses were proverbially red (Dent R177) and sweet (R178); for the use of roses in amorous poetry, see note on 'lily's white', above (l. 9).
11 **They** the lily and the rose.
   but. . . but merely.
   sweet pleasant, but also evoking the sense of 'sweet-smelling' (as in l. 5).
   figures images, representations (as opposed to the real thing); compare 'shadow' (l. 14).
12 **Drawn after you** copied from you; compare 53.6.
   pattern model (for lilies and roses); compare 19.12 and *Othello*, 5.2.11: 'Thou cunning'st pattern of excelling nature'. The friend is also made the epitome of beauty in Sonnet 53. In Sidney's *Astrophil and Stella* 91, Astrophil – separated from Stella ('in sorrow's night', l. 4) – explains how he finds pleasure in other women's beauty, 'because of you they models be' (l. 10).
   those the lily and the rose.
13 **Yet. . . still** Compare 97.1.
   you away you being absent; compare 97.12.
14 **shadow** 'delusive semblance or image . . . Often contrasted with *substance*' (OED 6a); compare 27.10; 37.10; 61.4.
   these the lily and the rose.

98

From you have I been absent in the spring,
When proud pied April (dressed in all his trim)
Hath put a spirit of youth in everything,
That heavy Saturn laughed and leapt with him.   4
Yet nor the lays of birds, nor the sweet smell
Of different flowers in odour and in hue
Could make me any summer's story tell,
Or from their proud lap pluck them where they grew.   8
Nor did I wonder at the lily's white,
Nor praise the deep vermillion in the rose;
They were but sweet, but figures of delight
Drawn after you, you pattern of all those.   12
    Yet seemed it winter still, and you away,
    As with your shadow I with these did play.

99

Benson combines Sonnets 97–99 under the title 'Complaint for his love's absence'. Sonnet 99 follows on from Sonnet 98, continuing the flower motif, to the extent that some editors (e.g. Malone) conclude Sonnet 98 with a colon, so that the violet and the marjoram are among 'these' flowers, with which the poet-speaker 'play[s]' (98.14). The governing motif of this sonnet is fairly conventional; see Petrarch *Rime Sparse* 127; however, there are particularly strong parallels with Constable's *Diana* 17 (1592):

> My lady's presence makes the roses red,
> Because they see her lips they blush for shame.
> The lily's leaves, for envy, pale became,
> And her white hands in them this envy bred.
> The marigold the leaves abroad doth spread,
> Because the sun's and her power is the same.
> The violet of purple colour came,
> Dyed in the blood she made my heart to shed.
> In brief, all flowers from her their virtue take;
> From her sweet breath their sweet smells do proceed;
> The living heat which her eyebeams doth make
> Warmeth the ground and quickeneth the seed.
>> The rain, wherewith she watereth the flowers,
>> Falls from mine eyes, which she dissolves in showers. (sig. D1r)

For other potential debts to Constable, see 24.7n, 106.9n, 128.12n.

Sonnet 99 is the only fifteen-line sonnet in *Shakespeare's Sonnets*, the first rhyming unit being five rather than four lines long (rhyming ababa). Unlike the other sonnets in this edition, line numbers have been inserted at ll. 5, 9, 13 to mark the end of the rhyming units. Whilst many sonnet collections (e.g. Barnes' *Parthenophil and Parthenophe*, 1593) include fifteen-line sonnets, and the term 'sonnet' was used rather loosely in the period (see Shrank 2008), such deviance from the form of fourteen decasyllabic lines is extremely unusual in Q. There are only two other examples: Sonnets 126 (six decasyllabic couplets, with the absence of a seventh couplet marked by brackets) and 145, with its fourteen octosyllabic lines. Otherwise, Shakespeare adheres to Gascoigne's strictures, which state that a sonnet is a poem 'of fourteen lines, every line containing ten syllables. The first twelve do rhyme in staves of four lines by cross metre, and the last two rhyming together do conclude the whole' ('Certain notes of instruction', *Posies* 1575: sig U1v). Some editors and critics (e.g. Beeching 1904) see Sonnet 99 as a draft; others (e.g.

G. Hammond 1981: 144–9) suggest that this is a deliberately hackneyed panegyric; others posit that the unusual length 'reinforces the sense of a potentially unlimited catalogue of flowers' (Duncan-Jones 1997a: 308; compare Burrow 2002: 578).

1 *forward* (i) 'of a plant, a crop, or the seasons: well advanced, early' (OED A5b); (ii) precocious (OED A7).
   violet a spring flower, particularly associated (i) with a sweet smell (see *Venus and Adonis*, l. 936); and (ii) youth and impermanence; see *Hamlet*, 1.3.5–8: 'For Hamlet, and the trifling of his favour, | Hold it a fashion and a toy in blood, | A violet in the youth of primy nature, | Forward, not permanent, sweet, not lasting'. 'Violet' is pronounced as three syllables.

2–5 *'Sweet. . . dyed.'* The speech marks are editorial.

2 *Sweet thief* Compare the description of the friend at 35.14.
   thy sweet fragrance (OED 6); used in the same sense in l. 15.

3–5 *The purple. . . dyed* There are similarities to *Venus and Adonis*, ll. 1165–70; however, the conceit is not entirely clear and does not exactly parallel ll. 2–3 (where the violet steals its odour from the friend) or ll. 7–11 (where the lily, marjoram and rose purloin qualities from the friend): in ll. 3–5, the exchange seems to work the other way, so that the violet stains (in an inexpert fashion) the friend's veins. The awkwardness of the conceit, which does not follow the pattern of the rest of the poem – where the flowers steal their beautiful qualities from the youth – may be the result of the sonnet being imperfectly revised (see headnote). Alternatively, as Blakemore Evans suggests, 'just possibly a thought may be developing in which the violet is accused of misrepresenting by too gross an imitation the delicacy of colour of the youth's veins' (1996: 208).

3 *breath?* Ending a sentence mid-way through the line is unusual in Shakespeare's sonnets, a syntactical rarity disguised by Q's punctuation at this point.
   purple In Elizabethan usage, 'purple' covers a range of shades, from blood-red to violet; as a colour associated with emperors, monarchs and cardinals it has a close association with 'pride'.
   pride splendour.

4 *complexion* 'a colouring preparation applied (by women) to "give a complexion" to a face' (OED 6).

99

The forward violet thus did I chide:
'Sweet thief, whence didst thou steal thy sweet that smells,
If not from my love's breath? The purple pride,
Which on thy soft cheek for complexion dwells,
In my love's veins thou hast too grossly dyed.'   5
The lily I condemnèd for thy hand,
And buds of marjoram had stol'n thy hair;
The roses fearfully on thorns did stand,
One blushing shame, another white despair;   9
A third, nor red nor white, had stol'n of both
And to his robbery had annexed thy breath;
But for his theft, in pride of all his growth,
A vengeful canker eat him up to death.   13
    More flowers I noted, yet I none could see,
    But sweet or colour it had stol'n from thee.

5 *grossly* thickly (OED 1); obviously (OED 2); compare 82.13, and *Lucrece*, l. 1173.

6–7 *The lily. . . hair* The syntax of these lines is compressed (perhaps a further sign that the sonnet is imperfectly revised); '*condemnèd*' applies to both the lily and the marjoram buds: the poet-speaker denounces the lily (for stealing the whiteness of the friend's hand) and the marjoram buds, which pilfer unspecified qualities from the friend's hair: fragrance, thickness and golden colour all seem relevant; John Gerard's *Herbal* describes sweet marjoram as 'of a whitish colour and marvellous sweet smell' (1597: 538).

6 *lily* See 98.9n.

6–15 *thy. . . thee* The addressee in ll. 6–15 is the friend (switching from the violet in ll. 2–5).

8 *roses. . . stand* The line combines two proverbs: 'No rose without a thorn' (Dent R182) and 'To stand upon thorns' (Dent T239), i.e. 'to be anxious', a state of trepidation also expressed pleonastically through 'fearfully'. The roses are fearful because they are guilty about the theft they have committed. For the use and significance of roses within the *Sonnets*, see also 1.2n.

9 *One* 'Our' in Q; 'one' and 'our' are easily mistaken when reading sixteenth-century handwriting, as can be seen by looking at printed lists of errata.

One blushing . . . despair The syntax of the line is compressed: one rose is blushing with shame; the other is white with despair.

10 *A third. . . both* a damasked rose, i.e. one that is both red and white; alternatively, it might indicate 'pink'. See 130.5n.

nor. . . nor neither. . . nor.

11 *robbery* pronounced as two syllables.

annexed appropriated.

12 *But* however.

for on account of, in punishment for.

in pride. . . growth in their 'prime' ('pride, *n*.1', OED[3] 10a); 'pride' also suggests arrogance and an inflated opinion of oneself.

13 *A vengeful. . . death* Compare the destructive canker-worms at 35.4, 70.7, 95.2; *Lucrece*, l. 848; *Romeo and Juliet*, 2.3.30: 'Full soon the canker death eats up that plant'. 'Eat' is past tense.

14 *flowers* pronounced as two syllables.

15 *But* except.

sweet sweet smell.

100

Benson combines Sonnets 100–101 under the title
'An invocation to his Muse'. In Q's sequence this
is the first of four sonnets (100–103) which, like
Sonnets 83 and 85–86, apologise for a period of
silence on the poet-speaker's part.

1, 5, 9 *Muse* creative faculty; for Shakespeare's use of
the word in the *Sonnets*, see 21.1n.

3 *Spend'st thou* are you expending, wasting;
compare 'spent' (l. 6).
fury the *furor poeticus* or poetic frenzy; compare
the 'poet's rage' (17.11) and King Ferdinand's
response to Berowne's poeticising in *Love's
Labours Lost*, 4.3.225: 'What zeal, what fury,
hath inspired thee now?'

4 *Darkening* (i) sullying; compare *Antony and
Cleopatra*, 1.4.10–11 ('I must not think there
are | Evils enow to darken all his goodness');
(ii) clouding, depriving of light; compare
Henry VIII, 1.1.224–6 ('I am the shadow of
poor Buckingham | Whose figure even this
instant cloud puts on | By darkening my clear
sun'). 'Darkening' is here pronounced as two
syllables.
power pronounced as one syllable.
base subjects inferior subject matter; a play
on the political meaning of the word further underscores the contrast between such
worthless subject matter and the friend, who
is treated elsewhere in the sequence as a 'sovereign' sun; see Sonnets 7, 33–34.

5 *straight* immediately.
redeem compensate for (OED[3] 11a); to
'redeem [...] time' has a Biblical resonance,
drawn from Ephesians 5:15–16: 'Take heed
therefore that ye walk circumspectly [...]
Redeeming the time, for the days are evil'.

6 *gentle numbers* noble verses, opposed to the
writing produced on 'base subjects'; compare
79.3 and note.
idly probably 'ineffectively' (OED 1a) rather
than 'lazily' (OED 2).
spent expended, wasted; compare 'spend'st'
(l. 3).

7 *lays* songs; see 98.5n.

8 *skill and argument* ability to write and something to write about (where 'argument' means
subject matter, OED 6).

9 *resty* 'sluggish' (*adj*.2, OED[3] 4a) rather than
'restless' (OED[3] 1); compare 'resty sloth'

(*Cymbeline*, 3.6.34), Shakespeare's only other
usage of the word.

9–10 *survey* | *If* inspect to see if.

10 *Time... there* Compare the effects of time at
2.2, 22.3, 60.10.

11 *If* if there are.
be... decay 'pillory the destructive effects of
time as a satirist would'; 'satire' is capitalised
and italicised in Q, which frequently indicates
a proper name or (as here) an unfamiliar or
'learned' term, usually etymologically derived
from Greek or Latin (see 1.2n). This is an
early use of 'satire' to mean 'satirist' (see OED[3]
4), an extension of the word which probably rests on the early modern connection
between 'satyr' and 'satire'; see Puttenham,
Art of English Poesy: 'the first and most bitter invective against vice and vicious men was
the satire: which to th' intent their bitterness
should breed none ill will, either to the poets,
or to the reciters (which could not have
been chosen if they had been openly known)
and besides to make their admonitions and
reproofs seem graver and of more efficacy,
they made wise as if the gods of the woods,
whom they called Satyrs or Silvans, should
appear and recite those verses of rebuke'
(1589: 24).

12 *spoils* acts of destruction: it is the destructiveness of time, not what is destroyed, which
should be 'despisèd'.

13 *my love* (i) my affection; (ii) my beloved.

14 *So* in this way.
prevent'st Most editors from Gildon on
emend Q's 'preuenst' (as here); Kerrigan
and Wells, however, retain 'prevene'st', on
the grounds that 'prevene' is a distinct verb
current from the fifteenth to eighteenth centuries; however, Shakespeare does not use the
verb 'prevene' elsewhere; nor (according to
searches on EEBO-TCP) is 'prevene' as common as Kerrigan (1986: 303) suggests; the
word (and its variants) appears in just 7 texts
(besides the *Sonnets*) between 1500 and 1609;
of these, 6 are Scottish in origin. Both 'prevent'st' and 'prevene'st' here mean 'forestall'.
scythe... crookèd knife The 'crookèd knife'
may refer to Time's sickle, or provide further description of his scythe; see 12.13n.
'Crooked' may suggest 'malicious' (as at 60.7)
as well as 'curved'.

100

Where art thou, Muse, that thou forget'st so long
To speak of that which gives thee all thy might?
Spend'st thou thy fury on some worthless song,
Darkening thy power to lend base subjects light?   4
Return, forgetful Muse, and straight redeem
In gentle numbers time so idly spent;
Sing to the ear that doth thy lays esteem
And gives thy pen both skill and argument.   8
Rise, resty Muse, my love's sweet face survey,
If Time have any wrinkle graven there;
If any, be a satire to decay,
And make Time's spoils despisèd everywhere.   12
    Give my love fame faster than Time wastes life,
    So thou prevent'st his scythe and crooked knife.

101

Benson combines Sonnets 100–101 under the title
'An invocation to his Muse'. Despite Benson's reputation for altering male pronouns to female ones in
his 1640 *Poems* (see De Grazia 2000: 90), this is the
only sonnet in which he does so (see notes on ll. 11,
14); for Benson's other alterations to the gender of
the addressee, see 108.5n, and headnotes to Sonnets
113–15, 122, 125.

1 *O truant Muse* continues from Sonnet 100,
which also berates the poet-speaker's sluggish
Muse. 'Muse' here, and at ll. 5 and 13, means
'creative faculty'; for Shakespeare's use of the
word in the *Sonnets*, see 21.1n.
truant idle, lazy (OED, B1a).
amends reparation; compare 100.5.

2 *truth. . . dyed* truth steeped in and permeated
by beauty, playing on the Platonic notion that
truth is beauty, and beauty truth; see 14.11,
14; 54.1–2, 13–14; 'Let the bird of loudest
lay', ll. 62–4. 'Dye' does not necessarily imply
superficiality or deceit; compare 54.5 and
111.7.

3 *my love* (i) my affection; (ii) my beloved.
depends a singular verb ending after plural subjects is possible in early modern English (see
Abbott 1884: § 333); as Ingram and Redpath
note, 'The Platonic ideas of Truth and Beauty
are made to depend on the Friend, thus reversing the dependence of the temporal on the
eternal' (1985: 230).

4 *So. . . dignified* The poet-speaker's Muse is
exalted/honoured because she (like truth and
beauty) relies on 'my love' (l. 3).

5 *haply* perhaps.

6–8 *'Truth. . . intermixed'* proverbial; see Dent
T585 ('Truth needs no colours'); there is also
a possible play on *'colour'* as a rhetorical figure ('colour, *n*.1', OED[3] 15), and hence on the
proverb 'Truth has not need of rhetoric' (Dent
T575). The speech marks – indicating the
Muse's imagined response – are editorial.

6 *Truth. . . fixed* (i) Truth's colour is permanent
('fixed'), so it does not need further touching up
(where 'his' is 'its', i.e. truth's); (ii) Truth does not
need further rhetorical embellishment ('colour,
n.1', OED[3] 15) when made permanently beautiful by the friend's complexion (OED[3] 2a),
where 'his' refers to the friend.

7 *pencil* paintbrush; see 16.10 and note.
lay 'put upon a surface in layers; to arrange
(colours, a picture) on canvas' (*v*.1, OED 41a).

8 *intermixed* adulterated (Ingram and Redpath).

9 *he* the friend; Benson omits to alter this pronoun to a feminine one (see headnote).

11 *him* Benson changes this pronoun to 'her' (one
of three pronouns he changes; see l. 14n, below).
gilded tomb Compare 55.1; 'gilded' introduces a
sense of a superficial attractiveness; see 20.6n.

12 *ages yet to be* Compare 17.7.

13 *office* duty.

14 *him. . . he* altered by Benson to 'her' and 'she'.
shows appears.

101

O truant Muse, what shall be thy amends
For thy neglect of truth in beauty dyed?
Both truth and beauty on my love depends:
So dost thou too and therein dignified.   4
Make answer, Muse, wilt thou not haply say,
'Truth needs no colour with his colour fixed,
Beauty no pencil beauty's truth to lay,
But best is best, if never intermixed'?   8
Because he needs no praise, wilt thou be dumb?
Excuse not silence so, for 't lies in thee
To make him much outlive a gilded tomb
And to be praised of ages yet to be.   12
    Then do thy office, Muse, I teach thee how,
    To make him seem long hence, as he shows now.

102

Benson combines Sonnets 102–103 under the title 'Amazement'. Like Sonnets 100–101, 102 apologises for a period of silence on the poet-speaker's part, although in this poem he moves away from blaming his Muse.

1   *seeming* appearance.
2   *show* outward appearance (*n*.1, OED 2a), but may also have connotations of 'ostentatious display' (OED 4a).
    appear is evident.
3   *merchandised* made into a commodity for selling; Shakespeare's only use of the word as an adjective. For the notion that sincere love keeps silent, see headnote to Sonnet 85.
    rich esteeming high valuation (placed on it by its owner); compare 21.14; Dent P546 ('He praises who wishes to sell').
5   *but* only.
    in the spring in its early days; compare 'spring' at 63.8.
6   *wont* accustomed.
    lays songs; see 98.5n.
7   *Philomel* the nightingale; Philomel was raped by her brother-in-law Tereus, who cut out her tongue to prevent her disclosing what had happened; the gods later turned Philomel into a nightingale (giving her back her voice); see Ovid, *Metamorphoses* 6.422–74 (Golding, 6.540–853; sigs L2v–7r); Shakespeare alludes to the story in *Titus Andronicus*.
    summer's front at the beginning of summer; compare *Winter's Tale*, 4.4.2–3: 'Flora | Peering in April's front'.
8   *stops his pipe* ceases his singing; the male pronoun is problematic; although only male nightingales sing, Philomel is always depicted as female (in avine as well as human form), and the feminine pronoun 'her' is used in ll. 10, 13. As a result, editors (following Housman 1835) frequently emend 'his' to 'her'. However, 'his' is not easily mistaken for 'her' in sixteenth-century handwriting; the reading would therefore seem authorial

rather than compositorial, and for that reason should be allowed to stand. Burrow suggests that 'the inconsistency illustrates Shakespeare's instinctive association of certain locales with particular genders': in l. 8, 'pipe' suggests pastoral 'where pipers are invariably male, and often are allegorical projections of their poets. The nightingale's metamorphosis back into *her* in l. 10 occurs when the context of pious nocturnal unhappiness jogs Shakespeare into remembering her mythological past. Nocturnal hymn-singing tends to be a feminine activity in Shakespearean drama' (2002: 584).
growth of riper days as the summer matures (along with its fruits); the nightingale is migratory and leaves England in late summer; in the early modern period – before they knew about its migratory patterns – they simply thought that the nightingale stopped singing in July; see Philip Sidney, 'As I my little flock on Ister bank', ll. 13–14: 'As for the nightingale, wood-music's king, | It August was; he deigned not then to sing'. Since it is only the unpaired males who sing, nightingale song will also get rarer as the summer progresses (even before the birds migrate).
11 *But that* parallels 'Not that' (l. 9).
    wild music unrestrained, tumultuous music, which is made by wild birds.
    burdens 'burthens', in Q, an acceptable early modern variant of 'burdens'; the birdsong is so plentiful (occurring on 'every bough') that it seems to 'weigh down' the branches; there is also a play on the musical senses of the noun 'burden' (accompaniment, OED 9; chorus, OED 10).
12 *sweets. . . delight* Compare Sonnet 52.4; Dent P417: 'Pleasure the rarer used the more commendable'.
    sweets pleasures.
    common frequent; compare the criticism of the friend at 69.14.
13 *sometime* from time to time; compare 18.5.
14 *dull* (i) bore you; (ii) make you seem less lustrous; compare 103.8.

102

My love is strengthened, though more weak in seeming;
I love not less, though less the show appear:
That love is merchandised whose rich esteeming
The owner's tongue doth publish everywhere.   4
Our love was new and then but in the spring,
When I was wont to greet it with my lays,
As Philomel in summer's front doth sing
And stops his pipe in growth of riper days;   8
Not that the summer is less pleasant now
Than when her mournful hymns did hush the night,
But that wild music burdens every bough,
And sweets grown common lose their dear delight.   12
   Therefore, like her, I sometime hold my tongue,
   Because I would not dull you with my song.

103

Benson combines Sonnets 102–103 under the title 'Amazement'. In Q's sequence, this is the last of a group of four sonnets (100–103) apologising for a period of silence on the poet-speaker's part.

1 *poverty* poor stuff (Ingram and Redpath); compare 40.10.
   Muse creative faculty; for Shakespeare's use of the word in the *Sonnets*, see 21.1n.

2 *That* In that.
   scope opportunity; compare 29.7.
   pride splendour (compare 76.1); perhaps also pride in the friend.

3–4 *The argument. . . beside* 'The unadorned subject matter is more valuable than when it has my praise added to it as well'; compare the proverb 'The truth shows best being naked' (Dent T589). The friend is called a 'lovely argument' at 79.5.

5 *no more* (i) nothing better than I do; (ii) nothing better than the bare argument of l. 3; (iii) no longer.
   write! The exclamation mark is in Q (one of ten in the volume; see 92.12n).

6, 14 *glass* mirror.

6 *Look. . . glass* echoes 3.1, but in a eulogistic rather than admonitory vein; see also 77.1 (where the mirror served as a memento mori).

7 *overgoes* (i) surpasses; (ii) overpowers.
   blunt (i) dull, stupid (OED A1); (ii) rough, without refinement (OED A4a); (iii) plain-spoken, curt (OED 5); the knife imagery is continued by 'dulling' in l. 8.
   invention one of the five parts of classical rhetoric; see 38.8n.

8 *Dulling* making tedious, blunting (so that the verses lack sharpness and refinement); compare 102.14.

9–10 *striving. . . well* Compare *King Lear*, 1.4.346 ('Striving to better, oft we mar what's well'); *Lucrece*, l. 578; Dent M875.1 ('To mend and to mar').

11 *pass* outcome, end.

12 *graces* charms, attractions.
   tell The verb is attached to 'of', which appears earlier in the line, making its primary meaning 'speak (of)'; since the verb is, however, detached from its particle, it is also possible to hear a secondary resonance of 'count, number' (OED 20a).

14 *shows you* (i) reveals you to be; (ii) reveals to you.

103

Alack, what poverty my Muse brings forth
That, having such a scope to show her pride,
The argument all bare is of more worth
Than when it hath my added praise beside.   4
O blame me not if I no more can write!
Look in your glass and there appears a face
That overgoes my blunt invention quite,
Dulling my lines and doing me disgrace.   8
Were it not sinful then, striving to mend,
To mar the subject that before was well?
For to no other pass my verses tend
Than of your graces and your gifts to tell;   12
    And more, much more, than in my verse can sit
    Your own glass shows you, when you look in it.

104

Benson combines Sonnets 104–106 under the title 'Constant affection'.

1 *friend* Benson substitutes 'love'; De Grazia suggests (2000: 90) that this is because that is the predominant address used for the friend in Sonnet 105 (with which 104 is grouped by Benson); retaining 'friend' would thus disrupt the continuity, when three sonnets are combined into one.

2 *when. . . eyed* 'when first I saw you'; Booth (1977: 333) highlights the conjunction of three rhetorical figures: (i) pun (eye, I); (ii) *polyptoton* (with eye/eyed); and (iii) *epizeuxis*. Shakespeare uses the eye/I quibble on a number of occasions, including *Hamlet*, 2.2.290, in the mouth of its punning protagonist ('I have an eye of you'); and *Henry VIII*, 1.1.66–9 ('I cannot tell | What heaven hath given him – let some graver eye | Pierce into that – but I can see his pride | Peep through each part of him'). The latter example points to the way in which the homophone 'eye/I' suggests an idea of the self ('I'), which here activates a play on two neo-Platonic concepts: (i) the eye as the window of the soul; (ii) the idea that a beautiful soul resides in a beautiful body.

3 *seems* appears; considering the examination of the relationship between the friend's inner and outer beauty in Sonnets 93–96, it is possible to read some degree of irony into the word; see 93.3n.

  still: three The decisive break mid-line is unusual in Shakespeare's sonnets, but not without precedent; see 99.3. *Still*: 'even now'.

  winters cold Because of the lack of possessive apostrophes in early modern English, 'winters' cold' is a possible modernisation, but less likely (despite the parallel with 'summers' pride', l. 4), owing to the plural 'have' in l. 4; Shakespeare uses a singular verb form with a plural subject (see 101.3n), but not vice versa.

3–4 *three winters. . . pride* The apparently precise chronological reference to 'three' winters is seized on by those critics and editors interested in hunting for autobiographical readings. However, these lines are probably translated from Horace, *Epodes*, 11.5–6: 'The third December, since I ceased to lust after Inachia, now is shaking the glory from the forests' ['hic tertius December, ex quo destiti |

Inachia furere, silvis honorem decutit']. There is thus a certain conventionality about a three-year affair, and Horace's timescale is adopted by Ronsard, Desportes and Vauquelin de la Fresnaie (see Rollins 1944: 1.255–6), although Daniel changes the celebration of 'three years' witness' (*Delia* 26.6) to 'five years' in editions from 1601 onwards.

4 *shook* past participle of the verb 'shake' (where modern English would have 'shaken'); compare *Timon*, 2.2.137 ('I have shook my head, and wept').

  pride splendour; compare *Romeo and Juliet*, 1.2.10–11: 'Let two more summers wither in their pride, | Ere we may think her ripe to be a bride'.

5 *beauteous* pronounced as two syllables; the word is strongly associated with the friend; see 4.5n.

  yellow For the association of 'yellow' with autumn, see 73.2; *Macbeth*, 5.3.23 ('the yellow leaf' there indicating the autumn of life that Macbeth senses is denied him).

  autumn That autumn is italicised and capitalised in this sonnet in Q, where none of the other seasons are (and only 'Winter' is capitalised), exemplifies the occasional randomness of Q's italics, and warns against reading too much into either Q's italics or capitals; see 1.2n.

6 *process* 'the passing or lapsing of time, years, seasons, etc.' (OED³ 2a).

7 *Three. . . burned* The metre is awkward here, owing to the juxtaposition at the end of the line of four monosyllables all of which invite a stress.

8 *fresh* 'blooming, looking healthy or youthful' (*adj*.1, OED A9b); a word recurrently used of the friend in the procreation sonnets (1.9; 3.3; 11.3); at 17.6, the poet-speaker describes the 'fresh numbers' required 'to number all [his] graces'. In Q's sequence, its use here is the first in a cluster, once again describing the friend (see 107.10, 108.9).

  which who; see Abbott 1884: § 265.

  yet still.

  green fresh, youthful (compare 63.14), but also carries a possible hint of censure: 'immature' (OED³ A8).

9–10 *like a. . . perceived* Compare the proverb 'To move as the dial hand, which is not seen to move' (Dent D321); the 'dial's shady stealth' at 77.7; and Meres, *Palladis Tamia*: 'we perceive

104

To me, fair friend, you never can be old,
For as you were when first your eye I eyed,
Such seems your beauty still: three winters cold
Have from the forests shook three summers' pride,   4
Three beauteous springs to yellow autumn turned
In process of the seasons have I seen,
Three April perfumes in three hot Junes burned,
Since first I saw you fresh which yet are green.   8
Ah, yet doth beauty like a dial hand
Steal from his figure, and no pace perceived;
So your sweet hue, which methinks still doth stand,
Hath motion, and mine eye may be deceived;   12
    For fear of which, hear this, thou age unbred:
    Ere you were born was beauty's summer dead.

the shadow of a dial passed, but perceive it not passing' (1598: sig. 2L5v). As in Sonnet 77, the dial could be a pocketwatch or a sundial (see 77.2n). The minute hand was only invented *c.* 1577 (see *Lucrece*, 297n) and most timepieces still only had an hour hand, meaning that its movement would be slow and barely perceptible. As well as indicating slow or stealthy movement (*v.*1, OED 6a), '*steal*' also has a secondary sense of 'thieve' (OED 2), as if beauty were appropriating and carrying off some of the friend's beauty, hinting at the way in which his good looks are threatened by, and will diminish with, the passing of time; this double meaning of 'steal' is also in play at 63.8; 77.7–8; 92.1.
yet even so; continuously.
10 *figure* (i) number on the face of the dial; (ii) the friend's external appearance.
11 *hue* (i) appearance; (ii) complexion; see 20.7n.
methinks it seems to me.
still doth stand (i) remains motionless (contrast to 'pace', l. 10); survives even now (compare 60.13).
13 *age unbred* future generations; compare 81.10–11; this is the only citation in OED for 'unbred' as 'unborn' (OED 1); other early usages of 'unbred' suggest that it means more precisely 'not yet conceived'; see Richard Barnfield,

Lady Pecunia: 'When Saturn lived, and wore the kingly crown | (And Jove was yet unborn, but not unbred)' (1605: sig. A4v); Austin Saker, *Narbonus*: 'in my judgement, a man were better be unborn, than live untaught; unbred, than unmannered; not begotten, than without behaviour' (1580: sig. K2v). The OED does not record 'unbred' in its more usual sense 'ill-bred' until 1622 (OED 2a), and that is borne out by searches on EEBO-TCP. If that sense is emergent here, then the future generations are doubly unbred: not yet conceived and, once born, deprived of the refinement of the friend's unique beauty.
14 *you* members of the 'age unbred'; the pronoun switches from 'thou' (l. 13), for the collective noun 'age unbred', to the plural pronoun, addressing individual members of those future generations.
beauty's summer height of beauty (see 18.9); i.e. the youth (the epitome of beauty) in the peak of his perfections; the seeming compliment also reminds the friend that – although he will never seem old to the poet-speaker – his beauty is not impregnable to the ravages of time; compare Sonnet 63, which affirms the friend's beauty whilst simultaneously recognising its vulnerability to temporal forces.

105

Benson combines Sonnets 104–106 under the title
'Constant affection'.

Some editors note parallels with Nicholas Breton's
'An Odd Conceit' in *Melancholic Humours* (although
the direction of borrowing, if any, is not certain):

> Lovely kind, and kindly loving,
> Such a mind were worth the moving:
> Truly fair, and fairly true,
> Where are all these, but in you?
>
> Wisely kind, and kindly wise,
> Blessed life, where such love lies:
> Wise, and kind, and fair, and true,
> Lovely live all these in you.
>
> Sweetly dear, and dearly sweet,
> Blessed, where these blessings meet:
> Sweet, fair, wise, kind, blessed, true,
> Blessed be all these in you. (1600: sig. F2r)

1 *idolatry* The poet-speaker argues that his
worship of the friend does not constitute
idolatry (i.e. worship or immoderate vener-
ation of images), because he has only the one
god (his friend); he further asserts his ortho-
doxy by casting the friend as a Trinitarian
unity ('three themes in one', l. 12). What
the poet-speaker writes is, of course, idolatry, because these feelings are not directed to
the Christian God; he might be monotheis-
tic, but he still breaks the first commandment
('Thou shalt have none other gods before
me', Exodus 20:3); see also 110.12, where
the friend is described as 'a god in love', and
106.9n.
2 *show* appear.
3 *Since* because; critical opinion divides as to
whether this introduces and explains the
charge of idolatry, or the poet-speaker's
defence. Ingram and Redpath argue the former as what follows is 'a very poor counter to
an accusation of idolatry' (1985: 238), but, as
Burrow notes, 'that is the point' (2002: 590).
all alike Compare 76.5 (a sonnet which also
considers the repetitive style in which the
poet-speaker celebrates his friend).
4 *still. . . so* There are liturgical echoes of the
Gloria ('As it was in the beginning, is now,
and ever shall be') and, as Booth observes

(1977: 336), of the 1563 'Homily against
Idolatry': 'images in temples and churches be
indeed none other but idols, as unto which
idolatry hath been, is, and ever will be committed' (*Second Tome of Homilies*, sig. 2B8r).
5 *Kind. . . kind* Like 'fair' and 'true' (see l. 9n),
'kind' encompasses a range of meanings,
including generous, benevolent, gentle, affectionate, and true to one's kind or nature, i.e. a
type of constancy, which, as Booth points out
(1977: 337) is mirrored in the use of *epanalepsis*, as the line begins and ends with 'kind'.
my love my beloved (l. 2).
6 *constant* (i) the same; (ii) faithful.
7 *to constancy confined* The poet-speaker's
verse is restricted to representing constancy;
compare 'confined' in 110.12. The theme of
constancy is also underlined by the *polyptoton*
of 'constant' (l. 6) and 'constancy'. See also l.
5n, above.
8 *leaves out difference* (i) excludes other subjects; (ii) omits to talk of quarrels between the
poet-speaker and the friend.
9 *'Fair, kind, and true'* The quotation marks
here and at l. 10 are editorial. The three qualities that the friend displays are repeated three
times (ll. 9, 10, 13), three repetitions of the
three themes which play on the sonnet's evocation of Trinitarianism. As with 'kind' (see l.
5n), 'fair' and 'true' cover a range of meanings, including: beautiful, blonde, gentle, just,
benign, unblemished ('fair'); loyal, constant,
honourable, trustworthy, genuine ('true').
argument subject matter; compare 76.10.
10 *varying to other words* Variety of expression
was a key virtue of early modern composition; see 76.2n.
11 *change* variety of expression; compare l. 10,
above, and 76.2.
invention one of the five parts of classical
rhetoric; see 38.8n.
spent (i) used; (ii) used up, exhausted.
12 *Three themes in one* three topics in one
person.
scope opportunity (for composition); compare
29.7, 103.2.
13–14 *Fair. . . one* Compare the proverb 'Beauty
and chastity (honesty) seldom meet' (Dent
B163).
13 *alone* separately.
14 *kept seat* resided.

105

Let not my love be called idolatry,
Nor my belovèd as an idol show,
Since all alike my songs and praises be
To one, of one, still such, and ever so.   4
Kind is my love today, tomorrow kind,
Still constant in a wondrous excellence;
Therefore my verse, to constancy confined,
One thing expressing, leaves out difference.   8
'Fair, kind, and true' is all my argument,
'Fair, kind, and true', varying to other words,
And in this change is my invention spent,
Three themes in one, which wondrous scope affords.   12
    Fair, kind, and true have often lived alone,
    Which three till now never kept seat in one.

106

Benson combines Sonnets 104–106 under the title 'Constant affection'.

Versions of this sonnet are found in two manuscripts dating from the 1630s: Pierpoint Morgan MA 1057, p. 96, and Rosenbach MS 1083/16, p. 256, where it is entitled 'On his mistress' beauty'; see Appendix 4.

1–4 **When. . . knights** The allusions to knights, ladies and 'old rhyme' would have gained an added topicality, owing to the publication of Spenser's *Faerie Queene* (1590, 1596), with its deliberately archaic language; see also l. 2n, below.

1 **wasted time** ages past: Shakespeare often uses 'waste the time' to indicate 'pass the time'; see *As You Like It*, 2.4.95; *Merchant of Venice*, 3.4.12. However, the phrase also invokes a sense of destruction (of ages laid to waste); compare 15.11, 30.4, 100.13.

2, 7 **I see. . . I see** An example of *antanaclasis*: in l. 2 'I see' indicates 'I behold' (seeing with eyes); in l. 7, 'I perceive, I discern' (exercising one's mental faculty).

2 **wights** people; the word seems self-consciously archaic (and is a recurrent word in Spenser's *Faerie Queene*); as such, Shakespeare's choice of diction can be seen as a response to these old 'chronicles' and their imitators, like those in Daniel's *Delia* 46.1–2 who 'sing of knights and palladines, | In aged accents, and untimely words'. Of Shakespeare's eight other usages of 'wight', one is given to the medieval poet Gower (*Pericles*); one appears in *Troilus and Cressida* (a play influenced by the medieval poets Chaucer and Robert Henryson); two appear in *Othello* at moments when Iago is quoting something (a proverb, a ballad); one is used by Berowne of Armado, a figure of fun, in *Love's Labours Lost*; and the remaining three are given to Pistol (in *Henry V* and *Merry Wives*), a character who regularly uses archaic and bombastic language.

3 **beauty. . . rhyme** beautiful style makes beautiful verses, which are also beautified by the presence in them of the 'fairest wights'; style and subject matter thus work in symbiosis.

4 **lovely** 'loving, kind, affectionate' (OED³ A1a); 'lovable' (OED³ A2); beautiful (OED³ A3a).

5 **blazon** Catalogues of female beauty (breaking the subject into various body parts, as we see in l. 6) are conventional in love poetry by the 1590s, and are parodied in Sonnet 130.

sweet beauty's best Q's 'sweet beauties best' allows a range of possibilities that are flattened by modernisation, when editors need to decide whether Q's 'beauties' represents a plural or a possessive singular; most editors modernise as here, so that beauty is a single, abstract, near-personification, as opposed to its plural, concrete manifestations.

7 **antique pen** compare the 'antique book' of 59.7; Time has an 'antique pen' at 19.10.

8 **Even** pronounced as one syllable.

master possess (OED³ 6a); see *Lucrece*, l. 863 and note.

9 **praises. . . prophecies** Compare the version of Constable's *Diana* 4.1–4 (composed before 1591) found in National Art Library MS Dyce 44: 'Miracle of the world, I never will deny | That former poets praise the beauty of their days; | But all those beauties were but figures of thy praise, | And all those poets did of thee but prophesy' (fol. 21r). Interestingly, in light of Sonnet 105, Constable's sonnet ends 'thou that goddess art, | Which only we without idolatry adore' (ll. 13–14). There is another possible borrowing from the manuscript version of *Diana* at 128.12 (see note on that poem).

10 **prefiguring** foreshadowing; the old chronicles foreshadow the friend, just as typologically characters and episodes in the Old Testament were interpreted by Christian theologians as prefiguring counterparts in the New Testament.

11 **for** because.

but only.

divining prophesying.

12 **skill** knowledge (*n.*1, OED 7); Q has 'still'; most editors follow Capell and emend (as here) to 'skill'; Randall McLeod (1991, writing as Random Clod) defends Q's 'still' on the grounds that a compositor is unlikely to set 'sk' instead of 'st' because the latter is a ligature; however, a compositor could misread 'sk' as 'st'. Sisson (1953: 1.213) also defends 'still', which he read as 'as yet'; Tucker conjectures 'style' (of which 'still' is a potential variant), an argument

106

When in the chronicle of wasted time
I see descriptions of the fairest wights,
And beauty making beautiful old rhyme
In praise of ladies dead and lovely knights,   4
Then in the blazon of sweet beauty's best,
Of hand, of foot, of lip, of eye, of brow,
I see their antique pen would have expressed
Even such a beauty as you master now.   8
So all their praises are but prophecies
Of this our time, all you prefiguring,
And, for they looked but with divining eyes,
They had not skill enough your worth to sing: 12
    For we, which now behold these present days,
    Have eyes to wonder, but lack tongues to praise.

also taken up by Hammond (2012: 320), who notes that definition of 'style' as 'a form of words, phrase, or formula by which a particular idea or thought is expressed' (OED 16) 'fits the context precisely'. Early modern spelling is variable, and the same writer, or compositor, can spell a word in different ways within a relatively close proximity; nonetheless, the three examples of 'style' – at Q32.14, Q78.11, Q84.12 – are all spelled consistently as 'stile', and the secretary 'e' (often written backwards, or with two strokes which detach from each other) is not easily mistaken for 'l' by someone well-acquainted with the script; 'still' is also an extremely rare spelling of 'style' by Shakespeare's day: the fifteen other examples of Shakespeare's usage of the word are all spelled 'stile' (in both Quarto and Folio, in cases where there is more than one edition of the play).

13 *which* who; compare 104.8.

107

Benson combines Sonnets 107–108 under the title 'A monument to fame'. A copy of this sonnet survives in Folger MS V.a.148, fol. 22r (transcribed *c.* 1650s), where it is entitled 'A monument' (see Appendix 4). The reference to 'the mortal moon' (l. 5) and 'this most balmy time' (l. 9) have been used to try to date the poem. Proposed dates range from 1579 (unfeasibly early) to 1609; see Rollins (1944: 1.263–8, 2.59–61). However, recent stylistic analysis (Jackson 2001) points to an early seventeenth-century date of composition for Sonnets 104–126; for a discussion of dating, see headnote on the *Sonnets*.

1   *Not* neither.

1–2 *prophetic. . . world* Compare *Hamlet*, 1.5.40 ('O my prophetic soul!'); Dent S666.2 ('A prophetic (presaging) soul'). As the seat of the emotions and spiritual powers, the soul is where any intimations of the future would be felt; '*Of the wide world*' indicates a general, widespread anxiety (the reasons for which become apparent in ll. 5–7); alternatively, as Hammond (2012: 322) points out, there might be a Platonic allusion here, since Plato said the world itself had a soul (*Timaeus* 30b, 34b).

2   *dreaming on* Shakespeare uses 'dream on' where modern English would use 'dream of' or 'about'; compare *Richard III*, 5.3.146, where the ghost instructs Richard to 'dream on' his victims.

3   *yet* A problematic word: it is unclear whether it is (i) temporal ('as yet'); (ii) an intensifier ('even'); or (iii) 'nevertheless'.

   lease a period of (temporary) tenure.

   my true love (i) my faithful and genuine affection; (ii) my soul mate; (iii) my beloved, who is loyal and faithful.

   control (i) regulate (OED 1); (ii) challenge, censure (OED 3b); (iii) exercise power or authority over (OED 4a); (iv) curb (OED 4b); (v) overpower (OED 5a).

4   *Supposed. . . doom* A difficult line, which continues the legalistic imagery instigated by 'lease' (l. 3); the most convincing paraphrase is Kerrigan's (1986: 319): 'thought destined to expire after a limited period'.

   confined stressed on the first syllable.

5   *mortal moon. . . endured* variously taken as reference to (i) the Spanish Armada (drawn up in the shape of a crescent and defeated in 1588); (ii) an actual eclipse of the moon (between 1590 and the publication of the *Sonnets*, there

were fourteen partial lunar eclipses visible from England if weather conditions were right, and three total lunar eclipses, in December 1591, April 1595 and February 1599; see http://astro.ukho.gov.uk; moonblink.info/eclipse; the partial eclipses of February 1598, December 1601 and September 1605 would have been particularly striking due to the amount of the moon in shadow and the fact that they occurred in close proximity to solar eclipses); (iii) the 'grand climacteric' or 63rd year of Elizabeth I's life (believed to be an especially hazardous time; see headnote to Sonnet 63) in 1595–6; Elizabeth was often associated with Cynthia/Diana (goddess of the moon); (iv) a serious illness that Elizabeth was rumoured to have in 1599–1600; (v) Elizabeth's death in 1603 and the accession of James I. (i) and (v) demand that 'endured' means 'suffered, undergone'; (ii)–(iv), 'survived'. The case for a seventeenth-century date of composition (see headnote) makes (ii), (iv) and (v) the most likely candidates.

6   *sad* serious, mournful.

   augurs prognosticators, fortune-tellers.

   mock because the dire events foretold did not transpire; for the fearful (but unfulfilled) predictions of the chaos that would follow Elizabeth I's death, see Joseph Hall, *The King's Prophecy* (1603), noted by F. S. Boas: 'False stars and falser wizards that foreseen | By their aspects the state of earthly things: | How been your bold predictions proved vain' (*TLS* 7 July 1950: 421). The idea of augurs mocking their own predictions ('*presage*', OED 2) may also owe something to Cicero's *De Divinatione* II.xxiv.51–2: '"I wonder," said [Cato], "that a soothsayer doesn't laugh when he sees another soothsayer". For how many things predicted by them really come true?' ['mirari se aiebat quod non rideret haruspex, haruspicem cum vidisset. Quota enim quaeque res evenit praedicta ab istis?']; this anecdote is repeated, without the reference to Cato, in Cicero's *De Natura Deorum* I.71 (a standard school text in Shakespeare's day).

7   *Incertainties. . . assured* 'What was uncertain now invests itself as certain'; a possible reference to the unexpectedly peaceful accession of James I. Kerrigan (1986: 315–16) usefully quotes John Donne's 1617 sermon on the anniversary of James I's accession, in which he reflects on the anxiety at Elizabeth's death and the subsequent relief at the succession of James I: 'every one

107

Not mine own fears, nor the prophetic soul
Of the wide world, dreaming on things to come,
Can yet the lease of my true love control,
Supposed as forfeit to a confined doom.   4
The mortal moon hath her eclipse endured,
And the sad augurs mock their own presage;
Incertainties now crown themselves assured,
And peace proclaims olives of endless age.   8
Now with the drops of this most balmy time
My love looks fresh, and Death to me subscribes,
Since spite of him I'll live in this poor rhyme,
While he insults o'er dull and speechless tribes;   12
   And thou in this shalt find thy monument,
   When tyrants' crests and tombs of brass are spent.

of you in the city were running up and down like ants with their eggs bigger than themselves, every man with his bags, to seek where to hide them safely [...] in [Elizabeth's] death we were all under one common flood, and depth of tears. But the *Spirit of God moved upon the face of that depth*; and God said, "*Let there be light, and there was light, and God saw that light was good*." God took pleasure, and found a savour of rest, in our peaceful cheerfulness' (*XXVI Sermons* 1661: 351–2).

8 *olives* olive branches, symbolising peace; James I and his panegyrists promoted his regime as a peaceful one; Donne's 1617 sermon (cited above) continues, describing how James has 'the blessed spirit of peace so abundantly in him, as that by his counsels, and his authority, he should sheathe the swords of Christendom again' (1661: 352). James' reputation as a peacemaker was not unfounded: England had been at war with Spain since 1585, and there was almost continual conflict in Ireland; James quickly made peace with Spain and suspended the Irish campaigns.

8 *of endless age* everlasting.

9 *drops. . . time* 'Balmy' was not used to describe the weather until the eighteenth century; its use here evokes aromatic ointments used in healing, and/or the fragrant oil used in the coronation ceremony for anointing monarchs (topical, should the sonnet have been composed *c.* 1603); see *Richard II*, 3.2.54–5: 'Not all the water in the rough rude sea | Can wash the balm off from an anointed king'.

10 *My love* (i) my affection; (ii) my beloved; proponents of Southampton as the young man of the *Sonnets* point to his release on 10 April 1603 from the 'confined doom' (l. 4) of imprisonment in the Tower of London (where he had been imprisoned for his role in Essex's Rebellion); proponents of Pembroke as the young man note his release from the Fleet prison in April 1601.
fresh See 104.8n.
subscribes submits (OED³ 3b); there may be play on the etymology of the word ('writes under', from the Latin *subscribere*).

11 *spite* in spite of, despite.

12 *insults* 'exult[s] proudly or contemptuously' (OED 1).
dull. . . tribes peoples lacking ability to write (and thus the means to triumph over time); sixteenth-century antiquarians such as John Leland regretted that the inhabitants of ancient Britain had failed to leave written records of their history.

13 *in this* in this sonnet, in this volume.
monument Compare 81.9 and note (in contrast to 55.1).

14 *tyrants' crests* 'Crests' might indicate (i) crested helmets; (ii) heraldic devices. That they belong to tyrants epitomises how even overweening power is transient and subject to time.
tombs of brass For the durability of brass, but also its propounded impermanence in comparison to authorial fame, see 64.4 and note.
spent gone (OED 2).

108

Benson combines Sonnets 107–108 under the title 'A monument to fame'.

1 *character* write; compare *Hamlet*, 1.3.58–9: 'these few precepts in thy memory | Look thou character'.

2 *figured* represented; in a sonnet about writing, there may also be a play on 'figures' of speech.
true faithful; genuine; see 105.9n.
spirit here pronounced as two syllables (rhyming with 'merit', l. 4).

3 *now* Although Q makes sense, some editors (following Malone) emend to 'new', so that the phrase in which it appears parallels 'new to speak', and the repetition prefigures 'old... old' in l. 7.
register record.

5 *boy* Benson emends to 'love', which is often seen as an attempt on his part to efface any homoerotic charge; De Grazia (2000: 90) argues that the change arises from Benson's desire for consistency, this being the only Shakespeare sonnet included in the 1640 *Poems* that addresses the friend as 'boy' (the only other sonnet in Q which does so is 126, which Benson omits); see also 104.1n.
yet nevertheless; still.

6 *say... same* The poet-speaker keeps to the ritualistic and predetermined form of his devotions; compare the preface to the first *Book of Common Prayer* (1549), which lays out the desired uniformity of worship: 'And where heretofore, there hath been great diversity in saying and singing in churches within this realm [...] Now from henceforth, all the whole realm shall have but one use' (2011: 5).

7 *Counting... old* deeming no well-used phrase a worn-out cliché ('old thing').
thou... thine an example of an 'old thing'; in a sonnet which flirts with divine offices and texts, there is a possible echo of Song of Solomon 2:16: 'My well-beloved is mine, and I am his'.

8 *Even* pronounced as one syllable.
hallowed thy fair name an echo of the Lord's Prayer ('Hallowed be thy name'), establishing a daring equivalence between the poet-speaker's beloved and God; compare 105.1–2, 110.12.
hallowed made holy (*v.*1, OED 1); there may also be a pun on 'hallow' as 'shout aloud' (*v.*2, OED 3); see *Twelfth Night*, 1.5.272: 'hallow your name to the reverberate hills'.
fair (i) honourable; (ii) unblemished; (iii) renowned for its beauty; see 105.9n.

9 *love's... case* There are various ways of reading this phrase: (i) the body ('case, *n.*2', OED³ 7c), (ii) skin (OED³ 7b), or (iii) clothing (OED³ 7a) that houses or covers love; (iv) the occurrence ('case, *n.*1', OED³ 2a), (v) condition (OED³ 5a), or (vi) circumstance (OED³ 6a) of love; (vii) the argument (OED³ 7b) which is made for love (e.g. in these sonnets).
fresh new, different (*adj.*1, OED A1a, A1b); unfading (OED A8); blooming, youthful (OED A9a); vigorous (OED A10a). For its use as an adjective relating to the youth, see 104.8n.

10 *Weighs not* pays no attention to.
injury of age damage caused by old age.

11 *necessary* inevitable.
place 'To give place' was to cede position to someone of higher status in a procession or at table; see 79.4n. This sense of social hierarchy is enforced by the 'page' of l. 12.

12 *antiquity* old age.
for aye for ever.
page (i) 'boy or youth employed as the personal attendant and messenger of a person of high rank' (*n.*1, OED³ 2a), which gives the fact that 'antiquity' occupies this office a comic incongruity; (ii) a pun on paper, as in Thomas Nashe's *Unfortunate Traveller* (1594), where the narrator Jack Wilton introduces himself as 'a proper fellow page of yours' who 'hath bequeathed for waste paper here amongst you certain pages of his misfortunes' (2.207).

13 *conceit* (i) conception, notion (OED 1a); (ii) understanding (OED 2a); (iii) a literary conceit (OED 8c), i.e. the first one written by the poet-speaker about his 'sweet boy'.

13–14 *there... Where* both in the beloved and the works written to (and about) him.

108

What's in the brain that ink may character
Which hath not figured to thee my true spirit?
What's new to speak, what now to register,
That may express my love or thy dear merit?   4
Nothing, sweet boy, but yet like prayers divine
I must each day say o'er the very same,
Counting no old thing old, thou mine, I thine,
Even as when first I hallowed thy fair name.   8
So that eternal love in love's fresh case
Weighs not the dust and injury of age,
Nor gives to necessary wrinkles place,
But makes antiquity for aye his page,   12
    Finding the first conceit of love there bred,
    Where time and outward form would show it dead.

109

Benson combines Sonnets 109–110 under the title 'A lover's excuse for his long absence'.

2 *qualify* reduce the force of (OED³ 9a), diminish (OED³ 11b).

3 *easy* easily.

my self Whilst 'myself' is always written as two words in Q (as is usual in the period), here modernising as 'my self' helps convey the sense that the 'self' is a distinct entity, from which the poet-speaker cannot separate; compare 87.9 and note, and see note on modernisation (p. xiv).

depart separate; echoes the marriage service in the *Book of Common Prayer*: 'till death us depart' (2011: 159).

4 *soul. . . lie* For the trope of lovers exchanging hearts, see 22.7n.

5 *ranged* wandered ('range, *v.*1', OED³ 1a).

7 *Just to the time* exactly at the appointed moment.

not with the time exchanged (i) not changed by time; (ii) not corrupted by the times (described as 'so bad', 67.14, and 'the filching age', 75.6); the meaning of 'time' in this line thus seems to shift from a 'moment' to an 'age'.

8 *So that* in order that.

water for my stain water (possibly penitential tears) to wash away his fault; compare *Macbeth*, 2.2.64: 'A little water clears us of this deed'.

10 *all kinds of blood* all kinds of temperaments; compare *Much Ado*, 1.3.28–30: 'it better fits my blood to be disdained of all than to fashion a carriage to rob love from any'. Early modern medical theory held that everyone was predisposed to have a dominant humour, which affected their health and behaviour; each disposition – choleric, sanguine, melancholic, phlegmatic – was vulnerable to specific '*frailties*'; see 91.5 and note.

11 *it* 'my nature' (l. 9).

preposterously absurdly; quite literally unnatural (from the Latin *praeposterus*, where what is before, 'prae/pre', is put afterwards, 'posterus'); for the importance of placing words and concepts in the 'correct' order, see Parker 2007: 133–4, and Wilson, *Art of Rhetoric*: 'who is so foolish as to say the council and the king, but rather the king and his council, the father and the son, and not contrary' (1553: sig. Z1r).

stained disgraced, dishonoured, blotted.

12 *To leave. . . good* 'to abandon the totality of all your worth for something of no value' (which would be preposterous, since it puts the lesser thing over and above the greater).

14 *Save* except.

rose See 1.2n ('rose' is capitalised in Q, as it is at 1.2, but not italicised).

109

O never say that I was false of heart,
Though absence seemed my flame to qualify;
As easy might I from my self depart
As from my soul, which in thy breast doth lie: 4
That is my home of love; if I have ranged,
Like him that travels I return again,
Just to the time, not with the time exchanged,
So that myself bring water for my stain. 8
Never believe, though in my nature reigned
All frailties that besiege all kinds of blood,
That it could so preposterously be stained
To leave for nothing all thy sum of good: 12
   For nothing this wide universe I call,
   Save thou, my rose; in it thou art my all.

110

Benson combines Sonnets 109–110 under the title 'A lover's excuse for his long absence'.

1 *Alas. . .* The opening line picks up on, and confesses, to the charge raised at 109.5 ('if I have ranged').

2 *motley* fool, jester; see *As You Like It* where Touchstone, the fool, is called 'motley' (3.3.78).

to the view in the public eye; compare *Antony and Cleopatra*, 5.2.209–11: 'Mechanic slaves | With greasy aprons, rules, and hammers shall | Uplift us to the view'. In conjunction with Sonnet 111, 110.2 is often read as Shakespeare expressing shame about his role as an actor and playwright for the public stage (see Rollins 1944: 1.275–6).

3 *Gored* (i) wounded ('stab[bed] deeply', 'gore, *v*.1', OED 1a), or besmeared with blood ('gored, *adj*.2', OED); (ii) refers to 'gores', triangular pieces of cloth ('gore, *n*.2', OED 3a), such as would be used to make a fool's motley; (iii) dishonoured: in heraldic devices, a 'gore sinister' was a record of cowardice ('gore, *n*.2', OED 4).

dear exploits the dual meanings of 'dear' as (i) precious; (ii) beloved.

4 *Made. . . new* repeated old crimes (presumably of lust) by forming new attachments; as Burrow notes there may be a reference here to sodomy, euphemistically named 'old-fashioned love' (2002: 600); see John Donne, *Satire* 2.7 (*c*. 1594).

affections 'passion[s], lust[s]' (*n*.1, OED³ 1b); a stronger word than in modern usage; see Romans 1:26–7 (a passage which alludes to homosexuality): 'God gave them up unto vile affections [. . .] the men left the natural use of the woman, and burned in their lust one toward another'.

5 *truth* fidelity; the friend himself is elsewhere portrayed as an embodiment of 'truth'; see 101.3, 6; 105.

6 *Askance* askew ('*adv*.2', OED 1a), with a potential suggestion of suspicion or disdain (OED 2); spelled 'asconce' in Q, an acceptable sixteenth-century variant.

strangely as a stranger, in an unfriendly way; compare *2 Henry IV*, 5.2.63–4: 'You all look strangely on me [. . .] | You are, I think, assured I love you not'.

by all above by heaven.

7 *blenches* swervings (see *v*.1, OED 2a), i.e. turning aside the eyes, emphasising 'askance' in l. 6;

the word is not a common one (in Shakespeare's works or sixteenth-century English); Shakespeare uses 'blench' most often as a variant of 'blanch' (an etymologically unrelated sense clearly not relevant here); the closest parallel to the usage here is *Troilus and Cressida*, 2.2.67–8: 'There can be no evasion | To blench from this and to stand firm by honour'. 'Blench' can also mean 'trick, strategem' (*n*., OED 1), but that meaning seems obscure by the late sixteenth century (the last citation in OED is *c*. 1400); the only citation for this usage revealed through a full-text search of EEBO-TCP is in Richard Robinson, *The Reward of Wickedness*, where it is used to complete a rhyme: 'Yet would they say that with a mass they could Plegethon quench: | And all the souls that damned were, deliver with a blench' (1574: sig. D3r).

gave. . . youth rejuvenated my affections; but, as Booth notes (1977: 356), it is possible to read this as indicating a different boy.

8 *essays* trials, experiments (of inferior loves).

proved showed (through the 'essays'); for the significance of 'proof' in *Sonnets*, see 2.12n.

my best of love my best love, or the best object of my love.

9 *have* Malone emends to 'save' (adopting a conjecture made by Tyrwhitt); the long 's' in secretary hand could be misread as 'h', however Q's 'have' has been allowed to stand, on the grounds that the line does make sense, as an address to the friend: 'Now that those experiments are over, accept my love for you, which will not end'.

what i.e. his love; the demonstrative pronoun makes this declaration of undying love strangely muted.

10 *appetite* bodily cravings (including sexual desire).

grind sharpen (on the whetstone of 'newer proof', l. 11); as at 56.2 and 118.1, appetite is like a knife. The choice of word has sexual implications (see 'grind, *v*.1', OED 11).

11 *proof* experience (OED³ 6), test (OED³ 7a).

try put to the test.

12 *A god in love* 'one whom, in my love, I worship as a god'; compare Sonnet 105 and notes.

confined restricted; see 105.7.

13 *next. . . best* 'you, who are the next best thing to heaven'.

heaven pronounced as one syllable.

14 *Even* pronounced as one syllable.

110

Alas 'tis true, I have gone here and there
And made myself a motley to the view,
Gored mine own thoughts, sold cheap what is most dear,
Made old offences of affections new.   4
Most true it is that I have looked on truth
Askance and strangely; but, by all above,
These blenches gave my heart another youth,
And worse essays proved thee my best of love.   8
Now all is done, have what shall have no end;
Mine appetite I never more will grind
On newer proof, to try an older friend,
A god in love, to whom I am confined.   12
    Then give me welcome, next my heaven the best,
    Even to thy pure and most most loving breast.

111

Benson combines Sonnets 111–112 under the title 'A complaint'.

Like Sonnet 110, Sonnet 111 is often read as Shakespeare's comment on the low esteem in which playwrights and actors were held (see l. 4n, below). John Davies of Hereford reflects on the degrading nature of the profession in *Microcosmos*, in a section which shares ideas and vocabulary with this sonnet: 'Players, I love ye, and your quality, | As ye are men, that pastime not abused: | And some I love for painting, poesy, | And say fell Fortune cannot be excused, | That hath for better uses you refused: | [. . .] And though the stage doth stain pure gentle blood, | Yet generous ye are in mind and mood' (1603: sig. 2F4r). That Davies had Shakespeare in mind here is evident from the printed marginalia adjacent to this passage, which reads 'RB WS' (Richard Burbage, William Shakespeare).

1 **with** 'wish' in Q; most editors accept Gildon's emendation to 'with' (1710), although Randall McLeod (1981) attempts to defend Q's reading, on the grounds that 'sh' could not be mistakenly inserted for 'th', because the former is a ligature and the latter is not; nevertheless, (i) a compositor might misread 'sh' for 'th'; (ii) as Kerrigan notes (1986: 325), 'None of the senses that can be squeezed from Q['s *wish*] seems quite satisfactory'; (iii) elsewhere Shakespeare uses 'chide' + 'with': see *Othello*, 4.2.167 ('he does chide with you'); *Cymbeline*, 5.4.30–2 ('No more [. . .] With Mars fall out, with Juno chide').
   chide 'give loud or impassioned utterance to anger, displeasure, disapprobation, reproof' (OED 1); stronger than in modern usage; see, for example, *Tempest*, 1.2.476–7: 'Silence! one word more | Shall make me chide thee, if not hate thee'.
2 **guilty goddess** Fortune (l. 1), who is here held responsible for the things that the poet-speaker has done wrong.
3 **That** who.
   better (i) more generously; (ii) more honourably; for a similar complaint against fortune, see 25.1–3.

4 **Than. . . breeds** A line frequently taken as alluding to the low social status of being an actor and playwright for the public stage (see also headnote and 110.2). The 1572 Vagrancy Act had, for example, required that all 'common players in interludes' attach themselves to an aristocrat, in order to distinguish themselves from 'rogues, vagabonds and sturdy beggars'; in *The Scourge of Folly* (1611) John Davies of Hereford suggests Shakespeare was demeaned by his acting; see the epigram, 'To our English Terence', cited at 87.14n. Third person plurals ending in -*s* ('breeds') are possible in Elizabethan English; see 41.3n.
5 **brand** Until the nineteenth century, criminals were branded with a hot iron ('P' for perjurer, 'V' for vagabond, 'M' for those murderers who avoided hanging by claiming benefit of the clergy); Ben Jonson was branded with an 'M' on his thumb after killing the actor Gabriel Spencer in a duel in 1598. Compare 112.2, and *Lucrece*, l. 1091 and note. Philip Stubbes derided actors in *The Anatomy of Abuses* in the following terms: 'they carrying the note or brand of God his curse upon their backs, which way soever they go, are to be hissed out of all Christian kingdoms' (1583: sig. L6v).
6 **subdued** subjected.
7 **the dyer's hand** Regular exposure to the dyes of this period would cause a permanent stain; as the son of a glover, Shakespeare may well have seen this as a child.
8 **renewed** restored, revived.
10 **eisel** vinegar; frequently used as a base in medicines.
   infection See 67.1n; in close proximity to 'the dyer's hand' there may be a play on the etymological root of infection (from the Latin *inficere*, 'to dip in, stain'); see 94.11n.
11 **No bitterness** there is no bitterness.
12 **Nor. . . correction** 'Nor will I think it a double penance to amend what has already been amended.'
14 **Even** pronounced as one syllable.
   pity mercy, tenderness (OED³ 1); compassion, sympathy (OED³ 2b).

111

O for my sake do you with Fortune chide,
The guilty goddess of my harmful deeds,
That did not better for my life provide
Than public means which public manners breeds.   4
Thence comes it that my name receives a brand,
And almost thence my nature is subdued
To what it works in, like the dyer's hand.
Pity me then and wish I were renewed,   8
Whilst like a willing patient I will drink
Potions of eisel 'gainst my strong infection;
No bitterness that I will bitter think,
Nor double penance to correct correction.   12
    Pity me then, dear friend, and I assure ye
    Even that your pity is enough to cure me.

112

Benson combines Sonnets 111–112 under the title 'A complaint'.

1 *pity* picks up on 111.8, 13, 14; see 111.14n.
   doth plural; see Abbott 1884: § 334.
   impression the indentation caused by the brand at 111.5.

2 *vulgar* widely disseminated (OED 6), rather than 'ill-bred' (OED 13), a meaning that only developed later in the seventeenth century.
   stamped upon my brow Roman slaves were branded on the forehead, either as a punishment or as means of identification ('stigma, -atis, *n*.', Lewis & Short, *Latin Dictionary*).

4 *So* provided that.
   o'ergreen 'to make green in colour. Also *fig*.: to cover so as to conceal a defect' (OED³); a Shakespearean coinage; 'green' – a colour associated with youth, vitality and freshness (OED³ A10, A9, A5) – is used of the friend at 63.14; 104.8.
   allow commend (OED³ 2); acknowledge (OED³ 3a).

5 *my all-the-world* Compare 109.13–14; *King John*, 3.4.104: 'My life, my joy, my food, my all the world'.

7–8 *None. . . wrong* elliptical and cryptic; Malone conjectured emending Q's 'or changes' to 'e'er changes' (671n); Tucker followed in a similar vein with 'o'erchanges'. Of the suggested emendments, 'o'erchanges' is the most attractive; the poet-speaker's obduracy thus overwhelms, or transforms, right and wrong. There is no Shakespearean precedent for 'o'erchange'; but see Thomas Dekker, *2 Honest Whore* (performed 1605): 'It will so overchange her heart with grief' (1630: sig. D2v). Another possibility is that the compositor of both Q and Dekker's *Honest Whore* have misread 'charge' as 'change', so that 'overchange'/'o'erchange' (an emended verion of Q) should read 'overcharge'/'o'ercharge'. Q has 'ore-charg'd' at 23.8. However, Q's reading (which has been retained here) can make sense without emendation if 'or. . . or' are read as 'either. . . or' (as at 75.14). Read this way, ll. 7–8 mean: 'there is no one else alive who means so much – nor do I play that role for anyone – that they may alter my inflexible opinion either rightly or wrongly'; Shakespeare uses both 'right' and 'wrong' adverbially elsewhere; see *Winter's Tale*, 4.3.18 ('I then do most go right')

and *Antony and Cleopatra*, 3.6.80 ('you were wrong led'). Alternatively, 'changes' can be seen as a *zeugma* governing both 'steeled sense' and 'right or wrong', in which case ll. 7–8 would mean: 'there is no one else alive who means so much – nor do I play that role for anyone – that they may either alter my inflexible opinion or change right and wrong'.

8 *steeled* 'hardened like steel, insensible to impression, inflexible' (OED 5); Shakespeare often uses 'steel' as the epitome of hardness; see, for example, *Comedy of Errors*, 4.2.34 ('whose hard heart is buttoned up with steel'); *Coriolanus*, 1.9.45 ('when steel grows soft as the parasite's silk); 65.8.

9 *In* into.
   so intensifier.
   profound abysm deep abyss; '*Abisme*' is capitalised and italicised in Q (often an indication of an unfamiliar word; see 1.2n).

10 *Of* about.
   voices opinions (see OED³ 9).
   adder's sense Adders were proverbially associated with deafness; see Dent A32 ('As deaf as an adder'); *2 Henry VI*, 3.2.76: 'What? art thou like the adder waxen deaf?'. According to animal lore, adders could hear well, but could voluntarily make themselves deaf by turning one ear to the ground and blocking the other with their tail, just as in l. 11 the poet-speaker has 'stopped' his ears; see Psalm 58.4: 'like the deaf adder that stoppeth his ear'.

11 *critic* fault-finder; compare *Troilus and Cressida*, 5.2.130–3: 'do not give advantage | To stubborn critics, apt without a theme | For depravation, to square the general sex | By Cressid's rule'.
   flatterer pronounced as two syllables.

12 *neglect* This could refer (i) to the poet-speaker's slighting by others, including – possibly – the friend (OED³ 1b); (ii) to his indifference (OED³ 1a) to the opinions of others; (iii) the poet-speaker's neglect of the friend, discussed in Sonnets 109–10, which he now endeavours to gloss over.
   dispense: deal with ('dispense with', phrasal verb, OED 7, 8); Q has a full-stop after 'dispense' (and a colon after 'are', l. 11); the friend is, however, being asked to 'mark' how the poet-speaker justifies himself; this comes in what follows (ll. 13–14), not what precedes (ll. 9–11).

13 *purpose* intention (OED³ 1a), subject of discourse (OED³ 3).

112

Your love and pity doth th' impression fill
Which vulgar scandal stamped upon my brow,
For what care I who calls me well or ill,
So you o'er-green my bad, my good allow?   4
You are my all-the-world, and I must strive
To know my shames and praises from your tongue;
None else to me, nor I to none alive,
That my steeled sense or changes right or wrong;   8
In so profound abysm I throw all care
Of others' voices, that my adder's sense
To critic and to flatterer stoppèd are;
Mark how with my neglect I do dispense: 12
    You are so strongly in my purpose bred
    That all the world besides methinks th'are dead.

---

bred generated, implanted (as in a womb) (see 'breed, *v.*'); compare *Merchant of Venice*, 3.2.63–4: 'Tell me where is fancy bred | Or in the heart or in the head?'.

14 ***That. . . dead*** A challenging line, which divides editorial opinion, depending on how editors interpret Q's 'me thinkes' and 'y'are'. The version here follows Blakemore Evans, who adapts Malone (1790); ll. 13–14 thus mean 'You are so strongly implanted in my discourse that it seems to me that the rest of the world is dead'. This reading requires (i) modernising Q's 'me thinkes' as ***methinks*** (it seems to me); Q prints 'me thinks' as separate words at all four instances of 'methinks' (the others occur at Q14.2, Q62.5, Q104.11); (ii) emending Q's 'y'are' to ***th'are*** (i.e. they are); 'y' is often used in early modern texts to indicate 'th' (a leftover from the Old English thorn). 'Th'are' is preferable to Malone's 'they're' as it is a more common Shakespearean form, found in the Quarto versions of *Hamlet* (Q2, 4.7.11) and *Troilus and Cressida* (3.3.120),

whereas 'they're' appears only in posthumously printed plays and the problematic and probably corrupt text of *Pericles*. For the treatment of the collective noun phrase '***all the world***' as a plural subject, see *Julius Caesar*, 1.3.98–100 ('If I know this, know all the world besides, | That part of tyranny that I do bear | I can shake off at pleasure', where the syntax of the second part of l. 98 is inverted: all the world know); *Winter's Tale*, 5.1.13–14 ('If, one by one, you wedded all the world, | Or from the all that are took something good'); *2 Henry VI*, 4.10.74 ('exhort all the world to be cowards'). The alternative rendering of l. 14 keeps 'me thinks' as separate words and interprets 'y' as 'ye', so that the couplet means 'You are so strongly implanted in my discourse that everyone else, except me, thinks you're dead'; compare 'y' have' at 120.6. Whilst grammatically possible, this is logically suspect: however much the poet-speaker obsesses about the friend, this can have no impact on his visibility to others.

113

Benson combines Sonnets 113–115 under the title 'Self-flattery of her beauty', one of three instances in *Poems* where Benson uses titles to redirect sonnets from the pre-127 section of Q (generally taken as being addressed to a man) to a woman; see also head-notes to Sonnets 122 and 125.

1 *mine. . . mind* Parted from him, the poet-speaker sees the friend in his imagination, not his actual eye; Compare *Hamlet*, 1.2.184–5 (where Hamlet imagines his dead father): 'HAMLET My father – methinks I see my father. | HORATIO Where, my lord? | HAMLET In my mind's eye, Horatio'.

2 *that. . . about* the eye, which guides ('governs') the poet-speaker as he walks.

3 *part* (i) depart from; compare *Pericles*, 5.3.38 ('When we with tears parted Pentapolis'); (ii) divide; compare *Henry VIII*, 5.2.26–7 ('I had thought | They had parted so much honesty among 'em'); some editors also suggest a third alternative ('does part of'); however, the example they use to endorse this (*Othello*, 5.2.296: 'This wretch hath part confessed his villainy') is not syntactically analogous, because 'part' is an adverb in *Othello*. There is a play on 'part' throughout the sonnet: l. 3 displays *polyptoton* (between 'part and 'partly'); 'part' (ll. 3, 7) functions as *antanaclasis*.

3, 7, 8 *his* its (the eye's).

4 *effectually* in effect; pronounced as four syllables.
out extinguished, blind.

5 *form* image.
delivers. . . heart The heart was regarded as the seat of perception; compare 69.2; *Hamlet*, 1.5.121: 'Would heart of man once think it?'. For the relationship between the eye and heart, see Sonnets 24, 46–47.

6 *flower* pronounced as one syllable.
latch Q has 'lack', which makes a faulty rhyme with l. 8; most editors (as here) follow Capell's suggestion of 'latch' ('grasp'; *v.*1, OED 1a); compare *Macbeth*, 4.3.193–5: 'But I have words | That would be howled out in the desert air, | Where hearing should not latch them'. Graphically, 'latch' could feasibly be misread as 'lack' in secretary hand.

7 *quick* living (OED³ A1a), vivid (OED³ A9), fleeting (see OED³ A26).
part share; see l. 3n, above.

8 *Nor. . . catch* Nor does the eye ('it') retain an image of what it sees ('doth catch'); Gildon (1714) emends 'catch' to 'take', in order to repair Q's 'lack'/'catch' rhyme (see l. 6n, above).

9 *rud'st* most barbarous, most common (i.e. as opposed to 'gentle-born'), most ill-shapen, roughest; here used in antithesis to 'gentlest' in the first of five oppositional pairs (ll. 9–12).

10 *sweet-favoured* Q has 'sweet-fauor'; the hyphen suggests that the word is adjectival, qualifying 'creature'; this edition follows Duncan-Jones (1997a) (and a conjecture made by Nicolaus Delius in 1860) in emending to 'sweet-favoured'. This emendation has the following advantages: (i) it more closely parallels 'deformed'st', so that l. 10 repeats the zeugmatic structure of l. 9 in a sequence (ll. 9–12) which is dependent on a repetitive pattern; (ii) a compositor is more likely to omit a letter than insert a hyphen; (iii) it is possible that the compositor might have misread the final 'd' in his copy-text as a redundant terminal 'e' (a feasible mistake when reading secretary hand) and dropped it; the use of the terminal 'e' was becoming rarer in printed texts by the later sixteenth century: a search on EEBO-TCP reveals 1,280 instances of 'favore/fauore/favoure/fauoure/', i.e. with a terminal 'e', in 339 texts 1550–1575, as opposed to 761 instances in 252 texts 1576–1601, despite the greater production and survival rate of texts 1576–1601; the use of spellings without the terminal 'e' ('favor/fauor/favour/fauour') increased over the same period from 7,597 instances in 751 texts (1550–1575) to 24,432 instances in 1,929 texts (1576–1601).
creature living being, person (compare 1.1); alternatively, it could refer to any object ('a created thing', OED³ 1a), since Judeo-Christian thought held that everything was created by God.

12 *it. . . feature* 'it [the eye or the mind's eye] makes them [the images listed in ll. 9–12] resemble you'; 'feature' could be 'form' (OED 1a) rather than (more narrowly) 'face' (OED 3).

13 *Incapable* 'unable to take in, receive, contain, hold, or keep' (OED 1a, citing this line as the first usage).
replete sated, gorged.

113

Since I left you, mine eye is in my mind,
And that which governs me to go about
Doth part his function and is partly blind,
Seems seeing, but effectually is out,   4
For it no form delivers to the heart
Of bird, of flower, or shape which it doth latch;
Of his quick objects hath the mind no part,
Nor his own vision holds what it doth catch,   8
For if it see the rud'st or gentlest sight,
The most sweet-favoured or deformed'st creature,
The mountain, or the sea, the day, or night,
The crow, or dove, it shapes them to your feature.   12
   Incapable of more, replete with you,
   My most true mind thus maketh mine eye untrue.

14 ***My most true mind. . . mine eye untrue***
In Q, this reads 'My most true minde thus maketh mine vntrue'. Most editors (following Malone's conjecture, 673n, following Capell) insert 'eye' between 'mine' and 'untrue' (as here). The contrast between the 'mind' and 'eye' is present throughout the sonnet (and, in Q's sequence, in the succeeding sonnet, 114), and the sonnet has been building up to the idea that the loyal ('true') mind makes the eye perceive things wrongly ('untrue'); the emended line also echoes l. 1, providing a satisfying conclusion to the sonnet, and if Q's 'maketh' is elided into one syllable, the insertion of 'eye' does not need to disrupt the meter (although some editors, following Capell, alter 'maketh' to 'makes'). Sonnet 113 is certainly either carelessly copied or carelessly set (see emendations at ll. 6, 10). Booth argues for emending to 'm'eyne', using old plural of eyes (1977: 375). However, Shakespeare uses a singular 'eye' throughout this sonnet, and his usage of 'eyne' elsewhere tends either to indicate an archaism (as at *Pericles*, 3.0.5, in one of the prologues spoken by the medieval poet Gower), or to make a rhyme, often in a section which seems deliberately heightened or cliché-ridden poetry (as in the song in *Antony Cleopatra*, 2.7.114; the hackneyed amorous verse of *Love's Labours Lost*, 5.2.206, or *As You Like It*, 4.3.50; and the rude mechanicals' playlet in *Midsummer Night's Dream*, 5.1.177). The only 'straight' use of 'eyne' – in a non-rhyming position – is in *Lucrece*, l. 1229. Certainly, by the late sixteenth century 'eyne' is more frequently found in poetry rather than prose (as a keyword search on EEBO-TCP attests) and at the very least should be considered a poeticism.
true faithful (but significantly not 'honest' in this context).
maketh pronounced as one syllable.

114

Benson combines Sonnets 113–115 under the title 'Self-flattery of her beauty', one of three instances in *Poems* where Benson uses titles to redirect sonnets from the pre-127 section of Q (generally taken as being addressed to a man) to a woman; see also head-notes to Sonnets 122 and 125.

Sonnet 114 continues from 113, expounding the exploration of the relationship between the eye and the mind.

1–3 *Or whether . . . Or whether* holds up two alternatives (both dependent on 'Shall I say', l. 3); see
 Abbott 1884: § 136; modern usage would omit
 the first 'or'.
1 *being* here pronounced as one syllable.
 crowned with you made glorious by your love.
2 *the monarch's plague, this flattery,* Flattery was
 regarded a serious problem in a political system
 (such as that of early modern England) that was
 perceived to depend on counsel; see Elyot, *Pasquil
 the Plain* (1533), where Gnatho (the flatterer)
 and Harpocrates (complicitly silent) have the ear
 of their ruler, whilst the plain-speaking Pasquil
 is banished beyond the city walls. *King Lear* 1.1
 enacts a similar dynamic: the plain-speaking
 Kent and Cordelia are both banished; Goneril
 and Regan's flattery is rewarded; and, over the
 course of the play, Albany is revealed as being
 complicitly silent, uncomfortable about much
 that happens, but refraining (until Act 4) from
 decisive intervention. Q has question marks at
 the end of ll. 2, 4 and a colon at the end of l.
 8. Many editors retain the question mark at l.
 2, and then – recognising that ll. 5–8 amplify
 'alchemy' – postpone the second question mark
 until l. 8. However, that leaves ll. 1–2 looking
 like an isolated question, rather than one of two
 alternatives (described in ll. 1–2, 3–8).
 flattery here pronounced as three syllables (but
 two at l. 9).
4 *alchemy* the art of transforming base metals into
 gold, here used to suggest the art of transformation more generally; capitalised and italicised in
 Q, often an indication of an unfamiliar world
 (see 1.2n), although the fact that it is not capitalised or italicised at its other appearance in Q
 (33.4) illustrates the occasionally unsystematic

nature of Q's italics (see 104.5n), particularly as 33.4 and 114.4 were probably set by the same compositor, A.
5 *make of* make out of.
 monsters malformed things (see OED³ A3a); compare 'deformed'st creatures' (113.10).
 indigest immature, shapeless; compare the description of the hunch-backed Richard, Duke of Gloucester, at *2 Henry VI*, 5.1.157–8: 'Hence, heap of wrath, foul indigested lump, | As crooked in thy manners as thy shape!'. There may be an echo of Ovid's description of Chaos as 'rudis indigestaque moles' at *Metamorphoses*, 1.7 ('a huge rude heap', in Golding's translation, 1.7, sig. B1r).
6 *cherubins* strictly speaking, 'one of the second order of angels of the Dionysian hierarchy, reputed to excel specially in knowledge' (OED 2b); here used to indicate creatures who are supremely beautiful in intellect and/or form.
 resemble The monsters are transformed into angels, who look like ('resemble') the friend; how-ever the similarity is potentially only skin-deep.
7 *perfect best* pleonastic, for emphasis, but 'perfect' (etymologically derived from the Latin 'perfec-tus', 'completed') also play on its rhyme-pair 'indigest' (whose shapelessness and immaturity is the opposite of 'finished').
8 *his beams* (i) the beams of the poet-speaker's eye; for the belief that eyes emitted rays, see 43.4n; (ii) the beams which were supposed to irradiate from a monarch (likened as sovereigns were to the sun); the poet-speaker resembles a monarch because his mind is 'crowned with you' (l. 1).
9 *'tis the first* the first option, laid out in ll. 1–2.
 'tis flattery . . . seeing Compare *Twelfth Night*, 1.5.308–9: 'I do I know not what, and fear to find | Mine eye too great a flatterer for my mind'. 'Flattery' is here pronounced as two syllables (contrast l. 3); this is a case where Q's orthography might indicate the number of stresses required, the three-syllable pronuncia-tion being indicated by the spelling 'flattery' (l. 3), the two-syllable pronunciation by the spell-ing 'flatry' (l. 9), although when the word (set by the other compositor, B) appears at 42.14 – requiring a disyllabic pronunciation – it is given as 'flattery'.
 seeing vision.

114

Or whether doth my mind, being crowned with you,
Drink up the monarch's plague, this flattery,
Or whether shall I say mine eye saith true,
And that your love taught it this alchemy, 4
To make of monsters and things indigest
Such cherubins as your sweet self resemble,
Creating every bad a perfect best
As fast as objects to his beams assemble? 8
O 'tis the first, 'tis flattery in my seeing,
And my great mind most kingly drinks it up;
Mine eye well knows what with his gust is 'greeing,
And to his palate doth prepare the cup. 12
 If it be poisoned, 'tis the lesser sin
 That mine eye loves it and doth first begin.

10 ***great mind*** because 'crowned with you' (l. 1).
most kingly drinks it up Compare the dumb show before Act 2 of Thomas Norton and Thomas Sackville's influential play *Gorboduc*, in which a king refuses a glass of wine offered by 'a grave and aged gentleman', and takes instead 'a cup of gold filled with poison', presented by 'a brave and lusty young gentleman' (1565: sigs B3r–v): 'Hereby was signified that as glass by nature holdeth no poison, but is clear and may easily be seen through, nor boweth by any art, so a faithful counsellor holdeth no treason, but is plain & open, nor yieldeth to any indiscrete affection, but giveth wholesome counsel, which the ill-advised prince refuseth. The delightful gold filled with poison betokeneth flattery, which under fair seeming of pleasant words beareth deadly poison, which destroyeth the prince that receiveth it'. The repetition of 'drinks up'

here awakens what was a dead metaphor at its original occurrence in l. 2.
11 ***what. . . 'greeing*** what suits the mind's taste (***'gust'***, *n*.2, OED 2); 'greeing'(without the apostrophe) is an acceptable aphetic form of 'agreeing'; however, the apostrophe has been inserted here to aid modern readers.
12 ***to his palate. . . cup*** The eye mixes the drink to suit the mind's taste.
13 ***it*** the cup (i.e. the friend's appearance, as perceived by the eye).
14 ***mine eye. . . begin*** The line absolves the eye from the sin of regicide (which would be the greater sin), since the eye – as well as preparing the drink – has also been the first to taste it.
begin pledge or make a toast (*v*.1, OED 5), as in John Earle's *Microcosmography*, cited by OED, which describes the type of drinker 'That is kind o'er his beer, and protests he loves you, and begins to you again' (1629: sig. N7v).

115

Benson combines Sonnets 113–115 under the title 'Self-flattery of her beauty', one of three instances in *Poems* where Benson uses titles to redirect sonnets from the pre-127 section of Q (generally taken as being addressed to a man) to a woman; see also headnotes to Sonnets 122 and 125.

This is generally regarded by editors as a difficult sonnet; see notes on ll. 5, 8, 11, 13, 14. The overall thrust of the sonnet – that absolute protestations of love prove false, because love can increase with time – is often compared to John Donne's 'Spring' (1598–9?), aka 'Love's Growth' (incipit: 'I scarce believe my love to be so pure'): 'Methinks I lied all winter, when I swore | My love was infinite, if spring make't more' (ll. 5–6).

2   *Even* pronounced as one syllable.

3   *Yet* but; as yet.

4   *most full flame* Fire was a conventional image of a lover's ardour; see 109.2; *Romeo and Juliet* 1.1.190–1 (where Romeo still plays the stereotypical lover): 'Love is a smoke made with the fume of sighs, | Being purged, a fire sparkling in lovers' eyes'. See also George Turberville's mockery of Petrarchan cliché: 'Not God (friend Googe) the lover blames as worker of his woes: | But Cupid, that his fiery flames so franticly bestows' (*Epitaphs, Epigrams, Songs and Sonnets*, 1567: sig. C2r).

burn clearer 'A clear fire' is 'a fire in full combustion without flame or smoke' ('clear', OED A1b).

5   *reckoning Time* (i) Time, who calls everyone to account (compare Nature's 'audit', 126.11); 'reckoning' is thus a participial adjective, qualifying time; 'reckoning' indicates a final account: 'the action or act of accounting to God after death for (one's) conduct in life' (*n.*, OED[3] 1a), a meaning reflected in 'the day of reckoning' to connote the day of judgement; but see l. 8n, for a discussion of the problematic grammar of ll. 5–8, if Time is taken as the subject; (ii) it is also possible (like Beeching 1904) to read 'reckoning' as a present participle, meaning 'considering' (*v.*, OED[3] 6a) and referring to the poet-speaker ruminating on the destructive effects of time; although not a usual Shakespearean

construction, a verbal noun does appear as the subject of a sentence at 95.8. '*Reckoning*' is here pronounced as two syllables.

millioned 'numbering a million, countless'; first citation by OED[3] (by over a century); a full-text search of EEBO-TCP reveals no earlier instances.

accidents occurrences, chance events.

6   *'twixt vows* between vows and their fulfilment.

7   *Tan* darken (and hence make unattractive, since pallor was considered beautiful); compare 62.10. The tanning process would toughen as well as darken leather (just as skin grows coarser with age).

sacred beauty beauty that is worthy of being worshipped.

sharp'st intents keenest (sharpest) intentions.

8   *Diverts* Q (and most editors) have 'divert', rendering l. 8 the last in a list of the effects of the plural 'accidents' (l. 5) and thus leaving the sentence without a main verb. Shakespeare's syntax is often difficult, but it is rarely nonsensical, and whilst Shakespeare uses a singular verb form with a plural subject (see 101.3n), he does not use plural verb forms for singular subjects. This edition therefore agrees with Capell (and Burrow who picks up the suggestion) in emending 'divert' to 'diverts', an error which may have occurred because the compositor missed the final 's' before 'strong' (easily done when the same letter ends one word and begins the next); the error would not have been immediately obvious, when doing in-press corrections, because it continues the pattern of plural verbs from the preceding lines. Emended as here, 'Reckoning time [...] | Diverts strong minds' is thus the main clause of the sentence, with a parenthetical clause running from 'whose millioned accidents' to 'intents' (ll. 5–7).

to. . . things in the direction of changing circumstances; 'course', in proximity to 'diverts', constructs the mind as a river, whose direction of flow is being re-routed.

altering here pronounced as two syllables.

9   *fearing of* being afraid of.

Time's tyranny Compare 5.3, 16.2.

10   *then* (i) at that time (as in l. 3); (ii) therefore (as in l. 13).

'Now. . . best' Quotation marks are editorial.

115

Those lines that I before have writ do lie,
Even those that said I could not love you dearer;
Yet then my judgement knew no reason why
My most full flame should afterwards burn clearer.   4
But reckoning Time, whose millioned accidents
Creep in 'twixt vows and change decrees of kings,
Tan sacred beauty, blunt the sharp'st intents,
Diverts strong minds to th' course of altering things.   8
Alas why, fearing of Time's tyranny,
Might I not then say, 'Now I love you best',
When I was certain o'er incertainty,
Crowning the present, doubting of the rest?   12
    Love is a babe; then might I not say so,
    To give full growth to that which still doth grow.

11–12 *certain. . . present* Compare 107.7.
11 *When* (i) at that time; (ii) since.
certain o'er incertainty an ambiguous phrase; (i) certain beyond doubt; (ii) certain over something which was uncertain; (iii) as Booth notes, the phrase is also 'colored by its echoes of constructions like "victorious over" and "triumph over"' (1977: 382). Q's spelling ('in-certainty') seems to invite a stress on the initial syllable.
12 *Crowning the present* valuing the present above everything else.
doubting of uncertain about.
13 *Love is a babe* Cupid was frequently depicted as an infant; see 151; 154.1.
then therefore.
say so say thus (i.e. 'Now I love you best', l. 10); it is grammatically and logically possible to read 'so' as referring back to 'Love is a babe' (where saying so highlights the extent to which love grows in l. 14); nevertheless, this reading isolates the couplet from the rest of the sonnet.

14 *grow.* Eighteenth- and nineteenth-century editors (Gildon to Tyler) regularly insert a question mark (as editors to the present day generally do at l. 12). There has, however, been a move since Ingram and Redpath to return to Q's punctuation for l. 14, so – despite the inverted syntax ('might I not') – the couplet reads as a statement, contradicting l. 10 and explaining why the poet-speaker might not say at any point 'Now I love you best' (because love continues to increase). However, like many of the poet-speaker's most seemingly forceful statements, the shadow of a question remains (not least because of the inverted syntax of the main clause).

116

Printed by Benson as a single sonnet entitled 'The picture of true love'.

A version of this sonnet, set to music by Henry Lawes, appears in New York Public Library, Music Division, Drexel MS 4257, no. 33; see Appendix 4; McLung Evans 1936.

This sonnet echoes 1 Corinthians 13:4–8: 'Love suffereth long. It is bountiful. Love envieth not. Love doth not boast itself. It is not puffed up. It disdaineth not. It seeketh not her own things. It is not provoked to anger. It thinketh not evil. It rejoiceth not in iniquity, but rejoiceth in the truth. It suffereth all things. It believeth all things. It hopeth all things. It endureth all things. Love doth never fall away, though that prophecyings be abolished, or the tongues cease, or knowledge vanish away'.

116 Uncorrected imprints of Q have 119.

1–12 *marriage. . . impediments. . . edge of doom* echoes the marriage service in the *Book of Common Prayer*, where the priest addresses the bride and groom: 'I require and charge you (as you will answer at the dreadful day of judgement, when the secrets of all hearts shall be disclosed) that if either of you do know any impediment, why ye may not be lawfully joined together in matrimony, that ye confess it' (2011: 158).

2 *Admit* acknowledge.

2–4 *love. . . remove* True love does not change when it meets with a change in the beloved (of affection, appearance, circumstances), nor does it swerve ('bend') if the beloved proves unfaithful ('remove[s]'). The insistence on fixity is at odds with 115.8. John Davies parodies such assertions of constancy in *Gulling Sonnets* (*c.* 1594; Grosart 1876b), 3.5–10: 'I changes prove, yet still the same am I, | The same am I and never will remove, | Never remove until my soul doth fly, | My soul doth fly and I surcease to move; | I cease to move which now am moved by you, | Am moved by you that move all mortal hearts'.

5 *ever-fixèd mark* a beacon or lighthouse; see *Coriolanus*, 5.3.74 ('Like a great sea-mark, standing every flaw'); Greville, *Caelica* (composed *c.* 1590), 42.11: 'Because my faith doth like the sea-marks show' (*Works* 1633: 2D3v).

6 *looks on* looks at ('on' is the usual sixteenth- and early seventeenth-century preposition with the verb 'look').

7 *star* guiding star, probably the North or Pole Star, used by sailors as the most reliable means of getting their bearings; compare *Julius Caesar*, 3.1.60–2: 'But I am constant as the northern star, | Of whose true-fixed and resting quality | There is no fellow in the firmament'.
wandering bark reflects the tradition of representing the lover as a boat ('bark') tossed in stormy seas at night; see Petrarch, *Rime Sparse* 189, translated by Wyatt as 'My galley charged with forgetfulness' (*Tottel* [50]). 'Wandering' is here pronounced as two syllables.

8 *Whose worth* the value and quality of the star (i.e. love).
his its (the star's).
height be taken altitude measured; navigators used sextants to measure the height of a star above the horizon in order to find their bearings.

9 *Time's fool* The phrase conveys both the sense of a dupe or victim of Time, and someone/ something subservient to Time, like a fool would be to his master, there for the latter's amusement; compare 124.13 (a sonnet which also explores the idea of constancy); *1 Henry IV* 5.4.81: 'life, time's fool'.
rosy. . . cheeks emblematic of youth and beauty (see Phoebe's assessment of Ganymede's youthful attractions in *As You Like It*, 3.5.120–2: 'There was a pretty redness in his lip, | A little riper and more lusty red | Than that mixed in his cheek'), and of vitality; see *Romeo and Juliet*, 4.1.99–100, where Friar Lawrence explains to Juliet how, on taking the potion that will simulate death, 'The roses in thy lips and cheeks shall fade | To wanny ashes'.

10 *bending sickle's* Bending works twice: (i) it refers (pleonastically) to the curved shape of the sickle; (ii) it conveys the threatening action of the sickle, as it is directed against mortal things (see 'bend, *v.*', OED 17a: 'To direct, turn, aim, level, bring to bear (cannon, forces, etc.) against, upon, at'). For Time's sickle, see 12.13n.
compass within the sweep or range of Time's sickle; the choice of word – strongly suggestive of curvature – further emphasises 'bending'.

11 *his* refers to Time (whose hours and weeks are 'brief' compared to the longevity of

116

Let me not to the marriage of true minds
Admit impediments; love is not love
Which alters when it alteration finds,
Or bends with the remover to remove.   4
O no, it is an ever-fixèd mark
That looks on tempests and is never shaken;
It is the star to every wandering bark,
Whose worth's unknown, although his height be taken.   8
Love's not Time's fool, though rosy lips and cheeks
Within his bending sickle's compass come;
Love alters not with his brief hours and weeks,
But bears it out even to the edge of doom.   12
   If this be error and upon me proved,
   I never writ, nor no man ever loved.

---

true love; see Dent L539: 'A perfect love does last eternally').

12 **bears it out** endures.

  even here pronounced as one syllable.

  doom death; day of judgement.

13 **error** a mistaken notion, false belief; drawing on its etymological roots in the Latin *errare* (to wander), the word recalls 'wandering bark' (l. 7); its close proximity to 'writ' (l. 14) also activates its legal resonances, as 'a mistake in matter of law', a 'writ of error' being 'a writ brought to procure the reversal of a judgement, on the ground of error' ('error', OED 4c).

  upon me proved demonstrated in evidence against me; as with 'error', there are legal resonances; for significance of 'proved', see 2.12n.

never, nor no Kerrigan (1986: 53) draws attention to how 'the convoluted negatives [...] show the poet protesting too much, losing confidence in his protestations, or at least inviting disagreement with them (by anticipating rebuttal)'. Double negatives were allowable in early modern English, but educated readers would also be aware of the rule in Latin grammar that two negatives make a positive; see Sidney, *Astrophil and Stella* 63, where 'grammar rules' allow Astrophil to reinterpret Stella's 'No, no' as 'yes'; *Twelfth Night*, 5.1.21–2: 'your four negatives make your two affirmatives'.

nor. . . loved It is possible to read this as both (i) a general statement, with 'no man' as the subject, and (ii) as dependent on 'I' ('I never loved any man').

117

Benson combines Sonnets 117–119 under the title 'Trial of love's constancy'. Sonnet 117 picks up on Sonnet 116's concern with constancy, as well as sharing some of its vocabulary ('minds', 'unknown', 'error(s)', 'prove(d)') and metaphors (navigation, a law-trial, weaponry); note, too, the proximity of the couplet rhymes. Nevertheless, the tone and the effect of the two sonnets are very different: where Sonnet 116 is framed – until the last line – as a general rumination on love, from the opening phrase, Sonnet 117 is an intensely personal response to accusations of inconstancy.

1   *Accuse* initiates the image of a trial, picked up in l. 13 with 'appeal'; the self-accusation links Sonnet 117 with Sonnets 109–10, as well as Sonnets 118–121.

thus: Q has a comma after 'thus', which is explicated in the list of charges that follow, ll. 1–8. Many editors consequently place a colon after 'thus' (as here). Sonnet 117 is thus unusual within the *Sonnets* in having the sense require a strong break in the opening line (see 74.1n). *scanted* neglected ('scant, *v.*', OED 7; compare *King Lear*, 1.1.278: 'You have obedience scanted'.

2   *Wherein* by which.

3   *upon. . . to call* to invoke, possibly as you would a god; to appeal to ('call on or upon', phrasal verb, in 'call, *v.*', OED 2, 3a). *dearest* Considering 'repay' (l. 2), there may be a play on 'costliest'.

4   *bonds* emotional ties, but also, within the context of the sonnet, with the sense of legal obligations; compare 87.4.

5   *frequent been with* (i) often in company with ('frequent, *adj.*', OED 6c; the earliest citation for this usage); (ii) 'frequent' could be used quasi-adverbially (although OED gives 1614 as the earliest such usage). Shakespeare only uses the word in three other instances – twice as a verb (*Pericles*, 4.6.191; *Richard II*, 5.3.6); once as an adjective (*Winter's Tale*, 4.2.32) – so it is difficult to be conclusive about patterns of use. *unknown minds* strangers.

6   *given to time* wasted; 'given' is pronounced as one syllable. *your. . . right* the privilege (presumably of the poet-speaker's love and loyalty) which has

been acquired with much cost (to the beloved, the poet-speaker, or both); compare 110.3 ('sold cheap what is most dear'). There is a possible play on rite/right, as at 17.11, 23.6.

7   *hoisted sail* For the metaphor of the ship, compare 116.7. For the poet-speaker's wanderings, see 109.5, 110.1.

8   *should* would.

9   *Book. . . down* record; compare *2 Henry IV*, 4.3.46–7: 'let it be booked with the rest of this day's deeds'. *wilfulness* For the sexual connotations of 'will', see 40.8n. *errors* (i) transgressions (OED 5); (ii) wanderings (OED 1); see 116.13n.

10   *And on. . . accumulate* 'Pile up ['accumulate'] actual ['just'] proof on top of guesswork ['surmise']'; *surmise* is thus a noun (compare *Lucrece*, l. 1579) – meaning 'an allegation, charge, imputation; esp. a false, unfounded, or unproved charge or allegation' (OED 2) – used in contrast to 'just proof'. If left, Q's punctuation – 'surmise, accumulate' – transforms the phrase into two verbs, disrupting the sense.

10, 13   *proof. . . prove* For the significance of ideas of proof in the *Sonnets*, see 2.12n.

11   *level* line of fire, range (OED 9a), as if the frown were a weapon, anticipating 'shoot not', l. 12; compare *Winter's Tale*, 2.3.4–6: 'for the harlot King | Is quite beyond mine arm, out of the blank | And level of my brain, plot-proof'. Compare Constable, *Diana* (1592), 9.5–7: 'Thine eye the pile [pointed tip] is of a murdering dart, | Mine eye the sight thou tak'st thy level by | To hit my heart' (sig. C1r).

12   *wakened hate* Compare *Othello*, 3.3.363 ('waked wrath'), in a speech which famously begins with a desire for proof: 'Villain, be sure thou prove my love a whore; | Be sure of it. Give me the ocular proof' (ll. 359–60).

13   *appeal* plea; see l.1n, above. *prove* The poet-speaker's defence relies on this verb, as he endeavours to excuse his transgressions by saying that he was testing ('prov[ing]', OED³ 6a) and thus demonstrating (OED³ 1) the strength of the beloved's love.

14   *virtue* (i) strength; (ii) purity, moral excellence.

117

Accuse me thus: that I have scanted all
Wherein I should your great deserts repay,
Forgot upon your dearest love to call,
Whereto all bonds do tie me day by day;   4
That I have frequent been with unknown minds,
And given to time your own dear-purchased right;
That I have hoisted sail to all the winds
Which should transport me farthest from your sight.   8
Book both my wilfulness and errors down,
And on just proof surmise accumulate;
Bring me within the level of your frown,
But shoot not at me in your wakened hate,   12
    Since my appeal says I did strive to prove
    The constancy and virtue of your love.

118

Benson combines Sonnets 117–119 under the title 'Trial of love's constancy'.

1 *Like as* Compare opening of Sonnet 60.
   appetites Compare 56.2, 110.10, 147.4; as in those instances, there is potential for a sexual resonance, as there clearly is at *Lucrece*, l. 9.

2 *eager compounds* mixtures which are 'pungent, acrid, keen to the taste or other senses. Of medicines: sharp or violent in operation' ('eager', OED 1a); compare *Hamlet*, 1.5.68–70: 'with a sudden vigour it doth posset | And curd, like eager [i.e. acidic] droppings into milk, | The thin and wholesome blood'. Early modern medicine was predominantly conducted through regulating the patient's diet, so the culinary and pharmaceutical were often very close, as here where strongly flavoured concoctions are being used to stimulate ('urge') the taste ('palate'); the medicinal motif anticipates ll. 3–4, 7–8, 11–12, 14.

3 *As* as also (introducing a second comparison before we get to 'so', l. 5).
   prevent forestall.

4 *We. . . purge* Early modern remedies often relied on violent purges (e.g. by taking emetics to induce vomiting).

5 *Even* pronounced as one syllable.
   being pronounced as one syllable.
   ne'er-cloying spelled 'nere cloying' in Q; Benson alters to 'neare cloying' in 1640, so the compliment to the friend verges on insult; however, 'ne'er' (never) is spelled 'nere' throughout Q, by both compositors ('nere' for 'ne'er' also occurs at Q17.8, Q89.14, Q144.13 and *Lover's Complaint*, ll. 182, 194), whereas 'near' is consistently spelled 'neere' (Q61.14, Q97.14, Q136.1, Q139.13, Q140.7; see also 'neerely', Q42.4). The line evokes the proverb 'Too much honey cloys the stomach' (Dent H560).

6 *bitter sauces* to counteract the friend's sweetness; see Dent M839: 'Sweet meat must have sour sauce'.
   frame fashion.

7 *sick of* (i) surfeited by; (ii) made ill by; see also l. 14.
   welfare (i) good diet, abundance of food; (ii) good health and happiness.
   meetness suitableness; pun on 'meat' (i.e. food, OED³ 1a).

8 *To be* in being.
   true needing a real need to be.

9 *policy* cunning, craftiness (*n*.1, OED³ 5a); see *Troilus and Cressida*, 5.4.9–10: 'the policy of those crafty swearing rascals'; compare also 124.9 and note.
   t'anticipate to pre-empt.

10 *ills* (i) illnesses; (ii) evils.
    grew. . . assured became real crimes; for the way in which pretended faults become ingrained, see Jonson, *Discoveries*, describing how 'children, that imitate the vices of stammerers so long, till at last they become such, and make the habit to another nature, as it is never forgotten' (7.537). Editors from Gildon onwards have habitually altered Q's punctuation (as here), since Q's positioning of the comma between 'were' and 'not' disrupts the sense of the line.

11 *brought. . . state* brought to the point of needing medicine from what had previously been a healthy condition.

12 *Which* the previously healthy condition.
    rank of abounding in (OED³ A7b).
    goodness the excellence of the friend.
    would wanted.

14 *sick of* See l. 7n, above. It was conventional to portray love as a sickness; see, for example, Daniel's *Complaint of Rosamond* (revised edn, 1594): 'Your lovesick heart, that overcharged hath been | With pleasure's surfeit, must be purged with art. | This potion hath a power, that will convert | To nought those humors that oppress you so' (sig. G4ʳ).

118

Like as to make our appetites more keen
With eager compounds we our palate urge,
As to prevent our maladies unseen
We sicken to shun sickness when we purge: 4
Even so, being full of your ne'er-cloying sweetness,
To bitter sauces did I frame my feeding,
And, sick of welfare, found a kind of meetness
To be diseased ere that there was true needing.   8
Thus policy in love, t'anticipate
The ills that were not, grew to faults assured
And brought to medicine a healthful state
Which, rank of goodness, would by ill be cured.   12
    But thence I learn and find the lesson true:
    Drugs poison him that so fell sick of you.

119

Benson combines Sonnets 117–119 under the title 'Trial of love's constancy'.

1 ***potions*** could be medicinal or venomous; the word picks up on the imagery of 118.14.
siren tears deceitful tears; sirens were monsters from classical mythology – half-bird, half-woman – which lured sailors to their deaths through their singing; see *Titus Andronicus*, 2.1.23–4: 'This siren that will charm Rome's Saturnine | And see his shipwreck and his commonweal's'. '*Syren*' is capitalised and italicised in Q, as is often the case for words of foreign origin even if, like siren, they are of established English usage. For italicisation and capitalisation, see 1.2n.

2 ***limbecks*** alembics, apparatus used in distilling; there is a long tradition of portraying eyes as 'limbecks'; see Chaucer, *Troilus and Criseyde*, 4.519–20: 'Troylus in teris gan distille, | As licour out of a lambyc ful faste'; Barnes, *Parthenophil and Parthenophe*, Sonnet 49.6–9: 'A siren which within thy breast doth bathe her [. . .] | From my love's limbeck still stilled tears, oh tears!' (1593: sig. E2v). Blakemore Evans (1996: 231) suggests that 'limbecks' holds a potential sexual allusion, thanks to their shape (like male or female genitalia), particularly when in close proximity to the reference to hell (see below).
foul as hell 'Hell' (a hot, dark pit) is often associated with female genitalia; see 129.14n. Kerrigan (1986: 338) draws attention to the similarity to 147.14, another sonnet that explores desire in terms of fever and madness.

3 ***Applying. . .fears*** 'Apply' has a medical sense: 'to place or spread (an ointment, remedy, dressing, etc.) on the skin or other body surface. In later use also: to administer (a treatment)' (OED³ 2a); see *Lover's Complaint*, 68n. Here, the poet-speaker acts in accordance with recommended early modern medical practice, which tried to achieve a balance of the bodily humours by treating a perceived excess of one humour with its opposite (e.g. the dry heat of the choleric person would be cooled and dampened; the cold wetness of the melancholic would be heated and dried). In this way, Shakespeare revitalises a by-now stale Petrarchan oxymoron of fearful hope and hopeful fear.

4 ***saw. . .win*** thought I would win.

4, 6, 8 ***?*** punctuated as in Q; a number of editors change these to exclamation marks. For the effect of question marks versus exclamation marks, see notes on 43.8, 12; 48.4; 97.2, 3 4.

5 ***errors*** A key word in this mini-sequence of sonnets (see 116.13, 117.9), during which – in the light of the poet-speaker's self-confessed absences – the Latin root of the word (*errare*, to wander) is close to the fore.
committed Duncan-Jones (1997a: 348) highlights the connotations of adultery, pointing to *King Lear*, 3.4.81–2 ('commit not with man's sworn spouse') and *Othello*, where Othello's interprets Desdemona's 'What ignorant sin have I committed?' (4.2.70) as a confession of adultery: 'Committed? O thou public commoner' (4.2.73).

6 ***so blessèd never*** never before so happy and/or fortunate.

7 ***How. . .fitted*** The poet-speaker imagines his eyes as planets, jolted out of their orbit by his feverish convulsions. Compare *Hamlet*, 1.5.17: 'Make thy two eyes like stars start from their spheres'; this instance is the OED's only citation for 'fit, *v*.2': '*trans*. To force by fits or paroxysms *out of* (the usual place)'. In the light of the poet-speaker's recurrent allusions to his social inferiority, there may also be some sense that – in loving the aristocratic youth – the poet-speaker is being pulled out of his social milieu; compare Polonius' advice to Ophelia at *Hamlet* 2.2.141: 'Lord Hamlet is a prince out of thy star'.

8 ***distraction*** 'violent perturbation or disturbance of mind or feelings, approaching to temporary madness' (OED 4); Shakespeare's *Antony and Cleopatra* (1606) is the first citation in OED, but compare the use of the word at *Twelfth Night*, 5.1.314 (first performed *c*. 1601), where Orsino's response to Malvolio's letter is that it 'savours not much of distraction', and *Troilus and Cressida* (*c*. 1602), 5.2.41, where Ulysses warns the tormented Troilus that he 'flow[s] to great distraction'.
madding frenzied; compare 147.10 ('frantic mad').

9 ***benefit of ill*** advantage that comes from (i) evil ('ill', OED B1); (ii) misfortune (OED B5a); (iii) disease (OED B6).
I find true I discover to be true; compare 118.13.

119

What potions have I drunk of siren tears
Distilled from limbecks foul as hell within,
Applying fears to hopes, and hopes to fears,
Still losing when I saw myself to win?   4
What wretched errors hath my heart committed,
Whilst it hath thought itself so blessèd never?
How have mine eyes out of their spheres been fitted
In the distraction of this madding fever?   8
O benefit of ill; now I find true
That better is by evil still made better,
And ruined love when it is built anew
Grows fairer than at first, more strong, far greater.   12
  So I return rebuked to my content,
  And gain by ills thrice more than I have spent.

10 *still* (i) constantly; (ii) even.

10–12 *That better. . . greater* Compare the proverbs 'A broken bone is the stronger when it is well set' (Dent B515), 'The falling-out of lovers is a renewing of love' (Dent F40), the latter of which derives from Terence's *Andria* ('amantium irae amoris integratio est'); see item 42 (by Richard Edwards) in *The Paradise of Dainty Devices* (1576: sigs F1v–F2r), which takes the Latin aphorism as its starting point and has the refrain 'The falling out of faithful friends is the renewing of love'. For the house as a metaphor for love, see *Two Gentlemen of Verona*, 5.4.7–10: 'O thou that dost inhabit in my breast, | Leave not the mansion so long tenantless, | Lest growing ruinous, the building fall | And leave no memory of what it was!'

13 *I. . . content* (i) 'I come back, chastised, to the source of my happiness [i.e. the youth]'; (ii) 'I come back, chastised in a way (or to such an extent) that makes me happy'. For the idea of returning to the friend as a homecoming, compare 109.5–6. 'Content' is stressed on the second syllable.

14 *spent* (i) expended, paid out; (ii) wasted.

120
Printed by Benson as a single sonnet entitled 'A good construction of his love's unkindness'.

1 ***once*** (i) on one occasion; (ii) earlier; the latter is more likely, considering the poet-speaker's recurrent allusions to the youth's neglect, emotional estrangement and/or transgressions (see Sonnets 33–36, 40–42, 57–58, 92–96).
  unkind stronger than in modern usage: 'lacking in natural gratitude' (OED 3a); 'contrary to nature' (OED 4); 'unnaturally cruel' (OED 5); 'lacking in kindness' (OED 6a).
  befriends favours, assists.
2 ***for*** because of.
3 ***bow*** a gesture of submission.
4 ***nerves*** sinews or tendons (OED³ 2).
  brass . . . steel used to epitomise hardness and durability; see 64.4n, 65.8n, 107.14n, 112.8n.
6 ***y' have*** you have; the elision is there in Q.
  a hell of time a hellish time; 'hell' also carries suggestions of eternal suffering. For the poet-speaker's experience of this relationship as 'hell', see 58.13, 119.2.
7 ***no leisure taken*** have not taken the time.
8 ***weigh*** consider.
  suffered in The choice of preposition is grammatically unusual, even in early modern English; it combines a sense of the poet-speaker suffering from the youth's transgressions, and suffering by sharing in them, such is the extent of the poet-speaker's identification with the friend (who is a second self; see 22.3n).
9 ***our night of woe*** The shared first person pronoun makes the grief mutual and simultaneously felt (see 'suffered in', l. 8n, above); 'night' is here used

figuratively, to indicate the darkest period (i.e. the depths of sorrow). Compare Sidney's portrayal of Stella's absence as 'night' in *Astrophil and Stella* 91.
  rememb'red reminded; compare *Tempest*, 1.2.243: 'Let me remember thee what thou hast promised'.
10 ***My deepest sense*** 'my innermost thoughts and feelings', playing on the ambiguity of 'sense' as both rational faculty and emotional perception.
11 ***tend'red*** The subject is 'night of woe'. The primary meaning is 'offered', but the financial imagery of ll. 13–14 retrospectively activates the legal meaning: 'to offer (money, etc.) in discharge of a debt or liability' (*v.*1, OED 1a).
12 ***The . . . fits!*** 'the healing ointment [e.g. of a meek apology or, as at 34.7, of tears], which is exactly suited ('fits') to soothing a wounded heart'; there may be echoes of Isaiah 57.15: 'I dwell in the high & holy place, with him also that is of a contrite and humble spirit to revive the spirit of the humble, and to give life to them that are of a contrite heart'. The final exclamation mark is in Q (one of ten in the volume; see 92.12n).
13 ***But that*** A problematic construction: 'except that' does not make sense in the context of the sonnet; most editors read 'that' as a demonstrative pronoun, qualifying 'your trespass'.
  fee payment.
14 ***Mine*** my transgression (l. 3).
  ransoms . . . ransom redeem(s), deliver(s); the verb holds a theological resonance: 'To deliver (a person, mankind, a soul, etc.) from sin, damnation, etc.; to redeem. Esp. with reference to the Passion of Christ' (OED³ 1a).
  yours your trespass (l. 13).

120

That you were once unkind befriends me now,
And for that sorrow which I then did feel
Needs must I under my transgression bow,
Unless my nerves were brass or hammered steel.   4
For if you were by my unkindness shaken,
As I by yours, y' have passed a hell of time,
And I, a tyrant, have no leisure taken
To weigh how once I suffered in your crime.   8
O that our night of woe might have rememb'red
My deepest sense how hard true sorrow hits,
And soon to you as you to me then tend'red
The humble salve which wounded bosoms fits!   12
    But that your trespass now becomes a fee:
    Mine ransoms yours, and yours must ransom me.

121

Printed by Benson as a single sonnet entitled 'Error in opinion'.

1–2 **'Tis better...being** Compare the proverb 'There is small difference to the eye of the world in being nought and being thought so' (Dent D336); '*vile*' has strongly moral connotations: 'of actions, conduct, character, etc.: Despicable on moral grounds; deserving to be regarded with abhorrence or disgust; characterized by baseness or depravity' (OED 1a).

3 **just** legitimate.

   so deemed i.e. considered vile.

4 **feeling** opinion (OED 7a).

   seeing perception; for this line, compare Tilley T140: 'It is an ill thing to be wicked but a worse to be known so'.

5 **false adulterate eyes** eyes (i.e. people) which perceive wrongly because they are themselves impure ('adulterate', OED[3] 1); both 'false' and 'adulterate' play on the idea of sexual betrayal; 'adulterate' is here pronounced as three syllables.

6 **Give salutation** greet, presumably in recognition, because they wrongly perceive the poet-speaker similar to their 'adulterate' selves.

   sportive dissolute, wanton; compare the use of 'sport' in a context of disapprobation at 95.6, 96.2.

   blood in early modern medical theory, the basis for determining character; see 109.10n. Blood was also the humour most associated with passions such as lust; see *Hamlet*, 1.3.115–17: 'I do know, | When the blood burns, how prodigal the soul | Lends the tongue vows'.

7 **frailties** moral weaknesses; compare 109.10.

   why are why are there.

   frailer more susceptible to temptation.

8 **Which** who.

   wills desires (*n*.1, OED 1a), including sexual ones (OED 2).

   count consider, esteem.

   think Through the choice of verb, the poet-speaker asserts his superiority over the 'frailer spies' (l. 7): he uses the higher faculty of thought, where they base their judgement on their own 'wills'.

9 **I am...am** Critics and editors have worried about the potential presumption of this phrase, since the poet-speaker seems to assume divine authority, rehearsing God's response to Moses in Exodus 3:14 ('And God answered Moses, "I am that I am"'). However, it is more likely that it is drawn from St Paul's echo of Exodus at 1 Corinthians 15:10 ('by the grace of God, I am that I am'), which also features in the *Book of Common Prayer*, read on the eleventh Sunday after Trinity (2011: 350–1). Far from being presumptuous, this follows on from a recognition of Paul's humility and fallibility in 1 Corinthians 15:9: 'For I am the least of the Apostles [...] because I persecuted the Church of God'.

   level (i) guess (as in *Merchant of Venice*, 1.2.36–8: 'I pray thee over-name them [Portia's suitors], and as thou namest them, I will describe them; and according to my description level at my affection'); (ii) take aim at (as in *3 Henry VI*, 2.2.19: 'Ambitious York did level at thy crown').

10 **abuses** transgressions; see *Lucrece*, l. 1075 and note.

   reckon up calculate; plays on 'count' (l. 8).

11 **straight** honest, upright; there may also be a play on 'strait' (narrow), another adjective used to indicate moral rectitude; see Matthew 7:13: 'Enter in at the strait gate: for it is the wide gate and the broad way that leadeth to destruction'.

   bevel oblique, sloping (OED 2), in contrast to 'straight'; this is the only usage in Shakespeare's works; apart from its use in making the rhyme, it may also have been chosen for its echo of 'be vile' (l. 1).

12 **By** (i) through the agency of; (ii) by analogy with.

   rank obscene (OED[3] A11), festering (OED[3] A12); compare 69.12, 118.12.

   must not (i) cannot; (ii) should not.

13 **this general evil** 'this universal maxim about evil' (which follows in l. 14).

14 **All...bad** an allusion to the doctrine of original sin, whereby all inherit Adam's guilt and are thereby inherently sinful; compare also 35.5.

   reign (i) exercise authority (OED[3] 6a); (ii) prosper (OED[3] 2c).

121

'Tis better to be vile than vile esteemed,
When not to be receives reproach of being,
And the just pleasure lost which is so deemed
Not by our feeling, but by others' seeing.   4
For why should others' false adulterate eyes
Give salutation to my sportive blood?
Or on my frailties why are frailer spies,
Which in their wills count bad what I think good?   8
No, I am that I am, and they that level
At my abuses reckon up their own;
I may be straight, though they themselves be bevel;
By their rank thoughts my deeds must not be shown,   12
    Unless this general evil they maintain:
    All men are bad and in their badness reign.

122

Printed by Benson as a single sonnet entitled 'Upon the receipt of a table book from his mistress', one of three instances in *Poems* where Benson uses titles to redirect sonnets from the pre-127 section of Q (generally taken as being addressed to a man) to a woman; see also headnotes to Sonnets 113–115 and 125.

1   *tables* probably a commonplace book ('a small, portable tablet for writing upon, esp. for notes or memoranda', 'table, *n.*', OED³ sense 2b); compare *Hamlet*, 1.5.107 (cited at 24.2n). In Sonnet 77, the poet-speaker had encouraged the friend to write in a blank notebook he had sent him (possibly with one of his own poems already inscribed in it; see 77.4n); here the situation is reversed. Editors often note the analogue in Pierre Ronsard's *Les Amours diverses* (1578), Sonnet 4: 'There was no need, mistress, for other notebooks to inscribe you, other than those of my heart, where with his hand, Love, our victor, has etched you, and your perfect graces' ['Il ne falloit, Maistresse, autres tablettes | Pour vous graver, que celles de mon coeur, | Où de sa main Amour nostre veinqueur | Vous a gravée, et vos graces parfaites']. As Ingram and Redpath point out, 'thy tables' could also be a blank book given to the poet-speaker by the friend, and either filled in – or not – before being given away (1985: 280); as they observe, a book 'would then have been a more valuable gift than it might seem now' (owing to the relative cost of paper). Although composing verses was a fairly usual aristocratic pastime, the friend is nowhere else described as a poet in the *Sonnets*, and – should the notebooks contain his compositions – the description of the writing therein as 'idle' (l. 3) is potentially problematic (see l. 3n).

1–2 *within. . . memory* The process of remembering is here likened to the process of writing; compare *Hamlet*, 1.3.58–9: 'these few precepts in thy memory | Look thou character'.

2   *Full charactered* inscribed at length.
    lasting memory an enduring record.

3   *that idle rank* (i) the rows ('rank') of letters written in the actual notebook; the description of the friend's writing as 'idle' ('worthless', OED A2a), whilst a commonplace description of poetry, jars in a sonnet which attempts to regain favour, and is out of kilter with the usual praise of the friend's talents (even if his morals are open to scrutiny). (ii) Possibly the adjective

is here being used to indicate 'inactive' (OED A5a): the inert words written on the page thus contrast with those living in the poet-speaker's memory. (iii) Alternatively, 'idle rank' could refer to the other thoughts that the poet-speaker possesses, and which are inferior to the friend's 'tables'; compare *Hamlet* 'wip[ing] away all trivial fond records', so that his brain has space to remember his father's words (*Hamlet*, 1.5.99).

4   *all date* every time limit; compare 14.14, 18.4, 38.12.
    even pronounced as one syllable.

5   *brain and heart* seats of thought and feeling; see 46.1n, 69.2.

6   *faculty by nature* natural capacity.
    subsist survive.

7   *each* i.e. brain and heart.
    razed evokes the destructiveness of time, which brings all things to oblivion: (i) by demolishing the strongest buildings (compare 64.3); (ii) by erasure, continuing the metaphor of memory as text (compare 25.11); 'oblivion' is three syllables.
    his its.

8   *thy record* memory of you; compare 55.8.
    missed be lost.

9   *retention* This usually abstract noun – indicating the ability to retain things (OED³ 2a) – has here been made concrete and refers to the actual notebook, which is being presented as inferior to the poet-speaker's memory and which, ironically, the poet-speaker has failed to retain.

10 *tallies. . . score* tangible records; a tally was a rod, marked or 'scored' on one side with notches to indicate the amount of a debt or payment. The rod was then split lengthwise, across the notches, and the debtor and creditor both retained one half, as proof to either party as to the amount owed. This was a system used by, and comprehensible to, illiterate people (see Jack Cade's enthusiasm for the system in *2 Henry VI*, 4.7.32–7: 'Thou hast most traitorously corrupted the youth of the realm in erecting a grammar school; and whereas, before, our forefathers had no other books but the score and the tally, thou has caused printing to be used, and [. . .] built a paper-mill'). Comparing the notebooks to 'tallies' thus further denigrates the status of the material records which the poet-speaker is here seeking to devalue.

11 *Therefore. . . bold* The poet-speaker begins to excuse himself for giving away the friend's gift (an excuse which culminates in ll. 13–14).

122

Thy gift, thy tables, are within my brain
Full charactered with lasting memory,
Which shall above that idle rank remain
Beyond all date even to eternity;   4
Or at the least so long as brain and heart
Have faculty by nature to subsist;
Till each to razed oblivion yield his part
Of thee, thy record never can be missed.   8
That poor retention could not so much hold,
Nor need I tallies thy dear love to score;
Therefore to give them from me was I bold
To trust those tables that receive thee more.   12
    To keep an adjunct to remember thee
    Were to import forgetfulness in me.

For the circulation of literary works between acquaintances (without the permission or knowledge of their originator), see the pseudo-excuses frequently found in the prefatory matter of printed collections of verse, as in Googe's *Epitaphs, Eclogues, and Sonnets*, where Googe explains 'myself being at that time out of the realm [...] a very friend of mine, bearing as it seemed better will to my doings than respecting the hazard of my name, committed them altogether unpolished to the hands of the printer' (1563: sig. A6r). The opening of Gascoigne's *Adventures of Master F.J.* (1573) tells a similar story, as H.W. passes a 'written book', compiled by G.T. and containing verses by F.J., to the printer A.B.

12 *those tables* the poet-speaker's memory.
   receive accept (OED³ III); take an impression (OED³ 11a), continuing the motif of memory as text.
13 *adjunct* external aid.
14 *import* imply.

123

Printed by Benson as a single sonnet entitled 'A vow'.

1 *No!* The exclamation is in Q (one of ten in the volume; see 92.12n). See Figure 4.2.

2 *pyramids* The allusion has prompted various attempts to date this sonnet: (i) by reading this as reference to the obelisks on the triumphal arches at James I's entry into the City of London on 15 March 1604 (Harbage 1950); pyramidal structures are depicted in Stephen Harrison's engravings in *The Arches of Triumph* (1604) and are described in the accompanying text (sigs C1r, D1r, E1r, F1r). Certainly, Sonnet 123 cannot refer to the Egyptian pyramids, since the edifices depicted have been 'built up with newer might'; the choice of the word 'might', however, does not quite suggest the very temporary structures created for a pageant. (ii) Hotson (1949) argues that this alludes to the obelisks that Pope Sixtus V had transferred from Egypt and re-erected in Rome in 1586-9, giving (if correct) a *terminus a quo* for the composition of the sonnet. Blakemore Evans suggests a way of reconciling the two theories (and overcoming the problem of 'might'), conjecturing that 'perhaps Shakespeare was reminded of the Egyptian obelisks by seeing the newly erected triumphal arches' (1996: 236). The allusion need not be to any specific event, however. Burrow (2002: 626) suggests a possible debt to Propertius 3.2: 'Not sumptuous Pyramids to skies upreared, | Nor Elean Jove's proud Fane, which heaven compeered, | Nor the rich fane of Mausoleus' tomb, | Are privileged from death's extremest doom' (trans. by John Weever, *Ancient Funeral Monuments*, 1631: sig. B2r); but see headnote to Sonnet 55. The quotation from Horace, *Odes* 3.30, cited in headnote to Sonnet 55, is also resonant here. 'Pyramid' was used in this period in a loose fashion, encompassing a range of structures – such as spires, pinnacles, obelisks and pediments – which rose up from a square or triangular base to meet in a point (OED³ 3a). Pyramids tended to be used to ridicule human ambition – as in Robert Greene's translation of Louise Labé's *Debat de folie et d'amour*: 'What made Rhodope build the Pyramids, and Artemisia frame the sumptuous sepulchre, but folly?' (*Gwydonius*, 1584: sig X1r) – or to explore the possibility and limits of immortality, often in relation to the immortalising powers of poetry, as in Drayton's *Idea, The Shepherd's*

Garland, Eclogue 8: 'And who erects the brave pyramids | Of monarchs or renowned warriors | Need bathe his quill for such attempts as these | In flowing streams of learned Maro's shores' (1593: sig. H4v); see also quotation from Thomas Andrewe at 65.6n, and Appendix 6 (the verses on the Stanley tomb at Tong).

4 *but* only, merely.

dressings reworkings; compare 76.11; Kerrigan (1986: 345) notes Shakespeare's recurrent use of clothing metaphors to express deceit.

of a former sight of something we have seen before.

5–8 *Our. . . told* The quatrain establishes what people (a collective 'we') believe, which contrasts with the perceptiveness of the poet-speaker ('I'), as indicated in the first and third quatrains.

5 *dates* life-spans.

admire wonder at (OED³ 1a).

6 *foist* palm off; the sixteenth-century usages of the word are firmly associated with cheating (see *v.*1, OED 1–3c, 4).

7–8 *rather. . . told* 'We would rather believe the old things to have been newly created to satisfy our wishes than acknowledge that they are something we encountered before'; compare 59.1–2 and note. Wyndham (1898) interprets Q's 'borne' as 'bourn' (limit), which is frequently spelled 'borne' in the First Folio. Whilst 'bourn' works for l. 7, however, it is less satisfactory for l. 8 (which establishes a contrast between old and new). As a noun 'bourn' also lacks an article; whilst not unprecedented, it does make l. 7 read more awkwardly than it need, if following Wyndham.

8 *told* (i) related; (ii) counted.

9 *registers* records.

10 *wondering* marvelling; here pronounced as two syllables.

11 *records* stressed on the second syllable.

doth plural, as at 112.1.

12 *Made. . . less* (i) With the passing of time, records accumulate, but they also diminish, as they perish or are destroyed; (ii) the perception of what is significant ('more or less') changes with time.

continual haste Time was proverbially swift; see 19.6n; 'continual' is three syllables.

13 *This* the statement (and opinion) that follows, but also these lines (compare 18.14).

14 *true* faithful, honest.

scythe For the portrayal of Time with a knife and/or reaping implement, see 12.13n.

123

No! Time, thou shalt not boast that I do change.
Thy pyramids built up with newer might
To me are nothing novel, nothing strange;
They are but dressings of a former sight.   4
Our dates are brief, and therefore we admire
What thou dost foist upon us that is old,
And rather make them born to our desire
Than think that we before have heard them told.   8
Thy registers and thee I both defy,
Not wondering at the present, nor the past,
For thy records, and what we see, doth lie,
Made more or less by thy continual haste.   12
   This I do vow, and this shall ever be:
   I will be true despite thy scythe and thee.

124

Continues from Sonnet 123 in asserting the poet-speaker's unalterable love for the friend. Printed by Benson as a single sonnet entitled 'Love's safety'.

1 *dear* heartfelt, precious, but also potentially something which comes at a cost.
love devotion.
but only.
child of state product of circumstance ('state, *n*.', OED³ 1a).

2 *for* as.
Fortune's bastard Fortune was often derided as a strumpet (see *Hamlet*, 2.2.235–6, 493; *King John*, 3.1.61; Dent F603.1); bearing a bastard is a potential consequence of promiscuity.
unfathered deprived of its father, denied its true paternity; Shakespeare also uses the word at 97.10 and *2 Henry IV*, 4.4.122 ('Unfathered heirs and loathly births of nature').

4 *Weeds. . . gathered* The weeds and flowers are emblematic (respectively) of Time's hate and Time's love, which dictates whether the 'child of state' is gathered up (and presumably cherished, at least temporarily) like flowers, or cast away with other weeds; either way, both flowers and weeds are cut down by time, so any favour enjoyed is merely transient. Metrically, the first '*flowers*' needs to be monosyllabic, the second disyllabic.

5, 6, 9, 12 *it* his love.

5 *builded* alternative form of 'built' (i.e. 'created'), chosen for metrical purposes.
accident chance; compare Time's 'millioned accidents', 115.5.

6–7 *It suffers. . . discontent* Lying behind this line is the image of fortune's wheel, raising people up, then casting them down; see also Dent F598.1: 'Fortune can both smile and frown'. 'The blow of thrallèd discontent' that threatens to bring low the 'child of state' could be (i) a sudden uprising of a discontented multitude, who have been kept in bondage ('thrallèd'); (ii) the mental strain of the frustration resulting from a lack of political advancement, in which case the adjective 'thrallèd' indicates 'enslaving' rather than 'enslaved'; for

the transference of properties from verb to agent, see Hope 2003: 46–8.

8 *Whereto* i.e. to 'discontent'; Kerrigan (1986: 347) suggests that this line can be read in the light of a *fin-de-siècle* vogue for melancholic discontent, which Shakespeare depicts in Jacques in *As You Like It*.
th' inviting time these alluring times.
our fashion 'men like us' (see OED 4); 'our behaviours' (see OED 6a).

9 *Policy* expediency and cunning; compare 118.9 and note. The word is closely associated with Machiavellianism; see, for example, *Timon*, 3.2.86–7: 'Men must learn now with pity to dispense, | For policy sits above conscience'. The word is not capitalised in Q, but its description as 'that heretic' tips it towards personification.
heretic This indicates more than someone who holds unorthodox beliefs; in Shakespearean usage it often implies someone of no beliefs; see the description of Benedick's imperviousness to female charms in *Much Ado*, 1.1.234–5 ('Thou wast ever an obstinate heretic in the despite of beauty'), and Ford's apology to the wife he has wrongly suspected in *Merry Wives*, 4.4.8–10: 'now doth thy honour stand, | In him that was of late an heretic, | As firm as faith'. 'Heretic' is italicised and capitalised in Q (see Figure 4.2), although the word was not a neologism; for the inconsistency of Q's italicisation and capitalisation, see 1.2n.

10 *works. . . hours* Most editors gloss this as 'acts according to the short-term view'; however, Burrow (2002: 628) demurs, arguing that 'lease' is never used to describe contracts of employment, only tenure of property, and that 'works on' implies 'deceptive corruption', as in *Othello*, 1.3.391: 'The better shall my purpose work on him'. He offers the alternative gloss: 'dissolves leases which are already of too short a date'.

11 *hugely* enormously, massively.
politic wise, prudent (in slightly uncomfortable distinction from 'policy', l. 9).

12 *That* so that.
nor. . . nor neither. . . nor.

124

If my dear love were but the child of state,
It might for Fortune's bastard be unfathered,
As subject to Time's love, or to Time's hate,
Weeds among weeds, or flowers with flowers gathered.   4
No, it was builded far from accident;
It suffers not in smiling pomp, nor falls
Under the blow of thrallèd discontent,
Whereto th' inviting time our fashion calls;   8
It fears not Policy, that heretic,
Which works on leases of short-numbered hours,
But all alone stands hugely politic,
That it nor grows with heat, nor drowns with showers.   12
    To this I witness call the fools of time,
    Which die for goodness, who have lived for crime.

      grows. . . showers glances back to the organic imagery of weeds and flowers in l. 4; for the use of the image of the sun and showers to describe favour and its subsequent loss, see Sonnet 34. 'Showers': pronounced as one syllable.

13 *this* this attitude, claim.

      I witness call call to give testimony, as in a court of law; compare the legal framework of 125.13–14.

      fools of time conveying both the sense of a dupe or victim of time, and someone/something subservient to time, as a fool would be to his master, there for the latter's amusement; compare 116.9, where true love is distinguished from 'Time's fool'.

14 *Which . . . crime* the fools of time who have lived immorally (presumably practising the Machiavellian policy of l. 9) but (i) die repentant, making a 'good death' and/or renouncing their crimes on the scaffold (as was customary for criminals and traitors); (ii) who acquire the reputation of martyrs posthumously; (iii) whose deaths, purging a disruptive element, are conducted for the greater good of the state. Critics and editors have tried to identify the 'fools of time' with various historical figures, favourites being Mary Queen of Scots (d. 1587), Robert Devereux, Earl of Essex (d. 1601) and Elizabethan Jesuits, such as Edmund Campion (d. 1581).

125

Printed by Benson as a single sonnet entitled 'An entreaty for her acceptance', one of three instances in *Poems* where Benson uses titles to redirect sonnets from the pre-127 section of Q (generally taken as being addressed to a man) to a woman; see also head-notes to Sonnets 113–115 and 122.

1 *Were 't. . . canopy* It would be a mark of honour to carry the canopy which was held over the chief persons in a procession; see, for example, the stage directions in *Henry VIII*, 4.1 ('The Order of the Coronation') and 5.4 (Princess Elizabeth's christening). Those critics and editors who favour a composition date of 1603–4 for Sonnets 123–125 read this as an allusion to James I's coronation on 25 July 1603 and its accompanying celebrations, such as his entry to the City of London (see also 123.2n); nevertheless, canopies were a standard feature in official processions.

2 *With. . . honouring* 'honouring with my outward appearance and behaviour the outward appearance of others'; an implicit contrast is established between mere external show and an inward, heartfelt sincerity. This line is the earliest citation in OED for the use of '*extern*' as a noun (B1); the only other early usage that shows up in a keyword search of EEBO-TCP is Daniel Price, *Praelium & Premium*: 'God requireth the extern and intern, soul & body, heart and face, words and works' (1608: sig. B3v).

3 *laid. . . eternity* established solid foundations (or magnificent pedestals) on which to place eternity (which is figured as a statue).

4 *Which proves* The antecedent could be (i) 'eternity' (thus forming a paradox); or (ii) 'great bases', since in early modern English verbs with a plural subject could end in *-s*; see Abbott 1884: § 333.
more short less lasting.
waste or ruining decay and destruction.

5 *dwellers. . . favour* those people who are fixated ('dwell') on (i) courtly manners and favour; (ii) beauty and outward appearance.

6–7 *Lose. . . savour* people who bankrupt themselves by living in expensive houses above their means and by rejecting plain wholesome ('simple') food for sweet but implicitly unwholesome concoctions ('compound[s]'). 'Compound' and 'simple' (often used to describe different types of payment) provide further play on 'rent', which retrospectively activates a meaning of 'dwellers' (l. 5) as 'inhabitants'. Q lacks a comma at the end of l. 6 and has a semi-colon after 'sweet' in l. 7, which (i) makes the 'dwellers on form and favour' pay rent 'for compound sweet'; and (ii) detaches 'compound sweet' from 'simple savour', with which it would seem to belong. Most editors (as here) follow Capell's emendment, providing a comma at the end of l. 6, and substituting a comma for Q's semi-colon in l. 7.

8 *Pitiful thrivers* people who appear successful, but who are really wretched and deserve pity.
in their gazing spent exhausted (and potentially bankrupted) by their love of spectacle.

9 *obsequious* dutiful (OED³ 1a), but perhaps also 'unduly or servilely compliant, [. . .] sycophantic' (OED³ 2a), pointing back to the 'dwellers on [. . .] favour' (l. 5); pronounced as three syllables.

10 *oblation* offering, with strong religious overtones; see the communion service in the *Book of Common Prayer*: 'Jesus Christ [did] suffer death upon the cross for our redemption, who made there (by his one oblation of himself once offered) a full, perfect and sufficient sacrifice, oblation, and satisfaction for the sins of the whole world' (2011: 136–7). Shakespeare uses the word in *Lover's Complaint*, l. 223 (where it also appears in close proximity to 'render', l. 221) and *Pericles*, 5.3.70. For the treatment of the friend as a god, see Sonnet 105; 110.12.
free generous (OED³ A17a); not given in return for something else (OED³ A17b); bearing in mind the echoes of court satire in this poem, the feudal resonances of this word – 'not in servitude to others' (OED³ AI) – are strong.

11 *not. . . seconds* pure, unadulterated; second pressings (of oil, honey) are inferior to the first.
art cunning.

12 *render* 'the action or an act of giving, handing over, or surrendering something' (*n.*1, OED³ 2).

13 *thou suborned informer* The couplet turns to address a hostile – but unidentified – third party: a bribed ('suborned') spy. 'Informer' is capitalised and italicised in Q (see Figure 4.2). For Q's use of italics, see 1.2n.

14 *impeached* accused, specifically used of treason and other serious crimes.
control power.

125

Were't aught to me I bore the canopy,
With my extern the outward honouring,
Or laid great bases for eternity,
Which proves more short than waste or ruining?   4
Have I not seen dwellers on form and favour
Lose all and more by paying too much rent,
For compound sweet forgoing simple savour,
Pitiful thrivers in their gazing spent?   8
No, let me be obsequious in thy heart,
And take thou my oblation, poor but free,
Which is not mixed with seconds, knows no art
But mutual render, only me for thee.   12
  Hence, thou suborned informer: a true soul
  When most impeached stands least in thy control.

126

Omitted by Benson from the 1640 *Poems*. Various explanations have been offered: (i) that Benson wanted to avoid the homoerotic charge of 'lovely boy' (see 108.5n, and l.1n, below; but see headnote to Sonnet 101); (ii) that Benson thought the poem was incomplete because of the missing couplet.

As six pairs of rhyming couplets, 126 departs from the usual rhyme scheme of *Shakespeare's Sonnets*. It is the last of the group traditionally read as being addressed to the young man. Its position in Q's sequence, at 126, may be numerologically appropriate, as twice the grand climacteric; see headnote to Sonnet 63.

1 *lovely boy* There are strong homoerotic resonances here. The epithet is frequently used in sixteenth- and early seventeenth-century poetry of male lovers from Greek mythology, such as Hyacinth, Apollo's lover; see Lewis Machin, 'Apollo's Hyacinth', appended to William Barksted, *Mirrha* (1607: sigs E5v, E7v); see also the description of Ganymede in Richard Barnfield's *Affectionate Shepherd* (1594: sig. A3r) and the homoerotic resonances in Marlowe's usages: 'Silvanus weeping for the lovely boy | That now is turned into a cypress tree' (*Hero and Leander*, ll. 154–5); and Gaveston's vision of 'a lovely boy in Dian's shape | With hair that gilds the water as it glides, | Crownets of pearl about his naked arms, | And in his sportful hands an olive tree | To hide those parts which men delight to see' (*Edward II*, 1.1.60–4). Philemon Holland's translation of Plutarch's *Moralia* deploys the phrase in a similarly erotic context (as evidence of the 'raging [...] affection' that can be experienced by 'those that are enamoured upon boys'): 'So often as these eyes of mine behold | That beardless youth, that smooth and lovely boy, | I faint and fall: then wish I him to hold | Within mine arms, and so to die with joy' (*Philosophy*, 1603: sig. 5E2r).
power pronounced as one syllable.

2 *glass* hour-glass.
sickle hour the moment when Time cuts us down with his sickle; Q punctuates as 'sickle, hour', making two nouns; however, a second

reference to the hour-glass seems illogical, and editors regularly emend this phrase, removing Q's comma to produce a noun phrase that mirrors 'fickle glass'. Punctuation (often unreliable in Q) is particularly erratic in this sonnet (see l. 7n on 'skill'). In early modern typography and secretary hand, the long 's' used for 'sickle' emphasises, visually, the syntactical parallel with 'fickle glass'.

3 *by waning grown* become more as (and because) he has grown older; *waning*: the passing of time.

4 *Thy lovers withering* Since early modern English lacks the possessive apostrophe, this can also be read as (i) 'thy lover's withering'; or (ii) 'thy lovers' withering', where 'withering' is a noun in both cases; 'withering' is here pronounced as two syllables.

5 *sovereign mistress* supreme ruler; compare *Othello*, 1.3.224–5: 'opinion, a sovereign mistress of effects'.
wrack destruction; see 65.6n.

6 *As thou . . . back* Nature will save ('pluck') the lovely boy from Time's destructive powers; '*still*' (continually) can qualify either 'goest onwards' or 'pluck'.

7 *to* for.
skill ability, cunning; Q's full-stop at the end of this line is clearly an error, since it disrupts the syntax.

8 *minutes* Q has 'mynuit'; most editors emend (as here), on the grounds that an error may have arisen (i) because the compositor misread an 'es' hook at the end of 'mynuites' as an 'e', which he then dropped as a redundant terminal letter (see 113.10n, and compare 55.1n); (ii) the compositor originally set 'mynuits kill' as 'mynuit skill' (possibly as the result of an eye-skip to the line above), and then – correcting the line – mistakenly removed the 's', rather than adjusting the spacing. Q's 'wretched mynuit' is not incomprehensible, but it is unusual for Shakespeare to omit the article before singular nouns, unless they are defined by another noun (see Abbott 1884: § 89; Sonnet 24.2), but that is not the case here.

9 *her* Nature.
minion 'a (usually male) favourite of a sovereign, prince, or other powerful person; a

126

O thou, my lovely boy, who in thy power
Dost hold Time's fickle glass, his sickle hour;
Who hast by waning grown, and therein show'st
Thy lovers withering, as thy sweet self grow'st;   4
If Nature (sovereign mistress over wrack)
As thou goest onwards still will pluck thee back,
She keeps thee to this purpose, that her skill
May Time disgrace and wretched minutes kill.   8
Yet fear her, O thou minion of her pleasure:
She may detain, but not still keep her treasure!
Her audit (though delayed) answered must be,
And her quietus is to render thee.   12
  (   )
  (   )

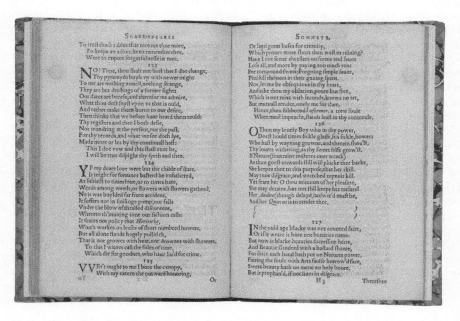

Figure 4.2 William Shakespeare, *Shakespeare's Sonnets* (London: George Eld, 1609), sigs H2v–H3r; Folger Shakespeare Library copy, classmark STC 22353. Used with permission of the Folger Shakespeare Library

person who is dependent on a patron's favour; a hanger-on' (OED[3] A1a); 'a man or woman kept for sexual favours' (OED[3] A1b).

10 *detain* withhold.

   still always.

11 *audit* official examination of financial accounts; sometimes used by Shakespeare to indicate the judgement that souls will receive after death; see *Hamlet*, 3.3.80–2: ''A took my father grossly, full of bread, | With all his crimes broad blown, as flush as May, | And how his audit stands who knows save heaven?'. The word is italicised and capitalised in Q; see 1.2n. The frequent arbitrariness of Q's use of italics and capitals is highlighted by the fact that this word is italicised when it occurs at 4.12 and here, but not at 49.4 (all these poems appear on pages set by Compositor B).

   answered paid ('answer, *v.*', OED 7c).

12 *quietus* 'acquittance or discharge granted on payment of a debt' (OED[3] 1), continuing the financial imagery of l. 11; 'quietus est' was a legal formula written at the closing of an account. 'To pay one's debt to nature' was a proverbial euphemism for death (see Dent D168), and Shakespeare's only other usage of the word connects it strongly with death; see *Hamlet*, 3.1.69–75: 'For who would bear the whips and scorns of time | [...] When he himself might his quietus make | With a bare bodkin'. The word is capitalised and italicised in Q; see 1.2n.

   render thee Since 'render' was often used of paying rent or taxation (OED[3] 10a), the verb continues the strain of financial imagery found in 'treasure' (l. 11) and 'audit' (l. 12). Here, the phrase could be read (i) as 'surrender you' (see OED[3] 6a). Shakespeare uses 'render' as a verb sixty times across his works in various senses ('give', 'make', 'surrender', 'recite'), usually in more syntactically complicated situations than here. The only two analogous situations to the construction Subject-Verb-Object required

by reading (i) are *Antony and Cleopatra*, 4.14.33 ('She rend'red life') and *Much Ado*, 4.1.29 ('unless you render her again'). Alternatively, if the empty parentheses are authorial (see note, below), the phrase could be read (ii) as 'make you...' (see OED[3] 18a); this reading requires an adjective (as in *Julius Caesar*, 2.1.303: 'Render me worthy of this noble wife!') that is supplied visually by the blank lines (and death's oblivion) that follow, as Nature's surrender of the lovely boy to Time causes him to become a void. Reading (ii) is problematised by Q's full-stop at the end of l. 12; however, this mark of punctuation may result from the compositors' habitual practice of ending the third quatrain (or indeed each sonnet) with a strong mark of punctuation (see headnote to the *Sonnets*, 'Printing Q').

13–14 *(...)* The parentheses (also italicised in Q) indicate that two lines are missing. The omission, and use of parentheses, might be authorial, invoking on the page the shape of a grave and thus the oblivion that comes with death; alternatively, they might originate with someone involved in the production of the text (copyist, compositor, editor), because they want to signal either (i) that they have noticed that the poem is shorter than the fourteen-line norm; or (ii) that the lines have been purposefully omitted (e.g. because they reveal the identity of the lovely boy). Visually, dark margins around a void, the parentheses also evoke an act of erasure, when letters are scraped off the page with a sharp implement, an action to which Shakespeare refers at 25.11; *2 Henry VI*, 1.1.100–1 ('Blotting your names from books of memory | Razing the characters of your memory'); *2 Henry IV*, 5.2.127–9 ('to rase out | Rotten opinion, who hath writ me down | After my seeming'); and *Macbeth*, 5.3.41–2 ('Pluck from the memory a rooted sorrow | Raze out the written troubles of the brain').

126

O thou, my lovely boy, who in thy power
Dost hold Time's fickle glass, his sickle hour;
Who hast by waning grown, and therein show'st
Thy lovers withering, as thy sweet self grow'st;   4
If Nature (sovereign mistress over wrack)
As thou goest onwards still will pluck thee back,
She keeps thee to this purpose, that her skill
May Time disgrace and wretched minutes kill.   8
Yet fear her, O thou minion of her pleasure:
She may detain, but not still keep her treasure!
Her audit (though delayed) answered must be,
And her quietus is to render thee.   12
    (   )
    (   )

127

Benson combines Sonnets 127 and 130–132 under
the title 'In praise of her beauty though black'.

Sonnet 127 is the first sonnet, in Q's sequence,
addressed to a dark-haired, dark-eyed mistress. The
mistresses of sonnet sequences were conventionally
blonde and fair-complexioned (see notes on Sonnet
130). Petrarch's Laura has 'golden tresses' ('le treccie
d'or', *Rime Sparse*, 37.81). The colour of her eyes is
less evident: they are recurrently described as 'lovely'
('begli'), as at *Rime Sparse*, 9.11, 37.74, 112.11; that
'gold and topaz in the sun [...] are vanquished by the
blonde locks next to those eyes' may indicate that her
eyes are blue ('L'auro e i topacii al sol [...] | vincon
le bionde chiome presso a gli occhi', *Rime Sparse*,
30.37–8); however, elsewhere he writes of Laura's
eyes as 'the lovely sweet mild white and black where
Love gilds and sharpens his arrows' ('del bel dolce
soave bianco et nero | in che in suoi strali Amor dora
et affina', *Rime Sparse*, 151.7–8). Sidney's *Astrophil and
Stella* provides a clear literary precedent for the celebration of a dark-eyed beauty, as in *Astrophil and
Stella*, 7.1–2: 'When Nature made her chief work,
Stella's eyes, | In colour black, why wrapped she
beams so bright?'. Daniel's revisions to the 1601
edition of *Delia* intriguingly alter the colour of the
beloved's hair from gold to sable (see 33.14 and 34.1,
revised as Sonnets 38 and 39 in 1601); as Ingram
and Redpath suggest this may indicate 'some general
shift in taste', although 'the tone of [127] and other
sonnets of the group (e.g. 131, 132) suggests that
Shakespeare is also, in part, attacking a convention
which had not yet died' (1985: 290).

Critics and editors since Malone generally see
Sonnet 127 as marking the beginning of a new section; it is probable that the sonnets in this section
were composed earlier than those preceding it (see
headnote to the *Sonnets*, 'Date'). Like the 'fair youth',
the identity of the mistress has been the source of
much speculation (see Rollins 1944: 2.242–76).
Candidates include (i) Mary Fitton, one of Elizabeth
I's maids of honour and the mistress of William
Herbert (a contender for the 'youth' of Sonnets
1–126; see headnote to *Sonnets*, 'W.H.'), although
her portrait reveals her to have the wrong colouring;
and (ii) the poet Emilia Lanier, the mistress of Henry
Carey, first Baron Hunsdon, the patron of the Lord
Chamberlain's Men, the playing company to which
Shakespeare belonged (see Rowse 1973). A number
of Shakespeare's heroines are specifically identified as
dark-eyed and/or dark-haired, including Anne Page

(*Merry Wives*, 1.1.47); Hero, who is 'too brown for a
fair praise' (*Much Ado*, 1.1.172); Katherina, 'as brown
in hue | As hazel-nuts' (*Taming of the Shrew*, 2.1.254–
5); and Rosaline in *Love's Labours Lost* (see below,
l. 1n). The recurrence of dark-complexioned beauties across Shakespeare's works does not, of course,
mean that these were all tributes to one particular
beauty; and even if an actual woman lies behind individual sonnets, it does not necessarily follow that the
same person inspired, or is addressed in, all the sonnets from 127 onwards: once gathered into and read
in one volume, however, the natural and dominant
impression created is that a single mistress is being
invoked (as also occurs with the youthful friend).

1   *old age* former times.
    black... fair 'Black was not formerly regarded
    as beautiful' (see headnote to this sonnet);
    'fair' puns on blonde. The assertion in Sonnet
    127 that black is beautiful is reminiscent of
    Berowne's description of the dark-haired
    Rosaline in *Love's Labours Lost*, 4.3.254–61:

    O, if in black my lady's brows be decked,
    It mourns that painting and usurping hair
    Should ravish doters with a false aspect:
    And therefore is she born to make
    black fair.
    Her favour turns the fashion of the days,
    For native blood is counted painting now;
    And therefore red, that would avoid
    dispraise,
    Paints itself black, to imitate her brow.

2   *Or... name* The line qualifies l. 1, stating
    that if dark colouring was regarded as beauti-
    ful in the past, it was not described as such (in
    poetry, for example); 'name' initiates a strand
    of vocabulary associated with legitimacy (see
    also 'heir', l. 3; 'bastard', l. 4).
3   *But... heir* 'Dark colouring is now rec-
    ognised as the true heir of beauty': *successive*
    invokes the idea of succession by inheritance
    (OED 3b); see also *2 Henry VI*, 3.1.49: 'next
    the King he was successive heir'.
4   *beauty... shame* Now that black is regarded
    as beautiful, fairness (which was previously
    seen as beautiful) has been discredited,
    because such fairness is presumed to be false,
    created by cosmetics (see ll. 5–8).
5–6 *nature's... art's* See 68.13–14n.
5–8 *For... disgrace* Beauty has been disgraced
    because of the way in which people (the

127

In the old age black was not counted fair,
Or if it were it bore not beauty's name;
But now is black beauty's successive heir,
And beauty slandered with a bastard shame: 4
For since each hand hath put on nature's power,
Fairing the foul with art's false borrowed face,
Sweet beauty hath no name, no holy bower,
But is profaned, if not lives in disgrace.   8
Therefore my mistress' eyes are raven black,
Her eyes so suited and they mourners seem
At such who, not born fair, no beauty lack,
Slandering creation with a false esteem.   12
    Yet so they mourn, becoming of their woe,
    That every tongue says beauty should look so.

implication is women) usurp ('**put on**') nature's creative power and counterfeit beauty through the use of cosmetics.

5 *since* probably means 'from that time' (OED A2), as 'because' (OED C4a) would make 'For' redundant.
power pronounced as one syllable.

6 *Fairing the foul* making the ugly beautiful; the play on these two opposites also occurs at 137.12, where it is directed against the mistress.

7 *name* (good) reputation; continues the play on lineage begun in l. 2; compare *All's Well*, 1.3.156–7: 'I am from humble, he from honoured name; | No note upon my parents, his all noble'.
bower OED cites this line as the first usage for sense 1b: 'a vague poetic word for an idealised abode' (*n*.1). However, the word was more current in late Elizabethan England than this suggests, and the choice of word (as well as completing the rhyme) continues the theme of noble lineage, being a word associated with elite dwellings; see Anthony Colynet, *The true history of the civil wars of France* – 'the bower, which is the king's house' (1591: sig. D6v) – and 'Thomas Newton to the loving reader'('The princely bower, that seat of mighty king') in Thomas Tymme's translation of Christiaan van Adrichem's *Brief Description*

of Jerusalem (1595: sig. A4r). As Burrow points out (2002: 634), the word also sustains the concern with bastardy; since 'bower' also indicates 'inner apartment [...] a bed-room' (OED 2a), the implication is that beauty's bedchamber (and her bed) have been violated. 'Bower' is here pronounced as one syllable.

8 *profaned* desecrated, treated without respect; compare *1 Henry IV*, 3.2.64: 'his great name profaned with their scorn'. The religious implications of this word resonate with the epithet 'holy' in l. 7.
disgrace 'disfavour' (OED 1b), with a play on 'disfigurement' (OED 6).

9 *Therefore. . . raven black* The mistress' eyes are said to be black because they mourn the abuse of beauty through the use of cosmetics. Black had been the colour of mourning in Western Europe since at least the time of the Roman Empire, when mourning was signalled by the 'toga pulla', made of dark-coloured wool (*Encyclopaedia Britannica*). Ravens are proverbially black (Dent R32.2).

9, 10 *eyes. . . eyes* Most editors since Capell have emended these lines, substituting 'brows' or 'hairs' for one of the occurrences of 'eyes' to avoid the repetition (see Ingram and Redpath 1985: 290, for a summary of the arguments for the various emendations). The most common emendation amongst editors since the mid-twentieth century, following Brooke (1936), is to substitute 'brows' for the second 'eyes'. This alteration is tempting. 'Brows' fits metrically (a monosyllable is required) and grammatically, since the plural 'they' that follows demands a plural subject (although that plural subject could comprise the 'eyes' of l. 9 along with a single 'brow' from l. 10). The image of black brows as mourners and the idea of a dark-complexioned mistress who will prove black beautiful ('fair') also appear in *Love's Labours Lost*, 4.3.254–7 (cited above, l. 1n). However, as Blakemore Evans (1996: 244) and Duncan-Jones (1997a: 368) argue, Q's text – although not so elegant as the revision – does make sense, and for that reason has been retained here. We do not know for sure whether Shakespeare intended 'brow(s)' or 'hairs' instead of 'eyes' in l. 10, but we do know what the original readers of Q would have read.

10 ***so suited*** dressed in this way (i.e. in 'raven black', l. 9).

and as if (OED³ A15); compare *A Midsummer Night's Dream*, 1.2.83–4 ('I will roar you and 'twere any nightingale') and *Troilus and Cressida*, 1.2.124–6 ('O, he smiles valiantly [. . .] and 'twere a cloud in autumn').

mourners Compare *Astrophil and Stella*, 7.13, which describes Stella's eyes in 'mourning weed' (although this apparent show of grief is for those who have died because of their beauty, not for the fate of beauty itself).

11–12 ***At such. . . esteem*** The mistress' eyes mourn the fact that those who have not been born beautiful/blonde manage to make themselves so through the use of cosmetics; this artificial beauty/blondeness gives nature ('***creation***') a bad name as what is real becomes indistinguishable from what is false. These lines repeat the idea expressed in ll. 5–8.

12 ***Slandering*** pronounced as two syllables.

esteem reputation (OED 4).

13 ***so*** in such a way ('that' comes in l. 14).

becoming of their woe The phrase works in multiple ways: the mistress' eyes are an appropriate colour for mourning ('become, *v*.', OED 8a); and they are 'comely' or 'beautiful' because of their mournful colour (OED 9a). As the mistress' beauty transforms others' sense of what is beautiful, 'becoming' also takes on the transformative sense of 'coming into being' (OED 6), i.e. her dark complexion becomes beautiful.

14 ***so*** like this (his mistress).

127

In the old age black was not counted fair,
Or if it were it bore not beauty's name;
But now is black beauty's successive heir,
And beauty slandered with a bastard shame: 4
For since each hand hath put on nature's power,
Fairing the foul with art's false borrowed face,
Sweet beauty hath no name, no holy bower,
But is profaned, if not lives in disgrace.   8
Therefore my mistress' eyes are raven black,
Her eyes so suited and they mourners seem
At such who, not born fair, no beauty lack,
Slandering creation with a false esteem.   12
   Yet so they mourn, becoming of their woe,
   That every tongue says beauty should look so.

128

Printed by Benson as a single sonnet entitled 'Upon her playing on the virginals'.

Music was integral to courtship and flirtation in the early modern period; the autobiography of the music teacher Thomas Whythorne (*c.* 1575) recounts how, in his youth, he was propositioned by a woman leaving love notes in his gittern strings; see also Hortensio's attempts in *Taming of the Shrew*, 3.1 to woo Bianca whilst disguised as a lute teacher. Lovers envying instruments played by their mistresses was a slightly tired conceit by the late sixteenth century. Jonson parodies it in *Every Man Out of his Humour* (1599), when the 'affecting Courtier' Fastidious Brisk observes his mistress playing the viola da gamba: 'You see the subject of her sweet fingers, there? Oh, she tickles it so, that [. . .] she makes it laugh most divinely [. . .] I have wished myself to be that instrument, I think, a thousand times' (3.3.91–5). See also John Marston, *Scourge of Villany*, Satire 8, which mocks a lover who would be 'his sweet lady's virginal | To clip her tender breech' (1598: sig. G4v).

Bodleian MS. Rawl. Poet. 152 contains a version of this sonnet, probably copied out in the first half of the seventeenth century; see Appendix 4.

1–8   *How oft. . . stand* This could be read as a question as well as statement.

1   *my music* The mistress is referred to as 'music' because she is a source of pleasure to the poet-speaker; compare 8.1, addressed to the youth.

2–12   *Upon. . . lips* From the combination of references to jacks (l. 5), chips (l. 10) and fingers walking over the instrument (l. 11), the instrument in question would seem to be the virginal, 'a keyed musical instrument (common in England in the 16th and 17th centuries), resembling a spinet, but set in a box or case without legs' (OED).

3   *With* both (i) as a result of, and (ii) in harmony with the fingers' motion.
sway'st set in motion, but the word also establishes the mistress as 'holding sway' over and 'controlling' the music ('sway, *v.*', OED 10, 9b).

4   *wiry* refers to the wires inside the virginal, which are plucked by the jacks to make the sound (see l. 5n).
concord harmony; compare 8.5.

confounds overwhelms; the sense of 'to throw into confusion of mind or feelings' (OED 4a) is also relevant, and extends the effect of the music from the poet-speaker's ear to his mind. For amorous passion as one of the 'perturbations of the mind', see Bullein, *Bulleins Bulwark* (1562: sigs ²M6v, ²N2v).

5   *envy* stressed on the second syllable.

5, 13   *jacks* 'In the virginal, spinet, and harpsichord' a jack is 'an upright piece of wood fixed to the back of the key-lever, and fitted with a quill which plucked the string as the jack rose on the key's being pressed down' ('Jack, *n.* 1', OED 14). The fact that the poet-speaker imagines the jacks kissing (i.e. touching) the player's hands would accord with the OED's subsequent suggestion that the word was wrongly applied by Shakespeare and others to the keys themselves. (The suggestion that the mistress is tuning the instrument, and thus touching the jacks themselves, does not fit with the obvious references to playing music in ll. 1–4.) The word 'jack' also plays on the sense of 'a lad, fellow, chap; esp. a low-bred or ill-mannered fellow, a "knave"' (OED 2a); see *Richard III*, 1.3.72–3: 'Since every Jack became a gentleman | There's many a gentle person made a Jack'. The keys are thus portrayed as presumptuous rival lovers.

6   *kiss. . . hand* The palm of the hand was considered an erogenous zone in this period; see, for example, the way Iago uses the image of Desdemona 'paddl[ing] with the palm of [Cassio's] hand' to incite Roderigo's jealousy (*Othello*, 2.1.254) or Leontes' similar reaction to the sight of his wife Hermione 'paddling palms and pinching fingers' with his friend Polixenes (*Winter's Tale*, 1.2.115); Leontes' 'still virginalling | Upon his palm?' (1.2.125–6) also links the sexual intimacy of paddling palms with the eroticism of playing a musical instrument.

8   *stand* strictly speaking, it is the lover's lips which 'stand'; however, in the erotic context of the poem, in which the lips come to represent the rest of the lover by *synecdoche*, 'stand' suggests an erection as well as the lover's location on his feet next to ('*by*') the mistress; compare 151.12 and note.

9   *tickled* The word is here used in both a technical sense (of playing or operating the keys

128

How oft, when thou, my music, music play'st
Upon that blessèd wood whose motion sounds
With thy sweet fingers when thou gently sway'st
The wiry concord that mine ear confounds,   4
Do I envy those jacks that nimble leap
To kiss the tender inward of thy hand,
Whilst my poor lips, which should that harvest reap,
At the wood's boldness by thee blushing stand.   8
To be so tickled they would change their state
And situation with those dancing chips,
O'er whom thy fingers walk with gentle gait,
Making dead wood more blest than living lips.   12
   Since saucy jacks so happy are in this,
   Give them thy fingers, me thy lips to kiss.

of a keyboard instrument; 'tickle, *v.*1', OED 6a) and an erotic one: 'be stirred or moved with a thrill of pleasure' (OED 1a). For the latter, see Abraham Fraunce's portrayal of Venus and Mars in the throes of passion, enjoying 'the sweet tickling joys of touching' (*Third Part of the Countess of Pembroke's Ivychurch*, 1592: fol. 38v), or the innuendo of John Bartlet's 'A pretty duck' describing 'A tickling part that maidens love | But I can never get' (*A Book of Airs*, 1606: sig. E2v).

9–10 *change their state | And situation* exchange their physical position ('situation') and position in the hierarchy of things ('state'), where the poet-speaker's lips (being animate) stand above the inanimate keys of the virginals.

10 *dancing chips* the wooden keys of the virginal ('unless otherwise specified, [chip is] understood to be of wood', 'chip, *n.*1', OED 1a).

11, 14 *thy fingers* Q reads 'their fingers' in both instances; for the thy/their error, see 26.12n; this sonnet is the last time in Q's sequence that this error appears.

12 *dead. . . lips* Grundy (1960: 225) notes a possible debt to one of Constable's sonnets (incipit: 'Not that thy hand is soft is sweet is white'), ll. 9–10: 'A lute of senseless wood by nature dumb | Touched by thy hand doth speak divinely well' (National Art Library MS Dyce 44, fol. 17v). Since this is sonnet is not printed during the early modern period, this raises the possibility that Shakespeare read Constable's work in manuscript; see 106.9n. Constable is also a possible influence on Sonnets 24, 46 and 99.

13 *saucy* impertinent (*adj.*1, OED 2a) or, more damningly, 'wanton, lascivious' (OED 2b).
happy (i) fortunate; (ii) contented.

129

Printed by Benson as a single sonnet, entitled 'Immoderate Lust'.

Kerrigan (1986: 356) points out that this is one of just two sonnets (the other being 94) which adopts this impersonal stance to the experience described; the process of generalisation here can be seen as another way in which the poem performs self-disgust as its speaker attempts to distance himself from the coital act. The central theme of the sonnet – the brevity, and tortured legacy, of sexual pleasure – is a recurrent theme of late sixteenth- and early seventeenth-century poetry. Compare, for example, verses in Thomas Lodge's *Rosalynde*, where 'lust' is seen to offer 'A heaven in show, a hell to them that prove [...] | A minute's joy to gain a world of grief' (1592: sig. E2r), or Ben Jonson, *Underwood*, 88.1–2: 'Doing a filthy pleasure is, and short; | And done, we straight repent us of the sport' (a translation of Petronius: 'Foeda est in coitu et brevis voluptas | Et taedet Veneris statim peractae'). See also *Lucrece*, ll. 211–12, 690–1, 694–700, 867–8.

1 *expense* loss (OED 1d), but also 'squandering' or 'wasteful expenditure' (OED 1a), a reading strengthened by its proximity to 'waste'; for the sexual connotations of the related verb 'spend', see 149.7–8n.
spirit 'vital power or energy' (OED 16b), bodily fluids including semen; 'spirit' can suggest an erect penis (see Booth 1977: 442–3, and Mercutio in *Romeo and Juliet*, 2.1.23–4: ''twould anger him | To raise a spirit in his mistress' circle'). Blakemore Evans (1996: 246) notes Timothy Bright's *A Treatise of Melancholy* as a possible source for Shakespeare's usage here: 'the excessive travail of animal actions, or such as spring from the brain, waste and spend that spirit [...] which spirit being consumed, or empaired, leaveth the massy parts more heavy, gross, and dull [...]. In othersome by lavish waste and prodigal expense of the spirit in one passion, which dispensed with judgement, would suffice the execution of many worthy actions beside' (1586: sigs Q5v–Q6r). It was believed that orgasm shortened the male life-span (see John Donne, 'Farewell to Love' (1592–5?), ll. 24–5: 'each such act, they say, | Diminisheth the length of life a day') and/or dimmed the eyesight: 'much use of Venus doth dim the sight [...]. The cause of dimness of sight [...] is the expense of spirits'

(Bacon, *Sylva Sylvarum* 1627: sig. Z2r). 'Spirit' can also denote the more rarefied 'immaterial [...] element [...] of a person, freq. in implied or express contrast to the body' (OED 11a) and 'vigour of mind' (OED 13a): the former risks corruption by the carnal act; the latter, dissipation (see Bright above).
waste of shame a shameful (disgraceful) waste; 'waste' can also mean 'desert, wilderness' (OED 1a). This is not a usage that occurs regularly in Shakespeare (usually the noun 'waste' connotes extravagance); however, that meaning would pre-empt the description of post-coital disgust as a place ('this hell') in l. 14. 'Waste' evokes its homophone 'waist' (for which 'waste' was an acceptable early modern spelling), a bodily region that includes the groin; see Bright, l. 2n above, and *Hamlet*, 2.2.232–6:

> HAMLET Then you live about [Fortune's] waist, or in the middle of her favours?
> GUILDENSTERN Faith, her privates we.
> HAMLET In the secret parts of Fortune? O, most true, she is a strumpet.

2 *action* sexual intercourse; see *Pericles*, 4.2.8–9: '[whores] with continual action are even as good as rotten'.
3 *perjured* 'false, deceitful' (OED³ A2); for the amorality of lust, compare the Latin motto 'penis erectus non habet conscientiam' ('an erect penis has no conscience'; Taylor 1931: 171); see also 151.1, 2, 13n.
murderous pronounced as two syllables; see 9.14n.
bloody 'addicted to bloodshed, bloodthirsty; cruel' (OED³ A4a).
full of blame full of accusations ('blame, n.', OED 2), full of culpability (OED 3).
4, 10 *extreme* 'severe or violent in the utmost degree', 'strict, severe, harsh' (OED A4c, A4e).
4 *rude* 'not gentle, violent, harsh; [...] marked by unkind or severe treatment of people or living things' (OED³ A2a).
not to trust not to be trusted; for this use of the infinitive, see Abbott 1884: § 359; Hope 2003: 169.
5 *Enjoyed* has a strongly sexual sense: 'to have one's will of (a woman)' (OED 4b); see also quotation at l. 6n, below.
straight immediately.

129

Th' expense of spirit in a waste of shame
Is lust in action; and, till action, lust
Is perjured, murderous, bloody, full of blame,
Savage, extreme, rude, cruel, not to trust,   4
Enjoyed no sooner but despisèd straight,
Past reason hunted, and no sooner had,
Past reason hated as a swallowed bait
On purpose laid to make the taker mad,   8
Mad in pursuit, and in possession so,
Had, having, and in quest to have, extreme,
A bliss in proof and proved, a very woe,
Before, a joy proposed; behind, a dream.   12
    All this the world well knows, yet none knows well
    To shun the heaven that leads men to this hell.

6, 7 **Past reason** beyond reason; love/desire are usually depicted as irrational in the early modern period; see, for example, *Midsummer Night's Dream*, 5.1.4–6: 'Lovers and madmen have such seething brains, | Such shaping fantasies, that apprehend | More than cool reason ever comprehends'. Here, the subsequent disgust is also represented as immoderate.

6 **hunted** The idea of the hunt as a metaphor for love/sexual pleasure recurs throughout medieval and early modern literature; see Bates 2013.

6, 10 **had** possessed sexually (compare 'enjoyed', l. 5); see *Merry Wives*, 3.5.135–8: 'the conclusion shall be crowned with your enjoying her. [...] You shall have her, Master Brook; Master Brook, you shall cuckold Ford'. This bawdy meaning is also in play, with varying degrees of intensity, at 42.1; 75.12; 87.13 (see 87.14n); 91.12; 134.13; 135.1; and 143.13.

7 **swallowed bait** The depiction of women entrapping men as anglers catch fish is commonplace in sixteenth-century love poetry; see, for example, 'The little fish' in Googe's *Eclogues, Epitaphs, and Sonnets*, which warns men 'that lovest [women's] wanton looks, | Feed on the bait, but yet beware the hooks' (1563: sig. F3r), or Spenser's *Amoretti* 47.1–3: 'Trust not the treason of those smiling looks | [...] For they are like but unto golden hooks' (1595: sig. D1r). See also *Antony and Cleopatra*,

2.5.11–14: 'I will betray | Tawny-finned fishes; my bended hook shall pierce | Their slimy jaws; and as I draw them up, | I'll think every one an Antony'. For the idea that something ingested can cause madness, see *Macbeth*, 1.3.83–4: 'Have we eaten on the insane root | That takes the reason prisoner?'. Kerrigan (1986: 358) notes a parallel with *Measure for Measure*, 1.2.129, where Claudio compares humans succumbing to sexual desire to 'rats that ravin down their proper bane [poison]'.

8 **On purpose laid** set deliberately.

8–9 **mad, / Mad** Q reads 'Made' in l. 9, an acceptable variant for 'mad'.

9 **so** (i) similarly (i.e. mad in possession as well as in pursuit); (ii) equally (i.e. as mad in possession as in pursuit).

11 **A bliss...woe** intensely pleasurable ('bliss') whilst being experienced ('in proof'); once experienced ('proved'), a source of intense ('very') wretchedness; for the concern with proof in the *Sonnets*, see 2.12n. This line poses one of the most problematic textual cruxes in the *Sonnets*. Q reads 'A blisse in proofe and proud and very wo'. Unemended, this line reads as a sequence of adjectival clauses, like those in ll. 3–4. McLeod (1991), a champion of unediting, argues against emending the second 'and' to 'a', asserting – like Graves and Riding (1949) – that early modern readers would have read 'proud' as an ocular pun on

proved and proud (thanks to interchangeability of *u* and *v* in early modern orthography). Unfortunately, Q's orthography does not offer clarity on whether 'proud' indicates an adjective or an elided verb form. Whilst the apostrophe is often used in Q to signal elision (see 'prou'd' at Q110.8), this practice is not consistent: in this sonnet not one of the other elisions ('periurd', 'murdrous', 'inioyd', 'proposd', ll. 3, 5, 12) is indicated by an apostrophe (contrast Q109, also set – like Q129 – by Compositor B, where all five unstressed *-ed* endings appear as -'*d*). The absence of an apostrophe consequently provides no evidence either way as to the reading of Q's 'proud'. Editors since Capell have usually revised the line as here, so that it parallels the structure of l. 12, which similarly divides into a first half before intercourse, and a second half post-intercourse. This requires reading the second 'and' in Q129.11 as a compositorial misreading of 'a'; the ampersand was a frequent manuscript brevigraph, in fair copies as well as drafts, and could in some hands resemble a minuscule 'a'. Blakemore Evans (1996: 247) cites a similarly structured phrase in Thomas Lodge's *A fig for Momus*: 'Divine in show, in proof, a subtle drift' (1595: sig. I1v).

12 *proposed* (i) 'put forward as something to be attained' ('propose, *v.*', OED³ 2c); (ii) anticipated, envisaged (OED³ 2d); for (i) compare *Hamlet*, 3.2.194–5 ('What to ourselves in passion we propose, | The passion ending, doth the purpose lose'); for (ii), see *2 Henry IV*, 5.2.92 ('Be now the father and propose a son').

13 *knows* Booth points to the potential play on 'knowing' as sexual experience (1977: 447); see *Venus and Adonis*, l. 525, where Adonis resists Venus' advances: 'Before I know myself seek not to know me'.
none no one.

14 *heaven* Resonates with 'bliss' (l. 11) as well as contrasting with 'hell' (l. 14). Booth (1977: 447) notes the possibility for sonic play on 'haven' (which is how the word appears in Benson's 1640 edition) and 'havin'' (as in sexual possession; see l. 6). 'Heaven' is pronounced as one syllable.
hell torment; may also suggest female genitalia, as at 144.12 and *King Lear*, 4.6. 124–9:

> Down from the waist they are Centaurs,
> Though women all above;
> But to the girdle do the gods inherit,
> Beneath is all the fiends': there's hell,
> there's darkness,
> There is the sulphurous pit, burning,
> scalding,
> Stench, consumption.

See also 'A description of Love' in R.S., *The Phoenix Nest*:

> It is that fountain and that well,
> Where pleasure and repentance dwell,
> It is perhaps that sauncing [unfailing] bell,
> That tolls all in to heaven or hell,
> And this is love as I hear tell. (1593: sig. N1v)

129

Th' expense of spirit in a waste of shame
Is lust in action; and, till action, lust
Is perjured, murderous, bloody, full of blame,
Savage, extreme, rude, cruel, not to trust,   4
Enjoyed no sooner but despisèd straight,
Past reason hunted, and no sooner had,
Past reason hated as a swallowed bait
On purpose laid to make the taker mad,   8
Mad in pursuit, and in possession so,
Had, having, and in quest to have, extreme,
A bliss in proof and proved, a very woe,
Before, a joy proposed; behind, a dream.   12
    All this the world well knows, yet none knows well
    To shun the heaven that leads men to this hell.

130

Benson combines Sonnets 127 and 130–132 under the title 'In praise of her beauty though black'.

The description of the mistress in this sonnet invokes a series of stereotypical descriptions of the archetypal mistress, many of which appear in ll. 1–12 of Watson's self-consciously emulative Passion 7 from *Hekatompathia* (1582: sig. A4r), in which 'he partly imitateth [...] Aeneas Silvius, who setteth down the like in describing Lucretia, the love of Euryalus; and partly he followeth Ariosto cant. 7, where he describeth Alcina; & partly borroweth from some others where they describe the famous Helen of Greece':

> Hark you that list to hear what saint I serve:
> Her yellow locks exceed the beaten gold;
> Her sparkling eyes in heaven a place deserve;
> Her forehead high and fair of comely mould;
>   Her words are music all of silver sound;
>   Her wit so sharp as like can scarce be found.
> Each eyebrow hangs like Iris in the skies;
> Her eagle's nose is straight of stately frame;
> On either cheek a rose and lily lies;
> Her breath is sweet perfume, or holy flame;
>   Her lips more red than any coral stone;
>   Her neck more white than aged swans that moan.

These clichés abound in late sixteenth-century English love poetry. See, for example, Richard Linche's *Diella*, Sonnet 3:

> Swift-footed Time, look back and here mark well
> Those rare shaped parts my pen shall now declare:
> My mistress' snow-white skin doth much excel
> The pure-soft wool Arcadian sheep do bear;
> Her hair exceeds gold forced in smallest wire,
> In smaller threads than those Arachne spun;
> Her eyes are crystal fountains, yet dart fire
> More glorious to behold then midday sun;
> Her ivory front (though soft as purest silk)
> Looks like the table of Olympic Jove;
> Her cheeks are like ripe cherries laid in milk,
> Her alabaster neck the throne of love;
> Her other parts so far excel the rest
> That, wanting words, they cannot be expressed.
> (1596: sig. B2r)

1 **My... sun** 'My' is probably stressed, to distinguish the poetic speaker's dark-haired, dark-eyed mistress from the usual blonde, blue-eyed mistress praised in love poetry. The comparison of one's mistress to the sun (because of her life-giving powers) is commonplace in love sonnets. See, for example, Watson, *Hekatompathia*, Passion 9, in which 'the author compareth himself with the marigold, and his love unto the sun' (1582: sig. B1r); Constable, *Diana* (1592), 13.9–10:'No, no, I flatter not, when I thee call | The sun' (sig. C3r). The poet-speaker compares the friend's eyes to the sun at 49.6, and at 132.5–9 comes close to doing likewise with his mistress'.
nothing in no way; compare 123.3.

2 **Coral. . . red** Coral red lips are a commonplace of Renaissance love poetry; see, for example, Watson's Passion 7.11 (cited above); *Venus and Adonis*, l. 542 and note; Lucentio's comically conventional praise of Bianca's 'coral lips' (*Taming of the Shrew*, 1.1.174); and the use of the same image in the troublingly Petrarchan blazon of Lucrece in the build-up to her rape by Tarquin (*Lucrece*, l. 420). Q's 'lips' can be modernised as either singular possessive ('lip's') or plural (as here, following Capell); however, Blakemore Evans points out that Q 'may equally well be taken to mean "than her lips (are) red", or even, possibly "lip's red" (i.e. "lip is red")' (1996: 248).

3 **If. . . dun** If snow is the standard by which whiteness is measured (as it was proverbially, see Dent S591, S591.1), then the mistress' breasts will appear dull brown ('dun') in comparison. Praising a mistress' breasts for their pallor was conventional poetic hyperbole; see, for example, Robert Chester's 'Rosalin's Complaint': 'Her breasts two crystal orbs of whitest white' (*Love's Martyr*, 1601: sig. B2v).

4 **wires** Hair was frequently described as golden wires in love poetry; see Amyntas' description of Phyllis' 'cheerful forehead with gold wire all to bedecked' (Abraham Fraunce, 'Phyllis' Funeral', *Countess of Pembroke's Ivychurch*, 1591: sig. G4r).

5 **damasked** Women's cheeks are conventionally described as 'damask' in Renaissance verse; see Barnes, *Parthenophil and Parthenophe*, Ode 10.16–17:'In her clear cheeks she closes | Sweet damask roses' (1593: sig. Q3r). Burrow (2002: 640) posits that this line alludes more specifically to *Rosa damascena versicolor* ('the York and Lancaster Rose'),'which has parti-coloured pink and white petals (and often also pure white or pure pink blooms)'. Ingram and Redpath also highlight its use to indicate a 'rich silk fabric [originally produced at Damascus] woven with elaborate

130

My mistress' eyes are nothing like the sun;
Coral is far more red than her lips' red;
If snow be white, why then her breasts are dun;
If hairs be wires, black wires grow on her head.   4
I have seen roses damasked, red and white,
But no such roses see I in her cheeks,
And in some perfumes is there more delight
Than in the breath that from my mistress reeks.   8
I love to hear her speak, yet well I know
That music hath a far more pleasing sound;
I grant I never saw a goddess go:
My mistress when she walks treads on the ground.   12
    And yet, by heaven, I think my love as rare
    As any she belied with false compare.

designs and figures' ('damask, *n.* and *adj.*', OED 3a), and suggest that – as well as evoking the variegated colours of pink and white cheeks – the word initiates 'a subsidiary train of associations [...] of the soft texture of both silk damask and of rose petals' (1985: 298–300). However, in the two instances in which Shakespeare's use of the word 'damask' can be calibrated more specifically, both indicate the colour pink: see *Coriolanus*, 2.1.216–17 ('the war of white and damask | In their nicely gawded [made-up] cheeks'), and *As You Like It*, 3.5.120–3: 'There was a pretty redness in his lip, | A little riper and more lusty red | Than that mixed in his cheek; 'twas just the difference | Betwixt the constant red and mingled damask'.

7 *in. . . delight* Sweet-smelling breath is another conventional attribute of the poetic mistress; see Watson, Passion 7.10 (cited above).

8 *reeks* not necessarily pejorative, as it is in modern English; whilst the first usage of 'reeks' meaning 'stinks' recorded in OED[3] is in 1609 (*v.*1, sense 7a), that meaning only becomes more common from the eighteenth century; the older meaning of 'reek' is 'emit or give off vapour or steam' (OED[3] 2). Compare *Venus and Adonis*, l. 555 and note, and *Love's Labours Lost*, 4.3.137–8: 'I heard your guilty rhymes, observed your fashion | Saw sighs reek from you'. However, that 'reek' (at least as a noun) could carry negative connotations in the early seventeenth century

is evident from *Coriolanus*, 3.3.120–1: 'You common cry of curs, whose breath I hate | As reek a' th' rotten fens'.

11 *goddess go* The idea that goddesses do not 'go' (walk) like humans do may stem back to Virgil's description of Venus at *Aeneid*, 1.405: 'et vera incessu patuit dea' ('and in her step she was revealed a very goddess'); compare *Venus and Adonis*, l. 1028.

12 *My mistress. . .ground* The line contrasts this mistress with those archetypal poetic mistresses: where she walks, like a human, 'on the ground', their movements are habitually described in almost divine terms; see, for example, Petrarch, *Rime Sparse*, 90.9–11: 'Her walk was not that of a mortal thing but of some angelic form, and her words sounded different from a merely human voice' ('Non era l'andar suo cosa mortale | ma d'angelica forma, et le parole | sonavan altro che pur voce umana').

13 *heaven* pronounced as one syllable.
my love the mistress.
rare exceptional (*adj.*1, OED[3] A4a), 'of uncommon excellence' (OED[3] A5a).

14 *she* woman; compare *As You Like It*, 3.2.10, where Orlando writes bad poetry to 'the fair, the chaste, and unexpressive she'.
belied slandered ('belie, *v.*2', OED[3] 2).
false erroneous (OED AI); mendacious, deceitful (OED AII).
compare comparison.

131

Benson combines Sonnets 127 and 130–132 under the title 'In praise of her beauty though black'.

1–2 **Thou. . . cruel** Petrarchan mistresses are typically described as tyrannous; see, for example Barnes, *Parthenophil and Parthenophe*, Elegy 16.15: 'She triumphs in beauty's tyranny' (1593: sig. M4v).

1 **so as thou art** i.e. lacking conventional beauty; the mistress of Sonnet 131 is equally ('as') tyrannous as those mistresses who are cruel because they are beautiful, but not because she shares their blonde, conventional beauty.

2 **proudly** Female pride is often attributed to beauty; see *3 Henry VI*, 1.4.128: ''Tis beauty that doth oft make women proud'.
cruel 'disposed to inflict suffering; indifferent to or taking pleasure in another's pain or distress; destitute of kindness or compassion; merciless, pitiless, hard-hearted' (OED 1a); frequently used of the typically unrelenting beloved in amorous verse; see, for example, Daniel, *Delia*, 6.1: 'Fair is my love, and cruel as she is fair'.

3 **dear** can be read as either an adjective (affectionate, loving, fond) or an adverb (affectionately, lovingly, fondly).
doting The primary sense of the verb – 'to be silly, deranged, or out of one's wits; to act or talk foolishly or stupidly' ('dote, doat, *v.*1', OED 1) – is pertinent here; the poet-speaker's delusion and distorted judgement are explored in Sonnets 147–150, 152. Compare also 141.4; 148.5, and see 20.10n.

4, 12 **fairest** The quibble on 'fair' as both beautiful and blonde (OED³ 1, OED³ 17) reminds us that the usual standards of beauty have been overturned; as with many of the sonnets about/addressed to the dark-eyed, dark-haired mistress, there is a hint that the poet-speaker's standards of judgement or ability to see or judge clearly have been disturbed (see Sonnets 147–150, 152).

4 **jewel** a conventional term of praise for one's mistress; compare Orlando's inept verses in *As You Like It*, 3.2.88–9: 'From the east to western Inde, | No jewel is like Rosalind'. See also the description of the youthful friend at 65.10.

5 **good faith** This could be an interjection ('yet, in good faith, some say. . .'), which is how some editors, following Capell and Malone, punctuate it. As punctuated here (as it appears in Q) it reads as a phrase qualifying 'some say'.

5–6 **some. . . groan** Some say, looking at her, that the mistress is not beautiful enough to make men groan (either with pain or erotic pleasure).

6 **power** here pronounced as one syllable.

7 **To say** i.e. declare publicly (in contrast to 'alone', in private, l. 8).
err The word was stronger in the sixteenth and seventeenth centuries than its modern sense and carried a sense of moral disapprobation; see 'err, *v.*', OED 4a: 'to go astray morally; to sin'. There was also a strong connection between erring and madness; as Feste tells Malvolio, 'Madman, thou errest' (*Twelfth Night*, 4.2.42).

8, 9 **swear** The first in a series of words ('witness', 'judgement', 'slander') which collectively suggest the proceedings in a court of law, where the charge is one of defamation.

10 **but** only.

11 **One. . . neck** in quick succession; for a contemporaneous use of 'one on another's neck', see Nashe, *The Unfortunate Traveller* (1594): 'Passion upon passion would throng one on another's neck' (2.262); see also the proverb 'One misfortune comes upon the neck of another' (Dent M1013). Nashe's use of the phrase comes in a passage preceding one of the sonnets written to Diamante by Jack Page's master (a fictionalised Henry Howard, Earl of Surrey).

12 **black** blackness.
fairest See ll. 4, 12 and note.
in my judgement's place (i) to my mind (the place of my judgement; compare *Romeo and Juliet*, 1.1.100–2: 'come you this afternoon, | To know our farther pleasure in this case, | To old Free-town, our common judgment-place'); (ii) according to the order in which my judgement would put it (i.e. that she is first in beauty); (iii) as Booth points out, potentially, 'The phrase also carries a self-mocking echo of "in place of my judgment" and suggests "which has displaced my judgment and now acts in its stead"' (1977: 456).

131

Thou art as tyrannous, so as thou art,
As those whose beauties proudly make them cruel,
For well thou know'st to my dear doting heart
Thou art the fairest and most precious jewel.   4
Yet in good faith some say, that thee behold,
Thy face hath not the power to make love groan;
To say they err I dare not be so bold,
Although I swear it to myself alone.   8
And to be sure that is not false, I swear
A thousand groans but thinking on thy face;
One on another's neck do witness bear
Thy black is fairest in my judgement's place.   12
    In nothing art thou black save in thy deeds,
    And thence this slander as I think proceeds.

13 ***In. . . deeds*** The mistress is only 'black' (i.e. reprehensible) because of what she does, not what she looks like. 'Deeds' could refer to her tyranny (l. 1); read in the wider context of these sonnets (e.g. Sonnets 133–138), it could also refer to her infidelity and promiscuity.

14 ***this slander*** that the woman is not beautiful enough to incite love/desire (see ll. 5–6).
as I think As in Sonnet 130 (l. 13), the phrase 'I think' introduces a contingent note in the final couplet by highlighting the subjective nature of this judgement.

132

Benson combines Sonnets 127 and 130–132 under the title 'In praise of her beauty though black'.

1   *as* as if.

   pitying pronounced as two syllables.

2   *Knowing. . . disdain* a parenthetical clause which explains why the mistress' eyes pity the poet-speaker (because they know that her heart disdains him).

   torment Benson alters to 'torments' (providing an easier reading followed by a handful of editors since), but 'torment' can function as an infinitive ('to torment').

   disdain a typical attribute of the mistress in sonnet sequences, for example, occurring no less than sixteen times in the fifty-five sonnets which comprise the 1594 version of Daniel's *Delia*. Benedick figures Beatrice as 'Lady Disdain' at *Much Ado*, 1.1.118.

3   *mourners* Her dark eyes resemble mourners, attired in black, replaying the idea raised in 127.10. For other poets' celebrations of dark-eyed mistresses, see headnote to Sonnet 127.

4   *with pretty ruth* with becoming pity; sonneteers often try self-interestedly to insist that there should be a co-relation between pity and beauty. See, for example, Daniel, *Delia*, 43.11: 'Pity and smiles do best become the fair'.

5   *morning* pun on 'mourning'; compare ll. 9, 11, and l. 9n (below).

5, 7   *heaven. . . even* See 28.10, 12n.

6   *grey cheeks* Compare *Romeo and Juliet*, 2.3.1 ('The grey-eyed morn') and 3.5.19 ('I'll say yon grey is not the morning's eye').

   the east where the sun rises; although Q has 'th' East', which invites elision, 'the' and 'East' need to be sounded as separate syllables, otherwise the line is left with only nine syllables. Editors from Gildon (1714) onwards have generally emended as here.

7   *that full star. . . even* Hesperus, the evening star (really the planet Venus, which can be seen at dusk); 'full' because 'intense' (OED 9b; see Burrow 2002: 644).

   even evening.

8   *sober* 'subdued in tone' (OED 9a), because the west is where the sun sets. The west is also emblematic of the afterlife, and the choice of adjective thus fits with the play on mourning that runs through the sonnet.

8–9   *west* | *As* Unusually for Shakespeare's sonnets, the syntax carries on over the border between the second and third quatrains.

9   *mourning* spelled 'morning' in Q and modernised to 'mourning' by Malone (following Capell); modernising the spelling flattens the pun that began in l. 5.

   become suit.

10   *as well* also.

   beseem suit (synonymous with 'become' in the line above); the mistress' heart is being asked to pity the speaker, as her eyes already do (l. 1). 'Beseem' and its derivatives drop out of Shakespearean usage in the plays after the 1590s, aside from one late appearance as the verbal noun ('beseeming') in *Cymbeline* (1609–10), 5.5.409.

11   *doth thee grace* becomes you.

12   *suit* clothe.

   pity. . . part 'Pity' in the English sonnet tradition generally means acquiescing to the (male) lover's desires; see, for example, Sidney, *Astrophil and Stella*, 1.1–4: 'Loving in truth, and fain in verse my love to show, | That the dear She might take some pleasure of my pain; | Pleasure might cause her read, reading might make her know; | Knowledge might pity win, and pity grace obtain'. The fact that Sonnet 132 requests that the mistress extend her pity into 'every part' of her body (not simply her heart) further suggests that she is being asked to yield to the poet-speaker's desires for sexual gratification.

   like equally.

13–14   *Then. . . lack* Compare Berowne's praise of Rosaline in *Love's Labours Lost*, 4.3.246–49:

> O, who can give an oath? Where is a book?
> That I may swear beauty doth beauty lack,
> If that she learn not of her eye to look:
> No face is fair that is not full so black.

13   *Then* used as a causative; the promise made in the couplet – to pronounce that true beauty is of dark complexion – is made dependent on the mistress agreeing to grant (sexual) favours.

14   *And. . . lack* The poet-speaker will declare that everyone who is not dark like his mistress is ugly ('*foul*'), inverting the usual standard of beauty whereby the fair (blonde) are esteemed. See also Sonnets 127, 130, 131.

   complexion 'temperament' (OED 1a) and 'disposition' (OED 3) as well as skin colouring (OED 4a); as Kerrigan (1986: 362) notes, 'an important quibble'.

132

Thine eyes I love, and they, as pitying me,
Knowing thy heart torment me with disdain,
Have put on black and loving mourners be,
Looking with pretty ruth upon my pain.   4
And truly not the morning sun of heaven
Better becomes the grey cheeks of the east,
Nor that full star that ushers in the even
Doth half that glory to the sober west   8
As those two mourning eyes become thy face.
O let it then as well beseem thy heart
To mourn for me, since mourning doth thee grace,
And suit thy pity like in every part: 12
    Then will I swear beauty herself is black
    And all they foul that thy complexion lack.

133

Benson combines Sonnets 133 and 134 under the title 'Unkind abuse'.

This sonnet depicts a love triangle between the mistress, poet-speaker and friend; see also Sonnets 134, 144. As Hammond (2012: 87n) notes, 'Shakespeare was interested elsewhere in the complex dynamics of desire which attend an intense relationship between two men and one woman: e.g. Valentine-Proteus-Silvia in *Two Gentlemen of Verona*; Antonio-Bassanio-Portia in *The Merchant of Venice*; Antonio-Sebastian-Olivia in *Twelfth Night*; Othello-Iago-Desdemona in *Othello*; and Leontes-Polixenes-Hermione in *The Winter's Tale*. Each example is differently constituted emotionally and psychologically, but the motif proved abidingly productive dramatically'.

Sonnets 133 and 134 also form a pair which explores this triangular relationship through the metaphor of two conditional common law bonds: bail (Sonnet 133) and mortgage (Sonnet 134).

1   *Beshrew* curse; this imprecation is generally used fairly mildly in Shakespearean texts; see, for example, *Midsummer Night's Dream*, 5.1.290: 'Beshrew my heart, but I pity the man'.
that heart the woman's heart.
groan As at 131.6, the word carries an erotic connotation: to groan with pleasure as well as pain (particularly in the light of the *double entendre* in l. 2).
2   *For* because of.
deep wound The friend and the poet-speaker are both wounded deeply by Cupid's arrow; since 'wound' is also slang for vagina (see *Passionate Pilgrim*, 9.12–14; Appendix 3), it can also refer to the woman's promiscuity, as she offers her vagina to both men.
3   *alone* only.
4   *slave to slavery* The *pleonasm* increases the sense of the friend's servitude, but also suggests that the woman herself embodies 'slavery' (in this case, the power to enslave); the image of the lover as a slave was a Petrarchan commonplace; see Watson, *Hekatompathia*, Passion 55.10, in which the lover 'perforce became [Love's] captive slave' (1582: sig. G4r). The poet-speaker describes himself as the friend's slave in 57.11 and 58.1. 'Slavery' is here pronounced as two syllables.
5   *Me from myself* For the depiction of love as a force that alienates the lover from their

true self, see the poetry of Thomas Wyatt; for example, 'I find no peace' (*Tottel* [49]), a translation of Petrarch's *Rime Sparse* 134, which includes the line 'I love another, and thus I hate myself' (l. 11), where Wyatt – departing from the original – makes self-hatred the direct result of loving another.

6   *my next self* the friend; see 22.3n and 134.3.
harder more cruelly ('hard, *adv.*', OED³ 2a); more firmly (OED³ 3).
engrossed The original meaning of the verb is 'to write in large letters; chiefly [...] to write in a peculiar character appropriate to legal documents' (OED 1a); by the sixteenth century, the word had come to mean 'to buy up wholesale; *esp.* to buy up the whole stock, or as much as possible, of (a commodity) for the purpose of [...] retailing it at a monopoly price' (OED 3a). The woman is thus portrayed as an avaricious landowner or merchant. The evil of engrossing was a recurrent theme of agrarian complaints in the period, whereby landowners would buy up land and increase the rents (see, for example, Thirsk 1990: 200–55). 'Engross' also means 'To make thick or bulky; to increase in size' (OED 10); hence it can be read bawdily, i.e. she has given the friend an erection. A further meaning – 'To make (the mind) gross or dull' (OED 9b) – suggests that the friend's mental faculties, like those of the poet-speaker (see Sonnets 147–150, 152), have been befuddled by the mistress. 'Engrossed' is the first in a series of legal words ('prison', 'ward', 'bail', 'guard', 'jail') used in this sonnet; it also anticipates the legal vocabulary of Sonnet 134. It is possible that Q's spelling of 'engrossed' and 'crossed' (l. 8) indicates a stressed ending ('engrossèd', 'crossèd'). Certainly, the *-ed* ending usually indicates a final stress in Q; however, see 'yellowed' (Q17.9), 'tottered' (Q26.11) and 'flattered' (Q134.14), which metrically need to be two syllables and which – like Sonnet 133 – were probably set by Compositor B. Other examples of *-ed* endings in Q (e.g. Q25.13–14; Q27.2, 4; Q41.6, 8; Q45.9, 11) come in terminal, rhyming positions, as here, and although an additional stress is not necessary metrically (these lines are all already ten syllables), it can be accommodated. It is possible to rhyme 'engrossed' and 'crossed' without stressing the final syllable; see Appendix 7.

7   *myself* a parenthetical gloss on 'friend' ('he is myself'), but which also suggests the idea of

133

Beshrew that heart that makes my heart to groan
For that deep wound it gives my friend and me;
Is't not enough to torture me alone,
But slave to slavery my sweet'st friend must be?   4
Me from myself thy cruel eye hath taken,
And my next self thou harder hast engrossed;
Of him, myself, and thee I am forsaken,
A torment thrice threefold thus to be crossed.   8
Prison my heart in thy steel bosom's ward,
But then my friend's heart let my poor heart bail;
Whoe'er keeps me, let my heart be his guard;
Thou canst not then use rigour in my jail.   12
    And yet thou wilt, for I, being pent in thee,
    Perforce am thine, and all that is in me.

self-alienation raised in l. 5. The *tricolon* ('him, myself, and thee') prepares us for the 'thrice threefold' torment of l. 8. For the treatment of 'myself' and 'my self', see note on modernisation, p. xiv.

8 *A torment* elliptical; 'it is a torment'.
  thrice threefold three times three; compare the Trinitarian imagery of Sonnet 105.
  crossed thwarted ('cross, *v*.', OED 14a), but the proximity to the Trinitarian imagery of thrice threefold also evokes the meaning 'crucified' (OED 1).

9 *Prison* imprison (see *Lucrece*, l. 642 and note); here an imperative.
  ward prison (*n*.2, OED 17a).

10 *then* in that case; at that time.
  bail (i) 'procure the liberation of (any one) from prison or arrest, by becoming bail or security for him' (*v*.1, OED 3); (ii) OED cites this line as the first usage of the extremely rare 'bail, *v*.3' ('to confine', sense 1); this captures the meaning here, but is a definition which is actually present in the primary use of the term. Cormack points out (2009: 259) that, by law 'bail does not release the prisoner from confinement into freedom, but only into

alternative confinement'; as William Lambarde writes in *Eirenarcha*, his manual for Justices of the Peace, 'Bailment' is a 'live prison, for that the party thereby becometh prisoner to his friends that do undertake for him' (1581: sig. R4v).

11 *keeps* guards, preserves (OED 14a), holds captive (OED 25), retains possession of (OED 29a).
  his the friend's.
  guard protection (OED 2); but the friend's heart can also been read as having been placed in the poet-speaker's custody (OED 1a) or 'guard-room' (OED 17a), an idea developed in l. 12, where the poet-speaker's heart becomes a 'jail' containing the friend's heart.

12 *use rigour* be severe.

13 *pent* imprisoned, confined; not a common Shakespearean word (it is used eight times across all his works), it also appears at 5.10.

14 *Perforce* 'by force' (OED³ A1); 'of necessity, inevitably' (OED³ A2).
  and. . . me Everything in him belongs to the mistress, including the friend's heart; the temporary refuge of bail is thus annulled: as the poet-speaker is in the mistress' power, anything under his control is also subject to her.

134

Benson combines Sonnets 133 and 134 under the title 'Unkind abuse'.

1 *So* The word connects Sonnets 133 and 134, the poet-speaker having confessed that the friend belonged to the mistress at 133.14.

confessed acknowledged; the first in a series of legal terms, many of which – 'mortgaged' (l. 2), 'forfeit' (l. 3), 'surety' (l. 7), 'bond' (l. 8) – are connected with the transferring of property.

2 *mortgaged* bound, pledged; the poet-speaker here figures himself as a piece of property 'convey[ed...] to a creditor [i.e. the mistress] as security for a debt or loan' ('mortgage, *v.*', OED^3 1).

will (i) volition; (ii) lust; (iii) genitalia (see Sonnet 135 and notes); the word is neither capitalised nor italicised here in Q, as it is in Sonnets 135 and 136 when it seems to suggest a name.

3 *forfeit* give up, make subject to confiscation; as in Sonnet 133, the poet-speaker is giving himself in return for the friend; on the surface, it sounds as if the poet-speaker is offering to sacrifice himself, however – should the mistress agree – he would win in two ways: (i) his friend would be restored to him; (ii) he would remain where he wants to be, with the mistress (but without his rival).

so (i) in order that; (ii) provided that: the choice of word leaves the sequence of events unclear. In (i) the poet-speaker forfeits himself to win the friend's release; in (ii) the poet-speaker forfeits himself on condition that the mistress first release his friend.

that other mine the friend; compare 'Let the bird of loudest lay', l. 36. For idea of the friend as a second self, see 22.3n.

4 *restore to be* give back so that he may be.
still always.

5 *But. . .free* Since 'will' can contain a sense of volition as well as futurity, it is possible to read this as a reluctant admission – couched in a double negative – that the friend does not want to be free of the mistress.

6 *covetous* 'culpably or inordinately desirous of gaining wealth or possessions; *esp.* of that which belongs to another or to which one has no right' (OED 2); the word anticipates 'usurer' (l. 10), since money-lenders were characteristically depicted as avaricious (witness Barabas in Christopher Marlowe's *Jew of Malta*).

kind (i) 'having a gentle, sympathetic, or benevolent nature' (OED 5); (ii) sexually active (OED 6).

7–8 *He. . . . bind* The friend had originally meant to act as a guarantor for the poet-speaker, underwriting his debt, but – in signing the bond – it seems that he too committed himself to the mistress.

7 *but* only.

surety-like as a guarantor, 'a person who undertakes specific responsibility on behalf of another person who remains primarily liable for that responsibility [...] such as a payment of a debt or appearance in court' ('surety, *n.*', OED^3 2a); 'surety' is here disyllabic (sure-ty), not trisyllabic (sur-e-ty); the triangular relationship that we see enacted here, where the friend guarantees the lover's behaviour, is also found in *Merchant of Venice*, where Antonio stands 'surety' for Bassanio's safe-keeping of Portia's ring (5.1.254). The word is often used of Christ, 'undertaking to take upon himself the sins of mankind' (OED^3 2b).

8 *bond* See 87.4n.
fast firmly, tightly.

9 *statute* (i) 'decree or command made by a sovereign, ruler, or ruling body' (*n.*1, OED^3 1); (ii) 'a bond or recognizance by which the creditor had the power of seizing a debtor's lands in case of default' (OED^3 5a, citing this line in a figurative context). Since subjects are bound by laws whether or not they have consented to them, (i) conveys a sense of the power the mistress holds over the poet-speaker; (ii) links more closely to the motif of monetary bonds that structures the sonnet; the suggestion that the mistress is ready to claim ('*take*') what the statute entitles her to also anticipates the allusion to the practice of usurers in the following line (l. 10).

10 *usurer. . . use* The mistress is like a usurer; compare the depiction of the youth at 4.7. The vilification of usurers was such that it was not simply that they were seen as lending money for excessive interest: stereotypically, their ultimate plan was that their debtors would default on the payment, allowing them to seize the goods/land that had been offered as pledge (see, for instance, Quomodo in Thomas Middleton's *Michaelmas Term*, 1604). For the bawdy connotations of 'use', see 2.9n.

11 *sue* (i) 'institute legal proceedings against' (OED 13); (ii) 'woo' (OED 15).

134

So now I have confessed that he is thine,
And I myself am mortgaged to thy will;
Myself I'll forfeit, so that other mine
Thou wilt restore to be my comfort still.   4
But thou wilt not, nor he will not be free,
For thou art covetous, and he is kind;
He learned but surety-like to write for me
Under that bond that him as fast doth bind.   8
The statute of thy beauty thou wilt take,
Thou usurer that put'st forth all to use,
And sue a friend came debtor for my sake:
So him I lose through my unkind abuse.   12
    Him have I lost, thou hast both him and me;
    He pays the whole, and yet am I not free.

came debtor (i) came as debtor; (ii) became a debtor.

12 *So* so that.
   lose spelled 'loose' in Q, a variant spelling of 'lose' (see 18.10n), but one which also plays on the sense of bonds running through the sonnet; see 42.9, 10, 11n.
   unkind abuse (i) the poet-speaker's unnaturally cruel treatment at the hands of the mistress, who has taken the friend from him; (ii) the poet-speaker's unnaturally cruel treatment of the friend.

13 *hast* For the bawdy implications of the verb 'have', see 129.6, 10n.

14 *He. . .free* The friend pays the whole debt to the mistress, i.e. he satisfies her sexually (with a pun on 'whole' as in hole/vagina); despite this, the poet-speaker has not been released from his ties to the mistress. For the bawdy play on 'hole', see *Romeo and Juliet*, 2.4.91–3: 'this drivelling love is like a great natural [fool] that runs lolling up and down to hide his bable [bauble] in a hole'.
   yet (i) nevertheless; (ii) even now.

135

Benson combines Sonnets 135 and 136 under the title 'A Love-Suit'.

The sonnet is constructed around a series of puns on 'will', which appears thirteen times (along with one occurrence of 'wilt').There are at least six senses of 'will' in play: (i) wish (OED 1a); (ii) carnal desire (OED 2); (iii) intention (OED 5b); (iv) wilfulness (OED 9a); (v) the proper name 'Will[iam]'; (vi) male and female genitalia (see Partridge 1990: 218–19; Williams 1997: 338–9); it is this last, bawdy meaning which dominates. Blakemore Evans (1996: 253) cites Breton's 'A Waggery' as an analogue for this quibble on 'will':

> Children's ahs and women's ohs
> Do a wondrous grief disclose;
> Where a dug [nipple] the t'one will still,
> And the t'other but a will
> [. . .]
> Let the child then suck his fill;
> Let the woman have her will;
> All will hush, was heard before;
> 'Ah' and 'oh' will cry no more. (*Melancholic Humours*, 1600: sigs F1v–F2r)

This poem appears immediately before the poem from Breton's collection that is cited in the headnote to Sonnet 105.

Q capitalises and italicises seven of the occurrences of the word 'will' (ll. 1, 2 (twice), 11 (twice), 12, 14; see Figure 4.3), a standard way of indicating a proper name (see 1.2n). As is usual editorial practice for this sonnet, Q's capitals have been retained but the italic type changed to roman.

1 *Whoever. . . Will* echoes the proverb 'women will have their wills' (Dent W723).
    hast For the bawdy implications of 'have', see 129.6, 10n.
1–2 *thy Will. . . overplus* All three occurrences of 'Will' are italicised and capitalised in Q, suggesting that they here indicate a proper name. This seeming excess of Williams has led to speculation about how many men of this name the mistress is involved with (see Rollins 1944: 1.345–7). The poet-speaker declares his name 'is Will' at 136.14. Most commentators argue for there being one or two other Williams: the friend and/or the mistress' husband; see l. 11n, below.

For the suggestion the she is married, see 152.3 and note.
2 *to boot* in addition.
    overplus excess; aside from here, Shakespeare only uses the word in *Antony and Cleopatra*, a play notable for its exploration of sexual passion and ideas of abundance, where it appears at 3.7.50 ('Our overplus of shipping will we burn') and 4.6.19–21 ('Antony | Hath after thee sent all thy treasure, with | His bounty overplus').
3 *More than enough* The poet-speaker asserts his sexual prowess, that he can satisfy the mistress.
    am I probably plays on Will-I-am.
    vex trouble, agitate (OED 1a, 6a); the latter sense holds the possibility of sexual innuendo; a stronger word than now (see 92.9n).
4 *To. . . addition* 'filling your vagina ['*will*'] with my penis ['addition']'.
5 *large* The word describes the mistress' will as (i) generous, lavish (OED³ A1) or (ii) morally lax (OED³ 19); compare *Antony and Cleopatra*, 3.6.93–4: 'th' adulterous Antony, most large | In his abominations'; (iii) it might also suggest that her vagina has become enlarged ('capacious', OED³ A3a), thanks to her promiscuity. The word in all senses is pleonastic with '*spacious*', which Shakespeare uses both to suggest capaciousness (see the quotation from *Titus Andronicus*, below) and lavishness/generosity; for the latter sense, see *All's Well*, 2.1.50–1 ('Use a more spacious ceremony to the noble lords') and *Coriolanus*, 4.6.68–9: '[He] vows revenge as spacious as between | The young'st and oldest thing'.
5, 7 *spacious. . . gracious* both pronounced as three syllables; Shakespeare also uses these words trisyllabically, again in terminal positions, at *Titus Andronicus*, 2.1.114 ('The forest walks are wide and spacious') and *Much Ado*, 4.1.108 ('And never shall it more be gracious').
6 *vouchsafe. . . thine* 'Allow me to put my penis ['*will*'] in your vagina'.
7 *will in others* others' wills.
    gracious attractive.
8 *fair acceptance* courteous welcome.
    shine appear.
9 *The sea. . . still* proverbial; 'The sea refuses no river (is never full)' (Dent S181). Burrow (2002: 650) also points out the allusion to

135

Whoever hath her wish, thou hast thy Will,
And Will to boot, and Will in overplus;
More than enough am I that vex thee still,
To thy sweet will making addition thus.   4
Wilt thou, whose will is large and spacious,
Not once vouchsafe to hide my will in thine?
Shall will in others seem right gracious,
And in my will no fair acceptance shine?   8
The sea, all water, yet receives rain still
And in abundance addeth to his store;
So thou, being rich in Will, add to thy Will
One will of mine to make thy large Will more.   12
    Let no unkind no fair beseechers kill;
      Think all but one, and me in that one Will.

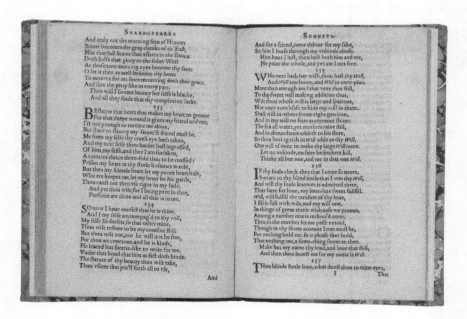

Figure 4.3 William Shakespeare, *Shakespeare's Sonnets* (London: George Eld, 1609), sigs H4v–I1r; Folger Shakespeare Library copy, classmark STC 22353. Used with permission of the Folger Shakespeare Library

Ecclesiastes 1:7: 'All the rivers go into the sea, yet the sea is not full'. Compare *Twelfth Night*, 1.1.11, where Orsino's love 'receiveth as the sea', and 2.4.100–1, where it 'is all as hungry as the sea, | And can digest as much'. The depiction of the sea as a 'sovereign' in *Lucrece* (ll. 650, 652) also opens up the possibility of hearing a pun in '*receive*', as here too the sea is figured as a monarch, admitting his subjects to his presence.

10 *in abundance* adverbial (abundantly).
his its.
store 'sufficient or abundant supply', 'plenty' (OED 4a, 4b).

11 *being* pronounced as a monosyllable.
rich in Will The mistress has abundant desires as well as abundant penises at her disposal; the capitalisation and italicisation in Q also suggests that this is a proper name, possibly indicating that the mistress has at least one other sexual partner also named Will (see note on ll. 1–2, above).

11–12 *add. . . more* 'Add my desire/penis to make your (already sizeable) sexual appetite/vagina even bigger.'

13 *Let. . . kill* This is a notoriously tricky line. Q punctuates it with a comma after 'unkind', although that indicates a caesura more than

a syntactical unit. A number of editors (e.g. Burrow and Kerrigan, following Ingram and Redpath) put speech marks around the first 'no', so that 'no' becomes an unkind utterance (i.e. a refusal). Other alternatives are (i) treating the second 'no' as the utterance (as Dowden conjectures); (ii) leaving the line unpunctuated (as here). In early modern English the double negative was a standard form of emphasis and 'adjectives could readily function as nouns' (Blake 2002: 50), so that 'unkind' would here stand for an unkind act or person; Blakemore Evans (1996: 254) notes Chapman's usage of 'unkind' as a noun in *Ovid's Banquet of Sense*: 'Not able to endure earth's rude unkinds' (1595: sig. B4v). Despite these different ways of reading the line, the sense is essentially the same: 'let no ungrateful/ungenerous act (e.g. a refusal) kill any upright/handsome suitors'. The power over the lover's life and death that is invested in the mistress is a Petrarchan commonplace. For the sexual potential of 'kind', see 134.6n.

14 *Think. . . Will* 'Think of all your lovers ['beseechers', l. 13] as one man and of me as (i) part of that collective desire; (ii) one penis among many; (iii) being in your vagina.'

135

Whoever hath her wish, thou hast thy Will,
And Will to boot, and Will in overplus;
More than enough am I that vex thee still,
To thy sweet will making addition thus.   4
Wilt thou, whose will is large and spacious,
Not once vouchsafe to hide my will in thine?
Shall will in others seem right gracious,
And in my will no fair acceptance shine?   8
The sea, all water, yet receives rain still
And in abundance addeth to his store;
So thou, being rich in Will, add to thy Will
One will of mine to make thy large Will more.   12
   Let no unkind no fair beseechers kill;
   Think all but one, and me in that one Will.

136

Benson combines Sonnets 135 and 136 under the title 'A Love-Suit'. This sonnet continues on from Sonnet 135, punning on 'will' (see headnote to Sonnet 135).

1 *check* reprimand (*v.*1, OED 11).
   come so near (i) draw so physically close; (ii) touch on the truth (because he has exposed her promiscuity), as in *Romeo and Juliet*, 1.5.18–20: 'which of you all | Will now deny to dance? She that makes dainty, | She I'll swear hath corns. Am I come near ye now?'

2, 5, 14 *Will* italicised and capitalised in Q (see Figure 4.3), suggesting a name.

2 *blind soul* The soul could be 'blind' (i) because, being internal, it cannot see out of the body; (ii) because it deliberately chooses to shut its eyes; or (iii) because it has been blinded by passion.
   thy Will The poet-speaker here refers to himself in the third person, reminding the mistress of their past liaison; Ingram and Redpath suggest (1995: 314) that this could also refer to the friend or (following J.Q. Adams, cited in Rollins 1944: 1.346) to the mistress' husband (see 135.1–2n); however, the past tense of '*was*' make both of these suggestions improbable: if the poet-speaker wants the mistress to delude herself that he is someone else – another Will, currently in favour – a present tense 'am' would be more likely ('Swear [. . .] I am thy Will').

3 *will* For the wordplay on desire and genitalia, see headnote to Sonnet 135.
   admitted In a political system where physical proximity to those in positions of authority was regulated, 'admitted' carries connotations of intimate or privileged access; see, for example, *Cymbeline*, 2.3.66–8 ('I know her women are about her; what | If I do line one of their hands? 'Tis gold | Which buys admittance'); *2 Henry VI*, 3.1.26–7 ('That he should come about your royal person, | Or be admitted to your Highness' Council').

4 *for love* 'out of charity'; the poet-speaker is calling on the mistress to show him the 'regard and consideration of one human being towards another prompted by a sense of a common relationship to God' ('love, *n.*1', OED³ 2).

sweet (i) either an adjective qualifying 'love-suit'; or (ii), as punctuated here (following Capell), a term of endearment applied to the mistress, as the poet-speaker requests that she 'fulfil' (i.e. grant) his 'love-suit'. Modernising the punctuation imposes a choice that is kept open in the original; the punctuation chosen here helps accentuate the fact that this line is an imperative, directed to the mistress. Compare note on 'sweet', l. 12, below.

5 *fulfil* fill up, fill full.
   treasure treasury (OED 3), but also – in the context of the *double entendres* and since 'will' is a penis as well as a name – the mistress' vagina. For the bawdy connotations of 'treasure', see 20.14n.

6 *Ay* 'I' in Q; editors since Capell recurrently emend 'I' to 'Ay'. I/ay puns are frequent in Shakespeare; see, for example, *Richard II*, 'Ay, no, no, ay; for I must nothing be' (4.1.201); in the 1623 Folio, this reads 'I, no: no I, for I must nothing be'. In Sonnet 136, retaining the spelling 'I' would make the potential parallel with the preceding line more obvious ('Will will fulfil'; 'I fill it full'); that rendering also conveys the sense of the poet-speaker attempting to assert himself sexually, in which he ('I') will be the one who fills her vagina; the fragility of this assertion is epitomised by the pun, however: by mid-line, it is apparent that the attempt to monopolise the mistress' vagina is unsustainable. His will becomes one among many, and 'I' is retrospectively heard as a resigned 'Ay' ('Go ahead, have sex with other men, me among many').
   fill it full pun on fulfil (l. 5).

7 *things* slang for genitalia; see 20.12 and note.
   of great receipt continues the financial imagery that began with 'treasure' (l. 5); see also 'store's account' (l. 10); the mistress' treasury (vagina) is of large capacity (see 135.5n) and/or it has received many men.
   prove demonstrate.

8 *Among. . . none* (i) when there is a large number (e.g. of other lovers), one more does not matter; (ii) mathematically and proverbially (Dent O54), 'one is no number' (this idea also lies behind 8.14 and 'Let the bird of loudest lay', l. 28); compare Christopher

136

If thy soul check thee that I come so near,
Swear to thy blind soul that I was thy Will,
And will, thy soul knows, is admitted there;
Thus far for love my love-suit, sweet, fulfil.   4
Will will fulfil the treasure of thy love,
Ay, fill it full with wills, and my will one;
In things of great receipt with ease we prove
Among a number one is reckoned none.   8
Then in the number let me pass untold,
Though in thy store's account I one must be;
For nothing hold me, so it please thee hold
That nothing me a something sweet to thee.   12
    Make but my name thy love, and love that still,
    And then thou lovest me for my name is Will.

Marlowe, *Hero and Leander*, where Leander uses this mathematical truth as one of his arguments in his seduction of Hero (l. 255).

9 *untold* uncounted (i.e. not included in the number); unrecounted, i.e. secret, unnoticed.

10 *store's account* reckoning of your (ample) possessions (i.e. the list of the mistress' lovers); compare the use of 'store' at 14.12 and 64.8. There may be a pun on 'cunt'.

11 *hold . . . hold* play on 'consider, value' and 'hold physically, embrace'; for the former sense, see *Hamlet*, 2.2.44: 'I hold my duty as I hold my soul'.
    so provided that.

12 *nothing* as punctuated here, an adjective qualifying 'me'; some editors (e.g. Duncan-Jones) punctuate with a comma afterwards, so that '*me*' glosses 'nothing' (a noun).
    sweet This could be either an adjective, qualifying 'something' (as punctuated here), or a term of endearment addressed to the mistress (as in l. 4, above); modernised punctuation imposes a choice that is kept open in the original. For the erotic connotations of 'sweet', see Nashe, *Choice of Valentines*,

ll. 121–2: 'O Gods! that ever anything so sweet | So suddenly should fade away, and fleet!'; 'sweet' and its derivatives also recur throughout *Venus and Adonis*.
    something play on 'thing', slang for 'penis'; see 20.12n.

13 *Make but* The phrase is ambiguous: it can both (i) constitute a demand that the mistress make his the 'only' name she loves, and (ii) figure as a more wheedling, desperate plea that she 'just' or 'merely' name him a lover, presumably one alongside other men.

14 *lovest* pronounced as one syllable.
    for my name is Will As Kerrigan points out (1986: 367), at the moment at which Shakespeare seems most autobiographical, he invokes a commonplace, as found in *The Book of Merry Riddles* (1617): 'My lover's will | I am content for to fulfil; | Within this rhyme his name is framed, | Tell me then how he is named. | *Solution:* | His name is William, for in the first line is *will*, and in the beginning of the second line is, *I am*, and then put them together, and that maketh *William*' (Riddle 51).

137

Benson combines Sonnets 137, 139 and 140 under the title 'His heart wounded by her eye'.

1 *blind fool love* Cupid was proverbially blind; see Dent L506 and *As You Like It*, 4.1.213–14: 'that blind rascally boy that abuses everyone's eyes because his own are out'. Editors frequently modernise this phrase as 'blind fool, Love', making it Cupid; leaving 'love' uncapitalised (as in Q) allows the possibility that this is the poet-speaker addressing their own deluded love, whilst 'fool' could – in early modern English – be an adjective rather than a noun, as in *Merchant of Venice*, 1.1.102 ('for this fool gudgeon [small fish]'), 2.9.26 ('the fool multitude').

2 *see. . . see* 'do not correctly perceive what they see'; compare 113.3–4 and Psalms 115:5: 'they have eyes and see not'. Sonnets 148–150 and 152 also discuss the problematic relationship between the poet-speaker's eyesight and his judgement. Eyes were regarded as the entry point for love. See Sidney, *Astrophil and Stella*, 36.1–6:

> Stella, whence doth this new assault arise,
> A conquered, yelden [yielding], ransacked heart to win?
> Whereto long since, through my long battered eyes,
> Whole armies of thy beauties entered in,
> And there long since, Love thy lieutenant lies,
> My forces razed, thy banners raised within.

3 *lies* (i) resides; (ii) deceives.

4 *Yet. . . be* Burrow (2002: 654) points to an analogy with Golding's translation of Ovid's *Metamorphoses* 7.19–21, where Medea declares: 'Love persuades me one, another thing my skill [knowledge]. | The best I see and like: the worst I follow headlong still' (Golding 7.24–5; sig. N8r).
take understand, suppose (OED 47b).

5 *corrupt* corrupted (past participle).
over-partial too favourable, prejudiced; it is ambiguous whose looks this adjective qualifies: the poet-speaker's (which look too favourably upon the mistress), or the mistress', who lures the poet-speaker by seeming to look favourably upon him.

6 *anchored. . . ride* another allusion to the mistress' promiscuity; compare Marlowe's translation of

Ovid's *Amores*, Book 3, Elegy 6, ll. 1–5 (printed, with poems by John Davies, in *Epigrams and Elegies*, 1599): 'Either she was foul, or her attire was bad | Or she was not the wench I wished t'have had | [. . .] Though both of us performed our true intent, | Yet could I not cast anchor where I meant' (sig. G1r).
ride (of ships) lie or float at anchor (OED³ 15a).

7 *forgèd hooks* made baits; for the commonplace that women's looks were baits to catch men's hearts, see 129.7n. However, here it could be the poet-speaker's own eyes. See also Sonnet 148, and contrast Sonnet 113, where his mind is accused of misleading his eyes.

9 *that* demonstrative ('that place', i.e. the mistress' body).
several plot private area of land, divided off by a wall or fence ('several': 'of land, *esp.* of enclosed pasture', OED A7a). 'Several' is here prounced as two syllables.

10 *wide. . . common place* reiterates the idea in l. 6: far from being his own private ('several') property (l. 9), the mistress is a 'common place', i.e. common land, to which everyone had access and where anyone could graze livestock; 'common' is often used to suggest sexual promiscuity (see OED A6b), whilst 'common place' could also indicate that the mistress is widely talked of ('commonplace', OED A5b), i.e. a subject of gossip.

11 *Or mine eyes* or why do my eyes.
seeing. . . not Despite seeing that the mistress is unfaithful, the poet-speaker's eyes deny it; compare 152.11–14.

12 *To put* in order to put; compare the proverb 'To set a good face [. . .] on a bad matter' (Dent F17).
fair. . . foul 'Foul' has ethical as well as aesthetic connotations; here the poet-speaker berates his eyes for projecting a virtuous (fair) character onto the mistress, who is as ugly in deeds (see 131.13) as she is unconventionally beautiful (see Sonnet 127). The threatening disruptiveness of this inversion is indicated by the witch's chant in *Macbeth*, 1.1.11: 'Fair is foul, and foul is fair'. The word 'foul' is used seven times in the *Sonnets* (119.2; 127.6, where it is also contrasted with 'fair'; 132.14; here at 137.12; 144.8; 148.14; 152.14); from this point on in Q's sequence, it is used exclusively to denigrate the mistress.

137

Thou blind fool love, what dost thou to mine eyes
That they behold and see not what they see?
They know what beauty is, see where it lies,
Yet what the best is, take the worst to be.　　　　　　　　4
If eyes corrupt by over-partial looks
Be anchored in the bay where all men ride,
Why of eyes' falsehood hast thou forgèd hooks
Whereto the judgement of my heart is tied?　　　　　　　8
Why should my heart think that a several plot,
Which my heart knows the wide world's common place?
Or mine eyes seeing this, say this is not,
To put fair truth upon so foul a face?　　　　　　　　　12
　　In things right true my heart and eyes have erred,
　　And to this false plague are they now transferred.

truth Meanings range from 'fidelity [...] constancy' (with implications of chastity) (OED 1a) to 'veracity [...], honesty [...], virtue' (OED 4).

13 ***In*** with regard to.

things right true (i) matters which are undoubtedly the case; (ii) as Kerrigan notes (1986: 369), a bawdy pun: 'chaste cunts', since 'thing' is slang for genitalia (see 20.12n, 136.7n).

erred The word has a stronger sense than in modern usage; see 131.7n.

14 ***this false plague*** Booth suggests a range of meanings, including 'this affliction of distorted perceptions' and 'the affliction of being false, telling falsehoods' (1977: 476). This overcomplicates the line: the most obvious meaning (also noted by Booth) is that it refers to the mistress, who is like a plague because she torments him but also possibly because she carries venereal disease (see Sonnets 153–154 and notes). The poet-speaker's inability to reject the mistress, which we see discussed from Sonnet 129 onwards, is here reflected in the sonnet's deictics, which move from the distal 'that' (l. 9) to the proximal 'this' in l. 14: even as he labels her a 'false plague', the use of 'this' signals his proximity (emotional or physical) to her.

they hearts and eyes (l. 13).

transferred handed over ('transfer, *v.*', OED 1a); conveyed or made over, like property (OED 2).

138

Printed by Benson, as a single sonnet entitled 'False belief', from the 1612 edition of *The Passionate Pilgrim*.

A version of this sonnet and of Sonnet 144 were first printed in 1599 in *The Passionate Pilgrim* (see Appendix 3). There is also a manuscript copy from the mid-seventeenth century in Folger MS V.a.339 (fol. 197v), which appears in a group of poems from *The Passionate Pilgrim* and probably derives from that text (see Appendix 4).

1 ***my love*** my mistress.
  made of truth is (i) faithful, (ii) honest; pun on the homophone 'maid' (virgin).
2 ***lies*** 'deceives'; by l. 13, a secondary meaning of 'lies down' (i.e. have sexual intercourse with other men) has been activated.
3 ***That*** so that.
  untutored unsophisticated, inexperienced in the lessons of love; Shakespeare's *3 Henry VI*, 5.5.32 and the dedication to *Lucrece* are cited by OED as the earliest usages of this word (senses 1a, 2); no earlier usage is returned using a keyword search of EEBO-TCP.
4 ***false subtleties*** deceitful tricks; 'false' carries connotations of sexual infidelity; see, for example, *Comedy of Errors*, 2.2.141–4: 'My blood is mingled with the crime of lust: | For if we too be one, and thou play false, | I do digest the poison of thy flesh, | Being strumpeted by thy contagion'.
5 ***Thus*** (i) in that way; (ii) therefore.
  vainly 'ineffectually' (OED 1); 'foolishly' (OED 2); it could also mean 'with personal vanity; conceitedly' (OED 3), although this sense was only emerging *c.* 1600 (the first citation in the OED is dated 1602) and, as Burrow points out (2002: 656), there is no precedent for Shakespeare using the adverb in this way; the closest Shakespeare gets is a pun on 'vanity' and 'vainly' in *All's Well*, 5.3.121–3: 'My fore-past proofs [. . .] | Shall tax my fears of little vanity, | Having vainly feared too little'.

6 ***Although. . . best*** This sonnet was first printed in 1599, when Shakespeare would have been 35, still within the category of 'youth' according to medical divisions of the ages of man (see Elyot, *Castle of Health* (1539), sigs B2v–B3r). The recurrent evocation of an aged persona (see in particular Sonnet 73) is one of the ways in which Shakespeare (i) plays around with aspects of his autobiography, and (ii) subverts cultural assumptions about sonnets as a young man's genre (see 22.1n).
7 ***Simply*** (i) 'unaffectedly, artlessly' (OED 1); (ii) 'in a foolish [. . .] manner' (OED 5); (iii) the rarer meaning of 'unconditionally' (OED 6c) may also be implied.
  credit believe (OED³ 4a).
8 ***suppressed*** (i) banished from one's mind ('suppress, *v.*', OED³ 2a); (ii) left unexpressed (OED³ 2b); (iii) kept secret (OED³ 3a).
9, 10 ***wherefore*** why.
9 ***unjust*** 'faithless, dishonest' (OED 2); compare *Passionate Pilgrim* 18.33 (Appendix 3). The sense of 'incorrect' and 'inaccurate' are also in play (OED 3, 4).
11 ***habit*** (i) apparel; (ii) regular practice.
  seeming trust both appearing to trust and appearing to be trustworthy.
12 ***And. . . told*** If 't' have' is elided, the line is only nine syllables long. To remedy this (i) either 'years' needs to be pronounced as two syllables; or (ii), despite the elision (present in Q), 't' have' needs to be pronounced as two syllables; compare 'th' East' (Q132.6).
  age aged people.
  told (i) counted; (ii) revealed (compare 136.9, 'untold').
13 ***lie*** (i) deceive; (ii) have sexual intercourse.
14 ***faults*** (i) sins, in having sexual intercourse with each other; (ii) weaknesses, in refusing to acknowledge the full truth.
  flattered (i) beguiled ('flatter, *v.*1', OED 6); (ii) gratified (OED 4). Compare Marlowe's translation of Ovid's *Amores*, Book 2, Elegy 11: 'I'll think all true, though it be feigned matter, | Mine own desires why should my self not flatter?' (*Ovid's Elegies*, 1603: sig. C8v).

138

When my love swears that she is made of truth,
I do believe her, though I know she lies,
That she might think me some untutored youth,
Unlearnèd in the world's false subtleties.   4
Thus vainly thinking that she thinks me young,
Although she knows my days are past the best,
Simply I credit her false-speaking tongue;
On both sides thus is simple truth suppressed.   8
But wherefore says she not she is unjust?
And wherefore say not I that I am old?
O love's best habit is in seeming trust,
And age in love loves not t' have years told.   12
    Therefore I lie with her, and she with me,
    And in our faults by lies we flattered be.

139

Benson combines Sonnets 137, 139 and 140 under the title 'His heart wounded by her eye'.

The central motif – of the mistress who can slay with her eyes – is a common conceit in Renaissance love poetry, and can be found in Sidney's *Astrophil and Stella*, 48:

> Soul's joy, bend not those morning stars from me,
> Where virtue is made strong by beauty's might,
> Where love is chasteness, pain doth learn delight,
> And humbleness grows one with majesty.
> Whatever may ensue, O let me be
> Co-partner of the riches of that sight;
> Let not mine eyes be hell-driven from that light.
> O look, O shine, O let me die and see,
> For though I oft myself of them bemoan
> That through my heart their beamy darts be gone,
> Whose cureless wounds even now most freshly bleed,
> Yet since my death-wound is already got,
> Dear killer, spare not thy sweet cruel shot:
> A kind of grace it is to slay with speed.

1 **call not me** 'do not ask me'.
2 **unkindness** unnaturalness, cruelty; see 134.12 and 135.13; conventionally, a sonnet mistress' unkindness is coldness towards her lover; however, by l. 5 it is clear that this mistress' unkindness is due to her infidelity, loving 'elsewhere'. For the sexual connotations of 'kind' (and thus, 'unkind'), see 134.6n.
lays upon imposes on (OED 28a), inflicts upon ('lay on' in 'lay, *v*.', OED 3).
3 **Wound. . . tongue** It was conventional for Petrarchan mistresses to wound their lovers with their eyes; see *Romeo and Juliet*, 2.4.13–14: 'Alas, poor Romeo, he is already dead, stabbed with a white wench's black eye'. For the idea that eyes emitted beams of light, see Sidney's *Astrophil and Stella*, 48.10 (cited in the head-note to this sonnet), and *Venus and Adonis*, 487n. This mistress is here being asked to hurt the poet-speaker, not by looking at him, but by talking to him (presumably about her other lovers).
4 **Use. . . power** 'Use your power [ability to hurt me] outright [strongly] rather than using underhand means ['*art*']'; compare 94.1. Both instances of 'power' are pronounced as one syllable.

5 **in my sight** 'when I can see you'.
6 **Dear heart** a term of affection used of the mistress.
forbear. . . aside 'restrain yourself from looking elsewhere' (i.e. at other men).
7 **What need'st thou** 'why do you need to'.
cunning. . . might recapitulates the distinction between 'art' and 'power' in l. 4.
8 **o'erpressed** oppressed, overburdened (OED³).
bide endure.
9 **Let me excuse thee** The poet-speaker sets about trying to do what he has said he refuses to do in l. 1.
9–12 **'Ah. . . injuries'** It is customary for editors to add speech marks to show that the poet-speaker is ventriloquising an excuse for his mistress' behaviour, which is 'couched in the language of the orthodox besotted sonneteer' (Burrow 2002: 658). The excuse framed is also a piece of ingenious and wishful thinking (where the mistress looking at other men is attributed to a desire not to wound the poet-speaker).
9 **my love** the mistress.
10 **pretty looks** her beauty and/or alluring glances.
11 **my foes** her eyes; a conventional Petrarchanism; see, for example, William Byrd: 'Ah, wanton eyes, my friendly foes' ('Though Amarillis', *Psalms, Sonnets and Songs*, 1588: sig. D1v).
12 **elsewhere** at other men.
dart. . . injuries plays with the Petrarchan idea that the beloved's eyes shoot arrows of love; see Sidney, *Astrophil and Stella*, 48.10 (cited above); Barnes, *Parthenophil and Parthenophe*, Sonnet 26.2: 'Love's golden darts take aim from her bright eyes' (1593: sig. C3r).
13 **Yet. . . so** 'But do not do what I have just told you' (i.e. look at other men, wounding them with love).
near slain The poet-speaker poses as an archetypal Petrarchan lover, half-dead with love; 'near' is adverbial ('nearly').
14 **Kill. . . looks** The mistress here figures as a basilisk, a mythical monster that could kill with looks; compare the depiction of the unkind mistress in Philip Sidney's 'I joy in grief', ll. 72–3: 'that crowned basilisk [. . .] | Whose footsteps I with kisses oft did trace'. The desire for a quick death was a commonplace pose of sonnet lovers; see Sidney, *Astrophil and Stella*, 48.14 (cited above).
outright immediately.
rid do away with.

139

O call not me to justify the wrong
That thy unkindness lays upon my heart;
Wound me not with thine eye but with thy tongue;
Use power with power and slay me not by art; 4
Tell me thou lov'st elsewhere; but in my sight,
Dear heart, forbear to glance thine eye aside.
What need'st thou wound with cunning when thy might
Is more than my o'erpressed defence can bide? 8
Let me excuse thee: 'Ah, my love well knows
Her pretty looks have been mine enemies
And therefore from my face she turns my foes,
That they elsewhere might dart their injuries.' 12
    Yet do not so, but since I am near slain,
    Kill me outright with looks and rid my pain.

140

Benson combines Sonnets 137, 139 and 140 under the title 'His heart wounded by her eye'.

1 *Be. . . cruel* (i) be equally wise as you are cruel; (ii) since you are cruel, be wise.

press (i) torture, referring to the punishment of *peine forte et dure*, which was 'used on prisoners who refused to plead' (*v.*1, OED³ 1c; 'peine', OED³ 1); compare *Measure for Measure*, 5.1.522–3: 'Marrying a punk [prostitute], my lord is pressing to death, whipping and hanging'; (ii) oppress (OED³ 11a); (iii) attack, beset (OED³ 11c); compare 139.8.

2 *tongue-tied* connects back to 'press' (see l. 1n, above): the poet-speaker – like the prisoner being pressed – is mute.

patience forbearance (*n.*1, OED³ 1b); the etymological origins in the Latin *patior* (I suffer) are also pertinent.

disdain scorn; typical quality of the cruel Petrarchan mistress; see 132.2 and note.

4 *pity-wanting* draws on the dual sense of 'want'; the mistress' pity is something the poet-speaker both lacks and needs ('want, *v.*', OED 1a, 4a). For the sexual resonances of 'pity', see 132.12n.

5 *wit* 'mental quickness' (OED 5a).

5–6 *better. . . so* 'It would be better, although you do not love me, nevertheless ['*yet*'] to enjoy telling me you do'. This line could also be punctuated with commas round '*love*', making it a term of endearment addressed to the mistress, rather than a verb. Modern punctuation imposes a choice which remains open in the original.

7 *testy* short-tempered (OED 2a).

8 *No. . . know* Their doctors only give them good news about their health.

9–10 *For. . . thee* reiterates the threat uttered in ll. 1–4.

11 *ill-wresting* twisting things to the worst interpretation.

12 *slanderers* here pronounced as two syllables.

ears synecdoche for hearers.

13 *be so* (i) be a slanderer; (ii) be believed.

belied be slandered.

13–14 *That. . . wide* The couplet restates the threat made in ll. 1–4, 9–10 (that if the mistress is not kinder to him, he will expose her); however, it is here tempered with the suggestion (similar to that made in Sonnet 138) that he is willing to enter knowingly into self-deception: it is enough that she pretends to be faithful.

14 *Bear. . . wide* 'Appear faithful, even if you are not' (wide = astray, OED 6); the image is from archery, picking up on the Petrarchan motif of the beloved's eyes as emitting arrows (see 139.12 and note); 'shooting straight' is a key element necessary for hitting the mark, as opposed to missing it, by going wide; see Roger Ascham, *Toxophilus* (1545: sig. N3r). Ascham also writes about archery in moral terms: 'By shooting also is the mind honestly exercised where a man always desireth to be best (which is a word of honesty) and that by the same way that virtue itself doth, coveting to come nighest a most perfect end or mean standing betwixt two extremes, eschewing short, or gone, or either side wide, for the which causes Aristotle himself sayeth that shooting and virtue be very like' (sig. B3r–v).

140

Be wise as thou art cruel; do not press
My tongue-tied patience with too much disdain,
Lest sorrow lend me words, and words express
The manner of my pity-wanting pain.   4
If I might teach thee wit, better it were,
Though not to love, yet love to tell me so,
As testy sick-men, when their deaths be near,
No news but health from their physicians know.   8
For if I should despair, I should grow mad
And in my madness might speak ill of thee;
Now this ill-wresting world is grown so bad,
Mad slanderers by mad ears believèd be.   12
   That I may not be so, nor thou belied,
   Bear thine eyes straight, though thy proud heart go wide.

141

Benson combines Sonnets 141 and 142 under the title 'A protestation'.

For the corrupted judgement of both eyes and heart, see Sonnet 137; here, the eyes are exempt from blame: faulty judgement lies with the heart alone.

1 ***In faith*** truly; since the mistress is unfaithful, this oath has an edge of sarcasm.

2 ***errors*** (i) physical blemishes; (ii) moral failings; for the moral seriousness of error/erring, see 131.7n.
  note notice (*v.*2, OED³ 5a), record (OED³ 8a); compare 99.14; *Lucrece*, l. 208.

3 ***they*** the speaker's eyes.
  despise view with contempt.

4, 11 ***Who*** which (his heart).

4 ***in despite of view*** despite what they see; possible pun on 'despite of you'.
  dote 'to bestow excessive love or fondness on or upon; to be foolishly in love' ('dote | doat, *v.*1', OED 3); see 20.10n.

5 ***thy tongue's tune*** your voice; compare 130.10; Burrow (2002: 662) points out that 'tune' is not necessarily complimentary (indicating melodiousness), citing Martius' words in *Coriolanus*, addressed to the citizens he despises: 'if it may stand with the tune of your voices that I may be consul' (2.3.85–6).

6 ***Nor*** nor is.
  tender feeling delicate sense of touch.
  base touches physical contact (presumably sexual) that is morally problematic ('base, *adj.*', OED³ A7a); compare *Measure for Measure*, 3.2.24, where the Duke describes sexual contact (purveyed by a bawd) as 'abominable and beastly touches'. 'Base' may also hint at touches which are 'low' on the body (i.e. around the genitals).
  prone disposed, inclined (OED³ 1); compare also *Lucrece*, 684n.

7 ***Nor*** nor do.

8 ***sensual feast*** the literary topos of the banquet of senses, which imagines the multiple delights of an amorous encounter by focussing on each sense in turn; see, for example, George Chapman's *Ovid's Banquet of Sense* (1595), where the erotic description is structured around 'auditus' (hearing), 'olfactus' (smell), 'visus' (sight), 'gustus' (taste) and

is interrupted just as the narrative reaches 'tactus' (touch). Sonnet 141 rejects the topos, even as it evokes it: the senses do not want to attend any such banquet; it is the heart alone which is in the mistress' sway, disregarding the often unfavourable information provided by the poet-speaker's sensory organs. 'Sensual' is disyllabic.
thee alone (i) with you and you only; (ii) alone with you, in private.

9 ***But*** but neither.
  five wits. . . five senses Sonnet 141 here shows the continued influence of medieval philosophy, which divided the five outer senses (sight, hearing, taste, touch, smell) from the five inner wits, described by Stephen Hawes as 'invention', 'imagination', 'fantasy', 'estimation' (judgement) and 'memory' (*Pastime of Pleasure*, printed 1554: sigs C4v–D1v). Shakespeare invokes the five wits at *King Lear*, 3.4.58, 3.6.57; *Much Ado*, 1.1.66; *Romeo and Juliet*, 1.4.47, 2.4.73; *Twelfth Night*, 4.2.86.

10 ***foolish heart*** Compare 'dote', l. 4.
  serving Petrarchan lovers habitually figure themselves as serving their lady; the word also has a sexual sense, pointed out by Duncan-Jones (1997a: 396), 'referring to the copulation of animals' ('serve, *v.*1', OED 52).

11 ***Who. . . man*** The subject of this clause is the poet-speaker's heart, which abandons its proper authority over the body in order to become the mistress' slave, thus leaving the body 'uncontrolled' ('***unswayed***', OED 1), without any faculty in command; the poet-speaker is thus been reduced to the '***likeness***' or mere semblance '***of a man***'. Compare *Richard III*, 4.4.469–70: 'Is the chair empty? is the sword unswayed? | Is the King dead? the empire unpossessed?'

12 ***slave and vassal wretch*** Since vassal also means 'slave' (OED A3), the phrase employs *pleonasm*, for emotive effect. Compare 57.1 and 58.1 (where the poet-speaker is the young man's 'slave') and 58.4 (where he is his 'vassal'). For the use of 'vassal' as an adjective, see *Lucrece*, 608n.

13 ***Only. . . far*** (i) however, to this extent; (ii) to this extent only (and no further).
  plague fever of love (compare Sonnet 147); the proximity of 'plague' with 'sin' and 'pain' may hint at venereal disease (see 144.14n and Sonnet 153).

141

In faith, I do not love thee with mine eyes,
For they in thee a thousand errors note,
But 'tis my heart that loves what they despise,
Who in despite of view is pleased to dote.　　　　4
Nor are mine ears with thy tongue's tune delighted,
Nor tender feeling to base touches prone,
Nor taste nor smell desire to be invited
To any sensual feast with thee alone;　　　　8
But my five wits nor my five senses can
Dissuade one foolish heart from serving thee,
Who leaves unswayed the likeness of a man,
Thy proud heart's slave and vassal wretch to be.　　　　12
　　Only my plague thus far I count my gain,
　　That she that makes me sin awards me pain.

count consider (OED 3); its proximity to 'gain' also plays on the idea of 'calculate' (OED 1a).

14 *awards* 'Award' can mean both 'sentence', i.e. punish ('award, *v.*1', OED 4, 5), and 'give' (OED 3b), where punishment is seen as a reward because it will cut short the sufferings endured after death, a vision of the relationship between earthly punishment and spiritual reward which is endorsed by the Roman Catholic, but not the Protestant, Church; Booth (1977: 488) cites Samuel Butler's helpful gloss from *Shakespeare's Sonnets Reconsidered* (1899): 'I shall suffer less for my sin hereafter, for I get some of the punishment coincidentally with the offence'. Since the doctrine is here applied in an irreverent context, this line cannot be taken as evidence of Shakespeare's religious persuasion.

142

Benson combines Sonnets 141 and 142 under the title 'A protestation'.

1 **Love is my sin** glosses the last line of Sonnet 141, in which the poet-speaker confessed to sinning.

1–2 **Love. . . loving** The first two lines form an *antimetabole* (love. . . hate. . . hate. . . loving); the poet-speaker's sin is loving the mistress; the mistress appears to have '**virtue**' ('moral exellence', 'conformity to [. . .] accepted moral standards', OED[3] 1a, 2a) because she scorns him, showing '**hate**' of his '**sin**', i.e. his love.

2 **grounded** founded; it is unclear what 'grounded' qualifies: the mistress' hate, or the poet-speaker's sin.
sinful loving By l. 8 it is clear that this is adultery.

3 **but** only.
mine my state.

4 **merits not reproving** does not deserve reproach.

5 **Or if it do** 'Or if my sin [love] merits censure' (looking back to l. 4).

6 **scarlet ornaments** lips; Sidney describes Stella's lips as 'scarlet judges, threatening bloody pain' at *Astrophil and Stella*, 73.11; scarlet was associated with ceremonial occasions, but also with the whore of Babylon in Revelations 17:4 (cited at *Lucrece*, 1650n). The phrase 'scarlet ornaments' (describing blushing) appears in *Edward III*, 2.1.10, a play in which Shakespeare possibly had a hand; see 94.14n.

7 **sealed false bonds** The lips seal bonds with kissing, an image frequently used by Shakespeare; see *King John*, 2.1.19–20 ('Upon thy cheek lay I this zealous kiss | As seal to this indenture of my love'); *Measure for Measure*, 4.1.5–6 ('My kisses bring again [. . .] | Seals of love, but sealed in vain'); *Romeo and Juliet*, 5.3.114 ('seal with a righteous kiss'); *Two Gentlemen of Verona*, 2.2.7 ('seal the

bargain with a holy kiss'); *Venus and Adonis*, ll. 511–12. The fact that the lips that seal the bond are described as 'scarlet' (l. 6) evokes the red of sealing wax. The bonds are 'false' because they (i) are adulterous, and (ii) prove untrusty, since they are later broken.
as. . . mine 'as often as mine have done'; Tucker argues for removing Q's comma after 'mine', so that l. 8 then describes the poet-speaker's behaviour rather than that of the mistress, but this is a suggestion not generally taken up by editors. Ingram and Redpath punctuate with a dash, arguing (1985: 326) that ll. 9–10 act as a conditional clause, introducing ll. 11–12.

8 **Robbed. . . rents** The mistress has lured husbands away from their wives; in doing so, she cuts off the proper profits ('**revenues**') of marriage (namely, offspring). The imagery of estate management ('**rents**') recalls the procreation sonnets, especially Sonnets 3, 10, 13. The plural '**beds**' indicates the mistress' promiscuity. 'Revenues' is stressed on the second syllable.

9 **Be 't lawful** (i) 'let it be allowed'; (ii) 'if it is permissible'.

10 **Whom. . . woo** That the mistress has a roving eye is evident from Sonnet 139 (esp. ll. 5–6, 9–12) and 140.14.
as (i) in the same way (i.e. adulterously); (ii) even as; the latter interpretation suggests that even as the poet-speaker begs ('**importune[s]**') the mistress, she is looking enticingly at other men. 'Importunes' is stressed on the second syllable.

11 **Root** fix firmly, implant deeply (*v.*1, OED[3] 7b).

11, 12 **pity. . . pitied** In early modern love poetry, 'pity' frequently meant sexual favour; see 132.12 and note.

13 **what. . . hide** i.e. pity, which the addressee 'hide[s]', i.e. refuses to show.

14 **self-example** your own example.
mayst thou (i) I hope that you (optative); (ii) you might (hypothetical).
denied denied pity.

142

Love is my sin, and thy dear virtue hate,
Hate of my sin, grounded on sinful loving.
O, but with mine compare thou thine own state
And thou shalt find it merits not reproving,   4
Or if it do, not from those lips of thine
That have profaned their scarlet ornaments
And sealed false bonds of love as oft as mine,
Robbed others' beds' revenues of their rents.   8
Be 't lawful I love thee as thou lov'st those
Whom thine eyes woo as mine importune thee;
Root pity in thy heart that, when it grows,
Thy pity may deserve to pitied be.   12
    If thou dost seek to have what thou dost hide,
    By self-example mayst thou be denied.

143

Printed by Benson as a single sonnet entitled 'An allusion'.

1 *careful* (i) anxious (OED 2); (ii) attentive (OED 4a); modernising Q's 'carefull' diminishes some of the force of this play on words.
   housewife The early modern pronunciation is reflected in Q's spelling ('huswife'); compare the Folio spelling at *As You Like It*, 1.2.31. Whilst the primary meaning is household manager (OED³ 1), the mistress' dubious morals mean that secondary sense of 'disreputable woman [...], hussy' is also pertinent (OED 2).

2 *feathered creatures* domestic fowl, probably hens; Kerrigan (1986: 374) and Booth (1977: 494) also suggest that the phrase evokes Elizabethan dandies, wearing fashionable feathered hats (figuring the rivals of whom the poet-speaker is jealous), but the allusion is not necessary: the extended conceit is clearly about chasing domesticated fowls (a mock-heroic scaling down of the conventional motif of love as a hunt; see 129.6n).
   broke away that has broken away (from the rest of the flock) or escaped (from an enclosure).

3 *all swift dispatch* the greatest possible speed; since 'dispatch' means haste (OED 6b), 'swift' is pleonastic (for emphasis).

4 *pursuit* stressed on the first syllable.

5 *holds. . . chase* chases after her.

6 *bent* directed, intent on; turned (i.e. away from the child).

7 *flies. . . face* flees just before her, but also flapping about just above the ground, at face level with someone who is stooping to catch them, as chickens do when trying unsuccessfully to get airborne.

8 *Not prizing* not caring about.

10 *thy babe* For the comparison of the poet-speaker to a child, see Greville, *Caelica* (composed *c.* 1590),

42.13–14 ('I, like the child, whom Nurse hath overthrown, | Not crying, yet am whipped, if you be known') and 60.5, where the frustrated lover is like 'the child in swaddling bands' (*Works*, 1633: sigs 2D3v, 2F2v).

11 *if. . . hope* 'if you get what you want' (i.e. other lovers, in particular the friend); 'hope' is here the object hoped for (*n.*1, OED 4c).

12 *play. . . part* act as a mother should; but, as Blakemore Evans points out, 'in terms of common theatrical idiom, [...] the phrase suggests that she should at least "play the role of a mother" even if she is only acting a "part"' (1996: 261).
   be kind be 'gentle' or 'favourably disposed to' ('kind, *adj.*', OED 5, 5b); behave naturally (OED 1a), i.e. as mother should treat her child; be 'sexually compliant' (OED 6).

13 *have* possess; enjoy sexually; for the sexual connotations of 'have', see 129.6, 10n.
   Will as in Sonnets 135 and 136, italicised and capitalised in Q, suggesting a proper name, and punning on the meaning of will as 'desire' ('I'll pray that you get Will, who is the one you desire'). As in 135.11, there is a hint that the poet-speaker and rival lover (the friend) are both called William. Here, in order to win the mistress' attention, the poet-speaker is prepared to say that he wishes that she may possess the other man whom she pursues; of course, if she does 'turn back' to kiss the poet-speaker, she will be forced to leave off chasing the other man, at least temporarily. The argument is also casuistry: the poet-speaker is not lying when he promises to 'pray that [she] mayst have [her] Will', it is just that he will really pray that she might have him, rather than the other object of her desire (will) who may or may not be also called Will. As at 135.1, the line evokes the proverb 'Women will have their wills' (Dent W723).

14 *still* quieten; see Breton's poem (l. 3), cited in the headnote to Sonnet 135.

143

Lo, as a careful housewife runs to catch
One of her feathered creatures broke away,
Sets down her babe and makes all swift dispatch
In pursuit of the thing she would have stay,   4
Whilst her neglected child holds her in chase,
Cries to catch her whose busy care is bent
To follow that which flies before her face,
Not prizing her poor infant's discontent;   8
So runn'st thou after that which flies from thee,
Whilst I, thy babe, chase thee afar behind;
But if thou catch thy hope, turn back to me
And play the mother's part: kiss me, be kind.   12
    So will I pray that thou mayst have thy Will,
    If thou turn back and my loud crying still.

144

Printed by Benson, as a single sonnet entitled 'A temptation', from the 1612 edition of *The Passionate Pilgrim*.

A version of this sonnet and of Sonnet 138 were first printed in 1599 in *The Passionate Pilgrim* (see Appendix 3). Most commentators read this sonnet as referring to the same situation as in Sonnets 40–42, a love triangle that also features in 133–134; J.Q. Adams (see Rollins 1944: 1.370) suggests that this sonnet is imitated by Samuel Rowlands in *The Letting of Humours' Blood*, Epigram 15:

> Amorous Austin spends much balleting,
> In rhyming letters and love sonneting.
> She that loves him, his inkhorn shall bepaint her,
> And with all Venus' titles he'll acquaint her,
> Vowing she is a perfect angel right,
> When she by weight is many grains too light.
> Nay, all that do but touch her with the stone
> Will be deposed that angel she is none.
> How can he prove her for an angel then,
> That proves herself a devil, tempting men,
> And draweth many to the fiery pit,
> Where they are burned for their entering it?
> I know no cause wherefore he terms her so,
> Unless he means she's one of them below,
> Where Lucifer, chief Prince, doth domineer.
> If she be such, then, good my hearts, stand clear;
> Come not within the compass of her flight,
> For such as do are haunted with a spright.
> This angel is not noted by her wings
> But by her tail, as full of pricks and stings;
> And know this lust-blind lover's vein is led
> To praise his devil in an angel's stead. (1600: sig. B3r)

At the very least, as Duncan-Jones points out (1997a: 404), Rowlands' epigram, Sonnet 144, and the sections of *King Lear* (cited at 129.14n) 'all draw on a shared traditional association of the female genitalia with a fiery "hell"'. Drayton also plays on the dichotomy between angelic and diabolic spirits in *Idea*, 22.14, but there it is the mistress who embodies both contrarieties: 'this good wicked spirit, sweet angel devil' (1599: sig. P7v).

1   **Two loves** two lovers, who bring two kinds of love.
     comfort As Ingram and Redpath note (1985: 330), 'modern usages seem to have lost the etymological element of *support*, present, for instance, in Psalm 23:4' ('thy rod and thy staff, they comfort me'). God is recurrently depicted as a source of 'comfort' (Psalm 71:21, 86:17 and Isaiah 49:13, 51:3 are just some of many such references; see also John 14.16–26 for the depiction of Christ and the Holy Ghost as 'comforters' sent by God). As comfort is contrasted with '*despair*' – a sin, since to lack hope is to manifest a failure to believe in God (see Spenser, *Faerie Queene*, I.ix.37–51) – the opening line introduces the religious idiom that becomes more firmly established from l. 3 onwards.

2   **spirits** unearthly beings, often 'conceived as troublesome, terrifying, or hostile to mankind' (OED 3a); the stage directions in the 1616 text of Christopher Marlowe's *Faustus* rename the 'Good Angel' and 'Bad Angel' of the 1604 text 'Angel' and 'Spirit' (where the choice of noun alone provides adequate differentiation between the two).
     suggest 'prompt (a person) to evil; [...] tempt *to* or *to do* something' (OED 2a); compare *Merry Wives*, 3.3.215–16 ('What spirit, what devil suggests this imagination?'); *Richard II*, 3.4.75: 'What Eve, what serpent hath suggested thee[?]'.
     still continually; even now.

3–7 **better... devil** These lines initially seem to suggest a conventional situation from morality drama (such as that explored, and tested, in Marlowe's *Doctor Faustus*, 1.1) in which good and bad supernatural forces compete to persuade the protagonist (here, the poet-speaker) to act in some way. See also Henry Porter, *The Two Angry Women of Abington*: 'They say every man hath two spirits attending on him, either good or bad' (1599: sig. E4r). In this sonnet, the narrative takes an unexpected turn in l. 6, since it is not the protagonist who falls prey to temptation, but the 'better angel'; perhaps as readers we should have been alerted to the unconventional nature of this encounter by the use of the comparative ('better'), which betrays the fact that the moral qualities described are relative, rather than absolute (as would be expected of an angel), although see quotation from *Othello*, l. 3n (below).

3   **better angel** The man is here detached from the negative associations of 'spirit' (see l. 2n) and is instead connected with angels (who carry predominantly positive connotations). Compare *Othello*, 5.2.207–10: 'This sight would make him do a desperate turn, | Yea, curse his better angel from his side, | And fall to reprobance'.

144

Two loves I have, of comfort and despair,
Which like two spirits do suggest me still:
The better angel is a man right fair,
The worser spirit a woman coloured ill.   4
To win me soon to hell, my female evil
Tempteth my better angel from my side
And would corrupt my saint to be a devil,
Wooing his purity with her foul pride.   8
And whether that my angel be turned fiend
Suspect I may, yet not directly tell,
But being both from me, both to each friend,
I guess one angel in another's hell.   12
    Yet this shall I ne'er know, but live in doubt,
    Till my bad angel fire my good one out.

right fair very beautiful and/or very blonde.

4 *spirit* here pronounced as one syllable; see 56.8n.

coloured ill of dark complexion; see Sonnets 127, 130.

5 *hell* place of suffering.

5, 7 *evil. . . devil* This rhyme pair is fairly common in Shakespeare's works, appearing in *Love's Labours Lost* (4.3.282–4, 5.2.105–6), *Twelfth Night*, 3.4.369–70, and five times in *Lucrece* (ll. 85–7, 846–7, 972–3, 1245–6, 1513–15); for the rhyme, see Appendix 7.

6 *side* Q here reads 'sight'; this is either (i) left over from an uncorrected, earlier draft, or (ii) a compositorial error (although it is difficult to see how a 'd', which has an ascender, might be read as a 'gh' ligature, both of which – in a secretary hand – have distinct descenders). Most editors adopt *Passionate Pilgrim*'s 'side' in order to make the full rhyme with 'pride' (Lintott, retaining Q's 'sight', is a rare exception). Shakespeare nowhere uses –ide/-ight in a rhyming position. The occasional appearance of an -ide/-ight within blank verse (e.g. *All's Well*, 2.5.25–6; *Titus Andronicus*, 4.2.125–6) would suggest that Shakespeare did not regard this as a viable rhyme, a position further strengthened by the appearance of -ide/-ight rhymes in positions where they are clearly meant to contrast with each other (e.g. *Midsummer Night's Dream*,

3.2.185–8, 5.1.379–81; *Lucrece*, ll. 484–8; Sonnet 139.5–8).

7 *my saint* the good angel (i.e. the man); saints are not usually synonymous with angels, but the exact theology is less important than (i) associating the man with positive religious imagery; (ii) finding a word that does that which fits metrically (one syllable is needed).

8 *foul* For the association of this word with the mistress, see 137.12n.

pride (i) arrogant behaviour (*n*.1, OED³ 2); (ii) ostentatious display (of the mistress' beauty) (OED³ 6a); (iii) 'sexual desire, esp. in a female animal' (OED³ 11); compare *Othello*, 3.3.403–4: 'Were they [women] as prime as goats, as hot as monkeys, | As salt as wolves in pride'. As the sin which caused Lucifer's fall (Isaiah 14:12–15), pride was often seen as the most heinous of the seven deadly sins; see, for example, Spenser, *Faerie Queene*, I.iv.18–35, where the other six deadly sins are Lucifera's counsellors in the House of Pride.

9 *whether that* whether or not.

10 *Suspect I may* 'I may be suspicious'; l. 10 echoes the proverb 'suspicion is no proof' (Dent S1019).

directly (i) 'straightforwardly' (OED 1b); (ii) 'completely[. . .], precisely' (OED 4); (iii) 'immediately' (OED 5).

tell know (OED 7b).

11 **But. . .friend** Both the woman and man are absent from the poet-speaker ('*from me*'), and both are friends (i.e. lovers, OED³ A6) to each other.

12 **hell** slang for vagina; see 129.14n and Rowland's epigram in the headnote above. A number of commentators also find here a reference to the game of barley-break (see Rollins 1944: 1.371), often regarded as a preamble to, and pretext for, sexual intimacy. Ringler describes the game as follows: 'In the country game of barley-break the two couples at either end attempt to change partners without being caught by the couple in the middle (called hell). The couple in the middle must hold hands while chasing the others, and if they catch any one member of an opposing couple before they meet as partners, that pair must take their place in hell' (Sidney 1962: 495, glossing Sidney's 'A shepherd's tale', ll. 208–416, which describes a game of barley-break).

13 **know** know for sure; l. 13 reiterates l. 10.

14 **Till. . . out** (i) until the woman (the '**bad angel**') drives away the male friend, propelling him into the hell of despair experienced by a rejected lover; (ii) until the woman repulses the friend's penis from the 'hell' of her vagina; (iii) the allusion to heat also suggests venereal disease (see also Sonnets 153–154), i.e. the poet-speaker will find proof of the friend's liaison with the mistress once the young man contracts venereal disease from her. Commentators often find an allusion to smoking out animals from their lair, as in *King Lear*, 5.3.22–3: 'He that parts us shall bring a brand from heaven, | And fire us hence like foxes'. However, in order for this analogy to work it would need to be the poet-speaker doing the 'fir[ing. . .] out', not – as here – the 'bad angel'.

144

Two loves I have, of comfort and despair,
Which like two spirits do suggest me still:
The better angel is a man right fair,
The worser spirit a woman coloured ill.   4
To win me soon to hell, my female evil
Tempteth my better angel from my side
And would corrupt my saint to be a devil,
Wooing his purity with her foul pride.   8
And whether that my angel be turned fiend
Suspect I may, yet not directly tell,
But being both from me, both to each friend,
I guess one angel in another's hell.   12
    Yet this shall I ne'er know, but live in doubt,
    Till my bad angel fire my good one out.

145

Printed by Benson as a single sonnet entitled 'Life and death'.

The only octosyllabic sonnet in Q; its authorship by Shakespeare has been challenged (e.g. Pooler 1931), and its quality derided: 'These trivial octosyllables scarcely deserve reprinting', Ingram and Redpath declare (1985: 334). More recent editors generally follow Gurr (1971) in regarding this as an early work. The order of sonnet sequences does not necessarily reflect the order of composition and, as Kerrigan notes (1986: 376) in the case of 145, 'thematic links with what precedes and what follows the poem in Q are evident: *fiend, heaven,* and *hell* in lines 11–12 help it blend into context'. He further suggests that its position in the sequence is authorial, arguing that 'whoever located it between 144 and 146 had a knowledge of the sequence superior to anything that the average scribe (who gets to know a text while copying) or compositor – who reads while printing, having already "cast off" or allotted the material to particular pages (an arrangement not easily altered once printing begins) – might be likely to possess' (376-7).

1   ***Love's own hand*** with the hand of either Cupid or Venus; the implication is that the woman is so beautiful that she must have had divine help; compare 20.1.

1–4   ***make. . . state*** As Blakemore Evans notes, 'the first quatrain has been criticised for its monosyllabic rhymes, all rhyming on the vowel sound, an infelicity that has been seen as another indication of early work. Perhaps so, but the same kind of vowel repetition in monosyllabic rhymes, though rare, may be paralleled elsewhere in the Sonnets' (1996: 264); see, for example, 9.1–4; 12.1–4.

2, 9, 13   ***'I hate'*** The quotation marks are editorial.

3   ***languished. . . sake*** pined because of her; compare Oberon's charm in *Midsummer Night's Dream*, 2.2.27–9: 'What thou seest when thou dost wake, | Do it for thy true-love take; | Love and languish for his sake'.

6–7   ***Chiding. . . doom*** Mercy reproves the woman's tongue, which has usually been kind ('***ever sweet***') or melodious ('sweet, *adj.*', OED 4a), giving mild judgement ('***gentle doom***'); for the use of 'doom' to mean 'judgement', compare *Lucrece*, l. 1849.

10–11   ***followed. . . night*** Compare the proverb 'After night comes the day' (Dent N164); see also Polonius' use of this commonplace at *Hamlet*, 1.3.79.

12   ***heaven*** pronounced as one syllable.

13   ***hate away*** possibly a pun on Hathaway; Shakespeare married the pregnant Ann Hathaway in 1582, when he was 18 and she was 26.

14   ***And*** Booth (1977: 501) suggests a play on 'Ann' ('and' can be pronounced 'an', without sounding the final *-d*).

'not you' The speech marks are editorial.

145

Those lips that Love's own hand did make
Breathed forth the sound that said 'I hate'
To me that languished for her sake;
But when she saw my woeful state,   4
Straight in her heart did mercy come,
Chiding that tongue, that ever sweet
Was used in giving gentle doom,
And taught it thus anew to greet: 8
'I hate' she altered with an end
That followed it as gentle day
Doth follow night, who like a fiend
From heaven to hell is flown away.   12
    'I hate' from hate away she threw
    And saved my life, saying 'not you'.

146

Printed by Benson as a single sonnet entitled 'A consideration of death'.

Sonnet 146 belongs to the literary tradition of debates between soul and body; compare Francis Davison, 'A Dialogue between the Soul the Body' in *A Poetical Rhapsody* (1602), which begins with the Soul's lament ('Ay me, poor Soul, whom bound in sinful chains | This wretched body keeps against my will!', sig. I12r), or Bartholomew Griffin, *Fidessa* (1596), Sonnet 28: 'Well may my soul, immortal and divine, | That is imprisoned in a lump of clay, | Breathe out laments, until this body pine, | That from her takes her pleasures all away' (sig. C6v). Like many of those poems, Sonnet 146 is infused with Pauline idiom from the New Testament, from those passages in which St Paul discusses the proper relationship between the body and soul and the need to restrain fleshly appetites in order to nurture the spirit. See, for example, Romans 7:22–4: 'I delight in the law of God, concerning the inner man. But I see another law in my members [limbs], rebelling against the law of my mind, and leading me captive unto the law of sin, which is in my members. O wretched man that I am, who shall deliver me from the body of this death?'. The sonnet has traditionally been read as expressing orthodox Christian values: it even appeared, set to music, in the 1926 edition of *Songs of Praise* (p. 746). Later twentieth-century criticism has found a greater degree of ambiguity, however, or even ambivalence in its treatment of Christian doctrine (on the latter, see Southam 1960). As Vendler observes, 'The gloominess of this sonnet has little of the radiance of Christian hope' (1997: 614).

1 ***Poor soul*** the addressee of the sonnet; the possession of a soul was believed to distinguish humans from the rest of God's creation; see Genesis 2:7: 'The Lord God also made the man of the dust of the ground, and breathed in his face breath of life, and the man was a living soul'. ***Poor***: deserving of pity, but also – in light of 'dearth' in l. 3 – punning on 'impoverished'.
the centre. . . earth 'earth' works both literally – indicating the human body (*n*.1, OED 14; see *Lucrece*, l. 487 and note) – and metaphorically. 'Centre' could be read as (i) at the mid-point of that microcosm ('centre, *n*.', OED A1b, citing this line); (ii) as the stable point around which the earth spins (OED 4); or (iii) the point to which things are attracted (OED 6b), as in *Troilus*

and Cressida, 4.2.103–5: 'The strong base and building of my love, | Is as the very centre of the earth, | Drawing all things to it'. For a similar conjunction of 'earth' and 'centre', see *Romeo and Juliet*, 2.1.2 ('Turn back, dull earth, and find thy centre out'), where Romeo's body is the 'dull earth' and Juliet the 'centre' attracting him.

2 [   ] Q has 'My sinful earth', a repetition of the end of l. 1, an error, since it makes the line uncharacteristically hypermetrical (comprising twelve syllables rather than ten). Emending editors, searching for a two-syllable phrase to substitute, tend to follow one of three metaphors:

  (i) trickery: e.g. 'Fooled by' (Malone), 'Gulled by' (Seymour-Smith), 'Foiled by' (Ingram and Redpath); Ricks (2003: 145n) – an article on wordplay in *Shakespeare's Sonnets* – follows Quentin Skinner's suggestion of 'Tricked by', as a phrase which puns on the imagery of both deception and clothing (trick = 'to dress, array' (OED 5a), as in *Hamlet*, 2.2.457–8: 'horridly tricked | With blood of fathers');
  (ii) consumption, linking with the imagery of ll. 3–8: e.g. 'Feeding' (Duncan-Jones, following Vendler), 'Starved by' (Steevens);
  (iii) battle: e.g. 'Leagued with' (Hudson), 'Pressed by' (Dowden), 'Hemmed with' (Furnivall), 'Spoiled by' (Burrow). This last alternative manages to pick up on the imagery of both military attack (l. 2) and decomposition (ll. 6ff), and has precedent in *Lucrece*, l. 1172.

However, any emendation is necessarily conjecture: it therefore seems more appropriate to leave the corrupted foot blank.
rebel powers rebellious forces, namely the flesh (the body) that encloses the soul and which brings with it earthbound qualities (i.e. passions) which distract the soul from more spiritual affairs. Compare Samuel Daniel, *Cleopatra*, 5.2: 'And sharply blaming of her rebel powers, | "False flesh" (sayeth she), "and what dost thou conspire | With Caesar too?"' (1594: sig. N4v). See also 'rebel will', *Lucrece*, l. 625. 'Powers': here pronounced as one syllable.
array Whilst the dominant meaning of array here is 'dress' (OED 8), the juxtaposition with

146

Poor soul, the centre of my sinful earth,
[   ] these rebel powers that thee array,
Why dost thou pine within and suffer dearth,
Painting thy outward walls so costly gay?   4
Why so large cost, having so short a lease,
Dost thou upon thy fading mansion spend?
Shall worms, inheritors of this excess,
Eat up thy charge? Is this thy body's end?   8
Then, soul, live thou upon thy servant's loss
And let that pine to aggravate thy store;
Buy terms divine in selling hours of dross;
Within be fed, without be rich no more: 12
   So shalt thou feed on Death, that feeds on men,
   And Death once dead, there's no more dying then.

the military image of 'rebel powers' means that the word retains some of its primary sense of drawing up ready for battle (OED 1).

3 **pine** starve, waste away (OED³ 3a, 4a).
dearth lack of food (OED 3a).

3–6 **Why. . . spend?** 'Why do you lavish so much on outward appearance when you are spiritually bankrupt and when you will actually occupy your increasingly decrepit [*fading*] body for so short a time?' The allusion to the proper management of an estate and family seat recalls the first seventeen sonnets, especially 13. For the futility of 'costly' expenditure in a transient world, subject to time, see 64.2.

4 **Painting. . . gay** In this line, the soul is not – as in ll. 1–2 – merely the victim of the 'rebel powers' that assault it, but is here made complicit with its own situation, since it is responsible for adorning the body ('thy outward walls') with extravagant display. For the negative connotations of (i) 'painting', see 21.2, 67.5, 82.13, 83.1–2 and notes; and (ii) 'gay', see 68.8n.
costly (i) with great expense; (ii) 'involving loss or sacrifice' (OED A1b), i.e. the detriment caused by this display is not necessarily simply financial; compare the play on 'dear' in 37.3, 42.2, 117.6 and notes.

5 **so large cost** such great expense.
so short a lease continues the metaphor of the house begun in l. 3; the soul will only occupy

the body for a short amount of time; it is therefore foolish to lavish expenditure upon it. For Shakespeare's use of 'lease', see 13.5n.

6 **fading mansion** the body; compare *Lucrece*, ll. 1170–2.
spend (i) expend; (ii) waste, squander.

7 **worms. . . excess** evokes the conventional idea that, after death, our bodies are consumed by worms (compare 6.14, 71.4, 74.10), underscoring the futility of all the extravagance ('excess') bestowed on the body.

8 **charge** (i) 'expense' (*n*.1, OED 10a); (ii) 'responsibility' (OED 12); possibly also used in the sense of 'burden [. . .] (of trouble, inconvenience, etc.)' (OED 8a).
end (i) fate (end of life); (ii) 'purpose' (OED 14a). The orthodox response to the question 'Is this thy body's end?' should be 'no', since it was believed that the body and soul would be reunited on the day of judgement; see 1 Corinthians 15.20–58, which also formed part of the Burial Service in the *Book of Common Prayer* (2011: 172–3).

9 **live. . . loss** (i) 'nourish yourself on what you have previously squandered on your body' ('thy servant'); (ii) 'nourish yourself by reflecting on the imminent loss of the body' (such mental preparations for death were seen as good spiritual practice).

10 **that** the body (refers to 'thy servant', l. 9).

pine 'starve' (OED³ 3a); compare *Love's Labours Lost*, 1.1.25: 'The mind shall banquet, though the body pine'.

aggravate 'increase' (OED³ 5).

store 'sufficient or abundant supply', 'plenty' (OED 4a, 4b).

11 *Buy terms divine* 'Purchase eternal life' (where 'terms' indicates 'portion[s] of time', OED 4a); the advice concurs with that in Matthew 6:20: 'But lay up treasures for yourselves in heaven, where neither the moth nor canker corrupteth, and where thieves neither dig through, nor steal'. An alternative interpretation put forward by some editors (e.g. Booth), where the soul is encouraged to secure favourable contractual terms from God, seems less likely, since the notion of making a deal with God is doctrinally presumptuous.

dross scum; worthless, impure pleasures (OED 1, 4); compare *Merchant of Venice*, 2.7.20: 'A golden mind stoops not to shows of dross'.

12 *Within. . . without* inside (i.e. spiritually). . . outside (i.e. in appearance).

rich splendidly dressed (see OED³ A5a).

13 *feed. . . men* Compare Psalm 49:14: 'death shall feed on them' (KJV).

14 *And. . . then* echoes 1 Corinthians 15:26 ('The last enemy that shall be destroyed is death') and 15:54 ('Death is swallowed up into victory'), passages included in the service for the Burial for the Dead from the *Book of Common Prayer* (2011: 172–3). This idea is also found in John Donne, 'Death, be not proud' (1609–10), l. 14: 'Death, thou shalt die'.

146

Poor soul, the centre of my sinful earth,
[   ] these rebel powers that thee array,
Why dost thou pine within and suffer dearth,
Painting thy outward walls so costly gay?   4
Why so large cost, having so short a lease,
Dost thou upon thy fading mansion spend?
Shall worms, inheritors of this excess,
Eat up thy charge? Is this thy body's end?   8
Then, soul, live thou upon thy servant's loss
And let that pine to aggravate thy store;
Buy terms divine in selling hours of dross;
Within be fed, without be rich no more: 12
    So shalt thou feed on Death, that feeds on men,
    And Death once dead, there's no more dying then.

147

Printed by Benson as a single sonnet entitled 'Immoderate passion'.

1 *fever* The sonnet is a sustained metaphor whereby love is imagined as sickness (both physical and mental). As such, the sonnet shares some of the imagery, and concerns, of 118, 119 and 129. Describing love as an illness was a common motif of amorous verse. See, for example, Gynecia's lament in Sidney's *Old Arcadia* ('Like those sick folks'), ll. 7–8: 'Bitter grief tastes me best, pain is my ease | Sick to the death, still loving my disease'.
still incessantly.

1–2 *longing. . . longer nurseth* The poet-speaker craves something which will protract his sickness; the perverse nature of this desire is emphasised by the *polyptoton* of 'longing' and 'longer'.
nurseth nourishes.

2, 3 *that which* the poet-speaker's desire ('love') for his mistress.

3 *ill* disease, evil.

4 *Th' uncertain sickly appetite* the fitful appetite of someone who is ill.

5–12 *My reason. . . expressed* Compare 129.6–9.

6 *prescriptions* physician's instructions (OED 2).

7 *desperate* 'despairing' (OED 1a); a stronger word than in modern usage, since despair is a condition which arises when someone has lost faith in God and is a condition strongly associated with self-slaughter; see, for example, *Lucrece*, ll. 739, 1038, and its recurrent use by, or about, the suicidal protagonists of *Romeo and Juliet* – the play in which the word appears most within Shakespeare's works – where it occurs at 3.3.108 ('Hold thy desperate hand'), 4.3.54 ('Dash out my desperate brains'), 5.1.36 ('the thoughts of desperate men'), 5.3.59 ('tempt not a desperate man'), 5.3.117–18 ('Thou desperate pilot, now at once run on | The dashing rocks thy sea-sick weary bark'), 5.3.263 ('She, too desperate, would not go with me'). 'Desperate': here pronounced as two syllables.
approve 'prove', 'find by experience' (*v*.1, OED 1, 9): the poet-speaker is both demonstrating this for others and discovering this for himself. For the idea that the poet-speaker's experience demonstrates a truth or provides a lesson, see also 136.7 and the controversial l. 11 in 129.

8 *Desire. . . except* 'Desire, which was forbidden ['except'] on doctor's orders, is fatal'; for the dangers of desire, see Romans 8:6: 'For the wisdom of the flesh is death'.

9 *Past cure. . . past care* invokes the proverb 'Past cure past care' (Dent C921). In Sonnet 147, however, it is the poet-speaker's reason which has given up caring, leaving the poet-speaker without a remedy, so rather than evoking a sense of (peaceful?) resignation, the line conveys instead a sense of abandonment. See also *Love's Labours Lost*, 5.2.28: 'past care is still past cure'.
now now that.

10 *And . . . unrest,* Some editors, following Capell, place a semi-colon at the end of this line (in place of Q's comma), making ll. 9–10 and 11–12 separate utterances, rather than – as here – one sentence, in which 'frantic mad with ever more unrest' is a parenthetical comment, qualifying and introducing 'my thoughts and my discourse' (l. 11).
frantic mad Q has 'madde', a feasible early modern spelling of both 'made' and 'mad', making 'frantic made' a possible reading; however, the spelling of 'mad' favoured by Compositor B, who probably set this sonnet (see Jackson 1975) is 'madde' (Q140.9, 12 (twice)), whereas 'made' is invariably spelled, by both compositors, with a single 'd' ('made'). The primary meaning of 'frantic' is 'insane' (OED A1); in part, the phrase typifies Shakespeare's use of *pleonasm* for emphasis (compare 'false forgeries' in *Passionate Pilgrim*, 1.4, Appendix 3); however, 'frantic' also indicates a particular type of mad excitement (OED A2a). This line is cited by OED as the first instance of 'frantic' as quasi-adverbial (OED A4).
evermore (i) continually increasing; (ii) perpetual.
unrest echoes the proverb 'Desire has no rest' (Dent D211).

11 *discourse* conversation.

12 *At. . . expressed* wandering haphazardly ('at random') from the truth and articulating all this ineffectually ('vainly'). Derived from the Old French 'randon' (meaning force or rapid movement), 'random' shares characteristics with 'frantic', and in *1 Henry VI*, random speech is also associated with madness: 'He talks at randon; sure the man is mad' (5.3.85). '*Vainly expressed*' could qualify 'truth' or 'thoughts and [. . .] discourse'.

147

My love is as a fever, longing still
For that which longer nurseth the disease,
Feeding on that which doth preserve the ill,
Th' uncertain sickly appetite to please.   4
My reason, the physician to my love,
Angry that his prescriptions are not kept,
Hath left me, and I desperate now approve
Desire is death, which physic did except.   8
Past cure I am, now reason is past care,
And, frantic mad with evermore unrest,
My thoughts and my discourse as madmen's are,
At random from the truth, vainly expressed: 12
   For I have sworn thee fair and thought thee bright,
   Who art as black as hell, as dark as night.

13 *fair* beautiful (despite the mistress' dark complexion); the poet-speaker challenges the association between beauty and a fair complexion in Sonnets 127, 130 and 132; see also 152.13–14.
bright 'beautiful' (OED A3), but – used here in distinction to darkness – it also contains a sense of moral worth.

14 *black. . . night* The line draws on two proverbs: (i) 'black (dark) as hell' (Dent H397); see *Love's Labours Lost*: 'Black is the badge of hell' (4.3.250); (ii) 'dark as night' (Dent N164.1). In 140.9–10, the poet-speaker threatens to speak ill of his mistress if she drives him mad with despair. If the sonnets are read sequentially, in Q's order, that threat is realised in this sonnet.

148

Benson combines Sonnets 148–150 under the title 'Love's powerful subtlety'.

1 *O me!* The exclamation mark is in Q (one of ten in the volume; see 92.12n).

1–4 *what. . . aright?* The sonnet revisits the idea (also found in Sonnets 137, 147, 149–150, 152) that love (or desire) has distorted the poet-speaker's judgement; like Cupid, who is often figured as blind, the poet-speaker's eyesight is compromised. Q does not capitalise 'love', but it is possible to read 'love' as the god of love in this sonnet.

2 *no correspondence. . . sight* What the poet-speaker sees bears no relation to what is really there.

3 *where. . . fled* Compare 147.5–7.

4 *censures* judges (OED 1); in the late sixteenth/early seventeenth centuries, the word did not have the pejorative connotations that dominate its modern usage.
falsely (i) untruthfully (OED 1); (ii) erroneously (OED 2); (iii) treacherously (OED 4).

5 *that* the mistress.
fair (i) beautiful (OED³ A1); (ii) free from moral imperfections (OED³ 12).
dote have excessive or foolish affection for; see 20.10n.

6 *the world* people in general, public opinion (OED³ 14).

7 *denote* 'indicate (a fact, state of things, etc.)' (OED 3).

8 *true* (i) 'reliable' (OED 1d); (ii) 'representing the thing as it is' (OED 3a); like 'falsely' (l. 4), the word has connotations of both accuracy and honesty.
all men's: no Q's punctuation (followed here) places a strong caesura late in the line, which

is unusual in *Shakespeare's Sonnets*. Along with the loss of a potential pun, in which 'love's eye/ ay' is contrasted with 'all men's no', this has led some editors (e.g. Kerrigan) to follow Lettsom's suggestion in Dyce 1857 (672) and to alter the punctuation so that the line reads 'Love's eye is not so true as all men's "no"'.

10 *vexed* (i) troubled ('vex, v.', OED 1a); (ii) afflicted (OED 2); a stronger word than in modern usage, see 92.9n.
watching 'wakefulness; often, wakefulness from disinclination or incapacity for sleep' (OED 2). Love is often associated with insomnia in amorous verse; see, for example, Sonnet 27 and Humfrey Gifford's description of stereotypical lovers who 'toss in restless bed, | With hammers working in their head' ('A renouncing of love', in *A Posy of Gillyflowers* (1580), sig. K4v).

11 *No marvel* It is not surprising; see *Venus and Adonis*, l. 390.
I Bearing in mind the focus on eyesight in this sonnet, the pronoun invokes the homophone 'eye'.

12 *The sun. . . clears* Even the sun is obscured until the clouds dissipate; the sun is frequently referred to as 'the eye of heaven' in early modern poetry and drama, an idea that lies behind this line (see, for example, 18.5; *Richard II*, 3.2.37–8: 'when the searching eye of heaven is hid | Behind the globe, that lights the lower world').

13 *cunning* (i) 'skilful' (OED 2a); (ii) 'crafty, [. . .] sly' (OED 5a).
love here suggests both Cupid and the manipulative mistress.

14 *eyes well-seeing* eyes which can see properly ('aright', l. 4).
foul The word is recurrently used to describe the mistress and contains both aesthetic and moral failings; see 137.12n.

148

O me! what eyes hath love put in my head,
Which have no correspondence with true sight,
Or if they have, where is my judgement fled
That censures falsely what they see aright? 4
If that be fair whereon my false eyes dote,
What means the world to say it is not so?
If it be not, then love doth well denote
Love's eye is not so true as all men's: no, 8
How can it? O, how can love's eye be true
That is so vexed with watching and with tears?
No marvel then though I mistake my view:
The sun itself sees not till heaven clears. 12
   O cunning love, with tears thou keep'st me blind,
   Lest eyes well-seeing thy foul faults should find.

149

Benson combines Sonnets 148–150 under the title 'Love's powerful subtlety'.

1 ***O cruel*** the mistress; Petrarchan mistresses are conventionally described as cruel (see 131.2n). Burrow notes (2002: 678) that this is the first time within Q's sequence that this adjective is used explicitly and specifically of the mistress, although the word has been brought recurrently into play from Sonnet 131 onwards (see also 133.5, 140.1). As Burrow states, the only time the friend is accused of being cruel is in 1.8, where he is told not to be cruel to himself. Where 'cruel' is used elsewhere in the sonnets to, or about, the young man, it is used to describe the effects of time (60.14, 63.10).

2 ***partake*** 'take sides' (OED³ 1a); compare 88.3 and 89.13–14, where the poet-speaker takes sides with the young man, against his own interests.

3–4 ***Do. . . sake?*** The punctuation followed here is that in Q; punctuated thus, these lines suggest that love for another results in alienation of the self (see also 133.5 and note) and that, because of his infatuation with the mistress, the poet-speaker has become a surrogate tyrant, masochistically torturing himself. Malone puts commas around 'all tyrant', making it a vocative, addressing the mistress. As Kerrigan suggests (1986: 382), it is also possible to read 'forgot' (l. 3) parenthetically ('forgotten by the mistress'). Q's punctuation has been retained, however, since the reading is both coherent and consistent with conceptions of love/desire expressed both within *Shakespeare's Sonnets* and early modern amorous verse more generally.

5 ***Who*** who is there who?

5–6 ***Who. . . upon?*** Compare *Henry VIII*, 2.4.29–34: 'which of your friends | Have I not strove to love, although I knew | He were mine enemy? What friend of mine | That had to him derived your anger did I | Continue in my liking?'

7 ***lour'st*** 'scowls, looks sullen' (OED 1a); compare *Venus and Adonis*, l. 75.

7–8 ***spend | Revenge upon myself*** punish myself; 'spend' can imply waste, squander (*v.*1, OED 10a), i.e. the poet-speaker's self-punishment

has been futile, since he remains enthralled to his mistress. Booth (1977: 523) calls the phrase 'most unidiomatic'; Burrow (2002: 678) draws out a *double entendre* on 'spend' (to mean 'ejaculate', OED 15c), particularly when placed in proximity to moan: understood thus, the poet-speaker protests his love by pointing out that even when she is angry, he is still capable of reaching orgasm, which can be seen as inflicting revenge upon himself since it was believed every orgasm shortened one's life-span (see 6.4n). The first citation in OED for 'spend' as 'ejaculate' is 1662; however, the extension of the earlier meaning – 'suffer the loss of (blood, life)' (OED 6a) – to include bodily fluids such as semen was clearly in use before the late seventeenth century; see, for example, Nashe's depiction of premature ejaculation in *The Choice of Valentines* (*c.* 1592): 'Her arms are spread, and I am all unarmed | Like one with Ovid's cursed hemlock charmed, | So are my limbs unwieldy for the fight, | That spend their strength in thought of her delight' (ll. 123–6). Compare 4.1–2; 129.1.

8 ***present*** immediate (OED³ A9a).

9–11 ***What. . . defect*** This excessive self-abjection ('is there anything that I value about myself that is so proud that it scorns to serve you?') is tempered by the poet-speaker's insistence that it is her 'defect' that he adores; defect (= lack or absence, deficiency, OED 1a) here puns on female genitalia (the woman lacks a penis), so that what the poet-speaker adores is both the woman's sinfulness (the 'imperfection' of her moral character', OED 2a) and her vagina. 'Defect' is stressed on the second syllable.

11 ***all my best*** all my best qualities/assets.

12 ***Commanded. . . eyes?*** The conceit of the woman's eyes having power to command is commonplace of amorous verse. See, for example, Daniel, *Delia*, 17.5–6: '[I] cannot leave her love that holds me hateful, | Her eyes exact it, though her heart disdains me'.

13 ***hate on*** keep hating me.
thy mind what you think, how you think.

14 ***Those. . . blind*** The poet-speaker has concluded that the mistress favours those who can see things clearly (including her faults) and despises those who are blindly besotted (a group which includes him).

149

Canst thou, O cruel, say I love thee not,
When I against myself with thee partake?
Do I not think on thee when I forgot
Am of myself, all tyrant for thy sake? 4
Who hateth thee that I do call my friend?
On whom frown'st thou that I do fawn upon?
Nay, if thou lour'st on me, do I not spend
Revenge upon myself with present moan? 8
What merit do I in myself respect
That is so proud thy service to despise,
When all my best doth worship thy defect,
Commanded by the motion of thine eyes? 12
    But, love, hate on, for now I know thy mind:
    Those that can see thou lov'st, and I am blind.

150

Benson combines Sonnets 148–150 under the title 'Love's powerful subtlety'.

1   *power* (i) authority (with perhaps a hint of a supernatural authority, such as the god of love; see 151.1); (ii) capacity; here pronounced as one syllable.
   powerful might pleonasm, for emphasis; also forms a *polyptoton* with 'power'; 'powerful' is here pronounced as two syllables.

2   *insufficiency* unfitness (OED 1a); compare 149.11 and 150.13, where the poet-speaker's love/desire is also aroused by the mistress' faults. The word is used by Shakespeare in only one other instance, in *Midsummer Night's Dream*, 2.2.128, where Helena describes the 'insufficiency' of her beauty.
   sway control (OED 9b); compare 149.12, where the mistress' eyes 'command'.

3   *To. . . sight* rehearses the idea (found in Sonnets 137, 147–149, 152) that the poet-speaker's judgement has been distorted by his infatuation with the mistress;
   give the lie to: accuse of lying; see *Coriolanus*, 5.6.105–6, where Martius refutes Aufidius' description of him as a 'boy of tears': 'Your judgments, my grave lords, | Must give this cur the lie'.

4   *And. . . day* The poet-speaker realises that his judgement is so distorted – since he has sworn his 'black' mistress 'fair' (147.13–14) – that he is prepared to profess that brightness does not make the day beautiful ('grace, *v.*', adorn, OED³ 3a). See also 28.9–10, where the friend's 'bright[ness]' was said to 'grace' the day.

5   *Whence* from where, from what source.
   this. . . ill 'this ability to make ugly or wicked things appealing'; the friend has the same power in 40.13 and 96.7–8.

becoming 'the action of benefitting or gracing' (OED, citing only Shakespearean instances); compare *Antony and Cleopatra*, 1.3.96–7 ('my becomings kill me when they do not | Eye well to you') or its use as a verb in the description of Cleopatra at 2.2.237–8: 'vilest things | Become themselves in her'.

6   *refuse of thy deeds* 'Refuse' indicates 'rubbish, waste, residue' (*n.*1, OED³ 1a); the phrase can (i) imply that everything the mistress does is despicable (all her deeds are 'refuse'); or (ii) distinguish her basest actions from other, more honourable ones. Burrow (2002: 680) draws attention to the way in which the proximity to '*warrantise of skill*' ('guarantee of expertise', l. 7) might activate a reading of 'refuse' as 'seconds': 'items of manufacture of poor quality which have been rejected for sale at full price. That sense appears to have been current in the seventeenth-century cloth trade'.

8   *thy. . . exceeds* Compare the description of the friend's powers at 114.7.

11 *abhor* probably puns on 'whore'; the name of Abhorson, the executioner in *Measure for Measure*, suggests that he is, in the seamy world of Shakespeare's Vienna, the son of a whore; Desdemona puns on whore/abhor in *Othello*: 'I cannot say "whore". | It does abhor me now I speak the word' (4.2.161–2).

12 *With others* along with others (the poet-speaker presents himself as someone whom others 'abhor').

13–14 *raised love* a possible innuendo; see 151.8–9, 12–14, and notes.

14 *worthy* (i) The poet-speaker is worthy of the mistress' love because of his generosity in loving her, despite her unworthiness; (ii) he is a worthy (suitable) lover because, in loving her, he has shown that he is *un*worthy (just as she is).

150

O, from what power hast thou this powerful might
With insufficiency my heart to sway,
To make me give the lie to my true sight
And swear that brightness doth not grace the day? 4
Whence hast thou this becoming of things ill,
That in the very refuse of thy deeds
There is such strength and warrantise of skill
That in my mind thy worst all best exceeds? 8
Who taught thee how to make me love thee more,
The more I hear and see just cause of hate?
O, though I love what others do abhor,
With others thou shouldst not abhor my state. 12
    If thy unworthiness raised love in me,
    More worthy I to be beloved of thee.

151

Benson combines Sonnets 151 with 152 under the title 'Perjury'.

1 **Love. . . young** Cupid is often represented iconographically as a boy or even an infant (see 115.13).

1, 2, 13 **conscience** a sense of right and wrong (OED³ 1a), with a bawdy pun (Partridge 1990: 84–5), made either (i) by *con*, the French for 'cunt' + science (knowledge); or (ii) an etymological reading of 'conscience' as 'knowledge with' (where 'knowledge' can mean sexual knowledge; see 129.13n). The conscience that is 'born of love' (l. 2) is thus not the moral kind but carnal knowledge. That love is 'too young' to know conscience possibly reflects legal concepts: of the age of reason (seven years old) under which – in canon law – no one can be held morally responsible; and the age of discretion (puberty), before which – in both canon and civil law – no one can be regarded as being capable of making crucial decisions for themselves. According to Booth (1977: 526), citing Taylor (1931: 171), the Latin axiom 'Penis erectus non habet conscientiam' ('The erect penis has no conscience') may also lie behind l. 2.

2 **not** not that.

3 **gentle cheater** the mistress, to whom the sonnet is addressed; for the use of endearments in potentially pejorative or ironic ways, see 35.14, 40.9; for the sexual potential of 'gentle', see 20.3n.

urge. . . amiss (i) 'do not accuse me of wrongdoing'; (ii) 'do not incite me to wrongdoing'.

4 **Lest. . . prove** (i) 'lest you transpire to be guilty of the same faults as me' (compare 142.3–4); (ii) 'lest you be responsible for my faults (by luring me into them)'; as Burrow points out (2002: 682), Q's spelling 'least' could lead a reader (seeing the text in old spelling) to interpret this line as an attempt to excuse the mistress. However, both of Q's compositors regularly spell 'lest' as 'least' (Q36.10; Q71.13; Q72.1, 9; Q89.11; Q140.3; Q148.14), and the context of the sonnet as a whole makes 'lest' the better reading.

5 **thou betraying me** In the context of the lines that follow, this describes the mistress, leading the poet-speaker into lust.

5–6 **I. . . treason** The poet-speaker sacrifices his soul ('his nobler part') by succumbing to his bodily desires; compare 146.1–2.

7 **he** the body.

8 **flesh** the body with its sensual appetites; by *metonymy*, the penis.

stays. . . reason Having been told by the soul that he 'may | Triumph in love', the body does not wait for further argument, but – understanding love in physical terms – becomes sexually active.

9 **rising . . . thee** describes the penis growing erect; the phrase is also resonant of conjuring (compare the quotation from *Romeo and Juliet* at 129.1n).

10 **triumphant prize** spoils of victory.

pride evokes the sense of animals 'in pride', i.e. sexually excited (*n*.1, OED³ 11); see *Lucrece*, l. 705; *Venus and Adonis*, l. 260 and note.

11 **contented** Booth (1977: 526) suggests another echo of 'cunt', drawing parallels with the sexually voracious Venus in *Venus and Adonis*, l. 513.

drudge slave.

12–14 **stand. . . fall. . . rise** describes cycles of tumescence, detumescence and retumescence. Compare Donne, 'The Canonization', ll. 26–7: 'We die and rise by the same, and prove | Mysterious by this love'. The image of the penis 'stand[ing]' and 'fall[ing]' also invokes the sense of sexual intercourse as a military engagement.

12 **affairs** (i) business (the word did not then mean 'love affairs'); (ii) vagina (Partridge 1990: 57); Hotspur makes a bawdy pun along these lines at *1 Henry IV*, 4.1.58–9: 'If that the devil and mischance look big | Upon the maidenhead of our affairs'.

13 **want** lack.

hold consider.

14 **'love'** The quotation marks are editorial.

dear (i) precious; (ii) costly (the affair with the mistress exacts a spiritual and emotional toll).

151

Love is too young to know what conscience is,
Yet who knows not conscience is born of love?
Then, gentle cheater, urge not my amiss,
Lest guilty of my faults thy sweet self prove;   4
For, thou betraying me, I do betray
My nobler part to my gross body's treason;
My soul doth tell my body that he may
Triumph in love; flesh stays no farther reason,   8
But, rising at thy name, doth point out thee
As his triumphant prize; proud of this pride,
He is contented thy poor drudge to be,
To stand in thy affairs, fall by thy side.   12
    No want of conscience hold it that I call
    Her 'love', for whose dear love I rise and fall.

152

Benson combines Sonnets 151 with 152 under the title 'Perjury'.

1 *am forsworn* have broken an oath (to another lover, or perhaps to a wife).

3–4 *In act. . . bearing* The mistress has behaved even worse than the poet-speaker because she has broken not one but two oaths: the first, the marriage vow ('*bed-vow*' in 'bed, *n.*', OED) by embarking on an extra-marital affair; the second, by declaring that she hates the poet-speaker, when she had previously sworn that she loved him. Q places a comma after 'torn'; leaving a comma there suggests that the two lines should be read in parallel, each separate line referring to one of the two broken vows. However, logically, '*vowing new hate*' does not in itself constitute a breach of an oath: it only becomes that when vowing hate violates a previously made pledge ('*faith*', l. 3). For Q's insertion of commas at the ends of lines which modern readers would enjamb, see headnote to *Sonnets* ('Printing Q').

3 *In act* reference to sexual intercourse; see *Othello*, 2.1.227 ('act of sport'), 5.2.211 ('act of shame').

   torn Compare *Love's Labours Lost*, 4.3.281: 'Our loving lawful, and our faith not torn'. As Brooke (1936) notes, the verb invokes the sense of a paper contract being ripped up.

4 *new love* may refer to (i) the love she conceived for the poet-speaker (betraying her husband); (ii) a more recent love (e.g. for the friend).

   bearing having, but also contains a more sexual sense, of bearing the weight of a lover; see, for example, *Romeo and Juliet*, 1.4.92–3 ('This is the hag, when maids lie on their backs, | That presses them and learns them first to bear') and *Taming of the Shrew*, 2.1.200–1:

> PETRUCCIO Women are made to bear, and so are you.
> KATE No such jade as you, if me you mean.

5 *two oaths' breach* breaking the two vows described in ll. 3–4.

6 *twenty* For 'twenty' as a numerical measure of hyperbole, see *Venus and Adonis*, l. 22 and note.

   am perjured have deliberately broken an oath (*adj.*, OED³ A1).

7 *but* only.

   misuse This line is cited by OED as the only example of the verb 'misuse' to mean 'to speak falsely of, misrepresent' (OED³ 6); however, there are a number of other meanings of the verb also in play, namely: 'to use wrongly or improperly' (OED³ 1a); 'to treat badly' (OED³ 2a); 'to violate (a woman)' (OED³ 2b); 'to deceive, delude' (OED 3³); 'to speak evil of; to abuse verbally; to deride' (OED³ 5).

8 *all. . . lost* (i) 'my faith in you, which was open and sincere ['*honest*'] has been lost'; (ii) because of the affair, the poet-speaker's capacity for moral integrity has been lost.

9 *deep oaths* solemn promises; see *Love's Labours Lost*, 1.1.23: 'Subscribe to your deep oaths, and keep it, too'. Where in l. 5, oaths were those sworn between lovers/partners, the oaths sworn in l. 9 have changed into oaths sworn about the mistress' character and behaviour, as if the poet-speaker were appearing in a court of law.

   kindness As at 143.12, 'kindness' holds a sexual resonance; see *Pericles*, 4.6.6–7: 'do me the kindness of our profession [i.e. prostitution]'.

11 *enlighten* make bright (i.e. less morally flawed); compare 147.13.

11–12 *And. . . see* rehearses the idea that the poet-speaker's infatuation with the mistress distorts either his eyesight (as in l. 11) or his judgement, which overrides the evidence of his eyes (l. 12); for this running theme in the sonnets to/about the mistress, see also 137, 147–150. Giving 'eyes to blindness' also evokes the representation of Cupid as blind (see 137.1); the poet-speaker has allowed himself to see the mistress through love's eyes, i.e. blindly.

12 *thing* may be intended contemptuously; compare *Tempest*, 5.1.275 ('this thing of darkness'), *Troilus and Cressida*, 2.1.49 ('thou thing of no bowels, thou!').

13 *For. . . fair* repeats verbatim, and in the same position, the opening words of the couplet from Sonnet 147.

152

In loving thee thou know'st I am forsworn,
But thou art twice forsworn to me love swearing:
In act thy bed-vow broke, and new faith torn
In vowing new hate after new love bearing.   4
But why of two oaths' breach do I accuse thee,
When I break twenty? I am perjured most,
For all my vows are oaths but to misuse thee,
And all my honest faith in thee is lost;   8
For I have sworn deep oaths of thy deep kindness,
Oaths of thy love, thy truth, thy constancy,
And to enlighten thee gave eyes to blindness,
Or made them swear against the thing they see: 12
    For I have sworn thee fair: more perjured eye,
    To swear against the truth so foul a lie.

perjured 'deceitful' (OED³ A2).

eye puns on 'I'; the play on words, whilst seeming to deflect blame onto the eye, also confesses the poet-speaker's complicity ('more perjured I'). There is an editorial tradition (following Sewell, and taken up by Malone and Dyce) of altering 'eye' to 'I' to clarify the pun; however, 'eye' must have been the reading in the manuscript, since a compositor would be unlikely to convert 'I' to 'eye'.

13–14 *fair. . .foul* For the recurrent play on these opposites, and the association of 'foul' with the mistress, see 137.12n.

14 *so* Benson corrects Q's 'fo', where the compositor has mistaken a long 's' for 'f' (a common mistake when reading secretary hand).

153

Benson combines Sonnets 153 and 154 under the title 'Cupid's treachery'.

Sonnet 153 is a companion piece to 154; Hutton argues that 154 was composed first on the grounds that 153 is 'more original in the sense that more of it is wholly given up to the poet's added inventions' (1941: 400). Both sonnets are versions of an almost commonplace epigram, going back to at least the fifth century CE and Marianus Scholasticus' six-line epigram:

> Beneath these plane trees, detained by gentle slumber, Love slept, having put his torch in the care of the Nymphs; but the Nymphs said one to another: 'Why wait? Would that together with this we could quench the fire in the heart of men.' But the torch set fire even to the water, and with the hot water thenceforth Love-Nymphs fill the bath. (Translated by Hutton 1941: 386)

As Hutton points out, Shakespeare did not need to have read Marianus' Greek original, and he traces numerous versions in modern European languages as well as Latin to which Shakespeare may have had access. These analogues include Giles Fletcher's *Licia* 27:

> The crystal streams wherein my love did swim
> Melted in tears, as partners of my woe.
> Her shine was such as did the fountain dim;
> The pearl-like fountain, whiter than the snow,
> Then like perfume resolved with a heat.
> The fountain smoked, as if it thought to burn.
> A wonder strange, to see the cold so great
> And yet the fountain into smoke to turn.
> I searched the cause, and found it to be this:
> She touched the water, and it burned with love,
> Now by her means, it purchased hath that bliss
> Which all diseases quickly can remove.
>   Then, if by you, these streams thus blessed be,
>   (Sweet) grant me love, and be not worse to me. (1593: sig. E3v)

As Scott 1929 has shown, Fletcher's sonnet also demonstrates the complex transmission of this tradition, derived as it is from Giralmo Angeriano's Italian epigram, 'De Caeliae Balneo', first printed in his *Erotopaegnion* (1512).

The more blatantly bookish, ultimately classically derived source material for Sonnets 153 and 154 signals a departure from the previous sonnets, as Shakespeare adopts a more Jonsonian manner.

Duncan-Jones tentatively suggests (1997a: 422) that the epigram may have reached Shakespeare via 'an English version [...] by Jonson himself, now lost, perhaps part of his projected Book II of *Epigrammes*'; Jonson is known to have owned a copy of Eilhard Lubinus' *Greek Anthology*, first printed in 1603, which contains a Latin translation of Marianus' epigram. A date of composition post-1603 for Sonnets 153 and 154 would not be out of keeping with the allusions to venereal disease that pervade these two sonnets as they do *Measure for Measure* (1604) and *Troilus and Cressida* (c. 1602). Despite their differences in source and mode, 153 and 154 are nevertheless connected to the preceding sonnets as they continue the attack on the mistress by suggesting that she has given the poet-speaker venereal disease (see 153.7n, 154.14n).

Sonnets 153 and 154 are often seen as a pivotal section of Q, between the sonnet sequence and *A Lover's Complaint*. See, for example, Duncan-Jones (1983), which argues that Q has a tri-partite structure, comprising (i) Sonnets 1–152; (ii) Sonnets 153 and 154, which are 'Anacreontic' in their amorous subject matter and bawdy tone, although they do not adopt Anacreontic form and metre; and (iii) *A Lover's Complaint*. As such, it follows a pattern that would be familiar to readers of 1590s collections, such as Daniel's *Delia* (1592), Spenser's *Amoretti* (1595), Fletcher's *Licia* (1593), Barnfield's *Cynthia* (1595) and Linche's *Diella* (1596), the latter of which, like Q, uses a sonnet (rather than an ode) to divide the sonnet sequence from the narrative poem that follows.

1 ***brand*** Cupid was sometimes depicted with a flaming torch; see, for example Ovid's description of Cupid with a 'fax' or 'lampas' (firebrand, torch) in *Remedia Amoris*, ll. 38, 552, 700, or Watson, *Hekatompathia*, Passion 100.5: 'His brand had lost his force' (1582: sig. N3r). The brand has clear phallic implications.

2 ***maid of Dian's*** Diana was the Roman goddess of the hunt, famed for her chastity, virginity which she also expected of her female followers.
advantage opportunity (OED³ 2d).

3 ***his*** 'His' is both masculine and neuter pronoun in early modern English; it thus refers to both Cupid's 'love-kindling fire' and to that of his brand.
steep 'soak', 'plunge [...] in water' (*v*.1, OED 2a, 1c).

4 ***valley-fountain*** fountain in a valley; hyphenated in Q; there is a probable sexual innuendo here; compare Venus' description of her genitalia in *Venus and Adonis*, l. 234.
of that ground in that area, vicinity.

153

Cupid laid by his brand and fell asleep;
A maid of Dian's this advantage found
And his love-kindling fire did quickly steep
In a cold valley-fountain of that ground,   4
Which borrowed from this holy fire of love
A dateless lively heat, still to endure,
And grew a seething bath, which yet men prove
Against strange maladies a sovereign cure.   8
But at my mistress' eye love's brand new fired,
The boy for trial needs would touch my breast;
I, sick withal, the help of bath desired
And thither hied, a sad distempered guest,   12
    But found no cure; the bath for my help lies
    Where Cupid got new fire: my mistress' eyes.

---

5 **borrowed** took (the brand is extinguished, so the water does not return the heat).

5, 9 **love. . . love's** The personification of Love as Cupid lies behind these images, but 'love' can also be here understood as the emotion.

6 **dateless** 'having no time limit of fixed term; endless' (OED³ A1); see *Richard II*, 1.3.151–2: 'The dateless limit of thy dear exile; | The hopeless word of "never to return"'. The insertion of '*still*' makes the line pleonastic, emphasising the everlasting nature of the heat.
    lively (i) life-giving (OED³ A2a); (ii) intense (OED³ A3b).

7 **grew a seething bath** became a hot bath, of the type used for treating venereal disease and other disorders; see *Measure for Measure*, 3.2.57 (where the bawd, Mistress Overdone, 'is herself in the tub'), *Troilus and Cressida*, 5.10.55 (where the diseased Pandarus says that he will 'sweat and seek about for eases').
    seething boiling.
    prove 'find out [. . .] by experience' (OED³ 7); for the recurrent interest in proof in the *Sonnets*, see 2.12n.

8 **strange** 'unusual'; the sense of 'foreign' may also be relevant, since venereal disease was often seen as a 'French' or 'Spanish' affliction; see, for example, Edward Topsell, *History of Serpents* for details of 'Ointments that are prepared against the French or Spanish-pox' (1608: sig. D5v). Although Q's 'strang' (a variant spelling of 'strange') could also be modernised as 'strong',

'strange' seems more likely: of the numerous printed works using the spelling 'strang' (over 180 for the years 1570–1609), only ones authored (or allegedly authored) by Scots use 'strang' to mean 'strong' (e.g. Robert Henryson's *Fables*; Elizabeth Melville Colville's *Ane Dream*; Alexander Hume's *Ane Treatise of Conscience*; Thomas Wilson's pseudo-Scots translation of George Buchanan's *Ane Detectioun*).
    sovereign 'of remedies, etc.: Efficacious or potent in a superlative degree' (OED B3); compare *Venus and Adonis*, l. 916.

9 **at. . . fired** evokes the idea, common to Petrarchan love poetry, that the beloved's eye was capable of igniting the lover's passion; see Barnes, *Parthenophil and Parthenophe*, Sonnet 94.5: 'Through mine eye, thine eye's fire inflames my liver' (1593: sig. H4v). There is a possible sexual innuendo here: 'eye' can indicate 'hole or aperture' (n.1, OED3 9), particularly one 'for the insertion of [. . .] some other object' (OED3 9d). Read thus, the lover's penis (the phallic 'brand') takes heat – be it of desire and/or disease – from the mistress' genitalia.
    new fired re-ignited.

10 **The boy** Cupid; see 115.13, 151.1 and notes.
    for trial. . . breast To test the strength of the newly relit brand, Cupid feels compelled ('**needs would**') to try it on the poet-speaker's heart.
    touch possibly carries the sense of 'infect' (OED 7); compare *King John*, 5.7.1–2: 'The life of all his blood | Is touched corruptibly'.

11 **withal** from that (as a result of being touched).
12 **hied** sped ('hie, *v.*1', OED 2).
   sad 'having had one's fill; satisfied, sated; weary or tired' (OED³ A1).
   distempered ill (because the heat has disturbed the balance of the four bodily humours which was believed to affect both physical and mental health).
14 **eyes** Q has 'eye'; first emended to 'eyes' by Benson; most editors accept this reading (for the sake of the rhyme with 'lies' in l. 13); the error probably arose from the compositor misreading the *-es* hook as an 'e'. Booth, however, prefers to follow Q, to keep live the innuendo of l. 9 (see note, above). There may be another play at work, on 'eye' as 'ay': the poet-speaker will thus be cured by his mistress saying 'yes'. The 'eyes/lies' rhyme echoes the couplet of Sonnet 152.

153

Cupid laid by his brand and fell asleep;
A maid of Dian's this advantage found
And his love-kindling fire did quickly steep
In a cold valley-fountain of that ground,   4
Which borrowed from this holy fire of love
A dateless lively heat, still to endure,
And grew a seething bath, which yet men prove
Against strange maladies a sovereign cure: 8
But at my mistress' eye love's brand new fired,
The boy for trial needs would touch my breast;
I, sick withal, the help of bath desired
And thither hied, a sad distempered guest,   12
    But found no cure; the bath for my help lies
    Where Cupid got new fire: my mistress' eyes.

154

Benson combines Sonnets 153 and 154 under the title 'Cupid's treachery'.

For the relationship between 153 and 154, and the literary tradition to which this sonnet belongs, see headnote to 153, above. The fact that both sonnets are versions of the same poem, with 154 being seen as comparatively inferior (see Blakemore Evans 1996: 274), has been used as an argument to suggest that its inclusion in Q is accidental, and that the publication of Q is unauthorised.

1 *little love-god* Cupid, often depicted as a young boy; see 115.13, 151.1, and notes.

2 *Laid by his side* Read literally, this implies that Cupid put aside his brand after falling asleep; the awkwardness (and illogical nature) of this construction is avoided in Sonnet 153, which compresses Cupid's actions into one line (153.1). *heart-inflaming brand* Cupid was sometimes represented with a firebrand (with possible phallic implications); see 153.1n.

4 *tripping* 'tread[ing] or step[ping] lightly or nimbly ('trip, *v.*', OED I).

5 *votary* 'one who has made, or is bound by, a special vow' (OED 1b); in this instance, the vow is one of chastity.

6 *legions* 'vast host[s] or multitude[s]' (OED 3a); the military origins of this word (denoting 'a body of infantry in the Roman army', OED 1a) are picked up by the militaristic connotations of 'general', 'disarmed' and 'thrall', which follow (ll. 7, 8, 12).

7 *general of hot desire* the one who commands passion, i.e. Cupid; 'general' is here pronounced as three syllables.

8 *disarmed* may suggest emasculation; see Tomalin's failure to get an erection in Nashe, *Choice of Valentines*, ll. 123–4 (cited at 149.7–8n).

9 *well* For the possible sexual innuendo, see 153.4n. *by* nearby.

11 *Growing* becoming. *bath* See 153.7n.

12 *thrall* 'one who is in bondage to a lord or master; a villein, serf, bondman, slave; also, in vaguer use, a servant, subject; transf. one whose liberty is forfeit; a captive, prisoner of war' (*n.*1, OED 1); the term captures the typical subjection of a Petrarchan lover to his mistress; see, for example, Barnes' *Parthenophil and Parthenope*, Sonnet 95.9–10: 'Thou that hast worlds of hearts with thine eye's glance | To thy love's pleasing bondage taken thrall' (1593: sig. I1r).

13 *for cure* to be cured. *this* the conclusion that follows in l. 14. *that* the action of coming to the bath for a cure (unsuccessfully, it transpires). *prove* 'demonstrate' (OED³ I), 'find out [...] by experience' (OED³ 7); for the preoccupation with proving in the *Sonnets*, see 2.12n.

14 *Love's. . . love* Compare *Venus and Adonis*, l. 94 and note. The statement 'Love's fire heats water' both summarises ll. 1–12 and suggests the burning urine ('*water*') that is a symptom of venereal disease. The final line thus balances the classicism of its chiasmic structure (*love. . . water. . . water. . . love*) against the wry bitterness of sexual experience as the poet-speaker indicates that his venereal disease (the fruits of love) has not been cured by its treatment. There is also a potential allusion to Song of Solomon 8:7: 'Much water cannot quench love, neither can the floods drown it: if a man should give all the substance of his house for love, they would greatly contemn it'. *FINIS* marks the end of the sonnets; in Q, *A Lover's Complaint* follows, beginning on the verso of the same leaf.

154

The little love-god, lying once asleep,
Laid by his side his heart-inflaming brand,
Whilst many nymphs, that vowed chaste life to keep,
Came tripping by; but in her maiden hand   4
The fairest votary took up that fire,
Which many legions of true hearts had warmed,
And so the general of hot desire
Was, sleeping, by a virgin hand disarmed.   8
This brand she quenchèd in a cool well by,
Which from love's fire took heat perpetual,
Growing a bath and healthful remedy
For men diseased; but I, my mistress' thrall,   12
    Came there for cure, and this by that I prove:
    Love's fire heats water; water cools not love.

FINIS

A Lover's Complaint

Publication

In Q, the *Sonnets* are followed by *A Lover's Complaint*, which begins on the verso (sig. K1v) of the leaf containing Sonnet 154, the catch-word of which ('A') links to the title of the poem that follows. In print, *A Lover's Complaint* can thus have only circulated with the *Sonnets*, and the volume must have been designed as a whole at the point of printing, although *A Lover's Complaint* is not mentioned by name in the entry made by Thorpe in the Stationers' Register on 20 May 1609. Certainly, the omission of *A Lover's Complaint* is at odds with entries for other bi- or tri-partite works, such as Samuel Daniel's 'Delia containing diverse sonnets with the Complaint of Rosamond' (4 Feb 1592; Arber, 2.604), Edmund Spenser's 'Amoretti and Epithalamion' (19 Nov 1594; Arber, 2.665), or Richard Barnfield's 'Cynthia, with certain sonnets, and the legend of Cassandra' (17 Jan 1595; Arber, 2.669). This may suggest that the manuscript containing *A Lover's Complaint* came to Thorpe separately from, and perhaps later than, that containing the *Sonnets*.

CELM lists just one manuscript containing lines from *A Lover's Complaint*: Folger Shakespeare Library MS V.a.150, 'the detached cover of an octavo book, [. . .] *c.* 1620s–30s', which includes part of ll. 41–2, 'partly erased'.

Authorship

A Lover's Complaint is attributed to Shakespeare by Thorpe in the 1609 Quarto: since no other copies of *A Lover's Complaint* exist, there is no external corroborating evidence of Shakespeare's authorship; it is not mentioned in Francis Meres' *Tamis Palladia*, for example, but that only lists works to 1598, and Hieatt et al. (1987) date the composition of the poem to *c.* 1600–3; Jackson (2014) to 1603–7.

Shakespeare's authorship of *A Lover's Complaint* has been contested, most notably by Vickers (2007; see also Eliott and Valenza 1997; Tarlinskaja 2004). The debate about Shakespeare's authorship is closely connected to the issue of whether or not Q was authorised, since Shakespeare would have been unlikely to countenance the inclusion, under his name, of a poem that he did not write; showing that Shakespeare was not its author would therefore indicate that Q was published without his sanction. However, the converse does not provide quite the same certainty: *A Lover's Complaint* could be by Shakespeare, and Thorpe could have printed it without his permission, as a number believe he did with the *Sonnets*.

The argument against Shakespeare's authorship rests on its omission from the entry for the *Sonnets* in the Stationers' Register (see above) and on analysis of its style and diction. Vickers, for example, disputes Shakespeare's authorship on the grounds that the poem is 'unShakespearean' in its reliance on the phrase 'many a' for 'iambic padding'; in its recycling of rhyme pairs; in its syntax;

and in its diction, which employs large numbers of archaic and Latinate words not used elsewhere by Shakespeare (2007: 2). He also reads the poem as 'an indictment of female sexuality [. . .], simultaneously moralizing and misogynistic' in a way that he finds uncharacteristic of Shakespeare (2007: 6). However, Shakespeare regularly recycles rhyming pairs: 'thee/me' appears fifteen times in the first sixty sonnets, for example; and Shakespeare's tendency to re-use rhymes is also evident from Appendix 7. Nor is the phrase 'many a' unShakespearean: 'many a' and 'many an' appear, in verse, over seventy times across the Shakespeare canon (besides *A Lover's Complaint*); in the overwhelming majority of cases – the exceptions being when the phrase appears in an emphatic position at the beginning of a line – it is elided into the disyllabic pronunciation employed in *A Lover's Complaint*, including a particularly dense cluster in Sonnets 30–33, where the phrase appears four times in forty-one lines (30.3, 8; 31.5; 33.1). Whether the poem is 'moralizing and misogynistic' is a matter of interpretation (and one challenged by Kerrigan, amongst others, in correspondence in *TLS* in September 2007); moreover, if misogyny is to be found in the poem, then it is voiced through a character, and Shakespeare's plays also contain vehemently misogynistic sentiments similarly voiced through others. Nor does unusual diction and syntax necessarily disprove Shakespeare's authorship: he was capable of writing in a wide variety of styles, as can be seen in the contrast between *Lucrece* and 'Let the Bird of Loudest Lay'; the latter also employs a high number of unusual and classically derived words such as 'threne' (three other pre-1609 instances in EEBO-TCP), 'precurrer' and 'defunctive' (no other instances).

Vickers' preferred candidate is John Davies of Hereford, who – according to Vickers – is the only Jacobean poet, besides the author of *A Lover's Complaint*, to use many of the unusual words and phrases that appear in *A Lover's Complaint* (2007: 4); Vickers here cites as proof words and phrases such as 'maund', 'fell rage', 'affectedly' and – oddly – 'particular', used as an adjective over forty times across Shakespeare's other works. 'Maund' is not used elsewhere by Shakespeare, but it is not in itself an unusual word: it was a standard dictionary definition, found in Thomas Cooper's *Thesaurus*, as a translation of the Latin 'alveolus' (1565: sig. C4v); and L.H.'s *Dictionary French and English*, as a translation of 'une banne & grand panier' (1571: sig. C4v); it regularly appears in practical handbooks such as N.F.'s *Fruiterer's Secret* (1604); and it is used in Arthur Golding's translation of *Ovid's Metamorphoses*, a work that Shakespeare knew well (5.493; sig. I7v). 'Fell rage' is also found in a number of works which Shakespeare must have known, including John Marston's *History of Antonio and Mellida* (1602, Act 1, sig. C1v), and Edmund Spenser's *Faerie Queene* (1596: IV.vi.10.4). 'Affectedly' was an unusual word before 1609 (the earliest citation in OED[3], and found in a keyword search of EEBO-TCP, is George Whetstone's *Heptameron of Civil Discourse*, 1582), but the adverb would have been encountered by anyone with an interest in English poetry, in George Puttenham's *Art of English Poesy* (1589: 211) and Meres' *Palladia Tamis* (1598: sig. 2K5v).

There is, meanwhile, a lot to recommend Shakespeare's authorship of *A Lover's Complaint*: see, for example, Jackson 2008, for connections between *A Lover's Complaint* and *Cymbeline*, usually dated 1609–10, and Jackson 2014, for a detailed study of collocations, spellings and neologisms, which strongly supports Shakespeare's authorship. Whilst compositors would alter the spelling and punctuation of their copy text, it is likely that some of the more unusual spellings would survive (Dover Wilson 1967), and the *Sonnets* and *A Lover's Complaint* share a number of distinctive spellings which may not be due to compositorial preference. These include the consistent choice of 'deu-' for 'divide' (and its related terms) in pages set by both compositors, and a preference for 'vsery' and 'vserer' over usury/usurer, words which only appear on pages set by Compositor B (note: it was usual practice in both manuscript and print for 'v' to stand for 'u' in the initial position in words, and for 'u' to stand for 'v' in a medial position). A search of EEBO-TCP of books printed in Eld's workshop for the years 1605–15 indicate that neither of these spellings would seem to reflect the preference of his compositors (unless he only employed A and B sporadically, which is improbable): 'vsery' appears once in one other text printed in Eld's printing house (aside from Q) – Thomas Dekker's *Northward Ho!* (1607) – as opposed to seventy-seven instances of 'vsury' (in twenty-two texts); 'vserer' appears four times in two texts (aside from Q), one of which is Dekker's *Northward Ho!*, in comparison with fifty-two occurrences of 'vsurer' across thirteen texts. The 'diu-' form of 'divide' also dominates, occurring 1,008 times in comparison to 277 instances of the 'deu-' form (six of which are in the two imprints of Q). In addition, as Jackson argues, a number of the rare spellings found in *A Lover's Complaint* also occur in 'good' quartos of Shakespeare's plays (2014: 141–59), as well as in the three pages of the manuscript of *Sir Thomas More*, written in Hand D, which may well have been Shakespeare's (159–60).

Furthermore, considering that the *Sonnets* must have had a very restricted manuscript circulation (see headnote to *Sonnets*, p. 272), it is extremely unlikely that anyone other than their author could have constructed the verbal and thematic echoes between that work and *A Lover's Complaint* (e.g. in the depiction of the woman's seducer who, in his universal attractiveness, androgyny and skilled horsemanship, has much in common with the young man of the *Sonnets*; see notes on ll. 101–3, 107, 127). This edition therefore sees no compelling need to disattribute the poem.

Genre

The poem belongs to the tradition of female-voiced complaint, a genre of poetry which – like the sonnet sequence – was in vogue in the mid-1590s; for an overview, and anthology, see Kerrigan 1991. A number of these female-voiced complaints were appended to sonnet sequences, where the (ventriloquised) female voice contrasts with the male perspective of the preceding sonnets: Daniel's *Rosamond* (1592) ends his *Delia* volume; Thomas Lodge's *Complaint of Elstred* is attached to *Phillis* (1593). Many of the Elizabethan female-voiced complaints (Daniel's *Rosamond*, Michael Drayton's *Matilda*, 1594) follow Thomas Churchyard's *Shore's Wife* (printed in the 1563 volume of *The Mirror for Magistrates*) and use rhyme royal, the verse form (rhyming *ababbcc*) also used in *A Lover's Complaint*. These female complainants also regularly give an account of how they were assailed by honeyed-tongued speeches (see *A Lover's Complaint*, ll. 182–280), be they those of their seducers (e.g. Churchyard, *Elstred*, sigs K1v–K2r) or their proxy (e.g. Daniel, *Rosamond*, ll. 225–301; Drayton, *Matilda*, sigs D1r–D3r).

However, *A Lover's Complaint* differs from most Elizabethan female-voiced complaints in a number of ways.

1 Its protagonist is unnamed and thus remains fictional, whereas the other poets feature historical persons: Jane or Elizabeth Shore, mistress to Edward IV (Churchyard); Rosamund Clifford, mistress to Henry II (Daniel); Elstred, mistress to the legendary British king, Locrine (Lodge); Matilda Fitzwalter, whom King John allegedly poisoned after she rejected his advances (Drayton). The position occupied by three of these women as royal mistresses means that their fall is as much about the loss of political influence as it is about a personal fall from a state of grace and purity; Churchyard's complaint (which instigated the Elizabethan vogue for female-voiced complaint) sets the pattern for this political edge, since it belongs to a volume – *The Mirror for Magistrates* – in which a series of male protagonists lament their fall from power.

2 The female-voiced complaints of the 1590s self-consciously situate themselves alongside their predecessors in the genre. Daniel's Rosamond enviously compares her continued ill-fame with the rehabilitation of Shore's wife who now, thanks to Churchyard's poem, 'passes for a saint' (l. 25); Drayton's Matilda contrasts her obscurity with the current fame enjoyed by Rosamond, Shore's wife, and Elstred (sigs B1v–B2r) as well as Shakespeare's Lucrece, 'lately revived to live another age' (sig. B2r); and Lodge uses his 'Induction' to place the entire

volume alongside 'modern poets' such as Daniel (who is described as Delia's 'sweet prophet', sig. A4v). *A Lover's Complaint*, in contrast, eschews this obvious use of inter-textuality.

3   Unlike these other contemporaneous examples, Shakespeare's female-voiced complainant does not directly address a poet, whom she requires to tell her story and set the record straight; rather, the woman in *A Lover's Complaint* is overheard by the narrator, unbeknownst to her. As such, it resembles the fifteenth-century *Lament of the Duchess of Gloucester* (another female-voiced complaint, which may have influenced George Ferrers' 'Elianor Cobham', first printed in the 1578 *Mirror for Magistrates*), which begins with the voice of the narrator: 'Throughout a palace as I can pass, | I heard a lady make great moan' (Robbins 1959: 176–80, ll. 1–2). Duncan-Jones (1997a: 431) draws attention to the similarity of the scenario with the folk-song 'Early one morning, just as the day was dawning, | I heard a maid sing in the valley below: | O, don't deceive me, O, never leave me, | How could you use a poor maiden so?'.

Structure

A Lover's Complaint comprises a series of embedded narratives. The male narrator overhears a woman's complaint about her seduction and abandonment; her voice first appears in direct speech at ll. 52–4; the bulk of the poem (ll. 71ff) is told in her words, but includes the words of others at several points:

ll. 107–9: other people's comments about her lover's skill at horse-riding;
ll. 183–280: her lover's speech of seduction.

A Lover's Complaint There is nothing intrinsically male about the word 'lover' in the sixteenth and early seventeenth century; see, for example, Antony's speech in *Antony and Cleopatra*, 4.14.99–101: 'I will be | A bridegroom in my death, and run into 't | As to a lover's bed'.

By William Shakespeare The attribution is in Q; for a discussion of Shakespeare's authorship of the poem, see headnote, above.

1 *concave womb* (i) naturally hollowed hillside; (ii) cave; for the echo created by the concavity, compare *Venus and Adonis*, ll. 829–31, and *Julius Caesar*, 1.1.44–7: 'Have you not made an universal shout, | That Tiber trembled underneath her banks | To hear the replication of your sounds | Made in her concave shores?'. For the figurative use of 'womb', compare *Venus and Adonis*, l. 268 and note.
   reworded re-echoed; the earliest citation for this usage in OED ('reword, *v.*', OED³ 1b); EEBO-TCP reveals no prior usages in this sense; Shakespeare uses the verb in one other instance, at *Hamlet*, 3.4.143 ('I the matter will reword'), where it means repeat.

2 *plaintful* 'mournful'; the word also draws attention to the genre of the poem as a complaint. Not used elsewhere by Shakespeare, the word is relatively unusual: in a keyword search of EEBO-TCP, it appears ten times in six other texts before 1609, used most frequently by Thomas Wyatt (*Quiet of Mind*, 1528, twice) and Philip Sidney (*Certain Sonnets*, once; *Arcadia*, three times). The word also appears in Golding's translation of Ovid's *Metamorphoses* at 7.663–4: 'At that the king did sigh, and thus with plaintful voice did say, | A sad beginning afterward in better luck did stay' (sig. N1r).
   sistering neighbouring; a coinage, not used elsewhere by Shakespeare, although 'sister' is used as a verb (another apparent coinage) at *Pericles*, 5.0.7: 'Her art sisters [i.e. resembles] the natural roses'. 'Sistering' is pronounced as two syllables.

3 *spirits* pronounced as one syllable; see Sonnet 56.8n.
   attend listen.

double voice because echoed; for a discussion of doubleness in *A Lover's Complaint*, see Kerrigan 1986: 15–17.
   accorded agreed ('accord, *v.*', OED³ 2); perhaps also with a sense of being 'in harmony' (OED³ 4) with the plaintive voice.

4 *list* listen to; Burrow (2002: 695) suggests that the verb 'had an archaic flavour by 1609'; however, the word appears in this sense (with and without the preposition 'to') in twenty-four other instances in plays by, or partly by, Shakespeare, from works at various stages of his career, including later plays such as *Coriolanus* (1607–8), *Winter's Tale* (1611) and *Two Noble Kinsman* (1613–14).

5 *Ere long espied* 'before long I espied'; the compressed syntax is characteristic of *A Lover's Complaint*.
   fickle inconstant (OED 2); Hudson (1881) suggests that this is a misreading of 'fitful', but the choice of word may reflect the judgemental attitude of the narrator, who has come to this conclusion because the woman is busy destroying stereotypical love tokens.
   full very; Shakespeare frequently uses this intensifier; see Blake (2002: 154).

6 *a-twain* in two.

7 *Storming. . . rain* Q reads 'sorrowes, wind and raine'. Early modern English lacks the possessive apostrophe, and editors from Gildon (1714) onwards have generally modernised as here; Q's comma may be an instance of the common use of a comma in early modern print to emphasise the preceding word, and the line is more cohesive if 'sorrows' is taken as the possessive, rather than the first in a sequence of three, where – as an emotion – it would sit as the odd-one-out alongside the elements 'wind and rain'. Compare the description of Lear at *King Lear*, 3.1.10–11, as he 'strives in his little world of man to outscorn | The to-and-fro conflicting wind and rain'.

8 *plaited hive of straw* woven straw hat, of a sort worn by country folk; see the shepherds' hats in many of the woodcuts in Spenser's *Shepheardes Calender* (1579), and compare *Tempest*, 4.1.134–6: 'You sunburned sicklemen, of August weary, | Come hither from the furrow and be merry. | Make holiday; your rye-straw hats put on'. 'Hive' is not a term generally used to describe

A Lover's Complaint

By William Shakespeare

> From off a hill whose concave womb reworded
> A plaintful story from a sistering vale,
> My spirits t' attend this double voice accorded,
> And down I laid to list the sad-tuned tale;
> Ere long espied a fickle maid full pale,   5
> Tearing of papers, breaking rings a-twain,
> Storming her world with sorrow's wind and rain.
>
> Upon her head a plaited hive of straw,
> Which fortified her visage from the sun,
> Whereon the thought might think sometime it saw   10
> The carcass of a beauty spent and done;
> Time had not scythèd all that youth begun,
> Nor youth all quit but, spite of heaven's fell rage,
> Some beauty peeped through lattice of seared age.

headgear, but is possibly chosen here because the hat resembles Elizabethan beehives, which were usually conical and made of straw.

9 *fortified* protected.

10 *the thought might think* 'Thought' here suggests 'mind'; compare *Merchant of Venice*, 1.1.36–7: 'Shall I have the thought | To think on this [...]?'. The construction increases the uncertainty of what the narrator perceives: (i) by detaching 'thought' from himself; (ii) by introducing the hypothetical 'might'.

11 *carcass* used metaphorically, to suggest 'remnants'; compare *2 Henry IV*, 1.1.192–3: 'My lord your son had only but the corpse, | But shadows and the shows of men, to fight'.
   spent and done exhausted and finished.

12 *Time... begun* Compare the depiction of time in Sonnets 12.13, 60.12, 100.14, 123.14.

13 *all quit* completely gone.
   spite of in spite of.
   heaven's pronounced as one syllable.
   fell fierce, destructive; compare the description of time at Sonnet 64.1.

14 *Some... age* The woman's face is criss-crossed with wrinkles, like a lattice window criss-crossed with lead; through these wrinkles some evidence of youthful beauty can still be glimpsed; compare Sonnet 3.11 and note. See also John Donne, 'Second Anniversary' (1611–12), ll. 296–7, in which the dead child is imagined avoiding the degeneration of old age: 'Thou shalt not peep through lattices of eyes | Nor hear through labyrinths of ears'.

seared withered; there is a potential analogy with *Cymbeline*, 2.4.6, if F's 'these fear'd hope' is emended, since the compositor seems to have made a number of errors at this point in F: (i) misreading the '-*es*' hook which would have appeared at the end of 'hope', supplying the necessary plural to match 'these'; and (ii) mistaking the long 's' for 'f' (a common error, when reading secretary hand): certainly 'seared' makes much better sense than 'feared' in *Cymbeline*'s context, as Posthumous laments his exile and fall from favour.

15 *heave* lift; the modern sense of 'to lift with exertion (something heavy)' (OED 1b) does not come into use until the eighteenth century, and Shakespeare's habitual usage does not suggest undue effort; see, for example, *Henry V*, 5.0.8: 'Heave him away upon your winged thoughts', or *Venus and Adonis*, l. 351.

napkin handkerchief.

eyne eyes; the word was becoming archaic by the end of the sixteenth century (keyword searches in EEBO-TCP indicate a steady decline in its usage from 1580s onwards, despite the increased number of extant texts). Shakespeare tends to use the form, which appears in twelve other instances, either to indicate an archaism (as at *Pericles*, 3.0.5, in one of the prologues spoken by the medieval poet Gower), or (as here) to make a rhyme, often – but not always – in poetry which seems deliberately heightened or hackneyed (as in the song in *Antony and Cleopatra*, 2.7.114; the amorous verse of *Love's Labours Lost*, 5.2.206, or *As You Like It*, 4.3.50; and the rude mechanicals' playlet in *Midsummer Night's Dream*, 5.1.177; but see also *Venus and Adonis*, l. 633). Certainly, by the late sixteenth century 'eyne' is found in poetry more frequently than in prose (as a keyword search in EEBO-TCP attests) and at the very least should be considered a poeticism.

16 *conceited characters* ingenious, complicated symbols; l. 19 indicates that these designs are of a textual nature (i.e. letters); 'conceited' does not bear the disapproving resonance it now holds; it was frequently used, for example, on title-pages (including Shakespeare's plays) to advertise their contents; see *An excellent conceited tragedy of Romeo and Juliet* (1597), *A most pleasant and excellent conceited comedy, of Sir John Falstaff, and the merry wives of Windsor* (1602).

17 *Laundering* pronounced as two syllables.

silken figures the 'characters' of l. 16, embroidered with silk onto the napkin of l. 15.

18 *seasoned* (i) matured (because of its long duration); (ii) salted (playing on 'brine', l. 17); compare *Lucrece*, l. 796.

pelleted shaped into pellets; first usage cited in OED[3] ('pellet, *v.*', OED[3] 1); compare the adjectival use at *Antony and Cleopatra*, 3.13.165: 'this pelleted storm'. There may also be a sense of being discharged like pellets (OED[3] 2), although OED[3] does not record this usage until the eighteenth century.

19 *contents* stressed on the second syllable.

20 *undistinguished* indistinguishable (the narrator being unable to decipher what she is saying).

21 *of all size. . . low* loud and soft (with a degree of pleonasm); there may also be a suggestion of high and low pitch. Compare *Winter's Tale*, 4.4.191–2: 'He hath songs for man or woman, of all sizes'.

22 *levelled. . . ride* The woman's eyes are here compared to a cannon, aimed ('levelled') at a target, and resting on a '*carriage*', 'the wheeled support on which a piece of ordnance is mounted' (OED 27); compare the use of 'level/levelled' at ll. 282, 309; Sonnets 117.11, 121.9.

23 *As* as if.

battery assault, bombardment (continuing the metaphor of artillery); pronounced as two syllables. See also l. 277 and note.

spheres celestial bodies.

intend purpose, design; Kerrigan (1986: 399) draws attention to the way the verb 'enriches the aiming imagery, implying (through the Latin idiom *intendere oculos*) "strain towards, direct at"'.

24 *poor balls* eyeballs (continuing, through the idea of cannonballs, the metaphor of artillery); compare *Henry V*, 5.2.15–17: 'Your eyes, which hitherto have borne in them | Against the French that met them in their bent | The fatal balls of murdering basilisks'.

24–5 *tied. . . earth* The woman's gaze is turned downwards, to the ground, but the image also conveys the sense of the beams of the eyes as strings; compare John Donne: 'Our eye-beams twisted, and did thread | Our eyes upon one double string' ('The Ecstasy' (1605–13?), ll. 7–8).

26 *right on* straight ahead.

anon straightaway.

28 *distractedly* 'Distracted' and its related terms are frequently used by Shakespeare to indicate madness, including madness caused by love; see the Folio SD at *Hamlet*, 4.5.20: 'Enter Ophelia distracted'; and *Twelfth Night*, 2.2.21–2, where Viola correctly diagnoses Olivia's affliction: 'she did speak in starts distractedly. | She loves me sure.' Compare also 'distract', l. 231.

commixed mixed together.

29 *Her hair. . . plait* Dishevelled hair was often used poetically and dramatically to signal intense grief and/or madness; see SDs at *Richard III*, 2.2.33 ('Enter the Queen with her

Oft did she heave her napkin to her eyne,   15
Which on it had conceited characters,
Laundering the silken figures in the brine
That seasoned woe had pelleted in tears,
And often reading what contents it bears;
As often shrieking undistinguished woe   20
In clamours of all size, both high and low.

Sometimes her levelled eyes their carriage ride,
As they did battery to the spheres intend;
Sometime diverted their poor balls are tied
To th' orbèd earth; sometimes they do extend   25
Their view right on; anon their gazes lend
To every place at once and nowhere fixed,
The mind and sight distractedly commixed.

Her hair, nor loose nor tied in formal plait,
Proclaimed in her a careless hand of pride,   30
For some untucked descended her sheaved hat,
Hanging her pale and pinèd cheek beside;
Some in her threaden fillet still did bide
And true to bondage would not break from thence,
Though slackly braided in loose negligence.   35

A thousand favours from a maund she drew,
Of amber, crystal, and of beaded jet,
Which one by one she in a river threw,

hair about her ears'); the Folio SD at *Troilus and Cressida*, 2.2.100 ('Enter Cassandra raving with her hair about her ears'); and Q1's SD at *Hamlet*, 4.5.20 ('Enter Ophelia, playing on a lute, and her hair down, singing').
formal orderly (Schmidt, 1)
30 *a careless. . . pride* a hand careless of (i.e. without regard for) pride.
31 *descended* descended from.
   sheaved made of straw (*adj*.1, OED 2; only citation); see l. 8n; not used elsewhere by Shakespeare.
32 *pinèd* showing the effects of pining (e.g. pallor, emaciation, dark circles under the eyes from sleepless nights).
33 *threaden* made of thread; used by Shakespeare in one other instance, at *Henry V*, 3.0.10: 'behold the threaden sails'.
   fillet ribbon.

35 *slackly. . . in negligence* a pleonasm; compare the description of the 'slackly guarded' children as 'negligence' in *Cymbeline*, 1.1.64, 66 (the only other instance of Shakespeare's use of the adverb 'slackly', although he uses the word in nominal, adjectival and verbal forms eighteen times across his works).
36 *favours* love-tokens.
   maund basket with handles; like 'plait' (l. 29) and 'fillet' (l. 33) – also words from a quotidian, feminine domain – there is no other occurrence of this word (in this form, with this meaning) elsewhere in Shakespeare's works; see also the discussion of unique or unusual words in the headnote, above.
37 *beaded* Q has 'bedded', which might be a variant spelling of 'beaded', but could also indicate 'embedded' (i.e. the jet has been inlaid into something, or set in jewellery).

39 **weeping** The woman's grief has been transferred to the river (with its wet banks); compare the 'weeping brook' in which Ophelia drowns (*Hamlet*, 4.7.175); 'weeping' may also invoke willow trees, traditionally associated with lost love; see Desdemona's 'Willow Song' at *Othello*, 4.3.40–57.
margent margin, bank.

40 **Like usury** adds money to money, by charging interest (just as, through her tears, the woman adds water to the river, which is already wet); usury is a recurring motif in the procreation sonnets (see Sonnets 4, 6, 9 and notes).
applying. . . wet Compare Sonnet 135.9–10.

41–2 **monarch's. . . all** Enforces the image of l. 40, where more is given to what already has abundance; as early modern English lacks the possessive apostrophe, Q's 'Monarches' could indicate either *monarchs'* (where the behaviour critiqued is emblematic of monarchs in general) or *monarch's*; it has here been modernised in the singular because that sits better – in modern English – with the verb 'lets', although in early modern English –*s* could function as a plural verb form; see Abbott 1884: §§ 333, 335–7.

42 **want** neediness, penury.

43 **schedules** sheets of paper with writing on (OED 1); in this case, letters or poems; compare *Lucrece*, l. 1312.

43, 45 **many a** elided into two syllables.

44 **sighed** sighed over.
flood river.

45 **posied** It was customary to inscribe rings with mottoes; see Thomas Whythorne, *Autobiography* (*c.* 1576): 'At this time I made me a ring of gold, in the which I caused to be graven this sentence following: "Where wily whisperers wait work wisely, quod W."' (1962: 38). The word, a coinage, is not used elsewhere by Shakespeare, and is rare. A keyword search of EEBO-TCP reveals just one other work which uses it: Joshua Poole's *English Parnassus, or a help to English poesy* (1657), where it appears in lists of adjectives recommended for pairing with 'rosemary' and 'thimble' (173, 205).
bone Jewellery made from animal bone was a cheaper alternative to metal; here gold seems to be inset in bone: compare the early seventeenth-century ring in the V&A collections (http://collections.vam.ac.uk/item/

O119774/signet-ring-unknown/; museum number M.273-1962). That might also explain why these rings can be described as being '**cracked**', as – unlike gold rings – bone ones can be broken if sufficient force is applied, or if the different components of bone and metal are snapped apart.

46 **sepulchres** Compare *Venus and Adonis*, l. 622 and note.

47 **mo** more.
sadly seriously, mournfully.
penned in blood Writing in blood is used to signal the apparent sincerity of the words.

48 **sleided silk** According to the OED, this is a variant of 'sleaved silk', i.e. silk which has been divided into filaments, for embroidery; Shakespeare also uses the term at *Pericles*, 4.0.21: 'Be't when they weaved the sleided silk'. A keyword search of EEBO-TCP produces no other usages.
feat elegantly; Shakespeare uses 'feat' (albeit as an adjective) in one other instance, at *Cymbeline*, 5.5.85–8: 'Never master had | A page so kind, so duteous, diligent, | So tender over his occasions, true, | So feat, so nurse-like'.
affectedly a double-edged word, able to mean both (i) lovingly; and (ii) artificially, with affectation; the adverb was a relatively recent coinage (the first citation in OED is 1582; see headnote, 'Authorship'); The adverb appears nowhere else in Shakespeare's works, but he uses the verb in both senses (i) and (ii). See (i) *Love's Labours Lost*, 1.2.88 ('He surely affected her for her wit'); (ii) *Coriolanus*, 5.3.149–50 ('Thou hast affected the fine strains of honour, | To imitate the graces of the gods').

49 **Enswathed** wrapped in; a coinage; a keyword search of EEBO-TCP search reveals no other usages.
sealed to sealed in, sealed in order to achieve secrecy; the unusual choice of preposition encourages readers to anticipate that the papers are sealed to prevent them being read by inquisitive ('**curious**') eyes; readers are then required to revise their initial interpretation of 'curious' when it becomes apparent that it qualifies 'secrecy', not (as expected) 'eyes'. Letters were habitually sealed in this period with wax and silk thread (Bloom 1906: 9).

Upon whose weeping margent she was set,
Like usury applying wet to wet,
Or monarch's hands that lets not bounty fall   40
Where want cries some, but where excess begs all.

Of folded schedules had she many a one,
Which she perused, sighed, tore, and gave the flood;
Cracked many a ring of posied gold and bone,   45
Bidding them find their sepulchres in mud;
Found yet mo letters sadly penned in blood,
With sleided silk feat and affectedly
Enswathed and sealed to curious secrecy.

These often bathed she in her fluxive eyes,   50
And often kissed, and often gave to tear,
Cried, 'O false blood, thou register of lies,
What unapprovèd witness dost thou bear!
Ink would have seemed more black and damnèd here!'

---

curious careful, elaborate; but see note on 'sealed to' (above).
50 *These* the letters of l. 47.
fluxive flowing (with tears); a recent coinage; the first citation in OED is Michael Drayton's 'Man in Moon' from *Poems* (1606?), sig. H5v ('In fluxive humour, which is ever found | As I do wane or wax unto my round'), although a keyword search of EEBO-TCP reveals one other, earlier usage, in Joseph Hall's *Two guides to good life* (1604), sig. C1r ('Pride [. . .] is flux-ive, momentary, and very uncertain'). The word is not used elsewhere by Shakespeare.
51 *often gave to tear* The woman repeatedly con-signs ('give', OED 12) or sacrifices (OED 11a) the letters to being torn up. Many edi-tors follow Malone's emendation ''gan to tear'; Gildon offers the slightly banal alterna-tive 'gave a tear'. However, Q's reading makes sense and can be left as it stands.
52 *O false blood* refers to the blood in which the letters have been penned (l. 47), but also antic-ipates the woman's narrative, in which she has been betrayed by her blood (the humour held responsible for passions, such as lust); see Sonnet 121.6n.
register record.

53 *unapprovèd* 'not demonstrated; unproved' (OED 2); not used elsewhere by Shakespeare, but compare the description of Fortinbras in *Hamlet*, 1.1.96 as being 'Of unimproved met-tle hot and full', where 'unimproved' (another of Shakespeare's unique words) could be interpreted as 'untried' (*Riverside Shakespeare*, 2nd edn: 1190n).
witness. . . bear echoes the Ninth Command-ment: 'Neither shalt thou bear false witness against thy neighbour' (Deuteronomy 5:20).
53, 54 *!* The exclamation marks are in Q (two of ten in the volume; see 92.12n).
54 *Ink. . . here* The papers are penned in blood (l. 47); the woman suggests that black ink would be more appropriate, as the colour associated with sin; see Thomas Middleton, *Microcynicon* (1599), Satire 1, where he depicts the present, degenerate age 'ranging the briary deserts of black sin' (sig. B1v). Ironically, the young man's letters are more diabolical than the woman seems to apprehend, since contracts with the devil were conventionally signed in blood, as seen in Christopher Marlowe's *Dr Faustus*, 2.1.35, where Faustus is required to 'write a deed of gift with [his] own blood', in which he bequeaths his soul to Lucifer.

55   ***in top of*** at the height of.
    rents tears.

56   ***Big*** violent, fierce (OED³ 2a), a much stronger word than in modern usage; see, for example, *Othello*, 3.3.349–50: 'Farewell the plumed troop and the big wars | That makes ambition virtue!'
    contents rhetorical play on 'discontent' earlier in the line; stressed on the second syllable.

57   ***reverend*** venerable, an adjective denoting respect; pronounced as two syllables.

58   ***Sometime*** once, formerly.
    blusterer braggart; a coinage, not elsewhere used by Shakespeare; a keyword search of EEBO-TCP reveals no earlier usages. Pronounced as two syllables.
    ruffle commotion; Shakespeare does not use the word as a noun in this sense elsewhere, but the verb appears in a similar context at *Titus Andronicus*, 1.1.311–13: 'A valiant son-in-law thou shalt enjoy, | One fit to bandy with thy lawless sons, | To ruffle in the commonwealth of Rome'.

59–60   ***had. . .flew*** The old man has had a misspent youth, letting slip by the '***swiftest hours***' of his younger days (when time passes quickest) rather than putting them to good use; however, he has gained some profit by this, because he '***observèd***' (noted) their passing and – presumably – has subsequently learned from his folly. The swiftness of time is proverbial; see Dent T327 ('Time flees away without delay') and Sonnet 19.6.

61   ***Towards*** pronounced as one syllable.
    afflicted distressed.
    fancy The woman is synonymous with her feelings; compare 'wounded fancies' (l. 197), used to describe the other women who pursue the youth. 'Fancy' in l. 61 indicates both 'love' (OED 8b) and a 'changeful mood' (OED 7a), as the woman destroys the tokens of her former affection.
    fastly (i) quickly (OED 4); (ii) close (OED 3); perhaps also 'steadfastly; with confidence' (OED 2a); the adverbial form does not appear elsewhere in Shakespeare's works. The word is probably chosen for its alliteration with 'afflicted fancy'.

63   ***motives of*** reasons for.

64   ***slides. . .bat*** The old man uses his walking stick ('bat, *n*.2', OED 1) to ease himself down to the ground; '***grainèd***' may indicate (i) the texture of the wood ('grained, *adj*.2', OED 2); (ii) that the stick is forked (*adj*.3). Shakespeare uses the adjective in sense (i) in a description of old age at *Comedy of Errors*, 5.1.312–13: 'this grained face of mine be hid | In sap-consuming winter's drizzled snow'. The man's stick thus mirrors his age (as the 'weeping margent' mirrored the woman's grief at l. 39). 'Bat' is used in this sense at *Coriolanus*, 1.1.55–6 ('Where go you | With bats and clubs?') and 161 ('your stiff bats and clubs').

65   ***comely distant*** at an appropriate, decorous distance.

67   ***divide*** share, drawing on the proverbial wisdom that 'grief is lessened when imparted to others' (Dent G447).

68   ***applied*** a verb often used of administering medical treatments (OED³ 2a); compare Sonnet 119.3 and note; *Midsummer Night's Dream*, 3.2.450–2 ('I'll apply | To your eye, | Gentle lover, remedy'); *Much Ado*, 1.3.10–12 ('I wonder that thou [. . .] goest about to apply a moral medicine to a mortifying mischief').

69   ***suffering*** pronounced as two syllables.
    ecstasy 'the state of being "beside oneself", thrown into a frenzy or a stupor, with anxiety, astonishment, fear, or passion' (OED 1); compare Ophelia's description of the distracted, much-altered Hamlet: 'That unmatched form and stature of blown youth | Blasted with ecstasy' (*Hamlet*, 3.1.159–60).

70   ***charity of age*** compassion that comes with the experience of age.

71   ***Father*** respectful term of address; as an epithet used of the clergy (see the disguised duke in *Measure for Measure*; Friar Lawrence in *Romeo and Juliet*), the word may, as Kerrigan notes, anticipate the 'confessional nature' of what follows, and establish the 'reverend man' in the role of confessor (1986: 404).

72   ***injury*** hurt.
    many a elided into two syllables.
    blasting blighting, harmful; the word also appears in close proximity to 'ecstasy' at *Hamlet*, 3.1.160; see l. 69n (above). In light of the narrative that follows, a further sense – 'defaming' (OED 1) – may also be relevant.

74, 75   ***power. . .flower*** pronounced as one syllable.

75   ***spreading*** flourishing (i.e. with the petals unfurling).

This said, in top of rage the lines she rents,
Big discontent so breaking their contents.   55

A reverend man that grazed his cattle nigh,
Sometime a blusterer that the ruffle knew
Of court, of city, and had let go by
The swiftest hours observèd as they flew,   60
Towards this afflicted fancy fastly drew,
And, privileged by age, desires to know
In brief the grounds and motives of her woe.

So slides he down upon his grainèd bat
And comely distant sits he by her side,   65
When he again desires her, being sat,
Her grievance with his hearing to divide;
If that from him there may be aught applied
Which may her suffering ecstasy assuage,
'Tis promised in the charity of age.   70

'Father,' she says, 'though in me you behold
The injury of many a blasting hour,
Let it not tell your judgement I am old;
Not age, but sorrow, over me hath power.
I might as yet have been a spreading flower,   75
Fresh to myself, if I had self-applied
Love to myself, and to no love beside.

'But woe is me, too early I attended
A youthful suit – it was to gain my grace –
O one by nature's outwards so commended   80

76–7 **Fresh. . . beside** Compare Sonnet 94.9–10; see also the youth's propensity for self-love in Sonnet 1.
78 **early** young.
   attended paid attention to.
79 **it was. . . grace** The suit was intended to win the woman's favour, but this can also be read as predictive: it would succeed in winning her favour. 'Grace' can suggest sexual favour. Compare Astrophil's endeavour to acquire Stella's 'grace' throughout Sidney's *Astrophil and Stella*, as outlined in 1.1–4: 'Loving in truth, and fain in verse my love to show, | That the dear She might take some pleasure of my pain: | Pleasure might cause her read, reading might make her know, | Knowledge might pity win, and pity grace obtain'.
80 **O** Some editors, following Malone, amend to 'Of'; 'O' could also indicate the abbreviated form of 'Of' (*O'*); however, Q's ejaculation fits the woman's emotional state and there is no need to amend it.
   nature's outwards The youth of *A Lover's Complaint* – like that of the *Sonnets* – is blessed with natural good looks; compare Sonnets 4.1–4; 11.9–14; 20; 67.9–14; 68. 13–14; 126.5–10.

81 **stuck over** lingered over ('stick, *v*.1', OED 6c); as Burrow points out (2002:700), 'Shakespeare talks of eyes "sticking" to their objects usually in contexts which suggest sycophantic adoration'; see *Measure for Measure*, 4.1.59–60 ('O place and greatness! millions of false eyes | Are stuck upon thee'), and *Timon*, 4.3.261–4 ('The mouths, the tongues, the eyes and hearts of men | At duty, more than I could frame employment; | That numberless upon me stuck as leaves | Do on the oak').

82 **Love** Venus, the goddess of love (because of the feminine pronoun 'her' that follows), rather than Cupid; compare *Venus and Adonis*, 241–6n (where it is a male Cupid who makes a dwelling place in Adonis' face); see also Sonnet 109.5.

85–95 **His browny locks. . . wear** The description of the youth deploys some of the commonplace standards of male, youthful beauty. See Charis' depiction of her ideal lover in Ben Jonson's 'Her man by her own dictamen':

> Young I'd have him too, and fair,
> Yet a man with crispèd hair,
> Cast in thousand snares and rings,
> For Love's fingers, and his wings:
> Chestnut colour, or more slack,
> Gold, upon a ground of black. [. . .]
> Chin as woolly as the peach;
> And his lip should kissing teach,
> Till he cherished too much beard,
> And made Love or me afeared.
> He would have a hand as soft
> As the down, and show it oft;
> Skin as smooth as any rush,
> And so think to see a blush
> Rising through it ere it came. (*Underwood*, 2.9, ll. 9–29)

85 **browny** 'inclining to brown' (OED); not used elsewhere by Shakespeare, but probably chosen here as a two-syllable word for the sake of the metre.

86 **every. . . wind** at each occurrence of a gentle breeze ('occasion, *n*.1', OED 2a); '*light*' can mean 'wanton, unchaste' (*adj*.1, OED 14b); '*occasion*' also suggests 'opportunity' (*n*.1, OED³ 1a).

87 **their silken parcels** his curls ('parcel' = 'item', Schimdt, 1); 'parcels' recurs at l. 231.

88 **What's. . . find** 'What's pleasant to do will be done readily' ('to do' is the subject of 'will [. . .] find'); refers in the first instance to the curls, which want to be kissed by the youth, but that desire transfers to all those who look at him; compare the description of Lucrece's hair, 'play[ing] with her breath' (*Lucrece*, l. 400).

89 **Each. . . mind** Everyone who saw him was enchanted by him; compare the effect of the youth in Sonnet 20.7–8. '**Enchant**' and its derivatives are closely associated with witchcraft and magic in Shakespearean usage, used for example of La Pucelle in *1 Henry VI* (3.3.40; 5.3.42), of the herbs the sorceress Medea gathers (*Merchant of Venice*, 5.1.13), of Prospero's art (*Tempest*, Epilogue.14).

90–1 **For. . . sawn** The youth's face reflects, in miniature, a vision of Paradise; 'largeness' works twice, indicating: (i) the great extent of what God created in Paradise; (ii) the extent of human imagination in perceiving it. 'Sawn' seems to be an unusual form of 'seen' (adopted for the purposes of rhyme), although some editors follow Boswell's suggestion that this is a form of 'sown' (carrying on the vegetative imagery of the Garden of Eden). A difficult pair of lines, in which 'largeness' contrasts with 'in little', although the parallel is not grammatical.

92 **Small. . . chin** i.e. he was almost entirely beardless, a sign of his youth.

93 **phoenix** The adjective hyperbolically confers the mythical bird's beauty and uniqueness on the youth's nascent beard; the beard may also be phoenix-like because it regrows after being shaved (like the phoenix regenerating from the ashes).

94 **unshorn velvet** Velvet was finished by shaving it; unshaved velvet is even softer than the final product.

termless (i) indescribable (OED 2, with this line as the only citation); compare 'phrase-less', l. 225; (ii) since 'term' indicates a period of time (OED 4a), 'termless' could also suggest 'untouched by time'; the word is not used elsewhere by Shakespeare; a keyword search of EEBO-TCP reveals no other, non-Shakespearean examples. For Shakespeare's use of the *-less* suffix in *Lucrece*, see 2n on that poem.

95 **bare** bare skin (OED C1).

out-bragged surpassed; compare Sonnets 94.12 ('outbraves') and 18.11 ('nor shall Death brag').

the web i.e. the emergent beard.

seemed introduces a note of doubt as to whether the spectator's perception is accurate; compare l. 10n.

That maidens' eyes stuck over all his face.
Love lacked a dwelling and made him her place,
And when in his fair parts she did abide,
She was new lodged and newly deified.

'His browny locks did hang in crookèd curls,   85
And every light occasion of the wind
Upon his lips their silken parcels hurls;
What's sweet to do, to do will aptly find;
Each eye that saw him did enchant the mind,
For on his visage was in little drawn   90
What largeness thinks in Paradise was sawn.

'Small show of man was yet upon his chin;
His phoenix down began but to appear
Like unshorn velvet on that termless skin,
Whose bare out-bragged the web it seemed to wear,   95
Yet showed his visage by that cost more dear,
And nice affections wavering stood in doubt
If best were as it was, or best without.

'His qualities were beauteous as his form,
For maiden-tongued he was and thereof free;   100
Yet if men moved him, was he such a storm
As oft 'twixt May and April is to see,
When winds breathe sweet, unruly though they be.
His rudeness so with his authorised youth
Did livery falseness in a pride of truth.   105

96 **cost** a coinage, meaning 'side, edge, fringe' (i.e. the incipient beard), drawn from the Latin *costa* (rib or side), perhaps via the French *côte*, the sixteenth-century meanings of which included 'partie de sallainte de divers objets' [the projecting part of various things] (*Le Grand Robert*, 2.650). The word seems to be closely related to cloth ('*velours de côte*' and '*velours côtelé*' are terms for corduroy), which fits with the earlier description of this beard using vocabulary from textiles ('velvet', 'web', ll. 94, 95).

97 **nice** fastidious, refined, precise.
affections inclinations.
wavering pronounced as two syllables.

98 **If best. . . without** whether he looked better with or without his emerging beard.

99 **qualities** attributes, accomplishments.
beauteous a word frequently associated with the youth of the *Sonnets*; see 4.5n; pronounced as two syllables.

100 **maiden-tongued** (i) soft-spoken, like a woman; (ii) chaste in his language, like a maiden.
free the meaning here is probably 'innocent' (OED³ A8); compare *Hamlet*, 2.2.564: 'Make mad the guilty, and appal the free'.

101 **moved** angered.

101–3 **such. . . be** Compare 18.3. The inversion of 'May and April' is for the metre.

104 **His rudeness. . . youth** His discourtesy or lack of polish is licensed, or excused, by his youth; for the notion that different behaviour is acceptable at different life-stages, compare 'privileged by age', l. 62.
authorised three syllables, stressed on the second syllable.

105 **livery** dress, disguise; pronounced as two syllables; probably plays on 'pride' (see below); 'pride' and 'livery' appear in close conjunction in Sonnet 2.3 ('proud livery').
pride display (*n*.1, OED³ 6a).

107–9 **"That. . . makes"** The insertion of speech marks is editorial, showing the direct speech that the woman repeats (where 'that' is read as a demonstrative); however, 'that' could also introduce the lines which follow as indirect speech.

107 **mettle** disposition, eagerness; for the ideal sympathy between horse and rider (which marks good horsemanship), see Sonnet 50.7n.

108 **Proud. . . sway** Paradoxically, the horse is ennobled by being subjected to the youth's control.

109 **rounds** circuits; like 'bounds', 'course' and 'stop', the term refers to techniques perfected in 'manage' (see l. 112n); see Thomas Blundeville, *Art of Riding* (1561).

bounds leaps; difficult manoeuvres, for which you need both skill and a suitable, well-trained horse; see Blundeville, *Art of Riding*: 'if your horse be light, a stirrer, and nimble of nature, you may [. . .] for pleasure's sake teach him many other proper feats, as to bound aloft [. . .], whereof I purpose here somewhat to entreat, thinking it now meet so to do, and not before, because that unless your horse be first perfect in the former lessons, it were in vain to teach him any of the lessons following' (1561: sigs L6v–L7r).

course gallop (OED 1).

stop Blundeville devotes a whole chapter to training a horse to stop (1561: E5v–E7r).

110 **controversy. . . takes** *Controversia* (topics for debate) and *questiones* (points to be investigated, an expression from forensic rhetoric) are both terms from formal disputation (see Skinner 2014). Here the issue under debate is whether the rider (l. 111) or the horse (l. 112) is responsible for the skill which they together display.

111 **became his deed** (i) graced or befitted the feats the horse was undertaking; (ii) the horse was so exact in its execution of the manoeuvre that he almost seemed to be the manoeuvre.

111, 112 **by** owing to, because of.

112 **Or. . . manage** elliptical; 'became' is understood from l. 111; Q's 'mannad'g' is an acceptable variant of 'manage', namely: 'The movements in which a horse is trained in a riding school; any of the separate movements characteristic of a horse so trained', 'The training, handling, and directing of a horse' ('manage, *n*.2', OED³ 2a, b). Compare *Venus and Adonis*, l. 598; *Pericles*, 4.6.63–4: 'My lord, she's not paced yet, you must take some pains to work her to your manage'.

113 **this side** i.e. the first option (that the rider is responsible for the horsemanship).

114 **real habitude** 'Regal manner' is more likely than 'actual manner' ('real, *adj*.1', OED³ A1; 'habitude, *n*.', OED 1). 'Habitude' is not used elsewhere by Shakespeare. 'Real' is pronounced as two syllables.

115 **appertainings** belongings, appurtenances; not used as a noun elsewhere in Shakespeare (and this line is the only citation in OED for 'appertaining' as a noun), but it is used as an adjective from the late fourteenth century; see *Romeo and Juliet*, 3.1.62–4: 'Tybalt, the reason that I have to love thee | Doth much excuse the appertaining rage | To such a greeting'.

ornament decoration, display (OED³ 3a, 3b); compare *Merchant of Venice*, 3.2.73–4: 'So may the outward shows be least themselves − | The world is still deceived with ornament'.

116 **case** clothes, outfit (*n*.2, OED³ 7a).

118 **Came for additions** came to improve or augment him; Q's 'Can' is retained by some editors, who read 'Can' in its old sense of 'have the power, ability or capacity' ('can, *v*.1', OED 4a); however, l. 119 denies the efficacy of these aids, and the same error, mistaking 'can' for 'came', can be found in the Folio *Macbeth*, 1.3.98. The emendation to 'Came' was first made by Sewell (1726).

purposed trim the ornamentation they intended to supply.

119 **Pieced** supplemented; compare *Coriolanus*, 2.3.211–12:

SECOND CITIZEN	I'll have five hundred voices of that sound.
FIRST CITIZEN	I twice five hundred, and their friends to piece 'em.

'Well could he ride, and often men would say,
"That horse his mettle from his rider takes,
Proud of subjection, noble by the sway;
What rounds, what bounds, what course, what stop he makes."
And controversy hence a question takes,   110
Whether the horse by him became his deed,
Or he his manage by th' well-doing steed.

'But quickly on this side the verdict went:
His real habitude gave life and grace
To appertainings and to ornament,   115
Accomplished in himself, not in his case.
All aids, themselves made fairer by their place,
Came for additions; yet their purposed trim
Pieced not his grace, but were all graced by him.

'So on the tip of his subduing tongue   120
All kind of arguments and question deep,
All replication prompt and reason strong,
For his advantage still did wake and sleep.
To make the weeper laugh, the laugher weep,

120 *subduing* that which subdues. The verb 'subdue' encompasses conquest (OED³ 1a) and seduction (OED³ 2g); both senses are relevant here (since militaristic imagery is deployed throughout the woman's account of her seduction); not used elsewhere by Shakespeare in this adjectival form. The first citation in OED³ for the adjective is 1608, Daniel Tuvill's *Essays, Politic and Moral* – 'To polish and fashion out his then rough-hewn fortune, with the edge of his subduing sword' (sig. 2K5v) – but the adjective was in use from the late 1590s, e.g. 'this all-subduing power' (Samuel Daniel, *The Civil Wars*, 1595, sig. S2v), 'that subduing power' (Daniel, 'A Letter from Octavia', *Poetical Essays*, 1599, sig. ³B3r); 'your subduing looks' (John Dickenson, *Greene in Conceipt*, 1598, sig. E2r). Shakespeare often uses the term 'subdue' about seductive encounters; see, for example, *Measure for Measure*, 2.2.184–5 (describing Isabella's inadvertent conquest of Angelo: 'this virtuous maid | Subdues me quite') and *Othello*, 1.3.111–12 ('Did you [...] | Subdue and poison this young maid's affections?').

121 *arguments* proofs, evidence (OED 1).
question a term from forensic rhetoric; see l. 110n.

122 *replication* reply; bearing in mind the forensic terms deployed in l. 121, the legal sense may be resonant: 'In traditional English pleadings: a claimant's answer to a defendant's plea' (OED 5a).

123 *For. . . sleep* The rhetorical strategies listed in ll. 121–2 were active ('did wake') or passive ('did [...] sleep'), as best suited the youth's persuasive tactics.

125 ***dialect*** (i) manner of speaking, idiom (OED³ 3a); compare *King Lear*, 2.2.109, where Kent describes his ornate speech to Cornwall (2.2.105–7) as 'go[ing] out of [his] dialect'; (ii) dialectic (OED 1), i.e. the art of logic; see Thomas Wilson, *Rule of Reason*: 'Logic, otherwise called dialect (for they are both one) is an art to try the corn from the chaff, the truth from every falsehood, by defining the nature of any thing, by dividing the same, and also by knitting together true arguments and untwining all knotty subtleties that are both false and wrongfully framed together' (1551: sig. B2v).
　　different skill (i) The youth knows how to use variety in his speech (variety was highly valued stylistically in this period); (ii) the youth's skill distinguishes him from others.

126 ***Catching all passions*** (i) capturing all emotions; (ii) ensnaring everyone's feelings.
　　his craft of will Both words articulate positive and negative qualities: 'craft' encompasses 'skill' as well as 'cunning' and 'deceit'; 'will', 'volition' as well as 'lust' and 'desire'. The meaning of the phrase consequently stretches from (i) his skilful moulding of (others') desires and/or volition to (ii) his lustful cunning. For the opacity and doubleness of language in *A Lover's Complaint*, see Kerrigan 1986: 15–17.

127 ***the general bosom*** in everyone's affections; compare 'the general tongue' (*Antony and Cleopatra*, 1.2.105), 'the general ear' (*Hamlet*, 2.2.563). See also the universal attractiveness of the young man of the *Sonnets*, as expressed (for example) at 5.2 and 20.8.

128 ***enchanted*** See l. 89n.

129 ***To dwell. . . thoughts*** to think continually about the young man; 'dwell' – 'to abide or continue for a time'; 'to linger'; 'to remain (in a house, country, etc.) as in a permanent residence' (OED 4a, 5, 7) – indicates that these are not passing thoughts.

129–30 ***remain. . . duty*** to attend him in person (like a servant).

130 ***personal. . . following*** Both words are pronounced as two syllables.
　　haunted frequented; the word does not necessarily carry supernatural overtones in the sixteenth and early seventeenth century; see, for example, *Measure for Measure*, 1.3.8–9: 'How I have ever loved the life removed | And held in idle price to haunt assemblies'.

131 ***Consents. . . granted*** 'People who have been bewitched by him consent to his wishes

even before he has formulated them himself'; people are here represented by their action in agreeing; compare use of 'fancies', l. 197 and note. Q's rendering of the line as 'Consent's [i.e. 'consent is'] bewitcht, ere he desire haue granted' opens up the possibility of a different reading, that consent is bewitched (i) before he desires the person consenting; (ii) before he has instilled desire for him in them. However, this is the only instance in Q where an apostrophe marks an elision of 'is', and the plural pronoun ('their') in l. 133 requires a plural subject. Most editors have therefore followed Malone in selecting 'Consents' over 'Consent's'.

132 ***dialogued for him*** scripted what he wants to say (OED³ 2); Shakespeare uses dialogue as a verb (meaning 'to hold [. . .] a conversation', OED³ 1a) at *Timon*, 2.2.51 ('Dost dialogue with thy shadow?').

133 ***wills*** inclinations, desires.

134–5 ***Many. . . mind*** Many acquire the young man's portrait, simply to look at, but then project their own desires onto it; Pooler (1931) suggests amending to 'put it in their mind' (i.e. committing the portrait to memory), but Q's reading should stand (i) in the spirit of the principle of *lectio difficilior* (whereby the more unusual or difficult reading is probably correct, because copyists and compositors are more likely to amend – consciously or not – to something familiar); (ii) because of the simile which follows, in which 'fools' take possession, in their imagination, of things which do not belong to them.

137 ***objects*** things 'placed before or presented to the eyes or other senses' (OED³ 1a).
　　abroad in the wider world.

138 ***theirs. . . assigned*** thinking them to be their own; 'assign' has a legal application: 'to transfer or formally make over to another' (OED 2).

139 ***mo*** more, as at l. 47.

139–40 ***labouring. . . them*** The syntax is contorted: '***mo pleasures***' attaches to 'bestow them', i.e. the people seeing these lands spend effort imagining how they might put them to more pleasurable uses than the gouty landlord who really owns them ('bestow' = employ, lay out, Schmidt, 2); however, because of its position in the line, the phrase 'more pleasures' also helps imply that there is pleasure to be had in having such

He had the dialect and different skill,   125
Catching all passions in his craft of will.

'That he did in the general bosom reign
Of young, of old, and sexes both enchanted
To dwell with him in thoughts, or to remain
In personal duty, following where he haunted.   130
Consents bewitched, ere he desire, have granted
And dialogued for him what he would say,
Asked their own wills and made their wills obey.

'Many there were that did his picture get
To serve their eyes, and in it put their mind,   135
Like fools that in th' imagination set
The goodly objects which abroad they find
Of lands and mansions, theirs in thought assigned,
And labouring in mo pleasures to bestow them
Than the true gouty landlord which doth owe them.   140

'So many have that never touched his hand
Sweetly supposed them mistress of his heart.
My woeful self that did in freedom stand
And was my own fee-simple (not in part),
What with his art in youth and youth in art,   145
Threw my affections in his charmèd power,
Reserved the stalk and gave him all my flower.

musings. 'Pleasure' may evoke 'pleasure ground' (OED³ 3b). The condition of being '*gouty*' is associated in Shakespeare with age, riches and miserliness (see *Lucrece*, ll. 855–6) and enforces the idea that the pleasurable potential of this land is currently unfulfilled, owing to the age and/ or penny-pinching ways of the man who owns it. 'Labouring' is two syllables; '*owe*' is an old form of 'own' (see Sonnet 18.10n).

142 *them* themselves.

144 *my own fee-simple* 'absolute possession of myself'; land held 'in fee-simple' belonged 'to the owner and his heirs for ever, without limitation to any particular class of heirs', as opposed to land in 'fee-tail', which came with conditions of inheritance attached. Compare *Romeo and Juliet*, 3.1.31–3: 'And I were so apt to quarrel as thou art, any man should buy the fee-simple of my life for an hour and a quarter'.
(not in part) not in part-ownership.

145 *art* probably implies deception (compare l. 295).

146, 147 *power. . . flower* pronounced as one syllable.

147 *Reserved. . . flower* The second half of the line has clear sexual connotations of 'deflowering'; OED finds a similarly bawdy reading in the first part of the line, citing this as an example of '*stalk*, *n*.1' sense 4d: '*coarse slang*. A penis, esp. one which is erect'; see also *Pericles*, 4.6.41–2 (where the bawd advertises the charms of the virginal Marina): 'Here comes that which grows to the stalk, never plucked yet, I can assure you'. The fact that the woman in *A Lover's Complaint* here hints that she has given herself sexually, but then draws back from that suggestion in the lines immediately following is symptomatic of her narrative and rhetorical strategies, where her fall is confessed (e.g. at ll. 78–9) and then partially retracted, as she seeks to distinguish herself from others who responded to his seduction more readily still. These strategies of confession mixed with self-justification are also common to female-voiced complaint; see, for example, Churchyard, *Shore's Wife* (Baldwin et al. 1960), ll. 92–154.

148   **equals** peers (socially and/or in age).

149   **nor. . . yielded** 'nor did I submit (i.e. have sex with him) the moment he asked me'; 'desired' works in two senses: 'request[ed]' ('desire, *v.*' OED 5) and 'crave[d]' (OED 1), with a strong sense of sexual longing.

    being pronounced as one syllable.

150   **Finding. . . forbid** 'finding that my sense of honour forbad it'.

151   **With . . . shielded** The woman preserves her virginity (honour) by keeping her distance; as at l. 237, 'distance' could be either literal or figurative (although OED cites both lines as examples of the latter; see OED 8a). There is a potential pun on 'honour' as genitalia; compare the bawdy exchange between Hero and Margaret on the morning of the former's wedding:

> MARG   [Your heart] will be heavier soon by the weight of a man.
> HERO   Fie upon thee, art not ashamed?
> MARG   Of what, lady? of speaking honourably? (*Much Ado*, 3.4.26–9)

152   **Experience** pronounced as three syllables.

153   **proofs new bleeding** fresh evidence of the injuries done to others; there was a superstitious belief that the bodies of victims bled in the presence of their murderers; see *Richard III*, 1.2.55–8: 'O gentlemen, see, see dead Henry's wounds | Open their congealed mouths and bleed afresh! | Blush, blush, thou lump of foul deformity, | For 'tis thy presence that exhales this blood'. Since the young man's crimes are of a sexual nature, the image of bleeding may evoke the blood shed when a woman's hymen is ruptured for the first time.

    foil The defensive, militaristic imagery of ll. 151–2 encourages an initial reading of 'repulse' or 'baffling check' (*n.*2, OED 2a), often used of wrestling (see *As You Like It*, 1.1.130, 1.2.187, 2.2.14). However, with the introduction of 'false jewel' in l. 154, 'foil' can also be read as 'a thin leaf of some metal placed under a precious stone to increase its brilliancy or under some transparent substance to give it the appearance of a precious stone' (*n.*1, OED 5a); compare *Hamlet*, 5.2.255–7 ('I'll be your foil, Laertes; in

mine ignorance | Your skill shall like a star i' th' darkest night | Stick fiery off indeed'); *1 Henry IV*, 1.2.213–15 ('My reformation, glittering o'er my fault, | Shall show more goodly and attract more eyes | Than that which hath no foil to set it off'). As the meaning slides, 'foil' thus epitomises the doubleness of the language in *A Lover's Complaint*; see Kerrigan 1986: 15–17. In terms of the psychological portrait of the woman, these lines suggest that it is the youth's reputation as a seducer which ultimately proves attractive; see ll. 169–75 (where the woman confesses that she knew his past history) and the youth's seduction speech, where he boasts of his conquests.

154   **amorous** pronounced as two syllables; compare l. 205.

    spoil (i) plunder (in the youth's campaigns of seduction); (ii) despoliation (pointing to the damage wreaked by these campaigns). Compare *Venus and Adonis*, l. 553 and note.

155   **precedent** previous example; compare Daniel, *Rosamond*, ll. 372–410 (where Rosamond sees the stories of Io and other victims of the rapacity of the classical gods engraved on a casket, and disregards their warning examples): 'These precedents presented to my view, | Wherein the presage of my fall was shown, | Might have forewarned me well what would ensue | And others' harms have made me shun mine own' (ll. 407–10).

156   **destined ill** Like Daniel's Rosamond, the woman frames her fall as something predestined; see *Rosamond*, ll. 411–13: 'But fate is not prevented though foreknown. | For that must hap decreed by heavenly powers, | Who work our fall, yet make the fault still ours'. Angelo in *Measure for Measure* tries to coerce Isabella into sexual relations by appealing to her womanhood as her 'destined livery' (2.4.138).

    assay try by experience.

157   **forced. . . content** 'whoever pressed home examples which warned against what she wanted to do?'; ironically, 'force' is often used to mean 'to violate, ravish' (*v.*1, OED 1), the very fate from which these examples could protect her; see *2 Henry VI*, 5.1.186: 'To force a spotless virgin's chastity'.

158   **by-passed** (i) because experienced by others; (ii) because they are now in the past.

'Yet did I not, as some my equals did,
Demand of him, nor being desirèd yielded;
Finding myself in honour so forbid,
With safest distance I mine honour shielded.   150
Experience for me many bulwarks builded
Of proofs new-bleeding, which remained the foil
Of this false jewel and his amorous spoil.

'But ah, who ever shunned by precedent   155
The destined ill she must herself assay,
Or forced examples 'gainst her own content
To put the by-passed perils in her way?
Counsel may stop awhile what will not stay;
For when we rage, advice is often seen   160
By blunting us to make our wits more keen.

'Nor gives it satisfaction to our blood
That we must curb it upon others' proof,
To be forbod the sweets that seems so good
For fear of harms that preach in our behoof.   165
O appetite from judgement stand aloof!
The one a palate hath that needs will taste,
Though reason weep and cry "It is thy last".

159 **Counsel. . . stay** The restraining effects of advice prove only temporary; '*will not*' may express volition as well as futurity.

160 *rage* are passionate; behave wantonly (OED³ 1a, citing this example); Kerrigan notes (1986: 412) the way in which the 1623 Folio uses 'raging' as a synonym for the quartos' 'lustful' at *Richard III*, 3.5.83.

161 **By. . . keen** Such counsel, attempting to dull the appetite, only manages to sharpen it; compare *Lucrece* ll. 645–6, where Tarquin's lust is further enflamed by Lucrece's attempts at dissuasion. Maxwell (1966) amends '*wits*' to 'wills' (i.e. passions, desires); however, retaining Q's reading helps convey the self-delusion of the victim, who chooses to ignore all warning precedents. For the sexual connotations of 'wit', see *Othello*, 2.1.131–3:

DESDEMONA [. . .] How if she be black and witty?
IAGO   If she be black, and thereto have a wit,
    She'll find a white that shall her blackness hit.

162 *blood* desire; blood was the humour held responsible for passions, such as lust; see l. 52n (above), Sonnet 121.6n.

163 *it* our blood (i.e. our desire).
upon others' proof on the grounds of others' experience; for 'proof' as sexual experience; see Sonnet 129.11 and note.

164 *forbod* an older form of 'forbade' which was still current in the early seventeenth century; compare *Lucrece*, l. 1648.
seems Plural verbs could take the *-s* form in early modern English; see Abbott (1884: §§ 333, 335–7).

165 *behoof* benefit, advantage.

166 **O appetite. . . aloof!** Appetite is requested to keep its distance from judgement (i.e. reason), so that it does not befuddle it. The exclamation mark is in Q (one of ten in the volume; see 92.12n).

167 **The one** i.e. appetite.

168 **"It. . . last".** 'It will be the end of you' (i.e. your undoing); the speech marks are editorial.

169 *further* (i) 'more' (i.e. 'I could say more about this man's infidelity'); (ii) 'moreover', whereby the stanza that follows distinguishes the 'precedent[s]' of others (l. 155) from what the woman herself observes; note the shift from the received wisdom, expressed through shared first person pronouns ('we', 'our', 'us') and generalised pronouns ('she', 'her') to the expression of first-hand experience: what 'I' 'knew' (l. 170), 'heard' (l. 171) and 'saw' (l. 172).

170 *patterns* examples, instances; the word also suggests that the youth's seductive strategies are formulae, which he repeats time after time (see also l. 221n).

171 *where. . . . grew* The youth has impregnated various women. That these women are married is indicated by the fact that these orchards belong to 'others' (wives being the legal possession of their husbands). For the image of women's bodies as horticultural spaces, compare Sonnets 16.6–7, 137.9–10, and notes.

172 *gilded* lent a specious attractiveness as a form of concealment; compare *Hamlet*, 3.3.58: 'Offence's gilded hand may shove by justice'.

173 *brokers* pimps, panders (OED 4); Pandarus is called a 'broker' at *Troilus and Cressida*, 5.10.33; compare also *Hamlet*, 1.3.127: 'Do not believe his vows, for they are brokers'. There may be a pun on 'broken vows'.

174 *characters* writing (of the type that the woman tears at ll. 55–6).
    merely but art Compare l. 295.

175 *bastards* illegitimate offspring; the phrase also recapitulates the organic imagery of l. 171, a 'bastard' being 'a shoot or sucker springing of its own accord from the root of a tree, or where not wanted' (OED B3b).
    foul adulterate heart Compare 'false adulterate eyes', Sonnet 121.5. 'Adulterate' (pronounced as three syllables) both indicates 'impure' (i.e. sinful), and underscores the adulterous liaisons of l. 171.

176 *city* Compare *Lucrece*, l. 469.

177 *'gan* began.

178 *feeling pity* Compare Sonnet 132.4.

179 *holy vows* (i) The youth swears his love in religious terms (e.g. invoking God to bear witness); (ii) the youth depicts his love (and the object of his love) as something pure and holy. From Ophelia's perspective, Hamlet's sincerity in love is proven by the fact that he 'hath given countenance to his speech [. . .] | With almost all the holy vows of heaven' (*Hamlet* 1.3.113–14).

180 *That's. . . sworn* what is sworn to you.

181 *feasts of love* Compare the 'sensual feast' of Sonnet 141.8; the phrase may also be reminiscent of George Chapman's erotic poem *Ovid's Banquet of Sense* (1595).

182 *woo* Q has vovv (i.e. vow, where – owing to a shortage of type – the 'w' has been supplied by two 'v's). The repetition in close proximity to 'vows' in l. 179 is unlikely, and 'woo' (first suggested by Capell) works much better in terms of the rhyme. Cercignani (1981: 197) highlights the unusualness of the 'know: woo' rhyme (equivalent to 'unto: vow') at *Midsummer Night's Dream*, 5.1.136–8; in contrast, the 'unto: woo' pair makes a full rhyme in *Venus and Adonis*, ll. 5–6, 307–9. The theory that the mistake results from an eye-skip from l. 179 is unconvincing, as the word does not appear in the same position in the line, and – in addition – is three lines back. In secretary hand, however, 'v' and 'w' both have a closed bowl (the second bowl, in the case of 'w'); 'woo' could thus be mistaken for 'vow'.

183 *that. . . see* i.e. which are public knowledge.

184 *errors. . . blood* For the belief that 'blood' was the humour which governed passions (such as lust), see l. 52n (above).

185 *with acture. . . be* 'They can be regarded as actions (where . . .)'; 'acture' is a coinage, used nowhere else in Shakespeare's works; nor does it appear elsewhere in a search of

'For further I could say this man's untrue,
And knew the patterns of his foul beguiling,   170
Heard where his plants in others' orchards grew,
Saw how deceits were gilded in his smiling,
Knew vows were ever brokers to defiling,
Thought characters and words merely but art,
And bastards of his foul adulterate heart.   175

'And long upon these terms I held my city,
Till thus he 'gan besiege me: "Gentle maid,
Have of my suffering youth some feeling pity
And be not of my holy vows afraid.
That's to ye sworn to none was ever said,   180
For feasts of love I have been called unto,
Till now did ne'er invite nor never woo.

'"All my offences that abroad you see
Are errors of the blood, none of the mind.
Love made them not; with acture they may be   185
Where neither party is nor true nor kind.
They sought their shame that so their shame did find,
And so much less of shame in me remains
By how much of me their reproach contains.

'"Among the many that mine eyes have seen,   190
Not one whose flame my heart so much as warmed,

EEBO-TCP. Burrow (2002: 707) suggests that 'the young man is inventing legalese terms to obscure a bogus argument'; note also the legal resonance of 'neither party', l. 186.

186 **neither. . . nor. . . nor** Multiple negatives are often used for emphasis in Elizabethan English, and were not – as in modern English – seen as grammatically incorrect.
true. . . kind These qualities are central to the depiction of love in the *Sonnets*, reaching their apogee in Sonnet 105.

187 **They. . .find** The youth makes the women responsible for their own downfall: as they sought it, so they reaped.

188–9 **And so. . .contains** 'The more they reproach me, the less I am to blame'; the logic is spurious.

191 **Not one** 'There is not one' (typical of the often elliptical syntax of *A Lover's Complaint*).

191, 193, 194 **warmed. . .charmed. . .harmed** When the *-ed* ending comes at the end of a line, scansion does not help determine pronunciation; Q's use of '-ed' (rather than the elided '-d') may suggest that the *-ed* endings should be stressed, producing eleven-syllable lines, each of which concludes in a feminine rhyme; however, few orthographic rules in Q are entirely consistent (see Sonnet 41.6n), and these lines would also work with a masculine rhyme (see Appendix 7).

192 *affection* feelings.

teen affliction (OED 3a); Burrow (2002: 707) and Kerrigan (1986: 413) suggest that by the late sixteenth century 'teen' was a poeticism, in Burrow's words 'favoured especially by the archaizing Spenser'. Certainly, a keyword search of EEBO-TCP reveals thirty-eight texts printed 1590–9 which use the word: of these, only three are prose (false results removed). Shakespeare uses the word in four other instances (*Love's Labours Lost*, 4.3.162; *Richard III*, 4.1.96; *Venus and Adonis*, l. 808; *Tempest*, 1.2.64); all bar the latter are used to make a rhyme.

193 *leisures* periods of free time; compare *Merchant of Venice*, 1.1.68 ('We'll make our leisures to attend on yours'); *Timon*, 2.2.128 ('At many leisures').

195 *Kept. . . free* The hearts of his other lovers were subject to his own, like servants or feudal retainers dressed in distinctive livery as a mark of their service (and obedience) to their master; in contrast, his heart is 'free', i.e. not subject to another; compare the woman's description of her former freedom at ll. 143–4; '*liveries*' is pronounced as two syllables.

196 *his* its (the young man's heart).

197 *Look here* The deictics throughout the youth's speech of seduction indicate that he is producing material evidence of his lovers' devotion; see also ll. 204 ('these talents'), 218 ('these trophies'), 223 ('these'), 227 ('these similes'), 232 ('this device').

tributes The choice of word continues the feudal register of ll. 195–6, tribute being 'rent or homage paid in money or an equivalent by a subject to his sovereign or a vassal to his lord' (OED 1a).

wounded by Cupid's arrow, but possibly also by the young man's mistreatment of them.

fancies adoring women; see l. 61 and note.

197, 199 Depending on pronunciation, this could be a triple – rather than a double – rhyme; see Appendix 7 (BY/DIE rhymes).

198 *pallid* Q's 'palyd' has been modernised both as 'palèd' (Malone) and (following Gildon 1714) as 'pallid', a word apparently coined by Spenser in *Faerie Queene* (1590) III.ii.28.1; Shakespeare uses 'pallid' nowhere else, but – as Burrow (2002: 708) notes – Spenser is 'a poet to whom *A Lover's Complaint* is more deeply indebted than to any other'. 'Pallid' is also more suggestive of the permanent pallor of pearls than 'palèd', which conveys instead the process of growing pale.

199 *Figuring* signifying (in the symbolic language of gem-stones); compare the description of Amphialus in Sidney's *Arcadia*: 'About his neck, he wore a broad and gorgeous collar, whereof, the pieces interchangeably answering, the one was of diamonds and pearl set with a white enamel [. . .] and the other piece, being of rubies and opals, had a fiery glistering, which he thought pictured the two passions of fear and desire, wherein he was enchained' (1590: sigs K5r–v). In *A Lover's Complaint*, ll. 201–2 clarify what the white pearls and red rubies symbolise. 'Figuring' is pronounced as two syllables.

200 *aptly understood* 'appropriately conceived'; the symbolism relies on an understanding shared between donor and recipient.

201 *encrimsoned* first recorded instance, although 'crimsoned' occurs in Thomas Heywood's *Troia Britannica* (1609) and Shakespeare's *Julius Caesar* (first performed in 1599), 3.1.206.

202 *Effects* manifestations, signs (OED³ 4a).

203 *Encamped. . . outwardly* situated in the heart, but manifested externally; the use of military metaphors in erotic poetry is conventional; Burrow (2002: 708) and Kerrigan (1986: 414) read 'fighting outwardly' as suggesting that the women put up a mere pretence of resistance, but external shows of emotion are not necessarily insincere.

204 *talents* 'Talent' was a 'denomination of weight' (OED 1a), i.e. a means of establishing value (the hair here having been enriched, and weighted down, with the metal with which it is 'impleached', l. 205). Duncan-Jones (1997a: 444) amends to 'talons', on the grounds that the word

Or my affection put to th' smallest teen,
Or any of my leisures ever charmed;
Harm have I done to them but ne'er was harmed,
Kept hearts in liveries, but mine own was free,   195
And reigned commanding in his monarchy.

'"Look here what tributes wounded fancies sent me
Of pallid pearls and rubies red as blood,
Figuring that they their passions likewise lent me
Of grief and blushes, aptly understood   200
In bloodless white and the encrimsoned mood,
Effects of terror and dear modesty,
Encamped in hearts but fighting outwardly.

'"And lo, behold these talents of their hair,
With twisted metal amorously impleached,   205
I have received from many a several fair,
Their kind acceptance weepingly beseeched,
With th' annexions of fair gems enriched,

was often spelled 'talents' in Elizabethan English.

205 **amorously** not used elsewhere by Shakespeare in this adverbial form; pronounced as three syllables; for the adjectival use of the word, see l. 154.

impleached interwoven; a coinage, formed from 'pleach': 'to interlace or intertwine (the [. . .] stems and branches of young trees and brushwood) so as to form a hedge, lattice, etc.' (OED³ 1); compare *Henry V*, 5.2.42 ('her hedges even-pleached) or its metaphorical use in *Antony and Cleopatra*, 4.14.72–3, where it describes the way in which a prisoner would be bound, with arms twisted behind their back: 'Wouldst thou [. . .] see | Thy master thus with pleached arms'. 'Impleached' appears nowhere else in Shakespeare's work; a search of EEBO-TCP reveals no other usages.

206 **many. . .fair** many different beautiful women ('fair' is used as a noun; see 16.11n).

many a elided into two syllables.
several pronounced as two syllables.

207 **weepingly** The adverbial form is rare before 1609 (and is not used elsewhere by Shakespeare); a full-text search of EEBO-TCP reveals seven other examples, three of them in different works by Thomas Lodge (*Phillis*, 1593; *William Longbeard*, 1593; *Prosopopeia*, 1596).

208 **th' annexions** the additions (OED 2); the elision is marked in Q and has worried some editors because it seems to make the line unmetrical; however, in late sixteenth-century pronunciation, 'annexions' could be four syllables (an-nex-i-on); see Cercignani on scanning 'incision' (1981: 295–9). Shakespeare does not use the word elsewhere; the word, derived from the Latin *annectere* (to bind), was a late Elizabethan coinage: a full-text search of EEBO-TCP reveals three other usages prior to 1609: in William Cornwallis, *Essays* (1600–1; twice), and Richard Carew, *Survey of Cornwall* (1602).

209 **deep-brained** clever; the term perhaps suggests 'overly ingenious', as in John Weever, *Mirror of Martyrs*, where the protagonist (Sir John Oldcastle) tells how 'Before these deep-brained, all-fore-seeing doctors, | These reverend fathers, purgatory teachers, | I was complained of' (1601: sig. D2r).

sonnets a form of poetry stereotypically written by lovers; see Armado's words on finding that he is in love at *Love's Labours Lost*, 1.2.181–4: 'Adieu, valour, rust, rapier, be still, drum, for your manager is in love; yea, he loveth. Assist me, some extemporal god of rhyme, for I am sure I shall turn sonnet [i.e. sonneteer]'.

amplify enlarge upon; 'amplification' was a rhetorical term indicating 'the extension of a simple statement by all such devices as tend to increase its rhetorical effect, or to add importance to the things stated; making the most of a thought or circumstance' (OED 4); see Thomas Wilson, *Art of Rhetoric*: 'Among all the figures of rhetoric, there is no one that so much helpeth forward an oration, and beautifieth the same with such delightful ornaments as doth amplification. For if either we purpose to make our tale appear vehement, to seem pleasant, or to be well-stored with much copy, needs must it be that here we seek help, where help chiefly is to be had, and not elsewhere' (1553: sig. Q4r). Compare *Coriolanus*, 5.2.14–16: 'I have been | The book of his good acts, whence men have read | His fame unparalleled, happily amplified'.

210 **dear** precious.

212 **his** Whilst 'his' could be either a neuter or masculine pronoun (referring respectively to the diamond or the youth), the former (its) is more likely, because (i) the rest of the stanza concentrates exclusively on the precious stones; (ii) this part of the poem is in the voice of the youth, who does not elsewhere refer to himself in the third person.

invised The meaning is obscure, as there is no other record of the word. Duncan-Jones (1997a: 444) conjectures that the compositor (or copyist) has misread 'invied' or 'invi'd' (i.e. envied). However, OED surmises that the word derives from the Latin 'invisus' (unseen); the invisible properties of the diamond thus contribute to its beauty and hardness, which makes the diamond exactly analogous to the youth.

213–14 **in whose. . . amend** It was believed that emeralds had the power to cure eyestrain; see Philemon Holland's translation of Pliny's *History of the World*: 'if the sight hath been wearied and dimmed by intentive [assiduous] poring upon anything else, the beholding of this stone doth refresh and restore it again, which lapidaries well know, that cut and engrave fine stones; for they have not a better means to refresh their eyes than the emerald, the mild green that it hath doth so comfort and revive their weariness and lassitude' (1601: sig. 3F6r). '*Emerald*' is pronounced as two syllables.

215 **heaven-hued** because blue, like the sky; 'heaven' is elided into one syllable.

215–16 **blend. . . . manifold** 'Blend' could be (i) a plural verb; interpreted this way, the sapphire and opal merge with many varied ('manifold') things presented to the view (see gloss on 'objects', l. 137n); (ii) a past-participle ('blended'), serving the same adjectival function as 'heaven-hued'; read this way, it is the opal which is composed of many varied things. (ii) seems more likely, as the opal is an iridescent stone, combining a wide variety of colours; see Holland's translation of Pliny's *History*: 'in the opal you shall see the burning fire of the carbuncle or ruby, the glorious purple of the amethyst, the green sea of the emerald, and all glittering together mixed after an incredible manner' (1601: sig. 3G1v).

216 **several** separate; pronounced as two syllables.

217 **well-blazoned** appropriately described (OED 4), in the 'deep-brained sonnets' (l. 209); see Sonnet 106.5 and note.

smiled. . . . moan Most editors gloss this as indicating that the stones appear to respond to the descriptions of themselves; however, it seems more likely that the youth here describes (and mocks) the poetic conceits of the lovers' sonnets which invest the stones with emotions and anthropomorphic characteristics. See, for example, the address to the diamond in John Davies, *Wit's Pilgrimage*, 34.9–10: 'And thou relentless diamond, too dear, | (Too dear for me, that offered me for thee)' (1605: sig. D2v).

218 **trophies** reawakens the militaristic metaphors of amorous conquest found in ll. 151–3, 176–7, 203.

affections passions.

219 **Of. . . tender** The syntax is inverted ('the tender of pensived and subdued desires').

And deep-brained sonnets that did amplify
Each stone's dear nature, worth, and quality.   210

'"The diamond? Why, 'twas beautiful and hard,
Whereto his invised properties did tend;
The deep green emerald in whose fresh regard
Weak sights their sickly radiance do amend;
The heaven-hued sapphire and the opal blend   215
With objects manifold; each several stone,
With wit well-blazoned, smiled, or made some moan.

'"Lo, all these trophies of affections hot,
Of pensived and subdued desires the tender,
Nature hath charged me that I hoard them not,   220
But yield them up where I myself must render:

---

pensived saddened; the unusual passive form (a coinage) is not necessary for metrical purposes ('pensive' and Q's 'pensiu'd' both having two syllables); however, it captures the sense that the desires (and the women from whom these desires emanate) have been made melancholic, presumably because of their mistreatment by the youth. Shakespeare's use elsewhere of 'pensive' suggests a high degree of mental distress. See *Romeo and Juliet*, where the desperate Juliet is described as 'pensive' (4.1.39) as she deals with Romeo's banishment and her impending marriage to Paris; and *Henry VIII*, 2.2.62, where Suffolk glosses the preceding SD ('*the King [. . .] sits reading pensively*') with 'How sad he looks! Sure he is much afflicted'.

subdued The usual meaning of 'subdued' in the early modern period is 'subjugated, overcome' (OED⁴ A1); however, this does not seem to fit in this context; most editors gloss as 'humble' (i.e. submitting voluntarily to the youth). 'Brought low' ('subdue, *v.*', OED³ 2e) is a possible reading; see *King Lear*, 3.4.70–1: 'Nothing could have subdued nature | To such a lowness but his unkind daughters'. See also l. 120n, for the seductive associations of 'subdue'. *Much Ado* offers another comparison, describing Don John as 'out of measure sad' (1.3.2) and 'discontent[ed]' (1.3.38). The scene concludes with Don John heading off to supper,

observing that 'their cheer is the greater that I am subdued' (1.3.71–2); this may refer to Don John's sense of having been eclipsed by Claudio ('that young start-up hath all the glory of my overthrow', 1.3.66–7), but the overall thrust of the scene, with its focus on Don John's moroseness, imbues the word with a sense close to 'dejected'.

tender offer (*n.*2, OED 2); compare *Hamlet*, 1.3.99–100 ('He hath, my lord, of late made many tenders | Of his affection to me') and Sonnet 83.4. The word has strong legal connotations.

220 **Nature. . . *not*** The youth echoes the arguments of Sonnets 4 and 11; however, where the law of nature would decree ('charge') that he should not hoard up his gifts (but should disseminate them through procreation), here the youth conflates desire with the material gifts which display it (and which he will go on to offer the woman, l. 221).

221 **render** surrender, relinquish (OED³ 6a); however, there may be an ironic play on 'render' as 'recite' or 'repeat' (OED³ 1), the youth having made similar seductive speeches previously (see l. 170n); for this usage of 'render', see *Cymbeline*, 5.5.135–6 ('My boon is, that this gentleman may render | Of whom he had this ring'); *Henry V*, 1.2.237–8 ('May't please your Majesty to give us leave | Freely to render what we have in charge?').

222 **origin and ender** beginning and end; the youth (i) transfers to the woman the attributes of nature (where all things begin and end); (ii) identifies her with God, described (in the person of Jesus) as 'Alpha and Omega, the beginning and the ending' (Revelations 1:8) and 'the author and finisher of our faith' (Hebrews 12:2). 'Ender' is not used elsewhere by Shakespeare.

223 **these** the trophies of l. 218.
of force of necessity.
oblations offerings (with a religious resonance); see Sonnet 125.10 and note.

224 **Since. . . altar** 'Since I am their altar' (another elliptical phrase).
enpatron stand as patron to; considering that the object in question is an altar, this figures the woman as a patron saint, to whom the altar is dedicated. The verb is a coinage and the only pre-1900 citation in OED, although 'impatron, v.' is treated as a separate entry (with one citation, from 1642); a full-text search of EEBO-TCP produces one further instance, spelled 'impatron', in George Mackenzie's 1660 romance *Aretina*.

225 **advance** stretch out; Shakespeare uses the verb in this sense in at least three other instances: *1 Henry VI*, 1.6.1 (where the victorious La Pucelle orders her troops to 'Advance our waving colours [banners] on the walls' of captured Orleans) and 2.2.4–5 ('Bring forth the body of old Salisbury, | And here advance it in the market-place'); *Merry Wives*, 3.4.81 ('I must advance the colours of my love'). The verb thus has a military resonance, which accords with the youth's perception of erotic encounters between the sexes; see ll. 203, 218 and notes.
of yours. . . hand 'that hand of yours, which surpasses description in words'; compare 'termless' (l. 94). As at l. 219, the genitive phrase has been inverted. '**Phraseless**' is not used elsewhere by Shakespeare, nor does it show up prior to 1609 in a full-text search of EEBO-TCP.

226 **Whose. . . praise** The line exemplifies why the hand is 'phraseless': it is so white that it is beyond praise; '**airy**' hints that the praise is

insubstantial (OED³ 6a) as well as celestial (OED³ 2a), an ambiguity which is no doubt inadvertent on the youth's part.

227 **these similes** presumably the comparisons made in the 'deep-brained sonnets' (l. 209), with their elaborate conceits about the properties of the jewels described; 'similes' is pronounced as two syllables.

228 **Hallowed** Q has 'Hollowed'; if Q is correct, as Porter argues it is (1912: 272), the image that follows is of glass-blowing; it is more probable that the compositor (or an earlier copyist) misread the first vowel (an easy mistake in secretary hand), and most editors follow Malone's emendation to 'Hallowed', i.e. made holy (a suggestion first made by Capell), and a word from the Lord's Prayer in *Book of Common Prayer* ('hallowed be thy name'); as such, the line continues the religious metaphor of l. 224, with the lovers' sighs portrayed as incense, rising from the fires of passion.

229–30 **What. . . under you** 'whoever obeys me, obeys you'; 'what' is here equivalent to 'who' (see Abbott 1884: § 252); '**minister**' suggests both (i) agent (OED³ 1a), anticipating the financial imagery of ll. 230–1; (ii) a member of the clergy, or someone authorised to administer liturgical duties (OED³ 2c, 2b), thus looking back to the religious imagery that has preceded this.

230 **audit** (i) final account; (ii) hearing.

231 **distract** (i) separate (OED 1); (ii) since the '**parcels**' ('items', Schmidt, 1) come from the youth's lovers, the use of the word to indicate madness (including that arising from disappointed love) is also relevant; see the description of Ophelia at *Hamlet*, 4.5.2–3: 'She is importunate, indeed distract. | Her mood will needs be pitied'; compare l. 28 and note.

232 **device** 'a fancifully conceived design or figure' (OED 8).

233 **Or sister sanctified** The youth's gloss (i) clarifies that the woman he describes is not a prostitute (for which 'nun' was Elizabethan slang); (ii) establishes that she is not a novice – as Isabella is in *Measure for Measure* –

That is to you, my origin and ender;
For these of force must your oblations be,
Since, I their altar, you enpatron me.

"'O then advance of yours that phraseless hand,   225
Whose white weighs down the airy scale of praise.
Take all these similes to your own command,
Hallowed with sighs that burning lungs did raise.
What me, your minister, for you obeys,
Works under you, and to your audit comes   230
Their distract parcels in combinèd sums.

"'Lo, this device was sent me from a nun,
Or sister sanctified of holiest note,
Which late her noble suit in court did shun,
Whose rarest havings made the blossoms dote;   235
For she was sought by spirits of richest coat,
But kept cold distance, and did thence remove
To spend her living in eternal love.

"'But, O my sweet, what labour is 't to leave
The thing we have not, mastering what not strives,   240

but has taken her full vows. The phrase also amplifies 'nun', stressing the way in which this woman should be beyond reach, and thus further demonstrating the youth's attractiveness and powers of seduction.
of holiest note renowned for being very holy.
234 *Which* who (see note on ll. 229–30).
late recently.
her noble suit in court attendance at court ('suit, *n.*', OED 2a), where – owing to her social status – she held an elevated position.
235 *rarest havings* most excellent attributes.
blossoms (i) the most eligible young men ('the flower') at court; compare Venus' description of Adonis, *Venus and Adonis*, l. 8; or (ii) a hyperbolic way of stressing the nun's excellence (that she affects even the natural world as she passes).
dote The verb suggests a foolish or excessive infatuation; see Sonnet 20.10n.

236 *spirits* men (of spirit); here pronounced as a monosyllable; see Sonnet 56.8n.
richest coat most splendid robes (i.e. those of the highest rank).
237 *cold distance* chaste distance; see l. 151 and note.
remove depart.
238 *living* life; the proximity with '*spend*' also produces a quibble on property (which – theoretically – she would have had to renounce on entering holy orders, although many nuns of high social status managed to retain their personal property, despite vows of poverty).
eternal love because devoted to God.
239–40 *what. . . have not* 'How difficult is it to abandon something we do not have?'
240 *mastering. . . strives* 'overpowering something that puts up no fight'; the phrase is elliptical. 'Mastering' is here pronounced as two syllables.

241 **Paling** Q has 'Playing'. Most editors (as here) follow Malone's emendation 'Paling' (which connects this line to the one that follows, through the shared imagery of hunting). Both Malone's 'Paling' and 'Planing' (first suggested by Capell) are feasible: their similarity to 'Playing', which appears in the same position in the line below, would increase the likelihood of an eye-skip, although it may be that mistaking 'Planing' for 'Playing' results, not from an eye-jump, but from the compositor (or an earlier copyist) missing a tilde over the 'y' ('Plaȳing') or 'a' ('Plāyng'), which would have supplied the 'n' to make 'Planning' or 'Planyng'.
did. . . receive (i) If the line is read as opening with 'paling' (enclosing), then *'form'* could indicate 'the nest or lair in which a hare crouches. Also rarely, of a deer' (there being little point in fencing off an area that such animals do not frequent), although this is not a sense which appears elsewhere in Shakespeare; (ii) more simply, 'form' could indicate the 'image' of the lover ('form, *n.*', OED 2); (iii) if we accept Capell's 'planing' as the verb on which the following action depends, the line depicts the action of (unnecessarily) smoothing a surface which has no image impressed on it; there may even be a specific reference to the 'form' ('the body of type, secured in a chase, for printing at one impression') used in printing (OED 20).

242 **Playing. . . gyves** feigning patience, because the fetters ('gyves') have been voluntarily adopted (**'unconstrained**, *adj.*', OED 1a). Compare *Cymbeline*, 5.4.14–15: 'I cannot do it better than in gyves, | Desired more than constrained'. Although Q has 'unconstraind' (a spelling which usually suggests an unstressed ending), the metre requires that the final syllable is stressed; 'Playing' is slurred into one syllable.

243 **She. . . contrives** 'she who works to keep her own reputation secure (by keeping herself to herself)'.

245 **And. . . might** Compare the proverb 'Discretion is the better part of valour' (Dent D354). Falstaff infamously uses this aphorism to justify his cowardice in *1 Henry IV*, 5.4.119–20.

246 **in that** since; from the youth's perspective, the factual basis of his story should excuse any moral failings on his part.
my boast The boast follows (ll. 246–52).

247 **accident** chance.

248 **Upon the moment** at once, immediately.
subdue For the erotic connotations of this word, see l. 120n.

249 **cagèd** This may refer to the fact that, after the Council of Trent (1545–63), nunneries were required to have grilles separating the nuns from the world.

250 **Religious love** (i) the love of a religious (i.e. a nun); (ii) a love which resembles religious devotion in its zeal and commitment; compare Sonnet 31.6 and note.
put out religion's eye blinded her religious scruples; the phrase is ironically indebted to Matthew 18:9: 'if thine eye cause thee to offend, pluck it out, and cast it from thee' (see also Mark 9:47).

251 **immured** walled in; compare Sonnet 84.3. Q has 'enur'd', and whilst the idea of becoming 'habituated' to not being tempted is an acceptable reading ('inure/enure, *v.*1', OED 1a), 'immured' better fits the immediate context of the 'cagèd cloister' (l. 249); moreover, 'emured' is an acceptable Elizabethan spelling of 'immured' (used, for example, in Q1 of *Love's Labours Lost* at 3.1.124); the mistake in *A Lover's Complaint* would thus arise from a misreading of one letter ('em' and 'en' being easily mistaken in a secretary hand).

252 **to tempt. . . procured** (i) 'in order to tempt (me) she obtained complete freedom (from her vows)'; (ii) 'to try all kinds of freedoms, she obtained her freedom'. Q has 'procure', but the emendation to 'procured' is necessary for the rhyme (and a secretary 'd' is easily mistaken for 'e' in a terminal position, especially if the hand is cramped and the letter form squat).

254 **bosoms** hearts; as the youth offers the woman all the broken hearts he possesses (as he would trophies), he resembles the poet-speaker in Sonnet 31, who finding the beloved's 'bosom [. . .] endearèd with all hearts' (31.1) recognises 'That due of many now is thine alone' (31.12); see also l. 266n.

255–6 **Have. . . among** The woman becomes the recipient of all the love that the youth has acquired from his unfortunate devotees ('the broken bosoms', l. 254) in addition to the love of the youth himself. For the use of the image of tributaries flowing into the sea, see Sonnet 135.9–10. '**Fountains**' hold erotic potential; see *Venus and Adonis*, ll. 231–4; Thomas

Paling the place which did no form receive,
Playing patient sports in unconstrainèd gyves?
She that her fame so to herself contrives,
The scars of battle scapeth by the flight,
And makes her absence valiant, not her might.   245

"'O pardon me in that my boast is true:
The accident which brought me to her eye
Upon the moment did her force subdue,
And now she would the cagèd cloister fly.
Religious love put out religion's eye: 250
Not to be tempted would she be immured,
And now to tempt all liberty procured.

"'How mighty then you are, O hear me tell:
The broken bosoms that to me belong
Have emptied all their fountains in my well,   255
And mine I pour your ocean all among.
I strong o'er them, and you o'er me being strong,
Must for your victory us all congest,
As compound love to physic your cold breast.

"'My parts had power to charm a sacred nun,   260
Who disciplined, ay, dieted in grace,

Nashe, *Choice of Valentines* (c. 1591): 'A pretty rising womb without a weam [blemish], | That shone as bright as any silver stream; | And bare out like the bending of an hill, | At whose decline a fountain dwelleth still, | That hath his mouth beset with ugly briars | Resembling much a dusky net of wires' (ll. 109–14). 'Ocean' is used as an image of expanse and worth at Sonnet 80.5.

257 *being* pronounced as one syllable.

258 *Must* The subject is 'I'.

congest gather together, heap up (OED 1); not used elsewhere in Shakespeare. The word, a mid-sixteenth-century neologism, from Latin, was still relatively rare in 1609 (EEBO-TCP reveals six other instances, aside from *A Lover's Complaint*).

259 *As. . . breast* This love, compounded (i.e. made up) of different elements (as were many early modern remedies), will be used to treat ('*physic*') her emotional coldness; the cure works on principles of early modern medicine, where one extreme (coldness) is brought

to a moderate and healthful state by the application of its opposite (here, passion, which is always regarded as hot).

260 *parts* attributes; physical body parts; compare Sonnet 17.4.

power pronounced as one syllable.

nun Q reads 'Sunne'; the emendation – first suggested by Capell and adopted by Dyce (1857) – has been followed by most modern editors. It would be feasible to mistake a capital 'N' for a capital 'S' in secretary hand.

261 *disciplined* trained (OED³ 2), with the suggestion of scourging, or flogging 'to mortify (the flesh) by way of penance' (OED³ 1a).

ay 'I' in Q (an acceptable Elizabethan spelling of 'ay', and sometimes used by Shakespeare for punning purposes; see Sonnet 136.6n).

dieted in grace followed a regulated regimen (e.g. restricting intake of food, or avoiding particular foodstuffs) in order to achieve a state of divine grace (favour); emphasises 'disciplined', and continues the medicinal imagery.

262 **t'assail** to attack; as is conventional in love poetry of the period, the onslaught on the nun's heart begins through her eyes, which present the beautiful outward form of the youth (which she then believes to reflect an inner, moral beauty); see Sonnet 46.1n.

263 **consecrations** acts or ceremonies which mark something apart and as belonging to God (in this case, probably the body of the nun herself); not used elsewhere by Shakespeare.
giving place yielding room.

264 **potential** powerful; used by Shakespeare in two other instances: *King Lear*, 2.1.76 ('very pregnant and potential spirits'); *Othello*, 1.2.13–14 ('[He] hath in his effect a voice potential | As double as the Duke's').

264–5 **vow. . . confine** Oaths have no hold over Love's conscience (such as would provide a 'sting'; compare Sonnet 151.1), obligations have no tie, and space has no restrictions or limits. The points of reference here are the nun's vows, her obligations to the Church, and the cloister which should confine her.

266 **For. . . thine** Compare Sonnet 31.14.

267 **thou** The subject is still 'love' (l. 264).
impressest force someone into service (*v.*2, OED 1a); see *1 Henry IV*, 1.1.20–1: 'under whose blessed cross | We are impressed and engaged to fight'.

267–8 **what. . . example?** 'What is the value of rules for conduct based on old examples?' The syntax is inverted (as it frequently is in *A Lover's Complaint*).

269 **coldly** unenthusiastically (as if the impediments were soldiers, stepping forward).
impediments obstacles (those listed in l. 270); there may be an echo of the marriage service in the *Book of Common Prayer*: 'if either of you do know any impediment, why ye may not be lawfully joined together in matrimony' (2011: 158); see also Sonnet 116.1–2.

270 **filial fear** a child's dread of disobeying a parent; 'filial' is two syllables.
law Marriages would be forbidden by civil law if the bride and groom were too closely related, if one of them was already married to someone else, or if one partner was not of age.
kindred fame Punctuated as in Q, where 'kindred fame' mirrors 'filial fear' and works

as an uninflected genitive, indicating 'the reputation of the family'; compare the 1597 Quarto of *Richard II*, 2.1.182: 'His hands were guilty of no kinred blood', amended in 1623 Folio to 'kindred's blood'. Q's reading was amended to 'kindred, fame' in Benson's 1640 edition, punctuation which has been adopted by numerous editors since.

271 **peace** Malone emends to 'proof'; but Q's reading works, since love's weapons are (paradoxically) those of peace.
'gainst. . . shame Tricolon is a well-tried and effective rhetorical device.

272 **sweetens** a singular verb (see 'it beats', which follows), the subject having shifted from 'love's arms' to 'love'.
suffering pronounced as two syllables.

273 **aloes** 'a drug made from the concentrated or dried juice of plants of the genus *Aloe*, having a bitter taste and unpleasant odour' (OED³ 3a).

275 **bleeding groans** Sighs were believed to draw blood from the heart; see *Midsummer Night's Dream*, 3.2.97 ('With sighs of love, that costs the fresh blood dear'); *2 Henry VI*, 3.2.60–1 ('Might liquid tears or heart-offending groans | Or blood-consuming sighs recall his life').

276 **supplicant** in supplication, as a suppliant (OED³ B).
extend stretch out (an imploring gesture).

277 **leave** leave off.
battery bombardment; compare l. 23 and *Venus and Adonis*, l. 426 and note. The word returns us to the militaristic imagery of ll. 176–7, only here it is the female speaker who is placed in the role of assailant. 'Battery' is pronounced as two syllables.

278 **Lending** giving.
audience hearing, attention (OED³ 3b).
design plan; the word is often used of plans made by Shakespeare's villains, such as Iachimo and Cloten in *Cymbeline* (2.2.23; 3.5.153; 5.5.192); see also *Macbeth*, 2.1.52–6, where 'withered Murder [...] | With Tarquin's ravishing strides, towards his design | Moves like a ghost'.

279 **credent** believing, with a strong sense of being gullible; also used at *Hamlet*, 1.3.29–30: 'weigh

Believed her eyes when they t' assail begun,
All vows and consecrations giving place.
O most potential love; vow, bond, nor space
In thee hath neither sting, knot, nor confine,   265
For thou art all, and all things else are thine.

'"When thou impressest, what are precepts worth
Of stale example? When thou wilt inflame,
How coldly those impediments stand forth
Of wealth, of filial fear, law, kindred fame.   270
Love's arms are peace 'gainst rule, 'gainst sense, 'gainst shame,
And sweetens in the suffering pangs it bears
The aloes of all forces, shocks, and fears.

'"Now all these hearts that do on mine depend,
Feeling it break, with bleeding groans they pine,   275
And supplicant their sighs to you extend
To leave the battery that you make 'gainst mine,
Lending soft audience to my sweet design,
And credent soul to that strong bonded oath
That shall prefer and undertake my troth."   280

'This said, his watery eyes he did dismount,
Whose sights till then were levelled on my face,
Each cheek a river running from a fount
With brinish current downward flowed apace.
O how the channel to the stream gave grace!   285

what loss your honour may sustain | If with too credent ear you list his songs'.
strong bonded Many editors, following Malone, render this a hyphenated adjective. As Burrow notes (2002: 714), this dilutes the sense that these can be distinct qualities: an oath can be strong; it can also be tied to a legal oath. In this case, the oath is both.
280 **prefer** advance, promote (OED³ 1a).
undertake my troth act as surety for my pledge; the use of 'troth' invokes the marriage service in the *Book of Common Prayer*: 'And thereto to I plight thee my troth' (2011: 159).
281–2 **his. . .face** The description of the youth lowering his eyes deploys the terminology of gunnery (compare the description of the

woman's eyes at ll. 22–3, and the young man of the *Sonnets* at 117.11–12); '*dismount*' means remove a gun from its carriage or other support (OED 6); '*sights*' are 'gun-sights'; '*levelled on*' means 'aimed at'.
281 **watery** pronounced as two syllables.
283–7 **Each. . . encloses** Compare the description of the weeping youth with that of Venus in *Venus and Adonis*, ll. 955–60.
fount See *Lucrece*, 850n.
284 **brinish** salty; also used to describe tears at *Lucrece*, l. 1213; *3 Henry VI*, 3.1.41.
285 **the channel** his cheeks (which beautify the stream of tears that runs down them).
grace! The exclamation mark is in Q (one of ten in the volume; see 92.12n).

286 **Who** which (the 'stream' of tears, l. 285); see Abbott 1884: § 264.
     gate barrier.
     glowing roses his cheeks; a conventional image of beauty; see Shakespeare's rebuttal of this motif in Sonnet 130.5–6.

286, 287 Both lines end in a feminine rhyme; if the 'g' of glowing is dropped (a pronunciation favoured by Crystal 2005: 70–1) a triple, rather than a double, rhyme is possible.

288 **father** the woman's auditor; see l. 71 and note.

288–9 **what. . . tear** Compare Sonnet 119.1–2.

289 **orb** globe.
     particular individual (emphasising 'one'); pronounced as three syllables.

290 **But** merely.
     inundation Compare *Romeo and Juliet*, 4.1.12: 'To stop the inundation of her tears'.

291 **to. . . wear** be worn down by water; proverbial: 'Constant dropping will wear the stone' (Dent D618). See also *Venus and Adonis*, l. 200; *Lucrece*, ll. 560, 592, 959.

293 **O** 'Or' in Q; possibly the compositor (or an earlier copyist) misread as 'r' the 'h' in 'Oh' (a frequently used variant spelling of 'O'); this is possible in secretary hand, where 'h' can become very loosely formed, and where 'r' can be formed in a number of ways.
     cleft divided, two-fold (because tears warm up modesty, but chill anger).

294 **from hence** from the 'inundation of the eyes' (l. 290).
     extincture extinction; a coinage, not used elsewhere in Shakespeare's works; a full-text search of EEBO-TCP produces no other examples (apart from Benson's 1640 edition, which reprints *A Lover's Complaint*).

295 **passion** emotion, but also 'a literary composition or passage marked by deep or strong emotion; a passionate speech or outburst' (OED³ 6d); see 20.2n.
     but merely.
     art of craft artful display of artifice; the phrase is pleonastic, for emphasis. Both 'art' and 'craft' are often associated with deceit; see Sonnets 125.11, 139.4; *Merry Wives*, 5.5.225–6: 'Th' offence is holy that she hath committed, | And this deceit loses the name of craft'.

296 **Even** pronounced as one syllable.
     resolved dissolved; compare *Hamlet*, 1.2.129–30 ('O that this too too sallied flesh would melt, | Thaw, and resolve itself into a dew!'); *Timon*, 4.3.439–40 ('The sea's a thief, whose liquid surge resolves | The moon into salt tears').

297 **stole** long robe.
     daffed 'daft' in Q, a variant of 'doffed' (took off); although an unusual spelling, it is distinctively Shakespearean (see Jackson 2014: 155): Shakespeare uses 'daff' (in a variety of grammatical forms) a total of six times across his works, usually to mean 'thrust aside'. The word only appears in a rhyming position in this instance, so his habitual use of this variant is not for the purpose of rhyme.

298 **guards** defences, reactivating the recurrent imagery of military attack and defence; the word – in its sense of 'an ornamental border or trimming on a garment' (OED 11a) – also connects to the imagery of clothes immediately preceding. Compare Thomas Wyatt's *Defence* (1541), cited at Sonnet 76.6n.
     civil fears There was a strong association, inherited from classical writers such as Cicero, between civility and the restraint of sexual relations to within wedlock; see Wilson's paraphrase of Cicero's *De Inventione*, 1.2.2 in *The Art of Rhetoric*, where the fact that 'none remembered the true observation of wedlock' is one of the key indicators of a barbaric (pre-civil) society (1553: sig. A3r).

299 **Appear. . . appears** The woman slips into the historic present as she recalls this crucial moment in her seduction. Compare the change of tense at *Venus and Adonis*, l. 45.

300 **melting** i.e. tearful; compare 'thy melting tears' at *3 Henry VI*, 1.4.174.
     drops teardrops.

301 **His. . . restore** Kerrigan (1986: 422) draws attention to 'Shakespeare's interest in the ambivalence of drugs, and in the Platonic idea of the *pharmakon* (that which is interchangeably "poison" and "medicine")': here, the same substance (tears) poisons the woman (compare Sonnet 119.1–2), but brings the youth back to health ('restore, *v.*1', OED³ 4b). Compare also Juliet's wordplay

Who glazed with crystal gate the glowing roses
That flame through water which their hue encloses.

'O father, what a hell of witchcraft lies
In the small orb of one particular tear?
But with the inundation of the eyes   290
What rocky heart to water will not wear?
What breast so cold that is not warmèd here?
O cleft effect! Cold modesty, hot wrath:
Both fire from hence and chill extincture hath.

'For lo, his passion, but an art of craft,   295
Even there resolved my reason into tears;
There my white stole of chastity I daffed,
Shook off my sober guards and civil fears,
Appear to him as he to me appears,
All melting, though our drops this difference bore: 300
His poisoned me, and mine did him restore.

'In him a plenitude of subtle matter,
Applied to cautels, all strange forms receives,
Of burning blushes, or of weeping water,
Or sounding paleness; and he takes and leaves   305
In either's aptness as it best deceives,
To blush at speeches rank, to weep at woes,
Or to turn white and sound at tragic shows.

in *Romeo and Juliet*, 5.3.165–6: 'Haply some poison yet doth hang on them, | To make me die with a restorative'.

302–5 **In him. . . paleness** The woman catalogues the vast array of cunning tricks ('plenitude of subtle matter') that the youth uses to deceive his victims.

302 **plenitude** not used elsewhere by Shakespeare.
subtle cunning; the adjective is traditionally applied to a fox (see Dent F629, and translations of Aesop's fables from 1484–1646); both the fox and the adjective are strongly associated with Machiavellian statecraft. See also *Merry Wives*, 3.1.101: 'Am I politic? am I subtle? am I a Machiavel?'

303 **cautels** tricks; compare *Hamlet*, 1.3.15–16: 'And now no soil nor cautel doth besmirch | The virtue of his will'.

all. . . receives 'takes on a great number of novel and surprising shapes' (i.e. blushing, weeping, fainting).

305 **sounding** swooning; an old-fashioned spelling by 1600; compare *Lucrece*, l. 1486.

305–6 **he. . . deceives** 'uses this and avoids that, according to whichever best suits his deceptions'.

307 **rank** highly offensive, obscene (OED³ A11a).

308 **turn white** a precursor of fainting as the blood leaves his face; a measure of the control that the youth has over his expression, able both to blush and blench at will; see Sonnet 20.7n.
sound See above, l. 305n.
tragic shows things which appear tragic; possibly, tragic drama (as in T.N.'s *Pleasant Dialogue* (1579), 2B4r).

309 **level** aim; the word returns to the gun imagery of ll. 281–2 (especially in proximity to 'hail', l, 310); see l. 22n. The word accentuates a play on **heart**/hart (i.e. deer) that is a conventional trope of medieval and early modern love poetry.

310 **'scape** escape.
  hail volley of shot.

311 **Showing. . . tame** 'Demonstrating that an agreeable disposition is both affectionate and pliant'; compare Thomas Wyatt, 'They Flee from Me' (*Tottel* [52]): 'Once have I seen them gentle, tame, and meek' (l. 3). The meaning of 'fair' as 'free from moral stain' (OED 9) is also relevant: these women are easily manipulated because they are innocent; see l. 318n. '**Kind**' may also pun on these women as being sexually available; compare Sonnet 134.6 and note.

312 **veiled in them** disguised in the 'strange forms' (l. 303) described in the previous stanza.

313 **Against. . . exclaim** The youth denounces the very thing that he desires (namely sexual intimacy); ll. 314–15 expand on this statement.

314 **heart-wished** desired from the bottom of his heart (the seat of passion; see Sonnet 46.1n).
  luxury lust (OED 1); see the Ghost's injunctions at *Hamlet*, 1.5.82–3: 'Let not the royal bed of Denmark be | A couch for luxury and damned incest'. The word was not used to describe other forms of material indulgence before the 1630s.

315 **pure maid** most chastely; compare *As You Like It*, 3.2.214–15: 'Speak sad brow [i.e. seriously] and true maid'.

316 **merely** both (i) entirely (*adv.*2, OED³ 2a); and (ii) only (OED³ 3).
  garment. . . grace outward covering of charm/sanctity; there are strong echoes in ll. 316–17 of Barnabe Barnes' *Parthenophil and Parthenophe* Sonnet 49.7: 'A fiend which doth in grace's garments grath [clothe] her' (1593: sig. E2v). Barnes' poem also has parallels with Sonnet 119; see 119.2n and Jackson 1972.

317–18 **fiend. . . the tempter** both words used of the devil (and used in contrast with 'cherubin', l. 319).

318 **That** so that.
  unexperient inexperienced; a coinage which does not appear elsewhere in Shakespeare's

works; 'experient' is, however, in use from the early fifteenth century. For the idea that the women are susceptible because they are innocent and inexperienced, see l. 311n. Pronounced as four syllables.
  gave. . . place See l. 263 and note.

319 **cherubin** strictly speaking, the plural form ('cherubim' is the singular), but this distinction is not widely upheld in Elizabethan and Jacobean English; see, for example, *Othello*, 4.2.63: 'Patience, thou young and rose-lipped cherubin'.

320 **simple** (i) innocent, free from guile (OED A1); (ii) foolish (OED 10a); compare Sonnet 66.11.
  lovered provided with a lover ('*adj.*2', OED³, with this line as the first citation); not used elsewhere in Shakespeare's works; a keyword search of EEBO-TCP reveals no other instances of the word in this sense. The word shares a close and ironic resemblance to 'lowered'.

323 **infected** both infectious and infected (OED³ A2a, A2b); see *Macbeth*, 4.1.138–9: 'Infected be the air whereon they [the witches] ride, | And damned all those that trust them!'.

323–7 **O** These repeated exclamations are used as a way of indicating extreme emotion, a rhetorical figure known as *ecphonesis*, 'when through affection either of anger, sorrow, gladness, marvelling, fear, or any such like, we break out in voice with an exclamation and outcry to express the passions of our mind, after this manner. O lamentable estate, O cursed misery, O wicked impudency, O joy incomparable, O rare and singular beauty [etc.]' (Henry Peacham, *Garden of Eloquence* (1577), sig. K4r). Bearing in mind the sense of contagion established by 'infection' in l. 323, the healthful effects of such 'vociferation' are also pertinent; for the medical efficacy of vociferation (particularly for the physically weak, such as women and old people), see Thomas Elyot, *Castle of Health* (1539: sigs G4v–G5r); Philip Barrough, *The Method of Physic* (1583: sigs K4r, K6r).

325 **from** that from.

326 **spongy** 'having a soft elastic or porous texture resembling that of a sponge' (OED 1); used in Shakespeare's works to describe things which are able to suck in and/or exude a substance (e.g. air, water); see

'That not a heart which in his level came
Could 'scape the hail of his all-hurting aim,   310
Showing fair nature is both kind and tame,
And, veiled in them, did win whom he would maim.
Against the thing he sought he would exclaim:
When he most burned in heart-wished luxury,
He preached pure maid and praised cold chastity.   315

'Thus merely with the garment of a grace
The naked and concealèd fiend he covered,
That th' unexperient gave the tempter place,
Which like a cherubin above them hovered.
Who, young and simple, would not be so lovered?   320
Ay me, I fell, and yet do question make
What I should do again for such a sake.

'O that infected moisture of his eye,
O that false fire which in his cheek so glowed,
O that forced thunder from his heart did fly,   325
O that sad breath his spongy lungs bestowed,
O all that borrowed motion, seeming owed,
Would yet again betray the fore-betrayed,
And new pervert a reconcilèd maid.'

FINIS.

Hamlet, 4.2.20–1 ('It is but squeezing you, and, sponge, you shall be dry again'); *Troilus and Cressida*, 2.2.11–12: 'There is no lady of more softer bowels, | More spongy to suck in the sense of fear'.

327 **borrowed** feigned.
motion (i) 'agitation (of the mind or feelings)' (OED³ 2); (ii) passion (OED³ 12a); (iii) gesture, facial expression (OED³ 4a). The context – of simulated emotion – also activates (iv) the sense of 'a show, an entertainment, *spec.* a puppet show' (OED³ 8a).
seeming owed apparently genuine; 'owed' ('possessed') is used in contrast to 'borrowed'.
328 **yet** nevertheless, even now.
329 **new pervert** corrupt again; 'pervert' has a strong religious resonance, the primary meaning of the verb being 'to turn aside from a correct course' (OED³ 1); see Acts 13:10: 'wilt thou not cease to pervert the straight ways of the Lord?'.
reconcilèd repentant; like 'pervert', the word has a strong religious resonance: 'to bring back, restore, or readmit to the Church' ('reconcile, *v.*', OED³ 4a); see Richard Taverner's 1536 translation of Philip Melancthon's *Confession of the Faith of the Germans* (cited in OED under 'reconciled, *n.*'): 'The reconciled be reputed righteous and the children of God, not for their own cleanness, but through mercy for Christ' (sig. C6r).
maid The woman overlooks the fact that maidenhood, once lost, cannot be recovered.

Appendix 1

Venus and Adonis: principal source

Ovid's *Metamorphoses*, Book 10, translated by Arthur Golding

Arthur Golding published four books of his translation in 1565, and then the complete *The XV Books of P. Ovidius Naso, Entitled Metamorphosis, Translated out of Latin into English Metre* (London: William Seres, 1567). Further editions followed in 1575, 1584, 1587, 1593, 1603 and 1612. It is generally agreed that Shakespeare knew the translation well (Taylor 1994/95; Bate 1993), even if it was not his only feasible access to Ovid and his stories. The 1567 edition has a dedicatory epistle to Robert Dudley, the Earl of Leicester, which outlines a moralising method for reading the *Metamorphoses*. Its account of Book 10 (213–23) is included here:

> The tenth booke cheefly dooth containe one kynd of argument
> Reproving most prodigious lusts of such as have bene bent
> Too incest most unnatural. And in the latter end   215
> It sheweth in Hippomenes how greatly folk offend,
> That are ingrate for benefits which God or man bestow
> Uppon them in the time of neede. Moreover it dooth show
> That beawty (will they nill they) aye dooth men in daunger throw:
> And that it is a foolyshnesse too stryve ageinst the thing   220
> Which God before determineth too passe in tyme too bring.
> And last of all Adonis death dooth shew that manhod strives
> Against forewarning though men see the perill of theyr lyves.

There is also a Preface 'Too the Reader' that offers a more simplistic moralisation, including a brisk typology of the gods (57–78, part of which is included here):

> Then must wee thinke the learned men that did theis names frequent,
> Some further things and purposes by those devises ment.
> By Jove and Juno understand all states of princely port:
> By Ops and Saturne auncient folke that are of elder sort: 60
> By Phoebus yoong and lusty brutes of hand and courage stout:
> By Mars the valeant men of warre that love too feight it out:
> [. . .]
> By Bacchus all the meaner trades and handycraftes are ment:
> By Venus such as of the fleshe too filthie lust are bent.
> By Neptune such as keepe the seas: By Phebe maydens chast,
> And Pilgrims such as wandringly theyr tyme in travell waste.   70

The translation of the Adonis section itself, like the translation in general, may not be very significantly inflected by this moralising premise (see Lyne 2001: 29–52; but also Wallace 2012). Book 10 starts with the story of the death of Eurydice and Orpheus' mourning, his descent into Hell and his failure to bring his wife out safely. He then sings, attended by a crowd of trees (including the cypress, once Cyparissus, who asks for death when he kills his beloved stag, and Apollo changes him into a tree). He tells the stories of (i) Hyacinthus (accidentally killed by Apollo and turned into a flower), (ii) the Cerastae (who fail to worship Venus and are turned into bullocks), (iii) the Propoetides (who shamelessly prostitute themselves and are turned to stone), (iv) Pygmalion (who prays to Venus and is rewarded by his beautiful statue coming to life), (v) Myrrha (Pygmalion's great-grand-daughter, who consummates her incestuous love for her father, becomes pregnant, and is turned into a myrrh-tree), and finally (vi) Adonis, Myrrha's son. Book 10 ends with the death of Adonis, and Book 11 starts with the death of Orpheus.

581 **want** lack.
582 **Lucina** Roman goddess of childbirth.
587 **cranye** 'open in crannies or chinks' (OED 1).
591 **condicions** respects.
592 **tables** paintings.
593 **too thentent** in order that.
598 **imp** child.
599 **alate** lately.
602 **stripling** 'a youth, one just passing from boyhood to manhood' (OED 1).
605 **revenge** Perhaps the most striking difference with Shakespeare's version: Ovid presents the story as vengeance (it is unclear whose) for the incestuous passion felt by Myrrha.
611 **Cythera** Greek island (modern Kythira), sacred to Aphrodite (Venus).
612 **Paphos** in Cyprus; mythically the birthplace of Aphrodite.
613 **Gnyde** Greek island (modern Cnidus/Knidos), also associated with Aphrodite.
    Amathus in Cyprus; also associated with Aphrodite.
619 **Lawnds** glades (see *Venus and Adonis*, l. 813).
621 **Phebe** another name for Diana/Artemis, goddess of hunting and chastity.

The misbegotten chyld
Grew still within the tree, and from his mothers womb defyld
Sought meanes too bee delyvered. Her burthened womb did swell
Amid the tree, and stretcht her out. But woordes wherwith to tell   580
And utter foorth her greef did want, She had no use of speech
With which Lucina in her throwes shee might of help beseech.
Yit like a woman labring was the tree, and bowwing downe
Gave often sighes, & shed foorth teares as though shee there should drowne.
Lucina to this wofull tree came gently downe, and layd   585
Her hand theron, and speaking woordes of ease the midwife playd.
The tree did cranye, and the barke deviding made away,
And yeelded out the chyld alyve, which cryde and wayld streyght way.
The waternymphes uppon the soft sweete hearbes the chyld did lay,
And bathde him with his mothers teares. His face was such as spyght   590
Must needes have praysd. For such he was in all condicions right,
As are the naked Cupids that in tables picturde bee.
But too thentent he may with them in every poynt agree,
Let eyther him bee furnished with wings and quiver light,
Or from the Cupids take theyr wings and bowes and arrowes quight.   595
    Away slippes fleeting tyme unspyde and mocks us too our face,
    And nothing may compare with yeares in swiftnesse of theyr pace.
That wretched imp whom wickedly his graundfather begate,
And whom his cursed suster bare, who hidden was alate
Within the tree, and lately borne, became immediatly   600
The beawtyfullyst babe on whom man ever set his eye.
Anon a stripling hee became, and by and by a man,
And every day more beawtifull than other he becam.
That in the end Dame Venus fell in love with him: wherby
He did revenge the outrage of his mothers villanye.   605
For as the armed Cupid kist Dame Venus, unbeware
An arrow sticking out did raze hir brest uppon the bare.
The Goddesse being wounded, thrust away her sonne. The wound
Appeered not too bee so deepe as afterward was found.
It did deceyve her at the first. The beawty of the lad   610
Inflaamd her. Too Cythera Ile no mynd at all shee had.
Nor untoo Paphos where the sea beats round about the shore,
Nor fisshy Gnyde, nor Amathus that hath of mettalls store.
Yea even from heaven shee did absteyne. Shee lovd Adonis more
Than heaven. To him shee clinged ay, and bare him companye.   615
And in the shadowe woont shee was too rest continually,
And for too set her beawtye out most seemely too the eye
By trimly decking of her self. Through bushy grounds and groves,
And over Hills and Dales, and Lawnds and stony rocks shee roves,
Bare kneed with garment tucked up according too the woont   620
Of Phebe, and shee cheerd the hounds with hallowing like a hunt,
Pursewing game of hurtlesse sort, as Hares made lowe before.
Or stagges with loftye heades, or bucks. But with the sturdy Boare

627 **shoonne** shun.
632 **Encounter** fight (see *Venus and Adonis*, l. 672).
633 **For dowt** for fear.
     scath harm.
647 **for a fault** (i) as a result of a sin (of Atalanta and Hippomenes); or perhaps (ii) as a result of an error (on Venus' part).
648 **in tyme** opportunely, in a timely way.
652 **in her tale. . . among** continuously during her tale.
     bussed kissed.

835 **a skew** askew, i.e. not a clean or fatal hit.
836 **groyne** snout (OED 'groyne, *n. 1*', 2a).
839 **hyding** burying.
840 **all along** flat on the ground.
842 **a farre** afar.
844 **Beehilld** beheld.
     beweltred smeared.
845 **brist** breast.

And ravening woolf, and Bearewhelpes armd with ugly pawes, and eeke
The cruell Lyons which delyght in blood, and slaughter seeke,   625
Shee meddled not. And of theis same shee warned also thee
Adonis for too shoonne them, if thou wooldst have warned bee.
Bee bold on cowards (Venus sayd) for whoso dooth advaunce
Himselfe against the bold, may hap too meete with sum mischaunce.
Wherfore I pray thee my sweete boy forbeare too bold too bee.   630
For feare thy rashnesse hurt thy self and woork the wo of mee
Encounter not the kynd of beastes whom nature armed hath,
For dowt thou buy thy prayse too deere procuring thee sum scath.
Thy tender youth, thy beawty bryght, thy countnance fayre and brave
Although they had the force too win the hart of Venus, have   635
No powre ageinst the Lyons, nor ageinst the bristled swyne.
The eyes and harts of savage beasts doo nought too theis inclyne.
The cruell Boares beare thunder in theyr hooked tushes, and
Exceeding force and feercenesse is in Lyons too withstand.
And sure I hate them at my hart. Too him demaunding why?   640
A monstrous chaunce (quoth Venus) I will tell thee by and by,
That hapned for a fault. But now unwoonted toyle hath made
Mee weerye: and beholde, in tyme this Poplar with his shade
Allureth, and the ground for cowch dooth serve too rest uppon.
I prey thee let us rest heere. They sate them downe anon.   645
And lying upward with her head uppon his lappe along,
Shee thus began: and in her tale shee bussed him among.

[653–830: The inset story is as follows. Atalanta is very fast and beautiful; a prophecy warns her off marriage; she ends up testing suitors in a foot-race; she is taken with Hippomenes and pities him; he prays to Venus, who gives him golden apples; with these he distracts Atalanta and wins the race, and they are married; but the lovers do not honour Venus enough and she takes revenge; they are overcome with lust in the ancient mother goddess Cybele's temple; Cybele turns them into lions; lions now hate Venus and she thus warns Adonis not to fight them.]

This warning given, with yoked swannes away through aire she goth.
But manhod by admonishment restreyned could not bee.
By chaunce his hounds in following of the tracke, a Boare did see,
And rowsed him. And as the swyne was comming from the wood,
Adonis hit him with a dart a skew, and drew the blood.   835
The Boare streyght with his hooked groyne the huntingstaffe out drew
Bestayned with his blood, and on Adonis did pursew
Who trembling and retyring back, too place of refuge drew.
And hyding in his codds his tuskes as farre as he could thrust
He layd him all along for dead uppon the yellow dust.   840
Dame Venus in her chariot drawen with swannes was scarce arrived
At Cyprus, when shee knew a farre the sygh of him depryved
Of lyfe. Shee turnd her Cygnets backe, and when shee from the skye
Beehilld him dead, and in his blood beweltred for to lye:
Shee leaped downe, and tare at once hir garments from her brist,   845
And rent her heare, and beate uppon her stomack with her fist,

852 **Persephonee. . . Mints** In one myth Perse-
phone turned the nymph Menthe into the
plant that shares her name.
rank sented pungent-smelling (with strong
implications of unpleasantness).

856 **sheere** translucent, transparent.

858 **that same tree** i.e. the pomegranate.

861–2 **For why. . . As that** because. . . therefore.

And blaming sore the destnyes, sayd. Yit shall they not obteine
Their will in all things. Of my greefe remembrance shall remayne.
(Adonis) whyle the world doth last. From yeere too yeere shall growe
A thing that of my heavinesse and of thy death shall showe   850
The lively likenesse. In a flowre thy blood I will bestowe.
Hadst thou the powre Persephonee rank sented Mints too make
Of womens limbes? and may not I lyke powre upon mee take
Without disdeine and spyght, too turne Adonis too a flowre?
This sed, shee sprinckled Nectar on the blood, which through the powre   855
Therof did swell like bubbles sheere that ryse in weather cleere
On water. And before that full an howre expyred weere,
Of all one colour with the blood a flowre she there did fynd
Even like the flowre of that same tree whose frute in tender rynde
Have pleasant graynes inclosde. Howbeet the use of them is short.   860
For why the leaves doo hang so looce through lightnesse in such sort,
As that the windes that all things perce, with every little blast
Doo shake them of and shed them so as that they cannot last.

Appendix 2

Lucrece: principal sources

1. *Ovid's Fasti*, Book 2, translated by John Gower (1640)

The six books of Ovid's *Fasti* were published in 8 CE; the poem seems to have been unfinished, and was probably interrupted by Ovid's exile. It explains, month-by-month, the origins of the festivals and customs of the Roman year. The last section of Book 2 concerns the 'Regifugium', which commemorated the flight of the last king, Tarquinius Superbus, from Rome. Ovid tells the story of Lucretia as the main incident in the fall of Tarquin. The first translation of the *Fasti* into English was not published until 1640. Although this is after Shakespeare's death we include it here as the most proximate early modern version of the Ovidian story. John Gower's *Ovids Festivalls, or Romane Calendar* set itself the difficult task of translating 'equinumerally' (as it says on the title-page), line by line, which explains its compressed style. The Lucrece section therefore covers the same line-range in both Latin and English (ll. 721–852; sig. E5v–E7v in Gower).

721 **Eagles** standards (an Eagle was traditionally carried by Roman legions).

723 **couch'd** hid.

728 **countrey-fanes** homeland's temples.

732 **frollick** merry.

734 **But come to triall** let us just put it to the test.

736 **Carier** gallop.
Content there is general agreement.

741 **post** ride
out of hand at once; see OED³ 'hand, *n.*', P1.j.(b).

745 **plie** work hard, apply yourselves (OED³ 'ply, *v.*2').

751 **high** (i) lofty, honourable (OED³ 9a); perhaps
(ii) haughty, heated (OED³ 11); but the point is
that Collatine is courageous.

755 **period** conclusion, end.

760 **sweets** pleasure(s).

761 **furiall** furious, raging (OED).

763 **deluding** mocking.

767 **horn-mouth'd harbinger** i.e. the cockerel, with
its beak.

768 **frollick** merry.

Romes conquering Eagles in the mean time over
The city Ardea in a long siege hover.
The foe, not daring battel, couch'd in forts:
Our souldiers revel in their tents with sports.
Young Tarquine makes a feast to all his lords: 725
'Mongst whom in mirth he falls into these words;
Whiles in dull warre this Ardea us deteins
From carrying tropheys to our countrey-fanes,
Do any of our wives mind us? or are
They carefull of us who for them take care?   730
Each prais'd his own, and very earnest grow:
The frollick bowls make lungs and tongues to glow.
Up starts Lord Collatine, *Few words are best:*
But come to triall; night's not yet deceast:
Mount we our steeds and to the citie all   735
Carier. Content: They for their horses call;
And straight were gallop'd by their speedy feet
To th' royall court. No watch was in the street:
Lo there the King's sonnes joviall wives they find
With garlands crown'd, at midnight up, well win'd.   740
Thence to fair Lucrece post they out of hand;
By whose bed-side the wooll and baskets stand.
At little lights their task her maidens spun:
To whom she softly thus these words begun;
Maids, we must make (plie, plie your bus'nesse faster)   745
A coat to send in hast unto your master.
What news heare you? for more then I you heare:
How long will't be e're warres be ended there?
Well, Ardea, thou that keep'st our Lords from home,
Thy betters thou affront'st, thy fall will come.   750
Be they but safe! but my Lords bloud's so high,
That with his sword he anywhere doth flie.
My heart doth fail quite chill'd with frozen fear
When-e're I think of his encounters there.
Tears were the period: She lets fall her thread,   755
And in her bosome hangeth down her head.
This was a grace; her tears became her well:
Her beauty was her minds true parallel.
Fear not, sweet wife; I'm come, cries he. She meets
And hangs on's neck, a burden full of sweets.   760
Meanwhile the young Prince furiall lust doth move;
His boyling spirits are fir'd in secret love.
Her lilie skin, her gold-deluding tresses,
Her native splendour slighting art him pleases.
Her voice, her stainlesse modesty h' admires: 765
And hope's decay still strengthens his desires.
Day's horn-mouth'd harbinger proclaim'd the morn;
The frollick gallants to their tents return.

769 *mazing* bewildering.
　　fansie desire.
773 *still'd* issued; the word (OED *v.*2) suggests liquids exuding or distilling.
775 *billows* sea-swells.
777 *tane* taken.
781 *event* outcome.
782 *vent'rous* adventurous.
　　sprite spirit.
783 *slav'd* enslaved.
　　Gabines The inhabitants of Gabii, about ten miles east of Rome.
784 *girts. . . on* equips himself with.
785 *ports* gates.
786 *Sol* the sun.

788 *a kind* kin.
792 *housen* houses.
793 *gilded* gold-coloured, shining; in Ovid the scabbard from which Tarquin draws his sword is 'aurata', gilded or golden.
798 *stupid* stupefied.
805 *profers* beseeches (OED³ *v.* 1); modern punctuation would have a comma before this word.
806 *no whit* in no way.
　　intreats entreaties.
807 *damne. . . for* condemn. . . for being.
809 *bruit* report.
810 *fame* rumour, (bad) reputation.
812 *bought'st* paid.

His mazing fansie on her picture roves;
The more he muses still the more he loves: 770
Thus did she sit, thus drest, thus did she spin,
Thus plaid her hair upon her necks white skin;
These looks she had, these rosie words still'd from her;
This eye, this cheek, these blushes did become her.
As billows fall down after some great blast,   775
Yet make some swelling when the wind is past:
So though her person from his sight was tane,
Yet did that love her person bred remain.
He burns; and prick'd with spurs of basest lust,
Against her chast bed plots attempts unjust.   780
Th' event's ambiguous, yet we'll throughly try't:
That she shall see. Fate helps the vent'rous sprite.
We slav'd the Gabines by a daring deed.
Thus girts he on his sword and mounts his steed.
Into Collatia's brasen ports he came   785
About the time Sol hides his glowing flame.
A foe the Court doth enter as a friend,
And there was welcome: For they were a kind.
Ah blind mankind! she thinking nought, good woman!
Provides good chear to entertain her foeman.   790
The supper's ended: time to sleep invites;
In all the housen now are seen no lights.
Up starts he, and draws forth his gilded blade,
And chast Lucretia's chamber doth invade.
Laid on the bed; *Lucretia, no deniall:*   795
Here is my sword: I'm Tarquine of bloud royall.
Nought she replies; nor had she power to say
Or plead, but stupid and quite senselesse lay.
And like a lamb that from the sheepfold rambles,
Now caught in claws of ravening wolf, she trembles.   800
What dares she? fight? ah, he could overmatch her!
Cry out? alas! his sword would soon dispatch her.
Fly? how? his arm is link'd about her wast:
Her wast then first by strangers hand embrac'd!
The Lecher pleads with profers, threats, intreats: 805
She's no whit mov'd with gifts, intreats, nor threats,
Yield, or I'll damne thee for a whore, cries he,
And thee accuse for base adulterie:
I'll kill the man, with whom I'll bruit thy shame.
She yielded, conquer'd by the fear of fame.   810
Why triumph'st thou? thy conquest is thy fall:
Ah, what a price bought'st thou that night withall!
Now day appear'd: with scatter'd hairs she lies,
As doth a mother when her deare sonne dies.
For her old father and deare husband home   815
She sends: To her without delay they come.

818   **Whom** i.e. Tarquin; the answer to their asking after the 'cause'.

    smit she has been smitten.

822   **Pray** beg.

824   **shamed** was ashamed.

827   **period** conclusion.

832   **pow'rs** pours.

834   **Express'd a care** took care.

835   **self-carelesse** with no thought of appearances. The Latin is 'obliti decoris', 'forgetful of what is fitting'.

837   **Brute** Brutus.

    at length at last.

    deceiv'd contradicted.

838   **repriev'd** withdrew.

842   **as my God** like a god to me.

843   **seed** descendants.

846   **as** as if.

847   **exequies** funeral rites.

848   **Endow'd with** accompanied by.

    emulation competition (in grief and vengefulness); the Latin word is 'invidiam', envy.

849   **States** citizens; the word suggests the powerful people in the city (OED³ 'state, *n.*', 23a, 23b) but translates 'quirites', an early name for Rome's citizens.

851   **sway** hold power.

Whose grief they seeing ask the cause of it,
Whom she laments, and with what evil smit.
She veils her modest face, nor any thing
Would utter; tears as from a fountain spring.   820
Her sire, her husband comfort her sad tears,
Pray her to speak, and weep in hidden fears.
Thrice she assay'd to speak, thrice stopt; yet tries
Once more, but shamed to lift up her eyes.
Shall we ow Tarquine this too? ah! shall I,   825
Shall I here publish my own infamie?
Something she tells, and for the period weeps,
And her grave cheeks in pure vermilion steeps.
They both forgive her forc'd adultery.
That pardon you give, I, cries she, *deny.*   830
Forthwith her self she stabs with hidden knife,
And at their feet pow'rs forth her crimson life;
And even in Fate's last act, as she did die,
Express'd a care to fall with modestie.
Her Sire, her Lord self-carelesse both fall down,   835
And o're her corps their common losse bemone.
Brute came, whose mind at length his name deceiv'd,
And from her dying breast the knife repriev'd:
There holds it spuing of her noble bloud,
And dauntlesse threatnings breath'd forth as he stood;   840
By this chast noble bloud I vow to thee
And thy dear ghost, which as my God shall be,
Proud Tarquine with his seed for this shall pay:
No longer I the counterfeit will play.
She at his words her sightlesse eyes doth move,   845
And shook her head as seeming to approve.
The manly matrone's exequies are done,
Endow'd with tears and emulation.
The wound lies open: Brute calls all the States,
And to their ears the Kings base act relates.   850
Proud Tarquine's house all flie. Two Consuls sway:
And that became the last Monarchick day.

In the tyme of the siege of that citee Holland gives a more elaborate context for the feasting of the young gentlemen: 'During this siege, and the standing campe lying there, (as it falleth out commonly, when the warre is rather long and late than hote and cruell) there were granted large licences and pasports to and fro betweene the campe and Rome, with much liberty: and yet more to the Principals of the armie than to the common soldiers'.

severall own particular.

quod he i.e. quoth he, said he.

livelihod Holland: 'lustinesse'; Livy: 'vigor' (i.e. not primarily implying anything sexual).

whiche of our wives doth surmount Holland explains the test further: 'as they shalbe found and seene, taken of a sodaine, and not looking for their husbands coming'.

in poste in haste, at speed (OED³ 'post, *n. 3*', phrase P4).

late in the night Holland's extra detail 'by candle light' is suggestive given how much Shakespeare's poem plays on light, but it is not in Livy.

Wolle wool.

construprate and defloure Holland: 'to offer violence and villanie'; Livy: 'libido...per vim stuprandae', i.e. closer to the violence of Painter's version. The OED lemma is 'constuprate', after Latin *constuprare*; Painter's word is a mis-spelling.

2. Livy's *Ab Urbe Condita* (*From the Founding of the City*), 1.57–9, trans. William Painter (1566)

The first books of Livy's history of Rome were written at some point in the years around the beginning of Augustus's principate (27 BCE). Book 1 covers the earliest period, from the founding of the city by Aeneas to the overthrow of its kings and the institution of a republic. The story of Lucretia is its climactic episode. The surviving books of Livy were first translated into English by Philemon Holland in 1600, and printed by Adam Islip with a dedication to the Queen. This was the first of Holland's great translations: the Livy was followed by Pliny's *History of the World* (1601), Plutarch's *Morals* (1603), Suetonius's *History of the Twelve Caesars* (1606), among others. The Lucretia section appears on E2v–E3r.

While it seems likely that Shakespeare attended to Latin sources in order to undertake the 'graver labour' of *Lucrece*, he had also read the story in the translation (looser at times than Holland's, but also less elaborated and paraphrased at others) in William Painter's collection of stories *The Palace of Pleasure*. It is likely at least that the Argument (see headnote) is written in the light of Painter (Culhane 2004). The first edition was printed by John Kingston and Henry Denham for Richard Tottel and William Jones in 1566, and contained sixty stories. Subsequent expansions followed, in 1567 and 1575. The work was widely read and provided the material from which plays by Shakespeare and others were adapted, e.g. *Appius and Virginia*, *All's Well That Ends Well* and *The Duchess of Malfi*. The Lucretia section, B1r–B2v, is included here. The notes record significant differences from Holland's translation.

Greate preparacion was made by the Romanes, against a people called Rutuli, who had a citie named Ardea, excellyng in wealth and richesse, whiche was the cause that the Romane kyng, beyng exhausted and quite voide of money, by reason of his sumptuous buildynges, made warres upon that countrie. In the tyme of the siege of that citee the yong Romane gentlemen banqueted one another, emonges whom there was one called Collatinus Tarquinius, the sonne of Egerius. And by chaunce thei entred in communicacion of their wives, every one praisyng his severall spouse. At length the talke began to growe hotte, where upon Collatinus said, that wordes wer vaine. For within fewe howers it might be tried, how muche his wife Lucrecia did excell the rest, wherfore (quod he) if there be any livelihod in you: Let us take our horse, to prove whiche of our wives doth surmount. Whereupon thei rode to Rome in poste. At their coming thei found the kynges doughters, sportyng themselfes with sundrie pastymes: From thence thei went to the house of Collatinus, where thei founde Lucrece, not as the other before named, spendyng the time in idlenes, but late in the night occupied and busie, emonges her maides in the middes of the house spinning of Wolle. The victorie and praise wherof was given to Lucretia who when she sawe her husbande, gently and lovingly interteigned hym, curteously biddyng the Tarquinians welcome. Imediatlie Sextus Tarquinius the sonne of Tarquinius Superbus, that tyme the Romane kyng was attached and incensed with a libidious desire, to construprate and defloure Lucrece. When the yong gentlemen had bestowed that night pleasantlie with their wives, thei retourned to the Campe. Not long after Sextus Tarquinius with one man returned to Collatia unknowen to Collatinus, and ignoraunte to Lucrece, and the reste of her houshold, for what purpose he came. Who beyng right hartely interteigned, after supper was conveighed to his chamber. Tarquinius burnyng with the love of Lucrece, after he perceived the housholde to bee at reste, and all thynges in quiet, he with his naked sworde in his hande, goeth to Lucrece beyng a slepe, and kepyng her doune with his lefte hande, saied. Holde thy peace Lucrece (quod he) I am Sextus Tarquinius, my sworde is in my hande, if thou crie, I will kill thee. The gentlewoman beyng sore a fraied, newlie awaked out of her slepe, and seyng iminent death, could not tell what to doe. Then Tarquinius

his love Holland: 'his amorous passion'; Livy: 'amorem', i.e. closer to Painter than to Holland's elaboration.

vanquished having been vanquished.

whiche doen he departed Holland adds the detail 'in great pride and jolitie'. This translates Livy's 'ferox': it seems apt to see this as an exultant kind of 'fierce', as Holland's paraphrase implies.

Sp. i.e. Spurius.

P. i.e. Publius.

L. i.e. Lucius.

made haste to Lucrece Holland includes the detail, present also in Livy, that Collatine and Brutus were 'both together by chance going backe to Rome', and they 'encountred in the way his wives messenger'.

steppes Holland: 'print'; Livy: 'vestigia', i.e. footprints. The translators handle the metaphor differently. See OED 'step, *n. 1*', 9b, 'trace', after 'step' as 'footprint'.

pestiferous joye Holland: 'deadly pleasure'; Livy: 'pestiferum. . . gaudium', damaging/pestilent joy (so Painter is very close here). Holland spells out more methodically, as Livy does, that the deadliness of the sin is now to be transferred to Tarquin: 'a deadly pleasure, I may say, to me: & to himselfe also no lesse, if yee be men of courage'.

every every one.

kirtle gown.

ne nor.

straungenesse i.e. because Brutus concealed his sharp mind (his name suggests slow wits), and his grievances against the Tarquins, until this moment.

Thes al swore that othe Holland's translation follows Livy by being more detailed here about the consent of the other men, and the plan to expel the Tarquins.

facinorous wicked.

shewe themselves like men Holland, following Livy, elaborates that they would be fighting against 'them that demeaned themselves no better, nay worse than ordinarie enemies'.

lustiest and moste desperate Holland: 'bravest and tallest'; Livy: 'ferocissimus', modifying the singular pronoun 'quisque', anyone. See OED 'desperate, *adj., n., and adv.*', 4a, 'driven to desperation, reckless or infuriated from despair' (*OED* A4a).

preste willing, prepared (OED³ 'prest, *adj.* and *adv.*', 2a, 1a). Livy's 'voluntarius' is translated by both 'preste' and 'readie'.

confessed his love, and began to intreate her, and therewithall used sundrie menacyng woordes, by all meanes attemptyng to make her quiet: when he sawe her obstinate, and that she would not yelde to his requeste, notwithstandyng his cruell threates, he added shamefull and villanous woordes, saiyng. That he would kill her, and when she was slaine, he would also kill his slave, and place hym by her, that it might be reported she was slain, beyng taken in adulterie. She vanquished with his terrible and infamous threat. His fleshly and licencious enterprise, overcame the puritie of her chast harte, whiche doen he departed. Then Lucrece sente a poste to Rome to her father, and an other to Ardea to her housbande, requiryng them that thei would make speede to come unto her, with certaine of their trustie frendes, for that a cruell facte was chaunced. Then Sp. Lucretius with P. Valerius the soonne of Volesius, & Collatinus with L. Junius Brutus, made haste to Lucrece. Where thei founde her sittyng, verie pensife and sadde, in her chamber. So sone as she sawe theim, she began pitiouslie to weepe. Then her housebande asked her, whether all thynges were well, unto whom she saied these woordes.

No dere housebande, for what can bee well or safe unto a woman, when she hath loste her chastitie. Alas Collatine, the steppes of an other man, be now fixed in thy bedde. But it is my bodie onely that is violated, my minde God knoweth is giltles, whereof my death shalbe witnesse. But if you be men, give me your handes, and trouthe, that the adulterer maie not escape unrevenged. It is Sextus Tarquinius who beyng an enemie, in stede of a frende, the other night came unto me, armed with his sworde in his hand, and by violence caried a waie from me, and tooke to himself a pestiferous joye. Then every of them gave her their faith, and comforted the pensife and languishyng ladie, imputing the offence, to the aucthor and doer of the same, affirmyng that her bodie was polluted, and not her mynde, and where consente was not, there the crime was absent. Whereunto she added. I praie you consider with your selves, what punishment is due for the malefactour. As for my parte, though I clere my self of the offence, my bodie shall feele the punishemente: for no unchast or ill woman, shall hereafter take example of Lucrece. Then she drew out a knife, whiche she had hidden secretly, under her kirtle, and stabbed her self to the harte. Whiche doen, she fell doune grovelyng upon her wounde, and so died. Whereupon her father and housebande made greate lamentacion, and as thes were bewailyng the death of Lucrece, Brutus plucked the knife out of the wounde, whiche gushed out with abundance of blood, and holdyng it up saied. I swere by the chaste blood of this bodie here deade, and I take you the immortall goddes to witnesse, that I wil drive and extirpate out of this Citie, bothe L. Tarquinius Superbus, and his wicked wife, with all the race of his children and progenie, so that none of them, ne yet any others shall raigne any longer in Rome. Then he delivered the knife to Collatinus. Lucretius and Valerius merveilyng at the straungenesse of his woordes: And from whence he should conceive that determinacion. Thes al swore that othe. And followed Brutus as their capitaine, in his conceived purpose. The bodie of Lucrece was brought into the markette place, where the people wondred at the vilenesse of that facte, every man complainyng upon the mischief of that facinorous rape, committed by Tarquinius. Whereupon Brutus perswaded the Romanes, that thei should cease from teares, and other childishe lamentacions, and take weapons in their handes, and shewe themselves like men. Then the lustiest and moste desperate persones within the citie, made theimselves preste and readie, to attempt any enterprise.

Appendix 3

The Passionate Pilgrim

The Passionate Pilgrim is an octavo pamphlet of twenty poems, first printed by Thomas Judson for William Jaggard in 1599.

Shakespeare's authorship

The title-page attributes the entire volume to Shakespeare, testimony to the marketability of his name by 1599: in 1598 he had been named, for the first time, on the title-pages of the quartos of *Richard II*, *Richard III* and *Love's Labours Lost*. The title 'Passionate Pilgrim' may also be an allusion to *Romeo and Juliet* (printed in 1597), where at their first meeting Juliet addresses Romeo as 'good pilgrim', responding to Romeo's description of his lips as 'blushing pilgrims' (1.5.97, 95). However, only five of the poems in *PP* can be securely attributed to Shakespeare: *PP* 1 and 2, which appear as 138 and 144 in the 1609 Quarto of *Shakespeare's Sonnets*; *PP* 3, 5 and 16 reproduce – with some substantive variants – wooing sonnets from *Love's Labours Lost*: *PP* 3 is Longueville's sonnet to Maria (4.3.58–71); *PP* 5 is Berowne's to Rosaline (4.2.105–18); *PP* 16 reproduces most of Dumaine's twenty-line 'sonnet' to Katherine (4.3.99–118).

Other authors

Bartholomew Griffin

Of the remaining fifteen poems, one sonnet (*PP* 11) is almost certainly by Griffin, since a version of it appeared as Sonnet 3 in his *Fidessa* (1596: sig. B2r). *PP* 4 and 6 have also been attributed to Griffin, on the grounds that (i) *PP* 4 follows *PP* 11 in Folger MS V.b.43, where it is headed 'Second part' (fol. 22r); and (ii) *PP* 4 and 6 would seem to be companion pieces: both feature an amorous, physically passionate 'Cytherea' (another name for Venus, although not one used in Griffin's *Fidessa*) and her young, and somewhat bashful, mortal lover Adonis, and *PP* 6 precedes *PP* 4 in Folger MS V.a.339 (compiled in 1630s and 40s), where the two poems appear on fol. 197r, immediately before *PP* 1, *PP* 7, and *PP* 11 (fol. 197v). Nonetheless, the evidence linking *PP* 4 and 6 to Griffin is slight, and the scenario they play out is also found in *PP* 9.

Richard Barnfield

Two poems (*PP* 8, 20) are by Barnfield and were first printed by Jaggard's brother John in 'Poems: in diverse humours' appended to *The Encomion of Lady Pecunia* (1598: sigs E2r, E2v–E3v). *PP* 17, a version of which first appeared, anonymously, in Thomas Weelkes' *Madrigals to 3, 4, 5, & 6 Voices* (1597: sigs B1v–B2r), has also been attributed to Barnfield (Grosart 1876a: 197), on the grounds that in *England's Helicon* (1600) it is followed by *PP* 20, which is there entitled 'Another of the same shepherd's' (sigs H1v–H2v); but the anthologist's title may reflect the presence of a similarly unfortunate pastoral speaker in both poems (although the tone of the latter is more bitter), rather than knowledge of their actual authorship.

Thomas Deloney

Deloney is the probable author of *PP* 12, which appears as the first stanza of 'A Maiden's Choice twixt Age and Youth' in his *Garland of Good Will*, entered into the Stationers' Register on 5 March 1593; although the earliest surviving edition is from 1628 (where it appears on sig. G4r), the collection was certainly available in the mid-1590s, since Thomas Nashe refers to it in *Have with you to Saffron Walden* (3.84).

'R.P.'

PP 18 appears in BL Harleian MS 7392(2), fols 43r–v, where it is attributed to 'R.P.' (fol. 43v); two other entries in that miscellany carry the same initials: 'Yf Fortune may enforce, the carefull hart to cry' (unattributed in Richard Edwards' *Paradise of Dainty Devices* (1585), sigs F3r–F4v), here attributed to 'Ro Poo' (fol. 20v); and 'Come Sorrow com, Sitte down & morne with mee', attributed to 'R.P.' (fol. 32r). Whether all three attributions indicate the same person is unclear; Marotti (2008: 88) suggests that 'Ro Poo' may be the spy Robert Pooley, who worked for Francis Walsingham in the late 1580s.

Christopher Marlowe and Walter Ralegh

PP 19 comprises four stanzas of 'Come live with me and be my love' (aka 'The Passionate Shepherd') – one of the most copied and imitated Elizabethan poems (*PP* is the earliest surviving version, in manuscript or print), which is attributed in *England's Helicon* to Marlowe (1600: sig. 2A2r) – along with the first stanza of its equally famous response, usually attributed to Ralegh. The attribution of 'The Passionate Shepherd' to Marlowe is further strengthened by his commemoration as the 'dead shepherd' in *As You Like It* (3.5.81). A garbled version of 'Come live with me', jumbled up with lines from Psalm 137 ('By the rivers of Babel'), is sung by the parson Hugh Evans in *Merry Wives*, 3.1.17–26: that much of the humour derives from an audience realising that the parson is combining secular and Biblical lyrics further indicates the popularity of the poem.

Anon

The remaining six poems (*PP* 7, 9, 10, 13, 14, 15) are of unknown authorship; of these six, *PP* provides the only known copies for all but *PP* 7 (which also appears alongside other *PP* poems in Folger MS V.a.339).

There were later attempts to tie some of the *PP* poems more firmly to the Shakespeare canon. It was probably the renowned Shakespeare forger J.P. Collier who inserted the initials 'W.S.' beside versions of *PP* 4, 6, 7, 11 and 18 in Folger MS V.a.339, fols 197r–v (see Dawson 1971). *The Gentleman's Magazine* (November 1750 and January 1760) twice printed a version of *PP* 13, 'Beauty's Value, by W. Shakespeare', which purportedly derived from 'a corrected manuscript' (20.521; 30.39). The poem appears, with the same title and attributed to Shakespeare, in *The Chester Miscellany* (1750: 289), where it is decreed as coming 'from a very correct manuscript'.

The handwritten copy of poem – probably drawn from one of these eighteenth-century printed sources and with the same title ('Beauty's Value') – is inscribed in one of the Folger library copies of the first volume of Shakespeare's *Plays* (1733), ed. Lewis Theobald (Folger shelfmark PR 2752 1733, copy 5).

Publication history and reception

PP proved popular. There were two editions in 1599 (STC 22341.5 and 22342), and a third, expanded edition of 1612, when Jaggard added nine excerpts from Thomas Heywood's *Troia Britannica*, which Jaggard had printed in 1609. The scarcity of copies (ESTC lists three copies of the first edition; three of the second; two of the third) and the fragmentary nature of the first edition (of which no complete copies survive) would suggest that – like many pamphlets and small items – the book was quite literally read to pieces. Versions of *PP* 16, 17, 19 and 20 also appear in *England's Helicon*; and John Benson reprinted all of *Passionate Pilgrim* (from the 1612 edition) in *Shakespeare's Poems* (1640), where he interspersed them with poems from the 1609 *Sonnets*.

Jaggard has come under fire for publishing *PP*. Thomas Heywood reports in his *Apology for Actors* (1612) that Shakespeare was 'much offended with M[aster] Jaggard (that altogether unknown to him) presumed to make so bold with his name' (sig. G4v), whilst Arthur Swinburne's assessment of both Jaggard and *PP* exemplifies the tone of much nineteenth- and twentieth-century scholarship. Swinburne calls Jaggard an 'infamous pirate, liar, and thief', and *PP* 'a worthless little volume of stolen and mutilated poetry, patched up and padded with dirty and dreary doggerel, under [a] senseless and preposterous title' (1894: 90). Later twentieth- and twenty-first-century evaluations (with Marotti 1990 in the vanguard) have been kinder, arguing that it is anachronistic to critique Jaggard for conduct which was entirely in line with Elizabethan printing practices. Literary property belonged to printers and publishers, not authors, and Jaggard had every right to print extracts from *Troia Britannica*, for example, since he owned the copyright. Passing off a miscellaneous collection as the work of one author was also quite usual: 'A friend's just excuse' at the end of Robert Toft's *Laura* (1597) draws attention to this practice, when 'R.B.' describes how he 'came at the last sheet's printing, and f[ou]nd more than thirty sonnets not his [Toft's], intermixed with his', and invites the reader to try to 'distinguish between them' (sig. E7r).

We also need to be careful about taking at face value Heywood's comments about Shakespeare's displeasure. Heywood was himself angry with Jaggard, not merely because he believed that Jaggard done him a 'manifest injury [. . .] by taking the two epistles of Paris to Helen, and Helen to Paris, and printing them in a less volume, under the name of another', but also because Jaggard had refused to print a list of *errata* for 'the infinite faults escaped in my book [*Troia Britannica*], by the negligence of the printer' since he 'would not publish his own disworkmanship, but rather let his own fault lie up on the neck of the author' (*Apology*, sig. G4r). Moreover, these complaints against his previous printer are made in a prefatory letter to his new printer, Nicholas Okes, and may be read as a way of prescribing the kind of relationship that Heywood wants with his new printer (careful printing, a list of *errata* if need be, due recognition of his authorship) rather than as an accurate reflection of how things actually worked in the Jacobean print trade. Heywood also suggests that *PP* was a prompt to Shakespeare publishing the sonnets 'in his own name' (sig. G4r); yet there is a ten-year gap between the first edition of *PP* and the 1609 Quarto, hardly a sign that Shakespeare was eager to stake a claim to his literary property (however, see the registration of '*Amours* [. . .] with certain other sonnets', discussed below). Nor is Heywood strictly accurate when he claims that his verse epistles have been passed off as Shakespeare's, since they are mentioned after the attribution to Shakespeare, and as a supplement to the original volume. As the 1612 title-page reads:

The Passionate Pilgrim, or Certain Amorous Sonnets, between Venus and Adonis, newly corrected and augmented. By W. Shakespeare. The third Edition. Whereunto is newly added two Love-Epistles, the first from Paris to Helen, and Helen's answer back again to Paris. Printed by W. Jaggard. 1612.

There is another version of the 1612 title-page, which omits Shakespeare's name. Rollins (1940: xxviii) has suggested that either 'Shakespeare or his friends' put pressure on Jaggard to remove his name. If that is the case, and the appropriation of Shakespeare's name so riled him, it is odd that he and/or his friends should wait until the third edition was in press to secure its removal. It is equally possible that that title-page without Shakespeare's name was a mistake, which was then corrected. The Bodleian copy of the 1612 *PP* (which belonged to the Shakespeare scholar Edmond Malone) contains both title-pages, the first of which omits Shakespeare's name, and which ESTC suggests was 'probably intended as a cancel'; this theory is backed up by Burrow's observation that 'The title-page without the name of Shakespeare [. . .] is noticeably less worn than that which includes Shakespeare's name. This suggests that the volume was originally circulated with Shakespeare's name on the outermost leaf of the volume, and that Malone had the pages bound in their present order, having found the cancelled title-page originally inside the volume' (2002: 79n).

However, it is possible that Shakespeare did respond to Jaggard's pamphlet, as Heywood suggests. Duncan-Jones (1997a: 3) draws attention to an entry in the Stationers' Register on 3 January 1600 by Eleazar Edgar for 'a book called *Amours* by J.D. with certain *other sonnets* by W.S.' (This would have been Edgar's first known publication; he would go on to print a number of works by Shakespeare's fellow playwrights, including Thomas Dekker's *The Double PP*, 1606; Francis Beaumont's *The Woman Hater*, 1607; and Thomas Middleton's *A Mad World My Masters*, 1608.) The book, if it was ever printed, is now lost, and 'W.S.' might well be someone other than Shakespeare (e.g. William Smith, author of the sonnet sequence *Chloris*, printed in 1596). Even if Shakespeare was 'W.S.', the entry can be interpreted in different ways, since the entry – rather than being a preamble to printing – could have been a staying entry, designed to prevent Jaggard reissuing *PP* (Duncan-Jones 1997a: 5). If that was the case, then it may have had some success, since Jaggard did not produce another edition of *PP* until 1612, thirteen years later.

PP was not a high-quality volume. The faulty nature of *PP* 9 (missing l. 2) goes unnoticed by the compositors of all three editions, and the compositor of the first edition may even be responsible for its omission (there is no other extant copy against which to check it). Certainly, *England's Helicon* is noticeably more careful in those poems (*PP* 16 and 17) which must derive from the same or a related source (if not copied from *PP*), due to the minimal number of substantive differences between them: the *EH* version (sig. H1r) corrects the 'throne/thorn' error found at *PP* 16.12, and substitutes the more probable 'ruthlesse beasts' for 'ruthlesse beares' at *PP* 20.22 (sig. H2r). The second 1599 edition of *PP* is particularly careless: there are a number of instances of turned type (*PP* 17.12; 18.7, 28, 36), and the order of stanzas in *PP* 18 is disrupted: the third and fourth stanzas in the second edition appear as stanzas five and six (and vice versa) in every other version: the first and third editions, and the two manuscript copies (Folger MSS. V.a.89, fol. 25r–v; V.a.339, fol. 185v). This compositor also misunderstands the unusual and extravagant practice, adopted in the first edition, of beginning each new poem on a recto. In the first edition, this lavish use of paper may have resulted from a desire to pad out the volume to three sheets, since the previous year (1598) the Court of Assistants of the Stationers' Company had set a maximum price of one pence for books without illustrations comprising two sheets or less, printed in pica or English type (Smith 2010: 29): the seemingly wasteful layout on materials would thus appear to be an attempt to maximise profits. In the second edition, however, until the final leaves of the volume (when he must have realised that he was running short of space), the compositor only uses the recto of each leaf, leaving the versos blank, meaning that the inattentive reader risks mistaking a new leaf for a new poem.

In the second and third editions at least (these pages do not survive in copies of the first edition), *PP* 15–20 appear after an internal title-page, which introduces them as *Sonnets to Sundry Notes of Music*. This title-page does not, however, denote a work that can be sold separately, since the title-page comes in the middle of a gathering (sig. C3 in both editions); nor can this internal title-page (which makes no mention of Shakespeare) be used to demarcate the end of a section of poems that Jaggard believed, or wished to present as, Shakespeare's, since the second poem that follows this title-page (*PP* 16) is by Shakespeare: the third of the extracts from *Love's Labours Lost*, acknowledged on its 1598 title-page as being 'newly corrected and augmented by W. Shakespeare'. This internal title-page may have been added to try to eke out the work to four full gatherings, and as such it would be further evidence of the incompetence of the compositor of the second edition, since – after using up paper in this profligate way – he ends up having to cram *PP* 18–20 into the remaining space, setting the last three stanzas of *PP* 18 onto one page (stanzas 1–6 appear two stanzas to a page), and *PP* 19–20 on verso as well as recto. The 1612 edition follows the second, in printing on the recto only (regardless of whether the poem is a continuation), until the beginning of *PP* 18 (sig. D1r), after which point both recto and verso are used to the end of the volume. The 1612 compositor does, however, correct the instances of turned type, and the nonce-word 'nenying' (*PP²* 17.4), which is emended to 'denying' (sig. C6r), which is how it also appears in the first edition.

The form in which Jaggard acquired the poems in *PP* is unclear: did they come as a pre-assembled collection, or did he get hold of two of Shakespeare's sonnets as separates? Jaggard was a canny businessman, as indicated by his later enterprises as a printer of playbills and the monopoly-holder of printing the Ten Commandments for use in church (*ODNB*). He was bound to have recognised the commercial value of the sonnets: Shakespeare's name was marketable, and Francis Meres' *Palladis Tamia* (1598) would surely have whetted the appetite of its readers for a glimpse of Shakespeare's 'sugared sonnets' then circulating in manuscript 'among his private friends' (fols 281v–2r). In light of the order of the Court of Assistants in 1598, to obtain maximum profit from these two sonnets, he would need to accrue other poems, to take the subsequent volume over the two-sheet margin. That two of the poems, *PP* 8 and 20, were certainly supplied by Jaggard's brother lends credibility to this second scenario, of Jaggard assembling poems from a variety of sources. However, although eight of the *PP* poems have versions in print by 1599, only the Barnfield poems, *PP* 8 and 20, would seem to derive from a printed source: there are no substantive variants between these two poems and their appearance in *The Encomion of Lady Pecunia*, and there is also a striking concordance in the use of capitalisation and punctuation (brackets, apostrophes, hyphens) across the two volumes. The remaining six poems (the *Love's Labours Lost* verses, *PP* 3, 5, 16; *PP* 11, by Griffin; *PP* 12, by Deloney; and *PP* 17, found in Weelkes' *Madrigals*) cannot derive from printed copies: that in Weelkes is a song-setting, which only uses half of each line of *PP* 17. It is difficult to assess *PP* 12, because the earliest surviving version post-dates *PP*, but there are four differences between it and *PP* 12, as well as an extra line in *PP* (l. 4: here Deloney 1628 would seem to be at fault, since the omission leaves l. 2 without a rhyming pair). The remaining four poems each contain between five and seven substantive differences in the lines that *PP* shares with other witnesses; *PP* 16 also omits two lines from Dumaine's 'sonnet', and Griffin's sonnet, as printed in *Fidessa*, has a different third quatrain from *PP* 11.

Ovidian verse

Despite its miscellaneity in terms of authorship, poetic forms and likely provenance, *PP* is nonetheless a cohesive publication. The volume comprises amorous verse, the ardour of which is repeatedly cut through with a sardonic note: a world in which mistresses prove 'not so fair as fickle' (*PP* 7.1); where love is physical rather than chaste and idealised (the poems are often bawdy, as in *PP* 9, where Adonis flees from the sight of Venus' 'wounds', l. 13); and where one lover can cynically and misogynistically counsel another how to seduce his 'chose[n] dame' (*PP* 18.1). The ambiance of these poems is frequently pastoral (*PP* 4, 6, 9, 11, 12, 17, 19 and 20 evoke rural settings), and the love affair between Venus and Adonis is recurrently invoked (*PP* 4, 6, 9, 11): these 'Venus and Adonis' sonnets replay the dynamic found in Shakespeare's narrative poem, where Adonis is figured as a naïve and reluctant lover ('the tender nibbler' who 'would not touch the bait', *PP* 4.11), and Venus as his lustful pursuer, 'hot' with desire (*PP* 6.7). Linking *PP* to Shakespeare's *Venus and Adonis* (a bestseller) must have been strategic on Jaggard's part (the sixth edition of *Venus and Adonis* appeared in 1599), and it is striking that he chose William Leake as the bookseller in 1599 (he is named on the 1599 title-page), since Leake had acquired the right to sell Shakespeare's *Venus and Adonis* by that date: the two works would thus have been sold side-by-side. Customers also seem to have made this link between the two volumes (or been persuaded to do so in Leake's shop in St Paul's Churchyard), since two of the extant copies of the second edition of *PP* are bound up with Shakespeare's poem (Folger Library shelfmark 22341.8; Huntington Library shelfmark 59000-2; see Knight 2009: 328).

The juxtaposition of material from a variety of sources – and in particular the presence of the 'Venus and Adonis' sonnets – brings out new and different meanings in the assembled poems. The emphasis that the speaker of *PP* 1 (Sonnet 138) puts on his (false) appearance as 'some untutored youth', for example, resonates with, and changes our impression of, Adonis' 'unripe[ness]' (*PP* 4.9): his seeming naivety becomes knowing and strategic. Likewise, the hints that the mistress of *PP* 1 is not necessarily in the first flush of youth (l. 9) further tarnishes her irreverent portrayal in both Shakespeare's narrative poem and the 'Venus and Adonis' sonnets in *PP*, whilst in conjunction with the 'Venus and Adonis' sonnets that follow, lying 'with Love' (*PP* 1.13) starts to sound like personification: lying with the goddess of Love herself. These readings are encouraged by additional verbal links between the 'Venus and Adonis' sonnets and the other *PP* poems, particularly towards the start of the volume; the references to the beloved as a 'goddess' (*PP* 3.6) and 'celestial' (*PP* 5.13) take on a quite different resonance when placed in close proximity to poems which explicitly invoke an actual goddess, a reminder that the context in which poems are read, and the company they keep, can affect their meaning and interpretation.

The Ovidian element of *PP* is foregrounded in Jaggard's third, expanded edition, where a new title-page provides a subtitle ('The Passionate Pilgrim, Or Certaine Amorous Sonnets, between Venus and Adonis') and announces the addition of 'two Love-Epistles, the first from Paris to Helen, and Helen's answer back again to Paris'. The material added comprises:

i 'The amorous epistle of Paris to Helen' (incipit: 'Health unto Leda's daughter, Priam's son', sigs D5r–F3v);

ii 'Helen to Paris' (incipit: 'No sooner came mine eye unto the sight', sigs F4r–G6r);

iii 'That Menelaus was cause of his own wrongs' (incipit: 'When Menelaus from his house is gone', sig. G7r–v);

iv a poem 'in another place somewhat resembling this' (incipit: 'Orestes liked, but not loved dearly', sig. G7v);

v 'The tale of Cephalus and Pocris' (incipit: 'Beneath Hymetus hill well clothed with flowers', sigs G8r–H1v);

vi 'Mars and Venus' (incipit: 'This tale is blazed through heaven, how once unware', sigs H2r–H3r);

vii 'The history how the Minotaur was begot' (incipit: 'Ida of cedars and tall trees stand full', sigs H3v–H4r);

viii a poem on 'the curious arts–master Daedalus' (incipit: 'When Daedalus the labyrinth had built', sigs. H4v–H6v);

  ix 'Achilles his concealment of his sex in the court of Lycomedes' (incipit: 'Now from another world doth sail with joy', sig. H7r–v).

Collectively, this material – along with the new subtitle – strengthens the Ovidian strain of the first two editions.

Note on the text

The version of the text given below is from the second edition of 1599, the earliest remaining complete copy. Although original spelling and punctuation have been retained, the text has been lightly edited: turned type has been corrected ('women' for 'wowen' at 17.12; 'thou' for 'thon' at 18.7; 'ringing' for 'ringiug' at 18.28; 'though' for 'thongh' at 18.36); the error at *PP* 17.4 ('neny-ing') has been emended; the missing letters (n/m) provided by tildes have been silently provided ('argument', *PP* 3.2; 'them', *PP* 18.40); and some punctuation which is obviously missing has been supplied: the closing brackets at *PP* 2.10, 10.10; the full-stops at the end of *PP* 5.12 (present in the first edition, but lost in the second because of 'thunder', which has been dropped down from the previous over-running line) and *PP* 12.6. The faulty rhymes found in all three editions ('eares' for 'ear' at *PP* 4.5; 'throne' for 'thorne' at *PP* 16.12, an error also found in the 1598 quarto of *Love's Labours Lost*, sig. F4r) – testimony to the imperfect state in which these poems circulated in *PP* – have also been amended.

In *PP* 1 and 2, words in bold indicate variants from Q; for glosses on lines and phrases common to the sonnets in Q, see notes at the appropriate place in the main text.

PP 1

Sonnet 138 in Q; printed by Benson from the third edition of *PP*, as a single sonnet entitled 'False belief'. There is also a version in Folger MS V.a.339 (fol. 197v), taken from either *PP* or Benson's 1640 *Poems*.

Roe (1992: 238–9) proposes that *PP*'s version has been 'contaminated' in the process of memorial reconstruction, since '(1) some of the readings make poor sense in the *PP* version (see especially 1.8), (2) they present a simpler, less interesting version of the theme and reduce the imaginative wordplay of 1609'. Booth – whom Roe cites in support of the contamination theory – is less decided: for him, the first part of *PP* 1.8 ('Outfacing faults in love') suggests 'an earlier version', whilst the second part ('with love's ill rest') 'sounds like a filler provided by someone who has forgotten everything about the line except that its final syllable rhymed with *best*' (1977: 479). Particularly in the light of the time-lag between *PP* and the 1609 Quarto, it seems likely that the *PP* version would have been revised over the intervening decade, so that Burrow's compromise position – it may be 'a mistranscribed or poorly remembered version of an early draft of 138, since some of its variants have parallels in other works by Shakespeare' (2002: 341) – seems both logical and sensible.

4 *false forgeries* The pleonasm is not unShakespearean. Burrow (2002: 341) points out the parallel with 'false perjury' in *Love's Labours Lost* (4.3.60, *PP* 3.3). Burrow also highlights Shakespeare's use of the word 'forgeries' in works of the 1590s (e.g. *Midsummer Night's Dream*, 2.1.81; *Lucrece*, l. 460) to denote 'delusions of the mind, especially of those in love'.

8 *Outfacing. . . rest* 'denying defects (including transgressions) in love/the beloved with the unease (insecurity) felt by someone who is in love'; see also headnote to *PP* 1 above.

9 *young* In contrast to Sonnet 138, both the poet-speaker and the mistress are here said to be old.

11 *soothing* flattering (OED 1).

14 *smother'd* 'suppressed, concealed, restrained, kept down or under in some manner' (OED 2a).

PP 2

Sonnet 144 in Q; printed by Benson from the third edition of *PP*, as a single sonnet entitled 'A temptation'.

8 *faire* less hostile than Q's 'foul'; as well as being less abusive towards the woman, it also makes the male friend's attraction to her less perverse.

11 *For. . .friend* Two different monosyllables ('for', 'to') completely alter the meaning from 144.11. In Q, the poet-speaker is estranged from the woman and male friend, who are friends of each other; here, the amorous triangle remains in place: the man and woman are friends of one another, but also friends to the poet-speaker.

THE PASSIONATE PILGRIME.
By W. Shakespeare

AT LONDON
Printed for W. Iaggard, and are
to be sold by W. Leake, at the Greyhound in Paules Churchyard.
1599.

[sig. A3r [sic]]   [*PP* 1]
When my Loue sweares that she is made of truth,
I doe beleeue her (though I know she lies)
That she might thinke me some vntutor'd youth,
Vnskilfull in the worlds false **forgeries**.   4
Thus vainly thinking that she thinkes me young,
Although **I know** my **yeares be** past the best:
I smiling, credite her false speaking toung,
Outfacing faults in Loue, with loues ill rest.   8
But wherefore says **my Loue that** she is **young**?
And wherefore say not I, that I am old?
O, Loues best habite is **a soothing toung**,
And Age (in Loue) loues not to have years told.   12
    Therefore **Ile** lye with **Loue**, and **Loue** with me,
    Since that our faults **in Loue thus smother'd** be.

[sig. A4r]   [*PP* 2]
Two Loues I haue, of Comfort, and Despaire,
That like two Spirits, do suggest me still:
My better Angell is a Man (right faire)
My worser spirite a Woman (colour'd ill.)   4
To winne me soone to hell, my Female euill
Tempteth my better Angell from my **side**,
And would corrupt my Saint to be a Diuell,
Wooing his purity with her **faire** pride.   8
And whether that my Angell be turnde feend,
Suspect I may (yet not directly tell):
For being both **to** me: both, to each friend,
I ghesse one Angell in anothers hell: 12
    The truth I shall not know, but liue in doubt,
    Till my bad Angell fire my good one out.

PP 3

A version also appears in *Love's Labours Lost*, 4.3.58–71. Printed by Benson from the third edition of *PP* entitled 'Fast and loose'.

PP 4

Copies appear in Folger MS V.b.43 (fol. 22r) and Folger MS V.a.339 (fol. 197r), where it is attributed, probably by the forger Collier, to 'W.S.'; it has also been ascribed to Griffin (see headnote to *PP*). It appears, in a musical setting by John Wilson, in Bodleian MS Mus.b.1 (fol. 60v), a mid-seventeenth collection of songs (see also *PP* 11). Printed by Benson from the third edition of *PP*, entitled 'A sweet provocation'.

1 *Cytherea* another name for Venus.

PP 5

A version also appears in *Love's Labours Lost*, 4.2.105–18. Printed by Benson from the third edition of *PP*, entitled 'A constant vow'.

4 *Osiers* willows; proverbially pliant (contrast the unmoving oak).

10 *this earth* the poetic speaker; may also indicate more precisely the speaker's body (*n.*1, OED 14; see *Lucrece*, l. 487 and note).

6 *fauors* probably bawdy: compare *Hamlet*, 2.2.232–3: 'Then you live about [Fortune's] waist, or in the middle of her favours?'
9 *conceit* understanding (OED³ 2b).
12 *ieast* jest.
13 *fell. . . backe* bawdy: see *Romeo and Juliet*, 1.3.42: 'Thou wilt fall backward when thou has more wit'. *queen* Bearing in mind the bawdy tone, a pun on 'quean' ('hussy [. . .] prostitute', OED³ 1) is probable. *toward* willing.
14 *froward* perverse, hard to please (OED 1).

5 *byas* bias; inclination, natural disposition (OED 3a).
13 *O. . . wrong* The reading in *Love's Labours Lost* – 'pardon, love, this wrong' – makes more immediate sense.

[sig. A5r]   [*PP* 3]

Did not the heauenly Rhetorike of thine eie,
Gainst whom the world could not hold argument,
Perswade my hart to this false periurie:
Vowes for thee broke deserue not punishment.   4
A woman I forswore: but I will proue
Thou being a Goddesse, I forswore not thee:
My vow was earthly, thou a heauenly loue,
Thy grace being gainde, cures all disgrace in me.   8
My vow was breath, and breath a vapor is,
Then thou faire Sun, that on this earth doth shine,
Exhale this vapor vow, in thee it is:
If broken, then it is no fault of mine.   12
    If by me broke, what foole is not so wise
    To breake an Oath, to win a Paradise?

[sig. A6r]   [*PP* 4]

Sweet Cytherea, sitting by a Brooke,
With young Adonis, louely, fresh and greene,
Did court the Lad with many a louely looke,
Such lookes as none could looke but beauties queen.   4
She told him stories, to delight his eare:
She shew'd him fauors, to allure his eie:
To win his hart, she toucht him here and there,
Touches so soft still conquer chastitie.   8
But whether vnripe yeares did want conceit,
Or he refusde to take her figured proffer,
The tender nibler would not touch the bait,
But smile, and ieast, at euery gentle offer: 12
    Then fell she on her backe, faire queen, & toward
    He rose and ran away, ah foole too froward.

[sig. A7r]   [*PP* 5]

If Loue make me forsworn, how shal I swere to loue?
O, neuer faith could hold, if not to beauty vowed:
Though to my selfe forsworn, to thee Ile constant proue,
those thoghts to me like Okes, to thee like Osiers bowed.   4
Studdy his byas leaues, and makes his booke thine eies,
where all those pleasures liue, that Art can comprehend:
If knowledge be the marke, to know thee shall suffice:
Wel learned is that toung that well can thee commend,   8
All ignorant that soule, that sees thee without wonder,
Which is to me some praise, that I thy parts admyre:
Thine eye Ioues lightning seems, thy voice his dreadfull thunder
which (not to anger bent) is musick & sweet fire.   12
    Celestiall as thou art, O, do not loue that wrong:
    To sing heauens praise, with such an earthly toung.

PP 6

A version appears in Folger MS V.a.339 (fol. 197r), where it is attributed, probably by the forger Collier, to 'W.S.'; it has also been ascribed to Griffin (see headnote to *PP*). Printed by Benson from third edition of *PP*, entitled 'Cruel deceit'.

3 *Cytherea* See *PP* 4.1n.

6 *spleene* The organ was associated with bad temper and lust, but it seems more likely that it is used here for the rhyme (within this sonnet – as in his portrayal in *PP* more generally – Adonis is notably chaste and self-contained).
14 *IOVE* Jove, king of the Roman gods.
   flood river.

PP 7

A version appears in Folger MS V.a.339 (fol. 197v), where it is attributed, probably by the forger Collier, to 'W.S.' (see headnote to *PP*). Printed by Benson from third edition of *PP*, entitled 'The unconstant lover'.

5 *damaske die* 'the colour [dye] of the damask rose; blush-coloured' (OED 8).

9 *coyned* invented, with a sense of counterfeiting (*v*.1, OED 5b).
12 *ieastings* jestings, jests.
15 *framd* contrived (but with a sense of falsity).
   foyld spoiled.
16 *bad* bade, commanded.
17 *whether* which of the two was she (a lover, or a 'letcher', someone given to sexual indulgence).

PP 8

Taken from Barnfield's 'Poems: in diverse humours' (see headnote to *PP*), where it is addressed to 'his friend Master R.L.', often identified as Richard Linche, author of the sonnet sequence *Diella*. The omission of the heading and its relocation within a series of poems about heterosexual relations removes the homoerotic dynamic of Barnfield's original. Printed by Benson from third edition of *PP*, entitled 'Friendly concord'.

2 *Sister and [. . .] brother* This would seem to indicate Apollo and his sister Diana (Artemis in the Greek). Whilst Apollo is usually depicted as the patron god of both music and poetry (as in *PP* 8.10), Diana-Artemis was sometimes depicted carrying a lyre.
5 *Dowland* John Dowland (1563?–1626), lutenist and composer. His works were printed from 1596, so this would be a voguish allusion in 1598 (when the poem was first printed).
7 *Spenser* The poet Edmund Spenser, the second, expanded edition of whose *Faerie Queene* had been printed in 1596.
7–8 *Conceit. . . conceit* a play on various meanings of 'conceit': 'his literary inventiveness surpasses understanding'.

[sig. A8r]   [*PP* 6]
Scarse had the Sunne dride vp the deawy morne,
And scarse the heard gone to the hedge for shade:
When Cytherea (all in Loue forlorne)
A longing tariance for Adonis made   4
Vnder an Osyer growing by a brooke,
A brooke, where Adon vsde to coole his spleene:
Hot was the day, she hotter that did looke
For his approch, that often there had beene.   8
Anon he comes, and throwes his Mantle by,
And stood starke naked on the brookes greene brim:
The Sunne look't on the world with glorious eie,
Yet not so wistly, as this Queene on him: 12
    He spying her, bounst in (whereas he stood)
    Oh IOVE (qouth she) why was not I a flood?

[sig. B1r]   [*PP* 7]
Faire is my loue, but not so faire as fickle.
Milde as a Doue, but neither true nor trustie,
Brighter then glasse, and yet as glasse is brittle,
Softer then waxe, and yet as Iron rusty:
    A lilly pale, with damaske die to grace her,   5
    None fairer, nor none falser to deface her.

Her lips to mine how often hath she ioyned,
Betweene each kisse her othes of true loue swearing:
How many tales to please me hath she coyned,
Dreading my loue, the losse whereof still fearing.   10
    Yet in the mids of all her pure protestings,
    Her faith, her othes, her teares, and all were ieastings.

She burnt with loue, as straw with fire flameth,
She burnt out loue, as soone as straw out burneth:
She framd the loue, and yet she foyld the framing,
She bad loue last, and yet she fell a turning.   15
    Was this a louer, or a Letcher whether?
    Bad in the best, though excellent in neither.

[sig. B2r]   [*PP* 8]
If Musicke and sweet Poetrie agree,
As they must needs (the Sister and the brother)
Then must the loue be great twixt thee and me,
Because thou lou'st the one, and I the other.   4
Dowland to thee is deere, whose heauenly tuch
Vpon the Lute, dooth rauish humane sense:
Spenser to me, whose deepe Conceit is such,
As passing all conceit, needs no defence.   8

10 **Phoebus** Apollo. Since Apollo is male '**Queene of Musicke**' must refer to the lute, which Phoebus here plays (rather than his usual instrument, the lyre).

13 **One God** Apollo. See *PP* 8.2n, above.
    faine feign.
14 **One Knight** an allusion to a patron, whose identity is now unknown.

PP 9

The only known version of this poem. Printed by Benson from third edition of *PP*, entitled 'Inhumanity'.

1 **Queene of loue** Venus.
3 **Doue** one of the symbols of Venus.
5 **stand** a term from hunting – 'the standing place from which a hunter or sportsman may shoot game' (*n*.1, OED 13) – thus evoking the 'hunt of love', a conventional motif of amorous verse.

Alternatively, it could figure Venus as standing in 'the post or station of a [...] sentinel' (OED 12a).
    steepe vp Compare Sonnet 7.5 and note.
7 **silly** unfortunate (OED³ A4).
10 **brakes** thickets; may also be an allusion to pubic hair; see *Venus and Adonis*, l. 237.
13 **more wounds then one** i.e. Venus' vagina, as well as her previous lover's wound, which she here evokes; **then** = than.

PP 10

The only known version of this poem. Printed by Benson from third edition of *PP*, entitled 'Love's loss'.

1, 2 **vaded** faded; compare Sonnet 54.14 and note.
3 **timely** early.

Thou lou'st to heare the sweet melodious sound,
That Phoebus Lute (the Queene of Musicke) makes:
And I in deepe Delight am chiefly drownd,
When as himselfe to singing he betakes.
    One God is God of both (as Poets faine)
    One Knight loues Both, and both in thee remaine.   12

[sig. B3r]   [*PP* 9]
Faire was the morne, when the faire Queene of loue,
[*1 line missing*   ]
Paler for sorrow then her milke white Doue,
For Adons sake, a youngster proud and wilde,   4
Her stand she takes vpon a steepe vp hill.
Anon Adonis comes with horne and hounds,
She silly Queene, with more then loues good will,
Forbad the boy he should not passe those grounds,   8
Once (quoth she) did I see a faire sweet youth
Here in these brakes, deepe wounded with a Boare,
Deepe in the thigh a spectacle of ruth,
See in my thigh (quoth she) here was the sore,   12
    She shewed hers, he saw more wounds then one,
    And blushing fled, and left her all alone.

[sig. B4r]   [*PP* 10]
Sweet Rose, faire flower, vntimely pluckt, soon vaded,
Pluckt in the bud, and vaded in the spring:
Bright orient pearle, alacke too timely shaded,
Faire creature kilde too soon by Deaths sharpe sting:
    Like a greene plumbe that hangs vpon a tree: 5
    And fals (through winde) before the fall should be.

I weepe for thee, and yet no cause I haue,
For why: thou lefts me nothing in thy will.
And yet thou lefts me more then I did craue,
For why: I craued nothing of thee still: 10
    O yes (deare friend) I pardon craue of thee,
    Thy discontent thou didst bequeath to me.

PP 11

A version – with a different third quatrain – is in Griffin's *Fidessa*; versions also appear in Folger MS V.a.339 (fol. 197v), where it is attributed, probably by the forger Collier, to 'W.S.' (see headnote to *PP*); in Folger MS V.b.43 (fol. 21v); and, set to music by John Wilson, in Bodleian MS Mus.b.1 (fol. 59v; see also *PP* 4). Printed by Benson from the third edition of *PP*, entitled 'Foolish disdain'.

> 1 **Venus with Adonis** The versions in *Fidessa* and Folger MS V.b.43 both read 'Venus, and young Adonis', making this an eleven-syllable

line, matching the form of l. 3, and in keeping with the predominance of hypermetric feminine-rhymed lines in this sonnet.

2 **Mirtle** plant associated with Venus.

3, 5 **Mars...the warlike god** Venus had an adulterous affair with Mars; see Ovid, *Metamorphoses*, 4.167–89.

6 **clipt** embraced.

8 **boy** Adonis.

13 **at this bay** a term from hunting, probably here indicating 'the final encounter between the hounds and the prey they have chased' (OED 2a).

PP 12

The first stanza of 'A maiden's choice twixt age and youth', from Deloney's *Garland of Good Will*; see headnote to *PP*. Printed by Benson from the third edition of *PP*, entitled 'Ancient antipathy'.

2 **pleasance** enjoyment, delight (*n*.1, OED³ 3); 'pleasure' in Deloney.

11 **hie** hurry.

PP 13

The only known version of this poem pre-1700; for mid-eighteenth-century printings, attributing it to Shakespeare, see headnote to *PP*. Printed by Benson from the third edition of *PP*, entitled 'Beauty's valuation'.

2, 6, 8 **vadeth...vaded** fades...faded; compare *PP* 10.1, 2.

3 **gins** begins.

4 **presently** (i) immediately (OED³ 1a); (ii) now (OED³ 2a).

5, 8 **glosse** lustre (*n*.2, OED) rather than explanatory note (*n*.1).

7 **seld** seldom.

10 **symant** cement.

12 **phisicke** medicine.
   paine effort.

PP 14

The only known version of this poem. Printed by Benson from the third edition of *PP*, entitled 'Loath to despir'.

2 **bad** said.

3 **daft** thrust aside (*v*.2, OED 2a).
   cabben temporary shelter (OED 1a) or rudimentary dwelling (OED 2a), expressive of the lover's woebegone state.

[sig. B5r]
[*PP* 11]

Venus with Adonis sitting by her,
Vnder a Mirtle shade began to wooe him,
She told the youngling how god Mars did trie her,
And as he fell to her, she fell to him. 4
Euen thus (quoth she) the warlike god embrac't me:
And then she clipt Adonis in her armes:
Euen thus (quoth she) the warlike god vnlac't me,
As if the boy should vse like louing charmes: 8
Euen thus (quoth she) he seized on my lippes,
And with her lips on his did act the seizure:
And as she fetched breath, away he skips,
And would not take her meaning nor her pleasure. 12
　　Ah, that I had my Lady at this bay:
　　To kisse and clip me till I run away.

[sig. B6r]
[*PP* 12]

Crabbed age and youth cannot liue together,
Youth is full of pleasance, Age is full of care,
Youth like summer morne, Age like winter weather,
Youth like summer braue, Age like winter bare.
Youth is full of sport, Ages breath is short, 5
Youth is nimble, Age is lame.
Youth is hot and bold, Age is weake and cold,
Youth is wild, and Age is tame.
　　Age I doe abhor thee, Youth I doe adore thee,
　　　O my loue my loue is young: 10
　　Age I doe defie thee. Oh sweet Shepheard hie thee:
　　　For me thinks thou staies too long.

[sig. B7r]
[*PP* 13]

Beauty is but a vaine and doubtfull good,
A shining glosse, that vadeth sodainly,
A flower that dies, when first it gins to bud,
A brittle glasse, that's broken presently.
　　A doubtfull good, a glosse, a glasse, a flower, 5
　　Lost, vaded, broken, dead within an houre.

And as goods lost, are seld or neuer found,
As vaded glosse no rubbing will refresh:
As flowers dead, lie withered on the ground,
As broken glasse no symant can redresse. 10
　　So beauty blemisht once, for euer lost,
　　In spite of phisicke, painting, paine and cost.

[sig. B8r]
[*PP* 14]

Good night, good rest, ah neither be my share,
She bad good night, that kept my rest away,
And daft me to a cabben hangde with care:

4 ***descant*** sing harmoniously (OED³ 1a), discourse at length, enlarge upon (OED³ 3); compare *Lucrece*, l. 1134.
doubts fears.

8 ***nill I conster whether*** 'I could not [or will not] work out which (whether she is smiling in scorn or friendship)'.

9 ***ioyd to ieast*** joyed to jest.

12 ***plucke the pelfe*** take the reward (pelf = booty, spoil, OED 1).

15 ***scite*** aphetic form of 'incite' (stir up).

16 ***daring trust*** daring to trust.

17 ***Philomela*** the nightingale; see Sonnet 107.7, 8 and notes.

18 ***lays*** songs; see Sonnet 98.5 and note.

19 ***she*** the lark.

21 ***packt*** sent packing.

21, 25 ***post*** hurry.

24 ***For why*** because.
sight sighed.
bad bade, ordered.

27 ***houre*** This is almost certainly the result of an eye-skip from the end of l. 26, as it means that the line does not rhyme, as required, with l. 25. Malone conjectures 'moon', i.e. month.

30 ***length*** lengthen.

To descant on the doubts of my decay.
   Farewell (quoth she) and come againe to morrow
   Fare well I could not, for I supt with sorrow.

Yet at my parting sweetly did she smile,
In scorne or friendship, nill I conster whether:
'Tmay be she ioyd to ieast at my exile,
'Tmay be againe, to make me wander thither.
   Wander (a word) for shadowes like my selfe,
   As take the paine but cannot plucke the pelfe.

[sig. C1r]
Lord how mine eies throw gazes to the East,
My hart doth charge the watch, the morning rise
Doth scite each mouing scence from idle rest,
Not daring trust the office of mine eies.
   While Philomela sits and sings, I sit and mark,
   And with her layes were tuned like the larke.

For she doth welcome daylight with her ditte,
And driues away darke dreaming night:
The night so packt, I post vnto my pretty,
Hart hath his hope, and eies their wished sight,
   Sorrow changd to solace, and solace mixt with sorrow,
   For why, she sight, and bad me come to morrow.

[sig. C2r]
Were I with her, the night would post too soone,
But now are minutes added to the houres:
To spite me now, ech minute seemes an houre,
   Yet not for me, shine sun to succour flowers.
   Pack night, peep day, good day of night now borrow
   Short night to night, and length thy selfe to morrow.

[sig. C3r]

SONNETS
To sundry notes of Musicke.

AT LONDON
Printed for W. Iaggard, and are
to be sold by W. Leake, at the Greyhound in Paules Churchyard.
1599.

5

10

15

20

25

30

PP 15

The only known version of this poem. Printed by Benson from the third edition of *PP*, entitled 'A duel'.

1 **Lordings** little lord; the form is probably chosen for metrical reasons, but it may be deliberately derogatory, as in George Puttenham's description of *meiosis* (dimunition) in the *Art of English Poesy*: 'Also such terms are used to be given in derision and for a kind of contempt, as when we say Lording for Lord' (1589: sig. 2B2v).

2 **maister** In the light of ll. 13–14, this must be 'tutor' (rather than employer).

5 **doubtfull** uncertain.

8 **silly** wretched, unfortunate.

9 **more mickle** the greater.

10 **That. . . gain** 'that nothing could be devised so that she could enjoy them both'.

PP 16

Versions appears in *Love's Labours Lost* (4.3.99–118, with two additional lines after *PP* 16.14, which refer to the situation in the play) and *England's Helicon*, under the heading 'The passionate shepherd's song' (1600: sig. H1r). Printed by Benson from the third edition of *PP*, entitled 'Lovesick'.

12 **thorne** The reading (from *England's Helicon*) is necessary for the rhyme; both *PP* and *Love's Labours Lost* here have 'throne'.

13 **vnmeet** unsuitable.

15 **Thou** The omission of the two lines from *Love's Labours Lost* means that there is an abrupt and slightly nonsensical shift from 'Youth' as the subject to 'Thou'.

15, 17 **Ioue** Jove; see *PP* 6.14n.

16 **Ethiope** Ethiopian, i.e. dark-skinned.

17 **deny. . . Ioue** deny that he was Jove.

PP 17

Versions appear in *England's Helicon*, under the heading 'The unknown shepherd's complaint' (1600: sigs. H1v–H2r) and in Weelkes' *Madgrials*; for the potential attribution to Barnfield, see headnote to *PP*. A version also appears in BL MS Harley 6910 (fol. 156r). Printed by Benson from the third edition of *PP*, entitled 'Love's labour lost'.

2 **speed** prosper.

5 **Iigges** jigs.

6 **wot** knows.

[sig. C4r]   [*PP* 15]
It was a Lordings daughter, the fairest one of three
That liked of her maister, as well as well might be,
Till looking on an Englishman, the fairest that eie could see,
    Her fancie fell a turning.
Long was the combat doubtfull, that loue with loue did fight   5
To leaue the maister louelesse, or kill the gallant knight,
To put in practise either, alas it was a spite
    Vnto the silly damsell.
But one must be refused, more mickle was the paine,
That nothing could be vsed, to turne them both to gain,   10
For of the two the trusty knight was wounded with disdain,
    Alas she could not helpe it.
Thus art with armes contending, was victor of the day,
Which by a gift of learning, did beare the maid away,
Then lullaby the learned man hath got the Lady gay,   15
    For now my song is ended.

[sig. C5r]   [*PP* 16]
On a day (alacke the day)
Loue whose month was euer May
Spied a blossome passing fair,
Playing in the wanton ayre,
Through the veluet leaues the wind   5
All vnseene gan passage find,
That the louer (sicke to death)
Wisht himselfe the heauens breath,
Ayre (quoth he) thy cheekes may blowe
Ayre, would I might triumph so   10
But (alas) my hand hath sworne,
Nere to plucke thee from thy thorne,
Vow (alacke) for youth vnmeet,
Youth, so apt to pluck a sweet,
Thou for whome Ioue would sweare,   15
Iuno but an Ethiope were
And deny hymselfe for Ioue
Turning mortall for thy Loue.

[sig. C6r]   [*PP* 17]
My flocks feede not, my Ewes breed not,
My Rams speed not, all is amis:
Loue is dying, Faithes defying,
Harts denying, causer of this.
All my merry Iigges are quite forgot,   5
All my Ladies loue is lost (god wot)
Where her faith was firmely fixt in loue,
There a nay is plac't without remoue.

9 *cross* misfortune (OED 10b).
16 *speeding* outcome (Burrow 2002: 360).
   gall bitterness.
17 *no deale* not a jot.
18 *weathers* wether's, i.e. belonging to his ram.
19 *curtaile dogge* dog whose tail has been docked.
26 *die* dye, colour.

27 *Heards* shepherds.
28 *backe peeping* The reading is taken from *England's Helicon*. *PP*'s 'blacke peeping' makes little sense.
35 *Coridon* The shepherd in Virgil's *Eclogue* 2, who laments his lost male lover, Alexis; more generally, an archetypal name for a shepherd in sixteenth-century poetry.

PP 18

There are versions in Folger MS V.a.89 (fols 25r-v); Folger MS V.a.339 (fol. 185v), where the forger Collier has tried to attribute it to Shakespeare; and BL Harleian MS 7392(2), fols 43r–v, where it is ascribed to 'R.P.', possibly Robert Pooley (see headnote to *PP*). Printed by Benson from the third edition of *PP*, entitled 'Wholesome counsel'.

2 *stalde the deare* stalled (stopped) the deer; deploys the conventional motif of the hunt-as-love, with a play on 'dear'.
4 *partyall* partial = biased (OED³ A4a).
8 *filed* polished.
12 *set. . . sale* praise her as if she were an item for sale; see the proverb cited at Sonnet 21.14n.

One silly crosse, wrought all my losse,
O frowning fortune cursed fickle dame,
For now I see, inconstancy,   10
More in women then in men remaine.

[sig. C7r]
In blacke morne I, all feares scorne I,
Loue hath forlorne me, liuing in thrall:
Hart is bleeding, all helpe needing,   15
O cruell speeding, fraughted with gall.
My shepheards pipe can sound no deale,
My weathers bell rings dolefull knell,
My curtaile dogge that wont to haue plaid,
Plaies not at all but seemes afraid.   20
    With sighes so deepe, procures to weepe,
    In howling wise, to see my dolefull plight,
    How sighes resound through hartles ground
    Like a thousand vanquisht men in blodie fight.

[sig. C8r]
Cleare wels spring not, sweete birds sing not,   25
Greene plants bring not forth their die,
Heards stands weeping, flocks all sleeping,
Nimphes backe peeping fearefully:
All our pleasure knowne to vs poore swaines:
All our merrie meetings on the plaines,   30
All our euening sport from vs is fled,
All our loue is lost, for loue is dead,
    Farewell sweet loue thy like nere was,
    For a sweet content the cause of all my woe,
    Poore Coridon must liue alone,   35
    Other helpe for him I see that there is none.

[sig. D1r]   [*PP* 18]
When as thine eye hath chose the Dame,
And stalde the deare that thou shouldst strike,
Let reason rule things worthy blame,
As well as fancy (partyall might)
    Take counsell of some wiser head,   5
    Neither too young, nor yet vnwed.

And when thou comst thy tale to tell,
Smooth not thy toung with filed talke,
Least she some subtill practise smell,
A Cripple soone can finde a halt,   10
    But plainly say thou loust her well,
    And set her person forth to sale.

14, 17   *yer* ere.

20   *ban* curse (OED 2a).

23–4   *Had. . . then* The poetic speaker ventriloquises the woman saying these words.

26   *spend* spend money or words on the woman, but perhaps also with a sexual sense, 'ejaculate'; see Sonnet 4.1–2n.

30   *golden bullet* money or eloquence ('golden' words).

34   *Prease* press, i.e. hurry (OED³ 8a).

35   *slacke* remiss.

40   *treads them* has sexual intercourse with them ('of the male bird: to copulate with the hen', OED 8a).

42   *A Womans. . . nought* invokes the misogynistic proverb 'A woman says nay and means aye' (Dent W660); 'nought' may also indicate female genitalia; see Sonnet 12.13n.

44   *saint* be good.

45   *There. . . heauen* 'Probably *there* refers to "in women", rather than making a general statement of atheism' (Burrow 2002: 364).
(by holy then) It is difficult to make sense of *PP* here. It is probable that Folger MS V.a.339 – 'Be holy then' (i.e. when women are old and ugly, as described in l. 46) – is the more reliable witness.

46   *attaint* infect, sully.

49   *soft* 'quiet!'

51   *stick* hesitate.
round. . . th' are clout me round the ear.

54   *bewraid* betrayed, divulged.

[sig. D2r]
What though her frowning browes be bent
Her cloudy lookes will calme yer night,
And then too late she will repent,   15
That thus dissembled her delight.
    And twice desire yer it be day,
    That which with scorne she put away.

What though she striue to try her strength,
And ban and braule, and say the nay: 20
Her feeble force will yeeld at length,
When craft hath taught her thus to say:
    Had women beene so strong as men
    In faith you had not had it then.

[sig. D3r]
And to her will frame all thy waies,   25
Spare not to spend, and chiefly there,
Where thy desart may merit praise
By ringing in thy Ladies eare,
    The strongest castle, tower and towne,
    The golden bullet beats it downe.   30

Serue alwaies with assured trust,
And in thy sute be humble true,
Vnlesse thy Lady proue vniust,
Prease neuer thou to chuse a new:
    When time shall serue, be thou not slacke,   35
    To proffer though she put thee back.

[sig. D4r]
The wiles and guiles that women worke,
Dissembled with an outward shew:
The tricks and toyes that in them lurke,
The Cock that treads them shall not know,   40
    Haue you not heard it said full oft,
    A Womans nay doth stand for nought.

Thinke Women still to striue with men,
To sinne and neuer for to saint,
There is no heauen (by holy then)   45
When time with age shall them attaint,
    Were kisses all the ioyes in bed,
    One Woman would another wed.

But soft enough, too much I feare,
Least that my mistresse heare my song.   50
She will not stick to round me on th' are,
To teach my toung to be so long:
    Yet will she blush, here be it said,
    To heare her secrets so bewraid.

PP 19

A longer version of the poem appears in *England's Helicon* (sigs. 2A1v–2r) and it was extensively copied in seventeenth-century manuscript miscellanies (CELM lists thirteen manuscripts for the poem attributed to Marlowe; twelve for the 'answer' attributed to Walter Ralegh). *England's Helicon* and Benson's 1640 *Poems* both give it the title 'The passionate shepherd to his love'.

10 *poses* posies.
11 *Kirtle* gown (OED 2a); skirt or outer petticoat (OED 2b).
12 *Mirtle* See *PP* 11.2n.
13 *Yuye* ivy.

PP 20

Taken from Barnfield's 'Poems: in diverse humours'; see headnote to *PP*. A shorter version also appears in *England's Helicon* (1600: sigs H2r–v), where it follows *PP* 17 and is entitled 'Another of the same shepherd'. Printed by Benson from the third edition of *PP*, entitled 'Sympathising love'.

4 *Myrtles* See *PP* 11.2n.
10 *vp-till* against; in poetry, nightingales are often depicted pressing their breasts against a thorn to induce their song; see Philip Sidney, *Certain Sonnets*, 4.1–4: 'The nightingale [. . .] | Sings out her woes, a thorn her song-book making'.
14 *Teru* Tereus, the brother-in-law who rapes Philomel and cuts out her tongue, setting in motion her revenge and the events which lead to her transfiguration into a nightingale; see Ovid, *Metamorphoses*, 6.424–674.

[sig. D5r]
Liue with me and be my Loue,
And we will all the pleasures proue
That hilles and vallies, dales and fields,
And all the craggy mountaines yeeld.

There will we sit vpon the Rocks,
And see the Shepheards feed their flocks,
By shallow Riuers, by whose fals
Melodious birds sing Madrigals.

5

There will I make thee a bed of Roses,
With a thousand fragrant poses,
A cap of flowers, and a Kirtle
Imbrodered all with leaues of Mirtle.

10

[sig. D5v]
A belt of straw and Yuye buds,
With Corall Clasps and Amber studs,
And if these pleasures may thee moue,
Then liue with me, and be my Loue.

15

    Loues answere.

If that the World and Loue were young,
And truth in euery shepheards toung,
These pretty pleasures might me moue,
To liue with thee and be thy Loue.

20

[sig. D6r]
As it fell vpon a Day,
In the merry Month of May,
Sitting in a pleasant shade,
Which a groue of Myrtles made,
Beastes did leape, and Birds did sing,
Trees did grow, and Plants did spring:
Euery thing did banish mone,
Saue the Nightingale alone.
Shee (poore Bird) as all forlorne,
Leand her breast vp-till a thorne,
And there sung the dolefulst Ditty,
That to heare it was great Pitty,
Fie, fie, fie, now would she cry
Teru, Teru, by and by:
[sig. D6v]
That to heare her so complaine,
Scarce I could from teares refraine:
For her griefes so liuely showne,

[*PP* 20]

5

10

15

21   **Senseless** unfeeling.

22   **Beares** *England's Helicon* has the more general
– and more probable – 'beasts'.

23   **Pandion** Philomel's father, who – as a result
of his grief over the fate of Philomel and her
sister Procne – died 'before his time' (Golding
1567: 6.845).

24   **lapt in Lead** buried in lead coffins.

34   **wherewith** the wherewithal, the means.

35   **Crownes** coins.

37–8 **prodigall | Bountifull** example of *paradiastole*.

40   **Pitty. . . King** 'He might as well be a king'; for
the association of kings and flattery, see Sonnet
114.2 and note.

41   **addict** addicted.

44   **They. . . Commaundement** They have women
at their command (to procure for him). The 'e'
before '-ment' is sounded for metrical purposes.

Made me thinke vpon mine owne.
Ah (thought I) thou mournst in vaine,
None takes pitty on thy paine: 20
Senslesse Trees, they cannot heare thee,
Ruthlesse Beares, they will not cheere thee.
King Pandion, he is dead:
All thy friends are lapt in Lead.
All thy fellow Birds doe sing,   25
Carelesse of thy sorrowing.
[sig. D7r]
Whilst as fickle Fortune smilde,
Thou and I, were both beguild.
Euery one that flatters thee,
Is no friend in miserie: 30
Words are easie, like the wind,
Faithfull friends are hard to find:
Euery man will be thy friend,
Whilst thou hast wherewith to spend:
But if store of Crownes be scant,   35
No man will supply thy want
If that one be prodigall,
Bountifull they will him call:
And with such-like flattering,
Pitty but he were a King.   40
[sig. D7v]
If he be addict to vice,
Quickly him, they will intice.
If to Women hee be bent,
They haue at Commaundement.
But if Fortune once doe frowne,   45
Then farewell his great renowne:
They that fawnd on him before.
Vse his company no more.
Hee that is thy friend indeede,
Hee will helpe thee in thy neede: 50
If thou sorrow, he will weepe:
If thou wake, hee cannot sleepe:
Thus of euery griefe, in hart
Hee, with thee, doeth beare a part.
These are certaine signes, to know   55
Faithfull friend, from flatt'ring foe.

Appendix 4

Shakespeare's sonnets in manuscript

The Catalogue of English Literary Manuscripts, 1450–1700 (CELM) lists twenty-one known manuscripts, which together contain versions of eleven complete sonnets: Sonnets 2 (thirteen copies), 8, 32, 33, 68, 71, 106 (two copies), 107, 116, 128 and 138, as well as traces of a further twenty individual sonnets left as excerpts and in composite poems, compiled from extracts (see item 8 in the list, below). None of these manuscripts pre-dates the 1609 Quarto, although at least some of Shakespeare's sonnets were circulating in manuscript, 'among his private friends' by 1598, when they are mentioned in Francis Meres' *Palladis Tamia* (fol. 282r). The majority of the manuscripts containing sonnets date from the 1630s. Although this figure may result from the higher numbers/survival rate of manuscript miscellanies from the mid-seventeenth century compared to those of earlier decades, the complete lack of manuscript copies of Shakespeare's sonnets from 1590s may indicate that (like Philip Sidney's *Astrophil and Stella* in the 1580s) their circulation – especially that of Sonnets 1–126 – was restricted (see Marotti 2010: 186).

Notable in the manuscript copies of Shakespeare's sonnets is the recurrent tendency to use headings ('To one that would die a maid'; 'On his mistress' beauty'; 'A lover to his mistress') to readdress to a woman poems which, read in Q's sequence, are to/about the young man; Benson's 1640 *Poems*, which does likewise, thus reflects a practice occurring in manuscript (see headnote to *Sonnets*, 'After the 1609 Quarto'). These sonnets are further heterosexualised by the contexts in which they occur, as they are positioned amongst amatory poems describing heterosexual love affairs (see Roberts 2003: 173). A number of the sonnets are also given a musical inflection: Sonnet 116 was substantially revised and set to music by Henry Lawes; one of the copies of Sonnet 2 carries the heading '*Spes Altera* A Song'; Sonnet 8 is broken (like Lawes' setting of Sonnet 116) into three stanzas and given a heading – 'In Laudem Musice et opprobrium Contemptorii [sic] eiusdem' ('In praise of music and in disapproval of he who despises it') – which 'recast[s the poem] as a eulogy to music' (Roberts 2003: 174); Sonnet 128 appears in company with a fragment of one of Dowland's airs.

As is usual in manuscript transmission (even for poems copied from print), most of the copies of Shakespeare's sonnets are unattributed (only four of the twenty-one manuscripts below acknowledge him by name or initials).

Manuscripts containing Shakespeare's sonnets

(Information on dating and provenance is drawn from CELM, supplemented with Marotti 2010; Roberts 2003: 172–9)

1. Bodleian, MS Rawl. poet. 152; collection of papers, bound into one volume. Contains a version of **Sonnet 128**, fol. 34r (possible dating is discussed below);
2. BL Add. MS 10309, Margaret Bellasis' miscellany, *c.* 1630. Contains a version of **Sonnet 2** (entitled 'Spes Altera'), fol. 143r;

3   BL Add. MS 15226, compiled *c.* 1627–*c.* 1673. Contains a version of **Sonnet 8** (entitled 'In laudem Musice et opprobrium Contemptorii eiusdem'), subscribed 'W. Shakespeare', fol. 4v;

4   BL Add. MS 21433, possibly associated with Inns of Court, *c.* 1620s–30s. Contains a version of **Sonnet 2** (entitled 'Spes Altera'), fol. 114v, copied from BL Add MS 25303 (see below);

5   BL Add. MS 25303, possibly associated with Inns of Court, *c.* 1620s. Contains a version of **Sonnet 2** (entitled 'Spes Altera'), fol. 119v;

6   BL Add. MS 30982, mainly compiled by Daniel Leare (cousin of the poet William Strode), probably at Christ Church, Oxford, *c.* early 1630s. Contains a version of **Sonnet 2** (entitled 'To one that would dy a maide'), fol. 18r;

7   BL Sloane MS 1792, compiled by 'I.A' of Christ Church, Oxford, *c.* early 1630s. Contains a version of **Sonnet 2** (entitled 'To one that would die a Mayd'), fol. 45r;

8   Folger MS V.a.148, possibly compiled by a member of Christ's College, Cambridge, *c.* 1650s. Under a heading 'Shakespeare', it reproduces excerpts from Benson's *Poems* (fols 22r–23r), including complete versions **Sonnets 33**, **68** and **107** as well as a series of extracts, which – from various elements of *mise-en-page* (spacing, indenting, rules), and (in one case) use of a title – seem to have been rearranged into composite poems. The compiler is writing freehand, rather than on ruled or pricked lines, so line spacing is sometimes hard to judge, particularly towards the bottom of a page, and particularly because the compiler does not always reproduce complete rhyming units. Ambiguities about what might comprise a poetic unit are recorded below, in the description of the contents of the 'Shakespeare' section, which consists of the following:

       fol. 22r

    (i)   Ben Jonson, 'To the Memory of my Beloved the Author, Mr William Shakespeare' (printed in 1623 Folio), ll. 47–8 (sig. A4v);

   (ii)   Sonnets 60.5–12 and 65.2–8 (distinguished by a line space from item i);

  (iii)   Sonnet 107, entitled 'A Monument' (the heading distinguishing it from item ii);

  (iv)   Sonnets 1.5–14, 2.1–4 and 54.5–6, entitled 'Cruel' (the heading, plus an indented first line, distinguishes the opening lines from item iii; it is less clear whether this item continues over the page and also comprises item v);

       fol. 22v

   (v)   Sonnet 68;

  (vi)   Sonnet 13.11–12 (probably distinguished from item v by the indented first line);

  (vii)   Sonnet 15.5–8 (distinguished from item vi by the line space and indented first line);

 (viii)   Sonnet 55.5–14 (distinguished from item vii by the line space and indented first line);

  (ix)   Sonnet 8.5–10 (distinguished from item viii by the line space);

  (x)   *PP* 3.1–2 (probably distinguished from item ix by the indented first line and a suggestion of a line space);

  (xi)   *PP* 3.13–14 (distinguished from item x by the line space and indented first line);

  (xii)   *PP* 5.11–12, Sonnet 20.6 and *PP* 5.13 (distinguished from item xii by a rule over the start of the first line);

       fol. 23r

 (xiii)   Sonnet 28.10–12, compressed into two lines, and 29.12;

 (xiv)   Sonnet 30.1–2 (distinguished from item xiii by the indented first line and a suggestion of a line space);

  (xv)   Sonnet 33 (distinguished from item xiv by a line space);

 (xvi)   Sonnet 62.10 (distinguished from item xv by a rule over the start of the line);

(xvii) Sonnet 116.11–12 (distinguished from item xvi by a rule over the start of the first line);

(xviii) Sonnet 82.9–10, compressed into one line (distinguished from item xvii by a rule over the start of the first line);

(xix) Sonnet 83.13 (distinguished from item xviii by a rule over the start of the line);

(xx) Sonnet 95.1–3 (distinguished from item xix by a rule over the start of the first line);

(xxi) Sonnet 97.2 (distinguished from item xx by a rule over the start of the line);

(xxii) Sonnet 107.2: two words only 'Summers front' (distinguished from item xxi by indentation);

(xxiii) Sonnet 112.1–4 (distinguished from item xxii by line spacing and a short rule over the start of the first line);

(xxiv) Sonnet 115.5–8 (distinguished from item xxiii by the indented first line, the suggestion of a line space, and a short rule over the start of the first line);

(xxv) Sonnets 121.5–6 and 124.6–7, 9 (distinguished from item xxiv by a rule over the start of the first line; the extracts from these two sonnets may also be intended as two different poetic units; line spacing is ambiguous);

(xxvi) Sonnet 132.5–6, 9 (seems to be distinguished from item xxv by a possible line space); fol. 23v

(xxvii) Sonnet 142.5–6; followed by more (non-Shakespearean) items from 1640 *Poems*;

9 Folger MS V.a.162, probably associated with Oxford University, *c.* 1650. Contains versions of **Sonnet 32** (entitled 'A sonnet'), fol. 26r, and **Sonnet 71** (also entitled 'A Sonnet'), fol. 12v;

10 Folger MS V.a.170, probably associated with Oxford University, *c.* 1630s–1655 (includes poems by the Christ Church poets Richard Corbett and William Strode). Contains a version of **Sonnet 2** (entitled 'To one that would dye a Mayd'), pp. 163–4;

11 Folger MS V.a.339, known as Joseph Hall's commonplace book, *c.* 1640s (note: this is not the bishop Joseph Hall; Hall is also a later owner, rather than the book's compiler). Contains a version of **Sonnet 138** (also *PP* 1), fol. 203v; although the manuscript contains copies of other *PP* poems (6, 7, 11, 18), they are not necessarily (all) copied from the printed copy: there are minor variants from *PP* 1, 6, 7 and 11, and substantive ones from *PP* 18;

12 Folger MS V.a.345, associated with Oxford University, possibly Christ Church, *c.* 1630s. Contains a version of **Sonnet 2** (entitled '*Spes Altera* A Song'), p. 145;

13 London Metropolitan Archives, ACC/1360/528, associated with the Clitherows, a London family, *c.* 1630s. Contains a version of **Sonnet 2** (entitled 'Spes Altera'), fol. 28v;

14 New York Public Library, Music Division, Drexel MS 4257, no. 33, a music book, compiled *c.* 1630s–50s, partly by the composer John Gamble (d. 1687). Contains a version of **Sonnet 116**, in a musical setting by Henry Lawes;

15 Pierpont Morgan Library, MA 1057, possibly compiled by William Holgate, Queens' College, Cambridge, *c.* 1630s. Contains a version of **Sonnet 106** (entitled 'On his Mistris Beauty'), p. 96;

16 Rosenbach Museum & Library, MS 1083/16, 'Collection of Divers Witty and pleasant Epigrams, Adages, Poems, Epitaphes &c', compiled by Robert Bishop, probably at Oxford University, *c.* 1630. Contains a version of **Sonnet 106** (entitled 'On his M^{ris} Beauty'), p. 256;

17 Rosenbach Museum & Library, MS 1083/17, compiled *c.* 1638–42. Contains a version of **Sonnet 2** (entitled 'The Benefitt of Mariage'), fols 132v–3r;

18 St John's College, Cambridge, MS S. 23, compiled *c.* 1630s–40s. Contains a version of **Sonnet 2** (untitled), subscribed 'W. Shakspere', fols 38r–v;

19 University of Nottingham, Pw V 37, possibly associated with Christ Church, Oxford, *c.* 1630s. Contains a version of **Sonnet 2** (entitled 'W. S./A Lover to his Mistres'), p. 69;

20 Westminster Abbey, MS 41, associated with Christ Church, Oxford (*c.* 1620s–40s); owned and partly compiled by George Morley (1598–1684), later Bishop of Winchester, during his time at Oxford. Contains a copy of **Sonnet 2** in Morley's hand (entitled 'To one y^t would dye a Mayd'), fol. 49r;

21 Yale, Osborn MS b 205, compiled *c.* 1630s; reproduces a large number of poems by Christ Church poets (Richard Corbett, George Morley and – in particular – William Strode). Contains a version of **Sonnet 2** (entitled 'To one that would die a maide'), fol. 54v.

At first glance, the seeming paucity of manuscript copies might suggest that Shakespeare's sonnets did not prove popular and that the 1609 Quarto had little impact (see Marotti 2010: 186). Certainly, despite the marketability of Shakespeare's name, Thorpe did not issue a subsequent edition of *Shakespeare's Sonnets*, to which he held the copyright, and they did not reappear in print until John Benson's 1640 edition of *Shakespeare's Poems*. However, the number of individual sonnets circulating in manuscript stands up very favourably in comparison to the printed sonnet sequences of his contemporaries, and the number of known copies of Sonnet 2 would indicate that it had a strong appeal for the compilers of mid-seventeenth-century miscellanies. CELM lists no manuscripts containing Thomas Lodge's *Phyllis* sonnets; six manuscripts which together contain versions of six poems (from a possible total of sixty-seven) from Michael Drayton's *Idea*; nine manuscripts which together contain four sonnets (from a total of eighty-nine) from Edmund Spenser's *Amoretti*; and five manuscripts which together contain six sonnets (from a possible total of fifty-seven) from Daniel's *Delia* (in addition to one manuscript which contains a run of forty-six sonnets). Sidney's *Astrophil and Stella* – which did so much to catalyse the Elizabethan vogue for sonnet sequences – fares even worse: aside from the three manuscripts containing much of the sequence (two of which definitely pre-date the print publication) and two manuscripts containing short extracts, only six sonnets (from a total of 108) appear as individual items across four different manuscripts; the songs from *Astrophil and Stella* were markedly more popular: seven of its eleven songs appear across twelve manuscripts. The high number of Henry Constable's sonnets in manuscript, meanwhile, relies on the reproduction of substantial portions of the *Diana* sequence in four main manuscripts (Arundel Harington MS Temp Eliz, Bodleian MS Ashmole 38, National Art Library MS Dyce 44 and Marsh Library, Dublin MS Z.3.5.21). Spenser's *Amoretti* 8, which appears in six manuscripts, is the closest that any of these Elizabethan sonnets comes to the popularity of Shakespeare's Sonnet 2.

   That all the copies of Shakespeare's sonnets post-date their print publication does not, of course, rule out the possibility (in theory) that some might descend from earlier versions. However, the following manuscripts can be easily disregarded on this count.

Folger MS V.a.148

The sonnets in this volume are copied in one hand, probably in one stint (judging from the uniformity of the colour of the ink, and size and general appearance of the handwriting). They almost certainly derive from print: there are no substantive differences in **Sonnets 68** and **107** from either the 1609 Quarto or Benson's 1640 *Poems*, and the only difference in **Sonnet 33** is the rendering of Q's/Benson's 'alack' (l. 11) as 'alas' (a minor variant); however, the fact that material from *PP* is included in this miscellany means that the 1640 *Poems*, rather than the 1609 Quarto is the likely source. The extracts also follow the order in which the sonnets appear in the 1640

Poems (Marotti 1990: 164), and the titles 'A Monument' and 'Cruel' may have been suggested by Benson's headings for the poems from which these sonnets are extracted: 'A monument to Fame' (for the poem comprising Sonnets 107 and 108, sig. F6r–v) and 'Loves Crueltie' (for the poem comprising Sonnets 1–3, sigs A5v–A6r). The compiler of the Folger manuscript takes considerable licence with their copy-text: where Benson fuses together entire sonnets, this compiler combines portions of sonnets and adapts the grammar to suit their repurposing, for example supplying a subject ('Love', fol. 23r) for the line which in Benson and Q reads 'It suffers not in smiling pomp, nor falls' (124.6). Some of the excerpts are fragments, probably collected 'as memorable poetic gems or felicitous expressions' (Marotti 2010: 189). At times, the Folger manuscript moves back towards the fourteen-line form of the sonnets in the 1609 Quarto: 'A Monument' detaches Sonnet 107 from Sonnet 108 (the company it keeps in the 1640 *Poems*), to reconstitute it as a fourteen-line sonnet; and the fusion of Sonnets 60.5–12 and 65.2–8 creates a fourteen-line 'sonnet', rhyming *ababcdcdefghgh*, by extracting these elements from the seventy-line poem ('Injurious Time'), comprising Sonnets 60 and 63–66, in which they appear in the 1640 *Poems*. Arguably, the composite poem 'Cruel' that follows could also be a fourteen-line sonnet, comprising Sonnets 1.5–14 and 2.1–4 (and thus rhyming *ababcdcdeefgfg*): as the compiler approaches the bottom of the page, it is unclear whether the next two lines (Sonnet 54.5–6) are meant to attach to this 'poem' or not. These lines do not rhyme, either with each other or the rest of the composite 'poem', but the compiler often disregards rhyming units (see the fusion of Sonnets 60 and 65, above). Although the versions in this manuscript have no claims to authority, they give insight into how readers used and appropriated the texts they encountered, and a selection of these composite, repurposed 'poems' and fragments appears at the very end of this appendix.

Folger MS. V.a.162

The sonnets included in this manuscript are fairly close to the 1609 Quarto, but perhaps at one or two removes, i.e. copied from a copy which derives from Q, the small number of errors making a longer genealogy unlikely. There no variants between Q and Benson in the sonnets that this manuscript contains; that Q is the likely copy-text is indicated by the fact that the miscellany does not contain other verses from the 1640 *Poems*, e.g. the *PP* poems that it reproduces, and by the fact that it distinguishes the two poems as 'sonnets' through the use of headings, a generic classification that the 1640 *Poems* suppresses. The four errors in the two sonnets are all careless ones, which disrupt the sense and therefore cannot be evidence of earlier readings. Of the two errors in **Sonnet 32**, 'high' at 32.8 may stem from a misreading of Q's 'hight' as 'highe', which is then 'corrected' by a scribe to remove the terminal 'e' that, by the mid-seventeenth century, was starting to be seen as redundant (see Sonnet 113.10n); the second slip might be down to an eye skip, so that Q's 'A dearer *birth* then this his loue had brought' (32.11) becomes 'a dearer *loue* then this his loue had brought' (emphases added). The Folger version of **Sonnet 71** also has very few differences from Q: a reversal of 'surly sullen' to 'sullen surly' (71.2) and a muddle with pronouns, which turns Q's 'make you woe' (71.8) to 'make me woe'.

Folger MS V.a.339

The version of **Sonnet 138** that this miscellany contains similarly derives from print, albeit from the version in *Passionate Pilgrim* (or Benson's 1640 *Poems*, which is itself based on *PP*) rather than the 1609 Quarto: there are two minor differences between *PP* 1 and the Folger version: a substitution of 'are' for 'be' at l. 6, and a misreading of 'soothing' as 'smoothinge' at l. 11.

Owing to their proximity to printed sources, the sonnets from Folger MSS V.a.162 and V.a.339 are not reproduced here. The remainder of this appendix provides a transcription of manuscript versions of Sonnets 2, 8, 106, 116 and 128 (following Q's numerical sequence), and considers the authority of each, before concluding with a sample of composite 'poems' from Folger MS V.a.148 (discussed above). The poems are given in original spelling and punctuation, and represent examples of the states in which Shakespeare's sonnets circulated in manuscript, acquiring both deliberate and accidental revisions. Text between angled brackets indicates <deleted text>; text between carets indicates ^inserted text^. Where abbreviations need expanding for sense (e.g. 8.14), the supplied letters are underlined; otherwise, the abbreviations have been represented as they appear in the manuscript, including the y-thorn (for 'th'), which has been retained (it serves as a reminder of how easily words deploying it can be misread). Where more than one manuscript version exists, a list of variants has been supplied.

[Sonnet 2]

Sonnet 2 is by far the most widely copied of Shakespeare's sonnets. Twelve of its thirteen manuscript witnesses fall into two distinct families. One is distinguished by the heading 'To one that would die a maid' (a title which transforms the poem into a *carpe diem* lyric, addressed to a woman), comprising:

> BL Add. MS 30982 (= BL4); BL Sloane MS 1792 (= BL5); Folger MS V.a.170 (= Fol2); Westminster Abbey, MS 41 (= W); Yale, Osborn MS b 205 (= Y).

The other grouping comprises:

> BL Add. MS 10309 (= BL1); BL Add. MS 21433 (= BL2), BL Add. MS 25303 (= BL3), London Metropolitan Archives, ACC/1360/528 (= LMA), all going under the heading 'Spes Altera', and Folger MS V.a.345 (= Fol3), headed 'Spes Altera A Song', as well as University of Nottingham, Pw V 37 (= N) and Rosenbach Museum & Library, MS 1083/17 (= R2), with which they share a reading of Q's 'Where' as 'Wheres' (l. 6).

The exception is St John's College, Cambridge, MS S. 23 (= SJC), which deviates from Q in just four places, two of which ('deserues' for 'deseru'd', l. 9; 'thy' for 'my', l. 11) are probably down to a straightforward misreading of a handwritten copy (it is easy to mistake a secretary 'd' as a sigma-style 's'); i.e. it is likely that the compiler of SJC was not copying directly from Q, but from a manuscript copy. The two other variants – 'say that' for Q's 'answere' (l. 10) and 'Making' for 'Proouing' (l. 12) – could result from cross-contamination (compilers of manuscripts often consulted more than one copy).

Despite falling into two groups, the twelve manuscripts (excluding SJC) show a remarkable consistency in their variants from the 1609 Quarto: fourteen variants from the 114 words in Q's Sonnet 2 are shared across all twelve manuscripts; a further seven appear in eleven out of the twelve manuscripts. This suggests that all twelve of these manuscripts share a common ancestor. What is less immediately apparent is whether this was (i) a copy deriving from Q, or (ii) an earlier alternative, authorial version. Many of the shared variants cannot be ascribed to mistranscription: it is not easy to mistake Q's 'digge deep trenches' for 'trench deep furrowes', 'beauties' for 'louely' (l. 2), or 'proud' for 'fair' (l. 3), for example. Taylor (1985b) argues that a number of these variants are reminiscent of vocabulary that Shakespeare was using in the 1590s (e.g. the deployment of 'trench' as a verb in *Two Gentleman of Verona*, 3.2.7 and *Venus and Adonis*, l. 1052), whilst others are closer to the epistle on marriage from Thomas Wilson's *Art of Rhetoric*, a source which Shakespeare periodically draws on in his procreation sonnets (see headnote to Sonnets 1–17): the substitution in many of the manuscripts of 'pretty child' for Q's 'faire child' (l. 10) and 'new borne' for 'new made' (l. 13) may, for example, reflect Wilson's 'you shall have a pretty little boy [. . .] by whom you shall seem to be new born' (1553: sig H3r). However, as Duncan-Jones points out (1997a: 453), it was not until the 1620s and 1630s that Sonnet 2 seems to have circulated widely, more than a decade after the 1609 Quarto, when it regularly appears alongside verses by the later Jacobean and Caroline poets Thomas Carew (1594/5–1640), William Strode (1601?–1645), Richard Corbett (1582–1635) and Robert Herrick (1591–1674). The company the poem consistently keeps with these later poems and the total absence of any sixteenth-century manuscripts make it much less likely that this version of the sonnet is descended from an Elizabethan original. Many of the variants that are shared across the manuscripts are the type of alterations that might occur through memorial reconstruction of the poem: for example, the compiler might have remembered the word 'trench' (l. 2), but mistaken its grammatical category (thus rendering it as a verb, not a noun); 'the *lustre* of thy youthfull dayes' might have been prompted by a vague memory of the adjective in Q's 'treasure of thy *lusty* daies' (l. 6, emphases added); or the compiler might have recalled that the sonnet uses financial imagery and consequently supplied 'accounted' (l. 3) for 'gaz'd on'. Many of the manuscripts in which Sonnet 2 circulated are closely connected to the University of Oxford (particularly Christ Church). It is thus entirely feasible that the manuscript tradition stems from a scribally altered version (drawn from the printed text) which circulated around Oxford and spread from there to London via the Inns of Court (which university students often attended after graduation). As Hobbs argues (1992: 116–29), George Morley probably played a key role in the transmission of the sonnet by lending his miscellany (W) to the Oxford students he tutored, who then copied that version into their own collections. The manuscript copies of Sonnet 2 thus stand as a witness to its reception, and both witting and unwitting reimagining, rather than its origin. The version below reproduces Westminster Abbey, MS 41 (W), supplying the letters that have almost certainly been cropped at the edge of the page at ll. 5, 8 and 10.

To one y^t would dye a Mayd

When forty wintres shall beseige thy brow
And trench deepe furrowes in y^t louely feild
Thy youths faire liuery so accounted now
Shall bee like rotten weeds of no worth held   4
  Then being askt where all thy bewty lye[s]
Where all y^e lustre of thy youthfull dayes
To say within these hollow sun\<c\>ken eyes
Were an all-eaten truth, & worthless prays[e]   8
  O how much better were thy bewtyes vse
If thou coulst say this pretty child of min[e]
Saues my account & makes my old excuse
Making his bewty by succession thine.   12
  This were to be new borne when thou art old
  And see thy bloud warme, when thou feelst it cold.

To one y^t would dye a Mayd] *Spes Altera* BL1, BL2, BL3, LMA; *Spes Altera* A song Fol3; A Lover to his Mistres N; The Benefitt of Mariage R2; *untitled in* SJC
1 forty] thre score BL1; to BL4
wintres] yeares R2

feild] cheek BL2, BL3
2 trench] drench R; digge Q, SJC
furrowes] trenches Q, SJC
y^t [i.e. that] louely] thy beauties Q, SJC
3 youths] youth BL5, Fol3
liurey] feild R2
accounted] esteemed N; gaz'd on Q, SJC
faire] proud Q, SJC; fairer R2
4 Shall] Wil Q, SJC
like] a Q, SJC; like like BL5
rotten] totter'd Q, SJC (tatterd)
weeds] cloaths Fol2; weed Q, SJC
no] smal Q, SJC
5 being askt] if wee aske BL2, BL3; askt R2
thy] this BL3
6 Where] Wheres BL1, BL2, BL3, Fol3, LMA, N, R2
y^e] y^t BL2, BL4
lustre] treasure Q, SJC
youthfull] lusty Q, SJC
7 these] thine Q, SJC; those Y
hollow] owne deepe Q, SJC
8 all–eaten] all–beaten Fol2; old eaten LMA; all–eating Q, SJC
truth] shame Q, SJC
worthlesse] thriftlesse Q, SJC
prayse] pleasure BL5
9 O how much better were] How better were BL5; How much more praise deseru'd Q; How much more prayse deserues SJC
bewtyes] bewtious Y
10 say] answere Q; say that SJC
pretty] little BL2, BL3; faire Q, SJC
11 Saues] Shall sum Q, SJC; Saud [i.e. Sav'd] Y
my account] mine account N; my count Q, SJC
makes my old] makes me old BL4; makes no old Fol2; yeilds mee an N; make my old Q; makes the old R2; make thy ould SJC; make no old Y
12 Making] Proouing Q
13 new borne] made younge BL2, BL3; new made Q, SJC

[Sonnet 8]

Like Sonnet 2, the copy of **Sonnet 8** in BL Add. MS 15226 has been scrutinised for any claims it might have to represent an alternative authorial version. Kerrigan (1986: 443) suggests that 'Sweete' at the start of l. 2 of could be a vocative, and hence an alternative rather than an erroneous reading. However, 'Sweete' could also result from a misreading of the terminal -es hook, common in early modern manuscripts in mixed or secretary hands, which can look like a large 'e'. This version of Sonnet 8 also has three other substantive variants: (i) Q's 'the parts that' is rendered as 'a parte, w^{ch}' (l. 8), which destroys the neat contrast in that line between 'singleness' and multiple parts, as well as the pun on the young man's attributes ('parts'), even as it makes the musical metaphor more exact (a musician can take one part, not many); (ii) Q's 'sier, and child' becomes 'Childe, & Syer' (l. 11); (iii) 'one pleasing note do' becomes 'this single note doth' (l. 12). These variants do not necessarily suggest that the BL version is descended from an earlier authorial manuscript, pre-dating Q: they are the type of errors that could creep in as scribes copied handwritten copies of handwritten copies, which might ultimately stem from a printed text. The picture is further complicated once the possibility of memorial reconstruction is allowed, a process which tends to simplify complicated syntax and substitute familiar words for unusual ones (see Marotti 1990: 151–2). The mistakes made here approximate Q's text; a scribe might remember that the rhyme word 'sing' in l. 12 picks up on a syllable earlier in the line, for example, but then makes sense of that through substituting 'single' for Q's 'pleasing'. The reversal of child and sire is also the type of error that can be explained by a memory slip; similarly the rationalisation of Q's multiple 'parts' to a single 'parte'. Other variants are minor slips or possibly conscious adjustments: (i) a tendency not to show the necessary metrical elisions ('hearest', 'louest', 'receauest', ll. 1, 3, 4); (ii) 'thy' for Q's 'thine' (l. 6); (iii) 'on' for Q's 'in' (l. 10); (iv) 'w^ch' [which] for Q's 'Who' (l. 12); (v) 'shalt' for Q's 'wilt'.

In laudem Musici et opprobrium Contemptorii eiusdem

1.

Musicke to heare, why hearest thou Musicke sadly
Sweeete wth sweetes warre not, Ioy delights in Ioy
Why louest y^u that wch thou receauest not gladly
or els receauest wth pleasure thine annoy.   4

2.

If the true Concord of well tuned Soundes
By Vnions maried doe offend thy eare
They doe but sweetlie chide thee, whoe conf<o>^e^undes
In singlenes a parte, wch thou shouldst beare   8

3.

Marke howe one stringe, sweet husband to another
Strikes each on each, by mutuall orderinge
Resemblinge *Childe*, & *Syer*, and happy *Mother*
wch all in one this single note doth singe   12
    whose speechles songe being many seeming one
    Singes this to thee, Thou single, shalt <u>proue</u> none.
                                                        W. Shakspeare

[Sonnet 106]

The versions of **Sonnet 106** which appear in Pierpont Morgan Library, MA 1057 (= P) and Rosenbach Museum & Library, MS 1083/16 (= R1) are closely related to each other and share the same deliberate changes, as in the opening line, which changes Q's 'Chronicle of wasted time' to 'Annalls of all-wasting time' (l. 1). This alteration cannot be the result of a misreading and possibly reflects the primacy of Tacitus' *Annals*, rather than *Holinshed's Chronicles*, as the model for history-writing by the early seventeenth century; the reviser thus substitutes a voguish word which then requires the addition of an extra syllable ('all') later in the line, to compensate for the syllable lost by the earlier revision. Q's error in l. 12 ('still' for 'skill') is also corrected, an indication that – at some point in the manuscript transmission – someone was paying close attention to the text. P is on the whole more careful than R1, having only one obvious error ('mine' for 'rime', l. 3); this slip is then corrected in the margin in another hand. A transcription of this version appears below. As well as containing more errors, which disrupt the sense (as with the misreading of Q's 'present' as 'pleasant', l. 13), R1 (Robert Bishop's miscellany) further adapts the sonnet, fusing it with an eighteen-line poem by William Herbert (incipit: 'When mine eyes first admiring of your beauty', first printed in Herbert's *Poems* in 1660), a conjunction that transforms the poem into an address to woman, ending 'Ile sit and view | your picture Mʳˢ, since I may not you' (for a transcription of the composite poem, see Marotti 2010: 197–8). It cannot be proved whether the composite poem that resulted was due to 'scribal inventiveness or [. . .] the association of Shakespeare's "papers" (sonnet 17.9) with Pembroke's' (Marotti 2010: 198). Sometimes such conflations do reflect a relationship between the two authors (as with the Thomas Churchyard/Earl of Oxford hybrid, 'In peascod time', found in British Library MS Harley 7392(2), fol. 51r); but this is not always the case; see, for example, Arthur Gorges' use of Pierre Ronsard in 'Would I were changed into that golden shower' (Gorges 1953: 201).

On his Mistris Beauty
When in the Annalls of all wastinge Time
I see discription of the fairest wights
And beauty makeinge beautifull old <u>mine</u>   rime
In praise of Ladyes dead and louely Knights   4
then in the Blazon of sweet beauties best
of face of hand, of lip, of eye, or brow
I see their antique pen would haue exprest
Eu'n such a beauty as you master now   8
Soe all their praises were but prophecies
of those our dayes, all you prefiguringe
And for they saw but with diuininge eyes
they had not skill enough thy worth to singe   12
for wee which now behould these present dayes
haue eyes to wonder, but no tongues to praise:

On his Mistris Beauty] 106 Q
1 Annals . . . wastinge] chronicle of wasted Q
2 discription] discriptions Q, R1
3 mine] rime Q, R1
6 Of face of hand] Of hand, of foote Q
of eye, or brow] of eye, of brow Q; or eye or brow R1
9 were] are Q
10 those our dayes] this our time Q; these our dayes R1
11 saw] look'd Q; say R1
diuininge] deceuing R1
12 skill] still Q [error]
thy] your Q
13 wee] me R1
present] pleasant R1
14 no] lack Q
tongues] tongue] R1

[Sonnet 116]

The rendition of **Sonnet 116** – a song setting – in New York Public Library, Drexel MS 4257 is (like the composite 'poems' in Folger MS V.a.148) an example of conscious creativity, rather than a witness to an earlier or alternative authorial version, and has been reproduced below.

Selfe blinding error seazeth all those mindes;
who with falce Appellations call that loue
wch alters when it alteration findes
or with the mouer hath a power to moue   4
not much vnlike ye hereticks pretence
that scites trew scripture but prevents ther sence: *Henry Lawes*

            2
Oh noe Loue is an euer fixed marke
That lookes on tempests but is neuer shaken   8
It is the starr to euery wandring barke
Whose worth's vnknowne although his height be taken
Noe mowntebanke with eie-deludeing flashes
But flameing Martyr in his holly ashes   12

            3
Loue's not tymes foole though Rosie lipps & Cheekes
Within his bynding Circle compas rownd
Loue alters not with his breife howers & weekes
But holds it out euen to the edge of doome   16
If this be errour & not truth approu'd
Cupids noe god nor Man nere lou'd

[Sonnet 128]

The version of **Sonnet 128** in Bodleian, MS Rawl. poet. 152 is one of four poems squeezed onto a single sheet of paper, written in the same, rather crude hand. As Duncan-Jones (1997a: 460) points out, the other poems all derive from printed sources: immediately above Shakespeare's sonnet is the first stanza of Song 12 from John Dowland's *First Book of Songs or Airs* (1597, with further editions in 1600, ?1603, 1606, 1613); on the verso, written out as prose, in order to squeeze them onto the page, appear William Browne's 'Love's Labyrinth', Song 3 from *Britannia's Pastorals* (1613), and Francis Davison's Sonnet 2, from *A Poetical Rhapsody* (1602, with further editions in 1608, 1611). All four poems are carelessly transcribed. The rendition of Q's 'swayst' as 'swaies' (l. 3) ruins the rhyme with 'plaiest' (l. 1); 'reped' (l. 7) breaks the rhyme it should make with 'leapes' (l. 5); nor does it make sense grammatically. The possessive is also missed in l. 8: Q's 'woods bouldness' becomes 'wood bouldnes' ('wood' might have also been understood as an adjective, and a synonym for 'mad'; OED 'wood, *adj*'). On the other hand, the copyist does not make the same slip with pronouns as found in Q's ll. 11 and 14, which have 'their fingers', not – as is needed – 'thy fingers'; this copyist changes both to 'your', but introduces a further error with pronouns, by missing the 'y' in 'they' in l. 9, which becomes (nonsensically) 'the'. The other changes could feasibly be ones that have been made consciously by a copyist: (i) where Q calls its addressee 'my musike', this version has 'deere deerist' (l. 1), possibly to avoid the juxtaposition of 'musike musike', which might have struck this, or an earlier, copyist as either inelegant or confusing; (ii) Q's 'Iackes' are called 'kies'/'keyes' (ll. 5, 13), a description which is both more musically correct (fingers touch the keys of a keyboard, not the jacks that strike the notes) and removes the innuendo; (iii) the innuendo is also reduced by the removal of Q's 'sausie' (l. 13). The substitution of 'tuched' for Q's 'tikled' (l. 9) may be due to a misreading of the second three letters (the 'ikl' ligature could well be mistaken for 'uch' in a secretary hand); alternatively, it may be a further attempt to reduce the innuendo, or to express the musical activity in more conventional terms (keys are touched, not tickled). Either way, the choice of verb (a monosyllable) affects the meter, which is then made good through the inclusion of 'faine'. It is possible that these variations may reflect an earlier version of the poem, before Shakespeare revised it and heightened its cheeky eroticism; however, its appearance with three other poems from sources which would all have been available in print, in fairly new editions, in 1613 makes it much more likely that Shakespeare's poem also derives from the printed source, Q, with its variants introduced through a mixture of carelessness and deliberate adaptation, to suit its copyist's taste. Robbins dates the hand 'before 1650' (1967: 137); the rest of the volume cannot provide clues for a more exact dating, since it was assembled from loose sheets. Duncan-Jones' suggestion of a date of 1613–20 seems sensible (1997a: 461), making it a candidate for the earliest known version of one of Shakespeare's sonnets in manuscript. A transcription appears below.

> how ouft when thow, deere deerist musick plaiest,
> vpon that blesed wood whose mocions sounds,
> with thy sweet fingers when thow gen^t^ly swaies,
> the wiry concord that myne eare confoun^d^es,   4
> o how I enuy those kies that nimble leapes,
> to kisse the tender inward of thy hand,
> whilst my poore lippes wich should that haruest reped,
> at the wood bouldnes by thee blushinge stand,   8
> to bee so tuched the faine would change there state,
> and situacion with those dancinge chippes,
> ouer whome youre fingers walke with gentle gate,
> makeinge de^e^d wood more blest then liuinge lipes,   12
> since then those keyes soe happy are in this,
> giue them youre fingers mee youre lipes to kisse.

Examples of the composite 'poems' in Folger MS V.a.148:

Cruel [item iv, fol. 22r]

> Thou Contracted to thine owne bright eys
> Feedst thy light flame with selfe substantial fewell
> Makeing a famine where aboundance lies
> Thy selfe thy foe to thy sweet selfe too cruell   4
> Thou that art now the worlds fresh ornament
> And onely herauld to ye Gaudy spring
> Within thine owne Bud Buriest thy Conten<d>t
> And Tender Churle makes wast in niggarding   8
> Pitty ye world orels this Glutton bee
> To eat ye worlds due by ye world & thee

When forty winters shall besie<g>^d^g thy brow
And Dig deep trenches in thy beautyes field
Thy youths Proud liuery so gazd on now
Wil be A totterd weed of small worth held
The Canker bloomes haue ful as deepe a dy
As ye Perfumed tincture of ye roses

12

[item xii, fol. 22v]
Thine ey Ioues lightening seemes thy voyce his dreadful thunder
Which not to anger Bent is musick & sweet fire
Gilding ye object wherupon It gazeth
Celestiall as thou art

[item xiii, fol. 23r]
Clouds blot ye heauen & make me flatter
The swart Complexiond night when sparkling stars twire
To sing from sullen earth h<i>^y^msnes at heauens Gate

[item xxiv, fol. 23v]
Why should Others fals adulterate eys
Giue salutation to my sportiue blood
Loue suffers not in smileing Pompe nor falls
Under the blow of thralling discontent
Nor fears It Heretick Policy

Appendix 5

Shakespeare's Sonnets and English sonnet sequences in print (to 1640)

Popularity

The 1609 Quarto of *Shakespeare's Sonnets* is often regarded as belated, appearing over a decade after the vogue for sonnet sequences in the 1590s, when the form was given profile and fashionability by the posthumous publication of Philip Sidney's *Astrophil and Stella* (1591). As the annotated bibliography below shows, the production of printed sonnet sequences certainly peaked in the early to mid-1590s: of the thirty-seven examples traced, twenty appear between 1592 and 1597. The rate of production does drop off after 1600: even the inveterate revisers Samuel Daniel and Michael Drayton stop adding new sonnets by 1602, and the new material that is printed in the first decade or so of the seventeenth century is primarily Scottish in origin (William Alexander, Alexander Craig, David Murray). Nonetheless, the sonnet sequence did continue in print, with another, smaller peak of popularity in the early 1630s (due to the posthumous publication of the works of older poets, John Donne and Fulke Greville, who had grown up during the Elizabethan period).

Dedications

One of the pieces of evidence used to argue that *Shakespeare's Sonnets* was unauthorised is the lack of an authorial dedication. Twelve of the works below (besides Shakespeare's) come without an authorial dedication or preface: of these publications, three are posthumous (Sidney 1591, Donne 1633, Greville 1633). Two are by authors resident abroad: Constable was in France after 1591; Spenser was in Ireland. Five are by authors who would seem to want to be discreet about their identities (R.L. 1596, T.W. 1593, Drummond 1616, Wroth 1621, I.B. 1632), although Drummond does not supply prefatory matter for *Flowers of Sion* (1623) either, although that work – unlike the 1616 *Poems* – was published under his full name. Nor can it have been distance that prevented Drummond supplying prefatory material, since he lived relatively close to Edinburgh, where his works were published. The final work is Barnes' *Parthenophil and Parthenophe*, which carries a preface by the printer, John Wolfe, 'To the learned gentlemen readers', although Barnes was probably lodging with Wolfe in 1593, when his collection was printed, and so would have been on hand to supply a dedication if he so desired (*ODNB*). Barnes' name is not on the title-page, but it does appear at the end of the work, so having Wolfe supply the dedication would seem to be an attempt to cultivate an air of discretion and pretend to step back from the act of publication, rather than a serious endeavour on Barnes' part to protect his identity (similar to the game played by 'R.T.' in 1597, where his friend 'R.B.' asserts that the work is unauthorised). Whilst unusual, then, the lack of an authorial dedication in *Shakespeare's Sonnets*, and its replacement with one from the publisher, does not on its own suggest that the work was unauthorised.

Titles and *mise-en-page*

As the bibliography below shows, the title of *Shakespeare's Sonnets* is unusual: most of the amorous (as opposed to religious or commemorative) sonnet sequences are named either after the mistress's pseudonym or the pair of lovers whose story they tell. The layout of *Shakespeare's Sonnets* – where individual poems frequently run over page-breaks – was also fairly atypical: most collections are laid out so as to have one or two complete sonnets per page. Nevertheless, the layout was not without precedent and may have much to do with the length of the sequence: the majority of the sequences which, like Shakespeare's, comprise over 100 poems, are laid out in this way, presumably to save paper (Sidney 1591, Barnes 1593, Alexander 1606, Greville 1633); the exceptions are Watson 1582 (which comprises longer sonnets as well as substantial descriptive headings, so that more use is made of each page) and Lok 1593, which is in a smaller format (sedicesimo).

Form

The definition of the sonnet was still flexible during this period. In 1575 George Gascoigne had sought to impose a strict classification on the sonnet, as a poem of 'fourteen lines, every line containing ten syllables. The first twelve [lines] do rhyme in staves of four lines by cross metre [*abab*], and the last two rhyming together do conclude the whole' ('Certain Notes of Instruction', in *Posies* (1575), sig. U1v). Nonetheless, Gascoigne's complaint that 'some think that all poems (being short) may be called sonnets' continued to hold true, long after 1575. Moreover, as the bibliography reveals, even those collections which adhere to fourteen-line versions of the sonnet are often miscellaneous in nature, with their sonnets interspersed, or collected up with, other poetic forms (such as complaints, elegies and odes). Shakespeare's consistent use of both the form and rhyme scheme outlined by Gascoigne (aside from one fifteen-line sonnet, 99; one of six couplets, 126; and one of fourteen octosyllabic lines, 145) is thus unusual, and is a feature of the sonnet sequences of the early and mid-1590s (Daniel 1592; Fletcher 1593; Anon 1594; Percy 1594; E.C. 1595; Griffin 1596; R.L. 1596; Smith 1596). A more experimental use of rhyme scheme is present at the birth of the Elizabeth sonnet 'boom', in Sidney's *Astrophil and Stella*, and Barnes (1593), Lodge (1593), T.W. (1593) and Drayton (1594) all employ a variety of rhyme schemes, and Spenser (1595) invents his own. However, the tendency to vary the rhyme scheme increases with time. Notably, Shakespeare's is the only sonnet sequence printed after 1600 which almost exclusively uses the 'English' form and rhyme-scheme delineated by Gascoigne.

In the bibliography below, 'English' denotes the fourteen-line form described by Gascoigne and used by Shakespeare: i.e. three quatrains, rhyming *abab cdcd efef*, and a final couplet, *gg*. 'Petrarchan sonnet' describes the fourteen-line form breaking into an octave, rhyming *abba abba*, and a sestet, comprising some variant of *cde* rhymes, although Petrarchan sonnets in English almost invariably end in a couplet, so the sestet often follows a scheme of either *cddcee*, or *cdcdee*. Some sonneteers (e.g. I.B. 1632) combine the Petrarchan and 'English' forms: in those cases, 'English' quatrain describes an alternately rhymed quatrain (*abab*), 'Petrarchan', an enclosed rhyme (*abba*).

Place of publication is London unless otherwise stated.

1560, A[nne] L[ok or Locke, *née* Vaughan], *A Meditation of a Penitent Sinner* (octavo), appended to John Calvin, *Sermons*: twenty-six 'English' sonnets, five prefatory, twenty-one paraphrasing Psalm 51; sonnets run on (including over page breaks), without headings or numbers. Printed by John Day.

1582, Thomas Watson, *Hekatompathia* (quarto): 100 eighteen-line sonnets and a Latin epilogue, divided into two parts: in the first part the poet-speaker pursues love; in the second, he rejects it; rhyme-scheme *ababccdedeffghghii*; one sonnet per page, each preceded by a Roman numeral and prose explanation. Printed by John Wolfe for Gabriel Cawood.

1591, Philip Sidney, *Astrophil and Stella* (quarto), posthumous printing: 108 fourteen-line sonnets, employing a variety of rhyme schemes, with ten songs appended (also entitled sonnets); the fourteen-line sonnets have no numbers or titles, and run over page-breaks. Both 1591 editions (the suppressed edition, printed by John Charlewood for Thomas Newman, with Thomas Nashe's preface; and the 'authorised' one, printed by John Danter for Thomas Newman, without it) employ the same *mise-en-page*. When appended to the 1598 *Arcadia* (printed by Richard Field for William Ponsonby), sonnets are numbered and, for the most part, arranged to avoid running over page-breaks; the songs are interspersed with the sonnets and labelled 'songs'.

1592, H[enry] C[onstable], *Diana* (quarto): twenty-two Petrarchan sonnets, plus one prefatory sonnet 'To his absent Diana'; one sonnet per page, each beneath a heading ('Sonnetto primo', etc.). Printed by John Charlewood for Richard Smith. The edition of 1595 (printed for Smith by James Roberts) rearranges the material into 'decades' of ten sonnets and adds more sonnets (it comprises seventy-six sonnets). Both the 1592 and 1595 editions lack either a dedicatory epistle or a preface from the author; the 1595 edition is introduced by an address from 'The printer to the reader' and a sonnet from the publisher, Richard Smith, 'Unto her Majesty's sacred honourable maids' (sig. A2v).

1592, Samuel Daniel, *Delia* (quarto): fifty 'English' sonnets, one sonnet per page, each with a numbered heading ('Sonnet I', etc.); an ode and *The Complaint of Rosamond* follow. Printed by John Charlewood for Simon Waterson. The *mise-en-page* remained the same as Daniel continued to add and revise material: the second edition of 1592 (also Charlewood for Waterson) had fifty-four sonnets; the third edition of 1594 (printed for Waterson by James Roberts and Edward Allde), fifty-five sonnets, as well as the tragedy of *Cleopatra*; when *Delia* appeared in Daniel's 1601 *Works* (printed for Waterson by Valentine Simms and William White), there were fifty-seven sonnets, laid out two per page.

1592, Gabriel Harvey, 'Greene's Memorial, or Certain Funeral Sonnets', appended to Harvey, *Four Letters* (quarto): twenty-two fourteen lines sonnets, using both 'English' and 'Petrarchan' quatrains + a rhyming couplet. Sonnets numbered ('Sonnet I', etc.) and titled, and run on, over page breaks. The volume concludes with two Latin epigrams and a commendatory sonnet by Edmund Spenser (in the 'Spenserian' form, rhyming *ababbcbccdcdee*). Printed by John Wolfe.

1593, Barnabe Barnes, *Parthenophil and Parthenophe* (quarto): 104 fourteen-line sonnets, using a variety of rhyme schemes, interspersed with madrigals; each sonnet introduced with a numbered heading ('Sonnet I', etc.) and divided from the preceding/subsequent poems with a lined rule; sonnets run over page breaks; sections of elegies, canzons and odes, and commendatory verses follow. The volume does not contain either a dedicatory epistle, or a preface from the author, but is introduced by a preface from the printer, John Wolfe.

1593, Giles Fletcher, *Licia* (quarto): fifty-three 'English' sonnets (plus one prefatory one, 'to Licia, the wise, kind, virtuous and fair'); one sonnet per page, with either a descriptive heading, or a number (Sonnet I, etc.); the sonnets are followed by other poetic forms (including an ode, a verse dialogue, three elegies, and a ghost complaint in the voice of Richard III). Printed at Cambridge by John Legat.

1593, Thomas Lodge, *Phillis* (quarto): thirty-nine fourteen-line sonnets, in both 'English' and Petrarchan rhyme schemes, and one twenty-four-line 'sonnet', along with eclogues, an elegy, an ode, and a female-voiced ghost complaint; sonnets laid out one per page, with a numbered heading ('Sonnet I', etc.). Printed by James Roberts for John Busby.

1593, Henry Lok, *Sundry Christian Passions* (sedicesimo): two parts, the first comprising 102 Spenserian sonnets (including one prefatory and one concluding poem); the second comprising 102 Petrarchan sonnets (including one prefatory and one concluding poem); two sonnets per page, each with a numbered heading ('Sonnet I', 'Son. II', etc.). Printed by Richard Field. Reprinted by Field in 1597 with Lok's *Ecclesiastes*, along with 102 'Sundry Affectionate Sonnets of a Feeling Conscience' (using a Petrarchan rhyme scheme) and twenty-two sonnets under the heading 'An Introduction to Peculiar Prayers' (mostly using a Petrarchan rhyme scheme); the same *mise-en-page* (two sonnets per page, with numbered headings) is employed throughout; the 'Introduction' sonnets also have explanatory headings. Henry was the son of Anne Vaughan Locke, believed to have authored the first known printed sonnet sequence in English (see above).

1593, T.W. [sometimes identified as Thomas Watson], *The Tears of Fancy* (quarto): sixty sonnets in 'English' and 'Petrarchan' forms, plus one envoi in sonnet form ('Go idle verse'), the only prefatory material from author or printer; two sonnets per page (except for the final two sonnets, on a page apiece), each with a numerical heading. Printed by John Danter for William Barley.

1594, Anon., *Zepheria* (quarto): forty 'canzon', mostly in the form of 'English' sonnets, one per page each with a numerical heading. No dedication from printer or author, aside from one prefatory poem 'Alli veri figlioli delle Muse' ('To the true children of the Muses'). Printed by Joan Orwin for Nicholas Ling and John Busby.

1594, Michael Drayton, *Idea's Mirror* (quarto): fifty-one 'Amours', mostly fourteen-line sonnets in both 'English' and Petrarchan rhyme schemes, with eclogues appended. Sonnets laid out one per page, each with a numerical heading. Printed by James Roberts for Nicholas Ling. Revised and printed (by Roberts for Ling), with *England's Heroical Epistles*, as *Idea* in 1599, with eight additional sonnets, laid out four to a page, with a numerical heading for each poem ('Sonnet 2', etc.), with dedicatory titles ('To. . .') accompanying the final sonnets. Later editions (also by Roberts for Ling) retain that more economical *mise-en-page*, as more material was added: seven extra sonnets in 1600; one in 1602.

1594, William Percy, *Sonnets to the Fairest Coelia* (quarto): twenty 'English' sonnets, and a 'madrigal', laid out one per page, each with a numerical heading ('Sonnet I', etc.); some come with an additional descriptive heading (e.g. 'Sonnet X. ¶ A Mystery'; 'Sonnet XI. ¶ To Polixena'). Printed by Adam Islip for William Ponsonby.

1595 Barnabe Barnes, *A Divine Century of Spiritual Sonnets* (quarto): 100 Petrarchan sonnets, two per page, each with a numerical heading ('Sonnet I', etc.) and surrounded by a decorative border; a hymn follows the hundredth sonnet. Printed by John Windet.

1595, Richard Barnfield, 'Certain Sonnets' in *Cynthia* (quarto): twenty Petrarchan sonnets, one per page, with a numerical heading ('Sonnet I', etc.); the sonnets are sandwiched between a panegyric to 'Cynthia' (Elizabeth I), and a narrative poem about the Trojan prophetess, Cassandra (which is itself preceded by an ode). Printed for Humfrey Lownes.

1595, E.C., *Emaricdulfe* (octavo): forty 'English' sonnets, one per page, with a numerical heading ('Sonnet I', etc.). Printed by Joan Orwin for Matthew Law.

1595, Edmund Spenser, *Amoretti* (octavo): eighty-nine Spenserian sonnets; laid out one per page, each with a numerical heading ('Sonnet I', etc.); the sonnets are followed by an ode, and Spenser's *Epithalamion*. The dedicatory epistle is provided by the publisher, William Ponsonby. Printed by Peter Short.

1596, Bartholomew Griffin, *Fidessa* (octavo): sixty-two sonnets, mostly in 'English' rhyme scheme, but with one Petrarchan example, and a number of mono-rhymed sonnets; laid out one per page, each with a numerical heading ('Sonnet I', etc.). Printed by Joan Orwin for Matthew Lownes.

1596, R.L. [possibly the translator Richard Linche], *Diella* (octavo): thirty-eight sonnets, mostly in the 'English' form, laid out one per page, each with a numerical heading ('Sonnet I', etc.), followed by a narrative poem about 'The love of Dom Diego and Ginevra'. The dedicatory epistle is provided by the publisher, Henry Olney. Printed by James Roberts.

1596, William Smith, *Chloris* (quarto): fifty sonnets, most in the 'English' form, laid out two per page with numerical headings ('Sonnet 1', etc.). Printed by Edmund Bollifant.

1597, Robert Parry, 'The Patron, His Pathetical Poesies', in *Sinetes' Passions* (octavo): includes a sequence of thirty-one sonnets, mostly – but not exclusively – of fourteen lines (in both 'English' and Spenserian forms). Sonnets are numbered ('Sonetto 1', etc.) and appear one per page, usually with decorative border above and below. Printed by Thomas Purfoot for William Holme.

1597, R[obert] T[ofte], *Laura* (octavo): three parts, each comprising forty ten- or twelve-line 'sonnets' (how they are described in 'A friend's just excuse' at the end of the volume) and a longer verse conclusion. These sonnets appear two per page, each introduced with a numbered heading ('I', etc.). Although the edition carries a dedicatory epistle from the author, the preface to the reader asserts that the publication is unauthorised, its publisher having chanced upon the manuscript. Printed by Valentine Simms.

1602, Nicholas Breton, *The Soul's Harmony* (octavo): one fifteen-line poem, one longer poem in six-line stanzas, and thirteen 'English' sonnets. Each sonnet takes up a double-spread; no numbering or headings. Printed by Simon Stafford for Randoll Bearkes. Later editions (in 1622, 1630, 1635, 1676) adopt a more economical layout, compressing all or most of the sonnets onto one per page.

1604, William Alexander (Earl of Stirling), *Aurora* (quarto): 106 sonnets, probably composed in the 1590s, mingled with other forms (madrigals, sestina, elegies, songs); sonnets in a variety of rhyme schemes (Spenserian; variations on Petrarchan sonnets, rhyming *abbaabbacddcee*, or *abbacddceffegg*); poems, including sonnets, run over page breaks; each comes with a generic, numbered heading ('Sonnet 1', 'Song 1', etc.). Printed by Richard Field for Edward Blount.

1604, Richard Nugent, *Cynthia* (quarto): divided into three parts, comprising (1) eighteen sonnets, mostly – but not exclusively – of fourteen lines (in both 'English' and Petrarchan forms) and a madrigal; (2) thirteen fourteen-line sonnets, along with a canzone and two madrigals; (3) a more miscellaneous third part, comprising poems (mostly entitled 'sonnets', but not always of fourteen lines) to and from various acquaintances, and concluding with two sonnets, one on the 'quiet life', and the other – in Italian – to Cynthia, in commendation of the author. Sonnets printed two per page, separated by numbered headings ('Sonnet I', etc.) and ruled lines. Prefatory material comprises a Latin quotation from Sophocles (probably via Cicero's *Tusculan Disputations*) and a dedicatory sonnet by Nugent. Printed by Thomas Purfoot for Henry Tomes.

1606, Alexander Craig, *Amorous Songs, Sonnets, and Elegies* (octavo): Not strictly speaking a sonnet sequence, but a collection of sonnets to various addressees, in a variety of rhyme schemes ('English', Spenserian, Petrarchan), and other poems; the sonnets (and other short poems) are laid out one per page, with descriptive heading ('To Idea', etc.). Printed by William White.

1609, William Shakespeare, *Shakespeare's Sonnets* (quarto): 154 sonnets, almost entirely in the 'English' form, and a female-voiced complaint; sonnets run over page-breaks, and are each headed by Arabic number. The publisher, Thomas Thorpe, supplies the dedication. Printed by George Eld.

1611, David Murray, 'Caelia', appended to Murray's *Tragical Death of Sophonisba* (octavo): twenty-four fourteen-line sonnets, in a variety of rhyme schemes, laid out two per page, with a numbered heading ('Sonnet 1', etc.); some come with additional, more descriptive titles (e.g. '19 Sonnet. Being accused by a gentleman for stealing of a book'). Followed by the 'Complaint of the shepherd Harpalus', and a variety of mourning poetry (an epitaph, and some commemorative sonnets). Printed by George Eld for John Smethwick.

1615, John Taylor, *The Muses Mourning: or Funeral Sonnets on the Death of John Moray, Esquire* (octavo). Fourteen fourteen-line sonnets (including one prefatory sonnet), in 'English' and Petrarchan forms, and variations on the two. Sonnets numbered ('Sonnet 1', etc) and printed one per page, on the recto only (versos have been inked out, in mourning black). No place of printing or printer mentioned.

1616, W[illiam] D[rummond], *Poems Amorous, Funeral, Divine, Pastoral, in Sonnets, Songs, Sextains, Madrigals* (quarto): fourteen-line sonnets, using variations on the '*ab*' rhyme in the octave (e.g. *ababbaab, ababbaab, abbaabab*), spread across three sections and interspersed with madrigals and other poetic forms: fifty-four in 'The first part', thirteen in 'The second part'; nine in 'Urania, or Spiritual Poems'. In the first and second parts, each poem is introduced with a generic heading (e.g. 'Son[net]'); in 'Urania', by an ornament. Sonnets do not run over page-breaks in any of the sections, but appear two per page (or one sonnet, matched with another short poem). No authorial preface or dedication. Printed in Edinburgh by Andrew Hart.

1621, Mary Wroth, 'Pamphilia to Amphilanthus', appended to her *Urania* (folio): eighty-three fourteen-line sonnets in various rhyme schemes, but consistently having an octave of '*ab*' rhymes (either *abbaabba* or *abababa*); sonnets, which are interspersed with songs, run on over page-breaks and are arranged into four numbered sequences of forty-eight, ten, fourteen ('A Crown of Sonnets, dedicated to love') and nine poems respectively; the remaining two sonnets (one entitled 'sonnet', the other untitled) appear in the poems between the first and second, and second and third sequences. No prefatory material. Printed by Augustine Matthews for John Mariott and John Grismand.

1623, William Drummond, *Flowers of Sion* (quarto): thirty-three fourteen-line sonnets and other poems, each separated by a fleuron; the sonnets appear two to a page, and use variations on '*ab*' rhymes in the octave (e.g. *abbaabba, abababba, ababbaba, abababab*). The sonnets are followed by 'A Hymn to the Fairest Fair' and Drummond's prose essay, 'The Cypress Grove'. No prefatory material. Printed in Edinburgh by the heirs of Andrew Hart.

1632, I.B. (or J.B.), *Virginalia, or Spiritual Sonnets* (octavo): forty-four fourteen-line sonnets in praise of the Virgin Mary; *mise-en-page* suggests a Petrarchan sonnet (two quatrains + sestet), but the sonnets comprise three quatrains (in both 'English' and Petrarchan forms, or a combination of the two) and a rhyming couplet. Sonnets are numbered ('Sonnet 1', etc.) and given a title, describing the Virgin Mary ('Sancta Maria', 'Sancta Dei Genitrix', etc.). One sonnet per page, with explanatory notes beneath. No prefatory material. Printed at Rouen by the widow of Nicholas Courant.

1633, John Donne, *Holy Sonnets* in *Poems* (quarto), possibly composed 1608–9, posthumous printing: two sequences of Petarchan sonnets: (i) 'Holy Sonnets, La Corona', comprising seven sonnets with explanatory headings ('Annunciation', etc.) and Arabic numbering; (ii) 'Holy Sonnets', comprising twelve sonnets, with Roman numerals, each sonnet divided from the others by a ruled line. Sonnets in both sequences run over page-breaks. No prefatory material in the first edition; printer's preface to the 'the understanders' added in second edition (1635). Both editions printed by Miles Flesher for John Marriott.

1633, Fulke Grevile, *Caelica*, composed *c.* 1590–1610, in *Certain Learned and Elegant Works* (folio), posthumous printing: 109 sonnets of differing lengths, each with a numbered heading ('Sonnet I', etc.); sonnets run over page-breaks, but are divided from each other with decorative borders. No prefatory material. Printed by Elizabeth Purslowe for Henry Seyle.

1634, William Habington, *Castara* (quarto); ninety poems in two parts, reflecting Araphil's courtship of, and marriage to, Castara; contains fourteen-line sonnets (seven sets of couplets) alongside other forms and poems to/about others besides Castara; poems have titles, and are separated from each other by a ruled line; poems run over page-breaks. Printed by Anne Griffin for William Cooke. A second edition of 1635 (printed for Cooke by Bernard Alsop and Thomas Fawcet) adds four poems to part one, fifteen to part two, and adds a third section comprising eight elegies. A third edition (printed for Cooke by Thomas Cotes) in 1640 adds a fourth part, comprising twenty-two religious poems. The later editions are in a smaller, duodecimo format.

Appendix 6

Poems posthumously attributed to Shakespeare

'Upon a Pair of Gloves'
Verses on the Stanley tomb
'Shall I die?'
'An Epitaph on Elias James'
'An Epitaph on John Combe'
Another epitaph on John Combe
'On Ben Jonson'
'Upon the King'
Shakespeare's epitaph on himself
'To the Queen'

The eleven poems below appear in the chronological order of their first extant attribution, so far as it can be ascertained. Many are of dubious attribution, and their brevity and often conventional nature makes it difficult (if not impossible) to ascertain their authorship. However, the fact that they were ascribed to Shakespeare – and the debates that prompts – tells us something of the way he has been constructed as an authorial entity, in both the seventeenth century and closer to our own time. Strikingly, many of the poems are epitaphs (both mock and serious), a form of often generic and usually anonymous poetry which would have been part of the quotidian cultural landscape. Whether or not Shakespeare did write them, the fact that his name is associated with the form tells us much about the type of poetry with which he was posthumously associated, and his subsequent fashioning both as a poet who might provide suitably serious reflections on the deceased, and as a Jacobean wit, weaving caustic and irreverent mock-memorials.

A Funeral Elegy has not been reproduced here. It was written in the immediate aftermath of the fatal stabbing of William Peter by Edward Drew on 25 January 1612; entered into the Stationers' Register by Thomas Thorpe on 13 February 1612; and printed by George Eld, attributed to 'W.S.' on the title-page. On the basis of these initials and stylometric analysis, Foster (1989) put forward two possible candidates for 'W.S': Shakespeare and William Strachey (author of the 1610 pamphlet about the wreck of the *Sea Venture*, which Shakespeare drew on when writing *The Tempest*). Abrams (1996) made a more forceful case for Shakespeare's authorship, based on analysis of Shakespearean 'rare words' in the poem and in plays revived by Shakespeare's company, the King's Men, around this period. This attribution prompted vigorous debate, conducted mainly in the *TLS* and in a special issue of *Shakespeare Studies*, vol. 25 (1997). The major stumbling blocks to ascribing this poem to Shakespeare include the fact that Thorpe and Eld did not attribute it to him, despite the fact that Shakespeare's name was immensely marketable: witness the prominence given to Shakespeare's name on the title-page of the *Sonnets*, printed by Eld for Thorpe in 1609. There are also biographical details that mitigate against Shakespeare's authorship: (i) the poem was written between 25 January and 13 February 1612, when Shakespeare would have been preoccupied with the death and funeral of his brother Gilbert, buried in Stratford-upon-Avon on 3 February that year; (ii) the poem alludes to its author as a 'youth' (Shakespeare was forty-seven when the poem was composed); and (iii) in the dedicatory epistle (sig. A2r), the poet claims 'love' and friendship with the dead man, an Oxford student from Devon: since there is no evidence that Shakespeare was closely connected to either of those places, it is hard to see how he might have developed such familiarity with the dead man. The statistical evidence supporting Shakespeare's authorship has also been challenged (e.g. Elliott and Valenza 1997). Various alternatives have been proposed: the clergyman William Sclater (Duncan-Jones 1997b), the schoolmaster Simon Wastell (Vickers 1996), and – despite the mismatch of initials – the playwright John Ford, who – like Peter – was from Devon (Monsarrat 2002; Vickers 2002). In 2002, following the case that Monsarrat made for Ford's authorship, both Abrams and Foster conceded that he, rather than Shakespeare, was the probable author (www.shakesper.net, 12 June 2002). A text of *A Funeral Elegy* can be found in *The Riverside Shakespeare*, 2nd edn (1997).

The poems below appear in original spelling and punctuation. For ease of comprehension, tildes suppling 'n' or 'm' have been silently expanded, but other abbreviations (e.g. w^t for 'with') remain unaltered.

'Upon a Pair of Gloves'

This item appears in Shakespeare Birthplace Trust MS ER 93/2, fol. 93v, a verse miscellany, begun *c.* 1629 by Sir Francis Fane (*c.* 1611–1681?), brother of the poet Mildmay Fane. Other poems associated with Shakespeare/Stratford – versions of the epitaphs on John Combe, Ben Jonson, and Shakespeare himself – appear on the same page (see below).

Transcriptions of this snippet of verse (e.g. Burrow 2002: 722; Wells and Taylor 2005: 808; Fripp 1938: 1.401) generally emend the final line to read 'Alexander Aspinall', the name of the schoolmaster at the grammar school in Stratford-upon-Avon, 1582–1624. However, as Foster (1999: 93) points out, the first part of that line actually reads 'A shey ander', which could be a mangled rendition of 'Alesaunder' (an acceptable, if slightly archaic, spelling of Alexander). Alternatively, 'A shey' may refer to his future wife, the widow Anne Shaw, whom he married in 1594, 'Shey' being a feasible variant of 'Shaw' (Foster 1999: 94), whilst 'ander' could be a misreading of 'under', playing on the conventional idea that a wife is under the authority of her husband or (more bawdily) under him in bed; this interpretation of the line also allows a sonic play ('A shey ander') on Aspinall's first name.

The ditty (whether or not it is by Shakespeare) is situated firmly within Shakespeare's Stratford circle: the Shaws lived in Henley Street; Anne's first husband, Ralph, dealt in wool, as did John Shakespeare – illegally – in 1570s (*ODNB*); and one of the Shaws' sons, William, was a glover (like John Shakespeare). Aspinall may thus have bought the gloves from Shakespeare's shop, with William Shakespeare supplying the epigram and punning on his own name in 1.2 (although, by 1594, Shakespeare's main base was in London). Gifts were often accompanied by verses in this period. The epigram echoes *Pericles*, 3.4.17–18 ('My recompense is thanks, that's all, | Yet my good will is great, though the gift is small'), but the sentiment and wording are commonplace; compare Richard Barnfield's dedicatory epistle to the *Cynthia* volume (1595): 'Small is the gift, but great is my good-will' (sig. A2r). 'Will' – if it is a pun – may also refer to Anne Shaw's son, William (and it may have been he who made the gloves, not John Shakespeare).

The gift is small:
The will is all:
A shey ander Asbenall:

Shaxpaire vpon a peaire of gloues that mas[t]er sent to his mistris

Verses on the Stanley tomb

The verses, which appear on the Stanley monument in St Bartholomew's church at Tong in Shropshire, are attributed to Shakespeare in three manuscripts: (i) Folger V.a.103 Pt 1 (compiled *c.* 1630–*c.* 1677), where they are included, fol. 8r, in section of 'Laudatory Epitaphs'; (ii) Nottingham Portland MS Pw.V.37, p. 12 (*c.* 1630s); and (iii) College of Arms MS C.35, Church Notes, p. 20 (based on the notebook, now lost, from the visitation of the church on 23 September 1663); another copy (with variants and unattributed) appears later in that same manuscript, p. 41. Variant versions also appear, unattributed, in Bodleian MS Rawl. poet. 117 (mid-17th-century), fol. 269v.

It is not clear which Stanley, or Stanleys, the poems commemorate. In the Folger and Nottingham MSS, 'Not monumental stone' [west end] is entitled 'An Epitaph on Sr Edward Standly Engraven on his Tomb in Tong Church'; the other ('Ask who lies' [east end]), 'On Sr Thomas Standly'. Thomas Stanley, second son of the third Earl of Derby, died in 1576 (when Shakespeare was in his early teens, before he became a poet or moved beyond Stratford); his son Edward died in 1632, after Shakespeare's death. However, wealthy people often commissioned monuments in their own lifetime (see heading to 'An epitaph on John Combe', below); the monument could thus have been erected in the early seventeenth century (*c.* 1602), in memory of Thomas and his wife Margaret (née Vernon, 1540–1596), and anticipating Edward's death.

As a player, Shakespeare may well have come into contact with the Stanley family. Ferdinando Stanley, Lord Strange, Edward's cousin, was the patron of Lord Strange's Men from the late 1570s to his death in 1594. Shakespeare's 'Let the Bird of Loudest Lay' appears in *Love's Martyr* (1601), dedicated to Sir John Salusbury, who married Ursula Stanley, the illegitimate daughter of Henry Stanley, fourth Earl of Derby, in 1586 (see headnote to that poem).

The Tong poems contain at least one distinctive, Shakespearean phrase, 'sky aspyring pyra-mids' ([west end], l. 2), a reference to the tall obelisks at each corner of the tomb and deploying a compound adjective probably coined by Shakespeare in *Richard II*, 1.3.130: 'Of sky-aspiring and ambitious thoughts' (an EEBO-TCP search produces just four other usages of the epithet, all after 1629). Campbell (1999) notes resonances between the Tong poems and John Milton's epitaph on Shakespeare, written in 1630 and later printed in Second Folio (1632), especially in Milton's echo of this phrase in his description of the 'starre-ypointing Pyramid' (l. 4). The attribution of the Tong epitaphs to Shakespeare was clearly known in the seventeenth century, and Milton may have deliberately alluded to a poem believed to be Shakespeare's when composing his own memorial to the poet. Compare, for example, the way that George Turberville's epitaph on Henry Howard, Earl of Surrey (*Epitaphs, Elegies, Songs, and Sonnets*, 1567, sig. C1r) echoes Surrey's own epitaph on Thomas Wyatt, 'Wyatt resteth here' (*Tottel* [31]).

The transcriptions below are from taken from the inscriptions on the Stanley monument.

[East End]

ASK WHO LYES HEARE, BVT DO NOT WEEP,
HE IS NOT DEAD, HE DOOTH BVT SLEEP
THIS STONY REGISTER, IS FOR HIS BONES
HIS FAME IS MORE PERPETVALL THEN THEISE STONES

AND HIS OWNE GOODNES W^T HIMSELF BEING GON   5
SHALL LYVE WHEN EARTHLIE MONAMENT IS NONE

[West End]

NOT MONVMENTALL STONE PRESERVES OVR FAME,
NOR SKY ASPYRING PIRAMIDS OVR NAME
THE MEMORY OF HIM FOR WHOM THIS STANDS
SHALL OVTLYVE MARBL, AND DEFACERS HANDS
WHEN ALL TO TYMES CONSVMPTION SHALL BE GEAVEN   5
STANDLY FOR WHOM THIS STANDS SHALL STAND IN HEAVEN

'Shall I die?'

The poem appears in Bodleian MS Rawl. poet. 160, fols 108r–109r (where it is attributed to Shakespeare) and Beinecke Library MS Osborn b.197 (compiled by a Norfolk teenager, Tobias Aston), p. 135 (where it is not).

Shakespeare's authorship was hotly disputed in the second half of the 1980s, after Gary Taylor championed 'Shall I die?' as a Shakespearean poem (in *New York Times*, *Sunday Times*, *Times Literary Supplement*) in advance of the publication of the Wells and Taylor *New Oxford Shakespeare* (1986), where it was included in the 'Various Poems' section. Taylor argued that it contains a significant proportion of rare words used by Shakespeare in the 1590s and that it is characteristic of Shakespeare's verbal innovation (e.g. Taylor 1985a). However, it is hard to derive statistically significant evidence from a poem of under 450 words and Taylor's arguments have been contested by many critics, including Peter Beal (*TLS*, 3 January 1986, p. 13) and Foster (1987b).

The Rawlinson scribe attributes a number of the poems that it contains fairly accurately, but not consistently so; certainly the attributions that the Rawlinson scribe makes for those few Elizabethan and earlier Jacobean poems that the manuscript contains follow tradition, whether or not that tradition is accurate (e.g. the ascriptions to Walter Ralegh, fols 57r, 117r, of poems – 'Give me my scallop shell of quiet', 'Wrong not, dear Empress of my heart' – now rejected from the Ralegh canon). As with the manuscript versions of Sonnet 2 (see Appendix 4), the context in which the two versions of 'Shall I die?' exist also problematises Taylor's claim that the lyric was one of Shakespeare's early poems, written before the mid-1590s. Both manuscripts date from the 1630s, almost two decades after Shakespeare's death, and (like Sonnet 2) the poem appears in the company of later Jacobean and Caroline poets (e.g. Thomas Carew, Richard Corbett, Robert Herrick, William Strode). Nor do its style and content point convincingly to a sixteenth-century origin. The poem is generic, beginning with a direct address that commands the reader's/auditor's attention and is obviously suited to both secular and religious lyric: the Folger Union First Line Index of English Verse lists well over a hundred separate items beginning 'Shall I?', the most popular of which in terms of copies are 'Shall I go force an elegy' (eight manuscript copies currently listed), by Sir John Roe (1581–1608) on the death of Mrs Boulstrode in 1602, and George Wither's 'Shall I wasting [or wrestling] in despair', printed in *Fidelia* in 1615, sig. C8r–v (twelve manuscript copies currently listed; CELM records fifteen copies, all bar one in manuscripts compiled in 1620s or later). Much of the imagery of 'Shall I die?' is also commonplace – the smooth high forehead, fair brows, star-like eyes, red lips (ll. 56–60, 66) – as is the blazon, starting with the woman's hair, and moving downwards (ll. 46–85). Foster (1987b: 71–2) further draws attention to the poem's description of the woman's low-cut bodice ('a pretty bare') that reveals her nipples ('plotts', ll. 76–7), a style of dress which, although known in Elizabethan England, became much more popular in the Jacobean period, and a theme of both erotic and moralising verse from 1610 onwards ('plot, *n*.': 'a small portion of a surface differing in character or aspect from the remainder', OED[3] 2). However, Foster's assertion (1987b: 67–8) that the use of the 'is' contraction (e.g. that's, l. 73; she's, l. 85) also points to a later, seventeenth-century date for the poem does not stand up to scrutiny: the construction is used in both *Venus and Adonis* (e.g. ll. 419, 561, 610) and *Lucrece* (e.g. ll. 133, 1092), printed early in Shakespeare's career (1593, 1594).

The verse is written in anapaestic metre, most commonly a song metre (as in the refrain 'with a hey, and a ho, and a hey nonino', *As You Like It*, 5.3.16–33); as Beal points out, one way in which 'Shall I die?' might have become attached to Shakespeare's name is through being a song performed with one of his plays (*TLS*, 3 January 1986, p. 13).

The transcription below is from Bodleian MS Rawl. poet. 160.

1

Shall I dye, shall I flye
lovers baits, and deceipts
    sorrow breeding
Shall I tend* shall I send
shall I shewe, and not rue   5   * wait
    my proceeding
In all duty her beawty
Binds me her servant for ever
If she scorne I mourne
I retire, to despaire   10
    Ioying never.

2

Yet I must, vent my lust
and explaine, inward paine
    by my loue breeding
If she smiles, she exiles   15
all my moane, if she frowne
    all my hopes deceaving
Suspitious doubt, oh keepe out
For thou art my tormentor
Fly away, pack away   20
I will loue for hope
    bids me venter

3

T'were abuse to accuse
my faire loue, ere I prove
    her affection   25
therefore try her reply
gives thee Ioy or annoy
    or affliction
Yet how ere, I will beare
Her pleasure with patience for beawty   30
sure wit not seeme to blot
her deserts wronging him,
    doth her duty.

4

In a dreame it did seeme
but alas dreames doe passe   35
          as doe shaddowes
I did walke, I did talke
with my loue, with my dove
          through faire meadows
Still we past till at last   40
we sate to repose vs
          for o.pleasure
being set lips mett
armes twin'd & did bind
          my hearts treasure   45

5

Gentle wind sport did find
wantonly to make fly
          her gold tresses
As they shooke, I did looke
but her faire★, did impaire   50   ★ beauty
          all my senses
As amaz'd I gaz'd
On more then a mortall complection
    then that loue, can prove
Such force in beawties inflection   55

6

Next her haire forehead faire
Smooth and high next doth lye
          without wrinckle
Her faire browes vnder those
starlike eyes win loues prize   60
          when they twinckle
In her cheekes, whoe seekes
Shall find there displaid beawties banner
    Oh admiring, desiring
breeds as I looke still vpon her   65

7

Thin lips red, fancies fed
with all sweets when he meets
          and is granted
There to trade, and is made
happy sure, to endure   70
          still vndaunted
Pretty chinne, doth winne
Of all thats cald commendatious
    Fairest neck, noe speck
All her parts meritt high admiracons   75

8

A pretty bare★, past compare   ★ low-cut bodice
parts those plotts★ (which besots)   ★ nipples
        still asunder
It is meet, nought but sweet
should come nere, that soe rare   80
        tis a wonder
Noe mishap, noe scape★   ★ defect
Inferior to natures perfection
        noe blot, noe spot
Shees beawties queene in election   85

9

Whilst I dream't, I exempt
for all care seem'd to share
        pleasures in plenty
but awake care take
for I find to my mind   90
        pleasures scanty
Therefore I will trie
To compasse my hearts cheife contenting
        to delay, some saye
In such a case causeth repenting

William Shakespeare

'An Epitaph on Elias James'

The epitaph was engraved in the south aisle of St Andrew's by the Wardrobe, destroyed in the Great Fire of London in 1666. It appears unattributed in the expanded, 1633 edition of John Stow's *Survey of London*, sig. 4A3r, and, attributed to Shakespeare, in the same manuscript as one of the copies of 'Shall I die?' Bodleian MS. Rawl. poet. 160, fol. 41r (compiled *c.* 1637).

Between 1600 and September 1610, when he died (leaving £10 to the poor of the parish), James was the owner–occupier of a substantial brewery at the bottom of Puddle Dock Hill, close to the Blackfriars Theatre, where Shakespeare's company were resident from 1608 (Hilton Kelliher, Letters, *LRB*, 22 May 1986). That places Shakespeare in proximity to, and likely contact with, James; whether or not Shakespeare wrote his epitaph is open to question (and unlikely to be proven by statistical analysis of a poem of under fifty words).

The transcription below comes from the 1633 *Survey of London*, which would have been taken from the stone epitaph. In Stow, which is laid out in double columns, the poem is broken into half-lines, to fit the available space; here the lines have been reconstituted as three rhyming couplets.

When God was pleas'd (the world unwilling yet)
Helias Iames, to Nature paid his debt,
And here reposes: As he liv'd, he died,
The saying strongly in him verified,
Such life, such death: then a knowne truth to tell,   5
He liv'd a godly life, and died as well.

'An Epitaph on John Combe'

The epitaph was first attributed to Shakespeare in BL MS Landsowne 213, fol. 332v, by a soldier, Lieutenant Hammond, who visited Stratford in 1634 and saw the poem on Combe's tomb, although Hammond did not have time to copy it out (Schoenbaum 1978: 242–3). The epitaph is also attributed to Shakespeare in Bodleian MS Aubrey 6, fol. 109r; in Folger MS V.a.345 (*c.* 1630), p. 232 (which also contains a version of Sonnet 2); and in Bodleian MS Ashmole 38, p. 180 (*c.* 1650), where a two-line version appears on the page before 'On Ben Jonson' and is followed by a second epitaph on Combe (see below). The Ashmole heading ('Iohn Combe, A Coueteous rich man, mʳ wᵐ Shake-spear wright this att his request while hee was yett liueing for his Epitaphe') presents the first epitaph – like that on Jonson – as a composition made in a spirit of jocular friendship, whilst the subject was still living.

Robert Dobyns also claimed to have transcribed the epitaph from the tomb in 1673, before the Combe family had it removed (Folger MS V.a.147, fol. 72r). The epitaph appears, unattributed, in its earliest manifestation, Richard Braithwait's *Remains after Death* (1618), sig. L2v, and in two manuscripts compiled by Francis Fane: Folger MS V.a.180, fol. 79v (*c.* 1655, where it appears on the same page as Shakespeare's alleged epitaph 'On himself', see below) and Shakespeare Birthplace Trust MS ER 93/2, fol. 93v (begun *c.* 1629, which also contains copies of 'Upon a pair of gloves', 'On Ben Jonson' and Shakespeare's alleged self-epitaph on the same page). There are numerous differences between all seven versions, a reflection of its conventional nature.

John Combe was a wealthy landowner from Welcombe, five miles from Stratford-upon-Avon, who died on 10 July 1614. He was known to Shakespeare, who had bought land off John and his uncle William in 1602, and in 1614 (after Combe's death), Shakespeare seems to have sided with John Combe's nephews, William and Thomas, when the Stratford Corporation objected to the Combes' plan to enclose common land at Welcombe ('Barlichway hundred', *VCH*). John Combe left Shakespeare £5 in his will; Shakespeare in turn left his sword to John's nephew, the would-be encloser Thomas (Schoenbaum 1978: 245).

There is little in the style or vocabulary of this short piece which is distinctively Shakespearean. Irreverent or satirical epitaphs were a feature of many seventeenth-century miscellanies, and references to the steep, but legally acceptable, rate of 10 per cent interest ('ten in the hundred', l. 1) and to the usurer belonging to the devil (l. 4) are common to many such epitaphs, which were written about both specific usurers and their stock type; see, for example, Epigram 24 in Henry Peacham, *The More the Merrier* (1608): 'Ten in the hundred lies under this stone | And a hundred to ten but to th' Devil he's gone' (sig. C2r); these same lines were allegedly written on the tomb of Sir Edward Stanhope shortly after his funeral in June 1608 (Harrison 2013: 93).

The text is from the earliest version, which appears at the end of Richard Braithwait's *Remains after Death*, appended to Patrick Hannay's *Happy Husband* (1619, sig. L2v).

An Epitaph vpon one Iohn Combe of Stratford vpon Auen, a notable Vsurer, fastened vpon a Tombe that he had caused to be built in his life time.

Ten in the hundred must lie in his graue,
But a hundred to ten whether God will him haue?
Who then must be interr'd in this Tombe?
Oh (quoth the Diuell) my Iohn a Combe.

Another epitaph on John Combe

The epitaph, and its attribution, appear in Bodleian MS Ashmole 38 (*c.* 1650), p. 180, directly after the previous epitaph and the page before 'On Ben Jonson'. The poem (l. 4) and its prose introduction both refer to Combe's will, in which he made a number of charitable bequests, including £100 capital to be used to make loans to poor tradesmen, as well as money for two sermons a year and ten black gowns for the poor (National Archives PROB 11/126/415). The heading in Ashmole sets up a contrast between this more respectful epitaph (acknowledging the charity of the departed) and the preceding one (a shorter version of the satirical epitaph immediately above). Clearly, this second epitaph was written by someone who knew both Combe's reputation as a usurer and the nature of his posthumous bequests; the slightness of the poem, however, means that it reveals few clues about its actual authorship.

> but [Combe] being dead, and making the poor his heires, hee [Shakespeare] after
> wrightes this for his Epitaph
>> How ere he liued Iudge not
>> Iohn Combe shall neuer be forgott
>> while poor, hath Memmorye, for hee did gather★   ★ accumulate wealth
>> To make the poore his Issue; hee their father
>> As record of his tilth★ and seedes   5   ★ labour
>> Did Crowne him In his latter deedes.
>>> finis.   W: Shak.

'On Ben Jonson'

Theses verses are attributed to Jonson and Shakespeare in Bodleian MS Ashmole 38 (*c.* 1650), p. 181 (the page after the two epitaphs on John Combe), and Plume MS 25 (Maldon, Essex), where it appears twice: on fols 51r and 77r. The epitaph also appears, extracted from its anecdote, in Folger MS V.a.275, fol. 177r, and Francis Fane's miscellanies (where it appears on the same page as the epitaphs on John Combe and on Shakespeare himself): MS Folger V.a.180 (*c.* 1655), fol. 79v, and Shakespeare Birthplace Trust MS ER 93/2 (begun *c.* 1629), fol. 93v. Shakespeare and Jonson were close acquaintances, and eulogies to Jonson by men who knew him, as well as his own poetry, often situate him within a tavern environment (such as the Mermaid or Sun), which is presented as an epitome of male sociability and poetic wit (see Francis Beaumont, 'The sun which doth the greatest comfort bring', in Benson's 1640 *Poems*, sigs L4r–5r; Robert Herrick, 'Ode to Ben Jonson', in *Hesperides*, 1648, sigs Z3v–Z4r). Thomas Fuller's *The History of the Worthies of England* (1662) records 'many [. . .] wit-combats' between the two men, in which Jonson, 'like a Spanish great galleon, [. . .] built far higher in learning', was outsmarted by the 'quickness' of Shakespeare's 'wit and invention' (sig. 3Q3v). However, Fuller's account is at least second hand (Fuller was no more than eight years old when Shakespeare died) and, like the mock-epitaph below, tells us more about the type of repartee expected between these friendly rivals than what they actually did or said.

The copy below is from Bodleian MS Ashmole 38.

> Mr Ben Iohnson and Mr Wm: Shak-speare
> Being Merrye att a Tauern, mr Ionson haueing begune this for his Epitaph

Here lies Ben Iohnson that was once one
he giues ytt to m^r Shakspear to make vpp★ who p[re]sently wrightes   ★complete
Who while hee liu'de was a sloe things
And now being dead is Nothinge
finis

'Upon the King'

This short poem appears below a picture of James VI and I, engraved by Simon Passe, used by the king's printers, Robert Barker and John Bill, as the frontispiece to James' *Works* in 1616. The compiler of Bodleian MS Ashmole 38 (*c.* 1650) – which also contains copies of 'On Ben Jonson' and the two epitaphs on John Combes on pp. 180–1 (see above) – attributes the lines to the printer, Barker, heading the composition 'Certayne verses wrighten by mr Robert Barker vnder his ma^tis picture' and concluding it 'finis R.B.' (p. 39). It seems unlikely that Shakespeare would be writing verses to commission in 1616, when he seems to have been in poor health (although admittedly, he could have written them earlier): he drew up his will in January that year (an event often instigated by illness); his signature on the revised version of March 1616 is feeble (Schoenbaum 1978: 297); and he was dead by the end of April. Nonetheless, this conventional piece of royal eulogy is ascribed to Shakespeare in Folger MS V.a.160 (Matthew Day's commonplace book, *c.* 1650), Part 2, p. 2, and Folger V.a.262 (a miscellany associated with Oxford University, *c.* 1650), p. 131. As such, it is part of the history of Shakespeare's reception as a poet, perhaps reflecting a belief that the nation's premier poet would naturally write verses in commendation of his monarch.

The text below is taken from the 1616 *Works*.

Crounes have their compasse, length of dayes their date,
Triumphes their tombes, felictie her fate:
Of more then earth, can earth make none partaker,
But knowledge make the KING most like his maker.

Simon Passaeus sculp[sit]★: Lond[on]   Ioh[n] Bill excudit.★   ★carved   ★printed

Shakespeare's epitaph on himself

Attributed to Shakespeare in Francis Fane's miscellany, Folger MS V.a.180 (*c.* 1655), fol. 79v (where it appears on the same page as 'On Ben Jonson' and the satirical epitaph on John Combe; see above) and in Folger MS V.a.232, p. 63 (Henry Newcome's miscellany, begun 1669). An unattributed version also appears in Fane's 1629 miscellany, Shakespeare Birthplace Trust MS ER 93, fol. 93v, where it appears on the same page as three other poems associated with Shakespeare/Stratford: 'Upon a pair of gloves', 'On Ben Jonson' and the satirical epitaph on John Combe. Robert Dobyns' transcription – made on his visit to Stratford in 1673 – is in MS Folger V.a.147, fol. 72r.

Owing to the limited burial space within Holy Trinity Church, Stratford-upon-Avon, bones would periodically be dug up by the sexton and placed in the adjoining charnel house. It is that practice that the epitaph seeks to avert. As with many of the poems above, the poem is too brief and conventional to offer clues about authorship.

The text below is taken from the (badly eroded) slab in the chancel of Holy Trinity Church.

GOOD FREND FOR IESVS SAKE FORBEARE,
TO DIGG THE DVST ENCLOASED HEARE:
BLES[T]E BE Yᴱ MAN Yᵀ SPARES THES STONES,
AND CVRST BE HE Yᵀ MOVES MY BONES.

'To the Queen'

The lines below appear in Cambridge University Library MS Dd.5.75, fol. 46r, the private miscellany of Henry Stanford, chaplain and tutor to the household of Sir George Carey, the son of Henry Carey, Second Baron Hunsdon, Elizabeth I's Lord Chamberlain (then patron of the company of players to which Shakespeare belonged). Line 11 indicates that the poem was performed at Shrovetide (the days immediately before Lent); if we can accept Stanford's dating of 1598, then this refers to early spring 1599 (owing to old style dating, where the New Year began on 25 March, not 1 January).

The tentative attribution to Shakespeare made in Ringler and May (1972) has been accepted by Shapiro (2005: 74–5), who suggests it was written as an epilogue for a court performance of *A Midsummer Night's Dream* (it shares the catalectic trochaic tetrameter of the fairies' songs, 2.2.10–26; 5.1.371–422); and by Dusinberre (2006: 37–42), who argues for its connection with a performance of *As You Like It* at Richmond Palace, renowned for its spectacular sundial, on Shrove Tuesday 1599. The poem has also been included in several *Complete Works* (including the *Riverside*, and Bate and Rasmussen 2007). In contrast, Hattaway (2009) has argued for Thomas Dekker and Ben Jonson as possible authors: like Shakespeare, the two poets often used trochaic tetrameters for songs, and there are similarities between the dial hand poem and the epilogue to Dekker's *Old Fortunatus* (both are phrased as prayers). Dekker is also championed by Hackett (2012), who adds to Hattaway's pro-Dekker evidence, noting Dekker's fondness for the imagery of dials and temporal cycles and the fact that he composed royal panegyric more regularly than Shakespeare. She suggests that the epilogue was written for a court performance of Dekker's *Shoemaker's Holiday* (1599), Shrovetide being the 'Holiday' to which Dekker's title refers. Whether or not the author was Shakespeare, and whether or not these verses were performed with one his plays, the poem is indicative of the type of material that companies of players would have been required to produce for their court performances.

In Cambridge University Library MS Dd.5.75, Stanford compresses the poem into nine lines to save space, using a virgule to mark the two parts of each 'line'. The transcription below, taken from his manuscript, breaks the poem back into couplets.

to yᵉ Q. by yᵉ players. 1598.

As the diall hand tells ore
yᵉ same howers yt had before
still beginning in yᵉ ending
Circuler account still lending
So most mightie Q. we pray   5
like yᵉ diall day by day
you may lead yᵉ seasons on

making new when old are gon.
that the babe wch now is yong
& hathe yet no vse of tongue   10
many a shrouetyde here may bow
to y^t empresse★ I doe now   ★ Elizabeth I
that the children of these lordes
sitting at your counsell bourdes★   ★ tables
may be graue & aeged seene   15
of her y^t was ther fathers Quene
once I wishe this wishe again
heauen subscribe yt wth amen.

Appendix 7

Shakespeare's rhymes

Many of the rhymes which look like imperfect rhymes to twenty-first-century readers were valid full rhymes to Shakespeare and his contemporaries. Well over 10 per cent of Shakespeare's rhymes might be mistaken as imperfect by modern readers: *Sonnets*, up to 14.0 per cent; *Lucrece*, 15.8 per cent; 'Let the Bird of Loudest Lay', 16.1 per cent; *Venus and Adonis*, 17.4 per cent; *Lover's Complaint*, 17.7 per cent. (We say 'up to' because pronunciation varies across English dialects, and some of Shakespeare's rhymes which have fallen out of 'Received Pronunciation' (RP) are still available in other accents.) This would be an extraordinarily high number of imperfect rhymes, leaving entire stanzas without one exact rhyme (e.g. *Lucrece*, ll. 1639–45; *Venus and Adonis*, ll. 187–92, 427–32).

Working out how people spoke in the past is challenging, not least because English – then, as now – was spoken with a wide variety of accents, and underwent generational shifts. In such a phonologically fluid environment, in many cases different pronunciations of the same word would have been available to Shakespeare and his early readers; for example, 'again' can rhyme with both the short vowel of 'pen' (Sonnet 79.6–8) and with the diphthong of 'slain' (Sonnet 22.13–14). Furthermore, as David Crystal notes (2011), the evidence which allows us to reconstruct historical pronunciation is 'often mixed' and 'deductions by historical linguists can reach different conclusions about the quality of a sound'.

The sources used here (Kökeritz 1953; Cercignani 1981; Crystal 2011, 2016) draw for their evidence on sixteenth- and seventeenth-century grammar and spelling books (the treatises on phonetic spelling by Thomas Smith, *De recta et emendata linguae anglicae scriptione* (1568), and John Hart, *Orthography* (1569) and *Method or Comfortable Beginning* (1570), being particularly useful); on foreign language manuals (which teach pronunciation through pointing out English equivalents); on spelling habits and hononymic puns; and on rhymes, although Kökeritz is more likely than Cercignani and Crystal to conclude that at least some of Shakespeare's rhymes are influenced by the literary tradition. In Kökeritz's view, poets tend to 'use more or less the same rhymes as the preceding [generation] and continue to do so long after some of the syllables they coupled in rhyme had ceased to be pronounced alike' (31). That view is frequently challenged by Cercignani, who provides more thorough coverage than Kökeritz in the range of rhymes analysed, and by Crystal's practical application of Original Pronunciation (OP) in transcriptions produced for twenty-first-century acting companies; Crystal's OP version of the *Sonnets* is included in the transcriptions available at originalpronunciation.com.

The explanations that follow are only for those rhymes which might look strange to a twenty-first-century reader; they are certainly not a definitive guide to OP. Readers wanting to find out more about OP are directed to Kökeritz 1953; Cercignani 1981; Crystal 2005, 2011, 2016.

The explanations here are aimed at readers without knowledge of linguistics or the International Phonetic Alphabet (IPA); they use the lexical sets in Wells 1982 (1.xviii–xix), which are tied to a keyword (here given small capitals) and which are accompanied with representative examples from both RP and General American Pronunciation (GA). We use RP as a necessary reference point only for vowel sounds, on which rhymes mainly depend. The degree to which 'r' would have been articulated in OP is unclear. Crystal (2016: xlvi) suggests that 'when used in front of a vowel, it would seem to have been the same sound as in RP' (i.e. not rolled), but that after a vowel, it may well have been sounded, as in GA rather than RP 'start'.

Abbreviations
LBLL: 'Let the Bird of Loudest Lay'
LC: *Lover's Complaint*
RL: *Lucrece*
S: *Sonnets*
VA: *Venus and Adonis*

Note: for ease of comparison, the rhyming pairs are grouped by the vowel sound or diphthong on which they depend; at the end of the appendix come those rhymes which depend on consonants rather than vowels, or on stressing a particular syllable. Within each explanation, the rhyming words are given in alphabetical order, which is not necessarily the order in which the rhymes appear *in situ*. Words are in bold when they occur in more than one rhyming combination.

'A' sounds

ARE/CARE/COMPARE/PREPARE/RARE/SNARE/UNAWARE

There were two ways of pronouncing 'are' in Elizabethan English; the one used to make the rhymes below is the 'strong' or 'stressed' form (Cercignani 1981: 104; Kökeritz 1953: 180), which resembles RP 'square', but with 'r' sounded (see also Crystal 2011).

are. . . *care* (S 48.5–7; S 112.9–11; S 147.9–11)

are. . . *care*. . . *snare* (RL 926–9)

are. . . *compare* (S 35.6–8; VA 8–10)

are. . . *prepare* (S 13.1–3)

are. . . *rare* (S 52.5–7)

are. . . *unaware* (VA 823–5)

ART/CONVERT/DESERT/HEART/PART; GUARD/HEARD/WARD

A full rhyme is possible (Cercignani 1981: 65; Kökeritz 1953: 250–1), relying on the words being pronounced with vowel sound of RP 'start'. See:

art. . . *convert* (S 14.10–12)

art. . . *convert*. . . *heart* (RL 590–3)

*convert*est. . . *depart*est (S 11.2–4), double rhyme

desert. . . *impart* (S 72.6–8)

desert(s). . . *part(s)* (S 17.2–4; S 49.10–12)

guard. . . *ward* (S 133.9–11)

heard. . . *regard*. . . . *ward* (RL 303–6)

BAR/FAR/JAR/SCAR/WAR; ARM/CHARM/HARM/WARM

These rhymes rely on the late Middle English short '*a*' (Cercignani 1981: 90), so that 'war' and 'warm' moves closer to RP 'START', a pronunciation also supported by Crystal (2011). See:

afar. . . *scar*. . . *war* (RL 828–31)

bar. . . *war* (S 46.1–3)

charmed. . . *harmed*. . . *warmed* (LC 191–4); a double rhyme if the final syllable is stressed

disarmed. . . *warmed* (S 154.6–8)

harm. . . *warm* (VA 193–5)

jar. . . *war* (VA 98–100)

BEGAN/RAN/THEN (RL 1437–40)

The rhyme rests on pronouncing 'then' with a short '*a*' (RP 'TRAP'), so that it sounds like 'than', a common variant spelling, and older pronunciation, of 'then' (Cercignani 1981: 67; Kökeritz 1953: 164).

BLAST/FAST/HASTE/LAST/PAST/TASTE/WASTE

Although Crystal (2011) allows a more inexact rhyme, a full rhyme – with a short '*a*' (RP 'TRAP') – is possible in Elizabethan pronunciation (Cercignani 1981: 175–6; Kökeritz 1953: 176). See:

blast. . .*fast*. . . *haste* (RL 1332–5)

fast. . . *last*. . . *taste* (RL 891–4)

fast. . . *haste* (VA 55–7)

fast. . . *haste*. . . *past* (RL 1668–71)

fast. . . *taste* (VA 527–8)

haste. . . *past* (S 123.10–12)

last. . . *taste* (LC 167–8; S 90.9–11; VA 445–7)

past. . . *waste* (S 30.2–4)

CAN/ENCHANT/GRANT/PANT/SWAN/VAUNT/WANT

During the sixteenth century, the short '*a*' was starting to merge with a short '*o*' (RP 'CLOTH') in many cases where it was preceded by '*w*', but this process was in flux, and it is probable that the rhyme depended on a short '*a*' (Cercignani 1981: 86–7). This also accounts for the MATCH/WATCH rhyme (VA 584–6). See:

can. . . swan (LBLL 14–15)

*grant*eth. . . *pant*eth. . . *want*eth (RL 555–8), double rhymes

*grant*ing. . . *want*ing (S 87.5–7), double rhyme

vaunt. . . want (RL 41–2)

However, compare the 'ENCHANTED/GRANTED/HAUNTED' cluster ('"A" → diphthongs', below).

CHAT/GATE; GRAPES/MISHAPS

A full rhyme, reliant on a short '*a*' (RP 'TRAP'), is possible in Elizabethan pronunciation (Cercignani 1981: 174, 178; Kökeritz 1953: 165). See:

chat. . . gate (VA 422–4)

grapes. . . mishaps (VA 601–3)

FLATTER/MATTER/WATER

A full rhyme, dependent on a short '*a*' (RP 'TRAP'), is possible in Elizabethan pronunciation (Cercignani 1981: 89), although Kökeritz (1953: 171) sees this as a 'traditional' (i.e. eye) rhyme. See:

flatter. . . water (RL 1560–1)

matter. . . water (LC 302–4)

GATHERED/UNFATHERED (S 124.2–4)

A full rhyme is possible in Elizabethan pronunciation, but it is unclear whether it rests on a short or long '*a*' (Cercignani 1981: 94, 102); Crystal (2011) favours the long vowel (RP 'BATH').

GAVE/GRAVE/HAVE/SLAVE

The rhyme relies on 'have' being pronounced with a late Middle English long '*a*' (Cercignani 1981: 102; Kökeritz 1953: 177), so that it resembles RP 'FACE'. See:

gave. . . have (RL 1511–12)

grave (it). . . have (it) (S 81.5–7; VA 374–6, double rhyme; VA 757–9)

grave. . . have. . . slave (RL 198–201)

have. . . slave (RL 1000–1; VA 101–2)

GLASS/GRASS/PASS/WAS

As with the CAN/ENCHANT cluster above, the rhyme relies on a short '*a*' (Cercignani 1981: 87) combined with the pronunciation of the final syllable as '*s*' (as in 'glass') not '*z*' (as in 'rise').

However, Kökeritz is more sceptical, regarding these as 'traditional' (i.e. eye) rhymes (1953: 167). Crystal (2011) indicates the shared consonantal sound 's'; he allows an inexact rhyme, but moves the vowel sound of 'was' closer towards the long 'a' of 'glass'/'pass' (RP 'BATH'), and away from the vowel in RP 'CLOTH'.

> *glass. . .* ***was*** (S 5.10–12; RL 1763–4)
>
> *grass. . .* ***was*** (RL 393–5)
>
> *pass. . .* ***was*** (S 49.5–7)

HATH/WRATH (LC 293–4)

A full rhyme is possible in Elizabethan pronunciation, if 'wrath' is sounded with a short 'a' (RP 'TRAP') rather than a short 'o' (RP 'CLOTH').

SCRATCH/WRETCH (VA 703–5)

A full rhyme, reliant on a short 'a' in both words, as in RP 'TRAP', is possible in Elizabethan pronunciation (Cercignani 1981: 67; Kökeritz 1953: 164).

'A' → 'O'

DALLY/FOLLY; FOLLOW/HALLOW

The short 'o' was often unrounded in Elizabethan pronunciation, so that it moved closer to a short 'a' (Cercignani 1981: 114, who cites 'clat-pole' for 'clot-pole'; see Kökeritz 1953: 224–5). However, it may also be that the follow/hallow rhyme depends on the common variant spelling 'hollow' and is pronounced accordingly. See:

> *dally. . . folly* (RL 554–6)
>
> *follow. . . hallow* (VA 973–5)

'A' → 'U'

ADDER/SHUDDER (VA 878–80)

Kökeritz (1953: 241) attributes the rhyme to Shakespeare taking on the sixteenth-century London pronunciation of 'u', which brings it closer to RP 'TRAP'. Cercignani (1981: 120) is sceptical and considers this a possible imperfect rhyme.

'A' → diphthongs

ENCHANTED/GRANTED/HAUNTED (LC 128–31)

These double rhymes show the fluidity of early modern pronunciation, as the rhyme relies not on a short 'a' (as with CAN/ENCHANT cluster above), but on the late Middle English 'au' (Cercignani 1981: 214), approximating to the diphthong in RP 'THOUGHT'; this sound also accounts for the rhyme BALK/HAWK (RL 694–6), where the 'l' in 'balk' is silent (Cercignani 1981: 212).

FALL/GENERAL/PERPETUAL/THRALL/WALL

The rhyme depends on a late Middle English '*au*' (Cercignani 1981: 212–13, 302), approximating to the diphthong in RP 'THOUGHT'. The polysyllabic words ('general', 'perpetual') also require a stress on the final syllable. See:

fall. . . general (RL 1483–4)

perpetual. . . **thrall** (S 154.10–12)

perpetual. . . **thrall**. . . *wall* (RL 723–6)

'E' sounds

BACK/NECK (VA 593–4)

The short '*e*' in 'back' (RP 'DRESS'), where we would expect a short '*a*' (RP 'TRAP'), may owe something to Mercian and Kentish English (Cercignani 1981: 100). Kökeritz (1953: 164) also endorses this as a full rhyme.

BEARD/HERD (S 12.6–8)

The evidence is ambiguous. The full rhyme that is possible in Elizabethan pronunciation may rest on either a short vowel, as in RP 'NURSE', or a long vowel, as in RP 'NEAR' (Cercignani 1981: 79). Crystal (2011) opts for a long vowel, akin to that in RP 'SQUARE', a pronunciation suggested by Kökeritz as one of the available options (1953: 207).

BEAST/BLEST/EAST/FEAST/GUEST/JEST/LEAST/POSSESSED/WEST; CONFESS/DECEASE/EXCESS/LEASE

The rhyme is probably dependent on a short '*e*' (Cercignani 1981: 74, 168; Kökeritz 1953: 201), as in RP 'DRESS', pronunciation with which Crystal (2011) largely concurs. See:

beast. . . *blest* (VA 326–8)

beast. . . *jest* (VA 997–9)

confess. . . decease (VA 1001–2)

east. . . west (S 132.6–8)

excess. . . lease (S 146.5–7)

least. . . possessed (S 29.6–8)

feast. . . guest (S 47.5–7; VA 449–50)

possessing. . . releasing (S 87.1–3), double rhyme

BED/BLEED/DEED/DREAD/MEAD/PLEAD/PROCEED/SHED

Full rhymes are possible in Elizabethan pronunciation, with the vowel either sounded as a short '*e*' (RP 'DRESS') or with a long '*e*' (RP 'FLEECE'), and the same word might be pronounced differently by different readers, or in different rhyming situations even within the same poem (see Cercignani 1981: 77–8); so, for example, 'dread' might be pronounced with a short '*e*' to rhyme with 'bed' at RL 169–71, but with a long '*e*', rhyming with the verbs 'lead' and 'plead,' at RL 268–71. See:

> *bleeds. . . proceeds. . . **sheds*** (RL 1549–52)
>
> *dead. . . o'er-read* (S 81.10–12)
>
> *deeds. . . **sheds*** (S 34.13–14)
>
> ***dread**. . . mead* (VA 635–6)
>
> ***dread**eth. . . leadeth. . . pleadeth* (RL 268–71), double rhymes

BEQUEATH/BREATH/DEATH (RL 1178–81)

A full rhyme is possible in Elizabethan pronunciation (Cercignani 1981: 76), but it can depend on either a short '*e*' (RP 'DRESS') or long '*e*' (RP 'FLEECE').

BESEECHED/ENRICHED/IMPLEACHED (LC 205–8)

A full rhyme, dependent on a long '*e*' (RP 'FLEECE') is possible in Elizabethan pronunciation (Cercignani 1981: 160).

COUNTERFEIT/(UN)SET (S 16.6–8; S 53.5–7)

The final syllable of 'counterfeit' would have been pronounced with a short '*e*', as in RP 'DRESS' (Cercignani 1981: 269).

ENTER/VENTURE (VA 626–8)

A full rhyme was possible in Elizabethan pronunciation, with 'venture' pronounced like 'enter' (Q spelling: 'venter'), thus making a double rhyme (Cercignani 1981: 261; Kökeritz 1953: 271).

EVEN/HEAVEN

The rhyme is invariably monosyllabic in Shakespeare's poems and probably depends on 'heav'n' moving towards a long '*e*' (RP 'FLEECE'), rather than 'ev'n' moving towards the short '*e*', as in RP 'DRESS' (Cercignani 1981: 71). See:

> *even. . . heaven* (S 28.10–12; S 132.5–7; VA 493–5)

FRET/GET/GREAT/HEAT/SWEAT/TREAT; BETTER/GREATER

Cercignani and Kökeritz treat this cluster differently. Kökeritz (1953: 201–2) does not mention the get/great rhyme, but sees the others depending on a short '*e*', resembling RP 'DRESS'. Cercignani (1981: 168–9) agrees that better/greater, get/heat (as well as get/great) depend on a short '*e*', but argues that the remaining rhymes (asterisked below) probably rest on both words sharing a long '*e*', resembling RP 'FLEECE', although he acknowledges that a short '*e*' is feasible

(Cercignani 1981: 78–9). Following Cercignani would mean that the same word ('heat') is pronounced differently, in different rhyming situations, within the same poem (compare discussion of 'dread' in BED/BLEED cluster, above). See:

> *better. . . greater* (S 119.10–12), a double rhyme
>
> *get. . . great* (RL 876–8)
>
> *get. . . heat* (VA 91–3)
>
> *entreats. . . frets* (VA 73–5)★
>
> *heat. . . sweat* (VA 175–7)★

LEAPS/STEPS (VA 277–9)

As with the BEAST/BLEST cluster, the rhyme is probably dependent on a short 'e' (Cercignani 1981: 168; Kökeritz 1953: 202).

'E' ↔ 'I'

COMMISSION/IMPRESSION; CONTENTED/IMPRINTED; EXTENUATE/INSINUATE

The attested fluidity in Elizabethan pronunciation between short 'e' (RP 'DRESS') and short 'i' (RP 'KIT') means that a full rhyme is possible here (Kökeritz 1953: 212), although Cercignani (1981: 68) suggests that these are inexact rhymes; all three rhyming pairs are, however, polysyllabic, which softens the impact of the (potentially) imperfect rhyme. See:

> *commission. . . impression* (VA 566–8)
>
> *contented. . . imprinted* (VA 511–13)
>
> *extenuate. . . insinuate* (VA 1010–12)

END/FIEND/FRIEND

'Friend' and 'end' are usually rhymed on a short 'e' (RP 'DRESS'); however, the fiend/end and fiend/friend rhymes may be explained by either (i) pronouncing both with a short 'i' (RP 'KIT'), or (ii) lengthening the vowel in 'end' so that it resembles that in RP 'FLEECE' (Cercignani 1981: 81–2). Kökeritz (1953: 192–3) similarly attests to a vacillation in the vowel sound. See:

> *end. . . fiend* (LBLL 6–7; S 145.9–11)
>
> *fiend(s). . . friend(s)* (S 144.9–11; VA 638–40)

DEVIL/EVIL

According to Cercignani (1981: 82), the rhyme (which appears frequently in RL) probably relies on both words being sounded with a long 'e' (RP 'FLEECE'), although a short 'e' (RP 'DRESS') is a possibility; on the other hand, Kökeritz (1953: 188) sees this either as (i) a traditional (i.e. 'eye') rhyme, or (ii) a rhyme made by pronouncing the first syllable of both words with a short '*i*' (RP '*kit*'). See:

> *devil. . . evil* (RL 85–7; RL 846–7; RL 972–3; RL 1245–6; RL 1513–15; S 144.5–7), double rhyme

FEVER/NEVER (S 119.6–8)

Kökeritz (1953: 203) and Cercignani (1981: 76) both agree that a full rhyme is possible in Elizabethan pronunciation: Cercignani proposes that both words could be pronounced with either a long '*e*' (RP '*fleece*') or a short '*e*' (RP '*dress*'); Kökeritz favours a short vowel, either short '*e*' or short '*i*' (RP '*kit*').

THITHER/TOGETHER/WEATHER/WHITHER

The full double rhyme that is possible in Elizabethan English depends on either (i) a short '*e*', as in RP '*dress*', or (ii) a short '*i*', as in RP '*kit*' (Cercignani 1981: 51). The rhyme pair NEITHER/TOGETHER (LBLL 42–3) would seem to be evidence for the former (Kökeritz 1953: 187) – Cercignani (1981: 72) proposes either a short '*e*' or long '*e*' (RP '*fleece*') for that rhyme – but compare the discussion of the variable pronunciation of 'dread' in the BED/BLEED cluster, above. See:

> *thither. . . weather* (RL 113–15), double rhyme
>
> *together. . . whither* (VA 902–4), double rhyme

'E' ↔ diphthongs

AFRAID/AID/ALLAYED/BEWRAYED/MAID/SAID/STAYED

The modern pronunciation of 'said' with a short '*e*' (to rhyme with 'bed') was available to Shakespeare, but for the most part he used the older form (Cercignani 1981: 83; Kökeritz 1953: 177), which makes a full rhyme with words like 'maid' (vowel sound of RP '*face*'). See:

> *afraid. . . maid. . . **said*** (LC 177–80)
>
> ***aid**. . . apaid. . . **said*** (RL 912–15)
>
> ***aid**. . . bewrayed. . . **said*** (RL 1696–9)
>
> ***aid**. . . **said*** (RL 1784–5)
>
> *allayed. . . **said*** (S 56.1–3)
>
> ***said**. . . stayed* (VA 331–3)

APPEAR/BEAR/CHEER/CLEAR/DEAR/EAR/–ER/FEAR/HAIR/HEAR/HERE/ NEAR/SPEAR/SWEAR/TEAR/THERE/WEAR/WERE/YEAR

This is a large rhyming cluster which constitutes 'a phonological situation which at first glance seems to border on the chaotic' (Kökeritz 1953: 204), with a large degree of vacillation between being sounded as something resembling RP '*near*' and something resembling RP '*square*'

(Cercignani 1981: 146–9; Kökeritz 1953: 204–9); the transcriptions in Crystal (2011) do not show perfect rhymes for all combinations, but those that do rhyme share the sound of RP 'square'.

appear. . . bear (S 80.6–8)

appear. . . dear. . . wear (LC 93–6)

appear. . . everywhere (S 102.2–4)

appear. . . fear. . . there (RL 114–17)

appear. . . tear [n.] (S 31.5–7)

appear. . . were (RL 631–3)

appear. . . year (S 53.9–11)

bear. . . dear. . . here (RL 1290–3)

bear. . . ear (S 8.6–8)

bear. . . ear. . . hear (RL 1325–8)

bear. . . ear. . . swear (RL 1416–19)

bear(s). . . fear(s) (LC 272–3; RL 610–12)

bear. . . hair*. . . tear* [n.] (RL 1129–32)

bear. . . here. . . tear [vb] (LC 51–4; RL 1472–5)

bear her*. . . clear* her*. . . hear* her (RL 1318–21), double rhymes

bearing. . . hearing (VA 428–30), double rhyme

bear it*. . . were* it (RL 1156–8), double rhyme

bear. . . swear (S 131.9–11)

bears. . . characters*. . . tears* [n.] (LC 16–19)

bears. . . clears. . . tears [n.] (RL 1710–13)

bear thee*. . . hear* thee*. . . tear* thee (RL 667–70), double rhymes

bear. . . were (S 13.6–8)

cheer*. . . fear. . .* worshipper (RL 86–9)

clear. . . everywhere (S 84.10–12)

dear. . . there (S 110.1–3)

ear. . . hair (VA 145–7)

ear. . . there (VA 779–80)

elsewhere. . . near (S 61.13–14)

everywhere. . . year (S 97.2–4)

fear. . . swear. . . there (RL 1647–50)

---

fear. . . tear [vb]. . . *there* (RL 737–40)

fear. . . there (RL 307–8; VA 320–2)

fear. . . wear (VA 1081–3)

forbear. . . there (S 41.9–11)

forbears. . . years (VA 524–6)

hairs. . . tears [n.] (VA 49–51; VA 191–2)

here. . . tear [n.]. . . *wear* (LC 289–92)

near. . . harbinger (LBLL 5–8)

near. . . there (S 136.1–3)

near. . . were (S 140.5–7)

spear. . . there (RL 1422–4; VA 1112–14)

swears. . . tears [n.] (VA 80–2)

tear [n.]. . . *there* (RL 1373–5)

tears [n.]. . . *wears* (RL 680–2)

tears [n.]. . . *years* (VA 1091–2)

wear. . . year (VA 506–8)

where. . . year (S 97.2–4)

BREAK/SPEAK; CREATE/DEFEAT/GREAT/SEAT; DEFEATURE/NATURE

Cercignani treats this group differently, favouring a long '*e*' (RP 'FLEECE') for the break/speak, great/defeat and great/seat rhymes (1981: 161), whilst acknowledging (1981: 158) that 'defeat' could be pronounced with a second vowel sound that resembles the diphthong in RP 'FACE' (see AFRAID/AID cluster, above). Kökeritz (1953: 198) and Crystal (2011) favour the diphthong: 'speak' thus sounds like 'spake'. See:

break(s). . . speak(s) (RL 566–7; RL 1268–70; RL 1716–18; S 34.5–7; VA 221–2)

created. . . defeated (S 20.9–11), double rhyme

defeat. . . great (S 61.9–11)

defeature. . . nature (VA 734–6)

great. . . seat (RL 69–70)

BY/DIE/EYE/HIGH/LIE/SPY/-LY/-Y; EYES/-IES

A full rhyme is possible in Elizabethan pronunciation, as '-ly' etc. and words like 'by' share the late medieval diphthong that approximates to RP 'PRICE' (Cercignani 1981: 304–5; Kökeritz 1953: 218–20). The length of the list below shows how frequently Shakespeare had recourse to this rhyme, particularly in RL, where it appears twenty times in 795 rhyming units (incidence: 0.025); compare S, where it appears fifteen times in 1077 rhyming units (incidence: 0.014). See:

advisedly. . . *by* (RL 1814–16)

advisedly. . . *eye*. . . *fly* (RL 177–80)

alchemy. . . *eye* (S 33.2–4)

amplify. . . *quality* (LC 209–10)

bastardy. . . *eye*. . . *obloquy* (RL 520–3)

beautify. . . *modesty*. . . *mortality* (RL 401–4)

by. . . *remedy* (S 154.9–11)

company. . . *eye*. . . *sky* (RL 1584–7)

cries. . . *enemies*. . . *tyrannise* (RL 674–7)

cry. . . *jollity* (S 66.1–3)

cry. . . *lustily* (VA 869–70)

cry. . . *patiently* (RL 1639–41)

destiny. . . *fly* (RL 1728–9)

die. . . *dignity* (S 94.10–12)

die. . . *infamy*. . . *livery* (RL 1052–5)

die. . . *iniquity* (RL 1686–7)

die. . . *memory* (S 1.2–4)

dignity. . . *eye* (RL 435–7)

dye. . . *wantonly* (S 54.5–7)

eye. . . *gravity* (S 49.6–8)

eye. . . *history* (S 93.5–7)

eye. . . *majesty*. . . *satisfy* (RL 93–6)

eye. . . *piety* (RL 540–2)

eye. . . *remedy* (S 62.1–3)

eye. . . *steadfastly* (VA 1063–5)

eye. . . *sky*. . . *sympathy* (RL 1227–30)

eyes. . . *enemies* (RL 1469–70)

eyes. . . *forgeries*. . . *lies* (RL 457–60)

eyes. . . *infamies* (RL 636–7)

eyes. . . *prophecies* (S 106.9–11)

eyes. . . *secrecies* (RL 99–101)

fly. . . **majesty** (S 78.6–8)

fly. . . *mutiny*. . . *readily* (RL 1150–3)

fortify. . . **memory** (S 63.9–11)

high. . . **majesty** (VA 854–6)

jealousy. . . *pry* (S 61.6–8)

jealousy. . . *spy* (VA 655–7)

lie. . . *rarity*. . . *simplicity* (LBLL 53–5)

lies. . . *subtleties* (S 138.2–4)

majesty. . . *under–eye* (S 7.2–4)

memory. . . **sky** (S 15.6–8)

perpetually. . . *purify* (RL 685–6)

quickly. . . *unlikely* (VA 989–90), double rhyme with the penultimate '*i*' both sounded short as in RP 'KIT' (Cercignani 1981: 256; Kökeritz 1953: 219)

KEY/SURVEY (S 52.1–3)

A full rhyme is possible in Elizabethan pronunciation (Cercignani 1981: 233; Kökeritz 1953: 178), as 'key' is pronounced to rhyme with 'may' (vowel in RP 'FACE').

'I' sounds

ACHIEVE/LIVE (S 67.1–3)

A full rhyme is possible in Elizabethan pronunciation, with the final syllable of 'achieve' pronounced with the shorter '*i*' of RP 'KIT', as Q's spelling ('atchiue') may suggest (Cercignani 1981: 57; Kökeritz 1953: 193; Crystal 2011).

BEEN/SIN; TEETH/WITH

A full rhyme is possible in Elizabethan pronunciation, with the long '*e*' (RP 'FLEECE') sounded as a short '*i*', as in RP 'KIT' (Cercignani 1981: 149; Kökeritz 1953: 191). See:

been. . . *sin* (RL 209–10)

teeth. . . *with* (VA 269–70)

BUILD/FIELD/GILD/HELD/KILLED/SHIELD/YIELD; KILL/SENTINEL

A full rhyme is possible in Elizabethan pronunciation, probably reliant on a short '*i*', as in RP 'KIT' (Cercignani 1981: 149–50, 295; Kökeritz 1953: 186, 192), a pronunciation also favoured by Crystal (2011). See:

   *builded. . . **shield**ed. . . **yield**ed* (LC 149–52)

   field**. . . gild. . . **shield (RL 58–61)

   field**. . . **held (S 2.2–4)

   field**. . . **killed**. . . **yield (RL 72–5)

   ***held**. . . fulfilled. . . **kill**ed* (RL 1255–8)

   ***kill**. . . sentinel* (VA 650–2)

PARASITES/WITS (VA 848–50)

A full rhyme, dependent on a short '*i*' (RP 'ᴋɪᴛ'), is possible in Elizabethan English (Cercignani 1981: 308; Kökeritz 1953: 219).

SHIFT/THEFT; WIT/YET

A full rhyme is possible in Elizabethan pronunciation, achieved by raising the short '*e*' of 'theft' and 'yet' to a short '*i*' (Cercignani 1981: 68), as in RP 'ᴋɪᴛ'. See:

   shift. . . theft (RL 918–20)

   wit. . . yet (VA 1007–8)

'I' ↔ diphthongs

DEPRIVED/DERIVED/UNLIVED (RL 1752–5)

'-Lived' is here sounded with the diphthong found in RP 'ᴘʀɪᴄᴇ' (Cercignani 1981: 256).

FIND/KIND/MIND/WIND

A full rhyme is possible in Elizabethan pronunciation, but owing to the fluctuation in pronunciation during this period, it is unclear whether the rhyme would have been made with a short '*i*', as in RP 'ᴋɪᴛ', or a diphthong, as in RP 'ᴘʀɪᴄᴇ' (Cercignani 1981: 59; Kökeritz 1953: 218); Crystal (2011) favours the diphthong.

   find**. . . **mind**. . . **wind (LC 86–9)

   find**. . . **wind (S 14.6–8; S 51.5–7)

   ***mind**(s). . . **wind**(s)* (S 117.5–7; VA 338–40)

   *unkind. . . **wind*** (VA 187–9)

GROIN/SWINE (VA 1115–16)

A full rhyme, dependent on the diphthong found in RP 'ᴄʜᴏɪᴄᴇ', is possible in Elizabethan pronunciation (Cercignani 1981: 246; Kökeritz 1953: 217).

'O' sounds

ALONE/ANON/BONE/GONE/GROAN/LOAN/MOAN/NONE/ON/ONE/
STONE/SUN

The rhyme probably relies on a long vowel (RP 'GOAT') – a pronunciation favoured by Crystal (2011) – but a short vowel (RP 'CLOTH') is also possible (Cercignani 1981: 115–16, 136). See:

alone. . .*anon* (S 75.5–7)

alone. . . *gone* (S 4.9–11; S 31.10–12; S 45.5–7; S 66.13–14; VA 380–2; VA 518–20)

alone. . . *one* (RL 1478–80; S 36.2–4; S 39.6–8; S 42.13–14; S 105.13–14)

bone. . . *one* (LC 43–5; VA 293–4)

bone. . . *gone* (VA 56–8)

foregone. . . *moan* (S 30.9–11)

gone. . . *groan*. . . *moan* (RL 1360–3)

gone. . . *moan* (S 44.10–12; S 71.13–14)

gone. . . *none* (VA 389–90)

gone. . . *one* (VA 227–8; VA 518–20; VA 1069–71)

gone. . . *sun* (VA 188–90)

groan. . . *on* (S 50.9–11)

loan. . . *one* (S 6.6–8)

moan. . . *upon* (S149.6–8)

none. . . *stone* (S 94.1–3)

BOAST/COST/LOST/MOST

Both words can be pronounced with a short 'o' (Cercignani 1981: 187; Kökeritz 1953: 228, 233). See:

boast. . . *cost* (S 91.10–12)

boast. . . *lost* (RL 1191–3; VA 1075–7)

lost. . . *most* (S 152.6–8)

BOTH/GROWTH/OATH/TROTH

Although Cercignani notes that 'troth' is 'phonologically ambiguous' (119) – even today, the pronunciation of this old-fashioned word varies between a short vowel (RP 'CLOTH') and a long one (RP 'GOAT') – the rhyme is most easily explained by adopting the long vowel sound.

both. . . *oath* (RL 883–5)

both. . . *oath*. . . *troth* (RL 569–72)

oath. . . *growth*. . . *troth* (RL 1059–62)

oath. . . *troth* (LC 279–80)

CROSSED/ENGROSSED (S 133.6–8)

Cercignani (1981: 187) considers it unclear as to whether the rhyme is made by lengthening the short '*o*' of 'cross' (RP 'CLOTH'), or by shortening the longer vowel sound 'gross' (RP 'GOAT'). Kökeritz (1953: 228–9) favours a short vowel sound (as does Crystal 2011), but also suggests that this type of rhyme was already becoming conventional (i.e. an eye rhyme). It is possible that the final syllable is meant to be stressed (crossèd/engrossèd); if it is, this makes a double rhyme.

DOTING/NOTHING (S 20.10–12)

The first syllable of both words is pronounced with a long vowel (RP 'GOAT'), and the '*th*' of 'nothing' as '*t*', producing a full double rhyme (Cercignani 1981: 137, 329; Kökeritz 1953: 132, 320; Crystal 2011).

STORY/GLORY/SORRY (RL 1521–4)

In this instance, the long vowel of 'story' and 'glory' (RP 'FORCE') is retained in the third rhyme, 'sorry'; see Cercignani (1981: 117), who draws attention to a similar vacillation in the pronunciation of the word 'sorrel'. Spenser uses these rhymes in *Faerie Queene*, 'Cantos of Mutabilite', 6.8.2–5. This does not preclude the possibility that these are conventional (i.e. 'eye') rhymes by the late sixteenth century, a position favoured by Kökeritz (1953: 235).

'O' ↔ 'U'

AMONG/LONG/SONG/STRONG/SUNG/THRONG/TONGUE/WRONG/YOUNG

The evidence suggests that there were different ways of making this full rhyme in Elizabethan pronunciation: either both words are pronounced with a short '*o*' (RP 'CLOTH'), or with a short '*u*' (RP 'STRUT'); see Cercignani (1981: 111, 130); Kökeritz (1953: 243). Crystal recommends the short '*o*'. See:

along. . . sung (VA 1093–5)

among. . . belong. . . strong (LC 254–7)

long. . . throng. . . tongue (RL 1780–3)

long. . . tongue (RL 1616–17)

long. . . tongue. . . wrong (RL 1465–8)

long. . . strong. . . young (RL 863–6)

song(s). . . tongue(s) (S 17.10–12; S 102.13–14; VA 775–7)

strong. . . tongue (LC 120–2)

strong. . . young (VA 419–20)

tongue. . . wrong (RL 78–80; RL 1462–3; RL 1465–8; S 89.9–11; S 112.6–8; S 139.1–3; VA 217–19; VA 329–30; VA 427–9; VA 1003–5)

wrong. . . young (S 19.13–14)

BLOOD/BROOD/COOLED/FLOOD/FOOD/FOOT/GOOD/MOOD/ROOT/SHOULD/STOOD/WOOD

It is ambiguous as to whether this rhyme is produced by lengthening the vowel (as in RP 'GOOSE') or shortening it ('*u*', as in RP 'STRUT'); see Cercignani (1981: 134, 198). Crystal (2011) favours the short sound (the same as that in his recommended pronunciation of the 'COME/TOMB' and 'LOVE/PROVE' clusters, below). See:

blood. . . *brood* (S 19.2–4)

blood. . .*flood*. . . **good** (RL 653–6)

blood. . .*flood*. . . **stood** (RL 1738–41)

blood. . . **good** (LC 162–4; RL 1028–9; S 109.10–12; S 121.6–8; VA 1181–2)

blood . . .*mood*. . . *under***stood** (LC 198–201)

blood. . . **stood** (VA 1121–2; VA 1169–70)

blood. . . **wood** (VA 740–2)

flood. . . **wood** (VA 824–6)

food. . . **good**. . .*flood* (RL 1115–18)

foot. . . *root* (RL 664–5)

mood. . . **good** (RL 1273–4)

should. . . *cooled* (VA 385–7)

stood. . .*flood* (RL 265–6)

COME/DOOM/DUMB/GROOM/ROME/TOMB

Cercignani suggests that the rhyme is probably made by lengthening the vowel sound of 'come' or 'dumb', so that it moves closer to the vowel sound of RP 'GOOSE', although he concedes that shortening the vowel in 'doom', 'tomb', 'groom etc.' to a '*u*' (RP 'STRUT') may also be possible (1981: 132, 184–5, 198). Crystal favours the short sound, rendering this vowel sound the same as that found in his recommended pronunciations for the 'BLOOD/BROOD' cluster (above) and 'LOVE/PROVE' (below). See:

come. . . **tomb** (S 17.1–3)

come. . . **doom** (RL 923–4; S 107.2–4; S 116.10–12; S 145.5–7)

doom. . . **Rome** (RL 715–17; RL 1849–51)

dumb. . . **tomb** (S 83.10–12; S 101.9–11)

dumb. . . *entomb* (RL 1121–3)

groom. . . **Rome** (RL 1644–5)

noon. . . *son* (S 7.13–14)

CORD/FORD/FORTH/LORD/SWORD/WORD/WORTH

There are different ways in which this rhyme might be made, depending on whether the vowel is pronounced as in RP 'FORCE' or RP 'NURSE' (Cercignani 1981: 112, 128–9, 192; Kökeritz 1953: 254). See:

accorded. . . re**word**ed (LC 1–3), a double rhyme

afford(s). . .**word**(s) (RL 1105–6; S 79.9–11; S 85.5–7; S 105.10–12)

fords. . . **word**s (RL 1329–30)

forth. . . worth (LC 267–9; S 38.9–11; S 72.13–14; S 103.1–3; VA 416–18)

lords. . . **word**s (RL 1609–10)

record. . . **sword**. . . **word** (RL 1640–3)

swords. . . **word**s (RL 1420–1)

GROVE/JOVE/LOVE/MOVE/PROVE; COVER/HOVER/LOVER/OVER

Ben Jonson's *English Grammar* (1640) records the pronunciation of 'love' and 'prove' with a 'short [. . .] more flat' sound, 'akin to *u*' (*Works*, vol. 2, sig. E4r). Cercignani endorses these as non-eye rhymes, but is more uncertain about the precise vowel sound they share, suggesting that the vowel in 'love' might be lengthened, rather than that in 'prove' shortened (1981: 130–2, 184, 198); Crystal champions the short sound, as in his favoured pronunciations of the 'BLOOD/BROOD' and 'COME/TOMB' clusters (above). See:

ap**prove**. . . **love** (S 70.5–7; S 147.5–7)

ap**prove** her. . . **love** her (S 42.6–8), double rhyme

be**love**d. . . re**move**d (S 25.13–14)

covered. . . hovered. . . **love**red (LC 317–20), double rhyme

grove. . . **love** (VA 865–7)

Jove. . . **love** (RL 568–70)

love. . . **move** (S 47.9–11; VA 433–5)

loveing. . . **move**ing (S 26.9–11), double rhyme

lover. . . over (VA 571–3), double rhyme

love. . . **prove** (S 10.10–12; S 32.13–14; S 39.9–11; S 72.2–4; S 117.13–14; S 136.5–7; S 151.2–4; S 153.5–7; S 154.13–14; VA 38–40; VA 595–7)

love thee. . . **prove** me (S 26.13–14), double rhyme

love. . . **prove**. . . re**move** (RL 611–14)

loved. . . **prove**d (S 116.13–14; VA 608–10)

love. . . re**move** (LC 237–8; S 116.2–4; VA 79–81; VA 185–6) *loving*. . . *removing*. . . *reproving* (RL 240–3), double rhyme

love. . . *reprove* (VA 787–9)

loving. . . *reproving* (S 142.2–4), double rhyme

NOON/SON (S 7.13–14)

This is part of the 'COME/DOOM' cluster, above.

'O' ↔ diphthongs

BOUND/CONFOUND/GROUND/HOUND/ROUND/SWOUND/WOUND

Cercignani (1981: 195–6) and Kökeritz (1953: 246–7) both accept this as a full rhyme, but the evidence is contradictory as to whether the rhyme relies on a diphthong (RP 'MOUTH') or a long vowel (RP 'GOOSE'). See:

bounds. . . *wounds* (VA 265–7)

confound. . . *ground*. . . *wound* (RL 1199–1202)

confounds. . . *sounds*. . . *wounds* (RL 1486–9)

hound. . . *wound* (VA 913–15)

round. . . *wound* (VA 368–70)

sound. . . *wound* (RL 1464–6)

sounding. . . *wounding* (VA 431–2), double rhyme

BOW/BROW/GLOW/GROW/KNOW/MOW

Cercignani (1981: 224) suggests that a full rhyme is possible in Elizabethan English as the vowel sound in 'grow' moves closer to the diphthong in 'brow' (RP 'MOUTH'), although Kökeritz (1953: 245) views this as a traditional (i.e. 'eye') rhyme. See:

bow. . . *know* (VA 14–16)

brow. . . *grow* (VA 139–41)

brow. . . *glow* (VA 337–9)

brow. . . *mow* (S 60.10–12)

COWARD/TOWARD (VA 1157–8), double rhyme

The first, stressed syllable of both words is sounded with a diphthong (Cercignani 1981: 224), as in RP 'MOUTH'.

OURS/PROGENITORS (RL 1756–7)

A full rhyme is possible in Elizabethan pronunciation (Cercignani 1981: 193), sounded either to resemble the vowel sound in RP 'GOOSE' or with a diphthong, as in RP 'MOUTH'.

'U' sounds

BUSHES/RUSHES (VA 629–30)

Cercignani (1981: 125) argues that the rhyme depends on a short '*u*' (RP 'STRUT'); see also Kökeritz (242–3).

COURAGE/FORAGE (VA 554–6), double rhyme

'Forage', deriving from the old French 'furrage', would have been pronounced with the short '*u*' of RP 'STRUT' (Cercignani 1981: 113; Kökeritz 1953: 244).

DULLNESS/FULLNESS (S 56.6–8), a double rhyme

Cercignani (1981: 125) proposes that the rhyme depends on a short '*u*', as with 'bushes/rushes' above.

Other diphthongs

VOICE/JUICE (VA 134–6)

Both Cercignani (1981: 246) and Kökeritz (1953: 217) agree that this is a full rhyme, created by the levelling of the diphthong, so that both words are pronounced to rhyme with RP 'PRICE'.

Consonants

BLISS/IS/KISS/MISS/THIS

In Elizabethan English, these would have been full rhymes, pronounced with '*s*', as in 'miss', rather than '*z*', as in 'rise' (Cercignani 1981: 343–5). This also accounts for the full rhyme NOISE/VOICE (VA 919–21). See:

> *amiss. . .* **is** (S 59.1–3; S 151.1–3)
>
> *bliss. . .* **is. . . kiss** (RL 387–90)
>
> **is. . . kiss** (VA 536–8)
>
> **is. . .** *this* (S 72.9–11; VA 613–15)

DEFACED/RAZED (S 64.1–3)

The ending of both words can be pronounced '*-st*' (Cercignani 1981: 345).

EYES/DESPISE/SUFFICE/SYMPATHISE

The full rhyme probably depends on a '*z*', as in 'rise' (Cercignani 1981: 345). See:

> *eyes. . .* **suffice** (RL 1679–80)
>
> *despised. . .* **suffice**d (S 37.9–11)
>
> **suffice**d. . . *sympathised* (RL 1112–13)

Stresses

The following rhymes all depend on the final syllable of the polysyllabic words being stressed.

AGE/-AGE

See:

    age. . . *equipage* (S 32.10–12)

    age. . . . ***pilgrimage*** (S 7.6–8; RL 960–2)

    age. . . *presage* (S 107.6–8)

    ambassage. . . *vassalage* (S 26.1–3)

    assuage. . . ***pilgrimage*** (RL 790–1)

    marriage. . . *rage*. . . *sage* (RL 219–22); 'marriàge' is trisyllabic in this instance.

-ATE

See:

    advocate. . . ***hate*** (S 35.10–12)

    compassionate. . . *gate* (RL 594–5)

    date. . . *temperate* (S 18.2–4)

    degenerate. . . ***hate***. . . *state* (RL 1003–6)

    estate. . . *inordinate* (RL 92–4)

EDGE/-EGE

    edge. . . *privilege* (S 95.13–14)

Glossary of rhetorical terms

anaphora the repetition of a word or phrase at the beginning of successive clauses (e.g. Son. 66.3–12; *Lucrece*, ll. 981–5).

antanaclasis repetition of the same word, in a different sense (e.g. Son. 78.13: 'thou art all my art'; *Lucrece*, l. 1131: 'So I at each sad strain will strain a tear').

antimetabole a figure in which words are repeated in inverse order (e.g. Son. 53.14: 'you like none, none you'; *Venus and Adonis*, l. 464: 'looks kill love, and love by looks reviveth'). This figure is a specific instance of the more general figure 'chiasmus'.

aposiopesis curtailment of speech, cutting it off before it is properly finished (as at *Lucrece*, ll. 666, 1534, 1716–18).

chiasmus reversal of word order in parallel clauses (e.g. *Venus and Adonis*, l. 108: 'Making my arms his field, his tent my bed'). 'Antimetabole' (see above) is a specific type of chiasmus where the same words are repeated.

chronographia a description of a particular time (e.g. of night, *Lucrece*, ll. 162–8).

correctio where the speaker rejects and corrects a developing idea (e.g. *Venus and Adonis*, l. 937: 'If he be dead – O no, it cannot be').

diacope repetition of a word with one or two in between, often deployed to express deep feeling (e.g. Son. 82.11: 'Thou, truly fair, were truly sympathised').

distinctio an artfully constructed contrast between two things (e.g. 'love' and 'lust' in *Venus and Adonis*, ll. 799–804).

epanalepsis repetition at the end of a clause or line of poetry of word(s) which appeared at the start (e.g. Son. 105.5: 'Kind is my love today, tomorrow kind').

epimone repetition of a phrase or question for emphatic effect (e.g. Son. 66.1, 13: 'Tired with all these').

epistrophe repetition of the final word or words in successive clauses (e.g. *Lucrece*, ll. 582–5).

epizeuxis repetition, without any intervening words (e.g. Son. 43.6: 'form form'; *Venus and Adonis*, ll. 963–4: 'sorrow, / Sorrow').

hendiadys expressing a single idea through the use of two nouns, joined by a conjunction, rather than a noun and an adjective qualifying it (e.g. Son. 61.7: 'shames and idle hours'; *Lucrece*, l. 1317: 'life and feeling').

metonymy reference to someone or something through something associated with it (e.g. the use of 'quill' to indicate 'writer' at Son. 83.7, or the use of Achilles' spear to represent the hero at *Lucrece*, l. 1424).

paradiastole a figure of speech in which something negative is represented positively (e.g. Son. 66.11: 'And simple truth miscalled simplicity'; *Lucrece*, ll. 251–2, where the trope is, in effect, described rather than enacted).

periphrasis circumlocution, expressing something in a roundabout way (e.g. 'thou shrieking harbinger,/ Foul precurrer of the fiend,/ Augur of the fever's end', 'Let the Bird', ll. 5–7).

pleonasm   the use of more words than is necessary to convey the meaning, for emphasis (the figure is related to tautology); typically the meaning of a noun will be repeated in an adjective (e.g. Son. 150.1: 'powerful might'; *Venus and Adonis*, l. 740: 'frenzies wood [mad]'; perhaps *Lucrece*, l. 1337: 'Extremity still urgeth such extremes').

polyptoton   repeating a word in a different grammatical form (e.g. Son. 78.12: 'graces gracèd be'; *Venus and Adonis*, l. 78: 'best is bettered'; *Lucrece*, l. 21: 'nor peer to such a peerless dame').

synecdoche   reference to the whole by naming one of the parts (e.g. the use of 'sail' to indicate 'ship' at Son. 80.6; the pictorial synecdoches of *Lucrece*, ll. 1427–8).

tricolon   a series of three parallel clauses (e.g. *Lover's Complaint*, l. 271: ''gainst rule, 'gainst sense, 'gainst shame').

zeugma   when one part of speech (usually the main verb) governs two or more parts of the sentence (e.g. Son. 55.7: 'Nor Mars his sword, nor war's quick fire shall burn'; *Venus and Adonis*, l. 223: 'Sometime she shakes her head, and then his hand').

Bibliography

Editions of Shakespeare

Quotations from Shakespeare's plays are based on *The Riverside Shakespeare*, ed. G. Blakemore Evans et al. 2nd edn, Boston: Houghton Mifflin, 1997.

Beeching, Henry Charles 1904. *The Sonnets of Shakespeare*. Boston, MA: Ginn & Co

Benson, John 1640. *Poems: Written by Wil. Sh.*

Blakemore Evans, G. 1996. *The Sonnets*. Cambridge: Cambridge UP

Booth, Stephen 1977. *Shakespeare's Sonnets*. New Haven, CT: Yale UP

Boswell, James 1821. *Plays and Poems*, vol. 20. London: F.C. and J. Rivington

Brooke, Tucker 1936. *Shakespeare's Sonnets*. New York: Oxford UP

Bullen, Arthur Henry 1934. *The Works of William Shakespeare*, one-volume edn. Oxford: Basil Blackwell

Burrow, Colin 2002. *Complete Sonnets and Poems*. Oxford: Oxford UP

Capell, Edward. Manuscript annotations in Lintott's reprint of 1609 Quarto of *Shakespeare's Sonnets*, Wren Library, Trinity College, Cambridge. Capell MS 4

Collier, J. P. 1878. *Plays and Poems of William Shakespeare*, vol. 8. London: privately printed

Craig, W. J. 1912. *The Histories and Poems of Shakespeare*, with introductory studies by Edward Dowden. London: Oxford UP

Dover Wilson, John 1966. *The Sonnets*. Cambridge: Cambridge UP

Dowden, Edward 1881. *The Sonnets of William Shakespeare*. London: Kegan Paul

Duncan-Jones, Katherine 1997a. *Shakespeare's Sonnets*. London: Arden, 3rd series

Duncan-Jones, Katherine 2010. *Shakespeare's Sonnets*, 2nd edn. London: Arden, 3rd series

Duncan-Jones, Katherine and Henry Woudhuysen 2007. *Shakespeare's Poems*. London: Arden, 3rd series

Dyce, Alexander 1857. *The Works of William Shakespeare*, vol. 6. London: Edward Moxon

Dyce, Alexander 1866. *The Works of William Shakespeare*, vol. 8. London: Edward Moxon

Gildon, Charles 1710. *The Works of Mr William Shakespeare*, vol. 7 (part of Nicholas Rowe's multi-volume edition). London: E. Curll

Gildon, Charles 1714. *The Works of Mr William Shakespeare*, vol. 9 (part of Nicholas Rowe's multi-volume edition). London: J. Tonson et al.

Hammond, Paul 2012. *Shakespeare's Sonnets, An Original-Spelling Text*. Oxford: Oxford UP

Housman, Robert F. 1835. *A Collection of English Sonnets*. London: Simpkin, Marshall & Co

Hudson, Henry N. 1881. *The Complete Works of William Shakespeare*. Boston, MA: Ginn

Ingram, W. G. and Theodore Redpath 1985. *Shakespeare's Sonnets*, 5th impression with minor amendments. London: Hodder and Stoughton (1st edn 1964)

Kerrigan, John 1986. *The Sonnets and A Lover's Complaint*. Harmondsworth: Penguin

Lintott, Bernard. 1710? *A Collection of Poems [. . .] being all the miscellanies of Mr. William Shakespeare*, 2 vols. London: Bernard Lintott

Malone, Edmond 1780. *Supplement to the Edition of Shakspeare's Plays*. London: C. Bathurst et al.

Malone, Edmond 1790. *Plays and Poems of William Shakspeare*, vol. 10. London: R. C. Rivington et al.

Maxwell, J. C. 1966. *The Poems*. Cambridge: Cambridge UP

Pooler, C. Knox 1927. *Shakespeare's Poems*, 2nd edn. London: Methuen

Pooler, C. Knox 1931. *Sonnets*, revised edn. London: Arden, 2nd series (1st edn 1918)
Porter, Charlotte E. 1912. *Sonnets and Minor Poems*. New York: Thomas Y. Crowell
Prince, F. T. 1960. *The Poems*. London: Arden, 2nd series
Roe, John 1992. *The Poems*. Cambridge: Cambridge UP
Rollins, Hyder E. 1938. *The Poems: A New Variorum Edition of Shakespeare*. Philadelphia: J. B. Lippincott
Rollins, Hyder E. 1944. *The Sonnets, A New Variorum Edition*, 2 vols. Philadelphia: J. B. Lippincott
Rowse, A. L. 1964. *Shakespeare's Sonnets*. London: Macmillan
Sewell, George 1726. *The Poems of Shakespear*. Dublin: George Grierson
Seymour-Smith, Martin 1963. *Shakespeare's Sonnets*. London: Heinemann
Sisson, Charles Jasper 1953. *William Shakespeare: The Complete Works*. London: Odhams P
Tucker, T. G. 1924. *The Sonnets of Shakespeare*. Cambridge: Cambridge UP
Vendler, Helen 1997. *The Art of Shakespeare's Sonnets*. Cambridge, MA: Harvard UP
Wells, Stanley 1985. *Shakespeare's Sonnets and A Lover's Complaint*. Oxford: Clarendon P
Wells, Stanley and Gary Taylor 2005. *The Complete Works*, 2nd edn. Oxford: Clarendon P (1st edn 1986)
Wright, William Aldis 1893. *The Works of William Shakespeare*, vol. 9. London: Macmillan
Wyndham, George 1898. *The Poems of Shakespeare*. London: Methuen

Other primary reading

As far as possible, texts have been cited from editions that would have been available to Shakespeare and his early reader: these primary texts, read in the original or on EEBO, are referenced *in situ* in the notes. The bibliography below lists modern critical editions, cited (i) for their commentary/ supporting material; or (ii) because the nature of the material is best brought together through a critically edited volume (e.g. because it is in manuscript, or because the publishing history is complex, as with the *Mirror for Magistrates* or Samuel Daniel's *Delia*). Where the edition is cited for the commentary, it is cited by the editor, rather than by the author.

Unless otherwise stated, editions of Latin and Greek writers are from the Loeb Classical Library and are not listed by individual volume below.

Alberi, Eugenio (ed.) 1853. *Le relazioni degli ambasciatori veneti al Senato*, serie 1, vol. 3. Florence: Società editrice fiorentina
Augustine 1998. *The City of God against the Pagans*, ed. and trans. R. W. Dyson. Cambridge: Cambridge UP
Bacon, Francis 1985. *The Essayes or Counsels, Civill and Morall*. Oxford: Oxford UP
Baldwin, William et al. 1960. *The Mirror for Magistrates*, ed. Lily B. Campbell. New York: Barnes & Noble
Bate, Jonathan and Eric Rasmussen 2007. *The RSC Shakespeare: Complete Works*. Basingstoke: Palgrave Macmillan
Bible. Unless otherwise stated, the version of the Bible cited is *The Geneva Bible, 1560 Edition*. Peabody, MA: Hendrickson Publishers, 2007, facsimile edn
The Book of Common Prayer 2011. *The Texts of 1549, 1559, and 1662*, ed. Brian Cummings. Oxford: Oxford UP
Brown, Carleton (ed.) 1913. *Poems by Sir John Salusbury and Robert Chester*. Bryn Mawr: Bryn Mawr College Monographs
Chapman, George 1962. *The Poems*, ed. Phyllis Brooks Bartlett. New York: Russell and Russell
Chaucer, Geoffrey 1988. *The Riverside Chaucer*, 3rd edn, ed. Larry D. Benson and F. N. Robinson. Oxford: Oxford UP
Clark, Sandra, ed. 1994. *Amorous Rites: Elizabethan Erotic Narrative Verse*. London: Everyman.
Daniel, Samuel 1592. *Delia and the Complaint of Rosamond*. Unless otherwise stated, this is cited from Arthur Colby Sprague's edition, *Poems and A Defence of Ryme* (Chicago: U of Chicago P, 1965; 1st edn 1930), based on the 1st edition of 1592, containing fifty sonnets (STC² 62432)
Davies, John 1941. *The Poems*, ed. Clare Howard. New York: Columbia UP
Donne, John 2010. *The Complete Poems*, revised edn, ed. Robin Robbins. Harlow: Longman (Annotated English Poets)
Donno, Elizabeth Story, ed. 1963. *Elizabethan Minor Epics*. New York: Routledge
Dusinberre, Juliet (ed.) 2006. *As You Like It*. London: Arden

Ficino, Marsilio 1985. *Commentary on Plato's Symposium on Love*, trans. Sears Jayne. Dallas, TX: Spring Publications

Gorges, Arthur 1953. *The Poems*, ed. Helen Eastbrook Sandison. Oxford: Clarendon P

Grosart, Alexander B. (ed.) 1876a. *Complete Poems of Richard Barnfield*. London: Roxburghe Club

Grosart, Alexander B. (ed.) 1876b. *Complete Poems of Sir John Davies*. London: Chatto and Windus

Grosart, Alexander B. (ed.) 1878. *Robert Chester's 'Loves Martyr, or Rosalins Complaint' (1601)*. London: N. Trubner

Grundy, Joan (ed.) 1960. *The Poems of Henry Constable*. Liverpool: Liverpool UP

Harrison, G. B. (ed.) 2013. *Elizabethan and Jacobean Journals, 1591–1610*, vol. 5. London: Routledge

Hooker, Richard 1977. *The Laws of Ecclesiastical Polity*, in *The Folger Library Edition of the Works of Richard Hooker*, 6 vols, general ed. W. Speed Hill. Cambridge, MA: Harvard UP, vols 1–2

Jerome 1963. *The Letters of St Jerome*, trans. Charles C. Mierow, vol 1. London: Longman

Jerome 1996. *Sancti Eusebii Hieronymi Epistulae, Pars I*, ed. I. Hilberg. Vienna: Austrian Academy of Sciences

Jonson, Ben 2012. *The Works of Ben Jonson*, ed. David Bevington et al. Cambridge: Cambridge UP, 7 vols

Kyd, Thomas 2016. *The Spanish Tragedy*, ed. Michael Neill. New York: Norton

Marlowe, Christopher 1986–. *The Complete Works*, ed. Roma Gill et al. Oxford: Clarendon P, 5 vols

Martindale, Charles and Colin Burrow 1992. 'Clapham's Narcissus: A Pre-Text for *Venus and Adonis*: Text, Translation, Commentary', *English Literary Renaissance* 22: 147–76

Muir, Kenneth 1963. *Life and Letters of Sir Thomas Wyatt*. Liverpool: Liverpool UP

Nashe, Thomas 1904–10. *The Works of Thomas Nashe*, ed. Ronald B. McKerrow. Oxford: Horace Hart (printer to the University), 5 vols

Ovid 2006. *The Metamorphoses*, trans. Arthur Golding, ed. Madeleine Forey. Harmondsworth: Penguin

Parnassus Plays 1949. *The Three Parnassus Plays*, ed. J. B. Leishman. London: Weidenfeld and Nicholson

Petrarch, Francesco 1976. *Petrarch's Lyric Poems*, ed. and trans. Robert M. Durling. Cambridge, MA: Harvard UP

Philostratus 1931. *Imagines*, ed. and trans. A. Fairbanks. Cambridge, MA: Harvard UP

Ralegh, Walter 1999. *The Poems of Sir Walter Raleigh*, ed. Michael Rudick. Tempe, AZ: Renaissance English Text Society

Robbins, R.H. (ed.) 1959. *Historical Poems of the XIVth and XVth Centuries*. New York: Columbia UP

Rollins, Hyder E. (ed.) 1931. *The Phoenix Nest*. Cambridge, MA: Harvard UP

Rollins, Hyder E. (ed.) 1940. *The Passionate Pilgrime by William Shakespeare, 3rd ed. (1612)*, facsimile edn. New York: Charles Scribner's Sons

Scott, William 2013. *The Model of Poesy*, ed. Gavin Alexander. Cambridge: Cambridge UP

Sidney, Philip 1962. *The Poems*, ed. William A. Ringler. Oxford: Clarendon P

Sidney, Philip 2004. *The Defence of Poesy*, in Gavin Alexander (ed.), *'The Defence of Poesy' and Selected Renaissance Literary Criticism*. Harmondsworth: Penguin

Spenser, Edmund 1989. *The Yale Edition of the Shorter Poems of Edmund Spenser*, ed. William Oram et al. New Haven, CT: Yale UP

Spenser, Edmund 2001. *The Faerie Queene*, ed. A. C. Hamilton and Yamashita Toshiyuki Susuki, revised edn. Harlow: Pearson (Annotated English Poets)

Tottel's Miscellany 1966, ed. Hyder E. Rollins, 2 vols, revised edn. Cambridge, MA: Harvard UP

Whythorne, Thomas 1962. *The Autobiography. Modern Spelling Edition*, ed. James M. Osborn. London: Oxford UP

Wright, Louis B. (ed.) 1962. *Advice to a Son: Precepts of Lord Burghley, Sir Walter Raleigh, and Francis Osborne*. Ithaca, NY: Cornell UP

Wyatt, Thomas 1969. *Collected Poems*, ed. Kenneth Muir and Patrician Thomson. Liverpool: Liverpool UP

Other works cited

Abbott, Edwin A. 1884. *A Shakespearian Grammar*, revised edn. London: Macmillan

Abrams, Richard 1996. 'W[illiam] S[hakespeare's] "Funeral Elegy" and the Turn from the Theatrical', *Studies in English Literature, 1500–1900* 36: 435–60

Adamson, Sylvia et al. 2001. *Reading Shakespeare's Dramatic Language: A Guide*. London: Arden

Alden, Raymond MacDonald 1916. 'The 1640 Text of Shakespeare's Sonnets', *Modern Philology* 14: 17–30

Arber, Edward 1875–94. *A Transcript of the Registers of the Stationers of London, 1564–1640*, 5 vols. London: privately printed

Axton, Marie 1977. *The Queen's Two Bodies: Drama and the Elizabethan Succession*. London: Royal Historical Society

Baker, David 1998. 'Cavalier Shakespeare: The 1640 *Poems* of John Benson', *Studies in Philology* 95: 152–73

Baldwin, T. W. 1950. *On the Literary Genetics of Shakspeare's Poems and Sonnets*. Urbana: U of Illinois P

Bate, Jonathan 1993. *Shakespeare and Ovid*. Oxford: Oxford UP

Bates, Catherine 2013. *Masculinity and the Hunt: Wyatt to Spenser*. Oxford: Oxford UP

Bates, Ronald 1955. 'Shakespeare's "Phoenix and the Turtle"', *Shakespeare Quarterly* 6: 19–30

Bednarz, James P. 2012. *Shakespeare and the Truth of Love: The Mystery of 'The Phoenix and the Turtle'*. Basingstoke: Palgrave Macmillan

Blake, N. F. 1998. 'Shakespeare's Sonnet 69', *Notes and Queries* 243: 355–7

Blake, N. F. 2002. *A Grammar of Shakespeare's Language*. Basingstoke: Palgrave Macmillan

Bland, Mark 2000. '"As far from all revolt": Sir John Salusbury, Christ Church MS 184, and Ben Jonson's First Ode', *English Manuscript Studies* 8: 43–78

Bloom, J. Harvey 1906. *English Seals*. London: Methuen

Borukhov, Boris 2009. 'Was the Author of *Love's Martyr* Chester of Royston?' *Notes and Queries* 56: 77–81

Bradbrook, Muriel C. 1936. *The School of Night: A Study in the Literary Relationships of Sir Walter Ralegh*. Cambridge: Cambridge UP

Bradbrook, Muriel C. 1951. *Shakespeare and Elizabethan Poetry: A Study of his Earlier Work in Relation to the Poetry of the Time*. London: Chatto & Windus

Buxton, John 1980. '"Two dead birds": A Note on *The Phoenix and Turtle*', in John Carey and Helen Peters (eds), *English Renaissance Studies Presented to Dame Helen Gardner*. Oxford: Clarendon P, 44–55

Campbell, Gordon 1999. 'Shakespeare and the Youth of Milton', *Milton Quarterly* 33: 95–105

Campbell, K. T. S. 1970. '"The Phoenix and the Turtle" as a Signpost of Shakespeare's Development', *British Journal of Aesthetics* 10: 169–79

Carter, Sarah 2011. *Ovidian Myth and Sexual Deviance in Early Modern English Literature*. Basingstoke: Palgrave Macmillan.

Caveney, Geoffrey 2015. '"Mr. W. H.": Stationer William Holme (d. 1607)', *Notes and Queries* 62: 120–4

Cercignani, Fausto 1981. *Shakespeare's Works and Elizabethan Pronunciation*. Oxford: Clarendon P

Cheney, Patrick 2008. *Shakespeare's Literary Authorship*. Cambridge: Cambridge UP

Connor, Francis X. 2012. 'More Press Corrections in *Lucrece* (1594)', *Notes and Queries*, 59: 530–1

Constable, John 1989. 'The Phoenix and the Turtle: "Either was the Other's Mine" – a New Reading', *Notes and Queries* 36: 327

Copland, Murray 1965. 'The Dead Phoenix', *Essays in Criticism* 15: 279–87

Cormack, Bradin 2009. 'On Will: Time and Voluntary Action in *Coriolanus* and the *Sonnets*', *Shakespeare* 5: 253–70

Crystal, David 2005. *Pronouncing Shakespeare*. Cambridge: Cambridge UP

Crystal, David 2011. *Original Pronunciation*, http://originalpronunciation.com/ [accessed 21/9/2015]

Crystal, David 2016. *The Oxford Dictionary of Original Shakespearean Pronunciation*. Oxford: Oxford UP

Culhane, Peter 2004. 'Livy in Elizabethan and Early Jacobean Literature'. PhD Dissertation, University of Cambridge

Cunningham, J. V. 1952. '"Essence" and the *Phoenix and Turtle*', *English Literary History* 19: 265–76

Davies, H. Neville 1995. '*The Phoenix and Turtle*: Requiem and Rite', *Review of English Studies* 46: 525–30

Dawson, Giles E. 1971. 'John Payne Collier's Great Forgery', *Studies in Bibliography* 24: 1–26

De Grazia, Margreta 2000. 'The Scandal of Shakespeare's Sonnets', in James Schiffer (ed.), *Shakespeare's Sonnets: Critical Essays*. New York: Garland, 89–112. First printed in *Shakespeare Survey* 47 (1994): 35–49

Dent, R. W. 1981. *Shakespeare's Proverbial Language: An Index*. Berkeley: U of California P

Donaldson, Ian 1982. *The Rapes of Lucretia: A Myth and Its Transformations*. Oxford: Oxford UP

Dover Wilson, John 1963. *An Introduction to the Sonnets of Shakespeare*. Cambridge: Cambridge UP

Dover Wilson, John 1967. 'Bibliographical Links between the Three Pages and the Good Quartos', in W. W. Greg (ed.), *Shakespeare's Hand in 'The Play of Sir Thomas More'*. Cambridge: Cambridge UP, 113–41

Dubrow, Heather 1987. *Captive Victors: Shakespeare's Narrative Poems and Sonnets*. Ithaca, NY: Cornell UP

Dubrow, Heather 1996. '"Uncertainties now crown themselves assur'd": The Politics of Plotting Shakespeare's Sonnets', *Shakespeare Quarterly* 47: 291–305

Duncan-Jones, Katherine 1983. 'Was the 1609 *Shake-speares Sonnets* Really Unauthorized?' *Review of English Studies* 34: 151–71

Duncan-Jones, Katherine 1993. 'Much Ado with Red and White: The Earliest Readers of Shakespeare's *Venus and Adonis*', *Review of English Studies* 44: 479–501

Duncan-Jones, Katherine 1997b. 'Who Wrote *A Funerall Elegie?*' *Shakespeare Studies* 25: 192–210

Duncan-Jones, Katherine 2001a. 'Ravished and Revised: The 1616 *Lucrece*', *Review of English Studies* 52: 516–23

Duncan-Jones, Katherine 2001b. *Ungentle Shakespeare: Scenes from his Life.* London: Arden

Elliott, W. E. Y. and R. J. Valenza 1997. 'Glass Slippers and Seven-League Boots: C-Prompted Doubts about Ascribing *A Funeral Elegy* and *A Lover's Complaint* to Shakespeare', *Shakespeare Quarterly* 48: 177–207

Ellrodt, Robert 1962. 'An Anatomy of "The Phoenix and the Turtle"', *Shakespeare Survey* 15: 99–110

Elton, G. R. (ed.) 1982. *The Tudor Constitution: Documents and Commentary*, 2nd edn. Cambridge: Cambridge UP

Eriksen, Roy T. 1981. '"Un certo amoroso martire": Shakespeare's "The Phoenix and the Turtle" and Giordano Bruno's *De gli eroici furori*', *Spenser Studies* 2: 193–215

Erne, Lukas 2013. *Shakespeare and the Book Trade.* Cambridge: Cambridge UP

Erne, Lukas and Tamsin Badcoe 2014. 'Shakespeare and the Popularity of Poetry Books in Print, 1583–1622', *Review of English Studies* 65: 33–57

Everett, Barbara 2001. '"Set upon a golden bough to sing": Shakespeare's Debt to Sidney in "The Phoenix and Turtle"', *TLS* 5107 (16 Feb): 13–15

Farr, Henry 1923. 'Shakespeare's Printers and Publishers, with Special Reference to the Poems and *Hamlet*', *The Library* 4th series, 3: 223–50

Fineman, Joel 1986. *Shakespeare's Perjured Eye: The Invention of Poetic Subjectivity in the Sonnets.* Berkeley: U of California P

Finnis, John and Andrew Martin 2003. 'Another Turn for the Turtle', *TLS* 5220 (18 April): 12–14

Fleissner, Robert F. 1980. 'The Case of the Embarrassing Lacuna: A Textual Approach to the W.H. Mystery', *Res Publica Litterarum* 3: 17–27

Foster, Donald W. 1987a. 'Mr W.H. RIP', *Proceedings of the Modern Language Association* 102: 42–54

Foster, Donald W. 1987b. '"Shall I Die" Post Mortem: Defining Shakespeare', *Shakespeare Quarterly* 38: 58–77

Foster, Donald W. 1989. *Elegy by W.S.: A Study in Attribution.* Newark: U of Delaware P

Foster, Donald W. 1999. '"The gift is small, / The will is all": Musings for Jay Halio', in Lois Potter and Arthur Kinney (eds), *Shakespeare, Text and Theater: Essays in Honor of Jay L. Halio.* Newark: U of Delaware P, 92–106

Fripp, E. I. 1938. *Shakespeare, Man and Artist*, 2 vols. Oxford: Oxford UP

Garber, Marjorie 1984. 'Two Birds with One Stone: Lapidary Re-inscription in *The Phoenix and Turtle*', *Upstart Crow* 5: 5–19

Gombrich, E. H. 1960. *Art and Illusion: A Study in the Psychology of Pictorial Representation.* London: Phaidon

Graves, Robert and Laura Riding 1949. 'A Study in Original Punctuation and Spelling', in Graves, *The Common Asphodel: Collected Essays on Poetry, 1922–1949.* London: Hamish Hamilton, 84–95

Graziani, René 1984. 'The numbering of Shakespeare's Sonnets: 12, 60, and 126', *Shakespeare Quarterly* 35: 79–82

Gurr, Andrew 1971. 'Shakespeare's First Poem: Sonnet 145', *Essays in Criticism* 21: 221–6

Hackett, Helen 2012. '"As the Diall Hand Tells Ore": The Case for Dekker, Not Shakespeare, as Author', *Review of English Studies* 63: 34–57

Halliday, F. E. 1964. *A Shakespearean Companion, 1564–1964.* Harmondsworth: Penguin

Halliwell, James O. 1848. *The Life of William Shakespeare.* London: John Russell Smith

Hammond, Gerald 1981. *The Reader and Shakespeare's Young Man Sonnets.* London: Macmillan

Hammond, Paul 2002. *Figuring Sex between Men from Shakespeare to Rochester.* Oxford: Clarendon P

Hammond, Paul 2008. 'A Textual Crux in Shakespeare's Sonnet 46', *Notes and Queries*, n.s. 55: 187–8

Harbage, Alfred 1950. 'Dating Shakespeare's Sonnets', *Shakespeare Quarterly* 1: 57–63

Harrison, Thomas P. 1951. '*Love's Martyr* by Robert Chester: A New Interpretation', *Texas Studies in English* 30: 66–85

Hattaway, Michael 2009. 'Dating *As You Like It*, Epilogues and Prayers, and the Problems of "As the Dial Hand Tells O'er"', *Shakespeare Quarterly* 60: 154–67

Heal, Felicity 2003. *The Reformation in Britain and Ireland*. Oxford: Oxford UP

Hieatt, A. K., et al. 1987. 'Shakespeare's Rare Words: "Lover's Complaint", *Cymbeline*, and Sonnets', *Notes and Queries*, n.s. 34: 219–24

Hill, Geoffrey 1984. *The Lords of Limit: Essays on Literature and Ideas*. London: Deutsch

Hobbs, Mary 1992. *Early Seventeenth-Century Verse Miscellany Manuscripts*. Aldershot: Scolar

Honigmann, E. A. J. 1985. *Shakespeare: The Lost Years*. Manchester: Manchester UP

Hope, Jonathan 2003. *Shakespeare's Grammar*. London: Arden

Hotson, Leslie 1949. *Shakespeare's Sonnets Dated and Other Essays*. Oxford: Oxford UP

Hulse, Clark 1978. 'Shakespeare's Myth of *Venus and Adonis*', *PMLA* 93: 95–105

Hulse, Clark 1981. *Metamorphic Verse: The Elizabethan Minor Epic*. Princeton, NJ: Princeton UP

Hume, Anthea 1989. '*Love's Martyr*, "The Phoenix and the Turtle", and the Aftermath of the Essex Rebellion', *Review of English Studies* 40: 48–71

Hutton, James 1941. 'Analogues of Shakespeare's Sonnets 153–4: Contributions to the History of a Theme', *Modern Philology* 38: 385–403

Hyland, Peter 2003. *An Introduction to Shakespeare's Poems*. Basingstoke: Palgrave Macmillan

Jackson, MacDonald P. 1972. 'Shakespeare's "Sonnets", "Parthenophil and Parthenophe", and "A Lover's Complaint"', *Notes and Queries* 217: 125–6

Jackson, MacDonald P. 1975. 'Punctuation and the Compositors of Shakespeare's *Sonnets*, 1609', *The Library*, fifth series, 30: 1–24

Jackson, MacDonald P. 1990. 'How Many Horses has Sonnet 51? Textual and Literary Criticism in Shakespeare's Sonnets', *English Language Notes* 27: 10–19

Jackson, MacDonald P. 1999a. 'Aspects of Organisation in *Shakespeare's Sonnets*', *Parergon* 17: 109–34

Jackson, MacDonald P. 1999b. 'Rhymes in Shakespeare's Sonnets: Evidence of Date of Composition', *Notes and Queries* 244: 213–19

Jackson, MacDonald P. 2001. 'Vocabulary and Chronology: The Case of Shakespeare's Sonnets', *Review of English Studies* 52: 59–75

Jackson, MacDonald P. 2005. 'Francis Meres and the Cultural Context of Shakespeare's Rival Poet Sonnets', *Review of English Studies* 56: 224–46

Jackson, MacDonald P. 2008. '*A Lover's Complaint*, *Cymbeline*, and the Shakespeare Canon: Interpreting Shared Vocabulary', *Modern Language Review* 103: 621–38

Jackson, MacDonald P. 2014. *Determining the Shakespeare Canon: Arden of Faversham and A Lover's Complaint*. Oxford: Oxford UP

Janakiram, Alur 1980. 'Leone Ebreo and Shakespeare: Love and Reason in *Dialoghi D'Amore* and "The Phoenix and the Turtle"', *English Studies* 61: 224–35

Jones, Norman 1989. *God and the Moneylenders: Usury and the Law in Early Modern England*. Oxford: Basil Blackwell

Kermode, Frank 2000. *Shakespeare's Language*. Harmondsworth: Penguin

Kerrigan, John 1991. *Motives of Woe: Shakespeare and "Female Complaint": A Critical Anthology*. Oxford: Clarendon P

Kiernan, Pauline 1995. 'Death by Rhetorical Trope: Poetry Metamorphosed in *Venus and Adonis* and the Sonnets', *Review of English Studies* 46: 475–501

Knight, G. Wilson 1955. *The Mutual Flame: On Shakespeare's Sonnets and 'The Phoenix and the Turtle'*. London: Methuen

Knight, Jeffrey Todd 2009. 'Making Shakespeare's Books: Assembly and Intertextuality in the Archives', *Shakespeare Quarterly* 60: 304–40

Kökeritz, Helge 1953. *Shakespeare's Pronunciation*. New Haven: Yale UP

Langley, Eric 2009. *Narcissism and Suicide in Shakespeare and His Contemporaries*. Oxford: Oxford UP

Le Grand Robert de la Langue Française 2001. Paris: Dictionnaire le Robert, 12th edn, 6 vols

Lewis, C. S. 1980. *Poetry and Prose in the Sixteenth Century*. Oxford: Oxford UP. Published in 1954 as *English Literature in Sixteenth Century Excluding Drama*

Lyne, Raphael 2001. *Ovid's Changing Worlds: English Metamorphoses 1567–1632*. Oxford: Oxford UP

Lyne, Raphael 2014. 'Thinking in Stanzas: *Venus and Adonis* and *The Rape of Lucrece*', in Elizabeth Scott-Baumann and Ben Burton (eds), *The Work of Form: Poetics and Materiality in Early Modern Culture*. Oxford: Oxford UP, 88–103

McCoy, Richard C. 1997. 'Love's Martyrs: Shakespeare's "The Phoenix and Turtle" and the Sacrificial Sonnets', in Claire McEachern and Deborah Shuger (eds), *Religion and Culture in Renaissance England*. Cambridge: Cambridge UP, 188–208

McGee, John 2012. 'Shakespeare's Narcissus: Omnipresent Love in *Venus and Adonis*', *Shakespeare Survey* 63: 272–81

McLeod, Randall 1981. 'Unemending Shakespeare's Sonnet 111', *Studies in English Literature* 21: 75–96

McLeod, Randall 1991 (writing as Random Clod). 'Information upon Information', *Text: Transactions of the Society for Textual Scholarship* 5: 241–78

McLung Evans, Willa 1936. 'Lawes's Version of Shakespeare's Sonnet CXVI', *Proceedings of the Modern Language Association* 51: 120–2

McMillan, Douglas J. 1972. 'The Phoenix in the Western World from Herodotus to Shakespeare', *D. H. Lawrence Review* 5: 238–67

Mahood, M. M. 1957. *Shakespeare's Wordplay*. London: Methuen

Marotti, Arthur F. 1990. 'Shakespeare's Sonnets as Literary Property', in Elizabeth D. Harvey and Katharine Eisaman Maus (eds), *Soliciting Interpretation: Literary Theory and Seventeenth-Century Poetry*. Chicago: U of Chicago P, 143–73

Marotti, Arthur F. 2008. 'Humphrey Coningsby and the Personal Anthologizing of Verse in Elizabethan England' in Michael Denbo (ed.), *New Ways of Looking at Old Texts IV*. Tempe, AZ: Renaissance English Text Society, 71–102

Marotti, Arthur F. 2010. 'Shakespeare's Sonnets and the Manuscript Circulation of Texts in Early Modern England', in Michael Schoenfeldt (ed.), *A Companion to Shakespeare's Sonnets*. Oxford: Blackwell, paperback edn., 185–203

Matchett, William H. 1965. *'The Phoenix and the Turtle': Shakespeare's Poem and Chester's 'Love Martyr'*. The Hague: Mouton

Minto, William 1874. *Characteristics of English Poets from Chaucer to Shirley*. Edinburgh: W. Blackwood

Monsarrat, G. D. 2002. '"A Funeral Elegy": Ford, W.S., and Shakespeare', *Review of English Studies* 53: 186–203

Mortimer, Anthony 2000. *Variable Passions: A Reading of Shakespeare's 'Venus and Adonis'*. New York: AMS Press

Moss, Ann 1982. *Ovid in Renaissance France: A Survey of the Latin Editions of Ovid and Commentaries Published before 1600*. London: The Warburg Institute

Moss, Daniel D. 2014. *The Ovidian Vogue: Literary Fashion and Imitative Practice in Late Elizabethan England*. Toronto: U of Toronto P

Oakeshott, Walter 1975. *'Love's Martyr'*, *Huntington Library Quarterly* 39: 29–49

Parker, Patricia 2007. 'Hysteron proteron: or the preposterous', in Sylvia Adamson et al. (eds), *Renaissance Figures of Speech*. Cambridge: Cambridge UP, 133–45

Partridge, Eric 1990. *Shakespeare's Bawdy*, 3rd edn. New York: Routledge

Petronella, Vincent 1975. 'Shakespeare's *The Phoenix and Turtle* and the Defunctive Music of Ecstasy', *Shakespeare Studies* 8: 311–31

Porter, Roy 1999. *The Greatest Benefit to Mankind: A Medical History of Humanity*. New York: W. W. Norton

Prynne, J.H. 2001. *They That Haue Powre to Hurt; A Specimen of a Commentary on Shakes-peares Sonnets, 94*. Cambridge: privately printed

Ricks, Christopher 2003. 'Shakespeare and the Anagram', *Proceedings of the British Academy* 121: 111–46

Ringler, William A. and Steven W. May 1972. 'An Epilogue Possibly by Shakespeare', *Modern Philology* 70: 138–9

Robbins, R. H. A. 1967. 'A Seventeenth-Century Manuscript of Shakespeare's Sonnet 128', *Notes & Queries* 212: 137–8

Roberts, Sasha 2003. *Reading Shakespeare's Poems in Early Modern England*. Basingstoke: Palgrave Macmillan

Rowse, A. L. 1965. 'Eminent Henrician: Part One. Thomas Wriothesley, First Earl of Southampton', *History Today* 15: 382–90

Rowse, A. L. 1973. *Shakespeare's Sonnets: The Problems Solved*. London: Macmillan

Schmidt, Alexander 1902. *Shakespeare Lexicon*, revised by Gregor Sarazin, 2 vols. Berlin: Georg Reimer

Schoenbaum, Samuel 1978. *A Compact Documentary Life*. Oxford: Oxford UP

Schwartz, Elias 1969. 'Shakespeare's Dead Phoenix', *English Language Notes* 7: 25–32

Scott, Janet 1929. *Les Sonnets élisabéthains: les sources et l'apport personnel*. Paris: H. Champion

Shahani, Ranjee G. 1946. 'The Phoenix and the Turtle', *Notes and Queries* 191: 99–101

Shapiro, James 2005. *A Year in the Life of William Shakespeare: 1599*. New York: Harper Collins

Shrank, Cathy 2008. '"Matters of love as of discourse": the English Sonnet, 1560–1580', *Studies in Philology* 105: 30–49

Shrank, Cathy 2009. 'Reading Shakespeare's Sonnets: John Benson and the 1640 *Poems*', *Shakespeare* 5: 271–91

Skinner, Quentin 2014. *Forensic Shakespeare*. Oxford: Oxford UP

Smith, Helen 2010. 'The Publishing Trade in Shakespeare's Time', in Andrew Murphy (ed.), *A Concise Companion to Shakespeare and the Text*. Oxford: Blackwell, 17–34

Sokol, B. J. and Mary Sokol 2000. *Shakespeare's Legal Language: A Dictionary*. London: Athlone P

Southam, B. C. 1960. 'Shakespeare's Christian Sonnet? Number 146', *Shakespeare Quarterly* 11: 67–71

Strong, Roy C. 1963. *Portraits of Queen Elizabeth*. Oxford: Clarendon P

Strype, John 1705. *The Life of the Learned Sir John Cheke*. London: John Wyat

Swinburne, Arthur 1894. *Studies in Prose and Poetry*. London: Chatto & Windus

Tarlinskaja, Marina 2004. 'The Verse of *A Lover's Complaint*: Not Shakespeare', in Brian Boyd (ed.), *Words That Count: Early Modern Authorship: Essays in Honor of MacDonald P. Jackson*. Newark: U of Delaware P, 141–60

Taylor, Anthony Brian 1994/5. 'Melting Earth and Leaping Bulls: Shakespeare's Ovid and Arthur Golding', *Connotations* 4: 192–206

Taylor, Archer 1931. *The Proverb*. Cambridge, MA: Harvard UP

Taylor, Gary 1985a. 'Shakespeare's New Poem', *New York Times Book Review*, 15 December

Taylor, Gary 1985b. 'Some Manuscripts of Shakespeare's Sonnets', *Bulletin of the John Rylands Library* 68: 210–46

Thirsk, Joan 1990. 'Enclosing and Engrossing', in J. Thirsk (ed.), *The Agrarian History of England and Wales: Volume 3, Agricultural Change: Policy and Practice, 1500–1750*. Cambridge: Cambridge UP, 200–55

Thomas, Vivian and Nicki Faircloth 2014. *Shakespeare's Plants and Gardens: A Dictionary*. London: Bloomsbury Arden Shakespeare

Tilley, Morris Palmer 1950. *A Dictionary of the Proverbs in England in the Sixteenth and Seventeenth Centuries*. Ann Arbor: U of Michigan P

Underwood, Richard Allan 1974. *Shakespeare's 'The Phoenix and Turtle': A Survey of Scholarship*. Salzburg: Institut für Englische Sprache und Literatur

Vickers, Brian 1989. *Returning to Shakespeare*. London: Routledge

Vickers, Brian 1996. 'Whose Thumbprints? A More Plausible Author for "A Funeral Elegy"', *TLS* 4849 (8 March): 16–18

Vickers, Brian 2002. *Counterfeiting Shakespeare: Evidence, Authorship, and John Ford's* Funerall Elegye. Cambridge: Cambridge UP

Vickers, Brian 2007. *Shakespeare,* A Lover's Complaint, *and John Davies of Hereford*. Cambridge: Cambridge UP

Walker, William Sidney 1860. *A Critical Examination of the Text of Shakespeare*. London: John Russell Smith

Wallace, Joseph 2012. 'Strong Stomachs: Arthur Golding, Ovid, and Cultural Assimilation', *Renaissance Studies* 26: 728–43

Weaver, William 2012. *Untutored Lines: The Making of the English Epyllion*. Oxford: Oxford UP

Wells, J. C. 1982. *Accents of English*. Cambridge: Cambridge UP, 3 vols

Williams, Gordon 1994. *A Dictionary of Sexual Language and Imagery in Shakespearean and Stuart Literature*. London: Athlone P

Williams, Gordon 1997. *A Glossary of Shakespeare's Sexual Language*. London: Athlone P

Williams, Gwyn 1981–2. 'Shakespeare's Phoenix', *National Library of Wales Journal* 22: 277–81

Withington, Phil 2010. *Society in Early Modern England: The Vernacular Origins of Some Powerful Ideas*. Cambridge: Polity

Wong, A. T. 2013. 'Sir Philip Sidney and the Humanist Poetry of Kissing', *Sidney Journal* 31: 1–30

Woodbridge, Linda 1991. 'Palisading the Elizabethan Body Politic', *Texas Studies in Literature and Language* 33: 327–54.

Wright, Joseph 1905. *English Dialect Dictionary*. Oxford: Oxford UP

Yates, Frances A. 1947. 'Queen Elizabeth as Astraea', *Journal of the Warburg and Courtauld Institutes* 10: 27–82

Young, Henry McClure 1937. *The Sonnets of Shakespeare: A Psycho-sexual Analysis*. Menasha, WI: G. Banta

Zurcher, Andrew 2010. *Shakespeare and Law*. London: Arden Shakespeare

Index of first lines and titles

A woman's face with Nature's own hand painted
(Sonnet 20) 329
Accuse me thus: that I have scanted all
(Sonnet 117) 535
Against my love shall be as I am now
(Sonnet 63) 421
Against that time (if ever that time come)
(Sonnet 49) 389
Ah, wherefore with infection should he live
(Sonnet 67) 431
Alack, what poverty my Muse brings forth
(Sonnet 103) 507
Alas 'tis true, I have gone here and there (Sonnet
110) 521
As a decrepit father takes delight (Sonnet 37) 365
As an unperfect actor on the stage (Sonnet 23) 337
As fast as thou shalt wane, so fast thou grow'st
(Sonnet 11) 311
As it fell upon a day (PP 20) 711
As the dial hand tells o'er 745
Ask who lies here but do not weep (Stanley tomb,
east) 737

Be wise as thou art cruel; do not press
(Sonnet 140) 589
Beauty is but a vain and doubtful good (PP 13) 701
Being your slave, what should I do but tend
(Sonnet 57) 409
Beshrew that heart that makes my heart to groan
(Sonnet 133) 573
Betwixt mine eye and heart a league is took
(Sonnet 47) 383
But be contented when that fell arrest
(Sonnet 74) 445
But do thy worst to steal thyself away
(Sonnet 92) 483
But wherefore do not you a mightier way
(Sonnet 16) 321

Canst thou, O cruel, say I love thee not
(Sonnet 149) 611
Clouds blot the heaven and make me flatter
(manuscript) 727

Crabbed age and youth cannot live together
(PP 12) 701
Crowns have their compass, length of days their
date 744
Cupid laid by his brand and fell asleep
(Sonnet 153) 619

Devouring Time, blunt thou the lion's paws
(Sonnet 19) 327
Did not the heavenly rhetoric of thine eye
(PP 3) 695

Even as the sun with purple-coloured face
(Venus and Adonis) 11

Fair is my love, but not so fair as fickle
(PP 7) 697
Fair was the morn, when the fair queen of love
(PP 9) 699
Farewell, thou art too dear for my possessing
(Sonnet 87) 473
For shame deny that thou bear'st love to any
(Sonnet 10) 309
From fairest creatures we desire increase
(Sonnet 1) 283
From off a hill whose concave womb reworded
(A Lover's Complaint) 631
From the besiegèd Ardea all in post
(Lucrece) 117
From you have I been absent in the spring
(Sonnet 98) 497
Full many a glorious morning have I seen
(Sonnet 33) 357

Good friend, for Jesu's sake forbear 745
Good night, good rest, ah, neither be my share
(PP 14) 701

Here lies Ben Jonson 744
How can I then return in happy plight
(Sonnet 28) 347
How can my Muse want subject to invent
(Sonnet 38) 367

How careful was I, when I took my way
  (Sonnet 48) 387
How heavy do I journey on the way
  (Sonnet 50) 391
How like a winter hath my absence been
  (Sonnet 97) 495
How oft, when thou, dear dearest, music play'st
  (Sonnet 128, manuscript) 726
How oft, when thou, my music, music play'st
  (Sonnet 128) 561
How sweet and lovely dost thou make the shame
  (Sonnet 95) 491
Howe'er he lived judge not 743

I grant thou wert not married to my Muse
  (Sonnet 82) 461
I never saw that you did painting need
  (Sonnet 83) 463
If love make me forsworn, how shall I swear to
  love? (PP 5) 695
If music and sweet poetry agree (PP 8) 697
If my dear love were but the child of state
  (Sonnet 124) 549
If that the world and love were young
  (PP 19.ii, 'Love's answer') 711
If the dull substance of my flesh were thought
  (Sonnet 44) 379
If there be nothing new, but that which is
  (Sonnet 59) 413
If thou survive my well-contented day
  (Sonnet 32) 355
If thy soul check thee that I come so near
  (Sonnet 136) 581
In faith, I do not love thee with mine eyes
  (Sonnet 141) 591
In laudem Musici (Sonnet 8, manuscript) 723
In loving thee thou know'st I am forsworn
  (Sonnet 152) 617
In the old age black was not counted fair
  (Sonnet 127) 557
Is it for fear to wet a widow's eye (Sonnet 9) 307
Is it thy will thy image should keep open
  (Sonnet 61) 417
It was a lording's daughter, the fairest one of three
  (PP 15) 705

Let me confess that we two must be twain
  (Sonnet 36) 363
Let me not to the marriage of true minds
  (Sonnet 116) 533
Let not my love be called idolatry (Sonnet 105) 511
Let the bird of loudest lay (aka *The Phoenix and the
  Turtle*) 261
Let those who are in favour with their stars
  (Sonnet 25) 341
Like as the waves make towards the pebbled shore
  (Sonnet 60) 415

Like as to make our appetites more keen
  (Sonnet 118) 537
Live with me and be my love (PP 19.i) 711
Lo, as a careful housewife runs to catch
  (Sonnet 143) 595
Lo, in the orient when the gracious light
  (Sonnet 7) 303
Look in thy glass and tell the face thou viewest
  (Sonnet 3) 289
Lord of my love, to whom in vassalage
  (Sonnet 26) 343
Love is my sin, and thy dear virtue hate
  (Sonnet 142) 593
Love is too young to know what conscience is
  (Sonnet 151) 615
A Lover's Complaint 625
Lucrece 105

Mine eye and heart are at a mortal war
  (Sonnet 46) 383
Mine eye hath played the painter and hath stelled
  (Sonnet 24) 339
Music to hear, why hear'st thou music sadly?
  (Sonnet 8) 305; manuscript 723
My flocks feed not, my ewes breed not
  (PP 17) 705
My glass shall not persuade me I am old
  (Sonnet 22) 335
My love is as a fever, longing still (Sonnet 147) 607
My love is strengthened, though more weak in
  seeming (Sonnet 102) 505
My mistress' eyes are nothing like the sun (Sonnet
  130) 567
My tongue-tied Muse in manners holds her still
  (Sonnet 85) 467

No longer mourn for me when I am dead
  (Sonnet 71) 439
No more be grieved at that which thou hast done
  (Sonnet 35) 361
No! Time, thou shalt not boast that I do change
  (Sonnet 123) 547
Not from the stars do I my judgement pluck
  (Sonnet 14) 317
Not marble, nor the gilded monuments
  (Sonnet 55) 403
Not mine own fears nor the prophetic soul
  (Sonnet 107) 515
Not monumental stone preserves our fame
  (Stanley tomb, west) 738

O call not me to justify the wrong
  (Sonnet 139) 587
O for my sake do you with Fortune chide
  (Sonnet 111) 523
O, from what power hast thou this powerful might
  (Sonnet 150) 613

O how I faint when I of you do write
(Sonnet 80) 457

O, how much more doth beauty beauteous seem
(Sonnet 54) 401

O how thy worth with manners may I sing
(Sonnet 39) 369

O lest the world should task you to recite
(Sonnet 72) 441

O me! what eyes hath love put in my head
(Sonnet 148) 609

O never say that I was false of heart (Sonnet 109)
519

O that you were yourself; but, love, you are
(Sonnet 13) 315

O thou, my lovely boy, who in thy power
(Sonnet 126) 553

O truant Muse, what shall be thy amends
(Sonnet 101) 503

On a day (alack the day) (*PP* 16) 705

On his mistress' beauty (Sonnet 106, manuscript) 724

Or I shall live your epitaph to make (Sonnet 81) 459

Or whether doth my mind, being crowned with
you (Sonnet 114) 529

The Passionate Pilgrim 685

The Phoenix and the Turtle, i.e. Let the Bird of
Loudest Lay, 261

Poor soul, the centre of my sinful earth
(Sonnet 146) 603

The Rape of Lucrece 105

Say that thou didst forsake me for some fault
(Sonnet 89) 477

Scarce had the sun dried up the dewy morn
(*PP* 6) 697

Shakespeare's Sonnets 269

Self-blinding error seizeth all those minds
(Sonnet 116, manuscript) 725

Shall I compare thee to a summer's day?
(Sonnet 18) 325

Shall I die, shall I fly 739

Sin of self-love possesseth all mine eye
(Sonnet 62) 419

Since brass, nor stone, nor earth, nor boundless sea
(Sonnet 65) 425

Since I left you, mine eye is in my mind
(Sonnet 113) 527

So am I as the rich whose blessèd key (Sonnet 52) 395

So are you to my thoughts as food to life
(Sonnet 75) 447

So is it not with me as with that Muse
(Sonnet 21) 333

So now I have confessed that he is thine
(Sonnet 134) 575

So oft have I invoked thee for my Muse
(Sonnet 78) 453

So shall I live, supposing thou art true (Sonnet 93) 485

Some glory in their birth, some in their skill
(Sonnet 91) 481

Some say thy fault is youth, some wantonness
(Sonnet 96) 493

Sweet Cytherea, sitting by a brook (*PP* 4) 695

Sweet Love, renew thy force; be it not said
(Sonnet 56) 407

Sweet rose, fair flower, untimely plucked, soon
vaded (*PP* 10) 699

Take all my loves, my love, yea take them all
(Sonnet 40) 371

Ten in the hundred must lie in his grave 742

Th' expense of spirit in a waste of shame (Sonnet
129) 563

That god forbid, that made me first your slave
(Sonnet 58) 411

That thou are blamed shall not be thy defect
(Sonnet 70) 437

That thou hast her, it is not all my grief
(Sonnet 42) 375

That time of year thou mayst in me behold
(Sonnet 73) 443

That you were once unkind befriends me now
(Sonnet 120) 541

The forward violet thus did I chide (Sonnet 99) 499

The gift is small 737

The little love-god, lying once asleep
(Sonnet 154) 623

The other two, slight air and purging fire
(Sonnet 45) 381

Then hate me when thou wilt, if ever, now
(Sonnet 90) 479

Then let not winter's ragged hand deface
(Sonnet 6) 301

They that have power to hurt and will do none
(Sonnet 94) 487

Thine eye Jove's lightning seems, thy voice his
dreadful thunder (manuscript) 727

Thine eyes I love, and they, as pitying me
(Sonnet 132) 571

Those hours, that with gentle work did frame
(Sonnet 5) 297

Those lines that I before have writ do lie
(Sonnet 115) 531

Those lips that Love's own hand did make
(Sonnet 145) 601

Those parts of thee that the world's eye doth view
(Sonnet 69) 435

Those pretty wrongs that liberty commits
(Sonnet 41) 373

Thou art as tyrannous, so as thou art (Sonnet 131) 569

Thou blind fool love, what dost thou to mine eyes
(Sonnet 137) 583

Thou contracted to thine own bright eyes
(manuscript) 726

Thus can my love excuse the slow offence
    (Sonnet 51) 393
Thus is his cheek the map of days outworn
    (Sonnet 68) 433
Thy bosom is endearèd with all hearts
    (Sonnet 31) 353
Thy gift, thy tables, are within my brain
    (Sonnet 122) 545
Thy glass will show thee how thy beauties wear
    (Sonnet 77) 451
Tired with all these, for restful death I cry
    (Sonnet 66) 427
'Tis better to be vile than vile esteemed
    (Sonnet 121) 543
To me, fair friend, you never can be old
    (Sonnet 104) 509
To one that would die a maid (Sonnet 2,
    manuscript) 721
Two loves I have, of comfort and despair
    (*PP* 2) 693; (Sonnet 144) 597

Unthrifty loveliness, why dost thou spend
    (Sonnet 4) 293

Venus and Adonis 1
Venus with Adonis sitting by her
    (*PP* 11) 701

Was it the proud full sail of his great verse
    (Sonnet 86) 469
Weary with toil, I haste me to my bed
    (Sonnet 27) 345
Were't aught to me I bore the canopy
    (Sonnet 125) 551
What is your substance, whereof are you made
    (Sonnet 53) 397
What potions have I drunk of siren tears
    (Sonnet 119) 539
What's in the brain that ink may character
    (Sonnet 108) 517
When as thine eye hath chose the dame
    (*PP* 18) 707

When forty winters shall besiege thy brow
    (Sonnet 2) 297; manuscript 721
When God was pleased (the world unwilling yet) 741
When I consider every thing that grows
    (Sonnet 15) 319
When I do count the clock that tells the time
    (Sonnet 12) 313
When I have seen by Time's fell hand defaced
    (Sonnet 64) 423
When in disgrace with Fortune and men's eyes
    (Sonnet 29) 349
When in the annals of all wasting time
    (Sonnet 106, manuscript) 724
When in the chronicle of wasted time
    (Sonnet 106) 513
When most I wink, then do mine eyes best see
    (Sonnet 43) 377
When my love swears that she is made of truth
    (*PP* 1) 693; (Sonnet 138) 585
When thou shalt be disposed to set me light
    (Sonnet 88) 475
When to the sessions of sweet silent thought
    (Sonnet 30) 351
Where art thou, Muse, that thou forget'st so long
    (Sonnet 100) 501
Whilst I alone did call upon thy aid
    (Sonnet 79) 455
Why should others' false adulterate eyes
    (manuscript) 727
Who is it that says most, which can say more
    (Sonnet 84) 465
Who will believe my verse in time to come
    (Sonnet 17) 323
Whoever hath her wish, thou hast thy Will
    (Sonnet 135) 577
Why didst thou promise such a beauteous day
    (Sonnet 34) 359
Why is my verse so barren of new pride
    (Sonnet 76) 449

Your love and pity doth th' impression fill
    (Sonnet 112) 525